A CRITICAL

CONCORDANCE

OF

THE NEW TESTAMENT.

PREPARED BY

CHARLES F. HUDSON,

UNDER THE DIRECTION OF

HORACE L. HASTINGS,

EDITOR OF "THE CHRISTIAN;"

REVISED AND COMPLETED BY

EZRA ABBOT, LL.D.,

ASSISTANT LIBRARIAN OF HARVARD UNIVERSITY.

SECOND EDITION—REVISED.

PHILADELPHIA:
J. B. LIPPINCOTT & CO.
1871.

PREFACE.

When the fulness of time had come, and the Gospel of grace and truth, the dispensation of the Spirit, was to take the place of the Mosaic Law, the language of the Old Testament had already become unintelligible to the common people in Palestine. Another tongue must therefore be selected, through which the New Covenant, founded upon better promises, might be made known to the human family. The Greek was then the choicest language of the globe. Copious, flexible, polished, and widely diffused, it had already done service for the Lord. Centuries before the Christian era, the writings of the Hebrew prophets were translated into the Greek, thus filling it with the aroma and energy of a divine inspiration, and sanctifying it as a chosen vessel to contain the treasures of eternal wisdom, and convey the truths of revelation to the scattered sons of men.

But in the changes of the eighteen centuries which have passed since the New Covenant was given to the world, the Greek has ceased to be the language of a living race, and it is only by means of translations into different tongues that the gospel of the kingdom can "be preached in all the world." And in making these translations, obstacles and difficulties present themselves, which cannot easily be surmounted.

If all nations possessed the same ideas and thoughts, and if each conception was invariably expressed by a single word, then, when once the different vocabularies had been learned, the work of translation would be but a simple, and almost a mechanical task. It might be illustrated by filling a thousand vessels of various forms and sizes with water, and placing beside them a thousand empty vessels of different form, but of exactly the same dimensions. To pour the water from vessel to vessel till the full were empty, and the empty full, would then be but a light undertaking. But there is no such correspondence between different languages, and this illustration does not represent the difficulties placed by the confusion of tongues in the path of the student of the Holy Scriptures.

If, however, we could regard the words of any language as ten thousand moulds of every imaginable figure and dimension; and if ideas could be represented as possessing material substance, like potter's clay, which, having been poured and pressed into these moulds and left to dry, had become rigid and inflexible;—and if beside these moulds were placed ten thousand others, capable of containing in the aggregate about the same amount of clay as the first series, but nearly all of them differing in length, breadth, depth, and capacity from the others;—and if we were then required to transfer the solid and unyielding masses from one class of moulds to the other, we should have a palpable illustration of the difficulties attending the accurate translation of the Holy Scriptures from the inspired originals into the languages of living men.

A transfer like that imagined would require time, labor, patience, judgment, and skill, and would often involve changes in form equivalent to the entire disintegration of the material of the masses which were to be transferred;—it would involve separations and re-combinations, transpositions and re-arrangements, so numerous that only he who had performed the task could fully appreciate its difficulties.

The necessary imperfections of translation must not, however, be exaggerated. The great fundamental truths of the Scriptures shine through the poorest and darkest translation which has ever been made. What is essential to salvation he that runs may read. The most important difficulties of the translator may be surmounted by patient, scholarly, critical toil. Still, the best translation of the Bible must, from the very nature of the case, often fail to express the full significance of the original. The delicate shades of meaning which distinguish one word from another, the precise force of some of the particles, the emphasis which rests on particular words as shown by their position or by some peculiarity of form, it is in many cases impossible to express. A translation is never exactly like an original, as the odor of a perfume is never like a fragrant rose. There is always room for study, research, and improvement; and he who reverently examines the Word of the Lord, will find it a treasury of hidden wealth, a light that shineth in a dark place, till the day dawn and the day-star arise.

Among the various helps to the investigations of the Biblical student, Concordances, or verbal indexes to the Holy Scriptures, hold perhaps the most important place. "If I could only have two books," said one of the most honored of American ministers, "they should be God's Bible and Cruden's Concordance."

By an arrangement of all the words in the English Bible in alphabetical order, and by the quotation, under each word, of every passage wherein that particular word occurs, a complete Concordance not only enables the student instantly to ascertain the location of any passage of which he can remember so much as a single word, but also to learn how frequently that word occurs in the Bible, and thus to study it in its connections, and in its various shades of meaning, and by comparing spiritual things with spiritual, to determine its true sense in many passages which might otherwise have seemed obscure.

But well and worthily as they have done, who, with pains and patience have prepared such aids for the readers of the common English version of the Bible, yet all their endeavors have left something more to be desired. For the best and most complete concordance of the English Bible, is a concordance, not of the inspired original, but of the uninspired, and consequently imperfect translation. And hence, though we may investigate and ascertain the entire Scriptural usage of any word found in the English Bible, we may still be in doubt as to the precise idea which the translators intended to convey, because,—

1. An English word may have several different meanings, and represent different Greek words, as the term 'master' may signify either a ruler, or a teacher; and the English reader may not be able to decide which kind of a 'master' is referred to in a given passage.[1]

2. Several synonymous English words may be employed to represent the same Greek word, when no variation of sense is intended. Indeed, King James's translators, in their address "To the Reader," say, "We wish to admonish thee that we have not tied ourselves to an uniformity of phrasing or an identity of words, . . . that we should express the same notion in the same particular word: as for example, if we translate the *Hebrew* or *Greek* word once by *purpose*, never to call it *intent;* if one where *think*, never *suppose;* if one where *pain*, never *ache;* if one where *joy*, never *gladness*, etc." —which is all very well stated, and has a certain weight, but the practice leaves the English reader involved in needless doubt and uncertainty. Who, for example, would imagine that the words 'conclude,' 'counted,' 'reckoned,' 'imputed,' 'accounted,' and 'esteem-

[1] See Index under the word Master, also pp. 79, 87. A similar instance may be noted in the case of the word Hell, see pp. 7, 68, 380.

eth,' (Rom. iii. 28, iv. 3, 4, 11, viii. 36, xiv. 14,) were translated from one and the same Greek word?[2] And many disputes, misunderstandings, and difficulties arise in consequence of such variations, which could at once be removed if the facts in such cases were made known.

3. More than one English word may be required to exhaust a single meaning of an original term, but as only one word can find place in the translation, the others must be dismissed to the margin, or perhaps be used in other passages as equivalents for the same Greek expression. This diversity of rendering is often a real benefit to the Greek scholar, furnishing him with new points of observation, and enabling him by a kind of mental triangulation to arrive at the precise signification of many difficult words.

Thus good old Myles Coverdale, in his preface to his translation of the Bible in 1535, says;—"Sure I am that there commeth more knowlege and vnderstondinge of the scripture by theyr sondrie translacyons, then by all the gloses of oure sophisticall doctours. For that one interpreteth somthynge obscurely in one place, the same translateth another, (or els he him selfe) more manifestly by a more playne vocable of the same meaning in another place."

But the difficulty of the English reader is, to ascertain what is the original word which is translated "somthynge obscurely in one place," and "more manifestly, by a more playne vocable in another place." Give him a knowledge of that word, and of all the places where it occurs, and he can study it with delight and profit; deprive him of this knowledge and he gropes in darkness.

The Greek scholar's remedy for all these difficulties is found in his Greek Testament or Greek Concordance. But the English reader, equally desirous of instruction, cannot avail himself of these important aids.

For the benefit of such students of the Holy Scriptures THE ENGLISHMAN'S GREEK CONCORDANCE OF THE NEW TESTAMENT was prepared under the direction, and at the munificent expense, of Mr. George V. Wigram, of London. In this goodly octavo of nearly eleven hundred pages, the Greek words of the New Testament are first presented in alphabetical order. After each word is placed every passage in which the word occurs, taken from the English Testament. The English words which in each passage represent the original word are printed in *italic type*, so that a person can readily ascertain how frequently the word in question occurs in the Greek Testament, and also in how many different ways our English translators have rendered it. To this is added an English

[2] See the Index, and page 243.

Index, similar to that found in the present volume, enabling a person who knows nothing of the original to find easily any word which he may desire to examine.

The value of The Englishman's Greek Concordance, as also of THE ENGLISHMAN'S HEBREW AND CHALDEE CONCORDANCE, prepared upon the same plan, can hardly be over-estimated, and but for their prior publication the present volume would probably never have been undertaken.

It was about the middle of October, 1863, that the writer sat one drizzly day beneath the shelter of The Bethel Tent, which had been pitched for special religious services, near Eaton Corners, a village in Eastern Canada, and while looking over the pages of the Greek New Testament, and consulting Bagster's pocket edition of Schmid's Greek Concordance to ascertain the usage of some original word, the thought arose, "I wish I had my Englishman's Greek Concordance here, so that I could see how this word is rendered in the English Testament in all the places where it occurs."

But the wish was a vain one, for the book was far too cumbrous for a travelling companion, and was standing quietly in my library, hundreds of miles away. And then arose another query: "Cannot a book be made which shall contain all the information which is absolutely necessary for the English reader, at a price within his means, and in a form so condensed that it can be made a constant companion of the Bible student in all his travels?" The writer had before him Bagster's edition of Cruden's Concordance, in which, by the omission of quotations after the references, a quarto was condensed into a very little space, and after brief consideration a plan was formed, and he determined, by divine permission, to place a book which should meet these requirements, in the hands of his brethren of the gospel ministry, and others who were interested in the careful study of the word of God.

The outlines of the plan having been thus determined, the next question was, "Who will execute it?" And while this matter was undecided, the writer received a visit from his friend, Charles Frederick Hudson, to whom he confided the project that he had formed. Mr. Hudson was favorably impressed by it, and after various discussions, submitted it to the judgment of Mr. Ezra Abbot, the accurate and accomplished Assistant Librarian of Harvard University, who approved the undertaking, and improved the plan by various important suggestions.

The result of mutual consultation was, that while the writer held fast his purpose to make the book available to the mere English reader, as an aid in the understanding of the English Bible, it was determined, at the suggestions of Messrs. Hudson and Abbot, to incorporate into its pages the various readings obtained by the careful comparison of hundreds of ancient Greek manuscripts, as laid down in the valuable critical editions published by Griesbach, Lachmann, Tischendorf, and Tregelles, as well as the confirmatory readings found in the recently discovered Sinaitic manuscript, thus making the book a repository of the results of the best critical scholarship of the age, and furnishing in a compact and inexpensive form, a mass of information which no scholar could afford to dispense with, and which could only be obtained elsewhere in cumbrous volumes, so numerous and costly, as to be entirely beyond the reach of most of those who would desire to possess them. For a full account of this, and other features of the work, the reader is referred to the Introduction by Mr. Hudson, which follows this Preface.

The plans being at last perfected, Mr. Hudson, whose critical scholarship and painstaking industry peculiarly qualified him for such a task, was induced to undertake its execution. And as the typographical difficulties were numerous, and as he, in his early days, had learned the printer's art in the office of a local paper conducted by his father, he chose to perform the typographical as well as the literary labor with his own hands.

On the twelfth of November, 1863, Mr. Hudson commenced his work by entering upon the margins of a copy of The Englishman's Greek Concordance all the various readings which were to be incorporated in the critical Concordance. A copy of Bruder's greatly improved edition of Schmid's Greek Concordance was procured, the most important critical editions of the Greek Testament were obtained, and all needful preparations for the work were made.

To secure accuracy of notation, every reference to chapter and verse in The Englishman's Greek Concordance was carefully compared with the references in Bruder's Greek Concordance, and every discrepancy and error noted, examined, and corrected. This collation, which revealed many inaccuracies in those valuable works, was performed partly by Mr. Hudson, but mainly by Miss Elizabeth A. Annable, to whose care in this department much is due.

When all was ready, a miniature printing office was fitted up within a few rods of Harvard University, where literary counsel could be conveniently obtained; fonts of type adapted to the necessities of the case were procured; and Mr. Hudson commenced his operations.

Having prepared a 'printer's stick,' containing several partitions, he laid his various Concordances and Testaments open before him, and selecting from the Englishman's Greek Concordance first a Greek word, and that translation which seemed most nearly to express the primary sense of the same, he set the translation in **bold-faced type**, and then followed it by references to all the passages in the New Testament where that Greek word was translated in that manner. Selecting then a translation which seemed to express a secondary meaning of the word most closely related to the primary sense, and placing it in another compartment of the 'stick,' he followed this by references to the places where the Greek word was so translated, continuing thus till all the different translations of the word were exhausted, inserting with each reference any various reading which occurred in the four above-mentioned editions of the Greek Testament, and so completing the article.

Thus from word to word the work proceeded. The book was never *written*. The arranging of the senses, the insertion of the various readings, the setting of the type, the proof-reading, correcting, and preparing the pages for the electrotyper, were all done by Mr. Hudson's own hands, Mr. Abbot giving constant counsel, and kindly assisting in the revision of the final proofs.

For nearly three years Mr. Hudson pursued this labor of love with unwearied patience and the most conscientious fidelity, and with as much continuity of application as his somewhat imperfect health allowed, until at length he seemed to see the end of his task at hand. The body of the work was completed, the Index finished, the Introduction drafted, and the Supplement begun.

At this time Mr. Hudson was offered a situation as corrector of the press, and considering the Concordance so nearly complete that it might be finished by the occasional labor of a few spare hours, he accepted the position. A few days demonstrated that the task was too severe, and a chronic pulmonary weakness soon culminated in a serious hemorrhage at the close of a hard day's work. He was urged to relinquish his position immediately, retire from the seaboard, and seek the restoration of his health; but with the self-deception characteristic of the victims of pulmonary disease, he endeavored to continue his labors until a recurrence of the hemorrhage rendered it impossible for him to proceed.

He then arranged his worldly affairs and started forth, too late, alas, in quest of health. Sojourning briefly with kind and loving friends in Worcester, Mass., and in West Killingly, Conn., he at last repaired to Haddonfield, New Jersey, in the hope that the milder climate might relieve his disease. Here he remained for several months, surrounded by friends who ministered to him with Christian fidelity and affection; hopeful and cheerful until the last, when he sweetly fell asleep May 26th, 1867, in the faith of that Redeemer whose service had been his labor and his joy.[3]

The work on The Critical Greek Concordance, suspended by Mr. Hudson's illness and decease, was only resumed after a considerable delay. Mr. Abbot, who had never lost his interest in the enterprise, undertook to revise and correct the proofs of the electrotype plates. He has also collated for the Supplement the latest edition of Tischendorf's Greek Testament, so far as it has been issued from the press, and has rendered such other assistance as was needful for the completion of the work.

Thus at last this Concordance, projected nearly seven years ago, and carried forward through the financial embarrassments incident to a terrible war, is ready for the public eye. It differs from other concordances in various respects. It leads the English reader to the Greek original and its various readings. It leads the Greek scholar to the common English translation, as given both in the text and in the margin. It saves space by omitting extended quotations, referring inquirers to the passages themselves for further information. It furnishes the Greek alphabet, with rules of pronunciation, which may be mastered by an hour's study, and thus obviates

[3] Charles Frederick Hudson, son of Timothy and Catherine Hudson, was born in Wadsworth, Medina county, Ohio, May 18th, 1821. His parents shortly after removed to Medina, the county seat, where he received the elements of a common school education.

After suitable preparation, he entered the Western Reserve College, and was graduated among the foremost of his class. Having in early life devoted himself to the service of the Savior, and believing that he was called to the work of the gospel ministry, he pursued the course of study prescribed at Lane Theological Seminary, receiving his certificate under the hands of Lyman Beecher, C. E. Stowe, and D. H. Allen, June 9th, 1847.

After spending some years as pastor of the Congregational church in Sycamore, Illinois, certain changes in his opinions regarding the nature and destiny of man, led to the dissolution of his ecclesiastical connections, and being released from pastoral responsibilities, he was free to employ his time in study and in writing, preaching meanwhile wherever an open door was set before him, without regard to denominational lines or connections.

During the latter part of his life he travelled extensively, visiting libraries and consulting with literary men; and some of the fruits of his patient research were given to the world in an elaborate volume entitled, "Debt and Grace, as related to the Doctrine of a Future Life;" which was followed by "Christ Our Life: The Scriptural Argument for Immortality through Christ Alone;" "Human Destiny, a Critique on Universalism," and other minor publications on kindred topics.

His last years were spent in the vicinity of Cambridge, Mass., and were devoted to these and other literary pursuits. The Critical Greek Concordance was the last and crowning labor of his life.

As a controversialist, Mr. Hudson was candid, patient, calm, and courteous; indefatigable in research, and temperate in expression. As a preacher, he was sober, diffident, and deliberate; yet instructive to the patient hearer. As a man, he was generous, cautious, honorable, self-reliant, and modest, even to bashfulness. As a Christian, he was circumspect, reverent, conscientious, and of good report. In person, he was tall, slightly stooping, of light, though swarthy complexion, having rather a thin face, and prominent nose, high, full forehead, and brown hair. His health was never very robust, but his powers of execution were considerable. Mr. Hudson never married. He is buried at Haddonfield, New Jersey, where he died May 26th, 1867, aged forty-six years and eight days.

the necessity of an imperfect representation of the Greek words in English characters. It classifies the passages where each Greek word occurs, reveals at a glance the number of ways in which it is translated in the New Testament, shows in what senses it is most frequently or more rarely used, exhibiting in their order, first the primary, and afterwards the several more remote senses of the different terms. It presents all the important various readings of the four best critical editions of the Greek Testament, confirmed by references to the Sinaitic manuscript. It combines with these peculiarities a cheapness of cost and convenience of form which bring it within the means of the student and enable him to have it always at his side. That the book is perfect is not to be imagined; but it is hoped that it may meet a want long felt, and fill a place which has never yet been occupied; and that it may be accepted and blessed of Him by whose kind providence it has been commenced and completed.

Though the first plan of the work was formed, and the financial responsibility borne by the writer, to whose decision every proposed improvement has been referred, and though its completion has been committed to other hands; yet the book itself will stand as a memorial of the patient industry and conscientious zeal of one to whom it was not granted to behold the consummation of his earthly labors, but who leaves this volume as a token of his devotion to that Master whose Word he has honored, and of love to His disciples for whose use it is prepared.

HORACE L. HASTINGS.

SCRIPTURAL TRACT REPOSITORY,
Office of THE CHRISTIAN, 19 Lindall St., Boston,
August, 1870.

*** Any errors which may be hereafter discovered in this Concordance will be thankfully corrected if sent to the above address.

NOTE TO SECOND EDITION.

In this edition the English Index has been thoroughly revised and corrected, and newly electrotyped. A few corrections have also been made in the body of the work, and the Supplement has been continued, so as to embrace the variations of Tischendorf's eighth edition from the seventh as far as it has been published. H. L. H.

BOSTON, July, 1871.

INTRODUCTION.

BY C. F. HUDSON.

A full account of the origin of the present work, and of the uses it is intended to serve, has already been given in the Preface of Mr. Hastings. Like the Englishman's Greek Concordance, it connects the Greek text of the New Testament with the common English version, though in a different way; but it is distinguished from that work by several important features, which, it is hoped, will make it a useful help in the critical study of the New Testament in the original. These features it is the object of the present Introduction briefly to describe; and in doing this, it will be necessary to give a concise history of the printed text of the Greek New Testament.

This Concordance, then, is offered as "critical" for several reasons. It names the grammatical forms which often appear in peculiar modes of translation. It gives adjunct words which in the Englishman's Greek Concordance often fail to appear as part of the rendering of the Greek. E. g., "these *things*" for ταῦτα, instead of simply "these;" and "blind *man*" instead of "blind," for τυφλός. It gives, with their renderings, Greek phrases which are not translated word for word. It notes the Greek text followed in our version, when it differs from the so-called "received text." This the Englishman's Greek Concordance often fails to do. Thus it gives "saw" as the rendering of εὑρίσκω, "to find," in Matt. ii. 11, where our translators read εἶδον, "saw." In James ii. 18 it gives "without" as the rendering of ἐκ, though it is really the rendering of χωρίς, ἐκ being represented by the word "by," which appears as a various reading in the margin. In a few instances it notes the fact that our version follows a text differing from that named in the Concordance itself; as ὑπὸ κρίσιν, "under condemnation," for εἰς ὑπόκρισιν, "into hypocrisy," James v. 12. But in all such instances there is an incongruity in seeming to give an erroneous translation of a word, "condemnation," for example, appearing improperly as the rendering of ὑπόκρισις in the passage referred to. Yet that Concordance, while not pretending to be critical, is still well worthy of the praise it has received as a general help to the study of the Scriptures.

But the passages just named suggest the inquiry, What text did our translators follow? The answer is, there was then no received text. This phrase originated in a boast[1] of the publishers of the second Elzevir edition (1633), twenty-two years after King James's version was printed. And the phrase is still employed by biblical scholars, not to denote an *accepted* and *authorized* text, but simply a current text which is conveniently taken as a standard for critical comparison or correction. In this sense the first Elzevir edition (Leyden, 1624), which varies very slightly from the edition just named, is the "received text" on the continent, while in England the phrase is oftener applied to the third edition of Robert Stephens, 1550. But the text of our translation seems to accord with Beza's fifth edition, 1598, more nearly than with any other. It agrees with this in opposition to the third edition of Stephens in about eighty places; with Stephens in opposition to Beza, in about half that number; and in about a dozen places it differs from both.

When the present work was proposed to the writer, he was well aware of the fact that the earlier printed Greek text was not now accepted by scholars. And it seemed proper, in preparing a concordance of the Greek words which lie at the basis of our Christian faith, to present with them the results of modern sacred criticism. He accordingly conferred with one of our first critical scholars, who at once took a lively interest in the work. He named the editors whose readings should be given, adding those of the newly discovered Sinaitic manuscript. He also suggested several other leading features of the work, and has ever followed it with his thoughts, cares, and not a few labors.

It is offered as critical, then, chiefly as giving the text of the best modern editions of the Greek, so far as this could be done in a manual concordance. In representing this text, and that of the translation itself, words appear in their simple forms, though notice is taken of any differences in grammatical form which may pertain to a new reading. And the account of the various readings is coextensive with that of the text, in which all the occurrences are given of every word in the Greek Testament except *αὐτός*, *δέ*, *καί*, *ὁ*, and *ὅς*, while even these words are amply treated.

In connection with this subject, it will be proper to give a brief

[1] "Textum ergo habes nunc ab omnibus receptum," i. e., "Thou hast, therefore, a text now received by all."

account of the text currently printed, and of the editions which now invite the attention of all biblical scholars.

The Greek Testament was first *printed* as part of the Complutensian Polyglot,[2] in 1514, under the direction of Cardinal Ximenes, from manuscripts not ancient, and with a manifest preference for the authority of the Vulgate. But its *publication* was delayed until 1522. Meanwhile an edition was undertaken by Erasmus, at the instance of Froben, the celebrated printer of Basle, who wished to anticipate that of Ximenes. Erasmus had made slight preparation for such a work, but the urgency of Froben brought it to completion in less than six months after the printing was begun, and it appeared early in 1516, making, with the Latin translation and notes, a folio volume of about 1000 pages. "It was driven headlong through the press rather than edited,"[3] says Erasmus in one of his letters. He used only five manuscripts, none of them containing the whole of the New Testament. They were all modern, and, with one exception, of very little critical value. For the Apocalypse he had but one manuscript, lacking the last six verses of the book, which he supplied by retranslating from the Vulgate. He published a second and more correct edition in 1519; a third in 1522, inserting 1 John v. 7 to redeem his promise that it should appear when a manuscript was found to contain it; a fourth in 1527, changing the text of the Apocalypse to that of the Complutensian Polyglot in about ninety places; and a fifth in 1535. The text of this, as compared with the first edition, was altered in about six hundred places, according to Mill, in more than one hundred of which this critic thinks there was no improvement.

In 1546 and 1549 Robert Stephens[4] printed at Paris two beautiful small editions; and in 1550 appeared his folio edition, in the margin of which were various readings collected by his son, Henry Stephens. These were from the Complutensian Polyglot and from fifteen manuscripts, and are known to be given very inaccurately. They "seem rather to be appended as an *ornament*," says Tregelles, the manuscripts being used little, if at all, for the improvement of the text. This differs but slightly from the fifth edition of Erasmus, except in the Apocalypse, where the Complutensian is chiefly followed. But the appearance of "annotations" offended the doctors of the Sorbonne. Stephens betook himself to Geneva, where he published, in 1551, a fourth edition, with the text of his third, but divided, for the first time, into our modern verses.[5]

2 So called from *Complutum*, the ancient name of Alcala, where the work was printed.

3 Præcipitatum fuit verius quam editum.

4 The vernacular form of his name is "Estienne," in Latin, "Stephanus."

5 This was in connection with a project for a Concordance.

Theodore Beza published five editions of the Greek Testament, in 1565, 1576, 1582, 1589, and 1598. Two ancient and valuable manuscripts were long in his possession. But he made very little use of them. He followed mostly the text of Stephens's third edition, and where he differed from it altered it often for the worse, sometimes introducing readings on mere conjecture, and frequently on very slight authority.

The editor of the Elzevir editions, 1624 and 1633, is unknown. Their text is that of Stephens, except in about 280 places (according to Scrivener's collation), in most of which Beza is followed. In many of these the difference is such as cannot be expressed in a translation.

Thus far almost nothing had been done to bring the text to the standard of earlier or better manuscripts. But in the Polyglot of Walton, 1657, important *materials* for criticism were collected, the fifth volume containing the readings of the Codex Alexandrinus, and the sixth volume giving other collations, including those of Stephens, and also of sixteen manuscripts, made under the direction of Archbishop Usher.

In 1707 appeared the edition of JOHN MILL, of whom it has been said, "This learned man did more in the labor of thirty years than all those who preceded him." His text is that of Stephens, correcting his errata. Of the various readings which he gives he often expresses an opinion in his Prolegomena (Introduction) and notes, and he frequently condemns those of Stephens.

But his collection of 30,000 various readings was censured by Whitby as unsettling the grounds of confidence in the words of the divine revelation. And his objections were employed by Anthony Collins, in his "Discourse of Free Thinking," in defense of his own rejection of the authority of Scripture. In reply to these writers, and in defense of Mill, appeared Richard Bentley. He shows from the case of the classics that the various readings of Scripture are no way to be feared. Of the manuscripts of Terence he says: "I have myself collated several; and do affirm that I have seen 20,000 various lections in that little author, not near so big as the whole New Testament; and I am morally sure that if half the number of manuscripts were collated for Terence with that niceness and minuteness which has been used in twice as many for the New Testament, the number of the variations would amount to above 50,000." Bentley also shows how unfortunate is the case of a work of which only one copy is preserved: the discovery of another copy would correct, by means of its varying readings, errors that are now without remedy. The growing number of these confirms the better text of an ancient author, instead of unsettling it.

Bentley proposed a new edition of the Greek Testament, with a specimen of his plan. It was attacked by Conyers Middleton. A controversy ensued, showing no good temper on either side. The edition was never published. The most valuable result of Bentley's labors was a collation of the Vatican manuscript of the fourth century, made for him by an Italian named Mico, and published by Ford in 1799.

The edition of John Albert Bengel appeared in 1734. Through excessive timidity he changes the text only in the Apocalypse, but gives in the margin those readings which he regards as genuine. And in an appendix he gives a selection of readings with the authorities for and against each, which had not been done before. His edition was the basis of a new German translation by Count Zinzendorf, and of an authorized Danish version, in 1745.

The edition of J. J. Wetstein was published in two folio volumes, Amsterdam, 1751–52. He had once designed to take the Alexandrian Codex as a basis; but various causes led him to undervalue the older manuscripts, and he took no pains to procure the collation which had been made of the Vatican manuscript. He printed the current text, giving in the margin the readings he preferred, and collations from the manuscripts, noted by a system which subsequent editors have followed. His most important contribution to criticism consists in his citations from the fathers, which are still highly valued. Compared with his predecessors, he has been praised with the words applied to Mill.

Among more recent contributions to our critical material, the following editions are worthy of note. (1.) That of Matthæi, in twelve volumes, 1782–88, with its collations of Moscow manuscripts. Matthæi also published a smaller edition in three volumes, 1803–07, containing some additional matter. (2.) That of the Gospels by Birch, 1788, with various readings from many manuscripts, and a partial collation of the Codex Vaticanus. (3.) That of Scholz, 1830–36, with much information about manuscripts, though the author's own collations are very imperfect. The separate publication of the oldest Greek manuscripts, as of the Alexandrian, by Woide, in 1786, the Codex Bezæ by Kipling in 1793, and Scrivener in 1864, and of various others by Hearne, Matthæi, Barrett, Rettig, Tregelles, Scrivener, and especially Tischendorf, has also been a most important aid to modern criticism. To this should be added editions of the ancient versions, Latin, Syriac, Coptic, Ethiopic, Gothic, Armenian, etc.

In the forty years of his critical labors, JOHN JAMES GRIESBACH published three editions of the Greek New Testament; the first in

1774–77, another in 1796–1806, and a manual edition in 1805, without the manuscript authorities, but which is regarded as giving generally his most matured judgment, and has been often reprinted. Besides the use which he made of earlier collations, he consulted about seventy manuscripts of various portions of the New Testament. He re-asserted the value of the ancient documents, and undertook to arrange the extant authorities in an intelligible order, and to apply them steadily and consistently to the emendation of the text. His doctrine of recensions, dividing the manuscripts into classes or families, each supposed to possess characteristic varieties of reading, was a modification of the views of Bentley, Bengel, and Semler, and has been held in other forms since Griesbach's time. That question is still unsettled. But the critics and opponents of Griesbach's theory do not regard it as having impaired his estimate of the value of single manuscripts. And the canons of criticism which he gave are generally accepted. "In acuteness, vigor, and candor," says the Rev. B. F. Westcott, "he stands below no editor of the New Testament, and his judgment will always retain a peculiar value."[6]

The care which he exercised in weighing evidence and pronouncing judgment is apparent in the various degrees of confidence with which he gave his readings, designating their different grades of probability by an elaborate system of notation. And it is worthy of remark that in hundreds of instances his cautious judgment as to what was probable has become the clear verdict of the other editors whose readings are here given.

The first edition of CHARLES LACHMANN appeared in 1831. It had no Preface. The principles on which it was prepared were indicated only in a note at the end, preceding a list of the places in which it differed from the current text. It was here stated that the editor had never followed his own judgment, but the custom of the most ancient Oriental churches; that when this was not uniform, he had preferred, as far as could be ascertained, what was supported by African and Italian consent; that where there was great uncertainty, this was indicated partly by the use of brackets, partly by marginal readings; and that no account was made of the current text of the last two centuries. In accordance with these views he sometimes gives a reading which he does not regard as the true one, —for it may be a palpable error,—but as *best attested* in the fourth century. Internal evidence, as well as private opinion, would be quite excluded by this method; though they are thought to appear in a very few instances, where his range of authorities was narrow.

6 Smith's *Dictionary of the Bible*, Art. "New Testament."

After some misapprehension of his design had passed away, a wish was expressed that he would prepare an edition with the authorities. This was undertaken with the aid of the younger Buttmann, who was to arrange those for the Greek readings only, the Latin appearing as a collateral text, based on ancient manuscripts. The citations of the earlier fathers were also employed. The new edition appeared in two volumes, Berlin, 1842–50. Lachmann is welcomed by Tregelles as having first edited the Greek Testament, "*wholly on ancient authorities, irrespective of modern traditions.*" And Mr. F. H. Scrivener, who censures the exclusive reliance on ancient manuscripts, yet speaks of him as "earnest, single-hearted," and "a true scholar, both in spirit and accomplishments."

The first edition of Lobegott Friedrich Constantin Tischendorf appeared at Leipsic, in 1841. This showed in several respects the influence of Lachmann's first edition. His next more important edition was published at Leipsic in 1849. Still more valuable is his seventh edition, 1856–59. This is far the most complete account of the various readings, with the authorities for and against,—manuscripts, versions, and patristic citations,—that has yet appeared. His eighth edition, incorporating the readings of more than twenty new manuscripts, including the Sinaitic, was begun in 1864, and is still in progress.

In his second Leipsic and his seventh editions, Tischendorf lays down the general principle that "the text is to be sought only from ancient evidence, and especially from Greek manuscripts, but without neglecting the evidence of versions and fathers. Those readings should hold the first place which are supported by the most ancient Greek manuscripts, i. e., those from the fourth to about the ninth century. And of these the older are of greatest authority." In the earlier portions of his seventh edition he was regarded by some as receding from his previous application of these views. But the changes in this edition from the Elzevir text are still more numerous than those in the edition of 1849. And in his eighth edition he professes to approach more nearly the principles of Bentley and Lachmann, in adherence to the oldest Greek and Latin bases of the text.

His travels for the collation and discovery of manuscripts are well known. And though Mr. Scrivener would rest his reputation largely on his editions of manuscripts, he still thinks he has well earned the name of "*the first biblical critic in Europe.*"

Samuel Prideaux Tregelles first became generally known by an edition of the Apocalypse, with an English version, in 1844. He published the Gospels of Matthew and Mark in 1857, and those of Luke and John in 1861.[7] He has also contributed largely to the materials of criticism, in the collation of above forty manuscripts, including the Codex Amiatinus of the Vulgate.

His leading maxim is that an ancient text is proved only by ancient evidence. Thus his principle in the selection of authorities is substantially the same with Lachmann's, and he approves the statement of Griesbach, that "readings which, looked at in themselves, we should judge to be the better, are not to be preferred unless authenticated by at least some ancient testimonies." In particular, he regards the arraying of mere *numbers* of manuscripts in behalf of any reading as fallacious. "His work," says Mr. Westcott, "must be regarded as one of the most important contributions, as it is perhaps the most exact, that has been made to the cause of textual criticism."

Of the Codex Sinaiticus, Tischendorf found a fragment in the Convent of St. Catherine, at the foot of Mt. Sinai, in 1844, and secured the remainder in a third journey in 1859. The whole was printed in fac-simile type at St. Petersburg in 1862, and the New Testament, with the epistle ascribed to Barnabas and a part of "The Shepherd" of Hermas, at Leipsic, in 1863.[8] It is regarded as a genuine document of the fourth century, of the same age as the Vatican manuscript, the readings of which it often confirms, while it is evidently independent of it. And though in its frequent omissions occasioned by the similar ending of words, and otherwise, it shows some carelessness of the scribe, it is still deemed a most important witness of the early state of the text. Tischendorf's new readings in his eighth edition rarely differ from it, though he seldom, if ever, concurs with it alone against the Vatican manuscript.

The readings here presented are taken, those of Griesbach from his manual edition of 1805, those of Lachmann, Tischendorf, and Tregelles from the careful compilation made by the Rev. F. H. Scrivener in his edition of the Greek Testament, 1862, (with a few corrections,) and those of the Sinaitic manuscript from the Leipsic edition. They have been also verified in the proof-reading, the last named by means of Mr. Scrivener's collation, in which a few errors have been detected. In the other portions of the work constant reference has been made to the Greek Concordance of Bruder, with which the Englishman's has been carefully collated. The proof-

7 Part III. of his edition, containing the Acts and Catholic Epistles, appeared in 1865, Part IV. (Romans—2 Thessalonians iii. 3) in 1869, and Part V., containing the remainder of the Epistles, in 1870. A.

8 A more convenient edition of the Sinaitic text of the New Testament only was published at Leipsic in 1865, with the various readings of the Elzevir edition of 1624 and the Vatican manuscript. A supplement containing corrections, particularly of the Vatican readings, appeared in 1870. A.

reading has been twice done, and it is believed that the remaining errata, so difficult wholly to avoid in a work of the kind, are the fewest possible.

Readings which affect the form or order of words, or the punctuation, are given for special reasons in the Appendix, but elsewhere only as occasion required. Such readings did not fall within the scope of a Concordance. A selection of all such as might be deemed important would be very difficult.

The text of the English version used is that of Bagster's Critical New Testament, which retains the italics of the edition of 1611. In most modern editions the italics have been considerably changed; sometimes carelessly, or by unauthorized persons, but mostly in the revision of 1769, under the charge of Dr. Blayney. In general, the principal variations of the common modern editions from the text of the edition of 1611 have been noted in the Concordance. Some of these variations are far from being improvements; e. g., the insertion of "not" in Matt. xii. 23; "broidered" for "broided," i. e., braided, 1 Tim. ii. 9. In several cases Dr. Blayney and later editors have wrongly put in italics words which represent Greek words found in some manuscripts and editions, and regarded by our translators as genuine, though they are omitted in the received text; e. g., John viii. 6; 1 John iii. 16.

Of the marginal renderings, which are all given, it need only be said that they are by some preferred to those in the text.

In the plan of giving the English words in their simple form, the order of the terms of a phrase is sometimes changed from that in which grammatical inflections have placed it, e. g., "furnish throughly" for "throughly furnished." And sometimes words occurring only in the passive voice are still given in the active form.

For the convenience of the English reader the Greek alphabet is appended. The Greek article has been so often employed that it is proper to explain as follows: ὁ, ἡ, τό, denote respectively the masculine, feminine, and neuter, singular; οἱ, αἱ, τά, the same in the plural number. Of grammatical forms, it need only be added that the Genitive case answers mostly to our Possessive, or is rendered by the preposition *of;* the Dative is rendered by *to*, *for*, and the like; the Accusative answers to our Objective; and the Middle Voice, primarily, to our reflexive form of the verb, though it is often to be translated by a simple active or neuter verb in English.

THE GREEK ALPHABET.

Characters.		Roman Letters.	Names.	
Α	α	a	Ἄλφα	Alpha
Β	β ϐ	b	Βῆτα	Beta
Γ	γ	g	Γάμμα	Gamma
Δ	δ	d	Δέλτα	Delta
Ε	ε	ĕ	Ἒ ψιλόν	Epsilon
Ζ	ζ ϛ	z	Ζῆτα	Zeta
Η	η	ē	Ἦτα	Eta
Θ	ϑ θ	th	Θῆτα	Theta
Ι	ι	i	Ἰῶτα	Iota
Κ	κ	k, c	Κάππα	Kappa
Λ	λ	l	Λάμβδα	Lambda
Μ	μ	m	Μῦ	Mu
Ν	ν	n	Νῦ	Nu
Ξ	ξ	x	Ξῖ	Xi
Ο	ο	ŏ	Ὂ μικρόν	Omicron
Π	π ϖ	p	Πῖ	Pi
Ρ	ρ ϱ	r	Ῥῶ	Rho
Σ	σ ς	s	Σίγμα	Sigma
Τ	τ ꞇ	t	Ταῦ	Tau
Υ	υ	u, y	Ὓ ψιλόν	Upsilon
Φ	φ ϕ	ph	Φῖ	Phi
Χ	χ	ch	Χῖ	Chi
Ψ	ψ	ps	Ψῖ	Psi
Ω	ω	ō	Ὦ μέγα	Omega

Pronunciation.

The English Method.

α and *ι*, in general, are sounded like *a* and *i* in English. *α* final, as *a* in *Columbia*. *ι* final, as *i* long.

ε and *ο*, like *e* in *met* and *o* in *not*. Final, as *e* and *o* in *be* and *go*.

η, *υ*, and *ω*, like *e* in *mete*, *u* in *tube*, and *o* in *note*.

αι is sounded as our affirmative *ay* (*ah'ee* as a diphthong). *αυ*, as *au* in *aught*. *ει*, as *ei* in *height*. *ευ* and *ηυ*, as *eu* in *Europe* or *neuter*. *οι*, as *oi* in *toil*. *ου* and *ωυ*, as *ou* in *thou*. *υι*, as *ui* in *quiet*. *υἱ*, as *whi* in *while*.

γ, *κ*, and *χ* are always hard. But *γ* before *γ*, *κ*, or *χ* is sounded as *ng* in *song*. *ϑ* has the sharp sound of *th* in *thin*. *σ*, the sound of *s* in *so*.

At the beginning of a word *ξ* is sounded as *z*; and of two consonants which can not be pronounced with ease the first is silent; thus Πτολεμαῖος, *Ptolemy*.

The rough breathing (ʽ) has the sound of *h*, as in ὁδός, *hŏdŏs*. The smooth (ʼ) has no sound.

In prepositions and some other particles final *α*, *ε*, *ι*, and *ο*, coming before a vowel, are dropped; thus, ἀπ' ἐμοῦ for ἀπὸ ἐμοῦ. And *π*, *κ*, and *τ*, thus brought before a rough breathing, are changed to *φ*, *χ*, and *ϑ*; as, καϑ' οὗ for κατὰ οὗ.

The *accent*, in words of two syllables, falls on the penult, or last syllable but one. In words of more than two syllables, the penult, if long, takes the accent; if short, it falls on the antepenult, or preceding syllable. But many now follow the Greek accent.

Continental or Erasmian Method.

This differs from the English chiefly in sounding *α* protracted as *a* in *father*, *η* as *ey* in *they*, *ι* protracted as *i* in *machine*, *αυ* as *ou* in *our*, *ου* as *ou* in *tour*, *υι* like our pronoun *we*, and *ζ* like a soft *dz*.

The Romaic or Modern Greek Method.

This accords mainly with the Continental where that differs from the English, but departs from both in various features. See the Grammars of Sophocles and Crosby.

Illustration.

2 Tim. iii. 15: ὅτι ἀπὸ βρέφους τὰ
English, *hot-i ap-o breph-ous ta*
Continent., *hŏt-ĭ ăp-o brĕph-oos ta*
ἱερὰ γράμματα οἶδας, τὰ δυνάμενά
hiera grammata oidas, ta dunamena
hĭĕra grammăta oidas, ta dunamĕna
σε σοφίσαι εἰς σωτηρίαν, διά, κ. τ. λ.
se sophisai eis soterian, dia, etc.
sĕ sophīsai eis sotērĭan, dĭa, etc.

ABBREVIATIONS AND OTHER SIGNS.

G signifies Griesbach, 1805.

G″, a reading thought by G hardly inferior, or equal, or even preferable to that retained in the text.

G′, a less probable reading.

G°°, words probably to be omitted, yet retained by G in the text.

G°, a less probable omission.

G^pr, an addition made to the text by G as *probably* correct.

G^ph, an addition *perhaps* to be made to the text.

L, Lachmann, 1842–50.

T, Tischendorf, 1859.

Tr, Tregelles, Gospels 1857–61, Apocalypse 1844.

^b, words inclosed in brackets by L, T, or Tr, as of doubtful authority.

^m, a reading given in the margin by L or Tr, as worthy of regard.

S, the Sinaitic Manuscript.

St, the edition of R. Stephens, 1550.

B, that of Beza, 1565.

E, the Elzevir edition, 1624.

–, words omitted, or given as doubtful, by the authorities following.

om, words omitted by G, L, T, and by Tr in the Gospels and Apocalypse.

omS, the same, adding the Sinaitic Manuscript.

S^c, an omission in *S*, with the context. (See page 422, note.)

ap refers to the Appendix.

C, the Common Version, 1611.

marg., a marginal translation in C.

Gr., a literal rendering of the Greek in the margin of C.

lit., literally.

t, a translation occurring twice in the same verse.

tr, the same, thrice.

f, the same, four times. Larger numbers are given in full.

t, a Greek word occurring twice in the same verse, rendered but once.

A number of the verse in the Greek text differing from that in the Common Version, is added in a parenthesis.

This sign also denotes a word occurring in one of two similar phrases, given in one expression.

^c denotes that the sense of a translating word is derived partly from the context; thus, **be preferred**^c, fr. *γίνομαι* (become, come to be), borrows from the preceding word *ἔμπροσθεν*, **before**, John i. 15, 27, 30.

^cc, a change of construction; thus the noun *ἀκοή* (hearing) is rendered by the verb **hear**^cc, 1 Thes. ii. 13; and the verb **have**^cc often represents the verb *εἰμί* (belong to).

^p, a participle, rendered by or with the aid of an adverb, conjunction, adjective, noun, or demonstrative pronoun. Thus in *ἀκούω*, Matt. ii. 3^p, the participle (hearing) yields the phrase "when . . had heard." See also *ὤν*, from *εἰμί*, p. 117.

art., the article, *ὁ*, *ἡ*, *τό*.

CASES: — *Nom.*, Nominative. *Gen.*, Genitive. *Dat.*, Dative. *Acc.*, Accusative.

NUMBERS: — *Sing.*, Singular. *Plur.*, *Pl.*, *or* ^pl, Plural.

VOICES: — *Act.*, Active. *Pass.*, Passive. *Mid.*, Middle.

MODES: — *Ind.*, Indicative. *Imper.*, Imperative. *Subj.*, Subjunctive. *Opt.*, Optative. *Inf.*, Infinitive. *Part.*, Participle.

TENSES: — *Pres.*, Present. *Imp.*, Imperfect. *Aor.*, Aorist.

Other signs are explained in the articles in which they occur.

A CRITICAL
GREEK AND ENGLISH CONCORDANCE
OF THE
NEW TESTAMENT.

A, or ἄλφα (LTTr*S*).
Alpha, Rev. i. 8, 11(*ap*). xxi. 6. xxii. 13.

ἀβαρής.
from° being burdensome (*lit.* not burdensome), 2 Cor. xi. 9.

ἀββᾶ.
Abba, Mark xiv. 36. Rom. viii. 15. Gal. iv. 6.

ἄβυσσος.
bottomless pit, Rev. ix. 11. xi. 7. xvii. 8. xx. 1, 3.
bottomless, Rev. ix. 1, 2(*ap*).
deep, Luke viii. 31. Rom. x. 7.

ἀγαθοεργέω.
do good, 1 Tim. vi. 18.
Add Acts xiv. 17, ἀγαθουργέω for ἀγαθοποιέω, G″LT*S*.

ἀγαθοποιέω.
do good, Mark iii. 4. Luke vi. 9, 33*t*, 35. Acts xiv. 17(ἀγαθουργέω G″LT*S*). 3 John 11.
do well, 1 Pet. ii. 20p. iii. 6p.
with well doing, 1 Pet. ii. 15p.
for well doing, 1 Pet. iii. 17p.

ἀγαθοποιΐα.
well doing, 1 Pet. iv. 19.

ἀγαθοποιός.
that doeth well, 1 Pet. ii. 14.

ἀγαθός.
good, Matt. v. 45. vii. 11, 17, 18. xii. 35*t*. xix. 16(-G°°LTTr*S*), 17*t* (*ap*). xx. 15. xxii. 10. xxv. 21, 23. Mark x. 17, 18*t*. Luke vi. 45*t*. viii. 8, 15. x. 42. xi. 13. xviii. 18, 19*t*. xix. 17. xxiii. 50. John vii. 12. Acts ix. 36. xi. 24. xxiii. 1. Rom. v. 7. vii. 12. xii. 2. xiii. 3. 2 Cor. v. 10. ix. 8. Gal. vi. 10. Eph. ii. 10. iv. 29. Phil. i. 6. Col. i. 10. 1 Thes. iii. 6. 2 Thes. ii. 16, 17. 1 Tim. i. 5, 19. ii. 10. v. 10. 2 Tim. ii. 21. iii. 17. Tit. i. 16. ii. 5, 10. iii. 1. Heb. xiii. 21. Jas. i. 17. iii. 17. 1 Pet. ii. 18. iii. 10, 16*t*, 21.
good, *subst.*, John v. 29. Rom. ii. 10. iii. 8. vii. 19. viii. 28. ix. 11. xii. 21. xiii. 4. xiv. 16. xv. 2. Gal. vi. 10. 1 Pet. iii. 11.
With art., **that which is good**, Luke vi. 45. Rom. vii. 13*t*. xii. 9. xiii. 3. xvi. 19. 1 Thes. v. 15. 1 Pet. iii. 13. 3 John 11.—**the thing which is good**, Eph. iv. 28.
good thing, Matt. vii. 11. xii. 34, 35. xix. 16. Luke i. 53. xvi. 25. John i. 46(47). Rom. vii. 18. x. 15. Gal. vi. 6. Eph. vi. 8. Phm. 6. Heb. ix. 11. x. 1.
goods, Luke xii. 18, 19.
benefit, Phm. 14.
well,°° Rom. ii. 7.

ἀγαθουργέω. See ἀγαθοεργέω.

ἀγαθωσύνη.
goodness, Rom. xv. 14. Gal. v. 22. Eph. v. 9. 2 Thes. i. 11.

ἀγαλλίασις.
gladness, Luke i. 14. Acts ii. 46. Heb. i. 9.
joy, Luke i. 44.
exceeding joy, Jude 24.

ἀγαλλιάω, ἀγαλλιάομαι.

be glad, Acts ii. 26.

be exceeding glad, Matt. v. 12.

rejoice, Luke i. 47. x. 21. John v. 35. viii. 56. Acts xvi. 34. 1 Pet. i. 8. Rev. xix. 7.

greatly rejoice, 1 Pet. i. 6.

with exceeding joy, 1 Pet. iv. 13p.

ἄγαμος.

unmarried, 1 Cor. vii. 8, 11, 32, 34.

Add 1 Cor. vii. 34(..wife), G'LS.

ἀγανακτέω.

have indignation, Matt. xxvi. 8. Mark xiv. 4.

with indignation, Luke xiii. 14p.

be moved with indignation, Matt. xx. 24.

be much displeased, Mark x. 14, 41.

be sore displeased, Matt. xxi. 15.

ἀγανάκτησις.

indignation, 2 Cor. vii. 11.

ἀγαπάω.

to love, Matt. v. 43, 44, 46*t*. vi. 24. xix. 19. xxii. 37, 39. Mark x. 21. xii. 30, 31, 33*t*. Luke vi. 27, 32*f*, 35. vii. 5, 42, 47*t*. x. 27. xi. 43. xvi. 13. John iii. 16, 19, 35. viii. 42. x. 17. xi. 5. xii. 43. xiii. 1*t*, 23, 34*tr*. xiv. 15, 21*f*, 23*t*, 24, 28, 31. xv. 9*t*, 12*t*, 17. xvii. 23*t*, 24, 26. xix. 26. xxi. 7, 15, 16, 20. Rom. viii. 28, 37. ix. 13. xiii. 8*t*, 9. 1 Cor. ii. 9. viii. 3. 2 Cor. ix. 7. xi. 11. xii. 15*t*. Gal. ii. 20. v. 14. Eph. ii. 4. v. 2, 25*t*, 28*tr*, 33. vi. 24. Col. iii. 19. 1 Thes. iv. 9. 2 Thes. ii. 16. 2 Tim. iv. 8, 10. Heb. i. 9. xii. 6. Jas. i. 12. ii. 5, 8. 1 Pet. i. 8, 22. ii. 17. iii. 10. 2 Pet. ii. 15. 1 John ii. 10, 15*t*. iii. 10, 11, 14*t*, 18, 23. iv. 7*t*, 8, 10*t*, 11*t*, 12, 19*t*, 20*tr*, 21*t*. v. 1*t*, 2*t*. 2 John 1, 5. 3 John 1. Rev. i. 5. iii. 9. xii. 11.

beloved, Rom. ix. 25*t*. Eph. i. 6. Col. iii. 12. 1 Thes. i. 4. 2 Thes. ii. 13. Rev. xx. 9.

Add John v. 20, for φιλέω, Lm. Jude 1, for ἁγιάζω, G'LTS.

ἀγάπη.

love, Matt. xxiv. 12. Luke xi. 42. John v. 42. xiii. 35. xv. 9, 10*t*, 13. xvii. 26. Rom. v. 5, 8. viii. 35, 39. xii. 9. xiii. 10*t*. xv. 30. 1 Cor. iv. 21. xvi. 24. 2 Cor. ii. 4, 8. v. 14. vi. 6. viii. 7, 8, 24. xiii. 11, 14(13). Gal. v. 6, 13, 22. Eph. i. 4, 15 (–LS). ii. 4. iii. 17(18), 19. iv. 2, 15, 16. v. 2. vi. 23. Phil. i. 9, 17. ii. 1, 2. Col. i. 4, 8. ii. 2. 1 Thes. i. 3. iii. 12. v. 8, 13. 2 Thes. ii. 10. iii. 5. 1 Tim. i. 14. vi. 11. 2 Tim. i. 7, 13. Phm. 5, 7, 9. Heb. vi. 10. x. 24. 1 John ii. 5, 15. iii. 1, 16, 17. iv. 7, 8, 9, 10, 12, 16*tr*, 17, 18*tr*. v. 3. 2 John 3, 6. Jude 2, 21. Rev. ii. 4.

charity, 1 Cor. viii. 1. xiii. 1, 2, 3, 4*tr*, 8, 13*t*. xiv. 1. xvi. 14. Col. iii. 14. 1 Thes. iii. 6. 2 Thes. i. 3. 1 Tim. i. 5. ii. 15. iv. 12. 2 Tim. ii. 22. iii. 10. Tit. ii. 2. 1 Pet. iv. 8*t*. v. 14. 2 Pet. i. 7. 3 John 6. Rev. ii. 19.

feast of charity, Jude 12.

dear (*Gr.* of love), Col. i. 13.

With κατά, **charitably** (*Gr.* according to love), Rom. xiv. 15.

Add 2 Pet. ii. 13, for ἀπάτῃ, G'L.

ἀγαπητός.

beloved, Mat. iii. 17. xii. 18. xvii. 5. Mark i. 11. ix. 7. Luke iii. 22. ix. 35(ἐκλελεγμένος, see ἐκλέγομαι, G'LmTTrS). xx. 13. Acts xv. 25. Rom. i. 7. xi. 28. xvi. 8, 9, 12(*ap*). 1 Cor. iv. 14, 17. xv. 58. Eph. vi. 21. Phil. ii. 12. Col. iv. 7, 9, 14. 1 Tim. vi. 2. Phm. 2(ἀδελφῇ G''LS), 16. Heb. vi. 9. Jas. i. 16, 19. ii. 5. 1 Pet. iv. 12. 2 Pet. i. 17. iii. 1, 8, 14, 15, 17. 1 John iii. 2, 21. iv. 1, 7, 11. 3 John 2, 5, 11. Jude 3, 17, 20.

well-beloved, Mark xii. 6. Rom. xvi. 5. 3 John 1.

dearly beloved, Rom. xii. 19. 1 Cor. x. 14. 2 Cor. vii. 1. xii. 19. Phil. iv. 1*t*. 2 Tim. i. 2. Phm. 1. 1 Pet. ii. 11.

dear, Eph. v. 1. Col. i. 7. 1 Thes. ii. 8.

Add 1 John ii. 7, for ἀδελφός, GLT*S*.

ἀγγαρεύω.

compel to go, Matt. v. 41.
compel, Matt. xxvii. 32. Mark xv. 21.

ἀγγεῖον.

vessel, Matt. xiii. 48(ἄγγος TTr*S*). xxv. 4.

ἀγγελία.

message, 1 John iii. 11 (*marg.* **commandment).**
Add 1 John i. 5, for ἐπαγγελία, GLT.

ἀγγέλλω, bring word, tell.

John xx. 18, for ἀπαγγέλλω, LTTr*S*.

ἄγγελος.

messenger, Matt. xi. 10. Mark i. 2. Luke vii. 24, 27. ix. 52. 2 Cor. xii. 7. Jas. ii. 25.
angel, Matt. i. 20, 24. ii. 13, 19. iv. 6, 11. xiii. 39, 41, 49. xvi. 27. xviii. 10. xxii. 30. xxiv. 31, 36. xxv. 31, 41. xxvi. 53. xxviii. 2, 5. Mark i. 13. viii. 38. xii. 25. xiii. 27, 32. Luke i. 11, 13, 18, 19, 26, 28(–TTr[b]), 30, 34, 35, 38. ii. 9, 10, 13, 15, 21. iv. 10. ix. 26. xii. 8, 9. xv. 10. xvi. 22. xxii. 43(*ap*). xxiv. 23. John i. 51(52). v. 4(*ap*). xii. 29. xx. 12. Acts v. 19. vi. 15. vii. 30, 35, 38, 53. viii. 26. x. 3, 7, 22. xi. 13. xii. 7, 8, 9, 10, 11, 15, 23. xxiii. 8, 9. xxvii. 23.
Rom. viii. 38. 1 Cor. iv. 9. vi. 3. xi. 10. xiii. 1. 2 Cor. xi. 14. Gal. i. 8. iii. 19. iv. 14. Col. ii. 18. 2 Thes. i. 7. 1 Tim. iii. 16. v. 21. Heb. i. 4, 5, 6, 7*t*, 13. ii. 2, 5, 7, 9, 16. xii. 22. xiii. 2. 1 Pet. i. 12. iii. 22. 2 Pet. ii. 4, 11. Jude 6. Rev. i. 1, 20. ii. 1, 8, 12, 18. iii. 1, 5, 7, 14. v. 2, 11. vii. 1, 2*t*, 11. viii. 2, 3, 4, 5, 6, 7 (*omS*), 8, 10, 12, 13(ἀετός GLTTr*S*), 13. ix. 1, 11, 13, 14*t*, 15. x. 1, 5, 7, 8, 9, 10. xi. 1(*ap*), 15. xii. 7*t*, 9. xiv. 6, 8, 9, 10, 15, 17, 18, 19. xv. 1, 6, 7, 8. xvi. 1, 3(–G[∞]LTTr*S*), 4(*omS*), 5, 8(*om*), 10(*omS*), 12(*om S*), 17(*omS*). xvii. 1, 7. xviii. 1, 21. xix. 17. xx. 1. xxi. 9, 12(*ap*), 17. xxii. 6, 8, 16.

ἄγγος, vessel.

Matt. xiii. 48, for ἀγγεῖον, TTr*S*.

ἄγε, imper. of ἄγω.

go to, Jas. iv. 13. v. 1.

ἀγέλη.

herd, Matt. viii. 30, 31, 32(–GLTr *S*), 32. Mark v. 11, 13. Luke viii. 32, 33.

ἀγενεαλόγητος.

without descent (*Gr.* without pedigree), Heb. vii. 3.

ἀγενής.

base thing, 1 Cor. i. 28.

ἁγιάζω.

hallow, Matt. vi. 9. Luke xi. 2.
sanctify, Matt. xxiii. 17, 19. John x. 36. xvii. 17, 19*t*. Acts xx. 32. xxvi. 18. Rom. xv. 16. 1 Cor. i. 2. vi. 11. vii. 14*t*. Eph. v. 26. 1 Thes. v. 23. 1 Tim. iv. 5. 2 Tim. ii. 21. Heb. ii. 11*t*. ix. 13. x. 10, 14, 29. xiii. 12. 1 Pet. iii. 15. Jude 1(ἀγαπάω G'LT*S*).
Pass., **be holy,** Rev. xxii. 11.

ἁγιασμός.

holiness, Rom. vi. 19, 22. 1 Thes. iv. 7. 1 Tim. ii. 15. Heb. xii. 14.
sanctification, 1 Cor. i. 30. 1 Thes. iv. 3, 4. 2 Thes. ii. 13. 1 Pet. i. 2.

ἅγιος.

holy, Matt. iv. 5. vii. 6. xxiv. 15. xxv. 31(*omS*). xxvii. 53. Mark vi. 20. viii. 38. Luke i. 49, 70, 72. ii. 23. ix. 26. John xvii. 11. Acts iii. 21. iv. 27, 30. vi. 13. vii. 33. x. 22. xxi. 28. Rom. i. 2. vii. 12*t*. xi. 16*t*. xii. 1. xvi. 16. 1 Cor. iii. 17. vii. 14, 34. xvi. 20. 2 Cor. xiii. 12. Eph. i. 4. ii. 21. iii. 5. v. 27. Col. i. 22. iii. 12. 1 Thes. v. 26, 27(–G[∞]L*S*). 2 Tim. i. 9. Heb. iii. 1. 1 Pet. i. 15*t*, 16*t*. ii. 5, 9. iii. 5. 2 Pet. i. 18, 21 (ἀπό T). ii. 21. iii. 2, 11. Jude 20. Rev. iii. 7. iv. 8*tr*. vi. 10. xi. 2. xiv. 10(–G[∞]T). xviii. 20. xx. 6. xxi. 2, 10. xxii. 6 (πνευμάτων τῶν GLTTr*S*), 11, 19.
Holy One, Mark i. 24. Luke iv. 34. Acts iii. 14. 1 John ii. 20.

Neut., **holy thing**, Luke i. 35. — **holy place**, Heb. ix. 12^{pl}, 24, 25^{pl}. — **sanctuary**, Heb. viii. 2^{pl} (*marg.* **holy things**). ix. 1, 2^{pl} (*marg.* **holy**; *ἁγία* St, *ἅγια. ἁγίων* L). xiii. 11^{pl}.

ἅγια, **holiest**, Heb. x. 19. — **holiest of all**, Heb. ix. 8.

ἅγια ἁγίων, **Holiest of all**, Heb. ix. 3.

With πνεῦμα, **Holy Ghost**, Matt. i. 18, 20. iii. 11. xii. 32. xxviii. 19. Mark i. 8. iii. 29. xii. 36. xiii. 11. Luke i. 15, 35, 41, 67. ii. 25, 26. iii. 16, 22. iv. 1. xii. 10, 12. John i. 33. vii. 39(–G^{oo}LTTr^{b}*S*). xiv. 26. xx. 22. Acts i. 2, 5, 8, 16. ii. 4, 33, 38. iv. 8, 31. v. 3, 32. vi. 3(*omS*), 5. vii. 51, 55. viii. 15, 17, 18(–LT*S*), 19. ix. 17, 31. x. 38, 44, 45, 47. xi. 15, 16, 24. xiii. 2, 4, 9, 52. xv. 8, 28. xvi. 6. xix. 2*t*, 6. xx. 23, 28. xxi. 11. xxviii. 25. Rom. v. 5. ix. 1. xiv. 17. xv. 13, 16. 1 Cor. ii. 13 (*omS*). vi. 19. xii. 3. 2 Cor. vi. 6. xiii. 14(13). 1 Thes. i. 5, 6. 2 Tim. i. 14. Tit. iii. 5. Heb. ii. 4. iii. 7. vi. 4. ix. 8. x. 15. 1 Pet. i. 12. 2 Pet. i. 21. 1 John v. 7(*ap*). Jude 20. — **Holy Spirit**, Luke xi. 13. Eph. i. 13. iv. 30. 1 Thes. iv. 8.

saint, Phil. iv. 21.

Plural, **saints**, Matt. xxvii. 52. Acts ix. 13, 32, 41. xxvi. 10. Rom. i. 7. viii. 27. xii. 13. xv. 25, 26, 31. xvi. 2, 15. 1 Cor. i. 2. vi. 1, 2. xiv. 33. xvi. 1, 15. 2 Cor. i. 1. viii. 4. ix. 1, 12. xiii. 13(12). Eph. i. 1, 15, 18. ii. 19. iii. 8(–G^{o}), 18. iv. 12. v. 3. vi. 18. Phil. i. 1. iv. 22. Col. i. 2, 4, 12, 26. 1 Thes. iii. 13. 2 Thes. i. 10. 1 Tim. v. 10. Phm. 5, 7. Heb. vi. 10. xiii. 24. Jude 3, 14. Rev. v. 8. viii. 3, 4. xi. 18. xiii. 7(*ap*), 10. xiv. 12. xv. 3(*ἔθνος* GLTTr, *αἰών* G'*S*). xvi. 6. xvii. 6. xviii. 24. xix. 8. xx. 9.

Add Luke x. 21(. . Spirit), LTr*S*. John vi. 69(*ap*). Acts iv. 25(*ap*). Rom. xv. 19, for *θεοῦ*, GL(–G^{oo}). Rev. xv. 4, *see ὅσιος*. xxii. 21, for *ὑμῶν*, GTr*S*(–G^{o}).

ἁγιότης.

holiness, Heb. xii. 10.

Add 2 Cor. i. 12, for *ἁπλότης*, L*S*.

ἁγιωσύνη.

holiness, Rom. i. 4. 2 Cor. vii. 1. 1 Thes. iii. 13.

ἀγκάλαι.

arms, Luke ii. 28.

ἄγκιστρον.

hook, Matt. xvii. 27.

ἄγκυρα.

anchor, Acts xxvii. 29, 30, 40. Heb. vi. 19.

ἄγναφος.

new (*marg.* **raw**, *or* **unwrought**), Matt. ix. 16. Mark ii. 21.

ἁγνεία.

purity, 1 Tim. iv. 12. v. 2.

ἁγνίζω.

purify, John xi. 55. Acts xxi. 24, 26. xxiv. 18. Jas. iv. 8. 1 Pet. i. 22. 1 John iii. 3.

ἁγνισμός.

purification, Acts xxi. 26.

ἀγνοέω.

know not, Acts xiii. 27^{p}. Rom. ii. 4. vi. 3. vii. 1.

unknown, 2 Cor. vi. 9. Gal. i. 22.

understand not, Mark ix. 32. Luke ix. 45. 2 Pet. ii. 12.

be ignorant, Rom. x. 3. xi. 25. 1 Cor. x. 1. xiv. 38*t*. 2 Cor. ii. 11. 1 Thes. iv. 13.

ignorant, Rom. i. 13^{inf}. 1 Cor. xii. 1^{inf}. 2 Cor. i. 8^{inf}. Heb. v. 2^{p}.

ignorantly, Acts xvii. 23^{p}. 1 Tim. i. 13^{p}.

ἀγνόημα.

error, Heb. ix. 7.

ἄγνοια.

ignorance, Acts iii. 17. xvii. 30. Eph. iv. 18. 1 Pet. i. 14.

ἁγνός.

pure, Phil. iv. 8. 1 Tim. v. 22. Jas. iii. 17. 1 John iii. 3.

clear, 2 Cor. vii. 11.

chaste, 2 Cor. xi. 2. Tit. ii. 5. 1 Pet. iii. 2.

ἁγνότης.
pureness, 2 Cor. vi. 6.
Add 2 Cor. xi. 3 (simplicity, καί τῆς ἁγνότητος), L*S*.

ἁγνῶς.
sincerely, Phil. i. 16.

ἀγνωσία.
not knowledge, 1 Cor. xv. 34.
ignorance, 1 Pet. ii. 15.

ἄγνωστος.
unknown, Acts xvii. 23.

ἀγορά.
market, Matt. xi. 16. xxiii. 7. Mark vii. 4. Luke xi. 43. xx. 46. Acts xvii. 17.
market-place, Matt. xx. 3. Mark xii. 38. Luke vii. 32. Acts xvi. 19 (*marg.* **court**).
street, Mark vi. 56.

ἀγοράζω.
buy, Matt. xiii. 44, 46. xiv. 15. xxi. 12. xxv. 9, 10. xxvii. 7. Mark vi. 36, 37. xi. 15. xv. 46. xvi. 1. Luke ix. 13. xiv. 18, 19. xvii. 28. xix. 45(*ap*). xxii. 36. John iv. 8. vi. 5. xiii. 29. 1 Cor. vi. 20. vii. 23, 30. 2 Pet. ii. 1. Rev. iii. 18. xiii. 17. xviii. 11.
redeem, Rev. v. 9. xiv. 3, 4 (*Gr.* buy).

ἀγοραῖος, or ἀγόραιος.
of the baser sort, Acts xvii. 5.
law (*marg.* **court days**), Acts xix. 38.

ἄγρα.
draught, Luke v. 4, 9.

ἀγράμματος.
unlearned, Acts iv. 13.

ἀγραυλέω.
abide in the field, Luke ii. 8.

ἀγρεύω.
catch, Mark xii. 13.

ἀγριέλαιος.
wild olive tree, Rom. xi. 17.
olive tree which is wild, Rom. xi. 24.

ἄγριος.
wild, Matt. iii. 4. Mark i. 6.
raging, Jude 13.

ἀγρός.
country, Mark v. 14. vi. 36, 56. xv. 21. xvi. 12(*ap*). Luke viii. 34. ix. 12. xxiii. 26.
field, Matt. vi. 28, 30. xiii. 24, 27, 31, 36, 38, 44*t*. xxiv. 18, 40. xxvii. 7, 8*t*, 10. Mark xiii. 16. Luke xii. 28. xv. 15. 25. xvii. 7, 31, 36(*ap*).
farm, Matt. xxii. 5.
land, Matt. xix. 29. Mark x. 29, 30. Acts iv. 37.
piece of ground, Luke xiv. 18.
Add Mark xi. 8, for δένδρον, TTr*S*.

ἀγρυπνέω.
to watch, Mark xiii. 33. Luke xxi. 36. Eph. vi. 18. Heb. xiii. 17.

ἀγρυπνία.
watching, 2 Cor. vi. 5. xi. 27.

ἄγω.
lead, Mark xiii. 11. Luke iv. 1, 29. xxii. 54. xxiii. 1, 32. John xviii. 28. Acts viii. 32. Rom. ii. 4. viii. 14. 1 Cor. xii. 2. Gal. v. 18.
lead away, 2 Tim. iii. 6.
bring, Matt. x. 18. xxi. 2, 7. Mark xi. 2 (φέρω G″TTr*S*), 7 (φέρω G″T Tr). Luke iv. 9, 40. x. 34. xviii. 40. xix. 27, 30, 35. xxi. 12 (ἀπάγω TTr*S*). John i. 42(43). vii. 45. viii. 3(*ap*). ix. 13. x. 16. xix. 4, 13. Acts v. 21, 26, 27ᵖ. vi. 12. ix. 2, 21, 27. xi. 26(25). xvii. 5(προάγω L*S*), 15, 19. xviii. 12. xix. 37. xx. 12. xxi. 16. xxii. 5, 24(εἰσάγω GLT *S*). xxiii. 10, 18*t*, 31. xxv. 6. 1 Thes. iv. 14. 2 Tim. iv. 11. Heb. ii. 10.
bring forth, Acts xxv. 17, 23.
carry, Acts xxi. 34.
Mid. **go**, Matt. xxvi. 46. Mark i. 38. xiv. 42. John xi. 7, 15, 16. xiv. 31.
beᶜᶜ, Luke xxiv. 21.
keep, Matt. xiv. 6(γίνομαι G″LTTr *S*).
be open (*marg.* **be kept**), Acts xix. 38.
Add Mark xv. 20, for ἐξάγω, L. John xviii. 13, for ἀπάγω, LTr*S*.

xix. 16, for ἀπάγω, G. Acts xiii. 23, for ἐγείρω, GLTS.
See also ἄγε.

ἀγωγή.

manner of life, 2 Tim. iii. 10.

ἀγών.

conflict, Phil. i. 30. Col. ii. 1(*marg.* **fear**, or **care**).
contention, 1 Thes. ii. 2.
fight, 1 Tim. vi. 12. 2 Tim. iv. 7.
race, Heb. xii. 1.

ἀγωνία.

agony, Luke xxii. 44(*ap*).

ἀγωνίζομαι.

strive, Luke xiii. 24. 1 Cor. ix. 25. Col. i. 29.
fight, John xviii. 36. 1 Tim. vi. 12. 2 Tim. iv. 7.
labor fervently (*marg.* **strive**), Col. iv. 12.
Add 1 Tim. iv. 10, for ὀνειδίζω, G′LS.

ἀδάπανος.

without charge, 1 Cor. ix. 18.

ἀδελφή.

sister, Matt. xii. 50. xiii. 56. xix. 29. Mark iii. 35. vi. 3. x. 29, 30. Luke x. 39, 40. xiv. 26. John xi. 1, 3, 5, 28, 39. xix. 25. Acts xxiii. 16. Rom. xvi. 1, 15. 1 Cor. vii. 15. ix. 5. 1 Tim. v. 2. Jas. ii. 15. 2 John 13.
Add Mark iii. 32(*ap*). Phm. 2, for ἀγαπητῇ, G′′LS.

ἀδελφός.

brother, *pl.* **brethren**, Matt. i. 2, 11. iv. 18*t*, 21*t*. v. 22*t*, 23, 24, 47(φίλος G′). vii. 3, 4, 5. x. 2*t*, 21*t*. xii. 46, 47, 48, 49, 50. xiii. 55. xiv. 3. xvii. 1. xviii. 15*t*, 21, 35. xix. 29. xx. 24. xxii. 24*t*, 25*t*. xxiii. 8. xxv. 40 (L[b]). xxviii. 10. Mark i. 16, 19. iii. 17, 31, 32, 33, 34, 35. v. 37. vi. 3, 17, 18. x. 29, 30. xii. 19*tr*, 20. xiii. 12*t*. Luke iii. 1, 19. vi. 14, 41, 42*tr*. viii. 19, 20, 21. xii. 13. xiv. 12, 26. xv. 27, 32. xvi. 28. xvii. 3. xviii. 29. xx. 28*tr*, 29. xxi. 16. xxii. 32. John i. 40(41), 41 (42). ii. 12. vi. 8. vii. 3, 5, 10. xi. 2, 19, 21, 23, 32. xx. 17. xxi. 23. Acts i. 14, 16. ii. 29, 37. iii. 17, 22. vi. 3(–L). vii. 2, 13, 23, 25, 26, 37. ix. 17, 30. x. 23. xi. 1, 12, 29. xii. 2, 17. xiii. 15, 26, 38. xiv. 2. xv. 1, 3, 7, 13, 22, 23*t*, 32, 33, 36, 40. xvi. 2, 40. xvii. 6, 10, 14. xviii. 18, 27. xx. 32(–G°LTS). xxi. 7, 17, 20. xxii. 1, 5, 13. xxiii. 1, 5, 6. xxviii. 14, 15, 17, 21.
Rom. i. 13. vii. 1. 4. viii. 12, 29. ix. 3. x. 1. xi. 25. xii. 1. xiv. 10*t*, 13, 15, 21. xv. 14, 15(–LS), 30 (–T). xvi. 14, 17, 23. 1 Cor. i. 1, 10, 11, 26. ii. 1. iii. 1. iv. 6. v. 11. vi. 5, 6, 8. vii. 12, 15, 24, 29. viii. 11, 12, 13*t*. ix. 5. x. 1. xi. 2(–LS), 33; xii. 1. xiv. 6, 20, 26, 39. xv. 1, 6, 50, 58. xvi. 11, 12*t*, 15, 20. 2 Cor. i. 1, 8. ii. 13(12). viii. 1, 18, 22, 23. ix. 3, 5. xi. 9. xii. 18. xiii. 11. Gal. i. 2, 11, 19. iii. 15. iv. 12, 28, 31. v. 11, 13. vi. 1, 18. Eph. vi. 10(–G°LTS), 21, 23. Phil. i. 12, 14. ii. 25. iii. 1, 13, 17. iv. 1, 8, 21. Col. i. 1, 2. iv. 7, 9, 15. 1 Thes. i. 4. ii. 1, 9, 14, 17. iii. 2, 7. iv. 1, 6, 10*t*, 13. v. 1, 4, 12, 14, 25, 26, 27. 2 Thes. i. 3. ii. 1, 13, 15. iii. 1, 6*t*, 13, 15. 1 Tim. iv. 6. v. 1. vi. 2. 2 Tim. iv. 21. Phm. 1, 7, 16, 20.
Heb. ii. 11, 12, 17. iii. 1, 12. vii. 5. viii. 11. x. 19. xiii. 22, 23. Jas. i. 2, 9, 16, 19. ii. 1, 5, 14, 15. iii. 1, 10, 12. iv. 11*tr*. v. 7, 9, 10, 12, 19. 1 Pet. v. 12. 2 Pet. i. 10. iii. 15. 1 John ii. 7(ἀγαπητός GLTS), 9, 10, 11. iii. 10, 12*t*, 13, 14, 14(–LTS), 15, 16, 17. iv. 20*t*, 21. v. 16. 3 John 3, 5, 10. Jude 1. Rev. i. 9. vi. 11. xii. 10. xix. 10. xxii. 9.
Add Acts i. 15, for μαθητής, G′LTS. 1 Cor. vii. 14, for ἀνήρ, LTS. xv. 31 (rejoicing, ἀδελφοί), LTS.

ἀδελφότης.

brotherhood, 1 Pet. ii. 17.
brethren, 1 Pet. v. 9.

ἄδηλος.
which appears not, Luke xi. 44.
uncertain, 1 Cor. xiv. 8.

ἀδηλότης.
uncertain (*Gr.* uncertainty), 1 Tim. vi. 17.

ἀδήλως.
uncertainly, 1 Cor. ix. 26.

ἀδημονέω.
be very heavy, Matt. xxvi. 37. Mark xiv. 33.
be full of heaviness, Phil. ii. 26.

ᾅδης.
hell, Matt. xi. 23. xvi. 18. Luke x. 15. xvi. 23. Acts ii. 27, 31. Rev. i. 18. vi. 8. xx. 13(*marg.* **grave**), 14.
grave, 1 Cor. xv. 55 (*marg.* **hell**; *θάνατος* LTS).
Add Acts ii. 24, for *θάνατος*, G′.

ἀδιάκριτος.
without partiality (*marg.* **without wrangling**), Jas. iii. 17.

ἀδιάλειπτος.
without ceasing, 2 Tim. i. 3.
continual, Rom. ix. 2.

ἀδιαλείπτως.
without ceasing, Rom. i. 9. 1 Thes. i. 3. ii. 13. v. 17.

ἀδιαφθορία.
uncorruptness, Tit. ii. 7 (ἀφθορία G′LTS).

ἀδικέω.
wrong, 2 Cor. vii. 2. Phm. 18.
do wrong, Matt. xx. 13. Acts vii. 26, 27. xxv. 10. 1 Cor. vi. 8. 2 Cor. vii. 12. Col. iii. 25*t*.
Pass., **suffer wrong,** Acts vii. 24. 2 Cor. vii. 12.
Mid., **take wrong,** 1 Cor. vi. 7.
be unjust, Rev. xxii. 11*t*.
be an offender, Acts xxv. 11.
injure, Gal. iv. 12.
hurt, Luke x. 19. Rev. ii. 11. vi. 6. vii. 2, 3, ix. 4, 10, 19. xi. 5*t*.

ἀδίκημα.
matter of wrong, Acts xviii. 14.
evil doing, Acts xxiv. 20.
iniquity, Rev. xviii. 5.

ἀδικία.
wrong, 2 Cor. xii. 13.
unjust (*lit.* of injustice), Luke xvi. 8. xviii. 6.
unrighteousness, Luke xvi. 9. John vii. 18. Rom. i. 18*t*, 29. ii. 8. iii. 5. vi. 13. ix. 14. 2 Thes. ii. 10, 12. Heb. viii. 12. 2 Pet. ii. 13, 15. 1 John i. 9. v. 17.
iniquity, Luke xiii. 27. Acts i. 18. viii. 23. 1 Cor. xiii. 6. 2 Tim. ii. 19. Jas. iii. 6.
Add Matt. xxiii. 25, for ἀκρασία, G.

ἄδικος.
unjust, Matt. v. 45. Luke xvi. 10*t*. xviii. 11. Acts xxiv. 15. 1 Cor. vi. 1. 1 Pet. iii. 18. 2 Pet. ii. 9.
unrighteous, Luke xvi. 11. Rom. iii. 5. 1 Cor. vi. 9. Heb. vi. 10.

ἀδίκως.
wrongfully, 1 Pet. ii. 19.

ἀδόκιμος.
reprobate, Rom. i. 28(*marg.* **void of judgment**). 2 Cor. xiii. 5, 6, 7. 2 Tim. iii. 8(*marg.* **of no judgment**). Tit. i. 16(*marg.* **void of judgment**).
rejected, Heb. vi. 8.
castaway, 1 Cor. ix. 27.

ἄδολος.
sincere, 1 Pet. ii. 2.

ἁδρότης.
abundance, 2 Cor. viii. 20.

ἀδυνατέω.
be impossible, Matt. xvii. 20. Luke i. 37.

ἀδύνατος.
weak, Rom. xv. 1.
impotent, Acts xiv. 8.
not possible, Heb. x. 4.
impossible, Matt. xix. 26. Mark x. 27. Luke xviii. 27. Heb. vi. 4, 18. xi. 6.
τὸ ἀδ. τοῦ νόμου, **what the law could not do,** Rom. viii. 3.

ᾄδω.
sing, Eph. v. 19. Col. iii. 16. Rev. v. 9. xiv. 3. xv. 3.

ἀεί.

ever, Mark xv. 8.
alway, 2 Cor. iv. 11. vi. 10. Tit. i. 12. Heb. iii. 10.
always, Acts vii. 51. 1 Pet. iii. 15. 2 Pet. i. 12.

ἀετός.

eagle, Matt. xxiv. 28. Luke xvii. 37. Rev. iv. 7. xii. 14.
Add Rev. viii. 13, for ἄγγελος, GL TTr*S*.

ἄζυμος.

unleavened, 1 Cor. v. 7.
unleavened bread, Matt. xxvi. 17. Mark xiv. 1, 12. Luke xxii. 1, 7. Acts xii. 3. xx. 6. 1 Cor. v. 8.

ἀήρ.

air, Acts xxii. 23 (οὐρανός G'). 1 Cor. ix. 26. xiv. 9. Eph. ii. 2. 1 Thes. iv. 17. Rev. ix. 2. xvi. 17.

ἀθανασία.

immortality, 1 Cor. xv. 53, 54. 1 Tim. vi. 16.

ἀθέμιτος.

unlawful thing, Acts x. 28.
abominable, 1 Pet. iv. 3.

ἄθεος.

without God, Eph. ii. 12.

ἄθεσμος.

wicked, 2 Pet. ii. 7. iii. 17.

ἀθετέω.

reject, Mark vi. 26. vii. 9(*marg.* **frustrate**). Luke vii. 30(*marg.* **frustrate**). John xii. 48.
cast off, 1 Tim. v. 12.
despise, Luke x. 16*f*. 1 Thes. iv. 8*t*(*marg.* **reject**). Heb. x. 28. Jude 8.
bring to nothing, 1 Cor. i. 19.
disannul, Gal. iii. 15.
frustrate, Gal. ii. 21.

ἀθέτησις.

put away[oo], Heb. ix. 26.
disannulling, Heb. vii. 18.

ἀθλέω.

strive, 2 Tim. ii. 5*t*.

ἄθλησις.

fight, Heb. x. 32.

ἀθροίζω, gather together.

Luke xxiv. 33, for συναθροίζω, LTTr*S*.

ἀθυμέω.

be discouraged, Col. iii. 21.

ἀθῷος, ἀθῷος LT.

innocent, Matt. xxvii. 4(*ap*), 24.

αἴγειος.

With δέρμα, **goatskin**, Heb. xi. 37.

αἰγιαλός.

shore, Matt. xiii. 2, 48. John xxi. 4. Acts xxi. 5. xxvii. 39, 40.

ἀΐδιος.

everlasting, Jude 6.
eternal, Rom. i. 20.

αἰδώς.

shamefacedness, 1 Tim. ii. 9.
reverence, Heb. xii. 28(δέος G''LT*S*).

αἷμα.

blood, Matt. xvi. 17. xxiii. 30, 35*tr*. xxvi. 28. xxvii. 4, 6, 8, 24, 25. Mark v. 25, 29. xiv. 24. Luke viii. 43, 44. xi. 50, 51*t*. xiii. 1. xxii. 20, 44(*ap*). John i. 13. vi. 53, 54, 55, 56. xix. 34. Acts i. 19. ii. 19, 20. v. 28. xv. 20, 29. xvii. 26 (–G°L*S*). xviii. 6. xx. 26, 28. xxi. 25. xxii. 20. Rom. iii. 15, 25. v. 9. 1 Cor. x. 16. xi. 25, 27. xv. 50. Gal. i. 16. Eph. i. 7. ii. 13. vi. 12. Col. i. 14(*ap*), 20. Heb. ii. 14. ix. 7, 12*t*, 13, 14, 18, 19, 20, 21, 22, 25. x. 4, 19, 29. xi. 28. xii. 4, 24. xiii. 11, 12, 20. 1 Pet. i. 2, 19. 1 John i. 7. v. 6*t*, 8. Rev. i. 5. v. 9. vi. 10, 12. vii. 14. viii. 7, 8. xi. 6. xii. 11. xiv. 20. xvi. 3, 4, 6*t*. xvii. 6*t*. xviii. 24. xix. 2, 13.

αἱματεκχυσία.

shedding of blood, Heb. ix. 22.

αἱμοῤῥοέω.

diseased with an issue of blood, Matt. ix. 20.

αἴνεσις.

praise, Heb. xiii. 15.

αἰνέω.

to praise, Luke ii. 13, 20. xix. 37.

xxiv. 53(*ap*). Acts ii. 47. iii. 8, 9. Rom. xv. 11. Rev. xix. 5.

αἴνιγμα.

With ἐν, **darkly** (*Gr.* in a riddle), 1 Cor. xiii. 12.

αἶνος.

praise, Matt. xxi. 16. Luke xviii. 43.

αἱρέομαι.

choose, Phil. i. 22. 2 Thes. ii. 13. Heb. xi. 25.

αἵρεσις.

sect, Acts v. 17. xv. 5. xxiv. 5. xxvi. 5. xxviii. 22.

heresy, Acts xxiv. 14. 1 Cor. xi. 19(*marg.* **sect**). Gal. v. 20. 2 Pet. ii. 1.

αἱρετίζω.

choose, Matt. xii. 18.

αἱρετικός.

that is an heretic, Tit. iii. 10.

αἴρω.

take up, Matt. ix. 6. xiv. 12, 20. xv. 37. xvi. 24. xvii. 27. Mark ii. 9, 11, 12. vi. 29, 43. viii. 8, 19, 20, 34. x. 21(-G∞LbTr*S*). xiii. 16. xvi. 18(*ap*). Luke v. 24, 25. ix. 17, 23(*ap*). xix. 21, 22. John v. 8, 9, 11, 12. viii. 59. Acts xx. 9. xxvii. 17. Rev. xviii. 21.

lift up, Luke xvii. 13. John xi. 41. Acts iv. 24. Rev. x. 5.

bear, Matt. xxvii. 32. Mark ii. 3. xv. 21.

bear up, Matt. iv. 6. Luke iv. 11.

carry, John v. 10.

take away, Matt. xiii. 12. xxii. 13 (-G″LTr*S*). xxiv. 39. xxv. 29. Mark ii. 21. iv. 15. Luke vi. 29, 30. viii. 12. xi. 52. xvii. 31. xix. 26. John i. 29(*marg.* **bear**). xi. 39, 41, 48. xv. 2. xix. 31, 38. xx. 1, 2, 13, 15. Acts viii. 33. 1 John iii. 5.

away with, Luke xxiii. 18. John xix. 15*t*. Acts xxi. 36. xxii. 22.

put away, Eph. iv. 31.

remove, Matt. xxi. 21. Mark xi. 23.

take, Matt. ix. 16. xi. 29. xx. 14. xxi. 43. xxiv. 17, 18. xxv. 28. Mark iv. 25. vi. 8. xiii. 15. xv. 24. Luke viii. 18. ix. 3. xi. 22. xix. 24. xxii. 36. John ii. 16. x. 18. xvi. 22. xvii. 15. xix. 38. Acts viii. 33. xxi. 11. 1 Cor. vi. 15. Col. ii. 24.

loose, Acts xxvii. 13.

With ψυχή, **make to doubt** (*marg.* **hold in suspense**), John x. 24.

Add Matt. x. 38, for λαμβάνω, Lm. John i. 36(*ap*). 1 Cor. v. 2, for ἐξαίρω, GLT*S*.

αἰσθάνομαι.

perceive, Luke ix. 45.

αἴσθησις.

judgment (*marg.* **sense**), Phil. i. 9.

αἰσθητήριον.

senses, Heb. v. 14.

αἰσχροκερδής.

greedy of filthy lucre, 1 Tim. iii. 3 (-GLT*S*), 8.

given to filthy lucre, Tit. i. 7.

αἰσχροκερδῶς.

for filthy lucre, 1 Pet. v. 2.

αἰσχρολογία.

filthy communication, Col. iii. 8.

αἰσχρός.

shame, 1 Cor. xi. 6. xiv. 35. Eph. v. 12.

filthy, Tit. i. 11.

αἰσχρότης.

filthiness, Eph. v. 4.

αἰσχύνη.

shame, Luke xiv. 9. Phil. iii. 19. Heb. xii. 2. Jude 13. Rev. iii. 18.

dishonesty (*Gr.* shame), 2 Cor. iv. 2.

αἰσχύνομαι.

be ashamed, Luke xvi. 3. 2 Cor. x. 8. Phil. i. 20. 1 Pet. iv. 16. 1 John ii. 28.

αἰτέω.

ask, Matt. v. 42. vi. 8. vii. 7, 8, 9, 10, 11. xiv. 7. xviii. 19. xx. 22. xxi. 22. xxvii. 20. Mark vi. 22, 23, 24, 25. x. 38. Luke i. 63. vi. 30.

xi. 9, 10, 11, 12, 13. xii. 48. John iv. 9, 10. xi. 22. xiv. 13, 14. xv. 7, 16. xvi. 23, 24*t*, 26. Acts iii. 2. Eph. iii. 20. Jas. i. 5, 6. iv. 2, 3*t*. 1 Pet. iii. 15. 1 John iii. 22. v. 14, 15, 16.

crave, Mark xv. 43.

beg, Matt. xxvii. 58. Luke xxiii. 52.

desire, Matt. xx. 20. Mark x. 35. xi. 24. xv. 6, 8. Luke xxiii. 25. Acts iii. 14. vii. 46. ix. 2. xii. 20. xiii. 21, 28. xxv. 3, 15. Eph. iii. 13. Col. i. 9. 1 John v. 15.

call for, Acts xvi. 29.

require, Luke xxiii. 23. 1 Cor. i. 22.

αἴτημα.

request, Phil. iv. 6.

require[cc], Luke xxiii. 24.

petition, 1 John v. 15.

αἰτία.

cause, Matt. xix. 3. Luke viii. 47. Acts x. 21. xiii. 28. xxiii. 28. xxviii. 18, 20. 2 Tim. i. 12. Heb. ii. 11.

With δι' ἥν, **wherefore**, Acts xxii. 24. 2 Tim. i. 6. Tit. i. 13.

case, Matt. xix. 10.

accusation, Matt. xxvii. 37. Mark xv. 26. Acts xxv. 18.

crime, Acts xxv. 27.

fault, John xviii. 38. xix. 4, 6.

αἰτίαμα.

complaint, Acts xxv. 7(*ap*).

αἴτιον.

cause, Luke xxiii. 22. Acts xix. 40.

fault, Luke xxiii. 4, 14.

αἴτιος.

author, Heb. v. 9.

αἰτίωμα. See αἰτίαμα.

αἰφνίδιος.

sudden, 1 Thes. v. 3.

unawares, Luke xxi. 34.

αἰχμαλωσία.

captivity, Eph. iv. 8(*marg.* **multitude of captives**). Rev. xiii. 10*t*.

αἰχμαλωτεύω.

lead captive, Eph. iv. 8. 2 Tim. iii. 6(αἰχμαλωτίζω GLT*S*).

αἰχμαλωτίζω.

lead away captive, Luke xxi. 24.

bring into captivity, Rom. vii. 23. 2 Cor. x. 5.

Add 2 Tim. iii. 6, for αἰχμαλωτεύω, GLT*S*.

αἰχμάλωτος.

captive, Luke iv. 18(19).

αἰών.

age, Eph. ii. 7. Col. i. 26.

course, Eph. ii. 2.

world, Matt. xii. 32. xiii. 22, 39, 40, 49. xxiv. 3. xxviii. 20. Mark iv. 19. x. 30. Luke xvi. 8. xviii. 30. xx. 34, 35. Rom. xii. 2. 1 Cor. i. 20. ii. 6*t*, 7[pl], 8. iii. 18. x. 11[pl]. 2 Cor. iv. 4. Gal. i. 4. Eph. i. 21. vi. 12 (-GLT*S*). 1 Tim. vi. 17. 2 Tim. iv. 10. Tit. ii. 12. Heb. i. 2. vi. 5. ix. 26[pl]. xi. 3.

eternal (*lit.* of the ages), Eph. iii. 11[pl]. 1 Tim. i. 17[pl].

With ἀπό, **since the world began**, Luke i. 70. Acts iii. 21(-G[oo]).—**from the beginning of the world**, Acts xv. 18. Eph. iii. 9[pl].

With ἐκ, **since the world began**, John ix. 32.

With εἰς, **for ever**, Matt. vi. 13[pl](*ap*). xxi. 19. Mark xi. 14. Luke i. 33[pl], 55(G', ἕως αἰῶνος G). John vi. 51, 58. viii. 35*t*. xii. 34. xiv. 16. Rom. i. 25[pl]. ix. 5[pl]. xi. 36[pl]. xvi. 27[pl]. 2 Cor. ix. 9. Heb. v. 6. vi. 20. vii. 17, 21. xiii. 8[pl]. 1 Pet. i. 23(*omS*), 25. 2 Pet. ii. 17(-G[oo]LT*S*). 1 John ii. 17. 2 John 2. Jude 13.—**for evermore**, 2 Cor. xi. 31[pl]. Heb. vii. 28.—**ever**, Heb. vii. 24.—**while the world standeth**, 1 Cor. viii. 13.

εἰς τὸν αἰῶνα τοῦ αἰῶνος, **for ever and ever**, Heb. i. 8.

εἰς αἰῶνας αἰώνων, **for ever and ever**, Rev. xiv. 11.

εἰς τοὺς αἰῶνας τῶν αἰώνων, **for ever and ever**, Gal. i. 5. Phil. iv. 20. 1 Tim.

i. 17. 2 Tim. iv. 18. Heb. xiii. 21 (–τῶν αἰ. G∞T). 1 Pet. iv. 11. v. 11 (–τῶν αἰ. T). Rev. i. 6(–τῶν αἰ. TS). iv. 9, 10. v. 13, 14(ap). vii. 12. x. 6. xi. 15. xv. 7. xix. 3. xx. 10. xxii. 5.—**for evermore**, Rev. i. 18.

τοῦ αἰῶνος τῶν αἰώνων, **world without end**, Eph. iii. 21(–τοῦ αἰ. G°).

εἰς πάντας τοὺς αἰῶνας, **ever**, Jude 25.

εἰς ἡμέραν αἰῶνος, **for ever**, 2 Pet. iii. 18.

With οὐκ εἰς, **never**, Mark iii. 29 (–εἰς τὸν αἰ. G°).

With οὐ μὴ εἰς, **never**, John iv. 14 (ap). viii. 51, 52(–εἰς τὸν αἰ. G°). x. 28. xi. 26. xiii. 8.

Add Rom. xvi. 27(εἰς τ. αἰ. τῶν αἰώνων), LS. Jude 25(ap). Rev. xv. 3, for ἁγίος, G′S.

αἰώνιος.

everlasting, Matt. xviii. 8. xxv. 41, 46. Luke xvi. 9. Rom. xvi. 26. 2 Thes. i. 9. ii. 16. 1 Tim. vi. 16. Heb. xiii. 20. 2 Pet. i. 11. Rev. xiv. 6.

eternal, Mark iii. 29. 2 Cor. iv. 17, 18. v. 1. 2 Tim. ii. 10. Heb. v. 9. vi. 2. ix. 12, 14, 15. 1 Pet. v. 10. Jude 7.

for ever, Phm. 15.

With ζωή, **everlasting life**, Matt. xix. 29. John iii. 16, 36. iv. 14. v. 24. vi. 27, 40, 47. Acts xiii. 46. Rom. vi. 22.—**life everlasting**, Luke xviii. 30. John xii. 50. Gal. vi. 8. 1 Tim. i. 16.—**eternal life**, Matt. xix. 16. Mark x. 17, 30. Luke x. 25. xviii. 18. John iii. 15. v. 39. vi. 54, 68. x. 28. xvii. 2. Acts xiii. 48. Rom. ii. 7. v. 21. vi. 23. 1 Tim. vi. 12, 19(ὄντως GLTS). Tit. i. 2. iii. 7. 1 John i. 2. ii. 25. iii. 15. v. 11, 13, 20. Jude 21.—**life eternal**, Matt. xxv. 46. John iv. 36. xii. 25. xvii. 3.

χρόνοις αἰωνίοις, **since the world began**, Rom. xvi. 25.

πρὸ χρόνων αἰωνίων, **before the world began**, 2 Tim. i. 9. Tit. i. 2.

Add John xx. 31(life..)LS.

ἀκαθαρσία.

uncleanness, Matt. xxiii. 27. Rom. i. 24. vi. 19. 2 Cor. xii. 21. Gal. v. 19. Eph. iv. 19. v. 3. Col. iii. 5. 1 Thes. ii. 3. iv. 7.

ἀκαθάρτης.

filthiness, Rev. xvii. 4(τὰ ἀκάθαρτα GLTTrS).

ἀκάθαρτος.

unclean, Matt. x. 1. xii. 43. Mark i. 23, 26, 27. iii. 11, 30. v. 2, 8, 13. vi. 7. vii. 25. Luke iv. 33, 36. vi. 18. viii. 29. ix. 42. xi. 24. Acts v. 16. viii. 7. x. 14, 28. xi. 8. 1 Cor. vii. 14. 2 Cor. vi. 17. Eph. v. 5. Rev. xvi. 13. xviii. 2.

foul, Mark ix. 25. Rev. xviii. 2.

Add Rev. xvii. 4, *see ἀκαθάρτης*.

ἀκαιρέομαι.

lack opportunity, Phil. iv. 10.

ἀκαίρως.

out of season, 2 Tim. iv. 2.

ἄκακος.

harmless, Heb. vii. 26.

simple, Rom. xvi. 18.

ἄκανθα.

thorns, Matt. vii. 16. xiii. 7*t*, 22. xxvii. 29. Mark iv. 7*t*, 18. Luke vi. 44. viii. 7*t*, 14. John xix. 2. Heb. vi. 8.

ἀκάνθινος.

of thorns, Mark xv. 17. John xix. 5.

ἄκαρπος.

unfruitful, Matt. xiii. 22. Mark iv. 19. 1 Cor. xiv. 14. Eph. v. 11. Tit. iii. 14. 2 Pet. i. 8.

without fruit, Jude 12.

ἀκατάγνωστος.

that cannot be condemned, Tit. ii. 8.

ἀκατακάλυπτος.

uncovered, 1 Cor. xi. 5, 13.

ἀκατάκριτος.

uncondemned, Acts xvi. 37. xxii. 25.

ἀκατάλυτος.

endless, Heb. vii. 16.

ἀκατάπαστος, unfed, hungry?
(Not found elsewhere; compare ἄπαστος.)
2 Pet. ii. 14, for ἀκατάπαυστος, L.

ἀκατάπαυστος.
that cannot cease, 2 Pet. ii. 14(ἀκατάπαστος L).

ἀκαταστασία.
commotion, Luke xxi. 9.
tumult, 2 Cor. vi. 5(*marg.* **tossing to and fro**). xii. 20.
confusion (*Gr.* tumult, *or* unquietness), 1 Cor. xiv. 33. Jas. iii. 16.

ἀκατάστατος.
unstable, Jas. i. 8.
Add Jas. iii. 8, for ἀκατάσχετος, LT*S*.

ἀκατάσχετος.
unruly, Jas. iii. 8 (ἀκατάστατος LT*S*).

ἀκέραιος.
simple (*marg.* **harmless**), Rom. xvi. 19.
harmless, Matt. x. 16 (*marg.* **simple**). Phil. ii. 15(*marg.* **sincere**).

ἀκλινής.
without wavering, Heb. x. 23.

ἀκμάζω.
be fully ripe, Rev. xiv. 18.

ἀκμήν.
yet, Matt. xv. 16.

ἀκοή.
hearing, Matt. xiii. 14. Rom. x. 17*t*. 1 Cor. xii. 17*t*. Gal. iii. 2, 5. Heb. v. 11. 2 Pet. ii. 8.
hearing, *part.*[cc], Acts xxviii. 26.
which . . hear[cc], 1 Thes. ii. 13.
audience, Luke vii. 1.
ears, Mark vii. 35. Acts xvii. 20. 2 Tim. iv. 3, 4.
preached (*Gr.* of hearing), Heb. iv. 2.
report, John xii. 38. Rom. x. 16 (*marg.* **preaching**; *Gr.* hearing).
rumor, Matt. xxiv. 6. Mark xiii. 7.
fame, Matt. iv. 24. xiv. 1. Mark i. 28.

ἀκολουθέω.
follow, Matt. iv. 20, 22, 25. viii. 1, 10, 19, 22, 23. ix. 9*t*, 19, 27. x. 38. xii. 15. xiv. 13. xvi. 24. xix. 2, 21, 27, 28. xx. 29, 34. xxi. 9. xxvi. 58. xxvii. 55. Mark i. 18. ii. 14*t*, 15. iii. 7(–G°). v. 24. vi. 1. viii. 34. ix. 38*t*(*ap*). x. 21, 28, 32[p], 52. xi. 9. xiv. 13, 51(συνακολουθέω G'LTTr*S*), 54. xv. 41. Luke v. 11, 27, 28. vii. 9. ix. 11, 23, 49, 57, 59, 61. xviii. 22, 28, 43. xxii. 10, 39, 54. xxiii. 27. John i. 37, 38, 40(41), 43(44). vi. 2. viii. 12. x. 4, 5, 27. xi. 31. xii. 26. xiii. 36*t*, 37. xviii. 15. xx. 6. xxi. 19, 20, 22. Acts xii. 8, 9. xiii. 43. xxi. 36. 1 Cor. x. 4(*marg.* **go with**). Rev. vi. 8. xiv. 4, 8, 9, 13. xix. 14.
reach, Rev. xviii. 5(κολλάομαι GLTTr*S*).
Add Mark v. 37, for συνακολουθέω, L. viii. 34, for ἐλθεῖν (ἔρχομαι), G TTr. xvi. 17, for παρακολουθέω, Tr.

ἀκούω.
hear, Matt. ii. 3[p], 9[p], 18, 22[p]. iv. 12[p]. v. 21, 27, 33, 38, 43. vii. 24, 26. viii. 10[p]. ix. 12[p]. x. 14, 27. xi. 2[p], 4, 5, 15(–TTr[b]), 15. xii. 19, 24[p], 42. xiii. 9(–TTr[b]*S*), 9, 13*t*, 14, 15, 16, 17*tr*, 18, 19[p], 20, 22, 23, 43(–L[b]TTr[b] *S*), 43. xiv. 1, 13[p]*t*. xv. 10, 12. xvii. 5, 6[p]. xviii. 15, 16. xix. 22[p], 25[p]. xx. 24[p], 30[p]. xxi. 16, 33, 45[p]. xxii. 7[p](–G''Tr*S*), 22[p], 33[p], 34[p]. xxiv. 6. xxvi. 65. xxvii. 13, 47[p]. Mark ii. 17[p]. iii. 8[p], 21[p]. iv. 9*t*, 12*t*, 15, 16, 18, 20, 23*t*, 24, 24(*ap*), 33. v. 27, 36 (Tr[m], παρακούω TTr*S*). vi. 2, 11, 14 16[p], 20[p], 20, 29[p], 55. vii. 16, 25, 37. viii. 18. ix. 7. x. 41[p], 47[p]. xi. 14, 18. xii. 28, 29, 37. xiii. 7. xiv. 11[p], 58, 64. xv. 35[p]. xvi. 11[p](*ap*).
Luke i. 41, 58, 66. ii. 18, 20, 46, 47. iv. 23, 28[p]. v. 1, 15. vi. 17(18), 27, 47, 49. vii. 3[p], 9[p], 22*t*, 29. viii. 8*t*, 10, 12, 13, 14[p], 15, 18, 21, 50[p]. ix. 7, 9, 35. x. 16*t*, 24*tr*, 39. xi. 28, 31. xii. 3. xiv. 15, 35*t*. xv. 1, 25.

xvi. 2, 14, 29, 31. xviii. 6, 22p, 23p, 26, 36. xix. 11p, 48. xx. 16p. xxi. 9, 38. xxii. 71. xxiii. 6p, 8. John i. 37, 40(41). iii. 8, 29, 32. iv. 1, 42, 47p. v. 24, 25*t*, 28, 30, 37. vi. 45, 60p, 60. vii. 32, 40p, 51. viii. 9(*ap*), 26, 40, 43, 47*t*. ix. 27*t*, 31*t*, 32, 35, 40. x. 3, 8, 16, 20, 27. xi. 4p, 6, 20, 29, 41, 42. xii. 12p, 18, 29, 34, 47. xiv. 24, 28. xv. 15. xvi. 13. xviii. 21, 37. xix. 8, 13p. xxi. 7p.

Acts i. 4. ii. 6, 8, 11, 22, 33, 37p. iii. 22, 23. iv. 4, 20, 24p. v. 5*t*, 11, 21p, 24, 32p. vi. 11, 14. vii. 12p. 34, 37(-G°LT*S*), 54p. viii. 6, 14, 30. ix. 4, 7, 13, 21, 38. x. 22, 33, 44, 46. xi. 1, 7, 18p. xiii. 7, 44, 48p. xiv. 9, 14. xv. 7, 24. xvi. 14, 38p. xvii. 8p, 21, 32p, 32. xviii. 8, 26p. xix. 2, 5p, 10, 26, 28p. xxi. 12, 20p, 22. xxii. 1, 2p, 7, 9, 14, 15, 26p. xxiii. 16p. xxiv. 4, 22p(G', *om S*), 24. xxv. 22*t*. xxvi. 3, 14, 29. xxviii. 15p, 22, 26, 27, 28.

Rom. x. 14*t*, 18. xi. 8inf. xv. 21. 1 Cor. ii. 9. xi. 18. 2 Cor. xii. 4, 6. Gal. i. 13, 23. iv. 21 (ἀναγινώσκω Lm). Eph. i. 13p, 15p. iii. 2. iv. 21. Phil. i. 27, 30. ii. 26. iv. 9. Col. i. 4p, 6, 9, 23. 2 Thes. iii. 11. 1 Tim. iv. 16. 2 Tim. i. 13. ii. 2. iv. 17. Phm. 5.

Heb. ii. 1, 3. iii. 7, 15. 16p. iv. 2, 7. xii. 19. Jas. i. 19. v. 11. 2 Pet. i. 18. 1 John i. 1, 3, 5. ii. 7, 18, 24*t*. iii. 11. iv. 3, 5, 6*t*. v. 14, 15. 2 John 6. 3 John 4. Rev. i. 3, 10. ii. 7, 11, 17, 29. iii. 3(*ap*), 6, 13, 20, 22. iv. 1. v. 11, 13. vi. 1, 3, 5, 6, 7. vii. 4. viii. 13. ix. 13, 16, 20. x. 4, 8. xi. 12. xii. 10. xiii. 9. xiv. 2*t*, 13. xvi. 1, 5, 7. xviii. 4, 22*t*, 23. xix. 1, 6. xxi. 3. xxii. 8*t*, 17, 18.

hearer, Eph, iv. 29p. 2 Tim. ii. 14p.
hearken, Mark iv. 3. vii. 14. Acts iv. 19. vii. 2. xv. 13. Jas. ii. 5.
give audience, Acts xiii. 16. xv. 12. xxii. 22.
in the audience ofcc, Luke xx. 45.
Pass., **be noised**, Mark ii. 1.—**be reported**, 1 Cor. v. 1.—**come to .. ears**, Matt. xxviii. 14(*with* ἐπί, ὑπό LTr).
With λόγος, **tidings come**, Acts xi. 22.
With βαρέως, **be dull of hearing**, Matt. xiii. 15. Acts xxviii. 27.
understand(*Gr.* hear), 1 Cor. xiv. 2.
Add John viii. 38, for ὁράω, G''LTr.

ἀκρασία.

incontinency, 1 Cor. vii. 5.
excess, Matt. xxiii. 25(G', ἀδικία G).

ἀκρατής.

incontinent, 2 Tim. iii. 3.

ἄκρατον.

without mixture, Rev. xiv. 10.

ἀκρίβεια.

perfect manner, Acts xxii. 3.

ἀκριβής.

most straitest, Acts xxvi. 5sup.

ἀκριβόω.

inquire diligently, Matt. ii. 7, 16.

ἀκριβῶς.

perfectly, Acts xviii. 26. xxiii. 15, 20. 1 Thes. v. 2.
perfectcc, Luke i. 3. Acts xxiv. 22.
diligently, Matt. ii. 8. Acts xviii. 25.
circumspectly, Eph. v. 15.

ἀκρίς.

locusts, Matt. iii. 4. Mark i. 6. Rev. ix. 3, 7.

ἀκροατήριον.

place of hearing, Acts xxv. 23.

ἀκροατής.

hearer, Rom. ii. 13. Jas. i. 22, 23, 25.

ἀκροβυστία.

uncircumcision, Rom. ii. 25, 26*t*, 27. iii. 30. iv. 9, 10*t*. 1 Cor. vii. 18, 19. Gal. ii. 7. v. 6. vi. 15. Eph. ii. 11. Col. ii. 13. iii. 11.
With ἔχω, **uncircumcised**, Acts xi. 3.
With ἐν, **uncircumcised**, Rom. iv. 11, 12.
With διά, **though not circumcised**, Rom. iv. 11.

ἀκρογωνιαῖος.

chief corner, Eph. ii. 20. 1 Pet. ii. 6.

ἀκροθίνιον.

spoils, Heb. vii. 4.

ἄκρον.

top, Heb. xi. 21.
tip, Luke xvi. 24.
uttermost part, Mark xiii. 27*t*.
ἀπ' ἄκρων ἕως ἄκρων, **from one end to the other**, Matt. xxiv. 31.

ἀκυρόω.

make of none effect, Matt. xv. 6. Mark vii. 13.
disannul, Gal. iii. 17.

ἀκωλύτως.

no man forbidding, Acts xxviii. 31.

ἄκων.

against one's will, 1 Cor. ix. 17.

ἀλάβαστρον.

alabaster box, Matt. xxvi. 7. Mark xiv. 3. Luke vii. 37.
box, Mark xiv. 3.

ἀλαζονεία, or ἀλαζονία.

boasting, Jas. iv. 16.
pride, 1 John ii. 16.

ἀλαζών.

boaster, Rom. i. 30. 2 Tim. iii. 2.

ἀλαλάζω.

wail, Mark v. 38.
tinkle, 1 Cor. xiii. 1.

ἀλάλητος.

which can not be uttered, Rom. viii. 26.

ἄλαλος.

dumb, Mark vii. 37. ix. 17, 25.

ἅλας.

salt, Matt. v. 13*t*. Mark ix. 50*tr*. Luke xiv. 34*t*. Col. iv. 6.

ἀλείφω.

anoint, Matt. vi. 17. Mark vi. 13. xvi. 1. Luke vii. 38, 46*t*. John xi. 2. xii. 3. Jas. v. 14.

ἀλεκτοροφωνία.

cock-crowing, Mark xiii. 35.

ἀλέκτωρ.

cock, Matt. xxvi. 34, 74, 75. Mark xiv. 30, 68(–L[b]*S*), 72*t*. Luke xxii. 34, 60, 61. John xiii. 38. xviii. 27.

ἄλευρον.

meal, Matt. xiii. 33. Luke xiii. 21.

ἀλήθεια.

truth, Matt. xxii. 16. Mark v. 33. xii. 14, 32. Luke iv. 25. xxii. 59. John i. 14, 17. iii. 21. iv. 23, 24. v. 33. viii. 32*t*, 40, 44*t*, 45, 46. xiv. 6, 17. xv. 26. xvi. 7, 13*t*. xvii. 17*t*, 19(*with* ἐν, *marg.* **truly**). xviii. 37*t*, 38. Acts iv. 27. x. 34. xxvi. 25.
Rom. i. 18, 25. ii. 2, 8, 20. iii. 7. ix. 1. xv. 8. 1 Cor. v. 8. xiii. 6. 2 Cor. iv. 2. vi. 7. vii. 14*t*. xi. 10. xii. 6. xiii. 8*t*. Gal. ii. 5, 14. iii. 1 (*ap*). v. 7. Eph. i. 13. iv. 21, 25. v. 9. vi. 14. Phil. i. 18. Col. i. 5, 6. 2 Thes. ii. 10, 12, 13. 1 Tim. ii. 4, 7. iii. 15. iv. 3. vi. 5. 2 Tim. ii. 15, 18, 25. iii. 7, 8. iv. 4. Tit. i. 1, 14.
Heb. x. 26. Jas. i. 18. iii. 14. v. 19. 1 Pet. i. 22. 2 Pet. i. 12. ii. 2. 1 John i. 6, 8. ii. 4, 21*t*. iii. 18, 19. iv. 6. v. 6. 2 John 1*t*, 2, 3, 4. 3 John 1(*with* ἐν, *marg.* **truly**), 3*t*, 4, 8, 12.
verity, 1 Tim. ii. 7.
With ἐπί, **truly** (*marg.* **of a truth**), Luke xx. 21.
Gen., **true** (*marg.* **of truth**), Eph. iv. 24.

ἀληθεύω.

tell the truth, Gal. iv. 16[p].
speak the truth, Eph. iv. 15.

ἀληθής.

true, Matt. xxii. 16. Mark xii. 14. John iii. 33. v. 31, 32. vii. 18. viii. 13, 14, 16(ἀληθινός LTTr), 17, 26. x. 41. xix. 35. xxi. 24. Acts xii. 9. Rom. iii. 4. 2 Cor. vi. 8. Phil. iv. 8. Tit. i. 13. 1 Pet. v. 12. 2 Pet. ii. 22. 1 John ii. 8. 3 John 12.
truth, 1 John ii. 27.
truly[cc], John iv. 18.
Add John vi. 55*t*, for ἀληθῶς, G″L TTr.

ἀληθινός.

true, Luke xvi. 11. John i. 9. iv.

23, 37. vi. 32. vii. 28. xv. 1. xvii. 3. xix. 35. 1 Thes. i. 9. Heb. viii. 2. ix. 24. x. 22. 1 John ii. 8. v. 20*tr*. Rev. iii. 7, 14. vi. 10. xv. 3. xvi. 7. xix. 2, 9, 11. xxi. 5. xxii. 6.

Add John viii. 16, for ἀληθής, LT Tr. Heb. ix. 14(living καί ἀ.), L.

ἀλήθω.

grind, Matt. xxiv. 41. Luke xvii. 35.

ἀληθῶς.

truly, Matt. xxvii. 54. Mark xv. 39.
in truth, 1 Thes. ii. 13.
of a truth, Matt. xiv. 33. Luke ix. 27. xii. 44. xxi. 3. John vi. 14. vii. 40.
verily, 1 John ii. 5.
very[cc], John vii. 26(*omS*).
surely, Matt. xxvi. 73. Mark xiv. 70. John xvii. 8.
of a surety, Acts xii. 11.
indeed, John i. 47(48). iv. 42. vi. 55*t*(ἀληθής G''LTTr). vii. 26. viii. 31.

ἁλιεύς.

fisher, Matt. iv. 18, 19. Mark i. 16, 17.
fisherman, Luke v. 2.

ἁλιεύω.

a fishing, John xxi. 3[p].

ἁλίζω.

to salt, Matt. v. 13. Mark ix. 49, 49(*ap*).

ἀλίσγημα.

pollution, Acts xv. 20.

ἀλλά.

but, Matt. iv. 4. v. 15, 17, 39. vi. 13, 18. vii. 21. viii. 4, 8. ix. 12, 13, 17, 18, 24. x. 20, 34. xi. 8, 9. xiii. 21. xv. 11. xvi. 12, 17, 23. xvii. 12. xviii. 22, 30. xix. 6. xx. 23, 26, 28. xxi. 21. xxii. 30, 32. xxiv. 6. xxvi. 39. xxvii. 24. Mark i. 44, 45. ii. 17*t*, 22(*ap*). iii. 26, 29. iv. 17, 22. v. 19, 26, 39. vi. 9. vii. 5, 15, 19. viii. 33. ix. 13, 22, 37. x. 8, 27, 40, 43, 45. xi. 23, 32. xii. 14, 25, 27. xiii. 7, 11*t*, 20, 24. xiv. 28, 49. xvi. 7.

Luke i. 60. iv. 4(*ap*). v. 14, 31, 32, 38. vi. 27. vii. 7, 25, 26. viii. 16, 27, 52. ix. 56(*ap*). xi. 4(*ap*), 13, 42. xii. 7, 51. xiii. 3, 5. xiv. 10, 13. xvi. 30. xviii. 13. xx. 21, 38. xxi. 9. xxii. 26, 36, 42, 53. xxiv. 6. John i. 8, 13, 31, 33. iii. 8, 15(*ap*), 16, 17, 28, 36. iv. 2, 14 (*ap*), 23. v. 18, 22, 24, 30, 34, 42. vi. 9, 22, 26, 27, 32, 36, 38, 39, 64. vii. 10, 12, 16, 22, 24, 28, 44, 49. viii. 12, 16, 26, 28, 37, 42, 49, 55. ix. 3, 31. x. 1, 5, 8, 18, 26, 33. xi. 4, 11, 22(-L[b]Tr*S*), 30, 42, 51, 52, 54. xii. 6, 9, 16, 27, 30, 42, 44, 47, 49. xiii. 9, 10*t*, 18. xiv. 24, 31. xv. 16, 19, 21, 25. xvi. 4, 6, 12, 13, 20, 25 (-GL[b]TTr*S*), 25, 33. xvii. 9, 15, 20. xviii. 28, 40. xix. 21, 24, 34. xx. 7, 27. xxi. 8, 23.

Acts i. 4, 8. ii. 16. iv. 17, 32. v. 4, 13. vii. 39. x. 35, 41. xiii. 25. xv. 11, 20. xvi. 37. xviii. 9, 21. xix. 26, 27. xx. 24. xxi. 13, 24. xxvi. 16, 20, 25, 29. xxvii. 10.

Rom. i. 21, 32. ii. 13, 29*t*. iii. 27. iv. 2, 4, 10, 12, 13, 16, 20, 24. v. 3, 11, 15. vi. 13, 14, 15. vii. 13, 15, 17, 19, 20. viii. 1(*ap*), 4, 9, 15, 20, 23, 26, 32. ix. 7, 8, 10, 11, 16, 24, 32. x. 2, 8, 16, 18, 19. xi. 4, 11, 18, 20. xii. 2, 3, 16, 19, 21. xiii. 3, 5, 14. xiv. 13, 17, 20. xv. 3, 21. xvi. 4, 18. 1 Cor. i. 17, 27. ii. 4, 5, 7, 9, 12, 13. iii. 1, 5(-GL *S*), 6, 7. iv. 14, 19, 20. v. 8. vi. 6, 11*tr*, 12*t*, 13. vii. 4*t*, 7, 10, 19, 21, 35. viii. 6(-L[b]). ix. 12, 21, 27. x. 5, 13, 20, 23*t*, 24, 29, 33. xi. 8, 9, 17. xii. 14, 24, 25. xiv. 2, 17, 22*t*, 33, 34. xv. 10*t*, 35, 37, 39, 40, 46. 2 Cor. i. 9*t*, 12, 19, 24. ii. 4, 5, 13, 17*t*. iii. 3*t*, 5, 6, 14, 15. iv. 2*t*, 5, 8, 9*t*, 16, 18. v. 4, 12, 15. vi. 4. vii. 5, 7, 9, 12, 14. viii. 5, 8, 10, 13, 19, 21. ix. 12. x. 4, 12, 13, 18. xi. 6, 17. xii. 14*t*. xiii. 3, 4, 7, 8.

Gal. i. 1, 8, 12, 17. ii. 3, 7, 14. iii. 12, 16, 22. iv. 2, 7, 14, 23, 29, 31. v. 6, 13. vi. 13, 15. Eph. i. 21. ii. 19. iv. 29. v. 4, 15, 17, 18, 27, 29. vi. 4, 6, 12. Phil. i. 20, 29. ii. 3, 4, 7, 12, 27*t*. iii. 7, 9. iv. 6, 17. Col. iii. 11, 22. 1 Thes. i. 5, 8. ii. 2, 4*t*, 7, 8, 13. iv. 7, 8. v. 6, 9, 15. 2 Thes. ii. 12. iii. 8, 9, 11, 15. 1 Tim. i. 13. ii. 10, 12. iii. 3. iv. 12. v. 1, 13, 23. vi. 2, 4, 17. 2 Tim. i. 7, 8, 9, 17. ii. 9, 20, 24. iii. 9. iv. 3, 8, 16. Tit. i. 8, 15. ii. 10 iii. 5. Phm. 14, 16.

Heb. ii. 16. iii. 13. iv. 2. v. 4, 5. vii. 16. ix. 24. x. 3, 25, 39. xi. 13. xii. 11, 22, 26. xiii. 14. Jas. i. 25, 26. iii. 15. iv. 11. 1 Pet. i. 15, 19, 23. ii. 16, 18, 20, 25. iii. 4, 14, 21. iv. 2, 13. v. 2*t*, 3. 2 Pet. i. 16, 21. ii. 4, 5. iii. 9*t*. 1 John ii. 2, 7, 16, 19*t*, 21, 27. iii. 18. iv. 1, 10, 18. v. 6, 18. 2 John 1, 5, 8, 12(G′, γάρ GL). 3 John 9, 11, 13. Jude 6, 9. Rev. ii. 6, 9, 14. iii. 9. ix. 5. x. 7, 9. xvii. 12. xx. 6.

save, Matt. xix. 11. Mark ix. 8 (εἰ μή L*S*).

howbeit, John vii. 27. Acts vii. 48. 1 Cor. viii. 7. xiv. 20. xv. 46. Gal. iv. 8. 1 Tim. i. 16. Heb. iii. 16.

yet, Mark xiv. 29. 1 Cor. iv. 4, 15. ix. 2. xiv. 19. 2 Cor. iv. 8, 16. v. 16. xi. 6. xiii. 4. Col. ii. 5.

nevertheless, Mark xiv. 36. John xi. 15. xvi. 7. Rom. v. 14. 1 Cor. ix. 12. 2 Cor. vii. 6. xii. 16. Gal. iv. 30. 2 Tim. i. 12. Rev. ii. 4.

notwithstanding, Rev. ii. 20.

nay, Rom. vii. 7. viii. 37. 1 Cor. vi. 8. xii. 22.

no, Luke xxiii. 15.

indeed, 2 Cor. xi. 1.

and rather, Luke xvii. 8.

yea, Luke xxiv. 22. John xvi. 2. Rom. iii. 31. 1 Cor. iv. 3. 2 Cor. vii. 11*six*. Gal. iv. 17. Phil. i. 18. ii. 17. iii. 8(–L[b]). Jas. ii. 18.

therefore, Acts x. 20. 2 Cor. viii. 7. Eph. v. 24.

ἀλλὰ καί, **moreover**, Luke xvi. 21. —**also**, Rom. vi. 5.

ἀλλά γε, **and**, Luke xxiv. 21.

ἀλλ' οὐδέ, **not so much as**, Acts xix. 2. —**neither**, 1 Cor. iii. 2.

ἀλλ'(–L[b]) ἤ, **than**, 2 Cor. i. 13.

Add Mark vi. 52, for 2d γάρ, Tr*S*. vii. 25, for γάρ, TTr*S*. John ix. 9, see ὅτι. Acts ix. 6 (. . arise), GLT*S*. Rom. xii. 20, see οὖν. 1 Pet. iii. 15 (. . with meekness), LT*S*. Rev. ii. 9, for δέ, GLTTr*S*. iii. 4 (. . thou hast), GLTTr*S*.

ἀλλάττω.

change, Acts vi. 14. Rom. i. 23. 1 Cor. xv. 51, 52. Gal. iv. 20. Heb. i. 12.

ἀλλαχόθεν.

some other way, John x. 1.

ἀλλαχοῦ, elsewhere.

Mark i. 38(Let us go . .), TTr*S*.

ἀλληγορέω.

Pass., **be an allegory**, Gal. iv. 24.

ἀλληλούϊα.

alleluia, Rev. xix. 1, 3, 4, 6.

ἀλλήλων,

ἀλλήλοις, ἀλλήλους.

one another, Matt. xxiv. 10*t*. xxv. 32. Mark iv. 41. ix. 50. Luke ii. 15. vi. 11. vii. 32. viii. 25. xii. 1. xxiv. 17, 32. John iv. 33. v. 44. xiii. 14, 22, 34*t*, 35. xv. 12, 17. Acts ii. 7(–LT*S*). vii. 26. xix. 38. xxi. 6. Rom. i. 27. ii. 15(*marg.* **themselves**[c]). xii. 5, 10*t*, 16. xiii. 8. xiv. 13, 19. xv. 5, 7, 14(ἄλλους G′). xvi. 16. 1 Cor. xi. 33. xii. 25. xvi. 20. 2 Cor. xiii. 12. Gal. v. 13, 15*t*, 26*t*. vi. 2. Eph. iv. 2, 25, 32. v. 21. Col. iii. 9, 13. 1 Thes. iii. 12. iv. 9, 18. Tit. iii. 3. Heb. x. 24. Jas. iv. 11. v. 9, 16*t*. 1 Pet. i. 22. iv. 9. v. 5, 14. 1 John i. 7. iii. 11, 23. iv. 7, 11, 12. 2 John 5. Rev. vi. 4. xi. 10.

one the other, Acts xv. 39. 1 Cor. vii. 5. Gal. v. 17.

each other, Phil. ii. 3. 2 Thes. i. 3.

yourselves[c], John vi. 43. xvi. 19. 1 Thes. v. 15.

yourselves[c] **together**, 1 Thes. v. 11.

themselves[c], Mark viii. 16. ix. 34. xv. 31. Luke iv. 36. John vi. 52. xi. 56. xvi. 17. xix. 24. Acts iv. 15. xxvi. 31. xxviii. 4, 25.

With ἐν, **mutual**[cc], Rom. i. 12.

With μετά, **together**, Luke xxiii. 12.

With πρός, **together**, Luke xxiv. 14.

Add Luke xx. 14, for ἑαυτούς, TTr *S*.

ἀλλογενής.

stranger, Luke xvii. 18.

ἅλλομαι.

leap, Acts iii. 8. xiv. 10.

spring up, John iv. 14.

ἄλλος.

(With the article, marked [a].)

other, Matt. iv. 21. v. 39[a]. xii. 13[a]. xiii. 8. xx. 3, 6. xxi. 8, 36, 41. xxii. 4. xxv. 16, 17, 20, 22. xxvii. 42, 61[a]. xxviii. 1[a]. Mark iii. 5[a](*om S*). iv. 8, 36, vi. 15*t*. vii. 8(*ap*). viii. 28. xi. 8. xii. 5, 9, 31, 32. xv. 31, 41. Luke v. 29. vi. 10[a] (*ap*), 29[a]. ix. 8, 19. xx. 16. xxiii. 35. John vi. 22, 23. vii. 12, 41. ix. 9, 16. x. 16, 21. xii. 29. xviii. 16[a], 34. xix. 18, 32[a]. xx. 2[a], 3[a], 4[a], 8[a], 25[a], 30. xxi. 2, 8[a]. Acts iv. 12(*ap*). xv. 2. 1 Cor. i. 16. iii. 11. ix. 2, 12, 27. xiv. 19, 29[a]. 2 Cor. xi. 8. 1 Thes. ii. 6. Heb. xi. 35. Jas. v. 12. Rev. ii. 24. xvii. 10[a].

another, Matt. ii. 12. viii. 9. x. 23[a] (ἕτερος G[pr]LTr*S*). xiii. 24, 31, 33. xix. 9. xxi. 33. xxvi. 71. Mark x. 11, 12. xii. 4, 5. xiv. 19(*ap*), 58. Luke vii. 8, 19(ἕτερος Tr*S*), 20. John v. 7, 32, 43. xiv. 16. xviii. 15[a].([a]–G[oo]L). xxi. 18. 1 Cor. iii. 10. xii. 8, 9, 10*f*. xiv. 30. xv. 39*tr*, 41*t*. 2 Cor. xi. 4. Gal. i. 7. Heb. iv. 8. Rev. vi. 4. vii. 2. viii. 3. x. 1 (–G[o]). xii. 3. xiii. 11. xiv. 6(G[oo]*S*), 8, 15, 17, 18. xv. 1. xvi. 7(*omS*). xviii. 1, 4. xx. 12.

otherwise[cc], Gal. v. 10.

another man's, 1 Cor. x. 29.

other man, John iv. 38. xv. 24. 2 Cor. viii. 13. Phil. iii. 4.

other things, Mark vii. 4. John xxi. 25. 2 Cor. i. 13.

more, Matt. xxv. 20.

some, Matt. xiii. 5, 7. xvi. 14(οἱ L). Mark iv. 5, 7. viii. 28. Luke ix. 19. John vii. 41(οἱ LTr, οἳ T). ix. 9.

ἄλλος τις, **another**, Luke xxii. 59.

ἄλλος . . ἄλλος, **one . . another**, John iv. 37. Acts ii. 12. 1 Cor. xv. 39, 41.

ἄλλοι ἄλλο τι, **some one thing, some another**, Acts xix. 32. xxi. 34.

Add Matt. x. 23(*ap*). Mark iv. 18, for οὗτος, GLTTr*S*. Rom. xv. 14, for ἀλλήλους, G′. Rev. xiv. 9(. . the third), GLTTr. xviii. 1(. . angel), GLTTr*S*.

ἀλλοτριοεπίσκοπος.

busybody in other men's matters, 1 Pet. iv. 15.

ἀλλότριος.

another man's, Luke xvi. 12. Rom. xiv. 4. xv. 20. 2 Cor. x. 15, 16. 1 Tim. v. 22.

of others, Heb. ix. 25.

strange, Acts vii. 6. Heb. xi. 9.

stranger, Matt. xvii. 25, 26. John x. 5*t*.

alien, Heb. xi. 34.

ἀλλόφυλος.

one of another nation, Acts x. 28.

ἄλλως.

otherwise, 1 Tim. v. 25.

ἀλοάω.

tread out [c]**the corn**, 1 Cor. ix. 9. 1 Tim. v. 18.

thresh, 1 Cor. ix. 10.

ἄλογος.

unreasonable, Acts xxv. 27.

brute, 2 Pet. ii. 12. Jude 10.

ἀλόη.

aloes, John xix. 39.

ἅλς.

salt, Mark ix. 49(*ap*).

ἁλυκός.

salt, *adj.*, Jas. iii. 12.

ἄλυπος.

less sorrowful, Phil. ii. 28comp.

ἅλυσις.

chain, Mark v. 3, 4*t*. Luke viii. 29. Acts xii. 6, 7. xxi. 33. xxviii. 20. 2 Tim. i. 16. Rev. xx. 1.
bonds (*marg.* **chain**), Eph. vi. 20.

ἀλυσιτελής.

unprofitable, Heb. xiii. 17.

ἄλφα. See *A*.

ἅλων.

floor, Matt. iii. 12. Luke iii. 17.

ἀλώπηξ.

fox, Matt. viii. 20. Luke ix. 58. xiii. 32.

ἅλωσις.

With εἰς, **to be taken** (*lit.* for capture), 2 Pet. ii. 12.

ἅμα.

together, Rom. iii. 12. 1 Thes. iv. 17. v. 10.
withal, Col. iv. 3. 1 Tim. v. 13. Phm. 22.
with, Matt. xiii. 29.
and, Acts xxvii. 40.
With καί, **also,** Acts xxiv. 26.
With πρωΐ, **early in the morning,** Matt. xx. 1.

ἀμαθής.

unlearned, 2 Pet. iii. 16.

ἀμαράντινος.

that fadeth not away, 1 Pet. v. 4.

ἀμάραντος.

that fadeth not away, 1 Pet. i. 4.

ἁμαρτάνω.

to sin, Matt. xviii. 21. xxvii. 4. Luke xv. 18, 21. John v. 14. viii. 11(*ap*). ix. 2, 3. Rom. ii. 12*t*. iii. 23. v. 12, 14, 16p(ἁμαρτήματος G′). vi. 15. 1 Cor. vi. 18. vii. 28*t*, 36. viii. 12*t*. xv. 34. Eph. iv. 26. 1 Tim. v. 20. Tit. iii. 11. Heb. iii. 17. x. 26. 2 Pet. ii. 4. 1 John i. 10. ii. 1*t*. iii. 6*t*, 8, 9. v. 16*t*, 18.
to trespass, Matt. xviii. 15. Luke xvii. 3, 4.
offend, Acts xxv. 8.
for yourc **faults,** 1 Pet. ii. 20p.

ἁμάρτημα.

sin, Mark iii. 28. iv. 12(–GooLbT Tr*S*). Rom. iii. 25. 1 Cor. vi. 18.
Add Mark iii. 29, for κρίσις, G″LT Tr*S*. Rom. v. 16, for ἁμαρτήσαντος (ἁμαρτάνω), G′. 2 Pet. i. 9, for ἁμαρτία, GT*S*.

ἁμαρτία.

sin, Matt. i. 21. iii. 6. ix. 2. 5, 6. xii. 31. xxvi. 28. Mark i. 4, 5. ii. 5, 7, 9, 10. Luke i. 77. iii. 3. v. 20, 21, 23, 24. vii. 47, 48, 49. xi. 4. xxiv. 47. John i. 29. viii. 21, 24*t*, 34, 34(–Goo), 46. ix. 34, 41*t*. xv. 22*t*, 24. xvi. 8, 9. xix. 11. xx. 23. Acts ii. 38. iii. 19. v. 31. vii. 60. x. 43. xiii. 38. xxii. 16. xxvi. 18.
Rom. iii. 9, 20. iv. 7, 8. v. 12*t*, 13*t*, 20, 21. vi. 1, 2, 6*t*, 7, 10, 11 12, 13, 14, 16, 17, 18, 20, 22, 2[illegible] vii. 5, 7*t*, 8*t*, 9, 11, 13*tr*, 14, 17, 2[illegible] 23, 25. viii. 2, 3(*marg.* **sacrifice f**[illegible] **sin**), 3, 10. xi. 27. xiv. 23. 1 Co[illegible] xv. 3, 17, 56*t*. 2 Cor. v. 21*t*. Ga[illegible] i. 4. ii. 17. iii. 22. Eph. ii. 1. Co[illegible] i. 14. ii. 11(*om S*). 1 Thes. ii. 1[illegible] 2 Thes. ii. 3. 1 Tim. v. 22, 2[illegible] 2 Tim. iii. 6.
Heb. i. 3. ii. 17. iii. 13. iv. 15. [illegible] 1, 3. vii. 27. viii. 12. ix. 26, 28*t*. x. 2, 3, 4, 6, 8, 11, 12, 17, 18, 26. xi. 25. xii. 1, 4. xiii. 11(–T). Jas. i. 15*t*. ii. 9. iv. 17. v. 15, 20. 1 Pet. ii. 22, 24*t*. iii. 18. iv. 1, 8. 2 Pet. i. 9(G′, ἁμάρτημα GT*S*). ii. 14. 1 John i. 7, 8, 9*t*. ii. 2, 12. iii. 4*t*, 5*t*, 8, 9. iv. 10. v. 16*t*, 17*t*. Rev. i. 5. xviii. 4, 5.
sinful (*lit.* of sin), Rom. viii. 3.
offence, 2 Cor. xi. 7.
Add Mark iii. 29, for κρίσις, G″. John i. 36 (*ap*). Jas. v. 16, for παράπτωμα, L*S*.

ἀμάρτυρος.
without witness, Acts xiv. 17.

ἁμαρτωλός.
sinner, Matt. ix. 10, 11, 13. xi. 19. xxvi. 45. Mark ii. 15, 16*t*, 17. xiv. 41. Luke v. 30(–T), 32. vi. 32, 33, 34*t*. vii. 34, 37, 39. xiii. 2. xv. 1, 2, 7, 10. xviii. 13. xix. 7. John ix. 16, 24, 25, 31. Rom. iii. 7. v. 8, 19. Gal. ii. 15, 17. 1 Tim. i. 9, 15. Heb. vii. 26. xii. 3. Jas. iv. 8. v. 20. 1 Pet. iv. 18. Jude 15.
sinful, Mark viii. 38. Luke v. 8. xxiv. 7. Rom. vii. 13.
Add Rev. xxi. 8(unbel. καὶ ἁμ.), G'.

ἄμαχος.
not a brawler, 1 Tim. iii. 3.
no brawler, Tit. iii. 2.

ἀμάω.
reap down, Jas. v. 4.

ἀμέθυστος.
amethyst, Rev. xxi. 20.

ἀμελέω.
regard not, Heb. viii. 9.
be negligent, 2 Pet. i. 12(*see* μέλλω).
neglect, 1 Tim. iv. 14. Heb. ii. 3^{p}.
make light of, Matt. xxii. 5.

ἄμεμπτος.
blameless, Luke i. 6. Phil. ii. 15. iii. 6.
unblamable, 1 Thes. iii. 13.
faultless, Heb. viii. 7.

ἀμέμπτως.
unblamably, 1 Thes. ii. 10.
blameless^{cc}, 1 Thes. v. 23.

ἀμέριμνος.
without carefulness, 1 Cor. vii. 32.
With ποιέω, **to secure,** Matt. xxviii. 14.

ἀμετάθετος.
immutable, Heb. vi. 18.
With art., **immutability,** Heb. vi. 17.

ἀμετακίνητος.
unmovable, 1 Cor. xv. 58.

ἀμεταμέλητος.
without repentance, Rom. xi. 29.
not to be repented of, 2 Cor. vii. 10.

ἀμετανόητος.
impenitent, Rom. ii. 5.

ἄμετρος.
With art., **things without measure,** 2 Cor. x. 13, 15.

ἀμήν.
verily, Matt. v. 18, 26. vi. 2, 5, 16. viii. 10. x. 15, 23. 42. xi. 11. xiii. 17. xvi. 28. xvii. 20. xviii. 3, 13, 18. xix. 23, 28. xxi. 21, 31. xxiii. 36. xxiv. 2, 34, 47. xxv. 12, 40, 45. xxvi. 13, 21, 34. Mark iii. 28. vi. 11(*ap*). viii. 12. ix. 1, 41. x. 15, 29. xi. 23. xii. 43. xiii. 30. xiv. 9, 18, 25, 30. Luke iv. 24. xii. 37. xiii. 35(*om*). xviii. 17, 29. xxi. 32. xxiii. 43. John i. 51(52)*t*. iii. 3*t*, 5*t*, 11*t*. v. 19*t*, 24*t*, 25*t*. vi. 26*t*, 32*t*, 47*t*, 53*t*. viii. 34*t*, 51*t*, 58*t*. x. 1*t*, 7*t*. xii. 24*t*. xiii. 16*t*, 20*t*, 21*t*, 38*t*. xiv. 12*t*. xvi. 20*t*, 23*t*. xxi. 18*t*.
amen, Matt. vi. 13(*ap*). xxviii. 20 (*omS*). Luke xxiv. 53(–GL^{b}TTr*S*). John xxi. 25(*omS*). Rom. i. 25. ix. 5. xi. 36. xv. 33(–G^{o}L^{b}). xvi. 20(*om*St*S*), 24(*ap*), 27. 1 Cor. xiv. 16. xvi. 24(–G^{o}L^{b}T). 2 Cor. i. 20. xiii. 14(13; *omS*). Gal. i. 5. vi. 18. Eph. iii. 21. vi. 24(C, 1617 seq.; *om*C*S*). Phil. iv. 20, 23(–G^{oo}L^{b}T). Col. iv. 18(*omS*). 1 Thes. v. 28 (*om*). 2 Thes. iii. 18 (–G^{oo}T*S*). 1 Tim. i. 17. vi. 16, 21 (*omS*). 2 Tim. iv. 18, 22(*omS*). Tit. iii. 15 (–GL^{b}T*S*). Phm. 25(*om*). Heb. xiii. 21, 25(–G^{o}*S*). 1 Pet. iv. 11. v. 11, 14 (*om*). 2 Pet. iii. 18(–G^{c}T). 1 John v. 21(*omS*). 2 John 13(*omS*). Jude 25. Rev. i. 6, 7, 18(*omS*). iii. 14. v. 14. vii. 12, 12(–LTTr^{b}). xix. 4. xxii. 20, 21(–GLTTr^{b}).
Add Matt. xviii. 19 (. . I say), G^{pb}TTr; for πάλιν, L. Mark xvi. 20 (at the end), CSt. 1 Thes. iii. 13 (saints . .), L*S*.

ἀμήτωρ.
without mother, Heb. vii. 3.

ἀμίαντος.
undefiled, Heb. vii. 26. xiii. 4. Jas. i. 27. 1 Pet. i. 4.

ἄμμος.

sand, Matt. vii. 26. Rom. ix. 27. Heb. xi. 12. Rev. xiii. 1 (xii. 18). xx. 8.

ἀμνός.

lamb, John i. 29, 36. Acts viii. 32. 1 Pet. i. 19.

ἀμοιβή.

With ἀποδίδωμι, **requite**, 1 Tim. v. 4.

ἄμπελος.

vine, Matt. xxvi. 29. Mark xiv. 25. Luke xxii. 18. John xv. 1, 4, 5. Jas. iii. 12. Rev. xiv. 18(–St), 19.

ἀμπελουργός.

dresser of one's vineyard, Luke xiii. 7.

ἀμπελών.

vineyard, Matt. xx. 1, 2, 4, 7, 8. xxi. 28, 33, 39, 40, 41. Mark xii. 1, 2, 8, 9*t*. Luke xiii. 6, xx. 9, 10, 13, 15*t*, 16. 1 Cor. ix. 7.

ἀμύνομαι.

defend, Acts vii. 24.

ἀμφιάζω L, ἀμφιέζω TTr, put round *or* on, clothe.

Luke xii. 28, for ἀμφιέννυμι.

ἀμφιβάλλω, cast around.

Mark i. 16, for βάλλω, GLTTr*S*.

ἀμφίβληστρον.

net, Matt. iv. 18. Mark i. 16(–T Tr*S*).

ἀμφιέννυμι.

clothe, Matt. vi. 30. xi. 8. Luke vii. 25. xii. 28(*see* ἀμφιάζω).

ἄμφοδον.

place where two ways meet, Mark xi. 4.

ἀμφότεροι.

both, Matt. ix. 17. xiii. 30. xv. 14. Luke i. 6, 7. v. 7, 38(–G°TTr^b*S*). vi. 39. vii. 42. Acts vii. 38. xxiii. 8. Eph. ii. 14, 16, 18.

Add Acts xix. 16, for αὐτοί, G″L T*S*.

ἀμώμητος.

without rebuke, Phil. ii. 15(ἄμωμος L*S*). 2 Pet. iii. 14(ἄμωμος G′).

ἄμωμον, amomum.

Rev. xviii. 13(cinnamon, καὶ ἄμ.), GLTTr*S*.

ἄμωμος.

without blemish, Eph. v. 27. 1 Pet. i. 19.

without spot (*marg.* **without fault**), Heb. ix. 14.

without fault, Rev. xiv. 5.

faultless, Jude 24.

without blame, Eph. i. 4.

unblamable, Col. i. 22.

See also ἀμώμητος.

ἄν, adv.

Often not apparent in translation: but used—

I. *In the apodosis* or conclusion of a conditional sentence, *with the Indicative*, (a) *Imperfect*, q. d. I *would* or *might* do: Matt. xxiii. 30. Luke vii. 39. xvii. 6. John v. 46. viii. 19, 39(–GTTr*S*), 42. ix. 41. xiv. 7. xv. 19. xviii. 36. 1 Cor. xi. 31. Gal. i. 10. iii. 21. Heb. iv. 8. viii. 4, 7. xi. 15.

(b) *Aorist*, q. d. I *would* or *might have* done: Matt. xi. 21, 23. xii. 7. xxiv. 22, 43. xxv. 27. Mark xiii. 20. Luke x. 13. xii. 39*t*. xvii. 6. xix. 23. John iv. 10*t*. xi. 32. xiv. 2, 28. xviii. 30. Acts xviii. 14. Rom. ix. 29*t*. 1 Cor. ii. 8. Gal. iv. 15(–LT*S*). Heb. x. 2.

(c) *Pluperfect*, q. d. I *would* or *might have* done: John xi. 21(*aor.* G″LTr *S*). 1 John ii. 19.

II. *With the Indicative*, denoting the *repetition* of an action from time to time, (a) *Present:* Mark xi. 24 (–G°°LTTr*S*).

(b) *Imperfect:* Mark vi. 56*t*. Acts ii. 45. iv. 35. 1 Cor. xii. 2.

III. *With the Subjunctive*, after relative pronouns and adverbs, which it renders *indefinite*, like Eng. *ever*,

(a) *Present:* Matt. vii. 12. xvi. 25 (ἐάν LTTr*S*). Mark iv. 25(*indic.* L TTr*S*). viii. 35(ἐάν TTr*S*). x. 44 (ἐάν GTTr). Luke viii. 18(ἐάν T), 18(ἐάν LT) ix. 24(ἐάν T*S*), 57(ἐάν LTTr). x. 5(*aor.* G″LTTr*S*), 8, 10 (*aor.* G″LTTr*S*). John ii. 5. v. 19 (*indic.* L^m; –LTr^b). Rom. ix. 15*t*.

xvi. 2. 1 Cor. xi. 25(ἐάν LTS), 26 (ἐάν LTS), 27. xvi. 2. 2 Cor. xi. 21. Gal. v. 10(ἐάν TS), 17(ἐάν L^b S). Col. iii. 17(ἐάν LT). 1 Thes. ii. 7(ἐάν LT). Jas. iii. 4. 1 John ii. 5. iii. 17. v. 15(ἐάν TS). Rev. xiv. 4 (*indic.* LT; ἐάν LTTr).

(b) *Aorist:* Matt. ii. 13. v. 18*t*, 19, 21, 22*t*, 26, 31, 32(-G'LTrS; *see* ὅς). vi. 5(-LTTrS). x. 11*t*, 23, 33(-LTr). xii. 20, 32(ἐάν LTTrS), 32, 50(*pres.* T). xv. 5. xvi. 25, 28. xviii. 6. xix. 9. xxi. 22(ἐάν TTr), 44(*ap*). xxii. 9(ἐάν LTTrS), 44. xxiii. 3(ἐάν T), 16*t*, 18, 39. xxiv. 34. xxvi. 48(ἐάν TS). Mark iii. 28(ἐάν TTr), 29, 35. iv. 25(-, and *indic.*, LTTrS). vi. 10, 11 (*ap*). viii. 35(*fut. indic.* TTrS), 38(ἐάν T TrS). ix. 1, 18(ἐάν LTTr), 41, 42 (ἐάν T). xi. 23. xii. 36. xiv. 9(ἐάν TS), 44. Luke ii. 35. ix. 4, 5(ἐάν T), 24, 26, 27. x. 35. xii. 8. xiii. 25, 35(-TTr). xx. 18, 43. xxi. 32. John i. 33. iv. 14. xi. 22. xiv. 13. xv. 16. xvi. 13(-LTTrS; *indic.* T Tr; *pres. ind.* S), 23 (ἄν τι for ὅσα ἄν, LTr). Acts ii. 21(ἐάν T), 35, 39. iii. 19(20), 22, 23(ἐάν TS). vii. 3. xv. 17. Rom. iii. 4. x. 13. 1 Cor. iv. 5. xi. 26(-GLTS), 34. xv. 25 (-G^{oo}LTS). 2 Cor. iii. 16. Phil. ii. 23. Heb. i. 13. Jas. iv. 4(ἐάν LTS). v. 7(-T). 1 John iv. 15. Rev. ii. 25. xiii. 15.

IV. *With the Optative,* (a) *Present:* Luke i. 62. ix. 46. John xiii. 24 (*ap*). Acts ii. 12(-LT). viii. 31. x. 17. xvii. 18, 20(-G^oLTS). xxi. 33.

(b) *Aorist:* Luke vi. 11. Acts v. 24. xxvi. 29.

V. *With the Infinitive?* 2 Cor. x. 9. (So Winer; but according to Buttmann, Green, and Meyer, ἄν here modifies ὡς.)

VI. *With a Verb understood,* 1 Cor. vii. 5.

Add, for ἐάν, Matt. x. 14, LTrS. 42, LTr. xi. 6, LTr. xiv. 7, LTr. xvi. 19, LTr. 19, Tr. xviii. 5, 18, LTr. xx. 26, LTr. 27, LTrS. xxiii. 18, LTrS. Mark vi. 10, LTr. ix. 37, LTTrS. 37, LTTr. x. 11, 15, 43, LTrS. xiii. 11, L. xiv. 14, LTr. Luke iv. 6, LTr. ix. 48, 1st, L. x. 22, LTr. xviii. 17, LTrS. John xv. 7, 2d, L. Acts vii. 7, L. viii. 19, St. Rom. xv. 24, 1st, LTS. 1 Cor. xvi. 3, L. Gal. vi. 7, L. Eph. vi. 8, G'. 1 John v. 14, L.—Matt. x. 38, *see* οὐ. xxvi. 36, *see* οὐ. Luke ii. 26, for ἤ, TrS. xv. 26(what . .), L^bTr. xviii. 36(what . .), L^bTr^b. 2 Cor. iii. 15(when . .), LS.

Comp. the compounds ἐάν, κἄν, ὅταν.

See also ἄχρις, ἕως, ἡνίκα, καθό, καθότι, ὅπου, ὅπως, ὅς, ὁσάκις, ὅσος, ὅστις, οὐ, πῶς, τις, ὡς.

ἄν, for ἐάν, conj.

John xx. 23(ἐάν L), 23(ἐάν LS).

Add John xiii. 20, for ἐάν, LTTr S. xvi. 23, ἄν τι for ὅσα ἄν, LTTr. 1 John v. 15, for ἐάν, L.

ἀνά.

With μέρος(ἀναμέρος St), **by course,** 1 Cor. xiv. 27.

With μέσον (ἀναμέσον St), **through the midst,** Mark vii. 31.—**in the midst,** Rev. vii. 17.—**among,** Matt. xiii. 25.—**between,** 1 Cor. vi. 5.

Used distributively.

apiece, Luke ix. 3(-Tr^bS). John ii. 6.

each, Rev. iv. 8.

every man, Matt. xx. 9, 10.

ἀνὰ εἷς ἕκαστος, **every several,** Rev. xxi. 21.

ἀνὰ δύο, **two and two,** Luke x. 1.

ἀνὰ πεντήκοντα, **by fifties,** Mark vi. 40(κατὰ π. LTTrS). Luke ix. 14.

ἀνὰ ἑκατόν, **by hundreds,** Mark vi. 40(κατὰ ἑκ. LTTrS).

ἀναβαθμός.

stair, Acts xxi. 35, 40.

ἀναβαίνω.

go up, Matt. iii. 16. v. 1. xiv. 23. xv. 29. xx. 17, 18. Mark iii. 13. vi. 51. x. 32, 33. Luke ii. 4, 42. ix. 28. xviii. 10, 31. John ii. 13.

v. 1. vii. 8*t*, 10*t*, 14. xi. 55. xxi. 11. Acts i. 13. iii. 1. x. 9. xv. 2. xviii. 22. xxi. 4 (ἐπιβαίνω LT*S*), 12, 15. xxiv. 11. xxv. 9. Gal. ii. 1, 2. Rev. xx. 9.
arise, Luke xxiv. 38. Rev. ix. 2.
rise up, Rev. xiii. 1. xix. 3.
come up, Matt. xvii. 27. Mark i. 10. John xii. 20. Acts viii. 31, 39. x. 4. xi. 2. Rev. iv. 1. xi. 12. xiii. 11.
come up again, Acts xx. 11.
ascend, John i. 51(52). xx. 17*t*. Acts ii. 34. xxv. 1. Rom. x. 6. Eph. iv. 9. Rev. vii. 2. xi. 7. xvii. 8.
ascend up, Luke xix. 28. John iii. 13. vi. 62. Eph. iv. 8, 10. Rev. viii. 4. xi. 12. xiv. 11.
climb up, Luke xix. 4. John x. 1.
grow up, Mark iv. 7, 32.
spring up, Matt. xiii. 7. Mark iv. 8.
enter, John xxi. 3(ἐμβαίνω GLTTr*S*). 1 Cor. ii. 9.
come, Acts vii. 23. xxi. 31.
With ἐπί, **go upon**, Luke v. 19.
Add Matt. xiv. 32, for ἐμβαίνω, LTr*S*. xv. 39, for ἐμβαίνω, GTTr. Mark xv. 8, for ἀναβοάω, LTTr*S*. Acts xxi. 6, for ἐπιβαίνω, T*S*.

ἀναβάλλομαι.
defer, Acts xxiv. 22.

ἀναβιβάζω.
draw, Matt. xiii. 48.

ἀναβλέπω.
look up, Matt. xiv. 19. Mark vi. 41. vii. 34. viii. 24, 25(*see* διαβλέπω). Luke ix. 16. xix. 5. xxi. 1. Acts xxii. 13.
look, Mark xvi. 4p.
see, Luke vii. 22.
receive sight, Matt. xi. 5. xx. 34. Mark x. 51, 52. Luke xviii. 41, 42, 43. John ix. 11, 15, 18*t*. Acts ix. 12, 17, 18. xxii. 13.

ἀνάβλεψις.
recovering of sight, Luke iv. 18.

ἀναβοάω.
cry aloud, Mark xv. 8(ἀναβαίνω L TTr*S*).
cry out, Luke ix. 38(βοάω LTr*S*).
cry, Matt. xxvii. 46(βοάω LmTr).

ἀναβολή.
delay, Acts xxv. 17.

ἀνάγαιον. See ἀνώγεον.

ἀναγγέλλω.
tell, Mark v. 14(ἀπαγγέλλω GLTTr*S*), 19 (ἀπαγγέλλω LTTr*S*). John iv. 25. v. 15(εἶπον Lm*S*). Acts xvi. 38(ἀπαγγέλλω LT*S*). 2 Cor. vii. 7p.
rehearse, Acts xiv. 27.
report, 1 Pet. i. 12.
declare, Acts xv. 4. xx. 27. 1 John i. 5.
show, John xvi. 13, 14, 15, 25(ἀπαγγέλλω LTTr*S*). Acts xix. 18. xx. 20.
speak of, Rom. xv. 21.

ἀναγεννάω.
beget again, 1 Pet. i. 3.
Pass., **be born again**, 1 Pet. i. 23.

ἀναγινώσκω.
read, Matt. xii. 3, 5. xix. 4. xxi. 16, 42. xxii. 31. xxiv. 15. Mark ii. 25. xii. 10, 26. xiii. 14. Luke iv. 16. vi. 3. x. 26. John xix. 20. Acts viii. 28, 30*t*, 32. xiii. 27. xv. 21, 31p. xxiii. 34p. 2 Cor. i. 13. iii. 2, 15. Eph. iii. 4p. Col. iv. 16*tr*. 1 Thes. v. 27. Rev. i. 3. v. 4(*om S*).
Add Gal. iv. 21, for ἀκούω, Lm.

ἀναγκάζω.
compel, Luke xiv. 23. Acts xxvi. 11. 2 Cor. xii. 11. Gal. ii. 3, 14.
constrain, Matt. xiv. 22. Mark vi. 45. Acts xxviii. 19. Gal. vi. 12.

ἀναγκαῖος.
necessary, Acts xiii. 46. 1 Cor. xii. 22. 2 Cor. ix. 5. Phil. ii. 25. Tit. iii. 14.
of necessity, Heb. viii. 3.
needful, Phil. i. 24.
near, Acts x. 24.

ἀναγκαστῶς.
by constraint, 1 Pet. v. 2.

ἀνάγκη.
necessity, 1 Cor. vii. 37. ix. 16.

2 Cor. vi. 4. ix. 7. xii. 10. Phm. 14. Heb. vii. 12.
must of necessity[cc], Heb. ix. 16.
necessary[cc], Heb. ix. 23.
distress, Luke xxi. 23. 1 Cor. vii. 26(*marg.* **necessity**). 1 Thes. iii. 7.
With ἐστίν, **it must needs be**, Matt. xviii. 7(–ἐστίν LTr).
With ἔχω, **must needs**, Luke xiv. 18. —**of necessity must**, Luke xxiii. 17(*ap*). —**to need**, Heb. vii. 27. —**be needful**[cc], Jude 3.
ἀνάγκη ὑποτάσσεσθαι, **must needs be subject**, Rom. xiii. 5(ὑποτάσσεσθε G).

ἀναγνωρίζομαι.

be made known, Acts vii. 13.

ἀνάγνωσις.

reading, Acts xiii. 15. 2 Cor. iii. 14. 1 Tim. iv. 13.

ἀνάγω.

lead up, Matt. iv. 1.
bring again, Heb. xiii. 20.
bring up again, Rom. x. 7.
bring forth, Acts xii. 4.
take up, Luke iv. 5.
lead, Luke xxii. 66(ἀπάγω Tr*S*).
bring, Luke ii. 22. Acts ix. 39. xvi. 34p.
offer, Acts vii. 41.
Mid. or *Pass.*, in navigation:
launch forth, Luke viii. 22.
launch, Acts xxi. 1. xxvii. 2, 4p.
set forth, Acts xxi. 2.
depart, Acts xxvii. 12. xxviii. 10p, 11.
loose, Acts xiii. 13p. xvi. 11. xxvii. 21.
sail, Acts xviii. 21. xx. 3. 13.

ἀναδείκνυμι.

show, Acts i. 24.
appoint, Luke x. 1.

ἀνάδειξις.

showing, Luke i. 80.

ἀναδέχομαι.

receive, Acts xxviii. 7. Heb. xi. 17.

ἀναδίδωμι.

deliver, Acts xxiii. 33p.

ἀναζάω.

live again, Rev. xx. 5(ζάω GLTTr).
be alive again, Luke xv. 24, 32 (ζάω TTr*S*).
revive, Rom. vii. 9. xiv. 9(ζάω GLT*S*).

ἀναζητέω.

seek, Luke ii. 44. Acts xi. 25.
Add Luke ii. 45, for ζητέω, G″L TTr.

ἀναζώννυμι.

Mid., **gird up**, 1 Pet. i. 13.

ἀναζωπυρέω.

stir up, 2 Tim. i. 6.

ἀναθάλλω.

flourish again[cc] (*marg.* **be revived**[cc]), Phil. iv. 10.

ἀνάθεμα.

accursed, Rom. ix. 3(*marg.* **separated**). 1 Cor. xii. 3(*marg.* **anathema**). Gal. i. 8, 9.
anathema, 1 Cor. xvi. 22.
With ἀναθεματίζω, **bind under a great curse**, Acts xxiii. 14.

ἀναθεματίζω.

to curse, Mark xiv. 71.
bind under a curse (*marg.* **bind with an oath of execration**), Acts xxiii. 12.
bind with an oath, Acts xxiii. 21.
With ἀνάθεμα, **bind under a great curse**, Acts xxiii. 14.

ἀναθεωρέω.

behold, Acts xvii. 23.
consider, Heb. xiii. 7.

ἀνάθημα.

gift, Luke xxi. 5.

ἀναίδεια.

importunity, Luke xi. 8.

ἀναίρεσις.

death, Acts viii. 1. xxii. 20(*omS*).

ἀναιρέω.

take up, Acts vii. 21.
take away, Heb. x. 9.
put to death, Luke xxiii. 32. Acts xxvi. 10p.
slay, Matt. ii. 16. Acts ii. 23. v.

33, 36. ix. 29. x. 39. xiii. 28. xxii. 20.
kill, Luke xxii. 2. Acts vii. 28*t*. ix. 23, 24. xii. 2. xvi. 27. xxiii. 15, 21, 27. xxv. 3.
Add 2 Thes. ii. 8. for ἀναλίσκω, G'L; ἀναλοῖ *S*.

ἀναίτιος.

guiltless, Matt. xii. 7.
blameless, Matt. xii. 5.

ἀνακαθίζω.

sit up, Luke vii. 15 (καθίζω L[m]). Acts ix. 40.

ἀνακαινίζω.

renew, Heb. vi. 6.

ἀνακαινόω.

renew, 2 Cor. iv. 16. Col. iii. 10.

ἀνακαίνωσις.

renewing, Rom. xii. 2. Tit. iii. 5.

ἀνακαλύπτω.

Pass., **open** (*lit.* unveiled), 2 Cor. iii. 18[p]. — *With* μή, **untaken away**, 2 Cor. iii. 14[p].

ἀνακάμπτω.

to return, Matt. ii. 12. Acts xviii. 21. Heb. xi. 15.
turn again, Luke x. 6.

ἀνάκειμαι.

lie, Mark v. 40(–GL[b]TTr*S*).
lean, John xiii. 23.
sit down, Matt. xxvi. 20. John vi. 11.
sit, Matt. xxvi. 7[p]. Mark xiv. 18[p].
sit at meat, Matt. ix. 10[p]. Mark xvi. 14[p](*marg.* **sit together**; *ap*). Luke vii. 37(κατάκειμαι LTTr*S*). xxii. 27*t*
at the table, John xiii. 28[p].
guest, Matt. xxii. 10[p], 11[p].
Add Mark vi. 26, for συνανάκειμαι, TTr. John xii. 2, *see* συνανάκειμαι.

ἀνακεφαλαιόομαι.

be briefly comprehended, Rom. xiii. 9.
Mid., **gather together in one**, Eph. i. 10.

ἀνακλίνω.

make sit down, Mark vi. 39 (ἀνακλιθῆναι L*S*). Luke ix. 15(κατακλίνω Tr*S*). xii. 37.
lay, Luke ii. 7.
Mid., **sit down**, Matt. viii. 11. xiv. 19. Luke vii. 36 (κατακλίνω LTTr; κατακείμαι *S*). xiii. 29.

ἀνακόπτω.

hinder (*marg.* **drive back**), Gal. v. 7(ἐγκόπτω GLT*S*).

ἀνακράζω.

cry out, Mark i. 23. vi. 49. Luke iv. 33. viii. 28. xxiii. 18.

ἀνακρίνω.

examine, Luke xxiii. 14. Acts iv. 9. xii. 19. xxiv. 8. xxviii. 18[p]. 1 Cor. ix. 3.
search, Acts xvii. 11.
ask question, 1 Cor. x. 25, 27.
discern, 1 Cor. ii. 14.
judge, 1 Cor. ii. 15*t*(*marg.* **discern**). iv. 3*t*, 4. xiv. 24.

ἀνάκρισις.

examination, Acts xxv. 26.

ἀνακυλίω, roll up *or* away.

Mark xvi. 4, for ἀποκυλίω, TTr*S*.

ἀνακύπτω.

lift up one's self, Luke xiii. 11. John viii. 7(*ap*), 10[p](*ap*).
look up, Luke xxi. 28.

ἀναλαμβάνω.

take up, Acts i. 2, 11, 22. vii. 43.
receive up, Mark xvi. 19(*ap*). Acts x. 16. 1 Tim. iii. 16.
take, Acts xxiii. 31. Eph. vi. 16. 2 Tim. iv. 11.
take unto, Eph. vi. 13.
take in, Acts xx. 13, 14.
ἀνελήμφθη for -λήφθη, LT*S*.

ἀνάληψις (-λημψις LTTr *S*).

that . . should be received up (*lit.* of taking up), Luke ix. 51.

ἀναλίσκω.

consume, Luke ix. 54. Gal. v. 15. 2 Thes. ii. 8(ἀναιρέω G'L; ἀναλοῖ *S*).

ἀναλογία.

proportion, Rom. xii. 6.

ἀναλογίζομαι.

consider, Heb. xii. 3.

ἄναλος.

With γίνομαι, **lose saltness**, Mark ix. 50.

ἀνάλυσις.

departure, 2 Tim. iv. 6.

ἀναλύω.

depart, Phil. i. 23.
return, Luke xii. 36.

ἀναμάρτητος.

without sin, John viii. 7(*ap*).

ἀναμένω.

wait for, 1 Thes. i. 10.

ἀναμιμνήσκω.

bring into remembrance, 1 Cor. iv. 17.
put in remembrance, 2 Tim. i. 6.
call to remembrance, Mark xi. 21. Heb. x. 32.
call to mind, Mark xiv. 72.
remember, 2 Cor. vii. 15.

ἀνάμνησις.

remembrance, Luke xxii. 19. 1 Cor. xi. 24, 25.
remembrance again, Heb. x. 3.

ἀνανεόομαι.

be renewed, Eph. iv. 23.

ἀνανήφω.

recover one's self (*Gr.* awake), 2 Tim. ii. 26.

ἀναντίρρητος.

With εἰμί, **can not be spoken against**, Acts xix. 36.

ἀναντιρρήτως.

without gainsaying, Acts x. 29.

ἀνάξιος.

unworthy, 1 Cor. vi. 2.

ἀναξίως.

unworthily, 1 Cor. xi. 27, 29(-G°° LT*S*).

ἀνάπαυσις.

rest, Matt. xi. 29. xii. 43. Luke xi. 24. Rev. xiv. 11.
With ἔχω, **to rest** (*Gr.* have rest), Rev. iv. 8.

ἀναπαύω.

give rest, Matt. xi. 28.
refresh, 1 Cor. xvi. 18. 2 Cor. vii. 13. Phm. 7, 20.
Mid., **take rest**, Matt. xxvi. 45. Mark xiv. 41. — **rest**, Mark vi. 31. 1 Pet. iv. 14. Rev. vi. 11. xiv. 13 (ἀναπαήσονται, *2d fut. pass.*, for ἀναπαύσωνται, LT*S*). — **take ease**, Luke xii. 19.

ἀναπείθω.

persuade, Acts xviii. 13.

ἀνάπειρος. See ἀνάπηρος.

ἀναπέμπω.

send again, Luke xxiii. 11. Phm. 12(πέμπω G').
send, Luke xxiii. 7, 15.
Add Acts xxv. 21, for πέμπω, LT*S*.

ἀναπηδάω, leap, spring up.

Mark x. 50, for ἀνίστημι, LTTr*S*.

ἀνάπηρος, ἀνάπειρος LTr*S*.

maimed, Luke xiv. 13, 21.

ἀναπίπτω.

sit down, Matt. xv. 35. Mark vi. 40. viii. 6. Luke xiv. 10. xxii. 14. John vi. 10*t*. xiii. 12.
sit down to meat, Luke xi. 37. xvii. 7.
lean, John xxi. 20.
Add John xiii. 25, for ἐπιπίπτω, G'LTTr.

ἀναπληρόω.

fill up, 1 Thes. ii. 16.
fulfill, Matt. xiii. 14. Gal. vi. 2.
supply, 1 Cor. xvi. 17. Phil. ii. 30.
occupy, 1 Cor. xiv. 16.

ἀναπολόγητος.

without excuse, Rom. i. 20.
inexcusable, Rom. ii. 1.

ἀναπτύσσω.

open, Luke iv. 17p(ἀνοίγω LTr).

ἀνάπτω.

kindle, Luke xii. 49. Acts xxviii. 2(ἅπτω L*S*). Jas. iii. 5.

ἀναρίθμητος.

innumerable, Heb. xi. 12.

ἀνασείω.
stir up, Luke xxiii. 5.
move, Mark xv. 11.

ἀνασκευάζω.
subvert, Acts xv. 24.

ἀνασπάω.
draw up, Acts xi. 10.
pull out, Luke xiv. 5.

ἀνάστασις.
rising again, Luke ii. 34.
resurrection, Matt. xxii. 23, 28, 30, 31. Mark xii. 18, 23. Luke xiv. 14. xx. 27, 33, 35, 36. John v. 29*t*. xi. 24, 25. Acts i. 22. ii. 31. iv. 2, 33. xvii. 18(*ap*), 32. xxiii. 6, 8. xxiv. 15, 21. Rom. i. 4. vi. 5. 1 Cor. xv. 12, 13, 21, 42. Phil. iii. 10. 2 Tim. ii. 18. Heb. vi. 2. xi. 35. 1 Pet. i. 3. iii. 21. Rev. xx. 5, 6.
With ἐκ, **raised to life again**, Heb. xi. 35.
πρῶτος ἐξ ἀναστάσεως, **the first that should rise**, Acts xxvi. 23.

ἀναστατόω.
turn upside down, Acts xvii. 6.
make an uproar, Acts xxi. 38.
trouble, Gal. v. 12.

ἀνασταυρόω.
crucify afresh, Heb. vi. 6p.

ἀναστενάζω.
sigh deeply, Matt. viii. 12.

ἀναστρέφω.
overthrow, John ii. 15.
return, Acts v. 22. xv. 16.
Pass. or *Mid.*, **be used**, Heb. x. 33. —**have one's conversation**, 2 Cor. i. 12. Eph. ii. 3. —**behave one's self**, 1 Tim. iii. 15. —**live**, Heb. xiii. 18. 2 Pet. ii. 18. —**abide**, Matt. xvii. 22p(συστρέφω LTr*S*). —**pass**, 1 Pet. i. 17.

ἀναστροφή.
conversation, Gal. i. 13. Eph. iv. 22. 1 Tim. iv. 12. Heb. xiii. 7. Jas. iii. 13. 1 Pet. i. 15, 18. ii. 12. iii. 1, 2, 16. 2 Pet. ii. 7. iii. 11.

ἀνατάσσομαι.
set forth in order, Luke i. 1.

ἀνατέλλω.
make to rise, Matt. v. 45.
rise, Luke xii. 54. Jas. i. 11.
risingco, Mark xvi. 2p.
arise, 2 Pet. i. 19.
be up, Matt. xiii. 6p. Mark iv. 6p.
spring up, Matt. iv. 16.
spring, Heb. vii. 14.

ἀνατίθεμαι.
declare, Acts xxv. 14.
communicate, Gal. ii. 2.

ἀνατολή.
day-spring (*marg.* **sun-rising**, or **branch**), Luke i. 78.
east, Matt. ii. 1, 2, 9. viii. 11. xxiv. 27. Luke xiii. 29. Rev. xxi. 13.
With ἡλίου, **east**, Rev. vii. 2. xvi. 12.

ἀνατρέπω.
overthrow, 2 Tim. ii. 18.
subvert, Tit. i. 11.

ἀνατρέφω.
nourish up, Acts vii. 20.
nourish, Acts vii. 21.
bring up, Acts xxii. 3.

ἀναφαίνομαι.
appear, Luke xix. 11.
discover, Acts xxi. 3p.

ἀναφέρω.
carry up, Luke xxiv. 51(*ap*).
bring up, Matt. xvii. 1.
lead up, Mark ix. 2.
bear, Heb. ix. 28. 1 Pet. ii. 24.
offer up, Heb. vii. 27, 27p. 1 Pet. ii. 5.
offer, Heb. xiii. 15. Jas. ii. 21p.

ἀναφωνέω.
speak out, Luke i. 42.

ἀνάχυσις.
excess, 1 Pet. iv. 4.

ἀναχωρέω.
give place, Matt. ix. 24.
withdraw one's self, Matt. xii. 15. Mark iii. 7.

depart, Matt. ii. 12, 13p, 14. iv. 12. xiv. 13. xv. 21. xxvii. 5. John vi. 15.
go aside, Acts xxiii. 19. xxvi. 31p.
turn aside, Matt. ii. 22.

ἀνάψυξις.
refreshing, Acts iii. 19(20).

ἀναψύχω.
refresh, 2 Tim. i. 16.

ἀνδραποδιστής.
menstealer, 1 Tim. i. 10.

ἀνδρίζομαι.
ἀνδρίζεσθε, **quit you like men**, 1 Cor. xvi. 13.

ἀνδροφόνος.
manslayer, 1 Tim. i. 9.

ἀνέγκλητος.
unreprovable, Col. i. 22.
blameless, 1 Cor. i. 8. 1 Tim. iii. 10. Tit. i. 6, 7.

ἀνεκδιήγητος.
unspeakable, 2 Cor. ix. 15.

ἀνεκλάλητος.
unspeakable, 1 Pet. i. 8.

ἀνέκλειπτος.
that faileth not, Luke xii. 33.

ἀνεκτός.
tolerable, Matt. x. 15. xi. 22, 24. Mark vi. 11(*ap*). Luke x. 12, 14.

ἀνελεήμων.
unmerciful, Rom. i. 31.

ἀνέλεος. See ἀνίλεως.

ἀνεμίζομαι.
be driven with the wind, Jas. i. 6.

ἄνεμος.
wind, Matt. vii. 25, 27. viii. 26, 27. xi. 7. xiv. 24, 30, 32. xxiv. 31. Mark iv. 37, 39*t*, 41. vi. 48, 51. xiii. 27. Luke vii. 24. viii. 23, 24, 25. John vi. 18. Acts xxvii. 4, 7, 14, 15. Eph. iv. 14. Jas. iii. 4. Jude 12. Rev. vi. 13. vii. 1*t*.

ἀνένδεκτος.
impossible, Luke xvii. 1.

ἀνεξερεύνητος(–ραύ–T S).
unsearchable, Rom. xi. 33.

ἀνεξίκακος.
patient (*marg.* **forbearing**), 2 Tim. ii. 24.

ἀνεξιχνίαστος.
unsearchable, Eph. iii. 8.
past finding out, Rom. xi. 33.

ἀνεπαίσχυντος.
that needeth not to be ashamed, 2 Tim. ii. 15.

ἀνεπίληπτος (-λημπτος LT S).
unrebukable, 1 Tim. vi. 14.
blameless, 1 Tim. iii. 2. v. 7.

ἀνέρχομαι.
go up, John vi. 3. Gal. i. 17(ἀπέρχομαι L), 18(*marg.* **return**).

ἄνεσις.
liberty, Acts xxiv. 23.
rest, 2 Cor. ii. 13(12). vii. 5. 2 Thes. i. 7.
be easedcc, 2 Cor. viii. 13.

ἀνετάζω.
examine, Acts xxii. 24, 29 (*marg.* **torture**).

ἄνευ.
without, Matt. x. 29. 1 Pet. iii. 1. iv. 9.

ἀνεύθετος.
not commodious, Acts xxvii. 12.

ἀνευρίσκω.
find, Luke ii. 16. Acts xxi. 4.

ἀνέχομαι.
forbear, Eph. iv. 2. Col. iii. 13.
bear with, Acts xviii. 14. 2 Cor. xi. 1*t*, 4.
suffer, Matt. xvii. 17. Mark ix. 19. Luke ix. 41. 1 Cor. iv. 12. 2 Cor. xi. 19, 20. Heb. xiii. 22.
endure, 2 Thes. i. 4. 2 Tim. iv. 3.

ἀνεψιός.
sister's son, Col. iv. 10.

ἄνηθον.
anise, Matt. xxiii. 23.

ἀνήκω.
be fit, Col. iii. 18.
be convenient, Eph. v. 4. Phm. 8.

ἀνήμερος.

fierce, 2 Tim. iii. 3.

ἀνήρ.

man, Matt. vii. 24, 26. xii. 41. xiv. 21, 35. xv. 38. Mark vi. 20, 44. x. 2. Luke i. 27, 34. v. 8, 12, 18. vii. 20. viii. 27, 38, 41. ix. 14, 30, 32, 38. xi. 31, 32. xiv. 24. xvii. 12. xix. 2, 7. xxii. 63. xxiii. 50*t*. xxiv. 4. John i. 13, 30. vi. 10. Acts i. 10, 11, 16, 21. ii. 5, 14, 22*t*, 29, 37. iii. 2, 12. iv. 4. v. 1, 14, 25, 35, 36. vi. 3, 5, 11. vii. 2. viii. 2, 3, 9, 12, 27. ix. 2, 7, 12, 13, 38(-G°). x. 1, 5, 17, 19, 21, 22, 28, 30. xi. 3, 11, 12, 13(*omS*), 20, 24. xiii. 7, 15, 16, 21, 22(-G°), 26, 38. xiv. 8. xv. 7, 13, 22*t*, 25. xvi. 9. xvii. 12, 22, 31, 34. xviii. 24. xix. 7, 35, 37. xx. 30. xxi. 11, 23, 26, 28, 38. xxii. 1, 3, 4, 12. xxiii. 1, 6, 21, 27, 30. xxiv. 5. xxv. 5, 14, 17, 23, 24. xxviii. 17.

Rom. iv. 8. vii. 3*t*. xi. 4. 1 Cor. vii. 16. xi. 3*t*, 4, 7*t*, 8*t*, 9*t*, 11*t*, 12*t*, 14. xiii. 11. Eph. iv. 13. v. 38. 1 Tim. ii. 8, 12. v. 9. Jas. i. 8, 12, 20, 23. ii. 2. iii. 2.

husband, Matt. i. 16, 19. Mark x. 12. Luke ii. 36. xvi. 18(-G°). John. iv. 16, 17*t*, 18*t*. Acts v. 9, 10. Rom. vii. 2*tr*, 3*t*. 1 Cor. vii. 2, 3*t*, 4*t*, 10, 11*t*, 13, 14, 14 (ἀδελφός LT*S*), 16, 34, 39*t*. xiv. 35. 2 Cor. xi. 2. Gal. iv. 27. Eph. v. 22, 23, 24, 25, 33. Col. iii. 18, 19. 1 Tim. iii. 2, 12. Tit. i. 6. ii. 5. 1 Pet. iii. 1, 5, 7. Rev. xxi. 2.

sir, Acts vii. 26. xiv. 15. xix. 25. xxvii. 10, 21, 25.

fellow, Acts xvii. 5.

ἀνὴρ προφήτης, **a prophet,** Luke xxiv. 19.

ἀνὴρ φονεύς, **a murderer,** Acts iii. 14.

Add Mark vi. 54(*ap*). Luke vi. 8, for ἄνθρωπος, G″TTr*S*. Acts xiii. 6(certain . .), LT*S*. 1 Cor. vii. 13, for αὐτόν, G″LT, αὐτὸν ἄνδρα *S*?.

ἀνθίστημι.

resist, Matt. v. 39. Luke xxi. 15. Acts vi. 10. Rom. ix. 19. xiii. 2*t*. 2 Tim. iii. 8. Jas. iv. 7. 1 Pet. v. 9.

withstand, Acts xiii. 8. Gal. ii. 11. Eph. vi. 13. 2 Tim. iii. 8. iv. 15.

ἀνθομολογέομαι.

give thanks, Luke ii. 38.

ἄνθος.

flower, Jas. i. 10, 11. 1 Pet. i. 24*t*.

ἀνθρακιά.

fire of coals, John xviii. 18. xxi. 9.

ἄνθραξ.

coal, Rom. xii. 20.

ἀνθρωπάρεσκος.

menpleaser, Eph. vi. 6. Col. iii. 22.

ἀνθρώπινος.

man's, 1 Cor. ii. 4(*omS*), 13. iv. 3.

of man, 1 Pet. ii. 13.

after the manner of men, Rom. vi. 19.

common to man (*marg.* **moderate),** 1 Cor. x. 13.

With φύσις, **mankind** (*Gr.* nature of man), Jas. iii. 7.

Add Acts xvii. 25, for ἄνθρωπος, G″LT*S*.

ἀνθρωποκτόνος.

murderer, Jo. viii. 44. 1 Jo. iii. 15*t*.

ἄνθρωπος.

man, Matt. iv. 4, 19. v. 13, 16, 19. vi. 1, 2, 5, 14, 15, 16, 18. vii. 9, 12. viii. 9, 27. ix. 8, 9, 32(-LTr^{b}*S*). x. 17, 32, 33, 35, 36. xi. 8, 19. xii. 10, 11, 12, 13, 31, 31(-LTr*S*), 35*t*, 36, 43, 45. xiii. 24, 25, 31, 44, 45, 52. xv. 9, 11*t*, 18, 20*t*. xvi. 13, 23, 26*t*. xvii. 14, 22. xviii. 7, 12. xix. 3 (-L*S*), 5, 6, 10, 12, 26. xx. 1. xxi. 25, 26, 28. xxii. 11, 16. xxiii. 4, 5, 7, 13(14), 28. xxv. 14, 24. xxvi. 24*t*, 72, 74. xxvii. 32, 57. Mark i. 17, 23. ii. 27*t*. iii. 1, 3, 5, 28. iv. 26. v. 2, 8. vii. 7, 8, 11, 15*t*, 18, 20*t*, 21, 23. viii. 24, 27, 33, 36, 37 (-T). ix. 31. x. 7, 9, 27. xi. 2, 30, 32. xii. 1, 14. xiii. 34. xiv. 13, 21*t*, 71. xv. 39.

Luke i. 25. ii. 14, 25*t*, 52. iv. 4,

33. v. 10, 18, 20. vi. 6, 8(ἀνήρ G''TTr *S*), 10(G', αὐτῷ GLTTr), 22, 26, 31, 45, 45(–G∞LbTTr*S*), 48, 49. vii. 8, 25, 31, 34. viii. 29, 33, 35. ix. 25, 44, 56(*ap*). x. 30. xi. 24, 26, 44, 46. xii. 8, 9, 14, 16, 36. xiii. 4, 19. xiv. 2, 16, 30. xv. 4, 11. xvi. 1, 15*t*, 19. xviii. 2, 4, 10, 11, 27. xix. 21, 22, 30. xx. 4, 6, 9. xxi. 26. xxii. 10, 22, 58, 60. xxiii. 4, 6, 14*t*, 47. xxiv. 7. John i. 4, 6, 9. ii. 10, 25*t*. iii. 1, 4, 19, 27. iv. 28, 29, 50. v. 5, 7, 9, 12, 15, 34, 41. vi. 10, 14. vii. 22, 23*t*, 46, 46(*ap*), 51. viii. 17, 40. ix. 1, 11, 16*t*, 24*t*, 30. x. 33. xi. 47, 50. xii. 43. xvi. 21. xvii. 6. xviii. 14, 17, 29. xix. 5. Acts iv. 9, 12, 13, 14, 16, 17, 22. v. 4, 28, 29, 35, 38*t*. vi. 13. ix. 33. x. 26, 28. xii. 22. xiv. 11, 15. xv. 17, 26. xvi. 17, 20, 35. xvii. 25 (ἀνθρώπινος G''LT*S*), 26, 29, 30. xviii. 13. xix. 16, 35. xxi. 28, 39. xxii. 15, 25, 26. xxiii. 9. xxiv. 16. xxv. 16, 22. xxvi. 31, 32. xxviii. 4.

Rom. i. 18, 23. ii. 1, 3, 9, 16, 29. iii. 4, 28 iv. 6. v. 12*t*, 15, 18*t*, 19. vi. 6. vii 1, 22, 24. ix. 20. x. 5. xii. 17, 18. xiv. 18, 20. 1 Cor. i. 25*t*. ii. 5, 9, 11*tr*, 14. iii. 21. iv. 1, 9. vi. 18. vii. 1, 7, 23, 26. xi. 28. xiii. 1. xiv. 2, 3. xv. 19, 21*t*, 39, 45(–L), 47*t*. 2 Cor. iii. 2. iv. 2, 16. v. 11. viii. 21. xii. 2, 3, 4. Gal. i. 1*t*, 10*tr*, 12. ii. 6, 16. iii. 12(*omS*), 15. v. 3. vi. 1, 7. Eph. ii. 15. iii. 5, 16. iv. 8, 14, 22, 24. v. 31. vi. 7. Phil. ii. 7, 8. iv. 5. Col. i. 28*tr*(–2d G°). ii. 8, 22. iii. 9, 23. 1 Thes. ii. 4, 6, 13, 15. iv. 8. 2 Thes. ii. 3. iii. 2. 1 Tim. ii. 1, 4, 5*t*. iv. 10. v. 24. vi. 5, 9, 11, 16. 2 Tim. ii. 2. iii. 2, 8, 13, 17. Tit. i. 14. ii. 11. iii. 2, 8, 10.

Heb. ii. 6. v. 1*t*. vi. 16. vii. 8, 28. viii. 2. ix. 27. xiii. 6. Jas. i. 7, 19. ii. 20, 24. iii. 8, 9. v. 17. 1 Pet. i. 24(G', αὐτῆς GLT, αὐτοῦ *S*). ii. 4, 15. iii. 4. iv. 2, 6. 2 Pet. i. 21*t*. ii. 16. iii. 7. 1 John v. 9. Jude 4. Rev. iv. 7. viii. 11. ix. 4, 5, 6, 7, 10, 15, 18, 20. xi. 13. xiii. 13, 18. xiv. 4. xvi. 2, 8, 9, 18, 21*t*. xviii. 13. xxi. 3, 17.

With υἱός, **Son of man**, Matt. viii. 20. ix. 6. x. 23. xi. 19. xii. 8, 32, 40. xiii. 37, 41. xvi. 13, 27, 28. xvii. 9, 12, 22. xviii. 11(*ap*). xix. 28. xx. 18, 28. xxiv. 27, 30*t*, 37, 39, 44. xxv. 13(*ap*), 31. xxvi. 2, 24*t*, 45, 64. Mark ii. 10, 28. viii. 31, 38. ix. 9, 12, 31. x. 33, 45. xiii. 26. xiv. 21*t*, 41, 62. Luke v. 24. vi. 5, 22. vii. 34. ix. 22, 26, 44, 56(*ap*), 58. xi. 30. xii. 8, 10, 40. xvii. 22, 24, 26, 30. xviii. 8, 31. xix. 10. xxi. 27, 36. xxii. 22, 48, 69. xxiv. 7. John i. 51(52). iii. 13, 14. v. 27. vi. 27, 53, 62. viii. 28. xii. 23, 34*t*. xiii. 31. Acts vii. 56. Rev. i. 13. xiv. 14.—**son of man**, Heb. ii. 6.

ἄνθρωπος βασιλεύς, **a certain king**, Matt. xviii. 23. xxii. 2.

ἄνθρωπος εὐγενής, **nobleman**, Luke xix. 12. [xiii. 28.

ἐχθρὸς ἄνθρωπος, **an enemy**, Matt.

ἄνθρωπος οἰκοδεσπότης, **a certain householder**, Matt. xxi. 33.

οἱ ἄνθρωποι οἱ ποιμένες, **the shepherds**, Luke ii. 15 (–οἱ ἄν. LbTrb*S*).

ἄνθρωποι Ῥωμαῖοι, **Romans**, Acts xvi. 37.

κατὰ ἄνθρωπον, **after man**, Gal. i. 11.—**after the manner of men**, 1 Cor. xv. 32. Gal. iii. 15.—**as a man**, Rom. iii. 5. 1 Cor. ix. 8.—**as men**, 1 Cor. iii. 3(*Gr.* according to man).

Add Mark vii. 15, for αὐτοῦ, LTTr *S*. John ix. 35, for θεός, G'*S*. Acts v. 34, for ἀπόστολος, G'LT*S*. 1 Cor. iii. 4, for σαρκικός, LT*S*. Rev. xvi. 9 (. . blasphemed), G'T.

ἀνθυπατεύω.

be deputy, Acts xviii. 12p (ἀνθυπάτου ὄντος G'L*S*).

ἀνθύπατος.

deputy, Acts xiii. 7, 8, 12. **xix. 38.**
Add Acts xviii. 12(*see* ἀνθυπατεύω).

ἀνίημι.

to loose, Acts xvi. 26. xxvii. 40.
leave, Heb. xiii. 5.
forbear (*marg.* **moderate**), Eph. vi. 9.

ἀνίλεως, ἀνέλεος G'LTS.

without mercy, Jas. ii. 13.

ἄνιπτος.

unwashen, Matt. xv. 20. Mark vii. 2, 5 (G'; κοινός GLTTrS).

ἀνίστημι.

raise, Acts xvii. 31.
raise up, Matt. xxii. 24. John vi. 40, 44, 54. Acts ii. 24, 30(*ap*), 32. iii. 22, 26. vii. 37. xiii. 34.
raise up again, John vi. 39. Acts xiii. 33(32).
lift up, Acts ix. 41.
stand up, Mark xiv. 60. Luke iv. 16. x. 25. Acts i. 15. v. 34p. x. 26. xi. 28. xiii. 16p.
stand upright, Acts xiv. 10.
rise, Matt. xii. 41. Mark ix. 9, 31. x. 50 (ἀναπηδάω LTTrS). xii. 23 (-GooLLTrS), 25. xvi. 9p(*ap*). Luke xi. 7, 8. xvi. 31. xxii. 45. xxiv. 46. Acts x. 13, 41. xxvi. 16. Rom. xiv. 9(*om*S). xv. 12. 1 Thes. iv. 16. Heb. vii. 11.
risingcc, Mark ix. 10p.
rise up, Mark i. 35. iii. 26. Luke iv. 29. v. 25, 28. xi. 32. xxii. 45p. xxiv. 33. John xi. 31. Acts v. 17, 36, 37. xiv. 20. xv. 7. xxvi. 30. 1 Cor. x. 7.
rise again, Matt. xvii. 9(ἐγείρω L TTr). xx. 19(ἐγείρω TTrS). Mark viii. 31. x. 34. Luke ix. 8, 19. xviii. 33. xxiv. 7. John xi. 23, 24. xx. 9. Acts xvii. 3. 1 Thes. iv. 14.
arise, Matt. ix. 9. xxvi. 62. Mark ii. 14. v. 42. vii. 24. ix. 27. x. 1. xiv. 57. Luke i. 39. iv. 38, 39. vi. 8. viii. 55. xv. 18, 20. xvii. 19. xxiii. 1. xxiv. 12(*ap*). Acts v. 6. vi. 9. vii. 18. viii. 26, 27. ix. 6, 11, 18, 34*t*, 39, 40. x. 20. xi. 7. xx. 30. xxii. 10, 16. xxiii. 9. Eph. v. 14. Heb. vii. 15.
arise up, Acts xii. 7.

Add, for ἐγείρω, Matt. xvii. 23, L. Mark vi. 14, T. Luke ix. 22, G'LT. 1 Cor. xv. 52, L.—Acts x. 23, ἀναστάς for ὁ Πέτρος, GLTS.

ἀνόητος.

unwise, Rom. i. 14.
foolish, Gal. iii. 1, 3. 1 Tim. vi. 9. Tit. iii. 3.
fool, Luke xxiv. 25.

ἄνοια.

folly, 2 Tim. iii. 9.
madness, Luke vi. 11.

ἀνοίγω.

to open, Matt. ii. 11p. iii. 16. v. 2. vii. 7, 8. ix. 30. xiii. 35. xvii. 27p. xx. 33. xxv. 11. xxvii. 52. Luke i. 64. iii. 21. xi. 9, 10. xii. 36. xiii. 25. John ix. 10, 14, 17, 21, 26, 30, 32. x. 3, 21. xi. 37. Acts v. 19, 23p. vii. 56(διανοίγω LTS). viii. 32, 35. ix. 8p, 40. x. 11, 34p. xii. 10, 14, 16p. xiv. 27. xvi. 26. xviii. 14. xxvi. 18. 1 Cor. xvi. 9. 2 Cor. ii. 12p. vi. 11. Col. iv. 3. Rev. iii. 7*t*, 20. iv. 1. v. 2, 3, 4, 5, 9. vi. 1, 3, 5, 7, 9, 12. viii. 1. ix. 2(*ap*). xi. 19. xii. 16. xiii. 6. xv. 5. xix. 11. xx. 12*t*.
open, John i. 51(52)p. Acts xvi. 27p. Rom. iii. 13p. Rev. iii. 8p. x. 2p, 8p.

Add Mark vii. 35, for διανοίγω, LTTrS. Luke iv. 17, for ἀναπτύσσω, LTr.

ἀνοικοδομέω.

build again, Acts xv. 16*t*.

ἄνοιξις.

With ἐν, **that .. may open,** Eph. vi. 19.

ἀνομία.

transgression of the law, 1 John iii. 4.
With ποιέω, **transgress the law,** 1 John iii. 4.
unrighteousness, 2 Cor. vi. 14.
iniquity, Matt. vii. 23. xiii. 41. xxiii. 28. xxiv. 12. Rom. iv. 7. vi.

19*t*. 2 Thes. ii. 7. Tit. ii. 14. Heb. i. 9. viii. 12. x. 17.

ἄνομος.

without law, 1 Cor. ix. 21*f*.
unlawful, 2 Pet. ii. 8.
lawless, 1 Tim. i. 9.
transgressor, Mark xv. 28. Luke xxii. 37.
wicked, Acts ii. 23. 2 Thes. ii. 8.

ἀνόμως.

without law, Rom. ii. 12*t*.

ἀνορθόω.

make straight, Luke xiii. 13.
set up, Acts xv. 16.
lift up, Heb. xii. 12.

ἀνόσιος.

unholy, 1 Tim. i. 9. 2 Tim. iii. 2.

ἀνοχή.

forbearance, Rom. ii. 4. iii. 25(26).

ἀνταγωνίζομαι.

strive against, Heb. xii. 4.

ἀντάλλαγμα.

in[co] **exchange**, Matt. xvi. 26. Mark viii. 37.

ἀνταναπληρόω.

fill up, Col. i. 24.

ἀνταποδίδωμι.

repay, Rom. xii. 19.
recompense, Luke xiv. 14*t*. 2 Thes. i. 6. Heb. x. 30.
recompense again, Rom. xi. 35.
render, 1 Thes. iii. 9.

ἀνταπόδομα.

recompense, Luke xiv. 12. Rom. xi. 9.

ἀνταπόδοσις.

reward, Col. iii. 24.

ἀνταποκρίνομαι.

answer again, Luke xiv. 6.
reply against (*marg.* **answer again**, or **dispute with**), Rom. ix. 20.

ἀντεῖπον.

say against, Acts iv. 14.
gainsay, Luke xxi. 15.

ἀντέχομαι.

hold to, Matt. vi. 24. Luke xvi. 13.
hold fast, Tit. i. 9.
support, 1 Thes. v. 14.

ἀντί.

in the room of, Matt. ii. 22.
for, Matt. v. 38*t*. xvii. 27. xx. 28. Mark x. 45. Luke xi. 11. John i. 16. Rom. xii. 17. 1 Cor. xi. 15. 1 Thes. v. 15. Heb. xii. 2, 16. 1 Pet. iii. 9*t*.
ἀντὶ τούτου, **for this cause**, Eph. v. 31.
ἀνθ' ὧν, **because**, Luke i. 20. xix. 44. Acts xii. 23. 2 Thes. ii. 10. — **therefore**, Luke xii. 3.
ἀντὶ τοῦ λέγειν, **for that . . ought to say** (*lit.* instead of saying), Jas. iv. 15.

ἀντιβάλλω.

have (*lit.* exchange), Luke xxiv. 17.

ἀντιδιατίθεμαι.

oppose one's self, 2 Tim. ii. 25.

ἀντίδικος.

adversary, Matt. v. 25*t*. Luke xii. 58. xviii. 3. 1 Pet. v. 8.

ἀντίθεσις.

opposition, 1 Tim. vi. 20.

ἀντικαθίστημι.

resist, Heb. xii. 4.

ἀντικαλέω.

bid again, Luke xiv. 12.

ἀντίκειμαι.

be contrary, Gal. v. 17. 1 Tim. i. 10.
oppose, 2 Thes. ii. 4.
adversary, Luke xiii. 17[p]. xxi. 15[p]. 1 Cor. xvi. 9[p]. Phil. i. 28[p]. 1 Tim. v. 14[p].

ἀντικρύ, ἄντικρυς LT*S*.

over against, Acts xx. 15.

ἀντιλαμβάνομαι.

to support, Acts xx. 35.
help, Luke i. 54.
partaker, 1 Tim. vi. 2[p].

ἀντιλέγω.

speak against, Luke ii. 34. John

xix. 12. Acts xiii. 45 (-G°L*S*).
xxviii. 19p, 22.
gainsay, Rom. x. 21.
gainsayer, Tit. i. 9p.
answer again (*marg.* **gainsay**), Tit.
contradict, Acts xiii. 45. [ii. 9.
With μή, **deny**, Luke xx. 27 (λέγω
LmTr*S*).

ἀντίληψις (-λημψις LT*S*).
help, 1 Cor. xii. 28.

ἀντιλογία.
gainsaying, Jude 11.
contradiction, Heb. vii. 7. xii. 3.
strife, Heb. vi. 16.

ἀντιλοιδορέω.
revile again, 1 Pet. ii. 23.

ἀντίλυτρον.
ransom, 1 Tim. ii. 6.

ἀντιμετρέω.
measure again, Matt. vii. 2 (μετρέω
GLTTr*S*). Luke vi. 38(μετρέω Lm).

ἀντιμισθία.
recompense, Rom. i. 27. 2 Cor. vi.
13.

ἀντιπαρέρχομαι.
pass by on the other side, Luke x.
31, 32.

ἀντιπέραν,
ἀντιπέρα G′′LTr*S*, ἀντίπερα T.
over against, Luke viii. 26.

ἀντιπίπτω.
resist, Acts vii. 51.

ἀντιστρατεύομαι.
war against, Rom. vii. 23.

ἀντιτάσσομαι.
oppose one's self, Acts xviii. 6p.
resist, Rom. xiii. 2. Jas. iv. 6. v.
6. 1 Pet. v. 5.

ἀντίτυπον.
like figure, 1 Pet. iii. 21.
figure, Heb. ix. 24.

ἀντίχριστος.
antichrist, 1 John ii. 18*t*, 22. iv. 3.
2 John 7.

ἀντλέω.
draw out, John ii. 8.
draw, John ii. 9. iv. 7, 15.

ἄντλημα.
With οὔτε, **nothing to draw with**,
John iv. 11.

ἀντοφθαλμέω.
bear up into, Acts xxvii. 15.

ἄνυδρος.
without water, 2 Pet. ii. 17. Jude
12.
dry, Matt. xii. 43. Luke xi. 24.

ἀνυπόκριτος.
without hypocrisy, Jas. iii. 17.
without dissimulation, Rom. xii. 9.
unfeigned, 2 Cor. vi. 6. 1 Tim. i.
5. 2 Tim. i. 5. 1 Pet. i. 22.

ἀνυπότακτος.
that is not put under, Heb. ii. 8.
disobedient, 1 Tim. i. 9.
unruly, Tit. i. 6, 10.

ἄνω.
up, John xi. 41. Heb. xii. 15.
above, John viii. 23. Acts ii. 19.
Gal. iv. 26. Col. iii. 1, 2.
high, Phil. iii. 14.
With ἕως, **up to the brim**, John ii. 7.
Add Rev. v. 3(heaven . .), G′.

ἀνώγεον, ἀνάγαιον GLTTr*S*.
upper room, Mark xiv. 15. Luke
xxii. 12.

ἄνωθεν.
from above, John iii. 31. xix. 11.
Jas. i. 17. iii. 15, 17.
from the beginning, Acts xxvi. 5.
from the very first, Luke i. 3.
again (*marg.* **from above**), John iii.
3, 7.
ἀπὸ ἄνωθεν, **from the top**, Matt.
xxvii. 51. Mark xv. 38.
ἐκ τῶν ἄνωθεν, **from the top**, John
xix. 23.
πάλιν ἄνωθεν, **again**, Gal. iv. 9.

ἀνωτερικός.
upper, Acts xix. 1.

ἀνώτερον.
higher, Luke xiv. 10.
above, Heb. x. 8.

ἀνωφελής.

unprofitable, Tit. iii. 9.

With art., **unprofitableness**, Heb. vii. 18.

ἀξίνη.

axe, Matt. iii. 10. Luke iii. 9.

ἄξιος.

worthy, Matt. x. 10, 11, 13*t*, 37*t*, 38. xxii. 8. Luke iii. 8(*marg.* meet). vii. 4. x. 7. xii. 48. xv. 19, 21. xxiii. 15. John i. 27. Acts xiii. 25. xxiii. 29. xxv. 11, 25. xxvi. 31. Rom. i. 32. viii. 18. 1 Tim. i. 15. iv. 9. v. 18. vi. 1. Heb. xi. 38. Rev. iii. 4. iv. 11. v. 2, 4, 9, 12. xvi. 6.

meet, Matt. iii. 8(*marg.* **answerable**). Acts xxvi. 20. 1 Cor. xvi. 4. 2 Thes. i. 3.

Plur. neut., **due reward**, Luke xxiii. 41.

With οὐ, **unworthy**, Acts xiii. 46.

ἀξιόω.

count worthy, 2 Thes. i. 11 (*marg.* **vouchsafe**). 1 Tim. v. 17. Heb. iii. 3.

think worthy, Luke vii. 7. Heb. x. 29.

think good, Acts xv. 38.

desire, Acts xxviii. 22.

ἀξίως.

as becometh, Rom. xvi. 2. Phil. i. 27.

worthy, Eph. iv. 1. Col. i. 10. 1 Thes. ii. 12.

ἀξίως τοῦ θεοῦ, **after a godly sort**, 3 John 6.

ἀόρατος.

invisible, Col. i. 15, 16. 1 Tim. i. 17. Heb. xi. 27.

τὰ ἀόρατα, **the invisible things**, Rom. i. 20.

ἀπαγγέλλω.

bring word, Matt. xxviii. 8.

bring word again, Matt. ii. 8.

report, Acts iv. 23. 1 Cor. xiv. 25.

tell, Matt. viii. 33. xiv. 12. xxviii. 9(*ap*), 10. Mark vi. 30. xvi. 10 (*ap*), 13(*ap*). Luke vii. 22. viii. 20, 34, 36. ix. 36. xiii. 1. xviii. 37. xxiv. 9. John iv. 51 (ἀγγέλλω Tr^b*S*). xx. 18 (ἀγγέλλω LTTr*S*). Acts v. 22, 25. xii. 14, xv. 27. xvi. 36. xxii. 26. xxiii. 16, 17, 19.

declare, Luke viii. 47. Heb. ii. 12. 1 John i. 3.

show, Matt. xii. 18. xxviii. 11. Luke vii. 18. xiv. 21. Acts xi. 13. xii. 17. xxvi. 20. xxviii. 21. 1 Thes. i. 9. 1 John i. 2.

show again, Matt. xi. 4.

Add, for ἀναγγέλλω, Mark v. 14, GLTTr*S*. 19, LTTr*S*. John xvi. 25, LTTr*S*. Acts xvi. 38, LT*S*.

ἀπάγχομαι.

hang one's self, Matt. xxvii. 5.

ἀπάγω.

lead away, Matt. xxvi. 57. xxvii. 2, 31. Mark xiv. 44, 53. xv. 16. Luke xiii. 15. xxiii. 26. John xviii. 13 (ἄγω LTr*S*). xix. 16 (17; ἄγω G; – G^{o}LTTr).

lead, Matt. vii. 13, 14.

take away, Acts xxiv. 7(*ap*).

put to death, Acts xii. 19.

carry away, 1 Cor. xii. 2.

bring, Acts xxiii. 17.

Add Luke xxi. 12, for ἄγω, TTr*S*. xxii. 66, for ἀνάγω, Tr*S*. Rev. xiii. 10, for συνάγω, G'.

ἀπαίδευτος.

unlearned, 2 Tim. ii. 23.

ἀπαίρω.

take away, Mark ii. 20. Luke v. 35.

take, Matt. ix. 15.

ἀπαιτέω.

be required^{cc}(*Gr.* do they require), Luke xii. 20.

ask again, Luke vi. 30.

ἀπαλγέω.

be past feeling, Eph. iv. 19.

ἀπαλλάσσω.

deliver, Luke xii. 58. Heb. ii. 15.

Mid., **depart**, Acts xix. 12.

ἀπαλλοτριόομαι.

be alienated, Eph. iv. 18.

With εἰμί, **be alienated,** Col. i. 21p.
—**be an alien,** Eph. ii. 12p.

ἁπαλός.

tender, Matt. xxiv. 32. Mark xiii. 28.

ἀπαντάω.

to meet, Matt. xxviii. 9 (ὑπαντάω TrS). Mark v. 2 (ὑπαντάω LTrS). xiv. 13. Luke xiv. 31 (ὑπαντάω LT TrS). xvii. 12. John iv. 51(ὑπαντάω LTTrS). Acts xvi. 16(ὑπαντάω TS).

ἀπάντησις.

With εἰς, **to meet,** Matt. xxv. 1 (ὑπάντησις LTrS), 6. Acts xxviii. 15. 1 Thes. iv. 17.

ἅπαξ.

once, 2 Cor. xi. 25. Phil. iv. 16. 1 Thes. ii. 18. Heb. vi. 4. ix. 7, 26, 27, 28. x. 2. xii. 26, 27. 1 Pet. iii. 18, 20(*see* ἀπεκδέχομαι). Jude 3, 5.

ἀπαράβατος.

unchangeable (*marg.* **not passing from one to another**), Heb. vii. 24.

ἀπαρασκεύαστος.

unprepared, 2 Cor. ix. 4.

ἀπαρνέομαι.

deny, Matt. xvi. 24. xxvi. 34, 35, 75. Mark viii. 34. xiv. 30, 31, 72. Luke ix. 23 (ἀρνέομαι GLTTrS). xii. 9. xxii. 61. John xiii. 38(ἀρνέομαι LTTr).
With μή, **deny,** Luke xxii. 34(–μή LTrS).

ἀπάρτι, ἀπ' ἄρτι GLTTr.

from henceforth, Rev. xiv. 13.

ἀπαρτισμός.

With εἰς, **to finish,** Luke xiv. 28.

ἀπαρχή.

first-fruit, Rom. xi. 16.
first-fruits, Rom. viii. 23. xvi. 5. 1 Cor. xv. 20, 23. xvi. 15. Jas. i. 18. Rev. xiv. 4.
Add 2 Thes. ii. 13, ἀπαρχήν for ἀπ' ἀρχῆς, L.

ἅπας.

every man, Mark viii. 25.
every one, Acts v. 16.
all, Mark xvi. 15(*ap*). Luke iv. 6. xix. 48. xxi. 4(πᾶς LTr).
whole, Luke viii. 37. xix. 37. xxiii. 1.
Plur., **all,** Matt. vi. 32. xxiv. 39. xxviii. 11. Mark v. 40(πᾶς GLTTr S). xi. 32 (πᾶς LS). Luke iii. 16, 21. v. 11 (πᾶς LTrS), 26, 28 (πᾶς LTr). vii. 16(πᾶς GTr). ix. 15. xv. 13(πᾶς LTr). xvii. 27(πᾶς LTr), 29 (πᾶς LTr). xix. 7 (πᾶς LTTrS). xxi. 4 (πᾶς L), 12 (πᾶς GLTTr). Acts ii. 1(πᾶς LT, –S), 4(πᾶς LS), 14(πᾶς LS). iv. 31. v. 12(πᾶς L). vi. 15(πᾶς LS). xi. 10. xiii. 29 (πᾶς GLTS). xvi. 3 (πᾶς L), 28. xxvii. 33. Eph. vi. 13. Jas. iii. 2.
—**all things,** Luke ii. 39 (πᾶς Tr). Acts ii. 44. iv. 32(πᾶς L). x. 8.
Add, for πᾶς, Mark i. 27, TTrS. Luke xx. 6, LmTTrS. xxi. 15, TTr. John iv. 25, TTrS. Acts ii. 7, 2d, LT. xxv. 24, 2d, LTS. 2 Thes. ii. 12, LmTS. 1 Tim. i. 16, LTS.

ἀπασπάζομαι, take leave of.

Acts xxi. 6, for ἀσπάζομαι, LTS.

ἀπατάω.

deceive, Eph. v. 6. 1 Tim. ii. 14, 14(ἐξαπατάω LTS). Jas. i. 26.

ἀπάτη.

deceit, Col. ii. 8.
deceiving, 2 Pet. ii. 13(ἀγάπη G'L).
deceitfulness, Matt. xiii. 22. Mark iv. 19. Heb. iii. 13.
deceitful(*lit.* of deceit), Eph. iv. 22.
deceivableness, 2 Thes. ii. 10.

ἀπάτωρ.

without father, Heb. vii. 3.

ἀπαύγασμα.

brightness, Heb. i. 3.

ἀπεῖδον,

ἀφεῖδον LTS, used as aor. of ἀφοράω.

ἀπείθεια.

unbelief, Rom. xi. 30, 32. Heb. iv. 6, 11(*marg.* **disobedience**).
disobedience, Eph. ii. 2. v. 6(*marg.* **unbelief**; *ap*). Col. iii. 6.

ἀπειθέω.

believe not, John iii. 36. Acts xvii. 5(-GL*S*). xix. 9. Rom. xi. 30 and 31 (*marg.* **obey not**). xv. 31(*marg.* **be disobedient**). Heb. iii. 18. xi. 31 (*marg.* **be disobedient**).

unbelieving, Acts xiv. 2p.

obey not, Rom. ii. 8. 1 Pet. iii. 1. iv. 17.

be disobedient, 1 Pet. ii. 7, 8. iii. 20.

disobedient, Rom. x. 21p.

ἀπειθής.

disobedient, Luke i. 17. Acts xxvi. 19. Rom. i. 30. 2 Tim. iii. 2. Tit. i. 16. iii. 3.

ἀπειλέω.

threaten, Acts iv. 17. 1 Pet. ii. 23.

ἀπειλή.

threatening, Acts iv. 29. ix. 1. Eph. vi. 9.

straitly (*lit.* with threatening), Acts iv. 17(-L*S*).

ἄπειμι.

be absent, 2 Cor. x. 1, 11p. xiii. 2, 10. Phil. i. 27. Col. ii. 5.

absent, 1 Cor. v. 3p.

ἄπειμι.

go, Acts xvii. 10.

ἀπεῖπον.

renounce, 2 Cor. iv. 2.

ἀπείραστος.

With εἰμί, **can not be tempted**, Jas. i. 13.

ἄπειρος.

unskilful (*Gr.* having no experience), Heb. v. 13.

ἀπεκδέχομαι.

wait for, Rom. viii. 19, 23, 25. 1 Cor. i. 7. Gal. v. 5.

look for, Phil. iii. 20. Heb. ix. 28.

Add 1 Pet. iii. 20, for ἅπαξ ἐκδέχομαι, GLT*S*.

ἀπεκδύομαι.

put off, Col. iii. 9.

spoil, Col. ii. 15.

ἀπέκδυσις.

putting off, Col. ii. 11.

ἀπελαύνω.

drive, Acts xviii. 16.

ἀπελεγμός.

Lit. refutation; *with* εἰς, **at nought**, Acts xix. 27.

ἀπελεύθερος.

freeman (*Gr.* made free), 1 Cor. vii. 22.

ἀπελπίζω.

hope for again, Luke vi. 35.

ἀπέναντι.

over against, Matt. xxi. 2(κατέναντι LTr*S*). xxvii. 61.

before, Matt. xxvii. 24 (κατέναντι LTr). Rom. iii. 18.

in the presence of, Acts iii. 16.

contrary to, Acts xvii. 7.

Add Mark xii. 41, for κατέναντι, Tr.

ἀπέραντος.

endless, 1 Tim. i. 4.

ἀπερισπάστως.

without distraction, 1 Cor. vii. 35.

ἀπερίτμητος.

uncircumcised, Acts vii. 51.

ἀπέρχομαι.

go away, Matt. viii. 31(*see* ἀποστέλλω). xix. 22. xxv. 46. xxvi. 42, 44. Mark x. 22. xiv. 39. Luke ii. 15. John iv. 8. vi. 22. x. 40. xvi. 7*t*. xx. 10.

go one's way, Matt. viii. 33. xiii. 25. xx. 4(5). xxii. 5, 22. Mark xi. 4. xii. 12. Luke viii. 39. xix. 32. xxii. 4. John iv. 28. ix. 7. xi. 28, 46. Acts ix. 17. Jas. i. 24.

go, Matt. ii. 22. iv. 24. viii. 19, 21, 32. x. 5. xiii. 28, 46. xiv. 15, 25 (ἔρχομαι G″LTr*S*). xvi. 21. xviii. 30. xxi. 29, 30. xxv. 10p, 18, 25. xxvi. 36. xxvii. 5. xxviii. 10. Mark i. 20. v. 24. vi. 27(28), 36, 37. vii. 24. ix. 43. xiv. 10, 12. xvi. 13(~*p*). Luke v. 14. viii. 34 (-GLTTr*S*). ix. 12(G′; πορεύομαι G LTTr*S*), 57, 59, 60. xvii. 23. xxii.

13. xxiv. 24. John iv. 47. vi. 1, 66, 68. ix. 11. xi. 54. xii. 19. xviii. 6. Acts v. 26p. Gal. i. 17. Jude 7. Rev. x. 9. xii. 17. xvi. 2.
depart, Matt. viii. 18. ix. 7. xiv. 16. xvi. 4. xxvii. 60. Mark i. 35, 42. v. 17, 20. vi. 32, 46. viii. 13. Luke i. 23, 38. v. 13, 25. vii. 24p. viii. 37. x. 30. xxiv. 12(*ap*). John iv. 3, 43(–G°LᵇTTr*S*). v. 15. xii. 36. Acts x. 7. xxviii. 29(*ap*). Rev. xviii. 14, 14(ἀπόλλυμι GLTTr*S*).
go aside, Acts iv. 15.
go out, Luke viii. 31.
pass away, Rev. xxi. 4.
pass, Rev. ix. 12. xi. 14.
come, Mark iii. 13. vii. 30p. Luke xxiii. 33(ἔρχομαι LTr*S*). Rom. xv. 28.
Add Matt. v. 30, for 2d βάλλω, LTTr*S*. Acts xvi. 39, *see* ἐξέρχομαι. xxiii. 32, for πορεύομαι, G'L*S*. 2 Cor. i. 16, for διέρχομαι, G'L. Gal. i. 17, for ἀνέρχομαι, L. Rev. xxi. 1, for παρέρχομαι, GLTTr*S*.

ἀπέχω.

have, Matt. vi. 2, 5, 16. Phil. iv. 18(*marg.* **have received**).
receive, Luke vi. 24. Phm. 15.
be, Matt. xv. 8. Mark vii. 6. Luke vii. 6p. xv. 20p. xxiv. 13.
Impers., **it is enough**, Mark xiv. 41.
Mid., **abstain**, Acts xv. 20, 29. 1 Thes. iv. 3. v. 22. 1 Tim. iv. 3. 1 Pet. ii. 11.
Add Matt. xiv. 24 (*ap*).

ἀπιστέω.

believe not, Mark xvi. 11(*ap*), 16 (*ap*). Luke xxiv. 11, 41p. Acts xxviii. 24. Rom. iii. 3. 2 Tim. ii. 13.

ἀπιστία.

unbelief, Matt. xiii. 58. xvii. 20 (ὀλιγοπιστία LTr*S*). Mark vi. 6. ix. 24. xvi. 14(*ap*). Rom. iii. 3. iv. 20. xi. 20, 23. 1 Tim. i. 13. Heb. iii. 12, 19.

ἄπιστος.

unbelieving, 1 Cor. vii. 14*t*, 15. Tit. i. 15. Rev. xxi. 8.
that believeth not, 1 Cor. vii. 12, 13. x. 27. xiv. 22*t*, 24.
which believeth not, 2 Cor. iv. 4.
unbeliever, Luke xii. 46. 1 Cor. vi. 6. xiv. 23. 2 Cor. vi. 14.
faithless, Matt. xvii. 17. Mark ix. 19. Luke ix. 41. John xx. 27.
infidel, 2 Cor. vi. 15. 1 Tim. v. 8.
thing incredible, Acts xxvi. 8.

ἁπλόος.

single, Matt. vi. 22. Luke. xi. 34.

ἁπλότης.

singleness, Eph. vi. 5. Col. iii. 22.
simplicity, Rom. xii. 8 (*with* ἐν, *marg.* **liberally**). 2 Cor. i. 12(ἁγιότης L*S*). xi. 3.
liberality, 2 Cor. viii. 2.
liberal[cc], 2 Cor. ix. 13.
bountifulness, 2 Cor. ix. 11.

ἁπλῶς.

liberally, Jas. i. 5.

ἀπό.

from, Matt. i. 17*tr*, 21, 24. ii. 1, 16. iii. 7, 13. iv. 17, 25. v. 18, 29, 30. vi. 13. vii. 23. viii. 1, 11, 30. ix. 15, 16, 22. xi. 12, 25. xii. 38. xiii. 12, 35. xiv. 2. xv. 8, 27, 28. xvii. 9 (ἐκ GLTTr*S*), 18. xviii. 8, 9, 35. xix. 1, 8. xx. 8, 29. xxi. 8, 43. xxii. 46. xxiii. 34, 35. xxiv. 1 (ἐκ L), 29. xxv. 28, 29 (*ap*), 32*t*, 34, 41. xxvi. 39, 42(–G°°LᵇTTr*S*), 47. xxvii. 40, 42, 45, 55, 64. xxviii. 2(–G°LTTr*S*), 7, 8. Mark i. 9, 42. ii. 20. iii. 7*t*, 8*t*, 22. iv. 25. v. 35. vii. 1, 4, 6, 17, 33. viii. 11. ix. 9(ἐκ L). x. 6. xi. 12. xii. 34. xiii. 19. xiv. 35, 36, 52(–G°Lᵇ Tr*S*). xv. 30, 32. xvi. 8.
Luke i. 2, 38, 52. ii. 4, 15, 36, 37 (–Tr; ἐκ *S*). iii. 7. iv. 1, 13, 42. v. 3, 8, 13, 35. vii. 6. viii. 18, 37. ix. 5, 33, 37, 39, 45, 54 (ἐκ L). x. 21, 30, 42. xi. 4(*ap*), 50, 51. xii. 58. xiii. 15, 16, 27, 29, 29 (–G°°LᵇTrᵇ*S*). xvi. 3, 18(–G°), 21, 30. xvii. 29. xviii. 34. xix. 24, 26, 26

(-Lᵇ*S*), 39, 42. xxi. 11. xxii. 41, 42, 43(*ap*), 45. xxiii. 5, 49. xxiv. 2, 9, 13, 51. John iii. 2. viii. 44. x. 5, 18. xi. 53. xii. 36. xiii. 3. xv. 27. xvi. 22, 30. xviii. 28. xix. 27. xxi. 8. Acts i. 4, 11, 12, 22*t*. ii. 40. iii. 19, 24, 26. v. 38, 41. viii. 10, 26, 33. ix. 3(ἐκ LT*S*), 8, 18. x. 17, 21(*ap*), 23, 37. xi. 11, 27. xii. 10, 19. xiii. 8, 13*t*, 14, 29, 31, 39. xiv. 15, 19. xv. 1, 18, 20 (-L*S*), 33, 38, 39. xvi. 11. xvii. 27. xviii. 2, 5, 6, 16, 21. xix. 9, 12*t*. xx. 6, 9, 17, 18, 26. xxi. 1, 7, 10. xxii. 22, 29, 30(-GLT*S*). xxiii. 21. xxiv. 18. xxv. 1, 7. xxvi. 18. xxvii. 21. xxviii. 23.

Rom. i. 7, 18, 20. v. 9, 14. vi. 7, 18, 22. vii. 2, 3, 6. viii. 2, 21, 35, 39. ix. 3. xi. 26. xv. 19, 31. 1 Cor. i. 3. vii. 10, 27. x. 14. xiv. 36. 2 Cor. i. 2. iii. 18. v. 6. vii. 1. xi. 3, 9. xii. 8. Gal. i. 3, 6. ii. 12. iv. 24. Eph. i. 2. iii. 9. iv. 31. vi. 23. Phil. i. 2, 5. iv. 15. Col. i. 2, 23, 26*t*. ii. 20. 1 Thes. i. 1(*ap*), 8, 9, 10. ii. 17. iii. 6. iv. 3, 16. v. 22. 2 Thes. i. 2, 7, 9*t*. ii. 13(*see* ἀπαρχή). iii. 2, 3, 6. 1 Tim. i. 2. vi. 5 (*ap*), 10. 2 Tim. i. 2, 3. ii. 19, 21. iii. 15. iv. 4, 18. Tit. i. 4. ii. 14. Phm. 3.

Heb. iii. 12. iv. 3, 4, 10*t*. vi. 1, 7. vii. 1, 26. viii. 11. ix. 14. x. 22. xi. 15. xii. 25. Jas. i. 17, 27. iv. 7. v. 19. 1 Pet. i. 12. iii. 10. 2 Pet. iii. 4. 1 John i. 1, 7, 9. ii. 7, 7(-G°°LT*S*), 13, 14, 20, 24*t*. iii. 8, 11, 17. iv. 21. v. 21. 2 John 5, 6. Jude 14. Rev. i. 4*t*, 5, 5(ἐκ LTr*S*). iii. 12. vi. 4(ἐκ GLTTr*S*, ἐκ -G°°), 16*t*. vii. 2, 17(G', ἐκ GLTTr). ix. 6. xii. 14. xiii. 8. xiv. 3, 4. xvii. 8. xviii. 14*t*. xx. 9(-G°LTTrᵇ*S*), 11. xxi. 2, 4 (ἐκ L*S*), 10(ἐκ T). xxii. 19.

from among, Acts xv. 19.

of, Matt. iii. 4. v. 42. vii. 15, 16*t*. x. 17. xi. 19, 29. xv. 1, 27. xvi. 6, 11, 12*t*, 21. xvii. 25*tr*, 26. xxi. 11. xxiv. 32. xxvii. 21, 24, 57. Mark v. 29, 34. vi. 43. vii. 28. viii. 15, 31 (ὑπό G''LTTr*S*). xii. 2, 38. xiii. 28. xv. 43, 45. Luke v. 15. vi. 13, 17, 30. vii. 21, 35. viii. 2, 3 (ἐκ G''LT Tr*S*). ix. 22, 38. xi. 50, 51. xii. 1, 4, 15, 20, 57. xvii. 25. xviii. 3. xx. 10, 46. xxi. 30. xxii. 18, 71. xxiii. 51. xxiv. 42(*ap*). John i. 44(45), 44(46). v. 19, 30. vii. 17, 18, 28. viii. 28, 42. x. 18. xi. 1, 51. xii. 21. xiv. 10. xv. 4. xvi. 13. xviii. 34. xix. 38. xxi. 2, 10. Acts ii. 17, 18, 22. v. 2, 3. vi. 9. viii. 22. x. 38. xii. 1. xiii. 23. xv. 5. xvii. 13. xix. 13 (καί G''LT*S*). xxi. 16, 27. xxiii. 34. xxvii. 44.

Rom. xiii. 1 (ὑπό G''L*S*). 1 Cor. i. 30. iv. 5. vi. 19. xi. 23. 2 Cor. ii. 3. iii. 5. x. 7. Gal. i. 1. ii. 6. iii. 2. Phil. i. 28. Col. i. 7. iii. 24. 1 Thes. ii. 6*t*. 1 Tim. iii. 7. Heb. vii. 2, 13. xi. 13. xii. 15 (*marg.* **from**). xiii. 24. Jas. i. 13. v. 4. 1 John i. 5. ii. 27. 3 John 7. Rev. ii. 17 (*om*, ἐκ *S*). xii. 6. xvi. 12.

they° of, Matt. xxvii. 9.

out of, Matt. iii. 16. vii. 4(ἐκ LTr *S*). viii. 34. xii. 43. xiii. 1(ἐκ L*S*, -Tr). xiv. 13, 29. xv. 22. xvii. 18. xxiv. 27. Mark i. 10(ἐκ G''LTTr*S*). v. 17. vi. 33. vii. 15(ἐκ LTTr). x. 46 (*see* ἐκεῖθεν). xv. 21. xvi. 9(παρά LTr, *ap*). Luke iv. 35, 41. v. 2, 36. vi. 17. viii. 2, 12, 29, 33, 35, 38, 46. ix. 5. xi. 24. xii. 54. xvii. 29. xxiii. 26. John vii. 42. Acts i. 9. ii. 5. xiii. 50. xvi. 18. xvii. 2. xix. 12 (-GLT*S*). xxviii. 21, 23. 2 Cor. i. 16. Heb. xi. 34. Rev. xvi. 17(ἐκ G'LTr*S*). xxii. 19.

because of, Matt. xviii. 7.

for, Matt. xiii. 44. xiv. 26. xxviii. 4. Luke xix. 3. xxi. 26. xxii. 45. xxiv. 41. John xxi. 6. Acts xii. 14. xxii. 11.

by, Matt. vii. 16, 20(ἐκ L). Acts ix. 13. xii. 20. 2 Cor. iii. 18(*marg.* **of**). vii. 13. Heb. v. 8. Jude 23. Rev. xviii. 15.

with, Luke xv. 16. xvi. 21. Acts xx. 9.
in, 2 Thes. ii. 2.
at, Matt. xix. 4. Luke xxiv. 27t, 47. John viii. 9(*ap*). Acts viii. 35. xxiii. 23. xxvi. 4. 1 Pet. iv. 17*t*.
before, Acts vii. 45. 1 John ii. 28.
on, Rev. vi. 10 (ἐκ G″LTTr*S*). xxi. 13*f*.
upon, Acts xi. 19.
since, Matt. xxiv. 21. Col. i. 6, 9. Heb. ix. 26.
ἀφ' ἧς (*sc.* ὥρας or ἡμέρας), since the time, Luke vii. 45. — since, Acts xxiv. 11. 2 Pet. iii. 4. — that, Acts xx. 18.
Add, for ἐκ, Mark i. 26, G″L. v. 8, L^m^. ix. 25, L. xvi. 3, LTr. Luke iv. 35, G″LTTr*S*. 38, G″TTr*S*. John vi. 38, LTTr. Acts i. 25, LT*S*. xviii. 2, LT*S*. xxvii. 34, LT. xxviii. 3, G′LT*S*. Rev. vii. 14, L. ix. 18, 1st, G′. xix. 5, G″LTTr. — For ἐν, Matt. viii. 13, L. — For παρά, Matt. xx. 20, LTTr. Luke viii. 49, L. Acts xxvi. 22, LT*S*. 1 John iii. 22, LT*S*. v. 15, LT*S*. — For ὑπό, Luke i. 26, TTr*S*. vi. 18, GLTTr*S*. viii. 43, LTTr. Acts iv. 36, LT*S*. x. 33, LT. xv. 4, T. Rom. xv. 24, LT. Rev. ix. 18, GLTTr*S*. — Matt. xiv. 24(*ap*). Mark ii. 21 (.. αὐτοῦ), LT*S*. viii. 3(from), T Tr*S*. xi. 13 (.. afar), G″LTTr*S*. Luke v. 36(1st of), G′LTTr*S*. xiii. 7, *see* οὐ. 12 (from), L*S*. xxii. 18, *see* νῦν. xxiii. 49(.. afar), L*S*. John xix. 36(of), G′*S*. Acts xvi. 39, *see* ἐξέρχομαι. 2 Pet. i. 21, for ἅγιοι, T. ii. 21(*ap*). Rev. xiv. 13, *see* ἀπάρτι.
See also αἰών, ἄκρον, ἄνωθεν, ἀποστασία, ἄρτι, ἄφαντος, εἰς, ἐκκλίνω, ἔτος, εὐλάβεια, καταργέω, κωλύω, λούω, μακρόθεν, μέρος, νῦν, οὐ, πέρυσι, πῆχυς, στάδιον, τέταρτος, τότε, φεύγω, φοβέομαι.

ἀποβαίνω.

go out, Luke v. 2.
turn, Luke xxi. 13. Phil. i. 19.
come, John xxi. 9.

ἀποβάλλω.

cast away, Mark x. 50. Heb. x. 35.
Add Rev. iii. 2^pass^, for ἀποθνήσκω, G′.

ἀποβλέπω.

have respect, Heb. xi. 26.

ἀπόβλητος.

to be refused, 1 Tim. i. 4.

ἀποβολή.

casting away, Rom. xi. 15.
loss, Acts xxvii. 22.

ἀπογίνομαι.

be dead, 1 Pet. ii. 24.

ἀπογραφή.

taxing, Luke ii. 2. Acts v. 37.

ἀπογράφω.

Pass., be written (*marg.* enrolled), Heb. xii. 23. — be taxed, Luke ii. 1 (*marg.* be enrolled), 3, 5.

ἀποδείκνυμι.

show, 2 Thes. ii. 4.
set forth, 1 Cor. iv. 9.
prove, Acts xxv. 7.
approve, Acts ii. 22.

ἀπόδειξις.

demonstration, 1 Cor. ii. 4.

ἀποδεκατόω.

pay tithe, Matt. xxiii. 23.
give tithes, Luke xviii. 12.
tithe, Luke xi. 42.
take tithes, Heb. vii. 5.

ἀπόδεκτος.

acceptable, 1 Tim. ii. 3. v. 4.

ἀποδέχομαι.

be received, Acts xv. 4 (παραδέχομαι LT*S*).
Mid., gladly receive, Luke viii. 40. Acts ii. 41. — receive, Acts xviii. 27. xxviii. 30. — accept, Acts xxiv. 3.
Add, for δέχομαι, Luke ix. 11, LT Tr*S*. Acts xxi. 17, G″LT*S*.

ἀποδημέω.

go into a far country, Matt. xxi. 33. Mark xii. 1. Luke xx. 9.
travel into a far country, Matt. xxv. 14.

take one's journey, Matt. xxv. 15. Luke xv. 13.

ἀπόδημος.

taking a far journey, Mark xiii. 34.

ἀποδίδωμι.

give, Matt. xii. 36. xx. 8. Luke xvi. 2. Acts iv. 33. xix. 40(*δίδωμι* G'T). 2 Tim. iv. 8. Heb. xiii. 17. 1 Pet. iv. 5. Rev. xxii. 12.
give again, Luke iv. 20.
deliver, Matt. xxvii. 58.
deliver again, Luke ix. 42.
sell, Acts v. 8. vii. 9. Heb. xii. 16.
pay, Matt. v. 26. xviii. 25, 26, 28, 29, 30, 34. Luke vii. 42. xii. 59.
payment be made, Matt. xviii. 25.
repay, Luke x. 35.
recompense, Rom. xii. 17.
With ἀμοιβάς, **requite**, 1 Tim. v. 4.
reward, Matt. vi. 4, 6, 18. xvi. 27. 2 Tim. iv. 14. Rev. xviii. 6.
restore, Luke xix. 8.
render, Matt. xxi. 41. xxii. 21. Mark xii. 17. Luke xx. 25. Rom. ii. 6. xiii. 7. 1 Cor. vii. 3. 1 Thes. v. 15. 1 Pet. iii. 9.
yield, Heb. xii. 11. Rev. xxii. 2.
perform, Matt. v. 33.
Add, for *δίδωμι*, Luke vii. 15, L[m]. Rom. xiv. 12, L.

ἀποδιορίζω.

to separate, Jude 19.

ἀποδοκιμάζω.

disallow, 1 Pet. ii. 4, 7.
reject, Matt. xxi. 42. Mark viii. 31. xii. 10. Luke ix. 22. xvii. 25. xx. 17. Heb. xii. 17.

ἀποδοχή.

acceptation, 1 Tim. i. 15. iv. 9.

ἀπόθεσις.

putting away, 1 Pet. iii. 21.
With ἐστί, **must put off**, 2 Pet. i. 14.

ἀποθήκη.

garner, Matt. iii. 12. Luke iii. 17.
barn, Matt. vi. 26. xiii. 30. Luke xii. 18, 24.

ἀποθησαυρίζω.

lay up in store, 1 Tim. vi. 19.

ἀποθλίβω.

to press, Luke viii. 45.

ἀποθνήσκω.

die, Matt. xxii. 24, 27. xxvi. 35. Mark xii. 19, 20, 21, 22. Luke xvi. 22*t*. xx. 28, 28 (ᾖ, fr. *εἰμί*, LTr), 29, 30(*ap*), 31, 32, 36. John iv. 49. vi. 50. viii. 21, 24*t*. xi. 16, 26, 32, 37, 50, 51. xii. 24*t*, 33. xviii. 32. xix. 7. xxi. 23*t*. Acts ix. 37. xxi. 13. xxv. 11. Rom. v. 6, 7*t*, 8. vi. 9, 10*t*. vii. 9(10). viii. 13, 34. xiv. 7, 8*tr*, 9, 15. 1 Cor. viii. 11. ix. 15. xv. 3, 22, 31, 32, 36. 2 Cor. v. 14 (15), 15*t*. vi. 9. Phil. i. 21. 1 Thes. iv. 14. v. 10. Heb. vii. 8. ix. 27. x. 28. xi. 13. Rev. iii. 2(*ἀποβάλλω* G'). viii. 9, 11. ix. 6. xiv. 13. xvi. 3.
be a dying, Heb. xi. 21[p].
lie a dying, Luke viii. 42.
μέλλω ἀποθνήσκειν, **be at the point of death**, John iv. 47.
be dead, Matt. ix. 24. Mark v. 35, 39. ix. 26. xv. 44. Luke viii. 52, 53. John vi. 49, 58. viii. 52, 53*t*. xi. 14, 25. Rom. v. 15. vi. 2, 7, 8. vii. 2, 3, 6(*ἀποθανόντες* StC[m]GLT*S*). 2 Cor. v. 14(15). Gal. ii. 19, 21. Col. ii. 20. iii. 3. Heb. xi. 4.
μετὰ τὸ ἀποθανεῖν, **when . . was dead**, Acts vii. 4.
dead, Jude 12[p].
perish, Matt. viii. 32.
ἀπ. φόνῳ, **be slain**, Heb. xi. 37.
Add, for *ἀπόλλυμι*, Matt. xxvi. 52, G''. John xviii. 14, G''LTr*S*.—John xi. 21, for *θνήσκω*, G''LTr*S*. 1 Pet. iii. 18, for *πάσχω*, G'L*S*.

ἀποκαθιστάνω.

restore again, Acts i. 6.
Add Mark ix. 12, for *ἀποκαθιστάω*, LTTr (*ἀποκαταστάνω* *S*).

ἀποκαθίστημι or -ιστάω.

restore, Matt. xii. 13. xvii. 11. Mark iii. 5. viii. 25. ix. 12(*see ἀποκαθιστάνω*). Luke vi. 10. Heb. xiii. 19.

ἀποκαλύπτω.

reveal, Matt. x. 26. xi. 25, 27 (*see* βούλομαι). xvi. 17. Luke ii. 35. x. 21, 22. xii. 2. xvii. 30. John xii. 38. Rom. i. 17, 18. viii. 18. 1 Cor. ii. 10. iii. 13. xiv. 30. Gal. i. 16. iii. 23. Eph. iii. 5. Phil. iii. 15. 2 Thes. ii. 3, 6, 8. 1 Pet. i. 5, 12. v. 1.

ἀποκάλυψις.

revelation, Rom. ii. 5. xvi. 25. 1 Cor. xiv. 6, 26. 2 Cor. xii. 1, 7. Gal. i. 12. ii. 2. Eph. i. 17. iii. 3. 1 Pet. i. 13. Rev. i. 1.
With ἐν, **when . . shall be revealed**, 2 Thes. i. 7. 1 Pet. iv. 13.
manifestation, Rom. viii. 19.
appearing, 1 Pet. i. 7.
coming(*Gr.* revelation), 1 Cor. i. 7.
With εἰς, **to lighten**, Luke ii. 32.

ἀποκαραδοκία.

earnest expectation, Rom. viii. 19. Phil. i. 20.

ἀποκαταλλάττω.

reconcile, Eph. ii. 16. Col. i. 20, 21.

ἀποκατάστασις.

restitution, Acts iii. 21.

ἀπόκειμαι.

be laid up, Luke xix. 20. Col. i. 5. 2 Tim. iv. 8.
be appointed, Heb. ix. 27.

ἀποκεφαλίζω.

behead, Matt. xiv. 10. Mark vi. 16, 27(28). Luke ix. 9.

ἀποκλείω.

shut, Luke xiii. 25.

ἀποκόπτω.

cut off, Mark ix. 43, 45. John xviii. 10, 26. Acts xxvii. 32. Gal. v. 12.

ἀπόκριμα.

sentence(*marg.* **answer**), 2 Cor. i. 9.

ἀποκρίνομαι.

to answer, Matt. iii. 15. iv. 4. viii. 8. xi. 4, 25. xii. 38, 39, 48. xiii. 11, 37. xiv. 28. xv. 3, 13, 15, 23, 24, 26, 28. xvi. 2, 16, 17. xvii. 4, 11, 17. xix. 4, 27. xx. 13, 22. xxi. 21, 24, 27, 29, 30. xxii. 1, 29, 46. xxiv. 4. xxv. 9, 12, 26, 37, 40, 44, 45. xxvi. 23, 25, 33, 62, 63(–Tr*S*), 66. xxvii. 12, 14, 21, 25. xxviii. 5.

Mark iii. 33. v. 9(G′, *om S*). vi. 37. vii. 6(–TTr*S*), 28. viii. 4, 28(εἶπον T*S*), 29. ix. 5, 12, 17, 19, 38(φημί TTr*S*). x. 3, 5(–Tr*S*), 20, 24, 29 (–T*S*), 51. xi. 14, 22, 29(–TTr*S*), 29, 30, 33, 33(Tr^{mb}, –L^{b}TTr*S*). xii. 17, 24(–TTr*S*),28, 29, 34, 35. xiii. 2(–TTr*S*), 5(–TTr*S*). xiv. 20(–G^{o} LTTr*S*), 40, 48, 60, 61. xv. 2, 4, 5, 9, 12.

Luke i. 19, 35, 60. iii. 11, 16. iv. 4, 8, 12. v. 5, 22(–LTr^{b}), 31. vi. 3. vii. 22, 40, 43. viii. 21, 50. ix. 19, 20, 41, 49. x. 27, 28, 41. xi. 7, 45. xiii. 2, 8, 14, 15, 25. xiv. 3, 5 (–G^{oo}LTr). xv. 29. xvii. 17, 20, 37. xix. 40. xx. 3, 7, 24, 34(–LTTr*S*), 39. xxii. 51, 68. xxiii. 3, 9, 40. xxiv. 18.

John i. 21, 26, 48(49), 49(50), 50 (51). ii. 18, 19. iii. 3, 5, 9, 10, 27. iv. 10, 13, 17. v. 7, 11, 17, 19. vi. 7, 26, 29, 43, 68, 70. vii. 16, 20, 21, 46, 47, 52. viii. 14, 19, 33, 34, 39, 48, 49, 54. ix. 3, 11, 20, 25, 27, 30, 34, 36. x. 25, 32, 33, 34. xi. 9. xii. 23, 30, 34. xiii. 7, 8, 26, 36, 38. xiv. 23. xvi. 31. xviii. 5, 8, 20, 22, 23, 30, 34, 35, 36, 37. xix. 7, 11, 15, 22. xx. 28. xxi. 5.

Acts iii. 12. iv. 19. v. 8, 29. viii. 24, 34, 37(*ap*). ix. 13. x. 46. xi. 9. xv. 13. xix. 15. xxi. 13. xxii. 8, 28. xxiv. 10, 25. xxv. 4, 9, 12, 16. Col. iv. 6. Rev. vii. 13.

Add Matt. xxiv. 2, for Ἰησοῦς, L TTr*S*. Mark ix. 6, for λαλέω, Tr*S*.

ἀπόκρισις.

answer, Luke ii. 47. xx. 26. John i. 22. xix. 9.

ἀποκρύπτω.

hide, Matt. xi. 25(κρύπτω LTTr*S*). xxv. 18(κρύπτω LTTr*S*). Luke x.

21. 1 Cor. ii. 7. Eph. iii. 9. Col. i. 26.

ἀπόκρυφος.

hid, Luke viii. 17. Col. ii. 3.
kept secret, Mark iv. 22.

ἀποκτείνω.

kill, Matt. x. 28*t*. xvi. 21. xvii. 23. xxi. 35, 38. xxiii. 34, 37. xxiv. 9. xxvi. 4. Mark iii. 4. vi. 19. viii. 31. ix. 31, 31p. x. 34. xii. 5*t*, 7, 8. Luke xi. 47, 48. xii. 4, 5. xiii. 31, 34. xx. 14, 15. John v. 18. vii. 1, 19, 20, 25. viii. 22, 37, 40. xvi. 2. Acts iii. 15. xxi. 31. xxiii. 12. xxvii. 42. Rom. xi. 3. 2 Cor. iii. 6. 1 Thes. ii. 15. Rev. ii. 23. vi. 8, 11. ix. 5, 18, 20. xi. 5, 7. xiii. 10*t*, 15.
slay, Matt. xxi. 39. xxii. 6. Luke ix. 22. xi. 49. xiii. 4. John v. 16 (*ap*). Acts vii. 52. xxiii. 14. Rom. vii. 11. Eph. ii. 16. Rev. ii. 13. ix. 15. xi. 13. xix. 21.
put to death, Mk. xiv. 1. Lk. xviii. 33. John xi. 53. xii. 10. xviii. 31. — θέλων . . ἀποκτεῖναι, **when he would have put . . to death**, Matt. xiv. 5.
Add Luke vi. 9, for ἀπόλλυμι, G.
ἀποκτέννω GLTTr*S* Mark xii. 5, Rev. vi. 11; do. LTTr*S* Matt. x. 28, Luke xii. 4, -κτένω G. — ἀποκταίνω L 2 Cor. iii. 6, Rev. xiii. 10.

ἀποκυέω.

bring forth, Jas. i. 15.
beget, Jas. i. 18.

ἀποκυλίω.

roll away, Mark xvi. 3, 4(ἀνακυλίω TTr*S*). Luke xxiv. 2.
roll back, Matt. xxviii. 2.

ἀπολαμβάνω.

receive, Luke vi. 34(λαμβάνω TTr*S*). xv. 27. xvi. 25. xviii. 30(λαμβάνω L). xxiii. 41. Rom. i. 27. Gal. iv. 5. Col. iii. 24. 2 John 8. 3 John 8(ὑπολαμβάνω G'LT*S*).
receive again, Luke vi. 34.
take, Mark vii. 33.
ἀπολήμψεσθε for ἀπολήψεσθε, LT*S*.

ἀπόλαυσις.

With εἰς, **to enjoy**, 1 Tim. vi. 17.
With ἔχω, **enjoy the pleasures**, Heb. xi. 25.

ἀπολείπω.

to leave, 2 Tim. iv. 13, 20. Jude 6.
Pass., **remain**, Heb. iv. 6, 9. x. 26.
Add Tit. i. 5, for καταλείπω, G'L T*S*.

ἀπολείχω.

lick, Luke xvi. 21(ἐπιλείχω LTTr*S*).

ἀπόλλυμι or -ολλύω.

destroy, Matt. ii. 13. x. 28. xii. 14. xxi. 41. xxii. 7. xxvii. 20. Mark i. 24. iii. 6. ix. 22. xi. 18. xii. 9. Luke iv. 34. vi. 9 (G'', ἀποκτείνω G). ix. 56(*ap*). xvii. 27, 29. xix. 47. xx. 16. John x. 10. Rom. xiv. 15. 1 Cor. i. 19. Jas. iv. 12. Jude 5.
Mid., **be destroyed**, 1 Cor. x. 9, 10. 2 Cor. iv. 9. —**perish**, Matt. v. 29, 30. viii. 25. ix. 17. xviii. 14. xxvi. 52 (ἀποθνήσκω G''). Mark iv. 38. Luke v. 37. viii. 24. xi. 51. xiii. 3, 5, 33. xv. 17. xxi. 18. John iii. 15, 16 (*ap*). vi. 27. x. 28. xi. 50. Acts v. 37. Rom. ii. 12. 1 Cor. i. 18. viii. 11. xv. 18. 2 Cor. ii. 15. 2 Thes. ii. 10. Heb. i. 11. Jas. i. 11. 1 Pet. i. 7. 2 Pet. iii. 6, 9. Jude 11. — **die**, John xviii. 14 (ἀποθνήσκω G''LTr*S*). — **be lost**, John vi. 12. xvii. 12. 2 Cor. iv. 3. — **be marred**, Mark ii. 22.
lose, Matt. x. 6, 39*t*, 42. xv. 24. xvi. 25*t*. xviii. 11(*ap*). Mark viii. 35*t*. ix. 41. Luke ix. 24*t*, 25. xv. 4p, 4, 6, 8, 9, 24, 32. xvii. 33*t*. xix. 10. John vi. 39. xii. 25. xviii. 9. 2 John 8.
Add Acts xxvii. 34, for πίπτω, G LT*S*. Rev. xviii. 14, for 2d ἀπέρχομαι, GLTTr*S*.

ἀπολλύων.

Apollyon (*marg.* **destroyer**), Rev. ix. 11.

ἀπολογέομαι.

speak for one's self, Acts xxvi. 24p.

answer for one's self, Acts xxv. 8p. xxvi. 1, 2.
answer, Luke xii. 11. xxi. 14. Acts xxiv. 10.
excuse one's self, 2 Cor. xii. 19.
excuse, Rom. ii. 15.
make defence, Acts xix. 33.

ἀπολογία.

to answer for one's self[cc], Acts xxv. 16.
answer, 1 Cor. ix. 3. 2 Tim. iv. 16. 1 Pet. iii. 15.
clearing of one's self, 2 Cor. vii. 11.
defence, Acts xxii. 1. Phil. i. 7, 17(16).

ἀπολούω.

wash away, Acts xxii. 16.
wash, 1 Cor. vi. 11.

ἀπολύτρωσις.

redemption, Luke xxi. 28. Rom. iii. 24. viii. 23. 1 Cor. i. 30. Eph. i. 7, 14. iv. 30. Col. i. 14. Heb. ix. 15.
deliverance, Heb. xi. 35.

ἀπολύω.

loose, Matt. xviii. 27. Luke xiii. 12.
release, Matt. xxvii. 15, 17, 21, 26. Mark xv. 6, 9, 11, 15. Luke xxiii. 16, 17(*ap*), 18, 20, 25. John xviii. 39*t*. xix. 10, 12.
forgive, Luke vi. 37*t*.
let go, Luke xiv. 4. xxii. 68(–T Tr[b]*S*). xxiii. 22. John xix. 12. Acts iii. 13. iv. 21, 23. v. 40. xv. 33. xvi. 35, 36. xvii. 9. xxviii. 18.
let depart, Luke ii. 29. Acts xxiii. 22.
Mid., **depart**, Acts xxviii. 25.
set at liberty, Acts xxvi. 32. Heb. xiii. 23.
send away, Matt. xiv. 15, 22, 23p. xv. 23, 32, 39. Mark vi. 36, 45. viii. 3, 9. Luke viii. 38. ix. 12. Acts xiii. 3.
dismiss, Acts xv. 30p. xix. 41.
put away, Matt. i. 19. v. 31, 32. xix. 3, 7, 8, 9*t*. Mark x. 2, 4, 11, 12. Luke xvi. 18*t*.
divorce, Matt. v. 32.

ἀπομάσσομαι.

wipe off, Luke x. 11.

ἀπονέμω.

give, 1 Pet. iii. 7.

ἀπονίπτομαι.

wash, Matt. xxvii. 24.

ἀποπίπτω.

fall from, Acts ix. 18.

ἀποπλανάω.

seduce, Mark xiii. 22.
Pass., **err**(*marg.* **be seduced**), 1 Tim. vi. 10.

ἀποπλέω.

to sail, Acts xiii. 4. xiv. 26. xx. 15. xxvii. 1.

ἀποπλύνω.

wash, Luke v. 2(ἔπλυνον, fr. πλύνω, LTr, ἔπλυναν G'*S*).

ἀποπνίγω.

choke, Matt. xiii. 7. Luke viii. 7, 33.

ἀπορέομαι.

be perplexed, 2 Cor. iv. 8.
stand in doubt(*marg.* **be perplexed**), Gal. iv. 20.
doubt, John xiii. 22. Acts xxv. 20 (*marg.* **be doubtful**).
Add Luke xxiv. 4, for διαπορέομαι, LTTr*S*.

ἀπορία.

perplexity, Luke xxi. 25.

ἀποῤῥίπτω.

cast one's self, Acts xxvii. 43.

ἀπορφανίζομαι.

be taken from (*lit.* be wholly bereaved of), 1 Thes. ii. 17.

ἀποσκευάζομαι.

take up one's carriage, Acts xxi. 15 (*lit.* pack away; ἐπισκευάζομαι C?G'LT*S*).

ἀποσκίασμα.

shadow, Jas. i. 17.

ἀποσπάω.

draw away, Acts xx. 30.

withdraw, Luke xxii. 41.
draw, Matt. xxvi. 51.
Pass., **be gotten from,** Acts xxi. 1p.

ἀποστασία.

falling away, 2 Thes. ii. 3.
With ἀπό, **to forsake,** Acts xxi. 21.

ἀποστάσιον.

divorcement, Matt. xix. 7. Mark x. 4.
writing of divorcement, Matt. v. 31.

ἀποστεγάζω.

uncover, Mark ii. 4.

ἀποστέλλω.

send away, Mark viii. 26. xii. 3, 4(*see* ἀτιμόω).
send forth, Matt. ii. 16. x. 5, 16. xiii. 41. xxii. 3, 4. Mark iii. 14. vi. 7, 17. xi. 1. xiv. 13. Luke x. 3. xx. 20. Heb. i. 14. Rev. v. 6.
send out, Matt. xiv. 35. xxii. 16.
send, Matt. x. 40. xi. 10. xv. 24. xx. 2. xxi. 1, 3, 34, 36, 37. xxiii. 34, 37. xxiv. 31. xxvii. 19. Mark i. 2. iii. 31. v. 10. vi. 27. ix. 37. xi. 3. xii. 2, 4, 5, 6, 13. xiii. 27. Luke i. 19, 26. iv. 18, 43. vii. 3, 20, 27. ix. 2, 48, 52. x. 1, 16. xi. 49. xiii. 34. xiv. 17, 32. xix. 14, 29, 32. xx. 10. xxii. 8, 35. xxiv. 49 (ἐξαποστέλλω TTr). John i. 6, 19, 24. iii. 17, 28, 34. iv. 38. v. 33, 36, 38. vi. 29, 57. vii. 29, 32. viii. 42. ix. 7. x. 36. xi. 3, 42. xvii. 3, 8, 18*t*, 21, 23, 25. xviii. 24. xx. 21. Acts iii. 20, 26. v. 21. vii. 14, 34, 35. viii. 14. ix. 17, 38 x. 8, 17, 20, 21(*ap*), 36. xi. 11, 13, 30. xiii. 15, 26(ἐξαποστέλλω LT*S*). xv. 27. xvi. 35, 36. xix. 22p. xxvi. 17. xxviii. 28. Rom. x. 15. 1 Cor. i. 17. 2 Cor. xii. 17. 2 Tim. iv. 12. 1 Pet. i. 12. 1 John iv. 9, 10, 14. Rev. i. 1. xxii. 6.
put in, Mark iv. 29.
set, Luke iv. 18.
Add Matt. viii. 31, for ἐπιτρέπω ἀπελθεῖν(G'), GLTTr*S*. Acts xv. 33, *see* ἀπόστολος. xxi. 25, for ἐπιστέλλω, L.

ἀποστερέω.

defraud, Mark x. 19. 1 Cor. vi. 7, 8. vii. 5.
keep back by fraud, Jas. v. 4.
Pass., **destitute,** 1 Tim. vi. 5p.

ἀποστολή.

apostleship, Acts i, 25. Rom. i. 5. 1 Cor. ix. 2. Gal. ii. 8.

ἀπόστολος.

he that is sent, John xiii. 16.
messenger, 2 Cor. viii. 23. Phil. ii. 25.
apostle, Matt. x. 2. Mark vi. 30. Luke vi. 13. ix. 10. xi. 49. xvii. 5. xxii. 14. xxiv. 10. Acts i. 2, 26. ii. 37, 42, 43. iv. 33, 35, 36, 37. v. 2, 12, 18, 29, 34 (ἄνθρωπος G'LT*S*), 40. vi. 6. viii. 1, 14, 18. ix. 27. xi. 1. xiv. 4, 14. xv. 2, 4, 6, 22, 23, 33 (G'; ἀποστείλαντας αὐτούς GLT, ἀπ. ἑαυτούς *S*). xvi. 4.
Rom. i. 1. xi. 13. xvi. 7. 1 Cor. i. 1. iv. 9. ix. 1, 2, 5. xii. 28, 29. xv. 7, 9*t*. 2 Cor. i. 1. xi. 5, 13. xii. 11, 12. Gal. i. 1, 17, 19. Eph. i. 1. ii. 20. iii. 5. iv. 11. Col. i. 1. 1 Thes. ii. 6. 1 Tim. i. 1. ii. 7. 2 Tim. i. 1, 11. Tit. i. 1. Heb. iii. 1. 1 Pet. i. 1. 2 Pet. i. 1. iii. 2. Jude 17. Rev. ii. 2. xviii. 20. xxi. 14.

ἀποστοματίζω.

provoke to speak, Luke xi. 53.

ἀποστρέφω.

turn away, Acts iii. 26. Rom. xi. 26. 2 Tim. iv. 4.
Mid., and Pass. aor., **turn away from,** Matt. v. 42. 2 Tim. i. 15. Tit. i. 14. Heb. xii. 25p.
pervert, Luke xxiii. 14.
put up again, Matt. xxvi. 52.
bring again, Matt. xxvii. 3(στρέφω TTr*S*).

ἀποστυγέω.

abhor, Rom. xii. 9.

ἀποσυνάγωγος.

With ποιέω, **put out of the synagogue,** John xvi. 2.

With γίνομαι, **be put out of the synagogue,** John ix. 22. xii. 42.

ἀποτάσσομαι.

take leave of, Acts xviii. 18p. 2 Cor. ii. 13.
bid farewell, Luke ix. 61. Acts xviii. 21.
forsake, Luke xiv. 33.
send away, Mark vi. 46p.

ἀποτελέω.

finish, Jas. i. 15p.
Add Luke xiii. 32, for ἐπιτελέω, LTTr*S*.

ἀποτίθεμαι.

put off, Eph. iv. 22. Col. iii. 8.
put away, Eph. iv. 25.
cast off, Rom. xiii. 12.
lay aside, Heb. xii. 1. 1 Pet. ii. 1.
lay apart, Jas. i. 21.
lay down, Acts vii. 58.
Add Matt. xiv. 3, for τίθεμαι, LTr *S*.

ἀποτινάσσω.

shake off, Luke ix. 5. Acts xxviii. 5.

ἀποτίω.

repay, Phm. 19.

ἀποτολμάω.

be very bold, Rom. x. 20.

ἀποτομία.

severity, Rom. xi. 22*t*.

ἀποτόμως.

sharply, Tit. i. 13.
sharpness[cc], 2 Cor. xiii. 10.

ἀποτρέπομαι.

turn away, 2 Tim. iii. 5.

ἀπουσία.

absence, Phil. ii. 12.

ἀποφέρω.

carry away, Mark xv. 1. Rev. xvii. 3. xxi. 10.
carry, Luke xvi. 22.
bring, 1 Cor. xvi. 3.
Add Acts xix. 12, for ἐπιφέρω, G″ LT*S*.

ἀποφεύγω.

to escape, 2 Pet. i. 4. ii. 18, 20p.

ἀποφθέγγομαι.

speak forth, Acts xxvi. 25.
utterance[cc], Acts ii. 4.
say, Acts ii. 14.

ἀποφορτίζομαι.

unlade, Acts xxi. 3.

ἀπόχρησις.

using, Col. ii. 22.

ἀποχωρέω.

depart, Matt. vii. 23. Luke ix. 39. Acts xiii. 13.

ἀποχωρίζομαι.

depart, Rev. vi. 14.
depart [c]**asunder,** Acts xv. 39.

ἀποψύχω.

ἀποψυχόντων ἀνθρώπων, **men's hearts failing them,** Luke xxi. 26.

ἀπρόσιτος.

which no man can approach unto, 1 Tim. vi. 16.

ἀπρόσκοπος.

without offence, Phil. i. 10.
void of offence, Acts xxiv. 16.
With γίνομαι, **give none offence,** 1 Cor. x. 32.

ἀπροσωπολήπτως (–λήμπτ-LT*S*).

without respect of persons, 1 Pet. i. 17.

ἄπταιστος.

With φυλάσσω, **keep from falling,** Jude 24.

ἅπτω.

kindle, Luke xxii. 55p (περιάπτω TTr*S*).
light, Luke viii. 16p. xi. 33p. xv. 8.
Mid., **touch,** Matt. viii. 3, 15. ix. 20, 21, 29. xiv. 36*t*. xvii. 7. xx. 34. Mark i. 41. iii. 10. v. 27, 28, 30, 31. vi. 56*t*. vii. 33. viii. 22. x. 13. Luke v. 13. vi. 19. vii. 14, 39. viii. 44, 45, 45(*ap*), 46, 47. xviii. 15. xxii. 51. John xx. 17. 1 Cor. vii. 1. 2 Cor. vi. 17. Col. ii. 21. 1 John v. 18.
Add Acts xxviii. 2, for ἀνάπτω, L*S*.

ἀπωθέομαι.
thrust from, Acts vii. 39.
thrust away, Acts vii. 27.
put from, Acts xiii. 46.
put away, 1 Tim. i. 19.
cast away, Rom. xi. 1, 2.

ἀπώλεια.
destruction, Matt. vii. 13. Rom. ix. 22. Phil. iii. 19. 2 Pet. ii. 1. iii. 16.
perdition, John xvii. 12. Phil. i. 28. 2 Thes. ii. 3. 1 Tim. vi. 9. Heb. x. 39. 2 Pet. iii. 7. Rev. xvii. 8, 11.
With εἰμί εἰς, **perish,** Acts viii. 20.
With εἰς, **to die,** Acts xxv. 16 (*om S*).
waste, Matt. xxvi. 8. Mark xiv. 4.
pernicious way, 2 Pet. ii. 2(ἀσελγεία C^mGLT*S*; *marg.* **lascivious way**).
damnation, 2 Pet. ii. 3.
damnable[cc], 2 Pet. ii. 1.

ἀρά.
cursing, Rom. iii. 14.

ἄρα.
then, Matt. xii. 28. xix. 25. xxiv. 45. Luke xii. 42. Rom. vii. 21. 1 Cor. xv. 14, 18. 2 Cor. v. 14(15). Gal. ii. 21. iii. 29. v. 11. Heb. xii. 8.
so then, Rom. x. 17. Gal. iv. 31 (-G[oo]; διό LT*S*).
therefore, Matt. xix. 27. Rom. viii. 1. Gal. iii. 7. Heb. iv. 9.
wherefore, 2 Cor. vii. 12.
no doubt, Luke xi. 20.
truly, Luke xi. 48.
ἄραγε, **then,** Matt. xvii. 26. Acts xi. 18(ἄρα L*S*).—**wherefore,** Matt. vii. 20.
ἄρα οὖν, **so then,** Rom. vii. 3, 25. ix. 16. xiv. 12(-οὖν L).—**now therefore,** Eph. ii. 19.—**therefore,** Rom. v. 18. viii. 12. ix. 18. xiv. 19. Gal. vi. 10. 1 Thes. v. 6. 2 Thes. ii. 15.
ἐπεὶ ἄρα, **for then,** 1 Cor. v. 10.—**else,** 1 Cor. vii. 14.
εἰ ἄρα, **if haply,** Mark xi. 13.—**if perhaps,** Acts viii. 22.
εἰ ἄραγε, **if haply,** Acts xvii. 27.
εἴπερ ἄρα, **if so be,** 1 Cor. xv. 15.
τίς ἄρα, **what manner of man,** Mark iv. 41. Luke viii. 25.—**what manner of,** Luke i. 66.
Also interrogatively, with εἰμί, Acts xxi. 38. *With* εἰ ἔχω, Acts vii. 1 (-G[oo]L*S*). *With* μήτι χράομαι, 2 Cor. i. 17. *With* τίς, Matt. xviii. 1. Luke xxii. 23. Acts xii. 18.
Add Gal. ii. 17, for ἆρα, **C?L.**

ἆρα.
Interrogative, **therefore,** Gal. ii. 17 (ἄρα C?L). *With* εὑρίσκω, Luke xviii. 8.
ἆρά γε, *with* γινώσκω, Acts viii. 30.

ἀραβών. See ἀρραβών.

ἄραφος. See ἄρραφος.

ἀργέω.
linger, 2 Pet. ii. 3.

ἀργός.
idle, Matt. xii. 36. xx. 3, 6(*omS*), 6. 1 Tim. v. 13*t*.
slow, Tit. i. 2.
barren, 2 Pet. i. 8.
Add Jas. ii. 20, for νεκρός, LT.

ἀργύριον.
silver, Acts iii. 6. xx. 33. 1 Pet. i. 18.
silver piece, Matt. xxvii. 6.
piece of silver, Matt. xxvi. 15. xxvii. 3, 5, 9. Acts xix. 19(pieces[c]).
money, Matt. xxv. 18, 27. xxviii. 12, 15. Mark xiv. 11. Luke ix. 3. xix. 15, 23. xxii. 5. Acts vii. 16. viii. 20.

ἀργυροκόπος.
silversmith, Acts xix. 24.

ἄργυρος.
silver, Matt. x. 9 (-T, *err.? S*). Acts xvii. 29. 1 Cor. iii. 12. Jas. v. 3. Rev. xviii. 12.

ἀργυροῦς.
of silver, 2 Tim. ii. 20. Rev. ix. 20.
silver, Acts xix. 24.

ἀρέσκεια.
pleasing, Col. i. 10.

ἀρέσκω.

please, Matt. xiv. 6. Mark vi. 22. Acts vi. 5. Rom. viii. 8. xv. 1, 2, 3. 1 Cor. vii. 32, 33, 34. x. 33. Gal. i. 10*t*. 1 Thes. ii. 4, 15. iv. 1. 2 Tim. ii. 4.

ἀρεστός.

With art., **those things that are pleasing**, 1 John iii. 22. — **those things that please**, John viii. 29.

With εἰμί, **please**, Acts xii. 3.

reason, Acts vi. 2.

ἀρετή.

virtue, Phil. iv. 8. 2 Pet. i. 3, 5*t*.

praise (*marg.* **virtue**), 1 Pet. ii. 9.

(ἀρήν) ἀρνός, gen.

lamb, Luke x. 3.

ἀριθμέω.

to number, Matt. x. 30. Luke xii. 7. Rev. vii. 9.

ἀριθμός.

number, Luke xxii. 3. John vi. 10. Acts iv. 4. v. 36. vi. 7. xi. 21. xvi. 5. Rom. ix. 27. Rev. v. 11 (*ap*). vii. 4. ix. 16*t*. xiii. 17, 18*tr*. xv. 2. xx. 8.

ἀριστάω.

dine, Luke xi. 37. John xxi. 12, 15.

ἀριστερός.

left, Matt. vi. 3. Luke xxiii. 33. 2 Cor vi. 7.

Add Mark x. 37, for εὐωνύμος, TTr.

ἄριστον.

dinner, Matt. xxii. 4. Luke xi. 38. xiv. 12.

Add Luke xiv. 15, for ἄρτος, G'.

ἀρκετός.

enough, Matt. x. 25.

sufficient, Matt. vi. 34.

With εἰμί *understood*, **suffice**, 1 Pet. iv. 3

ἀρκέω.

be enough, Matt. xxv. 9,

suffice, John xiv. 8.

be sufficient, John vi. 7. 2 Cor. xii. 9.

Mid., **be content**, Luke iii. 14. 1 Tim. vi. 8. Heb. xiii. 5. —**content**, 3 John 10p.

ἄρκτος, ἄρκος GLTTr*S*.

bear, Rev. xiii. 2.

ἅρμα.

chariot, Acts viii. 28, 29, 38. Rev. ix. 9.

ἁρμόζομαι.

espouse, 2 Cor. xi. 2.

ἁρμός.

joint, Heb. iv. 12.

ἀρνέομαι.

deny, Matt. x. 33*t*. xxvi. 70, 72. Mark xiv. 68, 70. Luke viii. 45p. xii. 9. xxii. 57. John i. 20. xviii. 25, 27. Acts iii. 13, 14. iv. 16. 1 Tim. v. 8. 2 Tim. ii. 12*t*, 13. iii. 5. Tit. i. 16. ii. 12. 2 Pet. ii. 1. 1 John ii. 22*t*, 23. Jude 4. Rev. ii. 13. iii. 8.

refuse, Acts vii. 35. Heb. xi. 24.

Add, for ἀπαρνέομαι, Luke ix. 23, GLTTr*S*. John xiii. 38, LTTr.

ἀρνίον.

lamb, John xxi. 15.

Said of Christ, **Lamb**, Rev. v. 6, 8, 12, 13. vi. 1, 16. vii. 9, 10, 14, 17. xii. 11. xiii. 8, 11. xiv. 1, 4*t*, 10. xv. 3. xvii. 14*t*. xix. 7, 9. xxi. 9, 14, 22, 23, 27. xxii. 1, 3.

ἀρνός. See ἀρήν.

ἀροτριάω.

to plow, Luke xvii. 7. 1 Cor. ix. 10.

ἄροτρον.

plow, Luke ix. 62.

ἁρπαγή.

spoiling, Heb. x. 34.

ravening, Luke xi. 39.

extortion, Matt. xxiii. 25.

ἁρπαγμός.

robbery, Phil. ii. 6.

ἁρπάζω.

take by force, Matt. xi. 12. John vi. 15. Acts xxiii. 10.

catch away, Matt. xiii. 19. Acts viii. 39.

catch, John x. 12.
catch up, 2 Cor. xii. 2, 4. 1 Thes. iv. 17. Rev. xii. 5.
pluck, John x. 28, 29.
pull, Jude 23.
Add, for *διαρπάζω*, Matt. xii. 29, LT, *ἁρπάζω* Tr. 29, LT.

ἅρπαξ.

ravening, Matt. vii. 15.
extortioner, Luke xviii. 11. 1 Cor. v. 10, 11. vi. 10.

ἀρραβών.

earnest, 2 Cor. i. 22 (*ἀραβών* L*S*). v. 5. Eph. i. 14.

ἄρραφος, *ἄραφος* TTr*S*.

without seam, John xix. 23.

ἄρρην, *ἄρσην* LT.

man, Rom. i. 27. Rev. xii. 5.
man child, Rev. xii. 13(*ἄρσην* *S*).

ἄρρητος.

unspeakable, 2 Cor. xii. 4.

ἄρρωστος.

sick, Matt. xiv. 14. Mark xvi. 18 (*ap*).
that is sick, Mark vi. 13.
Plural, **sick folk**, Mark vi. 5.
sickly, 1 Cor. xi. 30.

ἀρσενοκοίτης.

abuser of one's self with mankind, 1 Cor. vi. 9.
that defileth one's self with mankind, 1 Tim. i. 10.

ἄρσην.

male, Matt. xix. 4. Mark x. 6. Luke ii. 23. Gal. iii. 28.
man, Rom. i. 27*t*.
See also ἄρρην.

ἀρτέμων.

mainsail, Acts xxvii. 40.

ἄρτι.

even now, Matt. ix. 18.
now, Matt. iii. 15. xxvi. 53. John ix. 19, 25. xiii. 7, 33, 37. xvi. 12, 31. 1 Cor. xiii. 12*t*. xvi. 7. Gal. i. 9, 10. iv. 20. 1 Thes. iii. 6. 2 Thes. ii. 7. 1 Pet. i. 6, 8. Rev. xii. 10.

With ἀπό, **henceforth**, Matt. xxiii. 39. xxvi. 29. — **from henceforth**, John xiv. 7. — **hereafter**, Matt. xxvi. 64. John i. 51(52; -G″LTr*S*). — **now** (*marg.* **from henceforth**), John xiii. 19.

ἄχρι τῆς ἄρτι ὥρας, **even unto this present hour**, 1 Cor. iv. 11.

With ἕως, **until now**, Matt. xi. 12. John ii. 10. — **even until now**, 1 John ii. 9. — **unto this present**, 1 Cor. xv. 6. — **unto this day**, 1 Cor. iv. 13. — **unto this hour**, 1 Cor. viii. 7. — **hitherto**, John v. 17. xvi. 24.

Add Rev. xiv. 13 (*see ἀπάρτι*).

ἀρτιγέννητος.

new-born, 1 Pet. ii. 2.

ἄρτιος.

perfect, 2 Tim. iii. 17.

ἄρτος.

bread, Matt. iv. 3, 4. vi. 11. vii. 9. xv. 2, 26, 33. xvi. 5, 7, 8, 11, 12 (-T*S*). xxvi. 26. Mark iii. 20. vi. 8, 36(-G″L^bTr, *βρῶμα* *S*), 37. vii. 2, 5, 27. viii. 4, 14, 16, 17. xiv. 22. Luke iv. 3, 4. vii. 33(-G°). ix. 3. xi. 3, 11. xiv. 1, 15 (*ἄριστον* G′). xv. 17. xxii. 19. xxiv. 30, 35. John vi. 5, 7, 23, 31, 32*t*, 33, 34, 35, 41, 48, 50, 51*tr*, 58*t*. xiii. 18. xxi. 9, 13. Acts ii. 42, 46. xx. 7, 11. xxvii. 35. 1 Cor. x. 16, 17*t*. xi. 23, 26, 27, 28. 2 Cor. ix. 10. 2 Thes. iii. 8, 12.

ἄρτοι τῆς προθέσεως, **show-bread**, Matt. xii. 4. Mark ii. 26. Luke vi. 4. — *πρόθεσις τῶν ἄρτων*, **show-bread**, Heb. ix. 2.

loaf, Matt. xiv. 17, 19*t*. xv. 34, 36. xvi. 9, 10. Mark vi. 38, 41*t*, 44, 52. viii. 5, 6, 14, 19. Luke ix. 13, 16. xi. 5. John vi. 9, 11, 13, 26.

Add Mark viii. 20(seven . .), L*S*.

ἀρτύω.

to season, Mark ix. 50. Luke xiv. 34. Col. iv. 6.

ἀρχάγγελος.

archangel, 1 Thes. iv. 16. Jude 9.

ἀρχαῖος.

of old time, Matt. v. 21, 27(*omS*), 33.

ἀφ' ἡμερῶν ἀρχαίων, **a good while ago**, Acts xv. 7.

ἐκ γενεῶν ἀρχαίων, **of old time**, Acts xv. 21.

old, Luke ix. 8, 19. Acts xxi. 16. 2 Pet. ii. 5. Rev. xii. 9. xx. 2.

With art., **old things**, 2 Cor. v. 17.

ἀρχή.

beginning, Matt. xix. 4, 8. xxiv. 8, 21. Mark i. 1. x. 6. xiii. 8(9), 19. Luke i. 2. John i. 1, 2. ii. 11. vi. 64. viii. 25, 44. xv. 27. xvi. 4. Acts xi. 15. Phil. iv. 15. Col. i. 18. 2 Thes. ii. 13(*see* ἀπαρχή). Heb. i. 10. iii. 14. vii. 3. 2 Pet. iii. 4. 1 John i. 1. ii, 7, 7(-G°°LT*S*), 13, 14, 24*t*. iii. 8, 11. 2 John 5, 6. Rev. i. 8(*om*). iii. 14. xxi. 6. xxii. 13.

first[cc], Heb. v. 12.

With ἀπό, **at the first**, Acts xxvi. 4.

With λαμβάνω, **begin at the first**, Heb. ii. 3.

corner, Acts x. 11. xi. 5.

first estate (*marg.* **principality**), Jude 6.

principles[cc] (*marg.* **beginning**), Heb. vi. 1.

principality, Rom. viii. 38. Eph. i. 21. iii. 10. vi. 12. Col. i. 16. ii. 10, 15. Tit. iii. 1.

rule, 1 Cor. xv. 24.

power, Luke xx. 20.

magistrate, Luke xii. 11.

ἀρχηγός.

Prince, Acts iii. 15 (*marg.* **author**). v. 31.

captain, Heb. ii. 10.

author(*marg.* **beginner**), Heb. xii. 2.

ἀρχιερατικός.

of the high priest, Acts iv. 6.

ἀρχιερεύς.

chief priest, Matt. ii. 4. xvi. 21. xx. 18. xxi. 15, 23, 45. xxvi. 3, 14, 47, 59. xxvii. 1, 3, 6, 12, 20, 41, 62. xxviii. 11. Mark viii. 31. x. 33. xi. 18, 27. xiv. 1, 10, 43, 53, 55. xv. 1, 3, 10, 11, 31. Luke ix. 22. xix. 47. xx. 1(ἱερεύς G'T), 19. xxii. 2, 4, 52, 66. xxiii. 4, 10, 13, 23 (-L[b]Tr[b]*S*). xxiv. 20. John vii. 32, 45. xi. 47, 57. xii. 10. xviii. 3, 35. xix. 6, 15, 21. Acts iv. 23. v. 24. ix. 14, 21. xxii. 30. xxiii. 14. xxv. 15. xxvi. 10, 12.

chief of the priests, Acts xix. 14.

high priest, Matt. xxvi. 3, 51, 57, 58, 62, 63, 65. Mark ii. 26. xiv. 47, 53, 54, 60, 61, 63, 66. Luke iii. 2. xxii. 50, 54. John xi. 49, 51. xviii. 10, 13, 15*t*, 16, 19, 22, 24, 26. Acts iv. 6. v. 17, 21, 27. vii. 1. ix. 1. xxii. 5. xxiii. 2, 4, 5. xxiv. 1. xxv. 2. Heb. iv. 15. v. 1, 5. vii. 27, 28. viii. 3. ix. 7, 25. xiii. 11. — *Said of Christ*, Heb. ii. 17. iii. 1. iv. 14. v. 10. vi. 20. vii. 26. viii. 1. ix. 11.

Add Heb. x. 11, for ἱερεύς, L.

ἀρχιποίμην.

chief Shepherd, 1 Pet. v. 4.

ἀρχισυνάγωγος.

ruler of the synagogue, Matt. v. 22, 35, 36, 38. Luke viii. 49. xiii. 14. Acts xiii. 15.

chief ruler of the synagogue, Acts xviii. 8, 17.

ἀρχιτέκτων.

master-builder, 1 Cor. iii. 10.

ἀρχιτελώνης.

chief among the publicans, Luke xix. 2.

ἀρχιτρίκλινος.

governor of the feast, John ii. 8, 9.

ruler of the feast, John ii. 9.

ἄρχω.

rule over, Mark x. 42.

reign over, Rom. xv. 12.

Mid., **begin**, Matt. iv. 17. xi. 7, 20. xii. 1. xiv. 30. xvi. 21, 22. xviii. 24[p]. xx. 8. xxiv. 49. xxvi. 22, 37, 74. Mark i. 45. ii. 23. iv.

1. v. 17, 20. vi. 2, 7, 34, 55. viii. 11, 31, 32. x. 28, 32, 41, 47. xi. 15. xii. 1. xiii. 5. xiv. 19, 33, 65, 69, 71. xv. 8, 18. Luke iii. 8. iv. 21. v. 21. vii. 15, 24, 38, 49. ix. 12. xi. 29, 53. xii. 1, 45. xiii. 25, 25. xiv. 9, 18, 29, 30. xv. 14, 24. xix. 37, 45. xx. 9. xxi. 28p. xxii. 23. xxiii. 2, 5, 30. xxiv. 27, 47. John viii. 9(*ap*). xiii. 5. Acts i. 1, 22. ii. 4. viii. 35. x. 37. xi. 15. xviii. 26. xxiv. 2. xxvii. 35. 2 Cor. iii. 1. 1 Pet. iv. 17. —*With* εἰμί, **begin**, Luke iii. 23p. — **rehearse**[c] **from the beginning**, Acts xi. 4p.

ἄρχων.

prince, Matt. ix. 34. xii. 24. xx. 25. Mark iii. 22. John xii. 31. xiv. 30. xvi. 11. 1 Cor. ii. 6, 8. Eph. ii. 2. Rev. i. 5.

chief, Luke xi. 15. xiv. 1cc.

ruler, Matt. ix. 18, 23. Luke viii. 41. xviii. 18. xxiii. 13, 35. xxiv. 20. John iii. 1. vii. 26, 48. Acts iii. 17. iv. 5, 8, 26. vii. 27, 35*t*. xiii. 27. xiv. 5. xvi. 19. xxiii. 5. Rom. xiii. 3.

chief ruler, John xii. 42.

magistrate, Luke xii. 58.

ἄρωμα.

spices, Luke xxiii. 56. xxiv. 1. John xix. 40.

sweet spices, Mark xvi. 1.

ἀσαίνομαι. See σαίνομαι.

ἀσάλευτος.

unmovable, Acts xxvii. 41.

which cannot be moved, Heb. xii. 28.

ἄσβεστος.

unquenchable, Matt. iii. 12. Luke iii. 17.

that never shall be quenched, Mark ix. 43(*ap*), 45(*ap*).

ἀσέβεια.

ungodliness, Rom. i. 18. xi. 26. 2 Tim. ii. 16. Tit. ii. 12.

ungodlycc, Jude 15(–G°*S*), 18.

ἀσεβέω.

live ungodly, 2 Pet. ii. 6.

commit ungodly, Jude 15.

ἀσεβής.

ungodly, Rom. iv. 5. v. 6. 1 Tim. i. 9. 1 Pet. iv. 18. 2 Pet. ii. 5. iii. 7. Jude 15.

With art., **that is ungodly**, Jude 15.

ungodly man, Jude 4.

ἀσέλγεια.

lasciviousness, Mark vii. 22. 2 Cor. xii. 21. Gal. v. 19. Eph. iv. 19. 1 Pet. iv. 3. Jude 4.

wantonness, Rom. xiii. 13.

Plural, **much wantonness**, 2 Pet. ii. 18.

filthycc, 2 Pet. ii. 7.

Add 2 Pet. ii. 2, for ἀπωλεία, CmG LT*S*.

ἄσημος.

mean, Acts xxi. 39.

ἀσθένεια.

weakness, 1 Cor. ii. 3. xv. 43. 2 Cor. xii. 9. xiii. 4. Heb. xi. 34.

infirmity, Matt. viii. 17. Luke v. 15. viii. 2. xiii. 11, 12. John v. 5. Rom. vi. 19. viii. 26. 2 Cor. xi. 30. xii. 5, 9, 10. Gal. iv. 13. 1 Tim. v. 23. Heb. iv. 15. v. 2. vii. 28.

sickness, John xi. 4.

disease, Acts xxviii. 9.

ἀσθενέω.

be weak, Rom. iv. 19. viii. 3. xiv. 1, 2. 1 Cor. viii. 9p(ἀσθενής G''LT*S*). 2 Cor. xi. 21, 29*t*. xii. 10. xiii. 3, 4, 9.

be made weak, Rom. xiv. 21(*ap*).

weak, Acts xx. 35p. 1 Cor. viii. 11p, 12p.

impotent man, John v. 7p.

impotent folk, John v. 3p,pl.

be sick, Matt. xxv. 36. Luke vii. 10(–LTr*S*). John iv. 46. xi. 2, 3, 6. Acts ix. 37. Phil. ii. 26, 27. Jas. v. 14.

sick, Matt. x. 8p. Mark vi. 56p. Luke iv. 40p. ix. 2p(ἀσθενής G''LTrb *S*, –T). John xi. 1p. Acts xix. 12p. 2 Tim. iv. 20p.

be diseased, John vi. 2.

Add Matt. xxv. 39, for ἀσθενής,

LTTr. John v. 13, for ἰαθεὶς, fr. ἰάομαι, G'T.

ἀσθένημα.

infirmity, Rom. xv. 1.

ἀσθενής.

without strength, Rom. v. 6.
weak, Matt. xxvi. 41. Mark xiv. 38. 1 Cor. iv. 10. viii. 7, 10. ix. 22*tr*. xi. 30. 2 Cor. x. 10. Gal. iv. 9. 1 Thes. v. 14. 1 Pet. iii. 7.
With art., **weakness**, 1 Cor. i. 25. Heb. vii. 18.—**weak things**, 1 Cor. i. 27[pl](*ap*).
feeble, 1 Cor. xii. 22.
impotent, Acts iv. 9.
sick, Matt. xxv. 39(ἀσθενέω[p] LTTr), 43, 44. Luke x. 9. Acts v. 15.
sick folks, Acts v. 16[pl].
Add, for ἀσθενέω[p], Luke ix. 2, G″ LTr[b]*S*. 1 Cor. viii. 9, G″LT*S*.

ἀσιτία.

abstinence, Acts xxvii. 21.

ἄσιτος.

fasting, Acts xxvii. 33.

ἀσκέω.

to exercise, Acts xxiv. 16.

ἀσκός.

bottle, Matt. ix. 17*f*. Mark ii. 22*tr*, 22(*ap*). Luke v. 37*tr*, 38.

ἀσμένως.

gladly, Acts ii. 41(-G∞LT*S*). xxi. 17.

ἄσοφος.

fool, Eph. v. 15.

ἀσπάζομαι.

greet, Rom. xvi. 3, 6, 8, 11. 1 Cor. xvi. 20*t*. 2 Cor. xiii. 12. Phil. iv. 21. Col. iv. 14. 1 Thes. v. 26. 2 Tim. iv. 21. Tit. iii. 15(14). 1 Pet. v. 14. 2 John 13. 3 John 14(15).
salute, Matt. v. 47. x. 12. Mark ix. 15. xv. 18. Luke i. 40. x. 4. Acts xviii. 22[p]. xxi. 7, 19[p]. xxv. 13. Rom. xvi. 5, 7, 9, 10*t*, 11, 12, 12(*ap*), 13, 14, 15, 16*t*, 21, 22, 23*t*. 1 Cor. xvi. 19(18)*t*. 2 Cor. xiii. 13 (12). Phil. iv. 21, 22. Col. iv. 10, 12, 15. 2 Tim. iv. 19. Tit. iii. 15 (14). Phm. 23. Heb. xiii. 24*t*. 1 Pet. v. 13. 3 John 14(15).
embrace, Acts xx. 1. Heb. xi. 13.
take leave of, Acts xxi. 6[p](ἀπασπάζομαι LT*S*).

ἀσπασμός.

greeting, Matt. xxiii. 7. Luke xi. 43. xx. 46.
salutation, Mark xii. 38. Luke i. 29, 41, 44. 1 Cor. xvi. 21. Col. iv. 18. 2 Thes. iii. 17.

ἄσπιλος.

without spot, 1 Tim. vi. 14. 1 Pet. i. 19. 2 Pet. iii. 14.
unspotted, Jas. i. 27.

ἀσπίς.

asp, Rom. iii. 13.

ἄσπονδος.

implacable, Rom. i. 31(-G∞LT*S*).
truce-breaker, 2 Tim. iii. 3.

ἀσσάριον.

farthing, Matt. x. 29. Luke xii. 6,

ἆσσον, Ἄσσον St.

close by, Acts xxvii. 13.

ἀστατέω.

have no certain dwelling place, 1 Cor. iv. 11.

ἀστεῖος.

fair, Acts vii. 20.
proper, Heb. xi. 23.

ἀστήρ.

star, Matt. ii. 2, 7, 9, 10. xxiv. 29. Mark xiii. 35. 1 Cor. xv. 41*tr*. Jude 13. Rev. i. 16, 20*t*. ii. 1, 28. iii. 1. vi. 13. viii. 10, 11, 12. ix. 1. xii. 1, 4. xxii. 16.

ἀστήρικτος.

unstable, 2 Pet. ii. 14. iii. 16.

ἄστοργος.

without natural affection, Rom. i. 31(*marg.* **unsociable**). 2 Tim. iii. 3.

ἀστοχέω.

swerve from (*marg.* **not aim at**), 1 Tim. i. 6.
err, 1 Tim. vi. 21. 2 Tim. ii. 18.

ἀστραπή.
lightning, Matt. xxiv. 27. xxviii. 3. Luke x. 18. xvii. 24. Rev. iv. 5. viii. 5. xi. 19. xvi. 18.
bright shining, Luke xi. 36.

ἀστράπτω.
lighten, Luke xvii. 24.
shine, Luke xxiv. 4.

ἄστρον.
star, Luke xxi. 25. Acts vii. 43. xxvii. 20. Heb. xi. 12.

ἀσύμφωνος.
With εἰμί, **agree not**, Acts xxviii. 25[p].

ἀσύνετος.
without understanding, Matt. xv. 16. Mark vii. 18. Rom. i. 31.
foolish, Rom. i. 21. x. 19.

ἀσύνθετος.
covenant breaker, Rom. i. 31.

ἀσφαλεία.
safety, Acts v. 23. 1 Thes. v. 3.
certainty, Luke i. 4.

ἀσφαλής.
safe, Phil. iii. 1.
sure, Heb. vi. 19.
certain, Acts xxv. 26.
With art., **certainty**, Acts xxi. 34. xxii. 30.

ἀσφαλίζω.
make sure, Matt. xxvii. 64.
Mid., **make fast**, Acts xvi. 24.—**make sure**, Matt. xxvii. 65, 66.

ἀσφαλῶς.
safely, Mark xiv. 44. Acts xvi. 23.
assuredly, Acts ii. 36.

ἀσχημονέω.
behave one's self unseemly, 1 Cor. xiii. 5.
behave one's self uncomely, 1 Cor. vii. 36.

ἀσχημοσύνη.
that which is unseemly, Rom. i. 27.
shame, Rev. xvi. 15.

ἀσχήμων.
uncomely, 1 Cor. xii. 23.

ἀσωτία.
riot, Tit. i. 6. 1 Pet. iv. 4.
excess, Eph. v. 18.

ἀσώτως.
riotous[cc], Luke xv. 13.

ἀτακτέω.
behave one's self disorderly, 2 Thes. iii. 7.

ἄτακτος.
unruly (*marg.* **disorderly**), 1 Thes. v. 14.

ἀτάκτως.
disorderly, 2 Thes. iii. 6, 11.

ἄτεκνος.
without children, Luke xx. 28, 29.
childless, Luke xx. 30(*ap*).

ἀτενίζω.
look steadfastly, Acts i. 10 (*with* εἰμί). vi. 15. 2 Cor. iii. 13.
look up[c] **steadfastly**, Acts vii. 55.
look earnestly on, Acts iii. 12.
look earnestly upon, Luke xxii. 56.
look on, Acts x. 4[p].
behold steadfastly, Acts xiv. 9. 2 Cor. iii. 7 (*with* εἰς).
behold earnestly, Acts xxiii. 1.
fasten one's eyes, Acts iii. 4. xi. 6[p].
be fastened on, Luke iv. 20 (*with* εἰμί).
set one's eyes, Acts xiii. 9[p].

ἄτερ.
without, Luke xxii. 35.
in the absence of (*marg.* **without**), Luke xxii. 6.

ἀτιμάζω.
to dishonor, John viii. 49. Rom. ii. 23.—*Mid.*, Rom. i. 24.
despise, Jas. ii. 6.
entreat shamefully, Luke xx. 11.
Pass., **suffer shame**, Acts v. 41.

ἀτιμάω. See ἀτιμόω.

ἀτιμία.
dishonor, Rom. ix. 21. 1 Cor. xv. 43. 2 Cor. vi. 8. 2 Tim. ii. 20.
reproach, 2 Cor. xi. 21.
shame, 1 Cor. xi. 14.
vile[cc], Rom. i. 26.

ἄτιμος.
without honor, Matt. xiii. 57. Mark vi. 4.
less honorable, 1 Cor. xii. 23comp.
despised, 1 Cor. iv. 10.

ἀτιμόω.
handle shamefully, Mark xii. 4(ἠτίμησαν for ἀπέστειλαν ἠτιμωμένον LTr, ἠτίμασαν *S*).

ἀτμίς.
vapor, Acts ii. 19. Jas. iv. 14.

ἄτομος.
moment, 1 Cor. xv. 52.

ἄτοπος.
amiss, Luke xxiii. 41.
harm, Acts xxviii. 6.
unreasonable (*Gr.* absurd), 2 Thes. iii. 2.
wickedness, Acts xxv. 5 (τούτῳ ESt T,–G).

αὐγάζω.
shine, 2 Cor. iv. 4(καταυγάζω Lm).

αὐγή.
break of day, Acts xx. 11.

αὐθάδης.
selfwilled, Tit. i. 7. 2 Pet. ii. 10.

αὐθαίρετος.
willing of one's self, 2 Cor. viii. 3.
of one's own accord, 2 Cor. viii. 17.

αὐθεντέω.
usurp authority over, 1 Tim. ii. 12.

αὐλέω.
to pipe, Matt. xi. 17. Luke vii. 32. 1 Cor. xiv. 7.

αὐλή.
fold, John x. 16.
With τῶν προβάτων, **sheepfold,** John x. 1.
court, Rev. xi. 2.
hall, Mark xv. 16. Luke xxii. 55.
palace, Matt. xxvi. 3, 58, 69. Mark xiv. 54, 66. Luke xi. 21. John xviii. 15.

αὐλητής.
piper, Rev. xviii. 22.
minstrel, Matt. ix. 23.

αὐλίζομαι.
to lodge, Matt. xxi. 17.
abide, Luke xxi. 37.

αὐλός.
pipe, 1 Cor. xiv. 7.

αὐξάνω or αὔξω.
Trans., **increase,** 2 Cor. ix. 10.—**give the increase,** 1 Cor. iii. 6, 7.
Intrans., **grow,** Matt. vi. 28. Luke i. 80. ii. 40. xii. 27(*ap*). xiii. 19. Acts vii. 17. xii. 24. xix. 20. Eph. ii. 21. 2 Pet. iii. 18.—**grow up,** Eph. iv. 15.—**increase,** Mark iv. 8(*pass.* G''LTTr*S*). John iii. 30. Acts vi. 7.
Pass., **grow,** Matt. xiii. 32. 1 Pet. ii. 2.—**increase,** 2 Cor. x. 15p. Col. i. 10. ii. 19.
Add Col. i. 6(fruit, καί αὐ.)GLT*S*.

αὔξησις.
increase, Eph. iv. 16. Col. ii. 19.

αὔριον.
to-morrow, Matt. vi. 30. Luke xii. 28. xiii. 32, 33. Acts xxiii. 15(*om S*), 20. xxv. 22. 1 Cor. xv. 32. Jas. iv. 13.
morrow, Matt. vi. 34*t*. Luke x. 35. Acts iv. 5. Jas. iv. 14.
next day, Acts iv. 3.

αὐστηρός.
austere, Luke xix. 21, 22.

αὗται. See οὗτος.

αὐτάρκεια.
sufficiency, 2 Cor. ix. 8.
contentment, 1 Tim. vi. 6.

αὐτάρκης.
content, Phil. iv. 11.

αὕτη. See οὗτος.

αὐτοκατάκριτος.
condemned of one's self, Tit. iii. 11.

αὐτόματος.
of one's self, Mark iv. 28.
of one's own accord, Acts xii. 10.

αὐτόπτης.
eye-witness, Luke i. 2.

αὐτός.

An Adjective or Pronoun of constant occurrence. Its use is—

I. *Antithetical, discriminative,* or otherwise more or less *emphatic;* thus often joined with καί in the sense of *also, likewise,* or *even.*

(a) *Always so in the Nominative:*

Masc. sing., αὐτός.

With ἐγώ, **I myself,** Luke xxiv. 39. Acts x. 26. Rom. vii. 25. ix. 3cc. xv. 14. 2 Cor. x. 1. xii. 13.

Ic **myself,** Acts xxiv. 16cc. xxv. 22. 1 Cor. ix. 27. Phil. ii. 24.

thouc **thyself,** Luke vi. 42. Acts xxi. 24.—**thyself,** Acts xxiv. 8.

hec **himself,** Luke x. 1. John vi. 6, 15. vii. 4. Acts ii. 34. xviii. 19. xix. 22. 1 Cor. ii. 15. iii. 15. Heb. ii. 18. v. 2. 3 John 10. Rev. xix. 12.—**his**c **own self,** 1 Pet. ii. 24.

himself, Matt. vi. 4 (-GoLTr*S*). viii. 17. xxvii. 57. Mark vi. 17. xii. 36. Luke iii. 23. vi. 3. xx. 42. xxiv. 15, 36. John iv. 2, 12, 44, 53. v. 20, 37(ἐκεῖνος LmTTr*S*). xvi. 27. Acts viii. 13. xx. 13. 1 Cor. xv. 28. 2 Cor. xi. 14. 1 Thes. iii. 11. iv. 16. 2 Thes. ii. 16. iii. 16. 1 John ii. 6. Rev. xxi. 3.

he, Matt. i. 21. iii. 112d. viii. 24. xii. 31st(*omS*). xiv. 2. xvi. 202d. xxi. 27. xxv. 172d(-GoLTr*S*). Mark i. 8. ii. 251st (-GoLbTr*S*), 253d. iii. 132d. iv. 27, 38. vi. 162d(-GLbTTr*S*), 452d, 47. vii. 362d(-LTr*S*). viii. 29. xii. 21(*ap*). xiv. 15. Luke i. 17, 224th. ii. 28. iii. 15, 16. iv. 15, 30. v. 1, 14, 16, 17. vi. 81st, 20, 35. vii. 52d. viii. 1, 221st, 37, 411st (οὗτος LTr), 54. ix. 512d. x. 38. xi. 17, 28. xv. 142d. xvi. 241st. xvii. 112d, 16. xviii. 392d. xix. 9. xxii. 41. xxiii. 92d. xxiv. 21, 25, 281st, 31. John i. 27 (-GLbTTr*S*). ii. 122d, 25. vii. 10. ix. 212d(-TTr*S*), 213d. xii. 49. xiv. 10. xviii. 12d. Acts vii. 15. x. 42(οὗτος G′L). xiv. 12. xvi. 332d. xvii. 252d. xx. 35. 1 Cor. vii. 13 (οὗτος G′ LT*S*). 2 Cor. x. 72d. Eph. ii. 14. iv. 11. v. 23, 27. Col. i. 17, 18*t*. Heb. i. 5. ii. 141st. iv. 102d. viii. 5. Jas. i. 132d. 1 John i. 7. ii. 2, 25. iii. 242d. iv. 10, 131st, 15, 19(ὁ θεός L). Rev. iii. 20. xiv. 17. xvii. 11. xix. 152d, 153d. xxi. 72d.

this, Matt. xi. 14.

this man, Heb. x. 12(οὗτος CG″L*S*).

the same, Matt. iii. 4. xii. 50. Luke xxiii. 51(-LTr*S*). Eph. iv. 10. Rev. xiv. 10.

that same, Matt. xxvi. 48. Mark xiv. 44.

very, 1 Thes. v. 23.

With καί, **which,** Luke xix. 2.

it, John xii. 241st.

Not rendered, Mark xv. 43 (. . waited). Luke v. 37(. . be spilled). John ii. 24(. . Jesus). Acts xxii. 20(I . .). 1 Pet. v. 10(. . make).

Add, for οὗτος, Mark vi. 16, G′. Luke xix. 2, LTr. John i. 33, Lm. Acts iii. 10, L*S*.—Mark v. 40(he1st), LTr*S*. viii. 10(he), Lb. John vii. 9, for αὐτοῖς, G′T*S*. 1 Cor. ix. 20 (*ap*). Eph. v. 27, for αὐτήν, GLT*S*.

Plural, αὐτοί.

With ἡμεῖς, **we ourselves,** Rom. viii. 23.

wec **ourselves,** Luke xxii. 71. John iv. 42. 2 Cor. i. 4. Gal. ii. 17.

ourselves, Rom. viii. 28.

With ὑμεῖς, **ye yourselves,** Mark vi. 31. John iii. 28. 1 Thes. iv. 9.

yec **yourselves,** Luke xi. 46, 52. Acts ii. 22.

youc **yourselves,** Acts xx. 34.

yourselves, 1 Thes. ii. 1. iii. 3. v. 2. 2 Thes. iii. 7. Heb. xiii. 3.

With οὗτοι, **they themselves,** Acts xxiv. 15.

theyc **themselves,** John xviii. 28. Gal. vi. 13. 1 Thes. i. 9. 2 Pet. ii. 19.

themselves, Acts xv. 32. xvi. 37.

they, Matt. v. 4, 5, 6, 7, 8, 9(-Lb TrbS). xii. 27. xx. 102d. xxv. 44. Luke ii. 50. vi. 111st. ix. 361st. xi.

19, 48. xiv. 1, 12. xvi. 28. xvii. 13. xviii. 34[1st]. xxii. 23. xxiv. 14, 35, 52. John iv. 45. vi. 24. xvii. 8[1st], 19, 21[2d]. Acts xiii. 14[1st]. xxii. 19. xxvii. 36[2d]. xxviii. 28. Rom. xi. 31. 2 Cor. vi. 16. x. 12. Gal. ii. 9[2d]. 1 Thes. ii. 14. 2 Tim. ii. 10. Heb. i. 11. iii. 10[2d]. viii. 9, 10. xiii. 17[1st]. Jas. ii. 7. 1 John iv. 5[1st]. Rev. vi. 11[2d]. xii. 11[1st]. xxi. 3.

these same, Acts xxiv. 20.

Not rendered, Luke xi. 4(we . .). Acts xviii. 15(ye . .). Rom. xv. 14 (ye . .). 2 Cor i. 9(But we . .). Jas. ii. 6(. . draw). 1 Pet. i. 15 (ye . .). ii. 5(ye . .).

Add, for οὗτοι, Luke xiii. 4, LTTr *S*. Acts xiii. 4, LT*S*. 1 Cor. xvi. 17, LT.—Matt. xix. 28, for ὑμεῖς[2d], Tr*S*. xxiii. 4(*they themselves*), LTr*S*. Mark ii. 8 (they), G[pr]T. vii. 36 (they[2d]), LTTr*S*. 2 Pet. i. 5, for αὐτὸ τοῦτο, L.

Fem. sing., αὐτή.

herself, Heb. xi. 11.—**she**, Luke i. 36. 1 Cor. vii. 12(αὕτη LT). Rev. xviii. 6[1st](-LTTr*S*).

itself, Rom. viii. 21. 1 Cor. xi. 14 (-G°).

Add, for αὕτη, Rom. vii. 10, G″. xvi. 2, GLT.—Mark x. 12, for γυνή, Tr*S*.

Neut. sing., αὐτό.

itself, Rom. viii. 16, 26.—**it**, Luke xi. 14.

Plural, **the same**, John v. 36.

(b) *Rarely in Oblique cases*, mostly as an adjective.

Accusative.

αὐτόν, **himself**, Eph. i. 5. Col. i. 20. Heb. xii. 3.—**him**, Luke xxiv. 24. John ix. 21.—**itself**, John xxi. 25. Heb. ix. 24.

αὐτούς, **them**, Mark ix. 16(*marg.* **themselves**). Acts xiii. 36.

αὐτήν, **very**, Heb. x. 1.

αὐτό, Heb. ix. 19(book . .).

With τοῦτο, **this very thing**, Phil. i. 6.—**this selfsame thing**, 2 Cor. vii. 11.—**this same**, 2 Cor. ii. 3.—**the same**, Gal. ii. 10.—**besides this**[cc], 2 Pet. i. 5(αὐτοί L).

εἰς αὐτὸ τοῦτο, **upon this very thing**, Rom. xiii. 6.—**for the selfsame thing**, 2 Cor. v. 5.—**even for this same purpose**, Rom. ix. 17.—**for the same purpose**, Eph. vi. 22. Col. iv. 8.—**thereunto**, Eph. vi. 18(-τοῦτο G°°L T*S*).

αὐτά, **very**, John xiv. 11.—**themselves**, Heb. ix. 23.—**them**, Mark viii. 7(ταῦτα Tr, -G°).

Genitive.

αὐτοῦ, often written αὑτοῦ, **of himself**, Heb. ix. 26.—**of him**, John ix. 18.—**his**, Eph. ii. 10.—**same**, 2 Cor. viii. 19(-G°L).

his own, Matt. xiii. 54, 57, 57(-L Tr*S*). xvi. 26. xxvii. 60. Mark vi. 1, 4*t*. viii. 36. Luke i. 23, 56. v. 25, 29. ix. 26. John vii. 53(*ap*). 1 Cor. vi. 14. Eph. i. 11, 20. Heb. ii. 4. iii. 6. iv. 10. 1 Pet. ii. 24. Rev. i. 5.

With τούτου, **he himself**, Acts xxv. 25.

Add Mark vi. 4(own[2d]), L[b]TTr.

αὐτῶν(αὑτῶν), **their own**, Matt. ii. 12. xvii. 25. Mark viii. 3. Luke ii. 39. Acts vii. 41. xiv. 16. Heb. xii. 10. 2 Pet. ii. 12, 13. Jude 16.

αὐτῆς, **itself**, 3 John 12.—**the said**, Mark vi. 22.

Dative.

αὐτῷ(αὑτῷ), **himself**, Eph. i. 9.—**even him**, Eph. i. 10.—**that**, Luke xiii. 1.

αὐτοῖς (αὑτοῖς), **themselves**, John xvii. 13.—**them**, 1 Cor. i. 24.—Mark xvi. 14(. . the eleven; *ap*).

αὐτῇ, **her**, Luke i. 36.—**same**, Luke x. 7.

ἐν αὐτῇ τῇ ἡμέρᾳ, **that same day**, Luke xxiv. 13.—**the same day**, Luke xiii. 31. xxiii. 12.

ἐν αὐτῇ τῇ ὥρᾳ, **in that same hour**, Luke vii. 21(ἐκείνῃ L[m]TTr*S*).—**in that hour**, Luke x. 21.—**in the same hour**, Luke xii. 12.—**the same hour**, Luke xx. 19.

αὐτῇ τῇ ὥρᾳ, **the same hour,** Acts xvi. 18. xxii. 13.—**in that instant,** Luke ii. 38.

II. *With the Article, ὁ αὐτός, etc.*

the same, Matt. v. 46(οὕτως LTTr). xxvi. 44. xxvii. 44. Mark xiv. 39. Luke ii. 8. vi. 33, 38 (ᾧ LTr*S*). xxiii. 40. Rom. ix. 21. x. 12. xii. 4. 1 Cor. i. 10*t*. x. 3, 4. xii. 4, 5, 6, 8, 9, 9(τῷ ἑνί LT). xv. 39. 2 Cor. i. 6. iii. 14, 18. iv. 13. viii. 16. xii. 18*t*. Phil. i. 30. ii. 2. iii. 16. Heb. i. 12. ii. 14. iv. 11. vi. 11. x. 11. xi. 9. xiii. 8. Jas. iii. 10, 11. 1 Pet. iv. 1, 4. v. 9. 1 John ii. 27(τὸ αὐτοῦ G'T*S*).

the selfsame, 1 Cor. xii. 11.

the same thing, Acts xv. 27pl. Rom. ii. 1pl. 1 Cor. i. 10. Eph. vi. 9pl. Phil. iii. 1pl.

the same matter, Mark x. 10(τούτου LTTr, τούτων *S*).

for the same cause, Phil. ii. 18.

those, Heb. x. 1.

ταὐτά, **like things,** 1 Thes. ii. 14 (τὰ αὐτά GLT*S*).

ἐπὶ τὸ αὐτό, **in one place,** Acts ii. 1. —**together,** Matt. xxii. 34. Luke xvii. 35. Acts i. 15. ii. 44. iii. 1. iv. 26. 1 Cor vii. 5. (*See* ἐπί, III.).

κατὰ τὸ αὐτό, **together,** Acts xiv. 1.

τὴν αὐτὴν ἀντιμισθίαν, **for a recompense in the same,** 2 Cor. vi. 13.

With ἕν καί, **even all one as if,** 1 Cor. xi. 5.

With μεριμνάω, **have the same care,** 1 Cor. xii. 25.

With φρονέω, **mind the same thing,** Phil. iii. 16(*ap*).—**be of the same mind,** Rom. xii. 16. Phil. iv. 2.—**be of one mind,** 2 Cor. xiii. 11.—**be like-minded,** Rom. xv. 5. Phil. ii. 2.

Add, for ταῦτα, Luke vi. 23, 26, LT Tr; ταὐτά G''Lm. xvii. 30, TTr; ταὐτά GL.—Matt. v. 47, for οὕτω, LTTr*S*. 2 Pet. iii. 7, τῷ αὐτῷ for αὐτοῦ, CL.

III. *As a simple Pronoun, only in the oblique cases,* rendered by **he, she, it, they,** and their inflected forms; and the Genitive and Dative by the aid of prepositions, as **of, to,** and **unto.** *Passim.*

Without an antecedent, referring to Christ: Luke i. 17? John ix. 22. 1 John ii. 8, 12, 27, 28. iii. 5? 2 John 6. 2 Pet. iii. 4.

Other cases in which the subject is merely implied or presupposed to be known:—

him, John xx. 151st.—**his,** Rom. ii. 26.—**her,** Luke ii. 22(αὐτῶν GL TTr*S*, αὐτοῦ G').—**it,** John viii. 44.

them, Matt. xxv. 32. xxviii. 19. Luke v. 17. xviii. 152d. Acts viii. 5. xii. 21? xx. 2. 2 Cor. ii. 13. Eph. v. 12. Heb. iv. 8. viii. 8. xi. 28.—**their,** Matt. iv. 23. ix. 35. xi. 1. xii. 9. Luke iv. 15. Acts iv. 5. 1 Pet. iii. 14.—**of them,** Luke xxiii. 52.—**unto them,** Matt. viii. 4.

Add Luke ii. 21, αὐτόν for τὸ παιδίον, GLTTr*S*.

With διά, **thereat,** Matt. vii. 13.—**thereby,** John xi. 4. Heb. xi. 11.

With εἰς, **therein,** Mark x. 15. Luke xviii. 17.—**thereunto,** Luke xxi. 21.

With ἐν, **therein,** Luke x. 9. xix. 45(*ap*). Acts i. 20. xiv. 15. xvii. 24. Eph. vi. 20(*marg.* **thereof**). Col. ii. 7. 2 Pet. iii. 10. Rev. i. 3. x. 6*tr*. xi. 1. xii. 12. xxi. 22.—**thereon,** Mark xi. 13. Luke xiii. 6.—**thereby,** 1 Pet. ii. 2.—**therewith** Jas. iii. 9*t*.

With ἐπί, **thereon,** John xii. 14. Rev. vi. 4(*accus.* GLTTr*S*).

With περί, **thereof,** Matt. xii. 36.

IV. *Redundant:*—

(a) By Hebraism, *after* ὅς, Mark i. 7. vii. 25. Luke iii. 16. Acts xv. 17. 1 Pet. ii. 24(–GoL). Rev. iii. 8. vii. 2, 9. xiii. 12.

After ὅπου, Rev. xvii. 9.

Add Rev. xx. 8(ἀριθ. αὐτῶν), GL TTr*S*.

(b) By pleonasm, Matt. iv. 16. v. 40. viii. 5(*see below*). ix. 27(–LTrb), 28. xii. 36uc. xxv. 29. Luke xvii.

7. xix. 26. John ix. 13. xv. 2, 2(it). xviii. 11(it). Acts xxiii. 27[cc](–G[o]L *S*). Jas. iv. 17. Rev. ii. 7, 17. vi. 4.

Add Rev. xxi. 6(δώσω αὐτῷ), G′ TTr[b].

(c) By reduplication, Matt. viii. 1[ltr], 23, 28[ltrs]. xxi. 23[ltrs]. xxvi. 71 (–[1st] L[b]Tr*S*). Mark v. 2[ltrs]. ix. 28[ltrs]. Luke viii. 27(–[2d] Tr[b]*S*). Acts vii. 21[ls].

Add Matt. viii. 5(αὐτῷ for τῷ Ἰησοῦ), GT; but [ltrs].

[ltrs] Here L Tr and *S* read the first as a genitive absolute.

αὐτοῦ.

there, Acts xv. 34(*ap*). xviii. 19 (ἐκεῖ L*S*). xxi. 4.

here, Matt. xxvi. 36.

Add Luke ix. 27, for ὧδε, TTr*S*.

αὑτοῦ, αὑτῆς, etc.

L T Tr exclude this form from the Greek Testament, uniformly reading αὐτοῦ, etc. The oldest MSS. have no breathings. For the reading ἑαυτοῦ etc. instead of αὐτοῦ etc. see ἑαυτοῦ.

αὐτόφωρος. See ἐπαυτοφώρῳ.

αὐτόχειρ.

with one's own hand, Acts xxvii. 19.

αὐχέω. See μεγαλαυχέω.

αὐχμηρός.

dark, 2 Pet. i. 19.

ἀφαιρέω.

take away, Luke i. 25. x. 42. xvi. 3. Rom. xi. 27. Heb. x. 4. Rev. xxii. 19*t*.

cut off, Mark xiv. 47. Luke xxii. 50.

smite off, Matt. xxvi. 51.

ἀφανής.

that is not manifest, Heb. iv. 13.

ἀφανίζω.

disfigure, Matt. vi. 16.

corrupt, Matt. vi. 19, 20.

Pass., **vanish away,** Jas. iv. 14. — **perish,** Acts xiii. 41.

ἀφανισμός.

to vanish away[cc], Heb. viii. 13.

ἄφαντος.

With γίνομαι, **vanish out of sight** (*marg.* **cease to be seen**), Luke xxiv. 31.

ἀφεδρών.

draught, Matt. xv. 17. Mark vii. 19.

ἀφειδία, ἀφειδεία L.

neglecting (*marg.* **punishing,** or **not sparing**), Col. ii. 23.

ἀφελότης.

singleness, Acts ii. 46.

ἄφεσις.

deliverance, Luke iv. 18(19).

liberty, Luke iv. 18(19).

remission, Matt. xxvi. 28. Mark i. 4. Luke i. 77. iii. 3. xxiv. 47. Acts ii. 38. x. 43. Heb. ix. 22. x. 18.

forgiveness, Mark iii. 29. Acts v. 31. xiii. 38. xxvi. 18. Eph. i. 7. Col. i. 14.

ἁφή.

joint, Eph. iv. 16. Col. ii. 19.

ἀφθαρσία.

incorruption, 1 Cor. xv. 42, 50, 53, 54.

immortality, Rom. ii. 7. 2 Tim. i. 10.

sincerity, Eph vi. 24 (*marg.* **incorruption**). Tit. ii. 7(–GLT*S*).

ἄφθαρτος.

not corruptible, 1 Pet. iii. 4.

incorruptible, 1 Cor. ix. 25. xv. 52. 1 Pet. i. 4, 23.

uncorruptible, Rom. i. 23.

immortal, 1 Tim. i. 17.

ἀφθορία, incorruptness.

Tit. ii. 7, for ἀδιαφθορία, G′LT*S*.

ἀφίημι, ἀφέω, or ἀφίω.

send away, Matt. xiii. 36. Mark iv. 36[p].

put away, 1 Cor. vii. 11, 12.

lay aside, Mark vii. 8.

let go, Mark xi. 6.

let be, Matt. xxvii. 49.
let alone, Matt. xv. 14. Mark xiv. 6. xv. 36. Luke xiii. 8. John xi. 48. xii. 7.
let have, Matt. v. 40.
yield up, Matt. xxvii. 50.
With φωνὴν μεγάλην, **cry with a loud voice**, Mark xv. 37.
leave, Matt. iv. 11, 20, 22. v. 24. viii. 15. xviii. 12. xxii. 22, 25. xxiii. 23, 38. xxiv. 2, 40, 41. xxvi. 44. Mark i. 20, 31. viii. 13. x. 28, 29. xii. 12, 19, 20, 21(*ap*), 22. xiii. 2, 34. Luke iv. 39. x. 30. xi. 42. xiii. 35. xvii. 34, 35, 36(*ap*). xviii. 28, 29. xix. 44. xxi. 6. John iv. 3, 28, 52. viii. 29. x. 12. xiv. 18, 27. xvi. 28, 32. Acts xiv. 17. Rom. i. 27. 1 Cor. vii. 13. Heb. ii. 8. vi. 1. Rev. ii. 4.
forsake, Matt. xix. 27, 29. xxvi. 56. Mark i. 18. xiv. 50. Luke v. 11.
forgive, Matt. vi. 12*t*, 14*t*, 15*t*. ix. 2, 5, 6. xii. 31*t*, 32*t*. xviii. 21, 27, 32, 35. Mark ii. 5, 7, 9, 10. iii. 28. iv. 12. xi. 25*t*, 26*t*(*ap*). Luke v. 20, 21, 23, 24. vii. 47*t*, 48, 49. xi. 4*t*. xii. 10*t*. xvii. 3, 4. xxiii. 34 (*ap*). Acts viii. 22. Rom. iv. 7. Jas. v. 15. 1 John i. 9. ii. 12.
remit, John xx. 23*t*.
omit, Matt. xxiii. 23.
let, Matt. vii. 4. viii. 22. xiii. 30. Mark vii. 27. Luke vi. 42. ix. 60. John xi. 44. xviii. 8.
suffer, Matt. iii. 15. xix. 14. xxiii. 13(14). Mark i. 34. v. 19, 37. vii. 12. x. 14. xi. 16. Luke viii. 51. xii. 39. xviii. 16. Rev. xi. 9.
suffer it to be so, Matt. iii. 15.
Add, for ἐάω, Acts v. 38, G'L*S*. Rev. ii. 20, GLTTr*S*.

ἀφικνέομαι.
come abroad, Rom. xvi. 19.

ἀφιλάγαθος.
despiser of those that are good, 2 Tim. iii. 3.

ἀφιλάργυρος.
without covetousness, Heb. xiii. 5.
not greedy of filthy lucre, 1 Tim. iii. 3.

ἄφιξις.
departing, Acts xx. 29.

ἀφίστημι.
draw away, Acts v. 37.
depart from, Luke iv. 13. Acts xii. 10. xv. 38. xix. 9. xxii. 29. 2 Cor. xii. 8. 2 Tim. ii. 19. Heb. iii. 12.
refrain from, Acts v. 38.
fall away, Luke viii. 13.
Mid., **depart from**, Luke ii. 37. xiii. 27. 1 Tim. iv. 1. — **withdraw one's self**, 1 Tim. vi. 5(*ap*).

ἄφνω.
suddenly, Acts ii. 2. xvi. 26. xxviii. 6.

ἀφόβως.
without fear, Luke i. 74. 1 Cor. xvi. 10. Phil. i. 14. Jude 12.

ἀφομοιόομαι.
be made like, Heb. vii. 3.

ἀφοράω or ἀπεῖδον.
look, Heb. xii. 2.
see, Phil. ii. 23.

ἀφορίζω.
to separate, Matt. xxv. 32. Luke vi. 22. Acts xiii. 2. xix. 9. Rom. i. 1. Gal. i. 15. ii. 12.
divide, Matt. xxv. 32.
sever, Matt. xiii. 49.
Pass., **be separate**, 2 Cor. vi. 17.

ἀφορμή.
occasion, Rom. vii. 8, 11. 2 Cor. v. 12. xi. 12*t*. Gal. v. 13. 1 Tim. v. 14.

ἀφρίζω.
to foam, Mark ix. 18, 20.

ἀφρός.
With μετά, **that one foameth again**, Luke ix. 39.

ἀφροσύνη.
foolishness, Mark vii. 22.
With ἐν, **foolishly**, 2 Cor. xi. 17, 21.
folly, 2 Cor. xi. 1.

ἄφρων.

unwise, Eph. v. 17.
foolish, Rom. ii. 20. 1 Pet. ii. 15.
fool, Luke xi. 40. xii. 20. 1 Cor. xv. 36. 2 Cor. xi. 16*t*, 19. xii. 6, 11.

ἀφυπνόω.

fall asleep, Luke viii. 23.

ἄφωνος.

dumb, Acts viii. 32. 1 Cor. xii. 2. 2 Pet. ii. 16.
without signification, 1 Cor. xiv. 10.

ἀχάριστος.

unthankful, Luke vi. 35. 2 Tim. iii. 2.

ἀχειροποίητος.

made without hands, Mark xiv. 58. Col. ii. 11.
not made with hands, 2 Cor. v. 1.

ἀχλύς.

mist, Acts xiii. 11.

ἀχρειόομαι.

become unprofitable, Rom. iii. 12.

ἀχρεῖος.

unprofitable, Matt. xxv. 30. Luke xvii. 10.

ἄχρηστος.

unprofitable, Phm. 11.

ἄχρι or ἄχρις.

until, Matt. xxiv. 38. Luke i. 20. xvii. 27. xxi. 24. Acts i. 2. iii. 21. xxiii. 1. Rom. v. 13. viii. 22. 2 Cor. iii. 14. Gal. iv. 2. Phil. i. 5, 6. Rev. xvii. 17.
till, Acts xx. 11. Rev. xv. 8. xx. 3.
ἄχρις οὗ, **until**, Rom. xi. 25. Gal. iv. 19.—**till**, Acts vii. 18. 1 Cor. xi. 26. Gal. iii. 19. Rev. vii. 3(–οὗ LTTr*S*).—**while**, Acts xxvii. 33. Heb. iii. 13.
ἄχρις οὗ ἄν, **till**, 1 Cor. xv. 25(–ἄν G°°LT*S*). Rev. ii. 25.
as far as, Acts xxviii. 15.
as far as to, 2 Cor. x. 14.
unto, Acts ii. 29. xiii. 6. xxii. 4, 22. xxvi. 22. 1 Cor. iv. 11. 2 Cor. x. 13. Heb. vi. 11. Rev. ii. 10, 26. xii. 11. xiv. 20. xviii. 5.
even to, Acts xi. 5. Heb. iv. 12.
ἄχρι τοῦ δεῦρο, **hitherto**, Rom. i. 13.
into, Acts xx. 4.
in, Acts xx. 6.
for, Luke iv. 13. Acts xiii. 11.
Add Rev. xx. 5, for ἕως, GLTTr.

ἄχυρον.

chaff, Matt. iii. 12. Luke iii. 17.

ἀψευδής.

that can not lie, Tit. i. 2.

ἄψινθος.

wormwood, Rev. viii. 11.

ἄψυχος.

With art., **things without life**, 1 Cor. xiv. 7.

βαθέως, deeply? See βαθύς.

βαθμός.

degree, 1 Tim. iii. 13.

βάθος.

depth, Mark iv. 5. Rom. viii. 39. xi. 33. Eph. iii. 18. Rev. ii. 24(βαθύς GLTTr).
deepness, Matt. xiii. 5.
deep, *subst.*, Luke v. 4.
With κατά, **deep**, 2 Cor. viii. 2.
deep things, 1 Cor. ii. 10[pl].

βαθύνω, deepen.

σκάπτω καὶ β., **dig deep**, Luke vi. 48.

βαθύς.

deep, John iv. 11. Acts xx. 9.
ὄρθρου βαθεος(βαθέως LTTr*S*), **very early in the morning**, Luke xxiv. 1.
Add Rev. ii. 24, for βάθος, GLTTr.

βαΐον.

branch, John xii. 13.

βαλάντιον, βαλλάντιον LTTr*S*.

bag, Luke xii. 33.
purse, Luke x. 4. xxii. 35, 36.

βάλλω.

cast, Matt. iii. 10. iv. 6, 18. v. 13, 25, 29*t*, 30, 30(ἀπέρχομαι LTTr*S*). vi. 30. vii. 6, 19. xiii. 42, 47, 48, 50. xv. 26. xvii. 27. xviii. 8*t*, 9*t*, 30. xxi. 21. xxvii. 35, 35(*ap*). Mark i. 16(G′; ἀμφιβάλλω GLTTr*S*). iv. 26. vii. 27. ix. 22, 42, 45, 47. xi. 23. xii. 41*t*, 43*t*, 44*t*. xv. 24.

Luke iii. 9. **iv. 9. xii.** 28, 58. **xiii.** 19. xiv. 35. xxi. 1, 2, 3, 4*t*. xxiii. 19, 25, 34. John iii. 24. viii. 7(*ap*), 59. xv. 6*t*. xix. 24. xxi. 6*t*, 7. Acts xvi. 23, 37.
Rev. ii. 10, 14, 22. iv. 10. vi. 13. viii. 5, 7, 8. xii. 4, 13, 15, 16. xiv. 19. xviii. 19, 21. xix. 20. xx. 3, 10, 14, 15.
cast out, 1 John iv. 18. Rev. xii. 9*tr*.
throw, Mark xii. 42. Acts xxii. 23p.
throw down, Rev. xviii. 21.
send, Matt. x. 34*t*. Luke xii. 49.
thrust, John xx. 25, 27. Acts xvi. 24. Rev. xiv. 16, 19.
strike, Mark xiv. 65(λαμβάνω G'' LTTr*S*).
put, Matt. ix. 17*t*. xxv. 27. xxvii. 6. Mark ii. 22. vii. 33. Luke v. 37. John v. 7. xii. 6. xiii. 2. xx. 25. Jas. iii. 3. Rev. ii. 24.
put up, John xviii. 11.
With κόπρια, **dung,** Luke xiii. 8.
pour, Matt. xxvi. 12p. John xiii. 5.
lay, Matt. viii. 14. Mark vii. 30. Luke xvi. 20.
Pass., **lie,** Matt. viii. 6. ix. 2.
arise(*marg.* **beat**), Acts xxvii. 14.
Add, for ἐπιβάλλω, John vii. 30, Lm. 44, LTTr. For καταβάλλω, Rev. xii. 10, G''LTTr*S*.

βαπτίζω.

baptize, Matt. iii. 6, 11*t*, 13, 14, 16p. xx. 22*t*(*ap*), 23*t*(*ap*). xxviii. 19. Mark i. 4, 5, 8*t*, 9. x. 38*t*, 39*t*. xvi. 16(*ap*). Luke iii. 7, 12, 16*t*, 21*t*. vii. 29, 30. xii. 50. John i. 25, 26, 28, 31, 33*t*. iii. 22, 23*t*, 26. iv. 1, 2. x. 40. Acts i. 5*t*. ii. 38, 41. viii. 12, 13, 16, 36, 38. ix. 18. x. 47, 48. xi. 16*t*. xvi. 15, 33. xviii. 8. xix. 3, 4, 5. Rom. vi. 3*t*. 1 Cor. i. 13, 14, 15, 16*t*, 17. xii. 13. xv. 29*t*. Gal. iii. 27.
Mid., *and Pass. aor.*, **wash,** Mark vii. 4. Luke xi. 38.—**be baptized,** Acts xxii. 16. 1 Cor. x. 2.
Baptist, Mark vi. 14p.
Add **Mark vi. 24p, for** βαπτιστής, TTr*S*.

βάπτισμα.

baptism, Matt. iii. 7. xx. 22(*ap*), 23(*ap*). xxi. 25. Mark i. 4. x. 38, 39. xi. 30. Luke iii. 3. vii. 29. xii. 50. xx. 4. Acts i. 22. x. 37. xiii. 24. xviii. 25. xix. 3, 4. Rom. vi. 4. Eph. iv. 5. Col. ii. 12(βαπτισμός Lm). 1 Pet. iii. 21.

βαπτισμός.

washing, Mark vii. 4, 8(*ap*). Heb. ix. 10.
baptism, Heb. vi. 2.
Add Col. ii. 12, for βάπτισμα, Lm.

βαπτιστής.

Baptist, Matt. iii. 1. xi. 11, 12. xiv. 2, 8. xvi. 14. xvii. 13. Mark vi. 24(βαπτίζων TTr*S*), 25. viii. 28. Luke vii. 20, 28(-GoTTr*S*), 33. ix. 19.

βάπτω.

dip, Luke xvi. 24. John xiii. 26p (ἐμβάπτω L). Rev. xix. 13.
Add John xiii. 26, for ἐμβάπτω, LmTTr*S*.

βάρ.

Bar, Matt. xvi. 17(*lit.* son), joined with Ἰωνᾶ by LT.

βάρβαρος.

barbarian, Acts xxviii. 4. Rom. i. 14. 1 Cor. xiv. 11*t*. Col. iii. 11.
barbarous, Acts xxviii. 2.

βαρέομαι.

heavy, Matt. xxvi. 43p. Mark xiv. 40p(καταβαρύνομαι G''LTTr, καταβαρέομαι *S*). Luke ix. 32p.
be burdened, 2 Cor. v. 4.
be pressed, 2 Cor. i. 8.
be charged, 1 Tim. v. 16.
Add Luke xxi. 34, for βαρύνομαι, GLTTr*S*.

βαρέως, heavily. See ἀκούω.

βάρος.

weight, 2 Cor. iv. 17.
burden, Matt. xx. 12. **Acts xv. 28. Gal. vi. 2. Rev. ii. 24.**

ἐν βάρει εἶναι, **be burdensome**(*marg.* **use authority**), 1 Thes. ii. 6.

βαρύνομαι.

be overcharged, Luke xxi. 34(βαρέομαι GLTTr*S*).

βαρύς.

heavy, Matt. xxiii. 4.
weighty, 2 Cor. x. 10. — *Comp.*, **weightier matter**, Matt. xxiii. 23.
grievous, Acts xx. 29. xxv. 7. 1 John v. 3.

βαρύτιμος.

very precious, Matt. xxvi. 7(πολύτιμος L*S*).

βασανίζω.

to torment, Matt. viii. 6, 29. Mark v. 7. Luke viii. 28. Rev. ix. 5. xi. 10. xiv. 10. xx. 10.
pain, Rev. xii. 2.
vex, 2 Pet. ii. 8.
toss, Matt. xiv. 24.
Pass., **toil**, Mark vi. 48.

βασανισμός.

torment, Rev. ix. 5. xiv. 11. xviii. 7, 10, 15.

βασανιστής.

tormentor, Matt. xviii. 34.

βάσανος.

torment, Matt. iv. 24. Luke xvi. 23, 28.

βασιλεία.

kingdom, Matt. iv. 8, 23. vi. 10, 13(*ap*). viii. 12. ix. 35. xii. 25, 26. xiii. 19, 38, 41, 43. xvi. 28. xx. 21. xxiv. 7*t*, 14. xxv. 34. xxvi. 29. Mark iii. 24*t*. vi. 23. xi. 10. xiii. 8*t*. Luke i. 33. iv. 5. xi. 2, 17, 18. xii. 32. xix. 12, 15. xxi. 10*t*. xxii. 29, 30. xxiii. 42. John xviii. 36*tr*. Acts i. 6. Eph. v. 5. Col. i. 13. 1 Thes. ii. 12. 2 Tim. iv. 1, 18. Heb. i. 8. xi. 33. xii. 28. Jas. ii. 5. 2 Pet. i. 11. Rev. i. 9. xi. 15. xvi. 10. xvii. 12, 17.
With τοῦ θεοῦ, **kingdom of God**, Matt. vi. 33. xii. 28. xix. 24 (τῶν οὐρανῶν LTTr). xxi. 31, 43. Mark i. 14 (-β. G°°L*b*TTr*S*), 15. iv. 11, 26, 30. ix. 1, 47. x. 14, 15, 23, 24, 25. xii. 34. xiv. 25. xv. 43. Luke iv. 43. vi. 20. vii. 28. viii. 1, 10. ix. 2, 11, 27, 60, 62. x. 9, 11. xi. 20. xii. 31. xiii. 18, 20, 28, 29. xiv. 15. xvi. 16. xvii. 20*t*, 21. xviii. 16, 17, 24, 25, 29. xix. 11. xxi. 31. xxii. 16, 18. xxiii. 51. John iii. 3, 5. Acts i. 3. viii. 12. xiv. 22. xix. 8. xx. 25. xxviii. 23, 31. Rom. xiv. 17. 1 Cor. iv. 20. vi. 9, 10. xv. 24, 50. Gal. v. 21. Col. iv. 11. 2 Thes. i. 5. Rev. xii. 10.
With τῶν οὐρανῶν, **kingdom of heaven**, Matt. iii. 2. iv. 17. v. 3, 10, 19*t*, 20. vii. 21. viii. 11. x. 7. xi. 11, 12. xiii. 11, 24, 31, 33, 44, 45, 47, 52. xvi. 19. xviii. 1, 3, 4, 23. xix. 12, 14, 23. xx. 1. xxii. 2. xxiii. 13(14). xxv. 1.
With ἔχω, **to reign**, Rev. xvii. 18.
Add, for βασιλεῖς καί, Rev. i. 6, GL TTr*S*. For βασιλεῖς, v. 10, G′LT*S*.

βασίλειος.

royal, 1 Pet. ii. 9.
With art., **king's court**, Luke vii. 25.
Add Matt. xi. 8, for βασιλεύς, G′.

βασιλεύς.

king, Matt. i. 6, 6(-LTTr*S*). ii. 1, 3, 9. x. 18. xi. 8(βασίλειος G′). xiv. 9. xvii. 25. xviii. 23. xxii. 2, 7, 11, 13. Mark vi. 14, 22, 25, 26, 27. xiii. 9. Luke i. 5. x. 24. xiv. 31*t*. xxi. 12. xxii. 25. John vi. 15. xix. 12, 15. Acts iv. 26. vii. 10, 18. ix. 15. xii. 1, 20. xiii. 21, 22. xxv. 13, 14, 24, 26. xxvi. 2, 7, 13, 19, 26, 27, 30.
2 Cor. xi. 32. 1 Tim. ii. 2. Heb. vii. 1*t*. xi. 23, 27. 1 Pet. ii. 13, 17. Rev. i. 5, 6 (*see* βασιλεία). v. 10 (βασιλεία G′LT*S*). vi. 15. ix. 11. x. 11. xvi. 12, 14. xvii. 2, 10, 12*t*, 14, 18. xviii. 3, 9. xix. 16, 18, 19. xxi. 24.
Said of God or Christ, **King**, Matt. ii. 2. v. 35. xxi. 5. xxv. 34, 40. xxvii. 11, 29, 37, 42. Mark xv. 2, 9, 12, 18, 26, 32. Luke xix. 38.

xxiii. 2, 3, 37, 38. John i. 49(50). xii. 13, 15. xviii. 33, 37*t*, 39. xix. 3, 14, 15, 19, 21*t*. Acts xvii. 7. 1 Tim. i. 17. vi. 15. Heb. vii. 2*tr*. Rev. xv. 3. xvii. 14. xix. 16.

βασιλεύω.

to reign, Matt. ii. 22. Luke i. 33. xix. 14, 27. Rom. v. 14, 17*t*, 21*t*. vi. 12. 1 Cor. iv. 8*t*. xv. 25. Rev. v. 10. xi. 15, 17. xix. 6. xx. 4, 6. xxii. 5.
king, 1 Tim. vi. 15p.

βασιλικός.

royal, Acts xii. 21. Jas. ii. 8.
nobleman, John iv. 46(*marg.* **courtier,** or **ruler**), 49.
With art., **king's °country,** Acts xii. 20.

βασίλισσα.

queen, Matt. xii. 42. Luke xi. 31. Acts viii. 27. Rev. xviii. 7.

βάσις.

foot, Acts iii. 7.

βασκαίνω.

bewitch, Gal. iii. 1.

βαστάζω.

bear, Matt. iii. 11. viii. 17. xx. 12. Mark xiv. 13. Luke vii. 14. xi. 27. xiv. 27. xxii. 10. John xii. 6. xvi. 12. xix. 17. xx. 15. Acts ix. 15. xv. 10. xxi. 35. Rom. xi. 18. xv. 1. Gal. v. 10, vi. 2, 5, 17. Rev. ii. 2, 3.
carry, Luke x. 4. Acts iii. 2. Rev. xvii. 7.
take up, John x. 31.

βάτος, fem.

bramble bush, Luke vi. 44.
bush, Mark xii. 26. Luke xx. 37. Acts vii. 30, 35.

βάτος, masc.

measure, Luke xvi. 6.

βάτραχος.

frog, Rev. xvi. 13.

βαττολογέω.

use vain repetitions, Matt. vi. 7.

βδέλυγμα.

abomination, Matt. xxiv. 15. Mark xiii. 14. Luke xvi. 15. Rev. xvii. 4, 5. xxi. 27.

βδελυκτός.

abominable, Tit. i. 16.

βδελύσσομαι.

abhor, Rom. ii. 22.
abominable, Rev. xxi. 8p.

βέβαιος.

steadfast, 2 Cor. i. 7(6). Heb. ii. 2. iii. 14. vi. 19.
firm, Heb. iii. 6(*ap*).
sure, Rom. iv. 16. 2 Pet. i. 10, 19.
of force, Heb. ix. 17.

βεβαιόω.

establish, Heb. xiii. 9.
stablish, 2 Cor. i. 21. Col. ii. 7.
confirm, Mark xvi. 20(*ap*). Rom. xv. 8. 1 Cor. i. 6, 8. Heb. ii. 3.

βεβαίωσις.

confirmation, Phil. i. 7. Heb. vi. 16.

βέβηλος.

profane, 1 Tim. i. 9. iv. 7. vi. 20. 2 Tim. ii. 16.
profane person, Heb. xii. 16.

βεβηλόω.

to profane, Matt. xii. 5. Acts xxiv. 6.

βελόνη, needle.

Luke xviii. 25, for ῥάφις, G″LTTrS.

βέλος.

dart, Eph. vi. 16.

βελτίων.

Neut., **very well,** 2 Tim. i. 18.

βῆμα.

βῆμα ποδός, **to set one's foot on,** Acts vii. 5.
throne, Acts xii. 21.
judgment seat, Matt. xxvii. 19. John xix. 13. Acts xviii. 12, 16, 17. xxv. 6, 10, 17. Rom. xiv. 10. 2 Cor. v. 10.

βήρυλλος.

beryl, Rev. xxi. 20.

βία.

violence, Acts v. 26. xxi. 35. xxiv. 7(*ap*). xxvii. 41.

βιάζομαι.

suffer violence (*marg.* **be gotten by force**), Matt. xi. 12.
press, Luke xvi. 16.

βίαιος.

mighty, Acts ii. 2.

βιαστής.

violent(*marg.* **they that thrust men**), Matt. xi. 12pl.

βιβλαρίδιον.

little book, Rev. x. 2(βιβλίον G′), 8(βιβλίον LTr, βιβλιδάριον T), 9, 10.

βιβλίον.

scroll, Rev. vi. 14.
book, Luke iv. 17*t*, 20. John xx. 30. xxi. 25. Gal. iii. 10. 2 Tim. iv. 13. Heb. ix. 19. x. 17. Rev. i. 11. v. 1, 2, 3, 4, 5, 7(-G∞LTTr*S*), 8, 9. xvii. 8. xx. 12*tr*. xxi. 27. xxii. 7, 9, 10, 18*t*, 19.
bill, Mark x. 4.
writing, Matt. xix. 7.
Add, for βιβλαρίδιον, Rev. x. 2, G′. 8, LTr. For βίβλος, Rev. xiii. 8, GL TTr. xxii. 19^1st, GLTTr*S*.

βίβλος.

book, Matt. i. 1. Mark xii. 26. Luke iii. 4. xx. 42. Acts i. 20. vii. 42. xix. 19. Phil. iv. 3. Rev. iii. 5. xiii. 8(βιβλίον GLTTr). xx. 15. xxii. 19(βιβλίον GLTTr*S*). 19(ξύλον GLT Tr*S*).

βιβρώσκω.

eat, John vi. 13.

βίος.

life, Luke viii. 14. 1 Tim. ii. 2. 2 Tim. ii. 4. 1 Pet. iv. 3(-G∞LT*S*). 1 John ii. 16.
living, Mark xii. 44. Luke viii. 43. xv. 12, 30. xxi. 4.
good, *subst.*, 1 John iii. 17.

βιόω.

live, 1 Pet. iv. 2.

βίωσις.

manner of life, Acts xxvi. 4.

βιωτικός.

of this life, Luke xxi. 34.
of things pertaining to this life, 1 Cor. vi. 4.
things that pertain to this life, 1 Cor. vi. 3.

βλαβερός.

hurtful, 1 Tim. vi. 9.

βλάπτω.

to hurt, Mark xvi. 18(*ap*). Luke iv. 35.

βλαστάνω.

to bud, Heb. ix. 4.
spring up, Matt. xiii. 26. Mark iv. 27(βλαστάω LTTr).
bring forth, Jas. v. 18.

βλασφημέω.

speak evil of, Rom. xiv. 16. 1 Cor. x. 30. Tit. iii. 2. 1 Pet. iv. 4, 14 (*ap*). 2 Pet. ii. 2, 10, 12. Jude 8, 10.
revile, Matt. xxvii. 39.
rail on, Mark xv. 29. Luke xxiii. 39.
report slanderously, Rom. iii. 8.
defame, 1 Cor. iv. 13(δυσφημέω G″ T*S*).
blaspheme, Matt. ix. 3. Mark iii. 28, 29. Luke xii. 10(-G°). John x. 36. Acts xiii. 45. xviii. 6. xxvi. 11. Rom. ii. 24. 1 Tim. i. 20. vi. 1. Tit. ii. 5. Jas. ii. 7. Rev. xiii. 6. xvi. 9, 11, 21.
speak blasphemy, Matt. xxvi. 65.
blasphemously, Luke xxii. 65p.
blasphemer, Acts xix. 37p.
Add Mark ii. 7, for βλασφημίας, LT Tr*S*.

βλασφημία.

evil speaking, Eph. iv. 31.
railing, 1 Tim. vi. 4. Jude 9cc.
blasphemy, Matt. xii. 31*t*. xv. 19. xxvi. 65. Mark ii. 7(βλασφημέω LT Tr*S*). iii. 28. vii. 22. xiv. 64. Luke v. 21. John x. 33. Col. iii. 8. Rev. ii. 9. xiii. 1, 5(βλάσφημος G′LTr), 6. xvii. 3.

βλάσφημος.

railing, 2 Pet. ii. 11.
blasphemous, Acts vi. 11, 13(*omS*).
blasphemer, 1 Tim. i. 13. 2 Tim. iii. 2.
Add Rev. xiii. 5, for *βλασφημία*, G'LTr.

βλέμμα.

seeing, 2 Pet. ii. 8.

βλέπω.

look, Luke ix. 62. John xiii. 22. Acts iii. 4.
look on, Matt. v. 28. 2 Cor. x. 7. Rev. v. 3, 4.
look to, 2 John 8.
lie, Acts xxvii. 12. [Mark xii. 14.
With *εἰς*, **regard,** Matt. xxii. 16.
behold, Matt. vii. 3. xviii. 10. Luke vi. 41, 42p. xxiv. 12(*ap*). Acts i. 9p. iv. 14. 1 Cor. x. 18. Col. ii. 5. Rev. xvii. 8p.
take heed, Matt. xxiv. 4. Mark iv. 24. xiii. 5, 23, 33. Luke viii. 18. xxi. 8. 1 Cor. iii. 10. viii. 9. x. 12. Gal. v. 15. Heb. iii. 12.
take heed to, Mark xiii. 9. Col. iv. 17.
beware, Mark viii. 15. xii. 38. Acts xiii. 40. Col. ii. 8.
beware of, Phil. iii. 2*tr*.
see, Matt. vi. 4, 6, 18. xi. 4. xii. 22. xiii. 13*t*, 14*t*, 16, 17. xiv. 30p. xv. 31p, 31. xxiv. 2. Mark iv. 12*t*. v. 31. viii. 18, 23, 24. xiii. 2. Luke vii. 44. viii. 10*t*, 16. x. 23*t*, 24. xi. 33. xxi. 30. John i. 29. v. 19. ix. 7, 15, 19, 21, 25, 39*tr*, 41. xi. 9. xx. 1, 5. xxi. 9(*εἴδαν*, fr. *εἴδω*, Lm), 20. Acts ii. 33. viii. 6. ix. 8. xii. 9. xiii. 11. xxviii. 26*t*.
Rom. vii. 23. viii. 24*t*, 25. xi. 8inf, 10. 1 Cor. i. 26. xiii. 12. xvi. 10. 2 Cor. iv. 18*f*. xii. 6. Eph. v. 15. Heb. ii. 9. iii. 19. x. 25. xi. 1, 3, 7. xii. 25. Jas. ii. 22. Rev. i. 11, 12. iii. 18. vi. 1 (*ἴδε*, fr. *εἴδω*, G*S*, -GoLTTr), 3(*ἴδε* *S*, *om*), 5(*ἴδε* G*S*, -GoLTTr), 7(*ἴδε* G*S*, -GoLTTr). ix. 20. xi. 9. xvi. 15. xviii. 9. xxii. 8, 8(*ὅτε εἶδον* G', *ὅτε ἴδον* T).
sight, Luke vii. 21inf.
μὴ βλέπων, **without sight,** Acts ix. 9.
perceive, 2 Cor. vii. 8.
Add Rev. xviii. 18, for *ὁράω*, GLT Tr*S*.

βλητέος.

With *εἰμί* *understood*, **must be put,** Mark ii. 22(*ap*). Luke v. 38.

βοάω.

to cry, Matt. iii. 3. Mark i. 3. xv. 34. Luke iii. 4. xviii. 7, 38. John i. 23. Acts viii. 7. xvii. 6. xxi. 34 (*ἐπιφωνέω* G''LT*S*). Gal. iv. 27.
Add, for *ἀναβοάω*, Matt. xxvii. 46, LmTr. Luke ix. 38, LTr*S*. For *ἐπιβοάω*, Acts xxv. 24, L*S*.

βοή.

cry, Jas. v. 4.

βοήθεια.

help, Acts xxvii. 17.
With *εἰς*, **to help,** Heb. iv. 16.

βοηθέω.

to help, Matt. xv. 25. Mark ix. 22, 24. Acts xvi. 9. xxi. 28. Rev. xii. 16.
succor, 2 Cor. vi. 2. Heb. ii. 18.

βοηθός.

helper, Heb. xiii. 6.

βόθυνος.

pit, Matt. xii. 11.
ditch, Matt. xv. 14. Luke vi. 39.

βολή.

cast, Luke xxii. 41.

βολίζω.

to sound, Acts xxvii. 28*t*.

βολίς.

dart, Heb. xii. 20(*ap*).

βόρβορος.

mire, 2 Pet. ii. 22.

βορρᾶς.

north, Luke xiii. 29. Rev. xxi. 13.

βόσκω.

feed, Mark v. 14. Luke viii. 34. xv. 15. John xxi. 15, 17.

Mid., **feed**, Matt. viii. 30. Mark v. 11. Luke viii. 32.
keep, Matt. viii. 33.

βοτάνη.

herbs, Heb. vi. 7.

βότρυς.

cluster, Rev. xiv. 18.

βουλεύομαι.

take counsel, Acts v. 33(βούλομαι L).
consult, Luke xiv. 31. John xii. 10.
be minded, Acts xxvii. 39. 2 Cor. i. 17p(βούλομαι G″LS).
determine, Acts xv. 37(βούλομαι G″ LS).
purpose, 2 Cor. i. 17*t*.
Add John xi. 53, for συμβουλεύομαι, LTrS.

βουλευτής.

counsellor, Mark xv. 43. Luke xxiii. 50.

βουλή.

counsel, Luke vii. 30. xxiii. 51. Acts ii. 23. iv. 28. v. 38. xx. 27. xxvii. 42. 1 Cor. iv. 5. Eph. i. 11. Heb. vi. 17.
With τίθεμαι, **advise**, Acts xxvii. 12.
will, Acts xiii. 36.

βούλημα.

purpose, Acts xxvii. 43.
will, Rom. ix. 19.
Add 1 Pet. iv. 3, for θέλημα, G″LTS.

βούλομαι.

will, would, Matt. xi. 27(ἀποκαλύψῃ for βούληται ἀποκαλύψαι Lm). Mark xv. 15. Luke x. 22. John xviii. 39. Acts xvii. 20. xviii. 15. xix. 30p. xxii. 30p. xxiii. 28p. xxv. 20, 22. xxvii. 43. xxviii. 18. 1 Cor. xii. 11. Phil i. 12. 1 Tim. ii. 8. v. 14. vi. 9. Tit. iii. 8. Phm. 13. Heb. vi. 17. Jas. iv. 4. 2 Pet. iii. 9. 2 John 12. 3 John 10. Jude 5.
of one's own will, Jas. i. 18p.
be willing, Luke xxii. 42.
be minded, Matt. i. 19. 2 Cor. i 15.
be disposed, Acts xviii. 27p.
intend, Acts v. 28. xii. 4.
list, Jas. iii. 4.
Add, for βουλεύομαι, Acts v. 33, L xv. 37, G″LS. 2 Cor. i. 17, G″LS.

βουνός.

hill, Luke iii. 5. xxiii. 30.

βοῦς.

ox, Luke xiii. 15. xiv. 5, 19. John ii. 14, 15. 1 Cor. ix. 9*t*. 1 Tim. v. 18.

βραβεῖον.

prize, 1 Cor. ix. 24. Phil. iii. 14.

βραβεύω.

to rule, Col. iii. 15.

βραδύνω.

tarry, 1 Tim. iii. 15.
be slack, 2 Pet. iii. 9.

βραδυπλοέω.

sail slowly, Acts xxvii. 7p.

βραδύς.

slow, Luke xxiv. 25. Jas. i. 19*t*.

βραδυτής.

slackness, 2 Pet. iii. 9.

βραχίων.

arm, Luke i. 51. John xii. 38. Acts xiii. 17.

βραχύς.

Neut., **a little while**, Luke xxii. 58.
βραχύ τι, **a little**, John vi. 7. Heb. ii. 7(*marg.* **a little while**), 9.—**a little space**, Acts v. 34.
βραχὺ διίστημι, **go a little further**, Acts xxvii. 28.
διὰ βραχέων, **in few words**, Heb. xiii. 22.

βρέφος.

babe, Luke i. 41, 44. ii. 12, 16. 1 Pet. ii. 2.
infant, Luke xviii. 15.
young child, Acts vii. 19.
child, 2 Tim. iii. 15.

βρέχω.

send rain, Matt. v. 45.
rain, *trans.*, Luke xvii. 29.—*Intrans.*, Jas. v. 17inf, 17.
With ὑετός, **rain**, *intrans.*, Rev. xi. 6.
wash, Luke vii. 38, 44.

βροντή.

thunder, Mark iii. 17. Rev. vi. 1.

x. 3, 4*t*. xiv. 2. xvi. 18.
With γίνομαι, **to thunder,** John xii. 29.
thundering, Rev. iv. 5. viii. 5. xi. 19. xix. 6.

βροχή.
rain, Matt. vii. 25, 27.

βρόχος.
snare, 1 Cor. vii. 35.

βρυγμός.
gnashing, Matt. viii. 12. xiii. 42, 50. xxii. 13. xxiv. 51. xxv. 30. Luke xiii. 28.

βρύχω.
gnash, Acts vii. 54.

βρύω.
send forth, Jas. iii. 11.

βρῶμα.
meat, Mark vii. 19. Luke iii. 11[pl]. ix. 13[pl]. John iv. 34. Rom. xiv. 15*t*, 20. 1 Cor. iii. 2. vi. 13*t*. viii. 8, 13. x. 3. 1 Tim. iv. 3. Heb. ix. 10. xiii. 9.
victuals, Matt. xiv. 15[pl].

βρώσιμος.
Neut., **meat,** Luke xxiv. 41.

βρῶσις.
eating, 1 Cor. viii. 4.
rust, Matt. vi. 19, 20.
food, 2 Cor. ix. 10.
meat, John iv. 32. vi. 27*t*, 55. Rom. xiv. 17. Col. ii. 16 (*marg.* **eating**).
morsel of meat, Heb. xii. 16.

βρώσκω. See βιβρώσκω.

βυθίζω.
drown, 1 Tim. vi. 9.
Pass., **begin to sink,** Luke v. 7.

βυθός.
deep, *subst.*, 2 Cor. xi. 25.

βυρσεύς.
tanner, Acts ix. 43. x. 6, 32.

βύσσινος.
fine linen, Rev. xviii. 16. xix. 8, 8[neut], 14.
Add Rev. xviii. 12, *see* βύσσος.

βύσσος.
fine linen, Luke xvi. 19. Rev. xviii. 12 (βύσσινος GLTTr*S* [pl]).

βωμός.
altar, Acts xvii. 23.

γάγγραινα.
canker (*marg.* **gangrene**), 2 Tim. ii. 17.

γάζα.
treasure, Acts viii. 27.

γαζοφυλάκιον.
treasury, Mark xii. 41*t*, 43. Luke xxi. 1. John viii. 20.

γάλα.
milk, 1 Cor. iii. 2. ix. 7. Heb. v. 12, 13. 1 Pet. ii. 2.

γαλήνη.
calm, Matt. viii. 26. Mark iv. 39. Luke viii. 24.

γαμέω or γάμω.
marry a wife, Matt. xxii. 25[p]. Luke xvii. 27.
marry, Matt. v. 32. xix. 9*t*, 10. xxii. 30. xxiv. 38. Mark vi. 17. x. 11, 12. xii. 25. Luke xiv. 20. xvi. 18*t*. xx. 34, 35. 1 Cor. vii. 9*t*, 28*t*, 33, 34, 36, 39. 1 Tim. iv. 3. v. 11, 14.
married, 1 Cor. vii. 10[p].

γαμίζω, marry, give in marriage.
For ἐκγαμίζω, Matt. xxii. 30, G'L Tr*S*. Lk. xvii. 27, LTTr*S*. xx. 35, LTr*S*. 1 Cor. vii. 38(*ap*). 38, GL*S*. For γαμίσκω, Mark xii. 25, LTTr*S*.

γαμίσκω.
give in marriage, Mark xii. 25 (*see* γαμίζω).—*Add, see* ἐκγαμίσκω.

γάμος.
wedding, Matt. xxii. 3, 8, 10, 11[cc], 12[cc]. Luke xii. 36. xiv. 8.
marriage, Matt. xxii. 2, 4, 9. xxv. 10. John ii. 1, 2. Heb. xiii. 4. Rev. xix. 7, 9.

γάρ.
for, Matt. i. 20, 21. ii. 2, 5, 6, 13, 20. iii. 2, 3, 9, 15. iv. 6, 10, 17, 18.

v. 12, 18, 20, 29, 30, 46. vi. 7, 8, 14, 16, 21, 24, 32*t*, 34. vii. 2, 8, 12, 25, 29. ix. 5. 13, 16, 21, 24. x. 10, 17, 19(*ap*), 20, 23(–G^{o}), 26, 35. xi. 10(–L^{b}TTr^{b}*S*), 13, 18, 30. xii. 8, 33, 34, 37, 40, 50. xiii. 12, 15, 17. xiv. 3, 4, 24. xv. 2, 4, 19. xvi. 2, 3, 25, 26, 27. xvii. 15, 20. xviii. 7, 10, 11(*ap*), 20. xix. 12, 14, 22. xx. 1, 16(*ap*). xxi. 26, 32. xxii. 14, 16, 28, 30. xxiii. 3, 4(δέ G′LTTr*S*), 8, 9, 10(ὅτι G′LTTr), 13(14), 17, 19, 39. xxiv. 5, 6, 7, 21, 24, 27, 28 (–G^{o}LTr*S*), 38. xxv. 14, 29, 35, 42. xxvi. 9, 10, 11, 12, 28, 31, 43, 52. xxvii. 18, 19, 43. xxviii. 2, 5, 6.

Mark i. 16, 22, 38. ii. 15. iii. 10, 21, 35(–LTTr^{b}). iv. 22, 25, 28(–LTTr*S*). v. 8, 28, 42. vi. 14, 17, 18, 20, 31, 36(–G″L^{b}Tr*S*), 48, 50, 52, 52(ἀλλά Tr*S*). vii. 3, 8(–LTr*S*), 10, 21, 25(ἀλλά TTr*S*), 27. viii. 3 (καί LTTr*S*), 35, 36. ix. 6*t*, 31, 34, 39, 40, 41, 49. x. 14, 22, 27(*ap*). xi. 13, 18, 23(–LTTr^{b}*S*), 32. xii. 12, 14, 23, 25, 36(–L^{b}TTr^{b}*S*), 44. xiii. 6 (–TTr^{bm}*S*), 7(–TTr^{b}*S*), 8, 9(–TTr^{b}), 11, 19, 22, 33, 35. xiv. 5, 7, 40, 56. xv. 10. xvi. 4, 8.

Luke i. 15, 18, 30, 44, 48, 76. ii. 10. iii. 8. iv. 8(*omS*), 10. v. 9, 39. vi. 23*t*, 26, 38, 43, 44*t*, 45, 48 (*ap*). vii. 5, 6, 28(–Tr*S*), 33. viii. 17, 18, 29*t*, 40, 46. ix. 14, 24, 25, 26, 44, 48, 50, 56(*ap*). x. 7, 24. xi. 10, 30. xii. 12, 30, 34, 52, 58. xiv. 14, 24, 28. xvi. 2, 13, 28. xvii. 21, 24. xviii. 16, 23, 25, 32. xix. 5, 10, 21, 26(–L^{b}Tr^{b}*S*), 48. xx. 6, 19, 33, 36, 38. xxi. 4, 8, 9, 15, 23, 26, 35. xxii. 2, 16, 18, 27, 37, 71. xxiii. 8, 12, 15, 34, 41.

John ii. 25. iii. 2, 16, 17, 20, 24, 34*t*. iv. 8, 9, 18, 42, 44, 45, 47. v. 4(*ap*), 13, 19, 20, 21, 22, 26, 36, 46*t*. vi. 6, 27, 33, 55, 64, 71. vii. 1, 4, 5, 39. viii. 24, 42. ix. 22. xi. 39. xii. 8, 43, 47. xiii. 11, 13, 15, 29. xiv. 30. xvi. 7, 13, 27. xviii. 13. xix. 6, 31, 36. xx. 9, 17. xxi. 7, 8.

Acts i. 20. ii. 15, 25, 34, 39. iii. 22(*ap*). iv. 3, 12, 16, 20, 22, 27, 34. v. 26, 36. vi. 14. vii. 33, 40. viii. 7, 16, 21, 23. ix. 11, 16. x. 46. xiii. 8, 27, 36, 47. xv. 21, 28. xvi. 3, 28. xvii. 20, 23, 28*t*. xviii. 3(*ap*), 15 (–G^{o}LT*S*), 18, 28. xix. 24, 32, 37. xx. 10, 13, 16*t*, 27, 29(–G^{oo}L*S*). xxi. 3, 13, 22, 29, 36. xxii. 22, 26. xxiii. 5, 8, 11, 17, 21. xxiv. 5. xxv. 11(οὖν G″LT*S*), 27. xxvi. 16, 26*tr*. xxvii. 22, 23, 25, 34*t*. xxviii. 2, 22, 27.

Rom. i. 9, 11, 16*t*, 17, 18, 19, 20, 26. ii. 1*t*, 11, 12, 13, 14, 24, 25, 28. iii. 3, 7, 9, 20, 22, 23. iv. 2, 3, 9, 13, 14, 15(δέ G′L*S*). v. 6, 7, 10, 13, 15, 16, 17, 19. vi. 5, 7, 10, 14*t*, 19, 20, 21, 23. vii. 1, 2, 5, 7, 8, 11, 14 (δέ L^{n}), 15*t*, 18*t*, 19, 22. viii. 2, 3, 5, 6, 7, 13, 14, 15, 18, 19, 20, 22, 24*t*, 26, 38. ix. 3, 6, 9, 11, 15, 17, 19, 28, 32(–G^{oo}L*S*). x. 2, 3, 4, 5, 10, 11, 12*t*, 13, 16. xi. 1, 13(δέ L*S*), 15, 21, 23, 24, 25, 29, 30, 32, 34. xii. 3, 4, 19, 20. xiii. 1, 3, 4*tr*, 6*t*, 8, 9, 11. xiv. 3, 4, 6, 7, 8, 9, 10, 11, 17, 18. xv. 3, 4, 18, 24(–G), 26, 27. xvi. 18, 19.

1 Cor. i. 11, 17, 18, 19, 21, 26. ii. 2, 8, 10, 11, 14, 16. iii. 2, 3*t*, 4, 9, 11, 13, 17, 19*t*, 21. iv. 4, 7, 9, 15*t*, 20. v. 3, 12. vi. 16, 20. vii. 7(δέ G″LT*S*), 9, 14, 16, 22, 31. viii. 8(–LT*S*), 10. ix. 2, 9, 15, 16*t*, 17, 19. x. 4, 5, 17, 26, 28(–C to 1630; *ap*), 29. xi. 5, 6, 7, 8, 12, 18, 19, 21, 23, 26, 29, 31(δέ G″LT*S*). xii. 8, 12. xiii. 9(δέ G′T), 12(–G^{o}). xiv. 2*t*, 5 (δέ LT*S*), 9, 14(–L^{b}), 17, 31, 33, 34, 35. xv. 3, 9, 16, 21, 22, 25, 27, 32, 34, 41, 52, 53. xvi. 5, 7, 9, 10, 11, 18.

2 Cor. i. 8, 12, 13, 19, 20, 24. ii. 2, 4, 9, 11, 17. iii. 6, 9, 11, 14, iv. 5, 11, 15, 17, 18. v. 1, 2, 7, 10, 12 (–G^{oo}L*S*), 13, 14, 21(–G^{o}LT*S*). vi. 2, 14, 16. vii. 3, 8(–L^{b}), 9, 10, 11. viii. 9, 10, 12, 13. ix. 1, 2, 7. x. 3, 4, 8, 12, 14*t*, 18. xi. 2*t*, 4, 5(δέ L),

9, 13, 14, 19, 20. xii. 6*t*, 9, 10, 11*t*, 13, 14*t*, 20. xiii. 4, 8, 9.

Gal. i. 10, 10(–G″L*S*), 12, 13. ii. 6, 8, 12, 18, 19, 21. iii. 10*t*, 13(*ὅτί* G″LT), 18, 21, 26, 27, 28. iv. 15, 22, 24, 25, 27, 30. v. 5, 6, 13, 14, 17. vi. 3, 5, 7, 9, 13, 15, 17. Eph. ii. 8, 10, 14. v. 5, 6, 8, 9, 12, 13, 29. vi. 1. Phil. i. 8, 19, 21, 23(*δέ* GLT*S*). ii. 13, 20, 21, 27. iii. 3, 18, 20. iv. 11. Col. ii. 1, 5. iii. 3, 20, 24(–G″LT*S*). iv. 13.

1 Thes. i. 8, 9. ii. 1, 3, 5, 9, 9(*om* *S*), 14, 19, 20. iii. 3, 4, 9. iv. 2, 3, 7, 9, 14, 15. v. 2, 3(*δέ* L^{b}, –GT*S*), 7, 18. 2 Thes. ii. 7. iii. 2, 7, 10, 11. 1 Tim. ii. 3(–L*S*), 5, 13. iii. 13. iv. 5, 8, 10, 16. v. 4, 11, 15, 18. vi. 7, 10. 2 Tim. i. 7, 12. ii. 11, 16. iii. 2, 6, 9. iv. 3, 6, 10, 11, 15. Tit. i. 7, 10. ii. 11. iii. 3, 9, 12. Phm. 7, 15, 22.

Heb. i. 5. ii. 2, 5, 8, 10, 11, 16, 18. iii. 3, 4, 14, 16. iv. 3, 4, 8, 10, 12, 15. v. 1, 13*t*. vi. 4, 7, 10, 13, 16. vii. 1, 10, 11, 12, 13, 14, 17, 18, 19, 21, 26, 27, 28. viii. 3, 4(*οὐν* L*S*), 5, 7, 8. ix. 2, 13, 16, 17, 19, 24. x. 1, 4, 14, 15, 23, 26, 30, 36, 37. xi. 2, 5, 6, 10, 14, 16, 26, 27, 32. xii. 3, 6, 7, 10, 17*t*, 18, 20, 25. xiii. 2, 5, 9, 11, 14, 16, 17*t*, 18.

Jas. i. 6, 7, 11, 13, 20, 24. ii. 2, 10, 11, 13, 26. iii 2, 7, 16. iv. 14. 1 Pet. ii. 19, 20, 21, 25. iii. 5, 10, 17. iv. 3, 6. 2 Pet. i. 8, 10, 11, 16, 17, 21. ii. 4, 8, 18, 19, 20, 21. iii. 4, 5. 1 John ii. 19. iv. 20. v. 3. 2 John 11. 3 John 3. Jude 4.

Rev. i. 3. iii. 2. ix. 19*t*. xiii. 18. xiv. 4, 5(–G′LTr^{b}). xvi. 6(*om*, *ὅπερ* fr. *ὥσπερ* *S*), 14. xvii. 17. xix. 8, 10. xxi. 1, 22, 23, 25. xxii. 9(*om* *S*); 18(*ἐγώ* GLTTr*S*).

καὶ γάρ, **for**, Matt. viii. 9. xxvi. 73. Mark x. 45. xiv. 70. Luke vi. 32, 33, 34(–*γάρ* TTr^{b}*S*). vii. 8. xi. 4. xxii. 37(–*γάρ* $L^{b}Tr^{b}$), 59. John iv. 23. Acts xix. 40. Rom. xvi. 2. 1 Cor. v. 7. viii. 5. xii. 13, 14. xiv. 8. 2 Cor. ii. 10. iii. 10. v. 4. vii. 5. xiii. 4. Heb. iv. 2. v. 12. x. 34. xii. 29. xiii. 22.—**yet**, Matt. xv. 27. Mark vii. 28(–*γάρ* L^{b}Tr*S*).

because, John iii. 19. x. 26. Rom. iv. 15.

because that, Acts xxviii. 20. 3 John 7.

γὰρ ὅτι, **because that**, Rom. iii. 2 (–*γάρ* G′L).

therefore, Mark viii. 38.

seeing, Acts ii. 15.

indeed, Rom. viii. 7. 1 Thes. iv. 10.

verily, Acts xvi. 37. Rom. xv. 27.

no doubt, 1 Cor. ix. 10.

and, John iv. 37. Acts viii. 39. 2 Tim. ii. 7.

even, Jas. iv. 14(*marg.* **for**; –L*S*).

but, 1 Pet. iv. 15. 2 Pet. i. 9.

yet, Rom. v. 7.

why, John ix. 30.

what? 1 Cor. xi. 22.

τί γάρ, **why, what?** Matt. xxvii. 23. Mark xv. 14. Luke xxiii. 22.—**what then?** Phil. i. 18.

Not rendered, Matt. i. 18(–LTr*S*). Luke xii. 58. xx. 36. John vii. 41. viii. 42. Acts iv. 34. viii. 31. xix. 35. Rom. xv. 2(*om* *S*). 1 Cor. xi. 9. 2 Cor. xii. 1(*ap*). Phil. ii. 5(–G^{oo}L*S*).

Add. for *ἀλλά*, 2 John 12, GL.—For *δέ*, Matt. xxiii. 5, G′LTr*S*. xxiv. 37, LTr. Mark xiv. 2, LTTr*S*. xvi. 8, LTr*S*. Luke xx. 40, TTr*S*. John vi. 40, GLTTr*S*. Rom. ii. 2, L^{m}*S*. xiv. 15, G′LT*S*. xv. 8, G″LT*S*. 1 Cor. ii. 10, T. ix. 16, x. 1, xvi. 7, GLT*S*. Gal. i. 11, G′. iv. 25^{2d}, GLT*S*. v. 17^{2d}, L*S*. Col. iii. 25, G″LT*S*. Heb. xiii. 4, G L*S*. Rev. xiv. 13, G′LTr*S*.—For *ἤ*, Mark viii. 37, TTr*S*. Luke xviii. 14, *see* *ἤ*.—For *καί*, 1 Cor. viii. 11, LT.—Matt. xxv. 3, *see* *ὅστις*.—For *ὅτι*, Mark xi. 18, TTr*S*. Rev. xxii. 10, G′LTr*S*.—For *οὖν*, Rom. iii. 28, GLT*S*.

Mark ii. 17(. . I came), L^{m}. ix. 45 (. . it is better), L^{b}. Luke i. 66(*καί* ^{2d} . .), LTr*S*. viii. 52(*οὐκ* . .), LTr*S*.

xii. 23 (. . life), G′LᵇTr*S*. John xiii. 18 (. . I know), Lᵇ*S*. Acts x. 37 (. . and), Lᵇ. Rom. xiv. 5(. . one man), Lᵇ*S*. 2 Cor. viii. 21(. . providing), GLT*S*. Phil. i. 23 (. . which), GLT, –StG°ⁿ*S*. 1 Thes. v. 5 (. . ye are), GᵖʳLT*S*. 2 Tim. ii. 13 (. . he can), G′LT*S*. 1 Pet. ii. 20(. . this), LT.

γαστήρ.

belly, Tit. i. 12.
womb, Luke i. 31.
ἐν γαστρὶ ἔχω, **be with child**, Matt. i. 18p, 23. xxiv. 19. Mark xiii. 17. Luke xxi. 23. 1 Thes. v. 3p. Rev. xii. 2.

γέ.

An enclitic particle, used in antithesis, for emphasis.
(a) *With a noun, pronoun, or verb:*
yet, Luke xi. 8. xviii. 5.
Not rendered, Rom. viii. 32, *with ἴδιος υἱός*. 1 Cor. iv. 8, *with ὀφείλω*.
(b) *With other particles:*
ἀλλά γε, **yet doubtless**, 1 Cor. ix. 2.
ἀλλά γε σὺν, **and beside**, Luke xxiv. 21.
καί γε, **at least**, Luke xix. 42(–Lᵇ Tr*S*).—**and**, Acts ii. 18.
See also ἄρα, ἆρα, εἰ, εἰ δὲ μή, καίτοι, μὲν οὖν.

γέεννα.

hell, Matt. v. 29, 30. x. 28. xxiii. 15, 33. Mark ix. 43, 45. Luke xii. 5. Jas. iii. 6.
γέεννα τοῦ πυρός, **hell fire**, Matt. v. 22. xviii. 9. Mark ix. 47.

γείτων.

neighbor, Luke xiv. 12. xv. 6, 9. John ix. 8.

γελάω.

to laugh, Luke vi. 21, 25.

γέλως.

laughter, Jas. iv. 9.

γεμίζω.

fill, Luke xiv. 23. xv. 16. John ii. 7*t*. vi. 13. Rev. viii. 5. xv. 8.
fill full, Mark xv. 36.
Pass., **be full**, Mark iv. 37.

γέμω.

be full of, Matt. xxiii. 25, 27. Luke xi. 39. Rom. iii. 14. Rev. iv. 8.
Part., **full of**, Rev. iv. 6. v. 8. xv. 7. xvii. 3, 4. xxi. 9.

γενεά.

generation, Matt. i. 17*f*. xi. 16. xii. 39, 41, 42, 45. xvi. 4. xvii. 17. xxiii. 36. xxiv. 34. Mark viii. 12*t*, 38. ix. 19. xiii. 30. Luke i. 48. vii. 31. ix. 41. xi. 29, 30, 31, 32, 50, 51. xvi. 8. xvii. 25. Acts ii. 40. viii. 33. xiii. 36(*marg., q. v.*, **age**). Col. i. 26. Heb. iii. 10.
εἰς γενεὰς γενεῶν, **from generation to generation**, Luke i. 50(*εἰς γ. καὶ γενεάς* G′TTr, *εἰς γενεὰν κ. γενεάν* G″*S*).
nation, Phil. ii. 15.
age, Eph. iii. 5, 21.
time, Acts xiv. 16. xv. 21pl.
Add Luke xi. 29(This . .), LTTr*S*.

γενεαλογέομαι.

one's descent (*marg.* **pedigree**) **is counted**, Heb. vii. 6.

γενεαλογία.

genealogy, 1 Tim. i. 4. Tit. iii. 9.

γενέσια.

birthday, Matt. xiv. 6. Mark vi. 21.

γένεσις.

generation, Matt. i. 1.
nature, Jas. iii. 6.
naturalcc, Jas. i. 23.
Add, for *γέννησις*, Matt. i. 18, GLTTr*S*. Luke i. 14, GLTTr*S*.

γενετή.

birth, John ix. 1.

γένημα, produce, fruit.
See γέννημα.

γεννάω.

beget, Matt. i. 2*tr*, 3*tr*, 4*tr*, 5*tr*, 6*t*, 7*tr*, 8*tr*, 9*tr*, 10*tr*, 11, 12*t*, 13*tr*, 14*tr*, 15*tr*, 16. Acts vii. 8, 29. xiii. 33. 1 Cor. iv. 15. Phm. 10. Heb. i. 5. v. 5. 1 John v. 1*t*, 18.
gender, Gal. iv. 24. 2 Tim. ii. 23.
conceive, Matt. i. 20.
be delivered of, John xvi. 21.
bring forth, Luke i. 57.

bear, Luke i. 13. xxiii. 29.
Pass., **be born**, Matt. i. 16. ii. 1p, 4. xix. 12. xxvi. 24. Mark xiv. 21. Luke i. 35. John i. 13. iii. 3, 4*t*, 5, 6*t*, 7, 8. viii. 41. ix. 2, 19, 20, 32, 34. xvi. 21. xviii. 37. Acts ii. 8. vii. 20. xxii. 3, 28. Rom. ix. 11. Gal. iv. 23, 29. Heb. xi. 23p. 1 John ii. 29. iii. 9*t*. iv. 7. v. 1, 4, 18.—**spring**, Heb. xi. 12.—**be made**, 2 Pet. ii. 12(γίνομαι StC*S*).

γέννημα.

generation, Matt. iii. 7. xii. 34. xxiii. 33. Luke iii. 7.
fruit, Matt. xxvi. 29(γένημα LTTr*S*). Mark xiv. 25(γένημα G″TTr*S*). Luke xii. 18(γένημα StGLT*S*, σῖτον fr. σῖτος Tr). xxii. 18(γένημα LTTr*S*). 2 Cor. ix. 10(γένημα GLT*S*).

γέννησις.

birth, Matt. i. 18(G′, γένεσις GLT Tr*S*). Luke i. 14(γένεσις GLTTr*S*).

γεννητός.

that is born, Matt. xi. 11. Luke vii. 28.

γένος.

offspring, Acts xvii. 28, 29. Rev. xxii. 16.
generation, 1 Pet. ii. 9.
stock, Acts xiii. 26. Phil. iii. 5.
kindred, Acts iv. 6. vii. 13, 19.
one's own countrymen, 2 Cor. xi. 26.
Κύπριος τῷ γένει, **of the country of Cyprus**, Acts iv. 36.
Ποντικὸς τῷ γένει, **born in Pontus**, Acts xviii. 2.
Ἀλεξανδρεὺς τῷ γένει, **born at Alexandria**, Acts xviii. 24.
nation, Mark vii. 26. Gal. i. 14.
kind, Matt. xiii. 47. xvii. 21(*ap*). Mark ix. 29. 1 Cor. xii. 10. xiv. 10.
diversity(*marg.* **kind**), 1 Cor. xii. 28.

γερουσία.

senate, Acts v. 21.

γέρων.

old, John iii. 4.

γεύομαι.

to taste, Matt. xvi. 28. xxvii. 34p. Mark ix. 1. Luke ix. 27. xiv. 24. John ii. 9. viii. 52. Col. ii. 21. Heb. ii. 9. vi. 4, 5. 1 Pet. ii. 3.
eat, Acts x. 10. xx. 11p. xxiii. 14.

γεωργέομαι.

be dressed, Heb. vi. 7.

γεώργιον.

husbandry (*marg.* **tillage**), 1 Cor. iii. 9.

γεωργός.

husbandman, Matt. xxi. 33, 34, 35, 38, 40, 41. Mark xii. 1, 2*t*, 7, 9. Luke xx. 9, 10*t*, 14, 16. John xv. 1. 2 Tim. ii. 6. Jas. v. 7.

γῆ.

earth, Matt. v. 5, 13, 18, 35. vi. 10, 19. ix. 6. x. 34. xi. 25. xii. 40, 42. xiii. 5*t*. xvi. 19*t*. xvii. 25. xviii. 18*t*, 19. xxiii. 9, 35. xxiv. 30, 35. xxv. 18, 25. xxvii. 51. xxviii. 18. Mark ii. 10. iv. 5*t*, 28, 31, 31(*ap*). ix. 3. xiii. 27, 31. Luke ii. 14. v. 24. vi. 49. x. 21. xi. 2(*ap*), 31. xii. 49, 51, 56. xvi. 17. xviii. 8. xxi. 25, 33, 35. xxiii. 44(*marg.* **land**). xxiv. 5. John iii. 31*t*. xii. 32. xvii. 4. Acts i. 8. ii. 19. iii. 25. iv. 24, 26. vii. 49. viii. 33. ix. 4, 8. x. 11, 12(–G°). xi. 6. xiii. 47. xiv. 15. xvii. 24, 26. xxii. 22. xxvi. 14.
Rom. ix. 17, 28. x. 18. 1 Cor. viii. 5. x. 26, 28(*ap*). xv. 47. Eph. i. 10. iii. 15. iv. 9. vi. 3. Col. i. 16, 20. iii. 2, 5. Heb. i. 10. vi. 7. viii. 4. xi. 13, 38. xii. 25, 26*t*. Jas. v. 5, 7, 12, 17, 18. 2 Pet. iii. 5, 7, 10, 13. 1 John v. 8(*ap*). Rev. i. 5, 7. iii. 10. v. 3*t*, 6, 10, 13*t*. vi. 4, 8*t*, 10, 13, 15. vii. 1*tr*, 2, 3. viii. 5, 7, 13. ix. 1, 3*t*, 4. x. 2, 5, 6, 8. xi. 4, 6, 10*t*, 18. xii. 4, 9, 12, 13, 16*t*. xiii. 8, 11, 12, 13, 14*t*. xiv. 3, 6, 7, 15, 16*t*, 18, 19*t*. xvi. 1, 2, 14(*om S*), 18. xvii. 2*t*, 5, 8, 18. xviii. 1, 3*t*, 9, 11, 23, 24. xix. 2, 19. xx. 8, 9, 11. xxi. 1*t*, 24.
With ἐκ, **earthly**, John iii. 31.
ground, Matt. x. 29(–G°°). xiii. 8, 23. xv. 35. Mark iv. 8, 20, 23. viii.

6. ix. 20. xiv. 35. Luke viii. 8, 15. xiii. 7. xxii. 44(*ap*). John viii. 6 (*ap*), 8(*ap*). xii. 24. Acts vii. 33.

land, Matt. ii. 6, 20, 21. iv. 15*t*. ix. 26. x. 15. xi. 24. xiv. 34. xxvii. 45. Mark iv. 1. vi. 47, 53. xv. 33. Luke iv. 25. v. 3, 11. viii. 27. xiv. 35. xxi. 23. John iii. 22. vi. 21. xxi. 8, 9, 11. Acts vii. 3, 4*t*, 6, 11 (–G″L*S*), 29, 36(τῇ fr. ὁ L), 40. xiii. 17, 19*t*. xxvii. 39, 43, 44. Heb. viii. 9. xi. 9. Jude 5.

country, Matt. ix. 31. Acts vii. 3.

world, Rev. xiii. 3.

Add Matt. xiv. 24(*ap*). Heb. xi. 29(land), C?LT*S*. Rev. viii. 7(*ap*). xiv. 18, for αὐτῆς, G′T. xvii. 4, for αὐτῆς, G″T, αὐτῆς καὶ τῆς γῆς *S*.

γῆρας.

old age, Luke i. 36(*dat.* γήρει fr. γῆρος GLTTr*S*).

γηράσκω.

wax old, Heb. viii. 13.

be old, John xxi. 18.

γίνομαι.

become, Matt. xiii. 22, 32. xviii. 3. xxviii. 4. Mark i. 17. iv. 19, 32. ix. 3. John i. 12. Acts vii. 40. x. 10. xii. 18[cc]. Rom. iii. 19. iv. 18. vii. 13. 1 Cor. iii. 18. viii. 9. ix. 20, 22. xiii. 1, 11. xv. 20(*omS*). 2 Cor. v. 17. xii. 11. Gal. iv. 16. Phil. ii. 8. 1 Thes. i. 6. ii. 14. Phm. 6. Heb. v. 9, 12. x. 33[p]. xi. 7. Jas. ii. 4, 11. Rev. vi. 12*t*. viii. 8. xi. 15. xvi. 3, 4. xviii. 2.

With εἰς, **become**, Matt. xxi. 42. Mark xii. 10. Luke xx. 17. Acts iv. 11. Rev. viii. 11.—**be made**, 1 Cor. xv. 45.—**wax**, Luke xiii. 19.

be made, Matt. iv. 3. ix. 16. xxiii. 15. xxv. 6. xxvii. 24. Mark ii. 21, 27. xiv. 4. Luke iv. 3. viii. 17. xiv. 12. xxiii. 12, 19. John i. 3*tr*, 10, 14. ii. 9. v. 4(*ap*), 6, 9, 14. viii. 33. ix. 39. Acts vii. 13. xii. 5. xiii. 32. xiv. 5. xix. 26. xxi. 40[p]. xxvi. 6.

Rom. i. 3. ii. 25. vii. 13. x. 20. xi. 9. 1 Cor. i. 30. iii. 13. iv. 9, 13. vii. 21. ix. 22. xi. 19. xiv. 25. xv. 45. 2 Cor. v. 21. Gal. iii. 13. iv. 4*t*. Eph. ii. 13. iii. 7. Phil. ii. 7. Col. i. 23, 25. Tit. iii. 7. Heb. i. 4. iii. 14. v. 5. vi. 4, 20. vii. 12, 16, 21 (20), 22, 26. xi. 3. Jas. iii. 9. 1 Pet. ii. 7(*with* εἰς).

grow, Matt. xxi. 19. Acts v. 24.

wax, Heb. xi. 34.

draw[c], John vi. 19.

arise, Matthew viii. 24. xiii. 21[p]. Mark iv. 17[p], 37. Luke vi. 48[p]. xv. 14. John iii. 25. Acts vi. 1. xi. 19. xix. 23. xxiii. 7, 9, 10[p].

come, Matt. viii. 16[p]. xiv. 23[p]. xx. 8[p]. xxvi. 20[p]. xxvii. 1[p], 57[p]. Mark i. 11. iv. 35[p]. vi. 2[p], 21[p], 47[p]. ix. 21. xi. 19. xv. 33[p], 42[p]. Luke i. 65. iii. 2, 22. ix. 34, 35. xix. 9. xxii. 14. John i. 17. v. 14. vi. 16, 25. x. 35. xii. 30. xiii. 19. xxi. 4[p]. Acts ii. 2, 43. v. 5, 11. vii. 31. ix. 3. x. 13. xii. 11[p]. xvi. 29. xxi. 17[p], 35. xxvi. 22. xxvii. 7, 16, 27(ἐπιγίνομαι T). xxviii. 6.

2 Cor. i. 8. Gal. iii. 14. 1 Thes. i. 5. 1 Tim. vi. 4. 2 Tim. iii. 11. Heb. xi. 24[p]. Rev. xii. 10.

come to pass, Matt. vii. 28. ix. 10. xi. 1. xiii. 53. xix. 1. xxiv. 6. xxvi. 1. Mark i. 9. ii. 15, 23. iv. 4. xi. 23. xiii. 29. Luke i. 8, 23, 41, 59. ii. 1, 15*t*, 46. iii. 21. v. 1, 12, 17. vi. 1, 6, 12. vii. 11. viii. 1, 22, 40. ix. 18, 28, 33, 37, 51, 57 (–G″TTr*S*). x. 38. xi. 1, 14, 27. xii. 55. xiv. 1. xvi. 22. xvii. 11, 14. xviii. 35. xix. 15, 29. xx. 1. xxi. 7, 9, 28, 31, 36. xxiv. 4, 12(*ap*), 15, 18, 30, 51. John xiii. 19. xiv. 29*t*. Acts iv. 5. ix. 32, 37, 43. xi. 26, 28. xiv. 1. xvi. 16. xix. 1. xxi. 1. xxii. 6, 17. xxvii. 44. xxviii. 8, 17. 1 Thes. iii. 4. Rev. i. 1.

be brought to pass, 1 Cor. xv. 54.

fall, Rev. xvi. 2.

befall, Mark v. 16.

happen, Rom. xi. 25.

follow, Rev. viii. 7.

be wrought, Mark vi. 2. Acts v. 12.
be performed, Luke i. 20.
be done, Matt. i. 22. vi. 10. viii. 13. xi. 20, 21, 23*t*. xviii. 19, 31*t*. xxi. 4, 21. xxvi. 42, 56. xxvii. 54. xxviii. 11. Mark iv. 11. v. 14, 33. xiii. 30. Luke iv. 23. viii. 34, 35, 56. ix. 7. x. 13*t*, xi. 2 (*ap*). xiii. 17. xiv. 22. xxii. 42. xxiii. 8, 31, 47, 48. xxiv. 21. John i. 28. xv. 7. xix. 36. Acts ii. 43. iv. 16, 21, 28, 30. v. 7. viii. 13. x. 16. xi. 10. xii. 9. xiii. 12. xiv. 3. xxi. 14. xxiv. 2(3)[p]. xxviii. 9[p].
1 Cor. ix. 15. xiv. 26, 40. xvi. 14. Eph. v. 12. Rev. xvi. 17. xxi. 6. xxii. 6.
so[c] **be done**, Matt. viii. 13.
be one's doing, Matt. xxi. 42. Mark xii. 11.
be fulfilled, Matt. v. 18. xxiv. 34. Luke xxi. 32.
be finished, Heb. iv. 3.
be ended, John xiii. 2.
be past, Luke ix. 36. 2 Tim. ii. 18.
be had, Acts xxv. 26[p].
be kept[c], Mark iv. 22.
be found, 2 Cor. vii. 14.
be brought, Acts v. 36.
be showed, Acts iv. 22.
be published, Acts x. 37.
be ordained to be, Acts i. 22.
be preferred[c], John i. 15, 27(*ap*), 30.
be turned, John xvi. 20.
be divided, Rev. xvi. 19.
be taken, 2 Thes. ii. 7.
be assembled[c], Acts xv. 25.
be, Matt. v. 45. vi. 16. viii. 26. ix. 29. x. 16, 25. xii. 45. xiv. 15[p]. xv. 28. xvi. 2[p]. xvii. 2. xviii. 13. xix. 8. xx. 26. xxiii. 26. xxiv. 20, 21*t*, 32, 44. xxvi. 2, 5, 6[p], 54. xxvii. 45. xxviii. 2. Mark iv. 10, 39. vi. 26. ix. 7, 26, 33. x. 43, 44(εἰμί LTr*S*). xiii. 7, 18, 19*t*, 28. xv. 33. xvi. 10(*ap*).
Luke i. 2, 5, 38. ii. 2, 6, 13, 42. iv. 25, 42[p]. vi. 13, 16, 36, 49. viii. 24. x. 32[p](–Tr*S*[c]), 36. xi. 26, 30. xii. 40, 54. xiii. 2, 4. xv. 10. xvi. 11, 12. xvii. 26, 28. xviii. 23, 24(–TTr[b]*S*). xix. 17, 19. xx. 14 (ἔσται fr. εἰμί L[m]), 33. xxii. 24, 26, 40[p], 44*t* (*ap*), 66. xxiii. 24, 44. xxiv. 5[p], 19, 37. John i. 6. ii. 1. iii. 9. iv. 14. vi. 17, 21. vii. 43. viii. 58. ix. 27. x. 16, 19, 22. xii. 36. xiv. 22. xv. 8. xx. 27. Acts i. 16, 19, 20. iv. 4. v. 7. vii. 29, 38, 52. viii. 1, 8. ix. 19, 42. x. 4, 25. xii. 18[p], 23. xiii. 5[p]. xv. 7[p], 39. xvi. 26, 35[p]. xix. 17, 21, 28. xx. 16, 18. xxii. 9(–G[oo]L*S*), 17. xxiii. 12[p]. xxv. 15[p]. xxvi. 4, 19, 28(ποιέω L*S*), 29. xxvii. 36[p], 39, 42.
Rom. iii. 4. vi. 5. ix. 29. xi. 5, 6, 34. xii. 16. xv. 8, 16, 31. xvi. 2, 7. 1 Cor. ii. 3. iii. 18. iv. 16. vii. 23. ix. 23, 27. x. 6, 7. xi. 1. xiv. 20*t*. xv. 10, 37, 58. xvi. 2, 10. 2 Cor. i. 18(ἐστιν fr. εἰμί G' LT*S*), 19*t*. iii. 7. vi. 14. viii. 14*t*. Gal. iii. 17, 24. iv. 12. v. 26. Eph. iv. 32. v. 1, 7, 17. vi. 3. Phil. i. 13. ii. 15(εἰμί L). iii. 17, 21(*ap*). Col. iii. 15. iv. 11. 1 Thes. i. 5, 7. ii. 1, 7, 8. iii. 5. 1 Tim. ii. 14. iv. 12. v. 9. 2 Tim. i. 17[p]. iii. 9.
Heb. ii. 2, 17. v. 11. vi. 12. vii. 18. ix. 22. xi. 6. xii. 8. Jas. i. 12[p], 22, 25. ii. 10. iii. 1, 10. v. 2. 1 Pet. i. 15, 16(ἔσεσθε fr. εἰμί G'LT*S*). iii. 6, 13. iv. 12. v. 3. 2 Pet. i. 4, 16, 20. ii. 1, 20. 1 John ii. 18. 3 John 8. Rev. i. 9, 10, 18, 19. ii. 8, 10. iii. 2. iv. 1, 2. vi. 12. viii. 1, 5. xi. 13*t*, 15, 19. xii. 7. xvi. 10, 18, 18(–G[o] Tr), 18.
With εἰμί, **be**, Heb. vii. 23[p].
so be, Matt. xviii. 13.
Not rendered, *with* ἄμεμπτος, Phil. iii. 6[p].
μὴ γένοιτο, **God forbid** (*lit.* may it not be), Luke xx. 16. Rom. iii. 4, 6, 31. vi. 2, 15. vii. 7, 13. ix. 14. xi. 1, 11. 1 Cor. vi. 15. Gal. ii. 17. iii. 21. vi. 14.
ὅπως μὴ γένηται αὐτῷ, **because he would not**, Acts xx. 16.

have[cc] (*lit.* belonging to), Matt. xviii. 12. Acts xv. 2[p]. 1 Cor. iv. 5.

be married[c], Rom. vii. 3, 3[p], 4.

behave one's self, 1 Thes. ii. 10.

With ἐν, **to use**, 1 Thes. ii. 5.

With βαπτίζω[p], **baptize**, Mark i. 4.

continue[c], Acts xix. 10.

Add Matt. xiv. 6, for ἄγω[pass], G'L TTr*S*. Mark ix. 6, for εἰμί, G''LT Tr*S*. Luke viii. 42(*ap*). Acts x. 10, for ἐπιπίπτω, G''LT*S*. Heb. ix. 11, for μέλλω, L. 2 Pet. ii. 12, for γεννάω[pass], StC*S*. 2 John 12, for ἔρχομαι, G''LT*S*.

See also ἄναλος, ἀποσυνάγωγος, ἀπρόσκοπος, ἄφαντος, βροντή, γνώμη, ἐμφανής, ἔμφοβος, ἔντρομος, ἐξαρτίζω, ἔξυπνος, ἐπιβουλή, ἕτερος, εὐδοκία, εὔχομαι, θάμβος, θάνατος, κλαυθμός, κοινωνός, μέλλω, ὀφείλω, ὀψία, πολύς, πρηνής, πρωτεύω, συγκοινωνός, συνδρομή, ὑπήκοος, φανερός, φωνή.

γινώσκω.

know, Matt. i. 25. vi. 3. vii. 23. ix. 30. x. 26. xii. 7, 15[p], 33. xiii. 11. xxiv. 32, 33, 39, 43. xxv. 24. Mark iv. 11 (-G[oo]LTTr*S*), 13. v. 43. vi. 38[p]. vii. 24. viii. 17[p]. ix. 30. xii. 12. xiii. 28, 29. xv. 10, 45[p]. Luke i. 18, 34. ii. 43. vi. 44. vii. 39. viii. 10, 17. ix. 11[p]. x. 22. xii. 2, 39, 47, 48. xvi. 15. xviii. 34. xix. 15, 42, 44. xxi. 20, 30, 31. xxiv. 18, 35. John i. 10, 48(49). ii. 24, 25. iii. 10. iv. 1, 53. v. 6, 42. vii. 17, 26, 27, 49, 51. viii. 28, 32, 52, 55. x. 14*t*, 15*t*, 27, 38. xi. 57. xii. 9. xiii. 7, 12, 28, 35. xiv. 7, 7 (εἴδω Tr), 7, 9, 17*t*, 20, 31. xv. 18. xvi. 3, 19. xvii. 3, 7, 8(-L[b]*S*), 23, 25*tr*. xix. 4. xxi. 17. Acts i. 7. ii. 36. ix. 24. xvii. 19, 20. xix. 15, 35. xx. 34. xxi. 24, 34. xxii. 14, 30. xxiii. 28(ἐπιγινώσκω LT).

Rom. i. 21[p]. ii. 18. iii. 17. vi. 6. vii. 1, 7. x. 19. xi. 34. 1 Cor. i. 21. ii. 8*t*, 14, 16. iii. 20. iv. 19. viii. 2*t*, 3. xiii. 9, 12. xiv. 7, 9. 2 Cor. ii. 4, 9. iii. 2. v. 16*t*, 21. viii. 9. xiii. 6. Gal. iii. 7. iv. 9[p], 9. Eph. iii. 19. v. 5. vi. 22. Phil. ii. 19[p], 22. iii. 10. iv. 5. Col. iv. 8. 1 Thes. iii. 5. 2 Tim. i. 18. ii. 19. iii. 1. Heb. iii. 10. viii. 11. x. 34. xiii. 23. Jas. i. 3. ii. 20. v. 20. 2 Pet. i. 20. iii. 3. 1 John ii. 3*t*, 4, 5, 13*t*, 14, 18, 29. iii. 1*t*, 6, 19, 20, 24. iv. 2, 6*t*, 7, 8, 13, 16. v. 2, 20. 2 John 1. Rev. ii. 17(εἴδω GLTTr*S*), 23, 24. iii. 3, 9.

have knowledge, Acts xvii. 13.

perceive, Matt. xvi. 8[p]. xxi. 45. xxii. 18. Luke viii. 46. xx. 19. John vi. 15[p]. Acts xxiii. 6[p]. Gal. ii. 9[p]. 1 John iii. 16.

be aware of, Matt. xxiv. 50.

be aware, Luke xii. 46.

be sure of, Luke x. 11.

be sure, John vi. 69.

understand, Matt. xxvi. 10[p]. John viii. 27, 43. x. 6. xii. 16. Acts viii. 30. xxiv. 11(ἐπιγινώσκω LT*S*). Phil. i. 12.

can (*lit.* know how), Matt. xvi. 3.

With Ἑλληνιστί, **can speak Greek**, Acts xxi. 37.

allow(*Gr.* know), Rom. vii. 15.

feel, Mark v. 29.

be resolved, Luke xvi. 4.

Add, for εἴδω, 1 Cor. ii. 11[2d], G''LT*S*. viii. 2, LT*S*. For ἐπιγινώσκω, Mark vi. 33, LTr. For πιστεύω, John x. 38[3d], LTTr.

γλεῦκος.

new wine, Acts ii. 13.

γλυκύς.

sweet, Jas. iii. 11. Rev. x. 9, 10.

fresh, Jas. iii. 12.

γλῶσσα.

tongue, Mark vii. 33, 35. xvi. 17 (*ap*). Luke i. 64. xvi. 24. Acts ii. 3, 4, 11, 26. x. 46. xix. 6. Rom. iii. 13. xiv. 11. 1 Cor. xii. 10*t*, 28, 30. xiii. 1, 8. xiv. 2, 4, 5*t*, 6, 9, 13, 14, 18, 19, 22, 23, 26, 27, 39. Phil. ii. 11. Jas. i. 26. iii. 5, 6*t*, 8. 1 Pet. iii. 10. 1 John iii. 18. Rev. v. 9.

vii. 9. x. 11. xi. 9. xiii. 7. xiv. 6. xvi. 10. xvii. 15.

γλωσσόκομον.

bag, John xii. 6. xiii. 29.

γναφεύς.

fuller, Mark ix. 3.

γνήσιος.

own, 1 Tim. i. 2. Tit. i. 4.
true, Phil. iv. 3.
With art., **sincerity**, 2 Cor. viii. 8.

γνησίως.

naturally, Phil. ii. 20.

γνόφος.

blackness, Heb. xii. 18.

γνώμη.

mind, Phm. 14. Rev. xvii. 13.
judgment, 1 Cor. i. 10. vii. 25, 40.
ποιῆσαι γνώμην μίαν, **agree**, Rev. xvii. 17(*ap*).
advice, 2 Cor. viii. 10.
will, Rev. xvii. 17.
With γίνομαι, **to purpose**, Acts xx. 3.

γνωρίζω.

make known, Luke ii. 15. John xv. 15. Acts ii. 28. Rom. ix. 22, 23. xvi. 26. Eph. i. 9. iii. 3, 5, 10. vi. 19, 21. Phil. iv. 6. Col. i. 27. iv. 9. 2 Pet. i. 16.
do to wit, 2 Cor. viii. 1.
give to understand, 1 Cor. xii. 3.
declare, John xvii. 26*t*. 1 Cor. xv. 1. Col. iv. 7.
certify, Gal. i. 11.
wot, Phil. i. 22.
Add Luke ii. 17, for διαγνωρίζω, LTr*S*.

γνῶσις.

knowledge, Luke i. 77. xi. 52. Rom. ii. 20. xi. 33. xv. 14. 1 Cor. i. 5. viii. 1*t*, 7, 10, 11. xii. 8. xiii. 2, 8. xiv. 6. 2 Cor. ii. 14. iv. 6. vi. 6. viii. 7. x. 5. xi. 6. Eph. iii. 19. Phil. iii. 8. Col. ii. 3. 1 Pet. iii. 7. 2 Pet i. 5, 6. iii. 18.
science, 1 Tim. vi. 20.

γνώστης.

expert, Acts xxvi. 3.

γνωστός.

known, John xviii. 15, 16. Acts i. 19. ii. 14. iv. 10. ix. 42. xiii. 38. xv. 18(*ap*). xix. 17. xxviii. 28.
γνωστόν ἐστιν ἡμῖν **we know**, Acts xxviii. 22.
With art., **acquaintance**, Luke ii. 44pl. xxiii. 49pl. — **that which may be known**, Rom. i. 19.
notable, Acts iv. 16.

γογγύζω.

murmur, *trans.*, John vii. 32. — *Intrans.*, Matt. xx. 11. Luke v. 30. John vi. 41, 43, 61. 1 Cor. x. 10*t*.

γογγυσμός.

murmuring, John vii. 12. Acts vi. 1. Phil. ii. 14.—**grudging**, 1 Pet. iv. 9 pl (sing. G''LT*S*).

γογγυστής.

murmurer, Jude 16.

γόης.

seducer, 2 Tim. iii. 13.

γόμος.

burden, Acts xxi. 3.
merchandise, Rev. xviii. 11. 12.

γονεύς.

Plural, **parents**, Matt. x. 21. Mark xiii. 12. Luke ii. 27, 41. viii. 56. xviii. 29. xxi. 16. John ix. 2, 3, 18, 20, 22, 23. Rom. i. 30. 2 Cor. xii. 14*t*. Eph. vi. 1. Col. iii. 20. 2 Tim. iii. 2. [(*ap*).
Add Matt. xix. 29(*ap*). Luke ii. 43

γόνυ.

knee, Mark xv. 19. Luke v. 8. Rom. xi. 4. xiv. 11. Eph. iii. 14. Phil. ii. 10. Heb. xii. 12.
τίθημι τὰ γόνατα, **kneel**, Luke xxii. 41. Acts vii. 60. ix. 40. xx. 36. xxi. 5.

γονυπετέω.

kneel down to, Matt. xvii. 14. Mark i. 40(-LTrb).
kneel to, Mark x. 17.
bow the knee, Matt. xxvii. 29.

γράμμα.

letter, Luke xxiii. 38(*ap*). John vii. 15pl (*marg.* **learning**). Acts

xxviii. 21. Rom. ii. 27, 29. vii. 6. 2 Cor. iii. 6*t*. Gal. vi. 11.
writing, John v. 47.
ἐν γράμμασιν, **written**, 2 Cor. iii. 7.
scripture, 2 Tim. iii. 15.
bill, Luke xvi. 6, 7.
learning, Acts xxvi. 24[pl].

γραμματεύς.

scribe, Matt. ii. 4. v. 20. vii. 29. viii. 19. ix. 3. xii. 38. xiii. 52. xv. 1. xvi. 21. xvii. 10. xx. 18. xxi. 15. xxiii. 2, 13, 14(*ap*), 15, 23, 25, 27, 29, 34. xxvi. 3(–G°LTTr*S*), 57. xxvii. 41. Mark i. 22. ii. 6, 16. iii. 22. vii. 1, 5. viii. 31. ix. 11, 14, 16 (G'', *αὐτός* GLTTr*S*). x. 33. xi. 18, 27. xii. 28, 32, 35, 38. xiv. 1, 43, 53. xv. 1, 31. Luke v. 21, 30. vi. 7. ix. 22. xi. 44(*ap*), 53. xv. 2. xix. 47. xx. 1, 19, 39, 46. xxii. 2, 66. xxiii. 10. John viii. 3(*ap*). Acts iv. 5. vi. 12. xxiii. 9(*ap*). 1 Cor. i. 20.
town-clerk, Acts xix. 35.
Add Luke xxii. 4(priests, *καὶ τοὺς γ.*), L.

γραπτός.

written, Rom. ii. 15.

γραφή.

scripture, Matt. xxi. 42. xxii. 29. xxvi. 54, 56. Mark xii. 10, 24. xiv. 49. xv. 28(*ap*). Luke iv. 21. xxiv. 27, 32, 45. John ii. 22. v. 39. vii. 38, 42. x. 35. xiii. 18. xvii. 12. xix. 24, 28, 36, 37. xx. 9. Acts i. 6. viii. 32, 35. xvii. 2, 11. xviii. 24, 28. Rom. i. 2. iv. 3. ix. 17. x. 11. xi. 2. xv. 4. xvi. 26. 1 Cor. xv. 3, 4. Gal. iii. 8, 22. iv. 30. 1 Tim. v. 18. 2 Tim. iii. 16. Jas. ii. 8, 23. iv. 5. 1 Pet. ii. 6. 2 Pet. i. 20. iii. 16.

γράφω.

write, Matt. ii. 5. iv. 4, 6, 7, 10. xi. 10. xxi. 13. xxvi. 24, 31. xxvii. 37. Mark i. 2. vii. 6. ix. 12, 13. x. 4, 6. xi. 17. xii. 19 xiv. 21, 27. Luke i. 3, 63. ii. 23. iii. 4. iv. 4, 8, 10, 17. vii. 27. x. 20(*ἐγγέγραπται* fr. *ἐγγράφω* TTr*S*), 26. xvi. 6, 7. xviii. 31. xix. 46. xx. 17, 28. xxi. 22. xxii. 37. xxiii. 38(*ἐπιγράφω* L Tr[b], –T*S*). xxiv. 44, 46. John i. 45 (46). ii. 17, v. 46. vi. 31, 45. viii. 6(*ap*), 8(*ap*), 17. x. 34. xii. 14, 16. xv. 25, xix. 19, 20, 21, 22. xx. 30, 31. xxi. 24, 25*t*. Acts i. 20. vii. 42. xiii. 29, 33. xv. 15, 23. xviii. 27. xxiii. 5, 25. xxiv. 14. xxv. 26*t*.
Rom. i. 17. ii. 24. iii. 4, 10. iv 17, 23. viii. 36. ix. 13, 33. x. 15. xi. 8, 26. xii. 19. xiv. 11. xv. 3, 9, 15, 21. xvi. 22. 1 Cor. i. 19, 31. ii. 9. iii. 19. iv. 6, 14. v. 9, 11. vii. 1. ix. 9, 10, 15. x. 7, 11. xiv. 21, 37. xv. 45, 54. 2 Cor. i. 13. ii. 3, 4, 9. vii. 12. viii. 15. ix. 1, 9. xiii. 2(*om* *S*), 10. Gal. i. 20. iii. 10*t*, 13. iv. 22, 27. vi. 11. Phil. iii. 1. 1 Thes. iv. 9. v. 1. 2 Thes. iii. 17. 1 Tim. iii. 14. Phm. 19, 21.
Heb. x. 7. 1 Pet. i. 16. v. 12 2 Pet. iii. 1, 15. 1 John i. 4. ii. 1, 7, 8, 12, 13*tr*, 14*t*, 21, 26. 2 John 5, 12. 3 John 9, 13*t*. Jude 3*t*. Rev. i. 3, 11, 19. ii. 1, 8, 12, 17, 18. iii. 1, 7, 12, 14. v. 1. x. 4*t*. xiii. 8. xiv. 1, 13. xvii. 5, 8. xix. 9, 12, 16. xx. 12, 15. xxi. 5, 27. xxii. 18, 19.
κατὰ τὸ γεγραμμένον, **according as it is written**, 2 Cor. iv. 13.
ἦν γεγραμμένον, **the writing was** John xix. 19.
describe, Rom. x. 5.
Add, for *προγράφω*, Rom. xv. 4[1st]. L[m]. 4[2d], G''LT*S*.—Rev. xix. 12(*ap*).

γραώδης.

old wives', 1 Tim. iv. 7.

γρηγορέω.

watch, Matt. xxiv. 42, 43. xxv. 13. xxvi. 38, 40, 41. Mark xiii. 34, 35, 37. xiv. 34, 37, 38. Luke xii. 37, 39. Acts xx. 31. 1 Cor. xvi. 13. Col. iv. 2. 1 Thes. v. 6. Rev. iii. 3. xvi. 15.
watchful, Rev. iii. 2[p].
be vigilant, 1 Pet. v. 8.
wake, 1 Thes. v. 10.

γυμνάζω.

to exercise, 1 Tim. iv. 7. Heb. v. 14. xii. 11. 2 Pet. ii. 14.

γυμνασία.

exercise, 1 Tim. iv. 8.

γυμνητεύω, γυμνιτεύω LT*S*.

be naked, 1 Cor. iv. 11.

γυμνός.

naked, Matt. xxv. 36, 38, 43, 44. Mark xiv. 51, 52. John xxi. 7. Acts xix. 16. 2 Cor. v. 3. Heb. iv. 13. Jas. ii. 15. Rev. iii. 17. xvi. 15. xvii. 16.

bare, 1 Cor. xv. 37.

γυμνότης.

nakedness, Rom. viii. 35. 2 Cor. xi. 27. Rev. iii. 18.

γυναικάριον.

silly woman, 2 Tim. iii. 6.

γυναικεῖος.

wife[cc](*lit.* of woman), 1 Pet. iii. 7.

γυνή.

woman, Matt. v. 28. ix. 20, 22. xi. 11. xiii. 33. xiv. 21. xv. 22, 28, 38. xxii. 27. xxvi. 7, 10. xxvii. 55. xxviii. 5. Mark v. 25, 33. vii. 25, 26. x. 12(αὐτή Tr*S*). xii. 22. xiv. 3. xv. 40. Luke i. 28(*ap*), 42. iv. 26. vii. 28, 37, 39, 44*t*, 50. viii. 2, 43, 47. x. 38. xi. 27. xiii. 11, 12, 21. xv. 8. xx. 32. xxii. 57. xxiii. 27, 49, 55. xxiv. 22, 24. John ii. 4. iv. 7, 9*t*, 11, 15, 17, 19, 21, 25, 27, 28, 39, 42. viii. 3(*ap*), 4(*ap*), 9(*ap*), 10*t*(*ap*). xvi. 21. xix. 26. xx. 13, 15. Acts i. 14. v. 14. viii. 3, 12. ix. 2. xiii. 50. xvi. 1, 13, 14. xvii. 4, 12, 34. xxii. 4.

Rom. vii. 2. 1 Cor. vii. 1, 13. xi. 3, 5, 6*t*, 7. 8*t*. 9*t*, 10, 11*t*, 12*t*, 13, 15. xiv. 34, 35. Gal. iv. 4. 1 Tim. ii. 9, 10, 11, 12, 14. Heb. xi. 55. 1 Pet. iii. 5. Rev. ii. 20. ix. 8. xii. 1, 4, 6, 13, 14, 15, 16, 17. xiv. 4. xvii. 3, 4, 6, 7, 9, 18.

wife, Matt. i. 20, 24. v. 31, 32. xiv. 3. xviii. 25. xix. 3, 5, 8, 9, 10, 29(-LTTr). xxii. 24, 25, 28. xxvii. 19. Mark vi. 17, 18. x. 2, 7, 11, 29 (-G°LTTr*S*). xii. 19*t*, 20, 23*t*. Luke i. 5, 13, 18, 24. ii. 5(-LTr*S*). iii. 19. viii. 3. xiv. 20, 26. xvi. 18. xvii. 32. xviii. 29. xx. 28*t*, 29, 30 (*ap*), 33*t*. Acts v. 1, 2, 7. xviii. 2. xxi. 5. xxiv. 24.

1 Cor. v. 1. vii. 2, 3*t*, 4*t*, 10, 11, 12, 14*t*, 16*t*, 27*tr*, 29, 33, 34, 39. ix. 5(*marg.* **woman**). Eph. v. 22, 23, 24, 25, 28*t*, 31, 33*t*. Col. iii. 18, 19. 1 Tim. iii. 2, 11, 12. v. 9. Tit. i. 6. 1 Pet. iii. 1*t*. Rev. xix. 7. xxi. 9.

Add Luke xx. 33(. . therefore), T.

γωνία.

corner, Matt. vi. 5. xxi. 42. Mark xii. 10. Luke xx. 17. Acts iv. 11. xxvi. 26. 1 Pet. ii. 7. Rev. vii. 1.

quarter, Rev. xx. 8.

δαιμονίζομαι.

be possessed with a devil, Matt. ix. 32. xii. 22. Mark v. 15, 16, 18.

he that hath a devil, John x. 21p.

be possessed with devils, Matt. iv. 24. viii. 16, 28. Mark i. 32.

be possessed of the devils, Matt. viii. 33. Luke viii. 36(-G∞).

be vexed with a devil, Matt. xv. 22.

δαιμόνιον.

devil, Matt. vii. 22. ix. 33, 34*t*. x. 8. xi. 18. xii. 24*t*, 27, 28. xvii. 18. Mark i. 34*t*, 39. iii. 15, 22*t*. vi. 13. vii. 26, 29, 30. ix. 38. xvi. 9(*ap*), 17(*ap*). Luke iv. 33, 35, 41. vii. 33. viii. 2, 27, 30, 33, 35, 38. ix. 1, 42, 49. x. 17. xi. 14*t*, 15*t*, 18, 19, 20. xiii. 32. John vii. 20. viii. 48, 49, 52. x. 20, 21. 1 Cor. x. 20*t*, 21*t*. 1 Tim. iv. 1. Jas. ii. 19. Rev. ix. 20.

god, Acts xvii. 18.

Add, for δαίμων, Luke viii. 29, L*S*. Rev. xvi. 14, GLTTr*S*. xviii. 2, L*S*.

δαιμονιώδης.

devilish, Jas. iii. 15.

δαίμων.

devil, Matt. viii. 31. Mark v. 12

(–G°°LTrS). Luke viii. 29(δαιμόνιον LS). Rev. xvi. 14(δαιμόνιον GLTTrS). xviii. 2(δαιμόνιον LS).

δάκνω.

bite, Gal. v. 15.

δάκρυ or δάκρυον.

tear, Mark ix. 24(–LTTrS). Luke vii. 38, 44. Acts xx. 19, 31. 2 Cor. ii. 4. 2 Tim. i. 4. Heb. v. 7. xii. 17. Rev. vii. 17. xxi. 4.

δακρύω.

weep, John xi. 35.

δακτύλιος.

ring, Luke xv. 22.

δάκτυλος.

finger, Matt. xxiii. 4. Mark vii. 33. Luke xi. 20, 46. xvi. 24. John viii. 6(*ap*). xx. 25, 27.

δαμάζω.

to tame, Mark v. 4. Jas. iii. 7*t*, 8.

δάμαλις.

heifer, Heb. ix. 13.

δανείζω.

lend, Luke vi. 34*t*, 35.
Mid., **borrow,** Matt. v. 42.

δάνειον.

debt, Matt. xviii. 27.

δανειστής, δανιστής TS.

creditor, Luke vii. 41.

δαπανάω.

spend, Mark v. 26. Luke xv. 14p. 2 Cor. xii. 15.
be at charges, Acts xxi. 24.
consume, Jas. iv. 3.

δαπάνη.

cost, Luke xiv. 28.

δέ.

A particle denoting that the word or clause with which it stands is *to be distinguished* from something preceding. Its sense is —

I. *Adversative;* i. q. **but,** *on the contrary, etc.*

(a) In general. *Passim.*

(b) In the *apodosis* after εἰ, Acts xi. 17(–G°LS), not rendered.

(c) Often corresponding to μέν in a preceding clause. *See* μέν.

II. *Continuative* or *transitional;* i. q. **but, now, and, further, nevertheless.**

(a) In general. *Passim.*

(b) In explanation or example, **now,** Rom. xv. 8 (γάρ G″LTS). 1 Cor. x. 11. Gal. iv. 1. — **then,** Gal. v. 16. — **therefore,** 1 Cor. vii. 8. — **for,** Mark xvi. 8. — **even,** Rom. iii. 22. ix. 30. Phil. ii. 8. — **and,** 1 Cor. xv. 56. Gal. iii. 17. — **but,** Matt. xxiii. 5. Eph. v. 32. — Not rendered, 1 Cor. x. 29. xv. 56.

In parenthetic clauses, **now,** Matt. i. 22. — **but,** Matt. xxvi. 56. — Not rendered, Matt. xxi. 4.

In notation of number or time, **and,** John ix. 14. xv. 25. — **then,** Acts xii. 3. — Not rendered, Mark v. 13.

To introduce some new circumstance, **now,** John vi. 10. xix. 23. 1 Cor. xv. 50. Gal. i. 20. — **for,** Luke xxiii. 17. — **but,** 1 Cor. vii. 29. — **howbeit,** John vi. 23(–Tr, οὖν S). — **nevertheless,** Gal. iv. 20. — Not rendered, Mark vii. 26. John xi. 2.

(c) Resumptive, **and,** Matt. iii. 4. Luke iv. 1. — **but,** 2 Cor. x. 2.

(d) Καὶ δέ, **and also,** Matt. xvi. 18. Mark iv. 36(–δέ LTrS). John xv. 27. Acts xxii. 29. Rom. xi. 23. 1 Tim. iii. 10. — **and so also,** Acts v. 32(–δέ G°LS). — **also,** John viii. 17. — **and,** Matt. x. 18. Luke x. 8(–δέ G″LTrS). John vi. 51. Acts xxv. 25 (–καί LS). — **yea, and,** Acts iii. 24. 2 Tim. iii. 12. 3 John 12. — **yea, also,** Luke ii. 35(–δέ LbTrb). — **and truly,** 1 John i. 3. — **and yet,** John viii. 16. — **moreover,** Heb. ix. 21. — καὶ αὐτὸ τοῦτο δέ, **and besides this,** 2 Pet. i. 5 (*see* αὐτός).

See also εἰ δὲ μή, εἰ δὲ μή γε, ὁ δέ.

δέησις.

request, Phil. i. 4.
supplication, Acts i. 14(*omS*). Eph.

i. 18*t*. Phil. iv. 6. 1 Tim. ii. 1. v. 5.

prayer, Luke i. 13. ii. 37. v. 33. Rom. x. 1. 2 Cor. i. 11. ix. 14. Phil. i. 4, 19. 2 Tim. i. 3. Heb. v. 7. Jas. v. 16. 1 Pet. iii. 12

δεῖ.

Impersonal of δέω, commonly rendered by a change of construction; as "he *must* go," for "*it needs* that he go;" "ye *ought* to have done," for "*it behoved* you to do." The imperfect tense marked thus(²).

be needful, Acts xv. 5.

δέον ἐστίν, **be need,** 1 Pet. i. 6.—**ought,** Acts xix. 36.

must needs, Mark xiii. 7. John iv. 4². Acts i. 16². xvii. 3². xxi. 22. 2 Cor. xi. 30.

must, Matt. xvi. 21. xvii. 10. xxiv. 6. xxvi. 54. Mark viii. 31. ix. 11. xiii. 10. Luke ii. 49. iv. 43. ix. 22. xiii. 33. xvii. 25. xix. 5. xxi. 9. xxii. 7², 37. xxiv. 7, 44. John iii. 7, 14(-L^m), 30. iv. 24. ix. 4. x. 16. xii. 34. xx. 9. Acts i. 22(21). iii. 21. iv. 12. ix. 6, 16. xiv. 22. xvi. 30. xviii. 21(*ap*). xix. 21. xxiii. 11. xxvii. 24, 26.

1 Cor. xi. 19. xv. 25, 53. 2 Cor. v. 10. 1 Tim. iii. 2, 7. 2 Tim. ii. 6, 24. Tit. i. 7, 11. Heb. ix. 26². xi. 6. Rev. i. 1. iv. 1. x. 11. xi. 5. xiii. 10. xvii. 10. xx. 3. xxii. 6.

should, Matt. xviii. 33². xxvi. 35. Mark xiv. 31. Acts xxvii. 21².

ought, Matt. xxiii. 23². xxv. 27². Mark xiii. 14. Luke xi. 42². xii. 12. xiii. 14, 16². xviii. 1. xxiv. 26². John iv. 20. Acts v. 29. x. 6(*ap*). xx. 35. xxiv. 19². xxv. 10, 24. xxvi. 9. Rom. viii. 26. xii. 3. 1 Cor. viii. 2. 2 Cor. ii. 3². Eph. vi. 20. Col. iv. 4, 6. 1 Thes. iv. 1. 2 Thes. iii. 7. 1 Tim. iii. 15. Tit. i. 11. Heb. ii. 1. 2 Pet. iii. 11.

τὰ μὴ δέοντα, **things which they° ought not,** 1 Tim. v. 13.

be meet, Luke xv. 32². Rom. i. 27².

behove, Luke xxiv. 46²*t*(-G°L^bTTr*S*).

Add 2 Cor. xii. 1(*ap*).

δεῖγμα.

example, Jude 7.

δειγματίζω.

make a show of, Col. ii. 15.

Add Matt. i. 19, for παραδειγματίζω, G'LTTr.

δείκνυμι or δεικνύω.

show, Matt. iv. 8. viii. 4. xvi. 21. Mark i. 44. xiv. 15. Luke iv. 5. v. 14. xxii. 12. John ii. 18. v. 20*t*. x. 32. xiv. 8, 9. xx. 20. Acts vii. 3. x. 28. 1 Cor. xii. 31. 1 Tim. vi. 15. Heb. viii. 5. Jas. ii. 18*t*. iii. 13. Rev. i. 1. iv. 1. xvii. 1. xxi. 9, 10. xxii. 1, 6, 8.

Add, for ἐπιδείκνυμι, Luke xx. 24, GLTTr*S*. xxiv. 40, LTr*S*.—Luke xx. 24(*ap*).

δειλία.

fear, 2 Tim. i. 7.

δειλιάω.

be afraid, John xiv. 27.

δειλός.

fearful, Matt. viii. 26. Mark iv. 40. Rev. xxi. 8.

δεῖνα.

such a man, Matt. xxvi. 18.

δεινῶς.

vehemently, Luke xi. 53.

grievously, Matt. viii. 6.

δειπνέω.

sup, Luke xvii. 8. 1 Cor. xi. 25. Rev. iii. 20.

supper, Luke xxii. 20^inf.

δεῖπνον.

supper, Mark vi. 21. Luke xiv. 12, 16, 17, 24. John xii. 2. xiii. 2, 4. xxi. 20. 1 Cor. xi. 20, 21. Rev. xix. 9, 17.

feast, Matt. xxiii. 6. Mark xii. 39. Luke xx. 46.

Add Luke xi. 43(*ap*).

δεισιδαιμονία.

superstition, Acts xxv. 19.

δεισιδαίμων.
too superstitious, Acts xvii. 22comp.

δέκα.
ten, Matt. xx. 24. xxv. 1, 28. Mark x. 41. Luke xiv. 31. xv. 8. xvii. 12, 17. xix. 13*t*, 16, 17, 24, 25. Acts xxv. 6. Rev. ii. 10. xii. 3. xiii. 1*t*. xvii. 3, 7, 12*t*, 16.
δέκα καὶ ὀκτώ, **eighteen,** Luke xiii. 4, 11, 16.

δεκαέξ, sixteen. See χξς'.

δεκαδύο.
twelve, Acts xix. 7 (δώδεκα L*S*). xxiv. 11(δώδεκα L*S*).
Add Rev. xxi. 16, for δώδεκα, T.

δεκαπέντε.
fifteen, John xi. 18. Acts xxvii. 28. Gal. i. 18.

δεκατέσσαρες.
fourteen, Matt. i. 17*tr*. 2 Cor. xii. 2. Gal. ii. 1.

δεκάτη.
tenth part (*sc.* μερίς), Heb. vii. 2.
tenth, Heb. vii. 4.
tithe, Heb. vii. 8, 9.

δέκατος.
tenth, John i. 39(40). Rev. xi. 13. xxi. 20.

δεκατόω.
receive tithes of, Heb. vii. 6.
Pass., **pay tithes,** Heb. vii. 9.

δεκτός.
accepted, Luke iv. 24. Acts x. 35. 2 Cor. vi. 2.
acceptable, Luke iv. 19. Phil. iv. 18.

δελεάζω.
entice, Jas. i. 14.
beguile, 2 Pet. ii. 14.
allure, 2 Pet. ii. 18.

δένδρον.
tree, Matt. iii. 10*t*. vii. 17*t*, 18*t*, 19. xii. 33*tr*. xiii. 22. xxi. 8. Mark viii. 24. xi. 8(ἀγρός TTr*S*). Luke iii. 9*t*. vi. 43*t*, 44. xiii. 19. xxi. 29. Jude 12. Rev. vii. 1, 3. viii. 7. ix. 4.

δεξιολάβος.
spearman, Acts xxiii. 23.

δεξιός.
right, Matt. v. 29, 30, 39. Luke vi. 6. xxii. 50. John xviii. 10. xxi. 6. Acts iii. 7. Rev. i. 16, 17. x. 2. xiii. 16.
With χείρ *understood,* **right hand,** Matt. vi. 3. xxvii. 29. Acts ii. 33. v. 31. Rom. viii. 34. Gal. ii. 9. Eph. i. 20. Col. iii. 1. Heb. i. 3. viii. 1. x. 12. xii. 2. 1 Pet. iii. 22. Rev. i. 20. ii. 1. v. 1, 7.
With μέρη *understood,* **right side,** Mark xvi. 5. Luke i. 11.—**right hand,** Matt. xx. 21, 23. xxii. 44. xxv. 33, 34. xxvi. 64. xxvii. 38. Mark x. 37, 40. xii. 36. xiv. 62. xv. 27. xvi. 19(*op*). Luke xx. 42. xxii. 69. xxiii. 33. Acts ii. 25, 34. vii. 55, 56. 2 Cor. vi. 7. Heb. i. 13.
Add Rev. x. 5(. . hand), GLTTr*S*.

δέομαι.
make request, Rom. i. 10.
beseech, Luke v. 12. viii. 28, 38. ix. 38, 40. Acts xxi. 39. xxvi. 3. 2 Cor. x. 2. Gal. iv. 12.
pray, Matt. ix. 38. Luke x. 2. xxi. 36. xxii. 32. Acts iv. 31p. viii. 22, 24, 34. x. 2. 2 Cor. v. 20. viii. 4. 1 Thes. iii. 10.

δέος, fear.
Heb. xii. 28, for αἰδώς, G''LT*S*.

δέρμα.
With αἴγειος, **goatskin,** Heb. xi. 37.

δερμάτινος.
of a skin, Mark i. 6.
leathern, Matt. iii. 4.

δέρω.
beat, Matt. xxi. 35. Mark xii. 3, 5. xiii. 9. Luke xii. 47, 48. xx. 10, 11. Acts v. 40. xvi. 37. xxii. 19. 1 Cor. ix. 26.
smite, Luke xxii. 63. John xviii. 23. 2 Cor. xi. 20.

δεσμεύω.
bind, Matt. xxiii. 4. Acts xxii. 4.

δεσμέω.
bind[cc], Luke viii. 29.

δέσμη.
bundle, Matt. xiii. 30.

δέσμιος.
in bonds, Acts xxv. 14.
that is in bonds, Heb. xiii. 3.
prisoner, Matt. xxvii. 15, 16. Mark xv. 6. Acts xvi. 25, 27. xxiii. 18. xxv. 27. xxviii. 16(*ap*), 17. Eph. iii. 1. iv. 1. 2 Tim. i. 8. Phm. 1, 9.
Add Heb. x. 34, for δεσμοῖς μοῦ, GLT.

δεσμός.
(Neuter plural marked [n].)
band, Luke viii. 29[n]. Acts xvi. 26[n]. xxii. 30(*omS*).
string, Mark vii. 35.
bond, Luke xiii. 16. Acts xx. 23[n]. xxiii. 29. xxvi. 29, 31. Phil. i. 7, 13, 14, 16. Col. iv. 18. 2 Tim. ii. 9. Phm. 10, 13. Heb. x. 34 (*see* δέσμιος). xi. 36.
chain, Jude 6.

δεσμοφύλαξ.
keeper of the prison, Acts xvi. 27. 36.
jailor, Acts xvi. 23.

δεσμωτήριον.
prison, Matt. xi. 2. Acts v. 21, 23. xvi. 26.

δεσμώτης.
prisoner, Acts xxvii. 1, 42.

δεσπότης.
master, 1 Tim. vi. 1, 2. 2 Tim. ii. 21. Tit. ii. 9. 1 Pet. ii. 18.
Lord, Luke ii. 29. Acts iv. 24. 2 Pet. ii. 1. Jude 4. Rev. vi. 10.

δεῦρο.
ἄχρι τοῦ δεῦρο, **hitherto**, Rom. i. 13.
come hither, Rev. xvii. 1. xxi. 9.
come, Matt. xix. 21. Mark x. 21. Luke xviii. 22. John xi. 43. Acts vii. 3, 34.

δεῦτε.
come, Matt. xi. 28. xxi. 38. xxii. 4. xxv. 34. xxviii. 6. Mark i. 17. vi. 31. xii. 7. Luke xx. 14(–G[o]LTTr). John iv. 29. xxi. 12. Rev. xix. 17.
With ὀπίσω, **follow**, Matt. iv. 19.

δευτεραῖος.
the next day[cc], Acts xxviii. 13.

δευτερόπρωτος.
second after the first, Luke vi. 1 (–L[b]Tr[b]*S*).

δεύτερος.
second, Matt. xxi. 30(G′, ἕτερος G T*S*). xxii. 26, 39. Mark xii. 21, 31. Luke xii. 38. xix. 18. xx. 30. John iv. 54. Acts vii. 13. xii. 10. xiii. 33 (G′, πρῶτος GLT). 1 Cor. xv. 47. 2 Cor. i. 15. Tit. iii. 10. Heb. viii. 7. ix. 3, 7. x. 9. 2 Pet. iii. 1. Rev. ii. 11. iv. 7. vi. 3*t*. viii. 8. xi. 14. xvi. 3. xx. 6, 14. xxi. 8, 19.
Neut., **the second time**, John iii. 4. xxi. 16. 2 Cor. xiii. 2.—**secondarily**, 1 Cor. xii. 28.—**again**, Rev. xix. 3.—**afterward**, Jude 5.
ἐκ δευτέρου, **the second time**, Matt. xxvi. 42. Mark xiv. 72. Acts x. 15. Heb. ix. 28.—**again**, John ix. 24. Acts xi. 9.
Add Rev. xiv. 8(another..), LT*S*.

δέχομαι.
receive, Matt. x. 14. 40*f*, 41*t*. xi. 14. xviii. 5*t*. Mark vi. 11. ix. 37*f*. x. 15. Luke viii. 13. ix. 5, 11(ἀποδέχομαι LTTr*S*), 48*f*, 53. x. 8, 10. xvi. 4, 9. xviii. 17. John iv. 45. Acts iii. 21. vii. 38, 59. viii. 14. xi. 1. xvii. 11. xxi. 17(ἀποδέχομαι G″ LT*S*). xxii. 5. xxviii. 21. 1 Cor. ii. 14. 2 Cor. vi. 1. vii. 15. viii. 4(*om S*). xi. 16 (*marg.* **suffer**). Gal. iv. 14. Phil. iv. 18. Col. iv. 10. 1 Thes. i. 6. ii. 13. 2 Thes. ii. 10. Heb. xi. 31[p]. Jas. i. 21.
accept, 2 Cor. viii. 17. xi. 4.
take, Luke ii. 28. xvi. 6, 7. xxii. 17. Eph. vi. 17(–G[o]).

δέω.
bind, Matt. xii. 29. xiii. 30. xiv. 3, xvi. 19*t*. xviii. 18*t*. xxii. 13. xxvii. 2[p]. Mark iii. 27. v. 3, 4. vi. 17. xv. 1, 7. Luke xiii. 16. John xi. 44. xviii. 12, 24. Acts ix. 2, 14. 21.

xii. 6. xx. 22. xxi. 11*t*, 13, 33. xxii. 5, 29. xxiv. 27. Rom. vii. 2. 1 Cor. vii. 27, 39. 2 Tim. ii. 9. Rev. ix. 14. xx. 2.
Perf. pass., **be in bonds**, Col. iv. 3.
tie, Matt. xxi. 2. Mark xi. 2, 4. Luke xix. 30.
wind, John xix. 40.
knit, Acts x. 11(-G∞L*S*).

δή.

doubtless, 2 Cor. xii. 1(*ap*).
now, Luke ii. 15.
therefore, 1 Cor. vi. 20.
also, Matt. xiii. 23.
and, Acts xv. 36.
Not rendered, Acts xiii. 2.
Add Acts vi. 3, for οὖν, L. Rev. xi. 10(behold . .), Tr.
See also δήποτε, δήπου.

δῆλος.

manifest, 1 Cor. xv. 27.
With ποιέω, **bewray**, Matt. xxvi. 73.
evident, Gal. iii. 11.
certain, 1 Tim. vi. 7(-G°L*S*).

δηλόω.

declare, 1 Cor. i. 11. iii. 13. Col. i. 8.
show, 2 Pet. i. 14.
signify, Heb. ix. 8. xii. 27. 1 Pet. i. 11.

δημηγορέω.

make an oration, Acts xii. 21.

δημιουργός.

maker, Heb. xi. 10.

δῆμος.

people, Acts xii. 22. xvii. 5. xix. 30, 33.

δημόσιος.

common, Acts v. 18.
δημοσίᾳ, **publicly**, Acts xviii. 28. xx. 20.—**openly**, Acts xvi. 37.

δηνάριον.

penny, Matt. xviii. 28. xx. 2, 9, 10, 13. xxii. 19. Mark vi. 37. xii. 15. xiv. 5. Luke vii. 41. x. 35. xx. 24. John xii. 5. Rev. vi. 6*t*.
Genit. plural, **pennyworth**[cc], John vi. 7.

δήποτε or δή ποτε.

With ᾧ fr. ὅς, **whatsoever**, John v. 4(οἱῳδηποτοῦν L; *ap*).

δήπου or δή που.

verily, Heb. ii. 16.

διά.

I. With the Genitive.

through, Matt. xii. 1, 43. xix. 24. Mark ii. 23. ix. 30. x. 25. xi. 16. Luke iv. 30. v. 19. vi. 1. xi. 24. xvii. 1, 11. xviii. 25. John i. 7. iii. 17. iv. 4. viii. 59. xvii. 20. Acts i. 2. viii. 18. x. 43. xiii. 38. xiv. 22. xv. 11. xviii. 27. xx. 3. xxi. 4.
Rom. i. 8. ii. 23. iii. 24, 25, 30, 31. iv. 13*t*. v. 1, 9, 11, 21. vii. 25. viii. 3, 37. xi. 36. xii. 3. xv. 4. xvi. 27. 1 Cor. i. 1. iv. 15. x. 1. xiii. 12. xv. 57. 2 Cor. iii. 4. ix. 11. xi. 33. Gal. ii. 19. iii. 14. iv. 7(*ap*). Eph. i. 7. ii. 8, 18. iv. 6. Phil. i. 19. iii. 9. Col. i. 14(*ap*), 20, 22. ii. 8, 12. 2 Tim. i. 10. iii. 15. Tit. iii. 6. Phm. 22.
Heb. ii. 10, 14. vi. 12. ix. 14. x. 10, 20. xi. 33, 39. xiii. 21. 1 Pet. i. 5, 22(-G∞LT*S*). iv. 11. 2 Pet. i. 3. 1 John iv. 9.
throughout[c], John xix. 23. Acts ix. 32. xiii. 49. 2 Cor. viii. 18.
διὰ παντός (διαπαντός G), **always**, Matt. xviii. 10. Acts ii. 25. 2 Thes. iii. 16.
διὰ παντὸς τοῦ ζῆν, **all their**[c] **lifetime**, Heb. ii. 15.—δι' ὅλης τῆς νυκτός, **all the night**, Luke v. 5.—δι' ἡμερῶν τεσσ., **forty days**, Acts i. 3.
after, Acts xxiv. 17. Gal. ii. 1.
after [c]**some**, Mark ii. 1.
by, Matt. i. 22. ii. 5, 15, 23. iv. 14. viii. 17, 28. xii. 17. xiii. 35. xviii. 7. xxi. 4. xxiv. 15. xxvi. 24. xxvii. 9. Mark vi. 2. x. 1(καί for διὰ τοῦ LT Tr*S*). xiv. 21. Luke i. 70. v. 19 (*omS*). viii. 4. xviii. 31. xxii. 22. John i. 3, 10, 17*t*. x. 1, 2, 9. xiv. 6. Acts i. 16. ii. 16, 22, 23, 43. iii. 16, 18, 21. iv. 16, 25, 30. v. 12, 19.

vii. 25. **ix.** 25. **x.** 36. **xi.** 28, 30. xii. 9(ὑπό T). xiv. 3. **xv.** 7, 12, 23, 27. xvii. 10. xviii. 9, 28. xix. 11. xxi. 19. xxiii. 31. xxiv. 2*t*. xxviii. 25.

Rom. i. 2, 5, 12. ii. 12, 16, 27. iii. 20, 22, 27*t*. v. 2, 5, 10, 11, 12*t*, 16, 17*t*, 18*t*, 19*t*, 21. vi. 4*t*. vii. 4, 5, 7, 8, 11*t*, 13*t*. x. 17. xii. 1. xv. 18, 28, 32. xvi. 18, 26. 1 Cor. i. 9, 10, 21*t*. ii. 10. iii. 5, 15. vi. 14. viii. 6*t*. x. 1. xi. 12. xii. 8. xiv. 9. xv. 2, 21*t*. xvi. 3. 2 Cor. i. 1, 4, 5, 11, 16, 19*t*, 20. ii. 14. iv. 14(σύν G′LT*S*). v. 7*t*, 18, 20. vi. 7, 8*t*. viii. 5. ix. 12, 13. x. 1, 9, 11. xi. 33. xii. 17.

Gal. i. 1*t*, 12, 15. ii. 16, 21. iii. 18, 19, 26. iv. 23. v. 6, 13. vi. 14(δι' οὗ, *marg.* **whereby**). Eph. i. 1, 5. ii. 16. iii. 6, 9(*ap*), 10, 12, 16, 17. iv. 16. vi. 18. Phil. i. 11, 20*t*, 26. Col. i. 1, 16, 20, 20(–G∘L). ii. 19. iii. 17. 1 Thes. iii. 7. iv. 2. v. 9. 2 Thes. ii. 2*tr*, 14, 15t. iii. 12(ἐν G′LT*S*), 14. 1 Tim. iv. 5, 14. 2 Tim. i. 1, 6, 10, 14. iv. 17. Tit. iii. 5. Phm. 7.

Heb. i. 2, 3(–L*S*). ii. 2, 3, 10. iii. 16. vi. 18. vii. 11, 19, 21, 25. ix. 11, 12*t*, 26. xi. 4*t*, 7, 29. xiii. 11, 15. Jas. ii. 12. 1 Pet. i. 3, 12, 21, 23. ii. 5, 14. iii. 1, 20, 21. v. 12. 2 Pet. i. 4. 1 John v. 6. Rev. i. 1.

With αὐτός, **thereby**, John xi. 4. Heb. xii. 11.—**thereat**, Matt. vii. 13. *With* οὗτος, **thereby**, Heb xii. 15. xiii. 2.

With ὅς, **whereby**, Heb. xii. 28. 2 Pet. i. 4. iii. 6.

δι' ἄλλης ὁδοῦ, **another way**, Matt. ii. 12. —δι' ἐκείνης, **that way**, Luke xix. 4(δι' *omS*).

for, Rom. xv. 30.

for . . sake, Rom. xv. 30. 2 John 2.

from, 2 Thes. ii. 2.

of, Rom. xiv. 14.

out of[c], Matt. iv. 4.

by occasion of, 2 Cor. viii. 8.

with, Mark xvi. 20(*ap*). Acts viii. 20. **xv.** 32. **xix.** 26. **xx.** 28. Rom. viii. 25. xiv. 20. 1 Cor. **xiv.** 19(–G′L*S*). 2 Cor. ii. 4. Eph. vi. 18. 1 Tim. ii. 10. Heb. xii. 1. xiii. 12. 1 Pet. i. 7. 2 John 12. 3 John 13.

to, 2 Pet. i. 3 (*marg.* **by**; ἰδίᾳ G″LT*S*).

at, Matt. vii. 13. Luke xiii. 24.

in, Matt. **xxvi.** 61. Acts **xvi.** 9. 2 Cor. v. 10(ἰδια L[m]). 1 Thes. iv. 14. 1 Tim. ii. 15. Heb. vii. 9. xiii. 22. 2 Pet. iii. 5.

within, Mark xiv. 58.

among (*marg.* **by**), 2 Tim. ii. 2.

Add, for δύο, Matt. xi. 2, G′LTTr*S*. For ἐν, Rev. xxi. 24, GLTTr*S*. For ὑπό, Matt. ii. 17, iii. 3, G′LTTr*S*.—Mark vii. 31(. . Sidon), G′LTTr*S*. Rom. xv. 4(. . comfort), G″L*S*. 2 Cor. i. 20(*ap*). 2 Pet. i. 10(*ap*). Jude 25(*ap*).

See also ἀκροβυστία, διαπαντός, ὀλίγος, ὅλος.

II. With the Accusative.

because of, Matt. xiii. 21, 58. xvii. 20. xxvii. 19. Mark iii. 9. vi. 6. Luke v. 19. xi. 8. John iii. 29. iv. 41, 42. vii. 43. xi. 42. xii. 30, 42. xix. 42. Acts iv. 21. xvi. 3. xxviii. 2. Rom. vi. 19. viii. 10*t*. xv. 15. 1 Cor. xi. 10. Gal. ii. 4. Eph. iv. 18. v. 6. Heb. iii. 19. iv. 6.

With an Infinitive, **because**[cc], Matt. xiii. 5, 6. xxiv. 12. Mark iv. 5, 6. v. 4. Luke ii. 4. viii. 6. ix. 7. xi. 8. xviii. 5. xix. 11. xxiii. 8. John ii. 24. Acts xii. 20. xviii. 3. xxvii. 4, 9. xxviii. 18. Phil. i. 7. Heb. vii. 24. x. 2. Jas. iv. 2.—**because that**[cc], Acts viii. 11. xviii. 2.—**that**[cc], Acts iv. 2.—**by reason of**, Heb. vii. 23.

διὰ τοῦτο, **for this cause**, John xii. 18, 27. Rom. i. 26. xiii. 6. xv. 9. 1 Cor. iv. 17. xi. 10, 30. Col. i. 9. 1 Thes. ii. 13. iii. 5. 2 Thes. ii. 11. 1 Tim. i. 16. Heb. ix. 15.—**therefore**, Matt. vi. 25. xii. 27. xiii. 13, 52. xiv. 2. xviii. 23. xxi. 43. **xxiii. 14(13,** *ap***).**

xxiv. 44. Mark vi. 14. xi. 24. xii. 24. Luke xi. 19, 49. xii. 22. xiv. 20. John i. 31. v. 16, 18. vi. 65. vii. 22. viii. 47. ix. 23. x. 17. xii. 39. xiii. 11. xv. 19. xvi. 15. xix. 11. Acts ii. 26. Rom. iv. 16. 2 Cor. iv. 1. vii. 13. xiii. 10. 1 Thes. iii. 7. 2 Tim. ii. 10. Phm. 15. Heb. i. 9. ii. 1. 1 John iii. 1. iv. 5. Rev. vii. 15. xii. 12. xviii. 8. —**wherefore**, Matt. xii. 31. xxiii. 34. Rom. v. 12. Eph. i. 15. v. 17. vi. 13. 2 Tim. i. 6. 3 John 10.

δι' ἣν αἰτίαν, **wherefore**, Tit. i. 13.

δι' ἥν, **wherefore**, Acts x. 21. xxii. 24. xxiii. 28.—**wherein**, 2 Pet. iii. 12.

by reason of, John xii. 11. Rom. viii. 20. Heb. v. 14. 2 Pet. ii. 2.

διὰ ταύτην, **by reason hereof**, Heb. v. 3 (*δι' αὐτήν* LTS).

to avoid, *ital.* (*lit.* on account of), 1 Cor. vii. 2.

for, Matt. xxvii. 18. Mark ii. 4, 27*t*. vii. 29. xv. 10. Luke viii. 19, 47. xxiii. 19, 25. John iv. 39. vii. 13. x. 19, 32. xvi. 21. xix. 38. xx. 19. Acts xxi. 34, 35. xxviii. 20. Rom. iii. 25. iv. 24, 25*t*. xiii. 5. 1 Cor. vii. 5, 26. viii. 11. xi. 9*t*. 2 Cor. iii. 7. ix. 14. Eph. ii. 4. Phil. i. 24. ii. 30. iii. 7, 8*t*. Col. i. 5. iv. 3. 2 Tim. i. 12. Heb. i. 14. ii. 9(*marg.* **by**), 11. v. 12. vii. 18. 1 Pet. i. 20. ii. 19. Rev. i. 9, 9(–G° LTTr). ii. 3. iv. 11. vi. 9, 9(–L). xviii. 10. 15. xx. 4*t*.

for . . sake, Matt. x. 22. xiv. 3, 9. xix. 12. xxiv. 9, 22. Mark iv. 17. vi. 17, 26. xiii. 13, 20. Luke xxi. 17. John xi. 15. xii. 9, 30. xiv. 11. xv. 21. Rom. iv. 23. xi. 28*t*. xiii. 5. 1 Cor. iv. 6, 10. ix. 10*t*, 23. x. 25, 27, 28. 2 Cor. ii. 10. iv. 5, 11, 15. viii. 9. Col. iii. 6 (*see* διό). 1 Thes. i. 5. iii. 9. v. 13. 1 Tim. v. 23. 2 Tim. ii. 10. Phm. 9. 1 Pet. ii. 13. iii. 14. 1 John ii. 12. 2 John 2.

through, Luke i. 78. John xv. 3. Rom. ii. 24. 2 Cor. iv. 15(*genit.* G). Gal. iv. 13. Eph. iv. 18.

of, Phil. i. 15*t*.

by, Matt. xv. 3, 6. John vi. 57*t*. Rom. viii. 11 (*marg.* **because of**). Heb. vi. 7(*marg.* **for**). Rev. xii. 11*t*. xiii. 14.

with, Rom. xiv. 15.

Add Luke vi. 48(*ap*). xx. 5, *see* διατί. 2 Pet. iii. 9, for εἰς, G''LS.

διαβαίνω.

pass through, Heb. xi. 29.
pass, Luke xvi. 26.
come over, Acts xvi. 9.

διαβάλλω.

accuse, Luke xvi. 1.

διαβεβαιόομαι.

affirm constantly, Tit. iii. 8.
affirm, 1 Tim. i. 7.

διαβλέπω.

see clearly, Matt. vii. 5. Luke vi. 42.

Add Mark viii. 25, διέβλεψεν for ἐποίησεν αὐτὸν ἀναβλέψαι(–G°), TTrS.

διάβολος.

false accuser (*marg.* **makebate**), 2 Tim. iii. 3. Tit. ii. 3.
slanderer, 1 Tim. iii. 11.
devil, Matt. iv. 1, 5, 8, 11. xiii. 39. xxv. 41. Luke iv. 2, 3, 5(*ap*), 6, 13. viii. 12. John vi. 70. viii. 44. xiii. 2. Acts x. 38. xiii. 10. Eph. iv. 27. vi. 11. 1 Tim. iii. 6, 7. 2 Tim. ii. 26. Heb. ii. 14. Jas. iv. 7. 1 Pet. v. 8. 1 John iii. 8*tr*, 10. Jude 9. Rev. ii. 10. xii. 9, 12. xx. 2, 10.

διάγε.

Luke xi. 8, for διά γε, G.

διαγγέλλω.

declare, Rom. ix. 17.
preach, Luke ix. 60.
signify, Acts xxi. 26.

διαγίνομαι.

be past, Mark xvi. 1[p].
be spent, Acts xxvii. 9[p].
ἡμερῶν διαγενομένων τινῶν, **after certain days**, Acts xxv. 13[p].

διαγινώσκω.
know the uttermost, Acts xxiv. 22.
inquire, Acts xxiii. 15.

διαγνωρίζω.
make known abroad, Luke ii. 17 (γνωρίζω LTr*S*).

διάγνωσις.
hearing (*marg.* **judgment**), Acts xxv. 21.

διαγογγύζω.
murmur, Luke xv. 2. xix. 7.

διαγρηγορέω.
be awake, Luke ix. 32p.

διάγω.
lead a life, 1 Tim. ii. 2.
live, Tit. iii. 3.

διαδέχομαι.
come after, Acts vii. 45.

διάδημα.
crown, Rev. xii. 3. xiii. 1. xix. 12.

διαδίδωμι.
distribute, Luke xviii. 22 (δίδωμι L*S*). John vi. 11.
make distribution, Acts iv. 35.
divide, Luke xi. 22.
give, Rev. xvii. 13 (διδόασιν fr. δίδωμι GLTTr*S*).

διάδοχος.
With λαμβάνω,[co] **come into one's room** (*lit.* receive a successor), Acts xxiv. 27.

διαζώννυμι.
gird unto one's self, John xxi. 7.
gird, John xiii. 4, 5.

διαθήκη.
testament, Matt. xxvi. 28. Mark xiv. 24. Luke xxii. 20. 1 Cor. xi. 25. 2 Cor. iii. 6, 14. Heb. vii. 22. ix. 15*t*, 16, 17, 20. Rev. xi. 19.
covenant (*marg.* **testament**, marked [m]), Luke i. 72. Acts iii. 25. vii. 8. Rom. ix. 4[m]. xi. 27. Gal. iii. 15[m], 17. iv. 24[m]. Eph. ii. 12. Heb. viii. 6[m], 8, 9*t*, 10. ix. 4*t*. x. 16, 29. xii. 24[m]. xiii. 20[m].

διαίρεσις.
difference, 1 Cor. xii. 5.
diversity, 1 Cor. xii. 4, 6.

διαιρέω.
divide, Luke xv. 12. 1 Cor. xii. 11.

διακαθαρίζω.
throughly purge, Matt. iii. 12. Luke iii. 17.

διακατελέγχομαι.
convince, Acts xviii. 28.

διακονέω.
minister unto, Matt. iv. 11. viii. 15. xx. 28. xxv. 44. xxvii. 55. Mark i. 13, 31. x. 45. xv. 41. Luke iv. 39. viii. 3. Acts xix. 22. Rom. xv. 25. 2 Tim. i. 18. Phm. 13.
minister to, Heb. vi. 10.
minister, Matt. xx. 28. Mark x. 45. 2 Cor. iii. 3. Heb. vi. 10. 1 Pet. i. 12. iv. 10, 11.
administer, 2 Cor. viii. 19, 20.
serve, Luke x. 40. xii. 37. xvii. 8. xxii. 26, 27*t*. John xii. 2, 26*t*. Acts vi. 2.
use the office of a deacon, 1 Tim. iii. 10, 13(*marg.* **minister**).

διακονία.
ministering, Rom. xii. 7. 2 Cor. viii. 4. ix. 1.
ministration, Acts vi. 1. 2 Cor. iii. 7, 8, 9*t*. ix. 13.
With εἰς, **to minister**, Heb. i. 14.
serving, Luke x. 40.
service, Rom. xv. 31(δωροφορία L). Rev. ii. 19.
With πρός, **to do service**, 2 Cor. xi. 8.
relief, Acts xi. 29.
administration, 1 Cor. xii. 5. 2 Cor. ix. 12.
ministry, Acts i. 17, 25. vi. 4. xii. 25(*marg.* **charge**). xx. 24. xxi. 19. Rom. xii. 7. 1 Cor. xvi. 15. 2 Cor. iv. 1. v. 18. vi. 3. Eph. iv. 12. Col. iv. 17. 1 Tim. i. 12. 2 Tim. iv. 5, 11.
office, Rom. xi. 13.

διάκονος.
minister, Matt. xx. 26. Mark x. 43. Rom. xiii. 4*t*. xv. 8. 1 Cor. iii. 5. 2 Cor. iii. 6. vi. 4. xi. 15*t*, 23. Gal. ii. 17. Eph. iii. 7. vi. 21. Col. i. 7,

23, 25. iv. 7. 1 Thes. iii. 2(*ap*). 1 Tim. iv. 6.
servant, Matt. xxii. 13. xxiii. 11. Mark ix. 35. John ii. 5, 9. xii. 26. Rom. xvi. 1.
deacon, Phil. i. 1. 1 Tim. iii. 8, 12.

διακόσιοι.

two hundred, Mark vi. 37. John vi. 7. xxi. 8. Acts xxiii. 23*t*. xxvii. 37. Rev. xi. 3. xii. 6.

διακούω.

hear, Acts xxiii. 35.

διακρίνω.

make to differ, 1 Cor. iv. 7(*Gr.* distinguish).
put a difference, Acts xv. 9.
discern, Matt. xvi. 3. 1 Cor. xi. 29.
judge, 1 Cor. vi. 5. xi. 31. xiv. 29.

Mid., and Pass. aor.

make a difference, Jude 22.
be partial, Jas. ii. 4.
contend, Acts xi. 2. Jude 9.
doubt, Matt. xxi. 21. Mark xi. 23. Acts x. 20. xi. 12(−G°T). Rom. xiv. 23(*marg.* **discern, and put a difference between meats**).
waver, Jas. i. 6*t*.
stagger, Rom. iv. 20.

διάκρισις.

discerning, 1 Cor. xii. 10.
With πρός, **to discern**, Heb. v. 14.
disputation(*marg. with* εἰς, **to judge**), Rom. xiv. 1.

διακωλύω.

forbid, Matt. iii. 14.

διαλαλέω.

commune, Luke vi. 11.
noise abroad, Luke i. 65.

διαλέγομαι.

reason with, Acts xvii. 2. xviii. 19.
reason, Acts xviii. 4. xxiv. 25p.
dispute, Mark ix. 34. Acts xvii. 17. xix. 8, 9. xxiv. 12. Jude 9.
speak, Heb. xii. 5.
preach, Acts xx. 7, 9p.

διαλείπω.

cease, Luke vii. 45.

διάλεκτος.

language, Acts ii. 6.
tongue, Acts i. 19. ii. 8. xxi. 40. xxii. 2. xxvi. 14.

διαλλάττομαι.

be reconciled, Matt. v. 24.

διαλογίζομαι.

to reason, Matt. xvi. 7, 8. xxi. 25. Mark ii. 6, 8*t*. viii. 16, 17. Luke v. 21, 22. xx. 14.
consider, John xi. 50 (λογίζομαι G″ LTTr*S*).
think, Luke xii. 17.
muse(*marg.* **reason**, *or* **debate**), Luke iii. 15.
cast in one's mind, Luke i. 29.
dispute, Mark ix. 33.
Add Mark xi. 31, for λογίζομαι, G′LTTr, προσλογίζομαι *S*.

διαλογισμός.

reasoning, Luke ix. 46.
thought, Matt. xv. 19. Mark vii. 21. Luke ii. 35. v. 22. vi. 8. ix. 47. xxiv. 38. 1 Cor. iii. 20. Jas. ii. 4.
imagination, Rom. i. 21.
doubting, 1 Tim. ii. 8.
doubtfulcc(*marg.* **doubtful thoughts**), Rom. xiv. 1.
disputing, Phil. ii. 14.

διαλύω.

scatter, Acts v. 36.

διαμαρτύρομαι.

witness, Acts xx. 23.
testify, Luke xvi. 28. Acts ii. 40. viii. 25p. x. 42. xviii. 5. xx. 21, 24. xxiii. 11. xxviii. 23. 1 Thes. iv. 6. Heb. ii. 6.
charge, 1 Tim. v. 21. 2 Tim. ii. 14. iv. 1.

διαμάχομαι.

strive, Acts xxiii. 9.

διαμένω.

remain, Luke i. 22. Heb. i. 11.
continue, Luke xxii. 28. Gal. ii. 5. 2 Pet. iii. 4.

διαμερίζω.

divide, Luke xi. 17, 18. xii. 52, 53. xxii. 17.

part, Matt. xxvii. 35, 35(*ap*). Mark xv. 24. Luke xxiii. 34. John xix. 24. Acts ii. 45.
Pass., **cloven**, Acts ii. 3p.

διαμερισμός.

division, Luke xii. 51.

διανέμω.

Pass., **spread**, Acts iv. 17.

διανεύω.

With εἰμί, **beckon**, Luke i. 22p.

διανόημα.

thought, Luke xi. 17.

διάνοια.

mind, Matt. xxii. 37. Mark xii. 30. Luke x. 27. Eph. ii. 3. Col. i. 21. Heb. viii. 10. x. 16. 1 Pet. i. 13. 2 Pet. iii. 1.
understanding, Eph. i. 18 (καρδία GLTS). iv. 18. 1 John v. 20.
imagination, Luke i. 51.

διανοίγω.

to open, Mark vii. 34, 35(ἠνοίγησαν LTTr, ἠνύγησαν S, fr. ἀνοίγω). Luke ii. 23. xxiv. 31, 32, 45. Acts xvi. 14. xvii. 3.
Add Acts vii. 56, for ἀνοίγω, LTS.

διανυκτερεύω.

continue all night, Luke vi. 12.

διανύω.

finish, Acts xxi. 7p.

διαπαντός.

always *or* **alway**, Mark v. 5(διὰ παντός LT). Acts x. 2(διὰ π. LT). xxiv. 16(διὰ π. LT). Rom. xi. 10 (διὰ π. LT). Heb. ix. 6 (διὰ π. LT).
continually, Luke xxiv. 53. Heb. xiii. 15(διὰ π. LT).
See also διὰ παντός.

διαπαρατριβή, wrangling.
1 Tim. vi. 5, for παραδιατ., GLTS.

διαπεράω.

pass over, Matt. ix. 1. Mark v. 21p. vi. 53p.
canc **pass**, Luke xvi. 26.
go over, Matt. xiv. 34p.
sail over, Acts xxi. 2.

διαπλέω.

sail over, Acts xxvii. 5p.

διαπονέομαι.

be grieved, Acts iv. 2. xvi. 18.

διαπορεύομαι.

go through, Luke vi. 1. xiii. 22. Acts xvi. 4.
pass by, Luke xviii. 36.
in one's journey, Rom. xv. 24p.

διαπορέω.

be perplexed, Luke ix. 7.
Pass., **be much perplexed**, Luke xxiv. 4inf(ἀπορέω LTTrS).
be in doubt, Acts ii. 12.
doubt, Acts v. 24. x. 17.

διαπραγματεύομαι.

gain by trading, Luke xix. 15.

διαπρίομαι.

be cut to the heart, Acts v. 33.
be cut, Acts vii. 54.

διαρπάζω.

to spoil, Matt. xii. 29(ἁρπάζω LT, ἁρπάζω Tr), 29(ἁρπάζω LT). Mark iii. 27*t*.

διαρρήσσω or διαρρήγνυμι.

rend, Matt. xxvi. 65. Mark xiv. 63. Acts xiv. 14.
break, Luke viii. 29.
Mid., **break**, Luke v. 6.

διασαφέω.

tell, Matt. xviii. 31.
Add Matt. xiii. 36, for φράζω, LTrS.

διασείω.

do violence to (*marg.* **put in fear**), Luke iii. 14.

διασκορπίζω.

scatter abroad, Matt. xxvi. 31. John xi. 52.
scatter, Mark xiv. 27. Luke i. 51.
disperse, Acts v. 37.
waste, Luke xv. 13. xvi. 1.
strew, Matt. xxv. 24, 26.

διασπάω.

pluck asunder, Mark v. 4.
pull in pieces, Acts xxiii. 10.

διασπείρω.

scatter abroad, Acts viii. 1, 4. xi. 19.

διασπορά.

With ἐν, **which are scattered abroad,** Jas. i. 1.

scattered[cc], 1 Pet. i. 1.

dispersed[cc], John vii. 35.

διαστέλλομαι.

Mid., **charge,** Matt. xvi. 20 (ἐπιτιμάω G"L). Mark v. 43. vii. 36*t*. viii. 15. ix. 9.—**give commandment,** Acts xv. 24.

Pass., **be commanded,** Heb. xii. 20.

διάστημα.

space, Acts v. 7.

διαστολή.

distinction, 1 Cor. xiv. 7.

difference, Rom. iii. 22. x. 12

διαστρέφω.

turn away, Acts xiii. 8.

pervert, Luke xxiii. 2. Acts xiii 10.

Pass. part., **perverse,** Matt. xvii. 17. Luke ix. 41. Acts xx. 30. Phil. ii. 15.

διασώζω.

bring safe, Acts xxiii. 24.

save, Acts xxvii. 43. 1 Pet. iii. 20.

Pass., **escape safe,** Acts xxvii. 44. —**escape,** Acts xxviii. 1p, 4p.

make perfectly whole, Matt. xiv. 36.

heal, Luke vii. 3.

διαταγή.

disposition, Acts vii. 53.

ordinance, Rom. xiii. 2.

διάταγμα.

commandment, Heb. xi. 23(δόγμα L).

διαταράσσω or -ττω.

to trouble, Luke i. 29.

διατάσσω.

give order, 1 Cor. xvi. 1.—**ordain,** 1 Cor. ix. 14. Gal. iii. 19.—**appoint,** Luke iii. 13. Acts xx. 13(*pass., with* εἰμί). — **command,** Matt. xi. 1. Luke viii. 55. xvii. 9, 10. Acts xviii. 2. xxiii. 31. . . . *Mid.*, **set in order,** 1 Cor. xi. 34.—**ordain,** 1 Cor. vii. 17.—**appoint,** Acts vii. 44. Tit. i. 5.—**command,** Acts xxiv. 23.

διατελέω.

continue, Acts xxvii. 33.

διατηρέω.

keep, Luke ii. 51. Acts xv. 29p.

διατί.

wherefore? Luke xix. 23. Rom. ix. 32. 2 Cor. xi. 11. Rev. xvii. 7.

why? Matt. ix. 11, 14. xiii. 10. xv. 2, 3. xvii. 19. xxi. 25. Mark ii. 18. vii. 5. xi. 31. Luke v. 30, 33(-TTr[b]). xix. 31. xx. 5(διὰ τί LT Tr). xxiv. 38. John vii. 45. viii. 43, 46. xii. 5. xiii. 37. Acts v. 3. 1 Cor. vi. 7*t*.

διατίθεμαι.

appoint, Luke xxii. 29*t*.

make[c], Acts iii. 25. Heb. viii. 10. x. 16.

testator, Heb. ix. 16p, 17p.

διατρίβω.

be (*lit.* spend), Acts xxv. 14.

tarry, John iii. 22. Acts xxv. 6p.

continue, John xi. 54. Acts xv. 35.

abide, Acts xii. 19. xiv. 3, 28. xvi. 12. xx. 6.

διατροφή.

food, 1 Tim. vi. 8.

διαυγάζω.

to dawn, 2 Pet. i. 19.

διαυγής, transparent.

Rev. xxi. 21, for διαφανής, GLTTr*S*.

διαφανής.

transparent, Rev. xxi. 21 (διαυγής GLTTr*S*).

διαφέρω.

With διά, **carry through,** Mark xi. 16.

drive up and down, Acts xxvii. 27p.

publish, Acts xiii. 49.

differ from, 1 Cor. xv. 41. Gal. iv. 1.

Impers., with οὐδέν, **it maketh no matter,** Gal. ii. 6.

be better, Matt. vi. 26. xii. 12. Luke xii. 24.

be of more value, Matt. x. 31. Luke xii. 7.

τὰ διαφέροντα, **things that are excellent**(*marg.* **differ**), Phil. i. 10p.—

the things that are more excellent (*marg.* . . **differ**), Rom. ii. 18p.

διαφεύγω.

to escape, Acts xxvii. 42.

διαφημίζω.

spread abroad one's fame, Matt. ix. 31.
blaze abroad, Mark i. 45.
commonly report, Matt. xxviii. 15.

διαφθείρω.

destroy, Rev. viii. 9. xi. 18, 18 (*marg.* **corrupt**).
Pass., **perish**, 2 Cor. iv. 16.—**corrupt**, *adj.*, 1 Tim. vi. 5p.
corrupt, Luke xii. 33.
Add Rev. xix. 2, for φθείρω, G''.

διαφθορά.

corruption, Acts ii. 27, 31. xiii. 34, 35, 36, 37.

διάφορος.

diverse, Heb. ix. 10.
differing, Rom. xii. 6.
Comp., **more excellent**, Heb. i. 4. viii. 6.

διαφυλάσσω or -ττω.

keep, Luke iv. 10.

διαχειρίζομαι.

slay, Acts v. 30.
kill, Acts xxvi. 21.

διαχλευάζω, deride utterly.
Acts ii. 13, for χλευάζω, GLT*S*.

διαχωρίζομαι.

depart, Luke ix. 33inf.

διδακτικός.

apt to teach, 1 Tim. iii. 2. 2 Tim. ii. 24.

διδακτός.

taught, John vi. 45.
which one teachethcc, 1 Cor. ii. 13t.

διδασκαλία.

teaching, Rom. xii. 7.
learning, Rom. xv. 4.
doctrine, Matt. xv. 9. Mark vii. 7. Eph. iv. 14. Col. ii. 22. 1 Tim. i. 10. iv. 1, 6, 13, 16. v. 17. vi. 1, 3. 2 Tim. iii. 10, 16. iv. 3. Tit. i. 9. ii. 1, 7, 10.

διδάσκαλος.

teacher, John iii. 2. Acts xiii. 1. Rom. ii. 20. 1 Cor. xii. 28, 29. Eph. iv. 11. 1 Tim. ii. 7. 2 Tim. i. 11. iv. 3. Heb. v. 12.
doctor, Luke ii. 46.
master, Matt. x. 24, 25. Luke vi. 40t. Jas. iii. 1.—*Said of Christ*, Matt. viii. 19. ix. 11. xii. 38. xvii. 24. xix. 16. xxii. 16, 24, 36. xxvi. 18. Mark iv. 38. v. 35. ix. 17, 38. x. 17, 20, 35. xii. 14, 19, 32. xiii. 1. xiv. 14. Luke iii. 12. vii. 40. viii. 49. ix. 38. x. 25. xi. 45. xii. 13. xviii. 18. xix. 39. xx. 21, 28, 39. xxi. 7. xxii. 11. John i. 38(39). iii. 10. viii. 4(*ap*). xi. 28. xiii. 13, 14. xx. 16.
Add Matt. xxiii. 8, for καθηγητής, G'LTTr.

διδάσκω.

teach, Matt. iv. 23. v. 2, 19t. ix. 35. xi. 1. xiii. 54. xv. 9. xxi. 23p. xxii. 16. xxvi. 55(-G∘*S*∘). xxviii. 15, 20. Mark i. 21. ii. 13. iv. 1, 2. vi. 2, 6, 30, 34. vii. 7. viii. 31. ix. 31. x. 1. xi. 17. xii. 14, 35. xiv. 49. Luke iv. 15. v. 3, 17. vi. 6. xi. 1t. xii. 12. xiii. 10, 22, 26. xx. 1p, 21t. xxi. 37. xxiii. 5. John vi. 59p. vii. 14, 28p, 35. viii. 2(*ap*), 20, 28. ix. 34. xiv. 26. xviii. 20. Acts i. 1. iv. 2, 18. v. 21. 25, 28, 42. xi. 26. xv. 1, 35. xviii. 11, 25. xx. 20. xxi. 21, 28. xxviii. 31.
Rom. ii. 21t. xii. 7. 1 Cor. iv. 17. xi. 14. Gal. i. 12. Eph. iv. 21. Col. i. 28. ii. 7. iii. 16. 2 Thes. ii. 15. 1 Tim. ii. 12. iv. 11. vi. 2. 2 Tim. ii. 2. Tit. i. 11. Heb. v. 12. viii. 11. 1 John ii. 27tr. Rev. ii. 14, 20.
With εἰμί, **teach**, Matt. vii. 29p. Mark i. 22p. Luke iv. 31p. xix. 47p.

διδαχή.

With κατά, **as he**c **hath been taught** (*marg.* **in teaching**), Tit. i. 9.
doctrine, Matt. vii. 28. xvi. 12. xxii. 33. Mark i. 22, 27. iv. 2. xi. 18. xii. 38. Luke iv. 32. John vii. 16, 17. xviii. 19. Acts ii. 42. v. 28.

xiii. 12. xvii. 19. Rom. vi. 17. xvi. 17. 1 Cor. xiv. 6, 26. 2 Tim. iv. 2. Heb. vi. 2. xiii. 9. 2 John 9*t*, 10. Rev. ii. 14, 15, 24.

δίδραχμον.

tribute money, Matt. xvii. 24pl.
tribute, Matt. xvii. 24pl.

δίδωμι.

give, Matt. iv. 9. v. 31, 42. vi. 11. vii. 6, 7, 11*t*. ix. 8. x. 1, 8, 19(*ap*). xii. 39. xiii. 11*t*, 12. xiv. 7, 8, 9, 11, 16, 19. xv. 36. xvi. 4, 19, 26. xvii. 27. xix. 7, 11, 21. xx. 4, 14, 23, 28. xxi. 23, 43. xxii. 17. xxiv. 24, 29, 45. xxv. 8, 15, 28, 29, 35, 42. xxvi. 9, 15, 26, 27, 48. xxvii. 10, 34. xxviii. 12, 18.

Mark ii. 26. iv. 11, 25. v. 43. vi. 2, 7, 22, 23, 25, 28*t*, 37*t*, 41. viii. 6, 12, 37(–T). x. 21, 40, 45. xi. 28. xii. 9, 14, 15(14)*t*. xiii. 11, 24, 34. xiv. 5, 11, 22, 23, 44. xv. 23.

Luke i. 32, 77. iv. 6*t*. vi. 4, 30, 38*t*. vii. 44, 45. viii. 10, 18, 55. ix. 1, 13, 16. x. 19, 35. xi. 3, 7, 8*t*, 9, 13*t*, 29, 41. xii. 32, 33, 42, 48, 51, 58. xiv. 9. xv. 12, 16, 29. xvi. 12. xvii. 18. xviii. 43. xix. 8, 15, 23, 24, 26. xx. 2, 10, 16, 22. xxi. 15. xxii. 5, 19*t*. xxiii. 2.

John i. 12, 17, 22. iii. 16, 27, 34, 35. iv. 5, 7, 10*t*, 12, 14, 14(*ap*), 15. v. 26, 27, 36. vi. 27, 31, 32*t*, 33, 34, 37, 39, 51, 51(*ap*), 52, 65. vii. 19, 22. ix. 24. x. 28, 29. xi. 22, 57. xii. 5, 49. xiii. 3, 15, 26, 29, 34. xiv. 16, 27*tr*. xv. 16. xvi. 23. xvii. 2*tr*, 4, 6*t*, 7, 8*t*, 9, 11, 12, 14, 22*t*, 24*t*. xviii. 9, 11. xix. 9, 11, xxi. 13.

Acts ii. 4, 19. iii. 6, 16. iv. 12. v. 31, 32. vii. 5*t*, 8, 10, 38. viii. 18, 19. ix. 41. xi. 17. xii. 23. xiii. 20, 21, 34. xiv. 17. xv. 8. xvii. 25p. xx. 32, 35. xxiv. 26.

Rom. iv. 20. v. 5. xi. 8. xii. 3, 6, 19. xiv. 12 (ἀποδίδωμι L). xv. 15. 1 Cor. i. 4. iii. 5, 10. vii. 25. xi. 15. xii. 7, 8, 24. xiv. 7*t*, 8. xv. 38, 57. 2 Cor. i. 22. v. 5, 12, 18. vi. 3. viii. 5, 10. ix. 9. x. 8. xii. 7. xiii. 10. Gal. i. 4. ii. 9*t*. iii. 21, 22. iv. 15. Eph. i. 17, 22. iii. 2, 7, 8. iv. 7, 8, 11, 27. vi. 19. Col. i. 25. 1 Thes. iv. 2, 8. 2 Thes. ii. 16. iii. 16. 1 Tim. ii. 6. iv. 14. v. 14. 2 Tim. i. 7, 9, 16. ii. 7, 25. Tit. ii. 14.

Heb. ii. 13. vii. 4. Jas. i. 5*t*. ii. 16. iv. 6*t*. v. 18. 1 Pet. i. 21. v. 5. 2 Pet. iii. 15. 1 John iii. 1, 23, 24. iv. 13. v. 11, 16, 20. Rev. i. 1. ii. 7, 10, 17*t*, 21, 23, 26, 28. iv. 9. vi. 2, 4*t*. 8, 11. vii. 2. viii. 2, 3. ix. 1, 3, 5. x. 9. xi. 1, 2, 3, 13, 18. xii. 14. xiii. 2, 4, 5*t*, 7(*ap*), 7, 15. xiv. 7. xv. 7. xvi. 6, 8, 9, 19. xvii. 17. xviii. 7. xix. 7. xx. 4. xxi. 6.

give up, Rev. xx. 13.
give forth, Acts i. 26.
ἵνα δῶσιν αὐτοῖς, **to receive**, Rev. xiii. 16(*Gr.* give).
Pass. with dat., **have power**, Rev. xiii. 14, 15.
grant, Mark x. 37. Luke i. 74(73). Acts iv. 29. xi. 18. xiv. 3. Rom. xv. 5. Eph. iii. 16. 2 Tim. i. 18. Rev. iii. 21. xix. 8.
bestow, 2 Cor. viii. 1. 1 John iii. 1.
minister, Eph. iv. 29.
yield, Mark iv. 7, 8.
bring forth, Matt. xiii. 8.
offer, Luke ii. 24. Rev. viii. 3 (*marg.* **add**).
suffer, Acts ii. 27. xiii. 35.
adventure, Acts xix. 31.
deliver, Luke vii. 15(ἀποδίδωμι Lm). xix. 13.
deliver up, Rev. xx. 13.
commit, John v. 22.
utter, 1 Cor. xiv. 9.
show, Mark xiii. 22(ποιέω T).
set, Rev. iii. 8.
put, Luke xv. 22. 2 Cor. viii. 16. Heb. viii. 10(*Gr.* give). x. 16. Rev. xvii. 17.
make, 2 Thes. iii. 9. Rev. iii. 9.
takec(*marg.* **yield**), 2 Thes. i. 8.
Add, for ἀποδίδωμι, Acts xix. 40, G'T. For διαδίδωμι, Luke xviii. 22,

LS. Rev. xvii. 13, GLTTrS. For πέμπω, Rev. xi. 10, G″. For ποιέω, Mark iii. 6, Tr. — John vii. 39(*given*), L. xiii. 26, *see* ἐπιδίδωμι. xiv. 31, *see* ἐντέλλομαι. Rev. xxi. 7, *see* κληρονομέω.

See also ἐγκοπή, ἐμφανής, ῥάπισμα, σωτηρία.

διεγείρω.

to awake, Mark iv. 38(ἐγείρω TrS). Luke viii. 24.

stir up, 2 Pet. i. 13. iii. 1.

raise, Matt. i. 24(ἐγείρω LTrS).

Pass., **arise,** Mark iv. 39. John vi. 18.

Add Luke viii. 24, for ἐγείρω, TTrS.

διενθυμέομαι, consider carefully. Acts x. 19, for ἐνθυμέομαι, GLTS.

διεξέρχομαι, pass out through. Acts xxviii. 3, for ἔρχομαι, G′T.

διέξοδος.

With τῶν ὁδῶν, **highway,** Matt. xxii. 9.

διερμηνεία, interpretation. 1 Cor. xii. 10, for ἑρμηνεία, L.

διερμηνευτής.

interpreter, 1 Cor. xiv. 28(ἑρμηνευτής L).

διερμηνεύω.

interpret, 1 Cor. xii. 30. xiv. 5, 13, 27. — *Pass.*, **by interpretation,** Acts ix. 36p.

expound, Luke xxiv. 27.

διέρχομαι.

go through, Acts xiii. 6p. xv. 41.

go throughout, Acts xvi. 6p.

go over, Luke viii. 22. Acts xx. 2p.

go over °**all,** Acts xviii. 23.

go every where, Acts viii. 4.

go about, Acts x. 38.

go abroad, Luke v. 15.

go, Luke ii. 15. Acts xi. 22(–LS). xx. 25.

With κατά, **go through,** Luke ix. 6.

With διά, **go through,** Matt. xix. 24(εἰσέρχομαι GTTrS). John iv. 4. viii. 59(*ap*). —**pass through,** Luke iv. 30. xvii. 11. 1 Cor. x. 1. — **pass throughout,** Acts ix. 32. —**walk through,** Matt. xii. 43. Luke xi. 24.

pass through, Luke xix. 1. Acts viii. 40. xv. 3. xix. 1, 21p. 1 Cor. xvi. 5*t*.

pass throughout, Acts xiv. 24p.

pass over, Mark iv. 35.

pass by, Acts xvii. 23p.

pass, Luke xix. 4. Acts xii. 10p. xviii. 27. Rom. v. 12. 2 Cor. i. 16 (ἀπέρχομαι G′L). Heb. iv. 14.

pierce through, Luke ii. 35.

come, Acts ix. 38.

depart, Acts xiii. 14p.

travel, Acts xi. 19.

Add, for εἰσέρχομαι, **Mark x. 25,** GLTTr. Luke xviii. 25, L.

διερωτάω.

make inquiry for, Acts x. 17.

διετής.

two years old, Matt. ii. 16.

διετία.

two years, Acts xxiv. 27. xxviii. 30.

διηγέομαι.

tell, Mark v. 16. ix. 9. Luke ix. 10. Heb. xi. 32.

declare, Acts viii. 33. ix. 27. xii. 17.

show, Luke viii. 39.

διήγησις.

declaration, Luke i. 1.

διηνεκής.

With εἰς τό, **continually,** Heb. vii. 3. x. 1. —**for ever,** Heb. x. 12, 14.

διθάλασσος.

where two seas meet, Acts xxvii. 41.

διϊκνέομαι.

pierce, Heb. iv. 12.

διΐστημι.

be parted, Luke xxiv. 51.

go further, Acts xxvii. 28p.

διαστάσης ὥρας μιᾶς, **the space of one hour after,** Luke xxii. 59p.

διϊσχυρίζομαι.

constantly affirm, Acts xii. 15.

confidently affirm, Luke xxii. 59.

δικαιοκρισία.

righteous judgment, Rom. ii. 5.

δίκαιος.

right, Matt. xx. 4, 7(*ap*). Luke xii. 57. Acts iv. 19. Eph. vi. 1.
meet, Phil. i. 7. 2 Pet. i. 13.
just, Matt. i. 19. v. 45. xiii. 49. xxvii. 19, 24(–G°L^{b}TTr^b). Mark vi. 20. Luke i. 17. ii. 25. xiv. 14. xv. 7. xx. 20. xxiii. 50. John v. 30. Acts iii. 14. vii. 52. x. 22. xxii. 14. xxiv. 15. Rom. i. 17. ii. 13. iii. 26. vii. 12. Gal. iii. 11. Phil. iv. 8. Col. iv. 1. Tit. i. 8. Heb. x. 38. xii. 23. Jas. v. 6. 1 Pet. iii. 18. 2 Pet. ii. 7. 1 John i. 9. Rev. xv. 3.
righteous, Matt. ix. 13. x. 41*tr*. xiii. 17, 43. xxiii. 28, 29, 35*t*. xxv. 37, 46. Mark ii. 17. Luke i. 6. v. 32. xviii. 9. xxiii. 47. John vii. 24. xvii. 25. Rom. iii. 10. v. 7, 19. 2 Thes. i. 5, 6. 1 Tim. i. 9. 2 Tim. iv. 8. Heb. xi. 4. Jas. v. 16. 1 Pet. iii. 12. iv. 18. 2 Pet. ii. 8*t*. 1 John ii. 1, 29. iii. 7, 12. Rev. xvi. 5, 7. xix. 2. xxii. 11.
Add Matt. xxvii. 4, for ἀθῷος, G'. 1 John iii. 10(*ap*).

δικαιοσύνη.

righteousness, Matt. iii. 15. v. 6, 10, 20. vi. 33. xxi. 32. Luke i. 75. John xvi. 8, 10. Acts x. 35. xiii. 10. xvii. 31. xxiv. 25. Rom. i. 17. iii. 5, 21, 22, 25, 26. iv. 3, 5, 6, 9, 11*t*, 13, 22. v. 17, 21. vi. 13, 16, 18, 19, 20. viii. 10. ix. 28(*ap*), 30*tr*, 31, 31 (–G°L*S*). x. 3, 3(–GL), 3, 4, 5, 6, 10. xiv. 17. 1 Cor. i. 30. 2 Cor. iii. 9. v. 21. vi. 7, 14. ix. 9, 10. xi. 15. Gal. ii. 21. iii, 6, 21. v. 5. Eph. iv. 24. v. 9. vi. 14. Phil. i. 11. iii. 6, 9*t*. 1 Tim. vi. 11. 2 Tim. ii. 22. iii. 16. iv. 8. Tit. iii. 5. Heb. i. 9. v. 13. vii. 2. xi. 7, 33. xii. 11. Jas i. 20. ii. 23. iii. 18. 1 Pet. ii. 24. iii. 14. 2 Pet. i. 1. ii. 5, 21. iii. 13. 1 John ii. 29. iii 7, 10(*ap*). Rev. xix. 11.
Add Matt. vi. 1, for ἐλεημοσύνη, GLTTr*S*. Rev. xxii. 11, *see* δικαιόω.

δικαιόω.

justify, Matt. xi. 19. xii. 37. Luke vii. 29, 35. x. 29. xvi. 15. xviii. 14. Acts xiii. 39*t*. Rom. ii. 13. iii. 4, 20, 24, 28, 30. iv. 2, 5. v. 1, 9. viii. 30*t*, 33. 1 Cor. iv. 4. vi. 11. Gal. ii. 16*tr*, 17. iii. 8, 11, 24. v. 4. 1 Tim. iii. 16. Tit. iii. 7. Jas. ii. 21, 24, 25.
justifier, Rom. iii. 26^p.
free(*Gr*. justify), Rom. vi. 7.
Pass., **be righteous**, Rev. xxii. 11 (δικαιοσύνην ποιησάτω GLTTr*S*).

δικαίωμα.

judgment, Rom. i. 32. Rev. xv. 4.
ordinance, Luke i. 6. Heb. ix. 1 (*marg*. **ceremony**), 10 (*marg*. **rite**, *or* **ceremony**).
righteousness, Rom. ii. 26. v. 18. viii. 4. Rev. xix. 8.
justification, Rom. v. 16.

δικαίως.

justly, Luke xxiii. 41. 1 Thes. ii. 10.
righteously, Tit. ii. 12. 1 Pet. ii. 23.
to righteousness, 1 Cor. xv. 34.

δικαίωσις.

justification, Rom. iv. 25. v. 18.

δικαστής.

judge, Luke xii. 14 (κριτής LTr*S*). Acts vii. 27, 35.

δίκη.

judgment, Acts xxv. 15 (καταδίκη G''L*S*).—**vengeance**, Jude 7.
Vengeance, Acts xxviii. 4.
With τίω, **be punished**, 2 Thes. i. 9.

δίκτυον.

net, Matt. iv. 20, 21. Mark i. 18, 19. Luke v. 2, 4, 5, 6. John xxi. 6, 8, 11*t*.

δίλογος.

double-tongued, 1 Tim. iii. 8.

διό.

for which cause, Rom. xv. 22. 2 Cor. iv. 16.
wherefore, Matt. xxvii. 8. Luke vii. 7. Acts xiii. 35 (διότι LT*S*). xv. 19. xx. 26. xxiv. 26. xxv. 26. xxvii. 25, 34. Rom. i. 24. xiii. 5.

xv. 7. 1 Cor. xii. 3. 2 Cor. ii. 8. v. 9. vi. 17. Eph. ii. 11. iii. 13. iv. 8, 25. v. 14. Phil. ii. 9. 1 Thes. ii. 18 (*διότι* G'LT*S*). iii. 1. v. 11. Phm. 8. Heb. iii. 7, 10. x. 5. xi. 16. xii. 12, 28. xiii. 12. Jas. i. 21. iv. 6. 1 Pet. i. 13. ii. 6(*see διότι*). 2 Pet. i. 10, 12. iii. 14.

and therefore, 2 Cor. iv. 13.

therefore, Luke i. 35. Acts x. 29. xx. 31. Rom. ii. 1. iv. 22. 2 Cor. iv. 13. xii. 10. Heb. vi. 1. xi. 12.

Add 1 Cor. xiv. 13, for *διόπερ*, L*S*. 2 Cor. i. 20 (*ap*). xii. 7 (.. *ἵνα*[1st]), L*S*. Gal. iv. 31, for *ἄρα*, LT*S*. Col. iii. 6, for *δι' ἅ*, L[m].

διοδεύω.

pass through, Acts xvii. 1[p].

go throughout, Luke viii. 1.

διόπερ.

wherefore, 1 Cor. viii. 13. x. 14. xiv. 13(*διό* L*S*).

Διοπετής.

which fell down from Jupiter, Acts xix. 35.

διόρθωμα, a making straight.

Acts xxiv. 3, for *κατόρθωμα*, G'L*S*.

διόρθωσις.

reformation, Heb. ix. 10.

διορύσσω.

break through, Matt. vi. 19, 20. Luke xii. 39.

break up, Matt. xxiv. 43.

διότι.

because that, Rom. i. 21. Phil. ii. 26. 1 Thes. iv. 6.

because, Luke ii. 7. Acts xvii. 31 (*καθότι* G''LT*S*). Rom. i. 19. viii. 7. 1 Cor. xv. 9. 1 Thes. ii. 8. Heb. xi. 5, 23. Jas. iv. 3. 1 Pet. i. 16.

for, Luke i. 13. xxi. 28. Acts x. 20 (G', *ὅτι* GLT*S*). xviii. 10*t*. xxii. 18. Gal. ii. 16(*ὅτι* G''L*S*). 1 Pet. i. 24 (*marg.* **for that**).

therefore, Rom. iii. 20.

Add, for *διό*, Acts xiii. 35, LT*S*. 1 Thes. ii. 18, G'LT*S*. For *διὸ καί*, 1 Pet. ii. 6, GLT*S*.

διπλοῦς.

double, 1 Tim. v. 17. Rev. xviii. 6*t*.

twofold more, Matt. xxiii. 15[comp].

διπλόω.

to double, Rev. xviii. 6.

δίς.

twice, Mark xiv. 30, 72. Luke xviii. 12. Jude 12.

again, Phil. iv. 16. 1 Thes. ii. 18.

δισμυριάδες. See μυριάς.

διστάζω.

to doubt, Matt. xiv. 31. xxviii. 17.

δίστομος.

two-edged, Heb. iv. 12. Rev. i. 16.

with two edges, Rev. ii. 12.

Add Rev. xix. 15(.. sword), G''.

δισχίλιοι.

two thousand, Mark v. 13.

διϋλίζω.

strain at (*lit.* strain out), Matt. xxiii. 24.

διχάζω.

set at variance, Matt. x. 35.

διχοστασία.

division, Rom. xvi. 17. 1 Cor. iii. 3(*marg.* **faction**; -G[oo]LT*S*).

sedition, Gal. v. 20.

διχοτομέω.

cut asunder (*marg.* **cut off**), Matt. xxiv. 51.—**cut in sunder** (*marg.* **cut off**), Luke xii. 46.

διψάω.

to thirst, Matt. v. 6. John iv. 13, 14(*ap*), 15. vi. 35. vii. 37. xix. 28. Rom. xii. 20. 1 Cor. iv. 11. Rev. vii. 16.

be thirsty, Matt. xxv. 35, 37[p], 42.

be athirst, Matt. xxv. 44[p]. Rev. xxi. 6. xxii. 17.

δίψος.

thirst, 2 Cor. xi. 27.

δίψυχος.

double-minded, Jas. i. 8. iv. 8.

διωγμός.

persecution, Matt. xiii. 21. Mark iv. 17. x. 30. Acts viii. 1. xiii. 50.

Rom. viii. 35. 2 Cor. xii. 10. 2 Thes. i. 4. 2 Tim. iii. 11*t*.

διώκτης.

persecutor, 1 Tim. i. 13.

διώκω.

persecute, Matt. v. 10, 11, 12, 44. x. 23. xxiii. 34. Luke xxi. 12. John v. 16. xv. 20*t*. Acts vii. 52. ix. 4, 5. xxii. 4, 7, 8. xxvi. 11, 14, 15. Rom. xii. 14. 1 Cor. iv. 12. xv. 9. 2 Cor. iv. 9. Gal. i. 13, 23. iv. 29. Phil. iii. 6. Rev. xii. 13.

Pass., **suffer persecution**, Gal. v. 11. vi. 12. 2 Tim. iii. 12.

follow after, Rom. ix. 30, 31. xiv. 19. 1 Cor. xiv. 1. Phil. iii. 12. 1 Tim. vi. 11.

follow, Luke xvii. 23. 1 Thes. v. 15. 2 Tim. ii. 22. Heb. xii. 14.

ensue, 1 Pet. iii. 11.

press toward, Phil. iii. 14.

given to, Rom. xii. 13p.

Add Matt. x. 23(*ap*).

δόγμα.

decree, Luke ii. 1. Acts xvi. 4. xvii. 7.

ordinance, Eph. ii. 15. Col. ii. 14.

Add Heb. xi. 23, for διάταγμα, L.

δογματίζομαι.

be subject to ordinances, Col. ii. 20.

δοκέω.

think, Matt. iii. 9. vi. 7. xxiv. 44. xxvi. 53. Luke xii. 40. xiii. 4. xix. 11. John v. 39, 45. xi. 13. xiii. 29. xvi. 2. Acts xii. 9. xxvi. 9. 1 Cor. iv. 9. vii. 40. viii. 2. x. 12. xii. 23. xiv. 37. 2 Cor. xi. 16. xii. 19. Gal. vi. 3. Phil. iii. 4. Jas. iv. 5.

suppose, Mark vi. 49. Luke xii. 51. xiii. 2. xxiv. 37. John xx. 15. Acts xxvii. 13. Heb. x. 29.

trow, Luke xvii. 9(–L[b]Tr*S*).

seem, Luke viii. 18 (*marg.* **think**). Acts xvii. 18. 1 Cor. iii. 18. xi. 16. xii. 22. 2 Cor. x. 9. Gal. ii. 6*t*, 9. Heb. iv. 1. xii. 11. Jas. i. 26.

τὸ δοκοῦν αὐτοῖς, **their own pleasure**, Heb. xii. 10p.

be accounted, Mark x. 42 (*marg.* **think good**). Luke xxii. 24.

be of reputation, Gal. ii. 2.

Impers., **it seemeth**, Acts xxv. 27. —**it seemeth good**, Luke i. 3. Acts xv. 25, 28.—**it pleaseth**, Acts xv. 22, 34(*ap*).—*With dative*, **think**,[cc] Matt. xvii. 25. xviii. 12. xxi. 28. xxii. 17, 42. xxvi. 66. Luke x. 36. John xi. 56.

Add John xi. 31, for λέγω, G'Tr*S*.

δοκιμάζω.

try, 1 Cor. iii. 13. 1 Thes. ii. 4. 1 Pet. i. 7p. 1 John iv. 1.

prove, Luke xiv. 19. Rom. xii. 2. 2 Cor. viii. 8, 22. xiii. 5. Gal. vi. 4. Eph. v. 10. 1 Thes. v. 21. 1 Tim. iii. 10. Heb. iii. 9(*ap*).

examine, 1 Cor. xi. 28.

discern, Luke xii. 56*t*.

approve, Rom. ii. 18 (*marg.* **try**). 1 Cor. xvi. 3. Phil. i. 10(*marg.* **try**).

allow, Rom. xiv. 22. 1 Thes. ii. 4.

like, Rom. i. 28.

δοκιμασία, trial, temptation. Heb. iii. 9 (*ap*).

δοκιμή.

trial, 2 Cor. viii. 2.

experiment, 2 Cor. ix. 13.

experience, Rom. v. 4*t*.

proof, 2 Cor. ii. 9. xiii. 3. Phil. ii. 22.

δοκίμιον.

trial, 1 Pet. i. 7.

trying, Jas. i. 3.

δόκιμος.

tried, Jas. i. 12.

approved, Rom. xiv. 18. xvi. 10. 2 Cor. x. 18. xiii. 7. 2 Tim. ii. 15.

which is approved, 1 Cor. xi. 9.

δοκός.

beam, Matt. vii. 3, 4, 5. Luke vi. 41, 42*t*.

δόλιος.

deceitful, 2 Cor. xi. 13.

δολιόω.

use deceit, Rom. iii. 13.

δόλος.

guile, John i. 47(48). 2 Cor. xii. 16. 1 Thes. ii. 3. 1 Pet. ii. 1, 22. iii. 10. Rev. xiv. 5(ψεῦδος GLTTrS).

deceit, Mark vii. 22. Rom. i. 29.

craft, Mark xiv. 1.

subtilty, Matt. xxvi. 4. Acts xiii. 10.

δολόω.

handle deceitfully, 2 Cor. iv. 2.
Add 1 Cor. v. 6, for ζυμόω, G′.

δόμα.

gift, Matt. vii. 11. Luke xi. 13. Eph. iv. 8. Phil. iv. 17.

δόξα.

glory, Matt. iv. 8. vi. 13(*ap*), 29. xvi. 27. xix. 28. xxiv. 30. xxv. 31*t*. Mark viii. 38. x. 37. xiii. 26. Luke ii. 9, 14, 32. iv. 6. ix. 26, 31, 32. xii. 27. xvii. 18. xix. 38. xxi. 27. xxiv. 26. John i. 14. ii. 11. vii. 18*t*. viii. 50. xi. 4, 40. xii. 41. xvii. 5, 22, 24. Acts vii. 2, 55. xii. 23. xxii. 11.

Rom. i. 23. ii. 7, 10. iii. 7, 23. iv. 20. v. 2. vi. 4. viii. 18. ix. 4, 23*t*. xi. 36. xv. 7. xvi. 27. 1 Cor. ii. 7, 8. x. 31. xi. 7*t*, 15. xv. 40, 41, 41 (–C 1611 *to* 1629, *err*.), 41*t*, 43. 2 Cor. i. 20. iii. 7, 9*t*, 10, 18*tr*. iv. 6, 15, 17. viii. 19, 23. Gal. i. 5. Eph. i. 6, 12, 14, 17, 18. iii. 13, 16, 21. Phil. i. 11. ii. 11. iii. 19. iv. 19, 20. Col. i. 27*t*. iii. 4. 1 Thes. ii. 6, 12, 20. 2 Thes. i. 9. ii. 14. 1 Tim. i. 17. iii. 16. 2 Tim. ii. 10. iv. 18.

Heb. i. 3. ii. 7, 9, 10. iii. 3. ix. 5. xiii. 21. Jas. ii. 1. 1 Pet. i. 7, 11[pl], 21, 24. iv. 13, 14. v. 1, 4, 10, 11 (–G°LT). 2 Pet. i. 3, 17*t*. iii. 18. Jude 24, 25. Rev. i. 6. iv. 9, 11. v. 12, 13. vii. 12. xi. 13. xiv. 7. xv. 8. xvi. 9. xviii. 1. xix. 1. xxi. 11, 23, 24, 26.

glorious[cc], Rom. viii. 21. 2 Cor. iv. 4. Phil. iii. 21. Col. i. 11. 1 Tim. i. 11. Tit. ii. 13.

With διά, **glorious**, 2 Cor. iii. 11.

With ἐν, **glorious**, 2 Cor. iii. 7, 8, 11.

praise, John ix. 24. xii. 43*t*. 1 Pet. iv. 11.

honor, John v. 41, 44*t*. viii. 54. 2 Cor. vi. 8. Rev. xix. 7.

worship, Luke xiv. 10.

dignity, 2 Pet. ii. 10. Jude 8.

δοξάζω.

glorify, Matt. v. 16. ix. 8. xv. 31. Mark ii. 12. Luke ii. 20. iv. 15. v. 25, 26. vii. 16. xiii. 13. xvii. 15. xviii. 43. xxiii. 47. John vii. 39. xi. 4. xii. 16, 23, 28*tr*. xiii. 31*t*, 32(*ap*), 32*t*. xiv. 13. xv. 8. xvi. 14. xvii. 1*t*, 4, 5, 10. xxi. 19. Acts iii. 13. iv. 21. xi. 18. xiii. 48. xxi. 20. Rom. i. 21. viii. 30. xv. 6, 9. 1 Cor. vi. 20. 2 Cor. ix. 13[p]. Gal. i. 24. 2 Thes. iii. 1. Heb. v. 5. 1 Pet. ii. 12. iv. 11, 14(*ap*), 16. Rev. xv. 4. xviii. 7.

Pass., **be made glorious**, 2 Cor. iii. 10.—**have glory**, Matt. vi. 2. 2 Cor. iii. 10.—**full of glory**, 1 Pet. i. 8[p].

honor, John viii. 54*t*. 1 Cor. xii. 26.

magnify, Rom. xi. 13.

δόσις.

giving, Phil. iv. 15.

gift, Jas. i. 17.

δότης.

giver, 2 Cor. ix. 7.

δουλαγωγέω.

bring into subjection, 1 Cor. ix. 27.

δουλεία.

bondage, Rom. viii. 15, 21. Gal. iv. 24. v. 1. Heb. ii. 15.

δουλεύω.

be in bondage, John viii. 33. Acts vii. 7. Gal. iv. 9, 25.

serve, Matt. vi. 24*t*. Luke xv. 29. xvi. 13*t*. Acts xx. 19. Rom. vi. 6. vii. 6, 25. ix. 12. xii. 11. xiv. 18. xvi. 18. Gal. v. 13. Phil. ii. 22. Col. iii. 24. 1 Thes. i. 9. Tit. iii. 3.

do service, Gal. iv. 8. Eph. vi. 7. 1 Tim. vi. 2.

δούλη.

handmaid, Luke i. 38.

handmaiden, Luke i. 48. Acts ii. 18.

δοῦλος, adj.

servant, Rom. vi. 19*t*.

δοῦλος, subst.

bondman, Rev. vi. 15.
bond, 1 Cor. xii. 13. Gal. iii. 28. Eph. vi. 8. Col. iii. 11. Rev. xiii. 16. xix. 18.
servant, Matt. viii. 9. x. 24, 25. xiii. 27, 28(–T). xviii. 23, 26, 27, 28, 32. xx. 27. xxi. 34, 35, 36. xxii. 3, 4, 6, 8, 10. xxiv. 45, 46, 48, 50. xxv. 14, 19, 21, 23, 26, 30. xxvi. 51. Mark x. 44. xii. 2, 4. xiii. 34. xiv. 47. Luke vii. 2, 3, 8, 10. xii. 37, 38(–G∾TTrᵇS), 43, 45, 46, 47. xiv. 17, 21*t*, 22, 23. xv. 22. xvii. 7, 9, 10. xix. 13, 15, 17, 22. xx. 10, 11. xxii. 50. John iv. 51. viii. 34, 35. xiii. 16. xv. 15*t*, 20. xviii. 10*t*, 18, 26.
Rom. vi. 16*t*, 17, 20. 1 Cor. vii. 21, 22, 23. 2 Cor. iv. 5. Gal. iv. 1, 7. Eph. vi. 5. Phil. ii. 7. Col. iii. 22. iv. 1. 1 Tim. vi. 1. Tit. ii. 9. Phm. 16*t*. 2 Pet. ii. 19.
With Θεοῦ, Χριστοῦ, *etc.*, **servant**, Luke ii. 29. Acts ii. 18. iv. 29. xvi. 17. Rom. i. 1. 1 Cor. vii. 22. Gal. i. 10. Eph. vi. 6. Phil. i. 1. Col. iv. 12. 2 Tim. ii. 24. Tit. i. 1. Jas. i. 1. 1 Pet. ii. 16. 2 Pet. i. 1. Jude 1. Rev. i. 1*t*. ii. 20. vii. 3. x. 7. xi. 18. xv. 3. xix. 2, 5. xxii. 3, 6.

δουλόω.

bring into bondage, Acts vii. 6.
make servant, 1 Cor. ix. 19.
Pass., **be brought in bondage**, 2 Pet. ii. 19.—**in bondage**, Gal. iv. 3ᵖ.—**be under bondage**, 1 Cor. vii. 15.—**become servant**, Rom. vi. 18, 22.—**given to**, Tit. ii. 3ᵖ.

δοχή.

feast, Luke v. 29. xiv. 13.

δράκων.

dragon, Rev. xii. 3, 4, 7*t*, 9, 13, 16, 17. xiii. 2, 4, 11. xvi. 13. xx. 2.

δράσσομαι or -ττομαι.

take, 1 Cor. iii. 19.

δραχμή.

piece of silver, Luke xv. 8.
piece, Luke xv. 8, 9.

δρέμω. See τρέχω.

δρέπανον.

sickle, Mark iv. 29. Rev. xiv. 14, 15, 16, 17, 18*t*. 19.

δρόμος.

course, Acts xiii. 25. xx. 24. 2 Tim. iv. 7.

δῦμι. See δύνω.

δύναμαι.

can, *with* οὐ, **can not**, Matt. v. 14, 36. vi. 24*t*, 27. vii. 18. viii. 2. ix. 15. xii. 29, 34. xvi. 3. xvii. 16, 19. xix. 25. xxvi. 53. xxvii. 42. Mark i. 40, 45. ii. 4ᵖ, 7, 19, 19(*ap*). iii. 20, 23, 24, 25, 26, 27. v. 3. vi. 5, 19. vii. 15, 18, 24. viii. 4. ix. 3, 23, 28, 29, 39. x. 26, 38, 39. xv. 31.
Luke i. 22. v. 12, 21, 34. vi. 39, 42. viii. 19. ix. 40. xi. 7. xii. 25. xiii. 11. xiv. 20, 26, 27, 33. xvi. 13*t*, 26. xviii. 26. xix. 3. xx. 36. John i. 46(47). iii. 2, 3, 4*t*, 5, 9, 27. v. 19, 30, 44. vi. 44, 52, 60, 65. vii. 7, 34, 36. viii. 21, 22, 43. ix. 4, 16, 33. x. 21, 35. xi. 37. xii. 39. xiii. 33, 36, 37. xiv. 5(–LTTr), 17. xv. 4, 5. xvi. 12. Acts iv. 16, 20. v. 39. viii. 31. x. 47. xiii. 39. xv. 1. xxi. 34ᵖ. xxiv. 13. xxvii. 15ᵖ, 31, 43.
Rom. viii. 7, 8. 1 Cor. ii. 14. iii. 1, 11. x. 21*t*. xii. 3, 21. xv. 50. 2 Cor. iii. 7. Gal. iii. 21. 1 Thes. iii. 9. 1 Tim. v. 25. vi. 7, 16. 2 Tim. ii. 13.
Heb. iii. 19. iv. 15. v. 2. ix. 9. x. 1, 11. Jas. ii. 14. iii. 8, 12. iv. 2. 1 John iii. 9. iv. 20. Rev. ii. 2. iii. 8. vii. 9. ix. 20. xiv. 3.
can do, Mark ix. 22. 2 Cor. xiii. 8.
be able, Matt. iii. 9. ix. 28. x. 28*t*. xix. 12. xx. 22*t*. xxii. 46. xxvi. 61. Mark iv. 33. Luke iii. 8. xxi. 15. John x. 29. Acts xx. 32. Rom. viii. 39. 1 Cor. iii. 2*t*. vi. 5. x. 13*t*. 2 Cor. i. 4. Eph. iii. 20. vi. 11, 13,

16. Phil. iii. 31. 2 Tim. iii. 15. Heb. ii. 18. v. 7. vii. 25. Jas. i. 21. iv. 12. Jude 24. Rev. v. 3. vi. 17. xiii. 4(δυνατός G''). xv. 8.

able, Luke i. 20[p]. Rom. xv. 14[p]. 2 Tim. iii. 7[p].

be able to do, Luke xii. 26.

that is of power, Rom. xvi. 25[p].

be possible[cc], Acts xxvii. 39 (δυνατόν G'T).

may, Matt. xxvi. 9, 42. Mark iv. 32. xiv. 5, 7. Luke xvi. 2. Acts xvii. 19. xix. 40. xxiv, 8, 11[p]. xxv. 11. xxvi. 32. xxvii. 12. 1 Cor. vii. 21. xiv. 31. Eph. iii. 4. 1 Thes. ii. 6[p]. Rev. xiii. 17.

Add Heb. xi. 19, for δυνατός, L.

δύναμις.

power, Matt. vi. 13(*ap*). xxii. 29. xxiv. 29, 30. xxvi. 64. Mark ix. 1. xii. 24. xiii. 25, 26. xiv. 62. Luke i. 17, 35. iv. 14, 36. v. 17. ix. 1. x. 19. xxi. 26, 27. xxii. 69. xxiv. 49. Acts i. 8. iii. 12. iv. 7, 33. vi. 8. viii. 10. x. 38.

Rom. i. 4, 16, 20. viii. 38. ix. 17. xv. 13, 19. 1 Cor. i. 18, 24. ii. 4, 5. iv. 19, 20. v. 4. vi. 14. xv. 24, 43. 2 Cor. iv. 7. vi. 7. viii. 3*t*. xii. 9. xiii. 4*t*. Eph. i. 19. iii. 7, 20. Phil. iii. 10. 1 Thes. i. 5. 2 Thes. i. 11. ii. 9. 1 Tim. i. 7, 8. iii. 5. Heb. i. 3. vi. 5. vii. 16. 1 Pet. i. 5. iii. 22. 2 Pet. i. 3, 16. Rev. iv. 11. v. 12. vii. 12. xi. 17. xiii. 2. xv. 8. xvii. 13. xix. 1.

ability, Matt. xxv. 15.

strength, 1 Cor. xv. 56. 2 Cor. i. 8. xii. 9. Heb. xi. 11. Rev. i. 16. iii. 8. xii. 10.

might, Eph. i. 21. iii. 16. Col. i. 11. 2 Pet. ii. 11.

mighty[cc], Rom. xv. 19. 2 Thes. i. 7 (*Gr.* of power).

With ἐν, **mightily**, Col. i. 29.

mighty work, Matt. xi. 20, 21, 23. xiii. 54, 58. xiv. 2. Mark vi. 2, 5, 14. Luke x. 13. xix. 37.

mighty deed, 2 Cor. xii. 12.

wonderful work, Matt. vii. 22.

miracle, Mark ix. 39. Acts ii. 22. viii. 13. xix. 11. 1 Cor. xii. 10, 28. Gal. iii. 5. Heb. ii. 4.

worker of miracles (*marg.* **power**), 1 Cor. xii. 29.

abundance (*marg.* **power**), Rev. xviii. 3.

violence, Heb. xi. 34.

virtue, Mark v. 30. Luke vi. 19. viii. 46.

meaning, 1 Cor. xiv. 11.

Add 1 Pet. iv. 14 (glory καὶ δ.), G'L*S*.

δυναμόω.

strengthen, Col. i. 11.

Add Heb. xi. 34, for ἐνδυναμόω, L*S*.

δυνάστης.

Potentate, 1 Tim. vi. 15.

mighty, Luke i. 52.

of great authority, Acts viii. 27.

δυνατέω.

be mighty, 2 Cor. xiii. 3.

Add, for δυνατός ἐστιν, Rom. xiv. 4, G'LT*S*. For δυνατός, 2 Cor. ix. 8, L*S*.

δυνατός.

able, Luke xiv. 31. Acts xxv. 5. Rom. iv. 21. xi. 23. xiv. 4(*see* δυνατέω). 2 Cor. ix. 8 (δυνατεῖ L*S*). 2 Tim. i. 12. Tit. i. 9. Heb. xi. 19 (δύναται fr. δύναμαι L). Jas. iii. 2.

that I[c] **could**, Acts xi. 17.

strong, Rom. xv. 1. 2 Cor. xii. 10. xiii. 9.

mighty, Luke xxiv. 19. Acts vii. 22. xviii. 24. 1 Cor. i. 26. 2 Cor. x. 4.

that is mighty, Luke i. 49.

mighty man, Rev. vi. 15 (ἰσχυρός GLTTr*S*).

Neut., **possible**, Matt. xix. 26. xxvi. 39. Mark ix. 23. x. 27(*ap*). xiv. 35, 36. Luke xviii. 27. Acts ii. 24. xx. 16. — *With art.*, **power**, Rom. ix. 22.

εἰ δυνατόν, **if it be (were, had been) possible**, Matt. xxiv. 24. Mark xiii. 22. Rom. xii. 18. Gal. iv. 15.

Add, for δύναμαι, Acts xxvii. 39, G′T. Rev. xiii. 4, G″.

δύνω or δῦμι.

set, Mark i. 32.
be setting, Luke iv. 40p.

δύο.

two, Matt. iv. 18, 21. vi. 24. viii. 28. ix. 27. x. 10, 29. xi. 2(διά G′L TTr*S*). xiv. 17, 19. xviii. 8*t*, 9, 16*t*, 19, 20. xx. 21, 24, 30. xxi. 1, 28. xxii. 40. xxiv. 40, 41. xxv. 15, 17*t*, 22*tr*. xxvi. 2, 37, 60. xxvii. 38. Mark vi. 9, 38, 41*t*. ix. 43, 45, 47. xi. 1. xii. 42. xiv. 1, 13. xv. 27. xvi. 12(*ap*).
Luke ii. 24. iii. 11. v. 2. vii. 19, 41. ix. 13, 16, 30, 32. x. 35. xii. 6, 52*t*. xv. 11. xvi. 13. xvii. 34. xviii. 10. xix. 29. xxi. 2. xxii. 38. xxiii. 32. xxiv. 4, 13. John i. 35, 37, 40(41). iv. 40, 43. vi. 9. viii. 17. xi. 6. xix. 18. xx. 12. xxi. 2. Acts i. 10, 23, 24. vii. 29. ix. 38 (–G°). x. 7. xii. 6*t*. xix. 10, 22, 34. xxi. 33. xxiii. 23.
1 Cor. vi. 16. xiv. 27, 29. 2 Cor. xiii. 1. Gal. iv. 22, 24. Eph. v. 31. Phil. i. 23. 1 Tim. v. 19. Heb. vi. 18. x. 28. Rev. ix. 12, 16 (*see* μυριάς). xi. 2, 3, 4*t*, 10. xii. 14. xiii. 5, 11.
two men, Luke xvii. 36(*ap*).
two °**women**, Luke xvii. 35.
δύο δύο, **by two and two**, Mark vi. 7.
ἀνὰ δύο, **two and two**, Luke x. 1. —**two apiece**, Luke ix. 3. John ii. 6.
twain, Matt. v. 41. xix. 5, 6. xxi. 31. xxvii. 21, 51. Mark x. 8*t*. xv. 38. Eph. ii. 15.
both, John xx. 4. Rev. xix. 20.
Add Luke x. 1, 17(seventy . .), Lb.

δυσβάστακτος.

grievous to be borne, Matt. xxiii. 4 (–G°Trb*S*). Luke xi. 46.

δυσεντερία, δυσεντέριον LT*S*.

bloody flux, Acts xxviii. 8.

δυσερμήνευτος.

hard to be uttered, Heb. v. 11.

δύσκολος.

hard, Mark x. 24.

δυσκόλως.

hardly, Matt. xix. 23. Mark x. 23. Luke xviii. 24.

δυσμή.

Plural, **west**, Matt. viii. 11. xxiv. 27. Luke xii. 54. xiii. 29. Rev. xxi. 13.

δυσμυριάδες. See μυριάς.

δυσνόητος.

hard to be understood, 2 Pet. iii. 16.

δυσφημέω, speak evil, defame.

1 Cor. iv. 13, for βλασφημέω, G″T*S*.

δυσφημία.

evil report, 2 Cor. vi. 8.

δώδεκα.

twelve, Matt. ix. 20. xiv. 20. xix. 28*t*. xxvi. 53. Mark v. 25, 42. vi. 43. viii. 19. Luke ii. 42. viii. 42, 43. ix. 17. xxii. 30. John vi. 13. xi. 9. Acts vii. 8. Jas. i. 1. Rev. vii. 5*tr*, 6*tr*, 7*tr*, 8*tr*. xii. 1. xxi. 12, 12(*ap*), 12, 14, 16 (δεκαδύο T), 21. xxii. 2.—*Said of the Apostles*, Matt. x. 1, 2, 5. xi. 1. xx. 17. xxvi. 14, 20, 47. Mark iii. 14. iv. 10. vi. 7. ix. 35. x. 32. xi. 11. xiv. 10, 17, 20, 43. Luke vi. 13. viii. 1. ix. 1, 12. xviii. 31. xxii. 3, 14(–LTTr*S*), 47. John vi. 67, 70, 71. xx. 24. Acts vi. 2. 1 Cor. xv. 5. Rev. xxi. 14.
Add, for δεκαδύο, Acts xix. 7, xxiv. 11, L*S*.—Rev. xxi. 14(. . names), GLTTr*S*.

δωδέκατος.

twelfth, Rev. xxi. 20.

δωδεκάφυλον.

twelve tribes, Acts xxvi. 7.

δῶμα.

house-top, Matt. x. 27. xxiv. 17. Mark xiii. 15. Luke v. 19. xii. 3. xvii. 31. Acts x. 9.

δωρεά.

gift, John iv. 10. Acts ii. 38. viii. 20. x. 45. xi. 17. Rom. v. 15, 17 (–G°Lb). 2 Cor. ix. 15. Eph. iii. 7. iv. 7. Heb. vi. 4.

δωρεάν.

freely, Matt. x. 8*t*. Rom. iii. 24. 2 Cor. xi. 7. Rev. xxi. 6. xxii. 17.
for nought, 2 Thes. iii. 8.
without a cause, John xv. 25.
in vain, Gal. ii. 21.

δωρέω.

give, Mark xv. 45. 2 Pet. i. 3, 4.

δώρημα.

gift, Rom. v. 16. Jas. i. 17.

δῶρον.

gift, Matt. ii. 11. v. 23, 24*t*. viii. 4. xv. 5. xxiii. 18, 19*t*. Mark vii. 11. Luke xxi. 1. Eph. ii. 8. Heb. v. 1. viii. 3, 4. ix. 9. xi. 4. Rev. xi. 10.
offering, Luke xxi. 4.

δωροφορία, bringing of gifts.
Rom. xv. 31, for *διακονία*, L.

ἔα, imper. of ἐάω.

let alone, Mark i. 24 (–G[o]LTr*S*). Luke iv. 34(*marg.* **away**).

ἐάν.

(a) Without other particles.

I. *With the Indicative*, **if**, 1 John v. 15(ἀν L).

II. *With the Subjunctive*,

(a) *Present*, **if**, Matt. v. 23. vi. 22, 23. viii. 2. x. 13. xv. 14. xvii. 20. xxi. 21. Mark i. 40. ix. 43, 45, 47. xiv. 31. Luke v. 12. vi. 33, 34(*aor.* L; *ind. pres.* G″L[m]TTr). x. 6. xii. 38 (*κἀν* for *καὶ ἐάν* Tr). xix. 31. John v. 31. vi. 51. vii. 37. viii. 16, 54. ix. 31. xi. 9, 10. xii. 26*t*. xiii. 17, 35. xiv. 15, 23. xv. 14. xxi. 22, 23, 25. Acts v. 38. xxvi. 5.

Rom. ii. 25*t*, 26. xii. 20*t*. xiii. 4. xiv. 23. 1 Cor. v. 11. vi. 4. vii. 28, 36. viii. 8. xi. 14, 15. xiv. 14, 24. xvi. 4, 7. Col. iii. 13. 1 Thes. iii. 8 (*ind.* T). 1 Tim. i. 8. iii. 15. 2 Tim. ii. 5. Heb. x. 38. xiii. 23. Jas. ii. 15. 1 John i. 7, 9. ii. 3, 15, 29. iii. 20. iv. 12. v. 14(ἀν L).

and if, John vi. 62.

though, Acts xiii. 41. Rom. ix. 27. 1 Cor. iv. 15. ix. 16. xiii. 1, 2(*κἀν* for *καὶ ἐάν* L), 2. Jas. ii. 14.

(b) *Aorist*, **if**, Matt. iv. 9. v. 13, 46, 47. vi. 14. vii. 9 *and* 10 (–LTr*S*, *ind.* LTTr*S*). ix. 21. xii. 11. xvi. 26. xviii. 12, 13, 15*t*, 17*t*, 19. xxi. 3, 24, 25, 26. xxii. 24. xxiv. 23, 26. xxviii. 14. Mark iii. 24, 25. iv. 26(–Tr*S*). vii. 11. viii. 3, 36(–, *inf.*, T*S*). ix. 50. x. 12. xi. 3, 31, 32 (–G″LTTr*S*). xii. 19. xiii. 21.

Luke iv. 7. xi. 12(–Tr*S*, *ind.* TTr*S*). xiv. 34. xv. 8. xvi. 30. xvii. 3*t*, 4. xix. 40(*ind. fut.* LTTr*S*). xx. 5, 28. xxii. 67, 68. John iii. 12. v. 43. vii. 17. viii. 31, 36, 51, 52, 55 (*κἀν* for *καὶ ἐάν* LTr*S*). ix. 22. x. 9. xi. 40, 48, 57. xii. 24, 32, 47. xiv. 3, 14. xv. 7, 10. xvi. 7. xix. 12. Acts ix. 2.

Rom. vii. 2, 3*t*. x. 9. xi. 22. xv. 24. 1 Cor. iv. 19. vii. 8, 39, 40. viii. 10. x. 28. xii. 15, 16. xiv. 6, 8, 23, 30. xvi. 10. 2 Cor. v. 1. ix. 4. xiii. 2. Gal. v. 2. Col. iv. 10. 1 Tim. ii. 15. 2 Tim. ii. 21.

Heb. iii. 7, 15. iv. 7. Jas. ii. 2. iv. 15. v. 19. 1 Pet. iii. 13. 1 John i. 6, 8, 10. ii. 1, 24. iv. 20. v. 16. 3 John 10. Rev. iii. 20. xxii. 18, 19.

though, Luke xvi. 31. 1 Cor. xiii. 3*t*. 2 Cor. xii. 6.

when, 1 Cor. xiv. 16. 1 John iii. 2.

(b) With other particles.

With the Subjunctive, Present ([p]), *Aorist* ([a]).

καὶ ἐάν, **though**, Gal. i. 8[p]([a] L[m]*S*).

ἐὰν καί, **if** (*marg.* **although**), Gal. vi. 1[a].

ἐὰν δὲ καί, **but and if**, 1 Cor. vii. 11[a], 28[a].

ἐὰν δέ, **but and if**, Matt. xxiv. 48[a]. Luke xii. 45[a]. xx. 6[a].

ἐάνπερ, **if**, Heb. iii. 6[p](*ἐάν* L[b]T, *κἀν* *S*), 14[p]. vi. 3[p].

ἐάν τε, **whether**, Rom. xiv. 8[p], 8[p] (*ind.* L), 8[p]. —**or**, *ibid.*[p] (*ind.* L). —**though**, 2 Cor. x. 8[a].

ἐὰν μή, **if not**, Matt. vi. 15[a]. x. 13[p]. xviii. 16[a], 35[a]. John viii. 24[a].

xiii. 8ᵃ. xv. 6ᵃ. xvi. 7ᵃ. Rom. xi. 23ᵃ. 1 Cor. viii. 8ᵃ. ix. 16ᵖ. xiv. 11ᵖ. Jas. ii. 17ᵖ. 1 John iii. 21ᵖ. Rev. iii. 3ᵃ.—**if no**ᶜᶜ, 1 Cor. xiv. 28ᵖ.—**except**, Matt. v. 20ᵃ. xii. 29ᵃ. xviii. 3ᵃ. xxvi. 42ᵃ. Mark iii. 27ᵃ. vii. 3ᵃ, 4ᵃ. Luke xiii. 3ᵖ, 5ᵖ. John iii. 2ᵖ, 3ᵃ, 5ᵃ, 27ᵖ. iv. 48ᵃ. vi. 44ᵃ, 53ᵃ, 65ᵖ. xii. 24ᵃ. xv. 4tᵃ. xx. 25ᵃ. Acts viii. 31ᵃ. xv. 1ᵃ. xxvii. 31ᵃ. Rom. x. 15ᵃ. 1 Cor. xiv. 6ᵃ, 7ᵃ, 9ᵃ. xv. 36ᵃ. 2 Thes. ii. 3ᵃ. 2 Tim. ii. 5ᵃ. Rev. ii. 5ᵃ, 22ᵃ.—**but**, Mark x. 30ᵃ. John v. 19ᵃ. Gal. ii. 16.

*ἐὰν μὴ πρότερον*ᵃ, *see πρότερον*.

(c) After relative Pronouns and Adverbs.

Which it renders *indefinite*, like Eng. *ever*. Compare *ἄν*, where note the various readings. Used with the Subjunctive.

Add Luke xvii. 4(. . seven), LᵇS. 1 John ii. 28, for *ὅταν*, LS.

See also καθό, κἄν, ὅπου, ὅς, ὁσάκις, ὅσος, ὅστις, οὗ, τις, ὡς.

ἑαυτοῦ,

ἑαυτῆς, ἑαυτῶν, ἑαυτῷ, etc.

Masc. sing., ἑαυτοῦ.

his own, Luke xiv. 26. Rom. iv. 19. viii. 3. 1 Cor. vii. 2. x. 24. Gal. vi. 4. Eph. v. 29.

his, Luke xi. 21. xii. 47(*αὐτοῦ* LTrS). xiii. 19. xiv. 26(*αὐτοῦ* LTrS). xv. 5(*αὐτοῦ* TrS), 20(*αὐτοῦ* LTrS). xvi. 5. xix. 13. Rom. v. 8. 1 Cor. vii. 37. 2 Cor. iii. 13 (*αὐτοῦ* LT). Gal. vi. 8. Eph. v. 28, 33. 1 Thes. ii. 11, 12. iv. 4. 2 Thes. ii. 6. Rev. x. 7.

himself, Matt xii. 45t. Luke xi. 26. xxiv. 27(*αὐτοῦ* GLTTr). John v. 19. vii. 18. xi. 51. xvi. 13. Acts viii. 34. Rom. xiv. 12. 2 Cor. x. 7. Heb. i. 3(–LS). v. 3(*αὐτοῦ* L). vi. 13. ix. 7.

him, Mark xiv. 33(*αὐτοῦ* LTTrS).

of itself, Eph. iv. 16.

itself, John xv. 4. Rom. xiv. 14 (*αὐτοῦ* GLTS).

thineᶜ **own**, 1 Cor. x. 29.

thyself, John xviii. 34 (*σεαυτοῦ* L TrS).

Add, for *αὐτοῦ*, Matt. v. 28, L. Mark viii. 35²ᵈ, GTTr, –Gᵒ. Luke viii. 4, ix. 52, T. xiv. 27, LT. John ix. 21, TrS. Acts xxi. 11, G″LTS. Heb. xii. 16, LTS. Jas. i. 18, 26, T. 26²ᵈ, LT.—For *ἴδιος*, Luke ii. 3, LTr.

Fem., ἑαυτῆς.

her own, 1 Cor. xiii. 5.

her, Matt. xxiii. 37(*αὐτῆς* TTrᵇS, –L). Luke xiii. 34. 1 Cor. xi. 5(*αὐτῆς* L). 1 Thes. ii. 7.

With τὰ παρά, **that she had**, Mark v. 26(*τ. π. αὐτῆς* GLTTr).

of itself, Matt. vi. 34.

itself, Matt. xii. 25t.

Plural, ἑαυτῶν.

their own, Rom. xvi. 4, 18. Eph. v. 28. Phil. ii. 21. 2 Thes. iii. 12. Jude 13, 18.

hisᶜ **own**, Phil. ii. 4.

their, Matt. viii. 22. xxi. 8. xxv. 3(*αὐτῶν* GLTTr, –S). Luke ix. 60. xii. 36. xvi. 8. xix. 35(*αὐτῶν* LTr S). xxii. 66(*αὐτῶν* G′TrS). xxiii. 48(–GᵒᵒTTrS). Eph. v. 28. 1 Pet. iv. 19(*αὐτῶν* G′LTS). Jude 6. Rev. x. 3, 4(*om*S). xvii. 13 (*αὐτῶν* G″L TTrS).

themselves, Mark ix. 8. Phil. ii. 3.

them, Matt. xv. 30. xxv. 3. Mark ii. 19(*ap*). viii. 14. Acts xxi. 23.

ourᶜ **own**, 1 Thes. ii. 8.

of ᶜ**ourselves**, Heb. x. 25.

ourselvesᶜ, 2 Cor. iii. 5, 5 (*αὐτῶν* LT).

yourᶜ **own**, 1 Cor. vi. 19. Phil. ii. 12.

yourᶜ, Eph. v. 25(–LTS).

yourᶜ **own selves**, Luke xxi. 30.

yourselvesᶜ, Luke xii. 57.

youᶜ, Matt. xxvi. 11. Mark xiv. 7. John xii. 8.

one another, 1 Cor. vi. 7.

Add, for *αὐτῶν*, Matt. vi. 16¹ˢᵗ, L. xviii. 31, LTTrS. xxv. 1, LTTr.

4 2d, L*S*. 7, LTTr*S*. Luke ii. 39, LT Tr*S*. xvi. 4, TTr*S*. 2 Pet. ii. 11, Cm.

Dative sing., ἑαυτῷ.

to himself, Rom. xiv. 7*t*. 1 Cor. xi. 29. xiv. 28. 2 Cor. v. 18. x. 7. Eph. v. 27.

unto himself, 2 Cor. v. 19. Phil. iii. 21(αὐτῷ LT*S*). Tit. ii. 14. Heb. v. 4.

for himself, Luke xii. 21. xix. 12.

himself, Matt. xiii. 21. Mark v. 30. Luke vii. 39. xii. 17. xvi. 3. xviii. 4. John v. 26*t*. vi. 61. xi. 38. xiii. 32(αὐτῷ Tr). Acts x. 17. xii. 11. Rom. xv. 3. Eph. ii. 15(αὐτῷ L*S*). 1 John v. 10(αὐτῷ T).

him, Luke ix. 47. 1 Cor. xvi. 2.

Add, for αὐτῷ, 1 John iii. 15, L*S*.

Fem., ἑαυτῇ.

for her owncc, Acts vii. 21.

herself, Matt. ix. 21.

Plural, ἑαυτοῖς, ἑαυταῖς.

to themselves, Rom. xiii. 2. 1 Tim. iii. 13. 2 Tim. iv. 3. Heb. vi. 6.

unto themselves, Rom. ii. 14. 2 Cor. v. 15. 1 Pet. i. 12.

upon themselves, 2 Pet. ii. 1.

for themselves, 1 Tim. vi. 19.

among themselves, 2 Cor. x. 12.

themselves, Matt. ix. 3. xiv. 15. xvi. 7. xxi. 25, 38. Mark ii. 8. iv. 17. vi. 36, 51. Luke vii. 49. xviii. 9. Acts xxviii. 29(*ap*). Rom. i. 24 αὐτοῖς LT), 27. 2 Cor. x. 12.

among them, Matt. xxvii. 35(*ap*). John xix. 24.

ourselvesc, Rom. viii. 23. xv. 1. 2 Cor. i. 9*t*.

to c**yourselves,** Luke xvi. 9. Eph. v. 19.

unto c**yourselves,** Matt. xxiii. 31.

for c**yourselves,** Matt. xxv. 9.

among c**yourselves,** Luke xxii. 17 (εἰς ἑαυτούς LTTr, ἀλλήλοις *S*).

With παρά, **in your**c **own conceits,** Rom. xi. 25 (ἐν ἑ. T). xii. 16.

yourselvesc, Matt. iii. 9. xvi. 8. Mark ix. 50. Luke iii. 8. xii. 33. xvii. 3. xxi. 34. Acts v. 35. 1 Thes. v. 13 (αὐτοῖς G''*S*). Heb. x. 34. Jas. ii. 4.

youc, John v. 42. vi. 53.

one another, Eph. iv. 32. Col. iii. 13.

Add, for αὐτοῖς, John xvii. 14, Tr*S*.

Accus. masc., ἑαυτόν.

himself, Matt. xii. 26. xvi. 24. xviii. 4. xxiii. 12*t*. xxvii. 42. Mark iii. 26. v. 5. viii. 34. xii. 33. xv. 31. Luke ix. 23, 25. x. 29. xi. 18. xiv. 11*t*. xv. 17. xviii. 11, 14*t*. xxiii. 35. xxiv. 12(*ap*). John ii. 24 (αὐτόν LTTr*S*). v. 18. viii. 22. xiii. 4. xix. 7. xxi. 1, 7. Acts i. 3. v. 36. viii. 9. xiv. 17(αὐτόν L*S*). xvi. 27. xix. 31. xxviii. 16. Rom. xiv. 22. 1 Cor. iii. 18. xi. 28. xiv. 4. 2 Cor. x. 18. Gal. i. 4. ii. 12, 20. vi. 3, 4. Eph. v. 2, 25, 33. Phil. ii. 7, 8. 2 Thes. ii. 4. 1 Tim. ii. 6. 2 Tim. ii. 13, 21. Tit. ii. 14. Heb. v. 5. vii. 27. ix. 14, 25. Jas. i. 24, 27. 1 John iii. 3. v. 18(αὐτόν T).

he himselfcc, Luke xxiii. 2. Acts xxv. 4.

thyselfc, Rom. xiii. 9 (σεαυτόν LT *S*). Gal. v. 14(σεαυτόν GLT*S*).

Add, for αὐτόν, John xix. 12, GLT Tr*S*. Heb. xiii. 3, L, ἑαυτούς *S*. For σεαυτόν, Matt. xxii. 39, G'.

Fem., ἑαυτήν.

herself, Luke i. 24. Rev. ii. 20. xviii. 7(αὐτήν LTTr*S*). xix. 7.

itself, Mark iii. 24, 25. Luke xi. 17.

With κατά, **alone** (*Gr.* by itself), Jas. ii. 17.

Neut., ἐν καθ' ἑαυτό, **each of them,** Rev. iv. 8(*ap*).

Plural, ἑαυτούς, ἑαυτάς.

their own selves, 2 Cor. viii. 5.

themselves, Matt. xix. 12. Mark ix. 10. x. 26. xi. 31. xii. 7. xiv. 4. xvi. 3. Luke vii. 30. xx. 5, 14(ἀλλήλους TTr*S*), 20. xxii. 23. xxiii. 12(αὐτούς Tr*S*). John vii. 35. xi. 55. xii. 19. Acts xxiii. 12, 21. 1 Cor. xvi. 15. 2 Cor. x. 12*tr*. Eph. iv. 19. 1 Tim. ii. 9. vi. 10. 1 Pet.

iii. 5. Jude 12, 19(C? – StG°°LT*S*). Rev. vi. 15. viii. 6(αὐτούς L*S*).

With πρός, **unto their own home,** John xx. 10(π. αὐτούς TTr*S*).

they[cc], Rev. ii. 9. iii. 9.

ourselves[c], Acts xxiii. 14. 1 Cor. xi. 31. 2 Cor. iii. 1. iv. 2, 5*t*. v. 12. vi. 4. vii. 1. x. 12, 14. 2 Thes. iii. 9. 1 John i. 8.

your[c] **own selves,** 2 Cor. xiii. 5*t*. Jas. i. 22.

yourselves, Mark ix. 33 (– G°°LTr*S*). xiii. 9. Luke xvi. 15. xvii. 14. xxiii. 28. Acts xiii. 46. xv. 29. xx. 28. Rom. vi. 11, 13, 16. xii. 19. 2 Cor. vii. 11. xiii. 5. 1 Pet. iv. 8. 1 John v. 21 (ἑαυτά L*S*). 2 John 8. Jude 20, 21.

one another, Col. iii. 16. Heb. iii. 13. 1 Pet. iv. 10.

Add Mark i. 27, for αὐτούς, LTTr. Rev. ii. 2(*ap*).

See also προσέχω, ταράσσω, ὑπάρχω.

ἐάω.

let, Acts xxvii. 32.

suffer, Matt. xxiv. 43. Luke iv. 41. xxii. 51. Acts xiv. 16. xvi. 7. xix. 30. xxviii. 4. 1 Cor. x. 13. Rev. ii. 20(ἀφίημι GLTTr*S*).

let alone, Acts v. 38(ἀφίημι G′L*S*).

leave, Acts xxiii. 32.

commit (*marg.* **leave**), Acts xxvii. 40.

ἑβδομήκοντα.

seventy, Luke x. 1, 17.

three-score and ten, Acts xxiii. 23.

With πέντε, **three-score and fifteen,** Acts vii. 14.

With ἕξ, **three-score and sixteen,** Acts xxvii. 37.

ἑβδομηκοντάκις.

seventy times, Matt. xviii. 22.

ἕβδομος.

seventh, John iv. 52. Heb. iv. 4*t*. Jude 14. Rev. viii. 1. x. 7. xi. 15. xvi. 17. xxi. 20.

Ἑβραϊστί.

in (the) Hebrew, John xix. 13, 17, 20.

in the Hebrew tongue, John v. 2. Rev. ix. 11. xvi. 16.

Add John xx. 16(. . Rabboni), G′L[b]TTr*S*.

ἐγγίζω.

draw near, Matt. xxi. 34. Luke xv. 1. xxi. 8. xxii. 47. xxiv. 15.

draw nigh, Matt. xv. 8(*ap*). xxi. 1. Luke xv. 25. xxi. 28. xxii. 1. xxiv. 28. Acts vii. 17. x. 9[p]. Heb. vii. 19. Jas. iv. 8*t*. v. 8.

come near, Luke xviii. 40[p]. xix. 41. Acts ix. 3. xxi. 33. xxiii. 15.

come nigh, Mark xi. 1. Luke vii. 12. x. 9, 11. xviii. 35. xix. 29, 37[p]. Acts xxii. 6[p].

approach, Luke xii. 33. Heb. x. 25.

be nigh, Luke xxi. 20. Phil. ii. 30.

be at hand, Matt. iii. 2. iv. 17. x. 7. xxvi. 45, 46. Mark i. 15. xiv. 42. Rom. xiii. 12. 1 Pet. iv. 7.

ἐγγράφω, ἐνγ. T*S*.

write in, 2 Cor. iii. 2, 3.

Add Luke x. 20, for γράφω, TTr*S*.

ἔγγυος.

surety, Heb. vii. 22.

ἐγγύς.

near, Matt. xxiv. 33. Mark xiii. 28. Rom. xiii. 11.

near to, John iii. 23. xi. 54.

nigh, Matt. xxiv. 32. Mark xiii. 29. John vi. 4. Acts xxvii. 8. Rom. x. 8. Eph. ii. 13, 17.

nigh to, Luke xix. 11. John xix. 20. Acts ix. 38.

nigh unto, John vi. 19, 23. xi. 18. Heb. vi. 8.

from, Acts i. 12.

at hand, Matt. xxvi. 18. John ii. 13. vii. 2. Phil. iv. 5. Rev. i. 3. xxii. 10.

nigh at hand, Luke xxi. 30, 31. John xi. 55. xix. 42.

ready, Heb. viii. 13.

ἐγείρω.

awake, Matt. viii. 25.

raise, Matt. x. 8(– G°T). Luke vii. 22. ix. 22(ἀνίστημι G′LT). xx. 37.

John xii. 1, 9, 17. Acts iii. 15. iv. 10. xiii. 23(ἄγω GLT*S*), 30. xxvi. 8. Rom. vi. 9. vii. 4. x. 9. 1 Cor. xv. 16, 17, 42, 43*t*, 44, 52(ἀνίστημι L). 2 Cor. i. 9. Gal. i. 1. Eph. i. 20[p]. Col. ii. 12. 1 Thes. i. 10. 2 Tim. ii. 8.

raise up, Matt. iii. 9. xi. 5. Luke i. 69. iii. 8. John ii. 19. v. 21. Acts v. 30. x. 40. xii. 7. xiii. 22. Rom. iv. 24. vi. 4. viii. 11*t*. 1 Cor. vi. 14. xv. 15*t*, 35. 2 Cor. iv. 14*t*. Heb. xi. 19. Jas. v. 15. 1 Pet. i. 21.

raise again, Matt. xvi. 21. xvii. 23 (ἀνίστημι L). Acts xiii. 37. Rom. iv. 25.

rear up, John ii. 20.

lift up, Mark i. 31. ix. 27. Acts iii. 7.

lift out, Matt. xii. 11.

take up, Acts x. 26.

Mid., and Pass. aor.

awake, Rom. xiii. 11. Eph. v. 14 (*act.* GLT*S*).

arise, Matt. ii. 13, 14[p], 20, 21. viii. 15, 26. ix. 5(*act.* G″LTTr*S*), 6(*act.* LTr), 7, 19, 25. xvii. 7. xxiv. 24. xxv. 7. xxvii. 52. Mark ii. 9(*act.* GLT*S*), 11 (*act.* GLTTr*S*), 12. v. 41(*act.* GLTTr*S*). Luke v. 24(*act.* GLT*S*). vii. 14. viii. 24(διεγείρω T Tr*S*), 54(*act.* L). John vii. 52. xi. 29. xiv. 31. Acts ix. 8.

rise, Matt. xi. 11. xiv. 2. xxiv. 7, 11. xxvi. 46. xxvii. 64. xxviii. 6, 7. Mark iv. 27. vi. 14(ἀνίστημι T), 16. x. 49(*act.* GLTTr*S*). xii. 26. xiii. 8, 22. xiv. 28. xvi. 6, 14[p](*ap*). Luke ix. 7. xi. 8. xxi. 10. xxiv. 6, 34. John ii. 22. v. 8(*act.* LT*S*). xiii. 4. xxi. 14[p]. 1 Cor. xv. 12, 13, 14, 15, 16, 20, 29, 32. Rev. xi. 1(*act.* LT*S*).

rise up, Matt. xii. 42. Mark xiv. 42. Luke v. 23(*act.* GLT*S*). vi. 8 (*act.* GLT*S*). vii. 16. xi. 31. xiii. 25. Acts iii. 6(*act.* LT, -*S*).

rise again, Matt. xxvi. 32. xxvii. 63. Rom. viii. 34. 1 Cor. xv. 4. 2 Cor. v. 15.

ἔγειραι εἰς τὸ μέσον, **stand forth**, Mark iii. 3(*act.* GLTTr*S*).

Add, for διεγείρω, Matt. i. 24, LTr*S*. Mark iv. 38, Tr*S*. For ἀνίστημι, Matt. xvii. 9, LTTr. xx. 19, TTr*S*. For ἐπιφέρω, Phil. i. 16(17), G″LT*S*.

ἔγερσις.

resurrection, Matt. xxvii. 53.

ἐγκάθετος.

spy, Luke xx. 20.

ἐγκαίνια, ἐνκ. T*S*.

feast of the dedication, John x. 22.

ἐγκαινίζω.

consecrate (*marg.* **make new**). Heb. x. 20.

dedicate(*marg.* **purify**), Heb. ix. 18.

ἐγκακέω, be discouraged.

Luke xviii. 1, etc., *see* ἐκκακέω.

ἐγκαλέω.

call in question, Acts xix. 40.

implead, Acts xix. 38.

accuse, Acts xxiii. 28, 29. xxvi. 2, 7.

With κατά, **lay a thing to the charge of**, Rom. viii. 33.

ἐγκαταλείπω.

leave, Acts ii. 27. Rom. ix. 29.

forsake, Matt. xxvii. 46. Mark xv. 34. 2 Cor. iv. 9. 2 Tim. iv. 10, 16. Heb. x. 25. xiii. 5.

Add Acts ii. 31, for καταλείπω, G″LT*S*.

ἐγκαυχάομαι, pride one's self in.

2 Thes. i. 4, for καυχάομαι, LT*S*.

ἐγκατοικέω, ἐνκ. T*S*.

dwell among, 2 Pet. ii. 8.

ἐγκεντρίζω.

graff in, Rom. xi. 17, 19, 23*t*.

graff into, Rom. xi. 24*t*.

ἔγκλημα.

crime laid against one, Acts xxv. 16.

laid to one's charge, Acts xxiii. 29.

ἐγκομβόομαι.

be clothed with, 1 Pet. v. 5.

ἐγκοπή.

With δίδωμι, **hinder**, 1 Cor. ix. 12.

ἐγκόπτω.

hinder, Rom. xv. 22. 1 Thes. ii. 18.
be tedious unto, Acts xxiv. 4.
Add, for ἀνακόπτω, Gal. v. 7, GLT *S.* For ἐκκόπτω, 1 Pet. iii. 7, GL*S*

ἐγκράτεια.

temperance, Acts xxiv. 25. Gal. v. 23. 2 Pet. i. 6*t.*

ἐγκρατεύομαι.

can[c] **contain,** 1 Cor. vii. 9.
be temperate, 1 Cor. ix. 25.

ἐγκρατής.

temperate, Tit. i. 8.

ἐγκρίνω.

make of the number, 2 Cor. x. 12.

ἐγκρύπτω.

hide, Matt. xiii. 33 (κρύπτω G′). Luke xiii. 21 (κρύπτω TTr).

ἔγκυος.

great with child, Luke ii. 5.

ἐγχρίω.

anoint, Rev. iii. 18.

ἐγώ,

ἐμοῦ, μοῦ, etc., κἀγώ for καὶ ἐγώ, *etc.,* [k].

Nom., ἐγώ.

I, Matt. iii. 11, 14. v. 22, 28, 32, 34, 39, 44. viii. 7, 9. x. 16. xi. 10 (-L[b]). xii. 27, 28. xiv. 27. xviii. 33([k] LTTr*S*). xx. 15, 22, 22(*ap*), 23(*ap*). xxi. 27, 30. xxii. 32. xxiii. 34. xxiv. 5. xxv. 27. xxvi. 22, 25, 33, 39. xxviii. 20.

Mark i. 2(-LTTr), 8. vi. 16, 50. ix. 25. x. 38*t*, 39*t*. xi. 33. xii. 26. xiii. 6. xiv. 19, 19(*ap*), 29, 36, 58, 62. Luke i. 18, 19. iii. 16. vii. 8, 27(-LTTr*S*). viii. 46. ix. 9*t*. x. 3 (-LTTr*S*), 35. xi. 19. xv. 17. xix. 22, 23. xx. 8. xxi. 8, 15. xxii. 27, 32, 70. xxiii. 14. xxiv. 39, 49.

John i. 20, 23, 26, 27(-G[oo]L[b]Tr*S*), 30, 31. iii. 28. iv. 14, 26, 32, 38. v. 7, 30, 31, 34, 36, 36(-LTr*S*), 43, 45. vi. 20, 35, 40(-L[b]), 41, 44, 48, 51*t*, 51(*ap*), 54, 63, 70. vii. 7, 8, 17, 29, 34, 36. viii. 11(*ap*), 12, 14, 15, 16*t*, 18, 21*t*, 22, 23*t*, 24, 28, 29, 38, 42, 45, 49, 50, 54, 55, 58. ix. 9, 39. x. 7, 9, 10, 11, 14, 17, 18, 25, 30, 34. xi. 25, 27, 42. xii. 26, 46, 47, 49, 50. xiii. 7, 14, 15, 18, 19, 26, 33. xiv. 3, 4(-L[b]), 6, 10*t*, 11, 12*t*, 14(τοῦτο L[m]), 16([k] LTTr*S*), 19, 20, 21([k] LTTr*S*), 27, 28. xv. 1, 5, 10, 14, 16, 19, 20, 26. xvi. 4, 7*t*, 16(*ap*), 17 (-LTr, ᾧ for ὅτι ἐγώ *S*), 26, 27, 33. xvii. 4, 9, 11([k] LTTr*S*), 12, 14*t*, 16, 19(-L[b]*S*), 22([k] LTTr*S*), 23, 24, 25. xviii. 5, 6, 8, 20*t*, 21, 26, 35, 37(-Tr), 37(-L[b]*S*), 38. xix. 6.

Acts vii. 7, 32. ix. 5, 10, 16. x. 20, 21. xi. 5, 17. xiii. 25, 33, 41. xvii. 3, 23. xviii. 6, 10, 15. xx. 22, 25, 26(εἰμί L*S*), 29. xxi. 13, 39. xxii. 3, 8*t*, 19, 21, 28*t*. xxiii. 1, 6*t*. xxiv. 21. xxv. 18, 20, 25. xxvi. 9, 10, 15*t*. xxviii. 17.

Rom. vii. 9*t*, 14, 17, 20(-G[oo]L), 20, 24, 25. x. 19. xi. 1, 13, 19. xii. 19. xiv. 11. xv. 14. xvi. 4, 22. 1 Cor. i. 12*f*. ii. 3([k] L*S*). iii. 1([k] GLT*S*), 4*t*, 6. iv. 15. v. 3. vi. 12. vii. 10, 12, 28. ix. 6, 15, 26. x. 30*t*. xi. 23. xv. 9, 10, 11. xvi. 10([k] LT*S*). 2 Cor. i. 23. ii. 2, 10([k] LT*S*), 10. x. 1. xi. 23, 29. xii. 11, 13, 15, 16.

Gal. i. 12. ii. 19, 20. iv. 12. v. 2, 10, 11. vi. 17. Eph. iii. 1. iv. 1. v. 32. Phil. iii. 4*t*, 13. iv. 11. Col. i. 23, 25. 1 Thes. ii. 18. 1 Tim. i. 15. ii. 7. 2 Tim. i. 11. iv. 1(*omS*), 6. Tit. i. 5. Phm. 13, 19*t*.

Heb. i. 5*t*. ii. 13*t*. v. 5. x. 30. xii. 26. 1 Pet. i. 16. 2 Pet. i. 17. 2 John 1*t*. 3 John 1. Rev. i. 8, 9, 11(*ap*), 17. ii. 22(*omS*), 23. iii. 9(-G[oo]), 19. v. 4. xvii. 7. xxi. 2(*omS*), 6 (-G′), 6. xxii. 8, 13, 16*t*.

me[cc], Phm. 20.

With αὐτός, **myself,** Rom. ix. 3.

κἀγώ, **and I,** Matt. xi. 28. xxvi. 15. Luke ii. 48. xi. 9. xvi. 9(καὶ ἐγώ T Tr*S*). xxii. 29. John i. 31, 33, 34. v. 17. vi. 56, 57. viii. 26. x. 27, 28, 38. xii. 32. xiv. 20. xv. 4, 5. xvii. 21, 26. xx. 15. Acts xxii. 13, 19. Rom. xi. 3. 1 Cor. ii. 1. 2 Cor. vi. 17.

xii. 20. Gal. vi. 14. Phil. ii. 28. Heb. viii. 9. Jas. ii. 18*t*. —**I also,** Matt. ii. 8. x. 32, 33. xvi. 18. xxi. 24. Mark xi. 29(–TTr). Luke xx. 3. Acts x. 26. Rom. iii. 7. 2 Cor. xi. 18, 21. Eph. i. 15. Phil. ii. 19. Rev. ii. 6. iii. 10. —**also I,** 1 Cor. vii. 40. —**even I,** 1 Cor. vii. 8. x. 33. Rev. ii. 27. —**even I also,** 1 Cor. xi. 1. Rev. iii. 21. —**even so I,** John x. 15. xx. 21. —**so I,** John xv. 9. 2 Cor. xi. 22*tr*. —**even so I also,** John xvii. 18. —**I in like wise,** Matt. xxi. 24. —**I,** Acts xxvi. 29. 2 Cor. xi. 16. Gal. iv. 12. 1 Thes. iii. 5.

Add Luke xi. 20(I), Tr[b]. xxiv. 36 (*ap*). John xvi. 7(I[3d]), G'LT. Acts xxvi. 17, for νῦν, GLT*S*. xxvii. 23 (I[1st]), L*S*. Rev. xxii. 18, for γάρ, GLTTr*S*.

See also κρίνω, πιστεύω.

Genit., 1, ἐμοῦ.

of me, Rom. i. 12.

With αὐτός, **of myself,** Rom. xvi. 2.

my, Matt. v. 11. x. 18, 39. xvi. 25. Mark viii. 35. x. 29. xiii. 9. Luke ix. 24. John xiii. 38. Rom.

With παρά, **my,** Rom. xi. 27.

mine, Rom. xvi. 13.

me, Matt. vii. 23. xi. 29. xii. 30*tr*. xv. 5, 8. xvii. 27. xxv. 41. xxvi. 23, 38, 39, 40, 42 (–G[oo]L[b]TTr*S*). Mark vii. 6, 11. xiv. 18, 20, 36. Luke v. 8. viii. 46. x. 16. xi. 7, 23*tr*. xii. 13. xiii. 27. xv. 31. xvi. 3. xxii. 21, 28, 37, 42. xxiii. 43. xxiv. 44. John iv. 9. v. 7, 32*t*, 36, 37, 39, 46. viii. 18, 29. x. 8, 9, 18, 25. xiii. 8, 18(μοῦ Tr). xiv. 6. xv. 5, 26, 27. xvi. 32. xvii. 24. xviii. 34. xix. 11. Acts viii. 24. xi. 5. xx. 34. xxii. 18. xxiii. 11. xxv. 9.

Rom. xv. 18, 30. xvi. 7. 2 Cor. i. 19. ii. 2. vii. 7. xii. 6, 8. Gal. i. 11, 17. ii. 20. Eph. vi. 19. Phil. iv. 10. 2 Tim. i. 13. ii. 2. iv. 11, 17. Tit. iii. 15. Heb. x. 7. Rev. i. 12. iii. 4, 18, 20, 21. iv. 1. x. 8. xvii. 1. xxi. 9, 15. xxii. 12.

Add, for μοῦ, *see* μοῦ.

2, μοῦ.

of me, Matt. x. 37*t*, 38. Acts i. 4. 1 Cor. iv. 16. xi. 1. Phil. iii. 17.

my, Matt. ii. 6, 15. iii. 17. vii. 21. viii. 6, 8*t*, 9, 21. ix. 18. x. 22, 32, 33. xi. 10, 27, 29, 30*t*. xii. 18*f*, 44, 48*t*, 49*t*, 50*t*. xiii. 30, 35. xv. 13, 22. xvi. 17, 18. xvii. 5, 15. xviii. 5, 10, 19, 21, 35. xix. 20(–G[o]LTTr*S*), 29. xx. 21, 23*t*, 23 (–G[oo]LTTr*S*), 23. xxi. 13, 28(–G[oo]TTr*S*), 37. xxii. 4*t*, 44*t*. xxiv. 5, 9, 35, 36(–GLTr*S*), 48. xxv. 27, 34, 40(–L[b]). xxvi. 12, 18*t*, 26, 28, 29, 38, 39(–TTr[b]), 42, 53. xxvii. 35*t*(*ap*), 46*t*. xxviii. 10.

Mark i. 2, 11. iii. 33, 33(–TTr[b]), 34*t*, 35, 35(–LTr*S*). v. 23, 30. vi. 23. ix. 7, 17, 37, 39, 41(*om*). x. 20, 40, 40(*omS*). xi. 17. xii. 6, 36*t*. xiii. 6, 13, 31. xiv. 8, 14, 22, 24, 34. xv. 34*t*. xvi. 17(*ap*).

Luke i. 18, 20, 25, 43, 44, 46, 47*t*. ii. 49. iii. 22. vi. 47. vii. 6, 7, 8, 27, 44(μοί TTr), 44, 45, 46, 46(–G[o]). viii. 21*t*. ix. 35, 38, 48, 59, 61. x. 22, 29, 40. xi. 7, 24. xii. 4, 13, 17, 18, 18(–Tr), 18, 19, 45. xiv. 23, 24, 26, 27, 33. xv. 6, 17, 18, 24, 29. xvi. 3, 5, 24, 27. xviii. 21(–TTr[b]). xix. 8, 23, 46. xx. 13, 42*t*. xxi. 8, 12, 17, 33. xxii. 11, 19, 20, 28, 29, 30*t*, 42. xxiii. 46. xxiv. 39*t*, 49.

John ii. 16. iv. 49. v. 17, 24, 31, 43. vi. 32, 51, 54*t*, 55*t*, 56*t*, 65(–G[oo]LTTr*S*). viii. 14, 19*t*, 28(–LTTr*S*), 31, 38(–G[oo]LTTr), 49, 52, 54*t*. x. 15, 16, 17, 18, 25, 27, 28, 29, 29(–TTr[b]*S*), 32(–L[b]TTr[b]*S*), 37. xi. 21, 32. xii. 7, 27, 47, 48. xiii. 6, 8, 9, 37. xiv. 2, 7, 12(–G[oo]LTTr*S*), 13, 14, 20, 21*t*, 23*t*, 24, 26, 28(–G[o]L[b]TTr). xv. 1, 7, 8, 10*t*, 10(–LT), 14, 15, 16, 20, 21, 23, 24. xvi. 10(–G[oo]TTr*S*), 23, 24, 26. xviii. 37. xix. 24*t*. xx. 13, 17(–L[b]TTr), 17*tr*, 25*t*, 27*t*, 28*t*. xxi. 15, 16, 17.

Acts ii. 14, 17, 18*tr*, 25*t*, 26*tr*, 27, 34*t*. vii. 34, 49*t*, 50, 59. ix. 15, 16. x. 30. xi. 8. xiii. 22, 33. xv. 7, 17.

xvi. 15. xx. 24(–G°°LT*S*), 24, 25, 29, 34. xxii. 1. xxiv. 17. xxvi. 4. xxviii. 19.

Rom. i. 8, 9*t*, 9(10). ii. 16. vii. 4, 18, 23*tr*. ix. 1, 2, 3*t*, 17*t*, 25*t*, 26. x. 21. xi. 3, 14. xv. 14, 31. xvi. 3, 4, 5, 7*t*, 8, 9, 11, 21*t*, 25. 1 Cor. i. 4, 11. ii. 4*t*. iv. 14, 17*t*. viii. 13*t*. ix. 1, 15, 18, 27. x. 14, 29. xi. 24, 33. xiii. 3*t*. xiv. 14*t*, 18(*omS*), 19. xv. 58. xvi. 24. 2 Cor. ii. 13*t*. xii. 9, 9(–G°LT*S*), 9, 21. Gal. i. 14, 15. iv. 14(–G″, *see* ὑμῶν), 14, 19, 20. vi. 17. Eph. i. 16. iii. 4, 13, 14. vi. 10(–G°LT*S*), 19. Phil. i. 3, 7, 7(*marg.* **with**^{c} **me**), 8, 13, 14, 16, 20*t*. ii. 2, 12*tr*, 25*t*. iii. 1, 8(ἡμῶν L^{m}). iv. 1*t*, 3, 14, 19. Col. i. 24(*omS*), 24. ii. 1. iv. 10, 18. 2 Tim. i. 3, 6, 16. ii. 1, 8. iii. 10. iv. 16. Phm. 4*t*, 10(–G°°LT*S*), 20, 23, 24.

Heb. i. 5, 13. ii. 12. iii. 9, 10, 11*t*. iv. 3*t*, 5. v. 5. viii. 9, 10. x. 16, 34 (*see* δέσμιος), 38. xii. 5. Jas. i. 2, 16, 19. ii. 1, 3, 5, 14, 18(–G°°T*S*). iii. 1, 10, 12. v. 10(–LT), 12. 1 Pet. v. 13. 2 Pet. i. 14, 17. 1 John ii. 1. iii. 13 and 18(–G°°LT*S*). Rev. i. 20. ii. 3, 13*tr*, 16, 26, 27. iii. 5, 8*t*, 10, 12*five*, 16, 20, 21*t*. x. 10*t*. xi. 3. xviii. 4. xxii. 12.

mine, Mark ix. 24. Luke i. 44. ii. 30. xviii. 3. xix. 27. John ii. 4. ix. 11, 15, 30. Acts xxi. 13. Rom. xi. 13. xvi. 23. 2 Cor. xi. 30. xii. 5 (–L). Phil. i. 4. Rev. xxii. 16.

mine own, John viii. 50. Acts xiii. 22. xxvi. 4. Gal. i. 14.

of mine, Matt. vii. 24, 26. Luke xi. 6.

me, Matt. iii. 11. iv. 19. xvi. 23, 24. Mark i. 7, 17. v. 31. vii. 14. viii. 33, 34. Luke iv. 7(ἐμοῦ LTTr*S*), 8(*ap*). viii. 45, 45(*ap*), 46. ix. 23. xiv. 27. xix. 27. xxiii. 42. John i. 15*tr*, 27, 27(*ap*), 30*tr*. xi. 41, 42. xx. 17. Acts x. 30. xv. 7, 17. xxiv. 13. xxv. 11. xxvi. 3, 29. 1 Cor. xi. 2. xiv. 21. 2 Cor. xi. 1*t*, 28(μοί L*S*). Rev. i. 10.

to me, 2 Cor. xi. 9.

unto me, Matt. xvi. 23(ἐμοῦ LTr*S*). Acts xv. 13.

I^{co}, Matt. iii. 11. Mark i. 7. Luke iii. 16. xxii. 53. John xiv. 28. Acts xxii. 17. xxiv. 20. xxv. 15. 1 Cor. iv. 18. 2 Tim. i. 12. Heb. viii. 9.

Add, for ἐμοῦ, John xiii. 18, Tr. For μοί, Acts i. 8, LT*S*. 1 Cor. ix. 18, T*S*. 2 Cor. vi. 16, L*S*. For μέ, John vi. 40, G″LTTr*S*. 2 Cor. xii. 21, LT*S*. For ἐμός, 1 Cor. ix. 2, LT *S*. 2 Tim. iv. 6, L*S*. For ὑμῶν, Matt. xviii. 14, LTr. — Matt. iv. 10(ὀπίσω . .), G^{pr}L^{b}T. xx. 7(. . vineyard), L^{b}. xxv. 41(*ap*). Mark xiv. 14(. . guest c.), L^{b}TTr*S*. Luke xxiv. 44 (. . words), L^{b}TTr. 1 Cor. xiv. 39 (. . brethren), L^{b}*S*. Heb. viii. 10 (. . covenant), L^{b}. x. 38(t. just . .), LT*S*. Jas. v. 19(. . brethren), L*S*. 2 Pet. i. 17(υἱός μου ὁ ἀγαπητός . .), T. Rev. ii. 7(. . God), GT. 13(. . martyr), LT. iii. 2(. . God), GLT Tr*S*. vii. 14(. . Sir), GL^{b}TTr*S*.

Dative, 1, ἐμοί.

to me, Matt. xxv. 45. Rom. xiv. 11. Gal. ii. 6, 9. Phil. i. 21. iii. 1. 2 Tim. iv. 8. Phm. 11, 16.

τί ἐμοὶ καὶ σοί; **what have I to do with thee?** Mark v. 7. Luke viii. 28. John ii. 4.

unto me, Matt. xxv. 40. Luke iv. 6. John xviii. 35. xix. 10. Rom. vii. 13. Gal. vi. 14. Eph. iii. 8. Heb. x. 30.

for me, Phil. i. 7.

with me, Rom. vii. 21. 1 Cor. iv. 3.

at me, John vii. 23.

me, Matt. x. 32. xi. 6. xviii. 26 (ἐμέ Tr), 29(ἐμέ LTr). xxvi. 31. Mark xiv. 27(–G°°TTr*S*). Luke vii. 23. xii. 8. xv. 29. xxii. 37. John v. 46. vi. 56. viii. 12(μοί LTr). x. 38*t*. xii. 26*tr*. xiv. 10*t*, 11, 20, 30, xv. 2, 4*t*, 5, 6, 7. xvi. 33. xvii. 6 (^{k} TTr), 21, 23. Acts x. 28(^{k} LT*S*). xi. 12. xxii. 9. xxiv. 20 (–L*S*). xxvi. 13. xxviii. 18.

Rom. vii. 8, 17, 18, 20. 1 Cor. ix. 15. xiv. 11. xv. 10. xvi. 4. 2 Cor. i. 17. ix. 4. xi. 10. xiii. 3. Gal. i. 2, 16,* 24. ii. 3, 8(^{k} LT), 20. Phil. i. 26, 30*t*. ii. 22. iv. 9, 21. Col. i. 29. 1 Tim. i. 16.

my, Heb. xiii. 6.

mine, Rom. xii. 19.

I^{cc}, Rom. vii. 21. Gal. vi. 14.

κἀμοί, **to me also**, Luke i. 3.—**of me also**, 1 Cor. xv. 8. — **me also**, Acts viii. 19.

Add Mark xiv. 6, for *ἐμέ*, GLTTr*S*. *See also ἐλλογέω, καύχημα.*

2, *μοί.*

to me, Matt. vii. 22. xiv. 18. xvii. 17. Luke i. 43, 49. x. 22. xviii. 13. Acts ii. 28. vii. 42. xxii. 9. xxv. 27. Rom. xv. 15. 2 Cor. xii. 7. Gal. ii. 6. iv. 15. Phil. iii. 7. Col. i. 25. 2 Tim. iv. 11. Heb. i. 5. viii. 10. Rev. vii. 14.

unto me, Matt. vii. 21. xi. 27. xv. 8(*ap*). xxi. 2. xxv. 20, 22. xxviii. 18. Luke i. 38. iv. 23. xxii. 29. xxiii. 14. John i. 33. v. 11. ix. 11. xii. 50. Acts i. 8(*μοῦ* LT*S*). ix. 15. xi. 7. xxii. 7, 13, 18. xxvii. 21. Rom. ix. 19. xii. 3. 1 Cor. i. 11. iii. 10. vi. 12. vii. 1(–T*S*). ix. 16. xvi. 9. 2 Cor. ii. 12. xii. 9. Gal. ii. 9. Eph. iii. 3, 7. vi. 19. Col. iv. 11. 2 Tim. iii. 11. Phm. 13, 19. Heb. xiii. 6. Rev. i. 17(*omS*). v. 5. vii. 13. x. 4(*omS*), 9, 11. xiv. 13(*omS*). xvii. 1(*omS*), 7, 15. xix. 9*t*, 10. xxi. 5(–G^{oo}LTTr), 6. xxii. 6, 9, 10.

for me, Matt. xx. 15. 1 Cor. vi. 12. ix. 15. x. 23*t*(*omS*). 2 Cor. ix. 1. xii. 1(*ap*). 2 Tim. iv. 8.

with me, Luke i. 25. Rom. vii. 18. Phil. iv. 15.

in me, Rom. vii. 13.

me, Matt. ii. 8. iv. 9. viii. 21, 22. ix. 9. xiv. 8. xv. 25, 32. xvi. 24. xviii. 28(–G^{oo}LTTr*S*). xix. 21, 28. xx. 13. xxi. 24. xxii. 19. xxv. 35, 42. xxvi. 15, 53. xxvii. 10. Mark ii. 14. vi. 25. viii. 2(–LTr^{b}), 34. x. 21. xi. 29, 30. xii. 15. Luke v. 27. vii. 45. ix. 23, 59*t*, 61. x. 40. xi. 5, 7. xv. 6, 9, 12. xvii. 8. xviii. 5, 22. xx. 3, 24. xxii. 68(–TTr^{b}*S*). John i. 43(44). iii. 28. iv. 7, 10, 15, 21, 29, 39. v. 36. vi. 37, 39. viii. 45, 46. x. 27, 29, 37. xii. 49. xiii. 36, 36(–LTTr*S*). xiv. 11, 11(–G^{o}TTr^{b}), 31. xvii. 4, 6, 7, 8, 9, 11, 12, 22, 24*t*. xviii. 9, 11. xx. 15. xxi. 19, 22. Acts v. 8. vii. 7, 49. xi. 9(–LT*S*), 12. xii. 8. xiii. 2. xx. 19, 22. xxi. 39. xxii. 5, 11, 27. xxiii. 19, 30. xxv. 24. xxvii. 23, 25.

Rom. ix. 1. xv. 30. 1 Cor. ix. 16. xv. 32. 2 Cor. xii. 13. xiii. 10. Gal. iv. 21. vi. 17. Eph. iii. 2. Phil. ii. 18. iv. 3. 2 Tim. iv. 8, 14, 16, 17. Phm. 22. Heb. ii. 13. x. 5. Jas. ii. 18. 2 Pet. i. 14. Rev. x. 9. xi. 1. xxi. 10. xxii. 1, 8.

my, Mark v. 9. Acts vii. 49. 1 Cor. ix. 18(*μοῦ* T*S*). 2 Cor. vi. 16(*μοῦ* L*S*), 18. vii. 4*t*. Phil. i. 19, 22^{cc}. iv. 16. Rev. xxi. 7.

mine, Luke ix. 38.

I^{cc}, Acts iii. 6. xviii. 10. xxi. 37. xxii. 6, 17. Rom. vii. 10. ix. 2. 1 Cor. v. 12. ix. 16.

Not rendered, Acts xxiv. 11.

Add, for *ἐμοί*, John viii. 12, LTr. For *μοῦ*, Luke vii. 44, TTr. 2 Cor. xi. 28, L*S*.—Acts xx. 23(witnesseth . .), GLT*S*.

Accus., 1, *ἐμέ.*

myself, Phm. 17.

me, Matt. x. 37*t*, 40*t*. xviii. 5, 6, 21. xxvi. 10, 11. Mark ix. 37*tr*, 42 (–T*S*). xiv. 6 (*ἐμοί* GLTTr*S*), 7. Luke iv. 18. ix. 48*t*. x. 16*t*. xxii. 53. xxiii. 28. xxiv. 39. John vi. 35, 37, 47(–TTr^{b}*S*), 57. vii. 7, 38. viii. 19*t*, 42. xi. 25, 26. xii. 8, 30, 44*t*, 45, 46, 48. xiii. 18, 20*t*. xiv. 1, 9, 12. xv. 18, 20, 23, 24. xvi. 3, 9, 14, 23, 27, 32(^{k} TTr*S*). xvii. 18, 20, 23. xviii. 8. Acts iii. 22. vii. 37 (*marg.* **myself**). viii. 24. xiii. 25. xxii. 6. xxvi. 18.

Rom. i. 15. x. 20*t*. xv. 3. 1 Cor. ix. 3. xv. 10. 2 Cor. ii. 5. xi. 10.

xii. 6, 9. Phil. ii. 27. 2 Tim. i. 8. Phm. 17(μέ GLTS). Rev. i. 17.

κἀμέ, **both me**, John vii. 28.—**I**[co] **also**, 1 Cor. xvi. 4.

τὰ κατ' ἐμέ, **my affairs**, Eph. vi. 21. —**my state**, Col. iv. 7.—**the things which happened unto me**, Phil. i. 12.

τὰ περὶ ἐμέ, **how**[c] **it will go with me**, Phil. ii. 23.

I[cc], John iii. 30. ix. 4.

Add, for μέ, John vi. 35, Tr*S*. 44[1st], TTr. 45, Tr. x. 32, TTr*S*. Acts xiii. 25, xxii. 8, 13, L*S*. xxiv. 19, LT*S*. 1 Cor. xvi. 11, L. For ἐμοί, Matt. xviii. 26, Tr. 29, LTr.

2, μέ.

me, Matt. iii. 14. viii. 2. x. 33, 40. xi. 28. xiv. 28, 30. xv. 8, 9, 22. xviii. 32. xix. 14, 17. xxii. 18. xxiii. 39. xxv. 35*t*, 36*tr*, 42, 43*tr*. xxvi. 21, 23, 34, 46, 55*t*, 75. xxvii. 46. xxviii. 10.

Mark i. 40. v. 7. vi. 22, 23(–G°*S*). vii. 6, 7. viii. 38. ix. 19, 37, 39. x. 14, 18, 47, 48. xii. 15. xiv. 18, 30, 42, 48, 49, 72. xv. 34.

Luke i. 43, 48. ii. 49. iv. 18*t*. v. 12. vi. 46, 47. viii. 28. ix. 26, 48. x. 16, 40. xi. 6. xii. 9, 14. xiii. 35. xiv. 18, 19, 26. xv. 19. xvi. 4, 24. xviii. 3, 5, 16, 19, 38, 39. xx. 23 (*ap*). xxii. 21, 34, 61. xxiv. 39.

John i. 33, 48(49). ii. 17. iv. 34. v. 7, 11, 24, 30, 36, 37, 40, 43. vi. 26, 35(ἐμέ Tr*S*), 36(–L[b]*S*), 37, 38, 39, 40(μοῦ G''LTTr*S*), 44(ἐμέ TTr), 44, 45(ἐμέ Tr), 57*t*, 65. vii. 16, 19, 28, 29, 33, 34, 36, 37. viii. 16, 18, 21, 26, 28, 29*t*, 37, 40, 42, 46, 49, 54. ix. 4. x. 15, 17, 32(ἐμέ TTr*S*). xi. 42. xii. 27, 44, 45, 49. xiii. 13, 20, 21, 33, 38. xiv. 7, 9, 15, 19*t*, 21*t*, 23, 24*t*, 28. xv. 9, 16, 21, 25. xvi. 5*t*, 10, 16*t*, 17*t*, 19*t*. xvii. 5, 8, 21, 23, 24, 25, 26. xviii. 21, 23. xix. 11. xx. 21, 29. xxi. 15, 16, 17*t*.

Acts ii. 28. vii. 28. viii. 31, 36. ix. 4, 6(*ap*), 17. x. 29. xi. 11. xii. 11. xvi. 15. xx. 23. xxii. 7, 8(ἐμέ L*S*), 10, 13(ἐμέ L*S*), 21. xxiii. 3*t*, 18, 22. xxiv. 12, 18, 19(ἐμέ LT*S*). xxv. 11. xxvi. 5, 13, 14*t*, 21, 28. xxviii. 18.

Rom. vii. 11, 23, 24. viii. 2(σέ L[m] *S*). ix. 20. 1 Cor. i. 17. iv. 4. xvi. 6, 11(ἐμέ L). 2 Cor. ii. 2. xi. 16*t*, 32. xii. 6, 7, 11, 21(–St EG). Gal. i. 15. ii. 20. iv. 12, 14. Phil. ii. 30. iv. 13. 1 Tim. i. 12*t*. 2 Tim. i. 15, 16, 17. iii. 11. iv. 9, 10, 16, 17, 18. Tit. iii. 12. Heb. iii. 9(–G'LT*S*), 9 (*ap*). viii. 11. xi. 32. Rev. xvii. 3. xxi. 9(*om S*), 10.

τὸ ἐνταφιάσαι με, **my burial**, Matt. xxvi. 12.

I[cc], Matt. xvi. 13(–G°L[b]TTr*S*), 15. xxvi. 32, 35. Mark viii. 27, 29. x. 36(–G''LTr*S*[c]). xiv. 28, 31. Luke ii. 49. iv. 43. ix. 18, 20. x. 35. xi. 18. xiii. 33. xix. 5, 27. xxii. 15. John x. 16. Acts xi. 15. xiii. 25(ἐμέ L*S*). xvi. 30. xviii. 21(*ap*). xix. 21*t*. xxii. 17. xxv. 10. Rom. xv. 16, 19. 2 Cor. ii. 3, 13. vii. 7. xii. 21(μοῦ LT*S*). Gal. iv. 18. Eph. vi. 20. Phil. i. 7(*marg.* **me**). Col. iv. 4.

Not rendered, Acts xxiv. 13(*om S*).

κἀμέ, **both me**, John vii. 28.—**I**[co] **also**, 1 Cor. xvi. 4.

Add, for ἐμέ, Phm. 17, GLT*S*.—John vii. 34(me[2d]), 36(me[2d]), L. x. 14(*ap*). xiv. 14(ask . .), L[b]*S*. 1 Tim. i. 13(. . who was), L.

ἐδαφίζω.

lay even with the ground, Luke xix. 44.

ἔδαφος.

ground, Acts xxii. 7.

ἑδραῖος.

steadfast, 1 Cor. vii. 37(–G°). xv. 58.

settled, Col. i. 23.

ἑδραίωμα.

ground(*marg.* **stay**), 1 Tim. iii. 15.

ἐθελοθρησκεία.

will worship, Col. ii. 23.

ἐθέλω. See θέλω.

ἐθίζω.

Pass., **custom**, Luke ii. 27p.

ἐθνάρχης.

governor, 2 Cor. xi. 32.

ἐθνικός.

heathen man, Matt. xviii. 17.
With art., **the heathen**, Matt. vi. 7pl.
Add Matt. v. 47, for τελώνης, GL TTr*S*. 3 John 7, for ἔθνος, G'LT*S*.

ἐθνικῶς.

after the manner of Gentiles, Gal. ii. 14.

ἔθνος.

nation, Matt. xxi. 43. xxiv. 7*t*, 9, 14. xxv. 32. xxviii. 19. Mark xi. 17. xiii. 8*t*, 10. Luke vii. 5. xii. 30. xxi. 10*t*, 24, 25. xxiii. 2. xxiv. 47. John xi. 48, 50, 51, 52. xviii. 35. Acts ii. 5. vii. 7. x. 22, 35. xiii. 19. xiv. 16. xvii. 26. xxiv. 2, 10, 17. xxvi. 4. xxviii. 19.
Rom. i. 5. iv. 17, 18. x. 19. xvi. 26. Gal. iii. 8. 1 Pet. ii. 9. Rev. ii. 26. v. 9. vii. 9. x. 11. xi. 9, 18. xii. 5. xiii. 7. xiv. 6, 8. xv. 4(-G''). xvi. 19. xvii. 15. xviii. 3, 23. xix. 15. xx. 3, 8. xxi. 24, 26. xxii. 2.
people, Acts viii. 9. Rom. x. 19.
Plural, **Gentiles**, Matt. iv. 15. vi. 32. x. 5, 18. xii. 18, 21. xx. 19, 25. Mark x. 33, 42. Luke ii. 32. xviii. 32. xxi. 24*t*. xxii. 25. Acts iv. 27. vii. 45. ix. 15. x. 45. xi. 1, 18. xiii. 42(*om S*), 46, 47, 48. xiv. 2, 5, 27. xv. 3, 7, 12, 14, 17, 19, 23. xviii. 6. xxi. 11, 19, 21, 25. xxii. 21. xxvi. 17, 20, 23. xxviii. 28.
Rom. i. 13. ii. 14, 24. iii. 29*t*. ix. 24, 30. xi. 11, 12, 13*t*, 25. xv. 9*t*, 10, 11, 12*t*, 16*t*, 18, 27. xvi. 4. 1 Cor. v. 1. x. 20(-G''LT). xii. 2. Gal. ii. 2, 8, 12, 14, 15. iii. 14. Eph. ii. 11. iii. 1, 6, 8. iv. 17. Col. i. 27. 1 Thes. ii. 16. iv. 5. 1 Tim. ii. 7. iii. 16. 2 Tim. i. 11. iv. 17. 1 Pet. ii. 12. iv. 3. 3 John 7(ἐθνικός G'LT*S*). Rev. xi. 2.—**heathen**, Acts iv. 25. 2 Cor. xi. 26. Gal. i. 16. ii. 9. iii. 8.

Add 1 Cor. i. 23, for Ἕλληνpl, GL T*S*. Rev. xv. 3. for ἅγιοςpl, GLTTr.

ἔθος.

custom, Luke i. 9. ii. 42. Acts vi. 14 (*marg.* **rite**). xvi. 21. xxi. 21. xxvi. 3. xxviii. 17.
manner, John xix. 40. Acts xv. 1. xxv. 16. Heb. x. 25.
κατὰ τὸ ἔθος, **as one is wont**, Luke xxii. 39.

ἔθω, εἴωθα.

be wont, Matt. xxvii. 15. Mark x. 1.
κατὰ τὸ εἰωθός, **as his**c **custom was**, Luke iv. 16.—**as his**c **manner was**, Acts xvii. 2.

εἶ. See εἰμί.

εἰ.

With the Optative, marked opt; with the Subjunctive, sbj.

I. As a *conditional* particle,
if, Matt. iv. 3, 6. v. 29, 30. vi. 23, 30. vii. 11. viii. 31. x. 25. xi. 14, 21, 23. xii. 7, 26, 27, 28. xiv. 28. xvii. 4. xviii. 8, 9. xix. 10, 17, 21. xxii. 45. xxiii. 30. xxiv. 24, 43. xxvi. 24, 39, 42. xxvii. 40, 42(-G° TTr*S*), 43. Mark iii. 26. ix. 23. xi. 13, 26(*ap*). xiii. 22. xiv. 21, 35.
Luke iv. 3, 9. vi. 32. vii. 39. x. 13. xi. 13, 19, 20, 36. xii. 26, 28, 39, 49. xvi. 11, 12, 31. xvii. 6. xix. 42. xxii. 42. xxiii. 31, 35, 37(-Lb), 39 (οὐχί LmTTr*S*). John i. 25. iii. 12. iv. 10. v. 47. vii. 4, 23. viii. 19, 39, 42, 46. ix. 41. x. 24. 35, 37, 38. xi. 12, 21, 32. xiii. 14, 17, 32(*ap*). xiv. 7, 28. xv. 18, 19, 20*t*. xviii. 8, 23*t*, 36. xx. 15.
Acts iv. 9. v. 39. viii. 37(*ap*). xiii. 15. xvi. 15. xvii. 27opt. xviii. 14, 15. xix. 38, 39. xx. 16. xxiii. 9. xxv. 11*t*. xxvii. 39opt.
Rom. iii. 3, 5, 7. iv. 2, 14. v. 10, 15, 17. vi. 5, 8. vii. 16, 20. viii. 10, 11, 13*t*, 17, 25, 31. ix. 22. xi. 6, 6(*ap*), 12, 15, 16*t*, 18, 21, 24. xii. 18. xiv. 15. xv. 27.
1 Cor. vi. 2. vii. 9, 15. viii. 13. ix. 2, 11*t*, 12, 17*t*. x. 30. xi. 6*t*, 31.

xii. 17*t*, 19. xiv. 35. xv. 2, 12, 13, 14, 16, 17, 19, 29, 32*t*. 2 Cor. ii. 2. iii. 7, 9, 11. v. 14(15, -G°L*S*). viii. 12. xi. 4, 30.
Gal. i. 10. ii. 14, 17, 18, 21. iii. 18, 21, 29. iv. 7, 15. v. 11, 15, 18, 25. Phil. i. 22. Col. ii. 20. iii. 1. 1 Thes. iv. 14. 1 Tim. v. 10*five*. 2 Tim. ii. 11, 12*t*, 13. Phm. 17, 18.
Heb. ii. 2. iv. 3, 5, 8. vii. 11. viii. 4, 7. ix. 13. xi. 15. xii. 7(εἰς LT*S*), 8, 25. Jas. ii. 8, 9, 11. iii. 14. iv. 11. 1 Pet. i. 6, 17. ii. 19, 20*t*. iii. 17[opt]. iv. 14, 16, 17, 18. 2 Pet. ii. 4, 20. 1 John ii. 19. iii. 13. iv. 11. v. 9.

whether, Acts xvii. 11[opt]. xxv. 20[opt].

that, Mark ix. 42. Luke xvii. 2. Acts xxvi. 8, 23*t*.

for that, Heb. vii. 15.

forasmuch as, Acts xi. 17.

though, 2 Cor. xiii. 4(-L[b]*S*).

not, Heb. iii. 11(*Gr.* if).

no[cc], Mark viii. 12.

With τυγχάνω[opt], **it may chance,** 1 Cor. xv. 37.—**it may be,** 1 Cor. xiv. 10.

Not rendered, John v. 46. 1 Cor. ii. 8.

Add Luke xi. 11, for ἤ, St. Rom. ii. 17, *see* ἴδε. 1 Cor. xv. 44(. . there is a n.), LT. Heb. vi. 14, *see* ἦ μήν. Jas. iii. 3, *see* ἰδού. 1 Pet. ii. 3, for εἴ περ, L*S*.

II. In *interrogation*, direct or indirect,

whether, Matt. xxvi. 63. xxvii. 49. Mark iii. 2. xv. 36. Luke vi. 7. xiv. 28, 31. xxiii. 6. John ix. 25. Acts iv. 19. v. 8. x. 18. xix. 2. 1 Cor. vii. 16*t*. 2 Cor. ii. 9. xiii. 5. 1 John iv. 1.

if, Mark xv. 44. Acts viii. 22.

Not rendered, Matt. xii. 10. xix. 3. Mark x. 2. Luke xiii. 23. xiv. 3. xxii. 49, 67. Acts i. 6. vii. 1. xix. 2. xxi. 37. xxii. 25, 27(*omS*).

Add Matt. xx. 15, for ἤ[2d], StG'T. Luke vi. 9, for τί fr. τίς, LTTr*S*.

III. With other particles.

εἴγε or εἴ γε.

if so be that, 2 Cor. v. 3(εἴ περ L). Eph. iv. 21.

if, Eph. iii. 2. Col. i. 23.

εἴγε καί, **if yet,** Gal. iii. 4.

εἰ δὲ μή, εἰ δὲ μήγε².

and if not, Luke xiii. 9².

if not, Luke x. 6². John xiv. 2².

if otherwise, Luke v. 36². 2 Cor. xi. 16².

otherwise, Matt. vi. 1².

or else, Luke xiv. 32². John xiv. 11. Rev. ii. 5, 16.

else, Matt. ix. 17². Mark ii. 21, 22. Luke v. 37².

εἰ καί, εἰ δὲ καί², ἀλλ' εἰ καί³, καί εἰ⁴.

if also, Luke xi. 18². 2 Cor. xi. 15.

now if, 1 Cor. iv. 7.

if that, Phil. iii. 12[sbj].

but if, 1 Cor. vii. 21³. 2 Cor. iv. 3².

but and if, 1 Pet. iii. 14³.

yea, and if, Phil. ii. 17³.

though, Matt. xxvi. 33 (καί *omS*, -εἰ *S*). Luke xi. 8. xviii. 4. 2 Cor. vii. 8*tr*, 12. xii. 11, 15(-καί L*S*). Col. ii. 5. Heb. vi. 9.

although, Mark xiv. 29⁴(εἰ καί Tr*S*).

yea, though, 2 Cor. v. 16².

but though, 2 Cor. iv. 16³. xi. 6².

εἰ μή, ἐκτὸς εἰ μή².

if not, John ix. 33. xv. 22, 24. xviii. 30. Acts xxvi. 32.

unless, 1 Cor. xv. 2².

except, Matt. xix. 9(*ap*). xxiv. 22. John xix. 11. Rom. vii. 7. ix. 29. 1 Cor. xiv. 5². 2 Cor. xii. 13.

except that, Mark xiii. 20.

but, Matt. v. 13. xi. 27. xii. 4, 24, 39. xiv. 17. xv. 24. xvi. 4. xvii. 21(*ap*). xix. 17(*ap*). xxi. 19. xxiv. 36. Mark ii. 7, 26. vi. 4. ix. 29. x. 18. xi. 13. xiii. 32. Luke v. 21. vi. 4. x. 22*t*. xi. 29. John iii. 13. x. 10. xiv. 6. xvii. 12. xix. 15. Acts xi. 19.

Rom. vii. 7. xi. 15. xiii. 1, 8. xiv. 14. 1 Cor. i. 14. ii. 11. vii. 17. viii.

4. x. 13. xii. 3. 2 Cor. ii. 2. xii. 5. Gal. i. 7. Eph. iv. 9. Phil. iv. 15. 1 Tim. v. 19². Heb. iii. 18. 1 John ii. 22. v. 5. Rev. ix. 4. xiv. 3. xix. 12. xxi. 27.

save, Matt. xi. 27. xiii. 57. xvii. 8. Mark v. 37. vi. 8. Luke iv. 26. viii. 51. xvii. 18. xviii. 19. John vi. 22, 46. 1 Cor. ii. 2, 11. Gal. i. 19. vi. 14. Rev. xiii. 17.

saving, Luke iv. 27. Rev. ii. 17.

save that, Mark vi. 5.

save only that, Acts xxi. 25(*ap*).

or, 2 Cor. iii. 1(G', ἢ μή CGLT*S*).

more than, Mark viii. 14.

εἰ μὴ ὅταν, **till**, Mark ix. 9.

Add Mark ix. 8, for ἀλλά, L*S*. John xiii. 10, for ἤ, LTr.

εἰ μή τι.

except, Luke ix. 13sbj. 1 Cor. vii. 5. 2 Cor. xiii. 5.

εἴ περ or εἴπερ.

if so be that, Rom. viii. 9. 17. 1 Cor. xv. 15.

if so be, 1 Pet. ii. 3(εἰ L*S*).

seeing, 2 Thes. i. 6.

though, 1 Cor. viii. 5.

Add Rom. iii. 30, for ἐπείπερ, G'L*S*.

εἴ πως or εἴπως.

if by any means, Acts xxvii. 12opt. Rom. i. 10. xi. 14. Phil. iii. 11.

εἴ τε or εἴτε.

εἴτε . . εἴτε, **whether**w . . **or**o, Rom. xii. 6w, 7ot, 8o(-Go). 1 Cor. iii. 22, 22o*six*. viii. 5. x. 31, 31o. xii. 13*t*, 26(1st εἴ τι L). xiv. 7. xv. 11. 2 Cor. v. 9, 10. viii. 23. xii. 3. Eph. vi. 8. Phil. i. 18, 20, 27. Col. i. 16, 16o*t*, 20. 1 Thes. v. 10sbj. 2 Thes. ii. 15. 1 Pet. ii. 13 and 14.—**whether . . or whether**, 2 Cor. i. 6. v. 13. xii. 2.

whether, 1 Cor. xiii. 8*tr*.

if, 1 Cor. xiv. 27.

εἴ τις, *neut.* εἴ τι.

if any, Acts xxiv. 20(τί GLT*S*). xxv. 5. Rom. xiii. 9. 1 Cor. vii. 12. x. 27. 2 Cor. ii. 5. Phil. ii. 1*f*. iv. 8*t*. 2 Thes. iii. 10. 1 Tim. v. 4, 8. Tit. i. 6. Jas. i. 5, 23. 1 Pet. iii. 1. 2 John 10.

if some, Rom. xi. 17pl.

if any man, Matt. xvi. 24. Mark iv. 23. vii. 16. ix. 35. Luke ix. 23. xiv. 26. xix. 8. Rom. viii. 9. 1 Cor. iii. 12, 14, 15, 17, 18. vii. 36. viii. 2, 3. xi. 16, 34. xiv. 37, 38. xvi. 22. 2 Cor. v. 17. x. 7. Gal. i. 9. Phil. iii. 4. 2 Thes. iii. 14. 1 Tim. v. 16. vi. 3. Jas. i. 26. iii. 2. 1 Pet. iv. 11*t*. Rev. xi. 5*t*sbj(*ind.* GLTTr, 1st*S*). xiii. 9. xiv. 9.

if a man, 2 Cor. xi. 20*five*. Gal. vi. 3. 1 Tim. iii. 1, 5.

if any thing, Mark ix. 22. 2 Cor. ii. 10. vii. 14. Phil. iii. 15. 1 Tim. i. 10.

if aught, Mark viii. 23. xi. 25. Acts xxiv. 19opt.

whether any, 1 Cor. i. 16.

whosoever, Rev. xiv. 11. xx. 15.

he that, Rev. xiii. 10*t*.

that which, Eph. iv. 29.

Add, for ὅστις, Matt. xviii. 28, GLTTr*S*. Mark viii. 34, G'LTr*S*. For εἴτε, 1 Cor. xii. 26, L.

εἰδέα. See ἰδέα.

εἶδον; οἶδα.

I. εἶδον.

(For the present tense see ὁράω.)

see, Matt. ii. 2, 9, 10p, 11 (εὑρίσκω StE), 16p. iii. 7p, 16. iv. 16, 18, 21. v. 1, 16. viii. 14, 18p, 34p. ix. 2, 8p, 9, 11p, 22p, 23, 36p. xi. 8, 9. xii. 2p, 38. xiii. 15, 17*t*. xiv. 14, 26*t*. xvi. 28. xvii. 8. xviii. 31p. xx. 3. xxi. 15p, 19p, 20p, 32p, 38p. xxii. 11. xxiii. 39. xxiv. 15, 33. xxv. 37, 38, 39, 44. xxvi. 8p, 58, 71. xxvii. 3p, 24p, 49, 54. xxviii. 6, 17p.

Mark i. 10, 16, 19. ii. 5p, 12, 14, 16p. v. 6p, 14, 16, 22p, 32. vi. 33, 34, 38, 48, 49p, 50. vii. 2p. ix. 1, 8, 9, 14, 20p, 25p, 38. x. 14p. xi. 13, 20. xii. 15, 34p. xiii. 14, 29. xiv. 67p, 69. xv. 32, 36, 39p. xvi. 5.

Luke i. 12p, 29p(G', -GTTr*S*). ii. 15, 17p, 20, 26*t*, 30, 48p. v. 2, 8p,

12, 20p, 26. vii. 13p, 22, 25, 26, 39p. viii. 20, 28p, 34p, 35, 36, 47p. ix. 9, 27, 32, 49, 54p. x. 24t, 31p, 33p. xi. 38p. xii. 54. xiii. 12p, 35. xiv. 18. xv. 20. xvii. 14p, 15p, 22. xviii. 15p, 24p, 43p. xix. 3, 4, 5(–Tr*S*), 7p, 37. xx. 13p(–G^{oo}LTr*S*), 14p. xxi. 1, 2, 20, 31. xxii. 49p, 58. xxiii, 8p, 8t, 47p. xxiv. 24, 39.

John i. 33, 39t(40, 1st ὄψεσθε fr. ὁράω G'TTr), 46(47), 47(48), 48(49), 50(51). iii. 3. iv. 29, 48. v. 6p. vi. 14p, 22p, 24, 26, 30. viii. 56t. ix. 1. xi. 31p, 32, 33, 34. xii. 9, 21, 40, 41. xviii. 26. xix. 6, 26p, 33. xx. 8, 20p, 25, 29. xxi. 21.

Acts ii. 27, 31. iii. 3, 9, 12p. iv. 20. vi. 15. vii. 24, 31p, 34t, 55. viii. 39. ix. 12, 27, 35, 40p. x. 3, 17. xi. 5, 6, 13, 23p. xii. 3p, 16. xiii. 12p, 35, 36, 37, 45p. xiv. 11p. xvi. 10, 19p, 27, 40p. xix. 21. xxi. 32p. xxii. 14, 18. xxvi. 13, 16. xxviii. 4, 15p, 20, 27.

Rom. i. 11. 1 Cor. ii. 9. viii. 10. xvi. 7. Gal i. 19. ii. 7p, 14. vi. 11. Phil. i. 27, 30. ii. 28p. iv. 9. 1 Thes. ii. 17. iii. 6, 10. 1 Tim. vi. 16t. 2 Tim. i. 4. Heb. iii. 9. xi. 5, 13, 23. Jas. v. 11. 1 Pet. i. 8. iii. 10. 1 John v. 16. 3 John 14.

Rev. i. 2, 12, 17, 19, 20, 20(*omS*). iv. 4(*omS*). v. 1, 2. vi. 1, 2(–G^{oo}), 9. vii. 1, 2. viii. 2. ix. 1, 17. x. 1, 5. xii. 13. xiii. 1, 2, 3(*omS*). xiv. 6. xv. 1, 2. xvi. 13. xvii. 3, 6, 6p, 8. 12, 15, 16, 18. xviii. 1, 7. xix. 11, 17, 19. xx. 1, 4, 11, 12. xxi. 1, 2, 22.

perceive, Matt. xiii. 14. Mark iv. 12. Luke ix. 47. Acts xiv. 9. xxviii. 26.

behold, Mark ix. 15p. Luke xix. 41. xxi. 29. xxii. 56. xxiv. 39. John xx. 27. Acts xiii. 41. Rom. xi. 22. 1 John iii. 1. Rev. v. 6, 11. vi. 5 (–G^{oo}), 12. vii. 9. viii. 13. xiii. 11.

look, John vii. 52. Rev. iv. 1. vi. 8(–G^{oo}). xiv. 1, 14. xv. 5.

look on, Mark viii. 33. Luke x. 32.

consider, Acts xv. 6.

know, Matt. ix. 4 (οἶδα G'LTr).

Add, for βλέπω, John xxi. 9, L^{m}. Rev. vi. 1, 5, 7, G*S* (–G^{o}). xxii. 8, *see* βλέπω. For θεάομαι, Luke v. 27, L^{m}. Acts viii. 18, GLT*S*. — Phil. ii. 26 (longed . .), L^{b}*S*.

See also ἴδε, ἰδού, οἶδα.

II. οἶδα.

Literally *have seen;* hence,

know, Matt. vi. 8, 32. vii. 11. ix. 6. xii. 25. xv. 12. xx. 22, 25. xxii. 16, 29. xxiv. 36, 42, 43. xxv. 12, 13, 26. xxvi. 2. 70. 72, 74. xxvii. 18. xxviii. 5.

Mark i. 24, 34. ii. 10. iv. 13, 27. v. 33. vi. 20. x. 19, 38, 42. xii. 14, 15(εἶδον G'*S*), 24p. xiii. 32, 33, 35. xiv. 68, 71.

Luke iv. 34, 41. v. 24. vi. 8. viii. 53. ix. 33, 55(*ap*). xi. 13, 17. xii. 30, 39. xiii. 25, 27. xviii. 20. xix. 22. xx. 21. xxii. 34, 57, 60. xxiii. 34(*ap*).

John i. 26, 31, 33. ii. 9t. iii. 2, 11. iv. 10, 22t, 25, 42. v. 32. vi. 6, 42, 61p, 64. vii. 15, 27, 28*tr*, 29. viii. 14, 19*tr*, 37, 55*tr*. ix. 12, 20, 21t, 24, 25t, 29t, 30, 31. x. 4, 5. xi. 22, 24, 42, 49. xii. 35, 50. xiii. 1p, 3, 7, 11, 17, 18. xiv. 4, 4(–L^{b}TTr*S*), 5t. xv. 15, 21. xvi. 30. xviii. 2, 4, 21. xix. 10, 28(εἶδον G'), 35. xx. 2, 9, 13, 14. xxi. 4, 12, 15, 16, 17, 24.

Acts ii. 22, 30. iii. 16. v. 7. vii. 18. x. 37. xii. 11. xvi. 3. xix. 32. xx. 22, 25, 29. xxvi. 4, 27.

Rom. iii. 19. v. 3. vi. 9, 16. vii. 7, 14, 18. viii. 22, 26, 27, 28. xiii. 11. xiv. 14. 1 Cor. i. 16. ii. 2, 11, 11(γινώσκω G''LT*S*), 12. iii. 16. v. 6. vi. 2, 3, 9, 15, 16, 19. vii. 16t. viii. 1, 2(γινώσκω LT*S*), 4. ix. 13, 24. xi. 3. xii. 2. xiv. 11. xv. 58p. xvi. 15. 2 Cor. i. 7. iv. 14. v. 1, 6, 11, 16. ix. 2. xi. 11, 31. xii. 2t, 3t.

Gal. ii. 16. iv. 8p, 13. Eph. i. 18. vi. 8, 9, 21. Phil. i. 17, 19, 25. iv.

12*t*, 15. Col. ii. 1. iii. 24. iv. 1, 6. 1 Thes. i. 4, 5. ii. 1, 2, 5, 11. iii. 3, 4. iv. 2, 4, 5. v. 2, 12. 2 Thes. i. 8. ii. 6. iii. 7. 1 Tim. i. 8, 9. iii. 5, 15. 2 Tim. i. 12, 15. ii. 23. iii. 14, 15. Tit. i. 16. iii. 11. Phm. 21. Heb. viii. 11. x. 30. xii. 17. Jas. iii. 1. iv. 4, 17. 1 Pet. i. 18p. iii. 9 (–G∞LT*S*). v. 9. 2 Pet. i. 12, 14. ii. 9. 1 John ii. 11, 20, 21*t*, 29. iii. 2, 5, 14, 15. v. 13, 15*t*, 18, 19, 20. 3 John 12. Jude 5p, 10. Rev. ii. 2, 9, 13, 19. iii. 1, 8, 15, 17. vii. 14. xii. 12p. xix. 12.

know of, John iv. 32.

have knowledge, Acts xxiv. 22.

wis, (*imp.* **wist,**) Mark ix. 6. xiv. 40. Luke ii. 49. John v. 13. Acts xii. 9. xxiii. 5.

wot, Acts iii. 17. vii. 40. Rom. xi. 2.

understand, 1 Cor. xiii. 2. xiv. 16.

perceive, Mark xii. 28(εἰδὸν LTr*S*).

see, 1 Pet. i. 8(εἰδὸν LT*S*).

be aware, Luke xi. 44.

be sure, John xvi. 30. Rom. ii. 2. xv. 29.

can tell, Matt. xxi. 27. Mark xi. 33. Luke xx. 7. John iii. 8. viii. 14. xvi. 18. 2 Cor. xii. 2*t*, 3(–L).

can, Matt. xxvii. 65. Luke xii. 56.

Attic forms, ἴστε, Heb. xii. 17; ἴσασι, Acts xxvi. 4.

Add, for γινώσκω, John xiv. 7, Tr. Rev. ii. 17, GLTTr*S*.—ἴστε for ἐστε, Eph. v. 5, GLT*S*; for ὥστε, Jas. i. 19, G'L, ἴστω *S*.—Mark iii. 12(*ap*). Luke xii. 56, οἴδατε δοκιμάζειν for δοκιμάζετε, Tr*S*. Acts xxvi. 3p(because I know), C. *See also* εἰδον.

εἶδος.

sight, 2 Cor. v. 7.

appearance, 1 Thes. v. 22.

shape, Luke iii. 22. John v. 37.

fashion, Luke ix. 29.

εἴδω. See εἴδον.

εἰδωλεῖον.

idol's temple, 1 Cor. viii. 10.

εἰδωλόθυτον.

thing sacrificed unto idols, Rev. ii. 14, 20.

offered in sacrifice unto idols, 1 Cor. x. 28(ἱερόθυτον G''LT*S*).

that which is offered in sacrifice to idols, 1 Cor. x. 19.

thing that is offered in sacrifice unto idols, 1 Cor. viii. 4.

thing offered unto an idol, 1 Cor. viii. 7.

thing offered to idols, Acts xxi. 25.

thing offered unto idols, 1 Cor. viii. 1.

thing which is offered to idols, 1 Cor. viii. 10.

meat offered to idols, Acts xv. 29.

εἰδωλολατρεία.

idolatry, 1 Cor. x. 14. Gal. v. 20. Col. iii. 5. 1 Pet. iv. 3.

εἰδωλολάτρης.

idolater, 1 Cor. v. 10, 11. vi. 9. x. 7. Eph. v. 5. Rev. xxi. 8. xxii. 15.

εἴδωλον.

idol, Acts vii. 41. xv. 20. Rom. ii. 22. 1 Cor. viii. 4, 7. x. 19(*ap*). xii. 2. 2 Cor. vi. 16. 1 Thes. i. 9. 1 John v. 21. Rev. ix. 20.

εἴην, *etc.* See εἰμί.

εἰκῆ, εἰκῇ L.

without a cause, Matt. v. 22(–LTTrb*S*).

in vain, Rom. xiii. 4. 1 Cor. xv. 2. Gal. iii. 4*t*. iv. 11.

vainly, Col. ii. 18.

εἰκόνη, likeness, image.

For εἰκών, Rev. xiii. 14, LT.

εἴκοσι.

twenty, Luke xiv. 31. John vi. 19. Acts i. 15. xxvii. 28. 1 Cor. x. 8. Rev. iv. 4*t*, 10. v. 8, 14(*omS*). xi. 16. xix. 4.

εἰκοσιτρεῖς, -τέσσαρες, -πέντε, StG.

εἴκω.

give place, Gal. ii. 5.

εἴκω, ἔοικα.

be like, Jas. i. 6, 23.

εἰκών.

image, Matt. xxii. 20. Mark xii. 16. Luke xx. 24. Rom. i. 23. viii. 29. 1 Cor. xi. 7. xv. 49*t*. 2 Cor. iii. 18. iv. 4. Col. i. 15. iii. 10. Heb. x. 1. Rev. xiii. 14(εἰκόνη LT), 15*tr*. xiv. 9, 11. xv. 2. xvi. 2. xix. 20. xx. 4.

εἰλικρίνεια.

sincerity, 1 Cor. v. 8. 2 Cor. i. 12. ii. 17.

εἰλικρινής.

sincere, Phil. i. 10.
pure, 2 Pet. iii. 1.

εἱλίσσω, ἑλίσσω LTTr*S*.

roll together, Rev. vi. 14p.

εἰ μή. See **εἰ.**

εἰμί,

εἶ, ἦν, ἔσομαι, etc.

(With ἐγώ, marked [1]; σύ, [2]; ἡμεῖς, [4]; ὑμεῖς, [5].)

I. Present.

Indicative; 1, εἰμί.

I am (am I), Matt. iii. 11. viii. 8, 9[1]. xi. 29. xviii. 20[1]. xx. 15[1]. xxii. 32[1]. xxiv. 5[1]. xxvii. 24, 43. xxviii. 20. Mark i. 7. xiii. 6[1]. xiv. 62[1]. Luke i. 18[1], 19[1]. iii. 16. v. 8. vii. 6, 8. xv. 19, 21. xviii. 11. xxi. 8[1]. xxii. 27[1], 33, 58, 70[1].

John i. 20[1], 21, 27[1]. iii. 28[1], 28. iv. 26[1]. vi. 35[1], 41[1], 48[1], 51[1]. vii. 28, 29, 33, 34[1], 36[1]. viii. 12[1], 16, 18[1], 23*t*[1], 24[1], 28[1], 58[1]. ix. 5. 9[1]. x. 7[1], 9[1], 11[1], 14[1], 36. xi. 25[1]. xii. 26[1]. xiii. 13, 19[1], 33. xiv. 3[1], 6[1]. xv. 1[1], 5[1]. xvi. 32. xvii. 11, 14, 16, 24[1]. xviii. 5[1], 6[1], 8[1], 17, 25, 35[1], 37[1]. xix. 21.

Acts ix. 5[1]. x. 21[1], 26[1]. xiii. 25[1], 25. xviii. 10[1]. xxi. 39[1]. xxii. 3[1], 8[1]. xxiii. 6[1]. xxvi. 15[1], 29[1]. xxvii. 23.

Rom. i. 14. vii. 14[1]. xi. 1[1], 13[1]. 1 Cor. i. 12[1]. iii. 4[1]. ix. 1*t*, 2. xii. 15*t*, 16*t*. xiii. 2. xv. 9[1], 9, 10*t*. 2 Cor. xii. 10. Phil. iv. 11. Col. ii. 5. 1 Tim. i. 15[1]. 1 Pet. i. 16(–LT*S*)[1]. 2 Pet. i. 13. Rev. i. 8[1], 11[1](*ap*), 17[1], 18. ii. 23[1]. iii. 17. xviii. 7. xix. 10. xxi. 6(–G″*S*)[1]. xxii. 9, 13(*omS*)[1], 16[1].

With conj., **if I be**, 1 Cor. ix. 2. — **though I be**, 2 Cor. xii. 11.

it is I[1], Matt. xiv. 27. xxvi. 22, 25. Mark vi. 50. Luke xxiv. 39. John vi. 20.

have I been? John xiv. 9.

I °**was**, Luke xix. 22[1].

Add Luke xxiv. 36(*ap*). Acts xx. 26, for ἐγώ, L*S*.

See also ἔκφοβος, ἔντρομος, ἵστημι.

2, εἶ.

thou art (art thou), Matt. ii. 6[2]. v. 25. xi. 3[2]. xiv. 33. xvi. 16[2], 17, 18, 23. xxii. 16. xxv. 24. xxvi. 73[2]. xxvii. 11[2]. Mark i. 11[2], 24. iii. 11[2]. viii. 29[2]. xii. 14, 34. xiv. 61[2], 70*t*. xv. 2[2]. Luke iii. 22[2]. iv. 34, 41[2]. vii. 19[2], 20[2]. xv. 31. xix. 21. xxii. 58[2], 67(66)[2], 70[2]. xxiii. 3[2], 40.

John i. 19[2], 21*t*[2], 22, 42(43)[2], 49 (50)*t*[2]. iii. 10[2]. iv. 12[2], 19[2]. vi. 69[2]. vii. 52[2]. viii. 25[2], 48[2], 53[2]. ix. 28[2]. xi. 27[2]. xviii. 17[2], 25[2], 33[2], 37[2]. xix. 9[2], 12. xxi. 12[2].

Acts ix. 5. xiii. 33[2]. xxi. 38[2]. xxii. 8, 27[2]. xxvi. 15.

Rom. ii. 1. ix. 20[2]. xiv. 4[2]. Gal. iv. 7. Heb. i. 5[2], 12[2]. v. 5[2]. Jas. iv. 11, 12[2]. Rev. ii. 9. iii. 1, 15, 16, 17. iv. 11. v. 9. xvi. 5.

With εἰ, **if thou be**, Matt. iv. 3, 6. xxvii. 40. Luke iv. 3, 9. xxiii. 37[2], 39[2]. John i. 25[2]. x. 24[2]. — **if it be thou**, Matt. xiv. 28[2]. — **whether thou be**, Matt. xxvi. 63[2].

Add Rev. xv. 4, *see* ὅσιος.

3, ἐστί, ἐστίν.

is, Matt. i. 20, 23. ii. 2. iii. 3, 11, 17. v. 3, 10, 34, 35*t*, 48. vi. 13(*ap*), 21, 22, 25. vii. 9(–LTr), 12. viii. 27. ix. 5, 15. x. 10(–LTTr*S*), 11, 24, 26, 37*t*, 38. xi. 6, 10, 11, 14, 16, 30. xii. 6, 8, 23, 30, 48, 50. xiii. 19, 20, 22, 23, 31, 32*t*, 33, 37, 38, 39*t*, 44, 45, 47, 52, 55, 57. xiv. 2, 15, 26. xv. 26(*see* ἔξεστι). xvii.

4, 5. xviii. 1, 4, 8, 9, 14. xix. 14, 24, 26. xx. 1, 15. 23. xxi. 10, 11, 38, 42. xxii. 8, 32, 38, 42, 45. xxiii. 8, 9, 10(–G′), 16, 17, 18. xxiv. 6, 26, 33, 45. xxvi. 18, 26, 28, 38, 39, 48, 66, 68. xxvii. 6, 33, 37. xxviii. 6.

Mark i. 27(*ap*). ii. 9, 19, 28. iii. 17, 29, 33, 35. iv. 21, 26, 31(ὃν fr. ὢν LTr*S*), 41. v. 41. vi. 3, 4, 15, 15(–L^{b}TTr*S*), 16(–GL^{b}TTr*S*), 35. vii. 15, 27, 34. ix. 5, 7, 21, 39, 40, 42, 43, 45, 47. x. 14, 24, 25, 29, 40. xii. 7, 11, 27, 28, 29, 31, 32*t*, 33, 35, 37. xiii. 28, 29, 33. xiv. 14, 22, 24, 34, 44, 69. xv. 22, 34, 42. xvi. 6.

Luke i. 36, 61, 63. ii. 11. iv. 22, 24. v. 21, 23, 34, 39. vi. 5, 20, 35, 36, 40, 47, 48, 49. vii. 23, 27, 28*t*, 39, 49. viii. 11*t*, 17, 25(–LTTr*S*), 25, 26, 30. ix. 9, 33, 35, 38, 50*t*, 62. x. 7(–LTTr*S*), 22*t*, 29, 42. xi [illegible] 29, 34*t*. xii. 1, 2, 6, 23, [illegible] 18, 19, 21. xiv. 22, 35. xv. 31. xvi. 10*t*, 15(*om S*), 17. xvii. 1, 21. xviii. 16, 25, 29. xix. 9, 46(ἔσται L^{m}TTr, –*S*). xx. 2, 14, 17, 38, 44. xxi. 30, 31. xxii. 11, 19, 38, 53, 59, 64. xxiii. 15, 38(*ap*). xxiv. 6, 29.

John i. 19, 27 (–GL^{b}TTr*S*), 30, 33, 34, 42, 47(48). iii. 6*t*, 8, 19, 29, 31*t*, 31(*ap*), 33. iv. 10, 11, 18, 20, 22, 23, 29, 34, 37, 42. v. 2, 10, 12, 25, 27, 30, 31, 32*t*. 45. vi. 9, 14, 29, 31, 33, 39, 40, 42, 45, 50, 51, 55*t*, 58, 60, 63, 70. vii. 6, 11, 12, 16, 18*t*, 22, 25, 26, 27*t*, 28, 36, 40, 41. viii. 13, 14, 16, 17, 19, 26, 29, 34, 39, 44*t*, 50, 54*tr*. ix. 4, 8, 9*t*, 12, 16, 17, 19, 20, 24, 29, 30*t*, 36, 37. x. 1, 2, 13, 29, 34. xi. 4, 10. xii. 14, 31, 34, 35, 50. xiii. 10, 16, 25, 26. xiv. 21, 24, 28. xv. 1, 12, 20. xvi. 17, 18, 32. xvii. 3, 17. xviii. 36*t*, 38. xix. 35, 40. xx. 31. xxi. 7, 20, 24*t*.

Acts i. 7, 12. ii. 15, 16, 25, 29, 39. iv. 11, 12(*ap*), 12, 36. vi. 2. vii. 33, 37, 38. viii. 10, 21, 26. ix. 15, 20, 21, 22. x. 4, 6, 28, 34, 35, 36, 42. xii. 15. xvi. 12. xvii. 3. xix. 35. xx. 10, 35. xxi. 22, 28. xxii. 26. xxiii. 19. xxv. 14, 16. xxviii. 4.

Rom. i. 9, 12, 16, 19, 25. ii. 2, 11, 28. iii. 8, 10, 11*t*, 12*t*, 18, 22. iv. 15, 16. v. 14. vii. 3, 14. viii. 9, 24, 34. x. 1(*ap*), 8, 12. xi. 6*t*(*ap*), 23. xiii. 1, 4*t*. xiv. 4(*see* δυνατέω), 17, 23. xvi. 5.

1 Cor. i. 18*t*, 25*t*. iii. 5, 7, 11, 13, 17, 19. iv. 3, 4, 17. vi. 5(ἔνι), 7, 16, 17, 18, 19. vii. 8(*om S*), 9, 19*t*, 22*t*, 39, 40. ix. 3, 16, 18. x. 16*t*, 19 (*ap*), 19, 28. xi. 3, 5, 7, 8, 13, 14, 15, 20(*marg.* can^{cc}), 24, 25. xii. 6(*om S*), 12, 14, 15, 16. xiv. 14, 15, 25, 26, 33, 35. xv. 12, 13, 44*t*, 58. xvi. 15.

2 Cor. i. 12. ii. 2(–G^{o}LT*S*), 3. iii. 17. iv. 3, 4. vii. 15. ix. 1. x. 18. xi. 10. xii. 13. xiii. 5(–L^{b}T).

Gal. i. 7, 11. iii. 12, 16, 20*t*. iv. 1, 2, 24, 25, 26*t*. v. 3, 22, 23. Eph. i. 14, 18, 23. ii. 14. iii. 13. iv. 9, 10, 15, 21. v. 5, 10, 12, 13, 18, 23, 23 (–G^{oo}LT*S*), 32. vi. 1, 2, 9*t*, 17. Phil. i. 7, 8(–G^{o}L^{b}T*S*), 28. ii. 13. Col. i. 7, 15, 17, 18*t*, 24, 27. ii. 10. iii. 5, 14, 20, 25. iv. 9.

1 Thes. ii. 13. iv. 3. 2 Thes. i. 3. ii. 4, 9. iii. 3, 17. 1 Tim. i. 5, 20. iii. 15, 16. iv. 8, 10. v. 4, 8. vi. 6, 10. 2 Tim. i. 6, 12. ii. 17. iv. 11*t*. Tit. i. 13.

Heb. ii. 6. iv. 13. v. 13. vii. 2, 15. viii. 6. ix. 15. xi. 1, 6. xii. 7(–LT*S*). Jas. i. 17, 27. ii. 17, 19, 20, 26*t*. iii. 5, 17. iv. 4, 12, 14(ἔσται G′, ἐστέ LT), 16, 17. v. 11. 1 Pet. i. 25. ii. 15. iii. 4, 22. 2 Pet. i. 9, 17. iii. 4.

1 John i. 5*tr*, 7, 8, 9, 10. ii. 2, 4*t*, 7, 8, 9, 10, 11, 15, 16*t*, 18*t*, 21, 22*tr*, 25, 27*t*, 29. iii. 2, 3, 4, 5, 7*t*, 8, 10, 11, 15, 20, 23. iv. 2, 3*tr*, 4, 6, 7, 8, 10, 12, 15, 16, 17, 18, 20. v. 1, 3, 4, 5*t*, 6*tr*, 9*t*, 11*t*, 14, 16, 17*t*, 20. 2 John 6*t*, 7. 3 John 11, 12.

Rev. ii. 7. v. 2(–G^{oo}LTTr*S*), 12, 13 (–G^{oo}LTTr*S*). ix. 19(*ap*). xiii.

10, 18*t*. xiv. 12. xvii. 8*t*, 8(*see* πάρειμι), 10, 11*tr*, 14, 18. xix. 8, 10. xx. 2, 12, 14. xxi. 8, 16(*omS*), 17. xxii. 10.

With conj., . . **be**, Matt. vi. 23. xix. 10. xxvii. 42. Luke xi. 35. xiv. 31. xxiii. 35. John vii. 17. ix. 25. Acts iv. 19. v. 39. xviii. 15. xix. 2. xxv. 5, 11. 2 Cor. iv. 3. Tit. i. 6. Jas. i. 23. 1 Pet. i. 6(–T*S*).—**were**, Mark xiv. 35. Luke xxiii. 6. John xi. 57.

be, *imperat.*, 1 Pet. iv. 11.

be, *plural*, Luke xx. 6.

With ὅτι, **to be**, John xx. 15.

was[c], Matt. xvi. 20. Mark ii. 1. v. 14. vi. 55. x. 47. Luke vii. 4. xix. 3. John ii. 9, 17. v. 13, 15. vi. 24, 64. xii. 9. xx. 14. xxi. 4, 7, 12. Acts ix. 26, 38. xii. 9. xix. 34. xxii. 29. xxiii. 5, 27, 34. xxvi. 26. Rom. iv. 21. Rev. xvi. 21. xxi. 1.

had been[c], Luke xxiv. 21.

With neuter plural, **are**, Matt. x. [illegible] xv. 20. xix. 26(*omS*). Mark vii. 15. x. 27(*ap*). Luke xi. 21, 41. xiv. 17. xviii. 27. John iii. 21. vi. 9, 63*t*. vii. 7. x. 16, 21. xvi. 15. xvii. 7 (εἰσίν T Tr*S*), 10. xx. 30. xxi. 25. Acts xv. 18(*ap*). xxi. 24. 1 Cor. ii. 14. iii. 21, 22 (–G[oo]LT*S*). vi. 15, 20(*ap*). vii. 14. xii. 12, 22. xiv. 10 (εἰσίν LT*S*). Gal. iv. 24. v. 19*t*. Phil. iv. 8. Col. ii. 17, 22. 1 Tim. v. 25(–LT*S*). 2 Tim. ii. 20. Tit. iii. 8. 2 Pet. iii. 16. 1 John iii. 10. iv. 1. Rev. i. 4(–G[oo]LTTr*S*). v. 13. xxi. 12.—**be**, Mark vii. 4.—**were**[c], 1 Cor. vii. 14.

are, John iv. 35. 2 Tim. i. 15. Rev. xxi. 16, 22.

were[c], Acts xxiii. 6.

is to say, Mark vii. 11.

meaneth, Matt. ix. 13. xii. 7.

should mean, Mark ix. 10.

ὅ ἐστι, **called**, Mark xv. 16.

consisteth, Luke xii. 15.

make, Mark xii. 42.

cometh, Matt. v. 37.

belongeth to, Heb. v. 14.

With ἐκ, **belonged**[c] **unto**, Luke xxiii. 7.

With ἐν,[cc] **have**, Acts xiii. 15.

With genit.,[cc] **owneth** (**oweth** *ed.*1611), Acts xxi. 11.—**have**, Acts xix. 25.

With dative,[cc] **have**, Luke vi. 32, 33, 34. xii. 24. John xviii. 39. Acts viii. 21. xviii. 10. Rom. ix. 2. 1 Cor. ix. 16.

οὐκ ἔστι, **we**[c] **can not**, Heb. ix. 5.

Not rendered, John xiv. 10. Jas. iii. 15.

Add, for εἰσί, John x. 12, LTr*S*. 1 Cor. xiv. 37, LT*S*. Rev. iv. 5, *see* εἰσί. For ἦν, John i. 4, L*S*. For ἔσται, Matt. xx. 26, LTr. Mark x. 43, LT Tr*S*. Luke ix. 48, G″LTTr*S*. John xiv. 17, LTr. Rev. xxii. 12, LTTr. For ἐγένετο fr. γίνομαι, 2 Cor. i. 18, G″LT*S*. For ἰσχύω, Gal. vi. 15, GL T*S*.—Matt. xix. 17(*ap*). Mark v. 9 (is), L. xii. 29(*ap*). John xiii. 24 (*ap*). 1 Cor. iii. 5(is), LT*S*. xv. 17 [illegible] L[b]. 1 Thes. v. 18(is), L.

[illegible] ἀνάγκη, ἀπείραστος, ἀπόθεσις, ἀρεστός, γνωστός, δεῖ, δυνατέω, καθήμαι, καρποφορέω, λόγος, λοιπός, μετά, πάλη, παραδίδωμι, ποιέω, πρέπω, προσαναπληρόω, πρόσκαιρος, σπείρω, τεταρταῖος, ὠφέλιμος.

τοῦτ' ἔστι, τουτέστι L.

that is, Acts xix. 4. Rom. vii. 18. ix. 8. x. 6. 7, 8. Phm. 12. Heb. ii. 14. vii. 5. xi. 16. xiii. 15. 1 Pet. iii. 20.

that is to say, Matt. xxvii. 46. Mark vii. 11. Acts i. 19. Heb. ix. 11. x. 20.

4, ἐσμέν.

we are (**are we**), Mark v. 9. Luke ix. 12. xvii. 10. John ix. 28, 40[4]. xvii. 22[4](–TTr*S*). Acts ii. 32[4]. iii. 15[4]. v. 32[4]. x. 39(*omS*)[4]. xiv. 15[4]. xvi. 28. xvii. 28. xxiii. 15[4].

Rom. vi. 15. viii. 12, 16. xii. 5. xiv. 8. 1 Cor. iii. 9. x. 17, 22. xv. 19. 2 Cor. i. 14, 24. ii. 15, 17. iii. 5. x. 11. xiii. 6[4]. Gal. iii. 25. iv. 28[4] (ἐστέ LT), 31. Eph. ii. 10. iv. 25. v. 30. Phil. iii. 3[4]. 1 Thes. v. 5.

Heb. iii. 6[4]. x. 10, 39[4]. 1 John ii. 5. iii. 2, 19. iv. 6[4], 17[4]. v. 19, 20.

are, John x. 30.

we be, John viii. 33.

we have our being, Acts xvii. 28.

Add 2 Cor. vi. 15, for ἐστέ, L*S*. 1 John iii. 1(called καὶ ἐ.), L*S*.

See also ἐλπίζω, εὐαγγελίζω.

5, ἐστέ.

ye are (are ye), Matt. v. 11, 13[5], 14[5]. viii. 26. xv. 16[5]. xxiii. 8[5], 28, 31. Mark iv. 40. vii. 18[5]. Luke vi. 22. ix. 55[5](*ap*). xi. 44. xiii. 25, 27. xvi. 15[5]. xxii. 28. xxiv. 17(ἐστάθησαν fr. ἵστημι Tr[b]*S*), 38, 48[5](-TTr[b]). John viii. 23[5], 23, 31, 37, 44, 47. x. 26, 34. xiii. 10, 11, 17, 35. xv. 3[5], 14[5], 19. Acts iii. 25[5]. vii. 26[5]. xix. 15[5]. xxii. 3[5].

Rom. i. 6[5]. vi. 14, 16. viii. 9[5]. xv. 14. 1 Cor. i. 30[5]. iii. 3*t*, 4, 9, 16, 17[5]. iv. 8. v. 2, 7. vi. 2, 19. ix. 1[5], 2[5]. xii. 27[5]. xiv. 12. xv. 17. 2 Cor. i. 7. iii. 2[5]. vi. 16[5](ἐσμέν[4] L*S*). vii. 3. Gal. iii. 3, 26, 28[5], 29. iv. 6. v. 18. Eph. ii. 5, 8, 19. Col. ii. 10. 1 Thes. ii. 20[5]. iv. 9. v. 4, 5[5]. Heb. xii. 8. 1 John ii. 14. iv. 4.

it is ye,[5] Matt. x. 20. Mark xiii. 11.

With conj., . . **ye be**, 2 Cor. ii. 9. xiii. 5*t*. Heb. xii. 8.

ὅτι ἐστέ, **to be**, 2 Cor. iii. 3.

ye have been, John xv. 27.

With genitive, **ye belong to**, Mark ix. 41.

With γινώσκω[p], **ye know**, Eph. v. 5 (ἴστε fr. εἶδον GLT*S*).

Add Luke xi. 48, *see* μαρτυρέω. Eph. ii. 19 (. . fellow c.), G″LT*S*. *And see* ἐστίν, ἐσμέν, ἦτε.

6, εἰσί, εἰσίν.

are, Matt. ii. 18. vii. 15. x. 30. xi. 8. xii. 5, 48. xiii. 38*t*, 39, 56. xvii. 26. xviii. 20. xix. 6, 12*t*. xxii. 14, 30. Mark iv. 15, 16, 18(-G[oo]), 20. vi. 3. x. 8. xii. 25. Luke vii. 25, 31, 32. viii. 12, 14, 15, 21. xi. 7. xii. 38. xiii. 14, 30*t*. xvi. 8. xx. 36*t*. John iv. 35. v. 39. vi. 64. vii. 49. viii. 10(*ap*). x. 8, 12(ἐστίν LTr*S*). xi. 9. xiv. 2. xvii. 9, 11, 14, 16. Acts ii. 7, 13. v. 25. xiii. 31. xvi. 17. xix. 38. xxi. 20. xxiii. 21. xxiv. 11.

Rom. i. 32. ii. 14. viii. 14. ix. 4, 7. xiii. 1, 3, 6. xv. 27. xvi. 7. 1 Cor. i. 11. iii. 8, 20. x. 18. xii. 4, 5, 6. xiv. 22, 37(ἐστίν LT*S*). 2 Cor. xi. 22*tr*, 23. Gal. iii. 7, 10*t*. iv. 24. Eph. v. 16. Col. ii. 3. 1 Tim. v. 24. vi. 1, 2*t*. 2 Tim. iii. 6. Tit. i. 10. iii. 9. Heb. i. 10, 14. 2 Pet. ii. 17. iii. 7. 1 John iv. 5. v. 3, 7, 7(*ap*), 8(*ap*). Jude 12, 16. Rev. i. 19, 20*t*. ii. 2, 9. iii. 4, 9. iv. 5(ἅ ἐστιν for αἵ ἐ. T, -*S*), 11(ἦσαν GLTTr*S*). v. 6, 8. vii. 13, 14, 15. xi. 4. xiv. 4*t*, 4(-G[o] LTTr[b]*S*), 5. xvi. 6, 14. xvii. 9, 10, 12, 15. xix. 9. xxi. 5.

be, Matt. vii. 13, 14. xv. 14. xvi. 28. xix. 12. xx. 16. Mark ix. 1. Luke ix. 27. xxi. 22. Acts xix. 26. 1 Cor. viii. 5*t*. Gal. i. 7. Jude 19.

were[c], Luke xviii. 9. John vi. 64. Acts iv. 13. xvi. 38. Heb. vii. 21, 23. xi. 13. 1 John ii. 19.

With εἰς, **agree in**, 1 John v. 8.

With dative,[cc] **have**, Luke ix. 13. Acts xxi. 23.

Not rendered, Mark iv. 18(-C?G[oo]),

Add, for ἐστί, John xvii. 7, TTr*S*. 1 Cor. xiv. 10, LT*S*. Rev. ix. 19 (*ap*). For ἥκασιν fr. ἥκω, Mark viii. 3, T.

See also πρόσκαιρος.

Subjunctive, ὦ, ᾖς, ᾖ, *etc*.

be, Matt. vi. 22, 23. x. 13*t*. Luke x. 6. xiv. 8. John iii. 2, 27. ix. 31. xvii. 24. Acts v. 38. Rom. ii. 25. ix. 27. 1 Cor. i. 10*t*. v. 11(ᾖ St). vii. 29. xiv. 28. xvi. 4. 2 Cor. xiii. 7. Gal. v. 10. Eph. iv. 14. Tit. iii. 14.

may be, Matt. vi. 4. John xiv. 3. xvi. 24. xvii. 11, 21*t*, 22, 23, 26. 1 Cor. v. 7. vii. 34. xv. 28. 2 Cor. iv. 7. ix. 3. Phil. i. 10. ii. 28.

1 Tim. v. 7. 2 Tim. iii. 17. Tit. i. 9. Jas. i. 4. 1 John i. 4. 2 John 12.
might be, Mark v. 18. John xvii. 19.
should be, Mark iii. 14. Rom. xi. 25. 1 Cor. xii. 25. 2 Cor. i. 17. Eph. v. 27. Phm. 14.
were, John vi. 65.
am, John ix. 5.
is, Matt. xx. 4, 7(*ap*). xxiv. 28. Luke xi. 34*t*.
are, 2 Cor. xiii. 9.
should stand, 1 Cor. ii. 5.
Not rendered? Jas. ii. 15(-T*S*; *see* ὑπάρχω).
Add, for μένω, John xiv. 16, LTTr *S*. xv. 11, G″LTTr.—Luke xx. 28, for ἀποθνήσκω, LTr. 1 Cor. vii. 5, for συνέρχομαι, GLT*S*. Phil. ii. 15, for γίνομαι, L. Rev. iii. 15, for εἴην, GLTTr*S*.
See also πείθω, ποιέω, ὑπέρακμος, φανερός.

Optative, εἴην, εἴης, εἴη, *etc.*
might be, Luke viii. 9.
should be, Luke i. 29. ix. 46. John xiii. 24(*ap*).
wert, Rev. iii. 15(ἧς GLTTr*S*).
were, Luke iii. 15.
was, Luke xxii. 23. Acts xxi. 33.
should mean, Acts x. 17.
meant, Luke xv. 26. xviii. 36.
Add Acts xx. 16, for ἦν, L*S*.
See also ἀπώλεια.

Imperative, 1, ἴσθι.
be thou, Matt. ii. 13.
be, Mark v. 34.
ἴσθι ἐν, **give thyself wholly to,** 1 Tim. iv. 15.
See also εὐνοέω, ἔχω.

2, ἔστω, ἔστωσαν.
be, Acts ii. 14. iv. 10. xiii. 38. xxviii. 28.
let be, Matt. v. 37(ἔσται L). xviii. 17. xx. 26 and 27(ἔσται G″LTr*S*). Luke xii. 35. Gal. i. 8, 9. 1 Tim. iii. 12. Jas. i. 19. 1 Pet. iii. 3.
be so, 2 Cor. xii. 16.
See also κατοικέω.

3, ἤτω.
let be, 1 Cor. xvi. 22. Jas. v. 12.

Infinitive, εἶναι.
to be, Matt. xvii. 4. Mark ix. 5, 35. xiv. 64. Luke ix. 33. John vii. 4. Acts v. 36. xvi. 15. xvii. 18. Rom. i. 22. vi. 11(*omS*). xiv. 14. 1 Cor. iii. 18. vii. 25, 26. xi. 16. xii. 23. xiv. 37. 2 Cor. vii. 11. Gal. ii. 6, 9. iv. 21. vi. 3. Phil. i. 23. ii. 6. iv. 11. 1 Tim. i. 7. ii. 12. Tit. iii. 1, 2. Heb. v. 12. xii. 11. Jas. i. 26.
be, Matt. xix. 21. xx. 27. Luke ii. 49. xiv. 26, 27, 33. Acts xviii. 15. 1 Cor. xi. 19. 1 Tim. iii. 2. 2 Tim. ii. 24. Tit. i. 7. Jas. iv. 4.
to have been, Luke ii. 44. ix. 18. xi. 1.
have been, 1 Thes. ii. 6.
that (understood[s]) . . **am (art, is, are, be),** Matt. xvi. 13, 15. xxii. 23. Mark viii. 27, 29. xii. 18[s]. Luke ix. 18, 20. xx. 27, 41(-G°). xxiii. 2. Acts viii. 37(*ap*). xiii. 25. xvii. 7, 29. xxiii. 8. Rom. ii. 19. iii. 9. vii. 3. 2 Cor. x. 7. 1 Tim. vi. 5. Tit. ii. 2. 1 Pet. v. 12. 1 John ii. 9[s]. Rev. ii. 2[s], 9[s]. iii. 9[s].
that . . was (were), Luke iv. 41. xx. 6. John xvii. 5[s]. Acts iv. 32. viii. 9. xviii. 28. xxviii. 6. Rom. ix. 3. 1 Cor. vii. 7. Heb. xi. 4.
had been, Mark vi. 49[s].
that . . may (might, should) be, Luke viii. 38. Rom. iv. 13. 2 Cor. v. 9. ix. 5. Eph. i. 4. iii. 6.
τοῦ εἶναι, **that . . shouldest be,** Acts xiii. 47.
With διά, **because . . is (was, were),** Luke ii. 4. xi. 8. xix. 11. Acts xviii. 3. xxvii. 4.
With εἰς, **that . . might (should) be,** Rom. iii. 26. iv. 11, 16. viii. 29. xv. 16. Eph. i. 12. Jas. i. 18.—**so that . . are** (*marg.* **may be**), Rom. i. 20.
With ἐν, **as . . was,** Luke ix. 18. xi. 1.—**when . . was,** Luke v. 12.

—**while . . was (were),** Luke ii. 6. Acts xix. 1.

With ὥστε, **that . . might be,** 1 Pet. i. 21.

to be made, Acts xvi. 13.

come, John i. 46(47).

Not rendered, Luke xx. 20. xxii. 24. Rom. xvi. 19. 1 Cor. vii. 32. 2 Cor. xi. 16. Phil. iii. 8, 8(–L*S*).

Add Mark iii. 12(*ap*). x. 44, for γίνομαι, LTr*S*. Acts xviii. 5(that . . was), G'L*S*.

See also ἐπιθυμητής, εὐάρεστος, εὐμετάδοτος, θέλω, φίλανδρος.

Participle, ὤν, οὖσα, ὄν, *etc.*

being, Matt. i. 19. vii. 11. xii. 34. Mark viii. 1. xiv. 3. Luke ii. 5. iii. 23. xiii. 16. xx. 36. xxii. 3. John iv. 9. v. 13. vi. 71(–G∞LTr). vii. 50. x. 33. xi. 49, 51. xviii. 26. xix. 38. Acts xv. 32. xvi. 21. xxvii. 2. Rom. xi. 17. 1 Cor. viii. 7. ix. 21. xii. 12. Gal. ii. 3. Eph. ii. 20. iv. 18. Col. ii. 13. 1 Tim. iii. 10. Tit. i. 16. iii. 11. Phm. 9. Heb. i. 3. xiii. 3.

to be, Acts xxvi. 3.

that . . art (is, was, hast been), Acts vii. 12. viii. 23. xix. 35. xxiv. 10.

who (which, that) am (art, etc.), Matt. vi. 30. xii. 30. Mark xiii. 16 (–LTr*S*). Luke xi. 23. xii. 28. John i. 18. iii. 13(*ap*), 31. iv. 9. vi. 46. viii. 47. xviii. 37. Acts v. 17. Rom. i. 7. iv. 17. vii. 23. viii. 5, 8, 28. ix. 5. xii. 3. xiii. 1. xvi. 1, 11. 1 Cor. i. 2, 28*l*. viii. 10. 2 Cor. i. 1*l*. v. 4. xi. 31. Gal. iv. 8. Eph. i. 1. ii. 4. iv. 18. Phil. i. 1. Col. iv. 11. 1 Thes. ii. 14. v. 8. 1 Tim. ii. 2. 2 Tim. ii. 19. 2 Pet. ii. 11.

who (etc.) was (etc.), Mark ii. 26. Luke vi. 3(–LTr*S*). xxiii. 7. John ix. 40. xi. 31. xii. 17. Acts xi. 1. xiii. 1. xiv. 13. xvi. 3. xix. 31. xx. 34. xxi. 8. xxii. 5, 9. xxiv. 24. Eph. ii. 1, 13. Col. i. 21. 1 Tim. i. 13. Heb. iii. 2.

as . . was, Mark xiv. 66.

for all there were, John xxi. 11.

forasmuch as . . was, Acts ix. 38.

inasmuch as . . are, Phil. i. 7.

seeing . . are, 2 Cor. xi. 19.

seeing that there are, Heb. viii. 4.

though . . be, 1 Cor. ix. 19. Gal. iv. 1. Jas. iii. 4.

though . . was (were), 2 Cor. viii. 9. Heb. v. 8.

when . . is, John iii. 4. Rom. v. 13. Gal. vi. 3.

when . . was, Luke xxii. 53. xxiv. 6. John i. 48(49). xx. 1. Acts vii. 2. xxvii. 9. Rom. iv. 10. v. 6, 10. Eph. ii. 5. 2 Thes. ii. 5. 2 Pet. i. 18.

whereas . . was, John ix. 25.

while . . is, Luke xiv. 32.

while . . was (were), Luke xxiv. 44. Acts ix. 39. Rom. v. 8.

οὔσης ὀψίας, **at evening,** John xx. 19.

ὡς ὄντα, **as though they were,** Rom. iv. 17.

οὐκ ὄντος αὐτῷ, **when as yet he had no,** Acts vii. 5.

οὖσα ἐν, **having,** Luke viii. 43.—**which had,** Mark v. 25.

and was come, Mark xi. 11.

Not rendered, Mark xiv. 43(–G∞L Tr*S*). Luke xxiii. 12. John x. 12. Acts xvii. 16. xviii. 24. ix. 2. xxv. 23 (–G∞LT*S*). xxviii. 17. 2 Cor. viii. 22. Rev. v. 5(*omS*).

Add Mark iv. 31, for ἐστί, LTr*S*. Acts xviii. 12, *see* ἀνθυπατεύω. xx. 18(*ap*). 1 Cor. ix. 20(*ap*). 1 John iii. 10(*ap*).

See also ἀναντίρρητος, ἀσύμφωνος.

ὁ ὢν καὶ ὁ ἦν καὶ ὁ ἐρχόμενος.

which is, and which was, and which is to come, Rev. i. 4, 8.

which art, and wast, and art to come, Rev. xi. 17(καὶ ὁ ἐρχ. *omS*).

ὁ ἦν καὶ ὁ ὢν καὶ ὁ ἐρχ., **which was, and is, and is to come,** Rev. iv. 8.

ὁ ὢν καὶ ὁ ἦν καὶ ὁ ὅσιος (ἐσόμενος C), **which art, and wast, and shalt be,** Rev. xvi. 5(καί 2d *omS*, –ὁ 3d LTTr).

II. Imperfect.

1, ἦν, ἦς(ἦσθα), ἦν; ἦμεν, ἦτε, ἦσαν.

was (wast, were), Matt. i. 18. ii. 9, 15. iii. 4. iv. 18. vii. 27. viii. 30. xii. 4, 10(-G[o]LTTr*S*), 40. xiv. 21, 23, 24(*ap*), 24. xv. 38. xxi. 25, 33. xxii. 8, 25. xxiv. 38. xxv. 2. xxvi. 43, 69, 71. xxvii. 54, 55, 56, 61. xxviii. 3.

Mark i. 6, 13*t*, 16, 23, 33, 45(-L[b]). ii. 4, 6, 15. iii. 1(-LTr[b]). iv. 1, 36*t*, 38. v. 5, 11, 13(-G[oo]L[b]TTr*S*), 21, 40, 42. vi. 31, 34, 44, 47, 48, 52. vii. 26. viii. 9. ix. 4, 6(γίνομαι G″ LTTr*S*). x. 32. xi. 13, 30, 32. xii. 20. xiv. 1, 4, 21(-L[b]TTr[b]), 40, 67[2]. xv. 7, 25, 26, 39, 40, 40(-Tr[b]*S*), 41, 42, 46. xvi. 4.

Luke i. 6, 7*t*, 10, 66, 80. ii. 7, 8, 25*t*, 26, 36, 40, 51. iv. 16, 17, 20, 25, 27, 32, 33, 38. v. 3, 10, 17*f*, 18, 29. vi. 6*t*. vii. 2, 12(-GT), 12 (-StG[oo]TTr[b]), 37, 39. viii. 32, 40. ix. 14, 30, 32, 45, 53. xi. 14*t*. xiii. 10, 11(-LTTr), 11. xiv. 2. xv. 24, 24(-G[o]*S*), 25, 32, 32(-G[oo] LTTr). xvi. 1, 19, 20(-L[b]TTr*S*). xvii. 6. xviii. 2, 3, 23, 34. xix. 2, 2(-L[b]Tr), 3. xx. 4, 29. xxi. 37. xxii. 56, 59. xxiii. 8, 19, 38, 44, 47, 53, 54. xxiv. 10(ἦν for ἦσαν G″ T, -G″Tr[b]), 53.

John i. 1*tr*, 2, 4(ἐστίν L*S*), 4, 8, 9, 10, 15*t*, 24, 28, 30, 39(40), 40 (41), 44(45). ii. 1, 6, 13, 23, 25. iii. 1, 19, 23*t*, 24, 26. iv. 6*t*, 46. v. 1, 5, 9, 35. vi. 4, 10, 22, 62. vii. 2, 12, 39, 42. viii. 39(ἐστέ GLTTr*S*), 42, 44. ix. 8, 14, 16, 24, 33, 41. x. 6(ἦ Tr), 22, 41. xi. 1, 2, 6, 18, 30, 32, 38, 41(*ap*), 55. xii. 1, 2, 6, 16, 20. xiii. 5, 23, 30. xv. 19. xvii. 6. xviii. 1, 10, 13*t*, 14, 15, 16(ὁ for ὅς ἦν TTr), 18, 25, 28, 30, 36, 40. xix. 11, 14, 19, 20*t*, 23, 31*t*, 41, 42. xx. 7, 19, 24, 26. xxi. 2, 7, 8, 18.

Acts i. 15, 17. ii. 1, 2, 5, 24, 44. iii. 10. iv. 3, 6, 22, 31, 32, 33. v. 12. vii. 9, 20, 22, 44. viii. 1, 16, 28, 32. ix. 9, 10, 28, 33, 36*t*. x. 1(*omS*), 38. xi. 20, 21, 24. xii. 3, 5, 6, 12, 18, 20. xiii. 1, 7, 46, 48. xiv. 12. xvi. 1, 12. xvii. 1, 11. xviii. 3(*ap*), 14, 25. xix. 7, 14, 16, 32. xx. 8*t*, 16(εἴη L*S*). xxi. 3. xxiii. 13. xxvii. 8, 37(ἤμεθα LT*S*).

Rom. v. 13. vi. 17, 20*t*. vii. 5. 1 Cor. vi. 11. x. 1, 4. xii. 2, 19. xvi. 12. 2 Cor. v. 19. Gal. ii. 6, 11. iv. 3*t*. Eph. ii. 3, 12. v. 8. Phil. iii. 7. Col. ii. 14. 1 Thes. iii. 4. 2 Thes. iii. 10. Tit. iii. 3.

Heb. ii. 15. vii. 10, 11. viii. 4. xi. 38. xii. 21. Jas. i. 24. v. 17. 1 Pet. ii. 25. 2 Pet. iii. 5. 1 John i. 1, 2. ii. 19. iii. 12*t*. Rev. i. 4, 8. iv. 3 (*ap*), 8. v. 11. ix. 8, 10(καί LTTr*S*, -G′). x. 10. xi. 17. xiii. 2. xvi. 5. xvii. 8*t*, 11. xviii. 23. xxi. 18(-L), 21.

hast been, Matt. xxv. 21, 23.

had (hadst) been, Matt. xxiii. 30 (ἤμεθα GLTTr*S*). xxvi. 24. Luke iv. 16. viii. 2. John ix. 18. xi. 21, 32. Acts iv. 13. xiv. 26. Heb. viii. 7. 2 Pet. ii. 21. 1 John ii. 19.

With ἄν, **would have been**, Matt. xxiii. 30(ἤμεθα GLTTr*S*).—**should have been**, Gal. iii. 21.—**should be**, Heb. viii. 4.

is, Gal. iv. 15(-G[oo]LT*S*).

began to be, Luke iii. 23.

With dative,[cc] **had**, Luke i. 7. vii. 41. viii. 42. x. 39. Acts iv. 32. xxi. 9.

held[c], Acts xiv. 4.

With Participles, of

ἀκούω, **had heard**, Gal. i. 23. ἀτενίζω, **looked stedfastly**, Acts i. 10. βαπτίζω, **baptized**, John x. 40. δέω, **had bound**, Acts xxii. 29. διανυκτερεύω, **continued all night**, Luke vi. 12. ἐγγίζω, **drew near**, Luke xv. 1.

See also διανεύω, διατάσσω, διδάσκω, ἐκλύω, ἐπί, ἐπιποθέω, εὐαγγελίζω, ἔχω, θαυμάζω, ἴσος, ἵστημι, καίω, κατακεῖμαι, καταμένω, κηρύσσω, νηστεύω, παρατηρέω, πορεύομαι, προάγω, προοράω, προσδέχομαι, προσδοκάω, προσκαρτερέω, συγκάθημαι, συγκατατίθημι, συνομορέω, ὑποχωρέω.

Add John xix. 14, for δέ[2d], G''LT TrS. Acts iv. 34, for ὑπάρχω, LS. xi. 11, for ἤμην, LS. Rev. iii. 15, for εἴης, GLTTrS. iv. 11, for εἰσί, G LTTrS. xvii. 4, for ἤ[2d], GLTTrS.

2, ἤμην.

I was, Matt. xxv. 35, 36, 43. Mark xiv. 49. John xi. 15. xvi. 4. xvii. 12. Acts x. 30. xi. 5[1], 11(ἦμεν LS), 17. xxii. 19[1], 20. 1 Cor. xiii. 11. Gal. i. 22.

ἂν ἤμην, **I should be,** Gal. i. 10.

3, ἤμεθα.

For ἦμεν, Matt. xxiii. 30*t*, GLTTr S. Acts. xxvii. 37, LTS.

III. Future.

1, *Indicative,* ἔσομαι, ἔσῃ, ἔσται; ἐσόμεθα, ἔσεσθε, ἔσονται.

shall be, Matt. v. 21, 22*tr*. vi. 5, 22, 23. viii. 12. x. 15, 22. xi. 22, 24. xii. 11(–TTr), 27, 40, 45. xiii. 40, 42, 49, 50. xvi. 19*t*, 22. xvii. 17. xviii. 18*t*. xix. 5, 30. xx. 16, 26(ἐστίν LTr). xxii. 13, 28. xxiii. 11. xxiv. 3, 7, 9, 21, 27, 37, 39, 40, 51. xxv. 30. xxvi. 64.

Mark vi. 11(*ap*). ix. 19, 35. x. 8, 31, 43(ἐστίν LTTrS), 43, 44. xii. 7, 23. xiii. 4, 8*t*, 13, 19.

Luke i. 15, 20, 32, 33, 34, 45, 66. ii. 10. iv. 7. vi. 35*t*, 40. ix. 41, 48 (ἐστίν G''LTTrS). x. 12, 14. xi. 19, 30, 36. xii. 20, 52. xiii. 28, 30*t*. xiv. 14. xv. 7. xvii. 24, 26, 30, 31, 34, 35, 36(*ap*). xxi. 7, 11*t*, 17, 23, 24, 25. xxiii. 43.

John vi. 45. viii. 36, 55. xii. 26. xiv. 17 (ἐστίν LTr). xix. 24.

Acts i. 8. xiii. 11. xxii. 15. xxvii. 22, 25.

Rom. iv. 18. vi. 5. xv. 12. 1 Cor. vi. 16. xi. 27. xiv. 11. 2 Cor. iii. 8. vi. 16, 18. xi. 15. xii. 6. xiii. 11. Eph. v. 31. Phil. iv. 9. 1 Thes. iv. 17. 1 Tim. iv. 6. 2 Tim. ii. 2, 21. iii. 2, 9. Heb. i. 5. viii. 10. Jas. i. 25. v. 3. 2 Pet. ii. 1. 1 John iii. 2*t*. 2 John 2. Rev. x. 9. xx. 6. xxi. 3*t*, 4*t*, 7, 25. xxii. 3*t*, 4*t*, 5, 12(ἐστίν LTTr, –G°).

With εἰς, **shall be made,** Luke iii. 5.

should be, Jude 18 (ἐλεύσονται fr. ἔρχομαι G'). Rev. x. 6.

will be, Matt. vi. 21. Luke xii. 34, 55. 2 Cor. vi. 16, 18. Heb. i. 5. viii. 10, 12. Rev. xxi. 7.

be, Matt. v. 48. Mark xiv. 2. Heb. iii. 12. 2 John 3.

shall come to pass, Acts ii. 17, 21. iii. 23. Rom. ix. 26.

will come, 2 Tim. iv. 3.

With genitive,[∞] **may have,** Rev. xxii. 14.

With dative,[∞] **shall have,** Matt. xix. 27. Mark xi. 23, 24. Luke i. 14. xiv. 10. Rom. ix. 9.

Add, for ἐστίν, Luke xix. 46, L[m]T Tr. Jas. iv. 14, G'. For ἔστω, Matt. v. 37, L. xx. 26, 27, G''LTrS. For γένεσθε fr. γίνομαι, 1 Pet. i. 16, G' LTS.

See also ἐκπίπτω, ζωγρέω, κάθημαι, λαλέω, μακροχρόνιος, πάροικος, πείθω, συλαγωγέω.

2, *Infinitive,* ἔσεσθαι.

μέλλειν ἔσεσθαι,

that there shall be, Acts xxiv. 15.

that there should be, Acts xi. 28.

that . . will be, Acts xxvii. 10.

μέλλοντος ἐσ., **to come,** Acts xxiv. 25(–ἔσεσθαι GLS).

See also ἐπιβουλή.

3, *Participle,* ἐσόμενος.

With art., **which shalt be,** Rev. xvi. 5 (ὅσιος EGLTTrS). — **what would follow,** Luke xxii. 49.

εἵνεκεν. See ἕνεκα.

εἴπερ. See εἰ.

εἶπον.

(L, T, and Tr, following the older MSS., sometimes read εἶπαν for εἶπον.)

ἀποκριθεὶς εἶπε [1]. ἀπεκρίθη καὶ εἶπε [2].

say, Matt. ii. 5, 8. iii. 7, 15[1]. iv. 3, 4[1]. v. 11, 22*t*. viii. 10, 13, 19,

21, 22(*λέγω* LTTr*S*), 32. ix. 2, 3 (*εἶπα* LT), 4, 5*t*, 11(*λέγω* LTr*S*), 12, 15, 22. xi. 3, 4^1, 25^1. xii. 2, 3, 11, 24, 25, 39^1, 47, 48^1, 49. xiii. 10, 11^1, 27, 28(*λέγω* LTTr*S*), 37, 52(*λέγω* L), 57. xiv. 2, 16, 18, 28^1, 29. xv. 3^1, 5, 10, 12(*λέγω* LTTr), 13^1, 15^1, 16, 24^1, 26^1, 27, 28^1, 32, 34. xvi. 2^1, 6, 8, 14, 16^1, 17^1, 23, 24. xvii. 4^1, 7, 11^1, 13, 17^1, 19, 20(*λέγω* LTTr*S*), 22, 24. xviii. 3, 21. xix. 4^1, 5, 11, 14, 16, 17, 18, 23, 26, 27^1, 28. xx. 4, 13^1, 17, 21, 22, 25, 32. xxi. 3, 16, 21^1, 21, 24^1, 25, 26, 27^1, 28, 29^1, 30, 30^1, 38. xxii. 13, 18, 24, 29^1, 37(*φημί* GLTTr*S*), 44. xxiii. 39. xxiv. 2, 4^1, 23, 26, 48. xxv. 8, 12^1, 22, 24, 26^1. xxvi. 1, 10, 15, 18*t*, 21, 23^1, 25^1, 25, 26, 33^1, 35, 44, 49, 50, 55, 61, 62, 63^1, 64, 66, 73. xxvii. 4, 6, 17, 21^1, 21, 25^1, 43, 63, 64. xxviii. 5^1, 6, 7, 13.

Mark i. 17, 44. ii. 8(*λέγω* TTr*S*), 9*t*, 19. iii. 9, 32(*λέγω* LTTr*S*). iv. 39, 40. v. 7(*λέγω* G″LTTr*S*), 34. vi. 16(*λέγω* TTr*S*), 22, 24*t*, 31(*λέγω* T Tr*S*), 37^1. vii. 6^1, 10, 11, 27(*λέγω* L TTr*S*), 29. viii. 5, 20 (*λέγω* T*S*), 34. ix. 17^1(*ἀπεκρίθη* LTTr*S*), 21, 23, 29, 36, 39. x. 3^1, 4, 5^1, 14, 18, 20(*φημί* Tr*S*)^1, 21, 29^1(*φημί* T*S*), 36, 37, 38, 39*t*, 51, 52. xi. 3*t*, 6, 14^1, 23, 23(–G^{ou}TTr*S*), 29^1, 31, 32. xii. 7, 15, 16(*λέγω* L^m), 17^1, 24^1(*φημί* TTr *S*), 32*t*, 34, 36, 36(G′, *λέγω* GTTr). xiii. 2^1, 21. xiv. 6, 14, 16, 18, 20^1, 22, 24, 48^1, 62, 72. xv. 2(*λέγω* TTr*S*)^1, 12^1(*λέγω* Tr), 39. xvi. 7, 8, 15(*ap*).

Luke i. 13, 18, 19^1, 28, 30, 34, 35^1, 38, 42, 46, 60^1, 61. ii. 10, 15(*λαλέω* L^m*S*), 28, 34, 48, 49. iii. 12, 13, 14. iv. 3, 6, 8^1, 9, 12^1, 23, 24, 43. v. 4, 5^1, 10, 13(*λέγω* LTr*S*), 20, 22^1, 23*t*, 24, 27, 31^1, 33, 34. vi. 2, 3^1, 8, 9, 10. vii. 7, 9, 13, 14, 20, 22^1, 31(*ap*), 40^1, 40, 43^1, 43, 48, 50. viii. 10, 21, 22, 25, 28, 30, 45*t*, 46, 48, 52. ix. 3, 9, 12, 13*t*, 14, 19^1, 20, 20^1, 22, 33, 41, 43, 48, 49^1, 50, 54, 55(*ap*), 57, 58, 59*t*, 60, 61, 62. x. 10, 18, 21, 23, 26, 27^1, 28, 29, 30, 35, 37*t*, 40, 41^1. xi. 1, 2, 5, 5(*ἐρεῖ* fr. *εἴρω* L), 7^1, 15, 17, 27, 28, 39, 46, 49. xii. 11, 12, 13, 14, 15, 18, 20, 22, 41, 42, 45. xiii. 2^1, 7, 12, 15^1, 20, 23*t*, 32, 35. xiv. 5^1, 10(*ἐρεῖ* TTr*S*), 15, 16, 17, 18, 19, 20, 21, 22, 23, 25. xv. 11, 12, 17 (*φημί* T*S*), 21, 22, 27, 29^1, 31. xvi. 2, 3, 6*t*, 7*t*, 15, 24, 25, 27, 30, 31. xvii. 1, 5, 6, 14, 17^1, 19, 20^1, 22, 37. xviii. 4, 6, 16, 19, 21, 22, 24, 26, 27, 28, 29, 31, 41, 42. xix. 5, 8, 9, 12, 13, 17, 19, 24, 25, 30 (*λέγω* LTr*S*), 32, 33, 34, 39, 40^1. xx. 3^1, 5, 6, 8, 13, 16, 17, 23, 24^1, 25, 34^1, 39^1, 39, 41, 42, 45. xxi. 3, 5, 8. xxii. 8, 9, 10, 15, 17, 25, 31 (*ap*), 33, 34, 35*t*, 36, 38*t*, 40, 46, 48, 49, 51^1, 52, 56, 58, 60, 61, 67, 70, 71. xxiii. 4, 14, 22, 28, 43, 46*t*. xxiv. 5, 17, 18^1, 19*t*, 24, 25, 32, 38, 41, 44, 46.

John i. 22, 23, 25, 30, 33, 38(39), 42(43), 46(47), 48(49)^2, 50(51)^2, 50 (51). ii. 16, 18^2, 19^2, 20, 22. iii. 2, 3^2, 7, 9^2, 10^2, 26, 27^2, 28. iv. 10^2, 13^2, 17^2, 17, 27, 32, 48, 52, 53. v. 11, 12, 14, 19^2. vi. 10, 25, 26^2, 28, 29^2, 30, 32, 34, 35, 36, 41, 43^2, 53, 59, 60, 61, 67. vii. 3, 9^p, 16(–C 1611 to 1701, *err.*)^2, 20(–LTTr*S*)^2, 21^2, 33, 35, 36, 38, 42, 45, 52^2. viii. 7(*ap*), 10(*ap*), 11*t*(*ap*), 13, 14^2, 21, 23(*λέγω* LTTr*S*), 24, 25, 28, 39^2, 41, 42, 48^2 52, 55, 57, 58. ix. 7, 11 (–L^{b}TTr*S*)^2, 11, 12, 15, 17, 20^2, 23, 24, 25(–LTTr*S*)^2, 26, 28, 30^2, 34^2, 35, 36^2, 37, 39, 40, 41. x. 7, 26(*ap*), 34(*εἶπα* StGTTr, *εἶπον* L*S*), 36. xi. 4, 11, 12, 14, 16, 21, 25, 28^p, 28, 34, 37, 40, 41, 42, 49. xii. 6, 7, 19, 27, 30^2, 35, 39, 41, 44, 49. xiii. 7^2, 11, 12, 21^p, 21, 33. xiv. 23^2, 26, 28, 28(*om* *S*). xv. 20. xvi. 4, 15, 17, 19*t*. xvii. 1. xviii. 4(*λέγω* LTTr), 6, 7, 11, 21, 22, 25*t*, 29(*φησίν* fr. *φημί* TTr*S*), 30^2, 31*t*, 32, 33, 37, 38^p. xix. 21, 24, 30. xx. 14^p, 17(*λέγω* L^m), 20^p, 21, 22^p, 25, 26, 28^2. xxi. 6, 17*t*, 20, 23.

Acts i. 7, 11, 15, 24. ii. 34, 37. iii. 4, 6, 22. iv. 8, 19, 23, 24, 25. v. 3, 8, 9(-LT*S*), 19, 29[1], 35. vi. 2. vii. 1, 3, 7, 26, 27, 33, 35, 37, 40, 56, 60p. viii. 20, 24[1], 29, 30, 31, 34[1], 37[1](*ap*), 37(*ap*). ix. 5, 5(-G∞LT), 6(*ap*), 10*t*, 15, 17, 34, 40. x. 3, 4*t*, 14, 19, 21, 22, 34. xi. 8, 13. xii. 8, 11, 15, 17. xiii. 2, 10, 16, 22, 46. xiv. 10. xv. 7, 36. xvi. 18, 20, 31. xvii. 32. xviii. 6, 14, 21. xix. 2, 2(-G∞LT*S*), 3*t*, 4, 15[1], 21, 25. xx. 10, 18, 35. xxi. 11, 14, 20, 39. xxii. 8, 10*t*, 13, 14, 19, 21, 25, 27. xxiii. 1, 3, 4, 11, 14, 20, 23. xxiv. 20, 22. xxv. 9[1], 10. xxvi. 15(εἶπα LT), 15, 29(-G∞LT*S*). xxvii. 21, 31. xxviii. 21, 26, 29p(*ap*).

Rom. x. 6. 1 Cor. i. 15. x. 28. xi. 22, 24. xii. 3, 15, 16, 21. xv. 27. 2 Cor. vi. 16. Gal. ii. 14. Col. iv. 17. Tit. i. 12. Heb. i. 5. iii. 10. vii. 9. x. 7, 30. xii. 21. Jas. ii. 3*t*, 11*t*, 16. 1 John i. 6, 8, 10. iv. 20. Jude 9. Rev. vii. 14. xvii. 7. xxi. 5, 6. xxii. 6(λέγω G″), 17.

say on, Luke vii. 40.

speak, Matt. viii. 8. x. 27. xii. 32*t*. xvi. 11. xvii. 13. xxii. 1[1]. Mark i. 42p(-G°LTr*S*). iii. 9. ix. 18(εἶπα T Tr*S*). xii. 12, 26. xiv. 39. Luke vi. 26, 39. vii. 39. viii. 4. xii. 3, 13, 16. xiv. 3[1]. xv. 3. xviii. 9. xix. 11, 28p. xx. 2, 19. xxi. 29. xxiv. 40p(*ap*). John iv. 50. vii. 39. ix. 6p, 22. x. 6, 41. xi. 43p, 51. xii. 38. xiii. 28. xviii. 1p, 9, 16, 22p, 32. xx. 18. xxi. 19, 19p. Acts i. 9p. ii. 29. xviii. 9. xix. 41p. xx. 36p. xxi. 37. xxvi. 30p(*ap*). xxvii. 35p. xxviii. 25p.

speak of, John i. 15.

tell, Matt. viii. 4. xii. 48(λέγω LTr *S*). xvi. 20. xvii. 9. xviii. 17. xxi. 5, 24. xxii. 4, 17. xxiv. 3. xxvi. 63. xxviii. 7*t*. Mark v. 33. vii. 36(λέγω TTr*S*). viii. 26. ix. 12[1]. xiii. 4. xvi. 7. Luke v. 14. vii. 42(-G°LTr *S*). viii. 56. ix. 21(G′, λέγω GLTr *S*). xiii. 32. xx. 2. xxii. 67*t*. John iii. 12. iv. 29, 39. ix. 27. x. 24, 25. xi. 46. xiv. 2. xvi. 4. xviii. 8, 34. xx. 15. Acts v. 8.

tell of, John iii. 12.

bring word, Matt ii. 13.

answer, Luke xx. 3.

call, John x. 35.

bid, Matt. xvi. 12. xxiii. 3. Luke x. 40. Acts xi. 12. xxii. 24.

command, Matt. iv. 3. Mark v. 43. viii. 7. x. 49. Luke iv. 3. ix. 54. xix. 15. 2 Cor. iv. 6.

grant, Matt. xx. 21.

Add, for ἀναγγέλλω, John v. 13, Lm *S*. For ἀποκρίνομαι, Mark viii. 28, T*S*. For ἐντέλλομαι, Mark xi. 6, G″ LTTr*S*. For λαλέω, Acts xxiii. 7, L*S*. For λέγω, Matt. iv. 6, L. 9, L Tr*S*. xv. 4, G″LTr*S*. xvii. 26, LTr *S*. xxvii. 49, LTTr. Mark viii. 24, Lm*S*. 30, L. x. 51, TTr*S*. xii. 43[1st] GLTr*S*. Luke xxiii. 40, TTr*S*. Acts xii. 15, L. Rev. xvii. 15, L.—*Ap.*, Mark xii. 14. Luke x. 22. xx. 24. John xiii. 24.

For Future and Perfect, see ἐρῶ, *etc.*

εἴπως. See εἰ.

εἰρηνεύω.

have peace, Mark ix. 50.

be at peace, 2 Thes. v. 13.

live in peace, 2 Cor. xiii. 11.

live peaceably, Rom. xii. 18.

εἰρήνη.

peace, Matt. x. 13*t*, 34*t*. Mark v. 34. Luke i. 79. ii. 14, 29. vii. 50. viii. 48. x. 5, 6*t*. xi. 21. xii. 51. xiv. 32. xix. 38, 42. xxiv. 36(*ap*). John xiv. 27*t*. xvi. 33. xx. 19, 21, 26. Acts x. 36. xii. 20. xv. 33. xvi. 36.

Rom. i. 7. ii. 10. iii. 17. v. 1. viii. 6. x. 15(-L*S*). xiv. 17, 19. xv. 13, 33. xvi. 20. 1 Cor. i. 3. vii. 15. xiv. 33. xvi. 11. 2 Cor. i. 2. xiii. 11. Gal. i. 3. v. 22. vi. 16. Eph. i. 2. ii. 14. 15, 17. iv. 3. vi. 15, 23. Phil. i. 2. iv. 7, 9. Col. i. 2. iii. 15. 1Thes. i. 1. v. 3, 23. 2 Thes. i. 2.

iii. 16. 1 Tim. i. 2. 2 Tim. i. 2. ii. 22. Tit. i. 4. Phm. 3.

Heb. vii. 2. xi. 31. xii. 14. xiii. 20. Jas. ii. 16. iii. 18*t*. 1 Pet. i. 2. iii. 11. v. 14. 2 Pet. i. 2. iii. 14. 2 John 3. 3 John 14(15). Jude 2. Rev. i. 4. vi. 4.

rest, Acts ix. 31.

quietness, Acts xxiv. 2.

With εἰς, **at one**, Acts vii. 26.

Add Eph. ii. 17(. . to them that), G''LT*S*.

εἰρηνικός.

peaceable, Heb. xii. 11. Jas. iii. 17.

εἰρηνοποιέω.

make peace, Col. i. 20.

εἰρηνοποιός.

peacemaker, Matt. v. 9.

εἴρω. See ἐρῶ.

εἰς.

into, Matt. ii. 11, 12, 13, 14, 20, 21, 22. iii. 10, 12. iv. 1, 5, 8, 12, 18. v. 1, 20, 25, 29, 30. vi. 6, 13, 26, 30. vii. 19, 21. viii. 5, 12, 14, 23, 28, 31, 32*t*, 33. ix. 1*t*, 17*t*, 23, 26, 28, 38. x. 5*t*, 11, 12, 23. xi. 7. xii. 4, 9, 11, 29, 44. xiii. 2, 30, 36, 42, 47, 48, 50, 54. xiv. 13, 15, 22, 23, 32, 34(ἐπί Tr*S*), 35. xv. 11, 14, 17*t*, 21, 29, 39. xvi. 13. xvii. 1, 15*t*, 22, 25. xviii. 3, 8*t*, 9*t*, 30. xix. 1, 17, 23, 24. xx. 1, 2, 4, 7. xxi. 2, 10, 12, 17, 18, 21, 23, 31. xxii. 10, 13. xxiv. 38. xxv. 21, 23, 30, 41, 46*t*. xxvi. 18, 30, 32, 41, 45, 52, 71. xxvii. 6, 27, 53. xxviii. 7, 10, 11, 16*t*.

Mark i. 12, 14, 21*t*, 29, 35, 38, 45. ii. 1, 11, 22, 22(*ap*), 26. iii. 1, 13, 19(20, εἰς οἶκον, *marg.* **home**), 27. iv. 1, 37. v. 12*t*, 13*t*, 18. vi. 1, 10, 31, 32, 36, 45, 46, 51, 56. vii. 15, 17, 18, 19*tr*, 24*t*, 33. viii. 10*t*, 13(-G∞TTr*b*S), 26, 27. ix. 2, 22*t*, 25, 28, 31, 42, 43, 43(*ap*), 45, 45 (*ap*), 47*t*. x. 1, 17, 23, 24, 25. xi. 2*t*, 11*t*, 15, 23. xii. 41, 43. xiii. 15 (-L*b*S). xiv. 13, 16, 26, 28, 38, 41, 54, 68. xv. 41. xvi. 5, 7, 12(*ap*), 15(*ap*), 19(*ap*).

Luke i. 9, 39*t*, 40, 79. ii. 3, 4, 15, 27, 39. iii. 3, 9, 17. iv. 1(ἐν G''LT Tr*S*), 5(*ap*), 14, 16, 37, 38, 42. v. 3, 4, 19, 37, 38. vi. 4, 6, 12, 38, 39. vii. 1, 11, 24, 36, 44. viii. 22, 29, 30, 31, 32, 33*t*, 37, 41, 51. ix. 10, 12, 28, 34, 44*t*, 52. x. 1, 2, 5, 8, 10*t*, 38*t*. xi. 4. xii. 5, 28, 58. xiii. 19. xiv. 1, 5, 21, 23. xv. 13, 15. xvi. 4, 9, 16, 22, 28. xvii. 2, 12, 27. xviii. 10, 24, 25. xix. 12, 30, 45. xxi. 1, 24. xxii. 3, 10*t*, 33, 40, 46, 54, 66. xxiii. 19(ἐν TTr*S*), 25, 46. xxiv. 7, 26, 51(*ap*).

John i. 9, 43(44). iii. 4, 5, 17, 19, 22, 24. iv. 3, 14, 28, 38, 43, 45, 46, 47, 54. v. 7, 24. vi. 3, 14, 15, 17, 21, 22. vii. 3, 14. viii. 2 (*ap*). ix. 39. x. 1, 36, 40. xi. 7, 27, 30, 54. xii. 24, 46. xiii. 2, 3, 5. 27. xv. 6. xvi. 13(ἐν G'T*S*), 20, 21, 28. xvii. 18*t*. xviii. 1, 11, 15, 28, 33, 37. xix. 9, 17. xx. 6, 11, 25*t*, 27. xxi. 3, 7.

Acts i. 11*tr*, 13. ii. 20*t*, 34. iii. 1, 2, 3, 8. v. 21. vii. 3, 4, 9, 15(-T), 16, 34, 39, 55. viii. 38. ix. 6, 8, 17, 39. x. 16, 22, 24. xi. 8, 10, 12. xii. 17. xiii. 14. xiv. 1, 20, 22, 25. xvi. 9, 10, 15, 19, 23, 24, 34, 37, 40(πρός GLT*S*). xvii. 10. xviii. 7, 18, 19, 27. xix. 8, 22, 29, 31. xx. 1, 2, 3, 18. xxi. 3, 8, 11, 26, 28, 29, 34, 37, 38. xxii. 4, 10, 11, 23, 24. xxiii. 10, 16, 20, 28. xxv. 23. xxvii. 1, 6, 17, 30, 38, 39, 41. xxviii. 5, 17, 23.

Rom. i. 26. v. 2, 12. vi. 3*t*, 4. viii. 21. x. 6, 7, 18. xi. 24. xv. 24, 28. 1 Cor. xii. 13, 13(-G'LT*S*). xiv. 9. 2 Cor. i. 16. ii. 13. vii. 5. xi. 13, 14. xii. 4.

Gal. i. 17, 21. iii. 27. iv. 6. Eph. iv. 9, 15. Col. i. 13. 2 Thes. iii. 5*t*. 1 Tim. i. 3, 12, 15. iii. 6, 7. vi. 7, 9. 2 Tim. iii. 6.

Heb. i. 6. iii. 11, 18. iv. 1, 3*t*, 5, 10, 11. vi. 19. viii. 10. ix. 6, 7, 12, 24*t*, 25. x. 5, 31. xi. 8. xiii. 11. Jas.

i. 25. iv. 13. v. 4. 1 Pet. i. 12. ii. 9. iii. 22. 2 Pet. i. 11. 1 John iv. 1, 9. 2 John 7, 10. Jude 4.

Rev. ii. 10, 22*t*. v. 6. viii. 5, 8. xii. 6, 9, 14*t*. xiii. 10. xiv. 19*t*. xv. 8. xvi. 16, 17(G′, ἐπί GLTTr*S*), 19. xvii. 3, 8, 11. xviii. 21. xix. 20. xx. 3, 10, 14, 15. xxi. 24, 26, 27. xxii. 14.

to, Matt. ii. 1, 8. vii. 13. viii. 28. ix. 7, 13(*omS*). x. 17, 21, 22. xiv. 19. xvi. 5. xvii. 24, 27. xx. 17, 18. xxi. 1. xxii. 3, 5, 5 (ἐπί G′LTTr*S*), 9. xxiii. 34. xxv. 10. Mark ii. 17 (*omS*). v. 19, 38. vi. 41, 45. vii. 30, 34. viii. 3, 13, 22, 26. ix. 33. x. 32, 33, 46. xi. 1, 15, 27. xiii. 9, 12, 14. xiv. 8, 32.

Luke i. 23, 56. ii. 22, 39, 41, 42 (-G°°TTr[b]*S*), 45, 51. iv. 9, 16, 31. v. 25, 32. vii. 10. viii. 39. ix. 16, 51, 53, 56. x. 7, 30, 34. xiv. 8. xv. 17. xvi. 27. xvii. 11. xviii. 14, 31. xix. 28, 29. xxi. 12, 21. xxii. 33, 39. xxiv. 5, 13, 33, 50 (πρός LTr*S*), 52.

John ii. 2, 12, 13. iii. 13. iv. 5. v. 1. vi. 24. viii. 26. ix. 11. xi. 38, 55, 56. xii. 1, 12*t*. xvi. 32. xvii. 1. xx. 3, 4, 8. xxi. 9.

Acts i. 25. v. 21, 36. vi. 12. viii. 3, 5, 25, 27, 40. ix. 2, 26(ἐν G′LT), 30*t*. x. 5, 8, 32. xi. 2, 13, 20, 25. xii. 19. xiii. 4, 13*t*, 14, 31, 34, 46, 48. xiv. 20, 21, 24, 26. xv. 2, 4, 22, 30, 38. xvi. 1, 8, 11*t*, 12, 16. xvii. 1, 5, 20. xviii. 1, 19, 22, 24. xix. 1, 21. xx. 6, 14, 15, 17. xxi. 4, 7, 12, 15, 17. xxii. 5, 17. xxiii. 31, 32, 33. xxiv. 17. xxv. 1, 3, 9, 20. xxvi. 12, 14, 18. xxvii. 5, 12. xxviii. 6, 13*t*, 16.

Rom. i. 17, 24, 28. ii. 4. v. 16, 18. vii. 10. viii. 15. ix. 22, 31. xi. 36. xii. 10. xiii. 4(-G°), 14. xiv. 1. xv. 7, 16. xvi. 26. 1 Cor. iv. 6. x. 31. xiv. 8. xvi. 15. 2 Cor. ii. 12*t*. iii. 13, 18. iv. 15. vii. 9, 10. viii. 4, 24. ix. 1, 8, 11. x. 5. xi. 1. xiii. 10*t*.

Gal. i. 17, 18. ii. 1, 8, 11. iv. 24. vi. 8*t*. Eph. i. 5, 6, 12. iv. 32. Phil. i. 19. ii. 11. iv. 17. Col. i. 4. ii. 2. iii. 9, 15. 1 Thes. v. 9, 15. 2 Thes. ii. 13, 14. 1 Tim. i. 16. v. 24. 2 Tim. ii. 14(ἐπί LT*S*), 20*t*, 25. iii. 7. iv. 10, 12. Tit. iii. 12.

Heb. x. 39. xi. 7. Jas. i. 19. iv. 9*t*. 1 Pet. i. 4. iv. 4, 9, 10. 2 Pet. ii. 22. iii. 9. 3 John 5, 5 (*see* τοῦτο). Jude 4. Rev. ix. 9. x. 5. xi. 6, 12. xii. 4. xiii. 3. xvi. 14. xx. 8.

unto, Matt. iii. 11. vii. 14. viii. 4, 18. ix. 6. xii. 20. xiii. 52(ἐν L, -G TTr*S*). xiv. 22. xv. 24. xvi. 21. xxi. 1. xxii. 4. xxiv. 13. xxvi. 3, 36. xxvii. 33.

Mark iv. 35. v. 1, 21. xi. 1, 11. xiii. 13. xv. 41. Luke i. 26. ii. 4. iv. 26. v. 24. viii. 22. xi. 24. xvii. 24. xviii. 13, 35. xxiv. 28.

John i. 11. iv. 8, 36, 45. v. 24, 29*t*. vi. 27. vii. 8*t*, 10, 35, 53(*ap*). viii. 1(*ap*). xi. 31, 54. xii. 25. 27. xiii. 1. xviii. 28. xix. 27. xx. 1.

Acts i. 12. iv. 3. v. 16(-G°L*S*). viii. 26. ix. 2. xi. 18, 22, 26(25), 27. xii. 10. xiii. 4, 51. xiv. 6. xv. 39. xvii. 10. xviii. 6. xix. 3*t*. xx. 13(ἐπί LT*S*), 22, 38. xxi. 1*tr*, 2, 8. xxii. 5, 7, 21. xxv. 6, 13, 21. xxvi. 7, 11, 17. xxvii. 8, 40.

Rom. i. 1, 16, 26. iii. 7, 22. v. 15, 16, 18, 21. vi. 16(-G°°), 16, 19*t*, 22. vii. 10. ix. 21*t*, 23. x. 10*t*, 12, 18. xv. 25. xvi. 5, 19.

1 Cor. i 9. ii. 7. x. 2. xi. 34. xiv. 36. xvi. 3. 2 Cor. i. 23. ii. 4, 16*t*. iv. 11. viii. 2. ix. 5, 13*tr*. x. 14.

Gal. i. 6, 17. ii. 9*t*. iii. 23, 24. Eph. i. 5, 14, 15. ii. 21. iv. 13*t*, 16, 30. Phil. i. 11, 12. iii. 11. iv. 16 (-L[b]). Col. i. 6, 10, 11, 20. ii. 2. iv. 11. 1 Thes. i. 5(πρός G′L). ii. 9, 12. iv. 8, 15. 1 Tim. i. 6. ii. 4. 2 Tim. ii. 21*t*. iii. 15. iv. 10*t*, 18.

Heb. ii. 3, 10. vi. 6. ix. 28. x. 39. xi. 26. xii. 2. Jas. ii. 2. 1 Pet. i. 2, 3, 5, 7, 10, 22, 25. iii. 12. iv. 7. v. 10. 2 Pet. ii. 4, 9. 1 John iii. 14. Jude 6, 21. Rev. i. 11*seven*. vi. 13. ix. 1, 7. xii. 13. xix. 9, 17.

in unto, Luke xxi. 4. Acts xix. 30.
toward, Matt. xxviii. 1. Luke xii. 21. xiii. 22. John vi. 17. Acts i. 10. xx. 21. xxiv. 15. xxvii. 40. xxviii. 14. Rom. i. 27. v. 8. xii. 16. 2 Cor. i. 16. ii. 8. vii. 15. ix. 8. x. 1. xiii. 3, 4. Gal. ii. 8. Eph. i. 8, 19. iii. 2. 1 Thes. iii. 12*tr*. iv. 10. 2 Thes. i. 3. Phm. 5. Heb. vi. 10. 1 Pet. iii. 21. 2 Pet. iii. 9(G′, διά GL*S*).
towards, Rom. xiv. 19.
in at, Matt. xv. 17.
at, Matt. xii. 41. xviii. 29(-GLTr*S*). Luke viii. 26. ix. 61. xi. 32. John xi. 32. Acts iv. 6 (ἐν G″LT). viii. 40. xviii. 22. xx. 14, 15, 16. xxi. 3, 13. xxiii. 11. xxv. 15. xxvii. 3. xxviii. 12. Rom. iv. 20. 2 Tim. ii. 26.
before, Acts xxii. 30. Jas. ii. 6.
on, Matt. xxvii. 30. Mark iv. 8. viii. 23. xiv. 6 (ἐν GLTTr*S*). Luke vi. 20. viii. 23. xii. 49(ἐπί G″LTr*S*). xv. 22*t*. John i. 12. ii. 11. iii. 18, 36. iv. 39. vi. 29, 35, 40, 47 (-TTr[b]*S*). vii. 31, 38, 39, 48. viii. 6(*ap*), 8(*ap*), 30. ix. 35, 36. x. 42. xi. 45, 48. xii. 11, 37, 42, 44*tr*, 46. xiii. 22. xiv. 12. xvi. 9. xvii. 20. xix. 37. xxi. 4(ἐπί G′L*S*), 6. Acts vi. 15. xiii. 9. xiv. 23. xix. 4*t*.
Rom. xvi. 6. 2 Cor. xi. 20. Gal. iii. 14. Phil. i. 29. 1 John v. 10, 13 (*ap*), 13. Rev. xiii. 13.
upon, Matt. xxvi. 10. xxvii. 30. Mark xiii. 3. Luke viii. 43(*om S*). xviii. 13(-G[oo]LTr*S*). Acts iii. 4. xi. 6. xxii. 13. xxvii. 26, 29(κατά G″LT*S*). Rom. v. 12, 18*t*. xiii. 6. 1 Cor. x. 11. xv. 10. 2 Cor. i. 11. Gal. iv. 11. Rev. viii. 7. ix. 3. xvi. 1, 2(ἐπί G′LTTr*S*), 3, 4t(-[2d] LTr*S*).
in, Matt. ii. 23. iv. 13. x. 9, 27, 41*t*, 42. xii. 18(ἐν Tr, -L*S*). xiii. 30 (-G[oo]TTr[b]). 33. xviii. 6, 20. xxvi. 67. xxvii. 51. xxviii. 19.
Mark i. 9. ii. 1(ἐν LTr*S*). v. 14*t*, 34. vi. 8. ix. 42(-L*S*). xi. 8 (ἐν L[m]), 8(*ap*). xiii. 9, 16. xiv. 20, 60. xv. 38.
Luke i. 20, 44. ii. 28. iv. 35. vi. 8. vii. 1, 50. viii. 34*t*, 48. xi. 7, 33. xiii. 21. xiv. 8, 10. xvi. 8. xxi. 14 (ἐν LTTr*S*), 37. xxii. 19.
John i. 18. ii. 23. iii. 15(ἐν L[m]TTr, ἐπί L), 16, 18. v. 45. vii. 5. ix. 7. xi. 25, 26, 52. xii. 36. xiv. 1*t*. xvii. 23. xix. 13. xx. 7, 19, 26.
Acts ii. 27, 31. iv. 3. viii. 16, 23. x. 43. xii. 4. xiii. 29. xvi. 24. xvii. 21. xviii. 21(*ap*). xix. 5, 22. xxiii. 11. xxiv. 24. xxvi. 18.
Rom. viii. 18. x. 14. xi. 32. 1 Cor. i. 13, 15. viii. 6. xi. 24(*marg.* **for**), 25. xv. 54. 2 Cor. i. 5, 10, 21. viii. 6, 22. x. 16. xi. 3.
Gal. ii. 16. iii. 17(-G[oo]LT*S*). v. 10. vi. 4*t*. Eph. i. 10. iii. 16. iv. 13 (*marg.* **into**). Phil. i. 5. ii. 16, 22. Col. i. 10(G′, -GT*S*). ii. 5. iii. 10. 1 Thes. iv. 17. 2 Thes. ii. 4. 1 Tim. vi. 9. Phm. 6.
Heb. xi. 9. Jas. iii. 3. 1 Pet. i. 8, 21*t*. 2 Pet. i. 8, 17. 1 John v. 8. Rev. i. 11. vi. 15*t*. xi. 9. xiii. 6. xvii. 17.
among, Matt. xiii. 22. Mark iv. 7 (ἐπί L[m]), 18. viii. 19, 20. xiii. 10. Luke viii. 14. x. 36. xxiv. 47. John vi. 9. xxi. 23. Acts ii. 22. iv. 17. 2 Cor. xi. 6. 1 Thes. v. 15. 1 Pet. iv. 8.
in among, Acts xiv. 14. xx. 29.
throughout[c], Matt. iv. 24. Mark i. 28, 39. xiv. 9. Acts xxvi. 20(-L*S*). Eph. iii. 21.
by, Matt. v. 35. Acts vii. 53.
with, Eph. iii. 19.
for, Matt. v. 13. vi. 34. viii. 4. x. 10, 18. xxiv. 14. xxvi. 13, 28. xxvii. 10. Mark i. 4 (*marg.* **unto**), 44. vi. 8, 11. xiii. 9. xiv. 9. Luke ii. 34*t*. iii. 3. iv. 4, 14. ix. 3, 5, 13, 62(-LTTr*S*). xii. 19. xiv. 35*t*. xxi. 13. John i. 7. ix. 39. Acts ii. 38. vii. 5, 21. x. 4. xiii. 2, 47. xiv. 26. xxiii. 30.
Rom. i. 5. ii. 26. iv. 3, 5, 9, 22. viii. 28. ix. 8. x. 4. xiii. 4. xv. 2, 4, 26, 31(ἐν L). xvi. 26. 1 Cor. v. 5.

xi. 17*t*. xiv. 22. xvi. 1. 2 Cor. v. 5. viii. 14(13), 14. ix. 10. x. 8*t*. Gal. iii. 6. v. 13. Eph. ii. 22. iv. 12*t*. v. 2. vi. 22. Phil. i. 17, 25. Col. i. 16, 25. 2 Tim. iv. 11. Tit. iii. 14. Heb. iii. 5. vi. 16. ix. 9, 15. xi. 8. Jas. ii. 23. 1 Pet. i. 4. ii. 14. Rev. ix. 15 (*marg.* **at**). xxii. 2.

concerning, Acts ii. 25. Rom. xvi. 19. 2 Cor. viii. 23. Eph. v. 32t (–2d L). 1 Thes. v. 18.

of, Matt. v. 22. Acts xxv. 20. 2 Cor. x. 13, 15, 16. xii. 6. Heb. vii. 14. 1 Pet. i. 11.

against, Matt. xviii. 15(–L*S*), 21. Mark iii. 29. Luke vii. 30 (*marg.* **within**). xii. 10*t*. xv. 18, 21. xvii. 3 (–G∞LTTr*S*), 4. xxii. 65. John xii. 7. xiii. 29. Acts vi. 11. ix. 1. xxv. 8*tr*. Rom. viii. 7. 1 Cor. vi. 18. viii. 12*t*. 1 Tim. vi. 19. 2 Tim. i. 12. Heb. xii. 3. 2 Pet. iii. 7.

till, Phil. i. 10.

until, Eph. i. 14.

εἰς αὐτήν (αὐτό), **thereunto**, Luke xxi. 21. — **therein**, Mark x. 15. Luke xviii. 17. Acts xxvii. 6. Heb. iv. 6.

εἰς αὐτὸ τοῦτο, **for this same purpose**, Rom. ix. 17. — **for the same purpose**, Col. iv. 8. — **thereunto**, Eph. vi. 18.

εἰς ἥν (ὅ), **whereto**, Phil. iii. 16. — **whereunto**, John vi. 22(*ap*). Col. i. 29. 2 Thes. ii. 14. 1 Tim. ii. 7. vi. 12. 2 Tim. i. 11. 1 Pet. ii. 8.—**whither**, John vi. 21. — **wherein**, Acts vii. 4. 1 Pet. iii. 20. v. 12. — **wherefore**, 2 Thes. i. 11.

εἰς τί, **to what purpose?** Matt. xxvi. 8. — **wherefore?** Matt. xiv. 31. — **why?** Mark xiv. 4. xv. 34.

εἰς τοῦτο, **hereunto**, 1 Pet. ii. 21. — **thereunto**, 1 Thes. iii. 3. 1 Pet. iii. 9. — **to this end**, John xviii. 37. Rom. xiv. 9. 2 Cor. ii. 9. — **for this cause**, John xviii. 37. 1 Pet. iv. 6. — **for this purpose**, Acts xxvi. 16. 1 John iii. 8. — **for that intent**, Acts ix. 21. — **therefore**, Mark i. 38. Luke iv. 43(*ἐπί τ.* LTTr*S*). 1 Tim. iv. 10.

to becc, Acts xiii. 22, 47.

εἰς ἀθέτησιν, **to put away**, Heb. ix. 26.

εἰς τό, with an Infinitive.

to, Matt. xx. 19. xxvi. 2. xxvii. 31. Mark xiv. 55. Luke v. 17. Rom. vii. 5. xv. 8, 18. 1 Cor. viii. 10. xi. 22, 23. 2 Cor. vii. 3. Phil. i. 23. 1 Thes. ii. 16. iii. 2, 5. Heb. ii. 17. vii. 25. viii. 3. ix. 14, 28. xiii. 21. Jas. i. 19*t*.

for to, Rom. xi. 11.

to the end . . may (might), Acts vii. 19. Rom. i. 11. iv. 16. 1 Thes. iii. 13.

to the intent . . should, 1 Cor. x. 6.

that . . may (might), Luke iv. 29 (*see ὥστε*). Acts iii. 19. Rom. iii. 26. iv. 11*t*, 18. viii. 29. xii. 2. xv. 13. 2 Cor. i. 4. Eph. i. 18. Phil. i. 10. iii. 21(*ap*). 1 Thes. iii. 10. 2 Thes. i. 5. ii. 6, 10. Heb. xii. 10.

that so . . might, Luke xx. 20(*see ὥστε*).

that . . should, Rom. vi. 12. vii. 4. xv. 16. Gal. iii. 17. Eph. i. 12. 2 Thes. ii. 11. Jas. i. 18. 1 Pet. iv. 2. — *εἰς τὸ μή*, **lest . . should**, 2 Cor. iv. 4.

insomuch that, 2 Cor. viii. 6.

so that, Rom. i. 20 (*marg.* **that . . may**). Heb. xi. 3.

that, 1 Cor. ix. 18. 2 Thes. ii. 2. 1 Pet. iii. 7.

Not rendered, Matt. xix. 5. Mark x. 8. Luke xi. 49. Acts xi. 29. xiii. 42(*marg.* **in**). Rom. vi. 17. xi. 9*f*. xiv. 19. 1 Cor. iv. 3. vi. 16. xv. 45*t*(*see γίνομαι*). 2 Cor. vi. 18*t*. Eph. ii. 15. v. 31. Heb. i. 5*t*. viii. 10*t*. Jas. v. 3. 1 Pet. i. 11. ii. 7(*with γίνομαι*).

Add, for *εἰ*, Heb. xii. 7, LT*S*. For *ἐν*, Matt. xxvii. 5, Tr*S*. Mark i. 39, GLTTr*S*. x. 10, G''LTTr*S*. Luke

iv. 23, GLTTrS. 44, TTrS. xxiii. 42, Lm. xxiv. 18, G'. Acts vii. 12, ix. 28, xxv. 4, G''LTS. xxiv. 11, LTS. For ἐν fr. εἰς, Mark iv. 8tr, G'TTrS. For ἐπί, Matt. v. 39, LTr S. xviii. 6, G''T. xxiv. 16, LTr. Mark i. 10, LTTr. Luke viii. 8, GL TTrS. John xxi. 11, LTrS. Phil. iii. 14, LTS. 1 Pet. iii. 5, G'LT. Rev. xvi. 2, G''LTTrS. For κατά, Acts xvi. 7, GLTS. v. 15, *see* κατά. For πρός, Mark iii. 7, GLT. vii. 31, Luke xiv. 28, GLTTrS. Acts xxiii. 15, LTS. xxvi. 6, G''LTS. Phm. 5, L. Jas. iii. 3, LTS. For τήν, Rom. iv. 11, Lm. For ὡς, Matt. xxi. 46, G''LTTrS.

Matt. xiv. 34(. . Gennesaret), TrS. Mark vi. 56 (. . cities, . . country), LbTTrS. xi. 1(. . Bethany), G'LTS. Luke xxii. 10, *see* οὐ. 17, *see* ἑαυτοῦ. John xv. 21, *see* ὑμῖν. Acts xiv. 6(. . Lystra), L. 21(. . Iconium, . . Antioch), LTS. xvi. 1(. . Lystra), LS. xxvii. 2 (by), LS. Jas. v. 12, *see* ὑπόκρισις. 1 Pet. ii. 5 (. . holy), LS. Rev. xiii. 10 (into1st), G'LTTrS. — *Ap.*, Luke iii. 16. x. 11. 2 Pet. ii. 21.

See also αἰών, ἅλωσις, ἀνάντησις, ἀπελεγμός, ἀποκάλυψις, ἀπόλαυσις, ἀπώλεια, ἀτενίζω, βλέπω, βοήθεια, γενεά, γίνομαι, διακονία, διηνεκής, ἐγείρω, εἰρήνη, εἴσοδος, εἰσέρχομαι, ἐμβαίνω, ἐμβλέπω, ἔνδειξις, ἐργασία, ἔσται, εὐθύς, θλίψις, ἴασις, ἴδιος, καταβολή, καῦσις, καύχημα, κενός, κρίμα, λογίζομαι, λόγος, μακρός, μέλλω, μερίς, μετάληψις, οἶκος, ὀπίσω, πάλιν, περιποίησις, παντελής, παροξυσμός, περισσεία, περιτρέπω, πιστεύω, πρόσωπον, συμβάλλω, σωτηρία, σωφρονέω, ταφή, τέλος, ὑπακοή, ὑπάντησις, ὑπερβολή, ὕψος, φανερός, φθορά, φράσσω, χείρων.

εἷς.

Masc. εἷς, *neut.* ἕν.

one, Matt. v. 18, 29, 30. vi. 24t, 27, 29. x. 29, 42. xii. 11. xiii. 46. xvi. 14. xviii. 5, 6, 10, 12, 14, 16, 24, 28. xix. 16, 17. xx. 13. xxi. 24. xxii. 35. xxiii. 8, 9, 10(–G'), 15. xxv. 15, 17, 24, 40, 45. xxvi. 14, 21, 47, 51. xxvii. 48.

Mark v. 22. vi. 15. viii. 14, 28. ix. 17, 37, 42. x. 17, 18, 21. xi. 29. xii. 6, 28, 29, 32. xiii. 1. xiv. 10, 18, 20, 43, 47. xv. 6, 36(τις TrS).

Luke iv. 40. v. 3. vii. 41. ix. 8 (τις TTrS). xi. 46. xii. 6, 25(–TTrb S), 27, 52. xv. 4, 7, 10, 19, 26. xvi. 5, 13t. xvii. 2, 15, 34, 36(*ap*). xviii. 10, 19. xx. 3 (–G∞LTS). xxii. 47, 50. xxiii. 17(*ap*), 39. xxiv. 18.

John i. 40(41). vi. 8, 22, 70, 71. vii. 21, 50. viii. 41. x. 16, 30. xi. 49, 50, 52. xii. 2, 4. xiii. 21, 23. xvii. 11, 21, 21 (–G∞LbTTr), 22t, 23. xviii. 14, 22, 26, 39. xix. 34. xx. 24.

Acts i. 22. xi. 28. xvii. 26, 27. xx. 31. xxi. 26. xxiii. 6, 17. xxviii. 25.

Rom. iii. 10, 12, 30. v. 12, 15t, 16t, 17t, 18t, 19t. ix. 10. xii. 4, 5. xv. 6. 1 Cor. iii. 8. iv. 6t. vi. 16, 17. viii. 4, 6t. ix. 24. x. 17tr. xi. 5. xii. 11, 12, 12 (–G∞LTS), 12, 13tr, 14, 18, 19, 20, 26t. xiv. 27. 2 Cor. v. 14(15). xi. 2.

Gal. iii. 16, 20t, 28. v. 14. Eph. ii. 14, 15, 16, 18. iv. 4t, 5t, 6, 7. Phil. i. 27. ii. 2. Col. iii. 15. 1 Thes. ii. 11. 2 Thes. i. 3. 1 Tim. ii. 5t. v. 9. Heb. ii. 11. xi. 12. Jas. ii. 10, 19. iv. 12. 1 John v. 7(*ap*), 8. Rev. v. 5. vi. 1. vii. 13. xv. 7. xvii. 1, 10. xxi. 9, 21.

one man (*marg.* **one**), Rom. v. 17.

one thing, Luke x. 42. xviii. 22. John ix. 25. Phil. iii. 13(14). 2 Pet. iii. 8.

εἷς . . εἷς, **one . . other**, Matt. xx. 21. xxiv. 40. Mark x. 37. xv. 27. John xx. 12. Gal. iv. 22. — **one . . another**, Matt. xxvii. 38.

εἷς τὸν ἕνα, **one another**, 1 Thes. v. 11.

only, Mark ii. 7.

a certain, Matt. viii. 19.

a (an), Matt. v. 41. xxvii. 14, 15. Mark xiv. 51(-LTr*S*). Luke xv. 15. John vi. 9(-G°L^bTr*S*). xx. 7 (*see* χωρίς). 1 Cor. vi. 5(-G°, *see* οὐδείς). Jas. iv. 13(-L*S*). Rev. viii. 13. xviii. 21. xix. 17(-G°, ἄλλος [*S*).

any of them, Acts iv. 32.

any thing, John i. 3.

some, Mark iv. 8*tr* (ἐν G', εἰς TTr *S*), 20*tr* (ἐν G'TTr).

ὃν ἕνα, **whether**, Acts i. 24.

καθ' ἕνα, **one by one**, 1 Cor. xiv. 31.

καθ' ἕν, **every one**, John xxi. 25.

ἓν καθ' ἕν, **each**, Rev. iv. 8.

εἷς ἕκαστος, **every man**, Acts ii. 6. Col. iv. 6.—**every**, Eph. iv. 16. Rev. xxii. 2 (*with* κατά, εἰς *omS*).—**each**, Acts ii. 3.

καθ' ἕνα, ἕκαστος, **every one in particular**, Eph. v. 33.

καθ' ἓν ἕκαστον, **particularly**, Acts xxi. 19.

ἀνὰ εἷς ἕκαστος, **every several**, Rev. xxi. 21.

καθ' εἷς, καθεῖς St, **every one**, Rom. xii. 5.

εἷς καθ' εἷς, **one by one**, Mark xiv. 19(κατά for καθ' T*S*). John viii. 9 (καθεῖς for καθ' εἷς Tr, *ap*).

Add Matt. ix. 18(.. ruler), GLTr. xxvi. 22, εἷς ἕκαστος for ἐκ. αὐτῶν, G'LTTr*S*. 1 Cor. xii. 9, *see* ὁ αὐτός.

Fem. μία.

one, Matt. v. 18, 19, 36. xvii. 4*tr*. xix. 5, 6. xx. 12. xxvi. 40. Mark ix. 5*tr*. x. 8*t*. xiv. 37, 66. Luke ix. 33*tr*. xiii. 10. xv. 8. xvi. 17. xvii. 22, 34 (-L^b), 35. xx. 1. xxii. 59. John x. 16. Acts iv. 32. xii. 10. xix. 34. xxi. 7. xxiv. 21. xxviii. 13. 1 Cor. vi. 16. x. 8. 2 Cor. xi. 24. Gal. iv. 24. Eph. iv. 4. 5. v. 31. Phil. i. 27. 1 Tim. iii. 2, 12. Tit. i. 6. Heb. x. 12, 14. xii. 16. 2 Pet. iii. 8*t*. Rev. vi. 1. ix. 12. xiii. 3. xvii. 12. 13. xviii. 8, 10, 17(16), 19.

μία .. μία, **one .. other**, Matt. xxiv. 41.

ἀπὸ μιᾶς (*sc.* γνώμης), **with one consent**, Luke xiv. 18.

a, Matt. xxi. 19. xxvi. 69. Rev. ix. 13.

a certain, Mark xii. 42. Luke v. 12, 17. viii. 22.

first, 1 Cor. xvi. 2. Tit. iii. 10.

first day (*sc.* ἡμέρα), Matt. xxviii. 1. Mark xvi. 2. Luke xxiv. 1. John xx. 1, 19. Acts xx. 7.

See also γνώμη.

εἰσάγω.

With εἰς, **lead into**, Acts xxi. 37.—**bring into**, Luke xxii. 54. Acts ix. 8. xxi. 28, 29.

bring in, Luke ii. 27. xiv. 21. John xviii. 16. Acts vii. 45. Heb. i. 6.

Add Acts xxii. 24, for ἄγω, GLT*S*.

εἰσακούω.

hear, Matt. vi. 7. Luke i. 13. Acts x. 31. 1 Cor. xiv. 21. Heb. v. 7.

εἰσδέχομαι.

receive, 2 Cor. vi. 17.

εἴσειμι.

go in, Acts xxi. 18.

With εἰς, **go into**, Acts iii. 3. Heb. ix. 6.

enter, Acts xxi. 26.

εἰσέρχομαι.

come in, Matt. xxii. 11^p, 12. Mark v. 39^p. vi. 22^p, 25. Luke i. 28. vii. 45. xiv. 23. Acts i. 13. v. 7, 10. ix. 12. x. 3, 25. Rom. xi. 25. 1 Cor. xiv. 23, 24. Jas. ii. 2. Rev. iii. 20.

With εἰς, **come into**, Matt. x. 12^p. xvii. 25(*see* ἔρχομαι). xxi. 10^p. Mark ix. 28^p. Luke viii. 41, 51^p(ἔρχομαι GLTr*S*). Acts xiv. 20. xvi. 15. Heb. x. 5^p.—**come to**, Acts xi. 20^p (ἔρχομαι GLT*S*). xxiii. 33^p.—**come unto**, Jas. ii. 2.—**go into**, Matt. xv. 11. xxi. 12. xxvii. 53. Mark ii. 26. viii. 26. Luke i. 9. iv. 16. vi. 4. vii. 36. xix. 45. John xviii. 28. xix. 9. xx. 6. Acts ix. 6. xiii. 14. xiv. 1. xix. 8.

go in, Matt. vii. 13. ix. 25. xxiii. 13*t*. xxv. 10. Mark xiv. 14. xv. 43. Luke viii. 51. xi. 37. xv. 28. xxiv.

29. John x. 9. xx. 5, 8. Acts i. 21. ix. 6. x. 27. xi. 3. xvii. 2.
With ἔσω, **go in,** Matt. xxvi. 58.
enter, Matt. v. 20. vi. 6. vii. 21. viii. 5. x. 5, 11. xii. 4, 29. xviii. 3, 8, 9. xix. 17, 23, 24(-T*S*). xxiii. 13. xxiv. 38. xxv. 21, 23. xxvi. 41. Mark i. 21(-G°°TTr^b*S*), 45. ii. 1. iii. 1, 27. v. 12, 13. vi. 10. vii. 17, 24. ix. 25, 43, 45, 47. x. 15, 23, 24, 25. xi. 11. xiii. 15. xiv. 38(ἔρχομαι T*S*). xvi. 5(ἔρχομαι T).
Luke i. 40. iv. 38. vi. 6. vii. 1, 6, 44. viii. 30, 32, 33. ix. 4, 34, 52. x. 5, 8, 10, 38. xvii. 12p, 27. xviii. 17, 24(εἰσπορεύονται TTr), 25. xix. 1. xxi. 21. xxii. 3, 10p, 40, 46. xxiv. 26. John iii. 4, 5. iv. 38. x. 1. xiii. 27. xviii. 1, 33. Acts iii. 8. v. 21. ix. 17. x. 24. xi. 8, 12. xiv. 22. xvi. 40. xviii. 19. xxi. 8. xxiii. 16. xxv. 23p.
Rom. v. 12. Heb. iii. 11, 18. iv. 1, 3*t*, 5, 6, 10, 11. vi. 19, 20. ix. 24, 25. Jas. v. 4. 2 John 7(ἐξέρχομαι G″LT*S*). Rev. xi. 11. xv. 8. xxi. 27.
enter in, Matt. vii. 13. xii. 45. Luke xi. 26(ἔρχομαι G′T), 52*t*. xiii. 24*t*. xxiv. 3. John x. 2, 9. Acts xix. 30. xx. 29. xxviii. 8. Heb. iii. 19. iv. 6. ix. 12. Rev. xxii. 14.
come, Matt. viii. 8. Luke xvii. 7p.
go, Luke xix. 7.
With διά, **go through,** Mark x. 25 (StG″*S*, διέρχομαι δ. GLTTr). Luke xviii. 25(διέρχομαι δ. L).
arise, Luke ix. 46.
Add, for ἔρχομαι, Matt. ii. 21, L Tr*S*. ix. 18, T(for εἰς ἐλθών G′). Luke x. 1, L^m. Acts xviii. 7, L*S*. xxviii. 16, LT*S*. For διέρχομαι, Matt. xix. 24, GTTr*S*.

εἰσί. See εἰμί.

εἰσκαλέω.

call in, Acts x. 23.

εἴσοδος.

entrance, 2 Pet. i. 11.
entrance in, 1 Thes. ii. 1.
entering in, 1 Thes. i. 9.
With εἰς, **to enter into,** Heb. x. 19.
coming, Acts xiii. 24.

εἰσπηδάω.

spring in, Acts xvi. 29.
run in, Acts xiv. 14 (ἐκπηδάω GL T*S*).

εἰσπορεύομαι.

With εἰς, **go into,** Mark i. 21.
enter, Mark vi. 56. vii. 15, 18, 19. xi. 2p. xix. 30p. Acts iii. 2. viii. 3.
enter in, Matt. xv. 17. Mark iv. 19. v. 40. Luke viii. 16. xxii. 10.
come in, Luke xi. 33. Acts ix. 28. xxviii. 30.
Add Luke xviii. 24, for εἰσέρχομαι, TTr.

εἰστρέχω.

run in, Acts xii. 14.

εἰσφέρω.

bring in, Luke v. 18, 19.
With εἰς, **bring into,** 1 Tim. vi. 7. Heb. xiii. 11. —**bring to,** Acts xvii. 20. —**lead into,** Matt. vi. 13. Luke xi. 4.
Add Luke xii. 11, for προσφέρω, Tr*S*.

εἶτα.

then, Mark iv. 28. Luke viii. 12. John xix. 27. xx. 27. 1 Cor. xii. 28 (ἔπειτα LT*S*). xv. 5, 7(ἔπειτα L^mT *S*), 24. 1 Tim. ii. 13. iii. 10. Jas. i. 15.
afterward, Mark iv. 17.
after that, Mark iv. 28. viii. 25. John xiii. 5.
furthermore, Heb. xii. 9.

εἴτε. See εἰ.

εἴ τις. See εἰ.

εἴωθα. See ἔθω.

ἐκ, ἐξ.

out of, Matt. ii. 6, 15. vii. 5*t*. viii 28. xii. 34, 35*t*. xiii. 41, 52. xv. 11 18, 19. xvii. 5. xxi. 16. xxiv. 17 xxvii. 53. Mark i. 25, 26(ἀπό G″L) 29. v. 2*t*, 8(ἀπό L^m), 30. vi. 54. vii

20, 21, 26(-G∞), 29. ix. 7, 25(ἀπό L). xiii. 1, 15. xv. 46.

Luke i. 74. ii. 4. iv. 22. 35(ἀπό G″LTTr*S*), 38(ἀπό G″TTr*S*). v. 3, 17. vi. 42, 45*t*. viii. 27. ix. 35. xi. 54. xvii. 24. xix. 22.

John i. 46(47). ii. 15. iv. 30, 47, 54. vii. 38, 41, 52. viii. 59. x. 28, 29, 39. xi. 55. xii. 17, 34. xiii. 1. xv. 19. xvii. 6, 15. xx. 2.

Acts vii. 3, 4, 10, 40. viii. 39. xii. 11, 17. xiii. 17, 42(*ap*). xv. 14. xvi. 40. xix. 16, 33. xxii. 18. xxiv. 7(*ap*). xxvii. 29, 30*t*. xxviii. 3(ἀπό G′LT*S*).

Rom. ii. 18. xi. 24, 26. xiii. 11. 1 Cor. v. 10. 2 Cor. ii. 4. iv. 6. viii. 11. Eph. iv. 29. Col. ii. 14. iii. 8. 2 Thes. ii. 7. 1 Tim. i. 5. 2 Tim. ii. 22, 26. iii. 11. iv. 17.

Heb. iii. 16. vii. 5, 14. viii. 9. Jas. iii. 10, 13. 1 Pet. ii. 9. 2 Pet. ii. 9. iii. 5. 3 John 10. Jude 5, 23.

Rev. i. 16. ii. 5. iii. 5, 12, 16. iv. 5. v. 7, 9. vi. 14. vii. 14(ἀπό L). viii. 4. ix. 2, 3, 17, 18. x. 10. xi. 5, 7. xii. 15, 16. xiii. 1, 11. xiv. 15(-G°), 17, 20. xv. 6(-G∞TTr^b). xvi. 1(-G∞Tr^b), 7(*om S*), 13*tr*, 21. xvii. 8. xviii. 4. xix. 5(ἀπό G″LT Tr), 15, 21. xx. 7, 9, 12. xxi. 2, 3, 10. xxii. 1, 19(-L).

from, Matt. iii. 17. xii. 42. xiii. 49. xv. 18. xvi. 1. xvii. 9. xix. 12. xxi. 25*t*. xxiv. 31. xxviii. 2. Mark i. 11. vi. 14, 16(-TTr^b*S*). vii. 31. ix. 9. 10. x. 20. xi. 20, 30, 31. xii. 25. xiii. 27. xvi. 3(ἀπό LTr).

Luke i. 15, 71*t*, 78. iii. 22. ix. 7. x. 7, 18. xi. 16, 31. xii. 36. xvi. 31. xvii. 7. xx. 4, 5, 35. xxiii. 55. xxiv. 46, 49.

John i. 19, 32. ii. 22. iii. 13, 27, 31. v. 24. vi. 23, 31, 32*t*, 33, 38 (ἀπό LTTr), 41, 42, 50, 51, 58, 64. viii. 23*t*, 42. ix. 1. x. 32. xii. 1, 9, 17, 27, 28, 32. xiii. 4. xvii. 15. xviii. 3. xix. 23. xx. 1, 9. xxi. 14.

Acts i. 25(ἀπό LT*S*). ii. 2. iii. 2, 15. iv. 2, 10. x. 41. xi. 5, 9. xii. 7, 25. xiii. 30, 34. xiv. 8. xv. 24, 29. xvii. 3, 31, 33. xviii. 1, 2 (ἀπό LT *S*). xxii. 6. xxiii. 10. xxvi. 4, 17. xxvii. 34(ἀπό LT). xxviii. 17.

Rom. i. 17. iv. 24. vi. 4, 9, 13, 17. vii. 4, 24. viii. 11*t*. x. 7, 9. xi. 15. 1 Cor. v. 2. ix. 19. xv. 12, 20, 47. 2 Cor. i. 10. iii. 1. v. 2, 8. Gal. i. 1, 4, 8, 15. iii. 13. Eph. i. 20. iv. 16. v. 14. vi. 6. Phil. iii. 20. Col. i. 13, 18. ii. 12, 19. iv. 16. 1 Thes. i. 10*t*. 2 Tim. ii. 8.

Heb. v. 7. vii. 6. xi. 19. xiii. 20. Jas. v. 20*t*. 1 Pet. i. 3, 18, 21. 2 Pet. i. 18. ii. 21(*ap*). 1 John ii. 19. iii. 14. Rev. iii. 10. viii. 10. ix. 1, 13. x. 1, 4, 8. xi. 11, 12. xiii. 13. xiv. 2, 13*t*, 18. xv. 8*t*. xviii. 1, 4. xx. 1.

from .. up, Matt. xix. 20 (-G°LT Tr*S*). Luke xviii. 21.

from among, Acts iii. 23. 1 Cor. v. 13. Heb. v. 1.

among, Matt. xii. 11. John xii. 20, 42. Acts vi. 3. xxvii. 22.

off (of ed. of 1611), Mark xi. 8.

of, Matt. i. 3, 5*t*, 6, 16, 18, 20. iii. 9. v. 37. vi. 27. vii. 9. x. 29. xiii. 47. xviii. 12. xxi. 25, 26, 31. xxii. 35. xxiii. 25 (-LTr^b). xxv. 2, 8. xxvi. 21, 27, 29. xxvii. 29, 48. Mark ix. 17. xi. 14, 30, 32. xii. 44*t*. xiv. 18, 20(-Tr^b*S*), 23, 25. xvi. 12(*ap*).

Luke i. 5*t*, 27, 35 (ἐκ σοῦ BG^{ph}L^b). ii. 4, 35, 36. iii. 8. vi. 44*t*, 45. x. 11. xi. 5, 15, 27, 49. xii. 6, 13, 25. xiv. 28, 33. xv. 4*t*. xvi. 9. xvii. 7 (-Tr^b), 15. xx. 4, 6. xxi. 4*t*, 18. xxii. 3, 23, 50, 58. xxiv. 13, 18(-ἐξ αὐτῶν StGL^bTTr*S*), 22.

John i. 13*f*, 16, 24, 35, 40(41). ii. 15. iii. 1, 5, 6*t*, 8, 31*t*. iv. 7, 13, 14, 22, 39. vi. 8, 11, 13, 26, 51, 60, 64, 65, 70, 71. vii. 17, 19, 22*t*, 25, 31, 40, 42, 44, 48*t*, 50, 52. viii. 23*t*, 41, 44*t*, 46, 47*t*. ix. 6, 16. x. 16, 20, 26. xi. 19, 37, 45, 46, 49. xii. 4(-Tr), 9, 49. xiii. 21. xv. 19*t*. xvi. 5, 14, 15. xvii. 12, 14*t*, 16*t*. xviii. 9, 26, 36*t*, 37. xix. 2. xx. 24. xxi. 2.

Acts i. 24. ii. 30. iii. 22. iv. 6. v. 38, 39. vi. 9. vii. 37. x. 1, 45. xi. 2, 20, 28. xiii. 21. xv. 2, 21, 22, 23. xvii. 4, 12, 26. xx. 30. xxii. 14. xxiii. 21, 34. xxiv. 10.

Rom. i. 3. ii. 29*t*. iv. 12, 14, 16*tr*. v. 16. ix. 5, 6, 11*t*, 21, 24*t*, 30. x. 5, 6. xi. 1, 6, 6(*ap*), 14, 36. xiii. 3. xiv. 23*t*. xvi. 10, 11. 1 Cor. i. 30. ii. 12. vii. 7, viii. 6. ix. 7(–LT*S*), 7, 13, 14. x. 4, 17. xi. 8*t*, 12*t*, 28*t*. xii. 15*t*, 16*t*. xv. 6, 47. 2 Cor. ii. 17*t*. iii. 5*t*. iv. 7. v. 1, 18. ix. 7. xii. 6. Gal. ii. 12, 15. iii. 7, 9, 10, 12, 18*t*. iv. 4, 23*t*. v. 8. vi. 8*t*. Eph. ii. 8, 9. iii. 15. v. 30*t*(*ap*). Phil. i. 16, 17. iii. 5*t*, 9*t*. iv. 22. Col. iv. 11. 1 Thes. ii. 3*t*, 6. 2 Tim. ii. 8. iii. 6. Tit. i. 10, 12. ii. 8.

Heb. ii. 11. iii. 13. iv. 1. vii. 4, 5, 12. xi. 3. Jas. ii. 16. iv. 1. 1 Pet. i. 23. iv. 11. 1 John ii. 16*t*, 19*tr*, 21, 29. iii. 8, 9*t*, 10, 12, 19. iv. 1, 2, 3, 4, 5*t*, 6*t*, 7*t*, 13. v. 1*t*, 4, 18*t*, 19. 2 John 4. 3 John 11. Rev. i. 5(*omS*). ii. 7, 10, 11, 17, 21, 22. v. 5*t*. vi. 1*t*. vii. 4, 5*tr*, 6*tr*, 7*tr*, 8*tr*, 9, 13. viii. 11. ix. 20, 21*f*. xiv. 8, 10. xv. 7. xvi. 11. xvii. 1, 11. xviii. 3, 4, 12. xxi. 6, 21.

one of, Matt. xxvi. 73. Mark xiv. 69, 70. Luke xxii. 58. John xviii. 17, 25. Acts xxi. 8. Col. iv. 9, 12.—**some of**, Matt. xxiii. 34*t*. Luke xxi. 16. John ix. 40. xvi. 17. Rev. ii. 10. —**they (them)**[c] **of**, Rev. iii. 9. xi. 9.

ἐξ αὐτοῦ, **thereof**, Luke xxii. 16. John iv. 12. vi. 50.

μὴ ἐξ αὐτοῦ, **nothing of**, John vi. 39.

ἐξ οὗ (ὧν), **whereof**, 1 Tim. vi. 4. Heb. xiii. 10.

ἐκ τούτου, **from that time**, John vi. 66.—**from thenceforth**, John xix. 12. —**hereby**, 1 John iv. 6.

by the means of, 2 Cor. i. 11.

through, Gal. iii. 8. Rev. xviii. 3.

with, Matt. xxvii. 7. Mark xii. 30*f*, 33*t*, 33(*ap*), 33. Luke x. 27, 27*tr* (*ἐν* LTr*S*). John iv. 6. xii. 3. Acts i. 18. viii. 37(*ap*). 1 Cor. vii. 5. 1 Pet. i. 22. Rev. viii. 5. xvii. 2, 6*t*. xviii. 1. xix. 21.

by, Matt. xii. 33, 37*t*. xv. 5. Mark vii. 11. Luke vi. 44. John iii. 34. Acts xix. 25. Rom. i. 4, 17. ii. 27. iii. 20, 30. iv. 2. v. 1, 16. ix. 10, 32*t*. x. 17. 2 Cor. ii. 2. vii. 9. viii. 14(13). xi. 26*t*. xiii. 4*t*. Gal. ii. 16*f*. iii. 2*t*, 5*t*, 11, 21, 22, 24. iv. 22*t*. v. 5. Tit. iii. 5. Heb. x. 38. Jas. ii. 18, 21, 22, 24*t*, 25. 1 Pet. ii. 12. 1 John iii. 24. Rev. ix. 18 (*ἀπό* G'), 18*t* (*omS*).

by reason of, Rev. viii. 13. ix. 2. xviii. 19.

because of, Rev. xvi. 11t, 21.

for, Matt. xx. 2. Rev. xvi. 10.

in, Luke xi. 6 (*marg.* **out of**). Rev. iii. 18.

τὸ ἐξ ὑμῶν, **as much as lieth in you**, Rom. xii. 18.

at, John xvi. 4. Jas. iii. 11. Rev. xix. 2.

on, Matt. xxi. 19. Rev. xviii. 20.

over, Rev. xv. 2, 2(*ap*), 2*t*.

between[c] **some of**, John iii. 25.

betwixt[c], Phil. i. 23.

Not rendered, Luke xii. 15. John i. 44(45)? xi. 1? *see ἀπό*. Acts ix. 33. xxviii. 4 (*with διασώζω*).

Add, for *ἀπό*, Matt. vii. 4, LTr*S*. 20, L. xiii. 1, L*S*. xvii. 9, GLTTr*S*. xxiv. 1, L. Mark i. 10, G''LTTr*S*. vii. 15, LTTr*S*. ix. 9, L. Luke viii. 3, G''LTTr*S*. ix. 54, L. Acts ix. 3, LT*S*. Rev. i. 5, LTr*S*. vi. 4, GLTTr*S*, –G[oo]. 10, G''LTTr*S*. vii. 17, GLTTr. xvi. 17, G'LTr*S*. xxi. 4, L*S*. 10, T. For *ἐν*, Lk. i. 61, G'LTTr*S*. For *παρά*, John xvi. 28, LTTr. For *χωρίς*, Jas. ii. 18, StC[m]E.—For from, Acts xxvi. 17[2d], L*S*. For of, Mt. x. 14[2d], L*S*. xviii. 19[1st], LTr*S*. Mk. xiii. 1[2d], TTr. 25, LTTr*S*. Lk. xi. 11[2d], G''LTTr*S*. Jn. vi. 66, L[b]Tr[b]. xii. 2, T*S*. xiii. 23, GLTTr*S*. 2 Cor. ii. 16[1st], LT*S*. Rev. ii. 9, xiii. 3, GLTTr*S*. xxi. 9, G'LTTr*S*. For out of, Lk. xvi. 4, L[b]Tr*S*. For with, Rev. xv. 8, T. —Matt. x. 23 (*ap*). Mark ix. 21 (..*παιδιόθεν*), LTTr*S*. xvi. 14 (*ap*). Acts xxiii. 30, *see ἐξαυτῆς*. Phil. iii. 11 (*τὴν ἐκ* for *τῶν*), LT*S*.

See also αἰών, ἀνάστασις, γῆ, δεξιός, δεύτερος, ἐναντίος, ἐριθεία, ἐστί, εὐώνυμος, ἡμέρα, λύπη, μέρος, μέσος, οὐρανός, περισσός, πίστις, τρίτος, ὑμῶν, φωνή, χρόνος, ψυχή.

ἕκαστος.

every, Luke iv. 40. vi. 44. xvi. 5. John xix. 23. Acts xvii. 27. xx. 31. xxi. 26. 1 Cor. xii. 18. xv. 38. Eph. iv. 7, 16. 1 Thes. ii. 11. 2 Thes. i. 3. Rev. xxi. 21.

every one, Matt. xviii. 35. xxvi. 22. Luke ii. 3. John vi. 7. Acts ii. 38. iii. 26. Rom. xiv. 12. xv. 2. 1 Cor. i. 12. vii. 17. xi. 21. xiv. 26. xvi. 2. 2 Cor. v. 10. Eph. v. 33. 1 Thes. iv. 4. Heb. vi. 11. Rev. ii. 23. v. 8. vi. 11(αὐτοῖς GTTr, αὐτοῖς ἑκάστῳ LTr^b S).

every man, Matt. xvi. 27. xxv. 15. Mark xiii. 34. John vii. 53(*ap*). xvi. 32. Acts ii. 8. iv. 35. xi. 29. Rom. ii. 6. xii. 3. xiv. 5. 1 Cor. iii. 5, 8, 10, 13*t*. iv. 5. vii. 2^c, 7, 17, 20, 24. x. 24(*om S*). xii. 7, 11. xv. 23. 2 Cor. ix. 7. Gal. vi. 4, 5. Eph. iv. 25. Phil. ii. 4*t*. Heb. viii. 11*t*. Jas. i. 14. 1 Pet. i. 17. iv. 10. Rev. xx. 13. xxii. 12.

every ^c**woman**, 1 Cor. vii. 2.

each one, Luke xiii. 15.

καθ' ἓν ἕκαστον, **particularly**, Acts xxi. 19.

ἕκαστος τῶν, **both**, Heb. xi. 21.

any man, Eph. vi. 8.

See also εἷς, ἡμέρα.

ἑκάστοτε.

always, 2 Pet. i. 15.

ἑκατόν.

hundred, Matt. xviii. 12, 28. Mark iv. 8, 20. Luke xv. 4. xvi. 6, 7. John xix. 39. xxi. 11. Acts i. 15. Rev. vii. 4. xiv. 1, 3. xxi. 17.

ἀνὰ ἑκατόν, **by hundreds**, Mark vi. 40.

hundredfold, Matt. xiii. 8, 23.

ἑκατονταέτης.

an hundred years old, Rom. iv. 19.

ἑκατονταπλασίων.

hundredfold, Matt. xix. 29 (πολλαπλασίων LTTr). Mark x. 30. Luke viii. 8.

ἑκατοντάρχης.

centurion, Acts x. 1, 22. xxiv. 23. xxvii. 1, 31.

See also ἑκατόνταρχος.

ἑκατόνταρχος.

centurion, Matt. viii. 5, 8, 13(ἑκατοντάρχης GLTTrS). xxvii. 54. Luke vii. 2, 6. xxiii. 47(-χης TrS). Acts xxi. 32(-χης LTS). xxii. 25, 26(-χης LTS). xxiii. 17, 23. xxvii. 6(-χης LTS), 11(-χης G'LTS), 43 (-χης LTS). xxviii. 16(*ap*).

ἐκβαίνω, go out.

Heb. xi. 15, for ἐξέρχομαι, LTS.

ἐκβάλλω.

cast out, Matt. vii. 5*t*, 22. viii. 12, 16, 31. ix. 33^p, 34. x. 1, 8. xii. 24, 26, 27*t*, 28. xv. 17. xvii. 19. xxi. 12. Mark i. 34, 39. iii. 15, 22, 23. vi. 13. ix. 18, 28, 38. xi. 15. xvi. 17(*ap*). Luke vi. 22, 42. ix. 40, 49. xi. 14, 15, 18, 19*t*, 20. xiii. 32. xix. 45. xx. 12. John vi. 37. ix. 34 (*marg.* **excommunicate**), 35. xii. 31. Gal. iv. 30.

Mid., **cast out**, Acts xxvii. 38.

With ἀπό, **cast out of**, Mark xvi. 9 (*ap*).

With ἐκ, **cast out of**, 3 John 10.—**drive out of**, John ii. 15.

With ἔξω, **cast out of**, Mark xii. 8. Luke xx. 15. Acts vii. 58.—**cast out**, Matt. xxi. 39.—**thrust out of**, Luke iv. 29.—**thrust out**, Luke xiii. 28. — **leave out**, Rev. xi. 2 (*marg.* **cast out**).

cast forth, Mark vii. 26.

cast, Matt. xxii. 13. xxv. 30.

thrust out, Acts xvi. 37.

expel, Acts xiii. 50.

drive, Mark i. 12.

put out, Mark v. 40^p. Luke viii. 54(*ap*).

put forth, Matt. ix. 25. John x. 4. Acts ix. 40.

pluck out, Mark ix. 47.
pull out, Matt. vii. 4. Luke vi. 42*t*.
send out, Jas. ii. 25.
send forth, Matt. ix. 38. xii. 20. Luke x. 2.
send away, Mark i. 43.
take out, Luke x. 35.
bring forth, Matt. xii. 35*t*. xiii. 52.
Add Luke xi. 14, *pass.*, for ἐξέρχομαι, L.

ἔκβασις.

end, Heb. xiii. 7.
way to escape, 1 Cor. x. 13.

ἐκβολή.

Lit., a casting out; *with* ποιέω mid, lighten the ship, Acts xxvii. 18.

ἐκγαμίζω.

give in marriage, Matt. xxii. 30 (γαμίζω G'LTr*S*). xxiv. 38(γαμίσκω L, γαμίζω *S*). Luke xvii. 27(γαμίζω LTTr*S*). 1 Cor. vii. 38(*ap*), 38(γαμίζω GL*S*).—*Add, see* ἐκγαμίσκω.

ἐκγαμίσκω.

give in marriage, Luke xx. 34 (γαμίσκω LTr*S*, ἐκγαμίζω T), 35 (γαμίζω LTr*S*, ἐκγαμίζω T).

ἔκγονα.

nephews, 1 Tim. v. 4.

ἐκδαπανάομαι.

be spent, 2 Cor. xii. 15.

ἐκδέχομαι.

wait for, John v. 3(*ap*). Acts xvii. 16p. Jas. v. 7.
wait, 1 Pet. iii. 20(*see* ἀπεκδέχομαι).
expect, Heb. x. 13.
tarry for, 1 Cor. xi. 33.
look for, 1 Cor xvi. 11. Heb. xi. 10.

ἔκδηλος.

manifest, 2 Tim. iii. 9.

ἐκδημέω.

be absent, 2 Cor. v. 6, 8.
absent, 2 Cor. v. 9p.

ἐκδίδωμι.

let out, Matt. xxi. 33, 41. Mark xii. 1.
let forth, Luke xx. 9.

ἐκδιηγέομαι.

declare, Acts xiii. 41. xv. 3.

ἐκδικέω.

avenge, Luke xviii. 3, 5. Rom. xii. 19. Rev. vi. 10. xix. 2.
revenge, 2 Cor. x. 6.

ἐκδίκησις.

vengeance, Luke xxi. 22. Rom. xii. 19. 2 Thes. i. 8. Heb. x. 30.
With ποιέω, avenge, Luke xviii. 7, 8. Acts vii. 24.
revenge, 2 Cor. vii. 11.
punishment, 1 Pet. ii. 14.

ἔκδικος.

avenger, 1 Thes. iv. 6.
revenger, Rom. xiii. 4.

ἐκδιώκω.

persecute, Luke xi. 49. 1 Thes. ii. 15(*marg.* chase out).

ἔκδοτος.

being delivered, Acts ii. 23.

ἐκδοχή.

looking for, Heb. x. 27.

ἐκδύω.

take off from, Matt. xxvii. 31. Mark xv. 20.
strip, Matt. xxvii. 28(ἐνδύω L). Luke x. 30.
Mid., be unclothed, 2 Cor. v. 4.
Add 2 Cor. v. 3, for ἐνδύω, G'T.

ἐκεῖ.

there, Matt. ii. 13, 15. v. 24. vi. 21. viii. 12. xii. 45. xiii. 42, 50, 58. xiv. 23. xv. 29. xviii. 20. xix. 2. xxi. 17. xxii. 11, 13. xxiv. 28, 51. xxv. 30. xxvi. 71. xxvii. 36, 47, 55, 61. xxviii. 7. Mark i. 13 (-GLTr*S*). ii. 6. iii. 1. v. 11. vi. 5, 10. xi. 5. xiii. 21. xiv. 15. xvi. 7.
Luke ii. 6. vi. 6. viii. 32. ix. 4. x. 6. xi. 26. xii. 18, 34. xiii. 28. xv. 13. xvii. 21, 23. xxii. 12. xxiii. 33. John ii. 1, 6, 12. iii. 22, 23. iv. 6, 40. v. 5. vi. 3, 22, 24. x. 40, 42. xi. 15, 31. xii. 2, 9, 26. xix. 42.
Acts ix. 33. xiv. 28(*omS*). xvi. 1. xvii. 14. xix. 21. xxv. 9, 14. Rom.

ix. 26. 2 Cor. iii. 17(-G∞LT*S*). Tit. iii. 12. Heb. vii. 8. Jas. ii. 3. iii. 16. iv. 13. Rev. ii. 14. xii. 6. xxi. 25. xxii. 5(ἔτι GLTr^b*S*, -G∞T).

κἀκεῖ, **and there,** Matt. v. 23(καὶ ἐκεῖ T). x. 11. xxviii. 10. Mark i. 35 (καὶ ἐκεῖ L). John xi. 54. Acts xiv. 7. xxii. 10. xxv. 20. xxvii. 6. — **there also,** Mark i. 38. — **thither also,** Acts xvii. 13.

ὅπου . . ἐκεῖ, **where,** Mark vi. 55 (-ἐκεῖ LTr^b*S*). Rev. xii. 14.

thither, Matt. ii. 22. Mark vi. 33. Luke xvii. 37. xxi. 2. John xi. 8. xviii. 2, 3.

thitherward, Rom. xv. 24.

yonder, Matt. xxvi. 36.

to yonder place, Matt. xvii. 20.

Add Acts xviii. 19, for αὐτοῦ, L*S*. Rev. xii. 6(she hath . .), GTTr^b*S*. xxii. 3, for ἔτι, G′.

ἐκεῖθεν.

thence, Matt. v. 26. ix. 27. xi. 1. xii. 9. xiii. 53. xiv. 13. xv. 21. xix. 15. Mark i. 19(-G∞L^bTTr). vi. 11. ix. 30(κἀκεῖθεν for καὶ ἐκ. LTTr*S*). Luke ix. 4. xii. 59. John iv. 43. xi. 54. Acts xviii. 7.

κἀκεῖθεν, **and thence,** Acts xiv. 26. xx. 15. — **thence also,** Acts xxvii. 12(ἐκεῖθεν L*S*). — **and from thence,** Mark x. 1(καὶ ἐκ. LTr*S*). Acts vii. 4. xxi. 1. xxvii. 4. xxviii. 15. — **and afterward,** Acts xiii. 21. — *Add* Luke xi. 53(*ap*).

from thence, Matt. iv. 21. ix. 9. xii. 15. xv. 29. Mark vi. 1. vii. 24. Luke xvi. 26. Acts xiii. 4. xvi. 12 (κἀκεῖθεν for ἐκ. τε L*S*).

from that place, Mark vi. 10.

there, Acts xx. 13.

Add Mark x. 46, for ἀπὸ Ἰεριχώ, G′. Rev. xxii. 2, for ἐντεῦθεν, G″ LTTr.

ἐκεῖνος.

that (those), Matt. iii. 1. vii. 22, 25, 27. viii. 28. ix. 22, 26, 31. x. 14, 15. xi. 25. xii. 1, 45. xiii. 44. xiv. 1, 35*t*. xvii. 27. xviii. 7(-LTr*S*), 27 (-L), 32. xxi. 40. xxii. 7, 10, 46. xxiv. 19, 22*t*, 29, 36, 46, 48, 50. xxv. 7, 19. xxvi. 24*t*, 29. xxvii. 8, 19, 63.

Mark i. 9. ii. 20. iii. 24, 25. vi. 11 (*ap*), 55. vii. 15(-Tr^b*S*), 20. viii. 1. xii. 7. xiii. 11, 17, 19, 24*t*, 32. xiv. 21*t*, 25.

Luke ii. 1. iv. 2. v. 35. vi. 23, 48, 49. ix. 5, 36. x. 12*t*, 31. xi. 26. xii. 37, 38, 43, 45, 46, 47. xiii. 4. xiv. 21 (-G∞LTTr*S*), 24. xv. 14, 15. xvii. 9(-LTTr*S*), 31. xviii. 3. xix. 27. xx. 1(-G∞LTTr*S*), 18, 35. xxi. 23, 34, xxii. 22.

John i. 39(40). iv. 39. vi. 22(*ap*). viii. 10(*ap*). xi. 51, 53. xiv. 20. xvi. 23, 26. xviii. 15. xix. 27, 31. xxi. 3, 7, 23.

Acts i. 19. ii. 18. iii. 23. vii. 41. viii. 1, 8. ix. 37. xii. 1. xiv. 21. xvi. 3, 35. xix. 16. xx. 2. xxii. 11.

Rom. vi. 21. Eph. ii. 12. 2 Thes. i. 10. 2 Tim. i. 12, 18. iv. 8. Heb. iii. 10(οὗτος G″LT*S*). iv. 11. viii. 7, 10. x. 16. xi. 15. Jas. i. 7. iv. 15. Rev. ix. 6. xvi. 14(-G°LTr^b*S*).

he (she, it, they, etc.), Matt. xiii. 11. Mark iv. 11. xvi. 10(*ap*), 13 (*ap*), 20(*ap*). Luke viii. 32. ix. 34 (αὐτός TTr*S*).

John i. 8, 18. ii. 21. iii. 28, 30. iv. 25. v. 19, 35, 38, 39, 43, 46, 47. vi. 29. vii. 11, 45. viii. 42, 44. ix. 9, 11, 12, 25, 28, 36, 37. x. 6, 35. xi. 13, 29. xiii. 25, 26, 27, 30. xiv. 21, 26. xv. 26. xvi. 8, 13, 14. xviii. 17, 25. xix. 21. xx. 13, 15, 16.

Acts iii. 13. x. 9(αὐτός G″*S*), 10 (αὐτός G″LT*S*). xxi. 6. Rom. xi. 23 (κἀκεῖνος for καὶ ἐκ. GLT*S*). xiv. 14, 15. 1 Cor. ix. 25. x. 11, 28. xv. 11. 2 Cor. viii. 9, 14(13)*t*. x. 18. 2 Tim. ii. 13, 26. iii. 9. Tit. iii. 7. Heb. iv. 2. vi. 7. xii. 25. 2 Pet. i. 16. 1 John ii. 6. iii. 3, 5, 7, 16. iv. 17. v. 16.

κἀκεῖνος, **and he (etc.),** Matt. xv. 18. xx. 4. Mark xii. 4, 5. xvi. 11 (*ap*), 13(*ap*). Luke xi. 7. xxii. 12. John vii. 29. xix. 35(καὶ ἐκ. L). Acts xviii. 19. — **he (etc.) also,** Luke

xx. 11. John x. 16. xiv. 12. xvii. 24. Acts v. 37. 1 Cor. x. 6. 2 Tim. ii. 12. — **even he**, John vi. 57. — **they**, Acts xv. 11. — **them**, Heb. iv. 2. — **and the other**, Matt. xxiii. 23. Luke xi. 42. — *Add* Luke xx. 12, for καὶ οὗτος, L.

that very, Matt. xv. 28. xvii. 18.
that way (*sc.* ὁδός), Luke xix. 4.
that same, Matt. x. 19(*ap*). xxvi. 55. John xi. 49. xviii. 13.
same, Matt. xiii. 1. xv. 22. xviii. 1, 28(-L). xxii. 23. Mark iv. 35. John i. 33. iv. 53. v. 9, 11. x. 1. xii. 48. xx. 19. Acts ii. 41. xii. 6. xvi. 33. xix. 23. xxviii. 7. 2 Cor. vii. 8. Rev. xi. 13.
self-same, Matt. viii. 13.
the other, Luke xviii. 14.
this, Matt. xxiv. 43.
Peter[c], John xiii. 6(-LTTr[b]*S*).
Add, for αὐτός, Luke vii. 21, John v. 37, L[m]TTr*S*. For οὗτος, Mark iv. 20, TTr*S*. — Matt. xxii. 7(. . king), G'T. xxiv. 38(. . days), LTr[b]. Mark vi. 54(*ap*).

ἐκεῖσε.

there, Acts xxi. 3. xxii. 5.

ἐκζητέω.

seek after, Acts xv. 17. Rom. iii. 11.
seek diligently, Heb. xi. 6.
seek carefully, Heb. xii. 17.
inquire diligently, 1 Pet. i. 10.
require, Luke xi. 50, 51.

ἐκθαμβέομαι.

be greatly amazed, Mark ix. 15.
be sore amazed, Mark xiv. 33.
be affrighted, Mark xvi. 5, 6.

ἔκθαμβος.

greatly wondering, Acts iii. 11.

ἔκθετος.

With ποιέω, **cast out**, Acts vii. 19.

ἐκκαθαίρω.

purge out, 1 Cor. v. 7.
purge, 2 Tim. ii. 21.

ἐκκαίω, ἐκκαίομαι.

burn, Rom. i. 27.

ἐκκακέω.

to faint, Luke xviii. 1(ἐγκακέω LTr, ἐνκ. T*S*). 2 Cor. iv. 1 and 16(ἐγκ. LT*S*). Eph. iii. 13(ἐγκ. L*S*, ἐνκ. T).
be weary, Gal. vi. 9(ἐγκ. L*S*, ἐνκ. T). 2 Thes. iii. 13(*marg.* **faint**; ἐγκ. L*S*, ἐνκ. T).

ἐκκεντέω.

pierce, John xix. 37. Rev. i. 7.

ἐκκλάω, ἐκκλάζω.

break off, Rom. xi. 17, 19, 20(κλάζω L).

ἐκκλείω.

exclude, Rom. iii. 27. Gal. iv. 17.

ἐκκλησία.

assembly, Acts xix. 32, 39, 41.
church, Matt. xvi. 18. xviii. 17*t*. Acts ii. 47(-L*S*). v. 11. vii. 38. viii. 1, 3. ix. 31. xi. 22, 26. xii. 1, 5. xiii. 1. xiv. 23, 27. xv. 3, 4, 22, 41. xvi. 5. xviii. 22. xx. 17, 28.
Rom. xvi. 1, 4, 5, 16, 23. 1 Cor. i. 2. iv. 17. vi. 4. vii. 17. x. 32. xi. 16, 18, 22. xii. 28. xiv. 4, 5, 12, 19, 23, 28, 33, 34, 35. xv. 9. xvi. 1, 19*t*. 2 Cor. i. 1. viii. 1, 18, 19, 23, 24. xi. 8, 28. xii. 13. Gal. i. 2, 13, 22. Eph. i. 22. iii. 10, 21. v. 23, 24, 25, 27, 29, 32. Phil. iii. 6. iv. 15. Col. i. 18, 24. iv. 15, 16. 1 Thes. i. 1. ii. 14. 2 Thes. i. 1, 4. 1 Tim. iii. 5, 15. v. 16. Phm. 2.
Heb. ii. 12. xii. 23. Jas. v. 14. 3 John 6, 9, 10. Rev. i. 4, 11, 20*t*. ii. 1, 7, 8, 11, 12, 17, 18, 23, 29. iii. 1, 6, 7, 13, 14, 22. xxii. 16.

ἐκκλίνω.

go out of the way, Rom. iii. 12.
avoid, Rom. xvi. 17.
eschew, 1 Pet. iii. 11.

ἐκκολυμβάω.

swim out, Acts xxvii. 42.

ἐκκομίζω.

carry out, Luke vii. 12.

ἐκκόπτω.

cut out, Rom. xi. 24.
cut off, Matt. v. 30. xviii. 8. Rom. xi. 22. 2 Cor. xi. 12.

cut down, Luke xiii. 7, 9.
hew down, Matt. iii. 10. vii. 19. Luke iii. 9.
hinder, 1 Pet. iii. 7(ἐγκόπτω GL*S*).

ἐκκράζω, cry out.

Acts xxiv. 21, for κράζω, T*S*.

ἐκκρέμαμαι.

be very attentive (*marg.* **hang on**), Luke xix. 48.

ἐκλαλέω.

tell, Acts xxiii. 22.

ἐκλάμπω.

shine forth, Matt. xiii. 43.

ἐκλανθάνομαι.

forget, Heb. xii. 5.

ἐκλέγω.

choose, Acts xv. 22, 25.
Mid., **choose**, Mark xiii. 20. Luke vi. 13. x. 42. xiv. 7. John vi. 70. xiii. 18. xv. 16*t*, 19. Acts i. 2, 24. vi. 5. xiii. 17. xv. 7. 1 Cor. i. 27, 27(*ap*), 28. Eph. i. 4. Jas. ii. 5.
Add Luke ix. 35p, for ἀγαπητός, G′ LmTTr*S*.

ἐκλείπω.

fail, Luke xvi. 9. xxii. 32. Heb. i. 12.

ἐκλεκτός.

chosen, Matt. xx. 16(*ap*). xxii. 14. Luke xxiii. 35. Rom. xvi. 13. 1 Pet. ii. 4, 9. Rev. xvii. 14.
elect, Matt. xxiv. 22, 24, 31. Mark xiii. 20, 22, 27. Luke xviii. 7. Rom. viii. 33. Col. iii. 12. 1 Tim. v. 21. 2 Tim. ii. 10. Tit. i. 1. 1 Pet. i. 2(1). ii. 6. 2 John 1, 13.

ἐκλογή.

election, Rom. ix. 11. xi. 5, 7, 28. 1 Thes. i. 4. 2 Pet. i. 10.
chosencc, Acts ix. 15.

ἐκλύω.

Pass., **to faint**, Matt. xv. 32. Mark viii. 3. Gal. vi. 9. Heb. xii. 3, 5. —*With* εἰμί, Matt. ix. 36 (*marg.* **be tired and lie down**; σκύλλω GLTTr*S*).

ἐκμάσσω.

wipe, Luke vii. 38, 44. John xi. 2. xii. 3. xiii. 5.

ἐκμυκτηρίζω.

deride, Luke xvi. 14. xxiii. 35.

ἐκνεύω.

convey one's self away, John v. 13.

ἐκνήφω.

awake, 1 Cor. xv. 34.

ἑκούσιος.

Neut. with κατά, **willingly**, Phm. 14.

ἑκουσίως.

willingly, 1 Pet. v. 2.
wilfully, Heb. x. 26.

ἔκπαλαι.

of old, 2 Pet. iii. 5.
of a long time, 2 Pet. ii. 3.

ἐκπειράζω.

tempt, Matt. iv. 7. Luke iv. 12. x. 25. 1 Cor. x. 9.
Add 1 Cor. x. 9, for πειράζω, Lm*S*.

ἐκπέμπω.

send forth, Acts xiii. 4.
send away, Acts xvii. 10.

ἐκπερισσῶς, exceedingly.

Mark xiv. 31, for ἐκ περισσοῦ, G″ LTTr*S*.

ἐκπετάννυμι.

stretch forth, Rom. x. 21.

ἐκπηδάω, leap out, rush forth.

Acts xiv. 14, for εἰσπηδάω, GLT*S*.

ἐκπίπτω.

fall from, Gal. v. 4. 2 Pet. iii. 17.
fall off, Acts xii. 7. xxvii. 32.
fall away, 1 Pet. i. 24.
fall, Acts xxvii. 17, 29. Jas. i. 11. Rev. ii. 5(πίπτω GLT*S*). —*With* εἰμί, Mark xiii. 25(πίπτω LTTr*S*)
be cast, Acts xxvii. 26.
fail, 1 Cor. xiii. 8(πίπτω L*S*).
take none effect, Rom. ix. 6.

ἐκπλέω.

sail away, Acts xx. 6.
sail c**thence**, Acts xviii. 18.
sail, Acts xv. 39.

ἐκπληρόω.

fulfill, Acts xiii. 33(32).

ἐκπλήρωσις.

accomplishment, Acts xxi. 26.

ἐκπλήσσω, -ττω.

astonish, Matt. vii. 28. xiii. 54. xxii. 33. Mark i. 22. vi. 2. vii. 37. x. 26. xi. 18. Luke iv. 32. Acts xiii. 12.

amaze, Matt. xix. 25. Luke ii. 48. ix. 43.

ἐκπνέω.

give up the ghost, Mark xv. 37, 39. Luke xxiii. 46.

ἐκπορεύομαι.

go out, Matt. iii. 5. xvii. 21(*ap*). Mark i. 5. vii. 19. Luke iv. 37. Acts ix. 28.

go forth, Mark x. 17p. Rev. xvi. 14 (−Go).

With ἀπό, **go out of,** Mark x. 46p. —**come out of,** Mark vii. 15.

With ἐκ, **go out of,** Mark xiii. 1p. Rev. i. 16. xix. 15.—**come out of,** Matt. xv. 11. Mark vii. 20.

With ἔξω, **go out of,** Mark xi. 19.

proceed, Matt. iv. 4. xv. 18. Mark vii. 21. Luke iv. 22. John xv. 26. Eph. iv. 29. Rev. iv. 5. xi. 5. xix. 21(ἐξέρχομαι GLTTr*S*). xxii. 1.

depart, Matt. xx. 29p. Mark vi. 11p. Acts xxv. 4.

issue, Rev. ix. 17, 18.

come forth, Luke iii. 7. John v. 29.

With ἔσωθεν, **come from within,** Mark vii. 23.

Add Acts xix. 12, for ἐξέρχομαι, GLT*S*.

ἐκπορνεύω.

give one's self over to fornication, Jude 7.

ἐκπτύω.

reject, Gal. iv. 14.

ἐκριζόω.

root up, Matt. xiii. 29. xv. 13.

pluck up by the root, Luke xvii. 6. Jude 12.

ἔκστασις.

astonishment, Mark v. 42.

amazement, Acts iii. 10.

With ἔχω, **be amazed**cc, Mark xvi. 8. —*With* λαμβάνω, Luke v. 26.

trance, Acts x. 10. xi. 5. xxii. 17.

ἐκστρέφω.

subvert, Tit. iii. 11.

ἐκταράσσω, -ττω.

trouble exceedingly, Acts xvi. 20.

ἐκτείνω.

stretch out, Matt. xxvi. 51. Mark iii. 5.

stretch forth, Matt. xii. 13*t*, 49. xiv. 31. Mark iii. 5. Luke vi. 10. xxii. 53. John xxi. 18. Acts iv. 30. xxvi. 1.

put forth, Matt. viii. 3. Mark i. 41. Luke v. 13.

cast out, Acts xxvii. 30.

Add Luke vi. 10, for ποιέω, G′*S*.

ἐκτελέω.

finish, Luke xiv. 29, 30.

ἐκτένεια.

With ἐν, **instantly,** Acts xxvi. 7.

ἐκτενέστερον.

Comp. of ἐκτενῶς, **more earnestly,** Luke xxii. 44.

ἐκτενής.

fervent, 1 Pet. iv. 8.

without ceasing, Acts xii. 5 (*marg.* **instant and earnest**; ἐκτενῶς L*S*).

ἐκτενῶς.

fervently, 1 Pet. i. 22.

See also ἐκτενέστερον, ἐκτενής.

ἐκτίθημι.

cast out, Acts vii. 21p.

expound, Acts xi. 4. xviii. 26. xxviii. 23.

ἐκτινάσσω.

shake off, Matt. x. 14. Mark vi. 11. Acts xiii. 51.

shake, Acts xviii. 6.

ἕκτος.

sixth, Matt. xx. 5. xxvii. 45. Mark xv. 33. Luke i. 26, 36. xxiii. 44.

John iv. 6. xix. 14(τρίτος G''). Acts x. 9. Rev. vi. 13. ix. 12, 14. xvi. 12. xxi. 20.

ἐκτός.

out of, 2 Cor. xii. 2, 3(χωρίς LT).
without, 1 Cor. vi. 18.
With art., **the outside,** Matt. xxiii. 26.
other than, Acts xxvi. 22.
be excepted[oo], 1 Cor. xv. 27.
See also εἰ μή.

ἐκτρέπομαι.

turn aside, 1 Tim. i. 6. v. 15.
be turned out of the way, Heb. xii. 13.
be turned, 2 Tim. iv. 4.
avoid, 1 Tim. vi. 20.

ἐκτρέφω.

nourish, Eph. v. 29.
bring up, Eph. vi. 4.
Add Rev. xii. 6, for τρέφω, T.

ἔκτρωμα.

one born out of due time, 1 Cor. xv. 8(*marg.* **an abortive**).

ἐκφέρω.

carry out, Acts v. 6, 9. 1 Tim. vi. 7.
carry forth, Acts v. 10.
bring forth, Luke xv. 22. Acts v. 15.
bear, Heb. vi. 8.
Add Mark viii. 23, for ἐξάγω, TTr*S*.

ἐκφεύγω.

With ἐκ, **flee out of,** Acts xix. 16.
flee, Acts xvi. 27.
escape, Luke xxi. 36. Rom. ii. 3. 2 Cor. xi. 33. 1 Thes. v. 3. Heb. ii. 3.
Add Heb. xii. 25, for φεύγω, L*S*.

ἐκφοβέω.

terrify, 2 Cor. x. 9.

ἔκφοβος.

sore afraid, Mark ix. 6.
With εἰμί, **fear exceedingly,** Heb. xii. 21.

ἐκφύω.

put forth, Matt. xxiv. 32. Mark xiii. 28.

ἐκχέω.

pour out, John ii. 15. Acts ii. 17, 18. Rev. xvi. 1, 2, 3, 4, 8, 10, 12, 17.
shed forth, Acts ii. 33.
shed, Acts xxii. 20(ἐκχύνω LT*S*). Rom. iii. 15. Tit. iii. 6. Rev. xvi. 6.
spill, Mark ii. 22(–TTr).
Pass., **run out,** Matt. ix. 17.

ἐκχύνω.

(Regarded as a form of ἐκχέω.)
pour out, Acts x. 45.
shed abroad, Rom. v. 5.
shed, Matt. xxiii. 35. xxvi. 28. Mark xiv. 24. Luke xi. 50. xxii. 20.
spill, Luke v. 37.
Pass., **gush out,** Acts i. 18.—**run greedily,** Jude 11.
Add Acts xxii. 20, for ἐκχέω, LT*S*.

ἐκχωρέω.

depart out, Luke xxi. 21.

ἐκψύχω.

give up the ghost, Acts v. 5. xii. 23.
yield up the ghost, Act. v. 10.

ἑκών.

willingly (*lit.* willing), Rom. viii. 20. 1 Cor. ix. 17.

ἐλαία.

olive tree, Rom. xi. 17, 24. Rev. xi. 4.
olive berry, Jas. iii. 12.
Plural, **Olives,** Matt. xxi. 1. xxiv. 3. xxvi. 30. Mark xi. 1. xiii. 3. xiv. 26. Luke xix. 29, 37. xxi. 37. xxii. 39. John viii. 1(*ap*).

ἔλαιον.

oil, Matt. xxv. 3, 4, 8. Mark vi. 13. Luke vii. 46. x. 34. xvi. 6. Heb. i. 9. Jas. v. 14. Rev. vi. 6. xviii. 13.

ἐλαιών.

Olivet, Acts i. 12.

ἐλάσσων, -ττων.

less, Heb. vii. 7.
younger, Rom. ix. 12(*marg.* **lesser**).
Neut., **under,** 1 Tim. v. 9.

With art., **that which is worse,** John ii. 10.

ἐλαττονέω.

have lack, 2 Cor. viii. 15.

ἐλαττόω.

make lower, Heb. ii. 7(*marg.* **make inferior**), 9.

Pass., **decrease,** John iii. 30.

ἐλαύνω, ἐλάω.

drive, Luke viii. 29. Jas. iii. 4.

row, Mark vi. 48. John vi. 19p.

carry, 2 Pet. ii. 17.

ἐλαφρία.

lightness, 2 Cor. i. 17.

ἐλαφρός.

light, Matt. xi. 30. 2 Cor. iv. 17.

ἐλάχιστος.

least, Matt. ii. 6. v. 19*t*. xxv. 40, 45. Luke xvi. 10. 1 Cor. xv. 9.

that which is least, Luke xvi. 10.

that thing which is least, Luke xii. 26.

very little, Luke xix. 17.

smallest, 1 Cor. vi. 2.

very small, Jas. iii. 4.

very small thing, 1 Cor. iv. 3.

ἐλαχιστότερος.

less than the least, Eph. iii. 8.

ἐλάω. See ἐλαύνω.

ἐλεγμός, conviction, reproof.
2 Tim. iii. 16, for ἔλεγχος, LT*S*.

ἔλεγξις.

With ἔχω, **be rebuked,** 2 Pet. ii. 16.

ἔλεγχος.

reproof, 2Tim. iii. 16(ἐλεγμός LT*S*).

evidence, Heb. xi. 1.

ἐλέγχω.

convince, John viii. 46. 1 Cor. xiv. 24. Tit. i. 9. Jas. ii. 9.

convict, John viii. 9(*ap*).

tell one's fault, Matt. xviii. 15.

reprove, Luke iii. 19. John iii. 20 (*marg.* **discover**). xvi. 8(*marg.* **convince**). Eph. v. 11, 13(*marg.* **discover**). 2 Tim. iv. 2.

rebuke, 1 Tim. v. 20. Tit. i. 13. ii. 15. Heb. xii. 5p. Rev. iii. 19.

Add Jude 15, for ἐξελέγχω, G″LT*S*. 22(*ap*).

ἐλεεινός.

miserable, Rev. iii. 17.

Comp., **most**[c] **miserable,** 1Cor. xv. 19.

ἐλεέω.

have pity on, Matt. xviii. 33.

have compassion on, Matt. xviii. 33. Mark v. 19.

have compassion of, Jude 22(*ap*).

have mercy on, Matt. ix. 27. xv. 22. xvii. 15. xx. 30, 31. Mark x. 47, 48. Luke xvi. 24. xvii. 13. xviii. 38, 39. Rom. ix. 15*t*, 18. Phil. ii. 27.

have mercy upon, Rom. xi. 32.

show mercy, Rom. ix. 16. xii. 8.

Pass., **receive mercy,** 2 Cor. iv. 1.

—**obtain mercy,** Matt. v. 7. Rom. xi. 30, 31. 1 Cor. vii. 25. 1 Tim. i. 13, 16. 1 Pet. ii. 10*t*.

ἐλεάω, Rom. ix. 16, LT*S*; 18, T; Jude 22, LT*S*.

Add Jude 23(*ap*).

ἐλεημοσύνη.

alms, Matt. vi. 1(δικαιοσύνη GLTTr *S*), 2, 3, 4. Luke xi. 41. xii. 33. Acts iii. 2, 3, 10. x. 2, 4, 31. xxiv. 17.

alms-deed, Acts ix. 36.

ἐλεήμων.

merciful, Matt v. 7. Heb. ii. 17.

ἔλεος.

Generally neuter; masculine marked[m].

mercy, Matt. ix. 13[m](*neut.* G″LTTr *S*). xii. 7[m](*neut.* LTTr*S*). xxiii. 23[m](*neut.* LTTr*S*). Luke i. 50, 54, 58, 72, 78. x. 37. Rom. ix. 23. xi. 31. xv. 9. Gal. vi. 16. Eph. ii. 4. 1 Tim. i. 2. 2 Tim. i. 2, 16, 18. Tit. i. 4. iii. 5[m](*neut.* LT*S*). Heb. iv. 16[m](*neut.* LT*S*). Jas. ii. 13*t*. iii. 17. 1 Pet. i. 3. 2 John 3. Jude 2, 21.

ἐλευθερία.

liberty, Rom. viii. 21. 1 Cor. x. 29. 2 Cor. iii. 17. Gal. ii. 4. v. 1, 13*t*.

Jas. i. 25. ii. 12. 1 Pet. ii. 16. 2 Pet. ii. 19.

ἐλεύθερος.

free, Matt. xvii. 26. John viii. 33, 36. Rom. vi. 20. vii. 3. 1 Cor. vii. 21, 22. ix. 1, 19. xii. 13. Gal. iii. 28. iv. 26, 31. Eph. vi. 8. Col. iii. 11. 1 Pet. ii. 16. Rev. xiii. 16. xix. 18.
freeman, Rev. vi. 15.
free woman, Gal. iv. 22, 23, 30.
at liberty, 1 Cor. vii. 39.

ἐλευθερόω.

make free, John viii. 32, 36. Rom. vi. 18, 22. viii. 2. Gal. v. 1.
deliver, Rom. viii. 21.

ἔλευσις.

coming, Acts vii. 52.

ἐλεφάντινος.

of ivory, Rev. xviii. 12.

ἑλίσσω.

fold up, Heb. i. 12.
roll together, Rev. vi. 14p(εἱλ. StG).

ἕλκος.

sore, Luke xvi. 21. Rev. xvi. 2, 11.

ἑλκόω.

Pass., **full of sores**, Luke xvi. 20p.

ἑλκύω.

draw, John vi. 44. xii. 32. xviii. 10. xxi. 6, 11. Acts xvi. 19.

ἕλκω.

draw, Acts xxi. 30. Jas. ii. 6.

ἐλλογέω.

put on one's account, Phm. 18(-γάω LT*S*).
impute, Rom. v. 13(-γάω Lm).

ἐλπίζω.

to hope, Luke vi. 34. xxiii. 8. Acts xxiv. 26. xxvi. 7. 1 Cor. xiii. 7. 2 Cor. viii. 5. Phil. ii. 23. 1 Tim. iii. 14. 1 Pet. i. 13.
With εἰμί, **have hope**, 1 Cor. xv. 19.
hope for, Rom. viii. 24, 25.
thing hoped for, Heb. xi. 1p.
trust, Matt. xii. 21. Luke xxiv. 21. John v. 45. Rom. xv. 12, 24. 1 Cor. xvi. 7. 2 Cor. i. 10, 13. v. 11. xiii. 6. Phil. ii. 19. 1 Tim. iv. 10. v. 5. vi. 17. Phm. 22. 1 Pet. iii. 5. 2 John 12. 3 John 14.

ἐλπίς.

hope, Acts ii. 26. xvi. 19. xxiii. 6. xxiv. 15. xxvi. 6, 7. xxvii. 20. xxviii. 20. Rom. iv. 18*t*. v. 2, 4, 5. viii. 20, 24*tr*. xii. 12. xv. 4. 13*t*. 1 Cor. ix. 10*t*, 10(*ap*). xiii. 13. 2 Cor. i. 7(6). iii. 12. x. 15. Gal. v. 5. Eph. i. 18. ii. 12. iv. 4. Phil. i. 20. Col. i. 5, 23, 27. 1 Thes. i. 3. ii. 19. iv. 13. v. 8. 2 Thes. ii. 16. 1 Tim. i. 1. Tit. i. 2. ii. 13. iii. 7. Heb. iii. 6. vi. 11, 18. vii. 19. 1 Pet. i. 3, 21. iii. 15. 1 John iii. 3.
faith, Heb. x. 23.

Ἐλωΐ, Ἑλωΐ LT.

Eloi, Mark xv. 34*t*.

ἐμαυτοῦ, -τῷ, -τόν.

myself, Luke vii. 7. John v. 31. vii. 17, 28. viii. 14, 18, 28, 42, 54. x. 18. xii. 49. xiv. 3, 10, 21. xvii. 19. Acts xx. 24. xxiv. 10. xxvi. 2, 9. Rom. xi. 4. 1 Cor. iv. 4, 6. ix. 19. 2 Cor. ii. 1. xi. 7, 9. xii. 5. Gal. ii. 18. Phil. iii. 13.
Ico myself, 1 Cor. vii. 7.
mine own self, John v. 30. 1 Cor. iv. [3.
mine own, 1 Cor. x. 33.
me, Matt. viii. 9. Luke vii. 8. John xii. 32. Phm. 13.

ἐμβαίνω.

With εἰς, **go into**, Matt. xiii. 2. Luke viii. 22.—**go up into**, Luke viii. 37.—**come into**, Matt. xiv. 32p (ἀναβαίνω LTr*S*). Mark v. 18p.—**get into**, Matt. xiv. 22. Mark vi. 45.—**take**, Matt. xv. 39(ἀναβαίνω GTTr). John vi. 24.
step in, John v. 4p(*ap*).
enter, Matt. viii. 23p. ix. 1. Mark iv. 1. viii. 10, 13. Luke v. 3. John vi. 17, 22(*ap*).
Add John xxi. 3, for ἀναβαίνω, G LTTr*S*. Acts xxi. 6, for ἐπιβαίνω, L.

ἐμβάλλω.

With εἰς, **cast into**, Luke xii. 5.

ἐμβάπτω.
dip, Matt. xxvi. 23. Mark xiv. 20. John xiii. 26(βάπτω LᵐTTr*S*).
Add John xiii. 26, for βάπτω, L.

ἐμβατεύω.
intrude into, Col. ii. 18.

ἐμβιβάζω.
With εἰς αὐτό, **put therein**, Acts xxvii. 6(*lit.* cause to enter).

ἐμβλέπω.
look upon, Mark x. 27. xiv. 67. Luke xxii. 61. John i. 36.
behold, Matt. xix. 26. Mark x. 21. Luke xx. 17. John i. 42(43)ᵖ.
With εἰς, **behold**, Matt. vi. 26.
gaze up, Acts i. 11.
see, Mark viii. 25.
canᶜ see, Acts xxii. 11.

ἐμβριμάομαι.
murmur against, Mark xiv. 5.
charge straitly, Matt. ix. 30. Mark i. 43.
groan, John xi. 33, 38.

ἐμέ, ἐμοί. See ἐγώ.

ἐμέω.
spue, Rev. iii. 16.

ἐμμαίνομαι.
be mad against, Acts xxvi. 11.

ἐμμένω.
continue in, Acts xiv. 22. *With* ἐν, Gal. iii. 10. Heb. viii. 9.

ἐμμέσῳ. See μέσος.

ἐμός.
my (mine), Matt. xviii. 20. xx. 23. Mark viii. 38. x. 40. Luke ix. 26. John iii. 29. iv. 34. v. 30, 47. vii. 6, 8, 16*t*. viii. 16, 31, 37, 43*t*, 51, 56. x. 14*t*, 26, 27. xii. 26. xiii. 35. xiv. 15, 24, 27. xv. 8, 9, 11, 12. xvi. 14, 15*t*. xvii. 10*t*, 13, 24. xviii. 36*f*.
Rom. iii. 7. x. 1. 1 Cor. v. 4. vii. 40. ix. 2(μου LT*S*), 3. xi. 25. xvi. 18. 2 Cor. i. 23. ii. 3. viii. 23. Gal. i. 13. Phil. i. 26. 2 Tim. iv. 6(μου L*S*). Phm. 10. 2 Pet. i. 15. 3 John 4. Rev. ii. 20.
mine own, Matt. xx. 15. xxv. 27. John v. 30. vi. 38. 1 Cor. i. 15. xvi. 21. Gal. vi. 11. Phil. iii. 9. 2 Thes. iii. 17. Phm. 12, 19.
that I have, Luke xv. 31.
of me, Luke xxii. 19. 1 Cor. xi. 24, 25. Col. iv. 18.

ἐμοῦ. See ἐγώ.

ἐμπαιγμονή, mockery.
2 Pet. iii. 3(days ἐν ἐμπ.), GLT*S*.

ἐμπαιγμός.
mocking, Heb. xi. 36.

ἐμπαίζω.
mock, Matt. ii. 16. xx. 19. xxvii. 29, 31, 41. Mark x. 34. xv. 20, 31. Luke xiv. 29. xviii. 32. xxii. 63. xxiii. 11, 36.

ἐμπαίκτης.
mocker, Jude 18.
scoffer, 2 Pet. iii. 3.

ἐμπεριπατέω, ἐνπ. T.
walk in, 2 Cor. vi. 16.

ἐμπίπλημι, -πλάω.
fill, Luke i. 53. John vi. 12. Acts xiv. 17. Rom. xv. 24.
Pass., **be full**, Luke vi. 25.

ἐμπίπτω.
With εἰς, **fall into**, Matt. xii. 11. Luke xiv. 5(πίπτω LTr*S*). 1 Tim. iii. 6, 7. vi. 9. Heb. x. 31. — **fall among**, Luke x. 36.
Add Luke vi. 39, for πίπτω, LTTr.

ἐμπλέκω.
entangle in, 2 Pet. ii. 20.
Mid., **entangle one's self with**, 2 Tim. ii. 4.

ἐμπλήθω. See ἐμπίπλημι.

ἐμπλοκή.
plaiting, 1 Pet. iii. 3.

ἐμπνέω, ἐνπ. T*S*.
breathe out, Acts ix. 1.

ἐμπορεύομαι.
buy and sell, Jas. iv. 13.
make merchandise of, 2 Pet. ii. 3.

ἐμπορία.
merchandise, Matt. xxii. 5.

ἐμπορίον.
merchandise, John ii. 16.

ἔμπορος.
merchant, Matt. xiii. 45. Rev. xviii. 3, 11, 15, 23.

ἐμπρήθω.
burn up, Matt. xxii. 7.

ἔμπροσθεν.
before, Matt. v. 16, 24. vi. 1, 2. vii. 6. x. 32*t*, 33*t*. xi. 10. xvii. 2. xxv. 32. xxvi. 70. xxvii. 11, 29. Mark i. 2(*omS*). ix. 2. Luke v. 19. vii. 27. xii. 8*t*. xiv. 2. xix. 4, 27, 28. xxi. 36. John i. 15, 27(*ap*), 30. iii. 28. x. 4. xii. 37. Acts xviii. 17. 2 Cor. v. 10. Gal. ii. 14. Phil. iii. 13(14). 1 Thes. iii. 9, 13. 1 John iii. 19. Rev. iv. 6. xxii. 8.
in the presence of, 1 Thes. ii. 19.
in the sight of, 1 Thes. i. 3.
in one's sight, Matt. xi. 26. Luke x. 21.
at, Rev. xix. 10.
against, Matt. xxiii. 13(14).
of, Matt. xviii. 14.
Add, for ἐνώπιον, Luke xii. 9. L*S*. Acts x. 4, LT*S*.

ἐμπτύω.
spit on, Mark xiv. 65. Luke xviii. 32.
spit upon, Mark x. 34. xv. 19.
With εἰς, **spit in,** Matt. xxvi. 67.—**spit upon,** Matt. xxvii. 30.

ἐμφανής.
manifest, Rom. x. 20.
δίδωμι ἐμφανῆ γενέσθαι, **show openly,** Acts x. 40.

ἐμφανίζω.
to manifest, John xiv. 21, 22.
show, Acts xxiii. 22.
Pass., **appear,** Matt. xxvii. 53. Heb. ix. 24.
declare plainly, Heb. xi. 14.
inform, Acts xxiv. 1. xxv. 2, 15.
signify, Acts xxiii. 15.

ἔμφοβος.
afraid, Luke xxiv. 5. Acts x. 4. xxii. 9(-G∞L*S*).
affrighted, Luke xxiv. 37. Rev. xi. 13.
With γίνομαι, **tremble,** Acts xxiv. 25.

ἐμφυσάω.
breathe on, John xx. 22.

ἔμφυτος.
ingrafted, Jas. i. 21.

ἐν.
in, Matt. i. 20. ii. 1*t*, 2, 5, 9, 16*t*, 18, 19. iii. 1*t*, 3, 6, 12, 17. iv. 13, 16*t*, 21, 23. v. 12, 15, 16, 19*t*, 25, 28, 45, 48(*see* οὐράνιος). vi. 1, 2*t*, 4*t*, 5*t*, 6*t*, 9, 10, 18*t*, 20, 23, 29. vii. 3*t*, 4, 11, 15, 21, 22. viii. 10, 11, 13 (ἀπό L), 24, 32. ix. 4, 10, 31, 33, 35. x. 11, 15, 16, 17, 19, 20, 23, 27*t*, 28, 32, 33. xi. 1, 2, 6, 8*t*, 11, 16, 21*tr*, 23*t*, 24. xii. 5*t*, 19, 21(*om S*), 32*t*, 36, 40*t*, 41, 42, 50. xiii. 3, 10, 13, 19, 21, 24, 27, 30, 31, 32, 34, 35, 40, 43, 44, 54, 57*tr*. xiv. 2, 3, 10, 33. xv. 32, 33. xvi. 17, 19*t*, 27, 28. xvii. 5, 22. xviii. 1, 2, 4, 6, 10*t*, 14, 18*t*, 19, 20. xix. 21, 28. xx. 3, 17, 21. xxi. 8*t*, 9*t*, 12, 14, 15, 22, 28, 32, 33, 41, 42*t*. xxii. 15, 16, 28, 30*t*, 36, 43. xxiii. 6, 7, 9(*see* οὐράνιος), 30*t*, 34, 39. xxiv. 14, 15, 16, 18, 19, 26*t*, 30, 38, 40, 45, 48, 50*t*. xxv. 4, 18(-Tr*S*), 25, 31, 36, 39, 43, 44. xxvi. 6*t*, 13, 23, 29, 55*t*, 69. xxvii. 5(εἰς Tr*S*), 40, 60*t*. xxviii. 18.
Mark i. 2, 3, 4, 5, 9, 11, 13, 19, 20, 23, 39(εἰς GLTTr*S*), 45(ἐπί TTr*S*). ii. 6, 8, 15, 20. iii. 23. iv. 1, 2, 11, 15(*ap*), 17. 28, 36. v. 5*t*, 13, 20, 27, 30*t*. vi. 2, 4*t*, 11(*ap*), 14, 17, 27 (28), 29, 47, 48,51, 56. viii. 1, 14, 26, 38*t*. ix. 33, 36, 41, 50. x. 10(εἰς G″LTTr*S*), 21, 30*t*, 32, 37, 52. xi. 9, 10(*ap*), 10, 15, 23, 25, 26(*ap*), 27. xii. 11, 23, 25, 26, 35, 38*tr*, 39. xiii. 11, 14, 17, 24, 25, 26, 32. xiv. 3, 25. 30(-LTTr*S*), 49, 66. xv. 7, 29 (-LTTr), 41, 46. xvi. 12(*ap*) 17(*ap*).

Luke i. 5, 6, 7, 8, 17, 18, 21, 22, 25, 26, 31, 36, 39, 41, 44, 66, 69, 75, 79, 80. ii. 1, 7*t*, 8, 11, 12, 14, 16, 19, 21, 23, 24, 25, 29, 34, 38 (–G′LTTr*S*), 43, 44, 46*t*, 51. iii. 1, 2, 4*t*, 15, 17, 20, 22. iv. 2, 5, 14, 15, 20, 21, 23(G′, *εἰς* GLTTr*S*), 23, 24, 25*t*, 27, 28, 33, 44(*εἰς* TTr*S*). v. 7, 12, 22, 29, 35. vi. 12*t*, 23*t*, 41*t*, 42*tr*. vii. 9, 21, 23, 25*t*, 28, 32, 37*t*. viii. 10, 13, 15, 27*t*. ix. 12, 26, 31, 36, 57. x. 7, 12, 13*tr*, 20*t*, 21, 26. xi. 1, 2*t*(*ap*), 21, 31, 32, 35, 43*t*. xii. 1, 3*tr*, 12, 15, 27, 28, 33, 38*t*, 42, 45, 46, 52, 58. xiii. 4, 4(–Tr), 6, 10, 14*t*, 19, 26, 28, 29, 35. xiv. 15. xv. 4, 7, 25. xvi. 10*f*, 11, 12, 23*tr*, 24, 25. xvii. 6, 24(*ap*), 26*t*, 28, 31*tr*, 36(*ap*). xviii. 2, 3, 22, 30*t*. xix. 17, 20, 30, 36, 38*tr*, 42, 44, 47. xx. 1, 33, 42, 46*tr*. xxi. 6, 19, 21*tr*, 23, 25, 27, 37, 38. xxii. 16, 20, 28, 30, 37, 44(*ap*), 53, 55. xxiii. 4, 9, 14, 19, 22, 29, 31*t*, 40, 43, 53. xxiv. 4, 6, 18 (*εἰς* G′, –GTTr*S*), 18, 19, 27, 35*t*, 36, 38, 44, 49, 53.

John i. 1, 2, 4, 5, 10, 23, 28, 45 (46), 47(48). ii. 1, 11, 14, 19(–Tr^b), 20, 23, 23(–L^bTr), 25. iii. 13(*ap*), 14, 21, 23. iv. 14, 20*t*, 21, 23, 24, 31, 44, 53. v. 3, 13, 14, 26*t*, 28, 35, 38, 39, 42, 43*t*. vi. 10, 31, 45, 49, 53, 56*t*, 59*t*, 61. vii. 1*t*, 4, 9, 10, 18, 28, 37. viii. 3*t*(*ap*), 5(*ap*), 9 (*ap*), 12, 17, 20*t*, 21, 24*t*, 31, 35, 37, 44*t*. ix. 3, 5, 34. x. 23*t*, 25, 34, 38*t*. xi. 6, 9, 10*t*, 17, 20, 24, 30, 31, 38, 56. xii. 13, 25, 35, 46, 48. xiii. 1, 31, 32(*ap*), 32. xiv. 2, 10*tr*, 11*t*, 13*t*, 14, 17, 20*tr*, 26, 30. xv. 2, 4*f*, 5*t*, 6, 7*t*, 9, 10*t*, 11, 16, 25. xvi. 23*t*, 24, 25*t*, 26, 30, 33*t*. xvii. 10, 11*t*, 12 (–G^oLTTr*S*), 12, 13*t*, 21*tr*, 23*t*, 26*t*. xviii. 20*tr*, 26, 38. xix. 4, 6, 41*t*. xx. 12, 25, 30.

Acts i. 7, 8, 8(–LT), 10, 15*t*, 20. ii. 17, 18, 19, 22, 46. iii. 6, 26. iv. 7, 12(*ap*), 24. v. 4*t*, 12, 18, 20, 22, 25*t*, 34, 37, 42. vi. 1*t*, 7, 15. vii. 2*t*, 4, 5, 6, 7, 12(*εἰς* G″LT*S*), 16, 17, 20*t*, 22, 22(–G^{∞}LT*S*), 29, 30*t*, 34, 35, 36*tr*, 38*tr*, 41*t*, 42*t*, 44, 48. viii. 8, 9, 21, 33. ix. 10, 11, 12(–LT*S*), 17, 20, 21, 25, 27*t*, 29(28), 37*t*, 43. x. 1, 3, 17, 30*t*, 32, 35, 39, 39(–L^b T), 48. xi. 5*t*, 13, 22, 26, 27, 29. xii. 5, 7. xiii. 5, 17, 18, 19, 33, 35, 40, 41. xiv. 1, 16, 25. xv. 21, 35. xvi. 3, 6, 12, 18, 32, 36. xvii. 11, 16, 17*t*, 22, 24, 28, 31*t*. xviii. 4, 9, 10, 18, 24, 26. xix. 9, 16, 21, 39. xx. 8, 10, 16. xxi. 27, 29. xxii. 3*t*, 17*t*. xxiii. 6, 9, 35. xxiv. 12*t*, 14 (–StL), 18, 20(–L*S*). xxv. 5. xxvi. 10, 21, 26. xxvii. 21, 27, 31, 37. xxviii. 7, 9, 11*t*, 18, 30.

Rom. i. 2, 7, 9, 18, 19(*marg.* to), 21, 27*t*, 28(*see* ἐπίγνωσις). ii. 12, 15, 16, 19, 20, 28, 29. iii. 4, 16, 24, 25. iv. 10*f*. v. 2, 3, 5, 11, 13, 17. vi. 4, 12, 12(*ap*). vii. 5*t*, 6, 8, 17, 18, 20, 23*t*. viii. 1, 2, 3*tr*, 4, 8, 9*tr*, 10, 11*t*, 37, 39. ix. 1*t*, 7, 17, 25, 26, 28(*ap*), 33. x. 6, 8*t*, 9. xii. 4, 5. xiii. 9, 13. xiv. 5, 17, 18, 22. xv. 13*t*, 23, 27, 29, 30, 31. xvi. 2*t*, 3, 7, 8, 9, 10, 11, 12, 12(*ap*), 13, 22.

1 Cor. i. 2*t*, 5*t*, 6, 7, 8, 10*t*, 21, 30, 31. ii. 3*tr*, 4, 5*t*, 7, 11, 13. iii. 1, 16, 18, 19, 21. iv. 2, 6, 10, 15*t*, 17*tr*, 20*t*, 21. v. 4, 5, 9. vi. 4, 11, 19, 20, 20(*ap*). vii. 15, 17, 18, 20, 22, 37*t*, 39. viii. 4, 5, 7, 10. ix. 1, 2, 9, 18, 24. x. 2, 5, 8(–L*S*), 25. xi. 11, 13, 18, 21, 22, 25. xii. 6, 18, 25, 28. xiv. 10, 19*t*, 21, 25, 28, 33, 34, 35. xv. 17, 18, 19*t*, 22*t*, 23, 28, 31, 41, 42*t*, 43*f*, 52*t*, 58. xvi. 11, 13, 19, 24.

2 Cor. i. 1, 4, 6, 8, 9, 12*t*, 14, 19, 20, 20(*ap*), 22. ii. 1, 10, 14*t*, 15*t*, 17. iii. 2, 3*t*, 7(–G^{oo}LT*S*), 9(–L*S*), 10, 14. iv. 2, 4, 6*t*, 7, 10*t*, 11, 12*t*. v. 1, 2, 4, 6, 11, 12, 17, 19, 21. vi. 2, 3, 4*five*, 5*six*, 12*t*, 16. vii. 1, 3, 9, 11, 11(–$\mathrm{G}^o\mathrm{L}^b$T*S*), 14, 16*t*. viii. 2, 7*t*, 18, 20, 22. ix. 3, 4, 8, 11. x. 3, 6, 14, 16, 17. xi. 6, 9, 10*t*, 17, 23*f*, 25, 26*tr*, 27(–G^oLT*S*), 27*f*, 32, 33. xii. 2*t*, 3, 5, 9*t*, 10*five*, 12, 12(–LT

S), 19. xiii. 3*t*, 4(σύν L^{m}*S*; *marg.* **with**), 5*t*.

Gal. i. 13, 14*t*, 16, 22, 24. ii. 4, 20*t*. iii. 8, 10*t*, 12, 19, 26, 28. iv. 14, 18, 19, 25. v. 6, 14*t*. vi. 1*t*, 6, 12, 13, 14, 15(*ap*), 17.

Eph. i. 1, 3, 3(–St), 4*t*, 6, 7, 8, 9, 10, 10(ἐπί L*S*), 10, 11, 12, 13*t*, 15, 17 (*marg.* **for**), 18, 20*t*, 21*t*, 23. ii. 2, 3, 4, 6*t*, 7*t*, 10*t*, 11*t*, 12, 13, 15*tr*, 16, 21*t*, 22. iii. 3, 4, 5(*omS*), 6, 9, 10, 11, 12, 15, 17*t*, 20. iv. 2, 3, 4, 6, 15, 16*t*, 17*t*, 18, 21, 24. v. 2, 5, 8, 9, 19, 20, 21, 24. vi. 1(–G^{o}L), 4, 5, 9, 10*t*, 12, 13, 18, 20, 21, 24 (*marg.* **with**).

Phil. i. 1, 4, 6, 7*t*, 8, 9, 13(*marg.* **for**), 13, 14, 20*t*, 22, 24(–G^{oo}*S*), 26, 27, 28, 30*t*. ii. 1, 5*t*, 6, 7, 12*t*, 13, 15(–G″LT*S*), 15, 19, 24, 29. iii. 1, 3*t*, 4*t*, 6, 9, 14, 19, 20. iv. 1, 2, 3*t*, 4, 6, 9, 10, 11, 12, 15, 16, 19, 21.

Col. i. 2, 4, 5*t*, 6*tr*, 8, 9, 10, 12, 14, 16, 18(*marg.* **among**), 19, 20, 22, 24*t*, 27(*marg.* **amongst**), 28*t*, 29. ii. 1, 2, 3 (ἐν ᾧ, *marg.* **wherein**), 6, 7, 7(–LT), 9, 10, 11*t*, 12, 13(–G^{o}*S*), 15, 16*t*(*marg.* **for t**), 16, 18, 20, 23*t*. iii. 3, 4, 7*t*, 11, 15*t*, 16*t*, 17t, 17, 18, 22. iv. 1, 2, 5, 7, 12*t*, 13*t*, 15, 16, 17.

1 Thes. i. 1, 5*f*, 6, 7, 8*t*. ii. 2, 3, 13, 14*t*. iii. 2, 8, 13. iv. 4, 5, 6, 10, 16, 17. v. 2, 4, 12, 13, 18*t*.

2 Thes. i. 1, 4*tr*, 8, 10*tr*, 12*t*. ii. 6, 10(–G^{o}LT*S*), 12(–G^{o}L^{b}*S*), 17. iii. 4. 6, 17.

1 Tim. i. 2, 4, 13, 14, 16. ii. 2*t*, 7 (*omS*), 7, 9, 11, 12, 14, 15. iii. 4, 9, 11, 13*t*, 15, 16*tr*. iv. 1, 2, 12*tr*, 12 (–GLT), 12*t*, 14 .v. 17. vi. 17, 17(ἐπί L*S*), 18.

2 Tim. i. 1, 3, 5*tr*, 6, 9, 13*t*, 14, 15, 17, 18. ii. 1*t*, 7, 10, 20, 25. iii. 1, 12, 14, 15, 16. iv. 5.

Tit. i. 5, 13. ii. 3, 7, 9, 10, 12. iii. 3, 15. Phm. 6, 8, 10, 13, 16*t*, 20*t*, 23.

Heb. ii. 8, 12, 18. iii. 2, 5, 8*t*, 11, 12*t*, 15, 17. iv. 3, 5, 7. v. 6, 7. vi. 18. vii. 10. viii. 1, 5, 9*t*, 13. ix. 23. x. 3, 7, 22, 32, 34(*omS*), 34(–G^{o}LT*S*), 38. xi. 9, 18, 19, 26(G′, *omS*), 37t, 38(ἐπί LT*S*). xii. 23. xiii. 3, 4, 18, 21*t*.

Jas. i. 6, 8, 9, 10, 11, 23, 25, 27. ii. 2*t*, 4, 5, 10, 16. iii. 2, 14, 18. iv. 1, 5, 16. v. 5, 14.

1 Pet. i. 4, 5, 11, 14, 15, 17, 22. ii. 6(–L), 6, 12, 22, 24. iii. 4, 15*t*, 16, 19, 20. iv. 1(–G^{oo}LT*S*), 2, 3, 11, 19. v. 6, 9, 14.

2 Pet. i. 12, 13, 18, 19*t*. ii. 10, 12, 13, 18. iii. 1, 10(*omS*), 10, 11, 14, 16*tr*, 18.

1 John i. 5, 6, 7*t*, 8, 10. ii. 4, 5*t*, 6, 8*t*, 9*t*, 10*t*, 11*t*, 14, 15*t*, 16, 24*tr*, 24(–L), 27*t*, 28. iii. 5, 6, 9, 10, 14, 15, 17, 24*tr*. iv. 2, 3(*ap*), 3, 4*t*, 9, 12*t*, 13*t*, 15*t*, 16*tr*, 17*t*, 18*t*. v. 7(*ap*), 8(*ap*), 10, 11, 19, 20*t*.

2 John 1, 2, 3, 4, 6, 7, 9*t*. 3 John 1(*see* ἀλήθεια), 3, 4. Jude 10, 12, 18(ἐπί G″LT*S*), 20, 21.

Rev. i. 4, 5, 9, 9(*omS*), 9, 10, 11 (*omS*), 13(*see* ἐμμέσῳ), 15, 16*t*. ii. 1, 1(*see* ἐμμέσῳ), 7, 12, 13(–G^{oo}LT Tr), 18, 24. iii. 1, 4*t*, 5, 7, 12, 21*t*. iv. 1, 2*t*, 4, 6(*see* ἐμμέσῳ). v. 3, 6*t*(*see* ἐμμέσῳ), 13. vi. 5, 6 (*see* ἐμμέσῳ). vii. 9, 14, 15. viii. 1, 9. ix. 6, 10, 11, 17, 19, 19(*ap*). x. 2, 7, 8, 9, 10. xi. 6(:*mS*), 12, 13, 15, 19(–Tr^{b}), 19. xii. 1, 3, 7, 8, 10, 12. xiii. 6, 8. xiv. 5, 6, 13, 14, 17. xv. 1*t*, 5. xvi. 3. xvii. 3, 4. xviii. 6, 7, 8, 10(*om S*), 19, 22*tr*, 23(–L), 23, 24. xix. 1, 11, 14, 17*t*. xx. 6, 8, 12, 13*t*, 15. xxi. 8, 10, 14(ἐπί GLTTr*S*), 23(*om S*), 24(διά GLTTr*S*), 27. xxii. 2(*see* ἐμμέσῳ), 3, 18, 19.

ἐν αὐτῷ (αὐτῇ, αὐτοῖς), **therein**, Luke x. 9. xix. 45(*ap*). Acts i. 20. xiv. 15. xvii. 24. Rom. i. 17. vi. 2. Eph. vi. 20(*marg.* **thereof**). Col. ii. 7(–G^{o}*S*). 2 Pet. iii. 10. Rev. i. 3. x. 6*tr*. xi. 1. xiii. 12. xxi. 22.—**thereon**, Matt. xxi. 19. Mark xi. 13. Luke xiii. 6.—**thereby**, Eph. ii. 16 (*marg.* **in himself**). 1 Pet. ii. 2.—**therewith**, Jas.

iii. 9*t*. — **there**, Luke xxiv. 18. Acts ix. 38. xx. 22.

ἐν τούτῳ, **herein**, John iv. 37. ix. 30. xv. 8. Acts xxiv. 16. 2 Cor. viii. 10. 1 John iv. 10, 17. — **therein**, 1 Cor. vii. 24. Phil. i. 18. — **hereby**, 1 Cor. iv. 4. 1 John ii. 3, 5. iii. 16, 19, 24. iv. 2, 13.

ἐν ᾧ (ᾗ, οἷς, αἷς), **wherein**, Matt. xi. 20. xxv. 13(*ap*). John xix. 41. Acts ii. 8. x. 12. Rom. ii. 1. v. 2. vii. 6. 1 Cor. vii. 20, 24, xv. 1. 2 Cor. xi. 12. Eph. i. 6(ἧς G′T*S*). ii. 2. v. 18. Col. ii. 12. 2 Tim. ii. 9. Heb. vi. 17. ix. 2, 4. 1 Pet. i. 6. iv. 4. 2 Pet. iii. 13. Rev. ii. 13. xviii. 19. — **therein**[cc], Heb. xiii. 9. — **where**, Acts iv. 31. vii. 33(ἐπί for ἐν LT*S*). xi. 11. xv. 36. — **whereby**, Luke i. 78. Acts iv. 12. xi. 14. Rom. viii. 15. xiv. 21. Eph. iv. 30. — **wherewith**, Eph. vi. 16. Heb. x. 29. — **whereupon**, Acts xxiv. 18. xxvi. 12. — **when**, Luke xxii. 7. John iv. 52. — **while**, Mark ii. 19. Luke v. 34. John v. 7. — **whereas**, 1 Pet. ii. 12 (*marg.* **wherein**). iii. 16.

ἐν ᾧ ἄν, **whereinsoever**, 2 Cor. xi. 21.

within, Matt. iii. 9. ix. 3, 21. Mark ii. 8. Luke iii. 8. vii. 39, 49. xii. 17. xvi. 3. xviii. 4. xix. 44. xxiv. 32(-Tr[b]). Rom. viii. 23.

between, Rom. i. 24.

among, Matt. ii. 6. iv. 23. ix 35 (*om*). xi. 11. xvi. 7, 8. xx. 26*t*, 27. xxi. 38. xxvi. 5. xxvii. 56. Mark v. 3. vi. 4. x. 43*t*. xv. 40. Luke i. 1, 25, 28(*ap*), 42. ii. 44t ([2d] *omS*). vii. 16, 28. viii. 7. ix. 46, 48. x. 3. xvi. 15. xxii. 24, 26. John i. 14. vii. 12, 43. ix. 16. x. 19. xi. 54. xv. 24. Acts iv. 12, 34. v. 12. vi. 8. xii. 18. xiii. 26. xv. 7, 12, 22. xvii. 34. xviii. 11. xx. 25, 32. xxi. 19, 34. xxiv. 21. xxv. 5, 6. xxvi. 4, 18. xxviii. 29(*ap*).

Rom. i. 5, 6, 13 (*marg.* **in**), 13 ii. 24. viii. 29. xi. 17(*marg.* **for**). xii. 3. xv. 9. xvi. 7 1 Cor. i. 10, 11. ii. 2, 6. iii. 3, 18. v. 1*t*. vi. 5, 7(*omS*). xi. 18, 19*t*, 30. xv. 12. 2 Cor. i. 19. x. 1. xi. 26. xii. 12.

Gal. i. 16. ii. 2. iii. 1 (-G[oo]L*S*), 5. Eph. ii. 3. iii. 8(-L*S*). v. 3. Phil. ii. 15. Col. i. 27. 1 Thes. i. 5. ii. 7. v. 12, 13. 2 Thes. iii. 7, 11.

Jas. i. 26(G′, *omS*). iii. 6, 13. iv. 1. v. 13, 14. 1 Pet. ii. 12. v. 1, 2 (τὸ ἐν ὑμῖν, *marg.* **as much as in you is**). 2 Pet. ii. 1*t*, 8.

of, Luke i. 61(ἐκ G′LTTr*S*). Rom. ii. 17, 23. xi. 2. 2 Cor. ii. 12. 2 Cor. x. 15. Gal. iv. 20(*marg.* **for**). Eph. iv. 1(*marg.* **in**). Tit. iii. 5. Jas. v. 19. 2 Pet. ii. 12.

at, Matt. viii. 6. xi. 22, 25. xii. 1. xiii. 49. xiv. 1. xviii. 1. xxiii. 6. xxiv. 41. Mark vi. 3. xii. 39. Luke iv. 18(19). ix. 31. x. 14. xii. 46. xiii. 1. xiv. 14. xix. 5. xx. 10(-LT Tr*S*), 46. xxiii. 7*t*, 12. John iv. 21, 45*t*, 46, 53(-Tr[b]*S*). vi. 39(-Tr). vii. 11. x. 22. xi. 24. xii. 20. xiv. 20. xvi. 26. xviii. 39. xxi. 20.

Acts i. 6. ii. 5. vii. 13, 29. viii. 1, 14. ix. 10, 13, 19, 22, 27, 28(εἰς G″ LT*S*), 36. xi. 15. xiii. 1, 5, 27. xiv. 8. xvi. 2, 4. xvii. 13, 16. xix. 1. xx. 5, 15(*ap*). xxi. 11. xxv. 4 (εἰς G″LT*S*), 24. xxvi. 4.

Rom. i. 15. viii. 34. xi. 5. xv. 26. xvi. 1. 1 Cor. i. 2. xi. 34. xiv. 35. xv. 23, 32, 52. xvi. 8. 2 Cor. i. 1. viii. 14(13). Eph. i. 1(-T[b]*S*). ii. 12 (-G[oo]LT*S*). iii. 13. Phil. i. 1. ii. 10. Col. i. 2. ii. 1. 1 Thes. ii. 2, 19. iii. 1, 13. 1 Tim. i. 3. 2 Tim. i. 18. iii 11*tr*. iv. 8, 13, 16, 20*t*. Heb. xii. 2. 1 Pet. i. 7, 13. v. 13. 1 John ii. 28.

on, Matt. xxii. 40. xxiv. 20(*omS*). xxvi. 5. Mark ii. 23, 24(-G[oo]LTTr *S*). xiv. 2. xvi. 5. Luke i. 59. iv. 16, 31. v. 17. vi. 1, 2(-LTTr*S*), 6, 7. viii. 15, 22, 32. ix. 37(-Tr[b]*S*). xii. 51. xiii. 7, 10. xiv. 5(-L[b]Tr). xx. 1. John v. 9, 16. vii. 22(-L[b]), 23*t*. xiii. 23. xix. 31.

Rom. xii. 7*t*, 8. 2 Cor. iv. 8. vii.

5. viii. 1. Col. iii. 1. Heb. i. 3. viii. 1. x. 12. 1 Pet. iii. 22. iv. 16. Rev. i. 10. v. 13(ἐπί GLTTr*S*).

upon, Matt. xii. 2. Luke xxi. 23 (*omS*). Acts xx. 7. Jas. iv. 3.

over, Acts xx. 28.

under, Matt. vii. 6. Rom. iii. 19.

before, Acts v. 27.

about, Luke ii. 49.

into, Mark i. 16. Luke v. 16. xxiii. 42 (εἰς L[m]). John iii. 35. v. 4(*ap*). Acts vii. 45. Rom. i. 23, 25. 2 Cor. viii. 16. Gal. i. 6. 1 Tim. iii. 16.

to, Luke i. 17 (*marg.* **by**). John xiii. 35. Acts xii. 11. 1 Cor. vii. 15 (*marg.* **in**). 2 Cor. iv. 3. viii. 7. Col. i. 23. 2 Pet. i. 5*t*, 6*tr*, 7*t*. 1 John iv. 16.

toward, Luke ii. 14. Rom. xv. 5. 1 John iv. 9.

unto, Matt. xvii. 12. Acts xxvi. 20. Rom. v. 21. 1 Cor. ix. 15. xiv. 11. 2 Cor. v. 19 (*Gr.* in). 1 Thes. iv. 7. v. 23. 1 Tim. iii. 16.

against, Rom. ii. 5.

after, Heb. iv. 11.

with, Matt. iii. 11*t*. vii. 2*t*. xx. 15. xxii. 37*tr*. xxv. 16. xxvi. 52. Mark i. 8(-TTr[b]*S*), 8(-L[b]TTr[b]), 23. iv. 24, 30. v. 2. ix. 1, 50.

Luke i. 51. iii. 16. iv. 32, 36. viii. 15. xi. 20. xiv. 31. xxi. 25, 34. xxii. 49. John i. 26, 31, 33*t*. Acts i. 5. ii. 29, 46. v. 23. xi. 16, 26(*marg.* **in**).

Rom. i. 4, 9(*marg.* **in**), 12(*marg.* **in**), 27. ix. 22. x. 9. xii. 8*tr*, 21. xv. 32. xvi. 16. 1 Cor. i. 17. ii. 4. iv. 21. v. 8*tr*. x. 5. xiv. 21t. xvi. 14, 20. 2 Cor. i. 12. vii. 8. xiii. 12.

Eph. i. 3. iii. 12. iv. 19. v. 18. vi. 2, 14, 15, 18. Phil. i. 20. Col. i. 11. ii. 4, 7. iii. 16, 22. iv. 2, 6. 1 Thes. ii. 2, 17. iv. 16*tr*, 18. v. 26. 2 Thes. i. 11. ii. 9, 10. iii. 8. 1 Tim. ii. 9, 11. v. 2. 2 Tim. i. 3. iv. 2.

Heb. ix. 22, 25. xi. 37. Jas. i. 21. ii. 1. iii. 13. 1 Pet. i. 12(-G[o]LT). ii. 18. iii. 2. v. 14. 2 Pet. ii. 7, 13, 16. Jude 14. 23, 24. Rev. ii. 16, 23, 27. vi. 8*tr*. ix. 19. xii. 5. xiii. 10*t*. xiv. 2, 7(-L), 9, 10, 15. xvi. 8. xvii. 16. xviii. 8, 16(-G[∞]LTr[b]). xix. 2, 15*t*, 20*t*, 21.

ἐν τίνι, **wherewith**, Matt. v. 13. Mark ix. 50. Luke xiv. 34.—**by what means**, Acts iv. 9.

by, Matt. v. 34, 35, 36. xii. 24, 27*t*, 28. xiv. 13. xvii. 21(*ap*). xxi. 23, 24, 27. xxii. 1. xxiii. 16*t*, 18*t*, 20*tr*, 21*tr*, 22*tr*. Mark iii. 22. iv. 2. v. 21. viii. 3, 27. ix. 29*t*, 33, 34 (-L[b]). xi. 28, 29, 33. xii. 1, 36. xiv. 1.

Luke i. 77(*marg.* **for**). ii. 27. iv. 1. xi. 19*t*. xx. 2, 8. xxiv. 32. John xiii. 35. xvi. 30. Acts i. 3. iv. 7*t*, 10*t*, 30. vii. 35 (σύν G″LT). xiii. 39*t*. xvii. 31. xx. 19.

Rom. i. 10. v. 9, 10, 15. x. 5. xiv. 14. xv. 16, 19. 1 Cor. i. 4, 5. iii. 13. vi. 2, 11. vii. 14*t*. xii. 3*t*, 9*t*, 13. xiv. 6*f*. xvi. 7. 2 Cor. i. 12. vi. 6*six*, 7*t*. vii. 6, 7*t*. x. 12, 15(*marg.* **in**).

Gal. ii. 17, 20. iii. 11. v. 4. Eph. ii. 13, 18. iii. 5, 21. iv. 14t, 21. v. 26. Phil. iv. 19. Col. i. 16, 17, 21(*marg.* **in**). ii. 11. 1 Thes. iii. 3. iv. 1, 15. 2 Thes. iii. 16. 1 Tim. i. 18. Tit. i. 9. Phm. 6.

Heb. i. 1, 2(1). x. 10, 19. xi. 2. 1 Pet. i. 5. iii. 19. v. 10. 2 Pet. i. 13. 1 John v. 2, 6*t*. Jude 1. Rev. v. 9. ix. 20. x. 6. xviii. 23.

by way of, 2 Pet. iii. 1.

through, Matt. ix. 34. Luke x. 17. xi. 15, 18. John xvii. 11, 17, 19(*see* ἀλήθεια). xx. 31. Acts iv. 2. Rom. i. 24. iii. 7, 25(26). vi. 11, 23. xv. 13, 17, 19. 2 Cor. xi. 3. Gal. iii. 14. v. 10. Eph. ii. 7, 22. Phil. iv. 7, 13. 2 Thes. ii. 13, 16. Tit. i. 3. Heb. xiii. 20. 1 Pet. i. 2, 6. 2 Pet. i. 1, 2, 4. ii. 3, 18(-G*S*), 20. Rev. viii. 13.

throughout[c], Luke i. 65. vii. 17, 17(-L[b]Tr[b]*S*). Rom. i. 8. ix. 17.

for, Matt. vi. 7. Luke i. 44. Phil. i. 26. 1 Tim. v. 10. Jas. v. 3. 1 Pet. iv. 14.

for one's sake, Eph. iv. 32.

because of, Matt. xxvi. 31, 33. Mark xiv. 27(-G°°TTrS).

ἐν τῷ, **namely,** Rom. xiii. 9(-Lᵇ).

ἐν τῷ, *with an Infinitive,* **as,** Mark ii. 15(-TrᵇS). iv. 4. Luke ii. 43. v. 1. viii. 5, 42. ix. 18, 29, 33, 34. x. 38. xi. 1, 27, 37. xiv. 1. xvii. 11, 14. xviii. 35. xxiv. 4, 30. Acts ix. 3. xi. 15.—**that,** Luke i. 21.—**when,** Matt. xiii. 4. xxvii. 12. Luke ii. 27. iii. 21. v. 12. viii. 40. ix. 36, 51. x. 35. xix. 15. Acts ii. 1. Rom. iii. 4. Gal. iv. 18.—**while,** Matt. xiii. 25. Luke i. 8. ii. 6. xxiv. 15, 51. Acts xix. 1. Heb. iii. 15.

Not rendered (in notation of time ᵗ), Matt. xiii. 1ᵗ. xxii. 23ᵗ. xxvi. 31ᵗ, 34ᵗ. Mark iv. 35ᵗ. xiv. 27 (-G°°LᵇTTrS). Luke vii. 11ᵗ. xiii. 31ᵗ. xx. 19ᵗ. xxiii. 12ᵗ. xxiv. 13ᵗ. John xxi. 3ᵗ. Acts i. 21ᵗ, 21ᵗ (-LTS). vii. 14. viii. 6. xvi. 33ᵗ. xx. 26ᵗ. xxvii. 7ᵗ. Rom. xv. 6? (*see* ὁμοθυμαδόν). 1 Cor. xi. 23ᵗ. Heb. iv. 4ᵗ. 1 Pet. iv. 12. Rev. ii. 14(*om*S). xi. 13ᵗ. xiii. 3(-C?GLTTrS).

Add, for διά, 2 Thes. iii. 12, G'LTS. For εἰς, Matt. xii. 18, Tr. xiii. 52, L. Mark ii. 1²ᵈ, LTrS. xi. 8, Lᵐ. xiv. 6, GLTTrS. Luke iv. 1, G''LTTrS. xxi. 14, LTTrS. xxiii. 19, T TrS. John iii. 15, LᵐTTr. xvi. 13, G'TS. Acts iv. 5, G''LT. ix. 26, G'LT. Rom. xv. 31, L. For ἐκ, Luke x. 27*tr,* LTrS. For ἐν (fr. εἰς), Mark iv. 8*tr,* G'. 20*tr,* G'TTr. For ἐπί, Matt. iv. 4, G''LTTr. xxvii. 29²ᵈ, G''LTTrS. Mark iv. 38¹ˢᵗ, GLTTrS. Luke xvi. 26, LᵐS. Acts ii. 38, L. 1 Cor. viii. 11, G''LTS. Eph. vi. 16, LS. Rev. i. 20, L. xi. 11¹ˢᵗ, GLT. xxii. 16, LTr. For μετά, John xii. 35, GLTTrS. For παρά, Matt. xxi. 25, LTr. Rom. xi. 25, T. For σύν, Acts i. 17, GLTS. 2 Cor. viii. 19, G'LT.

Matt. iv. 23(. . all G.), TrS. xxvii. 59(in), TTr. Mark vi. 32(by), LS. ix. 38(in), C?LTrS. x. 44, *see* ὑμῶν. Luke xix. 13, *see* ἕως. xxiv. 19(. . word), Lᵇ. John vi. 40(at), LTS. 44(at), GLTTr. 54(at), LᵇT. ix. 14, *see* ὅτε. xvi. 29(. . παρρησίᾳ), LTTrS. xix. 40(in), G''T.

Acts ii. 41(. . the s. d.), LTS. 42 (in¹ˢᵗ), Lᵇ. iii. 25(in), GLTS. v. 32, *see* αὐτοῦ. vii. 16(of⁴ᵗʰ), LS. 22 (in¹ˢᵗ), TS. 39(in), LS. xxi. 20(ἐν τοῖς Ἰουδαίοις for Ἰουδαίων), G''LT. xxiv. 14(. . the prophets), GTS. xxvi. 10(in), GᵖʳLTS. 20(at), L.

Rom. v. 17(ἐν ἑνί for τῷ τοῦ ἑνός), G'LᵐT. vii. 23(to), TS. x. 20(of, *and* unto), Lᵇ. xv. 13(with), Lᵐ. 1 Cor. xiv. 39(with), LᵇT. 2 Cor. v. 12(in²ᵈ), LS. vii. 11(in¹ˢᵗ), Lᵇ. Eph. ii. 5(. . Christ), Lᵇ. v. 19 (in¹ˢᵗ), Lᵇ. Phil. i. 7(in³ᵈ), G''LᵇTS. Col. iii. 20(unto), GLTS. 1 Thes. i. 7(. . Achaia), G''LTS. 8(. . Achaia), G''LS. 1 Tim. iii. 14, *see* τάχιον.

Jas. v. 10 (in), LS. 2 Pet. iii. 3 (days ἐν ἐμπαιγμονῇ), GLTS. 1 John iii. 18(in³ᵈ), GLTS. v. 6(. . blood²ᵈ), LT. Rev. i. 9(of), G''LTTrS. ii. 1 (of²ᵈ), GLTTrS. 8(in), CGLTTrS. iii. 14 (of²ᵈ), CᵐGLTTrS. v. 2 (with), viii. 7(with), xi. 6(with), GLTTrS.

Ap., Mark xvi. 8. Luke vi. 35. xi. 43. Acts iv. 27. xiv. 10. Heb. iii. 9.

See also αἴνιγμα, ἀκροβυστία, ἄνοιξις, ἀποκάλυψις, ἀφροσύνη, βάρος, γαστήρ, γίνομαι, γράμμα, διασπορά, διδακτός, δόξα, δύναμις, εἰμί, ἐκτενεία, ἐπιγράφω, ἔχω, ἱματισμός, ἰσχύς, καθεξῆς, καιρός, κατηγορία, κρυπτός, λείπω, μέσος, ὁδός, ὀλίγος, ὁμολογέω, παροικία, παρρησία, πᾶς, πιστεύω, πολύς, προβαίνω, πρῶτος, τάχος, τόπος, ὑψηλός, φανερός, χρόνος.

ἐναγκαλίζομαι.

take in one's arms, Mark ix. 36ᵖ.
take up in one's arms, Mark x. 16.

ἐνάλιος.

Plur., **things in the sea,** Jas. iii. 7.

ἔναντι.

before, Luke i. 8(ἐναντίον G'S).
Add Acts viii. 21, for ἐνώπιον, GLTS.

ἐναντίον.

before, Mark ii. 12. Luke xx. 26. xxiv. 19. Acts viii. 32.
in the sight of, Acts vii. 10.
Add Luke i. 6, for ἐνώπιον, Tr*S*. 8, for ἔναντι, G'*S*.

ἐναντίος.

contrary, Matt. xiv. 24. Mark vi. 48. Acts xxvi. 9. xxvii. 4. 1 Thes. ii. 15. Tit. ii. 8.
against, Acts xxviii. 17.
ἐξ ἐναντίας, **over against,** Mark xv. 39.

ἐνάρχομαι.

begin, Gal. iii. 3. Phil. i. 6.

ἔνατος. See ἔννατος.

ἐνδεής.

that lacketh, Acts iv. 34.

ἔνδειγμα.

manifest token, 2 Thes. i. 5.

ἐνδείκνυμαι.

show forth, 1 Tim. i. 16.
show, Rom. ii. 15. ix. 17, 22. 2 Cor. viii. 24. Eph. ii. 7. Tit. ii. 10. iii. 2. Heb. vi. 10, 11.
do, 2 Tim. iv. 14.

ἔνδειξις.

With εἰς, **to declare,** Rom. iii. 25, 26.
evident token, Phil. i. 28.
proof, 2 Cor. viii. 24.

ἕνδεκα.

eleven, Matt. xxviii. 16. Mark xvi. 14(*ap*). Luke xxiv. 9, 33. Acts i. 26. ii. 14.

ἑνδέκατος.

eleventh, Matt. xx. 6, 9. Rev. xxi. 20.

ἐνδέχομαι.

Impers., **it can be,** Luke xiii. 33.

ἐνδημέω.

be at home, 2 Cor. v. 6p.
be present, 2 Cor. v. 8.
present, 2 Cor. v. 9p.

ἐνδιδύσκω.

Mid., **be clothed in,** Luke xvi. 19. —**wear,** Luke viii. 27.
Add Mark xv. 17, for ἐνδύω, LTTr*S*.

ἔνδικος.

just, Rom. iii. 8. Heb. ii. 2.

ἐνδόμησις.

building, Rev. xxi. 18.

ἐνδοξάζομαι.

be glorified, 2 Thes. i. 10, 12.

ἔνδοξος.

glorious, Luke xiii. 17. Eph. v. 27.
honorable, 1 Cor. iv. 10.
See also ἱματισμός.

ἔνδυμα.

clothing, Matt. vii. 15.
raiment, Matt. iii. 4. vi. 25, 28. xxviii. 3. Luke xii. 23.
garment, Matt. xxii. 11, 12.

ἐνδυναμόω.

strengthen, Phil. iv. 13. 2 Tim. iv. 17.
enable, 1 Tim. i. 12.
Pass. or Mid., **be made strong,** Heb. xi. 34 (δυναμόω L*S*). —**be strong,** Rom. iv. 20. Eph. vi. 10. 2 Tim. ii. 1.—**increase in strength,** Acts ix. 22.

ἐνδύνω.

With εἰς, **creep into,** 2 Tim. iii. 6.

ἔνδυσις.

putting on, 1 Pet. iii. 3.

ἐνδύω.

put on, Matt. xxvii. 31. Mark xv. 20. Luke xv. 22.
clothe with, Mark xv. 17 (ἐνδιδύσκω LTTr*S*).
Mid. or Pass., **put on,** Matt. vi. 25. xxii. 11. Mark vi. 9. Luke xii. 22. Rom. xiii. 12, 14. 1 Cor. xv. 53*t*, 54*t*. Gal. iii 27. Eph. iv. 24. vi. 11. Col. iii. 10, 12. 1 Thes. v. 8. —**have on,** Eph. vi. 14. —**be clothed in,** Rev. xv. 6. xix. 14. —**be clothed with,** Mark i. 6. Rev. i. 13. —**be clothed,** 2 Cor. v. 3 (ἐκδύω G'T). —**be endued with,** Luke xxiv. 49. —**be arrayed in,** Acts xii. 21.
Add Matt. xxvii. 28, for ἐκδύω, L.

ἐνέγκω. See φέρω.

ἐνέδρα.

With ποιέω, **lay wait,** Acts xxv. 3.
Add Acts xxiii. 16, for ἔνεδρον, G L*S*.

ἐνεδρεύω.

lie in wait for, Acts xxiii. 21.
lay wait for, Luke xi. 54(–G°°).

ἔνεδρον.

lying in wait, Acts xxiii. 16(G′, ἐνέδρα GL*S*).

ἐνειλέω.

wrap in, Mark xv. 46.

ἔνειμι.

ἔνι for ἔνεστι, **there is,** Gal. iii. 28*tr*. Col. iii. 11.—**is,** Jas. i. 17.
τὰ ἐνόντα, **such things as ye[c] have,** Luke xi. 41(*marg*. **as ye[c] are able**).
Add 1 Cor. vi. 5, for ἐστί, GLT*S*.

ἕνεκα, ἕνεκεν, εἵνεκεν.

for . . sake, Matt. v. 10, 11. x. 18, 39. xvi. 25. xix. 29. Mark viii. 35. x. 29. xiii. 9. Luke vi. 22. ix. 24. xviii. 29. xxi. 12. Rom. viii. 36.
for . . cause, Matt. xix. 5. Mark x. 7. Acts xxvi. 21. 2 Cor. vii. 12*t*.
for, Acts xxviii. 20. Rom. xiv. 20.
by reason of, 2 Cor. iii. 10.
οὗ ἕνεκεν, **because,** Luke iv. 18.
τίνος ἕνεκεν, **wherefore,** Acts xix. 32.
With Infinit., **that . . might,** 2 Cor. vii. 12.
Add Mark x. 29(. . the gospel's), GL[b]TTr.

ἐνενήκοντα. See ἐννενηκονταεννέα.

ἐνεός. See ἐννεός.

ἐνέργεια.

working, Eph. i. 19. Phil. iii. 21. Col. i. 29. 2 Thes. ii. 9.
effectual working, Eph. iii. 7. iv. 16.
operation, Col. ii. 12.
strong[cc], 2 Thes. ii. 11.

ἐνεργέω.

to work, 1 Cor. xii. 6, 11. Gal. iii. 5. v. 6. Eph. i. 11, 20. ii. 2. Phil. ii. 13.
work effectually in, Gal. ii. 8.
be mighty in, Gal. ii. 8.
do, Phil. ii. 13.
show forth one's self, Matt. xiv. 2. Mark vi. 14.
Mid., **work,** Rom. vii. 5. 2 Cor. iv. 12. Eph. iii. 20. Col. i. 29. 2 Thes. ii. 7.—**work effectually,** 1 Thes. ii. 13.—**be effectual** (*marg*. **be wrought**), 2 Cor. i. 6.—**effectual fervent,** Jas. v. 16[p].

ἐνέργημα.

working, 1 Cor. xii. 10.
operation, 1 Cor. xii. 6.

ἐνεργής.

effectual, 1 Cor. xvi. 9. Phm. 6.
powerful, Heb. iv. 12.

ἐνεστῶτα. See ἐνίστημι.

ἐνευλογέομαι.

be blessed, Acts iii. 25. Gal. iii. 8.

ἐνέχω.

have a quarrel (*marg*. **an inward grudge**) **against,** Mark vi. 19.
urge, Luke xi. 53.
Pass., **be entangled with,** Gal. v. 1.

ἐνθάδε.

hither, John iv. 15, 16. Acts xvii. 6. xxv. 17.
here, Luke xxiv. 41. Acts xvi. 28. xxv. 24.
there, Acts x. 18.

ἔνθεν, hence.

For ἐντεῦθεν, Matt. xvii. 20, LTTr. Luke xvi. 26, GLTTr*S*.

ἐνθυμέομαι.

think on, Matt. i. 20[p].
think, Matt. ix. 4. Acts x. 19[p](διενθυμέομαι GLT*S*).

ἐνθύμησις.

thought, Matt. ix. 4. xii. 25. Heb. iv. 12.
device, Acts xvii. 29.

ἔνι. See ἔνειμι.

ἐνιαυτός.

year, Luke iv. 19. John xi. 49, 51. xviii. 13. Acts xi. 26. xviii. 11. Gal. iv. 10. Heb. ix. 7, 25. x. 1(*see* κατά), 3. Jas. iv. 13. v. 17. Rev. ix. 15.

ἐνίστημι.
be at hand, 2 Thes. ii. 2.
come, 2 Tim. iii. 1.
Part., **present,** 1 Cor. vii. 26. Gal. i. 4. Heb. ix. 9.—ἐνεστῶτα, **things present,** Rom. viii. 38. 1Cor. iii. 22.

ἐνισχύω.
be strengthened, Acts ix. 19.
strengthen, Luke xxii. 43(*ap*).

ἐνκακέω. See ἐγκακέω.

ἔννατος or ἔνατος.
ninth, Matt. xx. 5. xxvii. 45, 46. Mark xv. 33, 34. Luke xxiii. 44. Acts iii. 1. x. 3, 30. Rev. xxi. 20.

ἐννέα.
nine, Luke xvii. 17.
See also ἐννενηκονταεννέα.

ἐννενηκονταεννέα,
ἐνενήκοντα ἐννέα LTTr*S*.
ninety and nine, Matt. xviii. 12, 13. Luke xv. 4, 7.

ἐννεός, ἐνεός G''LT*S*.
speechless, Acts ix. 7.

ἐννεύω.
make signs to, Luke i. 62.

ἔννοια.
intent, Heb. iv. 12.
mind, 1 Pet. iv. 1.

ἔννομος.
lawful (*marg.* **ordinary**), Acts xix. 39.
under the law, 1 Cor. ix. 21.

ἔννυχον, ἔννυχα G'LTTr*S*.
Lit. in the night; *with* λίαν, **great while before day,** Mark i. 35.

ἐνοικέω.
dwell in, Rom. viii. 11. 2 Cor. vi. 16. Col. iii. 16. 2 Tim. i. 5, 14.

ἐνόντα. See ἔνειμι.

ἑνότης.
unity, Eph. iv. 3, 13.

ἐνορκίζω, swear in, adjure.
For ὁρκίζω, 1 Thes. v. 27, LT.

ἐνοχλέω.
to trouble, Heb. xii. 15.
Add Luke vi. 18, for ὀχλέω, G'TTr[*S*.

ἔνοχος.
subject to, Heb. ii. 15.
in danger of, Matt. v. 21, 22*tr*. Mark iii. 29.
guilty of, Matt. xxvi. 66. Mark xiv. 64. 1 Cor. xi. 27. Jas. ii. 10.

ἔνταλμα.
commandment, Matt. xv. 9. Mark vii. 7. Col. ii. 22.

ἐνταφιάζω.
bury, John xix. 40.
Infinitive, **burial,** Matt. xxvi. 12.

ἐνταφιασμός.
burying, Mark xiv. 8. John xii. 7.

ἐντέλλομαι.
to command, Matt. xv. 4 (εἶπον G'' LTr). xix. 7. xxviii. 20. Mark x. 3. xi. 6(εἶπον G''LTTr*S*). xiii. 34. John viii. 5(*ap*). xv. 14, 17. Acts xiii. 47.
give commandment, John xiv. 31 (ἐντολὴν δίδωμι LTr). Acts i. 2p. Heb. xi. 22.
charge, Matt. xvii. 9.
give charge, Matt. iv. 6. Luke iv. 10.
enjoin, Heb. ix. 20.

ἐντεῦθεν.
hence, Matt. xvii. 20(ἔνθεν LTTr). Luke xiii. 31. John ii. 16. vii. 3. xiv. 31. Jas. iv. 1.
from hence, Luke iv. 9. xvi. 26(ἔνθεν LTTr*S*). John xviii. 36.
ἐντεῦθεν καὶ ἐντεῦθεν, **on either side,** John xix. 18. Rev. xxii. 2(ἐντ. καὶ ἐκεῖθεν G''LTTr, ἔνθεν καί *S*).

ἔντευξις.
intercession, 1 Tim. ii. 1.
prayer, 1 Tim. iv. 5.

ἔντιμος.
honorable, Luke xiv. 8.
With ἔχω, **hold in reputation,** Phil. ii. 29 (*marg.* **honor**).
dear, Luke vii, 2.
precious, 1 Pet. ii. 4, 6.

ἐντολή.
commandment, Matt. v. 19. xv. 3,

6 (λόγος LTr, νόμος TS), xix. 17. xxii. 36, 38, 40. Mark vii. 8, 9. x. 19. xii. 28, 29(*ap*), 30(*ap*), 31. Luke i. 6. xv. 29. xviii. 20. xxiii. 56. John x. 18. xi. 57. xii. 49, 50. xiii. 34. xiv. 15, 21. xv. 10*t*, 12. Acts xvii. 15.

Rom. vii. 8, 9, 10, 11, 12, 13. xiii. 9. 1 Cor. vii. 19. xiv. 37(–T). Eph. ii. 15. vi. 2. Col. iv. 10. 1 Tim. vi. 14. Tit. i. 14. Heb. vii. 5, 16, 18. 2 Pet. ii. 21. iii. 2. 1 John ii. 3, 4, 7*tr*, 8. iii. 22, 23*t*, 24. iv. 21. v. 2, 3*t*. 2 John 4, 5, 6*t*. Rev. xii. 17. xiv. 12. xxii. 14(*ap*).

precept, Mark x. 5. Heb. ix. 19.

Add John xiv. 31, *see* ἐντέλλομαι.

ἐντόπιος.

of that° place, Acts xxi. 12.

ἐντός.

within, Matt. xxiii. 26. Luke xvii. 21(*marg.* **among**).

ἐντρέπω.

to shame, 1 Cor. iv. 14. 2 Thes. iii. 14. Tit. ii. 8.

Mid., **regard,** Luke xviii. 2, 4.— **reverence,** Matt. xxi. 37. Mark xii. 6. Luke xx. 13. Heb. xii. 9.

ἐντρέφομαι.

be nourished up in, 1 Tim. iv. 6.

ἔντρομος.

trembling, Acts xvi. 29.

With γίνομαι, **tremble,** Acts vii. 32.

With εἰμί, **quake,** Heb. xii. 21.

ἐντροπή.

shame, 1 Cor. vi. 5. xv. 34.

ἐντρυφάω.

to sport one's self, 2 Pet. ii. 13.

ἐντυγχάνω.

deal with, Acts xxv. 24.

make intercession, Rom. viii. 27, 34. xi. 2. Heb. vii. 25.

ἐντυλίττω.

wrap in, Matt. xxvii. 59. Luke xxiii. 53.

wrap together, John xx. 7.

ἐντυπόω.

engrave, 2 Cor. iii. 7.

ἐνυβρίζω.

do despite unto, Heb. x. 29.

ἐνυπνιάζομαι.

to dream, Acts ii. 17.

filthy dreamer, Jude 8p.

ἐνύπνιον.

dream, Acts ii. 17.

ἐνώπιον.

in the presence of, Luke i. 19. xiv. 10. xv. 10. John xx. 30. Acts xxvii. 35. Rev. xiv. 10*t*.

in one's presence, Luke xiii. 26. 1 Cor. i. 29.

in the sight of, Luke i. 15. xvi. 15. Acts iv. 19. viii. 21(ἔναντι GLTS). x. 31. Rom. xii. 17. 2 Cor. iv. 2. vii. 12. viii. 21*t*. 1 Tim. ii. 3. vi. 13. Jas. iv. 10. 1 Pet. iii. 4. Rev. xiii. 13, 14.

in one's sight, Luke xv. 21. Rom. iii. 20. Heb. iv. 13. xiii. 21. 1 John iii. 22.

before, Luke i. 6(ἐναντίον TrS), 17, 75. v. 18, 25. viii. 47. xii. 6, 9(ἔμπροσθεν LS), 9. xv. 18. xvi. 15. xxiii. 14. xxiv. 43. Acts ii. 25. iv. 10. vi. 6. vii. 46. ix. 15. x. 4(ἔμπροσθεν LTS), 30, 33. xix. 9, 19.

Rom. xiv. 22. Gal. i. 20. 1 Tim. v. 4, 20, 21. vi. 12. 2 Tim. ii. 14. iv. 1. 3 John 6. Rev. i. 4. ii. 14. iii. 2, 5, 8. 9. iv. 5, 6, 10*t*. v. 8. vii. 9*t*, 11, 15. viii. 2, 3, 4. ix. 13. xi. 4, 16. xii. 4, 10. xiii. 12. xiv. 3*t*, 5(*ap*). xv. 4. xvi. 19. xix. 20. xx. 12.

to, Luke xxiv. 11.

Not rendered, Luke iv. 7, *with* προσκυνέω. Acts vi. 5, *with* ἀρέσκω.

Add Rom. xii. 17(*ap*).

ἐνωτίζομαι.

hearken to, Acts ii. 14.

ἐξ. See ἐκ.

ἕξ.

six, Matt. xvii. 1. Mark ix. 1. Luke iv. 25. xiii. 14. John ii. 6, 20.

xii. 1. Acts xi. 12. xviii. 11. Jas. v. 17. Rev. iv. 8. xiii.18(*see* χξς'). *See also* ἑβδομήκοντα.

ἐξαγγέλλω.

show forth, 1 Pet. ii. 9.

ἐξαγοράζω.

redeem, Gal. iii. 13. iv. 5. Eph. v. 16. Col. iv. 5.

ἐξάγω.

lead out, Mark viii. 23 (ἐκφέρω TTr *S*). xv. 20(ἄγω L). Luke xxiv. 50. John x. 3. Acts xxi. 38. Heb. viii. 9.

bring out, Acts vii. 36, 40. xii. 17. xiii. 17. xvi. 39.

bring forth, Acts v. 19.

fetch out, Acts xvi. 37.

ἐξαιρέω.

pluck out, Matt. v. 29. xviii. 9.

Mid., **rescue,** Acts xxiii. 27. — **deliver,** Acts vii. 10, 34. xii. 11. xxvi. 17. Gal. i. 4.

ἐξαίρω.

take away, 1 Cor. v. 2(αἴρω GLT*S*).

put away, 1 Cor. v. 13.

ἐξαιτέομαι.

to desire, Luke xxii. 31.

ἐξαίφνης.

suddenly, Mark xiii. 36. Luke ii. 13. ix. 39. Acts ix. 3. xxii. 6.

ἐξακολουθέω.

follow, 2 Pet. i. 16p. ii. 2, 15.

ἑξακόσιοι.

six hundred, Rev. xiii. 18. xiv. 20.

ἐξαλείφω.

blot out, Acts iii. 19. Col. ii. 14. Rev. iii. 5.

wipe away, Rev. vii. 17. xxi. 4.

ἐξάλλομαι.

leap up, Acts iii. 8.

ἐξανάστασις.

resurrection, Phil. iii. 11.

ἐξανατέλλω.

spring up, Matt. xiii. 5. Mark iv. 5.

ἐξανίστημι.

raise up, Mark xii. 19. Luke xx. 28.

rise up, Acts xv. 5.

ἐξαπατάω.

deceive, Rom. vii. 11. xvi. 18. 1 Cor. iii. 18. 2 Thes. ii. 3.

beguile, 2 Cor. xi. 3.

Add 1 Tim. ii. 14, for ἀπατάω, LT*S*.

ἐξάπινα.

suddenly, Mark ix. 8.

ἐξαπορέομαι.

in despair (*marg.* **altogether without help of means**), 2 Cor. iv. 8p.

to despair, 2 Cor. i. 8.

ἐξαποστέλλω.

send out, Acts vii. 12.

send forth, Acts ix. 30. xi. 22. Gal. iv. 4, 6.

send away, Luke i. 53. xx. 10, 11. Acts xvii. 14.

send, Acts xii. 11. xxii. 21.

Add, for ἀποστέλλω, Luke xxiv. 49, TTr. Acts xiii. 26, LT*S*.

ἐξαρτίζω.

With γίνομαι[cc], **accomplish,** Acts xxi. 5.

furnish throughly (*marg.* **perfect**), 2 Tim. iii. 17.

ἐξαστράπτω.

to glister, Luke ix. 29.

ἐξαυτῆς.

immediately, Acts x. 33. xi. 11. xxi. 32.

straightway, Acts xxiii. 30 (ἐξ αὐτῶν L*S*).

presently, Phil. ii. 23.

by and by, Mark vi. 25.

ἐξεγείρω.

raise up, Rom. ix. 17. 1 Cor. vi. 14.

ἔξειμι.

go out, Acts xiii. 42p.

depart, Acts xvii. 15. xx. 7.

get, Acts xxvii. 43.

ἐξελέγχω.

convince, Jude 15(ἐλέγχω G''LT*S*).

ἐξέλκομαι.

be drawn away, Jas. i. 14p.

ἐξέλω. See ἐξαιρέω.

ἐξέραμα.

vomit, 2 Pet. ii. 22.

ἐξερευνάω (–ραυ–TS).
search diligently, 1 Pet. i. 10.

ἐξέρχομαι.

(With ἀπό, [a]; with ἐκ, [e].)

go out, Matt. ix. 32p. xi. 7, 8, 9. xii. 14. xviii. 28. xx. 1, 3, 5, 6. xxii. 10. xxiv. 1. xxv. 6. xxvi. 30, 71p, 75. Mark i. 35, 45. iii. 21. iv. 3. v. 13, 14(ἔρχομαι G″LTTr). vi. 1, 12. vii. 30. viii. 27. xi. 11. xiv. 26, 48, 68. xvi. 8.
Luke ii. 1. iv. 14. vi. 12. vii. 24, 25, 26. viii. 5, 35. x. 10. xi. 14p (ἐκβάλλω pass L). xiv. 21, 23. xxi. 37. xxii. 62. John. viii. 9(*ap*). x. 9. xi. 31. xiii. 30, 31(30). xviii. 16, 29, 38. Acts i. 21. xii. 9, 10. xv. 24.
Heb. xi. 8*t*. 1 John ii. 19. iv. 1. Rev. iii. 12. vi. 4. xx. 8.

go out of, Matt. xii. 43a. xiii. 1a. Mark v. 30e. vii. 29e. Luke viii. 2a, 33a, 46a. ix. 5pa. xi. 24a. xvii. 29a. John iv. 30e. viii. 59e. Acts xvi. 40e. xix. 12a(ἐκπορεύομαι GLT*S*). 1 Cor. v. 10e.

With ἔξω, παρά[1], **go out of**, Matt. xxi. 17. Luke vi. 19[1]. Acts xvi. 13. —**come forth**, John xix. 5.

go forth, Matt. xiii. 3. xiv. 14. xxiv. 26. xxv. 1. Mark ii. 12, 13. iii. 6. vi. 24. xiv. 16. xvi. 20(*ap*). Luke v. 27. vii. 17. viii. 27p. John i. 43(44). xii. 13. xviii. 1, 4. xix. 4, 17. xx. 3. xxi. 3. Acts xvi. 3. Heb. xiii. 13. 3 John 7. Rev. vi. 2.

go abroad, Matt. ix. 26. John xxi. 23.

go away, Acts x. 23.

go c**thence**, Matt. x. 11.

go, Matt. xv. 21. Luke xiv. 18. xvi. 10, 19. Rom. x. 18. 2 Cor. ii. 13. viii. 17.

proceed, Matt. xv. 19. Jas. iii. 10.

proceed forth, John viii. 42.

spread abroad, Mark i. 28. 1 Thes. i. 8.

depart, Matt. ix. 31p. xxviii. 8(ἀπέρχομαι TTr*S*). Mark vi. 10. vii. 31. ix. 30. Luke iv. 42. v. 8. viii. 35, 38. ix. 4, 6. x. 35p(–GooLTr*S*). xii. 59. John iv. 43. Acts xi. 25. xii. 17. xiv. 20. xv. 40. xvi. 36, 40. xvii. 33. xviii. 23. xx. 1, 11. xxi. 5, 8. Phil. iv. 15.

depart out of, Matt. x. 14p. xvii. 18a. Acts xvi. 39(ἀπέρχομαι ἀπό LT*S*).

get out, Luke xiii. 31.

get out of, Acts vii. 3e. xxii. 18e.

escape, John x. 39.

come out, Matt. v. 26. viii. 32p, 34. xii. 44. xxvi. 55. xxvii. 32p. Mark vi. 34p. ix. 26. Luke i. 22p. iv. 36. xi. 24. xv. 28. xxii. 39, 52. John xvi. 27. xvii. 8. Acts xvi. 18. 1 Cor. xiv. 36. 2 Cor. vi. 17. Heb. xi. 15 (ἐκβαίνω LT*S*). Rev. xiv. 18(–GoL).

come c**thereout**, John xix. 34.

come out of, Matt. ii. 6e. viii. 28e. xv. 22a. xxiv. 27a. xxvii. 53e. Mark i. 25e, 26e, 29pe. v. 2pe, 8e. vi. 54pe. ix. 25e. Luke iv. 35*t*a, 41a. viii. 29a. Acts vii. 4e. viii. 7. xvi. 18a. xxviii. 3e (διεξέρχομαι G′T). Heb. iii. 16e. vii. 5e. Rev. ix. 3e. xiv. 15e, 17e, 20e. xv. 6e. xvi. 17a. xviii. 4e. xix. 5e.

come forth, Matt. xiii. 49. xv. 18. Mark i. 38(ἔρχομαι G′). viii. 11. ix. 29. John xi. 44. xvi. 28, 30. Acts vii. 7.

come, Mark xi. 12p. John xiii. 3. xix. 5. Acts xxviii. 15.

Add Luke xi. 53(*ap*). 2 John 7, for εἰσέρχομαι, G″LT*S*. Rev. xix. 21, for ἐκπορεύομαι, GLTTr*S*.

ἔξεστι.

it is lawful, Matt. xii. 10, 12. xiv. 4. xix. 3. xx. 15. xxii. 17. xxvii. 6. Mark iii. 4. vi. 18. x. 2. xii. 14. Luke vi. 4, 9. xiv. 3. xx. 22. John v. 10. xviii. 31. Acts xxii. 25. 2 Cor. xii. 4(*marg.* **it is possible**).

is (are) lawfulcc, Matt. xii. 2. Mark ii. 24, 26. Luke vi. 2. Acts xvi. 21. 1 Cor. vi. 12*t*. x. 23*t*.

Part., ἐξόν, **lawful**, Matt. xii. 4. —**let**cc, Acts ii. 29(*marg.* **may**).

maycc, Acts viii. 37(*ap*). xxi. 37.

Add Matt. xv. 26, for ἐστι καλόν, LT.

ἐξετάζω.
to search, Matt. ii. 8.
ask, John xxi. 12.
inquire, Matt. x. 11.

ἐξηγέομαι.
declare, John i. 18. Acts x. 8ᵖ. xv. 12, 14. xxi. 19.
tell, Luke xxiv. 35.

ἑξήκοντα.
sixty, Matt. xiii. 23. Mark iv. 8. 20.
sixty-fold, Matt. xiii. 8.
three-score, Luke xxiv. 13. 1 Tim. v. 9. Rev. xi. 3. xii. 6. xiii. 18(δεκαέξ for ἑξήκοντα ἕξ Lᵐ).

ἑξῆς.
next, Luke ix. 37.
With τῇ (*sc.* ἡμέρᾳ), **the next day**, Acts xxvii. 18.—**the day following**, Acts xxi. 1.—**the day after**, Luke vii. 11.—**on the morrow**, Acts xxv. 17.

ἐξηχέομαι.
sound out, 1 Thes. i. 8.

ἕξις.
use, Heb. v. 14 (*marg.* **habit**, or **perfection**).

ἐξίστημι.
make astonished, Luke xxiv. 22.
bewitch, Acts viii. 9, 11.
2nd Aor., and Mid., **be beside one's self**, Mark iii. 21. 2 Cor. v. 13.—**wonder**, Acts viii. 13.—**be astonished**, Mark v. 42. Luke ii. 47. viii. 56. Acts x. 45. xii. 16.—**be amazed**, Matt. xii. 23. Mark ii. 12. vi. 51. Acts ii. 7, 12. ix. 21.

ἐξισχύω.
be able, Eph. iii. 18.

ἔξοδος.
departing, Heb. xi. 22.
decease, Luke ix. 31. 2 Pet. i. 15.

ἐξολοθρεύω.
destroy, Acts iii. 23.

ἐξομολογέω.
to promise, Luke xxii. 6(–L*S*).
Mid., **confess**, Matt. iii. 6. Mark i. 5. Acts xix. 18. Rom. xiv. 11. xv. 9. Phil. ii. 11. Jas. v. 16. Rev. iii. 5(ὁμολογέω, *act.*, GLTTr*S*).—**thank**, Matt. xi. 25. Luke x. 21.

ἐξόν. See ἔξεστι.

ἐξορκίζω.
adjure, Matt. xxvi. 63.

ἐξορκιστής.
exorcist, Acts xix. 13.

ἐξορύσσω, -ττω.
pluck out, Gal. iv. 15.
break up, Mark ii. 4ᵖ.

ἐξουδενέω, set at nought.
For ἐξουδενόω, Mark ix. 12, LTr.
For ἐξουθενέω, 2 Cor. x. 10, L.

ἐξουδενόω.
set at nought, Mark ix. 12(-έω LTr).

ἐξουθενέω.
set at nought, Luke xxiii. 11. Acts iv. 11. Rom. xiv. 10.
despise, Luke xviii. 9. Rom. xiv. 3. 1 Cor. i. 28. xvi. 11. Gal. iv. 14. 1 Thes. v. 20.
Pass., **be least esteemed**, 1 Cor. vi. 4.—**contemptible**, 2 Cor. x. 10ᵖ(ἐξουδενέω L).

ἐξουσία.
power, Matt. ix. 6, 8. x. 1. xxviii. 18. Mark ii. 10. iii. 15. vi. 7. Luke iv. 6, 32. v. 24. x. 19. xii. 5, 11. xxii. 53. John i. 12(*marg.* **right**, or **privilege**). x. 18*t*. xvii. 2. xix. 10*t*, 11. Acts i. 7. v. 4. viii. 19. xxvi. 18.
Rom. ix. 21. xiii. 1*t*, 1(*omS*), 2, 3. 1 Cor. vii. 37. ix. 4, 5, 6, 12*t*, 18. xi. 10 (*see marg.*). 2 Cor. xiii. 10. Eph. i. 21. ii. 2. iii. 10. vi. 12. Col. i. 13, 16. ii. 10, 15. 2 Thes. iii. 9. Tit. iii. 1. Jude 25. Rev. ii. 26. vi. 8. ix. 3*t*, 10, 19. xi. 6*t*. xii. 10. xiii. 4, 5, 7, 12. xiv. 18. xvi. 9. xvii. 12. xviii. 1. xx. 6.
strength, Rev. xvii. 13.
liberty (*marg.* **power**), 1 Cor. viii. 9.
right, Heb. xiii. 10(–T). Rev. xxii. 14.
authority, Matt. vii. 29. viii. 9. xxi. 23*t*, 24, 27. Mark i. 22, 27. xi.

28*t*, 29, 33. xiii. 34. Luke iv. 36. vii. 8. ix. 1. xix. 17. xx. 2*t*, 8, 20. John v. 27. Acts ix. 14. xxvi. 10, 12. 1 Cor. xv. 24. 2 Cor. x. 8. 1 Pet. iii. 22. Rev. xiii. 2.
jurisdiction, Luke xxiii. 7.

ἐξουσιάζω.

have power of, 1 Cor. vii. 4*t*.
bring under power, 1 Cor. vi. 12.
exercise authority upon, Luke xxii. 25.

ἐξοχή.

κατ' ἐξοχὴν ὤν, **principal**, Acts xxv. 23.

ἐξυπνίζω.

awake out of sleep, John xi. 11.

ἔξυπνος.

With γίνομαι, **awake out of sleep**, Acts xvi. 27.

ἔξω.

without, Matt. xii. 46, 47. xxvi. 69. Mark i. 45. iii. 31, 32. xi. 4. Luke i. 10. viii. 20. xiii. 25. John xviii. 16. xx. 11(–L*S*). Acts v. 23 (*omS*). Heb. xiii. 11, 12, 13. Rev. xiv 20(ἔξωθεν GLTTr). xxii. 15.
With art., **one that is without**, Mark iv. 11. 1 Cor. v. 12, 13. Col. iv. 5. 1 Thes. iv. 12.
out, Matt. v. 13. xxvi. 75. Mark xiv. 68. Luke viii. 54(*ap*). xiii. 28. xiv. 35. xxii. 62. xxiv. 50(–G°L[b] Tr*S*). John vi. 37. ix. 34, 35. xii. 31. Acts xvi. 30. 1 John iv. 18. Rev. iii. 12. xi. 2 (ἔξωθεν L, ἔσω *S*).
outward, 2 Cor. iv. 16.
strange, Acts xxvi. 11.
out of, Matt. xxi. 17, 39. Mark v. 10. viii. 23. xi. 19. xii. 8. Luke iv. 29. xiii. 33. xx. 15. Acts iv. 15. vii. 58. xiv. 19. xvi. 13. xxi. 5, 30.
forth, John xi. 43. xv. 6. xix. 4*t*, 5, 13. Acts v. 34. ix. 40.
away, Matt. xiii. 48.
Add Matt. x. 14 (. . that house), LTr*S*. John xviii. 29(out), LTr*S*.

ἔξωθεν.

from without, Mark vii. 15, 18.
without, 2 Cor. vii. 5.
With art., **one (that) which is without**, Luke xi. 40. 1 Tim. iii. 7. Rev. xi. 2 (ἔσωθεν St*S*).—**the outside**, Matt. xxiii. 25. Luke xi. 39.
outward, Matt. xxiii. 27. 1 Pet. iii. 3.
outwardly, Matt. xxiii. 28.
Add Rev. v. 1, for ὄπισθεν, G′. xiv. 20, for ἔξω, GLTTr.

ἐξωθέω.

drive out, Acts vii. 45.
thrust in, Acts xxvii. 39.

ἐξώτερος.

outer, Matt. viii. 12. xxii. 13. xxv. 30.

ἑορτάζω.

keep the feast (*marg.* **holyday**), 1 Cor. v. 8.

ἑορτή.

feast, Matt. xxvi. 5. xxvii. 15. Mark xv. 6. Luke ii. 41, 42. xxii. 1. xxiii. 17(*ap*). John iv. 45*t*. v. 1. vi. 4. vii. 2, 8*t*, 10, 11, 14, 37. xi. 56. xii. 12, 20. xiii. 1, 29. Acts xviii. 21(*ap*).
feast day, Mark xiv. 2. John ii. 23.
holyday, Col. ii. 16.

ἐπαγγελία.

message, 1 John i. 5 (G′, ἀγγελία G LT, ἀπαγγελία *S*).
promise, Luke xxiv. 49. Acts i. 4. ii. 33, 39. vii. 17. xiii. 23, 32. xxiii. 21. xxvi. 6. Rom. iv. 13, 14, 16, 20. ix. 4, 8, 9. xv. 8. 2 Cor. i. 20. vii. 1. Gal. iii. 14, 16, 17, 18*t*, 21, 22, 29. iv. 23, 28. Eph. i. 13. ii. 12. iii. 6. vi. 2. 1 Tim. iv. 8. 2 Tim. i. 1. Heb. iv. 1. vi. 12, 15, 17. vii. 6. viii. 6. ix. 15. x. 36. xi. 9*t*, 13, 17, 33, 39. 2 Pet. iii. 4, 9. 1 John ii. 25.

ἐπαγγέλλομαι.

Mid. and Pass. perf., **to promise**, Mark xiv. 11. Acts vii. 5. Rom. iv. 21. Tit. i. 2. Heb. x. 23. xi. 11. xii. 26. Jas. i. 12. ii. 5. 2 Pet. ii. 19[p]. 1 John ii. 25.—**make promise**, Heb. vi. 13[p].—**profess**, 1 Tim. ii. 10. vi. 21.

Pass. Impers., **promise is made**, Gal. iii. 19.

ἐπάγγελμα.

promise, 2 Pet. i. 4. iii. 13.

ἐπάγω.

bring upon, Acts v. 28. 2 Pet. ii. 1.
bring in upon, 2 Pet. ii. 5.

ἐπαγωνίζομαι.

earnestly contend for, Jude 3.

ἐπαθροίζομαι.

be gathered thick together, Luke xi. 29p.

ἐπαινέω.

to praise, 1 Cor. xi. 2, 17, 22*t*.
laud, Rom. xv. 11.
commend, Luke xvi. 8.

ἔπαινος.

praise, Rom. ii. 29. xiii. 3. 1 Cor. iv. 5. 2 Cor. viii. 18. Eph. i. 6, 12, 14. Phil. i. 11. iv. 8. 1 Pet. i. 7. ii. 14.

ἐπαίρω.

take up, Acts i. 9.
lift up, Matt. xvii. 8p. Luke vi. 20. xi. 27. xvi. 23. xviii. 13. xxi. 28. xxiv. 50. John iv. 35. vi. 5p. xiii. 18. xvii. 1. Acts ii. 14. xiv. 11. xxii. 22. 1 Tim. ii. 8.
hoise up, Acts xxvii. 40.
Mid., **exalt one's self**, 2 Cor. x. 5. xi. 20.

ἐπαισχύνομαι.

be ashamed of, Mark viii. 38*t*. Luke ix. 26*t*. Rom. i. 16. vi. 21(*with* ἐπί). 2 Tim. i. 8, 16.
be ashamed, 2 Tim. i. 12. Heb. ii. 11. xi. 16.

ἐπαιτέω.

beg, Luke xvi. 3.
Add Luke xviii. 35, for προσαιτέω, LTTr*S*.

ἐπακολουθέω.

follow after, 1 Tim. v. 24.
follow, Mark xvi. 20(*ap*). 1 Tim. v. 10. 1 Pet. ii. 21.

ἐπακούω.

hear, 2 Cor. vi. 2.

ἐπακροάομαι.

hear, Acts xvi. 25.

ἐπάν.

when, Matt. ii. 8. Luke xi. 22, 34.

ἐπάναγκες.

necessarycc, Acts xv. 18.

ἐπανάγω.

to return, Matt. xxi. 8p.
In navigation, **thrust out**, Luke v. 3.—**launch out**, Luke v. 4.

ἐπαναμιμνήσκω.

put in mind, Rom. xv. 15.

ἐπαναπαύομαι.

With ἐπί, **rest upon**, Luke x. 6.
rest in, Rom. ii. 17.

ἐπανέρχομαι.

come again, Luke x. 35.
return, Luke xix. 15.

ἐπανίσταμαι.

rise up against, Matt. x. 21. Mark xiii. 12.

ἐπανόρθωσις.

correction, 2 Tim. iii. 16.

ἐπάνω.

above, John iii. 31, 31(*ap*). 1 Cor. xv. 6.
more than, Mark xiv. 5.
over, Matt. ii. 9. xxvii. 37. Luke iv. 39. xi. 44. xix. 17, 19.
upon, Matt. xxiii. 18. xxviii. 2. Rev. xx. 3.
on, Matt. v. 14. xxi. 7. Luke x. 19. Rev. vi. 8.
ἐπ' αὐτοῦ (αὐτῶν), **thereon**, Matt. xxi. 7. xxiii. 20, 22.

ἐπάρατος, accursed.

John vii. 49, for ἐπικατάρατος, LT Tr*S*.

ἐπαρκέω.

relieve, 1 Tim. v. 10, 16*t*.

ἐπαρχία.

province, Acts xxiii. 34. xxv. 1.

ἔπαυλις.

habitation, Acts i. 20.

ἐπαύριον.

With art. τῇ (*sc.* ἡμέρᾳ), **on the**

morrow, Mark xi. 12. Acts x. 9, 23. xx. 7. xxii. 30. xxiii. 32. xxv. 23. —**the morrow after**, Acts x. 24. —**on the next day**, John xii. 12. —**the next day**, Matt. xxvii. 62. John i. 29. Acts xiv. 20. xxi. 8. xxv. 6. —**the next day after**, John i. 35. —**the day following**, John i. 43(44). vi. 22.

ἐπαυτοφώρῳ.

in the very act, John viii. 4(*ap*).

ἐπαφρίζω.

foam out, Jude 13.

ἐπεγείρω.

stir up, Acts xiv. 2.
raise, Acts xiii. 50.

ἐπεί.

since, 2 Cor. xiii. 3.
seeing, Luke i. 34. Heb. iv. 6. v. 11.
seeing that, 2 Cor. xi. 18.
for then, Rom. iii. 6. 1 Cor. v. 10 (*with* ἄρα). Heb. ix. 26. x. 2.
when, Luke vii. 1(*see* ἐπειδή).
for that, Heb. v. 2.
forasmuch as, 1 Cor. xiv. 12. Heb. ii. 14.
because, Matt. xviii. 32. xxvii. 6. Mark xv. 42. John xiii. 29. xix. 31. Heb. vi. 13. xi. 11.
otherwise, Rom. xi. 6, 6(*ap*), 22. Heb. ix. 17.
else, 1 Cor. vii. 14. xiv. 16. xv. 29.
Add Matt. xxi. 46, for ἐπειδή, Tr*S*.

ἐπειδή.

since, 1 Cor. xv. 21.
seeing, Acts xiii. 46. 1 Cor. xiv. 16.
after that, 1 Cor. i. 21.
for that, 2 Cor. v. 4(ἐφ' ᾧ C?LT*S*).
forasmuch as, Acts xv. 24.
for, Luke xi. 6. 1 Cor. i. 22. Phil. ii. 26.
because, Matt. xxi. 46 (ἐπεί Tr*S*). Acts xiv. 12.
Add Luke vii. 1, for ἐπεὶ δέ, LTTr.

ἐπειδήπερ.

forasmuch as, Luke i. 1.

ἐπεῖδον.

look on, Luke i. 25(ἐφεῖδον T).
With ἐπί, **behold**, Acts iv. 29 (ἐφεῖδον LT).

ἔπειμι.

Participle, ἐπιών, ἐπιοῦσα.
following, Acts xxiii. 11.
next, Acts vii. 26.
With art. τῇ (*sc.* ἡμέρᾳ), **the day following**, Acts xxi. 18. —**the next day**, Acts xvi. 11. xx. 15.

ἐπείπερ.

seeing, Rom. iii. 30(εἴ περ G'L*S*).

ἐπεισαγωγή.

bringing in, Heb. vii. 19.

ἐπεισέρχομαι, come in upon.

Luke xxi. 35, for ἐπέρχ., LTTr*S*.

ἔπειτα.

afterward, 1 Cor. xv. 23, 46.
afterwards, Gal. i. 21.
after that, 1 Cor. xii. 28. xv. 6, 7. Heb. vii. 2.
then, Mark vii. 5 (καί G'LTTr*S*). Luke xvi. 7. John xi. 7. Gal i. 18. ii. 1. 1 Thes. iv. 17. Heb. vii. 27. Jas. iii. 17. iv. 14.
Add, for εἶτα, 1 Cor. xii. 28, LT*S*. xv. 7, L[m]T*S*.

ἐπέκεινα.

beyond, Acts vii. 43.

ἐπεκτείνομαι.

reach forth unto, Phil. iii. 13(14).

ἐπενδύομαι.

be clothed upon, 2 Cor. v. 2, 4.

ἐπενδύτης.

fisher's[c] coat, John xxi. 7.

ἐπέρχομαι.

come upon, Luke i. 35. xi. 22. Acts i. 8[p] (*see marg.*). viii. 24. xiii. 40. Jas. v. 1.
come on, Luke xxi. 35 (ἐπεισέρχομαι LTTr*S*).
With art., **those things which are coming on**, Luke xxi. 26[p].
come [c]thither, Acts xiv. 19.
come, Eph. ii. 7.

ἐπερωτάω.

ask of, Mark xi. 29. Acts i. 6(ἐρωτάω LT*S*).

ask, Matt. xii. 10. xvii. 10. xxii. 23, 35, 41, 46. xxvii. 11. Mark v. 9. vii. 5, 17. viii. 5(ἐρωτάω TTr*S*), 23, 27. ix. 11, 16, 21, 28, 32, 33. x. 2, 10, 17. xii. 18, 28, 34. xiii. 3. xiv. 60, 61. xv. 2, 4, 44. Luke iii. 10. vi. 9. viii. 9, 30. ix. 18. xviii. 18, 40. xx. 21, 27, 40. xxi. 7. xxii. 64. xxiii. 3 (ἐρωτάω TTr*S*), 6. John xviii. 7, 21*t* (ἐρωτάω LTTr*S*). Acts v. 27. xxiii. 34. 1 Cor. xiv. 35.
ask a question, Matt. xxii. 35.
ask questions, Luke ii. 46.
question with, Luke xxiii. 9.
ask after, Rom. x. 20.
desire, Matt. xvi. 1.
demand of, Luke iii. 14.
demand, Luke xvii. 20p.
Add Mark viii. 29, for λέγω, G′LT Tr*S*. Luke ix. 45, for ἐρωτάω, L.

ἐπερώτημα.

answer, 1 Pet. iii. 21.

ἐπέχω.

hold forth, Phil ii. 16.
take heed unto, 1 Tim. iv. 16.
give heed unto, Acts iii. 5.
mark, Luke xiv. 7p.
stay, Acts xix. 22.

ἐπηρεάζω.

use despitefully, Matt. v. 44(*ap*). Luke vi. 28.
accuse falsely, 1 Pet. iii. 16.

ἐπί.

I. With the Genitive.

upon, Matt. vi. 19. x. 27. xxiii. 9, 35. xxiv. 3. xxv. 31. Mark vi. 48, 49. vii. 30(*acc.* LTTr*S*). Luke v. 24. xii. 3. xvii. 31. xxi. 25. John xix. 31. Acts xii. 21. Rom. ix. 28. Col. iii. 5. Heb. vi. 7. Rev. iii. 10*t*. . 7, 13(*dat.* LTTr). vii. 10(*dat.* G′L Tr*S*). x. 1(*acc.* LTTr), 5*t*, 8*t*. xi. 0. xii. 1. xiii. 1, 8. xvi. 18. xvii. . xviii. 24. xix. 21. xxi. 5(*dat.* GL Tr*S*).
on, Matt. ix. 2, 6. xiv. 25(*acc.* LT r*S*). xvi. 19*t*. xviii. 18*t*, 19. xxiv. 7. xxvi. 12. xxvii. 19. Mark ii. 10. iv. 1. vi. 47. viii. 6. ix. 3, 20. xiii. 15. xiv. 35. Luke ii. 14. viii. 13, 16. xviii. 8. xxii. 21, 30. John vi. 2, 19. xvii. 4. xix. 19. Acts ii. 30(*acc.* LT*S*). v. 15, 30. x. 39. xxi. 23, 40. xxv. 6, 17. xxvii. 44.
1 Cor. xi. 10. Gal. iii. 13. Eph. i. 10. vi. 3. Col. iii. 2. Heb. viii. 4. xi. 13. xii. 25. Jas. v. 5, 17. Rev. iv. 2(*acc.* LT*S*), 9(*dat.* L*S*), 10. v. 1, 10. vi. 10, 16(*dat.* T*S*). vii. 1*t*, 15(*dat.* T). ix. 17. xi. 10. xiii. 14*t*. xiv. 6, 14(*acc.* LT), 15. xvii. 8, 9. xix. 4 (*dat.* G′LTTr*S*), 18 (*acc.* L, *dat.* *S*), 19. xx. 6, 11(*acc.* GT).
ἐφ᾽ οὗ, **whereon,** Luke iv. 29.
over, Matt. xxiv. 45. xxv. 21, 23. Luke xii. 42. Acts vi. 3. Rom. ix. 5. Rev. ii. 26. ix. 11. xi. 6. xiv. 18. xvii. 18.
With εἰμί, **have the charge of,** Acts viii. 27.
above, Eph. iv. 6.
before, Mark xiii. 9. Acts xxiii. 30. xxiv. 19, 20. xxv. 9, 26*t*. xxvi. 2. 1 Cor. vi. 1*t*, 6. 2 Cor. vii. 14. 1 Tim. v. 19(*marg.* **under**). vi. 13.
about, Mark xiv. 51. John xx. 7.
at, Luke xx. 37. xxii. 30, 40. John vi. 21. xxi. 1. Acts xxv. 10.
in, Matt. ii. 22(-G°LTrb*S*). iv. 6. vi. 10. xviii. 16. xix. 28. xxi. 19. xxiii. 2. xxiv. 30. xxvi. 64. xxviii. 18. Mark iv. 31, 31((*ap*). viii. 4. xii. 14, 26. Luke iv. 11. v. 18. vi. 17. xi. 2(*ap*). xvii. 34. xxi. 23. John xix. 13. Acts ii. 19. viii. 28. xx. 9. Rom. i. 9(10). 1 Cor. viii. 5. 2 Cor. xiii. 1. Eph. i. 16. Col. i. 16, 20. 1 Thes. i. 2. 1 Tim. vi. 17. Phm. 4. Heb. i. 2(1). viii. 10(*marg.* **upon**). x. 16(*acc.* L*S*). 1 Pet. i. 20. 2 Pet. iii. 3. Rev. i. 20(ἐν L). v. 13. ix. 4. xi. 8. xiii. 16, 16 (*acc.* GLTTr*S*). xiv. 1, 9. xviii. 17. xxii. 4.
ἐπὶ τοῦ ἀμφόδου, **in a place where two ways meet,** Mark xi. 4.
in the time of, Luke iv. 27.
in the days of, Mark ii. 26. Acts xi. 28.

ἐπὶ ἀρχιερέως Ἄννα καὶ Καϊάφα, **A. and C. being the high priests,** Luke iii. 2.

to, John xxi. 11(*εἰς* LTr*S*). Acts x. 11.

into, Mark iv. 26. Heb. x. 16.

of, Luke iv. 25. xxii. 59. Acts iv. 27. x. 34. Gal. iii. 16*t*. Heb. xi. 4. Rev. viii. 13.

Not rendered, Mark xii. 32. Eph. iii. 15?(*see* ἐν) Rev. xxi. 16(*acc.* G LTTr).

Add, for ἐν, Jude 18, G″LT*S*. Rev. v. 13, xxi. 14, GLTTr*S*. For ἐπάνω, Matt. xxi. 7, LTr*S*. For πρό, Acts v. 23, LT*S*. For ὑπό, Acts xxiv. 21, LT.

See also ἀλήθεια, ἀκούω, κοιτών, μετοικεσία.

II. With the Dative.

upon, Matt. xvi. 18. Mark vi. 39. xi. 7 (*acc.* G″LTTr*S*). xiii. 2 (*acc.* Tr*S*). Luke xix. 44(*acc.* Tr*S*). xxi. 6. John iv. 27. xi. 38. Acts viii. 16. Eph. ii. 20. iv. 26. Phil. i. 3. ii. 17, 27(*acc.* GLT*S*). Heb. viii. 6. Rev. xix. 14.

on, Mark ii. 21(*acc.* LTTr*S*). Luke vii. 13. John iv. 6. Acts xxvii. 44. Rom. ix. 33. x. 11. 1 Tim. i. 16. 1 Pet. ii. 6. Rev. vi. 2 and 5 (*acc.* GLTTr*S*).

ἐπ' αὐτῷ, **thereon,** Rev. vi. 4 (*acc.* GLTTr*S*).

ἐφ' ᾧ (ῇ, οἷς), **whereon,** Luke v. 25 (*acc.* G″TTr*S*). — **wherein,** Mark ii. 4(ὅπου G′LTr*S*). Luke xi. 22. Phil. iv. 10. — **wherefore,** Matt. xxvi. 50 (G′, *acc.* GLTTr*S*).— **for that,** Rom. v. 12 (*marg.* **in whom**). — **whereof,** Rom. vi. 21.

over, Matt. xxiv. 47. Luke xii. 44. xv. 7*t*, 10. xix. 41 (*acc.* LTTr*S*). xxiii. 38. Acts viii. 2. 1 Thes. iii. 7. Rev. xi. 10. xviii. 11(*acc.* TTr*S*).

above, Luke iii. 20. Eph. vi. 16(ἐν L*S*). Col. iii. 14.

beside, Matt. xxv. 20 and 22 (–G° LTr*S*). Luke xvi. 26 (ἐνLᵐ*S*).

at, Matt. vii. 28. xxii. 33. xxiv. 33. Mark i. 22. x. 22, 24. xi. 18. xii. 17. xiii. 29. Luke i. 14, 29 (–G′). ii. 33, 47. iv. 22, 32. v. 5, 9, 27. ix. 43*t*. xx. 26. John viii. 7 (*ap*). Acts iii. 10*t*, 12. v. 9. xiii. 12. 1 Cor. xiv. 16. Rev. xxi. 12(*ap*).

unto, Matt. ix. 16. Gal. v. 13. Eph. ii. 10. 1 Thes. iv. 7.

to, 2 Tim. ii. 14.

toward, Mark vi. 34(*acc.* LTTr*S*).

against, Luke xii. 52*t*, 53*t*, 53*t*(*acc.* LTTr*S*).

before, Rev. x. 11.

in, Matt. xiii. 14 (*omS*). xiv. 8, 11. xviii. 5. xxiv. 5. Mark iv. 38 (G′, ἐν GLTTr*S*). v. 33 (–LᵇTr*S*). vi. 25, 28, 55. ix. 37, 39. x. 24. xiii. 6. Luke i. 47. ix. 48, 49. xviii. 9. xxi. 8. xxiv. 47. Acts ii. 26, 38 (ἐν L). iii. 11. iv. 17, 18. v. 28, 40. xiv. 3.

Rom. iv. 18. v. 2. viii. 20. xv. 12. 1 Cor. ix. 10*t*. xiii. 6. 2 Cor. i. 4, 9*t*. iii. 14. vii. 4, 7, 13. ix. 14. 1 Thes. iii. 7. 1 Tim. iv. 10. v. 5. Tit. i. 2 (*marg.* **for**). Phm. 7. Heb. ii. 13. ix. 10, 26. 1 John iii. 3. Rev. ix. 4. xxii. 16(ἐν LTr, –G°T).

by, Matt. iv. 4, 4 (ἐν G″LTTr). Luke iv. 4, 4(*ap*) John v. 2. Rom. x. 19*t*. Phil. iii. 9.

with, Matt. xviii. 26(*acc.* Tr), 29 (*acc.* LTr). Luke xviii. 7. Acts xxi. 24. xxviii. 14(παρά L*S*). Rev. xii. 17(–L).

ἐπὶ τούτοις, **therewith,** 3 John 10.

through, Acts iii. 16. 1 Cor. viii 11(ἐν G″LT*S*).

under, Heb. vii. 11(*gen.* G′LT*S*) ix. 15. x. 28.

after, Luke i. 59. Rom. v. 14.

about, Acts xi. 19(*gen.* G″L).

as touching, Acts v. 35.

for, Matt. xix. 9. Mark iii. 5. Luk ii. 20. xiii. 17. Acts iv. 21. xv. 1 (–G°°LT*S*), 31. xx. 38. xxvi. 1 Cor. i. 4. 2 Cor. vii. 13. ix. 13, 1

Phil. i. 5. iii. 12. 1 Thes. iii. 9. Jas. v. 1, 7. Rev. xviii. 9(*acc.*TTr*S*).

on one's behalf, Rom. xvi. 19.

of, Matt. xviii. 13*t*. Mark vi. 52. John xii. 16. Acts iv. 9. 1 Cor. xvi. 17. 2 Cor. xii. 21. Heb. viii. 1. xi. 4.

Add, for ἐν, Mark i. 45, TTr*S*. Eph. i. 10[2d], L*S*. 1 Tim. vi. 17[2d], L*S*. Heb. xi. 38, LT*S*. — Matt. xxvii. 42 (believe . .), G′T. Mark vi. 27 (ἐπὶ πίνακι), L[b]. 2 Cor. v. 4, *see* ἐπειδή. Rev. x. 11(. . nations), T.

See also εὐλογία, κατάκειμαι, νεκρός, πιστεύω.

III. With the Accusative.

upon, Matt. iii. 16. vii. 24, 25, 26. ix. 18. x. 13. xi. 29. xii. 18. xiii. 5. xix. 28. xxi. 5. xxiii. 35, 36. xxiv. 2. xxvii. 29 (*gen.* TTr*S*), 35 (*ap*). Mark i. 10 (εἰς LTTr). viii. 25. x. 16. xv. 24.

Luke i. 12, 35. ii. 25, 40. iii. 22. iv. 18. v. 19, 36. vi. 48, 49(*ap*). viii. 6. ix. 38. x. 6. xi. 20. xiii. 4. xix. 35, 43. xx. 18. xxi. 34. xxiv. 49. John i. 32, 33, 51 (52). ix. 15. xviii. 4.

Acts i. 8, 26. ii. 3, 17. iv. 33. v. 11*t*, 28. vii. 57. viii. 24. x. 9. xiii. 11, 40(-LT*S*). xv. 10. xviii. 6. xxi. 35. xxvi. 16.

Rom. ii. 9. iii. 22(*ap*). iv. 9*t*. xv. 20. 1 Cor. iii. 12. 2 Cor. i. 23. iii. 15. xii. 9. Gal. vi. 16. Eph. v. 6. 1 Thes. ii. 16. Heb. xi. 21. Jas. ii. 21. 1 Pet. iv. 14. v. 7. Rev. i. 17. ii. 24. iii. 3, 12. iv. 4. viii. 3, 10*t*. x. 2 (*gen.* GLTTr*S*). xi. 11*t*, 16. xii. 3. xiii. 1(xii. 18), 1. xiv. 14. xvi. 2(εἰς G″LTTr), 8, 10, 12, 21. xvii. 3, 5, 16(καί GLTTr*S*). xix. 11. xx. 4*t*.

on, Matt. iv. 5. v. 15, 39(εἰς LTr*S*), 45*t*. x. 29 (-G[oo]), 34. xiii. 2. xiv. 19(*gen.* LTr*S*), 26 (*gen.* L*S*), 28, 29. xv. 32, 35. xvii. 6. xxi. 44*t* (*ap*). xxiii. 4. xxvi. 7(*gen.* LTr*S*), 39, 50. xxvii. 25*t*.

Mark iv. 5, 16, 20, 21, 38. viii. 2. ix. 22. xiv. 46 (-TTr*S*). xvi. 18 (*ap*). Luke i. 65. iv. 9. v. 12. vi. 29, 48. viii. 8(εἰς GLTTr*S*). x. 34, 35. xi. 33. xv. 5, 20. xvii. 16. xx. 18, 19. xxi. 12, 35*t*. xxiii. 30.

John i. 33. iii. 36. vii, 30, 44. xii. 15. xiii. 25. xxi. 20. Acts ii. 18*t*. iv. 5, 22. v. 5, 18. vii. 54. viii. 17. ix. 17. x. 44, 45. xi. 15*t*, 17. xiii. 11. xiv. 10. xvi. 31. xvii. 26 (*gen.* LT*S*). xix. 6, 16, 17. xx. 37. xxi. 5, 27. xxii. 19. xxviii. 3.

Rom. iv. 5, 24. ix. 23. xi. 22. xii. 20. xv. 3. 1 Cor. xiv. 25. Gal. vi. 16. Col. iii. 6(*ap*). 1 Tim. i. 18. Tit. iii. 6. 1 Pet. ii. 24(*marg.* **to**) Rev. iii. 3(-G[o]LTTr[b]). iv. 4. vi. 16. vii. 1*t*, 11, 16. ix. 7. x. 2 (*gen.* GLTTr*S*). xi. 16. xiv. 1, 16(*gen.* LTr*S*), 16. xv. 2. xviii. 19. xix. 12, 16*t*. xx. 9.

ἐπ' αὐτό, **thereon,** John xii. 14.

ἐφ' ὅν, **whereon,** Mark xi. 2. Luke xix. 30.

over, Matt. xxv. 21, 23. xxvii. 45. Mark xv. 33. Luke i. 33. ii. 8. ix. 1. x. 19. xii. 14. xix. 14, 27. xxiii. 44. Acts vii. 10, 11, 27(*gen.* LT*S*). xix. 13.

Rom. v. 14. 2 Cor. iii. 13. Heb. ii. 7(*ap*). iii. 6. x. 21. Jas. v. 14. 1 Pet. iii. 12. Rev. vi. 8. xiii. 7. xvi. 9. xviii. 20(*dat.* GLTTr*S*).

above, 2 Thes. ii. 4.

unto, Matt. vi. 27. xii. 28. xxvii. 27. Mark v. 21. xv. 22, 46. xvi. 2. Luke iii. 2. vi. 35. x. 9, 11(*om S*). xii. 11. xxiii. 1. xxiv. 1, 12(*ap*). John vi. 16. Acts viii. 26, 36. ix. 21. x. 11(*om S*). xi. 11, 21. xii. 10. xiv. 13, 15. xvi. 19. xvii. 6, 19. xix. 12. xxi. 32. xxiv. 8(*ap*). xxv. 12. xxvi. 18.

2 Thes. ii. 1. 2 Tim. ii. 16. iv. 4. Heb. vi. 1. 1 Pet. ii. 25. Rev. vii. 17. xvi. 14. xxii. 18.

to, Matt. iii. 7, 13. v. 23. xiii. 48. xxi. 19. Mark xi. 13. Luke i. 16, 17. v. 11. viii. 27. ix. 62. x. 6. xii. 25, 58. xvii. 4 (πρός LTr*S*, -GT). xix. 5. xxii. 44(*ap*), 52. xxiii. 33, 48. xxiv. 24. John xix. 33. Acts

viii. 32. ix. 4, 35. xii. 12. xv. 19. xvii. 14. xviii. 12. xx. 13. xxvi. 20. xxvii. 43, 44.
Gal. iv. 9. Jas. ii. 3. 2 Pet. ii. 22. Rev. xxi. 10. xxii. 14.
toward, Matt. xii. 49. xiv. 14(*dat.* GLTTr*S*). Rom. xi. 22. 1 Cor. vii. 36. Eph. ii. 7. Heb. vi. 1.
after, Luke xv. 4.
against, Matt. x. 21. xii. 26. xxiv. 7*t*. xxvi. 55. Mark iii. 24, 25, 26. x. 11. xiii. 8*t*, 12. xiv. 48. Luke ix. 5. xi. 17*t*, 18. xii. 53*t*. xiv. 31. xxi. 10*t*. xxii. 52, 53. John xiii. 18. Acts iv. 27. viii. 1. xiii. 50, 51.
Rom. i. 18. ii. 2. 2 Cor. x. 2. 1 Pet. iii. 12(*Gr.* upon).
at, Matt. ix. 9. Mark ii. 14. Luke v. 27. xxiv. 22. John viii. 59. Acts iii. 1. x. 25. Rev. iii. 20. viii. 3 (*gen.* G″T*S*).
into, Matt. xiii. 8, 20, 23. xviii. 12. xxii. 9. xxiv. 16(εἰς LTr). Mark vi. 53. Luke xix. 4, 23. Acts vii. 23. ix. 11. 1 Cor. ii. 9. Rev. xi. 11 (ἐν GLT, εἰς *S*, –Tr).
ἐπὶ τὸ αὐτό, **into one place**, 1 Cor. xi. 20. xiv. 23. (*See also* αὐτός, II.)
in, Matt. xxvii. 29(ἐν G″LTTr*S*), 43(*dat.* L). Mark xv. 1 (–LTTr*S*). Acts ix. 42. xxvii. 20. 2 Cor. ii. 3. 1 Tim. v. 5. 1 Pet. iii. 5(εἰς G′LT). Rev. ii. 17. v. 1. xiv. 9. xvii. 8. xx. 1, 4.
among, Matt. xiii. 7. Acts i. 21. 2 Thes. i. 10. Rev. vii. 15.
before, Matt. x. 18. Luke xxi. 12. Acts x. 17.
about, Matt. xviii. 6(εἰς G″T, περί LTr*S*).
with, Heb. viii. 8*t*.
touching, 2 Thes. iii. 4.
of, Mark ix. 12, 13. Heb. vii. 13.
because of, Rev. i. 7.
for, Luke vii. 44. xviii. 4. xxiii. 28*tr*. John xix. 24. Phil. iii. 14(εἰς LT*S*). Heb. xii. 10. 1 Pet. i. 13.
throughout[c], Luke iv. 25. Acts xi. 28.
for the space of, Acts xix. 8.
by the space of, Acts xix. 10.
the space of, Acts xix. 34.
Not rendered (in notation of time), Luke iv. 25 (–LTr). Acts xiii. 31. xvi. 18. xvii. 2. xviii. 20. Heb. xi. 30.
Add, for εἰς, Matt. xiv. 34, Tr*S*. xxii. 5[2d], G′LTTr*S*. Mark iv. 7, L[m]. Luke iv. 43, LTTr*S*. xii. 49, G″L Tr*S*. John iii. 15, L. xxi. 4, G′L*S*. Acts xx. 13, LT*S*. 2 Tim. ii. 14, L T*S*. Rev. xvi. 2, G′LTTr*S*. 17, GL TTr*S*. For πρός, Rev. xxii. 18, GL TTr*S*. — Matt. xxi. 5(. . a colt), LT Tr*S*. xxvii. 42 (believe . .), Tr*S*. John xix. 2 (on[1st]), L[m]. Acts vii. 18 (ἐπ' Αἴγυπτον), L*S*. Rev. xiv. 6 (unto), GLTTr*S*. xxii. 5(. . them), G[pr]LTTr[b]*S*.
See also ἐπεῖδον, ἐπιβλέπω, ἐπικαλέω, ἐπιπίπτω, ἐπιχρίω, θάμβος, ἱκανός, ὅσος, πλείων, πολύς, τρίς, χείρων, χρόνος.

ἐπιβαίνω.

come into, Acts xx. 18 (*with* εἰς). xxv. 1[p].
enter into, Acts xxvii. 2.
go aboard, Acts xxi. 2.
take ship, Acts xxi. 6 (ἐμβαίνω L, ἀναβαίνω T*S*).
Perf., with ἐπί, **sit upon**, Matt. xxi. 5.
Add Acts xxi. 4, for ἀναβαίνω, LT*S*.

ἐπιβάλλω.

cast upon, 1 Cor. vii. 35.
cast on, Mark xi. 7.
lay on, Acts iv. 3.
With ἐπί, **put upon**, Luke v. 36. — **put unto**, Matt. ix. 16. — **put to**, Luke ix. 62. — **lay on**, Matt. xxvi. 50. Mark xiv. 46. Luke xx. 19. xxi. 12. John vii. 30 (βάλλω L[m]), 44(βάλλω LTTr) Acts v. 18. xxi. 27.
With εἰς, **beat into**, Mark iv. 37.
stretch forth, Acts xii. 1(*marg., with* χείρ, **begin**).
fall to, Luke xv. 12. [κλαίω).
think [c]**thereon**, Mark xiv. 72[p] (*see*

ἐπιβαρέω.
be chargeable unto, 1 Thes. ii. 9.
be chargeable to, 2 Thes. iii. 8.
overcharge, 2 Cor. ii. 5.

ἐπιβιβάζω.
set on, Luke x. 34. xix. 35. Acts xxiii. 24.

ἐπιβλέπω.
With ἐπί, **look upon**, Luke ix. 38. —**have respect to**, Jas. ii. 3. —**regard**, Luke i. 48.

ἐπίβλημα.
piece, Matt. ix. 16. Mark ii. 21. Luke v. 36, 36(-G∞T).

ἐπιβοάω.
to cry, Acts xxv. 24(βοάω LS).

ἐπιβουλή.
laying await, Acts ix. 24.
lying in wait, Acts xx. 19.
With γίνομαι, **lay wait for**cc, Acts xx. 3p.
With μέλλειν ἔσεσθαι, **lay wait**cc, Acts xxiii. 30p(-μέλλειν LS).

ἐπιγαμβρεύω.
marry, Matt. xxii. 24.

ἐπίγειος.
in earth, Phil. ii. 10.
earthly, 2 Cor. v. 1. Jas. iii. 19.
Plur., with art., **earthly things**, John iii. 12. Phil. iii. 19.
terrestrial, 1 Cor. xv. 40*t*.

ἐπιγίνομαι.
to blow, Acts xxviii. 13.
Add Acts xxvii. 27, for γίνομαι, T.

ἐπιγινώσκω.
know well, 2 Cor. vi. 9.
know, Matt. vii. 16, 20. xi. 27*t*. xvii. 12. Mark v. 30. vi. 33(γινώσκω LTr), 54. Luke i. 4. vii. 37p. xxiii. 7p. xxiv. 16, 31. Acts iii. 10. ix. 30p. xii. 14p. xix. 34p. xxii. 24, 29p. xxv. 10. xxvii. 39. xxviii. 1. Rom. i. 32. 1 Cor. xiii. 12*t*. 2 Cor. xiii. 5. Col. i. 6. 1 Tim. iv. 3. 2 Pet. ii. 21, 21p.
perceive, Mark ii. 8p. Luke i. 22. v. 22p.
take knowledge of, Acts iv. 13. xxiv. 8.
have knowledge of, Matt. xiv. 35p.
acknowledge, 1 Cor. xiv. 37. xvi. 18. 2 Cor. i. 13*t*, 14.
Add, for γινώσκω, Acts xxiii. 28, xxiv. 11, LT*S*.

ἐπίγνωσις.
knowledge, Rom. i. 28 (*marg., with* ἔχω ἐν, **acknowledge**). iii. 20. x. 2. Eph. i. 17 (*marg.* **acknowledgment**). iv. 13. Phil. i. 9. Col. i. 9, 10. iii. 10. 1 Tim. ii. 4. 2 Tim. iii. 7. Heb. x. 26. 2 Pet. i. 2, 3, 8. ii. 20.
acknowledging, 2 Tim. ii. 25. Tit. i. 1. Phm. 6.
acknowledgement, Col. ii. 2.

ἐπιγραφή.
superscription, Matt. xxii. 20(*marg.* **inscription**). Mark xii. 16. xv. 26. Luke xx. 24. xxiii. 38.

ἐπιγράφω.
write c**thereon**, Rev. xxi. 12.
write over, Mark xv. 26.
write in, Heb. viii. 10. x. 16.
ἐν ᾧ ἐπεγέγραπτο, **with this inscription**, Acts xvii. 23.
Add Luke xxiii. 38, for γράφω, LTrb.

ἐπιδείκνυμι.
to show, Matt. xvi. 1. xxii. 19. xxiv. 1. Luke xvii. 14. xx. 24(δείκνυμι GLTTr*S*). xxiv. 40(*ap*). Acts xviii. 28. Heb. vi. 17.
Mid., **show**, Acts ix. 39.

ἐπιδέχομαι.
receive, 3 John 9, 10.

ἐπιδημέω.
be c**there**, Acts xvii. 21.
stranger, Acts ii. 10p.

ἐπιδιατάσσομαι, -ττομαι.
add c**thereto**, Gal. iii. 15.

ἐπιδίδωμι.
deliver, Luke iv. 17. Acts xv. 30.
Part., with φέρω, *pass.*, **let drive**, Acts xxvii. 15.
give, Matt. vii. 9, 10. Luke xi. 11*t*.

xxiv. 30, 42. John xiii. 26(καὶ δίδωμι αὐτῷ LTr).
offer, Luke xi. 12.

ἐπιδιορθόω.

Mid., **set in order,** Tit. i. 5.

ἐπιδύω.

With ἐπί, **go down upon,** Eph. iv. 26.

ἐπιείκεια.

gentleness, 2 Cor. x. 1.
clemency, Acts xxiv. 4.

ἐπιεικής.

With art., **moderation,** Phil. iv. 5.
gentle, Tit. iii. 2. Jas. iii. 17. 1 Pet. ii. 18.
patient, 1 Tim. iii. 3.

ἐπιζητέω.

seek after, Matt. vi. 32. xii. 39. xvi. 4. Mark viii. 12(ζητέω LTTr*S*). Luke xii. 30.
seek for, Acts xii. 19p. Rom. xi. 7.
seek, Luke xi. 29. Heb. xi. 14. xiii. 14.
desire, Acts xiii. 7. Phil. iv. 17*t*.
inquire, Acts xix. 39.
Add Luke iv. 42, for ζητέω, GLT Tr*S*.

ἐπιθανάτιος.

appointed (approved 1611, *err.*) **to death,** 1 Cor. iv. 9.

ἐπίθεσις.

putting on, 2 Tim. i. 6.
laying on, Acts viii. 18. 1 Tim. iv. 14. Heb. vi. 2.

ἐπιθυμέω.

to desire, Matt. xiii. 17. Luke xvi. 21. xvii. 22. xxii. 15. 1 Tim. iii. 1. Heb. vi. 11. 1 Pet. i. 12. Rev. ix. 6.
would fain, Luke xv. 16.
covet, Acts xx. 33. Rom. vii. 7. xiii. 9.
lust after, Matt. v. 28.
lust, 1 Cor. x. 6. Gal. v. 17. Jas. iv. 2.

ἐπιθυμητής.

With εἰμί, **lust after,** 1 Cor. x. 6.

ἐπιθυμία.

desire, Luke xxii. 15 (*dat.*, *marg.* **heartily**). Phil. i. 23. 1 Thes. ii. 17.
lust, Mark iv. 19. John viii. 44. Rom. i. 24. vi. 11(*ap*). vii. 7(*marg.* **concupiscence**). xiii. 14. Gal. v. 16, 24. Eph. ii. 3. iv. 22. 1 Tim. vi. 9. 2 Tim. ii. 22. iii. 6. iv. 3. Tit. ii. 12. iii. 3. Jas. i. 14, 15. 1 Pet. i. 14. ii. 11. iv. 2, 3. 2 Pet. i. 4. ii. 10, 18. iii. 3. 1 John ii. 16*t*, 17. Jude 16, 18.
that.. lusteth aftercc, Rev. xviii. 14.
concupiscence, Rom. vii. 8. Col. iii. 5. 1 Thes. iv. 5.

ἐπικαθίζω.

With ἐπάνω, **set on,** Matt. xxi. 7 (*sing. intrans.*, StGLTTr, καθίζω *S*).

ἐπικαλέω.

Mid., **call upon,** Acts vii. 59. Rom. x. 12, 13. 1 Cor. i. 2. — **call on,** Acts ii. 21. ix. 14, 21. xxii. 16. Rom. x. 14. 2 Tim. ii. 22. 1 Pet. i. 17. — **call,** 2 Cor. i. 23. — **appeal unto,** Acts xxv. 11, 12. xxvi. 32. xxviii. 19. — **appeal to,** Acts xxv. 25. — **appeal,** Acts xxv. 21p.
Pass., **be called upon,** Acts xv. 17 (*with* ἐπί . . ἐπί). — **be called by**cc, Jas. ii. 7(*with* ἐπί). — **be called,** Heb. xi. 16. — **be surnamed,** Luke xxii. 3 (καλέω TTr*S*). Acts i. 23. iv. 36. x. 18. xv. 22(καλέω LT*S*). — **be one's surname**cc, Matt. x. 3 (-G°LTTr*S*). Acts x. 5, 32. xi. 13. xii. 12, 25.
Add Matt. x. 25, for καλέω, GLT Tr*S*, *mid. S.*

ἐπικάλυμμα.

cloak, 1 Pet. ii. 16.

ἐπικαλύπτω.

to cover, Rom. iv. 7.

ἐπικατάρατος.

cursed, John vii. 49 (ἐπάρατος LT Tr*S*). Gal. iii. 10, 13.

ἐπίκειμαι.

lie upon, John xi. 38(*with* ἐπί).
lie on, Acts xxvii. 20p.
be laid upon, 1 Cor. ix. 16.
be laid c**thereon,** John xxi. 9p.
be imposed on, Heb. ix. 10.
press upon, Luke v. 1.
be instant, Luke xxiii. 23.

ἐπικέλλω, drive *or* thrust upon.
Acts xxvii. 41, for ἐποκέλλω, LT*S*.

ἐπικουρία.
help, Acts xxvi. 22.

ἐπικρίνω.
give sentence, Luke xxiii. 24(*marg.* **assent**).

ἐπιλαμβάνομαι.
take hold of, Luke xx. 20, 26.
take on, Heb. ii. 16*t*(*Gr.* take hold of).
take by, Mark viii. 23. Acts xxiii. 19. Heb. viii. 9[p].
take, Luke ix. 47. xiv. 4. Acts ix. 27. xvii. 19. xviii. 17. xxi. 30, 33.
lay hold upon, Luke xxiii. 26.
lay hold on, 1 Tim. vi. 12, 19.
catch, Matt. xiv. 31. Acts xvi. 19.

ἐπιλανθάνομαι.
forget, Matt. xvi. 5. Mark viii. 14. Luke xii. 6. Phil. iii. 13(14). Heb. vi. 10. xiii. 26. Jas. i. 24.
be forgetful, Heb. xiii. 2.

ἐπιλέγω.
to call, John v. 2.
Mid., **choose,** Acts xv. 40.

ἐπιλείπω.
fail, Heb. xi. 32.

ἐπιλείχω, lick over.
Luke xvi. 21, for ἀπολείχω, LTTr*S*.

ἐπιλησμονή.
forgetful[cc], Jas. i. 25.

ἐπίλοιπος.
rest of, 1 Pet. iv. 2.

ἐπίλυσις.
interpretation, 2 Pet. i. 20.

ἐπιλύω.
expound, Mark iv. 34.
determine, Acts xix. 39.

ἐπιμαρτυρέω.
testify, 1 Pet. v. 12.

ἐπιμέλεια.
Lit. care; *with* τυγχάνω, **refresh one's self,** Acts xxvii. 3.

ἐπιμελέομαι.
take care of, Luke x. 34, 35. 1 Tim. iii. 5.

ἐπιμελῶς.
diligently, Luke xv. 8.

ἐπιμένω.
abide in, Rom. xi. 23. Phil. i. 24 (*with* ἐν).
abide, Acts xv. 34(*ap*). Gal. i. 18.
tarry, Acts x. 48. xxi. 4, 10[p]. xxviii. 12, 14. 1 Cor. xvi. 7, 8.
continue in, Acts xiii. 43(προσμένω GLT*S*). Rom. vi. 1. xi. 22. Col. i. 23. 1 Tim iv. 16.
continue, John viii. 7 (*ap*). Acts xii. 16.

ἐπινεύω.
to consent, Acts xviii. 20.

ἐπίνοια.
thought, Acts viii. 22.

ἐπιορκέω.
forswear one's self, Matt. v. 33.

ἐπίορκος.
perjured person, 1 Tim. i. 10.

ἐπιοῦσα. See ἔπειμι.

ἐπιούσιος.
daily, Matt. vi. 11. Luke xi. 3.

ἐπιπίπτω.
With ἐπί, **fall upon,** Luke i. 12. Acts viii. 16.—**fall on,** Luke xv. 20. Acts x. 44 (πίπτω L). xi. 15. xiii. 11 (πίπτω L*S*). xix. 17 (πίπτω L). xx. 37. Rom. xv. 3.—**fall into**[cc], Acts x. 10(γίνομαι G″LT*S*).—**lie on,** John xiii. 25(ἀναπίπτω G′LTTr).
fall on, Acts xx. 10.
press(*marg.* **rush**) **upon,** Mark iii. 10.
Add Rev. xi. 11, for πίπτω; G″L TTr.

ἐπιπλήσσω, -ττω.
to rebuke, 1 Tim. v. 1.

ἐπιποθέω.
desire earnestly, 2 Cor. v. 2.
desire greatly, 1 Thes. iii. 6. 2 Tim. i. 4.
desire, 1 Pet. ii. 2.

long after, 2 Cor. ix. 14. Phil. ii. 26(p *with* εἰμί).
long after greatly, Phil. i. 8.
long, Rom. i. 11.
lust, Jas. iv. 5.

ἐπιπόθησις.

earnest desire, 2 Cor. vii. 7.
vehement desire, 2 Cor. vii. 11.

ἐπιπόθητος.

longed for, Phil. iv. 1.

ἐπιποθία.

great desire, Rom. xv. 23.

ἐπιπορεύομαι.

With πρός, **come to**, Luke viii. 4.

ἐπιῤῥάπτω.

With ἐπί, **sew on**, Mark ii. 21.

ἐπιῤῥίπτω.

With ἐπί, **cast upon**, Luke xix. 35. 1 Pet. v. 7.

ἐπίσημος.

of note, Rom. xvi. 7.
notable, Matt. xxvii. 16.

ἐπισιτισμός.

victuals, Luke ix. 12.

ἐπισκέπτομαι.

look out, Acts vi. 3.
visit, Matt. xxv. 36, 43. Luke i. 68, 78. vii. 16. Acts vii. 23. xv. 14, 36. Heb. ii. 6. Jas. i. 27.

ἐπισκευάζομαι, equip one's self for.

Acts xxi. 15, for ἀποσκευ., G'LT*S*.

ἐπισκηνόω.

With ἐπί, **rest upon**, 2 Cor. xii. 9.

ἐπισκιάζω.

overshadow, Matt. xvii. 5. Mark ix. 7. Luke i. 35. ix. 34. Acts v. 15.

ἐπισκοπέω.

take the oversight, 1 Pet. v. 2.
look diligently, Heb. xii. 15.

ἐπισκοπή.

visitation, Luke xix. 44. 1 Pet. ii. 12.
office of a bishop, 1 Tim. iii. 1.
bishopric, Acts i. 20(*marg.* **office**, *or* **charge**).

Add 1 Pet. v. 6(time . .), L.

ἐπίσκοπος.

overseer, Acts xx. 28.
bishop, Phil. i. 1. 1 Tim. iii. 2. Tit. i. 7. 1 Pet. ii. 25(*said of Christ*).

ἐπισπάομαι.

become uncircumcised, 1 Cor. vii. 18.

ἐπισπείρω, sow upon.

Matt. xiii. 25, for σπείρω, LTTr.

ἐπίσταμαι.

understand, Mark xiv. 68.
know, Acts x. 28. xv. 7. xviii. 25. xix. 15, 25. xx. 18. xxii. 19. xxiv. 10p. xxvi. 26. 1 Tim. vi. 4. Heb. xi. 8. Jas. iv. 14. Jude 10.

ἐπίστασις, stopping, concourse.

For ἐπισύστασις, Acts xxiv. 12, G' L*S*. 2 Cor xi. 28, L*S*.

ἐπιστάτης.

Said of Christ, **Master**, Luke v. 5. viii. 24*t*, 45. ix. 33, 49. xvii. 13.

ἐπιστέλλω.

write a letter unto, Heb. xiii. 22.
write unto, Acts xv. 20.
write, Acts xxi. 25(ἀποστέλλω L).

ἐπιστήμων.

endued with knowledge, Jas. iii. 13.

ἐπιστηρίζω.

confirm, Acts xiv. 22. xv. 32, 41.
strengthen, Acts xviii. 23 (στηρίζω L*S*).

ἐπιστολή.

epistle, Acts xv. 30. xxiii. 33. Rom. xvi. 22. 1 Cor. v. 9. 2 Cor. iii. 1, 2, 3. vii. 8. Col. iv. 16. 1 Thes. v. 27. 2 Thes. ii. 15. iii. 14, 17. 2 Pet. iii. 1, 16.
letter, Acts ix. 2. xxii. 5. xxiii. 25. 1 Cor. xvi. 3. 2 Cor. vii. 8. x. 9, 10, 11. 2 Thes. ii. 2.

ἐπιστομίζω.

stop the mouth of, Tit. i. 11.

ἐπιστρέφω.

With ἐπί, **turn unto**, Acts xi. 21. xiv. 15.—**turn to**, Luke i. 16, 17. Acts ix. 35. xv. 19. xxvi. 20.
With εἰς, **turn to**, Acts xxvi. 18.

With πρός, **turn to,** Acts ix. 40. 2 Cor. iii. 16. 1 Thes. i. 9.

turn again, Mark xiii. 16. Luke xvii. 4. Gal. iv. 9(*marg.* **turn back**). 2 Pet. ii. 22.

return, Matt. xii. 44. xxiv. 18. Luke ii. 20 (ὑποστρέφω GLTTr*S*). xvii. 31.

turn, Acts xvi. 18. 2 Pet. ii. 21 (*ap*). Rev. i. 12*t*.

convert, Jas. v. 19, 20.

be converted, Matt. xiii. 15. Mark iv. 12. Luke xxii. 32. Acts iii. 19. xxviii. 27.

come again, Luke viii. 55.

go again, Acts xv. 36.

Mid., and Pass. aor., **turn about,** Matt. ix. 22(στρέφω LTTr*S*). Mark v. 30. viii. 33p. John xxi. 20. — **return,** Matt. x. 13. 1 Pet. ii. 25. — **be converted,** John xii. 40 (στρέφω LTTr*S*).

ἐπιστροφή.

conversion, Acts xv. 3.

ἐπισυνάγω.

gather together, Matt. xxiii. 37. xxiv. 31. Mark i. 33. xiii. 27. Luke xii. 1. xiii. 34.

gather, Matt. xxiii. 37.

Add Luke xvii. 37, for συνάγω, T Tr*S*.

ἐπισυναγωγή.

gathering together, 2 Thes. ii. 1.

assembling together, Heb. x. 25.

ἐπισυντρέχω.

come running together, Mark ix. 25.

ἐπισύστασις.

ἐπ. ποιέω ὄχλον, **raise up the people,** Acts xxiv. 12(ἐπίστασις G'L*S*).

that which cometh upon, 2 Cor. xi. 28(ἐπίστασις L*S*).

ἐπισφαλής.

dangerous, Acts xxvii. 9.

ἐπισχύω.

be the more fierce, Luke xxiii. 5.

ἐπισωρεύω.

to heap, 2 Tim. iv. 3.

ἐπιταγή.

commandment, Rom. xvi. 26. 1 Cor, vii. 6, 25. 2 Cor. viii. 8. 1 Tim. i. 1. Tit. i. 3.

authority, Tit. ii. 15.

ἐπιτάσσω, -ττω.

enjoin, Phm. 8.

charge, Mark ix. 25.

command, Mark i. 27. vi. 27, 39. Luke iv. 36. viii. 25, 31. xiv. 22. Acts xxiii. 2.

ἐπιτελέω.

finish, 2 Cor. viii. 6.

accomplish, Heb. ix. 6. 1 Pet. v. 9.

perfect, 2 Cor. vii. 1.

make perfect, Gal. iii. 3.

perform, Rom. xv. 28p. 2 Cor. viii. 11. Phil. i. 6(*marg.* **finish**).

Inf., **performance,** 2 Cor. viii. 11.

do, Luke xiii. 32(ἀποτελέω LTTr*S*).

make, Heb. viii. 5.

ἐπιτήδειος.

With art., plur., **those things which are needful to,** Jas. ii. 16.

ἐπιτίθημι.

put upon, Mark vii. 32. viii. 23.

put on, Matt. xix. 13. John xix. 2. Acts ix. 12.

With ἐπί, **put upon,** Matt. xxvii. 29. Mark viii. 25 (τίθημι Tr). John ix. 15. Acts xv. 10. — **put on,** Acts ix. 17. — **set on,** Mark iv. 21(τίθημι L TTr*S*). Luke viii. 16 (τίθημι LTTr *S*).—**lay upon,** Matt. ix. 18. Rev. i. 17 (τίθημι GLTTr). — **lay on,** Matt. xxiii. 4. Mark xvi. 18 (*ap*). Luke xv. 5. Acts xxviii. 3. — **add unto,** Rev. xxii. 18*t*.

With ἐπάνω, **put on,** Matt. xxi. 7.

With ὄνομα, **surname,** Mark iii. 16, 17.

With πληγή, **wound,** Luke x. 30.

set on, Acts xviii. 10.

set up, Matt. xxvii. 37.

lay upon, Mark vi. 5. Acts xv. 28. xvi. 23p. xix. 6p.

lay on, Matt. xix. 15. Mark v. 23. Luke iv. 40. xiii. 13. xxiii. 26.

Acts vi. 6. viii. 17, 19. xiii. 3. xxviii. 3, 8. 1 Tim. v. 22.
Mid., **lade with**, Acts xxviii. 10.

ἐπιτιμάω.

to rebuke, Matt. viii. 26. xvi. 22. xvii. 18. xix. 13. xx. 31. Mark i. 25. iv. 39. viii. 32, 33. ix. 25. x. 13. Luke iv. 35, 39, 41. viii. 24. ix. 42, 55. xvii. 3. xviii. 15, 39. xix. 39. xxiii. 40. 2 Tim. iv. 2. Jude 9.
charge straitly, Luke ix. 21.
charge, Matt. xii. 16. Mark iii. 12. viii. 30. x. 48.
Add Matt. xvi. 20, for διαστέλλομαι, G″L.

ἐπιτιμία.

punishment, 2 Cor. ii. 6 (*marg.* **censure**).

ἐπιτοαυτό.

St, for ἐπὶ τὸ αὐτό, Acts i. 15. ii. 1, 44. iii. 1. (*See* ἐπί, III.)

ἐπιτρέπω.

permit, Acts xxvi. 1[cc]. 1 Cor. xiv. 34. xvi. 7. Heb. vi. 3.
give leave, Mark v. 13. John xix. 38.
give liberty, Acts xxvii. 3.
give license, Acts xxi. 40[p].
let, Luke ix. 61.
suffer, Matt. viii. 21, 31 (*see* ἀποστέλλω). xix. 8. Mark x. 4. Luke viii. 32*t*. ix. 59. Acts xxi. 39. xxviii. 16[cc]. 1 Tim. ii. 12.

ἐπιτροπή.

commission, Acts xxvi. 12.

ἐπίτροπος.

steward, Matt. xx. 8. Luke viii. 3.
tutor, Gal. iv. 2.

ἐπιτυγχάνω.

obtain, Rom. xi. 7*t*. Heb. vi. 15. xi. 33. Jas. iv. 2.

ἐπιφαίνω.

give light to, Luke i. 79.
appear, Acts xxvii. 20.
Pass., **appear**, Tit. ii. 11. iii. 4.

ἐπιφάνεια.

appearing, 1 Tim. vi. 14. 2 Tim. i. 10. iv. 1, 8. Tit. ii. 13.
brightness, 2 Thes. ii. 8.

ἐπιφανής.

notable, Acts ii. 20.

ἐπιφαύω, -αύσκω.

give light, Eph. v. 14.

ἐπιφέρω.

bring against, Jude 9.
bring, Acts xix. 12 (ἀποφέρω G″LT*S*). xxv. 18 (φέρω G″LT*S*).
add, Phil. i. 16 (17, ἐγείρω G″LT*S*).
take, Rom. iii. 5.

ἐπιφωνέω.

cry against, Acts xxii. 24.
cry, Luke xxiii. 21.
give a shout, Acts xii. 22.
Add Acts xxi. 34, for βοάω, G″LT*S*.

ἐπιφώσκω.

begin to dawn, Matt. xxviii. 1[p].
draw on, Luke xxiii. 54.

ἐπιχειρέω.

take in hand, Luke i. 1.
take upon, Acts xix. 13.
go about, Acts ix. 29.

ἐπιχέω.

pour in, Luke x. 34.

ἐπιχορηγέω.

minister unto, 2 Pet. i. 11.
minister to, 2 Cor. ix. 10. Gal. iii. 5.
Pass., **have nourishment ministered**, Col. ii. 19.
add, 2 Pet. i. 5.

ἐπιχορηγία.

supply, Phil. i. 19.
to supply[cc], Eph. iv. 16.

ἐπιχρίω.

With ἐπί, **anoint**, John ix. 6 (*marg.* **spread upon**), 11.

ἐποικοδομέω.

With ἐπί, **build upon**, 1 Cor. iii. 12. Eph. ii. 20.
build [c]**thereupon**, 1 Cor. iii. 10, 14.
build [c]**thereon**, 1 Cor. iii. 10.

build up on, Jude 20.
build up, Acts xx. 32(*οἰκοδομέω* G″ L*S*). Col. ii. 7.

ἐποκέλλω.

run aground, Acts xxvii. 41 (*ἐπικέλλω* LT*S*).

ἐπονομάζω.

to call, Rom. ii. 17.

ἐποπτεύω.

behold, 1 Pet. ii. 12[co]. iii. 2[p].

ἐπόπτης.

eye-witness, 2 Pet. i. 16.

ἔπος.

Lit., word; *ὡς ἔπος εἰπεῖν*, **as I may so say**, Heb. vii. 9.

ἐπουράνιος.

in heaven, Phil. ii. 10.
heavenly, Matt. xviii. 35 (*οὐράνιος* G″LTr*S*). 1 Cor. xv. 48, 49. Eph. i. 20 (*οὐρανός* L). 2 Tim. iv. 18. Heb. iii. 1. vi. 4. xi. 16. xii. 22.
With art., plural, masc., **they that are heavenly**, 1 Cor. xv. 48. *Neut.*, **heavenly things**, John iii. 12. Heb. viii. 5. ix. 23. — **heavenly places**, Eph. i. 3 (*marg.* **things**). ii. 6. iii. 10. — **high** (*marg.* **heavenly**) **places**, Eph. vi. 12.
celestial, 1 Cor. xv. 40*t*.

ἑπτά.

seven, Matt. xii. 45. xv. 34, 36, 37. xvi. 10. xviii. 22. xxii. 25, 28. Mark viii. 5, 6, 8, 20*t*. xii. 20, 22, 23. xvi. 9(*ap*). Luke ii. 36. viii. 2. xi. 26. xx. 29, 31, 33. Acts vi. 3. xiii. 19. xix. 14. xx. 6. xxi. 4, 8, 27. xxviii. 14.
Heb. xi. 30. Rev. i. 4*t*, 11 (–St), 12, 13(–G[oo]LTTr), 16, 20*six*. ii. 1*t*. iii. 1(–St), 1. iv. 5*t*. v. 1, 5, 6*t*, 6 (–LTr[b]). viii. 2*t*, 6*t*. x. 3. 4, 4(–Tr[b]). xi. 13. xii. 3*t*. xiii. 1. xv. 1*t*, 6*t*, 7*t*, 8*t*. xvi. 1. xvii. 1*t*, 3, 7, 9*t*, 10, 11. xxi. 9*tr*.
seventh, Matt. xxii. 26.
Add Rev. ii. 7 (. . churches), L. vi. 1 (. . seals), GLTTr*S*. xvi. 1 (. . vials), GLTTr*S*.

ἑπτάκις.

seven times, Matt. xviii. 21, 22. Luke xvii. 4*t*.

ἑπτακισχίλιοι.

seven thousand, Rom. xi. 4.

ἔπω. See εἶπον.

ἐραυνάω. See ἐρευνάω.

ἐργάζομαι.

to work, Matt. vii. 23. xxi. 28. xxvi. 10. Mark xiv. 6. Luke xiii. 14. John v. 17*t*. vi. 28, 30. ix. 4*t*. Acts x. 35. xiii. 41. xviii. 3. Rom. ii. 10. iv. 4, 5. xiii. 10. 1 Cor. iv. 12. xvi. 10. Eph. iv. 28. 1 Thes. iv. 11. 2 Thes. iii. 8, 10, 11, 12. Heb. xi. 23. 2 John 8(*marg.* **gain**).
With μή, **forbear working**, 1 Cor. ix. 6.
Pass., **be wrought**, John iii. 21.
labor, 1 Thes. ii. 9.
labor for, John vi. 27.
do, Gal. vi. 10. Col. iii. 23. 3 John 5.
commit, Jas. ii. 9.
trade by, Rev. xviii. 17.
trade, Matt. xxv. 16.
minister about, 1 Cor. ix. 13.
Add, for *κατεργάζομαι*, 2 Cor. vii. 10, LT*S*. Jas. i. 20, L*S*.

ἐργασία.

With εἰς, **to work**, Eph. iv. 19.
diligence, Luke xii. 58.
craft, Acts xix. 25.
gain, Acts xvi. 16. xix. 24.
gains, Acts xvi. 19.

ἐργάτης.

worker, Luke xiii. 27. 2 Cor. xi. 13. Phil. iii. 2.
workman, Matt. x. 10. Acts xix. 25. 2 Tim. ii. 15.
laborer, Matt. ix. 37, 38. xx. 1, 2, 8. Luke x. 2*t*, 7. 1 Tim. v. 18. Jas. v. 4.

ἔργον.

work, Matt. v. 16. xi. 2. xxiii. 3, 5. xxvi. 10. Mark xiii. 34. xiv. 6. John iv. 34. v. 20, 36*t*. vi. 28, 29. vii. 3, 7, 21. viii. 39. ix. 3, 4. x.

25, 32*t*, 33, 37, 38. xiv. 10, 11, 12. xv. 24. xvii. 4. Acts v. 38. vii. 41. ix. 36. xiii. 2, 41, 41(-G°). xiv. 26. xv. 18(*ap*), 38. xxvi. 20.
Rom. ii. 15. iii. 27. iv. 2, 6. ix. 11, 32. xi. 6, 6*tr* (*ap*). xiii. 3, 12. xiv. 20. 1 Cor. iii. 13*t*, 14, 15. ix. 1. xv. 58. xvi. 10. 2 Cor. ix. 8. xi. 15. Gal. ii. 16*tr*. iii. 2, 5, 10. v. 19. vi. 4. Eph. ii. 9, 10. iv. 12. v. 11. Phil. i. 6. ii. 30. Col. i. 10, 21. 1 Thes. i. 3. v. 13. 2 Thes. i. 11. ii. 17. 1 Tim. ii. 10. iii. 1. v. 10*t*, 25. vi. 18. 2 Tim. i. 9. ii. 21. iii. 17. iv. 5, 14, 18. Tit. i. 16*t*. ii. 7, 14. iii. 1, 5, 8, 14(*marg.* **trade**).
Heb. i. 10. ii. 7(*ap*). iii. 9. iv. 3, 4, 10. vi. 1, 10. ix. 14. x. 24. xiii. 21. Jas. i. 4, 25. ii. 14, 17, 18*tr*, 20, 21, 22*t*, 24, 25, 26. iii. 13. 1 Pet. i. 17. ii. 12. 2 Pet. iii. 10. 1 John iii. 8, 12. Rev. ii. 2, 5, 9 (-G°°LTTr), 13(*ap*), 19(-G°), 19, 23, 26. iii. 1, 2, 8, 15. ix. 20. xiv. 13. xv. 3. xviii. 6. xx. 12, 13. xxii. 12.

deed, Luke xi. 48. xxiv. 19. John iii. 19, 20, 21. viii. 41. Acts vii. 22. Rom. ii. 6. iii. 20, 28. xv. 18. 1 Cor. v. 2. 2 Cor. x. 11. Col. iii. 17. 2 Pet. ii. 8. 1 John iii. 18. 2 John 11. 3 John 10. Jude 15. Rev. ii. 6, 22. xvi. 11.

doing, Rom. ii. 7.

labor, Phil. i. 22.

Add Matt. xi. 19, for τέκνον, Tr*S*. Rom. xiii. 12, for ὅπλον L^m. 2 Pet. i. 10(*ap*).

ἐρεθίζω.

provoke, 2 Cor. ix. 2.

provoke to anger, Col. iii. 21 (παροργίζω G'L*S*).

ἐρείδω.

stick fast, Acts xxvii. 41.

ἐρεύγομαι.

utter, Matt. xiii. 35.

ἐρευνάω, -ραυ- T (exc. Rom.) Tr*S*.

to search, John v. 39. vii. 52. Rom. viii. 27. 1 Cor. ii. 10. 1 Pet. i. 11. Rev. ii. 23(ἐραυνάω L, not *S*).

ἐρέω. See ἐρῶ.

ἐρημία.

desert, Heb. xi. 38.

wilderness, Matt. xv. 33. Mark viii. 4. 2 Cor. xi. 26.

ἔρημος, adj.

desert, Matt. xiv. 13, 15. Mark i. 45. vi. 31, 32, 35. Luke iv. 42. ix. 10(*ap*), 12. Acts viii. 26.

desolate, Matt. xxiii. 38(-L). Luke xiii. 35(*om S*). Acts i. 20. Gal. iv. 27.

solitary, Mark i. 35.

ἔρημος, subst.

desert, Matt. xxiv. 26. Luke i. 80. John vi. 31.

wilderness, Matt. iii. 1, 3. iv. 1. xi. 7. Mark i. 3, 4, 12, 13. Luke iii. 2, 4. iv. 1. v. 16. vii. 24. viii. 29. xv. 4. John i. 23. iii. 14. vi. 49. xi. 54. Acts vii. 30, 36, 38, 42, 44. xiii. 18. xxi. 38. 1 Cor. x. 5. Heb. iii. 8, 17. Rev. xii. 6, 14. xvii. 3.

ἐρημόω.

bring to desolation, Matt. xii. 25. Luke xi. 17.

make desolate, Rev. xviii. 19.

desolate, Rev. xvii. 16^p.

Pass., **come to nought**, Rev. xviii. 17(16).

ἐρήμωσις.

desolation, Matt. xxiv. 15. Mark xiii. 14. Luke xxi. 20.

ἐρίζω.

strive, Matt. xii. 19.

ἐριθεία.

strife, 2 Cor. xii. 20. Gal. v. 20. Phil. ii. 3. Jas. iii. 14, 16.

contention, Phil. i. 16(17).

οἱ ἐξ ἐριθείας, **they that are contentious**, Rom. ii. 8.

ἔριον.

•**wool**, Heb. ix. 19. Rev. i. 14.

ἔρις.

strife, Rom. xiii. 13. 1 Cor. iii. 3. Phil. i. 15. 1 Tim. vi. 4.

contention, 1 Cor. i. 11. Tit. iii. 9.

debate, Rom. i. 29. 2 Cor. xii. 20.
variance, Gal. v. 20.

ἐρίφιον.

goat, Matt. xxv. 33.

ἔριφος.

kid, Luke xv. 29.
goat, Matt. xxv. 32.

ἑρμηνεία.

interpretation, 1 Cor. xii. 10 (*διερμηνεια* L). xiv. 26.

ἑρμηνευτής, interpreter.

1 Cor. xiv. 28, for *διερμηνευτής*, L.

ἑρμηνεύω.

interpret, John i. 38 (39, *μεθερμηνεύω* LTr).
Pass., **be by interpretation**, John i. 42(43). ix. 7. Heb. vii. 2.

ἑρπετόν.

creeping thing, Acts x. 12. xi. 6. Rom. i. 23.
serpent, Jas. iii. 7.

ἐρυθρός.

With *θάλασσα*, **Red sea**, Acts vii. 36. Heb. xi. 29.

ἔρχομαι.

come, Matt. ii. 2, 8, 9, 11p, 21 (*εἰσέρχομαι* LTr*S*), 23. iii. 7, 14. iv. 13. v. 17*t*, 24. vi. 10. vii. 15, 25, 27. viii. 2 (*προσέρχομαι* G′LTTr*S*), 7, 9*t*, 14p, 28p, 29. ix. 1, 10, 13, 15, 18 (*see* *εἰσέρχομαι*, *προσέρχομαι* L*S*), 18, 23p, 28p. x. 13, 23, 34*t*, 35. xi. 14, 18, 19. xii. 42, 44p. xiii. 4, 19, 25, 32, 54p. xiv. 28, 29, 33, 34. xv. 25, 29, 39. xvi. 5p, 13p, 24, 27, 28. xvii. 10, 11, 12, 14p, 24p. xviii. 7*t*, 11(*ap*), 31. xix. 1, 14. xx. 9p, 10p, 28. xxi. 1, 5, 19, 23p, 32, 40. xxii. 3. xxiii. 35. xxiv. 5, 30, 39, 42, 43, 44, 46p. xxv. 6 (–G°°LTTr*S*), 10, 11, 13 (*ap*), 19, 31, 36, 39. xxvi. 36, 40, 43, 45, 47, 64. xxvii. 33p, 49, 57, 64. xxviii. 1, 11, 13.

Mark i. 7, 9, 14, 24, 40, 45. ii. 3, 17, 18, 20. iii. 8, 31. iv. 4, 15, 22. v. 1, 15, 22, 23, 27, 33, 35, 38. vi. 1, 29, 31, 48, 53. vii. 1, 25, 31. viii. 10, 22, 34 (*ἀκολουθέω* GTTr), 38. ix. 1, 7, 11, 12, 13, 14p, 33. x. 1, 14, 30, 45, 46, 50. xi. 9, 10, 13, 13p, 15, 27*t*. xii. 9, 14p, 18, 42. xiii. 6, 26, 35, 36. xiv. 3, 16, 17, 32, 37, 41*t*, 45p, 62, 66. xv. 21, 36, 43. xvi. 1, 2.

Luke i. 43, 59. ii. 16, 27, 51(–G°). iii. 3, 12, 16. iv. 16, 34, 42. v. 7*t*, 17 (*συνέρχομαι* L), 32, 35. vi. 17, 47. vii. 3, 7, 8*t*, 33, 34. viii. 12, 17, 35, 41, 47, 49. ix. 23, 26, 56 (*ap*). x. 1 (*εἰσέρχομαι* Lm), 32 (–G° *S*c), 33. xi. 2, 25p, 31. xii. 36p, 37p, 38(–Tr*S*), 38, 39, 40, 43p, 49, 54. xiii. 6, 7, 14, 35. xiv. 9, 10, 17, 20, 26, 27, 31. xv. 6p, 17p, 20, 25, 30. xvi. 21, 28. xvii. 1*t*, 20*t*, 22, 27. xviii. 3, 8p, 16, 30. xix. 5, 10, 13, 18, 20. xx. 16. xxi. 6, 8, 27. xxii. 7, 18, 45. xxiii. 26, 42. xxiv. 1, 23.

John i. 7, 9, 11, 29, 30, 31, 39 (40)*t*, 46(47), 47(48). iii. 2, 2cc, 8, 19, 20, 21, 22, 26*t*. iv. 5, 7, 15, 16, 21, 23, 25*t*, 27, 30, 35, 40, 45, 46, 54p. v. 24, 40, 43*t*. vi. 5, 15, 17, 23, 24, 35, 37, 44, 45, 65. vii. 27, 28, 30, 31, 34, 36, 37, 41, 42, 45, 50. viii. 2(*ap*), 14*t*, 20, 21, 22, 42. ix. 4, 7, 39. x. 8, 10*t*, 12. xi. 17p, 19, 29, 30, 32, 34, 38, 45, 48, 56. xii. 1, 9, 12, 15, 22, 23, 27, 28, 46, 47. xiii. 1, 6, 33. xiv. 3, 6, 18, 23, 28, 30. xv. 22, 26. xvi. 2, 4, 7, 8p, 13*t*, 21, 25, 28, 32*t*. xvii. 1, 11, 13. xviii. 3, 4, 37. xix. 32, 33p, 38, 39*t*. xx. 1, 2, 3, 4, 6, 8, 18, 19, 24, 26. xxi. 8, 13, 22, 23.

Acts i. 11. ii. 20. iii. 19. vii. 11. viii. 27, 36, 40. ix. 17, 21. x. 29. xi. 5. xii. 10, 12. xiii. 13, 25, 51. xiv. 24. xv. 30(*κατέρχομαι* G″L*S*). xvi. 7p, 37, 39. xvii. 1, 13, 15. xviii. 1, 2, 21(*ap*). xix. 1, 6, 18. xx. 2, 6, 14, 15. xxi. 1, 8, 11p, 22. xxii. 11, 13. xxiv. 8(*ap*). xxv. 23p. xxvii. 8. xxviii. 13, 16 (*εἰσέρχομαι* LT*S*).

Rom. i. 10, 13. iii. 8. vii. 9p. ix. 9. xv. 23, 24(*ap*), 29p, 29, 32. 1 Cor.

ii. 1[p], 1. iv. 5, 18, 19, 21. xi. 26, 34. xiii. 10. xiv. 6. xv. 35. xvi. 2, 5, 10, 11, 12*tr*. 2 Cor. i. 15, 16, 23. ii. 1, 3[p], 12[p]. vii. 5[p]. ix. 4. xi. 4, 9. xii. 1, 14, 20[p], 21[p]. xiii. 2.

Gal. i. 21. ii. 11, 12*t*. iii. 19, 23, 25[p]. iv. 4. Eph. ii. 17. v. 6. Phil. i. 27. ii. 24. Col. iii. 6. iv. 10. 1 Thes. i. 10. ii. 18. iii. 6[p]. v. 2. 2 Thes. i. 10. ii. 3. 1 Tim. i. 15. ii. 4. iii. 14. iv. 13. 2 Tim. iii. 7. iv. 9, 13[p], 21. Tit. iii. 12.

Heb. vi. 7. viii. 8. xiii. 23. 2 Pet. iii. 3. 1 John ii. 18. iv. 2, 3(*ap*), 3. 2 John 7, 10, 12 (*γίνομαι* G″LT*S*). 3 John 3[p], 10. Jude 14. Rev. i. 7. ii. 5, 16. iii. 10, 11. v. 7. vi. 1, 3, 5, 7, 17. vii. 13, 14. viii. 3. ix. 12. xi. 14, 18. xiv. 7, 15. xvi. 15. xvii. 1, 10*t*. xviii. 10. xix. 7. xxi. 9. xxii. 7, 12, 17*tr*, 20*t*.

be coming, Luke xxiii. 29. John v. 7, 25, 28. xi. 20. xii. 12. 2 Cor. xiii. 1.

ὁ ἐρχόμενος, said of Christ, **that cometh,** Luke xix. 38. John xii. 13. —**he that cometh,** Matt. iii. 11. xxi. 9. xxiii. 39. John i. 15. iii. 31*t*. — **who coming,** John i. 27. — **he that shall come,** Heb. x. 37. — **that (which) should come,** John vi. 14. xi. 27.—**he that (which) should come,** Matt. xi. 3. Luke vii. 19, 20. Acts xix. 4. — **which is (art) to come,** Rev. i. 4, 8. iv. 8. xi. 17(*omS*). —*ὁ ἐλθών*, **he that came,** 1 John v. 6.

coming[cc], Matt. xxiv. 48 (–LTr*S*). xxv. 27[p]. Luke xii. 45. xviii. 5[p]. xix. 23[p]. Rom. xv. 22.

light, Matt. iii. 16.

be brought, Mark iv. 21.

go, Matt. xii. 9. xiii. 36. xiv. 12, 29. Mark iii. 19. Luke ii. 44. xiv. 1. John iv. 45. vi. 17. xxi. 3. Acts iv. 23. xxviii. 14. Heb. xi. 8.

With εἰς, **enter into,** Mark i. 29. Acts xviii. 7(*εἰσέρχομαι* L*S*).

With σύν, **accompany,** Acts xi. 12.

resort, Mark ii. 13. John x. 41.

pass by, Acts v. 15.

fall out, Phil. i. 12.

grow, Mark v. 26. [GLT*S*).

appear, Acts xxii. 30 (*συνέρχομαι*

next, Acts xiii. 44[p] (G′, *ἔχω mid.* GLT).

Add, for *ἀπέρχομαι*, Matt. xiv. 25, G″LTr*S*. Luke xxiii. 33, LTr*S*. For *εἰμί*, Mark i. 39, Tr*S*. Jude 18, G′. For *εἰσέρχομαι*, Mark xiv. 38, T*S*. xvi. 4, T. Luke viii. 51, GL Tr*S*. xi. 26, G′T. Acts xi. 20, GT T*S*. *ἐλθόντα* for *ὅτε εἰσῆλθεν*, Matt. xvii. 25, Tr. For *ἐξέρχομαι*, Mark i. 38, G′. v. 14, G″LTTr. Acts xxviii. 15, LT*S*. For *ἥκω*, Acts xxviii. 23, G″L*S*. For *συνέρχομαι*, 1 Cor. xiv. 23, L. For *καὶ πάλιν*, John xii. 22, LTTr, *καὶ π. ἐρχ. S*.

App., Mark vi. 33. xiv. 40. John xix. 2.

See also ἀπελεγμός.

ἦλθαν for *ἦλθον*, Matt. vii. 25, Tr. Acts xxviii. 15, T*S*. *ἤλθατε*, Matt. xxv. 36, LTTr*S*.

ἐρῶ, εἴρηκα.

(*Compare εἶπον, ῥέω.*)

say, Matt. vii. 4, 22. xiii. 30. xvii. 20. xxi. 3, 25. xxv. 34, 40, 41. xxvi. 75. Mark xi. 31. Luke ii. 24. iv. 12, 23. xii. 19. xiii. 25, 27. xiv. 9. xv. 18. xvii. 7, 8, 21, 23. xix. 31. xx. 5. xxii. 11, 13. xxiii. 29. John iv. 18. vi. 65. xii. 50. Acts xiii. 34. xvii. 28.

Rom. iii. 5. iv. 1. vi. 1. vii. 7. viii. 31. ix. 14, 19, 20, 30. xi. 19. 1 Cor. xiv. 16, 23. xv. 35. 2 Cor. xii. 6, 9. Phil. iv. 4. Heb. i. 13. iv. 3, 7(*προερῶ* G″LT*S*). x. 9. xiii. 5. Jas. ii. 18. Rev. vii. 14. xix. 3.

speak, Luke xii. 10. John xi. 13. Acts ii. 16. viii. 24. xx. 38. Rom. iv. 18. Heb. iv. 4.

speak of, Acts xiii. 40. xxiii. 5.

tell, Matt. xxi. 24. Mark xi. 29. John xiv. 29. Rev. xvii. 7.

call, John xv. 15.

Add, for *εἶπον*, Luke xi. 5[2d], L. xiv. 10, TTr*S*. For *προερῶ*, Heb. x. 15, G″L*S*.

ἐρωτάω.
ask, Matt. xvi. 13. xxi. 24. Mark iv. 10. Luke ix. 45 (ἐπερωτάω L). xix. 31. xx. 3. xxii. 68. John i. 19, 21, 25. v. 12. viii. 7(*ap*). ix. 2, 15, 19, 21, 23. xvi. 5, 19, 23, 30. xviii. 19. Acts iii. 3.
desire, Luke vii. 36. xiv. 32. John xii. 21. Acts xvi. 39. xviii. 20p. xxiii. 20.
pray, Luke v. 3. xiv. 18, 19. xvi. 27. John iv. 31. xiv. 16. xvi. 26. xvii. 9*t*, 15, 20. Acts x. 48. xxiii. 18. 1 John v. 16.
beseech, Matt. xv. 23. Mark vii. 26. Luke iv. 38. vii. 3. viii. 37. xi. 37. John iv. 40, 47. xix. 31, 38. 1 Thes. iv. 1(*marg.* **request**). v. 12. 2 Thes. ii. 1. 2 John 5.
entreat, Phil. iv. 3.
Add, for ἐπερωτάω, Mark viii. 5, TTr*S*. Luke xxiii. 3, TTr*S*. John xviii. 21*t*, LTTr*S*. Acts i. 6, LT*S*. —Matt. xix. 17(*ap*).

ἔσεσθαι. See εἰμί.

ἐσθής.
robe, Luke xxiii. 11.
raiment, Jas. ii. 2.
clothing, Acts x. 30. Jas. ii. 3.
apparel, Acts i. 10. xii. 21. Jas. ii. 2.

ἔσθησις.
garment, Luke xxiv. 4.

ἐσθίω.
eat, Matt. ix. 11. xi. 18, 19. xii. 1. xiv. 21. xv. 2, 27, 38. xxiv. 49. xxvi. 21p. Mark i. 6. ii. 16*t*. vii. 2, 3, 4, 5, 28. xiv. 18p, 18, 22p. Luke v. 30, 33. vi. 1. vii. 33, 34. x. 7, 8. xii. 45. xv. 16. xvii. 27, 28. xxii. 30. Acts xxvii. 35.
Rom. xiv. 2, 3*f*, 6*tr*, 20. 1 Cor. viii. 7, 10. ix. 7*t*. x. 18, 25, 27, 28, 31. xi. 22, 26, 27, 28, 29*t*, 34. 2 Thes. iii. 10, 12.
be eating, Matt. xxvi. 26p.
live (*marg.* **feed**) **of**, 1 Cor. ix. 13.
devour, Heb. x. 27.

ἐσμέν, ἔσομαι, ἐσόμενος. See εἰμί.

ἔσοπτρον.
glass, 1 Cor. xiii. 12. Jas. i. 23.

ἑσπέρα.
evening, Luke xxiv. 29. Acts xxviii. 23.
eventide, Acts iv. 3.

ἐστέ, ἐστί, ἔστω. See εἰμί.

ἔσχατος.
last, Matt. xix. 30*t*. xx. 8, 12, 14, 16*t*. xxvii. 64. Mark ix 35. x. 31*t*. xii. 6, 22(*adv.* G'LTr*S*). Luke xii. 59. xiii. 30*t*. John vi. 39, 40, 44, 54. vii. 37. viii. 9(*ap*). xi. 24. xii. 48. Acts ii. 17. 1 Cor. iv. 9. xv. 8(*adv.*), 26, 45, 52. 2 Tim. iii. 1. Heb. i. 2(1). Jas. v. 3. 1 Pet. i. 5, 20. 2 Pet. iii. 3. 1 John ii. 18*t*. Jude 18. Rev. i. 11 (*ap*), 17. ii. 8, 19. xv. 1. xxi. 9. xxii. 13.
τὰ ἔσχατα, **the last state**, Matt. xii. 45. Luke xi. 26.—**the latter end**, 2 Pet. ii. 20.
uttermost, Matt. v. 26.
uttermost part, Acts i. 8.
ends, Acts xiii. 47.
lowest, Luke xiv. 9, 10.

ἐσχάτως.
With ἔχω, **lie at the point of death**, Mark v. 23.

ἔσω.
into, Mark xiv. 54(*with* εἰς). xv. 16.
in, Matt. xxvi. 58.
within, John xx. 26. Acts v. 23. 1 Cor. v. 12.
inward, Rom. vii. 22.
inner, Eph. iii. 16.
Add 2 Cor. iv. 16, *see* ἔσωθεν.

ἔσωθεν.
from within, Mark vii. 21, 23. Luke xi. 7.
within, Matt. xxiii. 25, 27, 28. 2 Cor. vii. 5. Rev. iv. 8. v. 1.
inwardly, Matt. vii. 15.
With art., **the inward man**, 2 Cor. iv. 16 (ἔσω ἡμῶν L*S*).—**that which is within**, Luke xi. 40.—**inward part**, Luke xi. 39.
Add Rev. xi. 2, for ἔξωθεν, St*S*.

ἐσώτερος.
inner, Acts xvi. 24.
With art., **that within**, Heb. vi. 19.

ἑταῖρος.
fellow, Matt. xi. 16 (ἕτερος G''T TrS).
friend, Matt. xx. 13. xxii. 12. xxvi. 50.

ἑτερόγλωσσος.
of another tongue, 1 Cor. xiv. 21.

ἑτεροδιδασκαλέω.
teach otherwise, 1 Tim. vi. 3.
teach another doctrine, 1 Tim. i. 3.

ἑτεροζυγέω.
be unequally yoked together with, 2 Cor. vi. 14 (p *with* γίνομαι).

ἕτερος.
other, Matt. vi. 24*t*. xii. 45. xv. 30. xvi. 14. Luke iv. 43. v. 7. vii. 41. viii. 3. x. 1. xi. 16, 26. xvi. 13*t*. xvii. 34, 35, 36(*ap*). xviii. 10. xxiii. 32, 40. Acts ii. 4, 13, 40. iv. 12. viii. 34. xv. 35. xvii. 34. xxiii. 6. xxvii. 1.
Rom. viii. 39. xiii. 9. 1 Cor. viii. 4 (-G°°L*S*). x. 29. xiv. 17, 21. 2 Cor. viii. 8. Gal. i. 19. Eph. iii. 5. Phil. ii. 4. 2 Tim. ii. 2. Heb. xi. 36.
ἕτερος . . ἕτερος, **some t . . other**, Luke viii. 6, 7, 8.—**one . . another**, 1 Cor. xv. 40.
other thing, Luke iii. 18. xxii. 65. 1 Tim. i. 10.
other matter, Acts xix. 39(*see* περαιτέρω).
With γίνομαι, **be altered**, Luke ix. 29.
strange (*Gr.* other), Jude 7.
else, Acts xvii. 21.
another, Matt. viii. 21. xi. 3. Mark xvi. 12(*ap*). Luke vi. 6. ix. 56, 59, 61. xiv. 19, 20, 31. xvi. 7, 18. xix. 20. xx. 11. xxii. 58. John xix. 37. Acts i. 20. vii. 18. xii. 17. xvii. 7.
Rom. ii. 1, 21. vii. 3*t*, 4, 23. xiii. 8. 1 Cor. iii. 4. iv. 6. vi. 1. x. 24. xii. 9, 10. 2 Cor. xi. 4*t*. Gal. i. 6. vi. 4. Heb. vii. 11, 13, 15. Jas. ii. 25. iv. 12 (πλησίον G'LT*S*).
another °place, Heb. v. 6.
another °psalm, Acts xiii. 35.
next day (*sc.* ἡμέρᾳ), Acts xx. 15. xxvii. 3.
Add Matt. x. 23(*ap*). xi. 16, for ἑταῖρος, G''TTr*S*. xxi. 30, for δεύτερος, GT*S*. Luke vii. 20, for ἄλλος, Tr*S*.

ἑτέρως.
otherwise, Phil. iii. 15.

ἔτι.
yet, Matt. xii. 46. xvii. 5. xix. 20. xxvi. 47. xxvii. 63. Mark v. 35. viii. 17(-G°LTr*S*). xii. 6. xiv. 43. Luke viii. 49. ix. 42. xiv. 22, 32. xv. 20. xviii. 22. xxii. 37 (-G°LTr *S*), 47, 60. xxiv. 6, 41, 44. John iv. 35(-G°). vii. 33. xii. 35. xiii. 33. xiv. 19. xvi. 12. xx. 1. Acts ix. 1. x. 44. xviii. 18.
Rom. iii. 7. v. 6, 8. ix. 19. 1 Cor. iii. 2(-L[b]), 3. xii. 31. xv. 17. 2 Cor. i. 10(-L[m]). Gal. i. 10. v. 11*t*. Phil. i. 9. 2 Thes. ii. 5. Heb. vii. 10, 15. ix. 8. x. 37. xi. 4. Rev. vi. 11.
still, Rev. xxii. 11*f*.
longer, Luke xvi. 2.
any longer, Rom. vi. 2.
more, Matt. xviii. 16. Heb. viii. 12. x. 2, 17. xi. 32. Rev. iii. 12. vii. 16. ix. 12. xviii. 21, 22*t*, 23*t*. xx. 3. xxi. 1, 4. xxii. 3(ἐκεῖ G', -*S*).
yet more, Heb. xii. 26, 27.
any more, Luke xx. 36. Rev. vii. 16. xii. 8. xviii. 22. xxi. 4.
moreover, Acts ii. 26. Heb. xi. 36.
further, Matt. xxvi. 65. Acts xxi. 28. Heb. vii. 11.
any further, Mark v. 35. xiv. 63. Luke xxii. 71.
thenceforth, Matt. v. 13.
also, Luke xiv. 26.
even, Luke i. 15.
Add John xi. 39 (but was . .), L Tr*S*. Rom. v. 6(. . in due), G[pr]L*S*. Rev. xxii. 5, for ἐκεῖ, GLTr[b]*S*.
See also οὐκέτι.

ἑτοιμάζω.
make ready, Matt. xxvi. 19. Mark xiv. 15, 16. Luke i. 17. ix. 52.

xvii. 8. xxii. 12, 13. Acts xxiii. 23. Rev. xix. 7.

prepare, Matt. iii. 3. xx. 23. xxii. 4. xxv. 34, 41. xxvi. 17. Mark i. 3. x. 40. xiv. 12. Luke i. 76. ii. 31. iii. 4. xii. 47. xxii. 8, 9. xxiii. 56. xxiv. 1. John xiv. 2, 3. 1 Cor. ii. 9. 2 Tim. ii. 21. Phm. 22. Heb. xi. 16. Rev. viii. 6. ix. 7, 15. xii. 6. xvi. 12. xxi. 2.

provide, Luke xii. 20.

ἑτοιμασία.

preparation, Eph. vi. 15.

ἕτοιμος.

ready, Matt. xxii. 4, 8. xxiv. 44. xxv. 10. Luke xii. 40. xiv. 17. xxii. 23. John vii. 6. Acts xxiii. 15, 21. 2 Cor. ix. 5. Tit. iii. 1. 1 Pet. i. 5. iii. 15.

τὰ ἕτοιμα, **things made ready to** [c]**our hand**, 2 Cor. x. 16.

readiness, 2 Cor. x. 6.

prepared, Mark xiv. 15(-G[o]L[b]).

ἑτοίμως.

With ἔχω, **be ready**, Acts xxi. 13. 2 Cor. xii. 14. 1 Pet. iv. 5.

ἔτος.

year, Matt. ix. 20. Mark v. 25, 42. Luke ii. 36, 37, 41, 42. iii. 1, 23. iv. 25. viii. 42, 43. xii. 19. xiii. 7, 8, 11, 16. xv. 29. John ii. 20. v. 5. viii. 57. Acts iv. 22. vii. 6, 30, 36, 42. ix. 33. xiii. 20, 21. xix. 10. xxiv. 10, 17. Rom. xv. 23. 2 Cor. xii. 2. Gal. i. 18. ii. 1. iii. 17. 1 Tim. v. 9. Heb. i. 12. iii. 9, 17. 2 Pet. iii. 8*t*. Rev. xx. 2, 3, 4, 5, 6, 7.

εὖ.

well, Luke xix. 17 (*εὖγε* LTTr). Acts xv. 29. Eph. vi. 3.

well done, Matt. xxv. 21, 23.

good[cc], Mark xiv. 7.

εὐαγγελίζω.

I. Active.

declare to, Rev. x. 7.

preach [1]**unto. . .** [2]**to**, Rev. xiv. 6 (*with ἐπί*[1],[2] LTTrS, [2]G).

II. Middle.

bring good tidings of, Luke ii. 10. 1 Thes. iii. 6.

bring glad tidings of, Rom. x. 15.

declare glad tidings unto, Acts xiii. 32.

show glad tidings, Luke i. 19.

show the glad tidings of, Luke viii. 1.

preach the gospel, Luke iv. 18. ix. 6. xx. 1. Rom. i. 15. xv. 20. 1 Cor. i. 17. ix. 16*t*, 18[p]. 2 Cor. x. 16. Gal. iv. 13.

preach . . gospel, Gal. i. 8, 9.

preach the gospel of, Rom. x. 15 (-L*S*).

preach the gospel to, Acts xiv. 7 (*with εἰμί*), 21[p].

preach the gospel unto, Acts xvi. 10. 1 Pet. i. 12.

preach the gospel in, Acts viii. 25.

preach, Luke iv. 43. Acts v. 42. viii. 4, 12, 35, 40. x. 36. xi. 20. xv. 35. xvii. 18(*ap*). 1 Cor. xv. 1, 2. 2 Cor. xi. 7. Gal. i. 16, 23. Eph. ii. 17. iii. 8.

preach unto, Luke iii. 18. Acts xiv. 15.

III. Passive.

be preached by the gospel, 1 Pet. i. 25.

the gospel is preached, 1 Pet. iv. 6.

have the gospel preached to one's self, Matt. xi. 5.

the gospel is preached to[cc], Luke vii. 22.

it (*marg.* **the gospel**) **is preached to**[cc], Heb. iv. 6.

the gospel is preached unto[cc], Heb. iv. 2(*with εἰμί*).

be preached, Luke xvi. 16. Gal. i. 11.

εὐαγγέλιον.

(*With βασιλεία*, [k]. *θεός*, [g]. *χριστός*, *etc.*, [c]. *εἰρήνη*, [p]. *σωτηρία*, [s]. *χάρις*, [gr].)

gospel, Matt. iv. 23[k]. ix. 35[k]. xxiv. 14[k]. xxvi. 13. Mark i. 1[c], 14[kg], 15. viii. 35. x. 29. xiii. 10. xiv. 9. xvi. 15(*ap*). Acts xv. 7. xx. 24[gr]. Rom. i. 1[g], 9[c], 16[c]. ii. 16. x. 16.

xi. 28. xv. 16[g], 19[c], 29[c](*omS*). xvi. 25. 1 Cor. iv. 15. ix. 12[c], 14*t*, 18[e], 18, 23. xv. 1. 2 Cor. ii. 12[c]. iv. 3, 4[c]. viii. 18. ix. 13[c]. x. 14[c]. xi. 4, 7[g]. Gal. i. 6, 7[c], 11. ii. 2, 5, 7, 14. Eph. i. 13[s]. iii. 6. vi. 15[p], 19(–L[b]). Phil. i. 5, 7, 12, 17, 27[c], 27. ii. 22. iv. 3, 15. Col. i. 5, 23. 1 Thes. i. 5. ii. 2[g], 4, 8[g], 9[g]. iii. 2[c]. 2 Thes. i. 8[c]. ii. 14. 1 Tim. i. 11[g]. 2 Tim. i. 8, 10. ii. 8. Phm. 13. 1 Pet. iv. 17[g]. Rev. xiv. 6.

εὐαγγελιστής.

evangelist, Acts xxi. 8. Eph. iv. 11. 2 Tim. iv. 5.

εὐαρεστέω.

please, Heb. xi. 5, 6.

Pass., **be well pleased with**, Heb. xiii. 16.

εὐάρεστος.

well-pleasing, Phil. iv. 18. Col. iii. 20. — *With art.*, **that which is well-pleasing**, Heb. xiii. 21.

With εἰμί, **please well**, Tit. ii. 9. — **be accepted of**, 2 Cor. v. 9.

acceptable, Rom. xii. 1, 2. xiv. 18. Eph. v. 10.

εὐαρέστως.

acceptably, Heb. xii. 28.

εὖγε, well done.

Luke xix. 17, for εὖ, LTTr.

εὐγενής.

noble, Acts xvii. 11. 1 Cor. i. 26.

With ἄνθρωπος, **nobleman**, Luke xix. 12.

εὐδία.

fair weather, Matt. xvi. 2.

εὐδοκέω.

be well pleased, Matt. iii. 17. xii. 18. xvii. 5. Mark i. 11. Luke iii. 22. 1 Cor. x. 5. 2 Pet. i. 17.

have pleasure, 2 Thes. ii. 12. Heb. x. 6, 8, 38.

take pleasure, 2 Cor. xii. 10.

it pleaseth[cc], Rom. xv. 26, 27. 1 Cor. i. 21. Gal. i. 15. Col. i. 19.

be one's good pleasure[cc], Luke xii. 32.

think good, 1 Thes. iii. 1.

be willing, 2 Cor. v. 8. 1 Thes. ii. 8.

εὐδοκία.

good will, Luke ii. 14 (*gen.* LTTr *S*). Phil. i. 15.

good pleasure, Eph. i. 5, 9. Phil. ii. 13. 2 Thes. i. 11.

With γίνομαι, **seem good**, Matt. xi. 26. Luke x. 21.

desire, Rom. x. 1.

εὐεργεσία.

good deed done to, Acts iv. 9.

benefit, 1 Tim. vi. 2.

εὐεργετέω.

do good, Acts x. 38.

εὐεργέτης.

benefactor, Luke xxii. 25.

εὔθετος.

fit, Luke ix. 62. xiv. 35.

meet, Heb. vi. 7.

εὐθέως. (εὐθύς, [1].)

straightway, Matt. iv. 20, xiv. 22, 27([1] LTr*S*). xxi. 2, 3([1] Tr*S*). xxv. 15. xxvii. 48. Mark i. 10([1] TTr*S*), 18, 20([1] TTr*S*), 21. ii. 2(–L[b]Tr[b]*S*). iii. 6 ([1] TTr*S*). v. 29 ([1] TTr*S*), 42 ([1] TTr*S*). vi. 25 ([1] LTTr*S*, – G[o]), 45 ([1] TTr*S*), 54 ([1] TTr*S*). vii. 35 (–L[b] Tr*S*). viii. 10([1] LTTr*S*). ix. 15([1] T Tr*S*), 20([1] G'LTr*S*), 24([1] TTr, –*S*). xi. 3([1] LTTr*S*). xiv. 45([1] LTTr*S*). xv. 1([1] TTr*S*).

Luke v. 39(–TTr*S*). xii. 54. xiv. 5. Acts ix. 20. xxii. 29. Jas. i. 24.

immediately, Matt. iv. 22. viii. 3. xiv. 31. xx. 34. xxiv. 29. xxvi. 74 ([1] Tr). Mark i. 31(–Tr*S*), 42([1] TTr *S*). ii. 8([1] LTTr*S*), 12([1] TTr*S*). iv. 5([1] LTTr*S*), 15([1] TTr*S*), 16([1] LTTr *S*), 17 ([1] TTr*S*), 29 ([1] TTr*S*). v. 2 ([1] TTr[b]*S*, –L), 30 ([1] TTr*S*). vi. 27 ([1] TTr*S*), 50 ([1] LTTr*S*). x. 52 ([1] LT Tr*S*). xiv. 43 ([1] LTTr*S*).

Luke v. 13. vi. 49([1] TTr*S*). xii. 36. John v. 9. vi. 21. xiii. 30([1] LT Tr*S*). xviii. 27. Acts ix. 18, 34. xvi. 10. xvii. 10, 14. Gal. i. 16. Rev. iv. 2.

forthwith, Matt. xiii. 5. xxvi. 49. Mark i. 29(¹ LTTr*S*), 43(¹ LTTr*S*). v. 13(–LᵇTr*S*). Acts xii. 10. xxi. 30.
as soon asᶜᶜ, Mark v. 36 (–G°LᵇTr *S*). xi. 2(¹ TTr*S*).
anon, Mark i. 30(¹ LTTr*S*).
by and by, Luke xvii. 7. xxi. 9.
shortly, 3 John 14.
Add Mark xiv. 72(.. the sec.), Gᵖʰ.

εὐθυδρομέω.

come with a straight course, Acts xvi. 11.
with a straight course, Acts xxi. 1ᵖ.

εὐθυμέω.

be of good cheer, Acts xxvii. 22, 25.
be merry, Jas. v. 13.

εὔθυμος.

of good cheer, Acts xxvii. 36.

εὐθυμότερον.

more cheerfully, Acts xxiv. 10 (εὐθύμως G″LT*S*).

εὐθύμως, cheerfully. See above.

εὐθύνω.

make straight, John i. 23.
governor, Jas. iii. 4ᵖ.

εὐθύς, adj.

straight, Matt. iii. 3. Mark i. 3. Luke iii. 4, 5. Acts ix. 11.
right, Acts viii. 21. xiii. 10. 2 Pet. ii. 15.

εὐθύς, adv.

straightway, Matt. iii. 16. John xiii. 32.
immediately, Mark i. 12, 28(–Trᵇ *S*). John xxi. 3(–G°°LTTr*S*).
forthwith, John xix. 34.
anon, Matt. xiii. 20.
by and by, Matt. xiii. 21.
Add Mark i. 23(And . .), TTrᵐᵇ*S*. v. 42(. . they were), TTrᵇ*S*. vii. 25 (. . heard), TTr*S*. xiv. 72 (. . the sec.), LTr*S*. Acts x. 16, for πάλιν, LT*S*.
See also εὐθέως.

εὐθύτης.

righteousness (*Gr.* rightness, *or* straightness), Heb. i. 8.

εὐκαιρέω.

have convenient time, 1 Cor. xvi. 12.
have leisure, Mark vi. 31.
spend one's time, Acts xvii. 21.

εὐκαιρία.

opportunity, Matt. xxvi. 16. Luke xxii. 6.

εὔκαιρος.

in time of need, Heb. iv. 16.
convenient, Mark vi. 21.

εὐκαίρως.

in season, 2 Tim. iv. 2.
conveniently, Mark xiv. 11.

εὐκοπώτερος.

easier, Matt. ix. 5. xix. 24. Mark ii. 9. x. 25. Luke v. 23. xvi. 17. xviii. 25.

εὐλάβεια.

With ἐν, **in that one feareth** (*marg.* **for one's piety**), Heb. v. 7.
godly fear, Heb. xii. 28.

εὐλαβέομαι.

be moved with fear (*marg.* **be wary**), Heb. xi. 7.
fear, Acts xxiii. 10 (φοβέω G′L*S*).

εὐλαβής.

devout, Luke ii. 25. Acts ii. 5. viii. 2.
Add Acts xxii. 12, for εὐσεβής, LT*S*.

εὐλογέω.

bless, Matt. v. 44 (*ap*). xiv. 19. xxi. 9. xxiii. 39. xxv. 34. xxvi. 26 (εὐχαριστέω CᵐG″). Mark vi. 41. viii. 7. x. 16 (κατευλογέω TTr*S*). xi. 9, 10. xiv. 22. Luke i. 28(*ap*), 42*t*. ii. 28, 34. vi. 28. ix. 16. xiii. 35. xix. 38. xxiv. 30, 50, 51, 53 (*ap*). John xii. 13. Acts iii. 26. Rom. xii. 14*t*. 1 Cor. iv. 12. x. 16. xiv. 16. Gal. iii. 9. Eph. i. 3. Heb. vi. 14*t*. vii. 1, 6, 7. xi. 20, 21. Jas. iii. 9. 1 Pet. iii. 9.
praise, Luke i. 64.

εὐλογητός.

Said of God, **blessed**, Mark xiv. 61. Luke i. 68. Rom. i. 25. ix. 5. 2 Cor. i. 3. xi. 31. Eph. i. 3. 1 Pet. i. 3.

εὐλογία.

fair speeches, Rom. xvi. 18.
blessing, Rom. xv. 29. 1 Cor. x. 16. Gal. iii. 14. Eph. i. 3. Heb. vi. 7. xii. 17. Jas. iii. 10. 1 Pet. iii. 9. Rev. v. 12, 13. vii. 12.
bounty (*Gr.* blessing), 2 Cor. ix. 5.
matter of bounty, 2 Cor. ix. 5.
Plur., *with* ἐπί, **bountifully**, 2 Cor. ix. 6*t*.

εὐμετάδοτος.

ready to distribute, 1 Tim. vi. 18.

εὐνοέω.

agree, Matt. v. 25 (p *with* εἰμί).

εὔνοια.

good will, Eph. vi. 7.
benevolence, 1 Cor. vii. 3(*see* ὀφειλή).

εὐνουχίζω.

make eunuch, Matt. xix. 12*t*.

εὐνοῦχος.

eunuch, Matt. xix. 12*tr*. Acts viii. 27, 34, 36, 38, 39.

εὐοδόομαι, -οῦμαι.

have a prosperous journey, Rom. i. 10.
prosper, 1 Cor. xvi. 2cc. 3 John 2*t*.

εὐπάρεδρος, assiduous, devoted. 1 Cor. vii. 35, for εὐπρόσεδ., GLT*S*.

εὐπειθής.

easy to be entreated, Jas. iii. 17.

εὐπερίστατος.

which doth so easily beset c**us**, Heb. xii. 1.

εὐποιΐα.

to do goodcc, Heb. xiii. 16.

εὐπορέομαι.

With καθώς, **according to one's ability**, Acts xi. 29.

εὐπορία.

wealth Acts xix. 25.

εὐπρέπεια.

grace, Jas. i. 11.

εὐπρόσδεκτος.

acceptable, Rom. xv. 16. 1 Pet. ii. 5.
accepted, Rom. xv. 31. 2 Cor. vi. 2. viii. 12.

εὐπρόσεδρος.

πρὸς τὸ ε., **that one may attend upon**, 1 Cor. vii. 35 (εὐπάρεδρος GLT*S*).

εὐπροσωπέω.

make a fair show, Gal. vi. 12.

εὑρίσκω.

find, Matt. i. 18. ii. 8. vii. 7, 8, 14. viii. 10. x. 39*t*. xi. 29. xii. 43, 44. xiii. 44p, 46p. xvi. 25. xvii. 27. xviii. 13, 28. xx. 6. xxi. 2, 19. xxii. 9, 10. xxiv. 46. xxvi. 40, 43, 60, 60 (-GLbTTr*S*). xxvii. 32.
Mark i. 37p. vii. 30. xi. 2, 4, 13*t*. xiii. 36. xiv. 16, 37, 40, 55.
Luke i. 30. ii. 12, 45p, 46. iv. 17. v. 19p. vi. 7. vii. 9, 10. viii. 35. ix. 36. xi. 9, 10, 24, 25. xii. 37, 38, 43. xiii. 6, 7. xv. 4, 5p, 6, 8, 9*t*, 24, 32. xvii. 18. xviii. 8. xix. 30, 32. xxii. 13, 45. xxiii. 2, 4, 14, 22. xxiv. 2, 3. 23p, 24, 33.
John i. 41(42)*t*, 43(44), 45(46)*t*. ii. 14. v. 14. vi. 25p. vii. 34, 35, 36. ix. 35p. x. 9. xi. 17. xii. 14p. xviii. 38. xix. 4, 6. xxi. 6.
Acts iv. 21. v. 10, 22, 23*t*, 39. vii. 11, 46*t*. viii. 40. ix. 2, 33. x. 27. xi. 26(25)p. xii. 19. xiii. 6, 22, 28p. xvii. 6p, 23, 27. xviii. 2. xix. 1, 19. xxi. 2. xxiii. 9. xxiv. 5, 12, 18, 20. xxvii. 6, 28*t*. xxviii. 14.
Rom. iv. 1. vii. 10cc, 18 (-G″LT*S*), 21. x. 20. 1 Cor. iv. 2. xv. 15. 2 Cor. ii. 13(12). v. 3. ix. 4. xi. 12. xii. 20*t*. Gal. ii. 17. Phil. ii. 8. iii. 9. 2 Tim. i. 17, 18.
Heb. iv. 16. xi. 5. xii. 17. 1 Pet. i. 7. ii. 22. 2 Pet. iii. 14. 2 John 4. Rev. ii. 2. iii. 2. v. 4. ix. 6. xii. 8. xiv. 5. xvi. 20. xviii. 14, 21. 22, 24. xx. 11, 15.
can find, Luke xix. 48.
perceive, Acts xxiii. 29.
obtain, Heb. ix. 12.
get, Mark ix. 12.
Add Matt. ii. 11, for εἶδον, StE.

εὐρύχωρος.

broad, Matt. vii. 13.

εὐσέβεια.
godliness, 1 Tim. ii. 2. iii. 16. iv. 7, 8. vi. 3, 5, 6, 11. 2 Tim. iii. 5. Tit. i. 1. 2 Pet. i. 3, 6, 7. iii. 11.
holiness, Acts iii. 12.

εὐσεβέω.
show piety (*marg.* **kindness**) **at**, 1 Tim. v. 4.
worship, Acts xvii. 23.

εὐσεβής.
devout, Acts x. 2, 7. xxii. 12(εὐλαβής LT*S*).
godly, 2 Pet. ii. 9.

εὐσεβῶς.
godly, 2 Tim. iii. 12. Tit. ii. 12.

εὔσημος.
easy to be understood (*Gr.* significant), 1 Cor. xiv. 9.

εὔσπλαγχνος.
tender-hearted, Eph. iv. 32.
pitiful, 1 Pet. iii. 8.

εὐσχημόνως.
decently, 1 Cor. xiv. 40.
honestly, Rom. xiii. 13 (*marg.* **decently**). 1 Thes. iv. 12.

εὐσχημοσύνη.
comeliness, 1 Cor. xii. 23.

εὐσχήμων.
comely, 1 Cor. xii. 24.
With art., **that which is comely**, 1 Cor. vii. 35.
honorable, Mark xv. 43. Acts xiii. 50. xvii. 12.

εὐτόνως.
mightily, Acts xviii. 28.
vehemently, Luke xxiii. 10.

εὐτραπελία.
jesting, Eph. v. 4.

εὐφημία.
good report, 2 Cor. vi. 8.

εὔφημος.
of good report, Phil. iv. 8.

εὐφορέω.
bring forth plentifully, Luke xii. 16.

εὐφραίνω.
make glad, 2 Cor. ii. 2.
Mid., and Pass. aor., **rejoice**, Acts ii. 26. vii. 41. Rom. xv. 10. Gal. iv. 27. Rev. xii. 12. xviii. 20. — **be merry**, Luke xii. 19. xv. 23, 24. — **make merry**, Luke xv. 29, 32. Rev. xi. 10. — **fare**, Luke xvi. 19.

εὐφροσύνη.
gladness, Acts xiv. 17.
joy, Acts ii. 28.

εὐχαριστέω.
give thanks, Matt. xv. 36. xxvi. 27. Mark viii. 6. xiv. 23p. Luke xvii. 16. xxii. 17, 19. John vi. 11p, 23p (-G°). Acts xxvii. 35. Rom. xiv. 6*t*. xvi. 4. 1 Cor. x. 30. xi. 24p. xiv. 17. Eph. i. 16. v. 20. Col. i. 3, 12. iii. 17. 1 Thes. i. 2. v. 18. 2 Thes. ii. 13. Rev. xi. 17.
Pass., **thanks are given**, 2 Cor. i. 11.
thank, Luke xviii. 11. John xi. 41. Acts xxviii. 15. Rom. i. 8. vii. 25 (χάρις G''LT). 1 Cor. i. 4, 14. xiv. 18. Phil. i. 3. 1 Thes. ii. 13. 2 Thes. i. 3. Phm. 4.
be thankful, Rom. i, 21.
Add Matt. xxvi. 26, for εὐλογέω, CmG''.

εὐχαριστία.
thankfulness, Acts xxiv. 3.
thanksgiving, 2 Cor. iv. 15. ix. 11, 12. Phil. iv. 6. Col. ii. 7. iv. 2. 1 Tim. iv. 3, 4. Rev. vii. 12.
giving of thanks, 1 Cor. xiv. 16. Eph. v. 4. 1 Tim. ii. 1.
thanks, 1 Thes. iii. 9. Rev. iv. 9.

εὐχάριστος.
thankful, Col. iii. 15.

εὐχή.
prayer, Jas. v. 15.
vow, Acts xviii. 18. xxi. 23.

εὔχομαι.
pray, 2 Cor. xiii. 7. Jas. v. 16 (προσεύχομαι L).
wish, Acts xxvii. 29. 2 Cor. xiii. 9. 3 John 2(*marg.* **pray**).
can wish, Rom. ix. 3.
εὐξαίμην ἄν, **I would**, Acts xxvi. 29.

εὔχρηστος.
meet for use, 2 Tim. ii. 21.
profitable, 2 Tim. iv. 11. Phm. 11.

εὐψυχέω.

be of good comfort, Phil. ii. 19.

εὐωδία.

sweet smell, Phil. iv. 18.
sweet-smelling[cu], Eph. v. 2.
sweet savor, 2 Cor. ii. 15.

εὐώνυμος.

on the left hand, Acts xxi. 3.
left [c]**foot**, Rev. x. 2.
ἐξ εὐωνύμων, **on the (one's) left**, Matt. xx. 21, 23. xxv. 33. xxvii. 38. Mark xv. 27.—**on the (one's) left hand**, Matt. xxv. 41. Mark x. 37(ἀριστερός TTr), 40.

ἐφάλλομαι.

With ἐπί, **leap on**, Acts xix. 16.

ἐφάπαξ.

once for all, Heb. x. 10.
at once, 1 Cor. xv. 6.
once, Rom. vi. 10. Heb. vii. 27. ix. 12.

ἐφεῖδον. See ἐπεῖδον.

ἐφευρετής.

inventor, Rom. i. 30.

ἐφημερία.

course, Luke i. 5, 8.

ἐφήμερος.

daily, Jas. ii. 15.

ἔφιδε. See ἐπεῖδον.

ἐφικνέομαι.

reach unto, 2 Cor. x. 13(*with* ἄχρι), 14(*with* εἰς).

ἐφίστημι.

stand by, Luke xxiv. 4. Acts xxii. 20. xxiii. 11.
stand over, Luke iv. 39(*with* ἐπάνω).
stand before, Acts x. 17(*with* ἐπί).
stand, Acts xxii. 13.
come upon, Luke ii. 9. xx. 1. xxi. 34(*with* ἐπί). Acts iv. 1. vi. 12. xii. 7. 1 Thes. v. 3.
come unto, Acts xi. 11(*with* ἐπί).
come to, Luke x. 40.
come in, Luke ii. 38.
come, Acts xxiii. 27.
assault, Acts xvii. 5.
be instant, 2 Tim. iv. 2.
be at hand, 2 Tim. iv. 6.
present, Acts xxviii. 2[p].

ἐφοράω. See ἐπεῖδον.

ἐφφαθά.

ephphatha, Mark vii. 34.

ἐχθές, yesterday. See χθές.

ἔχθρα.

enmity, Luke xxiii. 12. Rom. viii. 7. Eph. ii. 15, 16. Jas. iv. 4.
hatred, Gal. v. 20.

ἐχθρός.

enemy, Matt. v. 43, 44. xiii. 25, 28, 39. xxii. 24. Mark xii. 36. Luke i. 71, 74. vi. 27, 35. x. 19. xix. 27, 43. xx. 43. Acts xiii. 10. Rom. v. 10. xi. 28. xii. 20. 1 Cor. xv. 25, 26. Gal. iv. 16. Phil. iii. 18. Col. i. 21. 2 Thes. iii. 15. Heb. i. 13. x. 13. Jas. iv. 4. Rev. xi. 5, 12.
foe, Matt. x. 36. Acts ii. 35.

ἔχιδνα.

viper, Matt. iii. 7. xii. 34. xxiii. 33. Luke iii. 7. Acts xxviii. 3.

ἔχω.

have, Matt. iii. 4, 9, 14. v. 23, 46. vi. 1, 8. vii. 29. viii. 9, 20*t*. ix. 6, 36. xi. 15, 18. xii. 10, 11. xiii. 5*t*, 6, 9, 12*tr*, 21, 27, 43, 44, 46. xiv. 4, 17. xv. 30, 32, 34. xvii. 20. xviii. 8, 9. 25[p], 25. xix. 16 (κληρονομήσω L[m]*S*), 21, 22(*with* εἰμί). xxi. 3, 21, 28. xxii. 12, 24, 25, 28. xxv. 25, 28, 29*tr*. xxvi. 7, 11*t*, 65. xxvii. 16, 65.
Mark i. 22. ii. 10, 17, 19(*ap*), 25. iii. 1, 3, 10, 15, 22, 26, 29, 30. iv. 5*t*, 6, 9, 17, 23, 25*tr*, 40. v. 3, 15 (-G[oo]). vi. 18, 34, 36(-G″L[b]Tr*S*), 38. vii. 16, 25. viii. 1, 2, 5, 7, 14, 16, 17*t*, 18*t*. ix. 17, 43, 45, 47, 50. x. 21*t*, 22(*with* εἰμί), 23. xi. 3, 13, 22, 25. xii. 6, 23, 44. xiv. 3, 7*t*.
Luke iii. 8, 11*tr*. iv. 33, 40. v. 24. vi. 8. vii. 8, 33, 40, 42[p]. viii. 8, 13, 18*tr*, 27. ix. 3, 11, 58*t*. xi. 5, 6, 36. xii. 4, 5, 17, 19, 50. xiii. 6. 11. xiv. 18, 19, 35. xv. 4, 8, 11. xvi.

1, 28, 29. xvii. 6, 7. xviii. 22*t*, 24. xix. 17 (*with* εἰμί), 24, 25, 26*tr*, 31, 34. xx. 24, 28, 33. xxi. 4. xxii. 36*t*, 37. xxiv. 39*t*, 41.

John ii. 3. iii. 15, 16, 29, 36. iv. 11*t*, 17*t*, 18*t*, 32, 44. v. 2, 5 (*with* ἐν), 7, 24, 26*t*, 36, 38, 39, 40, 42. vi. 9, 40, 47, 53, 54, 68. vii. 20. viii. 6(*ap*), 12, 26, 41, 48, 49, 52. ix. 41. x. 10*t*, 16, 18*t*, 20. xii. 6, 8*t*, 35, 36, 48. xiii. 8, 29*t*, 35. xiv. 21, 30. xv. 13, 22*t*, 34. xvi. 12, 15, 21, 22, 33*t*. xvii. 5, 13. xviii. 10. xix. 7, 10*t*, 11, 15. xx. 31. xxi. 5.

Acts ii. 44, 45, 47. iii. 6. iv. 35. ix. 14, 31. xiii. 5. xiv. 9. xv. 21. xviii. 18. xix. 13, 38. xxi. 23. xxiii. 17, 18, 19, 29. xxiv. 15, 16, 19, 23. xxv. 16, 19, 26*t*. xxviii. 9, 19, 29(*ap*).

Rom. i. 13. ii. 14*t*, 20. iv. 2. v. 1, 2. vi. 21, 22. viii. 9, 23. ix. 21. x. 2. xii. 4*t*, 6. xiii. 3. xiv. 22*t*. xv. 4, 17, 23*t*.

1 Cor. ii. 16. iv. 7, 15. v. 1. vi. 1, 4, 19. vii. 2*t*, 7, 12, 13, 25, 28, 29*t*, 37*t*, 40. viii. 1, 10. ix. 4, 5, 6, 17. xi. 4, 10, 16, 22. xii. 12, 21*t*, 23, 24, 30. xiii. 1, 2*tr*, 3. xiv. 26*five*. xv. 31, 34.

2 Cor. i. 9, 15. ii. 3, 4, 13. iii. 4, 12ᵖ. iv. 1ᵖ, 7, 13. v. 1, 12. vi. 10. vii. 1, 5. viii. 11, 12*t*. ix. 8. x. 6, 15.

Gal. ii. 4. iv. 22, 27. vi. 4, 10. Eph. i. 7. ii. 12, 18. iii. 12. iv. 28. v. 5, 27. Phil. i. 7, 23, 30. ii. 2, 20, 27. iii. 4, 9, 17. Col. i. 14. ii. 1, 23 (*with* εἰμί). iii. 13. iv. 1, 13. 1 Thes. i. 9. iii. 6. iv. 12, 13. v. 1. 2 Thes. iii. 9. 1 Tim. iii. 4, 7. iv. 8. v. 4, 12, 16. vi. 2, 8, 16. 2 Tim. i. 3. ii. 19. iii. 5. Tit. i. 6. ii. 8. Phm. 5, 7.

Heb. ii. 14. iii. 3. iv. 14ᵖ, 15. v. 12, 12ᵖ, 14. vi. 18, 19. vii. 3, 5, 6, 24, 28. viii. 1, 3. ix. 1, 4*t*. x. 1, 2, 19, 34, 35, 36. xi. 10, 15. xii. 9, 28 (*marg.* **hold fast**). xiii. 10*t*, 14, 18.

Jas. i. 4. ii. 1, 14*t*, 17, 18*t*. iii. 14. iv. 2*t*. 1 Pet. ii. 12. iii. 16. iv. 8. 2 Pet. i. 19. ii. 14*t*. 1 John i. 3, 6, 7, 8. ii. 1, 7, 20, 23, 28. iii. 3, 15, 17*t*, 21. iv. 16, 17, 18, 21. v. 10, 12*f*, 13, 14, 15. 2 John 5, 9*t*, 12. 3 John 4, 13. Jude 19.

Rev. i. 16, 18. ii. 3, 4, 6, 7, 10, 11, 12, 14*t*, 15, 17, 18, 20, 24, 25, 29. iii. 1*t*, 4, 6, 7, 8, 11, 13, 17, 22. iv. 4(*omS*), 7, 8. v. 6, 8. vi. 2, 5. vii. 2. viii. 3, 6, 9. ix. 3, 4, 8, 9, 10, 11*t*, 14, 17, 19. x. 2. xi. 6*t*. xii. 3, 6, 12*t*, 17. xiii. 1, 9, 11, 14, 17, 18. xiv. 1, 6, 11, 14, 17, 18*t*. xv. 1. 2, 6. xvi. 2, 9. xvii. 1, 3, 4, 7, 9, 13. xviii. 1, 19. xix. 10, 12, 16. xx. 1, 6*t*. xxi. 9, 11, 12*t*, 14, 15, 23.

μὴ ἔχω, **have not** (*marg.* **be poor**), 1 Cor. xi. 22. —**lack**, Luke viii. 6.

have sufficient, Luke xiv. 28.

can have, John xix. 11.

can, Mark xiv. 8. Luke xiv. 14. Acts iv. 14ᶜᶜ. Heb. vi. 13.

be able, 2 Pet. i. 15.

be possessed with, Acts viii. 7. xvi. 16.

be in ᶜ**that case**, John v. 6.

with, Acts xxvii. 39ᵖ.

hold, Matt. xxi. 26. Phil. ii. 29(*see* ἔντιμος). 1 Tim. i. 19. iii. 9. Rev. vi. 9.

hold fast, 2 Tim. i. 13.

keepᶜ, Luke xix. 20.

retain, Rom. i. 28 (*see* ἐπίγνωσις).

count, Matt. xiv. 5. Mark xi. 32. Acts xx. 24(-T*S*). Phm. 17.

take for, Matt. xxi. 46.

use, 1 Pet. ii. 16(*Gr.* have).

do, Acts xv. 36.

lie, John xi. 17.

In notation of space or time, **be**, Acts i. 12. —**be old**, John viii. 57.

be, Acts vii. 1. xii. 15. xvii. 11. xxiv. 9. 1 Tim. v. 25.

Mid., **accompany**, Heb. vi. 9.—**next**, Mark i. 38ᵖ. Acts xxi. 26ᵖ.—**next day**, Acts xx. 15ᵖ.—**day following**, Luke xiii. 33ᵖ.

Add Matt. xvi. 8, for λαμβάνω, L *S*. xvii. 15, for πάσχω, LTr*S*. xxi. 38, for κατέχω, G'LTTr*S*. Mark ix.

42, *see* πιστεύω. Acts xiii. 44, *mid.* for ἔρχομαι, GLT. xxiii. 25, for περιέχω, L*S*. Col. i. 4, ἣν ἔ. for τήν after ἀγάπην, G′LT*S*. 1 John ii. 23 (*ap*).

See also ἀκροβυστία, ἀνάγκη, ἀνάπαυσις, ἀπόλαυσις, βασιλεία, γάγγραινα, γαστήρ, ἔλεγξις, ἐσχάτως, ἑτοίμως, ἡλικία, κακῶς, καλῶς, κοιτή, κομψότερον, κρίμα, νῦν, παρρησία, περίκειμαι, στάσις, τρόμος, φόβος, χάρις, χρεία.

ἕως.

I. With a Verb.

(*With* ἄν, ^{1}. οὗ, ^{2}. ὅτου, ^{3}.)

till, Matt. i. 25^{2}. ii. 9. v. 18*t*^{1}, 26^{1}. x. 11^{1}, 23^{1}. xii. 20^{1}. xiii. 33^{2}. xvi. 28^{1}. xviii. 30^{2}(^{2}–LTTr*S*), 34^{2}(^{2}–L). xxii. 44^{1}. xxiii. 39^{1}. xxiv. 34^{1}. Mark vi. 10^{1}. ix. 1^{1}. xii. 36^{2}.

Luke ix. 27^{1}. xii. 50^{2}, 59^{2}. xiii. 8^{3}, 21^{2}. xv. 8^{3}. xvii. 8. xix. 13(ἐν ᾧ G″ LTTr*S*). xx. 43^{1}. xxi. 32^{1}. John xiii. 38^{2}. xxi. 22, 23. Acts xxiii. 12^{2}, 21^{2}. xxv. 21^{2}. 1 Tim. iv. 13. Heb. x. 13.

until, Matt. ii. 13^{1}. xvii. 9^{2}. xxiv. 39. Luke xv. 4. xxii. 16^{3}, 18^{3}. xxiv. 49^{2}. John ix. 18^{3}. Acts ii. 35^{1}. xxi. 26^{2}. xxiii. 14^{2}. 1 Cor. iv. 5^{1}. 2 Thes. ii. 7. Heb. i. 13^{1}. Jas. v. 7^{1}(^{1}–T). 2 Pet. i. 19^{2}. Rev. vi. 11(^{2}St). xx. 5 (ἄχρι GLTTr, –*S*^{c}).

until the time, Luke xiii. 35^{1}.

while, Matt. xiv. 22. xxvi. 36^{2} (ἕ. οὗ ἂν L). Mark vi. 45. xiv. 32. John ix. 4. xii. 35 (ὡς LTTr), 36 (ὡς LTTr*S*).

whiles, Matt. v. 25^{3}.

Add Luke xxii. 34, for πρὶν ἤ, LT Tr*S*.

II. With a Genitive.

till, Luke i. 80. Acts viii. 40(*inf.*). xxviii. 23.

until, Matt. i. 17. ii. 15. xi. 13. xxvi. 29. xxvii. 64. Mark xiv. 25. xv. 33. Luke xvi. 16(μέχρι TTr*S*). xxiii. 44. Acts xiii. 20. 1 Cor. xvi. 8.

to, Matt. i. 17. xi. 23. xxiv. 31. Mark xiii. 27. Luke x. 15*t*. Acts viii. 10. ix. 38. xxiii. 23. 2 Cor. i. 13. xii. 2. Heb. viii. 11.

unto, Matt. i. 17. xi. 23. xx. 8. xxii. 26. xxiii. 35. xxiv. 27. xxvi. 58. xxvii. 45. xxviii. 20. Mark vi. 23. xiv. 34. Luke ii. 15. iv. 29, 42. xi. 51. John viii. 9(*ap*). Acts i. 8, 22. vii. 45. xiii. 47. xvii. 15. Rom. xi. 8. 1 Cor. i. 8. Jas. v. 7.

even unto, Matt. xxvi. 38.

ἕως καὶ εἰς, **even unto**, Acts xxvi. 11.

as far as, Acts xi. 19, 22.

ἕως τούτου, **thus far**, Luke xxii. 51.

οὐκ ἔστιν ἕως ἑνός, **no, not one**, Rom. iii. 12.

Add Matt. xiii. 30, for μέχρι, LTr. Luke i. 55, for εἰς, G. ii. 37, for ὡς, LTTr*S*.

III. With other Particles.

till, Matt. xviii. 21. Acts xxi. 5.

until, Matt. xi. 12. xviii. 22*t*. John ii. 10.

unto, Matt. xxvii. 8.

even unto, 2 Cor. iii. 15.

as far as, Luke xxiv. 50.

ἕως ἔσω εἰς, **even into**, Mark xiv. 54.

ἕως τοῦ νῦν, **to this time**, Matt. xxiv. 21.—**unto this time**, Mark xiii. 19.

ἕως πότε; **how long?** Matt. xvii. 17*t*. Mark ix. 19*t*. Luke ix. 41. John x. 24. Rev. vi. 10.

ἕως ὧδε, **to this place**, Luke xxiii. 5.

Add Acts xvii. 14, for ὡς, L*S*.

See also ἄνω, ἄρτι, κάτω, ὅτου.

ζάω.

to live, Matt. iv. 4. ix. 18. xvi. 16. xxii. 32. xxvi. 63. Mark v. 23. xii. 27. Luke ii. 36. iv. 4. x. 28. xx. 38*t*. xxiv. 5. John iv. 10, 11, 50, 51, 53. v. 25. vi. 51*t*, 57*tr*, 58, 69 (*ap*). vii. 38. xi. 25, 26. xiv. 19*t*. Acts xiv. 15. xvii. 28. xxii. 22. xxv. 24. xxvi. 5. xxviii. 4.

Rom. i. 17. vi. 2, 10*t*. vii. 1, 2^{p}, 3^{p}. viii. 12, 13*t*. ix. 26. x. 5. xii. 1. xiv. 7, 8*tr*, 9, 11. 1 Cor. vii. 39. ix. 14. xv. 45. 2 Cor. iii. 3. iv. 11. v. 15*t*. vi. 9, 16. xiii. 4*t*.

Gal. ii. 14, 19, 20*f*. iii. 11, 12. v. 25. Phil. i. 21, 22. Col. ii. 20. iii. 7. 1 Thes. i. 9. iii. 8. v. 10. 1 Tim. iii. 15. iv. 10. v. 6p. vi. 17(-G∘LT *S*). 2 Tim. iii. 12. Tit. ii. 12. Heb. iii. 12. vii. 8, 25p. ix. 14, 17. x. 20, 31, 38. xii. 9, 22.

Jas. iv. 15. 1 Pet. i. 23. ii. 4, 24. iv. 6. 1 John iv. 9. Rev. i. 18. iii. 1. iv. 9, 10. v. 14 (*ap*). vii. 2, 17 (ζωῆς GLTTr*S*). x. 6. xiii. 14. xv. 7. xvi. 3(ζωῆς GLTTrb). xx. 4.

be alive, Matt. xxvii. 63p. Mark xvi. 11(*ap*). Luke xxiv. 23. Acts xxv. 19. Rom. vi. 13p. vii. 9. 1 Thes. iv. 15, 17. Rev. ii. 8.

Part., **alive**, Acts i. 3. ix. 41. xx. 12. xxv. 19. Rom. vi. 11. Rev. i. 18. xix. 20.—**lively**, Acts vii. 38. 1 Pet. i. 3. ii. 5. —**quick**, Acts x. 42. 2 Tim. iv. 1. Heb. iv. 12. 1 Pet. iv. 5.

ζῶν ἀσώτως, **with riotous living**, Luke xv. 13.

Inf., **life**, 2 Cor. i. 8.—**life-time**, Heb. ii. 15.

Add, for ἀναζάω, Luke xv. 32, TTr *S*. Rom. xiv. 9, GLT*S*. Rev. xx. 5, GLTTr.

ζβέννυμι. See σβέννυμι.

ζεστός.

hot, Rev. iii. 15*t*, 16.

ζεῦγος.

yoke, Luke xiv. 19.
pair, Luke ii. 24.

ζευκτηρία.

band, Acts xxvii. 40.

ζέω.

be fervent, Acts xviii. 25.
fervent, Rom. xii. 11p.

ζηλεύω, be zealous.

Rev. iii. 19, for ζηλόω, G''LTTr.

ζῆλος.

zeal, John ii. 17. Rom. x. 2. 2 Cor. vii. 11. ix. 2. Phil. iii. 6. Col. iv. 13(πόνος GLT*S*).
fervent mind, 2 Cor. vii. 7.
emulation, Gal. v. 20.
envy, Acts xiii. 45.
envying, Rom. xiii. 13. 1 Cor. iii. 3. 2 Cor. xii. 20. Jas. iii. 14, 15.
jealousy, 2 Cor. xi. 2.
indignation, Acts v. 17 (*marg.* **envy**). Heb. x. 27.

ζηλόω.

be zealous, Rev. iii. 19 (ζήλευε fr. ζηλεύω G''LTTr).
zealously affect, Gal. iv. 17, 18.
affect, Gal. iv. 17.
desire, 1 Cor. xiv. 1.
desire to have, Jas. iv. 2.
covet earnestly, 1 Cor. xii. 31.
covet, 1 Cor. xiv. 39.
be jealous over, 2 Cor. xi. 2.
envy, 1 Cor. xiii. 4.
be moved with envy, Acts vii. 9. xvii. 5(-GT).

ζηλωτής.

zealous, Acts xxi. 20. xxii. 3. 1 Cor. xiv. 12. Gal. i. 14. Tit. ii. 14.
Add 1 Pet. iii. 13, for μιμητής, G'' L*S*.

ζημία.

loss, Acts xxvii. 21. Phil. iii. 7, 8.
damage, Acts xxvii. 10.

ζημιόω.

Middle or Passive,

lose, Matt. xvi. 26. Mark viii. 36.
suffer loss, 1 Cor. xiii. 15.
suffer the loss of, Phil. iii. 8.
receive damage, 2 Cor. vii. 9.
be cast away, Luke ix. 25.

ζητέω.

seek, Matt. ii. 13, 20. vi. 33. vii. 7, 8. xii. 43. xiii. 45. xviii. 12. xxi. 46p. xxvi. 16, 59. xxviii. 5. Mark viii. 11. xi. 18. xii. 12. xiv. 1, 11. xvi. 6. Luke ii. 45 (ἀναζητέω G''LTTr), 48, 49. iv. 42(ἐπιζητέω G LTTr*S*). vi. 19. xi. 9, 10, 16, 24, 54(-G∘∘LTTrb*S*). xii. 29, 31. xiii. 6, 7, 24. xv. 8. xvii. 33. xix. 3, 10, 47. xx. 19. xxii. 2, 6. xxiv. 5.

John i. 38(39). iv. 23, 27 v. 16 (*ap*), 18, 30, 44. vi. 26. vii. 1, 4, 11, 18*t*, 25, 30, 34, 36. viii. 21, 37, 40, 50*t*. x. 39. xi. 8, 56. xiii. 33.

xviii. 4, 7, 8. xix. 12. xx. 15. Acts x. 19, 21. xiii. 8, 11. xvii. 5, 27. Rom. x. 20. xi. 3. 1 Cor. vii. 27t. x. 24, 33. xiii. 5. xiv. 12. 2 Cor. xii. 14. xiii. 3. Gal. i. 10. ii. 17p. Phil. ii. 21. Col. iii. 1. 1 Thes. ii. 6. 2 Tim. i. 17. 1 Pet. iii. 11. v. 8. Rev. ix. 6.

seek for, Mark i. 37. iii. 32. xiv. 55. John vi. 24. Rom. ii. 7. Heb. viii. 7.

seek after, 1 Cor. i. 22.

seek means, Luke v. 18.

go about, John vii. 19, 20. Acts xxi. 31p. Rom. x. 3.

be about, Acts xxvii. 30p.

endeavor, Acts xvi. 10.

desire, Matt. xii. 46, 47. Luke ix. 9.

inquire for, Acts ix. 11.

inquire, John xvi. 19.

require, Luke xii. 48. 1 Cor. iv. 2.

Add Mark vi. 19, for θέλω, L. viii. 12, for ἐπιζητέω, LTTr*S*.

ζήτημα.

question, Acts xv. 2. xviii. 15. xxiii. 29. xxv. 19. xxvi. 3.

ζήτησις.

question, John iii. 25. 1 Tim. i. 4. vi. 4. 2 Tim. ii. 23. Tit. iii. 9.

εἰς τὴν περὶ τούτου (τούτων G″LT*S*) ζήτησιν, **of such manner of questions**, Acts xxv. 20 (*marg.* **how to inquire hereof**).

Add Acts xv. 2, for συζήτησις, GL T*S*, -Goo.

ζιζάνιον.

Plur., **tares**, Matt. xiii. 25, 36, 27, 29, 30, 36, 38, 40.

ζόφος.

darkness, 2 Pet. ii. 4. Jude 6.

blackness, Jude 13.

mist, 2 Pet. ii. 17.

Add Heb. xii. 18, for σκότος, G″L T*S*.

ζυγός.

yoke, Matt. xi. 29, 30. Acts xv. 10. Gal. v. 1. 1 Tim. vi. 1.

pair of balances, Rev. vi. 5.

ζύμη.

leaven, Matt. xiii. 33. xvi. 6, 11, 12. Mark viii. 15t. Luke xii. 1. xiii. 21. 1 Cor. v. 6, 7, 8t, Gal. v. 9.

ζυμόω.

to leaven, Matt. xiii. 33. Luke xiii. 21. 1 Cor. v. 6(δολόω G′). Gal. v. 9.

ζωγρέω.

take captive, 2 Tim. ii. 26(*Gr.* take alive).

catch, Luke v. 10(*with* εἰμί).

ζωή.

life, Matt. vii. 14. xviii. 8, 9. xix. 17. Mark ix. 43, 45. Luke i. 75 (*omS*). xii. 15. John i. 4t. iii. 36. v. 24, 26t, 29, 40. vi. 33, 35, 48, 51, 53, 63. viii. 12. x. 10. xi. 25. xiv. 6. xx. 31. Acts ii. 28. iii. 15. v. 20. viii. 33. xi. 18. xvii. 25. Rom. v. 10, 17, 18. vi. 4. vii. 10. viii. 2, 6, 10, 38. xi. 15. 1 Cor. iii. 22. xv. 19. 2 Cor. ii. 16t. iv. 10, 11, 12. v. 4. Eph. iv. 18. Phil. i. 20. ii. 16. iv. 3. Col. iii. 3, 4. 1 Tim. iv. 8. 2 Tim. i. 1, 10. Heb. vii. 3, 16. Jas. i. 12. iv. 14. 1 Pet. iii. 7, 10. 2 Pet. i. 3. 1 John i. 1, 2. iii. 14, 15. v. 11, 12t, 16. Rev. ii. 7, 10. iii. 5. xi. 11. xiii. 8. xvii. 8. xx. 12, 15. xxi. 6, 27. xxii. 1, 2, 14, 17, 19.

life-time, Luke xvi. 25.

Add, for ζάωp, Rev. vii. 17, GLT Tr*S*. xvi. 3, GLTTrb.

See also αἰώνιος.

ζώνη.

girdle, Matt. iii. 4. Mark i. 6. Acts xxi. 11t. Rev. i. 3. xv. 6.

purse, Matt. x. 9. Mark vi. 8.

ζώννυμι, ζωννύω.

gird, John xxi. 18t.

Add Acts xii. 8, for περιζώννυμι, G″LT*S*.

ζωογονέω.

preserve, Luke xvii. 33.

Pass., **live**, Acts vii. 19.

Add 1 Tim. vi. 13, for ζωοποιέω, G′LT.

ζῶον.

beast, Heb. xiii. 11. 2 Pet. ii. 12. Jude 10. Rev. iv. 6, 7*f*, 8, 9. v. 6, 8, 11, 14. vi. 1, 3, 5, 6, 7. vii. 11. xiv. 3. xv. 7. xix. 4.

ζωοποιέω.

make alive, 1 Cor. xv. 22.

give life, 2 Cor. iii. 6 (*marg.* **quicken**). Gal. iii. 21.

quicken, John v. 21*t*. vi. 63. Rom. iv. 17. viii. 11. 1 Cor. xv. 36, 45. 1 Tim. vi. 13(ζωογονέω G'LT). 1 Pet. iii. 18.

ἤ.

A particle disjunctive, interrogative, or comparative.

I. Disjunctive.

(a) In general: —

or, Matt. v. 17, 18, 36. x. 11, 14, 19, 37*t*. xii. 25. xiii 21. xv 4, 5, 6 (5, *ap*). xvi. 14. xvii. 25. xviii. 8*tr*, 16*t*, 20 xix. 29*t*, 29*t*(*ap*), 29 (–LT Tr), 29*t*. xxiv. 23. xxv. 39, 44*five*. Mark vi. 15(*omS*), 56*t*. vii. 10, 11, 12. x. 29*f*, 29(–G°LTTr*S*), 29*t*. xiii. 21(–G°T*S*), 35*tr*.

Luke ii. 24. viii. 16. ix. 25. xii. 14. xiii. 15. xiv. 5, 12. xvii. 7, 21, 23(–G°°TTr, καί *S*). xviii. 11, 29*f*. John ii. 6. vi. 19. vii. 48. ix. 21. xiii. 29. Acts i. 7. iii. 12. iv. 7, 34. v. 38. x. 14 (καί LT*S*), 28*t* xi. 8. xvii. 29*t*. xviii. 14. xix. 12. xx. 33*t*. xxiii. 9, 29. xxiv. 23(–G°°LT *S*). xxvi. 31. xxviii. 6, 17, 21.

Rom. iv. 13. ix. 11. x. 7. xiv. 4, 10, 13, 21*t*(*ap*). 1 Cor. ii. 1. iv. 3. v. 10, 10 (καί G'LT*S*), 10, 11*five*. vii. 11, 15. xi. 4, 5, 6. xiii. 1. xiv. 7, 23, 24, 27, 29, 37. xv. 37. 2 Cor. i. 13. ix. 7. x. 12. xi. 4*t*. xii. 6.

Gal. i. 8. ii. 2. iii. 15. Eph. iii. 20. v. 3, 27*t*. Phil. ii. 3 (μηδὲ κατά LT *S*). Col. ii. 16*f*. iii. 17. 2 Thes. ii. 4. 1 Tim. ii. 9(καί LT*S*), 9*t*. v. 4, 16 (–G°L*S*), 19. Tit. i. 6. iii. 12. Phm. 18.

Heb. ii. 6. x. 28. xii. 16, 20(*ap*). Jas. ii. 3, 15. iv. 15. 1 Pet. i. 11. iii. 3, 9. iv. 15*tr*. Rev. iii. 15. xiii. 16, 17, 17(*om*), 17. xiv. 9.

or else, Acts xxiv. 20.

ἢ καί, **or else,** Rom. ii. 15. — **yea, and,** 1 Cor. xvi. 6.

either, Phil. iii. 12

and, Mark vi. 11(*ap*). 1 Cor. xi. 27(καί L[m]). 1 Pet. i. 18.

except it be, Acts xxiv. 21.

Answering to a negative, **neither,** Acts xxiv. 12. Rom. i. 21. Jas. i. 17. — **nor,** Luke xxii. 68 (–TTr[b]*S*). 1 Cor. xii. 21. Eph. v. 4, 5*t*.

(b) In contrast, repeated, ἢ . . ἤ: **either . . or else,** Matt. vi. 24. xii. 33. Luke xvi. 13.

either . . or*tr*, 1 Cor. xiv. 6.

ἤτοι . . ἤ, **whether . . or,** Rom. vi. 16.

Add, for καί, Mark x. 40, LTTr*S*. xiii. 32, GLTTr. John iii. 8[2d], L. viii. 14, TTr. Acts xvii. 21, LT*S*. 27, L. Eph. v. 4[1st], L. 4[2d], L*S*. Jas. iv. 11[1st], G'LT*S*. 13[1st], L*S*. For ᾖ fr. εἰμί, 1 Cor. v. 11, St. For οὐδέ, Luke xxi. 15, GTTr*S*. — Mark xiii. 35(. . at even), TTr*S*. Acts xxv. 6, ὀκτὼ ἢ δέκα for ἢ δέκα, G*S*.

II. Interrogative.

(a) In the latter clause of a double interrogation, also disjunctive: —

or, Matt. vi. 31*t*. vii. 4, 9, 16. ix. 5. xi. 3. xii. 5. xvi. 26. xvii. 25. xxi. 25. xxii. 17. xxiii. 17, 19. xxv. 37, 38. xxvii. 17. Mark ii. 9. iii. 4*t*, 33(καί LTr*S*). iv. 21, 30. viii. 37(γάρ TTr*S*). xi. 30. xii. 14, 15 (14).

Luke v. 23. vi. 9*t*. vii. 19, 20. xi. 12. xii. 11(–Tr), 11, 29(καί TTr*S*). 41. xiii. 4. xiv. 31. xx. 2, 4, 22. xxii. 27. John iv. 27. vii. 17. ix. 2. xviii. 34. Acts iii. 12. vii. 49. viii. 34.

Rom. ii. 4. iii. 1. iv. 9, 10. viii. 35*six*. xi. 34, 35. 1 Cor. i. 13. iv. 21. vii. 16. ix. 6, 7(–L). 8, 10. x. 19(*ap*). xi. 22. xiv. 36. 2 Cor. i. 17. iii. 1(εἰ StG'), 1. vi. 15. Gal. i. 10*t*. iii. 2, 5. 1 Thes. ii. 19*t*.

or else, Matt. xii. 29.
or if, Luke xi. 11(εἰ StC?).

(b) In direct interrogation: —

what? 1 Cor. vi. 16(–T), 19. xiv. 36.
either, Luke vi. 42(–TTrᵇ*S*). xv. 8. Jas. iii. 12.

Not rendered, Matt. xx. 15(–LTr), 15 (εἰ StG′T). xxvi. 53. Rom. iii. 29. vi. 3. vii. 1. ix. 21. xi. 2. 1 Cor. vi. 9. x. 22. xi. 14 (–G∞LT*S*). 2 Cor. xi. 7. xiii. 5. 1 Thes. ii. 19. Jas. iv. 5.

Add, for καί, Matt. vi. 25[1st], LTr. Mark x. 38, G″LTTr*S*. xi. 28, T*S*. For ἐάν, Matt. vii. 10, LTr*S*, ἢ καὶ ἐάν T. — Luke xiv. 3 (day? ἢ οὔ), LᵇTTr*S*. 1 Cor. vi. 2(. . do ye not), GLT*S*. 2 Cor. iii. 1, *see* εἰ μή. vi. 14, ἢ τίς for τίς δέ, G″LT*S*.

III. Comparative.

than, Matt. x. 15. xi. 22, 24. xviii. 13. xix. 24. xxvi. 53 (–LᵇTTr). Mark vi. 11(*ap*). ix. 43, 45, 47. x. 25. Luke x. 12, 14. xvi. 17. xvii. 2. xviii. 25. John iii. 19. iv. 1. Acts iv. 19. v. 29. xx. 35. xxv. 6 (*see* No. I.). xxvii. 11.
Rom. xiii. 11. 1 Cor. vii. 9. ix. 15. xiv. 5, 19. Gal. iv. 27. 1 Tim. i. 4. 2 Tim. iii. 4. Heb. xi. 25. 1 Pet. iii. 17. 2 Pet. ii. 21. 1 John iv. 4.

ἤπερ, **than,** John xii. 43.
more than, Luke xv. 7.
rather than, Matt. xviii. 8, 9. Luke xviii. 14(ἢ γάρ GT, παρά LTr*S*).
ἀλλ' ἤ, **but rather,** Luke xii. 51. — **but,** 1 Cor. iii. 5 (–GL*S*). — **than,** 2 Cor. i. 13.
but either, Acts xvii. 21.
but, Luke ix. 13.
οὐ πλείους ἤ, **yet but,** Acts xxiv. 11 (ἢ *om S*).
save, John xiii. 10(εἰ μή LTr, –G° *S*).
See also πρίν.

ἦ, truly, certainly.

ἦ (εἰ LT*S*) μήν, **surely,** Heb. vi. 14.

ἡγεμονεύω.

be governor, Luke ii. 2ᵖ. iii. 1ᵖ.

ἡγεμονία.

reign, Luke iii. 1.

ἡγεμών.

governor, Matt. x. 18. xxvii. 2, 11*t*, 14, 15, 21, 23 (–Tr*S*), 27. xxviii. 14. Luke xx. 20. Acts xxiii. 24, 26, 33, 34(*omS*). xxiv. 1, 10. xxvi. 30. 1 Pet. ii. 14.
ruler, Mark xiii. 9. Luke xxi. 12.
prince, Matt. ii. 6.

ἡγέομαι, ἡγοῦμαι.

be chief, Luke xxii. 26ᵖ.
chief, Acts xv. 22ᵖ.
ἡγούμενος τοῦ λόγου, **chief speaker,** Acts xiv. 12.
governor, Matt. ii. 6ᵖ. Acts vii. 10ᵖ.
have the rule over, Heb. xiii. 7 and 17 (*marg.* **be the guide**). 24 (*marg.* **guide**).
count, Phil. iii. 7, 8*t*. 2 Thes. iii. 15. 1 Tim. i. 12. vi. 1. Heb. x. 29. Jas. i. 2. 2 Pet. ii. 13. iii. 9.
account, 2 Pet. iii. 15.
judge, Heb. xi. 11.
esteem, Phil. ii. 3. 1 Thes. v. 13. Heb. xi. 26.
think, Acts xxvi. 2. 2 Cor. ix. 5. Phil. ii. 6. 2 Pet. i. 13.
suppose, Phil. ii. 25.

ἡδέως.

gladly, Mark vi. 20. xii. 37. 2 Cor. xi. 19.
ἥδιστα, **most gladly,** 2 Cor. xii. 9. — **very gladly,** 2 Cor. xii. 15.

ἤδη.

now, Matt. iii. 10. xiv. 15, 24. xv. 32. Mark iv. 37. vi. 35*t*. viii. 2. xi. 11. xv. 42. Luke iii. 9. vii. 6. xi. 7. xiv. 17. xxi. 30*t*. John iv. 51. v. 6. vi. 17. vii. 14. xiii. 2. xv. 3. xix. 28. xxi. 4, 14. Acts iv. 3. xxvii. 9. Rom. i. 10. iv. 19(–LᵇT). xiii. 11. 1 Cor. iv. 8*t*. vi. 7. Phil. iv. 10. 2 Tim. iv. 6. 2 Pet. iii. 1. 1 John ii. 8.
even now, Luke xix. 37.

already, Matt. v. 28. xvii. 12. Mark xv. 44. Luke xii. 49. John iii. 18. iv. 35. ix. 22, 27. xi. 17 (–T). xix. 33. 1 Cor. v. 3. Phil. iii. 12*t*. 2 Thes. ii. 7. 1 Tim. v. 15. 2 Tim. ii. 18. 1 John iv. 3.

καὶ ἤδη, **now already**, Acts xxvii. 9.

by this time, John xi. 39.

yet, Matt. xxiv. 32. Mark xiii. 28.

Add Mark xv. 44, for *πάλαι*, LTr. Luke xxiii. 44 (. . about), LTTr. xxiv. 29(. . far spent), L[b]Tr*S*.

ἤδιστα. See ἡδέως.

ἡδονή.

pleasure, Luke viii. 14. Tit. iii. 3. 2 Pet. ii. 13.

lust (*marg.* **pleasure**), Jas. iv. 1, 3.

ἡδύοσμον.

mint, Matt. xxiii. 23. Luke xi. 42.

ἦθος.

manner, 1 Cor. xv. 33.

ἥκω.

come, Matt. viii. 11. xxiii. 36. xxiv. 14, 50. Mark viii. 3(*εἰμί* T). Luke xii. 46. xiii. 29, 35. xv. 27. xix. 43. John ii. 4. iv. 47, vi. 37. viii. 42. Acts xxviii. 23 (*ἦλθον* fr. *ἔρχομαι* G″L*S*).

Rom. xi. 26. Heb. x. 7, 9, 37. 2 Pet. iii. 10. 1 John v. 20. Rev. ii. 25. iii. 3*t*, 9. xv. 4. xviii. 18.

Ἠλί, Ἡλί LT.

Eli (*i.e.* my God), Matt. xxvii. 46*t*.

ἡλικία.

age, Heb. xi. 11.

With ἔχω, **be of age**, John ix. 21, 23.

stature, Matt. vi. 27. Luke ii. 52 (*marg.* **age**). xii. 25. xix. 3. Eph. iv. 13(*marg.* **age**).

ἡλίκος.

how great, Jas. iii. 5.

what great, Col. ii. 1.

ἥλιος.

sun, Matt. v. 45. xiii. 6, 43. xvii. 2. xxiv. 29. Mark i. 32. iv. 6. xiii. 24. xvi. 2. Luke iv. 40. xxi. 25. xxiii. 45. Acts ii. 20. xiii. 11. xxvi. 13. xxvii. 20. 1 Cor. xv. 41. Eph. iv. 26. Jas. i. 11. Rev. i. 16. vi. 12. vii. 16. viii. 12. ix. 2. x. 1. xii. 1. xvi. 8. xix. 17. xxi. 23. xxii. 5 (–T).

See also ἀνατολή.

ἧλος.

nail, John xx. 25*t*.

ἡμεῖς,

ἡμῶν, ἡμῖν, ἡμᾶς.

Nominative, ἡμεῖς.

we, Matt. vi. 12. ix. 14. xvii. 19. xix. 27. xxviii. 14. Mark ix. 28. x. 28. xiv. 58. Luke iii. 14. ix. 13. xviii. 28. xxiii. 41. xxiv. 21. John i. 16. iv. 22. vi. 42, 69. vii. 35. viii. 41, 48. ix. 21, 24, 28, 29, 40. xii. 34. xvii. 11, 22. xix. 7. xxi. 3.

Acts ii. 8, 32. iii. 15. iv. 9, 20. v. 32. vi. 4. x. 33, 39, 47. xiii. 32. xiv. 15. xv. 10. xx. 6, 13. xxi. 7, 12, 25. xxiii. 15. xxiv. 8. xxviii. 21.

Rom. vi. 4. viii. 23(–LT*S*). xv. 1. 1 Cor. i. 23. ii. 12, 16. iv. 8, 10*tr*. viii. 6*t*. ix. 11*t*, 12, 25. xi. 16. xii. 13. xv. 13, 52. 2 Cor. i. 6. iii. 18. iv. 11, 13. v. 16, 21. ix. 4. x. 7, 13. xi. 12, 21. xiii. 4, 6, 7*t*, 9. Gal. i. 8. ii. 9, 15, 16. iv. 3, 28(*ὑμεῖς* L T). v. 5. Eph. ii. 3(2). Phil. iii. 3. Col. i. 9, 28. 1 Thes. ii. 13, 17. iii. 6, 12. iv. 15, 17. v. 8. 2 Thes. ii. 13. Tit. iii. 5.

Heb. ii. 3. iii. 6. x. 39. xii. 25. 2 Pet. i. 18. 1 John iii. 14, 16. iv. 6, 10, 11, 14, 16, 17, 19. 3 John 8, 12.

we ourselves, Tit. iii. 3.

us[cc], John xi. 16. Heb. xii. 1.

Add Rom. viii. 23, after *ἔχοντες*, L[b]*S*. 2 Cor. vi. 16, for *ὑμεῖς*. L*S*. 1 John i. 4, for *ὑμῖν*, G′*S*.

Genitive, ἡμῶν.

of us, Acts xvii. 27. Rom. iv. 16. xiv. 7, 12. xv. 2. Gal. iv. 26. Eph. iv. 7. 1 Thes. i. 6. iii. 6. 2 Pet. iii. 2(*ὑμῶν* LT*S*).

our, Matt. vi. 6, 9, 12*t*. viii. 17.

xx. 33. xxi. 42. xxiii. 30. xxv. 8. xxvii. 25. Mark ix. 40(ὑμῶν StGL). xi. 10. xii. 11, 29. Luke i. 55, 71, 72, 73, 74 (-LᵇTTr*S*), 74, 78, 79. vii. 5. xi. 2(*ap*), 3, 4. xiii. 26. xxiv. 20, 32. John iii. 11. iv. 12, 20. vi. 31. vii. 51. viii. 39, 53. ix. 20. xi. 11, 48. xii. 38. xix. 7(-LTr *S*).

Acts ii. 8, 39. iii. 13, 25. v. 30. vii. 2, 11, 12, 15, 19, 19(-LT*S*), 38, 39, 44, 45*t*. xiii. 17. xiv. 17(ὑμῶν G LT*S*). xv. 10, 25, 26, 36(*omS*). xvi. 20. xvii. 20. xix. 25(ἡμῖν LT*S*, ὑμῶν G″). xx. 21. xxii. 14. xxiv. 7 (*ap*). xxvi. 7. xxvii. 10. xxviii. 25 (ὑμῶν LT*S*).

Rom. i. 3(4), 7. iii. 5. iv. 1, 12, 24, 25*t*. v. 1, 5, 11, 21. vi. 6, 11 (*om*), 23. vii. 5, 25. viii. 16, 23, 26, 39. ix. 10. x. 16. xiii. 11. xv. 6. xvi. 1(ὑμῶν Lᵐ), 9, 18, 20, 24.

1 Cor. i. 2, 3, 7, 8, 9, 10. ii. 7. v. 4(-Lᵇ*S*), 4(-Lᵇ). vi. 11. ix. 1. x. 1, 6, 11. xii. 23, 24. xv. 3, 14, 31, 57. 2 Cor. i. 2, 3, 4, 5, 7(6), 8, 11 (ὑμῶν T), 12*t*, 18, 22. iii. 2, 5. iv. 3, 6, 10, 11, 16, 17. v. 1, 2, 12(ὑμῶν Lᵐ*S*). vi. 11*t*. vii. 3, 4, 5, 12 (Lᵐ, ὑμῶν StLT*S*), 14(ὑμῶν L). viii. 9, 22, 23, 24. ix. 3. x. 4, 8, 15. xi. 31(-LT*S*).

Gal. i. 3, 4*t*. ii. 4. iii. 24. vi. 14, 18. Eph. i. 2, 3, 14, 17. ii. 3, 14. iii. 11, 14(*ap*). v. 20. vi. 22, 24. Phil. i. 2. iii. 20, 21. iv. 20, 23 (-G°°LT*S*). Col. i. 2, 3, 7. iii. 4(ὑμῶν G″Lᵐ*S*). 1 Thes. i. 1(*ap*), 2, 3*t*, 5. ii. 1, 2, 3, 4, 9, 19*t*, 20. iii. 2, 2 (*ap*), 5, 7, 9, 11*t*, 13*t*. v. 9, 23, 28. 2 Thes. i. 1, 2(-G°LᵇT), 8, 10, 11, 12*t*. ii. 1*t*, 14*t*, 15, 16*t*. iii. 6(-LᵇT), 12 (-G′LT*S*), 14, 18. 1 Tim. i. 1*t*, 2 (-G°°LT*S*), 12, 14. ii. 3. vi. 3, 14. 2 Tim. i. 2, 8, 9, 10. Tit. i. 3, 4. ii. 10 (ὑμῶν St), 13. iii. 4, 6. Phm. 1, 2, 3, 25.

Heb. i. 3(-G°°LT*S*). iii. 1. iv. 15. vii. 14. xii. 9, 29. xiii. 20. Jas. ii. 1, 21. iii. 6. 1 Pet. i. 3. ii. 24. 2 Pet. i. 1(*ap*), 2, 8, 11, 14, 16. iii. 15*t*, 18. 1 John i. 1*t*, 9. ii. 2. iii. 5 (-G°°LT), 19, 20, 21(-L). iv. 10. v. 4. 2 John 12(ὑμῶν G″L). 3 John 12. Jude 4*t*, 17, 21, 25. Rev. i. 5. v. 10 (-T). vi. 10. vii. 3, 10(*ap*), 12. xi. 8(αὐτῶν GLTTr, -*S*), 15. xii. 10*tr*. xix. 1. 5. xxii. 21(*omS*).

μεθ' ἡμῶν, **our**, 1 John iv. 17 (*Gr.* with us).

ours, Mark xii. 7. Luke xx. 14. 1 Cor. i. 2. 2 Cor. i. 14.

our company, Luke xxiv. 22.

us, Matt. i. 23. xv. 23. Mark ix. 40(ὑμῶν StGL). Luke ix. 49, 50*t*(ὑμῶν GLTTr, ¹*S*). xvi. 26. xxiv. 29. Acts i. 22. vii. 40. xv. 9, 24. xxiv. 4. xxviii. 15. Rom. v. 8. viii. 26 (-G°LT*S*), 31*t*, 32, 34. 1 Cor. iv. 8. v. 7(-G°°LT*S*). 2 Cor. i. 11, 19, 20. ii. 14. iii. 3. iv. 7. v. 20, 21. vii. 9. viii. 4, 19*t*, 20. ix. 11.

Gal. iii. 13. Eph. v. 2 (ὑμῶν T). Col. ii. 14. iv. 3. 1 Thes. i. 9. ii. 13. iv. 1. v. 10, 25. 2 Thes. i. 7. ii. 2. iii. 1, 6. Tit. ii. 14. Heb. vi. 20. ix. 24. xi. 40*t*. xiii. 18. 1 Pet. ii. 21 (G″, ὑμῶν CᵐGL*S*). iv. 1 (-G°LT, ὑμῶν *S*), 17. 1 John i. 3. ii. 19*five*. iii. 16, 20, 21. iv. 6*t*. v. 14(ὑμῶν St, *err.*), 15. 2 John 2.

ψυχὴν ἡμῶν, **us**, John x. 24.

we[cc], Matt. xxviii. 13. Acts xvi. 16. xxi. 10 (-LT, αὐτῶν *S*), 17. xxvi. 14. xxvii. 18, 27. Rom. v. 6, 8. 2 Cor. iv. 18. vii. 5. Heb. x. 26.

Not rendered, Rom. xv. 30.

Add, for αὐτῶν, Acts ix. 38, LT*S*. For αὐτῶν ἡμῖν, Acts xiii. 32, L*S*. For ἡμᾶς, Acts vii. 27, LT*S*. Rev. i. 6, L. For τῶν μαθητῶν, Acts xx. 7, GLT*S*. For μοῦ, Phil. iii. 8, Lᵐ. For ὑμῶν, John viii. 54, G″TTr. 2 Cor. vii. 12, StLT. .. 13[1st], LT*S*. viii. 19, GLT*S*. Gal. iv 6, GLT*S*. Col. i. 7, G″L*S*. iv. 8[1st], G′L. Tit. ii. 8, GLT*S*. Heb. ix. 14, G″L. 1 John i. 4, StL*S*. 2 John 3, St*S*. Luke xxiii. 2(. . nation), LTTr*S*.

Acts xxvi. 6 (**our**) C? G''L*S*. 1 Cor. v. 5, *see* Ἰησοῦς. vi. 11 (. . Lord), L^b. 2 Cor. i. 14(. . Lord), L^b*S*. iv. 16, *see* ἔσωθεν. Heb. xiii. 23 (. . brother), L*S*. 2 Pet. ii. 20 (. . Lord), L*S*. Rev. xix. 7 (. . God), GTTr^b. — *Ap.*, Acts iv. 25. Jude 25. Rev. iv. 11.

Dative, ἡμῖν.

to us, Matt. xxv. 11. Luke xi. 4. xxiv. 32. Acts x. 41. xv. 28. Rom. xii. 6. 1 Cor. ii. 12. viii. 6. 2 Cor. i. 8(-G^{oo}L*S*). v. 18. x. 13. Col. ii. 14. Heb. x. 15. 1 John v. 11.

unto us, Matt. xiii. 36. xv. 15. xx. 12. xxi. 25. xxvi. 68. Mark x. 37. xii. 19. Luke i. 2, 74(73). ii. 15. x. 17. xiii. 25. xx. 28. xxiii. 18. John ii. 18. xiv. 22. xvi. 17. Acts vi. 14. vii. 38. xi. 17. xiii. 33(32, *see* ἡμῶν). xv. 8, 25.

Rom. v. 5. 1 Cor. i. 18, 30. ii. 10. 2 Cor. v. 5. viii. 5. Eph. i. 9. Col. i. 8. iv. 3. 1 Thes. ii. 8. Heb. i. 2 (1). 1 Pet. i. 12 (G', ὑμῖν GLT*S*). 2 Pet. i. 3, 4. 1 John i. 2.

for us, Matt. xxv. 9. Mark x. 35. xiv. 15. Luke i. 69. xx. 22(ἡμᾶς T Tr*S*. John xi. 50 (ὑμῖν TTr, -*S*). xviii. 31. Acts xvi. 21. 2 Cor. iv. 17. Heb. x. 20.

on us, Luke x. 11.

upon us, 1 John iii. 1.

with us, Luke xxiv. 32. 2 Pet. i. 1.

us, Matt. iii. 15. vi. 11, 12. viii. 31(G', ἡμᾶς GLTTr*S*). xxii. 17, 25. xxiv. 3. xxv. 8. xxvi. 63. Mark ix. 22, 38*t*(*ap*). xiii. 4. xvi. 3. Luke i. 1. vii. 5, 16. xi. 3, 4. xx. 2. xxii. 8, 67(66). xxiv. 24, 32(-Tr^b). John i. 14. iv. 12, 25. vi. 34, 52. viii. 5 (*ap*). x. 24. xiv. 8*t*, 9. xvii. 21.

Acts i. 17, 21, 22. ii. 29. iii. 12. vii. 40. x. 42. xi. 13. xiii. 47. xiv. 17 (ὑμῖν GLT*S*, -G^{oo}). xv. 7. xvi. 9, 16, 17, 17 (ὑμῖν T*S*). xx. 14. xxi. 16, 18. xxv. 24. xxvii. 2. xxviii. 2, 15.

Rom. viii. 4, 32. ix. 29. 1 Cor. iv. 6. xv. 57. 2 Cor. iv. 12. v. 19. vi. 12. vii. 7. viii. 7. x. 8 (-LT*S*). Eph. iii. 20. 1 Thes. iii. 6. 1 Tim. vi. 17. 2 Tim. i. 7, 9, 14.

Heb. vii. 26. xii. 1. Jas. iii. 3. iv. 5. 1 Pet. ii. 21 (ὑμῖν GLT*S*). iv. 3 (-G^oLT, ὑμῖν *S*). 1 John i. 8, 9, 10. ii. 25. iii. 23 (-T), 24*t*. iv. 9, 12*t*, 13*t*, 16. v. 20. 2 John 2.

our, Luke xvii. 5. Acts xix. 27.

τί ἡμῖν καὶ σοί; **what have we to do with thee?** Matt. viii. 29. Mark i. 24. Luke iv. 34.

we^{cc}, Matt. xv. 33. xix. 27. Luke ix. 13. Acts xxi. 23. xxviii. 22. Eph. vi. 12 (ὑμῖν L). Heb. iv. 13. v. 11. xii. 1. Jas. v. 17.

Add, for ἡμῶν, Acts xix. 25, LT*S*. For ὑμῖν, Eph. iv. 5, G (-G^{oo}). 32, G'L. Col. ii. 13, StGLT*S*. Phm. 6, GLT. 1 John ii. 8, G'. — Mark xii. 14 (*ap*). Luke xx. 5 (will say . .), L.

See also ποιέω.

Accusative, ἡμᾶς.

us, Matt. vi. 13*t*. viii. 25 (-LTTr *S*), 29, 31. ix. 27. xiii. 56. xvii. 4. xx. 7, 30, 31. xxvii. 4, 25. Mark i. 24. v. 12. vi. 3. ix. 5, 22. Luke i. 71, 78. iv. 34. vii. 20. ix. 33. xi. 1, 4, 4(*ap*), 45. xii. 41. xvi. 26. xvii. 13. xix. 14. xx. 6. xxiii. 30*t*, 39. xxiv. 22. John i. 22. ix. 34.

Acts i. 21. iii. 4. v. 28. vii. 27 (ἡμῶν LT*S*), 40. xi. 15. xiv. 11. xvi. 10, 15, 37*tr*. xx. 5. xxi. 5, 11, 17. xxvii. 6, 7. xxviii. 2, 7, 10.

Rom. iv. 24. v. 8. viii. 18, 35, 37, 39. ix. 24. xv. 7(ὑμᾶς GLT*S*). xvi. 6 (ὑμᾶς G''L*S*). 1 Cor. iv. 1, 9. vi. 14. vii. 15(ὑμᾶς T*S*). viii. 8. 2 Cor. i. 4, 5, 10, 11, 14, 21*t*, 22. ii. 14. iii. 6. iv. 14. v. 5, 14, 18. vii. 2, 6. viii. 20. x. 2. Gal. i. 4, 23. ii. 4. iii. 13. v. 1. Eph. i. 3, 4, 5, 6, 8, 19. ii. 4, 7. v. 2 (ὑμᾶς T*S*). Phil. iii. 17. Col. i. 12, 13. 1 Thes. i. 10. ii. 15 (ὑμᾶς St), 16, 18. iii. 6*t*. iv. 7, 8 (ὑμᾶς G''LT*S*). v. 9. 2 Thes. ii. 16. iii. 7, 9. 2 Tim. i. 9. ii. 12. Tit. ii. 12, 14. iii. 5, 6, 15.

Heb. ii. 3. Jas. i. 18. 1 Pet. i. 3. iii. 18 (ὑμᾶς T, –*S*), 21 (ὑμᾶς LT*S*). v. 10(ὑμᾶς G′LT*S*). 2 Pet. i. 3. iii. 9(ὑμᾶς G″LT*S*). 1 John i. 7, 9. iii. 1. iv. 10, 11, 19. 3 John 9, 10. Rev. i. 5*t*, 6 (ἡμῶν L). v. 9 (–G^{o}LT), 10 (αὐτούς GLTTr*S*). vi. 16*t*.

With διά, **for our sakes**, 1 Cor. ix. 10*t*.

we$^{\infty}$, Acts iv. 12. vi. 2. xiv. 22. xxi. 1, 5. xxvii. 1, 20, 26. Rom. iii. 8. vi. 6. vii. 6(–L^{b}). 1 Cor. x. 6. 2 Cor. i. 4, 8. v. 10. viii. 4(*omS*), 6. Eph. i. 4, 12. ii. 5. 1 Thes. i. 8. 2 Thes. i. 4. Heb. ii. 1. xiii. 6. Jas. i. 18.

Not rendered, Rom. xiii. 11.

Add, for ἡμῖν, Matt. viii. 31, GLTTr*S*. Luke xx. 22, TTr*S*. For ὑμᾶς, Gal. iv. 17, C^{m}. 2 Thes. ii. 14, L. 1 Pet. i. 4, StC^{m}. — Luke xxiii. 15 (*ap*).

ἡμέρα.

day, Matt. ii. 1. iii. 1. iv. 2. vi. 34. vii. 22. ix. 15. x. 15. xi. 12, 22, 24. xii. 36, 40*t*. xiii. 1. xv. 32. xvi. 21. xvii. 1, 23. xx. 2, 6, 12, 19. xxii. 23, 46. xxiii. 30. xxiv. 19, 22*t*, 29, 36, 37, 38*t*, 50. xxv. 13. xxvi. 2, 29, 61. xxvii. 40, 63, 64.

Mark i. 9, 13. ii. 1, 20*t*. iv. 27, 35. v. 5. vi. 11(*ap*), 21. viii. 1, 2, 31. ix. 2, 31. x. 34. xiii. 17, 19, 20*t*, 24, 32. xiv. 1, 12, 25, 58. xv. 29.

Luke i. 5, 20, 23, 24, 25, 39, 59, 75, 80. ii. 1, 6, 21, 22, 37, 43, 44, 46. iv. 2*t*, 16, 25, 42. v. 35*t*. vi. 12, 13, 23. ix. 12, 22, 28, 36, 37. x. 12. xii. 46. xiii. 14*t*, 16, 31(ὥρα G′T*S*). xiv. 5. xv. 13. xvii. 4, 4(–LTTr*S*), 22*t*, 24(*ap*), 26*t*, 27, 28, 29, 30, 31. xviii. 7, 33. xix. 42, 43. xx. 1. xxi. 6, 22, 23, 34. xxii. 7, 66. xxiii. 12, 29, 54. xxiv. 7, 13. 18, 21, 29, 46.

John i. 39(40). ii. 1, 12, 19, 20. iv. 40, 43. v. 9. vi. 39, 40, 44, 54. vii. 37. viii. 56. ix. 4. xi. 6, 9*t*, 17, 24, 53. xii. 1, 7, 48. xiv. 20. xvi. 23, 26. xix. 31. xx. 19, 26.

Acts i. 2, 3, 5, 15, 22. ii. 1, 15, 17, 18, 20, 29, 41. iii. 24. v. 36, 37. vi. 1. vii. 8, 26, 41, 45. ix. 9, 19, 23, 24, 37, 43. x. 3, 30, 40, 48. xi. 27. xii. 3, 18, 21. xiii. 14, 31, 41. xv. 36. xvi. 12, 18, 35. xvii. 31. xx. 6*tr*, 16, 18, 26, 31. xxi. 4, 5, 7, 10, 15, 26*t*, 27, 38. xxiii. 1, 12. xxiv. 1, 11, 24. xxv. 1, 6, 13, 14. xxvi. 7, 22. xxvii. 7, 20, 29, 33*t*, 39. xxviii. 7, 12, 13, 14, 17, 23.

Rom. ii. 5, 16. viii. 36. x. 21. xi. 8. xiii. 12, 13. xiv. 5*t*, 6, 6(*ap*). 1 Cor. i. 8. iii. 13. v. 5. x. 8. xv. 4. 2 Cor. i. 14. vi. 2*t*. Gal. i. 18. iv. 10. Eph. iv. 30. v. 16. vi. 13. Phil. i. 5, 6, 10. ii. 16. Col. i. 6, 9. 1 Thes. ii. 9. iii. 10. v. 2, 4, 5, 8. 2 Thes. i. 10. ii. 2. iii. 8. 1 Tim. v. 5. 2 Tim. i. 3, 12, 18. iii. 1. iv. 8.

Heb. i. 2(1). iii. 8. iv. 4, 7, 8. v. 7. vii. 3. viii. 8, 9, 10. x. 16, 25, 32. xi. 30. xii. 10. Jas. v. 3, 5. 1 Pet. ii. 12. iii. 10, 20. 2 Pet. i. 19. ii. 9, 13. iii. 3, 7, 8*t*, 10, 12. 1 John iv. 17. Jude 6.

Rev. i. 10. ii. 10, 13. iv. 8. vi. 17 vii. 15. viii. 12. ix. 6, 15. x. 7. xi 3, 6, 9, 11. xii. 6, 10. xiv. 11. xvi. 14. xviii. 8. xx. 10. xxi. 25.

μία τῶν ἡμερῶν, **a certain day**, Luke v. 17. viii. 22.

ἡμέρᾳ καὶ ἡμέρᾳ, **day by day**, 2 Cor. iv. 16.

ἡμέραν ἐξ ἡμέρας, **from day to day**, 2 Pet. ii. 8.

καθ' ἡμέραν, **daily**, Matt. xxvi. 55. Mark xiv. 49. Luke ix. 23(*ap*). xix. 47. xxii. 53. Acts ii. 46, 47. iii. 2. xvi. 5. xvii. 11. xix. 9. 1 Cor. xv. 31. 2 Cor. xi. 28. Heb. vii. 27. x. 11 — **day by day**, Luke xi. 3 (*marg.* **for the day**). — **every day**, Luke xvi. 19.

καθ' ἑκάστην ἡμέραν, **daily**, Heb. iii. 13.

κατὰ πᾶσαν ἡμ., **daily**, Acts xvii. 17.

ἡμέρας μέσης, **at mid-day**, Acts xxvi. 13.

τὰς ἡμέρας, **in the day-time**, Luke xxi. 37.

ἐν ταύταις ταῖς ἡμέραις, **at that time,** Luke xxiii. 7.
time, Luke ix. 51pl. Acts viii. 1.
judgment (*Gr.* day) 1 Cor. iv. 3.
ἡμέρας ἱκανάς, **a good while,** Acts xviii. 18.
πᾶσαν ἡμ., **daily**, Acts v. 42.—πάσας τὰς ἡμ., **alway,** Matt. xxviii. 20.
τῇ ἡμέρᾳ τῶν σαββάτων, **on the sabbath,** Acts xvi. 13.
Not rendered, Rom. xiv. 5.
Add, for ὥρα, Matt. xviii. 1, G″L. xxiv. 42, LTTr*S*. Rev. xi. 13, G″.—Matt. xxviii. 15(τῆς σήμερον . .), LTr. Luke xiii. 32(day2d), Lb. John ix. 14, *see* ὅτε. 2 Cor. iii. 14(τῆς σήμερον . .), G′LT*S*.
See also αἰών, ἀρχαῖος, προβαίνω.

ἡμέτερος.

our, Acts ii. 11. xxiv. 6(*ap*). xxvi. 5. Rom. xv. 4. 2 Tim. iv. 15. 1 John i. 3.
Plur., *with art.*, **ours,** Tit. iii. 14. 1 John ii. 2
Add 1 Cor. xv. 31, for ὑμέτερος, StCmG′.

ἤμην. See εἰμί.

ἡμιθανής.

half dead, Luke x. 30.

ἥμισυ.

half, Mark vi. 23. Luke xix. 8. Rev. xi. 9, 11. xii. 14.

ἡμιώριον, ἡμίωρον LTTr.

the space of half an hour, Rev. viii. 1.

ἦν, ἦς, ἦσθα. See εἰμί.

ἡνίκα.

when, 2 Cor. iii. 15, 16 (*with* ἄν).

ἤπερ. See ἤ, III.

ἤπιος.

gentle, 1 Thes. ii. 7 (νήπιος L*S*). 2 Tim. ii. 24.

ἤρεμος.

quiet, 1 Tim. ii. 2.

ἡσυχάζω.

be quiet, 1 Thes. iv. 11.
rest, Luke xxiii. 56.
hold one's peace, Luke xiv. 4(3). Acts xi. 18.
cease, Acts xxi. 14.

ἡσυχία.

quietness, 2 Thes. iii. 12.
silence, Acts xxii. 2. 1 Tim. ii. 11, 12.

ἡσύχιος.

quiet, 1 Pet. iii. 4.
peaceable, 1 Tim. ii. 2.

ἤτοι. See ἤ, I.

ἡττάομαι, -ῶμαι.

be inferior, 2 Cor. xii. 13.
be overcome, 2 Pet. ii. 19, 20.

ἥττημα.

diminishing, Rom. xi. 12(*marg.* **decay,** *or* **loss**).
fault, 1 Cor. vi. 7.

ἥττων, ἥσσων.

Neut., *with art.*, **the worse,** 1 Cor. xi. 17.
Adv., **the less,** 2 Cor. xii. 15.

ἤτω. See εἰμί.

ἠχέω.

to sound, 1 Cor. xiii. 1.
roar, Luke xxi. 25(G′; ἤχους fr. ἦχος *neut.* GLTTr*S*).

ἦχος, masc.

sound, Acts ii. 2. Heb. xii. 19.
fame, Luke iv. 37.

ἦχος (neut.), sound, noise.

For ἠχέωp, Luke xxi. 25, GLTTr*S*.

θάλασσα.

sea, Matt. iv. 15, 18*t*. viii. 24, 26, 27, 32. xiii. 1, 47. xiv. 24(*ap*), 25, 26. xv. 19. xvii. 27. xviii. 6. xxi. 21. xxiii. 15. Mark i. 16*t*. ii. 13. iii. 7. iv. 1*tr*, 39, 41. v. 1, 13*t*. 21. vi. 47, 48, 49. vii. 31. ix. 42. xi. 23. Luke xvii. 2, 6. xxi. 25. John vi. 1, 16, 17, 18, 19, 22, 25. xxi. 1, 7. Acts iv. 24. vii. 36. x. 6, 32. xiv. 15. xvii. 14. xxvii. 30, 38, 40. xxviii. 4.
Rom. ix. 27. 1 Cor. x. 1, 2. 2 Cor. xi. 26. Heb. xi. 12, 29. Jas. i. 6.

Jude 13. Rev. iv. 6. v. 13, vii. 1, 2, 3. viii. 8*t*, 9. x. 2, 5, 6(*ap*), 8. xii. 12. xiii. 1(xii. 18), 1. xiv. 7. xv. 2*t*. xvi. 3*t*. xviii. 17, 19, 21. xx. 8, 13. xxi. 1.

θάλπω.

cherish, Eph. v. 29. 1 Thes. ii. 7.

θαμβέω.

be astonished, Acts ix. 6(*ap*).
Pass., **be astonished**, Mark x. 24. —**be amazed**, Mark i. 27. x. 32.

θάμβος.

wonder, Acts iii. 10.
With περιέχω[cc], **be astonished**, Luke v. 9.
With γίνομαι ἐπί[cc], **be amazed**, Luke iv. 36.

θανάσιμος.

deadly thing, Mark xvi. 18[neut](*ap*).

θανατηφόρος.

deadly, Jas. iii. 8.

θάνατος.

death, Matt. iv. 16. x. 21. xv. 4. xvi. 28. xx. 18. xxvi. 38, 66. Mark vii. 10. ix. 1. x. 33. xiii. 12. xiv. 34, 64. Luke i. 79. ii. 26. ix. 27. xxii. 33. xxiii. 15, 22. xxiv. 20. John v. 24. viii. 51, 52. xi. 4, 13. xii. 33. xviii. 32. xxi. 19. Acts ii. 24(ᾅδης G'). xiii. 28. xxii. 4. xxiii. 29. xxv. 11, 25. xxvi. 31. xxviii. 18.

Rom. i. 32. v. 10, 12, 12(-G°T), 14, 17, 21. vi. 3, 4, 5, 9, 16(-G°°), 21, 23. vii. 5, 10, 13*t*, 24. viii. 2, 6, 38. 1 Cor. iii. 22. xi. 26. xv. 21, 26, 54, 55, 56. 2 Cor. i. 9, 10. ii. 16*t*. iii. 7. iv. 11, 12. vii. 10. xi. 23. Phil. i. 20. ii. 8*t*, 27, 30. iii. 10. Col. i. 22. 2 Tim. i. 10.

Heb. ii. 9*t*, 14*t*, 15. v. 7. vii. 23. ix. 16. xi. 5. Jas. i. 15. v. 20. 1 John iii. 14*t*. v. 16*tr*, 17. Rev. i. 18. ii. 10, 11, 23. vi. 8. ix. 6*t*. xii. 11. xiii. 3. xviii. 8. xx. 6, 13, 14*t*. xxi. 4, 8.

θανάτου γενομένου, **by means of death**, Heb. ix. 15.

Death, Rev. vi. 8.

deadly[cc], Rev. xiii. 3, 12.

Add 1 Cor. xv. 55, for ᾅδης, LT*S*.

θανατόω.

put to death, Matt. xxvi. 59. xxvii. 1. Mark xiv. 55. 1 Pet. iii. 18.
cause to be put to death, Matt. x. 21. Mark xiii. 12. Luke xxi. 16.
Pass., **become dead**, Rom. vii. 4.
mortify, Rom. viii. 13.
kill, Rom. viii. 36. 2 Cor. vi. 9.

θάπτω.

bury, Matt. viii. 21, 22. xiv. 12. Luke ix. 59, 60. xvi. 22. Acts ii. 29. v. 6, 9, 10. 1 Cor. xv. 4.

θαῤῥέω.

be bold, 2 Cor. x. 1, 2.
boldly, Heb. xiii. 6[p].
be confident, 2 Cor. v. 8.
confident, 2 Cor. v. 6[p].
have confidence, 2 Cor. vii. 16.

θαρσέω.

be of good cheer, Matt. ix. 2. xiv. 27. Mark vi. 50. John xvi. 33. Acts xxiii. 11.
be of good comfort, Matt. ix. 22. Mark x. 49. Luke viii. 48 (-G°LT Tr*S*).

θάρσος.

courage, Acts xxviii. 15.

θαῦμα.

admiration, Rev. xvii. 6.
Add 2 Cor. xi. 14, for θαυμαστόν, G'LT*S*.

θαυμάζω.

to wonder, Matt. xv. 31. Mark vi. 51(-GL[b]Tr*S*). Luke ii. 18. iv. 22. viii. 25. ix. 43. xi. 14. xxiv. 12 (*ap*), 41. Acts xiii. 41. Rev. xiii. 3 (*pass.* StLTr). xvii. 6.
Mid., **wonder**, Rev. xvii. 8.
wonder at, Acts vii. 31.
marvel, Matt. viii. 10, 27. ix. 8 (φοβέω[pass], G''LTTr*S*), 33. xxi. 20. xxii. 22. xxvii. 14. Mark v. 20. vi. 6. xii. 17. xv. 5, 44. Luke i. 21, 63. ii. 33 (*with* εἰμί) xi. 38. xx. 26. John iii. 7. iv. 27. v. 20. vii. 15, 21. Acts ii. 7. iii. 12. iv. 13. Gal. i. 6. 1 John iii. 13. Rev. xvii. 7.

marvel at, Luke vii. 9. John v. 28.
admire, 2 Thes. i. 10.
have in admiration, Jude 16.

θαυμάσιος.

wonderful thing, Matt. xxi. 15neut.

θαυμαστός.

marvelous, Matt. xxi. 42. Mark xii. 11. 1 Pet. ii. 9. Rev. xv. 1, 3.
Neut., **marvelous thing**, John ix. 30.—**marvel**, 2 Cor. xi. 14 (θαῦμα G'LT*S*).

θεά.

goddess, Acts xix. 27, 35 (*omS*), 37 (θεός GLT*S*).

θεάομαι.

see, Matt. xi. 7. xxii. 11. Mark xvi. 14(*ap*). Luke v. 27(εἶδον Lm). vii. 24. John i. 32, 38. vi. 5. viii. 10(*ap*). xi. 45. Acts i. 11. viii. 18p (εἶδον GLT*S*). xxi. 27p. xxii. 9. Rom. xv. 24. 1 John iv. 12(11), 14.
Pass., **be seen**, Matt. vi. 1. xxiii. 5. Mark xvi. 11(*ap*).
behold, Luke xxiii. 55. John i. 14.
look on, John iv. 35.
look upon, 1 John i. 1.

θεατρίζω.

make a gazing-stock, Heb. x. 33p.

θέατρον.

theatre, Acts xix. 19, 31.
spectacle (*Gr.* theatre), 1 Cor. iv. 9.

θεῖον.

brimstone, Luke xvii. 29. Rev. ix. 17, 18. xiv. 10. xix. 20. xx. 10. xxi. 8.

θεῖος.

divine, 2 Pet. i. 3, 4.
Neut., *with art.*, **the Godhead**, Acts xvii. 29.

θειότης.

Godhead, Rom. i. 20.

θειώδης.

of brimstone, Rev. ix. 17.

θέλημα.

will, Matt. vi. 10. vii. 21. xii. 50. xviii. 14. xxi. 31. xxvi. 42. Mark iii. 35. Luke xi. 2 (*ap*). xii. 47*t*. xxii. 42. xxiii. 35. John i. 13*t*. iv. 34. v. 30*t*. vi. 38*t*, 39, 40. vii. 17 ix. 31. Acts xxi. 14. xxii. 14.
Rom. i. 10. ii. 18. xii. 2. xv. 32. 1 Cor. i. 1. vii. 37. xvi. 12. 2 Cor. i. 1. viii. 5. Gal. i. 4. Eph. i. 1, 5, 9, 11. v. 17. vi. 6. Col. i. 1, 9. iv. 12. 1 Thes. iv. 3. v. 18. 2 Tim. i. 1. ii. 26. Heb. x. 7, 9, 10, 36. xiii. 21. 1 Pet. ii. 15. iii. 17. iv. 2, 3 (βούλημα G''LT*S*), 19. 2 Pet. i. 21. 1 John ii. 17. v. 14.
Plur., **will**, Acts xiii. 22.
pleasure, Rev. iv. 11.
desire (*Gr.* will), Eph. ii. 3.

θέλησις.

will, Heb. ii. 4.

θέλω.

will (would), Matt. i. 19. ii. 18. v. 40, 42. vii. 12. viii. 2, 3. xi. 14. xii. 38. xiii. 28. xiv. 5p. xv. 28, 32. xvi. 24, 25. xvii. 4. xviii. 23, 30. xix. 17, 21. xx. 14, 15, 21, 26, 27, 32. xxi. 29. xxii. 3. xxiii. 4, 37*t*. xxvi. 15, 17, 39. xxvii. 15, 17, 21, 34.
Mark i. 40, 41. iii. 13. vi. 19(ζητέω L), 22, 25, 26, 48. vii. 24. viii. 34, 35. ix. 30. x. 35, 36, 43, 44, 51. xiv. 7, 12, 36. xv. 9, 12(–Trb*S*).
Luke i. 62. iv. 6. v. 12, 13. vi. 31. ix. 23, 24, 54. x. 29. xii. 49. xiii. 31, 34*t*. xv. 28. xvi. 26. xviii. 4, 13, 41. xix. 14, 27. xxii. 9. xxiii. 20.
John i. 43(44). v. 6, 21, 40. vi. 11, 67. vii. 1, 17, 44. viii. 44. ix. 27*t*. xii. 21. xv. 7. xvii. 24. xxi. 18*t*, 22, 23.
Acts vii. 28, 39. x. 10. xiv. 13. xvii. 18. xviii. 21p. xix. 33. xxiv. 6 (*ap*), 27. xxv. 9*t*. xxvi. 5.
Rom. vii. 15, 16, 18, 19*t*, 20, 21p. ix. 16, 18*t*, 22. xi. 25. xiii. 3. xvi. 19. 1 Cor. iv. 19, 21. vii. 7, 32, 36, 39. x. 1, 20. xiv. 5, 35. xvi. 7. 2 Cor. i. 8. v. 4. viii. 11. xii. 20*t*.
Gal. i. 7. iii. 2. iv. 17. v. 17. Phil. ii. 13. Col. i. 27. ii. 1. 1 Thes. ii. 18. 2 Thes. iii. 10. 1 Tim. v. 11. 2 Tim. iii. 12. Phm. 14.

Heb. x. 5, 8. xii. 17p. xiii. 18. Jas. ii. 20. iv. 15. 1 Pet. iii. 10. 3 John 13. Rev. xi. 5t, 6. xxii. 17.
be willing, John v. 35.
willingly, John vi. 21cc. 2Pet. iii. 5p.
voluntarycc (*Gr.* being a voluntary), Col. ii. 18p.
will have, Matt. ix. 13. xii. 7. xxvii. 43. Acts ix. 6 (*ap*). xvi. 3. Rom. i. 13. 1 Cor. xi. 3. xii. 1. 1 Thes. iv. 13. 1 Tim. ii. 4.
list, Matt. xvii. 12. Mark ix. 13. John iii. 8.
be disposed, 1 Cor. x. 27.
desire, Mark ix. 35. Luke v. 39. viii. 20. x. 24. xx. 46. 2 Cor. xi. 12. xii. 6. Gal. iv. 9, 20, 21. vi. 12, 13. 1 Tim. i. 7.
be desirous, John xvi. 19.
desirous, Luke xxiii. 8p. 2 Cor. xi. 32p.
be forward (*Gr.* be willing), 2 Cor. viii. 10.
pleasecc, 1 Cor. xii. 18. xv. 38.
had ratherc, 1 Cor. xiv. 19.
intend, Luke xiv. 28.
With εἶναι, **mean**, Acts ii. 12. xvii. [20.
so bec, 1 Pet. iii. 17.
love, Mark xii. 38.
Add Rev. ii. 21 (*ap*).

θεμέλιος, θεμέλιον[1].

foundation, Luke vi. 48[1], 49[1]. xiv. 29[1]. Acts xvi. 26[1]. Rom. xv. 20. 1 Cor. iii. 10, 11, 12. Eph. ii. 20. 1 Tim. vi. 19. Heb. vi. 1. xi. 10. Rev. xxi. 14, 19t.

θεμελιόω.

lay the foundation of, Heb. i. 10.
found, Matt. vii. 25. Luke vi. 48 (*ap*).
ground, Eph. iii. 17(18). Col. i. 23.
settle, 1 Pet. v. 10(–GooL).

θεοδίδακτος.

taught of God, 1 Thes. iv. 9.

θεομαχέω.

fight against God, Acts xxiii. 9 (*om S*).

θεομάχος.

to fight against Godcc, Acts v. 39.

θεόπνευστος.

given by inspiration of God, 2 Tim. iii. 16.

Θεός.

Κύριος ὁ Θεός[1]. *Gen. with* υἱός[2].

God, Matt. i. 23. iii. 9, 16. iv. 3[2], 4, 6[2], 7[1], 10[1]. v. 8, 9[2], 34. vi. 24, 30, 33(–L*S*). viii. 29[2]. ix. 8. xii. 4, 28t. xiv. 33[2]. xv. 3, 4, 6, 31. xvi. 16[2], 23. xix. 6, 17(*ap*), 24(οὐρανόςpl LTTr), 26. xxi. 12 (–GoLTr *S*), 31, 43. xxii. 16, 21t, 29, 30(–GoL Tr), 31, 32*f*, 32(–LTr*S*), 37[1]. xxiii. 22. xxvi. 61, 63, 63[2]. xxvii. 40, 43. 43[2], 46t, 54[2].

Mark i. 1[2], 14, 15, 24. ii. 7, 12, 26. iii. 11[2], 35. iv. 11, 26, 30. v. 7[2], 7. vii. 8, 9, 13. viii. 33. ix. 1, 47. x. 6 (–LbTTr*S*), 9, 14, 15, 18, 23, 24, 25, 27, 27(*ap*). xi. 22. xii. 14, 17t, 24, 26*f*, 27, 27 (*omS*), 29, 30, 32 (*omS*), 34. xiii. 19. xiv. 25. xv. 34t, 39[2], 43. xvi. 19(*ap*).

Luke i. 6, 8, 16, 19, 26, 30, 32, 35[2], 37, 47, 64, 68[1], 78. ii. 13, 14, 20, 28, 40, 52. iii. 2, 6, 8, 38[2c]. iv. 3[2], 4(*ap*), 8[1], 9[2], 12[1], 34, 41[2], 43. v. 1, 21, 25, 26. vi. 4, 12, 20. vii. 16t, 28, 29, 30. viii. 1, 10, 11, 21, 28 (–Go)[2], 39. ix. 2, 11, 20, 27, 43, 60, 62. x. 9, 11, 27[1]. xi. 20t, 28, 42, 49. xii. 6, 8, 9, 20 (Κύριος Lm), 21, 24, 28, 31 (αὐτός G′′LTTr*S*). xiii. 13, 18, 20, 28, 29. xiv. 15. xv. 10. xvi. 13, 15t, 16. xvii. 15, 18, 20t, 21. xviii. 2, 4, 7, 11, 13, 16, 17, 19, 24, 25, 27, 29, 43t. xix. 11, 37. xx. 21, 25t, 36, 37tr, 38. xxi. 4 (–TTrb*S*), 31. xxii. 16, 18, 69, 70[2]. xxiii. 35, 40, 47, 51. xxiv. 19, 53.

John i. 1t, 2, 6, 12, 13, 18, 29, 34[2], 36, 49(50)[2], 51(52). iii. 2t, 3, 5, 16, 17, 18[2], 21, 33, 34t, 34 (–GoLbTTrb *S*), 36. iv. 10, 24. v. 18t, 25[2], 42, 44(–Lb). vi. 27, 28, 29, 33, 45, 46, 69[2]. vii. 17. viii. 40, 41, 42t, 47tr, 54. ix. 3, 16, 24, 29, 31, 33, 35(ἄνθρωπος G′*S*)[2]. x. 33, 35, 36[2]. xi. 4, 4[2], 22t, 27[2], 40, 52. xii. 43. xiii. 3t, 31, 32 (*ap*), 32. xiv. 1. xvi. 2, 27 (*πατήρ* Tr), 30. xvii. 3. xix. 7^{2}. xx. 17*t*, 28, 31^{2}. xxi. 19.

Acts i. 3. ii. 11, 17, 22*t*, 23, 24, 30, 32, 33, 36, 39^{1}, 47. iii. 8, 9, 13*t*, 15, 18, 21, 22^{1}, 25, 26. iv. 10, 19*t*, 21, 24, 24(–LT*S*), 31. v. 4, 29, 30, 31, 32, 39. vi. 2, 7, 11. vii. 2, 6, 7, 9, 17, 25, 32*t*, 32*t* (–LT*S*), 35, 37, 42, 45, 46, 46 (*οἶκος* L*S*), 55*t*, 56. viii. 10, 12, 14, 20, 21, 22 (Κύριος G′′LT*S*), 37^{2}(*ap*). ix. 20^{2}. x. 2*t*, 3, 4, 15, 22, 28, 31, 33, 33 (Κύριος G′′ LT*S*), 34, 38*t*, 40, 41, 42, 46. xi. 1, 9, 17*t*, 18*t*, 23. xii. 5, 23, 24. xiii. 5, 7, 16, 17, 21, 23, 26, 30, 33 (32), 36, 37, 43, 44(Κύριος G′LT*S*), 46. xiv. 15, 22, 26, 27. xv. 4, 7, 8, 10, 12, 14, 18(*ap*), 19, 40 (Κύριος G′ LT*S*). xvi. 14, 17, 25, 34. xvii. 13, 23, 24, 29, 30. xviii. 7, 11, 13, 21, 26 (–G^{oo}). xix. 8, 11, 20(Κύριος StEGLT*S*). xx. 21, 24, 25(–G^{oo}LT*S*), 27, 28 (G′, Κύριος GLT), 32. xxi. 19. xxii. 3, 14. xxiii. 1, 3, 4. xxiv. 14, 15, 16. xxvi. 6, 8, 18, 20, 22, 29. xxvii. 23, 24, 25, 35. xxviii. 15, 23, 28, 31.

Rom. i. 1, 4^{2}, 7*t*, 8, 9, 10, 16, 17, 18, 19*t*, 21*t*, 23, 24, 25, 26, 28*t*, 32. ii. 2, 3, 4, 5, 11, 13, 16, 17, 23, 24, 29. iii. 2, 3, 4, 5*t*, 6, 7, 11, 18, 19, 21, 22, 23, 25, 25 (26), 29, 30. iv. 2, 3, 6, 17, 20*t*. v. 1, 2, 5, 8, 10, 11, 15. vi. 10, 11, 13*t*, 17, 22, 23. vii. 4, 22, 25*t*. viii. 3. 7*t*, 8, 9, 14*t*, 16, 17, 19^{2}, 21, 27, 28, 31, 33*t*, 34, 39. ix. 5, 6, 8, 11, 14, 16, 20, 23, 26^{2}. x. 1, 2, 3*t*, 9, 17(Χριστός L*S*). xi. 1, 2*t*, 8, 21, 22, 23, 29, 30, 32, 33. xii. 1*t*, 2, 3. xiii. 1*t*, 2, 4*t*, 6. xiv. 3, 4, 6*t*, 11, 12(–L^{b}), 17, 18, 20, 22. xv. 5, 6, 7, 8, 9, 13, 15, 16, 17, 19 (G′, ἅγιος G(–^{oo})L, –T), 30, 32(Κύριος Ἰησοῦς L*S*), 33. xvi. 20, 26, 27.

1 Cor. i. 1, 2, 3, 4*t*, 9, 14, 18, 20, 21*tr*, 24*t*, 25*t*. 27, 27(*ap*), 28, 30. ii. 1, 5, 7*t*, 9, 10*t*, 11*t*, 12*t*, 14. iii. 6, 7, 9*tr*, 10, 16*t*, 17*tr*, 19, 23. iv. 1, 5, 9, 20. v. 13. vi. 9, 10, 11, 13, 14, 19, 20, 20 (*ap*). vii. 7, 15, 17 (Κύριος GLT*S*), 19, 24, 40. viii. 3, 4, 6, 8. ix. 9, 21. x. 5, 13, 20, 31, 32. xi. 3, 7, 12, 13, 16, 22. xii. 3, 6, 18, 24, 28. xiv. 2, 18, 25*t*, 28, 33, 36. xv. 9, 10*t*, 15*t*, 24, 28, 34, 38, 50, 57.

2 Cor. i. 1*t*, 2, 3*t*, 4, 9, 12, 18, 19^{2}, 20*t*, 21, 23. ii. 14, 15, 17*tr*. iii. 3, 4, 5. iv. 2*t*, 4, 6, 6(*αὐτός* G′′L), 7, 15. v. 1, 5, 11, 13, 18, 19, 20*t*, 21. vi. 1, 4, 7, 16*f*. vii. 1, 6, 12. viii. 1, 5, 16. ix. 7, 8, 11, 12, 13, 14, 15. x. 4, 5, 13. xi. 7, 11, 31. xii. 2, 3, 19, 21. xiii. 4*t*, 7, 11, 14(13).

Gal. i. 1, 3, 4, 10, 13, 15 (–G^{oo}L^{b} T), 20, 24. ii. 6, 19, 20^{2}, 21. iii. 6. 8, 11, 17, 18, 20, 21(–L^{b}), 26^{2}. iv. 4, 6, 7(*ap*), 8, 9*t*, 14. v. 21. vi. 7, 16.

Eph. i. 1, 2, 3, 17. ii. 4, 8, 10, 16, 19, 22. iii. 2, 7, 9, 10, 19. iv. 6, 13^{2}, 18, 24, 30, 32. v. 1, 2, 5, 6, 20, 21 (Χριστός GLT*S*). vi. 6, 11, 13, 17, 23.

Phil. i. 2, 3, 8, 11, 28. ii. 6*t*, 9, 11, 13, 15, 27. iii. 3 (*gen.* G′LT*S*), 9, 14, 15, 19. iv. 6, 7, 9, 18, 19, 20.

Col. i. 1, 2, 3, 6, 10, 15, 25*t*, 27. ii. 2, 12, 19. iii. 1, 3, 6, 12, 15 (Χριστός GLT*S*), 17, 22 (G′, Κύριος GLT*S*). iv. 3, 11, 12.

1 Thes. i. 1, 1(*ap*), 2, 3, 4, 8, 9*t*. ii. 2*t*, 4*t*, 5, 8, 9, 10, 12, 13*tr*, 14, 15. iii. 2, 9*t*, 11, 13. iv. 1, 3, 5, 7, 8, 14, 16. v. 9, 18, 23.

2 Thes. i. 1, 2, 3, 4, 5*t*, 6, 8, 11, 12. ii. 4, 4(*Gr.*^{3d}, *omS*), 4*t*, 11, 13*t*, 16. iii. 5.

1 Tim. i. 1, 2, 11, 17. ii. 3, 5*t*. iii. 5, 15*t*, 16 (ὅς GLT*S*, ὅ G′). iv. 3, 4, 5, 10. v. 4, 5, 21. vi. 1, 11, 13, 17.

2 Tim. i. 1, 2, 3, 6, 7, 8. ii. 9, 15, 19, 25. iii. 17. iv. 1.

Tit. i. 1*t*, 2, 3, 4, 7, 16. ii. 5, 10, 11, 13. iii. 4, 8. Phm. 3, 4.

Heb. i. 1, 6, 8, 9*t*. ii. 4, 9, 13, 17. iii. 4, 12. iv. 4, 9, 10, 12, 14^{2}. v. 1, 4, 10, 12. vi. 1, 3, 5, 6^{2}, 7, 10, 13, 17, 18. vii. 1, 3^{2}, 19, 25. viii. 10. ix. 14*t*, 20, 24. x. 7, 9(*omS*), 12, 21, 29^{2}, 31, 36. xi. 3, 4*t*, 5*t*, 6, 10, 16*t*,

19, 25, 40. xii. 2, 7, 15, 22, 23, 28, 29. xiii. 4, 7, 15, 16, 20. Jas. i. 1, 5, 13*t*, 20, 27. ii. 5, 19, 23*t*. iii. 9 (Κύριος G''LT*S*), 9. iv. 4*t*, 6, 7, 8.
1 Pet. i. 2, 3, 5, 21*t*, 23. ii. 4, 5, 10, 12, 15, 16, 17, 19, 20. iii. 4, 5, 15 (Χριστός G'LT*S*), 17, 18, 20, 21, 22. iv. 2, 6, 10, 11*tr*, 14, 16, 17*t*, 19. v. 2, 5, 6, 10, 12. 2 Pet. i. 1, 2, 17, 21. ii. 4. iii. 5, 12.
1 John i, 5. ii. 5, 14, 17. iii. 1, 2, 8^2, 9*t*, 10*t*, 16 (–StGLT*S*), 17, 20, 21. iv. 1, 2*t*, 3, 4, 6*tr*, 7*tr*, 8*t*, 9*t*, 10, 11, 12*t*, 15^2, 15*t*, 16*f*, 20*t*, 21. v. 1, 2*t*, 3, 4, 5^2, 9*t*, 10^2, 10(υἱός G'L), 10, 11, 12^2 (–C 1611 to 1629), 13^2 (*ap*), 13^2, 18*t*, 19, 20^2, 20.
2 John 3, 9. 3 John 11*t*.
Jude 1, 4, 4(*omS*), 21, 25.
Rev. i. 1, 2, 6, 9. ii. 7, 18^2. iii. 1, 2, 12*f*, 14. iv. 5, 8^1. v. 6, 9, 10(–T). vi. 9. vii. 2, 3, 10(*ap*), 11, 12, 15, 17. viii. 2, 4. ix. 4(–G°), 13. x. 7. xi. 1, 4 (Κύριος GLTTr*S*), 11, 13, 16*t*, 17^1, 19. xii. 5, 16, 10*t*, 17. xiii. 6. xiv. 4, 5(*ap*), 7(Κύριος G''), 10, 12, 19. xv. 1, 2, 3, 3^1, 7, 8. xvi. 1. 7^1, 9, 11, 14, 19, 21. xvii. 17*t*. xviii. 5, 8, 20. xix. 1^1 (Κύριος *omS*), 4, 5, 6^1, 9, 10, 13, 15, 17. xx. 4, 6, 9 (–G°LTTr^b*S*), 12(θρόνος GLTTr*S*). xxi. 2, 3*t*, 3 (–G°°*S*), 4 (–GTr^b*S*), 7, 10, 11, 22^1, 23. xxii. 1, 3, 5^1, 6^1, 9, 18, 19.

god, John x. 34, 35. Acts vii. 40, 43. xii. 22. xiv. 11. xix. 26. xxviii. 6. 1 Cor. viii. 5*t*. 2 Cor. iv. 4. Gal. iv. 8.

Gen., **godly**, 2 Cor. i. 12. xi. 2. 1 Tim. i. 4(–C 1611 to 1660, *err.*).

ἀξίως τοῦ Θεοῦ, **after a godly sort**, 3 John 6.

Dat., **exceeding**(*marg.* **to God**), Acts vii. 20.

κατὰ Θεόν, **after a godly manner**, 2 Cor. vii. 9(*marg.* **according to God**).
—**after a godly sort**, 2 Cor. vii. 11.
—**godly**, 2 Cor. vii. 10.

Add, for αὐτός, 1 Cor. i. 29, GLT*S*. 1 John iv. 19^{2d}, L, ^{1st}*S*. For θεά, Acts xix. 37, GLT*S*. For Κύριος, Luke ii. 38, LTr*S*. Acts xvi. 10, G'' L*S*. xvii. 27, xxi. 20, 1 Cor. vii. 17, Col. iii. 16, GLT*S*. Eph. v. 17, L^m. 2 Thes. iii. 3, L. 2 Tim. ii. 14, L^m*S*. For υἱός, John i. 18, L^{m}Tr*S*. For Χριστός, Rom. xiv. 10, G'LT*S*.

Acts iii. 13 (. . of Isaac, and . . of Jacob), L*S*. Rom. viii. 28, *after* συνεργεῖ, L. xi. 22 (the goodness . .), LT*S*. Phil. i. 14 (word . .), L *S*. 1 Pet. v. 2 (mind κατὰ Θεόν), L*S*. 1 John v. 10 (witness . .), L. Rev. i. 8^1 (the Lord . .), GLTTr*S*.
—*Ap.*, Rom. xii. 17. Rev. iv. 11^1.

θεοσέβεια.

godliness, 1 Tim. ii. 10.

θεοσεβής.

worshipper of God, John ix. 31.

θεοστυγής.

hater of God, Rom. i. 30.

θεότης.

Godhead, Col. ii. 9.

θεραπεία.

healing, Luke ix. 11. Rev. xxii. 2.
household, Matt. xxiv. 45 (οἰκετεία LTTr, οἰκία *S*). Luke xii. 42.

θεραπεύω.

to worship, Acts xvii. 25.
cure, Matt. xvii. 16, 18. Luke vii. 21. ix. 1. John v. 10.
heal, Matt. iv. 23, 24. viii. 7, 16. ix. 35. x. 1, 8. xii. 10, 15, 22. xiv. 14. xv. 30. xix. 2. xxi. 14. Mark i. 34. iii. 2, 10, 15(–TTr*S*). vi. 5, 13. Luke iv. 23, 40. v. 15. vi. 7, 18. viii. 2, 43. ix. 6. x. 9. xiii. 14*t*. xiv. 3. Acts iv. 14. v. 16. viii. 7. xxviii. 9. Rev. xiii. 3, 12.

θεράπων.

servant, Heb. iii. 5.

θερίζω.

reap, Matt. vi. 26. xxv. 24, 26. Luke xii. 24. xix. 21, 22. John iv. 36*t*, 37, 38. 1 Cor. ix. 11. 2 Cor. ix. 6*t*. Gal. vi. 7, 8*t*, 9. Jas. v. 4. Rev xiv. 15*t*, 16.

θερισμός.
harvest, Matt. ix. 37, 38*t*. xiii 30*t*, 39. Mark iv. 29. Luke x. 2*tr*. John iv. 35*t*. Rev. xiv. 15.

θεριστής.
reaper, Matt. xiii. 30, 39.

θερμαίνω.
Mid., **warm one's self**, Mark xiv. 54, 67. John xviii. 18*t*, 25. — **be warmed**, Jas. ii. 16.

θέρμη.
heat, Acts xxviii. 3.

θέρος.
summer, Matt. xxiv. 32. Mark xiii. 28. Luke xxi. 30.

θεωρέω.
look on, Mark xv. 40.
behold, Matt. xxvii. 55. Mark xii. 41. xv. 47. Luke x. 18. xiv. 29. xxi. 6. xxiii. 35, 48. John xvii. 24. Acts viii. 13. Rev. xi. 12.
consider, Heb. vii. 4.
see, Matt. xxviii. 1. Mark iii. 11. v. 15, 38. xvi. 4. Luke xxiv. 37, 39. John ii. 23p. vi. 19, 40, 62. vii. 3. viii. 51. ix. 8. x. 12. xii. 45*t*. xiv. 17, 19*t*. xvi. 10, 16, 17, 19. xx. 6, 12, 14. Acts iii. 6. iv. 13p. vii. 56. ix. 7. x. 11. xvii. 6p. xix. 26. xx. 38. xxi. 20. xxv. 24. xxviii. 6. 1 John iii. 17. Rev. xi. 11.
perceive, John iv. 19. xii. 19. Acts xvii. 22. xxvii. 10.
Add John vi. 2, for ὁράω, LTr.

θεωρία.
sight, Luke xxiii. 48.

θήκη.
sheath, John xviii. 11.

θηλάζω.
to suck, Luke xi. 27.
suckling, Matt. xxi. 16p.
give suck, Matt. xxiv. 19. Mark xiii. 17. Luke xxi. 23. xxiii. 29 (τρέφω LTTr*S*).

θῆλυς, θήλεια, θῆλυ.
θήλεια, **woman**, Rom. i. 26, 27.
θῆλυ, **female**, Matt. xix. 4. Mark x. 6. Gal. iii. 28.

θήρα.
trap, Rom. xi. 9.

θηρεύω.
to catch, Luke xi. 54.

θηριομαχέω.
fight with beasts, 1 Cor. xv. 32.

θηρίον.
wild beast, Mark i. 13. Acts x. 12 (–G∞LT*S*). xi. 6.
venomous beast, Acts xxviii. 4.
beast, Acts xxviii. 5. Tit. i. 12. Heb. xii. 20. Jas. iii. 7. Rev. vi. 8. xi. 7. xiii. 1, 2, 3, 4*tr*, 11, 12*t*, 14*t*, 15*tr*, 17, 18. xiv. 9, 11. xv. 2. xvi. 2, 10, 13. xvii. 3, 7, 8*t*, 11, 12, 13, 16, 17. xix. 19, 20*t*. xx. 4, 10.

θησαυρίζω.
treasure up, Rom. ii. 5.
lay up treasure, Luke xii. 21.
heap treasure together, Jas. v. 3.
lay up, Matt. vi. 19, 20. 2 Cor. xii. 14.
keep in store, 2 Pet. iii. 7.
in store, 1 Cor. xvi. 2p.

θησαυρός.
treasure, Matt. ii. 11. vi. 19, 20, 21. xii. 35*t*. xiii. 44, 52. xix. 21. Mark x. 21. Luke vi. 45, 45(*ap*). xii. 33, 34. xviii. 22. 2 Cor. iv. 7. Col. ii. 3. Heb. xi. 26.

θιγγάνω.
to touch, Heb. xi. 28. xii. 20.
handle, Col. ii. 21.

θλίβω.
Pass., **narrow** (*lit.* pressed, compressed), Matt. vii. 14p. — **suffer tribulation**, 1 Thes. iii. 4.
throng, Mark iii. 9.
afflict, 2 Cor. i. 6. 1 Tim. v. 10. Heb. xi. 37.
trouble, 2 Cor. iv. 8. vii. 5. 2 Thes. i. 6, 7.

θλῖψις.
burdened∞, 2 Cor. viii. 13.
anguish, John xvi. 21.
affliction, Mark iv. 17. xiii. 19. Acts vii. 10, 11. xx. 23. 2 Cor. ii. 4. iv. 17. vi. 4. viii. 2. Phil. i. 16. iv. 14.

Col. i. 24. 1 Thes. i. 6. iii. 3, 7. Heb. x. 33. Jas. i. 27.

With εἰς, **to be afflicted,** Matt. xxiv. 9.

tribulation, Matt. xiii. 21. xxiv. 21, 29. Mark xiii. 24. John xvi. 33. Acts xiv. 22. Rom. ii. 9. v. 3*t*. viii. 35. xii. 12. 2 Cor. i. 4. vii. 4. Eph. iii. 13. 2 Thes. i. 4, 6. Rev. i. 9. ii. 9, 10, 22. vii. 14.

persecution, Acts xi. 19.

trouble, 1 Cor. vii. 28. 2 Cor. i. 4, 8.

θνήσκω.

to die, John xi. 21 (ἀπέθανεν fr. ἀποθνήσκω G''LTr*S*).

be dead, Matt. ii. 20. Mark xv. 44. Luke viii. 49. John xi. 39 (τελευτάω G''LTTr*S*), 44. xii. 1 (–L^b^Tr^b^*S*). Acts xiv. 19. xxv. 19. 1 Tim. v. 6.

dead, Luke vii. 12^p^(–L^b^). John xi. 41^p^(*ap*). xix. 33^p^.

θνητός.

mortal, Rom. vi. 12. viii. 11. 1 Cor. xv. 53, 54. 2 Cor. iv. 11.

With art., **mortality,** 2 Cor. v. 4.

θορυβάζω, confuse by noise.

For τυρβάζω, Luke x. 41, LTr*S*.

θορυβέω.

set on an uproar, Acts xvii. 5.

Mid., **make a noise,** Matt. ix. 23. — **make this^c^ ado,** Mark v. 39. — **trouble one's self,** Acts xx. 10.

θόρυβος.

uproar, Matt. xxvi. 5. Mark xiv. 2. Acts xx. 1.

tumult, Matt. xxvii. 24. Mark v. 38. Acts xxi. 34. xxiv. 18.

θραύω.

to bruise, Luke iv. 18.

θρέμμα.

cattle, John iv. 12^pl^.

θρηνέω.

mourn, Matt. xi. 17. Luke vii. 32.

lament, Luke xxiii. 27. John xvi. 20.

θρῆνος.

lamentation, Matt. ii. 18 (–G^oo^LTTr*S*).

θρησκεία.

worshipping, Col. ii. 18.

religion, Acts xxvi. 5. Jas. i. 26, 27.

θρῆσκος.

religious, Jas. i. 26.

θριαμβεύω.

triumph over, Col. ii. 15.

cause to triumph, 2 Cor. ii. 14.

θρίξ, τριχός.

hair, Matt. iii. 4^pl^. v. 36. x. 30. Mark i. 6^pl^. Luke vii. 38, 44. xii. 7. xxi. 18. John xi. 2^pl^. xii. 3^pl^. Acts xxvii. 34. 1 Pet. iii. 3^pl^(–L). Rev. i. 14. ix. 8*t*^pl^.

θροέω.

Pass., **be troubled,** Matt. xxiv. 6. Mark xiii. 7. 2 Thes. ii. 2.

θρόμβος.

great drop, Luke xxii. 4(*ap*).

θρόνος.

seat, Luke i. 52. Rev. ii. 13. iv. 4*t*. xi. 16. xiii. 2. xvi. 10.

throne, Matt. v. 34. xix. 28*t*. xxiii. 22. xxv. 31. Luke i. 32. xxii. 30. Acts ii. 30. vii. 49. Col. i. 16. Heb. i. 8. iv. 16. viii. 1. xii. 2. Rev. i. 4. iii. 21*t*. iv. 2*t*, 3, 4, 5*t*, 6*tr*, 9, 10*t*. v. 1, 6, 7, 11, 13. vi. 16. vii. 9, 10(*ap*), 11*t*, 15*t*, 17. viii. 3. xii. 5. xiv. 3, 5(*ap*). xvi. 17. xix. 4, 5. xx. 4, 11. xxi. 5. xxii. 1, 3.

Add Rev. xx. 12, for Θεός, GLTTr*S*. xxi. 3, for οὐρανός, LT*S*.

θυγάτηρ.

daughter, Matt. ix. 18, 22. x. 35, 37. xiv. 6. xv. 22, 28. xxi. 5. Mark v. 34, 35. vi. 22. vii. 26, 29, 30 (παιδίον LTTr*S*). Luke i. 5. ii. 36. viii. 42, 48, 49. xii. 53*t*. xiii. 16. xxiii. 28. John xii. 15. Acts ii. 17. vii. 21. xxi. 9. 2 Cor. vi. 18. Heb. xi. 24.

θυγάτριον.

little daughter, Mark v. 23.

young daughter, Mark vii. 25.

θύελλα.

tempest, Heb. xii. 18.

θύϊνος.
thyine(*marg.* **sweet**), Rev. xviii. 12.

θυμίαμα.
incense, Luke i. 10, 11. Rev. viii. 3pl, 4pl.
odor, Rev. v. 8 (*marg.* **incense**). xviii. 13.

θυμιατήριον.
censer, Heb. ix. 4.

θυμιάω.
burn incense, Luke i. 9.

θυμομαχέω.
With εἰμί, **be highly displeased with** (*marg.* **bear an hostile mind intending war with**), Acts xii. 20.

θυμόω.
Pass., **be wroth**, Matt. ii. 16.

θυμός.
wrath, Luke iv. 28. Acts xix. 28. 2 Cor. xii. 20. Gal. v. 20pl. Eph. iv. 31. Col. iii. 8. Heb. xi. 27. Rev. xii. 12. xiv. 8 (-G°S°), 10, 19. xv. 1, 7. xvi. 1. xviii. 3.
indignation, Rom. ii. 8.
fierceness, Rev. xvi. 19. xix. 15.

θύρα.
door, Matt. vi. 6. xxiv. 33. xxv. 10. xxvii. 60. xxviii. 2 (-G°LTTr S). Mark i. 33. ii. 2. xi. 4. xiii. 29. xv. 46. xvi. 3. Luke xi. 7. xiii. 25*t*. John x. 1, 2, 7, 9. xviii. 16. xx. 19, 26. Acts v. 9, 19, 23. xii. 6, 13. xiv. 27. xvi. 26, 27. xxi. 30. 1 Cor. xvi. 9. 2 Cor. ii. 12. Col. iv. 3. Jas. v. 9. Rev. iii. 8, 20*t*. iv. 1.
gate, Acts iii. 2. [TrS. *Add* Luke xiii. 24, for πύλη, GLT

θυρεός.
shield, Eph. vi. 16.

θυρίς.
window, Acts xx. 9. 2 Cor. xi. 33.

θυρωρός.
With art., **that keepeth the door**, John xviii. 16, 17.
porter, Mark xiii. 34. John x. 3.

θυσία.
sacrifice, Matt. ix. 13. xii. 7. Mark ix. 49 (*ap*). xii. 33. Luke ii. 24. xiii. 1. Acts vii. 41, 42. Rom. xii. 1. 1 Cor. x. 18. Eph. v. 2. Phil. ii. 17. iv. 18. Heb. v. 1. vii. 27. viii. 3. ix. 9, 23, 26. x. 1, 5, 8, 11, 12, 26. xi. 4. xiii. 15, 16. 1 Pet. ii. 5.

θυσιαστήριον.
altar, Matt. v. 23, 24. xxii. 18, 19, 20, 35. Luke i. 11. xi. 51. Rom. xi. 3. 1 Cor. ix. 13*t*. x. 18. Heb. vii. 13. xiii. 10. Jas. ii. 21. Rev. vi. 9. viii. 3*t*, 5. ix. 13. xi. 1. xiv. 18. xvi. 7.

θύω.
to sacrifice, 1 Cor. v. 7 (*marg.* **slay**). x. 20*t*.
do sacrifice, Acts xiv. 13, 18.
kill, Matt. xxii. 4. Mark xiv. 12 (*marg.* **sacrifice**). Luke xv. 23, 27, 30. xxii. 7. John x. 10. Acts x. 13.
slay, Acts xi. 7.

θώραξ.
breastplate, Eph. vi. 14. 1 Thes. v. 8. Rev. ix. 9*t*, 17.

ἴαμα.
healing, 1 Cor. xii. 9, 28, 30.

ἰάομαι.
heal, Matt. viii. 8, 13. xiii. 15. Mark v. 29. Luke iv. 18 (*ap*). v. 17. vi. 17, 19. vii. 7. viii. 47. ix. 2, 11, 42. xiv. 4. xvii. 15. xxii. 51. John iv. 47. v. 13 (ἀσθενέω G'T). xii. 40. Acts iii. 11 (αὐτοῦ for τοῦ ἰαθέντος χωλοῦ GLTS). x. 38. xxviii. 8, 27. Heb. xii. 13. Jas. v. 16. 1 Pet. ii. 24.
make whole, Matt. xv. 28. Acts ix. 34.

ἴασις.
healing, Acts iv. 22.
With εἰς, **to heal**, Acts iv. 30.
cure, Luke xiii. 32.

ἴασπις.
jasper, Rev. iv. 3. xxi. 11, 18, 19.

ἰατρός.
physician, Matt. ix. 12. Mark ii. 17. v. 26. Luke iv. 23. v. 31. viii. 43. Col. iv. 14.

ἴδε.

(Imperative of εἶδον.)

see, Mark xiii. 1.
look, John vii. 52.
lo, Matt. xxv. 25. John vii. 26. xvi. 29.
behold, Matt. xxv. 20, 22. xxvi. 65. Mark ii. 24. iii. 34(ἰδού L). xi. 21. xv. 4. xvi. 6. John i. 29, 36, 47(48). iii. 26. v. 14. xi. 3, 36. xii. 19. xviii. 21. xix. 4, 5(ἰδού Tr*S*), 14. xx. 27. Rom. ii. 17 (εἰ δέ GLT *S*). Gal. v. 2 (ἰδέ G).

Add, for βλέπε fr. βλέπω, Rev. vi. 1, 5, 7, G, -G°. For ἰδού, Mark xiii. 21[1st], TTr*S*. 21[2d], LTTr*S*. xv. 35, TTr*S*. John xix. 26, GLTTr. 27, L TTr. Jas. iii. 3, G.

ἰδέα, εἰδέα TTr.

countenance, Matt. xxviii. 3.

ἴδιος.

one's own, Matt. ix. 1. xxv. 14. Mark xv. 20(αὐτοῦ L, -G°). Luke ii. 3(ἑαυτοῦ LTr*S*[pl]). vi. 41, 44. x. 34. John i. 11, 41(42). iv. 44. v. 43. vii. 18. viii. 44. x. 3, 4, 12. xiii. 1. xv. 19. Acts i. 7, 25. ii. 6, 8. iii. 12. iv. 32. xiii. 36. xx. 28. xxv. 19. xxviii. 30.

Rom. viii. 32. x. 3. xi. 24. xiv. 4, 5. 1 Cor. iii. 8*t*. iv. 12. vi. 18. vii. 2, 4*t*, 37. ix. 7. xi. 21. xv. 23, 38. Gal. vi. 5. Eph. v. 22, 24(-G°LT*S*). Col. iii. 18(*om**S*). 1 Thes. ii. 14, 15 (*om**S*). iv. 11(-G°°LT). 1 Tim. iii. 4, 5, 12. v. 8. vi. 1. 2 Tim. i. 9. iv. 3. Tit. i. 12. ii. 5, 9. Heb. vii. 27. ix. 12. xiii. 12. Jas. i. 14. 1 Pet. iii. 1, 5. 2 Pet. ii. 22. iii. 3, 16, 17. Jude 6.

Plur., **one's own company**, Acts iv. 23.—**one's acquaintance**, Acts xxiv. 23.

τὰ ἴδια, **one's own**, John i. 11. xvi. 32 (*marg.* **one's own home**). — **one's own home**, John xix. 27.—**one's own business**, 1 Thes. iv. 11.

εἰς τὰ ἴδια, **home**, Acts xxi. 6.

ὁ ἴδιος οἶκος, **home**, 1 Tim. v. 4.

his (their), Matt. xxii. 5. John v. 18. 1 Cor. xiv. 35. 1 Tim. iv. 2. vi. 15. Heb. iv. 10. 2 Pet. ii. 16.

private, 2 Pet. i. 20.

κατ' ἰδίαν, **privately**, Matt. xxiv. 3. Mark vi. 32. ix. 28. xiii. 3. Luke ix. 10. x. 23. Acts xxiii. 19. Gal. ii. 2 (*marg.* **severally**).—**apart**, Matt. xiv. 13, 23. xvii. 1, 19. xx. 17. Mark vi. 31. ix. 2. — **aside**, Mark vii. 33. —**when °they were alone**, Mark iv. 34.

°**his several**, Matt. xxv. 15.

ἰδίᾳ, **severally**, 1 Cor. xii. 11.

one's proper, Acts i. 19. 1Cor. vii. 7.

due, Gal. vi. 9. 1 Tim. ii. 6. Tit. i. 3.

Add, for αὐτοῦ, Mark iv. 34, T*S*. For διά, 2 Cor. v. 10, L[m]. 2 Pet. i. 3, G″LT*S*. — Luke xviii. 28, *see* πᾶς. Acts xxiv. 24 (. . wife), L. 1 Cor. vii. 37 (his . . heart[2d]), T*S*. Eph. iv. 28 (*his*), L*S*.

ἰδιώτης.

unlearned, 1 Cor. xiv. 16, 23, 24.
ignorant, Acts iv. 13.
rude, 2 Cor. xi. 6.

ἰδού.

(Imper. of εἶδον, aor. mid.)

see, Luke xvii. 23*t*. Acts viii. 36.
lo, Matt. ii. 9. iii. 16, 17. xxiv. 23. xxvi. 47. xxviii. 7, 20. Mark x. 28. xiii. 21(ἴδε TTr*S*), 21(ἴδε L TTr*S*). xiv. 42. Luke i. 44. ii. 9. ix. 39. xiii. 16. xv. 29. xvii. 21, 21 (-T*S*). xviii. 28. xxiii. 15. Acts xiii. 46. xxvii. 24. Heb. x. 7, 9. Rev. v. 6 (*om**S*). vi. 5, 12 (*om**S*). vii. 9(-LTr[b]). xiv. 1.
behold, Matt. i. 20, 23. ii. 1, 13, 19. iv. 11. vii. 4. viii. 2, 24, 29, 32, 34. ix. 2, 3, 10, 18, 20, 32. x. 16. xi. 8, 10, 19. xii. 2, 10, 18, 41, 42, 46, 47, 49. xiii. 3. xv. 22. xvii. 3, 5*t*. xix. 16, 27. xx. 18, 30. xxi. 5. xxii. 4. xxiii. 34, 38. xxiv. 25, 26*t*. xxv. 6. xxvi. 45, 46, 51. xxvii. 51. xxviii. 2, 7, 9, 11.

Mark i. 2. iii. 32. iv. 3. v. 22(-G°°

L^bTTrS). x. 33. xiii. 23(-L^bTTr). xiv. 41. xv. 35(ἴδε TTrS).
Luke i. 20, 31, 36, 38, 48. ii. 10, 25, 34, 48. v. 12, 18. vi. 23. vii. 12, 25, 27, 34, 37. viii. 41. ix. 30, 38. x. 3, 19, 25. xi. 31, 32, 41. xiii. 7, 11, 30, 32, 35. xiv. 2. xvii. 21. xviii. 31. xix. 2, 8, 20. xxii. 10, 21, 31, 38, 47. xxiii. 14, 29, 50. xxiv. 4, 13, 49.
John iv. 35. xii. 15. xvi. 32. xix. 26(G′, ἴδε GLTTr), 27(ἴδε LTTr, εἴδε S).
Acts i. 10. ii. 7. v. 9, 25, 28, vii. 56. viii. 27. ix. 10, 11. x. 17, 19, 21, 30. xi. 11. xii. 7. xiii. 11, 25. xvi. 1. xx. 22, 25.
Rom. ix. 33. 1 Cor. xv. 51. 2 Cor. v. 17. vi. 2t, 9. vii. 11. xii. 14. Gal. i. 20. Heb. ii. 13. viii. 8. Jas. iii. 3(ἴδε G, εἰ δέ G′LT, εἰ δὲ γάρ S), 4, 5. v. 4, 7, 9, 11. 1 Pet. ii. 6. Jude 14.
Rev. i. 7, 18. ii. 10, 22. iii. 8, 9t, 11(omS), 20. iv. 1, 2. v. 5. vi. 2, 8. ix. 12. xi. 14. xii. 3. xiv. 14. xv. 5(omS). xvi. 15. xix. 11. xxi. 3, 5. xxii. 7, 12.
Add, for ἴδε, Mark iii. 34, L. John xix. 5, TrS.

ἱδρώς.

sweat, Luke xxii. 24(*ap*).

ἱερατεία.

priest's office, Luke i. 9.
office of the priesthood, Heb. vii. 5.

ἱεράτευμα.

priesthood, 1 Pet. ii. 5, 9.

ἱερατεύω.

execute the priest's office, Luke i. 8

ἱερεύς.

priest, Matt. viii. 4. xii. 4, 5. Mark i. 44. ii. 26. Luke i. 5. v. 14. vi. 4. x. 31. xvii. 14. John i. 19. Acts iv. 1. vi. 7. xiv. 13.
Heb. v. 6. vii. 1, 3, 11, 15, 17, 21 (20), 21, 23. viii. 4, 4(-G^{oo}LTS). ix. 6. x. 11 (ἀρχιερεύς L), 21. Rev. i. 6. v. 10. xx. 6.

high priest, Acts v. 24(-LS).
Add Luke xx. 1, for ἀρχιερεύς, G′T. Heb. vii. 14, for ἱερωσύνη, G′LTS.

ἱερόθυτος, offered in sacrifice.

1 Cor. x. 28, for εἰδωλόθυτος, G″LTS.

ἱερόν.

temple, Matt. iv. 5. xii. 5, 6. xxi. 12t, 14, 15, 23. xxiv. 1t. xxvi. 55. Mark xi. 11, 15t, 16, 27. xii. 35. xiii. 1, 3. xiv. 49. Luke ii. 27, 37, 46. iv. 9. xviii. 10. xix. 45, 47. xx. 1. xxi. 5, 37, 38. xxii. 52, 53. xxiv. 53.
John ii. 14, 15. v. 14. vii. 14, 28. viii. 2 (*ap*), 20, 59. x. 23. xi. 56. xviii. 20. Acts ii. 46. iii. 1, 2t, 3, 8, 10. iv. 1. v. 20, 21, 24, 25, 42. xix. 27. xxi. 26, 27, 28, 29, 30. xxii. 17. xxiv. 6, 12, 18. xxv. 8. xxvi. 21. 1 Cor. ix. 13.

ἱεροπρεπής.

as becometh holiness (*marg.* **as becometh holy women**), Tit. ii. 3.

ἱερός.

holy, 2 Tim. iii. 15.
τὰ ἱερά, **holy things**, 1 Cor. ix. 13.

ἱεροσυλέω.

commit sacrilege, Rom. ii. 22.

ἱερόσυλος.

robber of churches, Acts xix. 37.

ἱερουργέω.

to minister, Rom. xv. 16.

ἱερωσύνη.

priesthood, Heb. vii. 11, 12, 14 (ἱερεύς p′ G′LTS), 24.

ἱκανός.

enough, Luke xxii. 38.
sufficient, 2 Cor. ii. 6, 16. iii. 5.
τὸ ἱκανόν, **security**, Acts xvii. 9.
τὸ ἱκανὸν ποιέω, **to content**, Mark xv. 15.
able, 2 Tim. ii. 2.
meet, 1 Cor. xv. 9.
worthy, Matt. iii. 11. viii. 8. Mark i. 7. Luke iii. 16. vii. 6.

large, Matt. xxviii. 12.
sore[cc], Acts xx. 37.
great, Acts xxii. 6.
great number of, Mark x. 46.
much, Luke vii. 12. Acts v. 37 (-G°LT*S*). xi. 24, 26. xix. 26. xxvii. 9.
Plur., **many**, Luke viii. 32. xxiii. 9. Acts ix. 23, 43. xii. 12. xiv. 21. xix. 19. xx. 8. xxvii. 7. 1 Cor. xi. 30.—**many of**, Luke vii. 11 (-G°L[b] Tr*S*).
ἐξ ἱκανοῦ, **of a long season**, Luke xxiii. 8(ἐξ ἱκανῶν χρόνων LTr*S*).
ἐφ' ἱκανόν, **a long while**, Acts xx. 11.
Add Rom. xv. 22, for πολύς, T.
See also ἡμέρα, χρόνος.

ἱκανότης.

sufficiency, 2 Cor. iii. 5.

ἱκανόω.

make able, 2 Cor. iii. 6.
make meet, Col. i. 12.

ἱκετηρία.

supplication, Heb. v. 8.

ἰκμάς.

moisture, Luke viii. 6.

ἱλαρός.

cheerful, 2 Cor. ix. 7.

ἱλαρότης.

cheerfulness, Rom. xii. 8.

ἱλάσκομαι.

make reconciliation for, Heb. ii. 17.
Pass., **be merciful**, Luke xviii. 13.

ἱλασμός.

propitiation, 1 John ii. 2. iv. 10.

ἱλαστήριος.

Neut., **propitiation**, Rom. iii. 25.—**mercy-seat**, Heb. ix. 5.

ἵλεως.

merciful, Heb. viii. 12.
ἵλεώς σοι, **be it far from thee**, Matt. xvi. 22.

ἱμάς.

latchet, Mark i. 7. Luke iii. 16. John i. 27.
thong, Acts xxii. 25.

ἱματίζω.

clothe, Mark v. 15. Luke viii. 35.

ἱμάτιον.

garment, Matt. ix. 16*t*, 20, 21. xiv. 36. xxi. 8. xxiii. 5 (-G°LTTr*S*). xxvii. 35, 35(*ap*). Mark ii. 21. v. 27. vi. 56. x. 50: xi. 7, 8. xiii. 16. xv. 24. Luke v. 36t. viii. 44. xix. 35. xxii. 36. John xiii. 4, 12. xix. 23. Acts ix. 39. xii. 8. Heb. i. 11. Jas. v. 2. Rev. iii. 4. xvi. 15.
clothes, Luke viii. 27.
Plural, **clothes**, Matt. xxi. 7. xxiv. 18(*sing.* G''LTr*S*). xxvi. 65. Mark v. 28, 30. xv. 20. Luke xix. 36. Acts vii. 58. xiv. 14. xvi. 22. xxii. 23. — **raiment**, Matt. xi. 8 (-L[b]TTr*S*). xvii. 2. xxvii. 31. Mark ix. 3. Luke vii. 25. xxiii. 34. John xix. 24. Acts xviii. 6. xxii. 20. Rev. iii. 5, 18. iv. 4. — **apparel**, 1 Pet. iii. 3.
vesture, Rev. xix. 13, 16.
cloak, Matt. v. 40. Luke vi. 29.
robe, John xix. 2, 5.
Add Heb. i. 12 (fold them up ὡς ἱμάτιον), L*S*.

ἱματισμός.

raiment, Luke ix. 29.
vesture, Matt. xxvii. 35(*ap*). John xix. 24.
apparel, Acts xx. 33.
οἱ ἐν ἱματισμῷ ἐνδόξῳ, **they which are gorgeously apparelled**, Luke vii. 25.
array, 1 Tim. ii. 9.

ἱμείρω, -ομαι.

be affectionately desirous of, 1 Thes. ii. 8 (G', ὁμείρομαι GLT*S*).

ἵνα.

A particle used, commonly with a Subjunctive, frequently with an Indicative ([1]), twice with an Optative ([2]), often rendered by *to* or *for to* with the Infinitive ([3]), —

I. In a *final* sense, to denote the end or purpose *for* or *on account of* which a thing is done,

to the intent that, Eph. iii. 10.
to the intent, John xi. 15.

that, Matt. ix. 6. xii. 10. xiv. 15. xviii. 16. xix. 13, 16. xxiii. 26. xxvii. 20. Mark i. 38. ii. 10. iii. 2, 14*t*. iv. 22. v. 12. vi. 36, 56. vii. 9. ix. 18. x. 13, 17. xi. 25. xii. 2, 15. xiv. 12. xv. 11, 32. xvi. 1.

Luke i. 4. v. 24. vi. 7. viii. 16. ix. 12. xi. 33, 54(*ap*). xii. 36. xiv. 23. xv. 29. xvi. 4, 9, 24. xviii. 15. xix. 15. xx. 10, 14, 20. xxi. 36. xxii. 8.

John i. 7, 22, 31. iii. 17, 21. v. 23, 34, 40. vi. 5, 28, 30, 40, 50. vii. 3. viii. 6(*ap*). ix. 3, 36, 39. x. 10, 17, 38. xi. 4, 11, 16, 42, 52. xii. 9, 36, 46. xiii. 15, 19. xiv. 3, 13, 16, 29, 31. xv. 2, 11, 16*t*. xvi. 4, 33. xvii. 1, 2 (¹TS), 11, 13, 19, 21*t*, 22, 23*t*. 24, 26. xviii. 28(-LTr*S*), 37. xix. 4, 31, 35. xx. 31*t*.

Acts v. 15. ix. 21. xxi. 24. xxii. 24. xxiii. 24.

Rom. i. 11, 13. iii. 8. iv. 16. v. 21. vi. 1, 4, 6. vii. 4, 13. viii. 4. ix. 11, 23. xi. 19, 32. xiv. 9. xv. 4, 16, 31, 31(-G∞LT*S*), 32. xvi. 2.

1 Cor. i. 31. ii. 12 iii. 18. iv. 6, 8. v. 5, 7. vii. 5, 34, 35. ix. 15, 19, 20*t*, 21, 22*t*, 23, 24. x. 33. xi. 19. xiv. 5, 19, 31. xv. 28. xvi. 2, 6, 11.

2 Cor. i. 11, 15, 27. ii. 4*t*, 9. iv. 10, 11. 15. v. 5, 10, 12, 15, 21. viii. 9, 14. ix. 3, 8. xi. 7, 12*t*, 16. xii. 9. xiii. 7*t*.

Gal. i. 16. ii. 4 (¹LT*S*), 5, 9, 16, 19. iii. 14*t*, 22, 24. iv. 5, 17¹. vi. 13. Eph. i. 17². ii. 7, 10. iii. 16² (*subj.* L), 17(18), 19. iv. 10, 14, 28, 29. v. 26, 27*t*. vi. 3(¹ 2*d verb*), 13, 19, 20, 21, 22. Phil. i. 27. ii. 10, 15, 19, 28. iii. 8. Col. i. 9, 18, 28. ii. 2. iv. 3, 4, 8, 12.

1 Thes. ii. 16. iv. 12 v. 10. 2 Thes. i. 11. ii. 12. iii. 1, 2, 14. 1 Tim. i. 3, 16, 18, 20. ii. 2. iii. 15. iv. 15. v. 7, 16, 20. vi. 19. 2 Tim. i. 4. ii. 4, 10. iii. 17. iv. 17. Tit. i. 5, 9, 13. ii. 4, 8, 10, 12, 14. iii. 7, 8, 13. Phm. 13, 15.

Heb. ii. 14, 17. iv. 16. v. 1. vi. 18. ix. 25. x. 9, 36. xi. 35. xiii. 12, 17, 19. Jas. iv. 3. 1 Pet. i. 7. ii. 2, 12, 21, 24. iii. 1 (¹G′LT*S*), 9, 16, 18. iv. 6, 11. v. 6. 2 Pet. i. 4.

1 John i. 3, 4. ii. 19, 28. iii. 1, 8. iv. 9. v. 13, 13(*omS*), 20. 2 John 6, 12. 3 John 8.

Rev. ii. 10. iii. 11, 18*tr*. viii. 3 (¹LT*S*). xii. 6, 14, 15. xvi. 12. xviii. 4. xix. 8, 15, 18. xxii. 14¹.

to,³ Matt. xxvi. 16. xxvii. 26. Mark iv. 21*t*. vi. 41. viii. 6. ix. 22. xi. 28. xii. 13. xiv. 10. xv. 15, 20. Luke vi. 34. xix. 4. John i. 7, 8, 19. iii. 17. iv. 8. v. 7, 36. vi. 15, 38. vii. 32. viii. 59. x. 31. xi. 19, 31, 55. xii. 20, 47*t*. xvii. 4. xix. 16. Acts xvi. 30, 36.

1 Cor. i. 27(*ap*), 27, 28. ix. 25. xiii. 3(¹T) 2 Cor. xii. 7. Gal. iv. 5. Phil. ii. 30. 2 Thes. iii. 9. 1 John iii. 5. Rev. iii. 9 (¹G″LTTr*S*). vi. 2. viii. 6. xxi. 15, 23.

for to,³ Mark iii. 10. John x. 10. Acts xvii. 15. xxii. 5. Eph. ii. 15. Rev. ix. 15. xii. 4.

so as, Rev. viii. 12.

ἵνα μή.

that not, Matt. vii. 1. xxvi. 41. John iii. 15, 16. iv. 15. vi. 50. vii. 23(*marg.* **without**ᶜᶜ). xi. 37. xii. 46. xvi. 1. xviii. 36. Acts xxiv. 4.

1 Cor. ii. 5. vii. 5. xi. 32. 34. 2 Cor. i. 9. ii. 5. vi. 3. ix. 4. x. 9. 1 Thes. iv. 13(¹LᵐT). 1 Tim. vi. 1. Tit. ii. 5. iii. 14. Phm. 14. Heb. vi. 12. xi. 40. 1 John ii. 1. 2 John 8. Rev. vii. 1. xi. 6. xviii. 4*t*.

that no, Acts iv. 17. 1 Cor. iv. 6¹. xii. 25. xvi. 2. Rev. xx. 3.

ἵνα μή τις, **that no man,** Rev. xiii. 17.

ἵνα μή τι, **that nothing,** John vi. 12.

albeit not, Phm. 19.

lest, Matt. xvii. 27. xxvi. 5. Mark iii. 9. xiv. 38. Luke viii. 12. xiv. 29. xvi. 28. xviii. 5. xxii. 46. John iii. 20. v. 14. xii. 35, 42. xviii. 28. Acts v. 26(-ἵνα L*S*).

Rom. xi. 25. xv. 20. 1 Cor. i. 15, 17. viii. 13. ix. 12. 2 Cor. ii. 3, 11. ix. 3. xii. 7, 7(*ap*). xiii. 10. Gal. vi. 12. Eph. ii. 9. Phil. ii. 27. Col. ii. 4(*see* μηδείς). iii. 21. 1 Tim. iii. 6, 7.

Heb. iii. 13. iv. 11. xi. 28. xii. 3, 13. Jas. v. 9, 12. Rev. xvi. 15.

Add Mark iv. 22, εἰ μὴ ἵνα G′, ἐὰν μὴ ἵνα L*S*, for ὃ ἐὰν μή. v. 23, for ὅπως, G″LTTr*S*. Luke vi. 37, for καὶ οὐ μή, L. 2 Pet. i. 10(¹ L, *ap*).

II. After verbs of causation, command, permission, counsel, or desire, or words denoting fitness or worthiness, in the sense of ὅτι,

that, Matt. iv. 3. v. 29, 30. vii. 12. viii. 8. x. 25. xiv. 36. xvi. 20. xviii. 6, 14. xx. 21, 33. xxvi. 4, 63. xxviii. 10. Mark iii. 9. v. 18, 43. vi. 8, 12, 25. vii. 26, 36. viii. 30. ix. 9, 12, 30. x. 35, 37, 48, 51. xi. 16. xii. 19. xiv. 35.

Luke i. 43. iv. 3. vi. 31. vii. 6, 36. viii. 32. x. 40. xvi. 27. xvii. 2. xviii. 39, 41. xx. 28.

John ii. 25. iv. 47. vi. 29. ix. 22. xi. 50, 57. xii. 10, 23. xiii. 1, 29, 34*t*. xv. 8, 12, 13, 17. xvi. 2, 7, 30, 32. xvii. 3, 15*t*, 21, 24. xviii. 39. xix. 31, 38. Acts xix. 4.

1 Cor. i. 10. iv. 2, 3. ix. 15(¹ LT*S*, *see* οὐδείς), 18. xiv. 1, 5, 12. xvi. 10, 16. 2 Cor. viii. 6, 7, 13. ix. 5. xii. 8. Gal. ii. 10. Phil. i. 9, 10. ii. 2. Col. iv. 16*t*, 17. 1 Thes. iv. 1. 2 Thes. iii. 12. 1 Tim. v. 21.

1 John ii. 27. iii. 11, 23. iv. 17, 21. v. 3, 16. 2 John 5, 6. Rev. vi. 4(¹ L TTr), 11(¹ T). ix. 5(¹ LTTr*S*). xiii. 15, 15(–T*S*).

so that, Rev. xiii. 13.

because, Matt. xx. 31.

to,[3] Matt. xxvii. 32. Mark vii. 32. viii. 22. xiii. 34. xv. 21. Luke ix. 40. John i. 27. iv. 34. viii. 56. ix. 22. xiii. 2. Acts xxvii. 42. 1 Cor. xvi. 12*t*. 1 John i. 9. 3 John 4. Rev. ii. 21. xiii. 12(¹ LTTr, –*S*, *inf.*), 16 (¹ GLTTr*S*).

for to,[3] John xi. 53.

ἵνα μή.

that not, Matt. xii. 16. xxiv. 20. Mark iii. 12. v. 10. xiii. 18. Luke viii. 31. xxii. 32. John vi. 50. 2 John 8. Rev. ix. 4(¹ LT), 5.

that nothing[c], John vi. 39.

lest, 2 Pet. iii. 17.

Not rendered, Mark v. 23.

Add Matt. viii. 34, for ὅπως, L. xx. 32 (that), L. xxii. 24¹(. . his brother), L. Luke xxii. 6, ἵνα παραδῷ for τοῦ παραδοῦναι, L[m]. John xii. 7, ἵνα . . τηρήσῃ for τετήρηκεν, LTTr *S*. 1 Thes. iv. 1 (that), G′LT.

III. To mark simply the *event* or *result* of an action, in the sense of ὥστε. (The instances are somewhat disputed. The following are taken mainly from Robinson.)

that, Matt. i. 22. ii. 15. iv. 14. xxi. 4. xxvi. 56. xxvii. 35(*ap*). Mark iv. 12. Luke xi. 50. xiv. 10. xxii. 30. John iv. 36. v. 20. vi. 7. ix. 2. xii. 38. xiii. 18. xv. 25. xvi. 24. xvii. 12. xviii. 9, 32. xix. 24, 28, 36. Acts viii. 19. Rom. iii. 19. v. 20. vii. 13. viii. 17. xi. 11, 31. xv. 6. 1 Cor. v. 2. vii. 29. xiv. 13. 2 Cor. iv. 7. vii. 9. Eph. v. 33. Phil. i. 26. 1 Thes. v. 4. Heb. xii. 27. Jas. i. 4. 1 Pet. iv. 13. Rev. ix. 20. xiv. 13 (¹ LTTr*S*).

must[cc], Mark xiv. 49.

ἵνα μή.

so that not, Gal. v. 17.

that not, Luke viii. 10. ix. 45. John xii. 40. Acts ii. 25. Rev. ix. 20 (¹ LTTr*S*).

Add Matt. xii. 17, for ὅπως, LTTr*S*.

ἱνατί or ἵνα τί.

wherefore? Matt. ix. 4.

why? Matt. xxvii. 46. Luke xiii. 7. Acts iv. 25. vii. 26. 1 Cor. x. 29.

ἰός.

rust, Jas. v. 3.

poison, Rom. iii. 13. Jas. iii. 8.

Ἰουδαΐζω.

to live as do the Jews, Gal. ii. 14.

'Ιουδαϊσμός.

Jews' religion, Gal. i. 13, 14.

ἱππεύς.

horseman, Acts xxiii. 23, 32.

ἱππικόν.

horsemen, Rev. ix. 16(ἵππος G').

ἵππος.

horse, Jas. iii. 3. Rev. vi. 2, 4, 5, 8. ix. 7, 9, 17*t*. xiv. 20. xviii. 13. xix. 11, 14, 18, 19, 21.

Add Rev. ix. 16, for ἱππικόν, G'. 19, for αὐτός[1st], GLTTr*S*.

ἶρις.

rainbow, Rev. iv. 3. x. 1.

ἰσάγγελος.

equal unto the angels, Luke xx. 36.

ἴσημι, ἴστε, ἴσασι. See εἶδον, II.

ἴσθι. See εἰμί.

ἶσος or ἴσος.

equal, Matt. xx. 12. John v. 18. Phil. ii. 6(*neut. plur.*). Rev. xxi. 16.

like, Acts xi. 17.

τὰ ἴσα, **as much**, Luke vi. 34.

With εἰμί, **agree**, Mark xiv. 56, 59.

ἰσότης.

equality, 2 Cor. viii. 14(13), 14.

With art., **that which is equal**, Col. iv. 1.

ἰσότιμος.

like precious, 2 Pet. i. 1.

ἰσόψυχος.

like-minded (*marg.* **so dear** [c]**unto me**), Phil. ii. 20.

ἵστημι.

I. Pres., 1st Aor., Fut., *transitive.*

make stand, Rom. xiv. 4.

set, Matt. iv. 5. xviii. 2. xxv. 33. Mark ix. 36. Luke iv. 9. ix. 47. John viii. 3[p](*ap*). Acts iv. 7[p]. v. 27. vi. 6. xxii. 30.

set up, Acts vi. 13.

establish, Rom. iii. 31. x. 3. Heb. x. 9.

present, Jude 24.

appoint, Acts i. 23. xvii. 31.

covenant with for, Matt. xxvi. 15.

lay to one's charge, Acts vii. 60.

ἱστάνω, Rom. iii. 31, G'LT*S*.

Add Mark vii. 9, for τηρέω, G''.

II. Aorist and Future Passive, and Future Middle.

stand, Matt. xii. 25, 26. Mark iii. 24, 25, 26(2*d aor.* LTTr*S*). Luke xi. 18. xviii. 11, 40. xix. 8. xxi. 36. Acts v. 20. xi. 13. xvii. 22. Rev. vi. 17. viii. 3. xiii. 1 (xii. 18). xviii. 15.

stand up, Acts ii. 14. xxv. 18[p].

stand forth, Acts xxvii. 21.

be holden up, Rom. xiv. 4.

be established, Matt. xviii. 16. 2 Cor. xiii. 1.

be brought, Mark xiii. 9.

Add Luke xxiv. 17, for ἐστέ, Tr[b]*S*.

III. Perfect, Pluperfect, and 2d Aorist, *intransitive.*

stand, Matt. ii. 9 (*aor. pass.* G''LT Tr*S*). vi. 5. xii. 46, 47. xiii. 2. xvi. 28. xx. 3, 6*t*. xxiv. 15. xxvii. 11, 47. Mark iii. 31. ix. 1. xi. 5. xiii. 14. Luke i. 11. v. 1(*with* εἰμί), 2. vi. 17. vii. 38. viii. 20. ix. 27. xiii. 25. xvii. 12. xviii. 13. xxiii. 10, 35, 49. xxiv. 36.

John i. 26, 35. iii. 29. vi. 22. vii. 37. viii. 9(*ap*). xi. 56[p]. xviii. 5, 16, 18, 18 (*with* εἰμί), 25. xix. 25. xx. 11, 14, 19, 26. xxi. 4. Acts i. 11. iii. 8. iv. 14. v. 23, 25. vii. 33, 55, 56. ix. 7. x. 30. xii. 14. xvi. 9(*with* εἰμί). xxi. 40. xxiv. 20[p], 21. xxv. 10 (*with* εἰμί). xxvi. 6, 16.

Rom. v. 2. xi. 20. 1 Cor. vii. 37. x. 12. xv. 1. 2 Cor. i. 24. Eph. vi. 11, 13, 14. Col. iv. 12. 1 Tim. ii. 19. Heb. x. 11. Jas. ii. 3. v. 9. 1 Pet. v. 12. Rev. iii. 20. v. 6. vii. 1, 9, 11. viii. 2. x. 5, 8. xi. 1(*ap*), 4, 11. xii. 4. xiv. 1. xv. 2. xviii. 10, 17. xix. 17. xx. 12.

stand forth, Luke vi. 8*t*.

stand by, Matt. xxvi. 73. John xii. 29. Acts xxii. 25.

stand still, Matt. xx. 32. Mark x. 49. Luke vii. 14. Acts viii. 38.

abide, John viii. 44.
continue, Acts xxvi. 22.
stanch[c], Luke viii. 44.
Compare στήκω.

ἱστορέω.

to see, Gal. i. 18.

ἰσχυρός.

strong, Luke xi. 22. 1 Cor. i. 25. iv. 10. x. 22. Heb. v. 7. vi. 18. 1 John ii. 14. Rev. v. 2. xviii. 8.
strong man, Matt. xii. 29*t*. Mark iii. 27*t*. Luke xi. 21.
mighty, Matt. iii. 11. Mark i. 7. Luke iii. 16. xv. 14. 1 Cor. i. 27. Rev. x. 1. xviii. 10, 21. xix. 6, 18.
powerful, 2 Cor. x. 10.
valiant, Heb. xi. 34.
boisterous (*marg.* **strong**), Matt. xiv. 30.
Add Rev. vi. 15, for δυνατός, GL TTr*S*. xviii. 2(*ap*).

ἰσχύς.

strength, Mark xii. 30, 33. Luke x. 27. Rev. v. 12.
might, Eph. vi. 10. Rev. vii. 12.
mighty (*Gr.* of might), Eph. i. 19.
With ἐν, **mightily**, Rev. xviii. 2(*ap*).
power, 1 Thes. i. 9. 2 Pet. ii. 11.
ability, 1 Pet. iv. 11.

ἰσχύω.

be of strength, Heb. ix. 17.
be able, Luke xiii. 24. xiv. 29, 30. John xxi. 6. Acts vi. 10. xv. 10.
can, Matt. xxvi. 40. Mark v. 4. ix. 18. xiv. 37. Luke vi. 48. viii. 43. xiv. 6. xvi. 3. xx. 26. Acts xxv. 7.
can do, Phil. iv. 13.
With μόλις, **have much work**, Acts xxvii. 16.
may, Matt. viii. 28.
avail, Gal. v. 6. vi. 15(G′, εἰμί GL T*S*). Jas. v. 16.
prevail, Acts xix. 16, 20. Rev. xii. 8.
be good, Matt. v. 13.
be whole, Matt. ix. 12. Mark ii. 17.

ἴσως.

it may be, Luke xx. 13.

ἰχθύδιον.

little fish, Matt. xv. 34.
small fish, Mark viii. 7.

ἰχθύς.

fish, Matt. vii. 10. xiv. 17, 19. xv. 36. xvii. 27. Mark vi. 38, 41*t*, 43. Luke v. 6, 9. ix. 13, 16. xi. 11*t*, xxiv. 42. John xxi. 6, 8, 11. 1 Cor. xv. 39.

ἴχνος.

step, Rom. iv. 12. 2 Cor. xii. 18. 1 Pet. ii. 21.

ἰῶτα.

jot, Matt. v. 18.

κἀγώ, κἀμοί, κἀμέ. See ἐγώ.

καθά.

as, Matt. xxvii. 10.

καθαίρεσις.

pulling down, 2 Cor. x. 4.
destruction, 2 Cor. x. 8. xiii. 10.

καθαιρέω.

take down, Mark xv. 36, 46. Luke xxiii. 53. Acts xiii. 29.
pull down, Luke xii. 18.
put down, Luke i. 52.
cast down, 2 Cor. x. 5.
destroy, Acts xiii. 19[p]. xix. 27.

καθαίρω.

purge, John xv. 2. Heb. x. 2(καθαρίζω L*S*).

καθάπερ.

as, Rom. xii. 4. 1 Cor. xii. 12. 2 Cor. iii. 13. viii. 11. 1 Thes. ii. 11. iii. 6. Heb. v. 4 (καθώς L, καθώσπερ T*S*).
even as, Rom. iv. 6. 2 Cor. i. 14. iii. 18. 1 Thes. iii. 12. iv. 5.
as well as, Heb. iv. 2.

καθάπτω.

fasten on, Acts xxviii. 3.

καθαρίζω.

make clean, Matt. viii. 2. xxiii. 25. Mark i. 40. Luke v. 12. xi. 39.
cleanse, Matt. viii. 3. x. 8. xi. 5.

xxiii. 26. Mark i. 42. Luke iv. 27. vii. 22. xvii. 14, 17. Acts x. 15. xi. 9. 2 Cor. vii. 1. Eph. v. 26. Jas. iv. 8. 1 John i. 7, 9.

Pass., **be clean**, Matt. viii. 3. Mark i. 41. Luke v. 13.

purify, Acts xv. 9. Tit. ii. 14. Heb. ix. 23.

purge, Mark vii. 19. Heb. ix. 14, 22.

Add Heb. x. 2, for καθαίρω, L*S*.

καθαρισμός.

cleansing, Mark i. 44. Luke v. 14.
purifying, John ii. 6. iii. 25.
purification, Luke ii. 22.
With ποιέω, **to purge**, Heb. i. 3p.
λήθην λαμβάνω τοῦ καθαρισμοῦ, **forget that one was purged**, 2 Pet. i. 9.

κάθαρμα.

filth, 1 Cor. iv. 13.

καθαρός.

clean, Matt. xxiii. 26. xxvii. 59. Luke xi. 41. John xiii. 10*t*, 11. xv. 3. Acts xviii. 6. Rev. xix. 8, 14.

clear, Rev. xxi. 18.

pure, Matt. v. 8. Acts xx. 26. Rom. xiv. 20. 1 Tim. i. 5. iii. 9. 2 Tim. i. 3. ii. 22. Tit. i. 15*tr*. Heb. x. 22(23). Jas. i. 27. 1 Pet. i. 22 (-LT). Rev. xv. 6. xxi. 18, 21. xxii. 1(*omS*).

καθαρότης.

purifying, Heb. ix. 13.

καθέδρα.

seat, Matt. xxi. 12. xxiii. 2. Mark xi. 15.

καθέζομαι.

sit, Matt. xxvi. 55. Luke ii. 46. John iv. 6. xi. 20. xx. 12. Acts vi. 15.

Add, for κάθημαι, Acts ii. 2, LT. xx. 9, LT*S*.

καθεῖς or καθ' εἷς. See εἷς.

καθεξῆς.

in order, Luke i. 3. Acts xviii. 23.
by order, Acts xi. 4.
afterward, Luke viii. 1. [iii. 24.
οἱ καθ., **those that follow after**, Acts

καθεύδω.

to sleep, Matt. ix. 24. xiii. 25. xxv. 5. xxvi. 45. Mark iv. 27. v. 39. xiii. 36. xiv. 37*t*, 41. Luke viii. 56. xxii. 46. Eph. v. 14. 1 Thes. v. 6, 7*t*, 10.

be asleep, Matt. viii. 24.

asleep, Matt. xxvi. 40p, 43p. Mark iv. 38p. xiv. 40p.

καθηγητής.

master, Matt. xxiii. 10.

Said of Christ, **Master**, Matt. xxiii. 8 (διδάσκαλος G'LTTr), 10.

καθήκω.

fit, Acts xxii. 22p(*ind.* GT*S*).
τὰ μὴ καθήκοντα, **those things which are not convenient**, Rom. i. 28.

κάθημαι.

sit down, Matt. xv. 29. xxvii. 19p, 36. Luke xxii. 55.

sit, Matt. iv. 16*t*. ix. 9. xi. 16. xiii. 1, 2. xx. 30. xxii. 44. xxiii. 22. xxiv. 3p. xxvi. 58, 64, 69. xxvii. 61. xxviii. 2. Mark ii. 6, 14. iii. 32, 34. iv. 1. v. 15. x. 46. xii. 36(κάθισον fr. καθίζω TTr). xiii. 3p. xiv. 62. xvi. 5.

Luke i. 79. v. 27. vii. 32. viii. 35. x. 13. xviii. 35. xx. 42. xxii. 56p, 69(*with* εἰμί). John ii. 14. vi. 3. ix. 8. xii. 15. Acts ii. 2(καθέζομαι LT), 34. iii. 10. viii. 28. xiv. 8. xx. 9 καθέζομαι LT*S*). xxiii. 3.

Col. iii. 1 (*with* εἰμί). Heb. i. 13. Jas. ii. 3*t*. Rev. iv. 2, 3(*ap*), 4, 9, 10. v. 1, 7, 13. vi. 2, 4, 5, 8, 16. vii. 10, 15. ix. 17. xi. 16. xiv. 14, 15, 16. xvii. 1, 3, 9, 15. xviii. 7. xix. 4, 11, 18, 19, 21. xx. 11. xxi. 5.

sit by, Luke v. 17. 1 Cor. xiv. 30.
dwell, Luke xxi. 35.

Add Rev. xiv. 6, for κατοικέω, GL TTr*S*.

καθημερινός.

daily, Acts vi. 1.

καθίζω.

set, 1 Cor. vi. 4. Eph. i. 20.

sit down, Matt. xiii. 48, Mark ix. 35. Luke iv. 20. v. 3. xiv. 28, 31. xvi. 6. John viii. 2 (*ap*). xix. 13. Acts xiii. 14. xvi. 13. 1 Cor. x. 7. Heb. i. 3. x. 12. xii. 2. Rev. iii. 21.
sit, Matt. v. 1p. xix. 28. xx. 21, 23. xxiii. 2. xxv. 31. xxvi. 36. Mark x. 37, 40. xi. 2, 7. xii. 41. xiv. 32. xvi. 19(*ap*). Luke xix. 30. xxii. 30. John xii. 14. Acts ii. 3, 30. viii. 31. xii. 21. xxv. 6, 17. 2 Thes. ii. 4. Heb. viii. 1. Rev. iii. 21. xx. 4.
Mid., **sit**, Matt. xix. 28.
tarry, Luke xxiv. 49.
continue, Acts xviii. 11(*marg.* **sit**).
Add Mark xii. 36, for κάθημαι, T Tr. Luke vii. 15, for ἀνακαθίζω, Lm.

καθίημι.

let down, Luke v. 19. Acts ix. 25. x. 11. xi. 5.

καθίστημι.

set, Heb. ii. 7(*ap*).
make, Matt. xxiv. 45, 47. xxv. 21, 23. Luke xii. 14, 42, 44. Acts vii. 10, 27, 35. Rom. v. 19*t*. Heb. vii. 28. 2 Pet. i. 8.
Pass., **be**, Jas. iii. 6. iv. 4.
appoint, Acts vi. 3.
ordain, Tit. i. 5. Heb. v. 1. viii. 3.
conduct, Acts xvii. 15.

καθό.

καθὸ ἄν, **according to that**, 2 Cor. viii. 12.
as, Rom. viii. 26.
inasmuch as, 1 Pet. iv. 13.

καθόλου.

at all, Acts iv. 18.

καθοπλίζω.

to arm, Luke xi. 21.

καθοράω.

see clearly, Rom. i. 20.

καθότι.

καθότι ἄν, **according as**, Acts iv. 35. —**as**, Acts ii. 45.
because that, Luke i. 7.
because, Acts ii. 24.
forasmuch as, Luke xix. 9.
Add Acts xvii. 31, for διότι, G″L T*S*.

καθώς.

according as, Rom. xi. 8. 1 Cor. i. 31. 2 Cor. ix. 7. Eph. i. 4.
as, Matt. xxi. 6. xxvi. 24. xxviii. 6. Mark iv. 33. ix. 13. xiv. 16, 21. xv. 8. xvi. 7. Luke i. 55, 70. ii. 20, 23. v. 14. vi. 31, 36. xi. 1, 30. xvii. 26. xxii. 13, 29. xxiv. 24, 39. John i. 23. iii. 14. v. 30. vi. 31, 57, 58. vii. 38. viii. 28. x. 15, 26(*ap*). xii. 14. xiii. 15, 33, 34. xiv. 27, 31. xv. 4, 9, 12. xvii. 2, 11, 18, 21, 23. xix. 40. xx. 21. Acts ii. 4, 22. vii. 42, 44, 48. xv. 8, 15. xxii. 3.
Rom. i. 13, 17. ii. 24, iii. 4, 8*t*, 10. iv. 17. viii. 36. ix. 13, 29, 33. x. 15. xi. 26. xv. 3, 7, 9, 21. 1 Cor. ii. 9. iv. 17. v. 7. viii. 2. x. 6, 7, 8, 9, 10, 33. xi. 2. xii. 11, 18. xiv. 34. xv. 38, 49. 2 Cor. i. 5, 14. iv. 1. vi. 16. viii. 5, 6, 15. ix. 3, 9. x. 7. xi. 12. Gal. ii. 7. v. 21. Eph. iii. 3. iv. 4, 17, 21, 32. v. 2, 3, 25, 29. Phil. ii. 12. iii. 17. Col. i. 6*t*, 7. ii. 7. iii. 13. 1 Thes. i. 5. ii. 2, 4, 5, 13, 14. iii. 4. iv. 1, 6, 11, 13. 2 Thes. i. 3. iii. 1. 1 Tim. i. 3.
Heb. iii. 7. iv. 3, 7. v. 3, 6. viii. 5. x. 25. xi. 12. 1 Pet. iv. 10. 2 Pet. i. 14. iii. 15. 1 John ii. 18. iii. 2, 12, 23. iv. 17. 2 John 4, 6.
even as, Mark xi. 6. Luke i. 2. xix. 32. John v. 23. xii. 50. xv. 10. xvii. 14, 16, 22. Rom. i. 28. 1 Cor. i. 6. xi. 1. xiii. 12. Gal. iii. 6. Phil. i. 7. 1 Thes. v. 11. 1 John ii. 6, 27. iii. 3, 7. 3 John 2, 3.
καθὼς (ὡς LT*S*) καί, **as well as**, Acts x. 47.
how, Acts xv. 14.—**when**, Acts vii. 17.
Add, for καθάπερ, Heb. v. 4, L. For καὶ ὡς, Luke xvii. 28, Tr*S*. For ὡς, Mark i. 2, TTr*S*. Acts vii. 51, L.—1 Thes. iv. 1(*ap*).
See also εὐπορέομαι.

καθώσπερ, even as.

Heb. v. 4, for καθάπερ, T*S*.

καί.

A particle having two distinct senses: I., *and*, II., *also*, *even*. Omitting the cases in which it merely couples words and sentences, Bruder gives over 3000 examples of its special uses, to which a few are added ([a]) in the following account.

I.

1. Uses somewhat peculiar.

(a). In the phrase ὁ Θεὸς καὶ πατήρ,

and, 2 Cor. xi. 31. Gal. i. 4. Eph. i. 3. iv. 6. v. 20. Phil. iv. 20. Col. i. 3. ii. 2 (*ap*). iii. 17 (–G°LT*S*). 1 Thes. i. 3. iii. 11. Jas. i. 27. iii. 9. 1 Pet. i. 3. Rev. i. 6.

even, Rom. xv. 6. 1 Cor. xv. 24. 2 Cor. i. 3. 1 Thes. iii. 13. 2 Thes. ii. 16(ὁ G′L*S*).

(b) πολλοὶ (πολλὰ) καὶ . . .

many and . ., Acts xxv. 7.

and many . ., Luke iii. 18. John xx. 30.

many . ., Tit. i. 10(–καί G°L*S*).

(c) A *rhetorical* use, in contrasted or concise expressions.

and, Matt. iii. 14. vii. 7*tr*. John i. 11[a]. Etc. B. gives 266 examples.

(d) Beginning the *apodosis* or conclusion of a conditional sentence.

then, Luke xix. 15. Jas. ii. 4(–G°° L*S*).

that, Luke x. 38. xiv. 1. xvii. 11.

and, Luke xiii. 25. Acts xiii. 19[cc]. Jas. iv. 15[2d,cc]. Rev. vi. 1, 12.

Not rendered, Matt. xxviii. 9. Mark ii. 15. Luke ii. 15 (–LTr*S*), 21. v. 1, 12. vii. 12. ix. 51. xxiv. 4, 15. Acts i. 10. x. 17(–L*S*). 2 Cor. ii. 2. Rev. xiv. 10.

Add Rev. iii. 20 (. . I will), G′*S*.

(e) With a negative, οὐ, μή, or οὔτε, in the preceding clause.

and, Matt. v. 25*t*. vii. 6. x. 26, 38. xiii. 15*tr*. xxvii. 65. Mark iv. 12. Luke xii. 58*t*. xiv. 9*t*. xxi. 34. John iv. 11. vi. 53. xii. 40*t*. xv. 22. Acts xxviii. 27*f*. Eph. v. 3. 1 Thes. iii. 5. 2 Thes. ii. 3. 1 Tim. vi. 1. 2 Tim. ii. 26. Heb. xii. 5, 15. 3 John 10. Rev. vi. 6, 10. xii. 9. xvi. 15. xviii. 12[13], 13[14](*and see* ἄμωμον).

nor, John xii. 40. Gal. iii. 28. Eph. v. 3.

neither, Eph. v. 3.

even, Rev. ii. 13(–G°°*S*).

so, Matt. xxvii. 64.

(f) Where some MSS. read ἤ.

Matt. vi. 25. vii. 10. Mark xi. 28. (*See* ἤ, II.) Jas. iv. 13. (ἤ, I.) Matt. x. 26 (οὐδέ various MSS.).

(g) καὶ . . καί. (Compare τε καί.)

both . . and, Matt. x. 28. xii. 22. Mark vi. 30 (–[1st] G°°LTr*S*). vii. 37. Luke ii. 46. v. 36. xxii. 33. John iv. 36. vii. 28. xi. 48, 57(–[1st] LTTr *S*). xii. 28. xv. 24. Acts ii. 29(28), 36. xxvi. 29.

Rom. xi. 33. xiv. 9*t*. 1 Cor. iv. 11. vi. 13. vii. 34. Phil. ii. 13. iv. 9, 12 ([1st] δέ St), 12*t*. 1 Thes. ii. 15. v. 15(–[1st] G°°L*S*). 2 Thes. iii. 4. 1 Tim. iv. 10 (–[1st] G°L*S*), 16. Tit. i. 9. Phm. 16. 2 Pet. iii. 18. 2 John 9. Rev. xiii. 15.

both . . and also, 1 Cor. vi. 14.

also . . and, Matt. xxii. 26. Luke xxiii. 27 (–[1st] G°LTr*S*). 1 Cor. vii. 34(–[1st] StG). xv. 40. Phil. iv. 3.

and . . also, Rom. xvi. 2.

even . . and, Matt. viii. 27. Mark iv. 41. Luke viii. 25. Tit. i. 15.

and . . and, Mark v. 38 (–[1st] StG°). xi. 9. John x. 9, 14. xvii. 26. xx. 17. Acts xxii. 20. 16 or. ii. 3, 4. iv. 9. xvi. 16. Col. ii. 2 (*ap*). Jas. iii. 6. 1 Pet. ii. 8. Rev. i. 19. ii. 26.

καὶ . . καὶ . . δέ, **and . . and also**, Acts v. 32(–δέ G°L*S*).

and (the first not rendered), Mark ix. 22. xv. 40. Luke x. 30. John xvii. 25. 1 Cor. i. 22. Phil. iv. 16. 1 Thes. ii. 18. iii. 4. Tit. i. 10 (–[1st] G°L*S*). Jude 25.

neither . . nor,[c] 1 Cor. x. 32.

With οὐ μή, **and neither . . nor**, Luke i. 15.

Add Matt. xii. 44 (. . swept and), L[b]*S*. Acts xvii. 18 (. . of the Epicureans and), G'LT*S*. Rev. xx. 10 (. . the beast and), GLTTr.

2. By Hebraism.

(a) In narrative, when an adverb of time might be used instead. B. gives about 1600 instances, all in the Gospels, Acts, or Apocalypse, except Gal. ii. 13; Heb. iv. 4.

Also (*) in connection with a note of time, place, or manner, —
Matt. v. 24. viii. 13. John iv. 27. Etc. 181 instances.

Also (**) with a note of time in the preceding clause, —
and, Matt. xxvi. 2, 45. Mark xv. 25. Luke xxiii. 44. John ii. 13[a]. v. 1[a]. x. 22(-G[o]T*S*). xi. 55[a].
and then, John iv. 35[a].
when, Acts v. 7. Heb. viii. 8.
that, Luke xix. 43.

(b) When the connection is logical. Matt. i. 21. v. 15. Luke vii. 23. Etc. 383 examples.

Also (*) *explicative*, —
and, Matt. i. 24[a]. viii. 33[a]. xiii. 41[a]. xvii. 2[a]. xxi. 5. xxiii. 14(13). Mark i. 15[a]. xii. 40. Luke i. 17, 36. ii. 12. vii. 12. viii. 41. xi. 14. xvii. 16. xx. 3[a]. xxiii. 41. John i. 16. ix. 31[a], 37. x. 10, 12[a]. xiii. 32. xvi. 3. Acts xxii. 25. xxvi. 10. xxvii. 41.

Rom. xiii. 11. 1 Cor. ii. 2. v. 1. vi. 6, 8, 11. xii. 28. xiv. 32. xv. 38. 2 Cor. v. 15. Gal. vi. 16. Eph. ii. 8. vi. 13. Phil. i. 9, 28. iii. 10[a]. Col. ii. 13. 1 Tim. iii. 16. Heb. v. 11[a]. x. 25. xi. 12. xii. 1. 1 John ii. 2. v. 4, 17. 3 John 5. Rev. xiii. 18.

καὶ ὅταν . . τότε, **when . . and then**, Luke v. 35[a].
and that, 1 Cor. xiv. 27.
even, 1 Cor. iii. 5. Eph. v. 23. Rev. xvii. 11.
also, Mark i. 19. Acts xv. 27.
though[c], Luke xviii. 7. [Tr*S*).
καί γε, **at least**, Luke xix. 42 (-L[b]
for, Rom. xi. 27. 1 John iii. 4[a].
but, John i. 20. Acts xvi. 7.
Add Mark x. 1, for *διὰ τοῦ*, LTTr*S*.
[[a] In *hendiadys*,
Luke vi. 48, *see βαθύνω*.
and, Acts xxiii. 6. Rom. i. 5. x. 20. Col. ii. 5.]

Also (**) *continuative*, Matt. i. 17*t*. v. 30. Etc. 145 times.

II.

With αὐτός, [1]; *with a comparative*, [2]. *δὲ καί, καὶ . . δέ, τε καί*, [3].

also, Matt. iii. 10(-G[o]LTTr*S*). v. 39, 40. vi. 14, 21. x. 4. xiii. 26. xv. 3, 16. xvii. 12. xviii. 33. xix. 28. xx. 4, 7. xxii. 26, 27. xxiii. 23. xxiv. 27 (-G[oo]LTTr*S*), 37 (-LTTr*S*), 39 (-LTTr), 44. xxv. 11, 17[1] (-G[o]LTr*S*), 22[1], 41, 44. xxvi. 13, 35([3]G[ph]), 69, 71, 73. xxvii. 41[3](-L[b]*S*, -*δέ* Tr[b]), 44, 57.

Mark i. 38. ii. 26, 28. iii. 19. iv. 36. vii. 18. viii. 7, 38. xi. 25. xii. 6, 22. xiv. 9, 31[3]. xv. 31[3], 40, 41, 43[1].

Luke i. 35, 36[1]. ii. 4. iii. 9[3], 12[3]. iv. 23, 43. v. 10, 36. vi. 4(-LTr), 5, 6(-LTr*S*), 13, 14, 16(-LTTr*S*), 29*t*, 31, 32, 34, 36 (-L[b]Tr[b]*S*). vii. 8, 49. viii. 36 (-G[oo]LTr*S*). ix. 61. x. 1(-Tr[b]), 17, 39. xi. 1, 4[1], 30, 34*t*, 40, 45, 46, 49. xii. 8, 24, 40, 54. xiii. 8. xiv. 12[3], 12[1]. xvi. 1, 10*t*, 14, 22, 28. xvii. 26, 28. xviii. 15. xix. 9[1], 19. xx. 12, 31, 32[3](-*δέ* G[oo]LTTr*S*). xxi. 2(-G[o]L[b]Tr*S*). xxii. 20, 24, 39, 56, 58, 59, 68. xxiii. 7, 27 (-G[o]LTr*S*), 32, 35, 36, 51 (-G[oo]LTr*S*), 55(-G[oo]LTTr*S*). xxiv. 23.

John iii. 23. iv. 45[1]. v. 18, 19, 27. vi. 36, 37. vii. 3, 10[1], 47, 52. viii. 17[3], 19. ix. 15, 27, 40. xi. 16, 52. xii. 9, 10, 18, 26, 32. xiii. 9, 14, 32, 34. xiv. 3, 7, 19. xv. 20*t*, 23. xvii. 1(-G[oo]LTTr*S*), 19[1], 20, 21[1]. xviii. 2, 5, 17, 25. xix. 39. xx. 8. xxi. 3, 20, 25.

Acts i. 3, 11. ii. 22[1](-G[oo]LT*S*), 26. iii. 17. v. 2, 16. vii. 45. viii. 13[1].

ix. 32. x. 45. xi. 1, 18, 30. xii. 3. xiii. 5, 9, 22, 33, 35. xiv. 15. xv. 32[1], 35. xvii. 6, 28*t*. xix. 21, 27. xx. 30. xxi. 13, 16[3], 24[1], 28. xxii. 5*t*, 20[1]. xxiii. 11, 30, 33, 35. xxiv. 6, 9, 15[1], 26. xxv. 22[1]. xxvi. 10, 26, 29. xxvii. 10. xxviii. 9, 10.

Rom. i. 6, 13, 15, 24(-G∞L*S*), 27. ii. 12. iii. 29[3] (δέ *omS*), 29. iv. 6, 9, 11[1], 12, 16, 21, 24. v. 2, 3, 11, 15. vi. 5, 8, 11. vii. 4. viii. 11, 17, 21[1], 23, 26[3], 29, 30*tr*, 32, 34. ix. 10, 24, 25. xi. 1, 16, 22, 31, 31[1]. xiii. 5, 6. xv. 7, 14*t*[1], 14, 22, 27. xvi. 4, 7.

1 Cor. i. 8, 16. ii. 13. iv. 8. v. 12 (-G∞L*S*). vii. 3, 4, 22(-LT*S*). ix. 8. x. 9 (-G∞LT*S*), 10(-G∞LT*S*), 13. xi. 6, 19, 23, 25. xii. 12. xiii. 12. xiv. 15*t*, 19, 34. xv. 1, 2, 3, 14, 18, 21, 28 (-L[b]), 42, 48, 49. xvi. 10 (κἀγώ for καὶ ἐγώ LT*S*).

2 Cor. i. 5, 6, 7, 11, 14*t*, 22. ii. 9, 10. iii. 6. iv. 10, 11, 13, 14. v. 5 (-G∞L*S*), 11. vi. 13. viii. 6*t*, 7, 10, 11, 14, 19. ix. 12. x. 11, 14. xi. 15. xiii. 4, 9.

Gal. ii. 1, 10, 13, 17[1]. v. 21, 25. vi. 1, 7. Eph. i. 11, 13*t*, 21. ii. 3, 22. iv. 9, 10. v. 2, 25. vi. 9(καὶ αὐτῶν (ἑαυτῶν *S*) καὶ ὑμῶν for καὶ ὑμῶν αὐτῶν C[m]G'LT*S*), 21. Phil. i. 15, 20, 29. ii. 4, 5, 9, 18, 24[1], 27. iii. 4, 12, 20. iv. 3, 10, 15. Col. i. 6, 7 (-G∞LT*S*), 8, 9, 29. ii. 11, 12. iii. 4, 7, 8, 13, 15. iv. 1, 3*t*, 16.

1 Thes. i. 5, 8 (-G∞LT*S*). ii. 8, 13*t*, 14. iii. 6. iv. 6, 8(-L). v. 11, 24. 2 Thes. i. 5, 11. 1 Tim. ii. 9 (-L*S*). v. 13, 20, 25. 2 Tim. i. 5, 12. ii. 2, 5, 10[1], 11, 12, 20. iii. 8, 9. iv. 8, 15. Tit. iii. 3, 13. Phm. 9, 21, 22.

Heb. i. 2. ii. 14[1]. iii. 2. iv. 10[1]. v. 2[1], 3, 5, 6. vii. 2*t*, 12, 25. viii. 3, 6. ix. 1. x. 15. xi. 11, 19. xii. 1, 26. xiii. 3[1], 12. Jas. i. 11. ii. 2, 11, 19, 25[3]. iii. 4. v. 8.

1 Pet. ii. 5, 8, 18, 21. iii. 1, 5, 18, 19, 21. iv. 6, 13. v. 1. 2 Pet. ii. 1. iii. 15, 16*t*. 1 John i. 3. ii. 2, 6[1], 24. iii. 4. iv. 11, 21. v. 1(-L[b]). 2 John 1. Jude 8, 14. Rev. ii. 15. vi. 11. xi. 8.

and also, Mark xiv. 67. Luke iv. 41[3]. Acts xxvii. 36[1]. Jas. iii. 2.

withal, Acts xxv. 27. 1 Tim. v. 13.

moreover, Acts xi. 30[3]. 1 Tim. iii. 7[3].

else, Rom. ii. 15.

yet, Luke iii. 20. John viii. 16. Gal. iii. 4.

so, John xiii. 33. Rom. xi. 16. 1 Pet. i. 15[1].

likewise, Matt. xviii. 35. xx. 10. xxiv. 33. Luke iii. 14[3]. xvii. 10. xix. 19. xxi. 31. Acts iii. 24. 1 Cor. xiv. 9. Col. iv. 16. 1 Pet. iv. 1.

in like manner, Mark xiii. 29.

both, Mark vii. 37. Luke xxi. 16. xxii. 23. John ii. 2. ix. 37. xi. 57 (-LTTr*S*). xv. 24*t*. 1 Cor. vii. 29. Phil. iv. 9. 1 Thes. ii. 15. 2 Thes. iii. 4.

even, Matt. v. 46, 47. vii. 12. viii. 27. xii. 8. xiii. 12. xviii. 33 (κἀγώ for καὶ ἐγώ LTTr*S*). xx. 14. xxv. 29. Mark i. 27. iv. 25, 41. vi. 2. xiii. 22. Luke viii. 18, 25. ix. 54. x. 11. xii. 41, 57. xviii. 11. xix. 26, 42. xx. 37. xxiv. 24 (-LTr). John v. 21. viii. 25. xi. 22, 37. Acts v. 39. xii. 4. xv. 8. xxvi. 11.

Rom. i. 13. v. 11, 14, 18, 21. vi. 4. viii. 23, 34(-G°L[b]*S*). ix. 24. xi. 5. xv. 3. 1 Cor. ii. 11. vii. 7. ix. 14. xiv. 12. xv. 22. xvi. 1. 2 Cor. i. 8, 13(-G∞L*S*). vii. 14. x. 7, 13. xi. 12. Gal. ii. 16. iv. 3, 29. v. 12. Eph. ii. 3. iv. 4, 32. v. 12, 23, 29, 33. Phil. i. 15. iii. 15, 18. . iv. 16. Col. iii. 13. 1 Thes. ii. 14[1], 19. iii. 4, 12. iv. 5, 13, 14. 2 Thes. iii. 1. Phm. 19.

Heb. vii. 4(-L). xi. 12, 19. Jas. ii. 17. iii. 5. 2 Pet. i. 14. ii. 1. Jude 23. Rev. ii. 13(-G∞*S*). xviii. 6[1].

even also, Matt. xii. 45. xxiii. 28. 1 Cor. xi. 12.

also even, Luke vi. 33.

and even, 1 John iv. 3.

even very, Luke xii. 7.

very, Matt. x. 30. xxiv. 24. Luke ix. 5(–L^{b}Tr*S*). xii. 59.

the same, Gal. ii. 8.

that^{c}, *pron.*, 2 Cor. xi. 12.

indeed, Mark ix. 13. Phil. ii. 27.

yea, Matt. xxvi. 60 (*omS*). John xvi. 32. Acts vii. 43. Rom. viii. 34^{3} (–*καί* G^{oo}L*S*). 1 Cor. ii. 10.

yea, and, 1 Cor. xv. 15^{3}. 2 Cor. viii. 3. 3 John 12^{3}.

ἀλλὰ καί, **yea, and,** Luke xxiv. 22. Phil. i. 18. ii. 17. — **and indeed,** 2 Cor. xi. 1. — **moreover,** Luke xvi. 21.

καὶ ἐάν, **or if,** Matt. vii. 10 (*ἤ καί* LTr*S*, *ἢ καὶ ἐάν* T). — **though,** Gal. i. 8.

ἐάν τε καί, **though,** 2 Cor. x. 8(–*τε* L^{b}, –*καί* L*S*).

εἰ καί, **if that,** Phil. iii. 12. — **though,** 2 Cor. iv. 16. vii. 8*tr*, 12. xi. 6. xii. 11, 15(–*καί* L*S*). Col. ii. 5. Heb. vi. 9.

καί εἰ, **although,** Mark xiv. 29 (*εἰ καί* Tr). — **though,** 2 Cor. xiii. 4.

εἰ γε καί, **if so be that,** 2 Cor. v. 3.

εἰ δὲ καί, **yea, though,** 2 Cor. v. 16.

ἔτι δὲ καί, **yea, and also,** Luke xiv. 26.

ἤ καί, **yea, and,** 1 Cor. xvi. 6.

and, Matt. x. 18. xi. 9^{2}. xxi. 27^{1}. xxv. 17 (–L^{b}Tr^{bm}*S*). Mark iii. 8. iv. 24(*ap*). vi. 41. viii. 7. xv. 26, 28, 32. Luke ii. 36, 38^{1}. v. 33. vii. 26^{2}. x. 32^{3}. xii. 29. xviii. 1^{3}, 9^{3} (–*καί* G^{o}L^{b}). xix. 47. xx. 30(*ap*). xxii. 36*t*, 65. xxiii. 38, 48, 54(–G^{oo}). xxiv. 14. John i. 16. iv. 23. v. 20^{2}, 25. vi. 11. vi. 11. vii. 4^{1}. viii. 53. x. 16. xiii. 10. xiv. 12^{2}. xvi. 22. xix. 19^{3}. xx. 30. Acts vii. 52. ix. 14. xii. 4. xviii. 8. xix. 27^{3}, 31^{3}. xxvii. 23. xxviii. 28.

Rom. xv. 27. 1 Cor. iii. 1(*κἀγώ* for *καὶ ἐγώ* GLT*S*). vii. 11, 28, 36. xii. 31. xv. 1, 30, 44. 2 Cor. i. 20. viii. 8, 10. xii. 3, 7, 15. Gal. i. 14. ii. 13. Phil. iii. 8. iv. 12. Col. i. 21. ii. 2, 13, 14^{1}. 1 Tim. ii. 5. 2 Tim. iii. 16. iv. 18(–G^{o}LT*S*).

Heb. i. 6. xii. 21. Jas. iii. 6. 1 Pet. iii. 14. 1 John iii. 16. 3 John 10. Rev. xviii. 14.

καὶ γάρ, **for,** Matt. viii. 9. xxvi. 73. 1 Cor. viii. 5.

καὶ ἤδη, **now already,** Acts xxvii. 9.

now, 1 Cor. iv. 7^{3}.

then, Matt. xxv. 24^{3}. Rom. viii. 17. 1 Cor. xv. 29. 2 Cor. vi. 1^{3}. Gal. iv. 7.

therefore, 2 Cor. viii. 11^{3}.

Not rendered, Matt. vi. 12. xviii. 17. Mark ix. 22. xv. 40. Luke ii. 28^{1}. xi. 11, 12. xiii. 7. John v. 26. Acts x. 29. xi. 15, 17, 28. xii. 25 (–L*S*). xvii. 13, 23, 34. xix. 12. xxii. 5, 28. xxiv. 6, 26. xxv. 10. xxvi. 12(–G^{oo}L*S*).

Rom. i. 32. iv. 22(–G^{o}L^{b}). v. 19. xi. 30(*omS*). xiv. 10. 1 Cor. iv. 5. vii. 21, 38. xv. 6(–L*S*), 48. xvi. 16. 2 Cor. i. 10, 13. iv. 3. v. 9. vii. 7. viii. 21. ix. 6*t*. Gal. vi. 1. Eph. iv. 17. v. 11, 24. Col. i. 6. 1 Thes. v. 6 (–L*S*). 1 Tim. v. 24. Heb. v. 4. vi. 6, 7. vii. 5, 6. xi. 11. xii. 17. Jas. ii. 26. 1 Pet. iii. 7. iv. 19. 2 Pet. ii. 19. Rev. vi. 11^{1}. x. 7. xiii. 13. xiv. 10^{1}. xxi. 16(–G^{oo}*S*).

Add, for *ἀπό*, Acts xix. 13, G′′LT*S*. For *δέ*, Acts xxiv. 16, G′′LT*S*. Phil. iv. 12, GLT*S*. Jas. iv. 14, LT*S*. — Luke vi. 39 (. . a parable), LTTr*S*. xxiv. 21, *after ἀλλά γε*, LTTr*S*. John xix. 35(that ye . .), GLTTr*S*. Acts v. 15, *καί εἰς* for *κατά*, L*S*. x. 39(. . slew), GLT*S*. xv. 37, for *τόν* 1st, GLT, *καὶ τόν* *S*. xvi. 1 (. . to Derbe), LT. xvii. 32(. . of this matter), LT*S*. 1 Cor. xv. 14 (. . our preaching), G′′L^{b}T*S*. Heb. vii. 26(. . became), G′L^{b}T). ix. 28 (. . Christ), GLT*S*. 2 Pet. ii. 12, *see καταφθείρω*. 1 John ii. 23 (*ap*). Rev. xx. 10(. . the beast), GLTTr.

Also (*) *ὡς, καθὼς . . καί*, **as . . even,** 1 John ii. 18.

even as, Rom. i. 13.
as . . even so, John xx. 21.
as . . so, Luke xi. 2(*ap*). John vi. 57. xiii. 33. xv. 9. Acts vii. 51. Gal. i. 9. Phil. i. 20. 1 John iv. 17.
as, Matt. vi. 10. John xiii. 15.
See also κἀγώ, καθώς, κἀκεῖ, κἀκεῖθεν, κἀκεῖνος, κἄν, ὡς.

καίγε. See γέ.

καινός.

new, Matt. ix. 17. xxvi. 28(-T*S*), 29. xxvii. 60. Mark i. 27. ii. 21, 22 (*ap*). xiv. 24(-G∞TTr*S*), 25. xvi. 17(*ap*). Luke v. 36*tr*, 38. xxii. 20. John xiii. 34. xix. 41. Acts xvii. 19, 21(*comp.*).
1 Cor. xi. 25. 2 Cor. iii. 6. v. 17*t*. Gal. vi. 15. Eph. ii. 15. iv. 24. Heb. viii. 8, 13. ix. 15. 2 Pet. iii. 13*t*. 1 John ii. 7, 8. 2 John 5. Rev. ii. 17. iii. 12*t*. v. 9. xiv. 3. xxi. 1*t*, 2, 5.
Neut. plur., **new things**, Matt. xiii. 52.

καινότης.

newness, Rom. vi. 4. vii. 6.

καίπερ.

and yet, Rev. xvii. 8 (*see* πάρειμι).
though, Phil. iii. 4. Heb. v. 8. vii. 5. xii. 17. 2 Pet. i. 12.

καιρός.

due season, Matt. xxiv. 45. Luke xii. 42.
convenient season, Acts xxiv. 25.
κατὰ καιρόν, **at a certain season**, John v. 4(*ap*).
season, Matt. xxi. 41. Mark xii. 2. Luke i. 20. iv. 13. xiii. 1. xx. 10. Acts i. 7. xiii. 11. xiv. 17. Gal. vi. 9. 1 Thes. v. 1.
παρὰ καιρὸν ἡλικίας, **past age**, Heb. xi. 11. [15.
opportunity, Gal. vi. 10. Heb. xi.
due time, Rom. v. 6 (*marg.* **time**). 1 Pet. v. 6.
time, Matt. viii. 29. xi. 25. xii. 1. xiii. 30. xiv. 1. xvi. 3. xxi. 34. xxvi. 18. Mark i. 15. x. 30. xi. 13. xiii. 33. Luke viii. 13. xii. 56. xviii. 30. xix. 44. xxi. 8, 24. John vii. 6*t*, 8. Acts iii. 19. vii. 20. xii. 1. xvii. 26. xix. 23.
Rom. iii. 26. viii. 18. ix. 9. xi. 5. xiii. 11. 1 Cor. iv. 5. vii. 5, 29. 2 Cor. vi. 2*t*. viii. 14(13). Gal. iv. 10. Eph. i. 10. ii. 12. v. 16. Col. iv. 5. 1 Thes. ii. 17. 2 Thes. ii. 6. 1 Tim. ii. 6[pl]. iv. 1. vi. 15. 2 Tim. iii. 1. iv. 3, 6. Tit. i. 3. Heb. ix. 9, 10. 1 Pet. i. 5, 11. iv. 17. Rev. i. 3. xi. 18. xii. 12, 14*tr*. xxii. 10.
while, Luke viii. 13.
ἐν παντὶ καιρῷ, **always**, Luke xxi. 36. Eph. vi. 18.
Add Rom. xii. 11, for Κύριος, StG.

καίτοι.

although, Heb. iv. 3.
καίτοιγε, **though**, John iv. 2. Acts xvii. 27(καίγε G″, καί γε LT).—**nevertheless**, Acts xiv. 17.

καίω.

to light, Matt. v. 15.
Pass., **be burned**, John xv. 6. 1 Cor. xiii. 3. —**burn**, Luke xii. 35. xxiv. 32 (*with* εἰμί). John v. 35. Heb. xii. 18. Rev. iv. 5. viii. 8, 10. xix. 20. xxi. 8.
Add Matt. xiii. 40, for κατακαίω, GTTr. Rev. ix. 2, *pass.*[p], for μέγας, G′.

κἀκεῖ. See ἐκεῖ.

κἀκεῖθεν. See ἐκεῖθεν.

κἀκεῖνος. See ἐκεῖνος.

κακία.

evil, Matt. vi. 34.
naughtiness, Jas. i. 21.
malice, 1 Cor. v. 8. xiv. 20. Eph. iv. 31. Col. iii. 8. Tit. iii. 3. 1 Pet. ii. 1.
maliciousness, Rom. i. 29. 1 Pet. ii. 16.
wickedness, Acts viii. 22.

κακοήθεια.

malignity, Rom. i. 29.

κακολογέω.

speak evil of, Mark ix. 39. Acts xix. 9.

curse, Matt. xv. 4. Mark vii. 10.

κακοπάθεια.

suffering affliction, Jas. v. 10.

κακοπαθέω.

suffer trouble, 2 Tim. ii. 9.
endure afflictions, 2 Tim. iv. 5.
be afflicted, Jas. v. 13.
endure hardness, 2 Tim. ii. 3 (*see* συγκακοπαθέω).

κακοποιέω.

do evil, Mark iii. 4. Luke vi. 9. 3 John 11.
for evil doing, 1 Pet. iii. 17[p].

κακοποιός.

evil-doer, 1 Pet. ii. 12, 14. iii. 16 (*ap*). iv. 15.
malefactor, John xviii. 30.

κακός.

evil, Matt. xxiv. 48. Mark vii. 21. Rom. xiii. 3. xiv. 20. 1 Cor. xv. 33. Phil. iii. 2. Col. iii. 5. Tit. i. 12.

Plur., **they which are evil,** Rev. ii. 2.

Neut., **evil,** *subst.*, Matt. xxvii. 23. Mark xv. 14. Luke xxiii. 22. John xviii. 23. Acts ix. 13[pl]. xxiii. 9. Rom. ii. 9. iii. 8[pl]. vii. 19, 21. ix. 11 (φαῦλος G″LTS). xii. 17*t*, 21*t*. xiii. 4. xvi. 19. 1 Cor. xiii. 5. 2 Cor. xiii. 7. 1 Thes. v. 15*t*. 1 Tim. vi. 10[pl]. 2 Tim. iv. 14[pl]. Heb. v. 14. Jas. i. 13[pl] (*marg.* **evils**). iii. 8. 1 Pet. iii. 9*t*, 10, 11, 12[pl]. — **ill,** Rom. xiii. 10.
harm, Acts xvi. 28. xxviii. 5. — *With art.*, **that which is evil,** Rom. xiii. 4. 3 John 11.

Neut. plur., **evil things,** Luke xvi. 25. Rom. i. 30. 1 Cor. x. 6.

bad, 2 Cor. v. 10 (φαῦλος G′TS).

noisome, Rev. xvi. 2.

wicked, Matt. xxi. 41.

κακοῦργος.

evil-doer, 2 Tim. ii. 9.
malefactor, Luke xxiii. 32, 33, 39.

κακουχέω.

Pass., **suffer adversity,** Heb. xiii. 3. — **be tormented,** Heb. xi. 37.

κακόω.

evil entreat, Acts vii. 6, 19.
hurt, Acts xviii. 10.
harm, 1 Pet. iii. 13.
vex, Acts xii. 1.
make evil affected, Acts xiv. 2.

κακῶς.

evil, John xviii. 23. Acts xxiii. 5.
amiss, Jas. iv. 3.
grievously, Matt. xv. 22.
sore, Matt. xvii. 15.
miserably, Matt. xxi. 41.
With ἔχω, **be diseased,** Matt. xiv. 35. Mark i. 32. — **be sick,** Matt. viii. 16. ix. 12. Mark i. 34. ii. 17. vi. 55. Luke v. 31. vii. 2. — **sick people,** Matt. iv. 24[p,pl].

κάκωσις.

affliction, Acts vii. 34.

καλάμη.

stubble, 1 Cor. iii. 12.

κάλαμος.

reed, Matt. xi. 7. xii. 20. xxvii. 29, 30, 48. Mark xv. 19, 36. Luke vii. 24. Rev. xi. 1. xxi. 15, 16.
pen, 3 John 13.

καλέω.

to call, Matt. i. 21, 23, 25. ii. 7, 15, 23. iv. 21. v. 9, 19*t*. ix. 13. x. 25 (ἐπικαλέω GLTTrS). xx. 8. xxi. 13. xxii. 3, 43, 45. xxiii. 7, 8, 9, 10. xxv. 14. xxvii. 8. Mark i. 20. ii. 17. xi. 17.

Luke i. 13, 31, 32, 35, 36, 59, 60, 61, 62, 76. ii. 4, 21, 23. v. 32. vi. 15, 46. vii. 11. viii. 2. ix. 10. x. 39. xiv. 13. xv. 19, 21. xix. 13, 29. xx. 44. xxi. 37. xxii. 25. xxiii. 33. John i. 42(43). ii. 2. x. 3 (φωνέω G″LTTrS). Acts i. 12, 19, 23. iii. 11. iv. 18. ix. 11. x. 1. xiii. 1. xiv. 12. xxvii. 8, 14, 16. xxviii. 1.

Rom. iv. 17. viii. 30*t*. ix. 7, 11, 24, 25, 26. 1 Cor. i. 9. vii. 15, 17,

18*t*, 20, 21, 22*t*, 24. xv. 9. Gal. i. 6, 15. v. 8, 13. Eph. iv. 1, 4. Col. iii. 15. 1 Thes. ii. 12. iv. 7. v. 24. 2 Thes. ii. 14. 1 Tim. vi. 12. 2 Tim. i. 9.

Heb. ii. 11. iii. 13. v. 4. ix. 15. xi. 8, 18. Jas. ii. 23. 1 Pet. i. 15. ii. 9, 21. iii. 6, 9. v. 10. 2 Pet. i. 3. 1 John iii. 1. Rev. i. 9. xi. 8. xii. 9. xvi. 16. xix. 9, 11, 13.

call forth, Acts xxiv. 2p.

bid, Matt. xxii. 3, 4, 8, 9. Luke vii. 39. xiv. 7, 8*t*, 9, 10*t*, 12, 16, 17, 24. 1 Cor. x. 27.

name, Luke xix. 2.

so[c] name, Luke ii. 21.

Pass., **be one's name**, Acts vii. 58. — **be one's surname**, Acts xv. 37.

Add, for ἐπικαλέω, Luke xxii. 3, TTr*S*. Acts xv. 22, LT*S*. For κληρόω, Eph. i. 11, G'L*S*. For φωνέω, Mark iii. 31, LTTr*S*. — Acts viii. 10pass(. . the great), GLT*S*. Col. i. 12(. . καί hath made), L.

καλλιέλαιος.

good olive tree, Rom. xi. 24.

κάλλιον. See καλῶς.

καλοδιδάσκαλος.

teacher of good things, Tit. ii. 3.

καλοποιέω.

in well doing, 2 Thes. iii. 13p.

καλός.

goodly, Matt. xiii. 45. Luke xxi. 5.

good, Matt. iii. 10. v. 16. vii. 17, 18, 19. xii. 33*t*. xiii. 8, 23, 24, 27, 37, 38, 48. xvii. 4. xxvi. 10, 24. Mark iv. 8, 20. ix. 5, 50. xiv. 6, 21. Luke iii. 9(–L[b]). vi. 38, 43*t*. viii. 15. ix. 33. xiv. 34. John ii. 10*t*. x. 11*t*, 14, 32, 33.

Rom. vii. 16. xiv. 21. 1 Cor. v. 6. vii. 1, 8, 26*t*. Gal. iv. 18. 1 Tim. i. 8, 18. ii. 3. iii. 1, 7, 13. iv. 4, 6*t*. v. 4(*omS*), 10, 25. vi. 12*t*, 13, 18, 19. 2 Tim. i. 14. ii. 3. iv. 7. Tit. ii. 7, 14. iii. 8*t*, 14(*marg.* **honest**). Heb. vi. 5. x. 24. xiii. 18. Jas. iii. 13. 1 Pet. ii. 12. iv. 10.

better[c], Matt. xviii. 8, 9. Mark ix. 42, 43, 45, 47. 1 Cor. ix. 15 (*with* μᾶλλον).

well[cc], Gal. vi. 9.

honest, Luke viii. 15. 1 Pet. ii. 12.

Neut., **honest thing**, Rom. xii. 17. 2 Cor. viii. 21. — **good thing**, Gal. iv. 18. Heb. xiii. 9. — **good**, Rom. vii. 21. Heb. v. 14. Jas. iv. 17.

τὸ καλόν, **that which is honest**, 2 Cor. xiii. 7. — **that which is good**, Rom. vii. 18. 1 Thes. v. 21.

meet, Matt. xv. 26 (*see* ἔξεστι). Mark vii. 27.

worthy, Jas. ii. 7.

Add 2 Pet. i. 10 (*ap*).

See also λιμήν.

κάλυμμα.

veil, 2 Cor. iii. 13, 14, 15, 16.

καλύπτω.

to cover, Matt. viii. 24. x. 26. Luke viii. 16. xxiii. 30. 1 Pet. iv. 8.

hide, 2 Cor. iv. 3*t*. Jas. v. 20.

καλῶς.

well, Matt. xii. 12. xv. 7. Mark vii. 6, 37. xii. 28, 32. Luke vi. 26. xx. 39. John iv. 17. viii. 48. xiii. 13. xviii. 23. Acts x. 33. xxviii. 25. Rom. xi. 20. 1 Cor. vii. 37, 38. xiv. 17. 2 Cor. xi. 4. Gal. iv. 17. v. 7. Phil. iv. 14. 1 Tim. iii. 4, 12, 13. v. 17. Jas. ii. 8, 19. 2 Pet. i. 19. 3 John 6.

full well, Mark vii. 9.

Comp., κάλλιον, **very well**, Acts xxv. 10.

good[cc], Matt. v. 44(*ap*). Luke vi. 27.

in a good place (*marg.* **well**, *or* **seemly**), Jas. ii. 3.

With ἔχω, **recover**, Mark xvi. 18 (*ap*).

honestly, Heb. xiii. 18.

Add Luke vi. 48 (*ap*).

κἀμέ. See κἀγώ.

κάμηλος.

camel, Matt. iii. 4. xix. 24. xxiii. 24. Mark i. 6. x. 25. Luke xviii. 25.

κάμινος.

furnace, Matt. xiii. 42, 50. Rev. i. 15. ix. 2.

καμμύω.

to close, Matt. xiii. 15. Acts xxviii. 27.

κάμνω.

be wearied, Heb. xii. 3.
faint, Rev. ii. 3(*ap*).
sick, Jas. v. 15p.

κἀμοί. See κἀγώ.

κάμπτω.

to bow, Rom. xi. 4. xiv. 11. Eph. iii. 14. Phil. ii. 10.

κἄν.

and if, Mark xvi. 18 (*ap*). Luke xiii. 9. Jas. v. 15.
and if so much as, Heb. xii. 20.
also if, Matt. xxi. 21.
if but, Mark v. 28. vi. 56.
though, Matt. xxvi. 35. John viii. 14. x. 38. xi. 25.
yet, 2 Cor. xi. 16.
at the least, Acts v. 15.
Add, for καὶ ἐάν, Luke xii. 38, Tr *S.* John viii. 55, LTr*S.* 1 Cor. xiii. 2st, 3*t*, L. — Matt. x. 23(*ap*). Luke xii. 38, for καί1st, Tr.

κανών.

rule, 2 Cor. x. 13 (*marg.* **line**), 15. Gal. vi. 16. Phil. iii. 16(*ap*).
line, 2 Cor. x. 16(*marg.* **rule**).

καπηλεύω.

to corrupt, 2 Cor. ii. 17 (*marg.* **deal deceitfully with**).

καπνός.

smoke, Acts ii. 19. Rev. viii. 4. ix. 2*tr*, 3, 17, 18. xiv. 11. xv. 8. xviii. 9, 18. xix. 3.

καρδία.

heart, Matt. v. 8, 28. vi. 21. ix. 4. xi. 29. xii. 34, 35(*omS*), 40. xiii. 15*t*, 19. xv. 8, 18, 19. xviii. 35. xxii. 37. xxiv. 48. Mark ii. 6, 8. iii. 5. iv. 15(*ap*). vi. 52. vii. 6, 19, 21. viii. 17. xi. 23. xii. 30, 33.
Luke i. 17, 51, 66. ii. 19, 35, 51. iii. 15. v. 22. vi. 45, 45(*ap*), 45. viii. 12, 15. ix. 47. x. 27. xii. 34, 45. xvi. 15. xxi. 14, 34. xxiv. 25, 32, 38. John xii. 40*t*. xiii. 2. xiv. 1, 27. xvi. 6, 22. Acts ii. 26, 37, 46. iv. 32. v. 3, 4. vii. 23, 39, 51, 54. viii. 21, 22, 37 (*ap*). xi. 23. xiii. 22. xiv. 17. xv. 9. xvi. 14. xxi. 13. xxviii. 27*t*.

Rom. i. 21, 24. ii. 5, 15, 29. v. 5. vi. 17. viii. 27. ix. 2. x. 1, 6, 8, 9, 10. xvi. 18. 1 Cor. ii. 9. iv. 5. vii. 37*t*. xiv. 25. 2 Cor. i. 22. ii. 4. iii. 2, 3, 15. iv. 6. v. 12. vi. 11. vii. 3. viii. 16. ix. 7. Gal. iv. 6. Eph, iii. 17. iv. 18. v. 19. vi. 5, 22. Phil. i. 7. iv. 7. Col. ii. 2. iii. 15, 16, 22. iv. 8. 1 Thes. ii. 4, 17. iii. 13. 2 Thes. ii. 17. iii. 5. 1 Tim. i. 5. 2 Tim. ii. 22.

Heb. iii. 8, 10, 12, 15. iv. 7, 12. viii. 10. x. 16, 22*t*. xiii. 9. Jas. i. 26. iii. 14. iv. 8. v. 5, 8. 1 Pet. i. 22. iii. 4, 15. 2 Pet. i. 19. ii. 14. 1 John iii. 19, 20*t*, 21. Rev. ii. 23. xvii. 17. xviii. 7.

Add Eph. i. 18, for διανοία, GLT*S*.
See also συντρίβω.

καρδιογνώστης.

which knoweth the hearts, Acts i. 24. xv. 8.

καρπός.

fruit, Matt. iii. 8, 10. vii. 16, 17*t*, 18*t*, 19, 20. xii. 33*tr*. xiii. 8, 26. xxi. 19, 34*t*, 41, 43. Mark iv. 7, 8, 29. xi. 14. xii. 2. Luke i. 42. iii. 8, 9. vi. 43*t*, 44. viii. 8. xii. 17. xiii. 6, 7, 9. xx. 10. John iv. 36. xii. 24. xv. 2*tr*, 4, 5, 8, 16*t*. Acts ii. 30.

Rom. i. 13. vi. 21, 22. xv. 28. 1 Cor. ix. 7. Gal. v. 22. Eph. v. 9. Phil. i. 11, 22. iv. 17. 2 Tim. ii. 6. Heb. xii. 11. xiii. 15. Jas. iii. 17, 18. v. 7, 18. Rev. xxii. 2*t*.

καρποφορέω.

bear fruit, Matt. xiii. 23.
bring forth fruit, Mark iv. 20, 28. Luke viii. 15. Rom. vii. 4, 5.

Mid., *with* εἰμί, **bring forth fruit,** Col. i. 6.
be fruitful, Col. i. 10.

καρποφόρος.

fruitful, Acts xiv. 17.

καρτερέω.

endure, Heb. xi. 27.

κάρφος.

mote, Matt. vii. 3, 4, 5. Luke vi. 41, 42*t*.

καρχηδών, carbuncle.

Rev. xxi. 19, for χαλκηδών, G′.

κατά.

I. With a Genitive.

down, Matt. viii. 32. Mark v. 13. Luke viii. 33.
on, Mark xiv. 3(–LTTr*S*).
upon, Jude 15.
covered[cc], 1 Cor. xi. 4.
against, Matt. v. 11, 23. x. 35*tr*. xii. 14, 25*t*, 30, 32*t*. xx. 11. xxvi. 59. xxvii. 1. Mark iii. 6. ix. 40. xi. 25. xiv. 55, 56, 57. Luke ix. 50. xi. 23. John xviii. 29. xix. 11. Acts iv. 26*t*. vi. 13. xiv. 2. xvi. 22. xix. 16. xxi. 28. xxiv. 1. xxv. 2, 3, 7 (*ap*), 15, 27. xxvii. 14.
Rom. viii. 31. xi. 2. 1 Cor. iv. 6. 2 Cor. x. 5. xiii. 8. Gal. iii. 21. v. 17*t*, 23. Col. ii. 14. 1 Tim. v. 19. Jas. iii. 14. v. 9. 1 Pet. ii. 11. 2 Pet. ii. 11. Jude 15. Rev. ii. 4, 14, 20. xii. 7 (μετά GLTTr*S*).
of, 1 Cor. xv. 15.
through, Luke iv. 14.
throughout[c], Luke xxiii. 5. Acts ix. 31, 42. x. 37.
by, Matt. xxvi. 63. Heb. vi. 13*t*, 16.
See also ἐγκαλέω, κατηγορέω.

II. With an Accusative.

through, Luke ix. 6. xiii. 22. Acts iii. 17. Phil. ii. 3.
throughout[c], Luke viii. 39. Acts viii. 1. xxiv. 5.
over against, Acts xxvii. 7*t*.
before, Luke ii. 31. Gal. iii. 1.
κατ' αὐτόν, **where he** [c]**was,** Lk. x. 33.
toward, Acts viii. 26. xxvii. 12t. Phil. iii. 14.
to, Acts xvi. 7. Rom. xiv. 22. 2 Cor. viii. 3. Gal. ii. 11.
into, Acts v. 15(καὶ εἰς L*S*; for *marg.*, *see* πλατεῖα). xvi. 7 (εἰς GLT*S*).
among, Acts xxi. 21. xxvi. 3.
about, Acts ii. 10. xii. 1. xxvii. 27.
at, Matt. xxvii. 15. Mark xv. 6. Luke x. 32. xxiii. 17(*ap*). Acts xvi. 25. Rom. ix. 9. 2 Tim. iv. 1(G′, καί GLT*S*).
in, Matt. i. 20. ii. 12, 13, 19, 22. xxvii. 19. Luke vi. 23. xv. 14. Acts iii. 13, 22. xi. 1. xiii. 1. xv. 23, 36. xvii. 22. xxiv. 12, 14. xxv. 3. xxvi. 11, 13. Rom. v. 6(*marg.* **according to**). xvi. 5. 1 Cor. xiv. 40. xvi. 19. 2 Cor. x. 1. Col. iii. 20, 22. iv. 15. Phm. 2. Heb. i. 10. ii. 17. iii. 8. iv. 15. ix. 9. xi. 13 (*Gr.* according to).
κατὰ πόλιν, **in every city,** Acts xv. 21. xx. 23. Tit. i. 5. — **throughout every city,** Luke viii. 1. — **out of every city,** Luke viii. 4.
κατ' ἐκκλησίαν, **in every church,** Acts xiv. 23.
κατὰ τόπους, **in divers places,** Matt. xxiv. 7. Mark xiii. 8. Luke xxi. 11.
κατ' ἐνιαυτόν, **year by year,** Heb. x. 1. — **every year,** Heb. ix. 25. x. 3.
κατ' ἔτος, **every year,** Luke ii. 41.
upon, 1 Cor. xvi. 2.
on, Acts viii. 36.
according to, Matt. ii. 16. ix. 29. xvi. 27. xxv. 15. Mark vii. 5. Luke i. 9, 38. ii. 22, 24, 29, 39. xxiii. 56. John vii. 24. xviii. 31. Acts ii. 30 (*ap*). vii. 44. xiii. 23. xxii. 3, 12. xxiv. 6(*ap*).
Rom. i. 3, 4. ii. 2, 6, 16. iv. 18. viii. 27, 28. ix. 3, 11. x. 2. xi. 5, 21. xii. 6*t*. xv. 5(*marg.* **after the example of**). xvi. 25*t*, 26. 1 Cor. iii. 8, 10. xv. 3, 4. 2 Cor. i. 17. x. 2, 13, 15. xi. 15. xiii. 10.
Gal. i. 4. iii. 29. Eph. i. 5, 7, 9,

11, 19. ii. 2*t*. iii. 7, 11, 16, 20. iv. 7, 16, 22. vi. 5. Phil. i. 20. iii. 21. iv. 19. Col. i. 11, 25, 29. iii. 22. 2 Thes. i. 12. 1 Tim. i. 11, 18. vi. 3. 2 Tim. i. 1, 8, 9*t*. ii. 8. iv. 14. Tit. i. 1, 3. iii. 5, 7.

Heb. ii. 5. vii. 4. viii. 4, 5, 9. ix. 19. Jas. ii. 8. 1 Pet. i. 2, 3, 17. iii. 7. iv. 6*t*, 19. 2 Pet. iii. 13 (καί L), 15. 1 John v. 14. Rev. ii. 23. xviii. 6. xx. 12, 13.

after, Matt. xxiii. 3. Luke ii. 27, 42. John viii. 15. Acts xiii. 22. xxiii. 3. xxiv. 14. xxvi. 5. Rom. ii. 5. vii. 22. viii. 1*t*(*ap*), 4*t*, 5*t*, 12, 13. 1 Cor. i. 26. vii. 40. x. 18. 2 Cor. v. 16*t*. x. 3, 7. xi. 17, 18. Gal. i. 11. iv. 23, 29*t*. Eph. i. 11. iv. 24. Col. ii. 8*tr*, 22. iii. 10. 2 Thes. ii. 9. iii. 6. 2 Tim. iv. 3. Tit. i. 1, 4. Heb. v. 6, 10. vi. 20. vii. 11*t*, 15, 16*t*, 17, 21(*ap*). xii. 10. Jas. iii. 9. 2 Pet. iii. 3. 2 John 6. Jude 16, 18.

after the manner of, John ii. 6.

κατὰ ταῦτα, **in the like manner**, Luke vi. 23. — **so**, Luke vi. 26. — **even thus**, Luke xvii. 30.

κατὰ τὸ διατεταγμένον, **as it was commanded**, Acts xxiii. 31.

κατὰ τὸν καλέσαντα, **as he which hath called**, 1 Pet. i. 15.

κατὰ Ἰσαάκ, **as I. °was**, Gal. iv. 28.

τὸ κατ' ἐμέ, **as much as in me is**, Rom. i. 15.

κατὰ λόγον, **reason would**, Acts xviii. 14.

with, Mark i. 27. 1 Cor. ii. 1. Eph. vi. 6.

by, Luke x. 4, 31. John x. 3. xix. 7. Acts xxvii. 2. xxviii. 16. Rom. ii. 7. iv. 16. xi. 24. 1 Cor. vii. 6. xii. 8. xiv. 27, 31. 2 Cor. viii. 8. Gal. ii. 2. Eph. iii. 3, 7. 2 Thes. ii. 3. 1 Tim. i. 1. v. 21. Heb. vii. 22. ix. 22. x. 8. xi. 7. 3 John 14(15).

κατὰ τί; **whereby?** Luke i. 18.

of, Acts xxvii. 2, 5. Rom. iv. 4*t*. 1 Cor. vii. 6. Phm. 14.

in respect of, Phil. iv. 11.

concerning, Eph. iv. 22. Phil. iii. 6.

as concerning, Rom. ix. 5. xi. 28. 2 Cor. xi. 21.

as pertaining to, Rom. iv. 1. Heb. ix. 9.

touching, Phil. iii. 6.

as touching, Rom. xi. 28. Phil. iii. 5.

τὰ κατὰ τὸν Παῦλον, **Paul's cause**, Acts xxv. 14.

on one's part, 1 Pet. iv. 4*t*(*ap*).

for, Matt. xix. 3.

Not rendered, Acts xiii. 27. xv. 21. xviii. 4. xix. 23. Rom. iii. 2. Rev. xxii. 2.

Add Mark vi. 40*t*, for ἀνά, LTTr*S*. Acts xvii. 25, for καὶ τά, St. xxvii. 29, for εἰς, G″LT*S*. Phil. ii. 3, *see* ἤ, I. 1 Pet. v. 2 (mind κατὰ Θεόν), L*S*.

See also ἀγάπη, ἄνθρωπος, τὸ αὐτό fr. αὐτός, βάθος, γράφω, διδαχή, ἑαυτήν fr. ἑαυτοῦ, ἐμέ fr. ἐγώ, ἔθος, ἔθω, εἰς, ἕκαστος, ἑκούσιος, ἐξοχή, ἡμέρα, Θεός, ἴδιος, καιρός, καταμόνας, κράτος, μέρος, οἶκος, ὁμοιότης, ὁρίζω, ὅσος, πλατεῖα, πρόσωπον, συναγωγή, τρόπος, ὑμᾶς fr. ὑμεῖς, ὑπερβολή, φύσις.

καταβαίνω.

go down, Mark xiii. 15. Luke ii. 51. x. 30. xviii. 14. John ii. 12. iv. 51ᵖ. v. 4(*ap*). vi. 16. Acts vii. 15. viii. 26, 38. x. 21. xiv. 25. xviii. 22. xx. 10. xxiii. 10. xxv. 6.

come down, Matt. viii. 1ᵖ. xiv. 29ᵖ. xvii. 9ᵖ. xxiv. 17. xxvii. 40, 42. Mark iii. 22. ix. 9ᵖ. xv. 30. Luke vi. 17. viii. 23. ix. 54. x. 31. xvii. 31. xix. 5, 6. John iii. 13. iv. 47, 49. vi. 33, 38, 41, 42, 50, 51, 58. Acts vii. 34. viii. 15ᵖ. xiv. 11. xvi. 8. xxiv. 22. xxv. 7. Jas. i. 17. Rev. iii. 12. x. 1. xii. 12. xiii. 13. xviii. 1. xx. 1, 9. xxi. 2.

step down, John v. 7.

descend, Matt. iii. 16. vii. 25, 27. xxviii. 2. Mark i. 10. xv. 32. Luke iii. 22. John i. 32, 33, 51(52). Acts x. 11. xi. 5. xxiv. 1. Rom. x. 7. Eph. iv. 9, 10. 1 Thes. iv. 16. Rev. xxi. 10.

get down, Acts x. 20.
fall down, Luke xxii. 44(*ap*).
fall, Rev. xvi. 21.
Add Matt. xi. 23, for καταβιβάζω, *pass.*, LTTr.

καταβάλλω.

cast down, 2 Cor. iv. 9. Rev. xii. 10(βάλλω G″LTTr*S*).
Mid., **lay,** Heb. vi. 1.

καταβαρέω.

to burden, 2 Cor. xii. 16.

καταβαρύνω, weigh down, oppress.

Mark xiv. 40, for βαρέω, G″LTTr.

κατάβασις.

descent, Luke xix. 37.

καταβιβάζω.

bring down, Matt. xi. 23 (*pass.*, καταβαίνω LTTr).
thrust down, Luke x. 15.

καταβολή.

foundation, Matt. xiii. 35. xxv. 34. Luke xi. 50. John xvii. 24. Eph. i. 4. Heb. iv. 3. ix. 26. 1 Pet. i. 20. Rev. xiii. 8. xvii. 8.
With εἰς, **to conceive,** Heb. xi. 11.

καταβραβεύω.

beguile of one's reward (*marg.* **judge against**), Col. ii. 18.

καταγγελεύς.

setter forth, Acts xvii. 18.

καταγγέλλω.

declare, Acts xvii. 23. 1 Cor. ii. 1.
show, Acts xvi. 17. xxvi. 23. 1 Cor. xi. 26.
speak of, Rom. i. 8.
preach, Acts iv. 2. xiii. 5, 38. xv. 36. xvii. 3, 13. 1 Cor. ix. 14. Phil. i. 16(17), 18. Col. i. 28.
teach, Acts xvi. 21.
Add Acts iii. 24, for προκαταγγέλλω, GLT*S*.

καταγελάω.

laugh to scorn, Matt. ix. 24. Mark v. 40. Luke viii. 53.

καταγινώσκω.

condemn, 1 John iii 20, 21.
Pass., **to be blamed,** Gal. ii. 11p.

κατάγνυμι.

to break, Matt. xii. 20. John xix. 31, 32, 33.

κατάγω.

bring down, Acts ix. 30. xxii. 30. xxiii. 15, 20. Rom. x. 6.
bring forth, Acts xxiii. 28.
bring, Luke v. 11p.
Pass., *in navigation*, **land,** Acts xxi. 3 (κατέρχομαι L*S*). xxviii. 12. — **touch,** Acts xxvii. 3.

καταγωνίζομαι.

subdue, Heb. xi. 33.

καταδέω.

bind up, Luke x. 34.

κατάδηλος.

evident, Heb. vii. 15.

καταδικάζω.

condemn, Matt. xii. 7, 37. Luke vi. 37*t*. Jas. v. 6.

καταδίκη, condemnation.

Acts xxv. 15, for δίκη, G″L*S*.

καταδιώκω.

follow after, Mark i. 36.

καταδουλόω.

bring into bondage, 2 Cor. xi. 20. Gal. ii. 4 (*mid.*, *act.* LT*S*).

καταδρέμω. See κατατρέχω.

καταδυναστέω.

oppress, Acts x. 38. Jas. ii. 6.

κατάθεμα, a curse.

Rev. xxii. 3, for κατανάθεμα, GLTTr.

καταθεματίζω, to curse.

Matt. xxvi. 74, for καταναθεματίζω, GLTTr*S*.

καταισχύνω.

to shame, 1 Cor. xi. 22.
make ashamed, Rom. v. 5.
Pass., **be ashamed,** Luke xiii. 17. Rom. ix. 33 (*marg.* **be confounded**).

x. 11. 2 Cor. vii. 14. ix. 4. 1 Pet. iii. 16.
confound, 1 Cor. i. 27 (*ap*), 27. 1 Pet. ii. 6.
dishonor, 1 Cor. xi. 4, 5.

κατακαίω.

burn up, Matt. iii. 12. 2 Pet. iii. 10. Rev. viii. 7*t*.
burn utterly, Rev. xviii. 8.
burn, Matt. xiii. 30, 40(καίω GTTr). Luke iii. 17. Acts xix. 19. 1 Cor. iii.15. Heb. xiii. 11. Rev. xvii. 16.
Add Rev. viii. 7(*ap*).

κατακαλύπτω.

Mid., **be covered,** 1 Cor. xi. 6*t*. — **cover,** 1 Cor. xi. 7.

κατακαυχάομαι.

boast against, Rom. xi. 18.
boast, Rom. xi. 18.
rejoice (*marg.* **glory) against,** Jas. ii. 13.
glory, Jas. iii. 14.

κατάκειμαι.

to lie, Mark i. 30. ii. 4. Luke v. 25. John v. 3, 6. Acts xxviii. 8.
With ἐπί, **keep,** Acts ix. 33.
sit down, Luke v. 29.
sit at meat, Mark ii. 15. xiv. 3. 1 Cor. viii. 10.
Add Luke vii. 37, for ἀνάκειμαι, LTTr*S*.

κατακλάω, -κλάζω.

to break, Mark vi. 41. Luke ix. 16.

κατακλείω.

shut up, Luke iii. 20. Acts xxvi. 10.

κατακληροδοτέω.

divide by lot, Acts xiii. 19 (κατακληρονομέω GLT*S*).

κατακληρονομέω, distribute by lot. *See* κατακληροδοτέω.

κατακλίνω.

make sit down, Luke ix. 14.
Mid., **sit down,** Luke xiv. 8. — **sit at meat,** Luke xxiv. 30.
Add, for ἀνακλίνω, Luke vii. 36, LTTr. ix. 15, Tr*S*.

κατακλύζω.

overflow, 2 Pet. iii. 6.

κατακλυσμός.

flood, Matt. xxiv. 38, 39. Luke xvii. 27. 2 Pet. ii. 5.

κατακολουθέω.

follow after, Luke xxiii. 55.
follow, Acts xvi. 17.

κατακόπτω.

to cut, Mark v. 5.

κατακρημνίζω.

cast down headlong, Luke iv. 29.

κατάκριμα.

condemnation, Rom. v. 16, 18. viii. 1.

κατακρίνω.

condemn, Matt. xii. 41, 42. xx. 18. xxvii. 3. Mark x. 33. xiv. 64. Luke xi. 31, 32. John viii. 10(*ap*), 11 (*ap*). Rom. ii. 1. viii. 3, 34. 1 Cor. xi. 32. Heb. xi. 7. Jas. v. 9 (κρίνω GLT*S*). 2 Pet. ii. 6.
damn, Mark xvi. 16 (*ap*). Rom. xiv. 23.

κατάκρισις.

condemnation, 2 Cor. iii. 9.
With πρός, **to condemn,** 2 Cor. vii. 3.

κατακυριεύω.

exercise lordship over, Mark x. 42.
be lord over (*marg.* **overrule),** 1 Pet. v. 3.
exercise dominion over, Matt. xx. 25.
overcome, Acts xix. 16.

καταλαλέω.

speak against, 1 Pet. ii. 12.
speak evil of, Jas. iv. 11*tr*. 1 Pet. iii. 16.

καταλαλία.

evil speaking, 1 Pet. ii. 1.
backbiting, 2 Cor. xii. 20.

κατάλαλος.

backbiter, Rom. i. 30.

καταλαμβάνω.

overtake, 1 Thes. v. 4.
take, Mark ix. 18. John viii. 3 (*ap*), 4(*ap*).

apprehend, Phil. iii. 12*t*, 13.
attain to, Rom. ix. 30.
obtain, 1 Cor. ix. 24.
come upon, John xii. 35.
comprehend, John i. 5.
Mid., **comprehend**, Eph. iii. 18.—**perceive**, Acts iv. 13. x. 34.—**find**, Acts xxv. 25p.

καταλέγω.

take (*marg.* **choose**) **into the number**, 1 Tim. v. 9.

κατάλειμμα.

remnant, Rom. ix. 27 (ὑπόλειμμα LT*S*).

καταλείπω.

to leave, Matt. iv. 13. xvi. 4. xix. 5. xxi. 17. Mark x. 7. xii. 19. xiv. 52. Luke v. 28. x. 40. xv. 4. xx. 31. John viii. 9(*ap*). Acts ii. 31(ἐγκαταλείπω G''LT*S*). vi. 2. xviii. 19. xxi. 3. xxiv. 27. xxv. 14. Eph. v. 31. 1 Thes. iii. 1. Tit. i. 5(ἀπολείπω G'LT*S*, *imperf.* T). Heb. iv. 1.
forsake, Heb. xi. 27. 2 Pet. ii. 15.
reserve, Rom. xi. 4.
Add Mark xii. 21(*ap*).

καταλιθάζω.

to stone, Luke xx. 6.

καταλλαγή.

reconciliation, 2 Cor. v. 18, 19.
reconciling, Rom. xi. 15.
atonement, Rom. v. 11.

καταλλάσσω, -ττω.

reconcile, Rom. v. 10*t*. 1 Cor. vii. 11. 2 Cor. v. 18, 19, 20.

κατάλοιπος.

Plur., **residue**, Acts xv. 17.

κατάλυμα.

inn, Luke ii. 7.
guest-chamber, Mark xiv. 14. Luke xxii. 11.

καταλύω.

dissolve, 2 Cor. v. 1.
throw down, Matt. xxiv. 2. Mark xiii. 2. Luke xxi. 6.
overthrow, Acts v. 39.
destroy, Matt. v. 17*t*. xxvi. 61. xxvii. 40. Mark xiv. 58. xv. 29. Acts vi. 14. Rom. xiv. 20. Gal. ii. 18.
Pass., **come to nought**, Acts v. 38.
lodge, Luke ix. 12.
be guest, Luke xix. 7.

καταμανθάνω.

consider, Matt. vi. 28.

καταμαρτυρέω.

witness against, Matt. xxvi. 62. xxvii. 13. Mark xiv. 60. xv. 4(κατηγορέω LTTr*S*).

καταμένω.

With εἰμί, **abide**, Acts i. 13.

καταμόνας, κατὰ μόνας LTTr.

alone, Mark iv. 10. Luke ix. 18.

κατανάθεμα.

curse, Rev. xxii. 3 (κατάθεμα GLT Tr, κατάγμα *S*).

καταναθεματίζω.

to curse, Matt. xxvi. 74(καταθεματίζω GLTTr*S*).

καταναλίσκω.

consume, Heb. xii. 29.

καταναρκέω.

be burdensome to, 2 Cor. xii. 13, 14.
be chargeable to, 2 Cor. xi. 9(8).

κατανεύω.

beckon unto, Luke v. 7.

κατανοέω.

perceive, Luke vi. 41. xx. 23.
discover, Acts xxvii. 39.
behold, Acts vii. 31, 32. Jas. i. 23, 24.
consider, Matt. vii. 3. Luke xii. 24, 27. Acts xi. 6. Rom. iv. 19. Heb. iii. 1. x. 24.

καταντάω.

With εἰς, **attain to**, Acts xxvii. 12.—**attain unto**, Phil. iii. 11.—**come to**, Acts xvi. 1. xviii. 19, 24. xxi. 7. xxviii. 13.—**come unto**, Acts xxv. 13. xxvi. 7. 1 Cor. xiv. 36. Eph. iv. 13.—**come upon**, 1 Cor. x. 11.
With ἀντικρύ, **come over against**, Acts xx. 15.

κατάνυξις.
slumber (*marg.* **remorse**), Rom. xi. 8.

κατανύσσω, -ττω.
to prick, Acts ii. 37.

καταξιόω.
count worthy, Acts v. 41. 2 Thes. i. 5.
account worthy, Luke xx. 35. xxi. 36 (*pass.*, κατισχύω Tr*S*).

καταπατέω.
tread down, Luke viii. 5.
tread under foot, Matt. v. 13. Heb. x. 29.
tread, Luke xii. 1.
trample, Matt. vii. 6.

κατάπαυσις.
rest, Acts vii. 49. Heb. iii. 11, 18. iv. 1, 3*t*, 5, 10, 11.

καταπαύω.
give rest, Heb. iv. 8.
restrain, Acts xiv. 18.
rest, Heb. iv. 4.
cease, Heb. iv. 10.

καταπέτασμα.
veil, Matt. xxvii. 51. Mark xv. 38. Luke xxiii. 45. Heb. vi. 19. ix. 3. x. 20.

καταπίνω.
swallow up, 1 Cor xv. 54. 2 Cor. ii. 7. v. 4. Rev. xii. 16.
swallow, Matt. xxiii. 24.
drown, Heb. xi. 29.
devour, 1 Pet. v. 8.

καταπίπτω.
fall down, Acts xxviii. 6.
fall, Acts xxvi. 14[p].

καταπλέω.
arrive, Luke viii. 26.

καταπονέω.
oppress, Acts vii. 24.
vex, 2 Pet. ii. 7.

καταποντίζω.
Mid. or Pass., **sink,** Matt. xiv. 30. —**be drowned,** Matt. xviii. 6.

κατάρα.
cursing, Heb. vi. 8. Jas. 3. 10.
curse, Gal. iii. 10, 13*t*.
Gen., **cursed,** 2 Pet. ii. 14.

καταράομαι.
to curse, Matt. v. 44(*ap*). Mark xi. 21. Luke vi. 28. Rom. xii. 14. Jas. iii. 9.
Pass., **be cursed,** Matt. xxv. 41.

καταργέω.
make without effect, Rom. iii. 3.
make of none effect, Rom. iv. 14. Gal. iii. 17.
Pass., **become of no effect,** Gal. v. 4[cc].—**come to nought,** 1 Cor. ii. 6. —**be to be done away,** 2 Cor. iii. 7. —**fail,** 1 Cor. xiii. 8.—**cease,** Gal. v. 11.—**vanish away,** 1 Cor. xiii. 8.
make void, Rom. iii. 31.
cumber, Luke xiii. 7.
deliver, Rom. vii. 6.
loose, Rom. vii. 2.
do away, 1 Cor. xiii. 10. 2 Cor. iii. 11, 14.
put away, 1 Cor. xiii. 11.
put down, 1 Cor. xv. 24.
abolish, 2 Cor. iii. 13. Eph. ii. 15. 2 Tim. i. 10.
destroy, Rom. vi. 6. 1 Cor. vi. 13. xv. 26. 2 Thes. ii. 8. Heb. ii. 14.
bring to nought, 1 Cor. i. 28.

καταριθμέω.
With ἐν, **number with,** Acts i. 17.

καταρτίζω.
mend, Matt. iv. 21. Mark i. 19.
restore, Gal. vi. 1.
make perfect, Heb. xiii. 21. 1 Pet. v. 10.
perfect, Matt. xxi. 16. 1 Thes. iii. 10.
Pass., **be perfect,** Luke vi. 40 (*marg.* **be perfected**). 2 Cor. xiii. 11. —**be perfectly joined together,** 1 Cor. i. 10.
fit (*marg.* **make up**), Rom. ix. 22.
prepare (*marg.* **fit**), Heb. x. 5.
frame, Heb. xi. 3.

κατάρτισις.
perfection, 2 Cor. xiii. 9.

καταρτισμός.
perfecting, Eph. iv. 12.

κατασείω.
beckon, Acts xii. 17. xiii. 16. xix. 33. xxi. 40.

κατασκάπτω.
dig down, Rom. xi. 2.
κατεσκαμμένα, **ruins**, Acts xv. 16.

κατασκευάζω.
prepare, Matt. xi. 10. Mark i. 2. Luke i. 17. vii. 27. Heb. xi. 7.
Pass., **be a preparing**, 1 Pet. iii. 20p.
build, Heb. iii. 3, 4*t*.
make, Heb. ix. 2.
ordain, Heb. ix. 6p.

κατασκηνόω.
to lodge, Matt. xiii. 32. Mark iv. 32. Luke xiii. 19.
rest, Acts ii. 26.

κατασκήνωσις.
nest, Matt. viii. 20. Luke ix. 58.

κατασκιάζω.
to shadow, Heb. ix. 5.

κατασκοπέω.
spy out, Gal. ii 4.

κατάσκοπος.
spy, Heb. xi. 31.

κατασοφίζομαι.
deal subtilely with, Acts vii. 19.

καταστέλλω.
appease, Acts xix. 35.
Pass., **quiet**, Acts xix. 36p.

κατάστημα.
behavior, Tit. ii. 3.

καταστολή.
apparel, 1 Tim. ii. 9.

καταστρέφω.
to overthrow, Matt. xxi. 12 Mark xi. 15.

καταστρηνιάω.
begin to wax wanton against, 1 Tim. v. 11.

καταστροφή.
overthrow, 2 Pet. ii. 6.
subverting, 2 Tim. ii. 14.

καταστρώννυμι.
to overthrow, 1 Cor. x. 5.

κατασύρω.
to hale, Luke xii. 58.

κατασφάζω, -άττω.
slay, Luke xix. 27.

κατασφραγίζω.
to seal, Rev. v. 1.

κατάσχεσις.
possession, Acts vii. 5, 45.

κατατίθημι.
lay, Mark xv. 46(τίθημι LTr*S*).
do, Acts xxv. 9.
show, Acts xxiv. 27.

κατατομή.
concision, Phil. iii. 2.

κατατοξεύω.
thrust through, Heb. xii. 20(*ap*).

κατατρέχω.
run down, Acts xxi. 32.

καταυγάζω, shine upon.
2 Cor. iv. 4, for αὐγάζω, Lm.

καταφάγω. See κατεσθίω.

καταφέρω.
give against, Acts xxvi. 10.
Pass., **sink down**, Acts xx. 9. — **fall**, Acts xx. 9.
Add Acts xxv. 7(*ap*).

καταφεύγω.
flee, Acts xiv. 16. Heb. vi. 18.

καταφθείρω.
Pass., **perish utterly**, 2 Pet. ii. 12 (καὶ φθείρω LT*S*). — **corrupt**, 2 Tim. iii. 8p.

καταφιλέω.
to kiss, Matt. xxvi. 49. Mark xiv. 45. Luke vii. 38, 45. xv. 20. Acts xx. 37.

καταφρονέω.
despise, Matt. vi. 24. xviii. 10. Luke xvi. 13. Rom. ii. 4. 1 Cor. xi. 22. 1 Tim. iv. 12. vi. 2. Heb. xii. 2. 2 Pet. ii. 10.

καταφρονητής.
despiser, Acts xiii. 41.

καταχέω.
pour, Matt. xxvi. 7. Mark xiv. 3.

καταχθόνιος.

under the earth, Phil. ii. 10.

καταχράομαι.

to abuse, 1 Cor. vii. 31. ix. 18.

καταψύχω.

to cool, Luke xvi. 24.

κατείδωλος.

wholly given to idolatry (*marg.* **full of idols**), Acts xvii. 16.

κατέναντι.

over against, Mark xi. 2. xii. 41 (ἀπέναντι Tr). xiii. 3. Luke xix. 30.

before (*marg.* **like unto**), Rom. iv. 17.

Add, for ἀπέναντι, Matt. xxi. 2, L Tr*S*. xxvii. 24, LTr. For κατενώπιον, 2 Cor. ii. 17, xii. 19, G″L*S*.

κατενώπιον.

in the sight of, 2 Cor. ii. 17 (κατέναντι G″L*S*).

in one's sight, Col. i. 22.

before the presence of, Jude 24.

before, 2 Cor. xii. 19 (κατέναντι G″ L*S*). Eph. i. 4.

κατεξουσιάζω.

exercise authority upon, Matt. xx. 25. Mark x. 42.

κατεργάζομαι.

work out, Phil. ii. 12.

work, Rom. i. 27. iv. 15. v. 3. vii. 8, 13. xv. 18. 2 Cor. iv. 17. v. 5. vii. 10 (ἐργάζομαι LT*S*), 10, 11. Jas. i. 3, 20 (ἐργάζομαι L*S*). 1 Pet. iv. 3.

be wrought, 2 Cor. xii. 12.

perform, Rom. vii. 18.

do, Rom. ii. 9. vii. 15, 17, 20. Eph. vi. 13 (*marg.* **overcome**).

With τοῦτο, **do this deed,** 1 Cor. v. 3.

cause, 2 Cor. ix. 11.

κατέρχομαι.

come down, Luke iv. 31. ix. 37p. Acts ix. 32. xv. 1. xxi. 10.

come, Acts xi. 27. xviii. 5. xxvii. 5.

go down, Acts viii. 5. xii. 19.

descend, Jas. iii. 15.

depart, Acts xiii. 4.

In navigation, **land,** Acts xviii. 22p.

Add Acts xv. 30, for ἔρχομαι, G″ L*S*. xxi. 3, for κατάγω, *pass.*, L*S*.

κατεσθίω.

2d Aorist, κατέφαγον.

eat up, John ii. 17. Rev. x. 9, 10.

devour up, Matt. xiii. 4. Mark iv. 4.

devour, Matt. xxiii. 14 (13, *ap*). Mark xii. 40. Luke viii. 5. xv. 30. xx. 47. 2 Cor. xi. 20. Gal. v. 15. Rev. xi. 5. xii. 4. xx. 9.

κατευθύνω.

to direct, 1 Thes. iii. 11. 2 Thes. iii. 5 (*marg.* **guide**).

guide, Luke i. 79.

κατευλογέω, bless much.

Mark x. 16, for εὐλογέω, TTr*S*.

κατεφίστημι.

make insurrection against, Acts xviii. 12.

κατέχω.

hold fast, 1 Thes. v. 21. Heb. iii. 6. x. 23.

withhold, 2 Thes. ii. 6 (*marg.* **hold**).

hold, Rom. i. 18. vii. 6. Heb. iii. 14.

retain, Phm. 13.

stay, Luke iv. 42.

let, 2 Thes. ii. 7.

keep, Luke viii. 15. 1 Cor. xi. 2.

keep in memory (*marg.* **hold fast**), 1 Cor. xv. 2.

take, Luke xiv. 9.

seize on, Matt. xxi. 38 (ἔχω G′LTTr*S*).

Pass., **have**cc, John v. 4 (*ap*).

possess, 1 Cor. vii. 30. 2 Cor. vi. 10.

In navigation, **make toward,** Acts xxvii. 40.

κατηγορέω.

accuse, Matt. xii. 10. xxvii. 12. Mark iii. 2. xv. 3. Luke xi. 54 (*ap*). xxiii. 2, 10, 14 (*with* κατά). John v. 45*t*. viii. 6 (*ap*). Acts xxii. 30. xxiv. 2, 8, 13. xxv. 5, 11, 16. xxviii. 19. Rom. ii. 15. Rev. xii. 10.

object, Acts xxiv. 19.

Add Mark xv. 4, for καταμαρτυρέω, LTTrS. Luke vi. 7, *inf.* for κατηγορία, Tr.

κατηγορία.

accusation, Luke vi. 7 (κατηγορέω Tr). John xviii. 29. 1 Tim. v. 19.
With ἐν, **accused,** Tit. i. 6.

κατήγορος.

accuser, John viii. 10 (*ap*). Acts xxiii. 30, 35. xxiv. 8(*ap*). xxv. 16, 18. Rev. xii. 10 (κατήγωρ GLTTr).

κατήγωρ, accuser.

Rev. xii. 10, for κατήγορος, GLTTr.

κατήφεια.

heaviness, Jas. iv. 9.

κατηχέω.

teach, 1 Cor. xiv. 19. Gal. vi. 6*t*.
instruct, Luke i. 4. Acts xviii. 25. Rom. ii. 18.
inform, Acts xxi. 21, 24.

κατ' ἰδίαν. See ἴδιος.

κατιόω.

to canker, Jas. v. 3.

κατισχύω.

prevail against, Matt. xvi. 18.
prevail, Luke xxiii. 23.
Add Luke xxi. 36, for καταξιόω, *pass.*, TrS.

κατοικέω.

dwell in, Matt. xxiii. 21. Acts ii. 9. iv. 16. xix. 10.
dweller in, Acts ii. 9p.
dwell at, Acts ii. 14. ix. 32, 35. xix. 17.
dweller at, Acts i. 19p.
dwell, Matt. ii. 23. iv. 13. xii. 45. Luke xi. 26. xiii. 4. Acts i. 20(*with* εἰμί). ii. 5. vii. 2, 4*t*, 48. ix. 22. xi. 29. xiii. 27. xvii. 24, 26. xxii. 12. Eph. iii. 17. Col. i. 19. ii. 9. Heb. xi. 9. Jas. iv. 5 (κατοικίζω LS). 2 Pet. iii. 13. Rev. ii. 13*t*. iii. 10. vi. 10. xi. 10*t*. xiii. 8, 12, 14*t*. xiv. 6(κάθημαι GLTTrS). xvii. 8.
inhabiter of, Rev. xii. 12p (–GLT Tr, εἰς S). xvii. 2p (1611 to 1769, now **-tant**).
inhabiter, Rev. viii. 13p.

κατοίκησις.

dwelling, Mark v. 3.

κατοικητήριον.

habitation, Eph. ii. 22. Rev. xviii. 2.

κατοικία.

habitation, Acts xvii. 26.

κατοικίζω, bring to dwell.

Jas. iv. 5, for κατοικέω, LS.

κατοπτρίζω.

Mid., **behold as in a glass,** 2 Cor. iii. 18.

κατόρθωμα.

very worthy deed, Acts xxiv. 2 (3, διόρθωμα G'LS).

κάτω.

down, Matt. iv. 6. Luke iv. 9. John viii. 6(*ap*), 8(*ap*). Acts xx. 9.
ἕως κάτω, **to the bottom,** Matt. xxvii. 51. Mark xv. 38.
beneath, Mark xiv. 66. Acts ii. 19.
τὰ κάτω, **beneath,** John viii. 23.
Comp., κατωτέρω, **under,** Matt. ii. 16.

κατώτερος.

lower, Eph. iv. 9.

καῦμα.

heat, Rev. vii. 16. xvi. 9.

καυματίζω.

scorch, Matt. xiii. 6. Mark iv. 6. Rev. xvi. 8, 9 (*marg.* **burn**).

καῦσις.

With εἰς, **to be burned,** Heb. vi. 8.

καυσόω.

Pass., **with fervent heat,** 2 Pet. iii. 10p, 12p.

καύσων.

burning heat, Jas. i. 11.
heat, Matt. xx. 12. Luke xii. 55.

καυτηριάζω.

sear with a hot iron, 1 Tim. iv. 2.

καυχάομαι.

to boast, 2 Cor. vii. 14. ix. 2. x. 8, 13(–G°), 15, 16. Eph. ii. 9.
boast one's self, 2 Cor. xi. 16.
make one's boast, Rom. ii. 17, 23.
glory, Rom. v. 3. 1 Cor. i. 29, 31*t*.

iii. 21. iv. 7. 2 Cor. v. 12. x. 17*t*. xi. 12, 18*t*, 30*t*. xii. 1, 5*t*, 6, 9. Gal. vi. 13, 14. 2 Thes. i. 4 (ἐγκαυχάομαι L*S*, ἐνκαυχάομαι T).
in glorying, 2 Cor. xii. 11p(*omS*).
rejoice, Rom. v. 2. Phil. iii. 3. Jas. i. 9(*marg.* **glory**). iv. 16.
joy, Rom. v. 11.

καύχημα.

boasting, 2 Cor. ix. 3.
glorying, 1 Cor. v. 6. ix. 15.
With οὐ, **nothing to glory of**, 1 Cor. ix. 16.
to glory, Rom. iv. 2. 2 Cor. v. 12.
rejoicing, 2 Cor. i. 14. Gal. vi. 4. Phil. i. 26. Heb. iii. 6.
εἰς κ. ἐμοί, **that I may rejoice**, Phil. ii. 16.

καύχησις.

boasting, Rom. iii. 27. 2 Cor. vii. 14. viii. 24. ix. 4(*omS*). xi. 10, 17.
glorying, 2 Cor. vii. 4.
whereof Ic **may glory**, Rom. xv. 17.
rejoicing, 1 Cor. xv. 31. 2 Cor. i. 12. 1 Thes. ii. 19 (*marg.* **glorying**). Jas. iv. 16.

κεῖμαι.

to lie, Matt. xxviii. 6. Luke ii. 12, 16. John xx. 5, 6, 7, 12. 1 John v. 19. Rev. xxi. 16.
there, John xxi. 9p.
be laid, Matt. iii. 10. Luke iii. 9. xxiii. 53. xxiv. 12(*ap*). John xi. 41(*ap*). 1 Cor. iii. 11.
be laid up, Luke xii. 19.
be set, Matt. v. 14. Luke ii. 34. John ii. 6. xix. 29. Phil. i. 17. Rev. iv. 2.
be appointed, 1 Thes. iii. 3.
be made, 1 Tim. i. 9.
be, 2 Cor. iii. 15.

κειρίαι.

grave-clothes, John xi. 44.

κείρω.

to shear, Acts xviii. 18. 1 Cor. xi. 6*t*.
shearer, Acts viii. 32p.

κέλευσμα.

shout, 1 Thes. iv. 16.

κελεύω.

to command, Matt. xiv. 9, 19. xv. 35 (παραγγέλλωv LTr*S*). xviii. 25. xxvii. 58, 64. Luke xviii. 40. Acts iv. 15p. v. 34. viii. 38. xii. 19. xvi. 22. xxi. 33, 34. xxii. 24, 30. xxiii. 3, 10, 35. xxiv. 8(*ap*). xxv. 6, 17, 21. xxvii. 43.
give commandment, Matt. viii. 18.
at one's commandment, Acts xxv. 23p.
bid, Matt. xiv. 28.

κενοδοξία.

vainglory, Phil. ii. 3.

κενόδοξος.

desirous of vain glory, Gal. v. 26.

κενός.

empty, Mark xii. 3. Luke i. 53. xx. 10, 11.
vain, 1 Cor. xv. 14*t*. Eph. v. 6. Col. ii. 8. Jas. ii. 20.
Neut. plur., **vain things**, Acts iv. 25.
in vain, 1 Cor. xv. 10, 58. 1 Thes. ii. 1.
εἰς κενόν, **in vain**, 2 Cor. vi. 1. Gal. ii. 2. Phil. ii. 16*t*. 1 Thes. iii. 5.

κενοφωνία.

Gen., **vain**, 1 Tim. vi. 20. 2 Tim. ii. 16.

κενόω.

make void, Rom. iv. 14. 1 Cor. ix. 15.
make of none effect, 1 Cor. i. 17.
Pass., **be in vain**, 2 Cor. ix. 3.
make of no reputation, Phil. ii. 7.

κέντρον.

prick, Acts ix. 5(*ap*). xxvi. 14.
sting, 1 Cor. xv. 55, 56. Rev. ix. 10.

κεντυρίων.

centurion, Mark xv. 39, 44, 45.

κενῶς.

in vain, Jas. iv. 5.

κεραία.

tittle, Matt. v. 18. Luke xvi. 17.

κεραμεύς.

potter, Matt. xxvii. 7, 10. Rom. ix. 21.

κεραμικός.

of a potter, Rev. ii. 27.

κεράμιον.

pitcher, Mark xiv. 13. Luke xxii. 10.

κέραμος.

tiling, Luke v. 19.

κεράννυμι, κεραννύω.

pour out, Rev. xiv. 10.
fill, Rev. xviii. 6*t*.

κέρας.

horn, Luke i. 69. Rev. v. 6. ix. 13. xii. 3. xiii. 1*t*, 11. xvii. 3, 7, 12, 16.

κεράτιον.

husk, Luke xv. 16.

κερδαίνω.

to gain, Matt. xvi. 26. xviii. 15. xxv. 17, 20, 22. Mark viii. 36. Luke ix. 25p. Acts xxvii. 21. 1 Cor. ix. 19, 20*t*, 21, 22.
get gain, Jas. iv. 13.
win, Phil. iii. 8. 1 Pet. iii. 1.
Add Matt. xxv. 16, for ποιέω, G' LTr.

κέρδος.

gain, Phil. i. 21. iii. 7.
lucre, Tit. i. 11.

κέρμα.

money, John ii. 15.

κερματιστής.

changer of money, John ii. 14.

κεφάλαιον.

sum, Acts xxii. 28. Heb. viii. 1.

κεφαλαιόω.

to wound in the head, Mark xii. 4.

κεφαλή.

head, Matt. v. 36. vi. 17. viii. 20. x. 30. xiv. 8, 11. xxi. 42. xxvi. 7. xxvii. 29, 30, 37, 39. Mark vi. 24, 25, 27, 28. xii. 10. xiv. 3. xv. 19, 29. Luke vii. 38, 44(*omS*), 46. ix. 58. xii. 7. xx. 17. xxi. 18, 28. John xiii. 9. xix. 2, 30. xx. 7, 12. Acts iv. 11. xviii. 6, 18. xxi. 24. xxvii. 34.
Rom. xii. 20. 1 Cor. xi. 3*tr*, 4*t*, 5*t*, 7, 10. xii. 21. Eph. i. 22. iv. 15. v. 23*t*. Col. i. 18. ii. 10. 1 Pet. ii. 7. Rev. i. 14. iv. 4. ix. 7, 17*t*, 19. x. 1. xii. 1, 3*t*. xiii. 1*t*, 3. xiv. 14. xvii. 3, 7, 9. xviii. 19. xix. 12.
Said of Christ, **Head,** Col. ii. 19.

κεφαλίς.

volume, Heb. x. 7.

κημόω, to muzzle.

1 Cor. ix. 9, for φιμόω, T.

κῆνσος.

tribute, Matt. xvii. 25. xxii. 17. Mark xii. 14.
Gen., **tribute,** *adj.,* Matt. xxii. 19.

κῆπος.

garden, Luke xiii. 19. John xviii. 1, 26. xix. 41*t*.

κηπουρός.

gardener, John xx. 15.

κηρίον.

With μελίσσιος, **honey-comb,** Luke xxiv. 42(*ap*).

κήρυγμα.

preaching, Matt. xii. 41. Luke xi. 32. Rom. xvi. 25. 1 Cor. i. 21. ii. 4. xv. 14. 2 Tim. iv. 17. Tit. i. 3.

κήρυξ.

preacher, 1 Tim. ii. 7. 2 Tim. i. 11. 2 Pet. ii. 5.

κηρύσσω.

proclaim, Luke xii. 3. Rev. v. 2.
publish, Mark i. 45. v. 20. vii. 36. xiii. 10. Luke viii. 39.
preach, Matt. iii. 1. iv. 17, 23. ix. 35. x. 7, 27. xi. 1. xxiv. 14. xxvi. 13. Mark i. 4, 7, 14, 38, 39(*with* ἦν (ἦλθεν fr. ἔρχομαι Tr*S*)). iii. 14. vi. 12. xiv. 9. xvi. 15(*ap*), 20(*ap*). Luke iii. 3. iv. 18, 19, 44(*with* ἦν). viii. 1. ix. 2. xxiv. 47. Acts viii. 5. ix. 20. x. 37, 42. xv. 21. xix. 13. xx. 25. xxviii. 31.
Rom. ii. 21. x. 8, 15. 1 Cor. i. 23. ix. 27p. xv. 11, 12. 2 Cor. i. 19. iv. 5. xi. 4*t*. Gal. ii. 2. v. 11. Phil. i. 15. Col. i. 23. 1 Thes. ii. 9. 1 Tim. iii. 16. 2 Tim. iv. 2. 1 Pet. iii. 19.

preacher, Rom. x. 14p.

κῆτος.

whale, Matt. xii. 40.

κιβωτός.

ark, Matt. xxiv. 38. Luke xvii. 27. Heb. ix. 4. xi. 7. 1 Pet. iii. 20. Rev. xi. 19.

κιθάρα.

harp, 1 Cor. xiv. 7. Rev. v. 8. xiv. 2. xv. 2.

κιθαρίζω.

to harp, 1 Cor. xiv. 7. Rev. xiv. 2.

κιθαρῳδός.

harper, Rev. xiv. 2. xviii. 22.

κινάμωμον, κιννάμωμον LTS.

cinnamon, Rev. xviii. 13.

κινδυνεύω.

be in danger, Acts xix. 27, 40.
be in jeopardy, Luke viii. 23.
stand in jeopardy, 1 Cor. xv. 30.

κίνδυνος.

peril, Rom. viii. 35. 2 Cor. xi. 26 *eight*.

κινέω.

move, Matt. xxiii. 4. Acts xxi. 30. Rev. vi. 14.
Mid., **move**, Acts xvii. 28.
mover of, Acts xxiv. 5p.
remove, Rev. ii. 5.
wag, Matt. xxvii. 39. Mark xv. 29.

κίνησις.

moving, John v. 3(*ap*).

κίχρημι. See χράω.

κλάδος.

branch, Matt. xiii. 32. xxi. 8. xxiv. 32. Mark iv. 32. xiii. 28. Luke xiii. 19. Rom. xi. 16, 17, 18, 19, 21.

κλάζω. See κλάω.

κλαίω.

weep, Matt. ii. 18. xxvi. 75. Mark v. 38, 39. xiv. 72 (*marg., with* ἐπιβάλλω, **weep abundantly**; *or* **begin to weep**, ἄρχομαι κλαίειν Cm). xvi. 10 (*ap*). Luke vi. 21, 25. vii. 13, 32, 38. viii. 52*t*. xix. 41. xxii. 62. xxiii. 28*t*. John xi. 31, 33*t*. xvi. 20. xx. 11*t*, 13, 15. Acts ix. 39. xxi. 13.
Rom. xii. 15*t*. 1 Cor. vii. 30*t*. Phil. iii. 18. Jas. iv. 9. v. 1. Rev. v. 4, 5. xviii. 11, 15, 19.
bewail, Rev. xviii. 9.

κλάσις.

breaking, Luke xxiv. 35. Acts ii. 42.

κλάσμα.

fragment, Matt. xiv. 20. Mark vi. 43. viii. 19, 20. Luke ix. 17. John vi. 12, 13.
Plur., **broken cmeat**, Matt. xv. 37. Mark viii. 8.

κλαυθμός.

weeping, Matt. ii. 18. viii. 12. xxii. 13. xxiv. 51. xxv. 30. Luke xiii. 28.
With γίνομαι, **weepcc**, Acts xx. 37.
wailing, Matt. xiii. 42, 50.

κλάω.

break, Matt. xiv. 19. xv. 36. xxvi. 26. Mark viii. 6, 19. xiv. 22. Luke xxii. 19. xxiv. 30. Acts ii. 46. xx. 7, 11. xxvii. 35p. 1 Cor. x. 16. xi. 24, 24 (-LTS).
Add Rom. xi. 20, for ἐκκλάζω, L.

κλείς.

key, Matt. xvi. 19. Luke xi. 52. Rev. i. 18 iii. 7. ix. 1. xx. 1.

κλείω.

shut, Matt. vi. 6p. xxv. 10. Luke xi. 7. John xx. 19p, 26. Acts v. 23. xxi. 30. Rev. iii. 7*t*, 8. xi. 6. xxi. 25.
shut up, Matt. xxiii. 13(14). Luke iv. 25. 1 John iii. 17. Rev. xx. 3.

κλέμμα.

theft, Rev. ix. 21.

κλέος.

glory, 1 Pet. ii. 20.

κλέπτης.

thief, Matt. vi. 19, 20. xxiv. 43. Luke xii. 33, 39. John x. 1, 8, 10. xii. 6. 1 Cor. vi. 10. 1 Thes. v. 2, 4.

1 Pet. iv. 15. 2 Pet. iii. 10. Rev. iii. 3. xvi. 15.

κλέπτω.

steal, Matt. vi. 19, 20. xix. 18. xxvii. 64. xxviii. 13. Mark x. 19. Luke xviii. 20. John. x. 10. Rom. ii. 21*t*. xiii. 9. Eph. iv. 28*t*.

κλῆμα.

branch, John xv. 2, 4, 5, 6.

κληρονομέω.

inherit, Matt. v. 5. xix. 29. xxv. 34. Mark x. 17. Luke x. 25. xviii. 18. 1 Cor. vi. 9, 10. xv. 50*t*. Gal. v. 21. Heb. vi. 12. xii. 17. 1 Pet. iii. 9. Rev. xxi. 7(δώσω αὐτῷ G').
obtain by inheritance, Heb. i. 4.
be heir of, Heb. i. 14.
be heir, Gal. iv. 30.
Add Matt. xix. 16, for ἔχω, L^m^*S*.

κληρονομία.

inheritance, Matt. xxi. 38. Mark xii. 7. Luke xii. 13. xx. 14. Acts vii. 5. xx. 32. Gal. iii. 18. Eph. i. 14, 18. v. 5. Col. iii. 24. Heb. ix. 15. xi. 8. 1 Pet. i. 4.

κληρονόμος.

heir, Matt. xxi. 38. Mark xii. 7. Luke xx. 14. Rom. iv. 13, 14. viii. 17*t*. Gal. iii. 29. iv. 1, 7. Tit. iii. 7. Heb. i. 2. vi. 17. xi. 7. Jas. ii. 5.

κλῆρος.

lot, Acts i. 26*t*. viii. 21.
lots, Matt. xxvii. 35, 35(*ap*). Mark xv. 24. Luke xxiii. 34(*plur*. L^m^T). John xix. 24.
part, Acts i. 17, 25 (τόπος G'LT).
inheritance, Acts xxvi. 18. Col. i. 12.
heritage, 1 Pet. v. 3.

κληρόω.

Pass., **obtain an inheritance**, Eph. i. 11 (καλέω G'L).

κλῆσις.

calling, Rom. xi. 29. 1 Cor. i. 26. vii. 20. Eph. i. 18. iv. 4. Phil. iii. 14. 2 Thes. i. 11. 2 Tim. i. 9. Heb. iii. 1. 2 Pet. i. 10.
vocation, Eph. iv. 1.

κλητός.

called, Matt. xx. 16(*ap*). xxii. 14. Rom. i. 1, 6, 7. viii. 28. 1 Cor. i. 1 (–G^o^L^b^), 2. Jude 1. Rev. xvii. 14.
which is called, 1 Cor. i. 24.

κλίβανος.

oven, Matt. vi. 30. Luke xii. 28.

κλίμα.

region, 2 Cor. xi. 10. Gal. i. 21.
part, Rom. xv. 23.

κλινάριον, a small bed.

Acts v. 15, for κλίνη, G'LT*S*.

κλίνη.

bed, Matt. ix. 2, 6. Mark iv. 21. vii. 30. Luke v. 18. viii. 16. xvii. 34. Acts v. 15 (κλινάριον G'LT*S*). Rev. ii. 22.
table (*marg*. **bed**), Mark vii. 4.

κλινίδιον.

couch, Luke v. 19, 24.

κλίνω.

to bow, John xix. 30.
bow down, Luke xxiv. 5.
lay, Matt. viii. 20. Luke ix. 58.
With ἡμέρα, **wear away**, Luke ix. 12.—**be far spent**, Luke xxiv. 29.
turn to flight, Heb. xi. 34.

κλισία.

Acc. plur., **in a company**, Luke ix. 14.

κλοπή.

theft, Matt. xv. 19. Mark vii. 22.

κλύδων.

wave, Jas. i. 6.
raging, Luke viii. 24.

κλυδωνίζομαι.

be tossed to and fro, Eph. iv. 14.

κνήθω.

Pass., *with* τὴν ἀκοήν, **have itching ears**, 2 Tim. iv. 3.

κοδράντης.

farthing, Matt. v. 26. Mark xii. 42.

κοιλία.

belly, Matt. xii. 40. xv. 17. Mark vii. 19. Luke xv. 16. John vii. 38.

Rom. xvi. 18. 1 Cor. vi. 13*t*. Phil. iii. 19. Rev. x. 9, 10.
womb, Matt. xix. 12. Luke i. 15, 41, 42, 44. ii. 21. xi. 27. xxiii. 29. John iii. 4. Acts iii. 2. xiv. 8. Gal. i. 15.

κοιμάω.

Passive, and Future Middle,
fall asleep, Acts vii. 60. 1 Cor. xv. 6, 18. 2 Pet. iii. 4.
fall on sleep, Acts xiii. 36.
sleep, Matt. xxvii. 52. xxviii. 13p. Luke xxii. 45. John xi. 11, 12. Acts xii. 6. 1 Cor. xi. 30. xv. 20, 51. 1 Thes. iv. 14.
be asleep, 1 Thes. iv. 13, 15.
be dead, 1 Cor. vii. 39.

κοίμησις.

taking of rest, John xi. 13.

κοινός.

common, Acts ii. 44. iv. 32. x. 14, 28. xi. 8. Tit. i. 4. Jude 3.
unclean, Rom. xiv. 14*t* (*marg.* **common**), 14.
defiled (*marg.* **common**), Mark vii. 2.
Neut., **unholy thing**, Heb. x. 29.
Add Mark vii. 5, for ἄνιπτος, and Rev. xxi. 27, for κοινόωp, GLTTr*S*.

κοινόω.

call common, Acts x. 15. xi. 9.
Pass., **unclean**, Heb. ix. 13p.
defile, Matt. xv. 11*t*, 18, 20*t*. Mark vii. 15*t*, 18, 20, 23. Rev. xxi. 27(p, κοινόν fr. κοινός GLTTr*S*).
pollute, Acts xxi. 28.

κοινωνέω.

be partaker of, Rom. xv. 27. 1 Tim. v. 22. Heb. ii. 14. 1 Pet. iv. 13. 2 John 11.
communicate, Gal. vi. 6. Phil. iv. 15.
distribute, Rom. xii. 13.

κοινωνία.

communion, 1 Cor. x. 16*t*. 2 Cor. vi. 14. xiii. 14(13).
communication, Phm. 6.
to communicatecc, Heb. xiii. 16.
fellowship, Acts ii. 42. 1 Cor. i. 9. 2 Cor. viii. 4. Gal. ii. 9. Eph. iii. 9 (οἰκονομία GLT*S*). Phil. i. 5. ii. 1. iii. 10. 1 John i. 3*t*, 6, 7.
contribution, Rom. xv. 26.
distribution, 2 Cor. ix. 13.

κοινωνικός.

willing to communicate (*marg.* **sociable**), 1 Tim. vi. 18.

κοινωνός.

partaker, Matt. xxiii. 30. 1 Cor. x. 18. 2 Cor. i. 7. 1 Pet. v. 1. 2 Pet. i. 4.
partner, Luke v. 10. 2 Cor. viii. 23. Phm. 17.
With γίνομαι, **have fellowship with**, 1 Cor. x. 20.
companion, Heb. x. 33.
Add Rev. i. 9, for συγκοινωνός, G'.

κοίτη.

bed, Luke xi. 7. Heb. xiii. 4.
With ἔχω, **conceive**, Rom. ix. 10.
Plur., **chambering**, Rom. xiii. 13.

κοιτών.

With ἐπί, **chamberlain** (*Gr.* over the bed-chamber), Acts xii. 20.

κόκκινος.

scarlet colored, Rev. xvii. 3.
scarlet, Matt. xxvii. 28. Heb. ix. 19 (*marg.* **purple**).
Neut., **scarlet color**, Rev. xvii. 4.—**scarlet**, Rev. xviii. 12, 16.

κόκκος.

grain, Matt. xiii. 31. xvii. 20. Mark iv. 31. Luke xiii. 19. xvii. 6. 1 Cor. xv. 37.
corn, John xii. 24.

κολάζω.

punish, Acts iv. 21. 2 Pet. ii. 9.
Add 2 Pet. ii. 4, κολαζομένους τηρεῖν for τηρουμένους fr. τηρέω, L*S*.

κολακεία.

Gen., **flattering**, 1 Thes. ii. 5.

κόλασις.

punishment, Matt. xxv. 46.
torment, 1 John iv. 18.

κολαφίζω.

buffet, Matt. xxvi. 67. Mark xiv.

65. 1 Cor. iv. 11. 2 Cor. xii. 7. 1 Pet. ii. 20p.

κολλάω.

Middle, and Passive Aorist,
cleave, Luke x. 11. Acts xvii. 34. Rom. xii. 9.
join one's self, Luke xv. 15. Acts v. 13. viii. 29. ix. 26.
be joined, 1 Cor. vi. 16, 17.
keep company, Acts x. 28.
Add Matt. xix. 5, for προσκολλάω, G″LTTr. Rev. xviii. 5, for ἀκολουθέω, GLTTr*S*.

κολλούριον, κολλύριον TTr*S*.

eye-salve, Rev. iii. 18.

κολλυβιστής.

money-changer, Matt. xxi. 12. Mark xi. 15.
changer, John ii. 15.

κολοβόω.

shorten, Matt. xxiv. 22*t*. Mark xiii. 20*t*.

κόλπος.

bosom, Luke vi. 38. xvi. 22, 23. John i. 18. xiii. 23.
creek, Acts xxvii. 39.

κολυμβάω.

swim, Acts xxvii. 43.

κολυμβήθρα.

pool, John v. 2, 4(*ap*), 7. ix. 7, 11 (*omS*).

κολωνία, κολώνεια T.

colony, Acts xvi. 12.

κομάω.

have long hair, 1 Cor. xi. 14, 15.

κόμη.

hair, 1 Cor. xi. 15.

κομίζω.

bring, Luke vii. 37.
Mid., **receive**, Matt. xxv. 27. 2 Cor. v. 10. Eph. vi. 8. Heb. x. 36. xi. 19, 39. 1 Pet. i. 9. v. 4. 2 Pet. ii. 13. —**receive for**, Col. iii. 25.

κομψότερον.

With ἔχω, **begin to amend**, John iv. 52.

κονιάω.

to white, Matt. xxiii. 27. Acts xxiii. 3.

κονιορτός.

dust, Matt. x. 14. Luke ix. 5. x. 11. Acts xiii. 51. xxii. 23.

κοπάζω.

cease, Matt. xiv. 32. Mark iv. 39. vi. 51.

κοπετός.

lamentation, Acts viii. 2.

κοπή.

slaughter, Heb. vii. 1.

κοπιάω.

Perf., **be wearied**, John iv. 6.
toil, Matt. vi. 28. Luke v. 5. xii. 27(*ap*).
labor, Matt. xi. 28. John iv. 38. Acts xx. 35. Rom. xvi. 12, 12(*ap*). 1 Cor. iv. 12. xv. 10. xvi. 16. Eph. iv. 28. Phil. ii. 16. Col. i. 29. 1 Thes. v. 12. 1 Tim. iv. 10. v. 17. 2 Tim. ii. 6. Rev. ii. 3(*ap*).
bestow labor (on[1]), John iv. 38[1]. Rom. xvi. 6. Gal. iv. 11.

κόπος.

weariness, 2 Cor. xi. 27.
Plur., *with* παρέχω, **to trouble**, Matt. xxvi. 10. Mark xiv. 6. Luke xi. 7. xviii. 5. Gal. vi. 17.
labor, John iv. 38. 1 Cor. iii. 8. xv. 58. 2 Cor. vi. 5. x. 15. xi. 23. 1 Thes. i. 3. ii. 9. iii. 5. 2 Thes. iii. 8. Heb. vi. 10(*omS*). Rev. ii. 2. xiv. 13.

κοπρία.

dunghill, Luke xiv. 35.
With βάλλω, **to dung**, Luke xiii. 8 (*see* κόπριος).

κόπριος, full of dung, filthy.

τὰ κόπρια, Luke xiii. 8, for κοπρία, GLTTr*S*.

κόπτω.

cut down, Matt. xxi. 8. Mark xi. 8.
Mid., **lament**, Matt. xi. 17. —**wail**, Rev. i. 7. —**bewail**, Luke viii. 52. xxiii. 27. Rev. xviii. 9. —**mourn**, Matt. xxiv. 30.

κόραξ.

raven, Luke xii. 24.

κοράσιον.

damsel, Matt. xiv. 11. Mark v. 41, 42. vi. 22, 28*t*.

maid, Matt. ix. 24, 25.

κορβᾶν, κορβανᾶς.

Corban, Mark vii. 11.

treasury, Matt. xxvii. 6.

κορέννυμι.

Pass. or Mid., **eat enough,** Acts xxvii. 38p. —**full,** 1 Cor. iv. 8p.

κόρος.

measure, Luke xvi. 7.

κοσμέω.

to trim, Matt. xxv. 7.

adorn, Luke xxi. 5. 1 Tim. ii. 9. Tit. ii. 10. 1 Pet. iii. 5. Rev. xxi. 2.

garnish, Matt. xii. 44. xxiii. 29. Luke xi. 25. Rev. xxi. 19.

κοσμικός.

worldly, Tit. ii. 12. Heb. ix. 1.

κόσμιος.

of good behavior (*marg.* **modest**), 1 Tim. iii. 2.

modest, 1 Tim. ii. 9.

κοσμοκράτωρ.

ruler, Eph. vi. 12.

κόσμος.

(*With* οὗτος, *marked* [1].)

adorning, 1 Pet. iii. 3.

world, Matt. iv. 8. v. 14. xiii. 35 (–LTTr), 38. xvi. 26. xviii. 7. xxiv. 21. xxv. 34. xxvi. 13. Mark viii. 36. xiv. 9. xvi. 15(*ap*). Luke ix. 25. xi. 50. xii. 30.

John i. 9, 10*tr*, 29. iii. 16, 17*tr*, 19. iv. 42. vi. 14, 33, 51. vii. 4, 7. viii. 12, 23[1]*t*, 26. ix. 5*t*, 39[1]. x. 36. xi. 9[1], 27. xii. 19, 25[1], 31[1]*t*, 46, 47*t*. xiii. 1[1], 1. xiv. 17, 19, 22, 27, 30[1] (οὗτος *om S*), 31. xv. 18, 19*five*. xvi. 8, 11[1], 20, 21, 28*t*, 33*t*. xvii. 5, 6, 9, 11*t*, 12 (–G°LTTr*S*), 13, 14*tr*, 15, 16*t*, 18*t*, 21, 23, 24, 25. xviii. 20, 36[1]*t*, 37. xxi. 25. Acts xvii. 24. Rom. i. 8, 20. iii. 6, 19. iv. 13. v. 12, 13. xi. 12, 15. 1 Cor. i. 20[1], 21, 27, 27(*ap*), 28. ii. 12. iii. 19[1], 22. iv. 9, 13. v. 10[1], 10. vi. 2*t*. vii. 31[1]*t*, 33, 34. viii. 4. xi. 32. xiv. 10. 2 Cor. i. 12. v. 19. vii. 10. Gal. iv. 3. vi. 14*t*. Eph. i. 4. ii. 2[1], 12. Phil. ii. 15. Col. i. 6. ii. 8, 20*t*. 1 Tim. i. 15. iii. 16. vi. 7.

Heb. iv. 3. ix. 26. x. 5. xi. 7, 38. Jas. i. 27. ii. 5[1] (οὗτος *om S*). iii. 6. iv. 4*t*. 1 Pet. i. 20. v. 9. 2 Pet. i. 4. ii. 5*t*, 20. iii. 6. 1 John ii. 2, 15*tr*, 16*t*, 17. iii. 1, 13, 17. iv. 1, 3, 4, 5*tr*, 9, 14, 17[1]. v. 4*t*, 5, 19. 2 John 7. Rev. xi. 15. xiii. 8. xvii. 8.

Add John i. 36(*ap*).

κοῦμι, κοῦμ TTr*S*.

cumi, Mark v. 41.

κουστωδία.

watch, Matt. xxvii. 65, 66. xxviii. 11.

κουφίζω.

lighten, Acts xxvii. 38.

κόφινος.

basket, Matt. xiv. 20. xvi. 9. Mark vi. 43. viii. 19. Luke ix. 17. John vi. 13.

κράββατος,

κράβαττος LTTr*S*, κράβακτος *S*.

couch, Acts v. 15.

bed, Mark ii. 4, 9, 11, 12. vi. 55. John v. 8, 9, 10, 11, 12 (–TTr[b]*S*). Acts ix. 33.

κράζω.

to cry, Matt. ix. 27. xiv. 30. xv. 23. xx. 31. xxi. 9, 15. xxvii. 50p. Mark i. 26(φωνέω TTr*S*). iii. 11. v. 5, 7. ix. 26. x. 48. xi. 9. Luke xviii. 39. John i. 15. vii. 28, 37. xii. 13 (κραυγάζω LTTr*S*), 44. Acts vii. 60. xvi. 17. xix. 32. xxi. 36. xxiv. 21 (ἐκκράζω T*S*). Rom. viii. 15. ix. 27. Gal. iv. 6. Jas. v. 4. Rev. vi. 10. vii. 2, 10. x. 3*t*. xii. 2. xiv. 15. xviii. 2, 18, 19. xix. 17.

cry out, Matt. viii. 29. xiv. 26. xx.

30. xxvii. 23. Mark ix. 24. x. 47. xv. 13, 14, 39(–Tr^b S). Luke iv. 41 (κραυγάζω LT). ix. 39. xix. 40. John xix. 12 (κραυγάζω LTTr, –S). Acts vii. 57. xiv. 14. xix. 28, 34. xxi. 28. xxiii. 6.

Add Matt. xv. 22, for κραυγάζω, L TrS.

κραιπάλη.

surfeiting, Luke xxi. 34.

κρανίον.

skull, Matt. xxvii. 33. Mark xv. 22. John xix. 17.

Calvary (*marg.* **the place of a skull**), Luke xxiii. 33.

κράσπεδον.

border, Matt. xxiii. 6. Mark vi. 56. Luke viii. 44.

hem, Matt. ix. 20. xiv. 36.

κραταιός.

mighty, 1 Pet. v. 6.

κρατιόω.

strengthen, Eph. iii. 16.

Pass., **wax strong,** Luke i. 80. ii. 40. —**be strong,** 1 Cor. xvi. 13.

κρατέω.

lay hold on, Matt. xii. 11. xiv. 3. xxvi. 55, 57. Mark iii. 21. xii. 12. xiv. 51. Rev. xx. 2.

lay hold upon, Mark vi. 17. Heb. vi. 18.

lay hands on, Matt. xviii. 28. xxi. 46.

take, Matt. xxii. 6. xxvi. 4, 50. Mark xiv. 1, 44, 46, 49. Acts xxiv. 6.

take by, Matt. ix. 25. Mark i. 31. v. 41. ix. 27. Luke viii. 54.

obtain, Acts xxvii. 13.

hold, Mark vii. 3, 4, 8. Luke xxiv. 16. Acts ii. 24. iii. 11p. Col ii. 19. 2 Thes. ii. 15. Rev. ii. 1, 14, 15. vii. 1.

hold fast, Matt. xxvi. 48. Heb. iv. 14. Rev. ii. 13, 25. iii. 11.

hold by, Matt. xxviii. 9.

keep, Mark ix. 10.

retain, John xx. 23*t*.

κράτιστος.

most excellent, Luke i. 3. Acts xxiii. 26.

most noble, Acts xxiv. 3. xxvi. 25.

κράτος.

strength, Luke i. 51.

With κατά, **mightily,** Acts xix. 20.

power, Eph. i. 19. vi. 10. Col. i. 11. 1 Tim. vi. 16. Heb. ii. 14. Rev. v. 13.

dominion, 1 Pet. iv. 11. v. 11. Jude 25. Rev. i. 6.

κραυγάζω.

to cry, Matt. xii. 19. xv. 22 (κράζω LTrS). John xi. 43. xviii. 40.

cry out, John xix. 6, 15. Acts xxii. 23p.

Add, for κράζω, Luke iv. 41, LT. John xii. 13, LTTrS. xix. 12, LTTr.

κραυγή.

cry, Matt. xxv. 5. Acts xxiii. 9. Rev. xiv. 18 (φωνή LTrS).

crying, Heb. v. 7. Rev. xxi. 4.

clamor, Eph. iv. 31.

Add Luke i. 42, for φωνή, TTr.

κρέας.

flesh, Rom. xiv. 21. 1 Cor. viii. 13.

κρείσσων, -ττων.

better, 1 Cor. vii. 9. xi. 17. Phil. i. 23. Heb. i. 4. vii. 7, 19, 22. viii. 6*t*. ix. 23. x. 34. xi. 35. 1 Pet. iii. 17. 2 Pet. ii. 21.

better °**country,** Heb. xi. 16.

Neut., **better thing,** Heb. vi. 9. xi. 40. xii. 24. —*Adv.*, **better,** 1 Cor. vii. 38.

best, 1 Cor. xii. 31 (μείζων LTS).

κρεμάννυμι, κρεμάω.

hang, Matt. xviii. 6. Luke xxiii. 39. Acts v. 30. x. 39.

Mid., **hang,** Matt. xxii. 40. Acts xxviii. 4. Gal. iii. 13.

κρημνός.

steep place, Matt. viii. 32. Mark v. 13. Luke viii. 33.

κριθή.

barley, Rev. vi. 6.

κρίθινος.

barley, *adj*., John vi. 9, 13.

κρίμα.

judgment, Matt. vii. 2. John ix. 39. Acts xxiv. 25. Rom. ii. 2, 3. v. 16. xi. 33. Gal. v. 10. Heb. vi. 2. 1 Pet. iv. 17. 2 Pet. ii. 3. Rev. xvii. 1. xx. 4.

Plur., *with* ἔχω, **go to law**, 1 Cor. vi. 7.

With κρίνω, **avenge**, Rev. xviii. 20.

condemnation, Luke xxiii. 40. 1 Cor. xi. 34(*marg*. **judgment**). 1 Tim. iii. 6. Jas. iii. 1(*marg*. **judgment**). Jude 4.

With εἰς, **to be condemned**, Luke xxiv. 20.

damnation, Matt. xxiii. 14(13, *ap*). Mark xii. 40. Luke xx. 47. Rom. iii. 8. xiii. 2. 1 Cor. xi. 29 (*marg*. **judgment**). 1 Tim. v. 12.

κρίνον.

lily, Matt. vi. 28. Luke xii. 27.

κρίνω.

to esteem, Rom. xiv. 5*t*.

think, Acts xxvi. 8.

determine, Acts iii. 13ᵖ. xx. 16. xxv. 25. xxvii. 1. 1 Cor. ii. 2. 2 Cor. ii. 1. Tit. iii. 12.

conclude, Acts xxi. 25.

judge, Matt. vii. 1, 2*t*. xix. 28. Luke vi. 37*t*. vii. 43. xii. 57. xix. 22. xxii. 30. John v. 22, 30. vii. 24*t*, 51. viii. 15*t*, 16, 26, 50. xii. 47*t*, 48*t*. xvi. 11. xviii. 31. Acts iv. 19. vii. 7. xiii. 46. xvi. 15. xvii. 31. xxiii. 3. xxiv. 6(*ap*). xxv. 9, 10, 20. xxvi. 6.

Rom. ii. 1*tr*, 3, 12, 16, 27. iii. 4, 6, 7. xiv. 3, 4, 10, 13*t*. 1 Cor. iv. 5. v. 3 (*marg*. **determine**), 12*t*, 13. vi. 2*t*, 3. x. 15, 29. xi. 13, 31, 32ᵖ. 2 Cor. v. 14ᵖ. Col. ii. 16. 2 Tim. iv. 1. Heb. x. 30. xiii. 4. Jas. ii. 12. iv. 11*tr*, 12. 1 Pet. i. 17. ii. 23. iv. 5, 6. Rev. vi. 10. xi. 18. xvi. 5. xviii. 8. xix. 2, 11. xx. 12, 13.

ἐγὼ κρίνω, **my sentence is**, Acts xv. 19.

decree, 1 Cor. vii. 37.

ordain, Acts xvi. 4.

condemn, John iii. 17, 18*t*. Acts xiii. 27ᵖ. Rom. xiv. 22.

damn, 2 Thes. ii. 12.

With κρίμα, **avenge**, Rev. xviii. 20.

call in question, Acts xxiii. 6. xxiv. 21.

Mid. or Pass., **sue at the law**, Matt. v. 40. —**go to law**, 1 Cor. vi. 1, 6.

Add Jas. v. 9, for κατακρίνω, GLT*S*.

κρίσις.

judgment, Matt. v. 21, 22. x. 15. xi. 22, 24. xii. 18, 20, 36, 41, 42. xxiii. 23. Mark vi. 11(*ap*). Luke x. 14. xi. 31, 32, 42. John v. 22, 27, 30. vii. 24. viii. 16. xii. 31. xvi. 8, 11. Acts viii. 33.

2 Thes. i. 5. 1 Tim. v. 24. Heb. ix. 27. x. 27. Jas. ii. 13*t*. 2 Pet. ii. 4, 9. iii. 7. 1 John iv. 17. Jude 6, 15. Rev. xiv. 7. xvi. 7. xviii. 10. xix. 2.

condemnation, John iii. 19. v. 24. Jas. v. 12 (*see* ὑπόκρισις).

damnation, Matt. xxiii. 33. Mark iii. 29(ἁμάρτημα G″LTTr*S* ἁμαρτία, G″). John v. 29.

accusation, 2 Pet. ii. 11. Jude 9.

κριτήριον.

judgment-seat, Jas. ii. 6.

judgment, 1 Cor. vi. 4.

Gen., **to judge**ᶜᶜ, 1 Cor. vi. 2.

κριτής.

judge, Matt. v. 25*t*. xii. 27. Luke xi. 19. xii. 58*t*. xviii. 2, 6. Acts xiii. 20. xviii. 15. xxiv. 10. Jas. ii. 4. iv. 11.

Said of God or Christ, **Judge**, Acts x. 42. Heb. xii. 23. —**judge**, 2 Tim. iv. 8. Jas. v. 9.

Add Luke xii. 14, for δικαστής, L Tr*S*. Jas. iv. 12(Lawgiver καὶ κρ.), GLT*S*.

κριτικός.

discerner, Heb. iv. 12.

κρούω.

to knock, Matt. vii. 7, 8. Luke xi. 9, 10. xii. 36. xiii. 25. Acts xii. 13ᵖ, 16. Rev. iii. 20.

κρυπτός.

hid, Matt. x. 26. Mark iv. 22. Luke xii. 2.
hidden, 1 Pet. iii. 4.
Neut., **hidden thing**, 1 Cor. iv. 5. 2 Cor. iv. 2.
secret, Luke viii. 17.
secret, *subst.*, Rom. ii. 16. 1 Cor. xiv. 25.
With ἐν, **in secret**, Matt. vi. 4*t*, 6*t*, 18*t* (κρυφαῖος G″LTTr*S*). John vii. 4, 10. xviii. 20.—**inwardly**, Rom. ii. 29.
εἰς κρυπτήν, **in a secret place**, Luke xi. 33.

κρύπτω.

to hide, Matt. v. 14. xiii. 44*t*. xxv. 25. Luke xviii. 34. xix. 42. Col. iii. 3. 1 Tim. v. 25. Heb. xi. 23. Rev. ii. 17. vi. 15, 16.
Pass., **hide one's self**, John viii. 59. xii. 36.
keep secret, Matt. xiii. 35.
secretly, John xix. 38p.
Add, for ἀποκρύπτω, Matt. xi. 25; xxv. 18, LTTr*S*. For ἐγκρύπτω, Matt. xiii. 33, G′. Luke xiii. 21, TTr.

κρυσταλλίζω.

clear as crystal, Rev. xxi. 11p.

κρύσταλλος.

crystal, Rev. iv. 6. xxii. 1.

κρυφαῖος, hidden, secret.
Matt. vi. 18*t*, for κρυπτός, G″LTTr*S*.

κρυφῇ.

in secret, Eph. v. 12.

κτάομαι.

obtain, Acts xxii. 28.
provide (*marg.* **get**), Matt. x. 9.
purchase, Acts i. 18. viii. 20.
possess, Luke xviii. 12. xxi. 19. 1 Thes. iv. 4.

κτῆμα.

possession, Matt. xix. 22. Mark x. 22. Acts ii. 45. v. 1.

κτῆνος.

beast, Luke x. 34. Acts xxiii. 24. 1 Cor. xv. 39. Rev. xviii. 13.

κτήτωρ.

possessor, Acts iv. 34.

κτίζω.

create, Mark xiii. 19. 1 Cor. xi. 9. Eph. ii. 10. iii. 9. iv. 24. Col. i. 16*t*. iii. 10. 1 Tim. iv. 3. Rev. iv. 11*t*. x. 6.
Creator, Rom. i. 25p.
make, Eph. ii. 15.
Add Matt. xix. 4, for ποιέω, Tr.

κτίσις.

creation, Mark x. 6. xiii. 19. Rom. i. 20. viii. 22(*marg.* **creature**). 2 Pet. iii 4. Rev. iii. 14.
creature, Mark xvi. 15(*ap*). Rom. i. 25. viii. 19, 20, 21, 39. 2 Cor. v. 17. Gal. vi. 15. Col. i. 15, 23. Heb. iv. 13.
building, Heb. ix. 11.
ordinance, 1 Pet. ii. 13.

κτίσμα.

creature, 1 Tim. iv. 4. Jas. i. 18. Rev. v. 13. viii. 9.

κτίστης.

Creator, 1 Pet. iv. 19.

κυβεία.

sleight, Eph. iv. 14.

κυβέρνησις.

government, 1 Cor. xii. 28.

κυβερνήτης.

ship-master, Rev. xviii. 17.
master, Acts xxvii. 11.

κυκλεύω, encircle, surround.
Rev. xx. 9, for κυκλόω, G′LTTr.

κυκλόθεν.

round about, Rev. iv. 3, 4. v. 11 (*see* κύκλος).
about, Rev. iv. 8.

κύκλος.

Dat., **round about**, Mark iii. 34. vi. 6, 36. Luke ix. 12. Rom. xv. 19. Rev. iv. 6. vii. 11.
Add Rev. v. 11, for κυκλόθεν, GL TTr*S*.

κυκλόω.

to compass, Luke xxi. 20.

compass about, Heb. xi. 30p. Rev. xx. 9 (κυκλεύω G'LTTr).
come round about, John x. 24.
stand round about, Acts xiv. 20p.

κύλισμα.

wallowing, 2 Pet. ii. 22.

κυλίω.

Mid., **wallow**, Mark ix. 20.

κυλλός.

maimed, Matt. xv. 30, 31. xviii. 8. Mark ix. 43.

κῦμα.

wave, Matt. viii. 24. xiv. 24. Mark iv. 37. Acts xxvii. 41(-LT*S*). Jude 13.

κύμβαλον.

cymbal, 1 Cor. xiii. 1.

κύμινον.

cummin, Matt. xxiii. 23.

κυνάριον.

dog, Matt. xv. 26, 27. Mark vii. 27, 28.

κύπτω.

stoop down, Mark i. 7.
stoop, John viii. 6(*ap*), 8(*ap*).

κυρία, Κυρία LT.

lady, 2 John 1, 5.

κυριακός.

Lord's, 1 Cor. xi. 20. Rev. i. 10.

κυριεύω.

be Lord of, Rom. xiv. 9.
lord, 1 Tim. vi. 15p.
exercise lordship over, Luke xxii. 25.
have dominion over, Rom. vi. 9, 14. vii. 1. 2 Cor. i. 24.

κύριος.

lord, Matt. x. 24, 25. xviii. 25, 26 (-LTTr), 27, 31, 32, 34. xx. 8. xxi. 40. xxiv. 45, 46, 48, 50. xxv. 11*t*, 18, 19, 20, 21*t*, 22, 23*t*, 24, 26. Mark xii. 9. Luke xii. 36, 37, 42, 43, 45, 46, 47. xiii. 8. xiv. 22, 23. xvi. 3, 5*t*, 8. xix. 16, 18, 20, 25. xx. 13, 15. John xiii. 16. xv. 15, 20. Acts xxv. 26. 1 Cor. viii. 5. Gal. iv. 1. 1 Pet. iii. 6. Rev. xvii. 14. xix. 16.

master, Matt. vi. 24. xv. 27. Mark xiii. 35. Luke xiv. 21. xvi. 13. Acts xvi. 16, 19. Rom. xiv. 4. Eph. vi. 5, 9. Col. iii.22. iv. 1.
owner, Luke xix. 33.
sir, Matt. xiii. 27. xxi. 30. xxvii. 63. Luke xiv. 21. John iv. 11, 15, 19, 49. v. 7. xii. 21. xx. 15. Acts xvi. 30. Rev. vii. 14.

Said of God or Christ, **Lord**, Matt. i. 20, 22, 24. ii. 13, 15, 19. iii. 3. iv. 7, 10. v. 33. vii. 21*t*, 22*t*. viii. 2, 6, 8, 21, 25. ix. 28, 38. xi. 25. xii. 8. xiii. 51 (-G°LTTr*S*). xiv. 28, 30. xv. 22, 25, 27. xvi. 22. xvii. 4, 15. xviii. 21. xx. 30, 31, 33. xxi. 3, 9, 42. xxii. 37, 43, 44*t*, 45. xxiii. 39. xxiv. 42. xxv. 37, 44. xxvi. 22. xxvii. 10. xxviii. 2, 6(-TTrb*S*).

Mark i. 3. ii. 28. v. 19. vii. 28. ix. 24(*omS*). xi. 3, 9, 10(*ap*). xii. 11, 29*t*, 30, 36, 37. xiii. 20. xvi. 19 (*ap*), 20(*ap*).

Luke i. 6, 9, 11, 15, 16, 17, 25, 28, 32, 38, 43, 45, 46, 58, 66, 68, 76. ii. 9, 9(-G°), 11, 15, 22, 23*t*, 24, 26, 38(θεός LTr*S*), 39. iii. 4. iv. 8, 12, 18, 19. v. 8, 12, 17. vi. 5, 46*t*. vii. 6, 13, 31(*ap*). ix. 54, 57(-G°LTr*S*), 59, 61. x. 1, 2, 17, 21, 27, 40. xi. 1, 39. xii. 41, 42. xiii. 8, 15, 23, 25, 25(-LbTTr*S*), 35. xvii. 5, 6, 37. xviii. 6, 41. xix. 8*t*, 31, 34, 38. xx. 37, 42*t*, 44. xxii. 31(*ap*), 33, 38, 49, 61*t*. xxiii. 42 (-LbTTr*S*). xxiv. 3 (-T), 34.

John i. 23. iv. 1. vi. 23(-G°), 34, 68. viii. 11(*ap*). ix. 36, 38. xi. 2, 3, 12, 21, 27, 32, 34(35), 39. xii. 13, 38*t*. xiii. 6, 9, 13, 14, 25, 36, 37. xiv. 5, 8, 22. xx. 2, 13, 18, 20, 25, 28. xxi. 7*t*, 12, 15, 16, 17, 20, 21.

Acts i. 6, 21, 24. ii. 20, 21, 25, 34*t*, 36, 39, 47. iii. 19, 22. iv. 26, 29, 33. v. 9, 14, 19. vii. 30(-G°LT*S*), 31, 33, 37 (-G°°LT*S*), 49, 59, 60. viii. 16, 24, 25, 26, 39. ix. 1, 5, 5(-G°°LT*S*), 6*t*(*ap*), 10*t*, 11, 13, 15, 17, 27, 29(28), 31, 35, 42. x. 4, 14, 36, 48 (Ἰησοῦς Χριστός G'L*S*). xi. 8,

16, 17, 20, 21*t*, 23, 24. xii. 7, 11, 17, 23. xiii. 2, 10, 11, 12, 47, 48, 49. xiv. 3, 23. xv. 11, 17*t*, 26, 35, 36. xvi. 10(*ϑεός* G″L*S*), 14, 15, 31, 32. xvii. 24, 27 (G″, *ϑεός* GLT*S*). xviii. 8, 9, 25, 25 (Ἰησοῦς LT*S*). xix. 5, 10, 13, 17. xx. 19, 21, 24, 35. xxi. 13, 14, 20 (*ϑεός* GLT*S*). xxii. 8, 10*t*, 16 (*αὐτός* GLT*S*), 19. xxiii. 11. xxvi. 15. xxviii. 31.

Rom. i. 3(4), 7. iv. 8, 24. v. 1, 11, 21. vi. 11(*om*), 23. vii. 25. viii. 39. ix. 28, 29. x. 9, 12, 13, 16. xi. 3, 34. xii. 11(G″, *καιρός* StG), 19. xiii. 14. xiv. 6, 6 (*ap*), 6*t*, 8*tr*, 11, 14. xv. 6, 11, 30. xvi. 2, 8, 11, 12, 12 (*ap*), 13, 18, 20, 22, 24(*ap*).

1 Cor. i. 2, 3, 7, 8, 9, 10, 31. ii. 8, 16. iii. 5, 20. iv. 4, 5, 17, 19. v. 4*t*, 5. vi. 11, 13*t*, 14, 17. vii. 10, 12, 17 (*ϑεός* GLT*S*), 22*t*, 25*t*, 32*t*, 34, 35, 39. viii. 6. ix. 1*t*, 2, 5, 14. x. 21*t*, 22, 26, 28(*ap*). xi. 11, 23*t*, 26, 27*t*, 29 (-LT*S*), 32. xii. 3, 5. xiv. 21, 37. xv. 31, 47(-G^{oo}LT*S*), 57, 58*t*. xvi. 7, 10, 19, 22, 23.

2 Cor. i. 2, 3, 14. ii. 12. iii. 16, 17*t*, 18*t*. iv. 5, 10(*omS*), 14. v. 6, 8, 11. vi. 17, 18. viii. 5, 9, 19, 21. x. 8, 17, 18. xi. 17, 31. xii. 1, 8. xiii. 10, 14(13).

Gal. i. 3, 19. v. 10. vi. 14, 17(-G^{oo}LT). Eph. i. 2, 3, 15, 17. ii. 21. iii. 11, 14(*ap*). iv. 1, 5, 17. v. 8, 10, 17(*ϑεός* L^m), 19, 20, 22, 29(*Χριστός* GLT*S*). vi. 1 (-G^oL), 4, 7, 8, 10, 21, 23, 24. Phil. i. 2, 14. ii. 11, 19 (*Χριστός* L), 24, 29. iii. 1, 8, 20. iv. 1, 2, 4, 5, 10, 23(24). Col. i. 2 (*ap*), 3, 10. ii. 6. iii. 16(G′, *ϑεός* GLT*S*), 17(-G^{oo}L), 18, 20, 23, 24*t*. iv. 7, 17.

1 Thes. i. 1, 1(*ap*), 3, 6, 8. ii. 15, 19. iii. 8, 11, 12(-G^o), 13. iv. 1, 2, 15*t*, 16, 17*t*. v. 2, 9, 12, 23, 27, 28. 2 Thes. i. 1, 2, 7, 8, 9, 12*t*. ii. 8, 13, 14, 16. iii. 1, 3(*ϑεός* L), 4, 6, 12, 16*t*, 18.

1 Tim. i. 1(*om*), 2, 12, 14. v. 21 (-G^{oo}LT*S*). vi. 3, 14, 15. 2 Tim. i. 2, 8, 16, 18*t*. ii. 7, 14 (*ϑεός* L^m*S*), 19, 22, 24. iii. 11. iv. 1(*omS*), 8, 14, 17, 18, 22. Tit. i. 4 (-LT*S*). Phm. 3, 5, 16, 20, 20(*Χριστός* GLT*S*), 25.

Heb. i. 10. ii. 3. vii. 14, 21. viii. 2, 8, 9, 10, 11. x. 16, 30 (-G^{oo}*S*), 30. xii. 5, 6, 14. xiii. 6, 20. Jas. i. 1, 7, 12(-G^oLT*S*). ii. 1. iv. 10, 15. v. 4, 7, 8, 10, 11, 11(-G^{oo}T), 14, 15.

1 Pet. i. 3, 25. ii. 3, 13. iii. 12*t*, 15. 2 Pet. i. 2, 8, 11, 14, 16. ii. 9, 11(-G^{oo}LT), 20. iii. 2, 8, 9, 10, 15, 18. 2 John 3(-G^{oo}LT). Jude 4, 5 (Ἰησοῦς G″L), 9, 14, 17, 21.

Rev. i. 8. iv. 8, 11. vii. 14. xi. 8, 15, 17. xiv. 13. xv. 3, 4(-G^o). xvi. 5(*omS*), 7. xvii. 14. xviii. 8(-Tr^b). xix. 1(*omS*), 6, 16. xxi. 22. xxii. 5, 6, 20, 21.

—**Master,** Eph. vi. 9. Col. iv. 1.

Add, for *αὐτός*, Rev. xi. 19, G. For *ϑεός*, Luke xii. 20, L^m. Acts viii. 22, x. 33, G″LT*S*. xiii. 44, xv. 40, G′LT*S*. xix. 20, StEGLT*S*. xx. 28, GLT. Rom. xv. 32, *see ϑεός*. 1 Cor. vii. 17, Col. iii. 22, GLT*S*. Jas. iii. 9, G″LT*S*. Rev. xi. 4, GLTTr*S*. xiv. 7, G″.

For Ἰησοῦς, Luke x. 39, LTTr*S*. 41, L^mT*S*. For ὅτι, Mark i. 40, L^m. For *Χριστός*, Rom. xvi. 9, L. 1 Cor. ii. 16, L. x. 9, G″L*S*. Col. iii. 13, L. 2 Thes. ii. 2, 2 Tim. ii. 19, GLT*S*. —John v. 4(angel . .), L^b. Acts xiv. 10(*ap*). xxvi. 15 (he), LT*S*. Jude 25(*ap*).

κυριότης.

dominion, Eph. i. 21. Col. i. 16. Jude 8.

government (*marg.* **dominion**), 2 Pet. ii. 10.

κυρόω.

confirm, 2 Cor. ii. 8. Gal. iii. 15.

κύων.

dog, Matt. vii. 6. Luke xvi. 21. Phil. iii. 2. 2 Pet. ii. 22. Rev. xxii. 15.

κῶλον.

carcass, Heb. iii. 17.

κωλύω.

to hinder, Luke xi. 52 (*marg.* **forbid**). Acts viii. 36.
let, Rom. i. 13.
keep from, Acts xxvii. 43.
withstand, Acts xi. 17.
suffer not, Heb. vii. 23.
forbid, Matt. xix. 14. Mark ix. 38, 39. x. 14. Luke ix. 49, 50. xviii. 16. xxiii. 2. Acts x. 47. xvi. 6. xxiv. 23. 1 Cor. xiv. 39. 1 Thes. ii. 16. 1 Tim. iv. 3. 2 Pet. ii. 16. 3 John 10.
With ἀπό, **forbid to take**, Luke vi. 29.

κώμη.

village, Matt. ix. 35. xiv. 15. xxi. 2. Mark vi. 6, 36, 56. xi. 2. Luke viii. 1. ix. 52, 56. x. 38. xiii. 22. xvii. 12. xix. 30. xxiv. 13, 28. Acts viii. 25.
town, Matt. x. 11. Mark viii. 23, 26*t*, 27. Luke v. 17. ix. 6, 12. John vii. 42. xi 1, 30.

κωμόπολις.

town, Mark i. 38.

κῶμος.

revelling, Gal. v. 21. 1 Pet. iv. 3.
rioting, Rom. xiii. 13.

κώνωψ.

gnat, Matt. xxiii. 24.

κωφός.

dumb, Matt. ix. 32, 33. xii. 22*t*. xv. 30, 31. Luke xi. 14*t*.
speechless, Luke i. 22.
deaf, Matt. xi. 5. Mark vii. 32, 37. ix. 25. Luke vii. 22.

λαγχάνω.

be one's lot, Luke i. 9.
cast lots, John xix. 24.
obtain, Acts i. 17. 2 Pet. i. 1.

λάθρα.

secretly, John xi. 28.
privily, Matt. i. 19. ii. 7. Acts xvi. 37.

λαῖλαψ.

storm, Mark iv. 37. Luke viii. 23.
tempest, 2 Pet. ii. 17.

λακέω. See λάσκω.

λακτίζω.

to kick, Acts ix. 5(*ap*). xxvi. 14.

λαλέω.

speak, Matt. ix. 18[p], 33. x. 19, 19 (*ap*), 20*t*. xii. 22, 34*t*, 36. xiii. 3, 10, 13, 33, 34*t*. xiv. 27. xv. 31. xvii. 5[p]. xxiii. 1. xxvi. 47[p]. xxviii. 18. Mark i. 34(*marg.* **say**). ii. 7. iv. 33, 34. v. 35[p], 36. vii. 35, 37. viii. 32. xiii. 11*tr*. xiv. 43[p]. xvi. 17(*ap*), 19(*ap*).
Luke i. 19, 20, 22, 55, 64, 70. ii. 33, 38, 50. iv. 41(*marg.* **say**). v. 4, 21. vi. 45. vii. 15. viii. 49[p]. ix. 11 xi. 14, 37. xii. 3. xxii. 47[p], 60[p]. xxiv. 6, 25, 36[p], 44.
John i. 37. iii. 11, 31, 34. iv. 26 vi. 63. vii. 13, 17, 18, 26, 46. viii 12, 20, 28, 30[p], 38, 44*t*. ix. 21, 29 x. 6. xii. 29, 36, 41, 48, 49*t*, 50*t* xiv. 10(λέγω TTr), 10, 25. xv. 3, 11 22. xvi. 1, 13*t*, 25*t*, 29, 33. xvii. 1 13. xviii. 20, 23. xix. 10.
Acts ii. 4, 6, 7, 11, 31. iii. 21, 24 iv. 1[p], 17, 20, 29, 31. v. 20, 40. vi 10, 11, 13. vii. 6, 38, 44. viii. 26 ix. 27, 29. x. 7, 32(*ap*), 44[p], 46. x 15, 20. xiii. 46. xiv. 1, 9. xvi. 13 14, 32. xvii. 19[cc]. xviii. 9, 25. xix 6. xx. 30. xxi. 39. xxii. 9. xxii 9. xxvi. 14 (λέγω L*S*), 26. xxvii 21, 25.
Rom. vii. 1. 1 Cor. ii. 6, 7, 13. ii 1. xii. 3, 30. xiii. 1, 11. xiv. 2*t* 3, 4, 5*t*, 6*t*, 9, 9 (*with* εἰμί), 11*t*, 1 18, 19, 21, 23, 27, 28, 29, 34, 3 39. 2 Cor. ii. 17. iv. 13*t*. vii. 1 xi. 17*t*, 23. xii. 19. xiii. 3.
Eph. iv. 25. v. 19. vi. 20. Phil. 14. Col. iv. 3, 4. 1 Thes. i. 8. ii. 4, 16. 1 Tim. v. 13. Tit. ii. 1, 15.
Heb. i. 1, 2(1). ii. 2, 3, 5. iv. vi. 9. vii. 14. ix. 19[cc]. xi. 4 (*pas* StC[m]G″; *marg.* **be spoken of**). x 24, 25. xiii. 7. Jas. i. 19. ii. 12.

10. 1 Pet. iii. 10. iv. 11. 2 Pet. i. 21. iii. 16. 1 John iv. 5. 2 John 12. 3 John 14. Jude 15, 16. Rev. i. 12. x. 8. xiii. 5, 11, 15.

speak of, Mark xiv. 9. Rom. xv. 18.

speak with, Matt. xii. 46, 47.

Fut. pass., **to be spoken after,** Heb. iii. 5p.

talk, Matt. xii. 46p. Mark vi. 50. John iv. 27*t*. ix. 37. xiv. 30. xvi. 4. Acts xxvi. 31. Rev. iv. 1. xvii. 1. xxi. 9, 15.

talk with, Luke xxiv. 32.

say, Mark ix. 6(ἀποκρίνομαι Tr*S*). John viii. 25, 26. xvi. 6, 18. xviii. 20, 21. Acts iii. 22. xxiii. 7p(εἶπον L*S*), 18. xxvi. 22. Rom. iii. 19. 1 Cor. ix. 8. Heb. v. 5. xi. 18.

tell, Matt. xxvi. 13. Luke i. 45. ii. 17, 18, 20. John viii. 40. Acts ix. 6. x. 6(*ap*). xi. 14. xxii. 10. xxvii. 25.

utter, 2 Cor. xii. 4. Rev. x. 3, 4*t*.

preach, Mark ii. 2. Acts viii. 25. xi. 19. xiii. 42. xiv. 25p. xvi. 6.

Add, for εἶπον, Luke ii. 15, Lm*S*. For λέγω, Mark xi. 23, xii. 1, xiv. 31, LTTr*S*. John viii. 26, G''LTTr *S*. Acts xiii. 45, L*S*. 1 Cor. vi. 5, 5. xv. 34, LT*S*.

λαλιά.

speech, Matt. xxvi. 73. Mark xiv. 70(*ap*). John viii. 43.

saying, John iv. 42.

λαμά, λαμμᾶ, λεμά, λημά, λιμά.

lama, Matt. xxvii. 46. Mark xv. 34.

λαμβάνω.

take, Matt. viii. 17. x. 38 (ἄρῃ fr. ἄρω Lm). xiii. 31, 33. xiv. 19. xv. 26, 36. xvi. 5, 7. xvii. 25, 27. xxi. 35. xxii. 15. xxv. 1, 3, 4. xxvi. 26*t*, 27, 52. xxvii. 1, 6, 7, 9, 24, 30, 48, 59p. xxviii. 12, 15. Mark vi. 41p. ii. 27. viii. 6, 14. ix. 36. xii. 8, 19, 20, 21. xiv. 22*t*, 23.

Luke v. 5. vi. 4(-Go*S*). ix. 16, 39. xiii. 19, 21. xx. 28, 29, 30(*ap*), 31. xxii. 17, 19. xxiv. 30, 43. John vi. 7, 11. x. 17, 18. xii. 3, 13. xiii. 4, 12. xvi. 15. xviii. 31. xix. 1, 6, 23, 27, 40. xxi. 13. Acts i. 20, 25. ii. 23 (-GooLT*S*). ix. 25. xv. 14. xvi. 3. xvii. 9p. xxvii. 35. xxviii. 15.

Rom. vii. 8, 11. 1 Cor. x. 13. xi. 23, 24(*omS*). 2 Cor. xi. 8, 20. Heb. v. 1, 4. ix. 19. Jas. v. 10. 3 John 7. Rev. iii. 11. v. 7, 8, 9. vi. 4. viii. 5. x. 8, 9, 10. xxii. 17.

take to one's self, Rev. xi. 17.

take upon one's self, Phil. ii. 7.

take up, Matt. xvi. 9, 10.

take away, Matt. v. 40.

catch, Matt. xxi. 39. Mark xii. 3. 2 Cor. xii. 16.

come on, Luke vii. 16.

receive, Matt. vii. 8. x. 8, 41*t*. xiii. 20. xvii. 24. xix. 29. xx. 7(*ap*), 9, 10*t*, 11p. xxi. 22, 34. xxiii. 14(13, *ap*). xxv. 16, 18, 20, 22(-GoLTTr), 24. Mark iv. 16. x. 30. xi. 24. xii. 2, 40. xv. 23.

Luke xi. 10. xix. 12, 15. xx. 47. John i. 12, 16. iii. 11, 27(*marg.* **take unto one's self**), 32, 33. iv. 36. v. 34, 41, 43*t*, 44. vi. 21. vii. 23, 39. x. 18. xii. 48. xiii. 20*f*, 30. xiv. 17. xvi. 14, 24. xvii. 8. xviii. 3. xix. 30. xx. 22. Acts i. 8. ii. 33, 38. iii. 5. vii. 53. viii. 15, 17, 19. ix. 19p. x. 43, 47. xvi. 24. xvii. 15. xix. 2. xx. 24, 35. xxvi. 10, 18.

Rom. i. 5. iv. 11. v. 11, 17. viii. 15*t*. xiii. 2. 1 Cor. ii. 12. iii. 8, 14. iv. 7*tr*. ix. 24. xiv. 5. 2 Cor. xi. 4*t*, 24. Gal. iii. 2, 14. Col. iv. 10. 1 Tim. iv. 4p.

Heb. ii. 2. vii. 5, 8, 9. ix. 15. x. 26. xi. 8, 11, 13(προσδέχομαι L, κομίζομαι *S*), 35. Jas. i. 7, 12. iii. 1. iv. 3. v. 7. 1 Pet. iv. 10. 2 Pet. i. 17. 1 John ii. 27. iii. 22. v. 9. 2 John 4, 10. Rev. ii. 17, 27. iii. 3. iv. 11. v. 12. xiv. 9, 11. xvii. 12*t*. xviii. 4. xix. 20. xx. 4.

obtain, 1 Cor. ix. 25. Heb. iv. 16.

attain, Phil. iii. 12.

accept, Luke xx. 21. Gal. ii. 6.

have, Mark xii. 22(-L^bTTr*S*). Acts xxv. 16. Heb. xi. 36.
hold, Matt. xii. 14(*marg.* **take**).
bring, Matt. xvi. 8 (ἔχετε fr. ἔχω L*S*).
call to^cc, 2 Tim. i. 5^p.
Not rendered, Acts iii. 3(-G^oo).
Add, for ἀπολαμβάνω, Luke vi. 34, TTr*S*. xviii. 30, L. For βάλλω, Mark xiv. 65, G″LTTr*S*. For παραλαμβάνω, Acts xxi. 32, L.—John xiii. 26(λαμβάνει καὶ gave), TTr.
See also ἀρχή, διάδοχος, ἔκστασις, λήθη, πεῖρα.

λαμμᾶ. See λαμά.

λαμπάς.

torch, John xviii. 3.
light, Acts xx. 8.
lamp, Matt. xxv. 1, 3, 4, 7, 8. Rev. iv. 5. viii. 10.

λαμπρός.

bright, Acts x. 30. Rev. xxii. 16.
white, Rev. xv. 6. xix. 8.
clear, Rev. xxii. 1.
gorgeous, Luke xxiii. 11.
gay, Jas. ii. 3.
goodly, Jas. ii. 2. Rev. xviii. 14.

λαμπρότης.

brightness, Acts xxvi. 13.

λαμπρῶς.

sumptuously, Luke xvi. 19.

λάμπω.

shine, Matt. v. 16. xvii. 2. Luke xvii. 24. Acts xii. 7. 2 Cor. iv. 6*t*.
give light, Matt. v. 15.

λανθάνω.

be hid (hidden), Mark vii. 24. Luke viii. 47. Acts xxvi. 26.
unawares^cc, Heb. xiii. 2.
be ignorant of^cc, 2 Pet. iii. 5, 8.

λαξευτός.

hewn in stone, Luke xxiii. 53.

λαός.

people, Matt. i. 21. ii. 4, 6. iv. 16, 23. ix. 35(*om*). xiii. 15. xv. 8. xxi. 23. xxvi. 3, 5, 47. xxvii. 1, 25, 64. Mark vii. 6. xi. 32. xiv. 2. Luke i. 10, 17, 21, 68, 77. ii. 10, 31^pl, 32. iii. 15, 18, 21. vi. 17. vii. 1, 16, 29. viii. 47. ix. 13. xviii. 43. xix. 47, 48. xx. 1, 6, 9, 19, 26, 45. xxi. 23, 38. xxii. 2, 66. xxiii. 5, 13, 14, 27, 35. xxiv. 19. John viii. 2(*ap*). xi. 50. xviii. 14.
Acts ii. 47. iii. 9, 11, 12, 23. iv. 1, 2, 8, 10, 17, 21, 25^pl, 27^pl. v. 12, 13, 20, 25, 26, 34, 37. vi. 8, 12. vii. 17, 34. x. 2, 41, 42. xii. 4, 11. xiii. 15, 17*t*, 24, 31. xv. 14. xviii. 10. xix. 4. xxi. 28, 30, 36, 39, 40. xxiii. 5. xxvi. 17, 23. xxviii. 17, 26, 27.
Rom. ix. 25*t*, 26. x. 21. xi. 1, 2. xv. 10, 11^pl. 1 Cor. x. 7. xiv. 21. 2 Cor. vi. 16. Tit. ii. 14. Heb. ii. 17. iv. 9. v. 3. vii. 5, 11, 27. viii. 10. ix. 7, 19*t*. x. 30. xi. 25. xiii. 12. 1 Pet. ii. 9, 10*t*. 2 Pet. ii. 1. Jude 5. Rev. v. 9. vii. 9^pl. x. 11. xi. 9^pl. xiv. 6. xvii. 15. xviii. 4. xxi. 3^pl.
Add Rev. xiii. 7 (καὶ λαὸν and tongues), GLTTr*S*.

λάρυγξ.

throat, Rom. iii. 13.

λάσκω.

burst asunder, Acts i. 18.

λατομέω.

hew, Matt. xxvii. 60. Mark xv. 46.

λατρεία.

service, John xvi. 2. Rom. ix. 4. xii. 1. Heb. ix. 6^pl.
divine service, Heb. ix. 1.

λατρεύω.

serve, Matt. iv. 10. Luke i. 74 ii. 37. iv. 8. Acts vii. 7. xxvi. 7. xxvii. 23. Rom. i. 9, 25. 2 Tim. i 3. Heb. viii. 5. ix. 14. xii. 28. xiii 10. Rev. vii. 15. xxii. 3.
do service, Heb. ix. 9.
worship, Acts vii. 42. xxiv. 14 Phil. iii. 3.
worshipper, Heb. x. 2^p.

λάχανον.

herb, Matt. xiii. 32. Mark iv. 32 Luke xi. 42^cc. Rom. xiv. 2.

λεγεών.

legion, Matt. xxvi. 53. Mark v. 15 (–G∞).
Legion, Mark v. 9. Luke viii. 30.
λεγιών, Mark v. 15, LTTr*S*.

λέγω.

(*Joined with ἀποκρίνομαι, εἶπον, ἐρῶ, ἐρωτάω, λαλέω, or φημί, marked* [a].)

put forth, Luke xiv. 7.
give out, Acts viii. 9.
show, 1 Cor. xv. 51.
describe, Rom. iv. 6.
tell, Matt. x. 27[a]. xxi. 27[a]. Mark i. 30. viii. 30 (εἶπον L). x. 32. xi. 33. Luke iv. 25. ix. 27. x. 24. xii. 51, 59. xiii. 3, 5, 27[a]. xvii. 34. xviii. 8, 14. xix. 40[a]. xx. 8[a]. xxii. 34[a]. xxiv. 10. John viii. 45. xii. 22*t*. xiii. 19. xvi. 7. Acts xvii. 21. xxii. 27[a]. Gal. iv. 21. Phil. iii. 18*t*. 2 Thes. ii. 5. Jude 18.
utter, Heb. v. 11.
say, Matt. i. 20, 22[a]. ii. 2, 13, 15[a], 17[a], 20. iii. 2, 3[a], 9*t*, 14, 17. iv. 6 (εἶπον L), 9 (εἶπον LTr*S*), 10, 14[a], 17, 19. v. 2, 18, 20, 22[a], 26, 28[a], 32[a], 34[a], 39[a], 44[a]. vi. 2, 5, 16, 25, 29, 31. vii. 21. viii. 2, 3, 4[a], 6, 7, 9, 10[a], 11, 17[a], 20, 25, 26, 27, 29, 31. ix. 6, 9, 14, 18[a], 21, 24(23), 27, 28*t*, 29, 30, 33, 34, 37. x. 5, 7, 15, 23, 42. xi. 7, 9, 11, 17, 18, 19, 22, 24. xii. 6, 10[a], 13, 17[a], 23, 31, 36, 38, 44. xiii. 3[a], 14, 17, 24, 31, 35[a], 36, 51(*ap*), 51, 54. xiv. 4, 15, 17, 26, 27[a], 30, 31, 33. xv. 1, 4 (*see* εἶπον), 5[a], 7, 22, 23, 25, 33, 34. xvi. 2[a], 7, 13[a], 13, 15*t*, 18, 22, 28. xvii. 5, 9[a], 10*t*, 12, 14, 20, 25[a], 25, 26 (*ap*). xviii. 1, 3[a], 10, 13, 18, 19, 22*t*, 26, 28, 29, 32. xix. 3, 7, 8, 9, 10, 18(ἔφη fr. φημί L*S*), 20, 23[a], 24, 25, 28[a]. xx. 6, 7*t*, 8, 12, 21, 22, 23, 30, 31, 33. xxi. 2, 4[a], 9, 10, 11, 13, 15, 16*t*, 19, 20, 21[a], 23, 25, 31*tr*, 37, 41, 42, 43. xxii. 1[a], 4[a], 8, 12, 16, 20, 21*t*, 23, 24[a], 31[a], 35[a] (–LTr*S*), 42[a], 42, 43*t*. xxiii. 2[a], 3, 16, 30, 36, 39[a]. xxiv. 2[a], 3[a], 5, 34, 47. xxv. 9[a], 11, 12[a], 20, 37[a], 40[a], 44[a], 45[a], 45. xxvi. 5, 8, 13, 17, 18[a], 21[a], 22, 25[a], 27, 29, 31, 34[a], 35, 36, 38, 39, 40, 42, 45, 48, 52, 64[a], 64, 65, 68, 69, 70*t*, 71. xxvii. 4, 9[a], 11[a], 11, 13, 19, 22[a], 22, 23, 24, 29, 40, 41, 46, 47, 49 (εἶπον LTr), 54, 63. xxviii. 9, 10, 13[a], 18[a].

Mark i. 7, 15, 24, 25, 27, 37, 38, 40, 41, 44. ii. 5, 10, 11, 12 (–L[b]), 14, 16, 17, 18, 24, 25, 27. iii. 3, 4, 5, 11, 21, 22, 23, 28, 30, 33[a], 34. iv. 2, 9, 11, 13, 21, 24, 26, 30, 35, 38, 41. v. 8, 9, 12, 19, 23, 28, 30, 31*t*, 35[a], 36[a], 39, 41*t*. vi. 2, 4, 10, 11(*ap*), 14, 15*t*, 18, 25, 35, 37, 38*t*, 50[a]. vii. 9, 11[a], 14, 18, 20, 28[a], 34, 37. viii. 1, 12*t*, 15, 16(–LTTr*S*), 17, 19, 21[a], 24(εἶπον L[m]*S*), 26, 27[a], 27, 29(ἐπηρώτα fr. ἐπερωτάω G′LTTr*S*), 29*t*, 33. ix. 1*t*, 5[a], 7(–GTTr*S*), 11[a], 11, 13, 19[a], 24, 25, 26, 31, 35, 38, 41. x. 11, 15, 23, 24[a], 26, 27, 28, 29[a], 35, 42, 47, 49, 51[a](εἶπον TTr*S*). xi. 2, 5, 9(–G°L[b]TTr*S*), 17, 21, 22[a], 23[a], 23(λαλέω LTTr*S*), 24, 28, 31[a], 33[a], 33. xii. 6, 14, 16[a], 18, 18[a], 26[a], 35[a], 35, 38, 43[a] (G′, εἶπον GLTr*S*), 43. xiii. 1, 5[a], 6, 30, 37*t*. xiv. 2, 4 (–TTr[b]*S*), 9[a], 12, 13, 14[a], 18[a], 19, 25, 27, 30*t*, 31, 32, 34, 36, 37, 41, 44, 45, 57, 58, 60[a], 61[a], 63, 65, 67, 68*t*, 69, 70. xv. 2, 4[a], 9[a], 14, 28(*ap*), 29, 31, 34 (–TTr*S*), 35, 36. xvi. 3, 6.

Luke i. 24, 63, 66, 67. ii. 13. iii. 4(–G∞LTTr*S*), 7, 8*t*, 10[a], 11[a], 14[a], 16[a], 22 (–G∞LTTr*S*). iv. 4[a] (–TTr *S*), 21, 22[a], 24[a], 34 (–TTr[b]*S*), 35, 36, 41. v. 8, 12, 21[a], 24[a], 26, 30, 39. vi. 5, 20, 27, 42, 46. vii. 4, 6, 8, 9[a], 14[a], 16, 19, 20[a], 26, 28, 32, 33, 34, 39, 47, 49. viii. 8[p], 9[a](–G° LTr*S*), 20(–LTr*S*), 24, 25, 30[a](–L *S*), 38, 45[a](*ap*), 49[a], 50[a](–LTTr*S*), 54. ix. 7, 18, 20, 23, 33, 35, 38. x. 2, 5, 9, 12, 17, 25. xi. 2[a], 8, 9, 18, 24, 29, 45[a], 45, 51, 53[p](*ap*). xii. 1, 4, 5, 8, 16[a], 17, 22[a], 27, 37, 44, 54*t*, 55. xiii. 8[a], 14[a], 17[p], 18, 24, 25[a],

26, 31, 35ᵃ. xiv. 3ᵃ(-Lᵇ), 7, 12, 24, 30. xv. 2, 3, 6, 7, 9, 10. xvi. 1, 5ᵃ, 7, 9, 29. xvii. 4, 6, 10, 13, 37. xviii. 2, 3, 6, 13, 17, 18, 29ᵃ, 38, 41 (-T Trᵇ*S*). xix. 7, 14, 16, 18, 20, 22, 26, 38, 42, 46. xx. 2ᵃ(-Tr), 5, 14, 21ᵃ, 21, 28ᵃ, 41, 42ᵃ. xxi. 3ᵃ, 7ᵃ, 8, 10, 32. xxii. 11ᵃ, 16, 18, 19, 20, 37, 42, 57, 59, 60, 64, 66ᵃ, 70ᵃ. xxiii. 2*t*, 3*t*, 5, 18, 21, 30, 34(*ap*), 35, 37, 39 (-TTrᵇ), 40 (ἔφη fr. φημί TTr*S*), 42, 43ᵃ, 47. xxiv. 7ᵃ, 23*t*, 29, 34, 36ᵃ(*ap*).

John i. 15ᵃ, 21, 22, 26ᵃ, 29, 32, 36, 38, 39(40), 41(42), 43(44), 45(46), 46(47)ᵃ, 47(48), 48(49)ᵃ, 49(50)ᵃ (-LᵇTTr, εἶπον *S*), 51(52)*t*. ii. 3, 4, 5*t*, 7, 8, 10, 22ᵃ. iii. 3ᵃ, 4, 5, 11ᵃ. iv. 7, 9, 10ᵃ, 11, 15, 16ᵃ, 17ᵃ, 19, 20, 21, 25, 26ᵃ, 28ᵃ, 31ᵃ, 33, 34, 35*t*, 42, 49, 50, 51. v. 6, 8, 10, 18, 19ᵃ. 24, 25, 34. vi. 5, 6, 8, 12, 14, 20, 26ᵃ, 32ᵃ, 42*t*, 47, 52, 53ᵃ, 65ᵃ. vii. 6, 11, 12*t*, 15, 25, 26, 28, 31, 37, 40, 41*t*, 50. viii. 4(*ap*), 5(*ap*), 6(*ap*), 12, 19, 22*t*, 25ᵃ, 31, 33, 34, 39ᵃ, 46, 48ᵃ, 51, 52ᵃ, 54, 58ᵃ. ix. 2, 8, 9*t*, 10, 12ᵃ, 16*t*, 17*t*, 19*t*, 41ᵃ. x. 1, 7ᵃ, 20, 21, 24, 33(-G∞LTTr*S*), 36ᵃ, 41ᵃ. xi. 3, 7, 8, 11ᵃ, 23, 24, 27, 31(δόξαντες fr. δοκέω G'Tr*S*), 32, 34(35)ᵃ, 36, 39*t*, 40ᵃ, 44, 47. xii. 4, 21, 23ᵃ, 24, 29, 29ᵃ, 33, 34. xiii. 6, 8, 9, 10, 13, 16, 20, 21ᵃ, 25, 27, 29, 31, 33ᵃ, 36, 37, 38. xiv. 5, 6, 8, 9*t*, 12, 22. xvi. 12, 17ᵃ, 18ᵃ, 18, 20, 23, 26ᵃ, 29. xviii. 5, 17*t*, 26, 34ᵃ, 37, 38*t*, 40. xix. 3, 4, 5, 6*t*, 9, 10ᵃ, 12, 14, 15, 21ᵃ, 24 (-L*S*), 26, 27, 28, 35, 37. xx. 2, 13*t*, 15*t*, 16*t*, 17, 19, 22, 25, 27ᵃ, 29. xxi. 3*t*, 5, 7, 10, 12, 15*tr*, 16*tr*, 17ᵃ, 17, 18. 19ᵃ, 21, 22.

Acts i. 6ᵃ. ii. 7, 12, 13, 17, 34ᵃ, 40. iii. 25. iv. 16, 32. v. 23, 25(*om S*), 28ᵃ, 38. vi. 11, 13, 14. vii. 48, 49, 59. viii. 10, 19, 26ᵃ. ix. 4, 21. x. 26. xi. 3, 4, 7, 16, 18. xii. 7, 8ᵃ, 15ᵃ (εἶπον L). xiii. 15, 25, 35. xiv. 11, 15. xv. 5, 13ᵃ, 17, 24(*ap*). xvi. 9, 15, 17, 28, 35. xvii. 7, 18*t*, 19. xviii. 13. xix. 4ᵃ, 13, 26, 28. xx. 23. xxi. 4, 11, 21, 23, 37ᵃ, 40. xxii. 7, 18, 22, 26. xxiii. 8, 9, 12, 30. xxiv. 2. xxv. 14. xxvi. 14ᵃ(-G'L*S*), 22ᵃ, 31ᵃ. xxvii. 10, 24, 33. xxviii. 4, 6, 17, 26ᵃ.

Rom. ii. 22. iii. 8ᵃ, 19ᵃ. iv. 3, 9. vii. 7ᵃ. ix. 1, 15, 17, 25. x. 8, 11, 16, 18, 19*t*, 20, 21. xi. 1, 2, 2(*om*), 4, 9, 11. xii. 3, 19. xiv. 11. xv. 8, 10, 12.

1 Cor. i. 12*t*. iii. 4. vii. 8. ix. 8ᵃ, 10. x. 29. xi. 25. xiv. 16ᵃ, 21ᵃ, 34ᵃ. xv. 12. 2 Cor. vi. 2, 17, 18. ix. 3, 4. xi. 16.

Gal. i. 9. iii. 16ᵃ, 17. iv. 1, 30. v. 2, 16. Eph. iv. 8, 17. v. 14. Col. ii. 4. 1 Thes. iv. 15. v. 3. 1 Tim. i. 7. v. 18. 2 Tim. ii. 7, 18. Tit. ii. 8. Phm. 19, 21.

Heb. i. 6, 7. ii. 6, 12. iii. 7, 15. iv. 7ᵃ. v. 6. vi. 14. vii. 21. viii. 8*t*, 9. 10, 11, 13. ix. 20. x. 5, 8ᵖ, 16, 30(-G∞*S*). xi. 14, 32. xii. 26. xiii. 6. Jas. i. 13. ii. 14, 23. iv. 5, 6, 13, 15. 2 Pet. iii. 4. 1 John ii. 4, 6, 9. v. 16. Jude 14.

Rev. i. 8, 11, 17. ii. 1, 7, 8, 9, 11, 12, 17, 18, 24, 29. iii. 1, 6, 7, 9, 13, 14, 17, 22. iv. 1ᵃ, 8, 10. v. 5, 9, 12, 13, 14. vi. 1, 3, 5, 6, 7, 10, 16. vii. 3, 10, 12, 13ᵃ. viii. 13. ix. 14. x. 4ᵃ, 8ᵃ, 9*t*, 11. xi. 1, 12, 15, 17. xii. 10. xiii. 4, 14. xiv. 7, 8, 9, 13*t*, 18. xv. 3. xvi. 1, 5, 7, 17. xvii. 1ᵃ, 15 (εἶπον L). xviii. 2, 4, 7, 10, 16, 18, 19, 21. xix. 1, 4, 5, 6, 9*t*, 10, 17. xxi. 3, 5ᵃ, 9ᵃ. xxii. 9, 10, 17ᵃ, 20.

With ταῦτα, **with these sayings**, Acts xiv. 18ᵖ.

Pass., **be to say**, John i. 38(39). xx. 16.—**to say**, Matt. xxvii. 33ᵖ (-G∘).

say on, Acts xiii. 15.

speak, Matt. xxi. 45. Mark xii. 1 (λαλέω LTTr*S*). xiv. 31 (λαλέω LT Tr*S*), 71. Luke v. 36. vii. 24. ix. 31, 34ᵖ. xi. 27ᵃ. xii. 41ᵃ. xiii. 6. xviii. 1. xx. 9. xxi. 5ᵖᵃ. xxii. 65.

John ii. 21. viii. 26 (*λαλέω* G″LT Tr*S*), 27. xi. 13[a], 56. xiii. 18, 22, 24. xvi. 29. Acts i. 3. ii. 25. viii. 34[a]. xxiv. 10. xxvi. 1.

Rom. iii. 5. vi. 19. x. 6[a]. xi. 13. 1 Cor. i. 10. vi. 5 (*λαλέω* L). vii. 6, 12, 35. x. 15[a]. xv. 34(*λαλέω* LT*S*). 2Cor. vi. 13. vii. 3. viii. 8. xi. 21*t*. Gal. iii. 15. Eph. v. 12, 32. Phil. iv. 11. 1 Tim. ii. 7. iv. 1. Heb. vii. 13. viii. 1. ix. 5. Rev. ii. 24. viii. 11.

τὰ λεγόμενα, **the (those) things which were spoken**, Luke xviii. 34. Acts xiii. 45 (*λαλέω* L*S*). xxvii. 11. xxviii. 24.—**the (those) things which . . spake (hath spoken)**, Acts viii. 6. Heb. viii. 1.

speak of, John vi. 71.

boast, Acts v. 36.

ask, Acts xxv. 20.

bid, 2 John 10, 11.

call, Matt. i. 16. ii. 23. iv. 18. x. 2. xiii. 55. xix. 17(*ap*). xxvi. 3, 14, 36. xxvii. 16, 17, 22, 33. Mark x. 18. xii. 37. xv. 12(–*ὃν λ.* LTr). Luke xviii. 19. xx. 37. xxii. 1, 47. John iv. 5, 25. ix. 11. xi. 16, 54. xv. 15. xix. 13, 17*t*. xx. 24. xxi. 2. Acts iii. 2. vi. 9. ix. 36. x. 28. xxiv. 14. 1 Cor. viii. 5. xii. 3[a]. Eph. ii. 11*t*. Col. iv. 11. 2 Thes. ii. 4. Heb. viii. 11. ix. 2, 3. xi. 24. Rev. ii. 20.

name, Matt. ix. 9. Mark xv. 7.

Add, for *ἀντιλέγω*, Luke xx. 27, L[m]Tr*S*. For *εἶπον*, Matt. viii. 22, xiii. 28, xvii. 20, LTTr*S*. ix. 11, xii. 48[a], LTr*S*. xv. 12, LTTr. Mark ii. 8, vi. 16, 31, vii. 36, TTr*S*. iii. 32, vii. 27, LTTr*S*. v. 7, G″LTTr*S*. xii. 16, L[m]. 36[a], GTTr. xv. 12, Tr. Luke v. 13, LTr*S*. ix. 21[a], GLTr*S*. xviii. 16, L[m]Tr*S*. xix. 30, LTr*S*. John viii. 23, LTTr*S*. xviii. 4, LT Tr. xxi. 17[a], L[m]*S*. Rev. xxii. 6, G″.

For *λαλέω*, John xiv. 10[a], TTr. Acts xxvi. 14, L*S*. For *φημί*, Matt. xix. 21, L. — Mark viii. 28[a] (answered . .), LTTr*S*. xv. 13 (. . Crucify), L*S*. John ix. 9(said[2d]), L[b]TTr*S*. xii. 13 (cried . .), L[b]*S*. xiii. 24[a](*ap*). Acts xiv. 10 (*ap*). Rom. xv. 11 (again . .), L. Rev. ii. 2(*ap*).

λεῖμμα.

remnant, Rom. xi. 5.

λεῖος.

smooth, Luke iii. 5.

λείπω.

to lack, Luke xviii. 22[cc].

be wanting, Tit. i. 5 (*marg.* **be left undone**). iii. 13.

Pass., **destitute**, Jas. ii. 15[p].—**lack**, Jas. i. 5. — *With ἐν*, **want**, Jas. i. 4.

λειτουργέω.

to minister, Acts xiii. 2[p]. Rom. xv. 27. Heb. x. 11.

λειτουργία.

service, 2 Cor. ix. 12. Phil. ii. 17, 30.

ministration, Luke i. 23.

ministry, Heb. viii. 6. ix. 21.

λειτουργικός.

ministering, Heb. i 14.

λειτουργός.

minister, Rom. xiii. 6. xv. 16. Heb. i. 7. viii. 2.

he that ministereth, Phil. ii. 25.

λέντιον.

towel, John xiii. 4, 5.

λεπίς.

scale, Acts ix. 18.

λέπρα.

leprosy, Matt. viii. 3. Mark i. 42. Luke v. 12, 13.

λεπρός.

leper, Matt. viii. 2. x. 8. xi. 5. xxvi. 6. Mark i. 40. xiv. 3. Luke iv. 27. vii. 22. xvii. 12.

λεπτόν.

mite, Mark xii. 42. Luke xii. 59. xxi. 2.

λευκαίνω.

to white, Mark ix. 3.

make white, Rev. vii. 14.

λευκός.

white, Matt. v. 36. xvii. 2. xxviii. 3. Mark ix. 3. xvi. 5. Luke ix. 29. John iv. 35. xx. 12. Acts i. 10. Rev. i. 14*t*. ii. 17. iii. 4, 5, 18. iv. 4. vi. 2, 11. vii. 9, 13. xiv. 14. xix. 11, 14*t*. xx. 11.

λέων.

lion, 2 Tim. iv. 17. Heb. xi. 33. 1 Pet. v. 8. Rev. iv. 7. ix. 8, 17. x. 3. xiii. 2.

Said of Christ, **Lion,** Rev. v. 5.

λήθη.

With λαμβάνω, **forget,** 2 Pet. i. 9.

ληκέω. See **λάσκω.**

ληνός.

wine-press, Matt. xxi. 33. Rev. xiv. 19, 20*t*. xix. 15 (*with* οἶνος).

λῆρος.

idle tales, Luke xxiv. 11.

λῃστής.

robber, John x. 1, 8. xviii. 40. 2 Cor. xi. 26.

thief, Matt. xxi. 13. xxvi. 55. xxvii. 38, 44. Mark xi. 17. xiv. 48. xv. 27. Luke x. 30, 36. xix. 46. xxii. 52.

λῆψις, λῆμψις LT*S*.

receiving, Phil. iv. 15.

λίαν.

greatly, Matt. xxvii. 14. 2 Tim. iv. 15. 2 John 4. 3 John 3.

ὑπὲρ λίαν, ὑπερλίαν GLT, **very chiefest,** 2 Cor. xi. 5. xii. 11.

sore, Mark vi. 51(-G°).

exceeding, Matt. ii. 16. iv. 8. viii. 28. Mark ix. 3. Luke xxiii. 8.

See also ἔννυχον, πρωΐ.

λίβανος.

frankincense, Matt. ii. 11. Rev. xviii. 13.

λιβανωτός.

censer, Rev. viii. 3, 5.

λιθάζω.

to stone, John x. 31, 32, 33. xi. 8. Acts v. 26. xiv. 19. 2 Cor. xi. 25. Heb. xi. 37.

λίθινος.

of stone, John ii. 6. 2 Cor. iii. 3. Rev. ix. 20.

λιθοβολέω.

cast stones, Mark xii. 4(-G°°LTr*S*).

stone, Matt. xxi. 35. xxiii. 37. Luke xiii. 34. John viii. 5(*ap*). Acts vii. 58, 59. xiv. 5. Heb. xii. 20.

λίθος.

stone, Matt. iii. 9. iv. 3, 6. vii. 9. xxi. 42, 44(*ap*). xxvii. 60, 66. xxviii. 2. Mark v. 5. xii. 10. xiii. 1. xv. 46. xvi. 3, 4. Luke iii. 8. iv. 3, 11. xi. 11. xix. 40. xx. 17, 18. xxi. 5. xxii. 41. xxiv. 2. John viii. 7(*ap*), 59. x. 31. xi. 38, 39, 41. xx. 1. Acts iv 11. xvii. 29.

1 Cor. iii. 12. 2 Cor. iii. 7. 1 Pet. ii. 4, 5, 6, 7, 8(7). Rev. iv. 3. xvii. 4. xviii. 12, 16, 21. xxi. 11*t*, 19.

λίθος ἐπὶ λίθῳ (*λίθον*), **one stone upon another,** Matt. xxiv. 2. Mark xiii. 2. Luke xix. 44. xxi. 6.

λίθος μυλικός, **millstone,** Mark ix. 42 (*μύλος ὀνικός* G′LTr*S*).

λίθος προσκόμματος, **stumbling-stone,** Rom. ix. 32, 33.

Add Luke xvii. 2, *λίθος μυλικός* for *μύλος ὀνικός*, G″LTTr*S*. Rev. xv. 6, for *λίνον*, L.

λικμάω.

grind to powder, Matt. xxi. 44(*ap*). Luke xx. 18.

λιμήν.

haven, Acts xxvii. 12*t*.

Καλοὶ Λιμένες, **The fair havens,** Acts xxvii. 8.

λίμνη.

lake, Luke v. 1, 2. viii. 22, 23, 33. Rev. xix. 20. xx. 10, 14, 15. xxi. 8.

Add Rev. xx. 14(*ap*).

λιμός.

hunger, Luke xv. 17. 2 Cor. xi. 27. Rev. vi. 8.

famine, Matt. xxiv. 7. Mark xiii. 8. Luke iv. 25. xv. 14. xxi. 11. Rom. viii. 35. Rev. xviii. 8.

dearth, Acts vii. 11. xi. 28.

λίνον.

flax, Matt. xii. 20.
linen, Rev. xv. 6 (λίθος L).

λιπαρός.

dainty, Rev. xviii. 14.

λίτρα.

pound, John xii. 3. xix. 39.

λίψ.

south west, Acts xxvii. 12.

λογία.

gathering, 1 Cor. xvi. 2.
collection, 1 Cor. xvi. 1.

λογίζομαι.

Middle and Passive.

to number, Mark xv. 28(*ap*).
account, Rom. viii. 36. Gal. iii. 6 (*marg.* **impute**). Heb. xi. 19.
account of, 1 Cor. iv. 1.
count, Rom. ii. 26. iv. 3, 5. ix. 8. Phil. iii. 13.
With εἰς οὐδέν (οὐθέν LT*S*), **despise**, Acts xix. 27.
lay to one's charge, 2 Tim. iv. 16.
reckon, Luke xxii. 37. Rom. iv. 4, 9, 10. vi. 11. viii. 18.
impute, Rom. iv. 6, 8, 11, 22, 23, 24. 2 Cor. v. 19. Jas. ii. 23.
reason, Mark xi. 31 (διαλογίζομαι G′LTTr, προσλογίζομαι *S*).
think, Rom. ii. 3. 1 Cor. xiii. 5, 11 (*marg.* **reason**). 2 Cor. iii. 5. x. 2, 7, 11. xii. 6.
think of (*marg.* **reckon**), 2 Cor. x. 2.
think on, Phil. iv. 8.
suppose, 2 Cor. xi. 5. 1 Pet. v. 12.
esteem, Rom. xiv. 14.
conclude, Rom. iii. 28.
Add John xi. 50, for διαλογίζομαι, G″LTTr*S*.

λογικός.

of the word, 1 Pet. ii. 2.
reasonable, Rom. xii. 1.

λόγιον.

oracle, Acts vii. 38. Rom. iii. 2. Heb. v. 12. 1 Pet. iv. 11.

λόγιος.

eloquent, Acts xviii. 24.

λογισμός.

thought, Rom. ii. 15.
imagination (*marg.* **reasoning**), 2Cor. x. 5(4).

λογομαχέω.

strive about words, 2 Tim. ii. 14.

λογομαχία.

strife of words, 1 Tim. vi. 4.

λόγος.

word, Matt. viii. 8, 16. x. 14. xii. 32, 37*t*. xiii. 19, 20, 21, 22*t*, 23. xv. 23. xxii. 46. xxiv. 35. Mark ii. 2. iv. 14, 15*t*, 16, 17, 18, 19, 20, 33. v. 36. vii. 13. viii. 38. x. 24. xiii. 31. xvi. 20(*ap*).

Luke i. 2, 20. iii. 4. iv. 22, 32, 36. v. 1. vii. 7. viii. 11, 12, 13, 15, 21. ix. 26(–T). x. 39. xi. 28. xii. 10. xxi. 33. xxii. 61. xxiii. 9. xxiv. 19, 44. John ii. 22. iv. 41, 50. v. 24, 38. viii. 31, 37, 43. x. 35. xii. 48. xiv. 24. xv. 3, 20, 25. xvii. 6, 14, 17, 20.

Acts ii. 22, 40, 41. iv. 4, 29, 31. v. 5. vi. 2, 4, 7. vii. 22. viii. 4, 14, 25. x. 36, 44. xi. 1, 19. xii. 24. xiii. 5, 7, 15, 26, 44, 46, 48, 49. xiv. 3, 25. xv. 7, 15, 24, 32, 35, 36. xvi. 6, 32. xvii. 11, 13. xviii. 11. xix. 10, 20. xx. 32, 35. xxii. 22.

Rom. ix. 6, 9. xv. 18. 1 Cor. ii. 4 (–G″), 13. iv. 20. xii. 8*t*. xiv. 19*t*, 36. 2 Cor. i. 18 (*marg.* **preaching**). ii. 17. iv. 2. v. 19. vi. 7. x. 11. Gal. v. 14. vi. 6. Eph. i. 13. v. 6. Phil. i. 14. ii. 16. Col. i. 5, 25. iii. 16, 17. 1 Thes. i. 5, 6, 8. ii. 13*tr*. iv. 15, 18. 2 Thes. ii. 2, 15, 17. iii. 1, 14. 1 Tim. iv. 5, 6, 12. v. 17. vi. 3. 2 Tim. i. 13. ii. 9, 15, 17. iv. 2, 15 (*marg.* **preaching**). Tit. i. 3, 9. ii. 5.

Heb. ii. 2. iv. 2, 12. v. 13. vii. 28. xii. 19. xiii. 7, 22. Jas. i. 18, 21, 22, 23. iii. 2. 1 Pet. i. 23. ii. 8. iii. 1*t*. 2 Pet. i. 19. ii. 3. iii.

5, 7. 1 John i. 10. ii. 5, 7, 14. iii. 18. 3 John 10. Rev. i. 2, 3, 9. iii. 8, 10. vi. 9. xii. 11. xx. 4. xxi. 5. xxii. 18, 19.

words, Matt. xxvi. 44. Mark xii. 13. xiv. 39. Luke xx. 20. John xiv. 23. Acts xv. 32. xviii. 15. xx. 38. 1 Cor. i. 17 (*marg.* **speech**). xiv. 9. 1 Thes. ii. 5.

Said of Christ, **Word**, John i. 1*tr*, 14. 1 John i. 1. v. 7(*ap*). Rev. xix. 13.

saying, Matt. vii. 24, 26, 28. xv. 12. xix. 1, 11, 22. xxvi. 1. xxviii. 15. Mark vii. 29. viii. 32. ix. 10. x. 22. Luke i. 29 (–G′). vi. 47. ix. 28 (*marg.* **thing**), 44. John iv. 37, 39. vi. 60. vii. 36, 40. viii. 51, 52, 55. x. 19. xii. 38. xiv. 24. xv. 20. xviii. 9, 32. xix. 8, 13. xxi. 23. Acts vi. 5. vii. 29. xvi. 36.

Rom. iii. 4. xiii. 9. 1 Cor. xv. 54. 1 Tim. i. 15. iii. 1. iv. 9. 2 Tim. ii. 11. Tit. iii. 8. Rev. xix. 9. xxii. 6, 7, 9, 10.

things to say, Heb. v. 11.

speech, Acts xx. 7. 1 Cor. ii. 1, 4. iv. 19. 2 Cor. x. 10. xi. 6. Col. iv. 6. Tit. ii. 8.

τίνι λόγῳ, **what**, 1 Cor. xv. 2 (*Gr.* by what speech).

talk, Matt. xxii. 15.

utterance, 1 Cor. i. 5. 2 Cor. viii. 7. Eph. vi. 19. Col. iv. 3.

mouth, Acts xv. 27.

show, Col. ii. 23.

tidings, Acts xi. 22.

preaching, 1 Cor. i. 18.

rumor, Luke vii. 17.

fame, Luke v. 15.

communication, Matt. v. 37. Luke xxiv. 17. Eph. iv. 29.

treatise, Acts i. 1.

question, Mark xi. 29(*marg.* **thing**).

account, Matt. xii. 36. xviii. 23. Luke xvi. 2. Acts xix. 40. Rom. xiv. 12. Phil. iv. 17. Heb. xiii. 17. 1 Pet. iv. 5.

With συναίρω, **reckon**, Matt. xxv. 19.

work, Rom. ix. 28 (*marg.* **account**), 28 (*marg.* **account**; *ap*).

With εἰς, **as concerning**, Phil. iv. 15.

ἡμῖν ὁ λόγος, **we have to do**, Heb. iv. 13.

thing, Matt. xxi. 24. Luke i. 4. xx. 3. Acts v. 24.

matter, Mark i. 45. Acts viii. 21. xv. 6. xix. 38.

doctrine (*marg.* **word**), Heb. vi. 1[cc].

reason, 1 Pet. iii. 15.

With κατά, **reason would**[cc], Acts xviii. 14.

intent, Acts x. 29.

cause, Matt. v. 32.

Add Matt. xv. 6, for ἐντολή, LTr. xix. 9(*ap*). Acts xviii. 5, for πνεῦμα, GLT*S*. Rev. xvii. 17, for ῥῆμα, GLTTr*S*.

See also ἡγέομαι, παρακαλέω, ποιέω.

λόγχη.

spear, John xix. 34.

λοιδορέω.

revile, John ix. 28. Acts xxiii. 4. 1 Cor. iv. 12. 1 Pet. ii. 23[p].

λοιδορία.

railing, 1 Pet. iii. 9*t*.

λοιδ. χάριν, **to speak reproachfully** (*Gr.* for railing), 1 Tim. v. 14.

λοίδορος.

railer, 1 Cor. v. 11.

reviler, 1 Cor. vi. 10.

λοιμός.

pestilence, Matt. xxiv. 7 (–LTr*S*). Luke xxi. 11.

pestilent fellow, Acts xxiv. 5.

λοιπός.

οἱ λοιποί, αἱ λοιπαί.

the remnant, Matt. xxii. 6. Rev. xi. 13. xii. 17. xix. 21.

the residue, Mark xvi. 13(*ap*).

the rest, Matt. xxvii. 49. Luke xxiv. 9. Acts ii. 37. v. 13. xxvii. 44. Rom. xi. 7. 1 Cor. vii. 12. Rev. ii. 24. ix. 20. xx. 5.

the other, Matt. xxv. 11. Acts xvii. 9. Gal. ii. 13. 2 Pet. iii. 16. Rev. viii. 13.

others, Luke viii. 10. xviii. 9. Acts xxviii. 9. Eph. ii. 3. 1 Thes. iv. 13. v. 6. 1 Tim. v. 20.
other, Luke xxiv. 10. Rom. i. 13. 1 Cor. ix. 5. 2 Cor. xii. 13. xiii. 2. Phil. i. 13(*marg.* **others**). iv. 3.
Add 2 Cor. ii. 17, for πολύς, G′.

τὰ λοιπά.

the things which remain, Rev. iii. 2.
the rest, Luke xii. 26. 1 Cor. xi. 34.
other things, Mark iv. 19.
other, 1 Cor. xv. 37. Eph. iv. 17 (-G°°LS).

τὸ λοιπόν, λοιπόν, ὁ λοιπόν.

With ἐστί, **it remaineth,** 1 Cor. vii. 29.
besides, 1 Cor. i. 16.
moreover, 1 Cor. iv. 2.
furthermore, 1 Thes. iv. 1.
henceforth, 2 Tim. iv. 8.
from henceforth, Heb. x. 13.
finally, 2 Cor. xiii. 11. Eph. vi. 10. Phil. iii. 1. iv. 8. 2 Thes. iii. 1.
now, Matt. xxvi. 45. Mark xiv. 41.
then, Acts xxvii. 20.
Gen., **from henceforth,** Gal. vi. 17.

λουτρόν.

washing, Eph. v. 26. Tit. iii. 5.

λούω.

wash, John xiii. 10. Acts ix. 37p. xvi. 33. Heb. x. 22(23)°°. 2 Pet. ii. 22. Rev. i. 5.

λύκος.

wolf, Matt. vii. 15. x. 16. Luke x. 3. John x. 12*t.* Acts xx. 29.

λυμαίνομαι.

make havoc of, Acts viii. 3.

λυπέω.

grieve, 2 Cor. ii. 5. Eph. iv. 30.
cause grief, 2 Cor. ii. 5.
make sorry, 2 Cor. ii. 2. vii. 8*t.*

Middle or Passive,

be grieved, Mark x. 22. John xxi. 17. Rom. xiv. 15. 2 Cor. ii. 4.
be made sorry, 2 Cor. ii. 2. vii. 9*t.*
be sorry, Matt. xiv. 9. xvii. 23. xviii. 31.
sorrow, 2 Cor. vii. 9, 11. 1 Thes. iv. 13.
be sorrowful, Matt. xxvi. 22, 37. Mark xiv. 19. John xvi. 20.
sorrowful, Matt. xix. 22p. 2 Cor. vi. 10p.
be in heaviness, 1 Pet. i. 6p.

λύπη.

grief, 1 Pet. ii. 19pl.
Gen., **grievous,** Heb. xii. 11.
With ἐκ, **grudgingly,** 2 Cor. ix. 7.
sorrow, Luke xxii. 45. John xvi. 6, 20, 21, 22. 2 Cor. ii. 3, 7. vii. 10*t.* Phil. ii. 27*t.*
heaviness, Rom. ix. 2. 2 Cor. ii. 1.

λύσις.

to be loosed°°, 1 Cor. vii. 27.

λυσιτελέω.

Impers., **it is better,** Luke xvii. 2.

λύτρον.

ransom, Matt. xx. 28. Mark x. 45.

λυτρόω.

redeem, 1 Pet. i. 18.—*Mid.,* Luke xxiv. 21. Tit. ii. 14.

λύτρωσις.

redemption, Luke ii. 38. Heb. ix. 12.
With ποιέω, **redeem,** Luke i. 68.

λυτρωτής.

deliverer, Acts vii. 35.

λυχνία.

candlestick, Matt. v. 15. Mark iv. 21. Luke viii. 16. xi. 33. Heb. ix. 2. Rev. i. 12, 13, 20*t.* ii. 1, 5. xi. 4.

λύχνος.

light, Matt. vi. 22. Luke xi. 34. xii. 35. John v. 35. 1 Pet. i. 19. Rev. xxi. 23.
candle, Matt. v. 15. Mark iv. 21. Luke viii. 16. xi. 33, 36. xv. 8. Rev. xviii. 23. xxii. 5.

λύω.

to loose, Matt. xvi. 19*t.* xviii. 18*t.* xxi. 2. Mark vii. 35. xi. 2, 4, 5. Luke xiii. 15, 16. xix. 30, 31, 33. John xi. 44. Acts ii. 24. xiii. 25. xxii. 30. xxiv. 26(*ap*). 1 Cor. vii.

27. Rev. v. 2, 5(*om*). ix. 14, 15. xx. 3, 7.
be loosing, Luke xix. 33p.
unloose, Mark i. 7. Luke iii. 16. John i. 27.
put off, Acts vii. 33.
Pass., **melt**, 2 Pet. iii. 10.
dissolve, 2 Pet. iii. 11, 12.
break, Matt. v. 19. John v. 18. vii. 23. x. 35. Acts xxvii. 41. Eph. ii. 14.
break up, Acts xiii. 43p.
destroy, John ii. 19. 1 John iii. 8.
Add Mark x. 3(*ap*).

μαγεία, μαγία T*S*.

sorcery, Acts viii. 11.

μαγεύω.

use sorcery, Acts viii. 9.

μάγος.

wise man, Matt. ii. 1, 7, 16*t*.
sorcerer, Acts xiii. 6, 8.

μαζός, breast.

Rev. i. 13, for μαστός, L.

μαθητεύω.

be a disciple, Matt. xxvii. 57(*pass.* LTr*S*).
teach, Matt. xxviii. 19. Acts xiv. 21.
instruct, Matt. xiii. 52.

μαθητής.

disciple, Matt. v. 1. viii. 21, 23, 25 (-LbTr*S*). ix. 10, 12, 14*t*, 19, 37. x. 1, 24, 25, 42. xi. 1, 2. xii. 1, 2, 49. xiii. 10, 36. xiv. 12, 15, 19*t*, 22, 26. xv. 2, 12, 23, 32, 33, 36*t*. xvi. 5, 13, 20, 21, 24. xvii. 6, 10, 13, 16, 19. xviii. 1. xix. 10, 13, 23, 25. xx. 17(-Tr*S*). xxi. 1, 6, 20. xxii. 16. xxiii. 1. xxiv. 1, 3. xxvi. 1, 8, 17, 18, 19, 26, 35, 36, 40, 45, 56. xxvii. 64. xxviii. 7, 8, 9(*ap*), 13, 16.
Mark ii. 15, 16, 18*tr*, 23. iii. 7, 9. iv. 34. v. 31. vi. 1, 29, 35, 41, 45. vii. 2, 5, 17. viii. 1, 4, 6, 10, 14 (-StE, *omS*), 27*t*, 33, 34. ix. 14, 18, 28, 31. x. 10, 13, 23, 24, 46. xi. 1, 14. xii. 43. xiii. 1. xiv. 12, 13, 14, 16, 32. xvi. 7.
Luke v. 30, 33. vi. 1, 13, 17, 20, 40. vii. 11, 18, 19(18). viii. 9, 22. ix. 1(-GTTr, ἀπόστολος *S*), 14, 16, 18, 40, 43, 54. x. 23. xi. 1*t*. xii. 1, 22. xiv. 26, 27, 33. xvi. 1. xvii. 1, 22. xviii. 15. xix. 29, 37, 39. xx. 45(*ap*). xxii. 11, 39, 45.
John i. 35, 37. ii. 2, 11, 12, 17, 22. iii. 22, 25. iv. 1, 2, 8, 27, 31, 33. vi. 3, 8, 11*t*(*ap*), 12, 16, 22(*ap*), 22*t*, 24, 60, 61, 66. vii. 3. viii. 31. ix. 2, 27, 28*t*. xi. 7, 8, 12(-T), 54. xii. 4, 16. xiii. 5, 22, 23, 35. xv. 8. xvi. 17, 29. xviii. 1*t*, 2, 15*t*, 16, 17, 19, 25. xix. 26, 27*t*, 38. xx. 2, 3, 4, 8, 10, 18, 19, 20, 25, 26, 30. xxi. 1, 2, 4, 7, 8, 12, 14, 20, 23, 24.
Acts i. 15 (ἀδελφός G'LT*S*). vi. 1, 2, 7. ix. 1, 10, 19, 25, 26*t*, 38. xi. 26, 29. xiii. 52. xiv. 20, 22, 28. xv. 10. xvi. 1. xviii. 23, 27. xix. 1, 9, 30. xx. 1, 7pl(ἡμῶν GLT*S*), 30, xxi. 4, 16*t*.
Add Matt. xxvi. 20 (twelve . .), LT*S*. Mark ii. 18 (and . . of the P.2), TTr*S*. Luke x. 22(*ap*).

μαθήτρια.

disciple, Acts ix. 36.

μαίνομαι.

be mad, John x. 20. Acts xii. 15. xxvi. 25. 1 Cor. xiv. 23.
be beside one's self, Acts xxvi. 24.

μακαρίζω.

count happy, Jas. v. 11.
call blessed, Luke i. 48.

μακάριος.

happy, John xiii. 17. Acts xxvi. 2. Rom. xiv. 22. 1 Cor. vii. 40. 1 Pet. iii. 14. iv. 14.
blessed, Matt. v. 3, 4, 5, 6, 7, 8, 9, 10, 11. xi. 6. xiii. 16. xvi. 17. xxiv. 46. Luke i. 45. vi. 20, 21*t*, 22. vii. 23. x. 23. xi. 27, 28. xii. 37, 38, 43. xiv. 14, 15. xxiii. 29. John xx. 29. Acts xx. 35. Rom. iv. 7, 8. 1 Tim. i. 11. vi. 15. Tit. ii. 13.

Jas. i. 12, 25. Rev. i. 3. xiv. 13. xvi. 15. xix. 9. xx. 6. xxii. 7, 14.

μακαρισμός.

blessedness, Rom. iv. 6, 9. Gal. iv. 15.

μάκελλον.

shambles, 1 Cor. x. 25.

μακράν.

(*With* ὁδόν *understood.*)

a great way off, Luke xv. 20.
a good way off, Matt. viii. 30.
far off, Eph. ii. 13.
With art., **that (which) is afar off,** Acts ii. 39. Eph. ii. 17.
far, Mark xii. 34. Luke vii. 6. John xxi. 8. Acts xvii. 27.
far °hence, Acts xxii. 21

μακρόθεν.

from far, Mark viii. 3.
afar off, Mark xi. 13 (ἀπὸ μ. G''LT TrS). Luke xviii. 13. xxii. 54. xxiii. 49 (ἀπὸ μ. LS).
ἀπὸ μακρόθεν, **afar off,** Matt. xxvi. 58. xxvii. 55. Mark v. 6(–ἀπό G°). xiv. 54. xv. 40. Luke xvi. 23. Rev. xviii. 10, 15, 17.

μακροθυμέω.

be long-suffering, 2 Pet. iii. 9.
bear long, Luke xviii. 7.
suffer long, 1 Cor. xiii. 4.
have long patience, Jas. v. 7.
have patience, Matt. xviii. 26, 29.
be patient, 1 Thes. v. 14. Jas. v. 7 (*marg.* **be long patient,** *or* **suffer with long patience**), 8.
endure patiently, Heb. vi. 15p.

μακροθυμία.

long-suffering, Rom. ii. 4. ix. 22. 2 Cor. vi. 6. Gal. v. 22. Eph. iv. 2. Col. i. 11. iii. 12. 1 Tim. i. 16. 2 Tim. iii. 10. iv. 2. 1 Pet. iii. 20. 2 Pet. iii. 15.
patience, Heb. vi. 12. Jas. v. 10.

μακροθύμως.

patiently, Acts xxvi. 3.

μακρός.

far, Luke xv. 13. xix. 12.
See also προσεύχομαι.

μακροχρόνιος.

With εἰμί, **live long,** Eph. vi. 3.

μαλακία.

disease, Matt. iv. 23. ix. 35. x. 1.

μαλακός.

soft, Matt. xi. 8. Luke vii. 25.
τὰ μαλακά, **soft °clothing,** Matt. xi. 8.
effeminate, 1 Cor. vi. 9.

μάλιστα.

most of all, Acts xx. 38.
chiefly, Phil. iv. 22. 2 Pet. ii. 10.
especially, Acts xxvi. 3. Gal. vi. 10. 1 Tim. v. 17. 2 Tim. iv. 13.
specially, Acts xxv. 26. Phil. iv. 22. 1 Tim. iv. 10. v. 8. Tit. i. 10. Phm. 16.

μᾶλλον.

more, Matt. vi. 30. vii. 11. x. 25. xviii. 13. Luke xi. 13. xii. 24, 28. John xii. 43. Acts iv. 19. xx. 35. xxvii. 11. Rom. v. 9, 10, 15, 17. xi. 12, 24. 1 Cor. xii. 22. xiv. 18. 2 Cor. iii. 9, 11. Gal. iv. 27°°. Phil. i. 9t. ii. 12. iii. 4. 2 Tim. iii. 4. Phm. 16. Heb. ix. 14. xii. 25.
the more, Mark xiv. 31(–G°°LTrS). John v. 18. xix. 8. Acts ix. 22. xxii. 2. 2 Cor. vii. 7, 13. Heb. x. 25.
so much the more, Luke v. 15.
πολλῷ μᾶλλον, **the more a great deal,** Mark x. 48. — **so much the more,** Luke xviii. 39. — **far,** Phil. i. 23.
With διαφέρω, **be much better,** Matt. vi. 26.
rather, Matt. x. 6, 28. xxv. 9. xxvii. 24. Mark v. 26. xv. 11. Luke x. 20(*om*S). John iii. 19. Acts v. 29. Rom. xiv. 13. 1 Cor. v. 2. vi. 7t. vii. 21. ix. 12. 2 Cor. ii. 7. iii. 8. v. 8. xii. 9. Gal. iv. 9. Eph. v. 4. Phil. i. 12. 1 Tim. i. 4. vi. 2. Phm. 9. Heb. xi. 25. xii. 9, 13.
the rather, 2 Pet. i. 10.
μᾶλλον δέ, **but rather,** 1 Cor. xiv. 1, 5. Eph. iv. 28. — **yea rather,** Rom. viii. 34. — **or rather,** Gal. iv. 9. — **and the more,** Acts v. 14.
μᾶλλον δὲ καί, **but rather,** Eph. v. 11.

See also καλός, περισσεύω, περισσός.

μάμμη.

grandmother, 2 Tim. i. 5.

μαμμωνᾶς, μαμωνᾶς GLTTr*S*.

mammon, Matt. vi. 24. Luke xvi. 9 and 11 (*marg.* **riches**), 13.

μανθάνω.

learn, Matt. ix. 13. xi. 29. xxiv. 32. Mark xiii. 28. John vi. 45. vii. 15. Rom. xvi. 17. 1 Cor. iv. 6. xiv. 31, 35. Gal. iii. 2. Eph. iv. 20. Phil. iv. 9, 11. Col. i. 7. 1 Tim. ii. 11. v. 4, 13. 2 Tim. iii. 7, 14*t*. Tit. iii. 14. Heb. v. 8. Rev. xiv. 3.

understand, Acts xxiii. 27.

μανία.

Lit. madness. *See* περιτρέπω.

μάννα.

manna, John vi. 31, 49, 58(–GTTr*S*). Heb. ix. 4. Rev. ii. 17.

μαντεύομαι.

by soothsaying, Acts xvi. 16p.

μαραίνω.

Pass., **fade away**, Jas. i. 11.

μαρὰν ἀθά.

Maran-atha, 1 Cor. xvi. 22.

μαργαρίτης.

pearl, Matt. vii. 6. xiii. 45, 46. 1 Tim. ii. 9. Rev. xvii. 4. xviii. 12, 16. xxi. 21*t*.

μάρμαρος.

marble, Rev. xviii. 12.

μάρτυρ. See μάρτυς.

μαρτυρέω.

be witness, Matt. xxiii. 31. Heb. x. 15.

witness, John v. 32. Rom. iii. 21. 1 Tim. vi. 13. Heb. vii. 8cc.

give witness, Acts x. 43.

bear witness, Luke iv. 22. xi. 48 (μάρτυς εἰμί TTr*S*). John i. 7, 8, 15. iii. 26, 28. v. 31, 32, 33, 36, 37. viii. 18*t*. x. 25. xv. 27. xviii. 23, 37. Acts xv. 8. xxii. 5. xxiii. 11. 1 John i. 2. v. 6, 8(*ap*). 3 John 6.

testify, John ii. 25. iii. 11, 32. iv. 39, 44. v. 39. vii. 7. xiii. 21. xv. 26. xxi. 24. Acts xxvi. 5. 1 Cor. xv. 15. Heb. vii. 17. xi. 4. 1 John iv. 14. v. 9. 3 John 3. Rev. xxii. 16, 20.

give testimony, Acts xiii. 22. xiv. 3.

bear record, John i. 32, 34. viii. 13, 14. xii. 17. xix. 35. Rom. x. 2. 2 Cor. viii. 3. Gal. iv. 15. Col. iv. 13. 1 John v. 7. 3 John 12. Rev. i. 2.

givec, 1 John v. 10.

Add Rev. xxii. 18, for συμμαρτυρέω, *mid.*, GLTTr*S*.

Passive or Middle,

obtain witness, Heb. xi. 4.

have testimony, Heb. xi. 5.

have good report, Acts xxii. 12. 3 John 12.

of good report, Acts x. 22p.

be well reported of, Acts xvi. 2. 1 Tim. v. 10.

obtain good report, Heb. xi. 2, 39.

of honest report, Acts vi. 3p.

witness, Acts xxvi. 22 (μαρτύρομαι LT*S*).

charge, 1 Thes. ii. 11 (12, μαρτύρομαι T*S*).

μαρτυρία.

witness, Mark xiv. 55, 56, 59. Luke xxii. 71. John i. 7. iii. 11. v. 31, 32, 36. Tit. i. 13. 1 John v. 9*tr*, 10. Rev. xx. 4.

testimony, John iii. 32, 33. v. 34. viii. 17. xxi. 24. Acts xxii. 18. Rev. i. 2, 9. vi. 9. xi. 7. xii. 11, 17. xix. 10*t*.

record, John i. 19. viii. 13, 14. xix. 35. 1 John v. 10, 11. 3 John 12.

report, 1 Tim. iii. 7.

μαρτύριον.

witness, Matt. xxiv. 14. Acts iv. 33. vii. 44. Jas. v. 3.

testimony, Matt. viii. 4. x. 18. Mark i. 44. vi. 11. xiii. 9. Luke v. 14. ix. 5. xxi. 13. 1 Cor. i. 6. ii. 1 (μυστήριον G*S*). 2 Cor. i. 12. 2 Thes. i. 10. 2 Tim. i. 8. Heb. iii. 5. Rev. xv. 5.

to be testified[cc] (*marg.* **testimony**), 1 Tim. ii. 6(-LT).

μαρτύρομαι.

take to record, Acts xx. 26.
testify, Gal. v. 3. Eph. iv. 17.
Add, see μαρτυρέω, *at the end.*

μάρτυς.

witness, Matt. xviii. 16. xxvi. 65. Mark xiv. 63. Luke xxiv. 48. Acts i. 8, 22. ii. 32. iii. 15. v. 32. vi. 13. vii. 58. x. 39, 41. xiii. 31. xxii. 15. xxvi. 16. Rom. i. 9. 2 Cor. xiii. 1. 1 Thes. ii. 5, 10. 1 Tim. v. 19. vi. 12. 2 Tim. ii. 2. Heb. x. 28. xii. 1. 1 Pet. v. 1. Rev. i. 5. iii. 14. xi. 3.
martyr, Acts xxii. 20. Rev. ii. 13. xvii. 6.
record, 2 Cor. i. 23. Phil. i. 8.
Add Luke xi. 48, *see* μαρτυρέω.

μασσάομαι.

gnaw, Rev. xvi. 10.

μαστιγόω.

to scourge, Matt. x. 17. xx. 19. xxiii. 34. Mark x. 34. Luke xviii. 33. John xix. 1. Heb. xii. 6.

μαστίζω.

to scourge, Acts xxii. 25.

μάστιξ.

scourging, Acts xxii. 24. Heb. xi. 36.
plague, Mark iii. 10. v. 29, 34. Luke vii. 21.

μαστός.

pap, Luke xi. 27. xxiii. 29. Rev. i. 13 (μαζός L).

ματαιολογία.

vain jangling, 1 Tim. i. 6.

ματαιολόγος.

vain talker, Tit. i. 10.

μάταιος.

vain, 1 Cor. iii. 20. xv. 17. Tit. iii. 9. Jas. i. 26. 1 Pet. i. 18.
Neut., **vanity**, Acts xiv. 15.

ματαιότης.

vanity, Rom. viii. 20. Eph. iv. 17. 2 Pet. ii. 18.

ματαιόω.

Pass., **become vain**, Rom. i. 21.

μάτην.

in vain, Matt. xv. 9. Mark vii. 7.

μάχαιρα.

sword, Matt. x. 34. xxvi. 47, 51, 52*tr*, 55. Mark xiv. 43, 47, 48. Luke xxi. 24. xxii. 36, 38, 49, 52. John xviii. 10, 11. Acts xii. 2. xvi. 27. Rom. viii. 35. xiii. 4. Eph. vi. 17. Heb. iv. 12. xi. 34, 37[cc]. Rev. vi. 4. xiii. 10*t*, 14.

μάχη.

fighting, 2 Cor. vii. 5. Jas. iv. 1 (*marg.* **brawling**).
strife, 2 Tim. ii. 23.
striving, Tit. iii. 9.

μάχομαι.

to fight, Jas. iv. 2.
strive, John vi. 52. Acts vii. 26[p]. 2 Tim. ii. 24.

μέ. See ἐγώ.

μεγαλαυχέω.

boast great things, Jas. iii. 5 (μεγάλα (fr. μέγας) αὐχέω LT).

μεγαλεῖος.

Neut., **great thing**, Luke i. 49 (μέγας LTrS). — **wonderful work**, Acts ii. 11.

μεγαλειότης.

magnificence, Acts xix. 27.
majesty, 2 Pet. i. 16.
mighty power, Luke ix. 43.

μεγαλοπρεπής.

excellent, 2 Pet. i. 17.

μεγαλύνω.

enlarge, Matt. xxiii. 5. 2 Cor. x. 15 (*marg.* **magnify**).
magnify, Luke i. 46. Acts v. 13. x. 46. xix. 17. Phil. i. 20.
show great, Luke i. 58.

μεγάλως.

greatly, Phil. iv. 10.

μεγαλωσύνη.

majesty, Jude 25.
Said of God, **Majesty**, Heb. i. 3. viii. 1.

μέγας,

μεγάλη, μέγα.

great, Matt. ii. 10. iv. 16. v. 19, 35. vii. 27. viii. 24, 26. xv. 28. xx. 26. xxii. 36, 38. xxiv. 21, 24, 31. xxvii. 60. xxviii. 2, 8. Mark iv. 32, 37, 39. v. 11(–G°), 42. x. 43. xiii. 2. xvi. 4.

Luke i. 15, 32. ii. 10. iv. 25, 38. v. 29. vi. 49. vii. 16. viii. 37. ix. 48. xiii. 19 (–G°L^bTr*S*). xiv. 16. xvi. 26. xxi. 11*t*, 23. xxiv. 52. John vi. 18. vii. 37. xxi. 11. Acts ii. 20. iv. 33*t*. v. 5, 11. vi. 8. vii. 11. viii. 1, 2, 8 (πολύς LT*S*), 9, 10. x. 11. xi. 5, 28. xv. 3. xvi. 26. xix. 27, 28, 34, 35. xxiii. 9. xxvi. 22.

Rom. ix. 2. 1 Cor. xvi. 9. Eph. v. 32. 1 Tim. iii. 16. vi. 6. 2 Tim. ii. 20. Tit. ii. 13. Heb. iv. 14. x. 35. xiii. 20. Jude 6.

Rev. i. 10. ii. 22. vi. 4, 12, 17. vii. 14. viii. 8, 10. ix. 2 (καιομένης fr. καίω G′), 14. xi. 8, 11, 12, 13, 15, 17, 18, 19. xii. 1, 3, 9, 12, 14. xiii. 2, 13, 16. xiv. 2, 8, 19. xv. 1, 3. xvi. 1, 9, 12, 14, 17(–G°L), 18*t*, 19*t*, 21*t*. xvii. 1, 5, 6, 18. xviii. 1, 2(*ap*), 10, 16, 18, 19, 21*t*. xix. 1, 2, 5, 17, 18. xx. 1, 11, 12. xxi. 3, 10, 10 (*om S*), 12.

οἱ μεγάλοι, **they that are great**, Matt. xx. 25.—**great ones**, Mark x. 42.

Neut., **great thing**, 1 Cor. ix. 11. 2 Cor. xi. 15. Rev. xiii. 5. [11.

greatest[c], Acts viii. 10. Heb. viii.

large, Mark xiv. 15. Luke xxii. 12.

mighty, Rev. vi. 13.

strong, Rev. xviii. 2(*ap*).

loud[c], Matt. xxvii. 46, 50. Mark i. 26. v. 7. xv. 34, 37. Luke i. 42. iv. 33. viii. 28. xvii. 15. xix. 37. xxiii. 23, 46. John xi. 43. Acts vii. 57, 60. viii. 7. xiv. 10. xvi. 28. xxvi. 24.

Rev. v. 2, 12. vi. 10. vii. 2, 10. viii. 13. x. 3. xii. 10. xiv. 7, 9, 15, 18. xix. 17.

high, John xix. 31. Heb. x. 21.

to years[c], Heb. xi. 24.

φόβον μέγαν, **exceedingly**, Mark iv. 41.—**sore**, Luke ii. 9.

Not rendered, Acts viii. 13(–G°°T).

Add Luke i. 49, for μεγαλεῖος, LTr *S*. Acts xxvi. 29, for πολύς, G′LT *S*. Jas. iii. 5, *see* μεγαλαυχέω.

Comparative, μείζων.

greater, Matt. xi. 11*t*. xii. 6. xxiii. 17, 19. Mark iv. 32. xii. 31. Luke vii. 28*t*. xii. 18. xxii. 27. John iv. 12. v. 20, 36. viii. 53. x. 29. xiii. 16*t*. xiv. 28. xv. 13, 20. xix. 11. 1 Cor. xiv. 5. Heb. vi. 13, 16. ix. 11. xi. 26. Jas. iii. 1. 2 Pet. ii. 11. 1 John iii. 20. iv. 4. v. 9.

Neut., **greater thing**, John i. 50(51).—**greater** [c]**work**, John xiv. 12.—*Adv.*, **the more**, Matt. xx. 31.

greatest, Matt. xiii. 32[cc]. xviii. 1, 4. xxiii. 11. Mark ix. 34. Luke ix. 46. xxii. 24, 26. 1 Cor. xiii. 13.

more, Jas. iv. 6.

elder (*marg.* **greater**), Rom. ix. 12.

Add 1 Cor. xii. 31, for κρείσσων, LT*S*.

μειζότερος, **greater**, 3 John 4.

Superlative, μέγιστος.

exceeding great, 2 Pet. i. 4.

μέγεθος.

greatness, Eph. i. 19.

μεγιστᾶνες.

great men, Rev. vi. 15. xviii. 23.

lords, Mark vi. 21.

μέγιστος. See μέγας.

μεθερμηνεύω.

interpret, Matt. i. 23. Mark v. 41 xv. 22, 34. Acts iv. 36.

Pass., **be by interpretation**, John i. 42. Acts xiii. 8.

Add John. i. 38(39), for ἑρμηνεύω, LTr.

μέθη.

drunkenness, Luke xxi. 34. Rom. xiii. 13. Gal. v. 21.

μεθίστημι, μεθιστάνω.

remove, Acts xiii. 22[p].

can[c] **remove**, 1 Cor. xiii. 2.

translate, Col. i. 13.
put out of, Luke xvi. 4.
turn away, Acts xix. 26.

μεθοδεία, -δία TS.

wile, Eph. vi. 11.
With πρός, **whereby one lieth in wait**, Eph. iv. 14.

μεθόριος.

Neut., **border**, Mark vii. 24 (ὅριον LTrS).

μεθύσκω.

Mid., **be drunk (drunken)**, Luke xii. 45. Eph. v. 18. 1 Thes. v. 7.

μέθυσος.

drunkard, 1 Cor. v. 11. vi. 10.

μεθύω.

be drunken, Matt. xxiv. 49. Acts ii. 15. 1 Cor. xi. 21. 1 Thes. v. 7. Rev. xvii. 6.
Mid., **have well drunk**, John ii. 10. —**be made drunk**, Rev. xvii. 2.

μεῖζων, μειζότερος. See μέγας.

μέλαν.

ink, 2 Cor. iii. 3. 2 John 12. 3 John 13.

μέλας.

black, Matt. v. 36. Rev. vi. 5, 12.

μέλει. See μέλω.

μελετάω.

meditate upon, 1 Tim. iv. 15.
premeditate, Mark xiii. 11 (-G∞Lb TrS).
imagine, Acts iv. 25.

μέλι.

honey, Matt. iii. 4. Mark i. 6. Rev. x. 9, 10.

μελίσσιος.

Lit. of honey. *See* κηρίον.

μέλλω.

be about, Acts xviii. 14p. xx. 3p. Heb. viii. 5p. Rev. x. 4.
about, Acts iii. 3p.
be yet, Rev. viii. 13.
tarry, Acts xxii. 16.
be ready, Luke vii. 2. Rev. iii. 2. xii. 4.
ready, Luke vii. 2p. Acts xx. 7p.
intend, Acts v. 35. xx. 13
mean, Acts xxvii. 2.
mind, Acts xx. 13.
be almost, Acts xxi. 27.
be, Matt. xi. 14. Luke xix. 4. Acts xxi. 37p. Rev. xii. 5.
be to come, Rom. v. 14. Eph. i. 21. 1 Tim. iv. 8.
Part., **to come**, Matt. iii. 7. xii. 32. Luke iii. 7. Acts xxiv. 25. Heb. ii. 5. vi. 5. ix. 11 (γίνομαι L). x. 1. xiii. 14. —**thing to come**, Rom. viii. 38. 1 Cor. iii. 22. Col. ii. 17. Heb. xi. 20. —**time to come**, 1 Tim. vi. 19.
With γίνεσθαι fr. γίνομαι, **be coming on**, Acts xxvii. 33.
begin, Rev. x. 7.
εἰς τὸ μέλλον, **after that**, Luke xiii. 9.
should hereafter, 1 Tim. i. 16.
should afterwards, Gal. iii. 23.
should after, Heb. xi. 8. 2 Pet. ii. 6.
τὰ μέλλοντα, **what things should**, Mark x. 32.
shall (should), Matt. xvi. 27. xvii. 12, 22. xx. 22. xxiv. 6. Mark xiii. 4. Luke ix. 31, 44. xix. 11. xxi. 7, 36. xxii. 23. xxiv. 21. John vi. 71. vii. 39. xi. 51. xii. 4, 33. xviii. 32. Acts xi. 28. xix. 27. xx. 38. xxii. 29. xxiii. 3. xxiii. 27. xxiv. 15. xxvi. 2p, 22, 23. xxviii. 6. Rom. iv. 24. viii. 13, 18. 1 Thes. iii. 4. 2 Tim. iv. 1. Heb. i. 14. x. 27. Jas. ii. 12. 1 Pet. v. 1. Rev. i. 19. ii. 10t. iii. 10. vi. 11. xvii. 8.
will (would), Matt. ii. 13. Luke x. 1. John vi. 6, 15. vii. 35t. xiv. 22. Acts xii. 6. xvi. 27. xvii. 31. xxiii. 15p, 20p. xxv. 4. xxvii. 10, 30p. Rev. iii. 16.
Not rendered, Acts xiii. 34. xxii. 26.
Add 2 Pet. i. 12, for οὐκ ἀμελέω, G'LTS.
See also ἀποθνήσκω, ἐπιβουλή.

μέλος.

member, Matt. v. 29, 30. Rom. vi. 13t, 19t. vii. 5, 23t. xii. 4t, 5. 1 Cor.

vi. 15*tr*. xii. 12*t*, 14, 18, 19, 20, 22, 25, 26*f*, 27. Eph. iv. 25. v. 30. Col. iii. 5. Jas. iii. 5, 6. iv. 1.

Add Eph. iv. 16, for μέρος, G'.

μέλω.

Impersonal, with a dative, **to care**[cc], Matt. xxii. 16. Mark iv. 38. xii. 14. Luke x. 40. John x. 13. xii. 6. Acts xviii. 17. 1 Cor. vii. 21. 1 Pet. v. 7.

take care[cc], 1 Cor. ix. 9.

μεμβράνα.

parchment, 2 Tim. iv. 13.

μέμφομαι.

find fault, Mark vii. 2(*omS*). Rom. ix. 19. Heb. viii. 8.

μεμψίμοιρος.

complainer, Jude 16.

μέν.

A particle expressing affirmation or concession, used in antithesis with δέ except when marked (¹). Frequently joined with οὖν (²).

indeed, Matt. iii. 11. xiii. 32. xx. 23. xxiii. 27. xxvi. 41. Mark i. 8 (-L[b]TTr*S*). x. 39 (-TTr*S*). xiv. 21. Luke iii. 16. xi. 48. xxiii. 41. Acts iv. 16. xi. 16. xxii. 9. Rom. vi. 11. xiv. 20¹. 1 Cor. xi. 7. 2 Cor. viii. 17. Phil. i. 15. iii. 1. Col. ii. 23. 1 Pet. ii. 4.

truly, Matt. ix. 37. xvii. 11. Mark xiv. 38. Luke x. 2. xxii. 22¹. John xx. 30². Acts i. 5. iii. 22. v. 23(-L T*S*). 2 Cor. xii. 12¹. Heb. vii. 23. xi. 15.

verily, Mark ix. 12¹(-TTr[b]). Acts xix. 4¹(-GL*S*). xxii. 3(-G[oo]L*S*). xxvi. 9¹². Rom. ii. 25. 1 Cor. v. 3. xiv. 17. Heb. iii. 5. vi. 16¹ (-L*S*). vii. 5, 18. ix. 1². xii. 10. 1 Pet. i. 20.

even, 1 Thes. ii. 18¹.

οἱ μέν, **some,** 1 Cor. xii. 28¹.

ὁ μὲν . . ὁ δέ, ὃς μὲν . . ὃς δέ, ἄλλος μὲν . . ἄλλος δέ.

the one . . the other, 2 Cor. ii. 16. Phil. i. 16 and 17.

one . . the other, Luke xxiii. 33.

one . . another, Matt. xxi. 35. xxii. 5. xxv. 15. Rom. ix. 21. xiv. 2. 1 Cor. vii. 7. xi. 21. xii. 8. xv. 39, 40.

one man . . another, Rom. xiv. 5.

some . . others, John vii. 12. Acts xvii. 32. Jude 22 and 23.

some . . some, Matt. xiii. 4 and 5, 8, 23. xvi. 14. Mark iv. 4 and 5. xii. 5. Luke viii. 5 and 6. Acts xix. 32². xxvii. 44. xxviii. 24. Eph. iv. 11. 2 Tim. ii. 20.

part . . part, Acts xiv. 4.

he (they, etc.) . . he (etc.), Acts i. 6² and 7. xxviii. 5². Rom. ii. 7 and 8. Gal. iv. 23(-μέν L[b]).

those . . this, Heb. vii. 21(20).

those things . . those things, Phil. iii. 13(14).

τοῦτο μὲν . . τοῦτο δέ, **partly . . partly,** Heb. x. 33.

ὅσα μὲν . . ὅσα δέ, **those things which . . but what,** Jude 10.

Not rendered, Matt. x. 13. xvi. 3. xxii. 8. xxiii. 28. xxv. 33. xxvi. 24. Mark xvi. 19² (*ap*). Luke iii. 18². x. 6(*omS*). xiii. 9. xxiii. 56. John x. 41. xi. 6¹. xvi. 9, 22². xix. 24¹², 32. Acts i. 1¹, 18¹². ii. 41¹². iii. 21¹. v. 41². viii. 4², 25². ix. 7, 31². xi. 19². xii. 5². xiii. 4¹², 36. xiv. 3², 12(-G[oo]LT*S*). xv. 3², 30². xvi. 5². xvii. 12², 17², 30¹². xviii. 14². xix. 38². xxi. 39. xxiii. 8(-L), 18², 22¹², 31². xxv. 4², 11. xxvi. 4¹². xxvii. 21¹, 41. xxviii. 22¹.

Rom. i. 8¹. ii. 8(-L*S*). iii. 2¹. v. 16. vii. 12, 25. viii. 10, 17. x. 1¹. xi. 13¹, 22, 28. xvi. 19 (-G[oo]LT). 1 Cor. i. 12, 18, 23. ii. 15(τά L[b]T, -G[o]). iii. 4¹. vi. 4², 7². ix. 24, 25². xi. 14, 18¹. xii. 20 (-L[b]). xv. 51 (-L[b]T). 2 Cor. iv. 12(*omS*). ix. 1. x. 1, 10. xi. 4¹. Gal. iv. 8, 24. Phil. i. 28 (*omS*). ii. 23². 2 Tim. i. 10. iv. 4. Tit. i. 15(-G[oo]LT*S*).

Heb. i. 7. vii. 2¹, 8, 11¹². viii. 4. ix. 6, 23. x. 11. xii. 9¹, 11. Jas. iii. 17. 1 Pet. ii. 14(*omS*). iii. 18. iv. 6, 14. Jude 8.

Add μὲν οὖν for μενοῦνγε, Luke xi. 28, Tr*S*. Phil. iii. 8, GLT.—Acts iii. 13[1](whom ye ..). GLT*S*. xxiii. 7 (.. divided), L. Rom. vi. 21[1](for ..), L. 2 Cor. xii. 1(*ap*). Gal. ii. 9 (we ..), GL[b].

μενοῦνγε.

yea rather, Luke xi. 28(*see* μέν).
yea doubtless, Phil. iii. 8(*see* μέν).
yes verily, Rom. x. 18.
nay but, Rom. ix. 20(-G[o]).

μέντοι.

yet, John iv. 27. xx. 5.
nevertheless, 2 Tim. ii. 19.
ὅμως μ., **nevertheless,** John xii. 42.
howbeit, John vii. 13.
but, John xxi. 4.
μέντοι καί, **also,** Jude 8.
Not rendered, Jas. ii. 8.

μένω.

remain, Matt. xi. 23. Luke x. 7. John i. 33. ix. 41. xv. 11 (εἰμί G''L TTr), 16. xix. 31. Acts v. 4[p]. xxvii. 41. 1 Cor. vii. 11. xv. 6. 2 Cor. iii. 11, 14. ix. 9. Heb. xii. 27. 1 John ii. 24. iii. 9.

abide, Matt. x. 11. Mark vi. 10. Luke i. 56. viii. 27. ix. 4. xix. 5. xxiv. 29. John i. 32. 39(40). iii. 36. iv. 40. v. 38. vii. 9. viii. 35*t*. x. 40. xi. 6. xii. 24, 34, 46. xiv. 16(εἰμί LTTr*S*). xv. 4*tr*, 5, 6, 10*t*. Acts xvi. 15. xviii. 3. xx. 23(*marg*. **wait for**). xxi. 7, 8. xxvii. 31. 1 Cor. iii. 14. vii. 8, 20, 24, 40. xiii. 13. Phil. i. 25. 2 Tim. ii. 13. iv. 20. Heb. vii. 3. 1 Pet. i. 23. 1 John ii. 6, 10. 14, 17, 24, 27*t*, 28. iii. 6, 14, 15, 24. 2 John 9*t*.

dwell, John i. 38(39, *marg*. **abide**), 39(40). vi. 56. xiv. 10, 17. Acts xxviii. 16, 30. 1 John iii. 17, 24. iv. 12, 13, 15, 16*t*. 2 John 2.

tarry, Matt. xxvi. 38. Mark xiv. 34. Luke xxiv. 29. John iv. 40. xxi. 22, 23. Acts ix. 43. xviii. 20. xx. 15(*ap*).

tarry for, Acts xx. 5.
be present[c], John xiv. 25.
continue, John ii. 12. viii. 31. xv. 9. 1 Tim. ii. 15. 2 Tim. iii. 14. Heb. vii. 24. xiii. 1, 14. 1 John ii. 19, 24. Rev. xvii. 10.
endure, John vi. 27. Heb. x. 34. 1 Pet. i. 25.
stand, Rom. ix. 11.
μένω σοί, **be thine own,** Acts v. 4.
Add 1 John iv. 16(.. in him), L[b]*S*.

μερίζω.

divide, Matt. xii. 25*t*, 26. Mark iii. 24, 25, 26. vi. 41. 1 Cor. i. 13.
Mid., **divide,** Luke xii. 13.
Pass., **be difference between**[cc], 1 Cor. vii. 34.
give part, Heb. vii. 2.
distribute, 1 Cor. vii. 17. 2 Cor. x. 13.
deal, Rom. xii. 3.

μέριμνα.

care, Matt. xiii. 22. Mark iv. 19. Luke viii. 14. xxi. 34. 2 Cor. xi. 28. 1 Pet. v. 7.

μεριμνάω.

be careful, Luke x. 41. Phil. iv. 6.
have care, 1 Cor. xii. 25.
care, 1 Cor. vii. 32, 33, 34*t*. Phil. ii. 20.
take thought, Matt. vi. 25, 27, 28, 31, 34*t*. x. 19. Luke xii. 11, 22, 26.
with taking thought, Luke xii. 25[p] (-T).

μερίς.

part, Luke x. 42. Acts viii. 21. xvi. 12(-G[o]). 2 Cor. vi. 15.
With εἰς, **to be partaker,** Col. i. 12.

μερισμός.

dividing asunder, Heb. iv. 12.
gift (*marg*. **distribution**), Heb. ii. 4.

μεριστής.

divider, Luke xii. 14.

μέρος.

part, Matt. ii. 22. Mark viii. 10. Luke xi. 36. John xiii. 8. xix. 23*t*. Acts ii. 10. v. 2. xx. 2. xxiii. 6, 9 (*ap*). Eph. iv. 9(-G[oo]T), 16 (μέλος G'). Rev. xvi. 19. xx. 6. xxi. 8. xxii. 19.
With ἀπό, **in part,** Rom. xi. 25.

2 Cor. i. 14. ii. 5. —**in some sort,** Rom. xv. 15. — **somewhat,** Rom. xv. 24.

With ἐκ, **in part,** 1 Cor. xiii. 9*t*, 10, 12. —**in particular,** 1 Cor. xii. 27.

With ἀνά, **by course,** 1 Cor. xiv. 27.

With κατά, **particularly,** Heb. ix. 5.

μέρος τι, **partly,** 1 Cor. xi. 18.

piece, Luke xxiv. 42.

portion, Matt. xxiv. 51. Luke xii. 46. xv. 12.

coast, Matt. xv. 21. xvi. 13. Acts xix. 1.

craft, Acts xix. 27.

τὰ δεξιὰ μέρη, **on the right side,** John xxi. 6.

behalf, 2 Cor. ix. 3. 1 Pet. iv. 16 (ὄνομα G''LT*S*).

respect, 2 Cor. iii. 10. Col. ii. 16 (*marg.* **part**).

μεσημβρία.

noon, Acts xxii. 6.

south, Acts viii. 26.

μεσιτεύω.

confirm (*Gr.* interpose one's self), Heb. vi. 7.

μεσίτης.

mediator, Gal. iii. 19, 20. 1 Tim. ii. 5. Heb. viii. 6. ix. 15. xii. 24.

μεσονύκτιον.

midnight, Acts xvi. 25. xx. 7.

Gen., **at midnight,** Mark xiii. 35. Luke xi. 5.

μέσος.

in the midst, Acts i. 18.

μέσον, **in the midst,** Matt. xiv. 24 (*ap*). Luke xxiii. 45. John xix. 18.

among, John i. 26.

ἀνὰ μέσον, **through the midst,** Mark vii. 31. —**in the midst,** Rev. vii. 17 (ἀναμέσον St). — **among,** Matt. xiii. 25. —**between,** 1 Cor. vi. 5.

ἐν μέσῳ, **among,** Luke viii. 7. x. 3. xxii. 27, 55. 1 Thes. ii. 7. —**before,** Matt. xiv. 6.

ἐκ μέσου, **from among,** Matt. xiii. 49. Acts xvii. 33. xxiii. 10. 1 Cor. v. 2. 2 Cor. vi. 17. —**out of the way,** Col. ii. 14. 2 Thes. ii. 7.

Mostly with διά, εἰς, *or* ἐν (ἐμμέσῳ for ἐν μέσῳ T, *marked* [t]),

. . **midst,** Matt. x. 16. xviii. 2, 20. Mark vi. 47. ix. 36. xiv. 60. Luke ii. 46. iv. 30, 35. v. 19. vi. 8. xvii. 11. xxi. 21. xxii. 55. xxiv. 36. John viii. 3(*ap*), 9(*ap*), 59. xx. 19, 26. Acts i. 15. ii. 22. iv. 7. xvii. 22. xxvii. 21. Phil. ii. 15 (μέσον G''LT*S*). Heb. ii. 12. Rev. i. 13[t] (μέσον *S*). ii. 1[t], 7(μέσῳ *omS*). iv. 6[t]. v. 6*t*[t]. vi. 6[t]. xxii. 2[t].

See also ἐγείρω, ἡμέρα, νύξ.

μεσότοιχον.

middle wall between, Eph. ii. 14.

μεσουράνημα.

midst of heaven, Rev. viii. 13. xiv. 6. xix. 17.

μεσόω.

about the midst[oo], John vii. 14[p].

μεστός.

full, Matt. xxiii. 28. John xix. 29. xxi. 11. Rom. i. 29. xv. 14. Jas. iii. 8, 17. 2 Pet. ii. 14.

Add John xix. 29(*ap*).

μεστόω.

Pass., **full,** Acts ii. 13[p].

μετά.

I. With a Genitive.

among, Luke xxii. 37. xxiv. 5. John vi. 43. xi. 56. xvi. 19.

ἐκ τῶν . . μετά, **between some of . . and,** John iii. 25.

with, Matt. i. 23. ii. 3, 11. iv. 21. v. 25, 41. viii. 11. ix. 11, 15. xii. 30, 41. 42, 45. xiii. 20. xiv. 7. xv. 30. xvi. 27. xvii. 3, 17. xviii. 16. xix. 10. xx. 2, 20. xxi. 2. xxii. 16. xxiv. 30, 31, 49, 51. xxv. 3, 4, 10, 19, 31. xxvi. 11, 18, 20, 23, 29, 36, 38, 40, 47*t*, 55, 58, 69, 71, 72. xxvii. 34, 41, 54. xxviii. 8, 12, 20.

Mark i. 13, 20, 29 ii. 16*t*, 19, 19 (*ap*), 25. iii. 5, 6, 7, 14. iv. 16, 36. v. 18, 24. vi. 25, 50. viii. 10, 14, 38. ix. 8, 24(-LTTr*S*). x. 30. xi. 11. xiii. 26. xiv. 7, 14, 17, 18, 20,

33, 43*t*, 48, 54, 67. xv. 1, 7, 28(*ap*), 31. xvi. 10(*ap*).
Luke i. 28, 39, 66. ii. 36, 51. v. 29, 30, 34. vi. 3, 17. vii. 36. viii. 13. ix. 49. x. 17. xi. 7, 23*t*, 31, 32. xii. 13, 46, 58. xiii. 1. xiv. 9, 31. xv. 29, 30, 31. xvii. 15, 20. xxi. 27. xxii. 11, 15, 21, 28, 33, 52, 53, 59. xxiii. 43. xxiv. 29, 30, 52.
John iii. 2, 22, 26. iv. 27*t*. vi. 3, 66. vii. 33. viii. 29. ix. 37, 40. xi. 16, 31, 54. xii. 8, 17, 35(ἐν GLTTr*S*). xiii. 8, 18(-Tr), 33. xiv. 9, 16, 30. xv. 27. xvi. 4, 32. xvii. 12, 24. xviii. 2, 3, 5, 18, 26. xix. 18, 40. xx. 7, 24, 26.
Acts i. 4 (Beza, -StE, *omS*), 26. ii. 28. iv. 29, 31. vii. 9, 38, 45. ix. 19, 28, 39. x. 38. xi. 21. xiii. 17. xiv. 23, 27. xv. 4, 35. xvii. 11. xviii. 10. xx. 18, 19, 24 (-G∞LT*S*), 31, 34. xxiv. 1, 3, 7(*ap*), 18*t*. xxv. 12, 23. xxvi. 12. xxvii. 10, 24. xxviii. 31.
Rom. xii. 15*t*, 18. xv. 10, 33. xvi. 20, 24(*ap*). 1 Cor. vi. 6, 7. vii. 12, 13. xvi. 11, 12, 23, 24. 2 Cor. vi. 15, 16. vii. 15. viii. 4, 18. xiii. 11, 14(13).
Gal. ii. 1, 12. iv. 25, 30. vi. 18. Eph. iv. 2*t*, 25. vi. 5, 7, 23, 24. Phil. i. 4. ii. 12, 29. iv. 3, 6, 9, 23. Col. i. 11. iv. 18. 1 Thes. i. 6. iii. 13. v. 28. 2 Thes. i. 7*t*. iii. 12, 16. 18. 1 Tim. i. 14. ii. 9, 15. iii. 4. iv. 3, 4, 14. vi. 6, 21. 2 Tim. ii. 10, 22. iv. 11*t*, 22, 22(*ap*). Tit. ii. 15. iii. 15. Phm. 25(24).
Heb. v. 7. vii. 21. ix. 19. x. 22. xi. 9, 31. xii. 14, 17, 28. xiii. 17, 23, 25. 1 Pet. iii. 15. 1 John i. 3*tr*, 6, 7. ii. 19. 2 John 2, 3. Rev. i. 7, 12. ii. 22. iii. 4, 20*t*, 21*t*. iv. 1. vi. 8(-G'*S*). xii. 9, 17. xiii. 4, 7(*ap*). xiv. 1, 4. xvii. 1, 2, 12, 14*t*. xviii. 3, 9. xix. 20. xx. 4, 6 (μετὰ ταῦτα for μετ' αὐτοῦ G''). xxi. 3*tr*, 9, 15. xxii. 12, 21.
With art., **he that (which) is with**, Matt. xii. 3, 4, 30. xxvi. 51. Mark i. 36. v. 40. Luke vi. 4. viii. 45 (σύν GLTTr*S*). — **that is with**, Tit. iii. 15.
οὐ μετά, **without**, Acts v. 26.
against, Rev. ii. 16. xi. 7. xix. 19*t*.
in, Mark xiv. 62. Acts xv. 33.
on, Luke x. 37.
upon, Luke i. 58.
unto, Rev. x. 8.
promised to[c], Luke i. 72.
of, Matt. xviii. 23.
and [c]**setting**, Matt. xxvii. 66.
Not rendered, Rev. xiv. 13.
Add Mark v. 37 (. . him), TTr*S*. Rev. xii. 7, for κατά, GLTTr*S*.
See also ἀλλήλων, ἀφρός, ἡμῶν, παρρησία, χαρά.

II. With an Accusative.
(Denoting time, except in Heb. ix. 3.)
after, Matt. i. 12[cc]. xvii. 1. xxiv. 29. xxv. 19. xxvi. 2, 32, 73. xxvii. 53, 63. Mark i. 14[cc]. viii. 31. ix. 2. xiii. 24. xiv. 1, 28[cc], 70[cc]. xvi. 12 (*ap*), 19(*ap*).
Luke i. 24. ii. 46. v. 27. ix. 28. x. 1. xii. 4[cc], 5. xv. 13[cc]. xxii. 20, 58. John ii. 12. iii. 22. iv. 43. v. 1, 4(*ap*). vi. 1. vii. 1. xi. 7, 11. xiii. 27. xix. 28, 38. xx. 26. xxi. 1.
Acts i. 3. v. 37. vii. 5, 7. x. 37, 41[cc]. xii. 4. xiii. 15, 20, 25. xv. 13[cc], 16, 36[cc]. xviii. 1. xix. 4, 21. xx. 1[cc], 6, 29. xxi. 15. xxiv. 1, 24. xxv. 1. xxviii. 11, 13, 17.
Gal. i. 18. iii. 17[cc]. Tit. iii. 10. Heb. iv. 7. viii. 10. ix. 3, 27. x. 15, 16, 26. 2 Pet. i. 15. Rev. iv. 1. vii. 1, 9. xi. 11. xv. 5. xviii. 1. xix. 1. xx. 3.
With ταῦτα, **hereafter**, John xiii. 7. Rev. i. 19. iv. 1. ix. 12. — **afterward**, Luke xvii. 8. xviii. 4. John v. 14. Heb. iv. 8. — **that should follow**, 1 Pet. i. 11.
since, Heb. vii. 28.
hence[cc], Acts i. 5.
With εἰμί, **follow**, Matt. xxvii. 62.
when[cc], Acts vii. 4. 1 Cor. xi. 25.
Add Mark ix. 31, x. 34, μετὰ τρεῖς

ἡμέρας for τῇ τρίτῃ ἡμέρᾳ, G″LTTr S. Rev. xx. 6, μ. ταῦτα for μ. αὐτοῦ, G″. 7, for ὅταν τελεσθῇ, G″. *See also* πολύς.

μεταβαίνω.

remove, Matt. xvii. 20*t*.
pass, John v. 24. 1 John iii. 14.
depart, Matt. viii. 34. xi. 1. xii. 9p. xv. 29. John vii. 3. xiii. 1. Acts xviii. 7.
go, Luke x. 7.

μεταβάλλω.

Mid., **change one's mind,** Acts xxviii. 6.

μετάγω.

turn about, Jas. iii. 3, 4.

μεταδίδωμι.

impart, Luke iii. 11. Rom. i. 11. 1 Thes. ii. 8.
give, Rom. xii. 8 (*marg.* **impart**). Eph. iv. 28 (*marg.* **distribute**).

μετάθεσις.

removing, Heb. xii. 27.
translation, Heb. xi. 5.
change, Heb. vii. 12.

μεταίρω.

depart, Matt. xiii. 53. xix. 1.

μετακαλέω.

Mid., **call for,** Acts xxiv. 25. — **call to one's self,** Acts vii. 14. — **call** °**hither,** Acts x. 32. — **call,** Acts xx. 17.

μετακινέω.

move away, Col. i. 23.

μεταλαμβάνω.

be partaker of, 2 Tim. ii. 6. Heb. xii. 10.
receive, Heb. vi. 7.
take, Acts xxvii. 33.
eat, Acts ii. 46.
have, Acts xxiv. 25p.
Add Acts xxvii. 34, for προσλαμβάνω, GLTS.

μετάληψις (–λημψις LTS).

With εἰς, **to be received,** 1 Tim. iv. 3.

μεταλλάσσω, -ττω.

to change, Rom. i. 25, 26.

μεταμέλομαι.

repent, Matt. xxi. 29, 32. 2 Cor. vii. 8*t*. Heb. vii. 21.
repent one's self, Matt. xxvii. 3.

μεταμορφόω.

Mid., **be transformed,** Rom. xii. 2. — **be transfigured,** Matt. xvii. 2. Mark ix. 2. — **be changed,** 2 Cor. iii. 18.

μετανοέω.

repent, Matt. iii. 2. iv. 17. xi. 20, 21. xii. 41. Mark i. 15. vi. 12. Luke x. 13. xi. 32. xiii. 3, 5. xv. 7, 10. xvi. 30. xvii. 3, 4. Acts ii. 38. iii. 19. viii. 22. xvii. 30. xxvi. 20. 2 Cor. xii. 21. Rev. ii. 5*t*, 16, 21*t*, 22. iii. 3, 19. ix. 20, 21. xvi. 9, 11.

μετάνοια.

repentance, Matt. iii. 8 (*marg.* **amendment of life**), 11. ix. 13(*omS*). Mark i. 4. ii. 17(*omS*). Luke iii. 3, 8. v. 32. xv. 7. xxiv. 47. Acts v. 31. xi. 18. xiii. 24. xix. 4. xx. 21. xxvi. 20. Rom. ii. 4. 2 Cor. vii. 9, 10. 2 Tim. ii. 25. Heb. vi. 1, 6. xii. 17 (*marg.* **to change one's mind**cc). 2 Pet. iii. 9.
Add Luke iii. 16(*ap*).

μεταξύ.

between, Matt. xviii. 15. xxiii. 35. Luke xi. 51. xvi. 26. Acts xii. 6. xv. 9.
mean while, John iv. 31. Rom. ii. 15 (*marg.* **between**).
next, Acts xiii. 42(*marg.* **between**).

μεταπέμπω.

send for, Acts x. 22, 29p, 29. xxiv. 24, 26. xxv. 3.
call for, Acts x. 5. xi. 13.

μεταστρέφω.

turn, Acts ii. 20. Jas. iv. 9.
pervert, Gal. i. 17.

μετασχηματίζω.

Mid., **transform one's self,** 2 Cor. xi. 13. — **be transformed,** 2 Cor. xi. 14, 15.
transfer in a figure, 1 Cor. iv. 6.

change, Phil. iii. 21.

μετατίθημι.

translate, Heb. xi. 5*t*.
carry over, Acts vii. 16.
remove, Gal. i. 6.
change, Heb. vii. 12.
turn, Jude 4.

μετέπειτα.

afterward, Heb. xii. 17.

μετέχω.

take part of, Heb. ii. 14.
be partaker of, 1 Cor. ix. 10, 12. x. 17, 21, 30.
pertain to, Heb. vii. 13.
use, Heb. v. 13.

μετεωρίζω.

Mid. or Pass., **be of doubtful mind**, Luke xii. 29 (*marg.* **live in careful suspense**).

μετοικεσία.

carrying away into, Matt. i. 17*t*.
With ἐπί, **about the time** °**they were**° **carried away to**, Matt. i. 11.
With μετά, **after** °**they were**° **brought to**, Matt. i. 12.

μετοικίζω.

carry away, Acts vii. 43.
remove into, Acts vii. 4.

μετοχή.

fellowship, 2 Cor. vi. 14.

μέτοχος.

partaker, Heb. iii. 1, 14. vi. 4. xii. 8.
partner, Luke v. 7.
fellow, Heb. i. 9.

μετρέω.

to measure, Mark iv. 24. 2 Cor. x. 12. Rev. xi. 1, 2. xxi. 15, 16, 17.
mete, Matt. vii. 2. Mark iv. 24. Luke vi. 38.
Add, for ἀντιμετρέω, Matt. vii. 2, GLTTr*S*. Luke vi. 38, L[m].

μετρητής.

firkin, John ii. 6.

μετριοπαθέω.

have compassion on (*marg.* **reasonably bear with**), Heb. v. 2.

μετρίως.

a little, Acts xx. 12.

μέτρον.

measure, Matt. vii. 2. xxiii. 32. Mark iv. 24. Luke vi. 38*t*. John iii. 34. Rom. xii. 3. 2 Cor. x. 13*t*. Eph. iv. 7, 13, 16. Rev. xxi. 17.
Add Rev. xxi. 15 (had . .), GLT Tr*S*.

μέτωπον.

forehead, Rev. vii. 3. ix. 4. xiii. 16. xiv. 1, 9. xvii. 5. xx. 4. xxii. 4.

μέχρι, μέχρις.

unto, Rom. xv. 19. Phil. ii. 8, 30. 2 Tim. ii. 9. Heb. iii. 6(*ap*), 14. xii. 4.
to, Rom. v. 14.
until, Matt. xi. 23. xiii. 30 (ἕως L Tr, ἄχρι *S*). xxviii. 15. Acts x. 30. xx. 7. 1 Tim. vi. 14. Heb. ix. 10.
till, Eph. iv. 13.
μέχρις οὗ, **till**, Mark xiii. 30.
Add Luke xvi. 16, for ἕως. TTr*S*.

μή.

A particle differing from οὐ in expressing negation dependent on the manner in which a thing is conceived; used

I. As a negative Adverb.

(*With an imperative, marked* [a].)

not, Matt. i. 19, 20[a]. ii. 12. iii. 9, 10. v. 17[a], 29, 30, 34, 39, 42[a]. vi. 1, 2[a], 3[a], 7[a], 8[a], 13, 16[a], 18, 19[a], 25[a]. vii. 1[a], 6[a], 19, 26. x. 5*t*[a], 26[a], 28*t*[a], 31[a], 34[a]. xii. 30*t*. xiii. 19. xiv. 27. xvii. 7[a]. xviii. 13, 25. xix. 6[a], 14[a]. xxi. 21[a]. xxii. 12, 29. xxiii. 3[a], 8[a], 23. xxiv. 17[a], 23[a], 26[a]*t*. xxv. 29. xxvi. 5. xxviii. 5[a], 10[a].
Mark ii. 4. iii. 20. iv. 12*t*. v. 36. vi. 9, 11, 34, 50. ix. 39[a]. x. 9[a], 14[a], 19, 19(-G°), 19*tr*. xi. 23. xii. 15 (14), 24. xiii. 7[a], 15[a], 16[a], 21[a]. xiv. 2. xvi. 6[a].
Luke i. 13[a], 20, 30[a]. ii. 10[a], 26, 45. iii. 8, 9. iv. 42. v. 10[a], 19. vi. 29[a], 30[a], 37*t*[a], 49. vii. 6[a], 13[a], 30. viii. 10*t*, 18, 28[a], 49[a](μηκέτι LTr*S*), 50[a]. 52[a]. ix. 5, 33, 50[a]. x. 7[a], 10, 20[a]. xi. 4, 7[a], 23*t*, 35, 42. xii. 4[a], 7[a], 21,

29[a], 32[a]. 33, 47, 48. xiii. 14. xiv. 8, 12[a], 29. xvi. 26. xvii. 23[a], 31*t*[a]. xviii. 1, 2, 16[a], 20*f*. xix. 26, 27. xx. 7. xxi. 8, 9[a], 14, 21[a]. xxii. 40, 42[a]. xxiii. 28[a]. xxiv. 16, 23.

John ii. 16[a]. iii. 7[a], 16 (*ap*), 18*t*. v. 23, 28[a], 45. vi. 20[a], 27[a], 43, 64. vii. 24[a], 49. viii. 6 (*see* προσποιέω). ix. 39. x. 1, 37[a], 38. xi. 37, 50. xii. 15[a], 47 (–G′), 48. xiii. 9. xiv. 1[a], 24, 27[a]. xv. 2. xviii. 17, 25, 40. xix. 21, 24. xx. 17[a], 27[a], 29.

Acts i. 4. iii. 23. iv. 18. v. 7, 28, 40. vii. 19, 60. ix. 26, 38. x. 15[a], 47. xi. 9[a]. xii. 19. xiii. 11. xiv. 18. xv. 19, 38*t*. xvii. 6. xviii. 9[a], 9. xix. 31. xx. 10[a], 16, 22, 29. xxi. 4, 12, 14, 21, 34. xxiii. 9 (*omS*), 21. xxv. 24, 27. xxvii. 7, 15, 21, 24.

Rom. i. 28, ii. 14*t*, 21, 22. iii. 8. iv. 5, 17, 19. v. 14 (–G[o]). vi. 12[a]. viii. 1 (*ap*), 4. ix. 30. x. 6, 20*t*. xi. 8*t*, 10, 18[a], 20[a]. xii. 2[a], 3, 11, 14[a], 16*t*, 19, 21[a]. xiii. 3, 13*tr*, 14[a]. xiv. 1, 3[a], 3, 3[a], 3, 6(*ap*), 6, 15[a], 16[a], 20[a], 22. xv. 1.

1 Cor. i. 28. iv. 7, 18. v. 8, 9, 11. vi. 9[a]. vii. 1, 5[a], 10, 11, 12[a], 13[a], 18*t*[a], 21[a], 23[a], 27*t*[a], 30*tr*, 31, 38. ix. 18, 21. x. 6, 28, 33. xi. 22 (*see* ἔχω), 29. xiii. 1, 2, 3. xiv. 20[a], 39[a]. xv. 33[a], 34[a].

2 Cor. ii. 1, 13. iii. 7, 13. iv. 2, 7, 18*tr*. v. 19. vi. 1, 9, 14[a], 17[a]. ix. 5, 7. x. 2, 14. xii. 21. Gal. iii. 1(*ap*). iv. 18. v. 1[a], 7, 13, 26. vi. 7[a], 9*t*. Eph. iii. 13. iv. 26[a]*t*, 30[a]. v. 7[a], 15, 17[a], 18[a], 27. vi. 4[a], 6. Phil. ii. 4, 12. iii. 9. Col. i. 23. ii. 18(–G[oo]L[b] *S*), 21. iii. 2, 9[a], 19[a], 21[a], 22.

1 Thes. i. 8. ii. 9, 15. iv. 5*t*. v. 6, 19[a], 20[a]. 2 Thes. i. 8*t*. ii. 2, 12. iii. 6, 8, 13[a], 15[a]. 1 Tim. i. 20. ii. 9. iii. 3, 3(*omS*), 6, 8*tr*, 11. iv. 14[a]. v. 1, 9[a], 13, 16[a], 19[a]. vi. 2[a], 3, 17. 2 Tim. i. 8. ii. 14. Tit. i. 6, 7*f*, 11, 14. ii. 3*t*, 9, 10.

Heb. iii. 8[a], 15[a], 18. iv. 2, 7[a], 15. vi. 1. vii. 6. ix. 9. x. 25, 35. xi. 3, 5, 8, 13, 27. xii. 5, 19, 27. xiii. 2[a], 9[a], 16, 17. Jas. i. 5, 7[a], 16[a], 22, 26. ii. 1[a], 11*t*, 14, 16. iii. 1[a], 14[a]. iv. 2, 11[a], 17. v. 9[a], 12[a], 17.

1 Pet. i. 8, 14. ii. 16. iii. 6, 7, 9, 14[a]. iv. 4, 12[a], 16[a]. v. 2. 2 Pet. ii. 21. iii. 8[a], 9. 1 John ii. 4, 15, 28. iii. 10*t*, 13[a], 14, 18, 21. iv. 1[a], 3, 8, 20. v. 10, 12, 16*t*. 2 John 7, 9, 10[a]. 3 John 10, 11[a]. Jude 5, 6, 19. Rev. i. 17[a]. iii. 18. v. 5[a]. vi. 6. vii. 3. viii. 12. x. 4. xi. 2. xiii. 15. xxii. 10.

thou do it[c] not, Rev. xix. 10[a]. xxii. 9[a].

no[cc], Matt. vi. 31[a], 34[a]. ix. 36. x. 19[a]. xiii. 5, 6. xxii. 23, 24, 25. xxiii. 9. Mark iv. 5, 6. vi. 8*tr*. xii. 18, 19. xiii. 11[a]. Luke xii. 11[a], 22[a]. xiii. 11. xxii. 36. Acts i. 20[a]. xxiii. 8.

Rom. v. 13. vii. 3. 1 Cor. i. 10. vii. 37. 2 Cor. v. 21. xiii. 7. Gal. iv. 8. Eph. ii. 12. v. 11[a]. 1 Thes. iv. 6, 13. 2 Thes. iii. 14[a]. 1 Tim. i. 3. iii. 3. Tit. i. 7. Jas. ii. 13. 1 Pet. iii. 10.

neither, Matt. x. 9[a]. xxiv. 18[a]. Luke x. 4[a]. xii. 29. xviii. 2. Rom. xiv. 21. 2 John 10.

nor, Matt. x. 10[a]. Luke x. 4[a].

that[cc] not, Matt. xxiv. 6[a]. Mark v. 7.

εἰς τὸ μή, **lest**, 2 Cor. iv. 4.

no man[cc], Rom. xiv. 13.

no one of you[cc], 1 Cor. iv. 6.

none[cc], Luke iii. 11. xi. 24. 1 Cor. vii. 29.

nothing[cc], Luke vii. 42.

μήτις, **none**, 1 Pet. iv. 15.—**no man**, Matt. viii. 28. 1 Cor. xvi. 11. 2 Cor. xi. 16. Col. ii. 16[a]. 2 Thes. ii. 3.

μή τι, **nothing**, 1 Cor. iv. 5.—**no**, Luke xi. 36. xii. 4.

μή τί, **nothing[cc]**, Mark viii. 1.

never, John vii. 15.

but, Luke xvii. 1. Acts iv. 20. xx. 20[cc].

any[c], Luke xx. 27.

With another negative, not rendered, Luke xxii. 34(–TTr*S*). Acts xx. 27. 1 Cor. i. 7. Phil. i. 28. 1 Tim. i. 7. Rev. vii. 16. *See also οὐ μή.*

Add, for ἤ, Matt. xi. 23, Luke x. 15, LTr*S*. — Matt. x. 38, *see* οὐ. xix. 9(*ap*). Mark xii. 21(*ap*). Luke xxiv. 36(*ap*). John vii. 31, for μήτι, G'LTr*S*. 1 Cor. ix. 20 (*ap*). 2 Cor. v. 12, for οὐ, L*S*. 1 Pet. v 3, for μηδέ, T. Rev. ii. 10[a], for μηδέν, G'LTr. vii. 16 (neither[1st] . .), L.

See also ἀνακαλύπτω, βλέπω, γίνομαι, ἐργάζομαι, ἔχω, πάρειμι, πᾶς. — *Also* ἐάν, εἰ, ἵνα.

II. As a Conjunction.

that not, Matt. xviii. 10. Mark v. 7. Luke xxi. 8. Gal. v. 15. 2 Tim. iv. 16. Heb. xii. 25.

μή τις, **that none,** 1 Thes. v. 15. — **that no man,** Matt. xxiv. 4. 2 Cor. viii. 20.

lest, Mark xiii. 5, 36. Acts xiii. 40. xxiii. 10. xxvii. 17, 42. 1 Cor. x. 12. 2 Cor. iv. 4. xii. 6, 21. Gal. vi. 1. Col. ii. 8. Heb. xii. 15*t*, 16.

III. As an Interrogative (expecting a negative answer).

Not rendered, Matt. vii. 9, 10. ix. 15. Mark ii. 19. Luke v. 34. xi. 11*t*, 12. xvii. 9. xxii. 35. John iii. 4. iv. 12. vi. 67. vii. 35, 41, 47, 51, 52. viii. 53. ix. 27, 40. x. 21. Acts vii 28, 42.

Rom. iii. 3, 5. ix. 14, 20. xi. 1, 11. 1 Cor. i. 13. ix. 8, 9. x. 22. xii. 29*f*, 30*tr*. 2 Cor. xii. 17. Jas. iii. 12.

IV. With other particles.

μὴ οὐκ ;

not? Rom. x. 18, 19. 1 Cor. ix. 4, 5. xi. 22.

οὐ μή.

Interrogative, [a]. With another negative, [2].

not in any wise, Mark xiv. 31.

in no wise, Matt. v. 18. x. 42. Luke xviii. 17. John vi. 37. Acts xiii. 41. Rev. xxi. 27.

in no case, Matt. v. 20.

by no means, Matt. v. 26.

by any means, Luke x. 19[2].

not at all, Rev. xxi. 25.

at all, Rev. xviii. 14[2].

With ἔτι, **no more at all,** Rev. xviii. 21, 22*t*, 23*t*. — **no more,** Heb. viii. 12. x. 17. Rev. iii. 12.

πᾶς οὐ μὴ ἔτι, **no more,** Rev. xviii. 22.

not, Matt. x. 23. xiii. 14*t*. xv. 6 (5). xvi. 22, 28. xviii. 3. xxiii. 39. xxiv. 2, 2 (μή *omS*), 34, 35. xxvi. 29, 35. Mark ix. 1, 41. x. 15. xiii. 2*t*, 30, 31. xvi. 18(*ap*). Luke vi. 37 (*see* ἵνα μή, I.), 37. ix. 27. xii. 59. xiii. 35. xviii. 7, 30. xxi. 18, 32, 33. xxii. 16, 18, 34(-μή TTr*S*), 67, 68. John iv. 48. viii. 12. x. 5. xi. 56. xiii. 38. xviii. 11[a]. xx. 25. Acts xxviii. 26*t*.

Rom. iv. 8. Gal. iv. 30. v. 16. 1 Thes. iv. 15. v. 3. Heb. viii. 11. 1 Pet. ii. 6. Rev. ii. 11. iii. 3, 5. xv. 4.

no[cc], 1 Cor. viii. 13. Rev. xviii. 7.

neither, Mark xiii. 19. Luke i. 15.

never, John vi. 35. Heb. xiii. 5.

οὐδ' οὐ μή, **no, nor ever,** Matt. xxiv. 21.

Not rendered, Mark xiv. 25[2]. Heb. xiii. 5[2].

Add, for οὐ, Matt. xii. 32, L*S*. xxv. 9, G''LTTr. Luke viii. 17, L Tr*S*. John xvi. 7, Tr. Rev. ix. 6, GLTTr*S*.

See also αἰών, πότε, πώποτε.

μή τις ; *or* μήτις ;

any man? John iv. 33.

any? John vii. 48.

μή τι ; *or* μήτι ;

any? John xxi. 5.

not? Matt. xii. 23(fr. 1660). John iv. 29.

With γε, **how much more?** 1 Cor. vi. 3.

Not rendered, Matt. vii. 16. xii. 23(*ed.* 1611, *etc.*). xxvi. 22, 25. Mark iv. 21. xiv. 19, 19(*ap*). Luke vi. 39. John vii. 31(μή G'LTr*S*). viii. 22. xviii. 35. Acts x. 47. 2 Cor. i. 17(*with* ἄρα). xii. 18. Jas. iii. 11.

μήγε. See εἰ δὲ μήγε.

μηδαμῶς.

not so, Acts x. 14. xi. 8.

μηδέ.

neither, Matt. vii. 6. x. 10*t*. xxiii. 10. xxiv. 20. Mark viii. 26. xii. 24. xiii. 11(–G^{oo}L^{b}Tr*S*), 15. Luke iii. 14. xii. 22, 47. xiv. 12(*ap*). xvi. 26. John iv. 15. xiv. 27. Acts xxi. 21. xxiii. 8(*μήτε* L*S*). Rom. vi. 13. ix. 11. 1 Cor. v. 8. x. 7, 8, 9, 10. 2 Thes. iii. 10. 1 Tim. i. 4. v. 22. 1 Pet. iii. 14. v. 3(*μή* T). 1 John ii. 15. iii. 18.
nor, Matt. x. 9(–T, *err.? S*), 9, 14. xxii. 29. Mark vi. 11. viii. 26. Luke x. 4. xiv. 12*t*. xvii. 23. Acts iv. 18. Rom. xiv. 21*t*. 2 Cor. iv. 2. 1 Tim. vi. 17. 2 Tim. i. 8. Heb. xii. 5.
nor yet, Matt. vi. 25. x. 10.
no, not, 1 Cor. v. 11.
not, Col. ii. 21*t*. 1 Pet. v. 2.
not once, Eph. v. 3.
no, not so much as, Mark ii. 2.
Add, for *μήτε*, Mark iii. 20, LTTr. Eph. iv. 27, 2 Thes. ii. 2, LT*S*. — Phil. ii. 3, *see ἤ*, I.

μηδείς, μηδεμία, μηδέν.

With another negative, ^{2}.

no man, Matt. viii. 4. ix. 30. xvi. 20. xvii. 9. Mark v. 43. vii. 36. viii. 30. ix. 9. xi. 14. Luke iii. 14. v. 14. viii. 56. ix. 21. x. 4. Acts ix. 7. xxiii. 22. Rom. xii. 17. xiii. 8. 1 Cor. iii. 18, 21. x. 24. Gal. vi. 17. Eph. v. 6. Col. ii. 18. 1 Thes. iii. 3. 1 Tim. iv. 12. v. 22. Tit. ii. 15. iii. 2 Jas. i. 13. 1 John iii. 7. Rev. iii. 11.
not any man, Acts x. 28.
any man, Mark i. 44^2.
none, John viii. 10(*ap*). Acts viii. 24. xi. 19. xxiv. 23. 1 Tim. v. 14.
no, Luke iii. 13. Acts iv. 17. xiii. 28. xv. 28. xvi. 28. xix. 40. xxi. 25(*ap*). xxviii. 6, 18. 1 Cor. i. 7. x. 25, 27. 2 Cor. vi. 3. xiii. 7. Heb. x. 2. Rev. ii. 10(*μή* G'LTr).
any, 2 Thes. ii. 3^2. 1 Pet. iii. 6^2.
no thing, Tit. ii. 8.
nothing, Matt. xxvii. 19. Mark i. 44(–LTr^{b}*S*). v. 26. vi. 8. Luke vi. 35. ix. 3. Acts iv. 21. x. 20. xi. 12 (–G^{o}T). xix. 36. xxiii. 14, 29. xxv. 25. xxvii. 33. 2 Cor. vi. 10. vii. 9. Gal. vi. 3. Phil. i. 28. ii. 3. iv. 6. 1 Thes. iv. 12 (*marg.* **no man**). 1 Tim. v. 21. vi. 4. Tit. iii. 13. Jas. i. 4, 6. 3 John 7.
any thing, Rom. xiii. 8^2. 2 Cor. vi. 3^2.
μηδεμίαν ποιησάμενος, **without any**, Acts xxv. 17.
not, Luke iv. 35. Acts x. 28.
not a whit, 2 Cor. xi. 5.
not at all, 2 Thes. iii. 11.
Add Col. ii. 4, for *μή τις*, LT*S*.

μηδέποτε.

never, 2 Tim. iii. 7.

μηδέπω.

not as yet, Heb. xi. 7.

μηκέτι.

With another negative, ^{2}.

no longer, 1 Thes. iii. 1, 5. 1 Tim. v. 23. 1 Pet. iv. 2.
any longer, Acts xxv. 24^2.
no more, Mark i. 45. ix. 25. John v. 14. viii. 11(*ap*). Acts xiii. 34. Rom. xv. 23. Eph. iv. 28.
not any more, Rom. xiv. 13.
not henceforth, 2 Cor. v. 15.
henceforth not, Rom. vi. 6. Eph. iv. 17.
henceforth no more, Eph. iv. 14.
henceforth, Acts iv. 17^2.
hereafter, Mark xi. 14^2.
no^{cc} . . **henceforward**, Matt. xxi. 19.
no^{cc}, Mark ii. 2.
Add Luke viii. 49, for *μή*, LTr*S*.

μῆκος.

length, Eph. iii. 18. Rev. xxi. 16*t*.

μηκύνω.

Mid., **grow up**, Mark iv. 27.

μηλωτή.

sheepskin, Heb. xi. 37.

μήν, adv. See ἤ.

μήν, subst.

month, Luke i. 24, 26, 36, 56. iv. 25. Acts vii. 20. xviii. 11. xix. 8. xx. 3. xxviii. 11. Gal. iv. 10. Jas.

v. 17. Rev. ix. 5, 10, 15. xi. 2. xiii. 5. xxii. 2(μήνη LT).

μήνη, moon, month.

Rev. xxii. 2, for μήν, LT.

μηνύω.

show, Luke xx. 37. John xi. 57. 1 Cor. x. 28.

tell, Acts xxiii. 30p.

μήποτε.

lest at any time, Matt. iv. 6. v. 25. xiii. 15. Mark iv. 12. Luke iv. 11. xxi. 34. Heb. ii. 1.

lest haply, Luke xiv. 29. Acts v. 39.

lest, Matt. vii. 6. xiii. 29. xv. 32. xxv. 9. xxvii. 64. Mark xiv. 2. Luke xii. 58. xiv. 8, 12. Acts xxviii. 27. Heb. iii. 12. iv. 1.

if peradventure, 2 Tim. ii. 25.

nocc . . **at all,** Heb. ix. 17.

whether or not, Luke iii. 15.

Interrogative, not rendered, John vii. 26.

μήπου, lest anywhere.

Acts xxvii. 29, for μήπως, G''T*S*.

μήπω.

not yet, Rom. ix. 11. Heb. ix. 8.

μήπως.

lest by any means, 1 Cor. viii. 9. 2 Cor. xi. 3. Gal. ii. 2.

lest that by any means, 1 Cor. ix. 27.

lest by some means, 1 Thes. iii. 5.

lest perhaps, 2 Cor. ii. 7.

lest haply, 2 Cor. ix. 4.

lest, Acts xxvii. 29 (μήπου G''T*S*). Rom. xi. 21(-GooL*S*). 2 Cor. xii. 20*t*. Gal. iv. 11.

μηρός.

thigh, Rev. xix. 16.

μήτε.

With another negative, [2].

neither, Matt. v. 34, 35, 36. xi. 18. Luke vii. 33. ix. 3*f*. Acts xxiii. 12, 21. xxvii. 20. Eph. iv. 27 (μηδέ LT *S*). 2 Thes. ii. 2. 1 Tim. i. 7. Heb. vii. 3. Jas. v. 12*tr*. Rev. vii. 3.

nor, Matt. v. 35. xi. 18. Luke vii. 33. ix. 3. Acts xxiii. 8, 21. xxvii. 20. 2 Thes. ii. 2*t*. 1 Tim. i. 7. Heb. vii. 3. Rev. vii. 1*t*, 3.

or, 2 Thes. ii. 2[2](μηδέ LT*S*).

so much as, Mark iii. 20[2] (μηδέ LT Tr).

Add Acts xxiii. 8, for μηδέ, L*S*.

μήτηρ.

mother, Matt. i. 18. ii. 11, 13, 14, 20, 21. x. 35, 37. xii. 46, 47, 48, 49, 50. xiii. 55. xiv. 8, 11. xv. 4*t*, 5, 6 (5, *ap*). xix. 5, 12, 19, 29(*ap*). xx. 20. xxvii. 56*t*.

Mark iii. 31, 32, 33, 34, 35. v. 40. vi. 24, 28. vii. 10*t*, 11, 12. x. 7, 19, 29, 30. xv. 40.

Luke i. 15, 43, 60. ii. 33, 34, 43 (*ap*), 48, 51. vii. 12, 15. viii. 19, 20, 21, 51. xii. 53*t*. xiv. 26. xviii. 20.

John ii. 1, 3, 5, 12. iii. 4. vi. 42. xix. 25*t*, 26*t*, 27.

Acts i. 14. iii. 2. xii. 12. xiv. 8, Rom. xvi. 13. Gal. i. 15. iv. 26, Eph. v. 31. vi. 2. 1 Tim. v. 2. 2 Tim. i. 5. Rev. xvii. 5.

μήτις, μήτι. See μή, IV.

μήτρα.

womb, Luke ii. 23. Rom. iv. 19.

μητραλῴας, μητρολῴας LT*S*.

murderer of a mother, 1 Tim. i. 9.

μία. See εἷς.

μιαίνω.

defile, John xviii. 28. Tit. i. 15*t*. Heb. xii. 15. Jude 8.

μίασμα.

pollution, 2 Pet. ii. 20.

μιασμός.

uncleanness, 2 Pet. ii. 10.

μίγμα.

mixture, John xix. 39.

μίγνυμι.

mingle, Matt. xxvii. 34. Luke xiii. 1. Rev. viii. 7. xv. 2.

μικρός.

little, Luke xii. 32. xix. 3. John

vii. 33. xii. 35. 1 Cor. v. 6. Gal. v. 9. Jas. iii. 5. Rev. iii. 8. vi. 11 (-GTTr[b]). xx. 3.
little one, Matt. x. 42. xviii. 6, 10, 14. Mark ix. 42. Luke xvii. 2.
less, Mark xv. 40.
least[c], Acts viii. 10. Heb. viii. 11.
small, Acts xxvi. 22. Rev. xi. 18. xiii. 16. xix. 5, 18. xx. 12.

Comp., μικρότερος.

less, Mark iv. 31.
least, Matt. xi. 11. xiii. 32. Luke vii. 28. ix. 48.

Adv., μικρόν.

a little, Matt. xxvi. 39. Mark xiv. 35, 70. 2 Cor. xi. 1, 16.
a little while, John xiii. 33. xiv. 19. xvi. 16*t*, 17*t*, 18, 19*t*. Heb. x. 37.
a while, Matt. xxvi. 73.

μίλιον.

mile, Matt. v. 41.

μιμέομαι.

follow, 2 Thes. iii. 7, 9. Heb. xiii. 7. 3 John 11.

μιμητής.

follower, 1 Cor. iv. 16. xi. 1. Eph. v. 1. 1 Thes. i. 6. ii. 14. Heb. vi. 12. 1 Pet. iii. 13 (ζηλωτής G''L*S*).

μιμνήσκω.

Mid., **be mindful of**, Heb. ii. 6. — **remember**, Heb. xiii. 3.

1st Aorist, ἐμνήσθην.

be mindful of, 2 Tim. i. 4. 2 Pet. iii. 2.
remember, Matt. v. 23. xxvi. 75. xxvii. 63. Luke i. 72. xvi. 25. xxiii. 42. xxiv. 6, 8. John ii. 17, 22. xii. 16. Acts xi. 16. 1 Cor. xi. 2. Heb. viii. 12. x. 17. Jude 17.
in remembrance of, Luke i. 54[inf].
Pass., **come in remembrance**, Rev. xvi. 19.—**be had in remembrance**, Acts x. 31.

μισέω.

to hate, Matt. v. 43, 44 (*ap*). vi. 24. x. 22. xxiv. 9, 10. Mark xiii. 13. Luke i. 71. vi. 22, 27. xiv. 26. xvi. 13. xix. 14. xxi. 17. John iii. 20. vii. 7*t*. xii. 25. xv. 18*t*, 19, 23, 24, 25. xvii. 14. Rom vii. 15. ix. 13. Eph. v. 29. Tit. iii. 3. Heb. i. 9. 1 John ii. 9, 11. iii. 13, 15. iv. 20. Jude 23. Rev. ii. 6*t*, 15(*see* ὁμοίως). xvii. 16.
Pass. part., **hateful**, Rev. xviii. 2.
Add Rev. xviii. 2[p](foul and . .), L.

μισθαποδοσία.

recompense of reward, Heb. ii. 2. x. 35. xi. 26.

μισθαποδότης.

rewarder, Heb. xi. 6.

μίσθιος.

hired servant, Luke xv. 17, 19.

μισθός.

hire, Matt. xx. 8. Luke x. 7. Jas. v. 4.
wages, John iv. 36. 2 Pet. ii. 15.
reward, Matt. v. 12. 46. vi. 1, 2, 5, 16. x. 41*t*, 42. Mark ix. 41. Luke vi. 23, 35. Acts i. 18. Rom. iv. 4. 1 Cor. iii. 8, 14. ix. 17, 18. 1 Tim. v. 18. 2 Pet. ii. 13. 2 John 8. Jude 11. Rev. xi. 18. xxii. 12.

μισθόω.

Mid., **to hire**, Matt. xx. 1, 7.

μίσθωμα.

hired [c]**house**, Acts xxviii. 30.

μισθωτός.

hired servant, Mark i. 20.
hireling, John x. 12, 13(*ap*), 13.

μνᾶ.

pound, Luke xix. 13, 16*t*, 18*t*, 20, 24*t*, 25.

μνάομαι. See μιμνήσκω.

μνεία.

remembrance, Phil. i. 3(*marg.* mention). 1 Thes. iii. 6. 2 Tim. i. 3.
mention, Rom. i. 9. Eph. i. 16. 1 Thes. i. 2. Phm. 4.

μνῆμα.

tomb, Mark v. 5. Luke viii. 27.
sepulchre, Luke xxiii. 53. xxiv. 1. Acts ii. 29. vii. 16.

grave, Rev. xi. 19.
Add Mark v. 3, for μνημεῖον, GLT Tr*S*.

μνημεῖον.

tomb, Matt. viii. 28. xxvii. 60. Mark v. 2, 3 (μνῆμα GLTTr*S*). vi. 29.
sepulchre, Matt. xxiii. 29. xxvii. 60. xxviii. 8. Mark xv. 46*t*. xvi. 2, 3, 5, 8. Luke xi. 47, 48(–G∞L[b] TTr*S*). xxiii. 55. xxiv. 2, 9, 12, 22, 24(*ap*). John xix. 41, 42. xx. 1*t*, 2, 3, 4, 6, 8, 11*t*. Acts xiii. 29.
grave, Matt. xxvii. 52, 53. Luke xi. 44. John v. 28. xi. 17, 31, 38. xii. 17.

μνήμη.

remembrance, 2 Pet. i. 15.

μνημονεύω.

remember, Matt. xvi. 9. Mark viii. 18. Luke xvii. 32. John xv. 20. xvi. 4, 21. Acts xx. 31, 35. Gal. ii. 10. Eph. ii. 11. Col. iv. 18. 1 Thes. i. 3. ii. 9. 2 Thes. ii. 5. 2 Tim. ii. 8. Heb. xiii. 7. Rev. ii. 5. iii. 3. xviii. 5.
be mindful of, Heb. xi. 15.
make mention, Heb. xi. 22 (*marg.*, *with* περί, **remember**).

μνημόσυνον.

memorial, Matt. xxvi. 13. Mark xiv. 9. Acts x. 4.

μνηστεύω.

Pass., **be espoused**, Matt. i. 18. Luke i. 27. ii. 5.

μογγιλάλος, speaking with a hoarse hollow voice.

Mark vii. 32, for μογιλάλος, G′′Tr.

μογιλάλος.

having an impediment in one's speech, Mark vii. 32 (μογγιλάλος G′′Tr).

μόγις.

hardly, Luke ix. 39.

μόδιος.

bushel, Matt. v. 15. Mark iv. 21. Luke xi. 33.

μοί. See ἐγώ.

μοιχαλίς.

adulteress, Rom. vii. 3*t*. Jas. iv. 4.
adulterous, Matt. xii. 39. xvi. 4. Mark viii. 38.
adultery (*Gr.* an adulteress), 2 Pet. ii. 14.

μοιχάω.

Mid., **commit adultery**, Matt. v. 32 (μοιχευθῆναι fr. μοιχεύω LTr*S*), 32. xix. 9*t*. Mark x. 11, 12.

μοιχεία.

adultery, Matt. xv. 19. Mark vii. 21. John viii. 3(*ap*). Gal. v. 19 (*omS*).

μοιχεύω.

commit adultery (with[1]), Matt. v. 27, 28[1]. xix. 18. Mark x. 19. Luke xvi. 18*t*. xviii. 20. Rom. ii. 22*t*. xiii. 9. Jas. ii. 11*t*. Rev. ii. 22.
Pass. as Mid., **in adultery**, John viii. 4[p](*ap*).
Add Matt. v. 32, *see* μοιχάω.

μοιχός.

adulterer, Luke xviii. 11. 1 Cor. vi. 9. Heb. xiii. 4. Jas. iv. 4(–LT*S*).

μόλις.

hardly, Acts xxvii. 8.
scarcely, Rom. v. 7. 1 Pet. iv. 18.
scarce, Acts xiv. 18. xxvii. 7.
See also ἰσχύω.

μολύνω.

defile, 1 Cor. viii. 7. Rev. iii. 4. xiv. 4.

μολυσμός.

filthiness, 2 Cor. vii. 1.

μομφή.

quarrel (*marg.* **complaint**), Col. iii. 13.

μονή.

abode, John xiv. 23.
mansion, John xiv. 2.

μονογενής.

only begotten (*said of Christ*), John i. 14, 18. iii. 16, 18. 1 John iv. 9.
only begotten son, Heb. xi. 17.
only child, Luke ix. 38.
only, Luke vii. 12. viii. 42.

μόνος.

only, Matt. iv. 10. xii. 4. xvii. 8. xxiv. 36. Mark ix. 8. Luke iv. 8. xxiv. 18. John v. 44. xvii. 3. Rom. xvi. 4, 27. 1 Cor. ix. 6. xiv. 36. Phil. iv. 15. Col. iv. 11. 1 Tim. i. 17. vi. 15, 16. 2 Tim. iv. 11. 2 John 1. Jude 4, 25. Rev. ix. 4 (*omS*). xv. 4.

alone, Matt. iv. 4. xiv. 23. xviii. 15. Mark vi. 47. Luke iv. 4. v. 21. vi. 4. ix. 36. x. 40. John vi. 15, 22. viii. 9(*ap*), 16, 29. xii. 24. xvi. 32*t*. Rom. xi. 3. Gal. vi. 4. 1 Thes. iii. 1. Heb. ix. 7.

by one's self, Mark ix. 2. Luke xxiv. 12(*ap*).

Add Mark xi. 13 (leaves . .), L[b].

See also καταμόνας.

Adv., μόνον.

only, Matt. v. 47. viii. 8. x. 42. xiv. 36. xxi. 19, 21. Mark v. 36. vi. 8. Luke viii. 50. John v. 18. xi. 52. xii. 9. xiii. 9. Acts viii. 16. xi. 19. xviii. 25. xix. 27. xxi. 13. xxvi. 29. xxvii. 10.

Rom. i. 32. iii. 29. iv. 12, 16. v. 3, 11. viii. 23. ix. 10, 24. xiii. 5. 1 Cor. vii. 39. xv. 19. 2 Cor. vii. 7. viii. 10, 19, 21. ix. 12. Gal. i. 23. ii. 10. iii. 2. iv. 18. v. 13. vi. 12. Eph. i. 21. Phil. i. 27, 29. ii. 12, 27. 1 Thes. i. 5, 8. ii. 8. 2 Thes. ii. 7. 1 Tim. v. 13. 2 Tim. ii. 20. iv. 8.

Heb. ix. 10. xii. 26. Jas. i. 22. ii. 24. 1 Pet. ii. 18. 1 John ii. 2. v. 6.

alone, John xvii. 20. Acts xix. 26. Rom. iv. 23.

but, Matt. ix. 21.

μονόφθαλμος.

with one eye, Matt. xviii. 9 Mark ix. 47.

μονόω.

Pass., **desolate**, 1 Tim. v. 5[p].

μορφή.

form, Mark xvi. 12(*ap*). Phil. ii. 6, 7.

μορφόω.

to form, Gal. iv. 19.

μόρφωσις.

form, Rom. ii. 20. 2 Tim. iii. 5.

μοσχοποιέω.

make a calf, Acts vii. 41.

μόσχος.

calf, Luke xv. 23, 27, 30. Heb. ix. 12, 19. Rev. iv. 7.

μοῦ. See ἐγώ.

μουσικός.

musician, Rev. xviii. 22.

μόχθος.

travail, 1 Thes. ii. 9. 2 Thes. iii. 8.

painfulness, 2 Cor. xi. 27.

μυελός.

marrow, Heb. iv. 12.

μυέω.

instruct, Phil. iv. 12.

μῦθος.

fable, 1 Tim. i. 4. iv. 7. 2 Tim. iv. 4. Tit. i. 14. 2 Pet. i. 16.

μυκάομαι.

to roar, Rev. x. 3.

μυκτηρίζω.

to mock, Gal. vi. 7.

μυλικός.

λίθος μυλικός, **millstone**, Mark ix. 42 (μύλος ὀνικός G'LTr*S*).

Add Luke xvii. 2, for ὀνικός, G''L TTr*S*.

μύλινος, of a mill?

Rev. xviii. 21, for μύλος, LTr.

μύλος.

millstone, Matt. xviii. 6. Luke xvii. 2 (λίθος G''LTTr*S*). Rev. xviii. 21 (μύλινος LTr, λίθος *S*), 22.

Add Matt. xxiv. 41, for μύλων, LT Tr*S*. Mark ix. 42, *see* λίθος.

μύλων.

mill, Matt. xxiv. 41 (μύλος LTTr*S*).

μυριάς.

ten thousand, Jude 14.

μυριάδες μυριάδων, **ten thousand times ten thousand**, Rev. v. 11(*ap*).

μυριάδες πέντε, **fifty thousand**, Acts xix. 19.

δύο μυριάδες (δισμυριάδες LT, δυσμυριάδες Tr) μυριάδων, **two hundred thousand thousand,** Rev. ix. 16.

Plural, **thousands,** Acts xxi. 20.— **an innumerable multitude,** Luke xii. 1.—**an innumerable company,** Heb. xii. 22.

μυρίζω.

anoint, Mark xiv. 8.

μύριοι, μυρίοι.

ten thousand, Matt. xviii. 24. 1 Cor. iv. 15. xiv. 19.

μύρον.

ointment, Matt. xxvi. 7, 9 (*omS*), 12. Mark xiv. 3, 4. Luke vii. 37, 38, 46. xxiii. 56. John xi. 2. xii. 3*t*, 5. Rev. xviii. 13.

Add Mark xiv. 5 (τοῦτο . .), G[pr]L TTr, for τοῦτο, *S*.

μυστήριον.

mystery, Matt. xiii. 11. Mark iv. 11. Luke viii. 10. Rom. xi. 25. xvi. 25. 1 Cor. ii. 7. iv. 1. xiii. 2. xiv. 2. xv. 51. Eph. i. 9. iii. 3, 4, 9. v. 32. vi. 19. Col. i. 26, 27. ii. 2. iv. 3. 2 Thes. ii. 7. 1 Tim. iii. 9, 16. Rev. i. 20. x. 7. xvii. 5, 7.

Add 1 Cor. ii. 1, for μαρτύριον, G''*S*.

μυωπάζω.

can not see afar off, 2 Pet. i. 9.

μώλωψ.

stripes, 1 Pet. ii. 24.

μωμάομαι, μωμέομαι.

to blame, 2 Cor. vi. 3. viii. 20.

μῶμος.

blemish, 2 Pet. ii. 13.

μωραίνω.

Pass., **lose savor,** Matt. v. 13. Luke xiv. 34.—**become a fool,** Rom. i. 22.

make foolish, 1 Cor. i. 20.

μωρία.

foolishness, 1 Cor. i. 18, 21, 23. ii. 14. iii. 19.

μωρολογία.

foolish talking, Eph. v. 4.

μωρός.

foolish, Matt. vii. 26. xxv. 2, 3, 8. 2 Tim. ii. 23. Tit. iii. 9.

fool, Matt. v. 22. xxiii. 17, 19(–G[o] L[b]TTr*S*). 1 Cor. iii. 18. iv. 10.

Neut., **foolish thing,** 1 Cor. i. 27.—**foolishness,** 1 Cor. i. 25.

ναί.

yea, Matt. v. 37*t*. ix. 28. xi. 9. xiii. 51. xxi. 16. Luke vii. 26. xii. 5. John xi. 27. xxi. 15, 16. Acts v. 8. xxii. 27. 2 Cor. i. 17*t*, 18, 19*t*, 20. Phm. 20. Jas. v. 12*t*. Rev. xiv. 13.

yes, Matt. xvii. 25. Mark vii. 28. Rom. iii. 29.

even so, Matt. xi. 26. Luke x. 21. Rev. i. 7. xvi. 7. xxii. 20(*omS*).

surely, Rev. xxii. 20.

verily, Luke xi. 51.

truth, Matt. xv. 27.

Add Phil. iv. 3, for καί, GLT*S*.

ναός.

temple, Matt. xxiii. 16*t*, 17, 21, 35. xxvi. 61. xxvii. 5, 40, 51. Mark xiv. 58. xv. 29, 38. Luke i. 9, 21, 22. xxiii. 45. John ii. 19, 20, 21. Acts vii. 48(*omS*). xvii. 24. 1 Cor. iii. 16, 17*t*. vi. 19. 2 Cor. vi. 16*t*. Eph. ii. 21. 2 Thes. ii. 4. Rev. iii. 12. vii. 15. xi. 1, 2, 19*t*. xiv. 15(–G[o]), 17 xv. 5, 6 (–G[oo]T Tr[b]), 8*t*. xvi. 1(–G[oo]Tr[b]), 17. xxi. 22*t*.

shrine, Acts xix. 24.

νάρδος.

With πιστικός, **spikenard,** Mark xiv. 3 (*marg.* **pure nard,** *or* **liquid nard**). John xii. 3.

ναυαγέω.

suffer shipwreck, 2 Cor. xi. 25.

make shipwreck, 1 Tim. i. 19.

ναύκληρος.

owner of the[c] ship, Acts xxvii. 11.

ναῦς.

ship, Acts xxvii. 41.

ναύτης.

shipman, Acts xxvii. 27, 30.

sailor, Rev. xviii. 17.

νεανίας.

young man, Acts vii. 58. xx. 9. xxiii. 17, 18 (νεανίσκος LT*S*), 22 (νεανίσκος LT*S*).

νεανίσκος.

young man, Matt. xix. 20, 22. Mark xiv. 51, 51(-G°°LTr*S*). xvi. 5. Luke vii. 14. Acts ii. 17. v. 10. 1 John ii. 13, 14.

Add Acts xxiii. 18, 22, for νεανίας, LT*S*.

νεκρός.

dead, *subst.*, Matt. viii. 22*t*. x. 8 (-G°T). xi. 5. xiv. 2. xvii. 9. xxii. 31, 32. xxvii. 64. xxviii. 7. Mark vi. 14, 16(-TTr[b]*S*). ix. 9, 10. xii. 25, 26, 27. Luke vii. 22. ix. 7, 60*t*. xvi. 30, 31. xx. 35, 37, 38. xxiv. 5, 46. John ii. 22. v. 21, 25. xii. 1, 9, 17. xx. 9. xxi. 14. Acts iii. 15. iv. 2, 10. x. 41, 42. xiii. 30, 34. xvii. 3, 31, 32. xxiii. 6. xxiv. 15 (-G°°LT*S*), 21. xxvi. 8, 23. Rom. i. 4. iv. 17, 24. vi. 4, 9, 13. vii. 4. viii. 11*t*. x. 7, 9. xi. 15. xiv. 9. 1 Cor. xv. 12*t*, 13, 15, 16, 20, 21, 29*t*, 29(αὐτός GLT*S*), 32, 35, 42, 52. 2 Cor. i. 9. Gal. i. 1. Eph. i. 20. v. 14. Phil. iii. 11. Col. i. 18. ii. 12. 1 Thes. i. 10. iv. 16. 2 Tim. ii. 8. iv. 1. Heb. vi. 2. xi. 19, 35. xiii. 20. 1 Pet. i. 3, 21. iv. 5. Rev. i. 5. xi. 18. xiv. 13. xx. 5, 12*t*, 13*t*.

one dead, Mark ix. 26.

dead man, Matt. xxiii. 27. xxviii. 4. Rev. xvi. 3.

he that is dead, Luke vii. 15. 1 Pet. iv. 6.

dead, *adj.*, Luke xv. 24, 32. Acts v. 10. xx. 9. xxviii. 6. Rom. vi. 11. vii. 8. viii. 10. Eph. ii. 1, 5. Col. ii. 13. Heb. vi. 1. ix. 14. Jas. ii. 17, 20 (ἀργός LT), 26*t*. Rev. i. 17, 18. ii. 8. iii. 1.

ἐπὶ νεκροῖς, **after men are dead**, Heb. ix. 17.

Add Mark xvi. 14(*ap*).

νεκρόω.

mortify, Col. iii. 5.

Pass., **dead**, Rom. iv. 19[p]. Heb. xi. 12[p].

νέκρωσις.

dying, 2 Cor. iv. 10.

deadness, Rom. iv. 19.

νεομηνία. See νουμηνία.

νέος.

new, Matt. ix. 17*t*. Mark ii. 22, 22 (-G°°LTTr*S*), 22(*ap*). Luke v. 37*t*, 38, 39. 1 Cor. v. 7. Heb. xii. 24.

new man, Col. iii. 10.

Fem., **young woman**, Tit. ii. 4.

Comp., νεώτερος.

younger, Luke xv. 12, 13. xxii. 26. 1 Tim. v. 2, 11, 14. 1 Pet. v. 5.

younger man, 1 Tim. v. 1.

young, John xxi. 18.

young man, Acts v. 6. Tit. ii. 6.

νεοσσός, νοσσός G'T*S*.

young, Luke ii. 24.

νεότης.

youth, Matt. xix. 20(-G°LTTr*S*). Mark x. 20. Luke xviii. 21. Acts xxvi. 4. 1 Tim. iv. 12.

νεόφυτος.

novice (*marg.* **one newly come to the faith**), 1 Tim. iii. 6.

νεύω.

beckon, John xiii. 24. Acts xxiv. 10[p].

νεφέλη.

cloud, Matt. xvii. 5*t*. xxiv. 30. xxvi. 64. Mark ix. 7*t*. xiii. 26. xiv. 62. Luke ix. 34*t*, 35. xii. 54. xxi. 27. Acts i. 9. 1 Cor. x. 1, 2. 1 Thes. iv. 17. 2 Pet. ii. 17(καὶ ὁμίχλη GLT *S*). Jude 12. Rev. i. 7. x. 1. xi. 12. xiv. 14*t*, 15, 16.

νέφος.

cloud, Heb. xii. 1.

νεφρός.

Plur., **reins**, Rev. ii. 23.

νεωκόρος.

worshipper (*Gr.* temple keeper), Acts xix. 35.

νεωτερικός.
youthful, 2 Tim. ii. 22.

νεώτερος. See νέος.

νή.
I^c protest by, 1 Cor. xv. 31.

νήθω.
spin, Matt. vi. 28. Luke xii. 27.

νηπιάζω.
be a child, 1 Cor. xiv. 20.

νήπιος.
babe, Matt. xi. 25. xxi. 16. Luke x. 21. Rom. ii. 20. 1 Cor. iii. 1. Heb. v. 13.
child, 1 Cor. xiii. 11*f*. Gal. iv. 1, 3. Eph. iv. 14.
Gen., **childish**, 1 Cor. xiii. 11.
Add 1 Thes. ii. 7, for ἤπιος, L*S*.

νησίον.
island, Acts xxvii. 16.

νῆσος.
island, Acts xxvii. 26. xxviii. 1, 7, 9. Rev. vi. 14. xvi. 20.
isle, Acts xiii. 6. xxviii. 11. Rev. i. 9.

νηστεία.
fasting, Matt. xvii. 21(*ap*). Mark ix. 29(–T*S*). Luke ii. 37. Acts xiv. 23. 1 Cor. vii. 5(*omS*). 2 Cor. vi. 5. xi. 27.
fast, Acts xxvii. 9.

νηστεύω.
to fast, Matt. iv. 2p. vi. 16*t*, 17p, 18. ix. 14*t*, 15. Mark ii. 18*t*, 19, 19 (*ap*), 20. Luke v. 33, 34, 35. xviii. 12. Acts x. 30(–L*S*). xiii. 2, 3p.
With ἦν, **used to fast**, Mark ii. 18p.

νῆστις.
fasting, Matt. xv. 32. Mark viii. 3.

νηφάλιος, νηφάλεος.
sober, 1 Tim. iii. 2, 11. Tit. ii. 2 (*marg.* **vigilant**).

νήφω.
be sober, 1 Thes. v. 6, 8. 1 Pet. v. 8.
sober, 1 Pet. i. 13p.
watch, 2 Tim. iv. 5. 1 Pet. iv. 7.

νικάω.
get the victory, Rev. xv. 2.
prevail, Rev. v. 5.
overcome, Luke xi. 22. John xvi. 33. Rom. iii. 4. xii. 21*t*. 1 John ii. 13, 14. iv. 4. v. 4*t*, 5. Rev. ii. 7, 11, 17. 26. iii. 5, 12, 21*t*. xi. 7. xii. 11. xiii. 7(*ap*). xvii. 14. xxi. 7.
conquer, Rev. vi. 2*t*.

νίκη.
victory, 1 John v. 4.

νῖκος.
victory, Matt. xii. 20. 1 Cor. xv. 54, 55, 57.

νιπτήρ.
basin, John xiii. 5.

νίπτω.
to wash, Matt. vi. 17. xv. 2. Mark vii. 3. John ix. 7(–Lb), 7, 11*t*, 15. xiii. 5, 6, 8*t*, 10, 12, 14*t*. 1 Tim. v. 10.

νοέω.
perceive, Mark vii. 18. viii. 17.
understand, Matt. xv. 17. xvi. 9, 11. xxiv. 15. Mark xiii. 14. John xii. 40. Rom. i. 20. Eph iii. 4. 1 Tim. i. 7. Heb. xi. 3.
think, Eph. iii. 20.
consider, 2 Tim. ii. 7.

νόημα.
thought, 2 Cor. x. 5.
device, 2 Cor. ii. 11.
mind, 2 Cor. iii. 14. iv. 4. xi. 3. Phil. iv. 7.

νόθος.
bastard, Heb. xii. 8.

νομή.
pasture, John x. 9.
With ἔχω, **eat**, 2 Tim. ii. 17.

νομίζω.
Pass., **be wont**, Acts xvi. 13.
think, Matt. v. 17. x. 34. Acts viii. 20. xvii. 29. 1 Cor. vii. 36.
suppose, Matt. xx. 10. Luke ii. 44. iii. 23. Acts vii. 25. xiv. 19. xvi. 27. xxi. 29. 1 Cor. vii. 26. 1 Tim. vi. 5.

νομικός.
about the law, Tit. iii. 9.
lawyer, Matt. xxii. 35. Luke vii. 30. x. 25. xi. 45, 46, 52. xiv. 3. Tit. iii. 13.

νομίμως.
lawfully, 1 Tim. i. 8. 2 Tim. ii. 5.

νόμισμα.
money, Matt. xxii. 19.

νομοδιδάσκαλος.
teacher of the law, 1 Tim. i. 7.
doctor of the law, Luke v. 17. Acts v. 34.

νομοθεσία.
giving of the law, Rom. ix. 4.

νομοθετέω.
Pass., **receive the° law,** Heb. vii. 11.
establish, Heb. viii. 6.

νομοθέτης.
lawgiver, Jas. iv. 12.

νόμος.
Without the article, [1].
law, Matt. v. 17, 18. vii. 12. xi. 13. xii. 5. xxii. 36, 40. xxiii. 23. Luke ii. 22, 23[1], 24[1], 27, 39. x. 26. xvi. 16, 17. xxiv. 44. John i. 17, 45(46). vii. 19*t*, 23, 49, 51. viii. 5 (*ap*), 17. x. 34. xii. 34. xv. 25. xviii. 31. xix. 7. Acts vi. 13. vii. 53. xiii. 15, 39. xv. 5, 24(*ap*). xviii. 13, 15. xxi. 20, 24, 28. xxii. 3, 12. xxiii. 3, 29. xxiv. 6(*ap*), 14. xxv. 8. xxviii. 23.
Rom. ii. 12[1]*t*, 13 (–*art.* LT*S*), 13 (–*art.* G°°LT*S*), 14[1], 14, 14[1]*t*, 15, 17 (–*art.* G°°LT*S*), 18, 20, 23[1], 23, 25[1]*t*, 26, 27, 27[1]. iii. 19*t*, 20[1]*t*, 21[1], 21, 27, 27[1], 28[1], 31[1]*t*. iv. 13[1], 14[1], 15, 15[1], 16. v. 13[1]*t*, 20[1]. vi. 14[1], 15[1]. vii. 1[1], 1, 2[1], 2, 3, 4, 5, 6, 7, 7[1], 7, 8[1], 9[1], 12, 14, 16, 21, 22, 23[1], 23*t*, 25[1]*t*. viii. 2*t*, 3, 4, 7. ix. 31[1]*t*, 32[1] (–G°°LT*S*). x. 4[1], 5. xiii. 8[1], 10[1].
1 Cor. vii. 39[1] (*om S*). ix. 8, 9, 20[1]*tr*. xiv. 21, 34. xv. 56. Gal. ii. 16[1]*tr*, 19[1], 21[1]. iii. 2[1], 5[1], 10[1], 10, 11[1], 12, 13, 17, 18[1], 19, 21*t*, 21[1], 23[1], 24. iv. 4[1], 5[1], 21[1], 21. v. 3, 4[1], 14, 18[1], 23[1]. vi. 2, 13[1]. Eph. ii. 15. Phil. iii. 5[1], 6[1], 9[1]. 1 Tim. i. 8, 9[1].
Heb. vii. 5, 12[1], 16[1], 19, 28*t*. viii. 4, 10[1]. ix. 19[1](*art.* L), 22. x. 1, 8 (–*art.* G°LT*S*), 16, 28[1]. Jas. i. 25[1]. ii. 8[1], 9, 10, 11[1], 12[1]. iv. 11[1]*f*.
Add Matt. xv. 6, for ἐντολή, T*S*. 1 Cor. ix. 20(*ap*).

νοσέω.
dote (*marg.* **sick**), 1 Tim. vi. 4[p].

νόσημα.
disease, John v. 4(*ap*).

νόσος.
sickness, Matt. iv. 23. viii. 17. ix. 35. x. 1. Mark iii. 15(–TTr*S*).
disease, Matt. iv. 24. Mark i. 34. Luke iv. 40. vi. 17. ix. 1. Acts xix. 12.
infirmity, Luke vii. 21.

νοσσιά.
brood, Luke xiii. 34 (*νοσσίον* [pl] L).

νοσσίον.
chicken, Matt. xxiii. 37.
Add Luke xiii. 34, *see νοσσιά.*

νοσσός. See νεοσσός.

νοσφίζω.
Mid., **keep back,** Acts v. 2, 3. — **purloin,** Tit. ii. 10.

νότος.
south wind, Luke xii. 55. Acts xxvii. 13. xxviii. 13.
south, Matt. xii. 42. Luke xi. 31. xiii. 29. Rev. xxi. 13.

νουθεσία.
admonition, 1 Cor. x. 11. Eph. vi. 4. Tit. iii. 10.

νουθετέω.
admonish, Rom. xv. 14. Col. iii. 16. 1 Thes. v. 12. 2 Thes. iii. 15.
warn, Acts xx. 31. 1 Cor. iv. 14. Col. i. 28. 1 Thes. v. 14.

νουμηνία, νεομηνία L*S*.
new moon, Col. ii. 16.

νουνεχῶς.
discreetly, Mark xii. 34.

νοῦς.

mind, Rom. i. 28. vii. 23, 25. xi. 34. xii. 2. xiv. 5. 1 Cor. i. 10. ii. 16*t*. Eph. iv. 17, 23. Col. ii. 18. 2 Thes. ii. 2. Tit. i. 15. Rev. xvii. 9.

minds[c], 1 Tim. vi. 5. 2 Tim. iii. 8.

understanding, Luke xxiv. 45. 1 Cor. xiv. 14, 15*t*, 19. Phil. iv. 7. Rev. xiii. 18.

νύμφη.

bride, John iii. 29. Rev. xviii. 23. xxi. 2, 9 (–G″). xxii. 17.

daughter-in-law, Matt. x. 35. Luke xii. 53*t*.

νυμφίος.

bridegroom, Matt. ix. 15*t*. xxv. 1, 5, 6, 10. Mark ii. 19(*ap*), 19, 20. Luke v. 34, 35. John ii. 9. iii. 29*tr*. Rev. xviii. 23.

νυμφών.

bride-chamber, Matt. ix. 15. Mark ii. 19. Luke v. 34.

νῦν.

now, Matt. xxvi. 65. xxvii. 42, 43. Mark x. 30. xv. 32. Luke ii. 29. vi. 21*t*, 25. xi. 39. xvi. 25. xix. 42. xxii. 36.

John ii. 8. iv. 18, 23. v. 25. viii. 40, 52. ix. 21, 41. xi. 22. xii. 27, 31*t*. xiii. 31, 36. xiv. 29. xv. 22, 24. xvi. 5, 22, 29, 30, 32 (–G∞LT Tr*S*). xvii. 5, 7, 13. xviii. 36. xxi. 10.

Acts ii. 33 (*omS*). iii. 17. vii. 4, 34, 52. x. 5, 33. xii. 11. xiii. 11. xv. 10. xvi. 36, 37. xx. 22, 25. xxii. 16. xxiii. 15, 21. xxiv. 13 (νυνί LT*S*). xxvi. 6, 17 (G′, ἐγώ GLT*S*).

Rom. iii. 21. v. 9, 11. vi. 19, 21. viii. 1, 22. xi. 30, 31. xiii. 11. xvi. 26. 1 Cor. iii. 2. vii. 14. xii. 20. 2 Cor. vi. 2*t*. vii. 9. xiii. 2. Gal. i. 23. ii. 20. iii. 3. iv. 9, 25, 29. Eph. ii. 2. iii. 5, 10. v. 8. Phil. i. 5, 20, 30. ii. 12. iii. 18. Col. i. 24. 1 Thes. iii. 8. 2 Thes. ii. 6. 2 Tim. i. 10.

Heb. ii. 8. ix. 5, 24, 26(νυνί LT*S*). xii. 26. Jas. iv. 13, 16. v. 1. 1 Pet. i. 12. ii. 10*t*, 25. iii. 21. 2 Pet. iii. 7, 18. 1 John ii. 18, 28. iii. 2. iv. 3. 2 John 5. Jude 25.

With art., **that now is**, 1 Tim. iv. 8. — **which I make**[c] **now**, Acts xxii. 1 (νυνί GLT*S*).

at this time, 1 Cor. xvi. 12.

this time, Matt. xxiv. 21. Mark xiii. 19.

τὸ νῦν ἔχον, **for this time**, Acts xxiv. 25.

ὁ νῦν καιρός, **this time**, Rom. iii. 26. — **this present time**, Rom. viii. 18. xi. 5. — *With* ἐν, **now at this time**, 2 Cor. viii. 14(13).

ὁ νῦν αἰών, **this world**, 1 Tim. vi. 17. — **this present world**, 2 Tim. iv. 10. Tit. ii. 12.

ἀπὸ τοῦ νῦν, **from henceforth**, Luke i. 48. v. 10. xii. 52. Acts xviii. 6. — **henceforth**, 2 Cor. v. 16. — **hereafter**, Luke xxii. 69.

νῦν οὐκέτι, **now henceforth no more**, 2 Cor. v. 16.

of late, John xi. 8.

Add Matt. xii. 32, for τούτῳ, G′. Luke vi. 25 (full . .), Tr[b]*S*. xxii. 18 (drink ἀπὸ τοῦ νῦν), Tr[b]*S*. John vi. 42, for οὖν, TTr. Acts xiii. 31 (who are . .), G′LT*S*. Rom. xi. 31 (they . .), L[b], for αὐτοί, *S*. Heb. xi. 16, for νυνί, GLT*S*.

τὰ νῦν, ταννῦν.

now, Acts iv. 29. v. 38. xx. 32. xxvii. 22.

but now, Acts xvii. 30.

νυνί.

now, Rom. vi. 22. vii. 6, 17. xv. 23, 25. 1 Cor. v. 11. xii. 18. xiii. 13. xiv. 6. xv. 20. 2 Cor. viii. 11, 22. Eph. ii. 13. Col. i. 21, 26. iii. 8. Phm. 9, 11. Heb. viii. 6. xi. 16 (νῦν GLT*S*).

Add, for νῦν, Acts xxii. 1, GLT*S*. xxiv. 13, LT*S*.

νύξ.

night, Matt. iv. 2. xii. 40*t*. xiv. 25. xxvi. 31, 34. Mark iv. 27. v. 5. vi. 48. xiv. 27 (–G∞L[b]TTr*S*),

30. Luke ii. 37. v. 5. xii. 20. xvii. 34. xviii. 7. xxi. 37. John ix. 4. xi. 10. xiii. 30. xxi. 3. Acts ix. 24. xii. 6. xvi. 9, 33. xvii. 10. xviii. 9. xx. 31. xxiii. 11, 23, 31. xxvi. 7. xxvii. 23, 27.
Rom. xiii. 12. 1 Cor. xi. 23. 1 Thes. ii. 9. iii. 10. v. 2, 5. 2 Thes. iii. 8. 1 Tim. v. 5. 2 Tim. i. 3. 2 Pet. iii. 10(*omS*). Rev. iv. 8. vii. 15. viii. 12. xii. 10. xiv. 11. xx. 10. xxi. 25. xxii. 5.
Gen., **by night**, Matt. ii. 14. xxvii. 64(*omS*). xxviii. 13. Luke ii. 8. John iii. 2. vii. 50(–LTTr*S*). xix. 39. Acts v. 19. ix. 25.—**in the night**, 1 Thes. v. 7*t*.
μέσης νυκτός, **at midnight**, Matt. xxv. 6.
μέσον τῆς νυκτός, **about midnight**, Acts xxvii. 27.

νύσσω, νύττω.

pierce, John xix. 34.

νυστάζω.

to slumber, Matt. xxv. 5. 2 Pet. ii. 3.

νυχθήμερον.

a night and a day, 2 Cor. xi. 25.

νωθρός.

slothful, Heb. vi. 12.
dull, Heb. v. 11.

νῶτος.

back, Rom. xi. 10.

ξενία.

lodging, Acts xxviii. 23. Phm. 22.

ξενίζω.

entertain, Heb. xiii. 2.
lodge, Acts x. 18, 23, 32. xxviii. 7.
Pass., **lodge**, Acts x. 6. xxi. 16.
strange thing, Acts xvii. 20p.
Mid., **think strange concerning**, 1 Pet. iv. 12.—**think strange**, 1 Pet. iv. 4.

ξενοδοχέω.

lodge strangers, 1 Tim. v. 10.

ξένος.

stranger, Matt. xxv. 35, 38, 43, 44. xxvii. 7. Acts xvii. 21. Eph. ii. 12, 19. Heb. xi. 13. 3 John 5.
strange, Acts xvii. 18. Heb. xiii. 9.
strange thing, 1 Pet. iv. 12.
host, Rom. xvi. 23.

ξέστης.

pot, Mark vii. 4, 8(*ap*).

ξηραίνω.

dry up, Mark v. 29. xi. 20. Rev. xvi. 12.
wither, Jas. i. 11.

Passive,

be withered, Mark iii. 1, 3p (ξηρός LTr*S*). John xv. 6.
wither, 1 Pet. i. 24.
wither away, Matt. xiii. 6. xxi. 19, 20. Mark iv. 6. xi. 21. Luke viii. 6.
pine away, Mark ix. 18.
be ripe (*marg.* **be dried**), Rev. xiv. 15.

ξηρός.

dry, Luke xxiii. 31.
dry land, Heb. xi. 29.
land, Matt. xxiii. 15.
withered, Matt. xii. 10. Luke vi. 6, 8. John v. 3.
Add Mark iii. 3, for ξηραίνω, *pass. part.*, LTr*S*.

ξύλινος.

of wood, 2 Tim. ii. 20. Rev. ix. 20.

ξύλον.

wood, 1 Cor. iii. 12. Rev. xviii. 12*t*.
staff, Matt. xxvi. 47, 55. Mark xiv. 43, 48. Luke xxii. 52.
stocks, Acts xvi. 24.
tree, Luke xxiii. 31. Acts v. 30. x. 39. xiii. 29. Gal. iii. 13. 1 Pet. ii. 24. Rev. ii. 7. xxii. 2*t*, 14.
Add Rev. xxii. 19, for βίβλος, GL TTr*S*.

ξυράω.

shave, 1 Cor. xi. 5p, 6.
Mid., **shave**, Acts xxi. 24.

ὁ, ἡ, τό.

A particle answering mainly to our article *the*, better to the French *le*, better still to the German *der*. Used generally where the noun refers to a person or thing as *well known*, either already mentioned or otherwise understood. Also commonly with *proper names*, as ὁ Ἰησοῦς, ὁ Παῦλος; and often with *abstract nouns*, as ἡ ἀγάπη, ἡ δικαιοσύνη. *Passim*.

Its peculiar uses are as follows:

I. As a *demonstrative pronoun*, once, in the quotation: τοῦ γὰρ καὶ γένος ἐσμέν,

his, Acts xvii. 28.

II. In distinctions and distribution, ὁ μὲν . . ὁ δέ. *See* μέν.

III. In narrative, by way of transition to another person or party, ὁ δέ without a preceding ὁ μέν.

and he, Matt. ii. 21. xii. 11.

οἱ δέ, **but they**, Matt. ix. 31.

he, Matt. xiii. 28. xiv. 18.

then he, Matt. xiii. 52.

Etc. Bruder gives 240 instances, all in the Gospels and Acts.

IV. With an ellipsis.

he that had received[c], Matt. xxv. 17. —*Add* ver. 22 (-λαμβάνω G°LTTr).

he that had . ., 2 Cor. viii. 15*t*.

who is . ., Acts xiii. 9.

to whom . ., Rom. xiii. 7*f*.

V. Followed by a genitive.

ὁ, **the son**, Matt. iv. 21. x. 2, 3. Mark i. 19. ii. 14. Luke vi. 15. John xxi. 2. Acts xiii. 22. — *In italics*, Mark iii. 17, 18. — *the father*, Acts vii. 16.

ἡ, **her . . the wife**, Matt. i. 6. — *the wife*, John xix. 25. — **the mother**, Mark xvi. 1.

οἱ, **they which are of the house**, 1 Cor. i. 11. — **they that are**, 1 Cor. xv. 23. Gal. v. 24. — **the disciples**, Luke v. 33.

οἱ ἐκ τῶν, **they which are (that be) of one's household**, Rom. xvi. 10, 11.

τῶν τοῦ λαοῦ, **the people's**, Heb. vii. 27.

τὴν τοῦ ἑτέρου, **of the other**, 1 Cor. x. 29.

τὸ τοῦ ἑτέρου, **another's wealth**, 1 Cor. x. 24.

τό, **the profit**[c], 1 Cor. x. 33. — **it . . according to**, 2 Pet. ii. 22. — **what . . on**, Jas. iv. 14 (τά L).

this . ., Matt. xxi. 21.

that . ., 1 John iv. 3.

which is, Rom. v. 15.

With a pronoun, **thine own, his, his own, etc., yours, etc.**, Acts xvi. 33. 1 Cor. x. 24, 29. xiii. 5. xvi. 18. 2 Cor. xii. 14. Phil. ii. 21. 2 Tim. iii. 9.

Neut. plural, τά.

the things, Matt. vi. 34 (-G''LTTrS). Rom. viii. 5*t*. 1 Cor. ii. 11*t*, 14. vii. 34*t*. Phil. ii. 4.

things, 1 Cor. xiii. 11. Phil. ii. 4.

the things that (which) are (be), Matt. xxii. 21*t*. Mark viii. 33*t*. xii. 17*t*. Luke xx. 25*t*. 1 Cor. vii. 33. Phil. ii. 21.

the things that (which) belong to (concern, make for), Rom. xiv. 19. 1 Cor. vii. 32. 2 Cor. xi. 30.

the things contained in, Rom. ii. 14.

the things (those) that . ., Matt. xvi. 23*t*.

what was befallen to, Matt. viii. 33.

business, Luke ii. 49.

τὰ τοῦ ἀδελφοῦ, **brother's**, 1 John iii. 12.

Not rendered, Matt. xvi. 13. xxvi. 28(-LTTrS). Mark ii. 18. viii. 27. xiv. 24 (-G°L[b]TS). Luke xvi. 8. 1 Cor. i. 18. x. 33. Gal. ii. 20. 1 Tim. vi. 3. Jas. i. 25.

Add Luke xxiv. 10(. . of James), LTTrS. Tit. ii. 10(. . of God), G'LTS.

See also οἰκοδομή.

VI. As the Prepositive Article.

1. Before Nouns, Adjectives, and Numerals.

Sometimes rendered **he that is**,

that which is; often with a neuter, . . **thing**. *See also* ἄλλος, ἀρχαῖος, αὐτός, διηνεκής, ἐπίγειος, ἔσχατος, ἴσος, καλός, κρυπτός, λοιπός, πᾶς, πολύς, φανερός, *etc*.

2. Before Participles.

Commonly rendered **he that, that which, etc.**, with the indicative of the verb; e. g.,

ὁ ἐρχόμενος, (*lit.* the one coming,) **he that cometh**, Matt. iii. 11.

τὸ ῥηθέν, **that which was spoken**, Matt. ii. 17. xxii. 31.

B. gives about 1200 instances.

* ὁ ὢν καὶ ὁ ἦν, κ. τ. λ. *See* ὢν fr. εἰμί.

3. Before Infinitives.

Which thus become nouns, with all their cases except the vocative.

Nominative, e. g., τὸ ἀναστῆναι, **the rising**, Mark ix. 10. But τό oftener not rendered, as

τὸ ζῆν, **to live**, Phil. i.21.

Genitive, τοῦ, often denotes the *design* or *purpose* of an action.

that . . may, might, would, should, Matt. xxi. 32. Luke iv. 42. v. 7. xxi. 22. xxii. 31. xxiv. 16, 45. Acts x. 47. xiii. 47. xxiii. 20. xxvi. 18. xxvii. 1. Rom. vi. 6. xi. 8*t*, 10. 1 Cor. x. 13. Phil. iii. 10. Heb. xi. 5. Jas. v. 17.

that, Acts xiv. 18. xv. 20. 1 Pet. iii. 10.

so that, Acts vii. 19. Rom. vii. 3?

from[c], Rom. xv. 22.

Not rendered, Matt. ii. 13. iii. 13. xiii. 3. xxiv. 45. Mark iv. 3 (-LTr[b] *S*). Luke i. 77, 79. ii. 24, 27. iv. 10. v. 1 (καί L[m]TTr*S*). viii. 5. ix. 51. xii. 42. xxiv. 29. Acts iii. 2, 12. ix. 15. xviii. 10. xx. 3, 20, 27, 30. xxi. 12. xxiii. 15. xxvi. 18. Rom. i. 24. viii. 12. 1 Cor. vii. 37(-LT*S*). Gal. iii. 10? Heb. x. 7, 9.

Denoting a *result*, or in other forms of expression,

so that, Rom. vii. 3?

that, 1 Cor. xvi. 4. Heb. v. 12.

that . . would, should, will, must, Luke i. 57, 74. ii. 6. xvii. 1. Acts xxvii. 20. 1 Pet. iv. 17.

whereby[cc], Phil. iii. 21.

for[cc], Luke ii. 21.

Not rendered, Luke i. 9. xxii. 6. xxiv. 25. Acts xiv. 9. Rom. xv. 23. 1 Cor. ix. 6(-L*S*). 2 Cor. i. 8. viii. 11. Gal. iii. 10? Rev. ix. 10. xiv. 15 (-G[oo]LTTr, τοῦ θερισμοῦ for τοῦ θερίσαι, *S*).

Add Acts x. 25 (. . εἰσελθεῖν), LT *S*. 1 Cor. ix. 10(*ap*). Rev. xii. 7, τοῦ πολεμῆσαι for ἐπολέμησεν, GLT Tr*S*.

In a few other cases τοῦ is preceded by ἐκ, ἕως, or πρό.

Dative, τῷ, *see* ἐν.

Accusative, τό, *see* διά, εἰς, μετά([cc]), πρός.

4. Before Adverbs and Prepositions.

Often rendered **he that is, that which is, the things, etc.** *See also* κατά, κάτω, μετά, νῦν, πλησίον, πρός, περί, σύν. B. gives 279 instances. Frequently not rendered.

5. Before quotations and other phrases.

this saying, namely, Rom. xiii. 9.

this, Rom. xiii. 9. Gal. v. 14.

τὸ δέ, **this**, Heb. xii. 27. —**now that**, Eph. iv. 9.

Not rendered, Matt. xix. 18. Mark ix. 23. Luke i. 62. ix. 46. xix. 48. xxii. 2, 4, 23, 24, 37 (ὅτι L). Acts iv. 21. xxii. 30. Rom. viii. 26. 1 Thes. iv. 1.

VII. Before nouns with defining words intervening.

Matt. vii. 3. xv. 1. Etc. B. gives 131 instances.

VIII. After nouns with defining words following. The article is thus commonly repeated, the second use often rendered **who is, etc.**, and often not rendered.

Matt. i. 16, 25. ii. 16. Mark vi. 11. Etc. B. gives 792 instances.

IX. Before a nominative used as a vocative. Rendered **thou** in Matt. xxvii. 40, etc., **ye** in Matt. vii. 23, etc.; but oftener not apparent in translation. 76 instances.

ὅ. See ὅς.

ὀγδοήκοντα.

fourscore, Luke ii. 37. xvi. 7.

ὄγδοος.

eighth, Luke i. 59. Acts vii. 8. 2 Pet. ii. 5. Rev. xvii. 11. xxi. 20.

ὄγκος.

weight, Heb. xii. 1.

ὅδε, ἥδε, τόδε.

ὅδε, **he,** Luke xvi. 25.

ἥδε, **she,** Luke x. 39. — **such,** Jas. iv. 13.

τάδε, **these things,** Rev. ii. 1, 8, 12, 18. iii. 1, 7, 14. — **thus,** Acts xxi. 11. — **after this manner,** Acts xv. 23 (-LTS).

Add 2 Cor. xii. 19, τάδε for τὰ δέ, G.

ὁδεύω.

to journey, Luke x. 33p.

ὁδηγέω.

to lead, Matt. xv. 14. Luke vi. 39. Rev. vii. 17.

guide, John xvi. 13. Acts viii. 31.

ὁδηγός.

leader, Matt. xv. 14.

guide, Matt. xxiii. 16, 24. Acts i. 16. Rom. ii. 19.

ὁδοιπορέω.

go on one's journey, Acts x. 9p.

ὁδοιπορία.

journeying, 2 Cor. xi. 26.

journey, John iv. 6.

ὁδοποιέω, make a road, make one's way, journey.

Mark ii. 23, for ὁδὸν ποιέω, L.

ὁδός.

way, Matt. ii. 12. iii. 3. iv. 15. v. 25. vii. 13, 14. viii. 28. x. 5. xi. 10. xv. 32. xx. 17. xxi. 8*t*, 19, 32. xxii. 16. Mark i. 2, 3. viii. 3, 27. ix. 33, 34(-Lb). x. 17, 32, 52. xi. 8, 8(*ap*). xii. 14.

Luke i. 76, 79. iii. 4, 5. vii. 27. ix. 57. x. 4. xii. 58. xix. 36. xx. 21. xxiv. 32, 35. John i. 23. xiv. 4, 5, 6. Acts ii. 28. viii. 26, 36, 39. ix. 2, 17, 27. xiii. 10. xiv. 16. xvi. 17. xviii. 25, 26. xix. 9, 23. xxii. 4. xxiv. 14, 22. xxv. 3. xxvi. 13.

Rom. iii. 16, 17. xi. 33. 1 Cor. iv. 17. xii. 31. 1 Thes. iii. 11. Heb. iii. 10. ix. 8. x. 20. Jas. i. 8. ii. 25. v. 20. 2 Pet. ii. 2, 15*t*, 21. Jude 11. Rev. xv. 3. xvi. 12.

ἐν τῇ ὁδῷ, **that way,** Luke x. 31.

With παρά, **by the way side,** Matt. xiii. 4, 19. xx. 30. Mark iv. 4, 15. Luke viii. 5, 12. xviii. 35. — **by the highway side,** Mark x. 46.

highway, Matt. xxii. 10. Luke xiv. 23.

journey, Matt. x. 10. Mark vi. 8. Luke ii. 44. ix. 3. xi. 6(*marg.* **way**). Acts i. 12.

With ποιέω, **go,** Mark ii. 23cc (ὁδοποιέω L).

See also διέξοδος.

ὀδούς.

tooth, Matt. v. 38. viii. 12. xiii. 42, 50. xxii. 13. xxiv. 51. xxv. 30. Mark ix. 18. Luke xiii. 28. Acts vii. 54. Rev. ix. 8.

ὀδυνάω.

Mid. or Pass., **be tormented,** Luke xvi. 24, 25. — **sorrow,** Luke ii. 48. Acts xx. 38.

ὀδύνη.

sorrow, Rom. ix. 2. 1 Tim. vi. 10.

ὀδυρμός.

mourning, Matt. ii. 18. 2 Cor. vii. 7.

ὄζω.

stink, John xi. 39.

ὅθεν.

whence, Luke xi. 24.

from whence, Matt. xii. 44. Acts xiv. 26. Heb. xi. 19.

from thence, Acts xxviii. 13.

where, Matt. xxv. 24, 26.

wherefore, Heb. ii. 17. iii. 1. vii. 25. viii. 3.
whereby, 1 John ii. 18.
whereupon, Matt. xiv. 7. Acts xxvi. 19. Heb. ix. 18.

ὀθόνη.

sheet, Acts x. 11. xi. 5.

ὀθόνιον.

linen cloth, Luke xxiv. 12 (*ap*). John xix. 40. xx. 5, 6, 7.

οἶδα. See εἶδον.

οἰκεῖος.

of the household, Gal. vi. 10. Eph. ii. 19.
of one's own house (*marg.* kindred), 1 Tim. v. 8.

οἰκετεία, household.

Matt. xxiv. 45, for θεραπεία, LTTr.

οἰκέτης.

household servant, Acts x. 7.
servant, Luke xvi. 13. Rom. xiv. 4. 1 Pet. ii. 18.

οἰκέω.

dwell, Rom. vii. 17, 18, 20. viii. 9, 11. 1 Cor. iii. 16. vii. 12, 13. 1 Tim. vi. 16.

οἴκημα.

prison, Acts xii. 7.

οἰκητήριον.

habitation, Jude 6.
house, 2 Cor. v. 2.

οἰκία.

house, Matt. ii. 11. v. 15. vii. 24, 25, 26, 27. viii. 14. ix. 10, 23, 28. x. 12, 13, 14. xii. 25, 29*t*. xiii. 1, 36, 57. xvii. 25. xix. 29. xxiii. 14 (13, *ap*). xxiv. 17, 43. xxvi. 6.
Mark i. 29. ii. 15. iii. 25*t*, 27*t*. vi. 4, 10. vii. 24. ix. 33. x. 10, 29, 30. xii. 40. xiii. 15(–L^b S), 15, 34. 35. xiv. 3.
Luke iv. 38. v. 29. vi. 48*t*, 49*t*. vii. 6, 36 (οἶκος LTTr), 37, 44. viii. 27, 51. ix. 4. x. 5, 7*tr*. xv. 8, 25. xvii. 31. xviii. 29. xx. 47. xxii. 10, 11.
John iv. 53. viii. 35. xi. 31. xii. 3. xiv. 2. Acts iv. 34. ix. 11, 17. x. 6, 17, 32. xi. 11. xii. 12. xvi. 32. xvii. 5. xviii. 7*t*.
1 Cor. xi. 22. xvi. 15. 2 Cor. v. 1*t*. 2 Tim. ii. 20. iii. 6. 2 John 10.
τὰς οἰκίας, from house to house°, 1 Tim. v. 13.
With ἐν, at home, Matt. viii. 6.
household, Phil. iv. 22.
Add Luke xxii. 54, for οἶκος, TTr*S*.

οἰκιακός.

of one's household, Matt. x. 25, 36.

οἰκοδεσποτέω.

guide the house, 1 Tim. v. 14.

οἰκοδεσπότης.

master of the house, Matt. x. 25. Luke xiii. 25. xiv. 21.
householder, Matt. xiii. 27, 52. xx. 1. xxi. 33.
goodman of the house, Matt. xx. 11. xxiv. 43. Mark xiv. 14. Luke xii. 39.
goodman, Luke xxii. 11.

οἰκοδομέω.

build, Matt. vii. 24, 26. xvi. 18. xxi. 33. xxiii. 29. xxvi. 61. xxvii. 40. Mark xii. 1. xiv. 58. xv. 29. Luke iv. 29. vi. 48, 49. vii. 5. xi. 47, 48. xii. 18. xiv. 28, 30. xvii. 28. Acts vii. 47, 49. Rom. xv. 20. Gal. ii. 18.
Pass., be in building, John ii. 20.
builder, Matt. xxi. 42^p. Mark xii. 10^p. Luke xx. 17^p. Acts iv. 11 (οἰκοδόμος G''LT*S*). 1 Pet. ii. 7^p.
build up, 1 Pet. ii. 5.
edify, Acts ix. 31. 1 Cor. viii. 1. x. 23. xiv. 4*t*, 17. 1 Thes. v. 11.
embolden (*Gr.* edify), 1 Cor. viii. 10.
Add Luke vi. 48 (*ap*). Acts xx. 32, for ἐποικοδομέω, G''L*S*.

οἰκοδομή.

building, Matt. xxiv. 1. Mark xiii. 1, 2. 1 Cor. iii. 9. 2 Cor. v. 1. Eph. ii. 21.
edifying, 1 Cor. xiv. 5, 12, 26. 2 Cor. xii. 19. Eph. iv. 12, 16, 29 (*marg.* edify°°).

τὰ τῆς οἰκοδομῆς, **the things wherewith one may edify**, Rom. xiv. 19.
edification, Rom. xv. 2. 1 Cor. xiv. 3. 2 Cor. x. 8. xiii. 10.
Add 1 Tim. i. 4, for οἰκοδομία, G''.

οἰκοδομία.

edifying, 1 Tim. i. 4 (E, οἰκονομία StGLT*S*, οἰκοδομή G'').

οἰκοδόμος, builder.

Acts iv. 11, for οἰκοδομέων, G''LT*S*.

οἰκονομέω.

be steward, Luke xvi. 2.

οἰκονομία.

stewardship, Luke xvi. 2, 3, 4.
dispensation, 1 Cor. ix. 17. Eph. i. 10. iii. 2. Col. i. 25.
Add Eph. iii. 9, for κοινωνία, GLT*S*. 1 Tim. i. 4, for οἰκοδομία, StGLT*S*.

οἰκονόμος.

steward, Luke xii. 42. xvi. 1, 3, 8. 1 Cor. iv. 1, 2. Tit. i. 7. 1 Pet. iv. 10.
chamberlain, Rom. xvi. 23.
governor, Gal. iv. 2.

οἶκος.

house, Matt. ix. 6, 7. x. 6. xi. 8. xii. 4, 44. xv. 24. xxi. 13*t*. xxiii. 38. Mark ii. 1, 11, 26. iii. 19 (20, *marg.*, *with* εἰς, **home**). v. 38. vii. 17, 30. viii. 3, 26. ix. 28. xi. 17*t*.
Luke i. 23, 27, 33, 40, 56, 69. ii. 4. v. 24, 25. vi. 4. vii. 10. viii. 39, 41. ix. 61. x. 5, 38. xi. 17*t*, 24. xii. 39, 52. xiii. 35. xiv. 1, 23. xvi. 4, 27. xviii. 14. xix. 5, 9, 46*t*. xxii. 54(οἰκία TTr*S*).
John ii. 16*t*, 17. vii. 53(*ap*). xi. 20. Acts ii. 2, 36. vii. 10, 20, 42, 47, 49. x. 2, 22, 30. xi. 12, 13, 14. xvi. 15, 31, 34. xviii. 8. xix. 16. xxi. 8.
Rom. xvi. 5. 1 Cor. xvi. 19. Col. iv. 15. 1 Tim. iii. 4, 5, 12, 15. 2 Tim. i. 16. Tit. i. 11. Phm. 2. Heb. iii. 2, 3, 4, 5, 6*t*. viii. 8*t*, 10. x. 21. xi. 7. 1 Pet. ii. 5. iv. 17.
With κατά, **from house to house**, Acts ii. 46 (*marg.* **at home**). xx. 20. — **in every house**, Acts v. 42. — **into every house**, Acts viii. 3pl.
With εἰς, **home**, Mark v. 19. Luke xv. 6.
With ἐν, **at home**, 1 Cor. xi. 34. xiv. 35.
With ἴδιος, **home**, 1 Tim. v. 4.
household, Acts xvi. 15. 1 Cor. i. 16. 2 Tim. iv. 19.
temple, Luke xi. 51.
Add Luke vii. 36, for οἰκία, LTTr. Acts vii. 46, for θεός, L*S*.

οἰκουμένη.

earth, Luke xxi. 26.
world, Matt. xxiv. 14. Luke ii. 1. iv. 5. Acts xi. 28. xvii. 6, 31. xix. 27. xxiv. 5. Rom. x. 18. Heb. i. 6. ii. 5. Rev. iii. 10. xii. 9. xvi. 14.

οἰκουργός, doing house-work.

Tit. ii. 5, for οἰκουρός, G'LT*S*.

οἰκουρός.

keeper at home, Tit. ii. 5 (οἰκουργός G'LT*S*).

οἰκτείρω.

have compassion on, Rom. ix. 15*t*.

οἰκτιρμός.

mercy, Rom. xii. 1. 2 Cor. i. 3. Phil. ii. 1. Col. iii. 12. Heb. x. 28.

οἰκτίρμων.

merciful, Luke vi. 36*t*.
of tender mercy, Jas. v. 11.

οἶμαι. See οἴομαι.

οἰνοπότης.

wine-bibber, Matt. xi. 19. Luke vii. 34.

οἶνος.

wine, Matt. ix. 17*tr*. Mark ii. 22*tr*, 22(*ap*). xv. 23. Luke i. 15. v. 37*t*, 38. vii. 33(−G°). x. 34. John ii. 3*t*, 9, 10*t*. iv. 46. Rom. xiv. 21. Eph. v. 18. 1 Tim. iii. 8. v. 23. Tit. ii. 3. Rev. vi. 6. xiv. 8, 10. xvi. 19. xvii. 2. xviii. 3(−LTrb), 13.
With ληνός, **wine-press**, Rev. xix. 15.
Add Matt. xxvii. 34, for ὄξος, G'' LTr*S*.

οἰνοφλυγία.

excess of wine, 1 Pet. iv. 3.

οἴομαι.
suppose, John xxi. 25. Phil. i. 16.
think, Jas. i. 7.

οἷος.
what manner, Luke ix. 55(*ap*).
what manner of man, 1 Thes. i. 5.
what, 2 Tim. iii. 11.
which, Phil. i. 30. 2 Tim. iii. 11.
such as, Matt. xxiv. 21. Mark xiii. 19. 2 Cor. x. 11. xii. 20*t*. Rev. xvi. 18.
as, 1 Cor. xv. 48*t*.
οἷα, **so as**, Mark ix. 3.
οἷον ὅτι, **as though**, Rom. ix. 6.
See also δήποτε.

οἴω. See φέρω.

ὀκνέω.
to delay (*marg.* **be grieved**), Acts ix. 38.

ὀκνηρός.
slothful, Matt. xxv. 26. Rom. xii. 11.
grievous, Phil. iii. 1.

ὀκταήμερος.
the eighth day, Phil. iii. 5.

ὀκτώ.
eight, Luke ii. 21. ix. 28. John v. 5. xx. 26. Acts ix. 33. 1 Pet. iii. 20.
Add Acts xxv. 6 (*ap*).
See also δέκα.

ὀλεθρεύω. See ὀλοθρεύω.

ὀλέθριος, destructive, deadly.
2 Thes. i. 9, for ὄλεθρος, L.

ὄλεθρος.
destruction, 1 Cor. v. 5. 1 Thes. v. 3. 2 Thes. i. 9(ὀλέθριος L). 1 Tim. vi. 9.

ὀλιγοπιστία, little faith.
Matt. xvii. 20, for ἀπιστία, LTr*S*.

ὀλιγόπιστος.
of little faith, Matt. vi. 30. viii. 26. xiv. 31. xvi. 8. Luke xii. 28.

ὀλίγος.
little, Luke vii. 47. 2 Cor. viii. 15. 1 Tim. v. 23. Jas. iii. 5 (ἡλίκος LT*S*).
small, Acts xii. 18. xv. 2. xix. 23, 24. xxvii. 20.
short, Rev. xii. 12.
With ἐν, **almost**, Acts xxvi. 28, 29.
—**in few words** (*marg.* **a little**), Eph. iii. 3.
With οὐ, **long**, Acts xiv. 28.
With πρός, **for a little time**, Jas. iv. 14. —**little** (*marg.* **for a little time**), 1 Tim. iv. 8.

Plural,
few, Matt. vii. 14. ix. 37. xv. 34. xx. 16(*ap*). xxii. 14. Mark vi. 5. viii. 7. Luke x. 2. xiii. 23. Acts xvii. 4, 12. Heb. xii. 10. 1 Pet. iii. 20. Rev. iii. 4.
few [c]**stripes**, Luke xii. 48.
Neut., **a few things**, Matt. xxv. 21, 23. Rev. ii. 14, 20.
δι' ὀλίγων, **briefly**, 1 Pet. v. 12.

Adv., ὀλίγον.
a little, Mark i. 19. Luke v. 3.
little, Luke vii. 47.
a short space, Rev xvii. 10.
for a season, 1 Pet. i. 6.
a while, Mark vi. 31. 1 Pet. v. 10.

ὀλιγόψυχος.
feeble-minded, 1 Thes. v. 14.

ὀλιγωρέω.
despise, Heb. xii. 5.

ὀλίγως.
2 Pet. ii. 18, for ὄντως, C[m]GLT, *marg.* **for a little**, *or* **a little**.

ὀλοθρευτής.
destroyer, 1 Cor. x. 10.

ὀλοθρεύω, ὀλεθρεύω LT.
destroy, Heb. xi. 28.

ὁλοκαύτωμα.
whole burnt-offering, Mark xii. 33.
burnt-offering, Heb. x. 6, 8.

ὁλοκληρία.
perfect soundness, Acts iii. 16.

ὁλόκληρος.
whole, 1 Thes. v. 23.
entire, Jas. i. 4.

ὀλολύζω.
to howl, Jas. v. 1.

ὅλος.
whole, Matt. v. 29, 30. vi. 22, 23. xiii. 33. xvi. 26. xxvi. 13. xxvii. 27. Mark vi. 55. viii. 36. xiv. 9. xv. 1, 16, 33. Luke viii. 39. ix. 25. xi. 34, 36*t*. xiii. 21. John iv. 53. xi. 50. Acts xi. 26. xv. 22. xix. 29 (-LT*S*). xxviii. 30.
Rom. i. 8. xvi. 23. 1 Cor. v. 6. xii. 17*t*. xiv. 23. Gal. v. 3, 9. Tit. i. 11. Jas. ii. 10. iii. 2, 3, 6. 1 John ii. 2. v. 19. Rev. xii. 9. xvi. 14.
all, Matt. i. 22. iv. 23, 24. ix. 26, 31. xiv. 35. xx. 6. xxi. 4(-G∞LTr *S*). xxii. 37*tr*, 40. xxiv. 14. xxvi. 56, 59. Mark i. 28, 33, 39. xii. 30*f*, 33*t*, 33(*ap*), 33, 44. xiv. 55.
Luke i. 65. iv. 14. v. 5. vii. 17. viii. 43. x. 27*f*. xxiii. 5, 44. Acts ii. 2, 47. v. 11. vii. 10, 11. viii. 37 (*ap*). ix. 31, 42. x. 22, 37. xi. 28. xiii. 49. xviii. 8. xix. 27. xxi. 30, 31. xxii. 30(πᾶς GLT*S*).
2 Cor. i. 1. Phil. i. 13. 1 Thes. iv. 10. Heb. iii. 2, 5. Rev. iii. 10. xiii. 3.
all . . long, Rom. viii. 36. x. 21.
altogether, John ix. 34.
With διά, **throughout,** John xix. 23.
every whit, John vii. 23. xiii. 10.
Add Acts xiii. 6 (. . the isle), GL T*S*. Rev. vi. 12 (. . the moon), G LTTr*S*.

ὁλοτελής.
wholly∞, 1 Thes. v. 23.

ὄλυνθος.
untimely fig (*marg.* **green fig**), Rev. vi. 13.

ὅλως.
utterly, 1 Cor. vi. 7.
at all, Matt. v. 34. 1 Cor. xv. 29.
commonly, 1 Cor. v. 1.

ὄμβρος.
shower, Luke xii. 54.

ὁμείρομαι, long for.
1 Thes. ii. 8, for ἱμείρομαι, GLT*S*.

ὁμιλέω.
commune together, Luke xxiv. 15.
commune with, Acts xxiv. 26.
talk, Luke xxiv. 14. Acts xx. 11.

ὁμιλία.
communication, 1 Cor. xv. 33.

ὅμιλος.
company, Rev. xviii. 17(*ap*).

ὁμίχλη, mist, fog.
2 Pet. ii. 17, *see* νεφέλη.

ὄμμα.
eye, Mark viii. 23.
Add Matt. xx. 34, for ὀφθαλμός, LTr.

ὄμνυμι, ὀμνύω.
swear, Matt. v. 34, 36. xxiii. 16*t*, 18*t*, 20*t*, 21*t*, 22*t*. xxvi. 74. Mark vi. 23. xiv. 71. Luke i. 73. Acts ii. 30. vii. 17(ὁμολογέω G″LT*S*). Heb. iii. 11, 18. iv. 3. vi. 13*t*, 16. vii. 21. Jas. v. 12. Rev. x. 6.

ὁμοθυμαδόν.
with one accord, Acts i. 14. ii. 1 (ὁμοῦ LT*S*), 46. iv. 24. v. 12. vii. 57. viii. 6. xii. 20. xv. 25. xviii. 12. xix. 29.
with one mind, Rom. xv. 6.

ὁμοιάζω.
agree °**thereto,** Mark xiv. 70(*ap*).
Add Matt. xxiii. 27, for παρομοιάζω, LTr.

ὁμοιοπαθής.
of like passions, Acts xiv. 15.
subject to like passions, Jas. v. 17.

ὅμοιος.
like, Matt. xi. 16. xiii. 31, 33, 44, 45, 47, 52. xx. 1. xxii. 39. Mark xii. 31(-T*S*) Luke vi. 47, 48, 49. vii. 31, 32. xii. 36. xiii. 18, 19, 21. John viii. 55. ix. 9. Acts xvii. 29.
Gal. v. 21. 1 John iii. 2. Jude 7. Rev. i. 13, 15. ii. 18. iv. 3, 3 (ὁμοίως G′ -*S*), 6, 7*tr*. ix. 7, 7 (G′, *see* χρύσεος), 10, 19. xi. 1. xiii. 2, 4, 11. xiv. 14. xvi. 13 (ὡς GLTTr, εἰ ὡσεί *S*). xviii. 18. xxi. 11, 18.

ὁμοιότης.
similitude, Heb. vii. 15.
With κατά, **like as**, Heb. iv. 15.

ὁμοιόω.
liken, Matt. vii. 24, 26. xi. 16. xiii. 24. xviii. 23. xxv. 1. Mark iv. 30. Luke vii. 31. xiii. 20.
make like, Rom. ix. 29. Heb. ii. 17.
Pass., **be like**, Matt. vi. 8. xxii. 2.
— **in the likeness of**, Acts xiv. 11p.
resemble, Luke xiii. 18.

ὁμοίωμα.
likeness, Rom. vi. 5. viii. 3. Phil. ii. 7.
made like tocc, Rom. i. 23.
similitude, Rom v. 14.
shape, Rev. ix. 7.

ὁμοίως.
likewise, Matt. xxii. 26. xxvi. 35. xxvii. 41. Mark iv 16. xv. 31. Luke iii. 11. v. 33. vi. 31. x. 32, 37. xiii. 5 (ὡσαύτως TTr*S*). xvi. 25. xvii. 28, 31. xxii. 36. John v. 19. vi. 11. xxi. 13.
Rom. i. 27. 1 Cor. vii. 3, 4, 22. Jas. ii. 25. 1 Pet. iii. 1, 7. v. 5. Jude 8. Rev. viii. 12.
so, Luke v. 10.
καὶ . . ὁμοίως, **moreover**, Heb. ix. 21.
Add Luke xiii. 3, for ὡσαύτως, L Tr*S*. Rev. ii. 15, for ὃ μισῶ, GLT Tr*S*. iv. 3, for ὅμοιος, G′.

ὁμοίωσις.
similitude, Jas. iii. 9.

ὁμολογέω.
confess, John i. 20*t*. ix. 22. xii. 42. Acts xxiii. 8. xxiv. 14. Rom. x. 9. Heb. xi. 13. 1 John i. 9. iv. 2, 3, 15. 2 John 7.
With ἐν, **confess**, Matt. x. 32*t*. Luke xii. 8*t*.
Pass., **confession is made**, Rom. x. 10.
give thanks (*marg.* **confess**), Heb. xiii. 15.
profess, Matt. vii. 23. 1 Tim. vi. 12. Tit. i. 16.
promise, Matt. xiv. 7.
Add Acts vii. 17, for ὄμνυμι, G″L T*S*. 1 John ii. 23(*ap*). Rev. iii. 5, for ἐξομολογέομαι, GLTTr*S*.

ὁμολογία.
confession (*marg.* **profession**), 1 Tim. vi. 13.
profession, 1 Tim. vi. 12. Heb. iii. 1. iv. 14. x. 23.
Gen., **professed**, 2 Cor. ix. 13.

ὁμολογουμένως.
without controversy, 1 Tim. iii. 16.

ὁμότεχνος.
of the same craft, Acts xviii. 3.

ὁμοῦ.
together, John iv. 36. xx. 4. xxi. 2.
Add Acts ii. 1, for ὁμοθυμαδόν, L T*S*. xx. 18(*ap*).

ὁμόφρων.
of one mind, 1 Pet. iii. 8.

ὀμόω. See ὄμνυμι.

ὅμως.
and even, 1 Cor. xiv. 7.
though it be but, Gal. iii. 15.
ὅμως μέντοι, **nevertheless**, John xii. 42.

ὄναρ.
dream, Matt. i. 20. ii. 12, 13, 19, 22. xxvii. 19.

ὀνάριον.
young ass, John xii. 14.

ὀνειδίζω.
revile, Matt. v. 11. Mark xv. 32.
upbraid, Matt. xi. 20. Mark xvi. 14 (*ap*). Jas. i. 5.
cast in one's teeth, Matt. xxvii. 44.
reproach, Luke vi. 22. Rom. xv. 3. 1 Pet. iv. 14.
Pass., **suffer reproach**, 1 Tim. iv. 10 (ἀγωνίζομαι G′L*S*).

ὀνειδισμός.
reproach, Rom. xv. 3. 1 Tim. iii. 7. Heb. x. 33. xi. 26. xiii. 13.

ὄνειδος.
reproach, Luke i. 25.

ὄνημι. See ὀνίνημι.

ὀνικός.

With μύλος, **millstone**, Matt. xviii. 6. Luke xvii. 2 (λίθος μυλικός G″L TTr*S*).

Add Mark ix. 42, *see* μυλικός.

ὀνίνημι.

Mid., **have joy**, Phm. 20.

ὄνομα.

name, Matt. i. 21, 23, 25. vi. 9. vii. 22*tr*. x. 2, 22, 41*t*, 42. xii. 21. xviii. 5, 20. xix. 29. xxi. 9. xxiii. 39. xxiv. 5, 9. xxvii. 32. xxviii. 19. Mark v. 9*t*, 22(-G°). vi. 14. ix. 37, 38, 39, 41. xi. 9, 10(*ap*). xiii. 6, 13. xvi. 17(*ap*).

Luke i. 5, 13, 27*t*, 31, 49, 59, 61, 63. ii. 21, 25. vi. 22. viii. 30. ix. 48, 49. x. 17, 20. xi. 2. xiii. 35 xix. 38. xxi. 8, 12, 17. xxiv. 18, 47. John i. 6, 12. ii. 23. iii. 18. v. 43*t*. x. 3, 25. xii. 13, 28. xiv. 13, 14, 26. xv. 16, 21. xvi. 23, 24, 26. xvii. 6, 11, 12, 26. xviii. 10. xx. 31.

Acts i. 15. ii. 21, 38. iii. 6, 16*t*. iv. 7, 10, 12, 17, 18, 30. v. 28, 40, 41. viii. 12, 16. ix. 14, 15, 16, 21, 27, 29(28). x. 43, 48. xiii. 6, 8. xv. 14, 17, 26. xvi. 18. xviii. 15. xix. 5, 13, 17. xxi. 13. xxii. 16. xxvi. 9. xxviii. 7.

Rom. i. 5. ii. 24. ix. 17. x. 13. xv. 9. 1 Cor. i. 2, 10, 13, 15. v. 4. vi. 11. Eph. i. 21. v. 20. Phil. ii. 9, 10. iv. 3. Col. iii. 17. 2 Thes. i. 12. iii. 6. 1 Tim. vi. 1. 2 Tim. ii. 19.

Heb. i. 4. ii. 12. vi. 10. xiii. 15. Jas. ii. 7. v. 10, 14. 1 Pet. iv. 14. 1 John ii. 12. iii. 23. v. 13(*ap*), 13. 3 John 7, 14(15).

Rev. ii. 3, 13, 17. iii. 1, 4, 5*t*, 8, 12*tr*. vi. 8. viii. 11. ix. 11*t*. xi. 18. xiii. 1, 6, 8, 17*t*. xiv. 1, 11. xv. 2, 4. xvi. 9. xvii. 3, 5, 8. xix. 12, 13, 16. xxi. 12, 14. xxii. 4.

Dat., or with αὐτῷ, *or* οὗ *or* ᾧ fr. ὅς, **named**[cc], Mark xiv. 32. Luke i. 5, 26. v. 27. viii. 41. x. 38. xvi. 20. xix. 2. xxiii. 50. John iii. 1. Acts v. 1, 34. ix. 10, 12, 33, 36. xi. 28. xii. 13. xvi. 1, 14. xvii. 34. xviii. 2, 7, 24. xix. 24. xx. 9. xxi. 10. xxvii. 1. — **called**, Luke xxiv. 13. Acts viii. 9. ix. 11. x. 1.

τοὔνομα for τὸ ὄνομα, **named**[cc], Matt. xxvii. 57.

Not rendered, Rev. xi. 13 (*Gr.* name).

Add Acts xiv. 10(*ap*). 1 Pet. iv. 16, for μέρος, G″LT*S*. Rev. xiv. 1 (*ap*). xix. 12(*ap*). xxi. 12(*names*), LTTr.

See also ἐπιτίθημι.

ὀνομάζω.

to name, Luke vi. 13, 14. Rom. xv. 20. 1 Cor. v. 1(*omS*). Eph. i. 21. iii. 15. v. 3. 2 Tim. ii. 19.

call, Acts xix. 13. 1 Cor. v. 11.

ὄνος.

ass, Matt. xxi. 2, 5, 7. Luke xiii. 15. xiv. 5 (υἱός G″LTTr) John xii. 15.

ὄντως.

indeed, Mark xi. 32. Luke xxiv. 34. John viii. 36. 1 Tim. v. 3, 5, 16.

certainly, Luke xxiii. 47.

verily, Gal. iii. 21.

of a truth, 1 Cor. xiv. 25.

clean, 2 Pet. ii. 18(ὀλίγως C[m]GLT).

Add 1 Tim. vi. 19, for αἰώνιος, GL T*S*.

ὄξος.

vinegar, Matt. xxvii. 34 (οἶνος G″ LTr*S*), 48. Mark xv. 36. Luke xxiii. 36. John xix. 29*t*, 30.

ὀξύς.

sharp, Rev. i. 16. ii. 12. xiv. 14, 17, 18*t*. xix. 15.

swift, Rom. iii. 15.

ὀπή.

cave, Heb. xi. 38.

place (*marg.* **hole**), Jas. iii. 11.

ὄπισθεν.

behind, Matt. ix. 20. Mark v. 27. Luke viii. 44. Rev. iv. 6.

on the backside, Rev. v. 1 (ἔξωθεν G′).

after, Matt. xv. 23. Luke xxiii. 26.

ὀπίσω.

behind, Matt. xvi. 23. Mark viii. 33. Luke iv. 8(*ap*). vii. 38. Rev. i. 10.

τὰ ὀπίσω, **those things which are behind**, Phil. iii. 13(14).

back, Matt. xxiv. 18.

εἰς τὰ ὀπίσω, **backward**, John xviii. 6.—**back**, Mark xiii. 16. Luke ix. 62. xvii. 31. John vi. 66. xx. 14.

after, Matt. iii. 11. x. 38. xvi. 24. Mark i. 7, 17, 20. viii. 34. Luke ix. 23. xiv. 27. xix. 14. xxi. 8. John i. 15, 27, 30. xii. 19. Acts v. 37. xx. 30. 1 Tim. v. 15. 2 Pet. ii. 10. Jude 7. Rev. xii. 15. xiii. 3.

Add Matt. iv. 10 (. . *μοῦ* G^{pr}L^{b}T). 2 Pet. ii. 21(*ap*).

See also δεῦτε.

ὁπλίζω.

Mid., **arm one's self with**, 1 Pet. iv. 1.

ὅπλον.

instrument, Rom. vi. 13(*pl.*, *marg.* **arms**, *or* **weapons**), 13.

weapon, John xviii. 3. 2 Cor. x. 4.

Plural, **armor**, Rom. xiii. 12 (*ἔργα* L^{m}). 2 Cor. vi. 7.

ὁποῖος.

of what sort, 1 Cor. iii. 13.

what manner of, 1 Thes. i. 9. Jas. i. 24.

such as, Acts xxvi. 29.

With πότε, **whatsoever**, Gal. ii. 6.

ὁπότε.

when, Luke vi. 3 (*ὅτε* LTr*S*).

ὅπου.

where, Matt. vi. 19*t*, 20*t*, 21. xiii. 5. xxv. 24, 26. xxvi. 57. xxviii. 6. Mark ii. 4. iv. 5, 15. v. 40. ix. 44 (*ap*), 46(*ap*), 48. xiii. 14. xiv. 14. xvi. 6. Luke xii. 33, 34. xxii. 11. John i. 28. iii. 8. iv. 20, 46. vi. 23, 62. vii. 42. x. 40. xi. 30, 32. xii. 1, 26. xvii. 24. xviii. 1. xix. 18, 20, 41. xx. 12, 19.

Acts xvii. 1. Rom. xv. 20. Col. iii. 11. Heb. ix. 16. x. 18. Jas. iii. 16. Rev. ii. 13*t*. xi. 8. xii. 6. xx. 10.

ὅπου . . ἐκεῖ, **where**, Mark vi. 55 (– *ἐκεῖ* LTr^{b}*S*). Rev. xii. 14 (*ὅπως* for *ὅπου* G′).

ὅπου . . ἐπ' αὐτῶν, **on which**, Rev. xvii. 9.

wheresoever, Luke xvii. 37.

where . . there, John xiv. 3.

where . . thither, John vii. 34, 36.

whither, John viii. 21, 22. xiii. 33, 36. xiv. 4. xviii. 20. xxi. 18*t*. Heb. vi. 20.

With ἄν^{1} *or ἐάν*^{2}, **wheresoever**, Matt. xxiv. 28^{2}. xxvi. 13^{2}. Mark ix. 18^{1}. xiv. 9^{1}(^{2}T*S*), 14^{2}(^{1}LTr).—**whithersoever**, Matt. viii. 19^{2}. Mark vi. 56^{1}. Luke ix. 57^{1}(^{2}LTTr). Jas. iii. 4^{1}. Rev. xiv. 4^{1}.—**in what place soever**, Mark vi. 10^{2}(^{1}LTr).

whereas, 1 Cor. iii. 3. 2 Pet. ii. 11.

Add Mark ii. 4, for *ἐφ' ᾧ*, G′LTr*S*.

ὀπτάνω.

see, Acts i. 3.

Compare also ὁράω.

ὀπτασία.

vision, Luke i. 22. xxiv. 23. Acts xxvi. 19. 2 Cor. xii. 1.

ὀπτός.

broiled, Luke xxiv. 42.

ὅπτω, ὄψομαι, ὤφθην. See ὁράω.

ὀπώρα.

fruits, Rev. xviii. 14.

ὅπως.

I. As a relative Adverb.

how, Luke xxiv. 20.

II. As a Conjunction.

that, Matt. ii. 8, 23. v. 16, 45. vi. 2, 4, 16, 18. viii. 17, 34 (*ἵνα* L). ix. 38. xii. 17 (*ἵνα* LTTr*S*). xiii. 35. xxiii. 35. Mark v. 23 (*ἵνα* G″LTTr*S*). Luke vii. 3. x. 2. xvi. 28. John xi. 57. Acts viii. 15, 24. ix. 2, 12, 17. xxiii. 15, 20. xxiv. 26 (*ap*). xxv. 3, 26.

Rom. ix. 17*t*. 1 Cor. i. 29. 2 Cor. viii. 11, 14. Gal. i. 4. 2 Thes. i. 12. Phm. 6. Heb. ii. 9. ix. 15. Jas. v. 16. 1 Pet. ii. 9.

ὅπως ἄν, **that**, Matt. vi. 5 (– *ἄν* LT

TrS). Luke ii. 35. Acts xv. 17. Rom. iii. 4. — **when,** Acts iii. 19.
so that, Luke xvi. 26.
to[cc], Matt. xxvi. 59. Luke xi. 37. Acts ix. 24. xxiii. 23.
because, Acts xx. 16.
how, Matt. xii. 14. xxii. 15. Mark iii. 6.
Add Rev. xii. 14, for ὅπου, G'.

ὅραμα.

sight, Acts vii. 31.
vision, Matt. xvii. 9. Acts ix. 10, 12(–LTS). x. 3, 17, 19. xi. 5. xii. 9. xvi. 9, 10. xviii. 9.

ὅρασις.

sight, Rev. iv. 3.
to look upon[cc], Rev. iv. 3.
vision, Acts ii. 17. Rev. ix. 17.

ὁρατός.

visible, Col. i. 16.

ὁράω,

Fut. ὄψομαι, *Aor. pass.* ὤφθην.

see, Matt. v. 8. viii. 4. ix. 30. xxiv. 6, 30. xxvi. 64. xxviii. 7, 10. Mark i. 44. viii. 15. xiii. 26. xiv. 62. xvi. 7. Luke i. 22. iii. 6. ix. 36. xiii. 28. xvi. 23. xvii. 22. xxi. 27. xxiv. 23.
John i. 18, 34, 50(51), 51(52). iii. 11, 32, 36. iv. 45. v. 37. vi. 2 (θεωρέω LTr), 36, 46*t*. viii. 38, 38 (ἀκούω G''LTr), 57. ix. 37. xi. 40. xiv. 7, 9. xv. 24. xvi. 16, 17, 19, 22. xix. 35. xx. 18, 25, 29. Acts ii. 17. vii. 44. xiii. 31. xx. 25. xxii. 15.
Rom. xv. 21. 1 Cor. ix. 1. xv. 5, 6, 7, 8. Col. ii. 1, 18. 1 Thes. v. 15. 1 Tim. iii. 16. Heb. ii. 8. viii. 5. xi. 27. xii. 14. xiii. 23. Jas. ii. 24. 1 Pet. i. 8p. 1 John i. 1, 2, 3. iii. 2, 6. iv. 20*t*. 3 John 11. Rev. i. 7. xi. 19. xviii. 18p (βλέπω GLTTrS). xix. 10. xxii. 4, 9.
see to, Matt. xxvii. 4, 24.
perceive, Acts viii. 23.
look to, Acts xviii. 15.
look, John xix. 37.
Pass., **appear,** Matt. xvii. 3. Mark ix. 4. Luke i. 11. ix. 31. xxii. 43 (*ap*). xxiv. 34. Acts ii. 3. vii. 2, 30, 35. ix. 17. xvi. 9. xxvi. 16*t*. Heb. ix. 28. Rev. xii. 1, 3. — **show one's self,** Acts vii. 26.
behold, Luke xxiii. 49.
take heed, Matt. xvi. 6. xviii. 10. Mark viii. 15. Luke xii. 15. Acts xxii. 26(*om*S).
Not rendered, Mark viii. 24(*ap*).
Add John i. 39(40), for εἶδον, G' TTr.
Compare also ὀπτάνω.

ὀργή.

anger, Mark iii. 5. Eph. iv. 31. Col. iii. 8.
indignation, Rev. xiv. 10.
wrath, Matt. iii. 7. Luke iii. 7. xxi. 23. John iii. 36. Rom. i. 18. ii. 5*t*, 8. iv. 15. v. 9. ix. 22*t*. xii. 19. xiii. 4(–G°), 5. Eph. ii. 3. v. 6. Col. iii. 6. 1 Thes. i. 10. ii. 16. v. 9. 1 Tim. ii. 8. Heb. iii. 11. iv. 3. Jas. i. 19, 20. Rev. vi. 16, 17. xi. 18. xvi. 19. xix. 15.
vengeance, Rom. iii. 5.

ὀργίζω.

Pass. or Mid., **be angry,** Matt. v. 22. Luke xiv. 21. xv. 28. Eph. iv. 26. Rev. xi. 18. — **be wroth,** Matt. xviii. 34. xxii. 7. Rev. xii. 17.

ὀργίλος.

soon angry, Tit. i. 7.

ὀργυιά.

fathom, Acts xxvii. 28*t*.

ὀρέγω.

Mid., **to desire,** 1 Tim. iii. 1. Heb. xi. 16. — **covet after,** 1 Tim. vi. 10p.

ὀρεινός.

hill, *adj.*, Luke i. 39, 65.

ὄρεξις.

lust, Rom. i. 27.

ὀρθοποδέω.

walk uprightly, Gal. ii. 14.

ὀρθός.

straight (*marg.* even), Heb. xii. 13.
upright, Acts xiv. 10.

ὀρθοτομέω.
divide rightly, 2 Tim. ii. 15.

ὀρθρίζω.
come early in the morning, Luke xxi. 38.

ὀρθρινός.
morning, Rev. xxii. 16 (πρωϊνός G LTr*S*, πρoϊνός T).
Add Luke xxiv. 22, for ὄρθριος, L TTr*S*.

ὄρθριος.
early, Luke xxiv. 22 (ὀρθρινός LT Tr*S*).

ὄρθρος.
Gen. or Acc., **early in the morning,** John viii. 2(*ap*). Acts v. 21.
See also βαθύς.

ὀρθῶς.
rightly, Luke vii. 43. xx. 21.
right, Luke x. 28.
plain, Mark vii. 35.

ὁρίζω.
to limit, Heb. iv. 7.
determine, Luke xxii. 22. Acts xi. 29. xvii. 26.
Pass., **determinate,** Acts ii. 23P.
ordain, Acts x. 42. xvii. 31.
declare (*Gr.* determine), Rom. i. 4.

ὅριον.
border, Matt. iv. 13.
coast, Matt. ii. 16. viii. 34. xv. 22, 39. xix. 1. Mark v. 17. vii. 31*t*. x. 1. Acts xiii. 50.
Add Mark vii. 24, for μεθόριος *neut.,* LTr*S*.

ὁρκίζω.
adjure, Mark v. 7. Acts xix. 13.
charge, 1 Thes. v. 27 (*marg.* **adjure,** ἐνορκίζω LT).

ὅρκος.
oath, Matt. v. 33. xiv. 7, 9. xxvi. 72. Mark vi. 26. Luke i. 73. Acts ii. 30. Heb. vi. 16, 17. Jas. v. 12.

ὁρκωμοσία.
oath, Heb. vii. 20, 21(*marg.* **swearing of an oath**), 21, 28.

ὁρμάω.
to rush, Acts xix. 29.
run violently, Matt. viii. 32. Mark v. 13. Luke viii. 33.
run, Acts vii. 57.

ὁρμή.
assault, Acts xiv. 5.
Not rendered, Jas. iii. 4.

ὅρμημα.
violence, Rev. xviii. 21.

ὄρνεον.
bird, Rev. xviii. 2.
fowl, Rev. xix. 17, 21.

ὄρνις.
hen, Matt. xxiii. 37. Luke xiii. 34.

ὁροθεσία.
bound, Acts xvii. 26.

ὄρος.
mountain, Matt. iv. 8. v. 1. viii. 1. xiv. 23. xv. 29. xvii. 1, 9, 20. xviii. 12. xxi. 21. xxiv. 16. xxviii. 16. Mark iii. 13. v. 5, 11(-G°*S*). vi. 46. ix. 2, 9. xi. 23. xiii. 14. Luke iii. 5. iv. 5(*ap*). vi. 12. viii. 32. ix. 28. xxi. 21. xxiii. 30. John iv. 20, 21. vi. 3, 15.
1 Cor. xiii. 2. Heb. xi. 38. xii. 20. Rev. vi. 14, 15, 16. viii. 8. xvi. 20. xvii. 9. xxi. 10.
mount, Matt. xxi. 1. xxiv. 3. xxvi. 30. Mark xi. 1. xiii. 3. xiv. 26. Luke xix. 29, 37. xxi. 37. xxii. 39. John viii. 1 (*ap*). Acts i. 12 vii. 30, 38. Gal. iv. 24, 25. Heb. viii. 5. xii. 18(-L*S*), 22. 2 Pet. i. 18. Rev. xiv. 1.
hill, Matt. v. 14. Luke iv. 29. ix 37.

ὀρύσσω, -ττω.
dig, Matt. xxi. 33. xxv. 18. Mark xii. 1.

ὀρφανός.
fatherless, Jas. i. 27.
comfortless (*marg.* **orphan**), John xiv. 18.

ὀρχέω.
Mid., **to dance,** Matt. xi. 17. xiv. 6. Mark vi. 22. Luke vii. 32.

ὅς, ἥ, ὅ.

Originally a demonstrative pronoun, like ὁ, ἡ, τό, but mostly used as a relative, and rendered **who, which, that.** Omitting the cases in which it simply refers to nouns preceding or following, Bruder gives its special uses as follows: —

I. As a demonstrative, only in distinctions and distribution, thus:

ὃς μὲν . . ὃς δέ (ὃς δέ repeated[2]),

the one . . and the other, 2 Cor. ii. 16.

one . . the other, Luke xxiii. 33.

one . . (and) another, Matt. xxi. 35[2]. xxv. 15[2]. Rom. ix. 21. xiv. 5. 1 Cor. vii. 7 (ὁ for ὃς LT*S*). xi. 21.

some . . and others, Jude 22.

some . . (and) some, Matt. xiii. 8[2]. Acts xxvii. 44. 2 Tim. ii. 20.

Add Matt. xxii. 5, for ὁ μὲν . . ὁ δέ, LTTr, ὁ μὲν . . ὃς δέ *S*.

ὃς μέν or ὃς δέ, with or without another corresponding term.

some, Matt. xiii. 4. Mark iv. 4. Luke viii. 5. 1 Cor. xii. 28.

one, Rom. xiv. 2. 1 Cor. xii. 8.

Add John v. 11 (he[1st]), L.

II. When not agreeing in gender or number with the preceding noun, but representing the sense. Sometimes[2] by *attraction* agreeing with a predicate following.

Mark xv. 16[2]. Luke vi. 17. John i. 13. Acts xv. 17, 36. xxii. 5. xxiv. 11. xxvi. 17. Rom. vi. 21. ix. 24[2]. 1 Cor. iii. 17[2]. Gal. iii. 16[2]. iv. 19. Eph. i. 14[2]. iii. 13[2]. vi. 17[2]. Phil. i. 28[2]. ii. 15. iii. 20. Col. i. 27(ὃ for ὃς L). ii. 29. 1 Tim. iii. 15[2]. Phm. 10. 2 Pet. iii. 1. 1 John ii. 8[2]. 2 John 1. Rev. v. 8[2].

Add ὃς for ὅ, John vi. 9, LTTr. Rev. xiii. 14, LT. — 1 Tim. iii. 16, *see* θεός. Rev. iii. 4, οἳ for ἅ, T. iv. 5[2], ἅ for αἵ, T.

* ὅ with ἐστί, λέγεται, or ἑρμηνεύεται, 25 times.

III. ὅ or ἅ referring to a sentence or clause.

which, Acts xi. 30. Gal. ii. 10. Col. ii. 17, 22. 1 Tim. i. 6. Rev. xxi. 8.

which thing, Acts xxvi. 10.

whom, Heb. v. 11.

whereof, Acts ii. 32. iii. 15.

With εἰς, **whereunto,** Col. i. 29.

With ἐν, **whereupon,** Acts xxiv. 18. xxvi. 12.

Add Matt. xii. 4, ὃ for οὓς, LTTr.

IV. In *attraction*, when the pronoun is made to agree in *case* with its antecedent. 81 instances.

* With prepositions. *See* ἀντί, ἀπό, ἄχρις, ἐν, ἕως, μέχρις, *etc.* 66 times.

V. Including the notion of a demonstrative pronoun, and commonly rendered **what.**

Matt. vii. 2*t*. x. 27. Etc.

what . . that, Matt. x. 27.

he that, Matt. x. 38. Mark ix. 40.

what things, Matt. vi. 8.

Etc. 179 instances.

* ὅ preceding a clause.

in that, Rom. vi. 10*t*.

the life° which, Gal. ii. 20.

VI. With ἂν[1] or ἐάν[2].

whosoever, Matt. v. 19[2], 19[1], 21[1], 22*t*[1], 31[1], 32[1](πᾶς G'LTr*S*), 32[2]. x. 14[2] ([1]LTr*S*), 42[2] ([1]LTr). xi. 6[2]([1]LTr), 27[2]. xii. 32[1] ([2]LTTr*S*), 32[1]. xv. 5[1]. xvi. 25[1]([2]LTTr), 25[1]. xix. 9[1]. xx. 26[2] ([1]LTr), 27[2] ([1]LTr*S*). xxi. 44[1]. xxii. 16[1]*t*, 18[2] ([1]LTr*S*), 18[1]. xxvi. 48[1] ([2]T*S*).

Mark iii. 35[1]. viii. 35[1] ([2]TTr*S*), 35[1], 38[1]([2]LTTr). ix. 37[2]([1]LTTr*S*), 37[2]([1]LTTr), 41[1], 42[1]([2]T). x. 11, 15, and 43,[2]([1]LTr*S*), 44[1] ([2]GTTr). xi. 23[1]. xiv. 44[1].

Luke iv. 6[2]([1]LTr). vii. 23[2]. viii. 18[1]([2]T), 18[1] ([2]LT). ix. 24[1] ([2]T*S*), 24[1], 26[1], 48[2]([1]L), 48[2]. xvii. 33*t*[2]. xviii. 17[2]([1]LTr*S*). xx. 18[1]. John iv. 14[1]. Acts ii. 21[1]([2]T). viii. 19[1] ([2]GLT*S*).

Rom. x. 13[1]. 1 Cor. xi. 27[1]. xvi.

3²(¹L). Jas. iv. 4¹(²LT*S*). 1 John iv. 15¹.

πᾶς ὃς ἄν, **whosoever,** Luke xii. 8.

whoso, Matt. xviii. 5²(¹LTr), 6¹. 1 John ii. 5¹. iii. 17.

who, Matt. vii. 9²(-²LTr*S*). Luke x. 22²(¹LTr). John i. 33¹. Acts vii. 7²(¹L). Rom. ix. 15*t*¹.

he that, Mark iii. 29¹. iv. 25¹(-¹LT Tr*S*).

whatsoever, Matt. x. 11¹. xiv. 7² (¹LTr). xv. 5². xvi. 19²(Lᵐ ὅσα), 19² (¹LTr). xx. 4², 7². Mark vi. 22², 23². vii. 11². x. 35². xi. 23²(-G∞TTr*S*). xiii. 11². Luke ix. 4¹. x. 5¹, 8¹, 10¹. Rom. xvi. 2¹. Gal. vi. 7²(¹L). 1 John iii. 22². v. 15¹(²T*S*). 3 John 5.

ὃ ἐάν τι, **whatsoever,** Eph. vi. 8 (ὃ ἄν G', ὃ ἐάν L, ἐάν τι Lᵐ, ἐάν *S*).

what things soever, John v. 19¹ (-¹ LTrᵇ).

ἐν ᾧ ἄν, **whereinsoever,** 2 Cor. xi. 21.

what, John xv. 7²(¹L).

which, Mark iv. 22². Acts vii. 3¹.

that, Matt. xii. 36² (-²LTTr*S*). xviii. 19². 1 Cor. vi. 18². Gal. v. 17¹ (²Lᵇ*S*).

VII. Followed by a demonstrative pronoun. Matt. iii. 12. Mark i. 7. Etc. 13 instances.

For the Genitive used as an Adverb of time or place, see οὗ.

ὁσάκις.

With ἄν¹ *or* ἐάν², **as often as,** 1 Cor. xi. 26¹(²LT*S*). Rev. xi. 6². — **as oft as,** 1 Cor. xi. 25¹(²LT*S*).

ὅσγε, ὅς γε LT.

he that, Rom. viii. 32.

ὅσιος.

holy, 1 Tim. ii. 8. Tit. i. 8. Heb. vii. 26. Rev. xv. 4(ἅγιος εἶ G'').

Said of Christ, **Holy One,** Acts ii. 27. xiii. 35.

τὰ ὅσια, **mercies** (*Gr.* holy or just things), Acts xiii. 34.

Add Rev. xvi. 5, for ἐσόμενος, EG LTTr*S*.

ὁσιότης.

holiness, Luke i. 75. Eph. iv. 24.

ὁσίως.

holily, 1 Thes. ii. 10.

ὀσμή.

odor, John xii. 3. Phil. iv. 18.

savor, 2 Cor. ii. 14, 16*t*. Eph. v. 2.

ὅσος.

Plural, ὅσοι, ὅσαι, ὅσα.

how much, Acts ix. 13. Heb. viii. 6. Rev. xviii. 7.

as much as, John vi. 11.

ἐφ' ὅσον, **inasmuch as,** Matt. xxv. 40, 45. Rom. xi. 13. — **as long as,** Matt. ix. 15. 2 Pet. i. 13.

καθ' ὅσον, **inasmuch as,** Heb. iii. 3. vii. 20. — **as,** Heb. ix. 27.

as large as, Rev. xxi. 16.

as, Heb. i. 4. x. 25.

the more, Mark vii. 36.

μικρὸν ὅσον ὅσον, **a little while,** Heb. x. 37.

as many as, Matt. xiv. 36. xxii. 10. Mark iii. 10. Luke xi. 8. John i. 12. Acts iii. 24. iv. 6, 34. v. 36, 37. x. 45 (οἱ L). xiii. 48. Rom. ii. 12*t*. viii. 14. Gal. iii. 10, 27. vi. 12, 16. Phil. iii. 15. Col. ii. 1. 1 Tim. vi. 1. Rev. ii. 24. xviii. 17.

so many as, Rom. vi. 3.

who, Heb. ii. 15.

how great things, Mark v. 19, 20. Luke viii. 39*t*. Acts ix. 16.

how many things, 2 Tim. i. 18.

what great things, Mark iii. 8(ἃ fr. ὅς Lᵐ).

whatsoever, Matt. xvii. 12. xxviii. 20. Mark ix. 13. x. 21. Luke iv. 23. xii. 3. John xv. 14(ὃ T, ἃ LTr*S*). xvii. 7. Acts iv. 28.

whatsoever things, Rom. xv. 4. Phil. iv. 8*six*.

what things soever, Rom. iii. 19.

all that, Luke ix. 10. Acts iv. 23. xiv. 27.

all things that, Acts xv. 4. 'Rev. i. 2.

that ever, John iv. 29, 39(ἃ Tr*S*). x. 8.

all, 2 Cor. i. 20.
that, Matt. xiii. 44, 46. xviii. 25. xxiii. 3(²T*S*). Mark xii. 44. Luke iv. 40. xviii. 12, 22. John x. 41. xvi. 15.
what, Mark vi. 30*t*. Acts xv. 12.
which, John xxi. 25. Acts ix. 39.

ὅσοι (ὅσαι, ὅσα) ἄν (ἐάν²).

as many as, Matt. xxii. 9 (²LTTr *S*). Mark vi. 56. Acts ii. 39(*οὓς ἄν* L). Rev. iii. 19². xiii. 15(²LTTr).
whosoever, Mark vi. 11(*ap*). Luke ix. 5.
whatsoever, Matt. vii. 12. xviii. 18² (*ἄν* LTr), 18². xxi. 22 (²TTr). xxiii. 3 (²T). John xi. 22. xvi. 13 (–*ἄν* LTTr*S*), 23 (*ἄν τι* LTTr, *ὅ τι ἄν* Lᵐ, *ὃ ἄν S*). Acts iii. 22.
what things soever, Mark xi. 24 (–*ἄν* G°°LTTr*S*).
wherewithᶜ **soever**, Mark iii. 28 (²TTr).
Add, for *ὅς*, Matt. xvi. 19¹ˢᵗ, Lᵐ. Jn. iv. 45, LTTr. 1 Cor. ii. 9²ᵈ, LT. Rev. iv. 1, L. For *ὡς*, Lk. xxiv. 6, Lᵐ.
See also μέν, χρόνος.

ὅσπερ.

whosoever, Mark xv. 6.

ὀστέον.

bone, Matt. xxiii. 27. Luke xxiv. 39. John xix. 36. Eph. v. 30(*ap*). Heb. xi. 22.

ὅστις,

Fem. ἥτις, Neut. ὅ τι.

With *ἄν*¹ or *ἐάν*².

whosoever, Matt. v. 39, 41. vii. 24. x. 32, 33¹ (–*ἄν* LTr). xii. 50¹. xiii. 12*t*. xviii. 4. xxiii. 12. Mark viii. 34 (*εἴ τις* G′LTr*S*). Luke xiv. 27. Gal. v. 4, 10¹(²T*S*). Jas. ii. 10.
whatsoever, Luke x. 35¹. John ii. 5¹. xiv. 13¹. xv. 16¹.
such as, Mark iv. 20. 1 Cor. v. 1.
who, which, Matt. vii. 15, 24, 26. xiii. 52. xvi. 28. xix. 12*tr*. xx. 1. xxi. 33, 41. xxii. 2. xxiii. 27. xxv. 1. xxvii. 55. Mark ix. 1. xii. 18. xv. 7.
Luke i. 20. ii. 4, 10. vii. 37. viii. 3, 15, 26, 43. ix. 30. x. 42. xii. 1. xv. 7. xxiii. 19, 55. John viii. 53. Acts vii. 53. viii. 15. x. 41, 47. xi. 20, 28. xii. 10. xiii. 31, 43. xvi. 12, 16, 17. xvii. 10. xxi. 4. xxiii. 21, 33. xxiv. 1. xxviii. 18.
Rom. i. 25, 32. ii. 15. ix. 4. xi. 4. xvi. 4, 6, 7, 12(*ap*). 1 Cor. iii. 17. vi. 20(*ap*). vii. 13. 2 Cor. viii. 10. ix. 11. Gal. ii. 4. iv. 24*t*, 26. v. 19. Eph. i. 23. iii. 13. iv. 19. vi. 2. Phil. i. 28. ii. 20. iv. 3. Col. iii. 5, 14 (*ὅ* fr. *ὅς* G″LT, *ὅς S*). iv. 11. 2 Thes. i. 9. 1 Tim. i. 4. iii. 15. vi. 9. 2 Tim. i. 5. ii. 2, 18. Tit. i. 11.
Heb. ii. 3. viii. 5, 6. ix. 2, 9. x. 8, 11, 35. xii. 5. xiii. 7. 1 Pet. ii. 11. 2 Pet. ii. 1. 1 John i. 2. Rev. ii. 24. ix. 4. xi. 8. xii. 13. xvii. 12. xix. 2. xx. 4.
the which, John xxi. 25.
which ᶜ**veil**, 2 Cor. iii. 14(*ὅτι* GLT).
which things, Col. ii. 23.
what things, Phil. iii. 7.
that, Matt. ii. 6. xviii. 28 (*εἴ τις* G LTTr*S*). xxvii. 62. Luke vii. 39. Rom. vi. 2. Rev. i. 12. xvii. 8 (*ὅτι* GLTTr).
the same that, John viii. 25(*ὅτι* St).
he (they) that (which), Matt. xxiii. 12. xxv. 3 (*αἱ δέ* L, *αἱ γάρ* Tr*S*). Rev. i. 7.
in that they, Acts xvii. 11.
and they, Acts v. 16. xxiii. 14.
and, Acts ix. 35.
whereas ᶜ**ye**, Jas. iv. 14.
as, 1 Cor. xvi. 2¹.

πᾶς ὅστις ἄν.

every . . which, Acts iii. 23(²T*S*).
whatsoever, Col. iii. 17 (*ἐάν* for *ἄν* LT), 23 (*πᾶν ὃ ἐάν* G″, *ὃ ἐάν* LT*S*).
Add, for *ὅς*, Matt. xix. 29, GᵖʰLT Tr*S*. For *ὅτι*, Mark ix. 11, 28, L. 1 John iii. 20², v. 14², L¹. For *τίς*, Acts ix. 6, G′LT*S*.
See also ὅτου.

ὀστράκινος.

earthen, 2 Cor. iv. 7.
of earth, 2 Tim. ii. 20.

ὄσφρησις.

smelling, 1 Cor. xii. 17.

ὀσφύς.

loins, Matt. iii. 4. Mark i. 6. Luke xii. 35. Acts ii. 30. Eph. vi. 14. Heb. vii. 5, 10. 1 Pet. i. 13.

ὅταν.

I. With the Subjunctive.

whensoever, Mark xiv. 7.

when, Matt. v. 11. vi. 2, 5, 6, 16. ix. 15. x. 19, 23. xii. 43. xiii. 32. xv. 2. xix. 28. xxi. 40. xxiii. 15. xxiv. 15, 32, 33. xxv. 31. xxvi. 29. Mark ii. 20. iv. 15, 16, 29, 31, 32. viii. 38. xi. 25. xii. 23 (–G∞LᵇTr *S*), 25. xiii. 4, 7, 11, 14, 28, 29.

Luke v. 35. vi. 22*t*, 26. viii. 13. ix. 26. xi. 2, 21, 24, 34, 36. xii. 11, 54, 55. xiii. 28. xiv. 8, 10*t*, 12, 13. xvi. 4, 9. xvii. 10. xxi. 7, 9, 20, 30, 31. xxiii. 42. John ii. 10. iv. 25. v. 7. vii. 27, 31. viii. 28, 44. x. 4. xiii. 19. xiv. 29. xv. 26. xvi. 4, 13, 21. xxi. 18. Acts xxiii. 35. xxiv. 22.

Rom. ii. 14. xi. 27. 1 Cor. xiii. 10. xiv. 26. xv. 24*t*, 27, 28, 54. xvi. 2, 3, 5, 12. 2 Cor. x. 6. xii. 10. xiii. 9. Col. iii. 4. iv. 16. 1 Thes. v. 3. 2 Thes. i. 10. 1 Tim. v. 11. Tit. iii. 12. Heb. i. 6. Jas. i. 2. 1 John ii. 28 (ἐάν L*S*). v. 2. Rev. ix. 5. x. 7. xi. 7. xvii. 10. xviii. 9. xx. 7 (*see* μετά).

while, 1 Cor. iii. 4.

as soon as, John xvi. 21. Rev. xii. 4.

as long as, John ix. 5.

εἰ μὴ ὅταν, **till,** Mark ix. 9.

that, Mark xiv. 25.

Add Mark ix. 10, ὅταν ἀναστῇ for τὸ ἀναστῆναι, G′. xi. 19, for ὅτε, TTr*S*.

II. With the Indicative.

when, Mark iii. 11. Rev. iv. 9.

Add Rev. viii. 1, for ὅτε, LTTr.

ὅτε.

when, Matt. vii. 28. ix. 25. xi. 1. xii. 3. xiii. 26, 48, 53. xvii. 25 (–L Tr*S*). xix. 1. xxi. 1, 34. xxvi. 1. Mark i. 32. ii. 25. iv. 10. vii. 17. viii. 19, 20. xi 1, 19 (ὅταν TTr*S*). xiv. 12. xv. 20, 41 Luke ii. 21, 22, 42. iv. 25. vi. 13. xiii. 35 (–Trᵇ*S*). xvii. 22. xxii. 14, 35. xxiii. 33.

John i. 19. ii. 22. iv. 21, 23, 45. v. 25. vi. 24. ix. 4, 14 (ἐν ᾗ ἡμέρᾳ LTTr*S*). xii. 16, 17 (G′, ὅτι GLT), 41 (ὅτι LTTr*S*). xiii. 31 (30) xvi. 25. xix. 6, 8, 23, 30. xx. 24. xxi. 15, 18. Acts i. 13. viii. 12, 39. xi. 2. xii. 6. xxi. 5, 35. xxii. 20. xxvii. 39. xxviii. 16.

Rom. ii. 16 (ᾗ fr. ὅς L). vi. 20. vii. 5. xiii. 11. 1 Cor. xiii. 11*t*. Gal. i. 15. ii. 11, 12, 14. iv. 3, 4. Phil. iv. 15. Col. iii. 7. 1 Thes. iii. 4. 2 Thes. iii. 10. 2 Tim. iv. 3.

Heb. vii. 10. 1 Pet. iii. 20. Jude 9 (τότε L). Rev. i. 17. v. 8. vi. 1, 3, 5, 7, 9, 12. viii. 1 (ὅταν LTTr). x. 3, 4. xii. 13. xxii. 8.

while, John xvii. 12. Heb. ix. 17.

after that, Matt. xxvii. 31. Tit. iii. 4.

after, John xiii. 12.

that, Mark vi. 21 (ὅ τε L).

as soon as, Luke xv. 30. Rev. x. 10.

Add Mark iv. 6 (when), LTTr*S*. Luke vi. 3, for ὁπότε, LTr*S*. 1 Cor. xii. 2 (. . ye were), G″LᵇT*S*. Jude 9, for ὁ δέ, L. Rev. xxii. 8, *see* βλέπω.

ὅ τε. See τέ.

ὅτι.

A Conjunction having two distinct uses, here classified according to Bruder, except when noted ([a]).

I. As a Demonstrative.

that, Matt. ii. 16, 22. iii. 9. iv. 12. v. 17, 20, 21, 22, 23, 27, 28, 32, 33, 38, 43. vi. 7, 29, 32. viii. 11, 27. ix. 6, 28. x. 34. xi. 24. xii. 6, 36. xiii. 17. xv. 12, 17. xvi. 11, 18, 20. xvii. 10, 12, 13. xviii. 10, 19. xix. 4, 23, 28. xx. 10, 25, 30. xxi. 31, 45. xxii. 16, 34. xxiii. 31. xxiv. 32, 33, 43, 47. xxv. 24, 26. xxvi. 2, 21, 34, 53, 54. xxvii. 3, 18, 24, 63. xxviii. 5, 7.

Mark ii. 1, 8, 10, 16. iv 38, 41. v 29. vi. 2(*omS*), 14, 15*t*. vii. 18. viii. 31. ix. 1, 11, 13, 25. x. 42, 47. xi. 3(–LTTr), 23*t*, 24, 32. xii. 12, 14, 26, 28, 34, 35, 43. xiii. 28, 29, 30. xiv. 30. xv. 10, 39. xvi. 4, 7, 11(*ap*).

Luke i. 22. ii. 49*t*. iii. 8. iv. 4. v. 24. vi. 5(–Tr^b*S*). vii. 4, 16*t*, 37, 43. viii. 47, 53. ix. 7, 8*t*, 19. x. 11, 12, 20, 21, 24, 40. xi. 38. xii. 30, 37, 39, 44, 51. xiii. 2, 4. xiv. 24. xv. 7. xvi. 25. xvii. 15. xviii. 8, 9 (*marg.*, *with* εἰσί, **as being**), 11, 37. xix. 7, 22, 26, 40 (–Tr^b). xx. 19, 21, 37. xxi. 3, 20, 30, 31. xxii. 37, 70. xxiii. 7. xxiv. 21, 39, 44.

John i. 34. ii. 17, 18, 22. iii. 2, 7, 19, 21, 28*t*, 33. iv. 1, 19, 20, 25, 27, 42, 44, 47, 53. v. 6, 15, 32, 36, 42, 45. vi. 15, 22*t*, 24, 36, 46, 61, 65, 69. vii. 26, 35, 42. viii. 17, 24*t*, 27, 28, 37, 48, 52, 54. ix. 8, 17, 18, 20*t*, 24, 25, 29, 30, 31, 32, 35. x. 38. xi. 6, 13, 15, 20, 22, 24, 27, 31, 40, 41, 42*t*, 50, 51, 56. xii. 9, 12, 16, 34, 50. xiii. 1, 3*t*, 19, 21, 29, 35. xiv. 10, 11, 20, 22, 31. xv. 18. xvi. 4, 15, 19, 20, 21, 26, 27, 30*t*. xvii. 7, 8*t*, 21, 23, 25. xviii. 8, 14, 37. xix. 4, 10, 21, 28, 35. xx. 9, 14, 18, 31. xxi. 4, 7, 12, 15, 16, 17, 23, 24.

Acts ii. 29, 30, 31, 36. iii. 10, 17. iv. 10, 13*t*, 16. v. 9, 41. vi. 14. vii. 6. viii. 14, 18. ix. 20, 22, 26, 27, 38. x. 34, 42. xi. 1. xii. 9, 11. xiii. 38. xiv. 9, 22. xv. 5, 24. xvi. 3, 10, 19, 38. xvii. 3*t*, 13. xix. 25, 26*t*, 34. xx. 23*t*, 25, 26, 29, 31, 34, 38. xxi. 21, 22, 24, 29, 31. xxii. 2, 19, 29. xxiii. 5, 6, 22, 27, 34. xxiv. 11, 14, 26. xxvi. 5, 27. xxvii. 10, 25. xxviii. 1, 22, 28.

Rom. i. 8, 13, 32. ii. 2, 3, 4. iii. 2, 19. iv. 9(–L^b*S*), 21, 23. v. 3. vi. 3, 6, 8, 9, 16, 17. vii. 14, 16, 18, 21. viii. 16, 18, 22, 28, 38. ix. 2, 30. x. 2, 5, 9*t*. xi. 25. xiii. 11. xiv. 14. xv. 14, 29.

1 Cor. i. 5, 11, 12, 14, 15. iii. 16, 20. iv. 9(–G^{oo}LT*S*). v. 6 vi. 2, 3, 9, 15, 16, 19. vii. 26. viii. 1, 4*t*. ix. 10, 13, 24. x. 19(*ap*), 20. xi. 2, 3, 14, 17, 23. xii. 2, 3. xiv. 23, 25, 37. xv. 4*t*, 5, 12*t*, 15, 27, 50, 58. xvi. 15.

2 Cor. i. 7, 8, 10(–L^b), 12, 14, 23. ii. 3. iii. 5. iv. 14. v. 1, 6, 14(15). vii. 3, 8, 9*t*, 16. viii. 9. ix. 2. x. 7, 11. xi. 31. xii. 13, 19. xiii. 2, 6*t*.

Gal. i. 6, 11, 23. ii. 7, 14, 16. iii. 7, 8, 11. iv. 15, 22. v. 2, 3, 10, 21. Eph. ii. 11, 12. iv. 9. v. 5. vi. 8, 9. Phil. i. 6, 12, 17, 19, 20, 25, 27. ii. 11, 16, 22, 24, 26. iv. 10, 15. Col. iii. 24. iv. 1, 13.

1 Thes. ii. 1. iii. 3, 4, 6. iv. 14, 15. v. 2. 2 Thes. ii. 2, 4, 5. iii. 4, 10. 1 Tim. i. 8, 9, 15. iv. 1. 2 Tim. i. 5, 12, 15. ii. 23. iii. 1, 15. Tit. iii. 11. Phm. 21, 22.

Heb. ii. 6*t*. iii. 19. vii. 8, 14. xi. 6, 13, 14, 18, 19. Jas. i. 3, 7. ii. 19, 20. iii. 1. iv. 4, 5. v. 11, 20. 1 Pet. i. 12, 18. ii. 3. iii. 9. 2 Pet. i. 14, 20. iii. 3, 5, 8.

1 John i. 5, 6, 8, 10. ii. 3, 5, 18*t*, 19, 22, 29*t*. iii. 2, 5, 14, 15, 19, 24. iv. 3, 10*t*, 13, 14, 15. v. 1, 2, 5, 11, 13, 14 (ὅ τι L), 15*t*, 18, 19, 20. 2 John 4. 3 John 12. Rev. ii. 6, 23. iii. 1*t*, 9, 15, 17. x. 6. xii. 12, 13.

ὡς ὅτι, **to wit, that,** 2 Cor. v. 19.— **as though,** 2 Cor. xi. 21.

οἷον δὲ ὅτι, **as though,** Rom. ix. 6.

as though, Phil. iii. 12.

how that, Matt. xii. 5. xvi. 12, 21. Luke vii. 22(–LTr^b*S*). Acts vii. 25. xiii. 32. xv. 7. xx. 35. Rom. vii. 1. 1 Cor. i. 26. x. 1. xv. 3. 2 Cor. viii. 2. xii. 4. xiii. 5. Gal. i. 13. Eph. iii. 3. Heb. xii. 17. Jas. ii. 24. Jude 5, 18.

how, Luke i. 58. xxi. 5. John iv. 1. xii. 19. xiv. 28. Acts xiv. 27. xx. 35. Gal. iv. 13. Phm. 19. Jas. ii. 22. Rev. ii. 2.

why, Mark ix. 11 and 28 (ὅ τι L).

because that, Acts x. 45. 2 Thes. i. 3. 1 John iv. 9.

because, Matt. xi. 25. Luke xi. 18. xiii. 14. xvi. 8. xvii. 9. xix. 11, 31. John vii. 23. viii. 45. xiv. 28. xvi. 17. xxi. 17. Acts ii. 6. xxii. 29. Rom. viii. 21. xiv. 23. 1 Cor. vi. 7. 2 Cor. vii. 13. xi. 7. 1 Thes. ii. 13. 2 Thes. ii. 13. 1 John iii. 16. iv. 13, 17. v. 6. Rev. ii. 4, 14 (–LTTr^{b}), 20. xi. 17.

for that, 1 Tim. i. 12.

for, Matt. vi. 26. Mark i. 27(*ap*). xii. 32. Luke i. 45(*marg.* **that**), 48. iv. 36. vii. 39. viii. 25. xii. 24. xv. 6, 9. John iv. 35. v. 28. vii. 52. xiv. 17. Acts viii. 33. xxii. 15. 1 Cor. xvi. 17. 2 Cor. i. 5. ii. 15. vii. 14. viii. 3. ix. 12. Gal. iii. 11. iv. 27. Eph. ii. 18. Phil. iv. 16. 1 Thes. i. 5. 2 Thes. iii. 7. 1 John iii. 2, 20 (ὅ τι L). iv. 8. Rev. xii. 12. xviii. 20. xix. 7. xxi. 5.

Not rendered, Matt. ii. 23. iv. 6. v. 31(–LTTr*S*). vi. 5 and 16 (–LT Tr*S*). vii. 23. ix. 18, 33(*omS*). x. 7. xiv. 26. xviii. 13. xix. 8, 9(–LT Tr). xx. 12(–LTTr*S*). xxi. 3, 16, 43. xxvi. 29 and 65 (–LTTr*S*), 72, 74, 75. xxvii. 43, 47. xxviii. 13.

Mark i. 15, 37, 40 (Κύριε L^{m}). ii. 12. iii. 11, 21, 22*t*, 28. v. 23, 28, 35. vi. 4, 16 (–G^{o}LTTr*S*), 18, 23, 35, 55. vii. 6(–L^{b}Tr^{b}*S*), 20. viii. 24(*ap*). ix. 26, 31. x. 33. xii. 6, 7, 19, 29. xiii. 6. xiv. 14, 18, 25, 27, 58*t*, 69, 71, 72.

Luke i. 25, 61. ii. 23. iv. 10, 11 (–G^{oo}), 12, 21, 24, 41, 43. v. 26, 36. viii. 49. ix. 22. xii. 55. xiii. 35(–L^{b} Tr*S*). xiv. 30. xv. 2, 27. xvii. 10 (–L). xviii. 29. xix. 9, 42. xx. 5. xxi. 8 (–L^{b}Tr^{b}*S*), 32. xxii. 16, 18 (–TTr), 61. xxiii. 5, 40. xxiv. 7, 34, 46.

John i. 20, 32. ii. 25. iii. 11. iv. 17, 21, 35, 37, 39, 42(–L^{b}), 51, 52, 53 (–LTr*S*). v, 24, 25. vi. 5, 14, 42. vii. 12, 31(–LTr*S*). viii. 33, 34, 55. ix. 9, 9 (L^{mb}, οὐχὶ, ἀλλά, L^{b}TTr*S*), 9, 17, 19, 23, 41. x. 7(–L^{b}Tr), 36, 41. xi. 31. xii. 34(–G^{oo}). xiii. 33. xv. 25. xvi. 19, 23 (–L^{b}TTr). xviii. 6 (–LTr*S*), 9. xx. 15^{oc}. xxi. 23.

Acts ii. 13. iii. 22. v. 4, 23, 25. vi. 11. xi. 3. xii. 3. xiii. 34. xv. 1. xvi. 36. xvii. 6. xviii. 13. xix. 21. xxiii. 20. xxiv. 21. xxv. 8, 16. xxvi. 31. xxviii. 25.

Rom. iii. 8, 10. iv. 17. ix. 12, 17. xiv. 11. 1 Cor. x. 19. xiv. 21. xv. 27 (–L^{b}). 2 Cor. i. 13, 18. iii. 3. vi. 16. xi. 10. Gal. i. 20. iii. 8. 1 Tim. vi. 7. Heb. vii. 17. x. 8. xiii. 18. Jas. i. 13. 1 John iii. 20. iv. 20. Jude 18 (–L*S*). Rev. iii. 17 (–G^{o}*S*).

Not rendered, Rom. viii. 36.

Add Matt. xvi. 28 (. . there be), L*S*. xxiii. 36(. . All), G^{pr}. xxiv. 34(. . this), LTr. Mark ii. 16, *ὅτι ἐσθίει* L, *ὅτι ἤσθιεν* Tr*S*, for *ἐσθίοντα.* iii. 12(*ap*). iv. 21 (. . Is), T. vii. 2(saw . .), Tr*S*. viii. 4(. . From), TTr. 28 (. . John), T*S*. 28, *ὅτι εἷς* for *ἕνα*, LTTr*S*. ix. 41, *ἐν ὀνόματι ὅτι* for *ἐν τῷ ὀνόματί μου, ὅτι*, GLTTr, *–τῷ, ἐμόν ἔσται* for *Χριστοῦ ἐστε*, *S*.

Luke xii. 27 (that). L^{b}*S*. 54 (. . There), L^{b}Tr*S*. xviii. 14(. . this), L^{b}. xix. 34 (said . .), LTr*S*. 46 (written . .), L. xxii. 37, for *τό*^{2d}, L. John i. 50(51, . . I saw), LTTr*S*. viii. 11 (. . Go), TTr. 25, for *ὅ τι*, St. x. 34(. . I said), LTTr*S*. xii. 17, for *ὅτε*, GLT. xiii. 11 (. . Ye), LTTr. xiv. 2(. . I go), LTTr*S*. Acts x. 20, for *διότι*, GLT*S*.

Rom. x. 9, *ὅτι κύριος Ἰησοῦς* for *Κύριον Ἰησοῦν*, L^{m}. Gal. iii. 10 (written . .), GLT*S*. Phil. i. 18(. . every), L*S*. 1 Pet. i. 16 (written . .), T. 1 John ii. 4(saith . .), L^{b}T*S*. v. 9, for [illegible], G″LT*S*. Rev. xvii. 8, for *ὅ τι*, GLTTr. xviii. 7(. . I sit), LTTr*S*.

II. As a Causal.

because, Matt. ii. 18. v. 36. vii. 14 (G′, *τί* C^{m}GLTr, *marg.* **how**). ix. 36. xi. 20. xii. 41. xiii. 11, 13. xiv. 5. xv. 32. xvi. 7, 8. xx. 7, 15. xxiii. 29. Mark i. 34 (*marg.* **that**). iii. 30. iv. 29. vi. 34. vii. 19. viii. 2, 16,

17. ix. 38(*ap*), 41(ᵃ, *see* No. I., *add.*). xi. 18 (γάρ TTrS). xvi. 14(*ap*).
Luke viii. 30. ix. 49, 53. xi. 18. xii. 17. xiii. 2. xv. 27. xix. 3, 17, 21. John i. 50(51). iii. 18, 23. v. 16, 18, 27, 30. vi. 2, 26*t*, 41. vii. 1, 7, 22, 30, 39. viii. 22, 37, 43, 44, 47. ix. 16, 22. x. 13, 17, 33, 36. xi. 9, 10. xii. 6, 11, 39. xiv. 12, 17, 19. xv. 19, 21, 27. xvi. 3, 4, 6, 9, 10, 11, 16(*ap*), 21, 27, 32. xvii. 14. xix. 7. xx. 13, 29. Acts ii. 27. vi. 1. viii. 20. xvii. 18(*ap*).
Rom. v. 5. vi. 15. viii. 27 (*marg.* **that**). ix. 7, 28(*ap*), 32. 1 Cor. i. 25. ii. 14. iii. 13. xii. 15, 16. xv. 15. 2 Cor. xi. 11. Gal. ii. 11. iv. 6. Eph. v. 16. Phil. ii. 30. iv. 17. 2 Thes. i. 10. iii. 9. 1 Tim. i. 13. iv. 10. v. 12. vi. 2*t*. Phm. 7.
Heb. viii. 9. Jas. i. 10. 1 Pet. ii. 21. v. 8(*ap*). 1 John ii. 8ᵃ, 12ᵃ, 13*tr*ᵃ, 14*t*ᵃ, 21*t*ᵃ. iii. 1, 9, 12, 14, 22. iv. 1, 4, 18, 19. v. 10.
Rev. iii. 10, 16. v. 4. viii. 11. xi. 10. xiv. 8 (ἡ fr. ὅς LTTr, –G°°S°). xvi. 5.

because that, 1 John ii. 11.

for, Matt. v. 3, 4, 5, 6, 7, 8, 9, 10, 12, 34, 35*t*, 45. vi. 5, 13(*ap*). vii. 13. xi. 21, 23, 26, 29. xii. 42. xiii. 16. xv. 23. xvi. 17, 23. xvii. 15. xxiii. 13(14), 14(13, *ap*), 15, 23, 25, 27. xxiv. 42, 44. xxv. 8, 13. Mark v. 9. vi. 17. viii. 33. xiv. 27.
Luke i. 37, 49, 68. ii. 11, 30. iv. 6, 32, 41 (*marg.* **that**), 43. v. 8. vi. 19, 20, 21*t*, 24, 25*t*, 35. vii. 47. viii. 37, 42. ix. 12, 38. x. 13, 21. xi. 31, 32, 42, 43, 44, 46, 47, 48, 52. xii. 15, 32, 40. xiii. 24, 31, 33. xiv. 11, 14, 17. xv. 24, 32. xvi. 3, 8, 15, 24. xviii. 14. xix. 4, 43. xxi. 22. xxiii. 29, 31. xxiv. 29, 39.
John i. 15, 17, 30. iv. 22. v. 38, 39. vi. 38. vii. 8, 29. viii. 14, 16, 20, 29, 44. x. 4, 5. xi. 47. xii. 49. xiv. 28. xv. 5, 15*t*. xvi. 14. xvii. 8, 9, 24. xviii. 2, 18. xix. 20, 42. Acts i. 5, 17. ii. 25. iv. 21. v. 38. ix. 15. x. 14, 38. xi. 8, 24. xiii. 41. xxii. 21.
Rom. viii. 29. xi. 36. 1 Cor. iv. 9. x. 17. xi. 15. 2 Cor. iv. 6. vii. 8. viii. 17. x. 10. Gal. iii. 11. iv. 12, 20. vi. 8. Eph. iv. 25. v. 23, 30. vi. 12. Phil. i. 29. Col. i. 16, 19. ii. 9. 1 Thes. ii. 14. iii. 8. iv. 16. v. 9. 2 Thes. ii. 3. 1 Tim. iv. 4. 2 Tim. i. 16.
Heb. viii. 10, 11, 12. Jas. i. 12, 23. v. 8. 1 Pet. i. 16. ii. 15. iii. 12, 18. iv. 1, 8, 14, 17. v. 5, 7. 1 John ii. 16. iii. 8, 9, 11. iv. 7. v. 4, 7, 9. 2 John 7. Jude 11.
Rev. iii. 4, 8. iv. 11. v. 9. vi. 17. vii. 17. xi. 2. xii. 10, 12. xiv. 7, 15*t*, 18. xv. 1, 4*tr*. xvi. 6, 21. xvii. 14. xviii. 3, 5, 7, 8, 10, 11, 17(16), 19, 23*t*. xix. 2*t*, 6. xxi. 4(–L). xxii. 5, 10 (γάρ G′LTrS, –GT).

for that, John xii. 18. 2 Cor. i. 24.

in that, Rom. v. 8.

as concerning that, Acts xiii. 34.

that, John xi. 42. Phil. iv. 11. 1 John ii. 21ᵃ.

Not rendered, Mark xi. 17(ᵃ?, –L). Luke xvii. 10 (–G°LTTrS). John ii. 25? (*see* διὰ τό, ver. 24).

Add, for γάρ, Matt. xxiii. 10, G′L TTr. Gal. iii. 13, G″LT. For καί, Luke xxii. 22, TTrS. John i. 16, GLTTrS. — Mark xiv. 21 (. . The Son), TTrᵇS. John xii. 41, for ὅτε, LTTrS. 2 Cor. iii. 14, for ὅ τι, GLT. Gal. ii. 16, for διότι, G″LS. Rev. xiii. 4, for ὅς, GLTTrS.

ὅ τι. See ὅστις.

ὅτου.

Genitive of ὅστις. *See* ἕως, *where read* οὗ for ὅτου, Luke xv. 8, xxii. 16, TrS.

Add Luke xii. 50, for οὗ, G″LTTrS.

οὗ.

Genitive of ὅς, *used as an Adverb.*

I. Of Place.

where, Matt. ii. 9. xviii. 20. xxviii. 16. Luke iv. 16, 17. xxii. 10(εἰς ἥν LTrS). John xi. 41(*ap*). Acts i. 13. ii. 2. vii. 29. xii. 12. xvi. 13. xx.

6, 8. xxv. 10. xxviii. 14. Rom. iv. 15. v. 20. ix. 26. 2 Cor. iii. 17. Col. iii. 1. Rev. xvii. 15.
wherein, Luke xxiii. 53.
whither, Luke x. 1. xxiv. 28.
οὐ ἐάν, **whithersoever**, 1 Cor. xvi. 6.
ἐξ οὐ, **from whence**, Phil. iii. 20.
when, Heb. iii. 9.

II. Of Time.

ἀφ' οὐ, **since**, Luke xxiv. 21.
ἀφ' οὐ ἄν, **when once**, Luke xiii. 25.
See also ἄχρις, ἕως, μέχρις.

οὐ, οὐκ, οὐχ.

Used interrogatively[1].
With another negative[2].

not, Matt. i. 25. ii. 18t. iii. 11. iv. 4, 7. v. 14, 17, 21, 27, 33, 36. vi. 5, 20, 24, 26, 26[1], 28, 30[1]. vii. 3, 18, 21, 22, 25, 29. viii. 8, 20. ix. 12, 13, 14, 24. x. 20, 24, 26t, 29, 34, 37t, 38 (ἂν μή L[m]), 38. xi. 11, 17t, 20. xii. 2, 3[1], 4, 5[1], 7t, 19, 20t, 24, 25, 31, 32. xiii. 5, 11, 12, 13t, 17t, 21, 34 (οὐδέν LTTrS), 55[1], 57, 58. xiv. 4, 16. xv. 2, 11, 13, 20, 23, 24, 26, 32. xvi. 3, 11t, 12, 17, 18, 23. xvii. 12, 16, 19, 21(ap), 24[1]. xviii. 14, 22, 30, 33[1]. xix. 4[1], 8, 10, 11, 18tr. xx. 15[1], 22, 23, 26, 28. xxi. 21, 25, 27, 29, 30, 32, 32 (οὐδέ LTr). xxii. 3, 8, 11, 16, 17, 31[1], 32. xxiii. 3, 4, 30, 37. xxiv. 2[1] (–G[oo]), 21, 29, 39, 42, 43, 44, 50t. xxv. 9 (οὐ μή G''LTTr), 12, 24t, 26t, 43tr, 44, 45. xxvi. 11, 24, 39, 40, 42, 53, 70, 72, 74. xxvii. 6, 13[1], 34, 42. xxviii. 6.

Mark i. 7, 22, 34. ii. 17, 18, 19 (ap), 24, 26, 27. iii. 24, 25, 26. iv. 5, 13[1], 21[1], 25, 27, 34, 38[1]. v. 19, 39. vi. 3[1]t, 4, 18, 19, 26, 52. vii. 3, 4, 5, 18[1], 18, 19, 24, 27. viii. 18[1]tr, 21 (οὔπω LTTrS), 33. ix. 6, 18, 28, 30, 37, 38t(ap), 40, 44t(ap), 46t (ap), 48t. x. 27, 38, 40, 43, 45. xi. 13, 16, 17[1], 26, 31, 33. xii. 14t, 24[1], 26[1], 27, 34. xiii. 11, 14, 19, 24, 33, 35. xiv. 7, 29, 36, 37, 49, 56, 68 (οὔτε LTrS), 71. xv. 23, 31. xvi. 6, 14(ap).

Luke i. 20, 22, 33, 34. ii. 37, 43. 49[1], 50. iii. 16. iv. 4, 12, 22[1], 41. v. 31, 32, 36. vi. 2. 4, 40, 41, 42, 43, 44, 46, 48. vii. 6t, 32t, 45, 46. viii. 17, 17 (οὐ μή LTrS), 19, 47, 52. ix. 40, 49, 50, 53, 55[1](ap), 56 (ap), 58. x. 24t, 40[1], 42. xi. 7, 8, 38, 40[1], 44, 46, 52. xii. 2t, 6, 10, 15, 27(ap), 39, 40, 46t, 56, 57. xiii. 15[1], 16[1], 24, 25, 27, 33, 34. xiv. 5[1], 6, 14, 20, 26t, 27t, 30, 33t. xv. 4[1], 13, 28. xvi. 3, 11, 12, 13, 31. xvii. 9 (–L[b]TrS[c]), 18, 20, 22. xviii. 4t, 11, 13[2]. xix. 3, 14, 21t, 22t, 23, 44t, 48. xx. 5, 26, 38. xxi. 6t, 9, 15. xxii. 26, 57, 58, 60. xxiii. 34(ap), 51. xxiv. 3, 6, 18, 24, 39.

John i. 5, 8, 10, 11, 13, 20t, 21, 25, 26, 27, 31, 33. ii. 9, 12, 24, 25. iii. 3, 5, 8, 10, 11, 12, 17, 18, 28, 34, 36. iv. 2, 18, 22, 32, 35[1]. v. 10, 13, 18, 23, 24, 30, 31, 34, 38t, 40, 41, 42, 43, 44, 47. vi. 7, 17(οὔπω L TrS), 22, 24, 26, 32, 36, 38, 42[1], 46, 58, 64, 70[2]. vii. 1, 7, 10, 16, 19[1], 22, 25[1], 28t, 34t, 35, 36t, 45. viii. 13, 14, 16, 21, 22, 23, 27, 29, 35, 40, 41, 43t, 44, 45, 46, 47t, 48[1], 49, 50, 55t. ix. 8[1], 12, 16t, 18, 21t, 25, 27, 29, 30, 31, 32. x. 5, 6, 8, 10, 12t, 13, 16, 21, 25, 26t, 33, 34[1], 35, 37. xi. 4, 9, 15, 21, 32, 37[1], 40[1], 51, 52. xii. 5, 6, 8, 9, 16, 30, 35, 37, 39, 42, 44, 47t, 49. xiii. 7, 10, 16, 18, 33, 36, 37. xiv. 5, 9. 10[1], 10, 17t, 18, 22, 24t, 27. xv. 4, 15, 16, 19, 20, 21, 22, 24. xvi. 3, 4, 7 (οὐ μή Tr), 9, 12, 13, 16 (οὐκέτι LS, οὐκ ἔτι Tr), 17, 18, 19, 26, 30, 32. xvii. 9, 14t, 15, 16t, 25. xviii. 17, 25, 26[1], 28, 30, 31[2], 36t. xix. 10[1]t, 12, 33, 36. xx. 2, 5, 7, 13, 14, 24, 30. xxi. 4, 8, 11, 18, 23tr.

Acts i. 5, 7. ii. 7[1](οὐχί T), 15, 24, 27, 31(οὔτε G''LTS), 34. iv. 16, 20. v. 4, 22, 28[1](–G[o]LTS), 39, 42. vi. 2, 10, 13. vii. 18, 25, 32, 39, 40, 48, 52, 53. viii. 21, 32. ix. 21[1]. x. 41. xii. 9, 14, 22, 23. xiii. 10[1], 25t, 35, 39. xiv. 17. xv. 1. xvi. 7, 21. xvii.

4, 12, 24, 27, 29. xviii. 20. xix. 26, 27, 30, 32, 35. xx. 12, 27, 31. xxi. 13, 38^1. xxii. 9, 11, 18, 22. xxiii. 5*t*. xxv. 7, 11, 16. xxvi. 19, 25, 26, 29. xxvii. 10, 14, 31, 39. xxviii. 4, 19.

Rom. i. 13, 16, 21, 28, 32. ii. 13, 21, 28, 29*t*. iii. 17. iv. 2, 4, 10, 12, 13, 16, 19 (–G^{oo}L*S*), 20, 23. v. 3, 5, 11, 13, 15, 16. vi. 14*t*, 15, 16^1. vii. 6, 7*tr*, 15*t*, 16, 18, 19*t*, 20. viii. 7, 8, 9*t*, 12, 15, 18, 20, 23, 24, 25, 26, 32. ix. 1, 6*t*, 8, 10, 11, 16, 21^1, 24, 25*t*, 26, 31, 32, 33. x. 2, 3, 11, 14*t*, 16. xi. 2, 2^1, 4, 7, 18, 21, 25. xii. 4. xiii. 3, 4, 5, 9*tr*, 9(*om*), 9. xiv. 6(*ap*), 6, 17, 23*t*. xv. 3, 18*t*, 20, 21*t*. xvi. 4, 18.

1 Cor. i. 16, 17*t*, 21, 26*tr*. ii. 1, 2, 4, 6, 8, 9, 12, 13, 14. iii. 1, 2, 16^1. iv. 4, 7, 14, 15, 19, 20. v. 6, 6^1, 10. vi. 2^1, 3^1, 5, 9^1, 9, 12*t*, 13, 15^1, 16^1, 19^1, 19. vii. 4*t*, 6, 9, 10, 12, 15, 28*t*, 35, 36. viii. 7, 8. ix. 1^1*tr*, 2, 6^1, 7, 7^1, 9, 12^1, 12, 13^1, 24^1, 26*t*. x. 1, 5, 13, 20*t*, 21*t*, 23*t*. xi. 6, 7, 8, 17*t*, 20, 22, 31. xii. 1, 14, 15*tr*, 16*tr*, 21. xiii. 4*tr*, 5*tr*, 6. xiv. 2, 16, 17, 22*t*, 23^1, 33, 34. xv. 9, 10*t*, 14, 15*t*, 16, 17, 29, 32, 36, 37, 39, 46, 50, 51 (*ap*), 58. xvi. 7, 12, 22.

2 Cor. i. 8, 12, 18, 19, 24. ii. 4, 5, 11, 17. iii. 3*t*, 5, 6, 13. iv. 1, 5, 8*t*, 9*t*, 16. v. 3, 4, 7, 12, 12 (*μή* L*S*). vi. 12. vii. 3, 7, 8, 9, 12, 14. viii. 5, 8, 10, 12, 13, 19, 21. ix. 12. x. 3, 4, 8*t*, 12, 12(–G^{oo}), 14(–L), 14, 15, 16, 18. xi. 4*tr*, 6. 11, 17, 29*t*, 31. xii. 1, 2*t*, 3 (–L), 4, 5, 6, 13, 14*tr*, 16, 18^1*t*, 20*t*. xiii. 2, 3, 5^1, 6, 7, 10.

Gal. i. 1, 7, 10, 11, 16, 19, 20. ii. 14*t*, 15, 16*t*, 21. iii. 10, 12, 16, 17, 20. iv. 8, 14, 17, 21, 27*t*, 31. v. 8, 18, 21. vi. 4, 7. Eph. i. 16, 21. ii. 8, 9. iii. 5. iv. 20. v. 4. vi. 7, 12. Phil. i. 16, 22, 29. ii. 6, 16, 21, 27. iii. 1, 12, 13 (*οὔπω* L^m*S*). iv. 11, 17. Col. i. 9. ii. 1, 8, 19, 23. iii. 23.

1 Thes. i. 5, 8. ii. 1, 3, 4, 8, 13, 17. iv. 7, 8, 9, 13. v. 4, 5, 9. 2 Thes. ii. 5, 10. iii. 2, 7, 9, 10, 14. 1 Tim. i. 9. ii. 7, 12, 14. iii. 5. v. 8, 13, 18, 25. 2 Tim. i. 7, 9, 12, 16. ii. 5, 9, 13, 20, 24. iv. 3, 8. Tit. iii. 5.

Heb. i. 12. ii. 5, 11, 16. iii. 10, 16, 19. iv. 2, 6, 8, 15. v. 4, 5, 12. vi. 10. vii. 11, 16, 20, 21, 27. viii. 2, 9*t*. ix. 5, 7, 11*t*, 24. x. 1, 2, 5, 8, 37, 39. xi. 1, 5, 16, 23, 31, 35, 38, 39. xii. 7, 8, 9, 18, 20, 25, 26. xiii. 6, 9*t*. Jas. i. 20, 23, 25. ii. 4^1, 5^1, 6^1, 7^1, 21^1, 24, 25^1. iii. 2, 10, 15. iv. 1^1, 2*tr*, 3, 4^1, 11, 14. v. 6, 17.

1 Pet. i. 8, 12, 18, 23. ii. 10*t*, 18, 23*t*. iii. 3, 21. 2 Pet. i. 12 (*see μέλλω*), 16, 21. ii. 3*t*, 4, 5, 10, 11. iii. 9. 1 John i. 6, 8, 10*t*. ii. 2, 4, 11, 15, 16, 19*t*, 21*t*, 27. iii. 1*t*, 6*t*, 9*t*, 10, 12. iv. 3, 6*t*, 8, 10, 18, 20. v. 3, 6, 10, 12, 16, 17, 18*t*. 2 John 1, 5, 9, 10, 12. 3 John 9, 11, 13. Jude 9, 10.

Rev. ii. 2*t*, 3(*ap*), 9, 13, 21, 24*t*. iii. 2, 4, 8, 9, 17. iv. 8. vi. 10. ix. 4, 6 (*οὐ μή* GLTTr*S*), 20. xi. 9. xii. 8, 11. xiii. 8. xiv. 4. xvi. 9, 11, 18, 20. xvii. 8*tr*, 11. xx. 4, 5, 15.

no, Luke xvi. 2. xx. 22. John i. 21. xxi. 5. Rom. iii. 9. 2 Tim. iii. 9. Rev. vii. 16. x. 6 (*see οὐκέτι*).

nay, Matt. v. 37*t*. xiii. 29. John vii. 12. Acts xvi. 37. 2 Cor. i. 17*t*, 18, 19. Jas. v. 12*t*.

no, *adj.*^{cc}, Matt. vi. 1. xii. 39. xvi. 4, 7, 8. xix. 18. xx. 13. xxv. 3, 42*t*. xxvi. 55. Mark ii. 17. iv. 7, 17, 40 (*ap*). viii. 16, 17. ix. 3. xii. 20, 22. xiii. 20. Luke i. 7, 33. ii. 7. vii. 44, 45. viii. 13, 14, 27. ix. 13. xi. 29. xii. 17, 33. xv. 7. xx. 31. xxii. 53. John i. 47(48). ii. 3. iv. 9, 17*t*, 38, 44. v. 7. vi. 53. vii. 18, 52. viii. 37, 44. ix. 41. xi. 10. xiii. 8. xv. 22. xix. 6, 9, 15. Acts vii. 5, 11. x. 34. xii. 18. xiii. 37. xv. 2. xviii. 15. xix. 23, 24, 26. xxi. 39. xxv. 26. xxvii. 20. xxviii. 2.

Rom. ii. 11. iii. 18, 20, 22. iv. 15. vii. 18. x. 12, 19. xiii. 1, 10. 1 Cor. vii. 25. x. 13. xi. 16. xii. 21*t*, 24.

xiii. 5. xv. 12, 13. 2 Cor. ii. 13. viii. 15. xi. 14, 15. Gal. ii. 6, 16. v. 23. Eph. v. 5. Phil. iii. 3. Col. iii. 25. 1 Thes. v. 1.

Heb. viii. 7. ix. 22. x. 6, 38. xii. 11, 17. xiii. 10, 14. Jas. i. 17. ii. 11. 1 Pet. ii. 22. 2 Pet. i. 20. 1 John i. 8. ii. 7, 21, 27. iii. 5, 15. iv. 18. 3 John 4. Rev. xiv. 5, 11. xviii. 7. xx. 6, 11. xxi. 1, 4, 22, 23, 25. xxii. 3, 5*t*.

no [c]**such**, Acts xv. 24.

none[cc], Matt. xii. 43. xxvi. 60, 60 (-GL[b]TTr*S*). Mark xii. 31, 32. xiv. 55. Luke xiii. 6, 7, John vi. 22. Acts iii. 6. vii. 5. Rom. iii. 10, 11*t*, 12. viii. 9. 2 Cor. i. 13. Gal. i. 19. 1 John ii. 10. Rev. ii. 24.

no man[cc], 2 Cor. xi. 10.

With οὐδείς (οὐδεμία, οὐδέν), **no . . at all**, John xix. 11. 1 John i. 5. — **nothing at all**, John xi. 49.

nothing[cc], Luke viii. 17. xi. 6. 1 Cor. ix. 16.

With καί, **neither**, Matt. xxii. 16². Mark viii. 14. xiv. 40. Luke viii. 27. xviii. 34. xx. 21. John iii. 20. x. 28. Acts iv. 12²(*ap*). 1 Cor. ii. 9, 14. xi. 9. Eph. vi. 9. Heb. iv. 13. Rev. ix. 21. xx. 4. — **nor**, Luke xviii. 4(οὐδέ LTr*S*). 1 Cor. ii. 9. vi. 10*t*.

With δέ, **neither**, 1 Cor. ix. 15.

neither, Matt. xxiii. 13(14). xxv. 13. Luke viii. 43². xii. 24 (οὔτε T *S*), 24. John xvii. 20. Acts viii. 21. ix. 9. xxiv. 18. Gal. iii. 28*tr*. Col. iii. 11. 2 Pet. i. 8.

never, Mark iii. 29. xiv. 21. Luke xxiii. 29*t*.

Not rendered², Matt. xiv. 17. xxvii. 14. Mark iii. 27 (-GLTr). v. 37. vi. 5. xii. 14. xiv. 60. xv. 4¹. Luke iv. 2. viii. 51. xxiii. 53. John iii. 27. v. 19, 30. vi. 63. viii. 15. ix. 33. xii. 19. xiv. 30. xv. 5. xvi. 23, 24. xviii. 9. Acts viii. 39. xxvi. 26. 1 Cor. vi. 10(-G[o]L*S*). 2 Cor. xi. 9(8) 1 John ii. 22. Rev. xxi. 4.

Add, for οὐδέ, 2 Cor. iii. 10, GLT*S*. For οὔπω, Matt. xv. 17, LTTr. John vii. 8[1st], GT*S*. Rev. xvii. 12, L. For οὔτε, 1 Cor. vi. 10[3d], T*S*. Rev. ix. 20[1st], GTTr. For οὐχί, Matt. xiii. 55, LTr*S*. Luke xvii. 17, John vii. 42, LTr. Rom. ii. 26, L*S*. 1 Cor. iii. 4, x. 18, LT*S*. ix. 8, G''LT*S*. 2 Cor. x. 13, LT*S*. For πῶς, 1 John iv. 20, L*S*.

Matt. xxi. 19(. . μηκέτι), LT. Mark xiv. 61(. . answered), TTr*S*. Luke xiv. 3 (day ἢ οὐ;), L[b]TTr*S*. Acts xxv. 6(*ap*). 1 Cor. ix. 15(. . used), GLT*S*. Rev. vii. 16(neither[2d] . .), T.

See also ἄξιος, μετά, μή, ὀλίγος, οὐκέτι, πᾶς, πλείων, πλεονάζω, τις, τίς, τυγχάνω.

οὐά.

ah, Mark xv. 29.

οὐαί.

woe, Matt. xi. 21*t*. xviii. 7*t*. xxiii. 13(14), 14(13, *ap*), 15, 16, 23, 25, 27, 29. xxiv. 19. xxvi. 24. Mark xiii. 17. xiv. 21. Luke vi. 24, 25*t*, 26. x. 13*t*. xi. 42, 43, 44, 46, 47, 52. xvii. 1. xxi. 23. xxii. 22. 1 Cor. ix. 16. Jude 11. Rev. viii. 13*tr*. ix. 12*t*. xi. 14*t*. xii. 12.

alas, Rev. xviii. 10*t*, 16*t*, 19*t*.

οὐδαμῶς.

not, Matt. ii. 6.

οὐδέ.

With another negative ².

also not, Rom. xi. 21.

not even, 1 Cor. xi. 14. — **even not**, Matt. vi. 29. John xxi. 25.

then not, 1 Cor. xv. 13, 16.

neither, Matt. v. 15. vi. 15, 26, 28. vii. 18. ix. 17. xi. 27. xii. 4, 19. xiii. 13. xvi. 9, 10. xxi. 27. xxii. 46. xxiii. 13(14). Mark iv. 22. viii. 17. xi. 26(*ap*), 33. xii. 21(*ap*). xiii. 32. xiv. 59, 68 (οὔτε LTTr*S*). xvi. 13(*ap*).

Luke vi. 43. vii. 7. viii. 17. xi. 33. xii. 33. xvi. 31. xvii. 21. xx. 8. John vi. 24. vii. 5. viii. 11(*ap*), 42. xiii. 16. xiv. 17. Acts ii. 27, 31

(οὔτε G″LT*S*). iv. 32, 34. xvi. 21. xvii. 25. xx. 24(–T*S*).
Rom. ii. 28. ix. 7. 1 Cor. xi. 16. xv. 50. Gal. i. 1, 12, 17. ii. 3. vi. 13. Phil. ii. 16. 2 Thes. iii. 8. Heb. ix. 12, 18. x. 8. 1 Pet. ii. 22. 1 John iii. 6. Rev. v. 3*t*. vii. 16, 16². ix. 4*t*. xxi. 23.
neither indeed, Rom. viii. 7.
nor, Matt. vi. 20, 26. x. 24. xii. 19. xxiv. 21². xxv. 13. Luke vi. 44. xii. 24 (οὔτε T*S*), 24. xxi. 15 (ἤ GT Tr*S*). John i. 13*t*. xi. 50. xvi. 3. Acts viii. 21. ix. 9. xxiv. 18. Rom. ix. 16. 1 Cor. ii. 6. 2 Cor. vii. 12. Gal. iii. 28*t*. iv. 14. 1 Thes. ii. 3. v. 5. 1 Tim. ii. 12. vi. 16. Heb. xiii. 5². 2 Pet. i. 8. Rev. v. 3. vii. 16.
no, nor, Luke xxiii. 15.
nor yet, Heb. ix. 25.
no, not, Matt. viii. 10 (παρ' οὐδενί LTr). xxiv. 36. Mark xiii. 32. Luke vii. 9. Acts vii. 5. Rom. iii. 10. 1 Cor vi. 5(–G°, *see* οὐδείς). Gal. ii. 5(–G°°).
not, Matt. xxv. 45. Mark xii. 10. Luke xii. 27 (*ap*), 27. xxiii. 40. John i. 3. 1 Cor. iv. 3. xiv. 21. Heb. viii. 4. 1 John ii. 23.
not so much as, Luke vi. 3. Acts xix. 2. 1 Cor. v. 1.
no . . so much as, Mark vi. 31.
so much as, Luke xviii. 13².
οὕτως οὐδέ, **no more**, John xv. 4.
never, Matt. xxvii. 14².
no[cc], Rom. iv. 15. 2 Cor. iii. 10(G′, οὐ GLT*S*).
Not rendered, John v. 22².
Add, for καὶ . . οὐκ, Luke xviii. 4, LTr*S*. For οὐ, Matt. xxi. 32[2d], LTr. For οὔτε, Mark v. 3, LTTr*S*. John i. 25*t*, LTTr*S*. Acts iv. 12, LT*S*. 1 Cor. iii. 2, GLT*S*. Rev. xii. 8, G LTTr*S*. — Matt. xxiv. 36(*ap*).
See also ἀλλά, τις.

οὐδείς,

Fem. οὐδεμία, *Neut.* οὐδέν.
With another negative².

no man, Matt. vi. 24. ix. 16. xi. 27. xvii. 8. xx. 7. xxii. 46. xxiv. 36. Mark ii. 21, 22. iii. 27². v. 3, 37². vii. 24. ix. 8², 39. x. 18 (until 1660; now **none**), 29. xii. 14², 34². xiii. 32. Luke v. 36, 37, 39. viii. 16, 51²(*ap*). ix. 36, 62. x. 22. xi. 33. xv. 16. xviii. 29.
John i. 18. iii. 2, 13, 32. iv. 27. v. 22. vi. 44, 65. vii. 4, 13, 27, 30, 44. viii. 10(*ap*), 11(*ap*), 15², 20. ix. 4. x. 18, 29. xiii. 28. xiv. 6. xv. 13. xvi. 22. Acts v. 13, 23. ix. 8 (*neut.* LT*S*). xviii. 10. xx. 33. xxv. 11.
Rom. xiv. 7. 1 Cor. ii. 11, 15. iii. 11. xii. 3*t*. xiv. 2. 2 Cor. v. 16. vii. 2*tr*. xi. 9(8, οὐθείς LT*S*). Gal. iii. 11, 15. Eph. v. 29. Phil. ii. 20. 1 Tim. vi. 16. 2 Tim. ii. 4. iv. 16. Heb. vii. 13. xii. 14. Jas. iii. 8. 1 John iv. 12. Rev. ii. 17. iii. 7*t*, 8. v. 3, 4. vii. 9. xiv. 3. xv. 8. xviii. 11². xix. 12.
οὐδεὶς ἀνθρώπων, **never man**, Mark xi. 2.
With καί, **neither any man**, Mark v. 4. Jas. i. 13. — **neither any thing**, Mark xvi. 8².
With οὐδέπω, **never man yet**, John xix. 41. — **never man before**, Luke xxiii. 53.
With πώποτε, **never man**, Luke xix. 30. — **never . . any man**, John viii. 33.
not a, Luke vii. 28.
not any, Acts xxvii. 34.
not any at all, Luke xx. 40².
any², Luke viii. 43. ix. 36. Acts iv. 12(*ap*).
any man², Matt. xxii. 16. Mark xvi. 8. John xviii. 31.
none, Matt. xix. 17(*ap*). Luke i. 61. iv. 26, 27. xiv. 24. xviii. 19, 34. John vii. 19. xv. 24. xvi. 5. xvii. 12. xviii. 9². xxi. 12. Acts viii. 16. xviii. 17. xxv. 11, 18. xxvi. 22, 26 (οὐθείς T*S*, –L). Rom. xiv. 7. 1 Cor. i. 14. ii. 8. viii. 4. ix. 15. xiv. 10. Gal. v. 10.
none of these things[cc], Acts xx. 24.
no, Mark vi. 5². Luke iv. 24. xvi.

13. xxiii. 4, 14, 22. John x. 41. xvi. 29. xix. 4. Acts xv. 9. xxiii. 9. xxv. 10. xxvii. 22. xxviii. 5. Rom. viii. 1. 2 Cor. vii. 5. 2 Tim. ii. 14. Phil. iv. 15. Heb. v. 13. Jas. iii. 12(*ap*).

no . . at all, John xviii. 38.

not at all, Gal. iv. 12.

nothing, Matt. v. 13. x. 26. xvii. 20. xxi. 19. xxiii. 16, 18. xxvi. 62. xxvii. 12, 24. Mark vii. 15. ix. 29. xi. 13. xiv. 60², 61. xv. 4, 5². Luke iv. 2². v. 5. x. 19². xii. 2. xxii. 35. xxiii. 9, 15, 41. John iii. 27. v. 19², 30. vi. 63². vii. 26. viii. 28, 54. ix. 33. xii. 19². xiv. 30². xv. 5². xvi. 23², 24². xviii. 20. xxi. 3. Acts iv. 14. xvii. 21. xx. 20. xxi. 24. xxvi. 31. xxviii. 17.

Rom. xiv. 14. 1 Cor. iv. 4. vii. 19*t*. viii. 2² (-G°L*S*), 4. xiii. 3. 2 Cor. xii. 11*t*. Gal. ii. 6. iv. 1. v. 2. Phil. i. 20. 1 Tim. iv. 4. vi. 7. Tit. i. 15. Phm. 14. Heb. ii. 8. vii. 14, 19. Rev. iii. 17.

nought, Acts v. 36.

aught, Mark vii. 12².

Add Matt. viii. 10, παρ' οὐδενί for οὐδέ, LTr. xiii. 34, for οὐ, LTTr*S*. 1 Cor. vi. 5, for οὐδὲ εἷς, L*S*. ix. 15, for ἵνα τις, L*S*. xiii. 2, for οὐθέν, G.

See also διαφέρω, λογίζομαι, οὐ.

οὐδέποτε.

neither at any time, Luke xv. 29.

With πᾶν, **nothing at any time**, Acts xi. 8 (πᾶν *omS*).

never, Matt. vii. 23. ix. 33. xxi. 16, 42. Mark ii. 12, 25. Luke xv. 29. John vii. 46. Acts x. 14. xiv. 8. 1 Cor. xiii. 8. Heb. x. 1, 11.

yet never, Matt. xxvi. 33.

οὐδέπω.

With another negative².

not yet, John vii. 39 (οὔπω LTr*S*).

as yet . . not, John xx. 9.

yet, 1 Cor. viii. 2² (οὔπω L*S*).

never yet, John xix. 41².

never before, Luke xxiii. 53².

Add Acts viii. 16, for οὔπω, G″LT*S*.

οὐθείς, οὐθέν.

nothing, 1 Cor. xiii. 2 (οὐδέν G).

Add, for οὐδείς, Acts xxvi. 26, T*S*. 2 Cor. xi. 9(8), LT*S*.

οὐκέτι, οὐκ ἔτι¹ St.

With another negative².

no more, Matt. xix. 6. Mark vii. 12². x. 8. xiv. 25². Luke xv. 19, 21. John vi. 66. xi. 54¹. xiv. 19¹. xvi. 10¹, 21¹, 25¹. xvii. 11¹. Acts viii. 39². xx. 25, 38. Rom. vi. 9¹*t*. vii. 17¹, 20¹. xi. 6¹*t*, 6¹*t*(*ap*). 2 Cor. v. 16¹. Gal. iii. 18¹. iv. 7¹. Eph. ii. 19. Heb. x. 18¹, 26¹.

With οὐ μή, **no more at all**, Rev. xviii. 14.

any more², Matt. xxii. 46. Mark ix. 8. Luke xxii. 16(-LᵇTrᵇ*S*). Rev. xviii. 11.

no longer, Gal. iii. 25¹.

hereafter . . not, John xiv. 30¹.

henceforth not, John xv. 15.

after that², Mark xii. 34. Luke xx. 40¹.

not as yet, 2 Cor. i. 23.

yet not, Gal. ii. 20¹.

yet², Mark xv. 5.

now . . not, John iv. 42. xxi. 6¹. Rom. xiv. 15¹.—**not now**, Phm. 16.

Add Mark v. 3 (could . .), LTTr*S*. John xvi. 16, for οὐ, LTr*S*. Rev. x. 6, for οὐκ . . ἔτι, GLTTr*S*.

οὐκοῦν.

then ? John xviii. 37.

οὐ μή. See μή.

οὖν.

then, Matt. vii. 11. xii. 12, 26. xiii. 27, 28, 56. xvii. 10. xix. 7. xxi. 25. xxii. 43, 45. xxvi. 54. xxvii. 22. Mark iii. 31 (καί LTr*S*). xi. 31(-LTTr). xv. 12. Luke iii. 7, 10. vi. 9 (δέ LTTr*S*). vii. 31. x. 37 (δέ GLTTr*S*, -G°). xi. 13. xii. 26. xiii. 15 (δέ LTr*S*). xx. 5(-G°LᵇTTr*S*), 17. xxii. 36 (δέ Tr*S*), 70.

John i. 21, 22(-L), 25. ii. 18, 20. iii. 25. iv. 5, 9, 11, 28, 30(-GLTTr), 45, 48, 52. v. 4(*ap*), 12(-G°LᵇTTrᵇ

S), 19. vi. 5, 14, 21, 28, 30, 32 (–G^{oo}), 34, 41, 42 (*νῦν* TTr), 53, 67, 68(*omS*). vii. 6(–G^{oo}*S*), 11, 25, 28, 30, 33, 35, 45, 47 (–T*S*). viii. 12, 19, 21, 22, 25, 28, 31, 41(–G^{o}LTTr *S*), 48(*omS*), 52(–LTTr*S*), 57, 59. ix. 12(–LTTr*S*), 15, 19, 24, 28(*om S*). x. 7, 24, 31(–Tr^{b}*S*). xi. 12, 14 (–L^{b}), 16, 17, 20, 21, 31, 32, 36, 41, 45, 47, 53, 56. xii. 1, 3, 4, 7, 28, 35. xiii. 6, 14, 22(–G^{oo}TTr^{b}), 27, 30. xvi. 17. xviii. 3, 6, 7, 10, 11, 12, 16, 17, 19, 27, 28(–G^{oo}), 29, 31 (–L^{b}), 33, 40. xix. 5, 10(–G^{oo}T*S*), 20, 21, 23, 32, 40. xx. 2, 6, 10, 19, 20, 21. xxi. 5, 9, 13(*omS*), 23.

Acts ii. 41^{2}. ix. 31^{2}. x. 23. xi. 17. xvii. 29. xix. 3, 36. xxii. 29. xxiii. 31^{2}.

Rom. iii. 1, 9, 27, 31. iv. 1, 9, 10. v. 9. vi. 1, 15, 21. vii. 7, 13. viii. 31. ix. 14, 19, 30. x. 14. xi. 1, 5, 7, 11, 19. xiv. 16. 1 Cor. iii. 5. vi. 4^{2}, 15. ix. 18. x. 19. xiv. 15, 26. 2 Cor. iii. 12. Gal. iii. 19, 21. iv. 15. Eph. v. 15. Col. iii. 1. 1 Thes. iv. 1. 1 Tim. iii. 2. Heb. ii. 14. iv. 14. ix. 1^{2}. 1 Pet. iv. 1. 2 Pet. iii. 11 (*οὕτως* T).

so then, Mark xvi. 19^{2}(*ap*).

so, Matt. i. 17. John iv. 40, 46, 53. vi. 10(–G^{oo}), 19. vii. 43. xiii. 12. xxi. 15. Acts xiii. 4. xv. 30^{2}. xxiii. 18^{2}, 22^{2}. xxviii. 9(*δέ* LT*S*).

οὕτως οὖν, **so likewise**, Luke xiv. 33.

now then, 2 Cor. v. 20.

now, Mark xii. 20 (E, –St, *omS*). Luke x. 36(–L^{b}TTr^{b}*S*). John xvi. 19 (–GTTr*S*). xviii. 24(ELTr^{b}, –StGT *S*). xix. 29(–LTr, *δέ S*). xxi. 7. Acts i. 18^{2}. xi. 19^{2}. xxv. 1. 1 Cor. ix. 25^{2}.

therefore, Matt. iii. 8, 10. v. 19, 23, 48. vi. 2, 8, 9, 22, 23, 31, 34. vii. 12, 24. ix. 38. x. 16, 26, 31, 32. xiii. 18, 40. xviii. 4, 26. xix. 6. xxi. 40. xxii. 9, 17, 21, 28. xxiii. 3, 20. xxiv. 15, 42. xxv. 13, 27, 28. xxvii. 17, 64. xxviii. 19 (–GL^{b}TTr^{b} *S*). Mark x. 9. xii. 6(–L^{b}TTr*S*), 9 (–T), 23 (–G^{o}TTr*S*), 27 (–TTr^{b}*S*), 37(–G^{o}L^{b}TTr*S*). xiii. 35.

Luke iii. 8, 9. iv. 7. vi. 36(–G^{oo}L Tr*S*). vii. 42. viii. 18. x. 2 (*δέ* G′L TTr*S*), 2, 40. xi. 34(–G^{o}LTTr*S*), 35, 36. xii. 7(–L^{b}TTr), 40(–LTr*S*). xiii. 14. xv. 28 (*δέ* LTTr*S*). xvi. 11, 27. xix. 12. xx. 15, 29, 33, 44. xxi. 8(–LTr*S*^{c}), 14, 36 (*δέ* LTTr*S*). xxiii. 16, 20 (*δέ* LTr*S*), 22.

John ii. 22. iii. 29. iv. 1, 6, 33. v. 10. vi. 13, 15, 24, 30, 43(–G L^{b}TTr), 45 (*omS*), 52, 60. vii. 3, 40. viii. 13, 24, 36. ix. 7, 8, 10, 16, 41 (–G^{oo}L^{b}TTr*S*). x. 19 (–G^{o}LTTr *S*), 39(–Tr^{b}). xi. 3, 6, 33, 38, 54. xii. 9, 17, 19, 21, 29 (–L^{b}Tr^{b}), 50. xiii. 24, 31(30, –StG). xvi. 18, 22. xviii. 4, 8, 25, 31(–LTTr), 37, 39. xix. 1, 4(*omS*), 6, 8, 13, 16, 24, 24^{2}, 26, 30, 31, 38, 42. xx. 3, 25. xxi. 6, 7.

Acts i. 6^{2}. ii. 30, 33, 36. iii. 19. viii. 4^{2}, 22. x. 29, 32, 33*t*. xii. 5^{2}. xiii. 38, 40. xiv. 3^{2}. xv. 2 (*δέ* T*S*), 10, 27. xvi. 11 (*δέ* T*S*), 36. xvii. 12^{2}, 17^{2}, 20, 23. xix. 32^{2}. xx. 28(–L^{b}*S*). xxi. 22, 23. xxiii. 15. xxv. 5, 17. xxvi. 22. xxviii. 20, 28.

Rom. ii. 21, 26. iii. 28(*γάρ* GL*S*). v. 1. vi. 4, 12. xi. 22. xii. 1, 20 (*ἀλλά* L*S*, –G$^{″}$). xiii. 7, 10, 12. xiv. 8, 13. xv. 17, 28. xvi. 19. 1 Cor. v. 7(*omS*). vi. 7^{2}. vii. 26. viii. 4. x. 31. xi. 20. xiv. 11, 23. xv. 11. xvi. 11, 18. 2 Cor. i. 17. v. 6, 11. vii. 1. ix. 5. xi. 15. xii. 9.

Gal. iii. 5. v. 1(*ap*). Eph. iv. 1, 17. v. 1, 7. vi. 14. Phil. ii. 1, 23^{2}, 28, 29. iii. 15. Col. ii. 6, 16. iii. 5, 12. 1 Tim. ii. 1, 8. v. 14. 2 Tim. i. 8. ii. 1, 3 (*see συγκακοπαθέω*), 21. iv. 1(*omS*). Phm. 17. Heb. iv. 1, 6, 11, 16. vii. 11^{2}. ix. 23. x. 19, 35. xiii. 15. Jas. iv. 4, 7, 17. v. 7. 1 Pet. ii. 7. iv. 7. v. 6. 2 Pet. iii. 17. 1 John ii. 24(–G^{oo}LT*S*). 3 John 8. Rev. ii. 5. iii. 3*t*, 19.

wherefore, Matt. xxiv. 26. Acts i. 21. vi. 3 (*δή* L, *δέ S*). xix. 38^{2}.

1 Cor. iv. 16. 2 Cor. viii. 24. Col. ii. 20(*om*). 1 Pet. ii. 1.
truly, John xx. 30².
verily, Acts xxvi. 9².
and, Matt. xviii. 29. Luke iii. 18². John vi. 62. xx. 11. Acts v. 41². viii. 25². xv. 3², 39(δέ LT*S*). xvii. 30². xxv. 23. xxviii. 5².
and so, Acts xvi. 5².
but, Luke xxi. 7. John viii. 5(*ap*). ix. 18. Acts xxiii. 21. xxv. 4².
Not rendered, John v. 18. viii. 38, 42(-GLTTr). ix. 25(-G°°). xii. 2. xx. 8. Acts xviii. 14²(-G°LT*S*). xxvi. 4². 1 Pet. ii. 13(-G°°L*S*).

Add, for γάρ, Acts xxv. 11, G″LT*S*. Heb. viii. 4, L*S*. For δέ, Matt. xviii. 31, LTr*S*. Luke xiii. 18, Lᵐ TTr*S*. John vi. 11¹ˢᵗ, LTTr. ix. 11, LTTr*S*. 26, LTTr. xix. 15, LᵐTTr. 16, LTTr. For καί, John iv. 52, T Tr. vii. 15, LTTr*S*. xiii. 26, LᵐT Tr*S*. For οὐ, 1 Cor. xv. 51², G′.

Matt. vii. 19 (every tree . .), Lᵇ. xiv. 15 (away . .), T*S*. Mark xii. 14 (*ap*). Luke xi. 28, *see* μενοῦνγε. xiii. 7 (. . cut it), L. xiv. 34 (Salt . .), TTrᵇ*S*. John i. 39(40, came . .), Lᵇ Tr*S*. vii. 16 (answered . .), G′LT Tr*S*. ix. 10 (How . .), LᵇT*S*. 17 (They say . .), LTr*S*. 20 (answered . .), L*S*. xiii. 26 (answered . .), LᵇT. xix. 29(*ap*). xxi. 11(. . went), Tr*S*. 21 (Peter . .), LTTr*S*.
Rom. ix. 19 (Why . .), LT. xi. 13²(. . am), L*S*. Phil. iii. 8, *see* μενοῦνγε. Jas. v. 16 (confess . .), LT*S*. 1 Pet. v. 1 (elders . .), L*S*, for τούς L. 1 John iv. 19 (We . .), L. Rev. i. 19 (Write . .). GLTTr*S*. ii. 16 (Repent . .), GLTTrᵇ.

² *With* μέν. *See also* ἄρα.

οὕπω.

not yet, Matt. xv. 17 (οὐ LTTr). xvi. 9. xxiv. 6. Mark viii. 17. xiii. 7. John ii. 4. iii. 24. vii. 6, 8 (οὐκ GT*S*), 8, 30, 39. viii. 20, 57. xi. 30. xx. 17. Heb. ii. 8. xii. 4. 1 John iii. 2. Rev. xvii. 10 (οὐκ L, οὕτω *S*).
hitherto . . not, 1 Cor. iii. 2.
noᶜᶜ **. . as yet**, Rev. xvii. 12.
With another negative, **as yet**, Acts viii. 16 (οὐδέπω G″LT*S*).
Add, for οὐ, Mark viii. 21, LTTr*S*. John vi. 17, LTr*S*. Phil. iii. 13, Lᵐ *S*. For οὐδέπω, John vii. 39, LTr*S*. 1 Cor. viii. 2, L*S*.—Mark iv. 40 (*ap*). xi. 2 (. . sat), LTr*S*.

οὐρά.

tail, Rev. ix. 10*t*, 19(*ap*). xii. 4.

οὐράνιος.

heavenly, Matt. vi. 14, 26, 32. xv. 13. Luke ii. 13. Acts xxvi. 19.
Add, for ἐν τοῖς οὐρανοῖς, Matt. v. 48, G″LTTr*S*. xxiii. 9, LTTr*S*. For ἐπουράνιος, Matt. xviii. 35 G″LTr*S*.

οὐρανόθεν.

from heaven, Acts xiv. 17. xxvi. 13.

οὐρανός.

The plural rendered by the singular ².
heaven, Matt. iii. 2², 16, 17². iv. 17². v. 3², 10², 12², 16², 18, 19²*t*, 20², 34, 45², 48²(*see* οὐράνιος). vi. 1², 9², 10, 20. vii. 11², 21²*t*. viii. 11². x. 7², 32², 33². xi. 11², 12², 23, 25. xii. 50². xiii. 11²(-G°), 24², 31², 33², 44², 45², 47², 52². xiv. 19. xvi. 1, 17², 19²*tr*. xviii. 1², 3², 4², 10²*t*, 14², 18²*t*, 19², 23². xix. 12², 14², 21, 23². xx. 1². xxi. 25*t*. xxii. 2², 30. xxiii. 9² (*see* οὐράνιος), 13(14)², 22. xxiv. 29*t*, 30*t*, 31², 35, 36². xxv. 1². xxvi. 64. xxviii. 2, 18.
Mark i. 10, 11². vi. 41. vii. 34. viii. 11. x. 21. xi. 25², 26²(*ap*), 30, 31. xii. 25². xiii. 25, 25², 27, 31, 32. xiv. 62. xvi. 19(*ap*). Luke ii. 15. iii. 21, 22. iv. 25. vi. 23. ix. 16, 54. x. 15, 18, 20², 21. xi. 2²(*ap*), 2(*ap*), 16. xii. 33. xv. 7, 18, 21. xvi. 17. xvii. 24*t*, 29. xviii. 13, 22. xix. 38. xx. 4, 5. xxi. 11, 26², 33. xxii. 43(*ap*). xxiv. 51(*ap*).
John i. 32, 51(52). iii. 13*t*, 13(*ap*), 27, 31. vi. 31, 32*t*, 33, 38, 41, 42, 50, 51, 58. xii. 28. xvii. 1. Acts i. 10, 11*tr*. ii. 2, 5, 19, 34. iii. 21. iv.

12, 24. vii. 42, 49, 55, 56. ix. 3. x. 11, 16. xi. 5, 9, 10. xiv. 15. xvii. 24. xxii. 6.

Rom. i. 18. x. 6. 1 Cor. viii. 5. xv. 47. 2 Cor. v. 1, 2. xii. 2. Gal. i. 8. Eph i. 10² (*Gr.* the heavens). iii. 15². iv. 10. vi. 9². Phil. iii. 20². Col. i. 5², 16², 20², 23. iv. 1² 1 Thes. i. 10². iv. 16. 2 Thes. i. 7.

Heb. i. 10. iv. 14. vii. 26. viii. 1. ix. 23, 24. x. 34²(–G°LT*S*). xii. 23², 25², 26. Jas. v. 12, 18. 1 Pet. i. 4², 12. iii. 22. 2 Pet. i. 18. iii. 5, 7, 10, 12, 13. 1 John v. 7(*ap*). Rev. iii. 12. iv. 1, 2. v. 3, 13. vi. 13, 14. viii. 1, 10. ix. 1. x. 1, 4, 5, 6, 8. xi. 6, 12*t*, 13, 15, 19(–Trᵇ). xii. 1, 3, 4, 7, 8, 10, 12. xiii. 6, 13. xiv. 2, 7, 13, 17. xv. 1, 5. xvi. 11, 17 (–G°°LTTrᵇ, θεοῦ for οὐρανοῦ ἀπὸ τοῦ θρόνου *S*), 21. xviii. 1, 4, 5, 20. xix. 1, 11, 14. xx. 1, 9, 11. xxi. 1*t*, 2, 3 (θρόνος LT*S*), 10.

With ἐκ, **heavenly**, Luke xi. 13.

sky, Matt. xvi. 2, 3*t*. Luke xii. 56. Heb. xi. 12.

air, Matt. vi. 26. viii. 20. xiii. 32. Mark iv. 4(*omS*), 32. Luke viii. 5. ix. 58. xiii. 19. Acts x. 12. xi. 6.

Add Matt. xix. 24ᵖˡ, for θεός, LT Tr. Luke vi. 35(*ap*). Acts xxii. 23, for ἀήρ, G′. Eph. i. 20, for ἐπουράνιος, L.

οὖς.

ear, Matt. x. 27. xi. 15. xiii. 9, 15*t*, 16, 43. Mark iv. 9, 23. vii. 16, 33. viii. 18. Luke i. 44. iv. 21. viii. 8. ix. 44. xii. 3. xiv. 35. xxii. 50. Acts vii. 51, 57. xi. 22. xxviii. 27*t*. Rom. xi. 8. 1 Cor. ii. 9. xii. 16. Jas. v. 4. 1 Pet. iii. 12. Rev. ii. 7, 11, 17, 29. iii. 6, 13, 22. xiii. 9.

οὖσα. See ὤν fr. εἰμί.

οὐσία.

substance, Luke xv. 13.

goods, Luke xv. 12.

οὔτε.

neither, Luke xx. 36. Acts xxiv. 12*t*, 13. xxv. 8*t*. Rom. viii. 38. 1 Cor. iii. 7*t*. vi. 9. Gal. i. 12. 1 Thes. ii. 6. 3 John 10. Rev. v. 4. ix. 20. xii. 8 (οὐδέ GLTTr*S*). xx. 4. xxi. 4*t*.

nor, Acts xxiv. 12. Rom. viii. 38 *six*, 39*tr*. 1 Cor. vi. 9*f*, 10*t*, 10 (οὐ T*S*). 1 Thes. ii. 3, 6. Rev. ix. 20*t*, 21*tr*. xxi. 4.

οὔτε . . οὔτε, **neither . . nor**, Matt. vi. 20. xxii. 30. Mark xii. 25. Luke xx. 35. John v. 37. viii. 19. ix. 3. Acts xv. 10. Gal. v. 6. vi. 15. 1 Thes. ii. 5. Rev. iii. 15, 16.—**neither . . nor yet**, Luke xiv. 35. John iv. 21. Acts xix. 37.—**nor . . neither**, John i. 25(οὐδὲ . . οὐδέ LTTr*S*).—**neither . . neither**, Matt. xii. 32. Acts xxviii. 21. 1 Cor. iii. 7. viii. 8. xi. 11.

ἀλλ' οὔτε (οὐδέ GLT*S*), **neither**, 1 Cor. iii. 2.

nor yet, Acts xxv. 8. 1 Thes. ii. 6.

yet not, Rev. ix. 20 (οὐ GTTr, οὐδέ *S*).

no, not, Mark v. 3 (οὐδέ LTTr*S*.)

not, Luke xii. 26.

noneᶜᶜ, Acts iv. 12 (οὐδέ LT*S*).

Add, for οὐ, Mark xiv. 68, LTr*S*. Luke xii. 24, T*S*. 27(*ap*). Acts ii. 31, G″LT*S*. For οὐδε, Mark xiv. 68, LTTr*S*. Luke xii. 24, T*S*. Acts ii. 31, G″LT*S*. For οὐδεμία, Jas. iii. 12(*ap*).

See also ἄντλημα.

οὗτος.

The demonstrative pronoun *this, etc.*

(a) *Nominative and Accusative.*

1. *Masc. Sing.*, οὗτος.

this, Matt. iii. 3, 17. vii. 12 (οὕτω G′). viii. 27. xi. 10. xii. 23, 24. xiii. 19, 55. xiv. 2. xv. 8. xvii. 5. xxi. 10, 11, 38. xxvi. 61. xxvii. 37, 54. xxviii. 15. Mark iv. 41. vi. 3. vii. 6. ix. 7. xii. 7. xiv. 69. Luke i. 29, 36. iv. 22, 36. v. 21. vii. 17, 27, 49. viii. 25. ix. 9, 35. xv. 24, 30, 32. xvii. 18. xviii. 11. xx. 14. xxiii. 38(*ap*), 47.

John i. 15, 30, 34. ii. 20. iv. 29.

42. vi. 14, 42, 50, 58, 60. vii. 25, 26, 36, 40, 41, 46(*ap*), 49. ix. 8, 9, 16, 19, 20, 24. xi. 47. xii. 34. xxi. 23, 24. Acts iv. 11. vi. 13, 14. vii. 37, 38, 40. ix. 21, 22. xvii. 3, 18. xix. 26. xxi. 28. xxii. 26. xxvi. 31, 32. xxviii. 4. Rom. iv. 9. ix. 9. Heb. iii. 3. vii. 1. 2 Pet. i. 17. 1 John v. 6, 20. 2 John 7. Rev. xx. 14.

this man, Matt. ix. 3. xxvii. 47. Mark ii. 7. xv. 39. Luke vii. 39. xiv. 30. xv. 2. xviii. 14. xxii. 56. xxiii. 41, 52. John vi. 52. vii. 15, 31. ix. 2, 3, 33. xi. 37*t*. xxi. 21. Acts i. 18. iv. 10. viii. 10. xviii. 25. Heb. vii. 4. Jas. i. 25.

this fellow, Matt. xxvi. 71. Luke xxii. 59. Acts xviii. 13.

this [c]**child,** Luke ii. 34.

this same, Acts i. 11.

the same, Matt. v. 19. xiii. 20. xviii. 4. xxi. 42. xxiv. 13. xxvi. 23. Mark iii. 35. viii. 35 (*omS*). xiii. 13. Luke ii. 25. ix. 24, 48. xvi. 1. xx. 17. xxiii. 51. John i. 2, 7, 33 (αὐτός L[m]). iii. 2, 26. vii. 18. xv. 5. Acts vii. 19. xiv. 9. 1 Cor. viii. 3. Jas. iii. 2. 1 Pet. ii. 7. Rev. iii. 5 (οὕτως LTr*S*).

he, Matt. xiii. 22, 23. xxvii. 58. Luke i. 32. xix. 2 (αὐτός LTr, –*S*). xx. 28, 30(*ap*). xxiii. 22, 35. John i. 41(42). iv. 47. vi. 42(–G°L[b]Tr), 46. vii. 35. xviii. 30. Acts iii. 10 (αὐτός L*S*). iv. 9. vii. 36. ix. 15, 20. x. 6, 6(*ap*), 32, 36. xvii. 24. xviii. 26. Rom. viii. 9. Jas. i. 23, 25 (–G°L*S*). 1 John ii. 22. 2 John 9.

With ἤμελλεν fr. μέλλω, **he it was that should,** John vi. 71.

who[cc], Acts xiii 7.

it, Mark vi. 16 (αὐτός G′).

Not rendered, Matt. x. 22. Mark xii. 10.

Add, for αὐτός, Luke viii. 4, LTr. Acts x. 42, G′L. 1 Cor. vii. 13, G″ LT*S*. Heb. x. 12, G″L*S*.

Accusative, τοῦτον.

this, Matt. xix. 11(–L[b]). xxi. 44 (*ap*). Mark vii. 29. xiv. 58, 71. Luke ix. 13. xii. 56. xvi. 28. xxiii. 14. John ii. 19. vi. 34, 58. ix. 39. xix. 20. Acts ii. 32. vi. 14. vii. 35. xxi. 28. xxiii. 17, 18, 25, 27. xxiv. 5. xxviii. 26. Rom. ix. 9. xv. 28. 1 Cor. iii. 12(–G°L*S*). xi. 26, 27(*om S*). 2 Cor. iv. 7.

this man, Luke xix. 14. xxiii. 18. John vii. 27. xviii. 40. xix. 12. Acts iii. 16. v. 37. xxv. 24. Heb. viii. 3.

this fellow, Luke xxiii. 2. John ix. 29.

him, Matt. xxvii. 32. Luke ix. 26. xii. 5. xx. 12(*see* κἀκεῖνος), 13. John v. 6. vi. 27. xxi. 21. Acts ii. 23. v. 31. x. 40. xiii. 27. xv. 38. xvi. 3. xvii. 23. 1 Cor. ii. 2. iii. 17 (αὐτόν G′L). Phil. ii. 23.

the same, Acts vii. 35.

that, John xix. 8, 13 (τούτων G″L TTr*S*).

that man, 2 Thes. iii. 14.

that same, Acts ii. 36.

Add Matt. xix. 22 (that), L[b].

2. *Masc. Plural,* οὗτοι.

these, Matt. iv. 3. xx. 12, 21(–L[b]). xxi. 16. xxv. 46. xxvi. 62. Mark iv. 15, 16, 18 (ἄλλοι GLTTr*S*, –G[oo]), 20 (ἐκεῖνοι TTr*S*). xii. 40. xiv. 60. Luke viii. 13, 21. xiii. 2. xix. 40. xxi. 4. xxiv. 17, 44. John vi. 5. xvii. 11, 25. Acts i. 14. ii. 7, 15. xi. 12. xvi. 17, 20. xvii. 6, 7, 11. xx. 5. xxv. 11. xxvii. 31. Rom. ii. 14 (οἱ τοιοῦτοι L[m]). xi. 24, 31. Col. iv. 11. 1 Tim. iii. 10. 2 Tim. iii. 8. Heb. xi. 13, 39. 2 Pet. ii. 12, 17. 1 John v. 7. Jude 8, 10, 12, 16, 19. Rev. vii. 13, 14. xi. 4, 6, 10. xiv. 4*tr*. xvii. 13, 14, 16. xix. 9. xxi. 5. xxii. 6.

they, Luke viii. 14, 15. xiii. 4(αὐτοί LTTr*S*). John xviii. 21. Acts xiii. 4 (αὐτοί LT*S*). Rom. viii. 14. ix. 6. 1 Cor. xvi. 17 (αὐτοί LT). Gal. vi. 12.

αὐτοὶ οὗτοι, **they themselves,** Acts xxiv. 15. — **these same here,** Acts xxiv. 20.

the same, Luke xx. 47. John xii. 21. Gal. iii. 7.
such as, Mark iv. 18 (–G°°).
Not rendered, Matt. xiii. 38.

Accusative, τούτους.

these, Matt. vii. 24(–LᵇTrᵇ), 26, 28. x. 5. xix. 1. xxvi. 1. Luke ix. 28, 44. xix. 15. xx. 16. John x. 19. xviii. 8. Acts ii. 22. v. 5, 24. x. 47. xix. 37.
these men, Mark viii. 4.
this, Acts xvi. 36(–L).
them, Acts xxi. 24. Rom. viii. 30*tr*. 1 Cor. vi. 4. xvi. 3. Heb. ii. 15.
such, 2 Tim. iii. 5.
Add Luke xix. 27, for ἐκείνους, TTr*S*.

3. *Fem. Sing.*, αὕτη.

this, Matt. xiii. 54. xxi. 42. xxii. 20, 38. xxiv. 34. xxvi. 8. Mark i. 27(*ap*). viii. 12. xii. 11, 16, 30(*ap*), 31 (αὐτῇ G″LTr), 43. xiii. 30. xiv. 4. Luke ii. 2. iv. 21. viii. 9, 11. xi. 29. xxi. 3, 32. xxii. 53. John i. 19. iii. 19, 29. viii. 4(*ap*). xi. 4. xii. 30. xv. 12. xvii. 3. Acts v. 38 (–G°). viii. 32. xvii. 19. xxi. 11.
Rom. xi. 27. 1 Cor. viii. 9. ix. 3. 2 Cor. i. 12. ii. 6. xi. 10. Eph. iii. 8. Tit. i. 13. Heb. viii. 10. x. 16. Jas. i. 27. iii. 15. 1 John i. 5. ii. 25. iii. 11, 23. v. 3, 4, 9, 11*t*, 14. 3 John 6*t*. Rev. xx. 5.
this woman, Matt. xxvi. 13. Luke vii. 45, 46. Acts ix. 36.
hereof[cc], Matt. ix. 26 (*marg.* **this**).
she, Matt. xxvi. 12. Mark xii. 44. xiv. 8(–LᵇTTrᵇ*S*), 9. Luke ii. 36, 37 (αὐτή TTr), 38(–LTr*S*). vii. 12 (St, αὐτή TTr), 44. viii. 42. xxi. 4. Rom. xvi. 2 (G′, αὐτή GLT).
the same, Acts xvi. 17.
which, Acts viii. 26.
Not rendered, Rom. vii. 10 (G″, αὐτή G).
Add Matt. xxii. 39, for αὐτῇ, G″. 1 Cor. vii. 12, for αὐτή, LT.

Accusative, ταύτην.

this, Matt. xi. 16. xv. 15(–LTr*S*). xxi. 23. xxiii. 36. Mark iv. 13. x. 5. xi. 28. xii. 10. Luke iv. 6, 23. vii. 44. xii. 41. xiii. 6. xv. 3. xviii. 5, 9. xx. 2, 9, 19. John ii. 11. vii. 8(–G°°LTTr), 8. x. 6, 18. xii. 27. Acts i. 16(–G°L*S*). iii. 16. vii. 4, 60. viii. 19. xxii. 4, 28. xxiii. 13. xxvii. 21. xxviii. 20*t*.
Rom. v. 2. 2 Cor. iv. 1. xii. 13. 1 Tim. i. 18. 2 Tim. ii. 19. 1 Pet. v. 12. 2 Pet. i. 18. iii. 1. 1 John iii. 3. iv. 21. 2 John 10. Rev. ii. 24.
this woman, Luke xiii. 16.
her, Rev. xii. 15 (αὐτήν GLTTr*S*).
it, 1 Cor. vi. 13.
the, Luke xxiv. 21.
the same, Acts xiii. 33. 2 Cor. viii. 6. ix. 5.
that, Luke xxiii. 48.
See also διά, II.

4. *Fem. Plural*, αὗται.

these, Luke xxi. 22. Acts xx. 34. Gal. iv. 24.

Accusative, ταύτας.

these, Matt. xiii. 53. Mark xiii. 2. Acts iii. 24. 2 Cor. vii. 1. Heb. ix. 23. Rev. xvi. 9.
those, Luke i. 24. Acts xxi. 15.
μετὰ πολλὰς ταύτας ἡμέρας, **many days hence**, Acts i. 5.

5. *Neut. Sing.*, τοῦτο.

this, Matt. i. 22. viii. 9. ix. 28. xiii. 28. xv. 11. xvi. 22. xvii. 21 (*ap*). xviii. 4. xix. 26. xxi. 4. xxiv. 14. xxvi. 9, 12, 13, 26, 28, 39, 42, 56. xxviii. 14. Mark i. 27(*ap*). ix. 21, 29. xi. 3(*ap*). xiv. 9(–LᵇTTr*S*), 22, 24, 36. Luke i. 18, 34, 43, 66. ii. 12, 15. iii. 20. v. 6. vi. 3. vii. 4. 8. ix. 45, 48. x. 11, 28. xii. 18, 39. xiii. 8. xvi. 2. xviii. 34. xx. 17. xxii. 15, 17, 19*t*, 20, 37, 42.
John ii. 12, 22. iv. 15, 54. v. 28. vi. 6, 29, 39, 40, 61. vii. 39. viii. 6(*ap*), 40. xi. 26, 51. xii. 5, 6, 18, 33. xiii. 28. xvi. 17, 18. xviii. 38. xix. 28. xx. 22. xxi. 14, 19*t*. Acts ii. 12, 14, 16, 33. iv. 7, 22. v. 4, 24, 38. vii. 60. viii. 34.

ix. 21. x. 16. xi. 10. xvi. 18. xix. 10, 17, 27. xx. 29(–G∞L*S*). xxi. 23. xxiv. 14. xxvii. 34.

Rom. ii. 3. vi. 6. xi. 25. xiv. 13. xv. 28. 1 Cor. i. 12. v. 2. vii. 6, 26, 29, 35. ix. 23 (πάντα fr. πᾶς G″LT *S*). x. 28. xi. 17, 24*t*, 25*t*, 26(–G∞ LT*S*). xv. 50, 53*t*, 54*t*. 2 Cor. ii. 1. viii. 10, 20. ix. 6. x. 7, 11. xiii. 1, 9.

Gal. iii. 2, 17. Eph. iv. 17. v. 5, 32. vi. 1. Phil. i. 7, 9, 19, 22, 25. ii. 5. iii. 15. Col. ii. 4. iii. 20. 1 Thes. iv. 3, 15. v. 18. 2 Thes. iii. 10. 1 Tim. i. 9. ii. 3. iv. 16. 2 Tim. i. 15. iii. 1. Heb. vi. 3. vii. 27. ix. 8, 20, 27. xiii. 19. Jas. iv. 15. 1 Pet. i. 25. ii. 19, 20. 2 Pet. i. 20. iii. 3, 5, 8. 1 John iv. 3. Jude 4, 5 (πάντα LT*S*, –G″). Rev. ii. 6.

this thing, Mark v. 32. Luke xxii. 23. John xviii. 34. Acts xxvi. 26. 1 Cor. ix. 17.

this [c]**deed**, 1 Cor. v. 3.

it, Matt. xii. 11. Mark v. 43. xiv. 5. Luke xviii. 36. Heb. xiii. 17.

the same, Eph. vi. 8.

that, Mark xiii. 11. John iii. 32 (–G∞*S*). iv. 18. xi. 7, 11. xiv. 13. Rom. i. 12. vii. 15(–G∘T), 15, 16, 19, 20. xiii. 11. 1 Cor. vi. 6. Gal. vi. 7. Eph. ii. 8. Phil. i. 28. 1 Tim. v. 4. Phm. 18. Heb. xiii. 17.

that thing, Luke ix. 21.

thus[cc], Luke xxiv. 40. 2 Cor. i. 17. v. 14. Phil. iii. 15.

so[cc], John xx. 20. Acts xix. 14. xxiii. 7. Rom. xii. 20. 1 Cor. vii. 37.

Not rendered, Acts iii. 6.

Add Matt. xx. 23 (. . is not mine), T. Mark x. 27 (it), L[b]. John xiv. 14, for ἐγώ, L[m]. Acts xxviii. 28(. . salvation), LT*S*. Rom. xi. 7, for τούτου, GLT*S*. 2 Cor. xii. 14(the[1st]), GLT*S*. 3 John 5, for εἰς τούς[2d], G′L T*S*. Rev. vii. 1, for ταῦτα, G″LT Tr*S*.

See also αὐτό fr. αὐτός, διά, εἰς, ἐστί fr. εἰμί, μέν, παρά.

6. *Neut. Plural*, ταῦτα.

these, Matt. x. 2. xv. 20. xxiii. 23. xxiv. 8. Mark vii. 23. x. 20. xiii. 8(9). xvi. 17(*ap*). Luke i. 19, 65. ii. 19, 51(–L[b]*S*). xi. 42. xviii. 21. John iii. 2. v. 19. vii. 9. viii. 20, 30. x. 21. xx. 31. Acts x. 44. xiii. 42(–G∘). xvi. 38. Rom. ix. 8. 1 Cor. xii. 11. xiii. 13. Gal. v. 17.

these things, Matt. i. 20. iv. 9. vi. 32, 33. ix. 18. xi. 25. xiii. 34, 51, 56. xix. 20. xxi. 23, 24, 27. xxiii. 36. xxiv. 2, 3, 33, 34. Mark ii. 8. vi. 2. xi. 28*t*, 29, 33. xiii. 4*t*, 29, 30. xvi. 17(*ap*). Luke i. 20. iv. 28. v. 27. vii. 9. viii. 8. x. 1, 21. xi. 27, 53 (*ap*). xii. 30, 31. xiii. 17. xiv. 6, 15, 21. xv. 26. xvi. 14. xviii. 22(–LTTr*S*). xix. 11. xx. 2, 8. xxi. 6, 7*t*, 9, 31, 36. xxiii. 31, 49. xxiv. 9, 10, 21, 26.

John i. 28. ii. 16, 18. iii. 9, 10, 22. v. 16, 34. vi. 1, 59. vii. 1, 4. viii. 28. xi. 11. xii. 16*tr*, 36, 41. xiii. 17. xiv. 25. xv. 11, 17, 21. xvi. 1, 3, 4*t*, 6, 25, 33. xvii. 13. xix. 24, 36. xx. 18. xxi. 1, 24. Acts i. 9. v. 5 (–G∞LT*S*), 11. vii. 1, 50, 54. xi. 18. xii. 17. xiv. 15. xv. 17. xvii. 8, 20. xviii. 1. xix. 21. xxi. 12. xxiii. 22. xxiv. 9, 22 (G′, *om S*).

Rom. viii. 31. 1 Cor. iv. 6, 14. ix. 8, 15. x. 6, 11. 2 Cor. ii. 16. xiii. 10. Eph. v. 6. Phil. iv. 8. 2 Thes. ii. 5. 1 Tim. iii. 14. iv. 6, 11, 15. v. 7, 21. vi. 2, 11. 2 Tim. i. 12. ii. 14. Tit. ii. 15. iii. 8. Heb. vii. 13. Jas. iii. 10. 2 Pet. i. 8, 9, 10. 1 John i. 4. ii. 1, 26. v. 13. Rev. vii. 1 (τοῦτο G″LTTr*S*). xviii. 1. xix. 1. xxii. 8*t*, 16, 18 (αὐτά GLTTr, αὐτόν *S*), 20.

these [c]**words**, John ix. 22, 40. xvii. 1. xviii. 1. Acts xxviii. 29(*ap*).

this, Luke xviii. 23. John v. 1. xix. 38. Acts xv. 16. Rev. iv. 1. vii. 9.

they, them, John vi. 9. x. 25. 1 Cor. vi. 13. Rev. x. 4(*αὐτά* G″LTTr*S*).
him[cc], Heb. xi. 12.
such, 1 Cor. vi. 11.
such things, John vii. 32. 2 Pet. iii. 14.
the things, Gal. ii. 18. v. 17.
the same, 1 Cor. ix. 8. 2 Tim. ii. 2.
those, Phil. iii. 7.
those things, John viii. 26. Acts xvii. 11. Phil. iv, 9.
that, Mark xvi. 12(*ap*). Luke xii. 4. Acts vii. 7. xiii. 20. 1 Cor. vi. 8 (*τοῦτο* G″LT*S*). Rev. xv. 5. xx. 3.
thus[cc], Luke ix. 34. xi. 45. xviii. 11. xix. 28. xxiii. 46. xxiv. 36. John ix. 6. xi. 43. xiii. 21. xviii. 22. xx. 14. Acts xix. 41. xx. 36. xxvi. 24, 30(*ap*). xxvii. 35. Rev. xvi. 5.
so[cc], John xi. 28.
Add Mark viii. 7 (blessed . .), LT. 7, for *αὐτά*, Tr. Luke xiii. 2, for *τοιαῦτα*, Tr*S*. xxiv. 11, for *αὐτῶν*, LTr*S*. Rev. xx. 6, for *αὐτοῦ*, G′. xxi. 7, for *πάντα*, GLTTr*S*.
See also κατά and αὐτός, II., *λέγω*, *μετά*.

(b) *Genitive.*

1. *Masc. and Neut. Sing.*, *τούτου.*

this, Matt. xiii. 15, 22 (–LTTr*S*), 40(–G°LTTr*S*). xxvi. 29. xxvii. 24. Mark iv. 19(*omS*). Luke ii. 17. ix. 45. xiii. 16. xvi. 8. xx. 34. John iv. 13. vi. 51. viii. 23*t*. xi. 9. xii. 31(–G°°), 31. xiii. 1. xiv. 30(*omS*). xvi. 11. xviii. 17, 29, 36*t*. Acts v. 28. vi. 13(*omS*). ix. 13. xiii. 17, xv. 2, 6. xxi. 28. xxii. 22. xxviii. 9, 27. Rom. vii. 24. 1 Cor. i. 20 (–G°°LT*S*), 20. ii. 6*t*, 8. iii. 19. v. 10. vii. 31. 2 Cor. iv. 4. Eph. ii. 2. vi. 12. Col. i. 27. Jas. ii. 5(*omS*). Rev. xxii. 7, 9, 10, 18.
this man's, Acts xiii. 23. Jas. i. 26.
this man, John x. 41. Acts xiii. 38.
this thing, 2 Cor. xii. 8.
this matter, Acts xvii. 32.
With ἕνεκα, **for this cause,** Matt. xix. 5. Mark x. 7.
him, John ix. 31. Rev. xix. 20(*αὐτοῦ* GLTTr*S*).
αὐτοῦ τούτου, **he himself**[cc], Acts xxv. 25.
it, John vi. 61.
that, John xvi. 19. Rom. xi. 7 (*τοῦτο* GLT*S*).
Add Matt. xxvii. 24 (. . just person), L. Mark x. 10, for *τοῦ αὐτοῦ*, LTTr*S*.
See also ἀντί, ἐκ, ἕως, ζήτησις, περί, χάρις.

2. *Fem. Sing.*, *ταύτης.*

this, Matt. xii. 41, 42. Luke vii. 31. xi. 31, 32, 50, 51. xvii. 25. John x. 16. xii. 27. xv. 13. Acts i. 17, 25. ii. 6, 29, 40. v. 20. vi. 3. viii. 22. x. 30. xiii. 26. xix. 25, 40. xxiii. 1. xxiv. 21. xxvi. 22. xxviii. 22. 2 Cor. ix. 12, 13. Heb. ix. 11. Rev. xxii. 19.
With διά, **thereby,** Heb. xii. 15(*αὐτῆς* L). xiii. 2.
same, Acts viii. 35.
Add Matt. x. 23(*ap*).

3. *Plural*, *τούτων.*

of these, Matt. vi. 29. xxv. 40, 45. Luke x. 36. xii. 27. Acts i. 24. 1 Cor. xiii. 13. Heb. x. 18.
of these things, Matt. vi. 32. Luke xii. 30. xviii. 34. xxiv. 48. Acts xxvi. 26. 1 Cor. ix. 15. Rev. xviii. 15.
than[c] **these,** Matt. v. 37. Mark xii. 31. John i. 50(51). v. 20. vii. 31 (–G°LTTr*S*). xiv. 12. xxi. 15.
these, Matt. iii. 9. v. 19. x. 42. xviii. 6, 10, 14. Luke iii. 8. xvii. 2. xxi. 12. John xvii. 20. Acts i. 21(22). v. 32, 36, 38. xiv. 15. xv. 28 (–G°°T). xxi. 38. xxvi. 29. 2 Tim. ii. 21. Heb. i. 2(1). 2 Pet. i. 4. Rev. ix. 18.
these things, Luke vii. 18. xxi. 28. xxiv. 14. John xxi. 24. Acts xix. 36. xxiv. 8. xxv. 9. xxvi. 26. Tit. iii. 8. Heb. ix. 6. 2 Pet. i. 12, 15. iii. 11, 16.

these matters, Acts xxv. 20.
this sort, 2 Tim. iii. 6.
With ἕνεκα, **for these causes,** Acts xxvi. 21.
their, Rom. xi. 30.
they[cc], Matt. xi. 7.
those, Heb. xiii. 11.
of those things, Acts xviii. 17.
Not rendered, 3 John 4.
such, 1 Thes. iv. 6. Rev. xx. 6.
of such matters, Acts xviii. 15.
Add Mark ix. 42 (these), TTr*S*. John vii. 40 (saying . .), LTr*S*. xix. 13, for τοῦτον, G″LTTr*S*. Acts xxv. 20, *see* ζήτησις.

(c) *Dative.*

1. *Masc. and Neut. Sing.*, τούτῳ.

to this, Acts xv. 15.
unto this, Matt. xx. 14.
this, Matt. xii. 32. xvii. 20. xxi. 21. Mark x. 30. xi. 33. Luke i. 61. iv. 3. x. 5, 20. xviii. 30. xix. 9. xxi. 23. xxiii. 4, 14. John iv. 20, 21, 27. xii. 25. xiii. 35. xvi. 30. xx. 30. Acts i. 6. iii. 12. iv. 17. v. 28. vii. 7, 29. viii. 21, 29. xxiii. 9. xxiv. 2(3), 10. Rom. xii. 2. xiii. 9. 1 Cor. iii. 18. vii. 31 (–LT*S*). xi. 22. xiv. 21. 2 Cor. iii. 10. v. 2. ix. 3. Gal. vi. 16. Eph. i. 21. 1 Pet. iv. 16. 2 Pet. i. 13. 1 John iii. 10. iv. 9, 17. v. 2. Rev. xxii. 18, 19.
to this man, Matt. viii. 9.
this man, Matt. xiii. 54[cc], 56[cc]. Mark vi. 2[cc]. Luke xiv. 9.
this [e]**place,** Heb. iv. 5.
of the same, 2 Pet. ii. 19.
the same, Acts xxi. 9[cc].
to him, Luke xix. 19. John x. 3. xiii. 24. Acts x. 43.
him, John v. 38. Acts iv. 10. xiii. 39. 1 John ii. 4, 5.
unto one, Luke vii. 8.
Add Acts xxv. 5, for ἄτοπον, StET. Rom. xiv. 18, for τούτοις, GLT*S*.
See also ἐν.

Plural, τούτοις.

upon these, 1 Cor. xii. 23.
with these, Heb. ix. 23.
these, Acts iv. 16. v. 35. Rom. xv. 23. 1 Thes. iv. 18. Jude 14.
these things, Rom. viii. 37. xiv. 18 (τούτῳ GLT*S*). Col. iii. 14.
this, Luke xvi. 26. xxiv. 21.
them, 1 Tim. iv. 15.
therewith, 1 Tim. vi. 8.
therein, 2 Pet. ii. 20.
those things, Jude 10.
such, Gal. v. 21.
Not rendered, Jude 7.
Add Col. iii. 7, for αὐτοῖς, G″LT*S*.
See also ἐπί, II.

2. *Fem. Sing.*, ταύτῃ.

this, Matt. x. 23. xii. 45. xvi. 18. xxvi. 31, 34. Mark viii. 12, 38. xiv. 27(–G[oo]L[b]TTr*S*), 30. Luke xi. 30. xii. 20. xiii. 7. xvi. 24. xvii. 6. xix. 42. Acts xviii. 10. xxii. 3. xxvii. 23. 1 Cor. ix. 12. xv. 19. 2 Cor. i. 15. viii. 7, 19, 20. xi. 17.
this same, 2 Cor. ix. 4.
the same, 1 Cor. vii. 20.
it, Heb. xi. 2.
that, Luke xiii. 32. xvii. 34. Acts xvi. 12 (αὐτῇ T).
Add Acts iv. 27(*ap*). Heb. iii. 10, for ἐκείνῃ, G″LT*S*. Rev. xviii. 18 (this), L.

Plural, ταύταις.

these, Matt. xxii. 40. Luke xxiv. 18. John v. 3. Acts xi. 27. 1 Thes. iii. 3. Rev. ix. 20.
them, Luke xiii. 14(αὐταῖς LTTr*S*).
those, Luke i. 39. vi. 12. Acts i. 15. vi. 1.
that, Luke xxiii. 7.

οὔτω, οὔτως.

thus, Matt. ii. 5. iii. 15. xxvi. 54. Mark ii. 7. Luke i. 25. ii. 48. xix. 31. xxiv. 46, 46(–G[o]L[b]TTr*S*). John iv. 6. xi. 48. Rom. ix. 20. 1 Cor. xiv. 25(*om S*). Heb. vi. 9. ix. 6. Rev. ix. 17. xviii. 21.
so, Matt. v. 12. 16, 19, 47 (τὸ αὐτό LTTr*S*). vi. 30. vii. 12. ix. 33. xi. 26. xii. 40. xiii. 40, 49. xviii. 35. xix. 8, 10, 12. xx. 16, 26. xxiv. 27, 33, 37, 39, 46. Mark ii. 8(–L).

iv. 26, 40(*ap*). vii. 18. x. 43. xiv. 59. xv. 39.
Luke vi. 10(–GTTr*S*). ix. 15. x. 21. xi. 30. xii. 21, 28, 38, 43, 54. xvii. 10, 24, 26. xxi. 31. xxii. 26. xxiv. 24. John iii. 8, 16. v. 21, 26. viii. 59(*ap*). xii. 50. xviii. 22. Acts i. 11. iii. 18. vii. 1, 8. viii. 32. xii. 8. xiii. 8, 47. xiv. 1. xvii. 11, 33. xix. 20. xx. 11, 13, 35. xxi. 11. xxii. 24. xxiii. 11. xxiv. 9, 14. xxvii. 17, 44. xxviii. 14.
Rom. i. 15. iv. 18. v. 12, 15, 18, 19 (*with καί*), 21. xi. 5, 26. xii. 5. xv. 20. 1 Cor. ii. 11. iii. 15. iv. 1. v. 3. vi. 5. vii. 17*t*, 26, 36, 40. viii. 12. ix. 14, 15, 24, 26*t*. xi. 28. xii. 12. xiv. 9, 12, 25. xv. 11*t*, 22, 42, 45. xvi. 1. 2 Cor. i. 5, 7. vii. 14. viii. 6, 11. x. 7. xi. 3(–G°L*S*).
Gal. i. 6. iii. 3. iv. 3, 29. vi. 2. Eph. iv. 20. v. 24(*with καί*), 28, 33. Phil. iii. 17. iv. 1. Col. iii. 13. 1 Thes. ii. 8. iv. 17. v. 2. 2 Thes. iii. 17. 2 Tim. iii. 8. Heb. v. 3, 5. vi. 15. ix. 28. x. 33. xii. 21. Jas. i. 11. ii. 12*t*, 17, 26. iii. 5, 6(–G°° LT*S*), 10, 12(*ap*). 1 Pet. ii. 15. 2 Pet. i. 11. 1 John ii. 6(–L). iv. 11. Rev. ii. 15. iii. 16. xvi. 18.

even so, Matt. vii. 17. xii. 45. xviii. 14. xxiii. 28. John iii. 14. xiv. 31. Acts xii. 15. Rom. vi. 4, 19 xi. 31. 1 Cor. xi. 12. 1 Thes. ii. 4. iv. 14.

even, Acts xxvii. 25.

in this manner, Rev. xi. 5.

after this manner, Matt. vi. 9. 1 Pet. iii. 5.

οὕτως . . οὕτως, **after this manner . . after that,** 1 Cor. vii. 7.

in like manner, Mark xiii. 29.

on this fashion, Mark ii. 12.

on this wise, Matt. i. 18. John xxi. 1. Acts vii. 6. xiii. 34. Rom. x. 6. Heb. iv. 4.

likewise, Matt. xvii. 12. Luke xv. 7, 10. Rom. vi. 11.

οὕτως ὡς, **like,** John vii. 46.

as °they were, 2 Pet. iii. 4.

for all that, 1 Cor. xiv. 21.

what, Matt. xxvi. 40.

Not rendered, 2 Cor. ix. 5.

Add, for τὸ αὐτό, Matt. v. 46, LTTr. For οὖν, 2 Pet. iii. 11, T. For οὗτος, Matt. vii. 12, G′*S*. Rev. iii. 5, LTr *S*. — Mark ix. 3 (can . .), G^ph TTr*S*. John xiii. 25 (lying . .), TTr^b. 1 Cor. vii. 8 (even . .), L^b.

See also οὐδέ, οὖν.

οὐχ. See οὐ.

οὐχί.

Interrogative, except when noted [1].

not, Matt. v. 46, 47. vi. 25. x. 29. xii. 11. xiii. 27, 55 (οὐ LTr*S*), 56. xviii. 12. xx. 13. Luke vi. 39. xii. 6. xiv. 28, 31. xv. 8. xvii. 8, 17 (οὐ L). xxii. 27. xxiv. 26, 32. John vii. 42 (οὐ L). xi. 9. xiii. 10[1], 11[1]. xiv. 22. Acts v. 4. vii. 50.
Rom. ii. 26 (οὐ L*S*). iii. 29. viii. 32. 1 Cor. i. 20. iii. 3, 4 (οὐ LT*S*). v. 2, 12. vi. 1, 7*t*. viii. 10. ix. 1, 8 (οὐ G″LT*S*). x. 16*t*, 18 (οὐ LT*S*), 29[1]. 2 Cor. iii. 8. x. 13[1] (οὐ LT*S*). 1 Thes. ii. 19. Heb. i. 14. iii. 17.

not so, Luke i. 60[1].

nay, Luke xii. 51[1]. xiii. 3[1], 5[1]. xvi. 30[1]. Rom. iii. 27[1].

Add Luke xxiii. 39, for εἰ, L^m TTr *S*. John ix. 9[1], *see* ὅτι. Acts ii. 7, for οὐκ, T.

ὀφειλέτης.

debtor, Matt. vi. 12. Rom. i. 14. viii. 12. xv. 27. Gal. v. 3.

which oweth, Matt. xviii. 24.

sinner (*marg.* **debtor**), Luke xiii. 4.

ὀφειλή.

debt, Matt. xviii. 32.

due, Rom. xiii. 7.

Add 1 Cor. vii. 3, for ὀφειλομένην εὔνοιαν, GLT*S*.

ὀφείλημα.

debt, Matt. vi. 12. Rom. iv. 4.

ὀφείλω.

be indebted, Luke xi. 4.

be a debtor, Matt. xxiii. 16.

Pass., **be due,** Matt. xviii. 34. —

due, 1 Cor. vii. 3p (*see* ὀφειλή). — **debt**, Matt. xviii. 30p.
owe, Matt. xviii. 28*t*. Luke vii. 41. xvi. 5, 7. Rom. xiii. 8. Phm. 18.
ought, John xiii. 14. xix. 7. Acts xvii. 29. Rom. xv. 1. 1 Cor. xi. 7, 10. 2 Cor. xii. 11, 14. Eph. v. 28. Heb. v. 3, 12p. 1 John ii. 6. iii. 16. iv. 11. 3 John 8.
should, 1 Cor. ix. 10.
be one's dutycc, Luke xvii. 10. Rom. xv. 27.
With γίνεσθαι fr. γίνομαι, **need so requireth**, 1 Cor. vii. 36.
must needs, 1 Cor. v. 10.
it behoveth onecc, Heb. ii. 17.
be bound, 2 Thes. i. 3. ii. 13.
be guilty (*marg.* **a debtor** *or* **bound**), Matt. xxiii. 18.

ὄφελον.

I would, Gal. v. 12. Rev. iii. 15.
I would to God, 1 Cor. iv. 8.
would to God, 2 Cor. xi. 1.

ὄφελος.

it profitethcc, Jas. ii. 14, 16.
it advantagethcc, 1 Cor. xv. 32.

ὀφθαλμοδουλεία.

eye-service, Eph. vi. 6. Col. iii. 22.

ὀφθαλμός.

eye, Matt. v. 29, 38. vi. 22*t*, 23. vii. 3*t*, 4*t*, 5*t*. ix. 29, 30. xiii. 15*t*, 16. xvii. 8. xviii. 9*t*. xx. 15, 33, 34 (ὄμμα LTr), 34 (-LTr*S*). xxi. 42. xxvi. 43. Mark vii. 22. viii. 18, 25. ix. 47*t*. xii. 11. xiv. 40. Luke ii. 30. iv. 20. vi. 20, 41*t*, 42*f*. x. 23. xi. 34*t*. xvi. 23. xviii. 13. xix. 42. xxiv. 16, 31. John iv. 35. vi. 5. ix. 6, 10, 11, 14, 15, 17, 21, 26, 30, 32. x. 21. xi. 37, 41. xii. 40*t*. xvii. 1. Acts ix. 8, 18, 40. xxvi. 18. xxviii. 27*t*.
Rom. iii. 18. xi. 8, 10. 1 Cor. ii. 9. xii. 16, 17, 21. xv. 52. Gal. iii. 1. iv. 15. Eph. i. 18. Heb. iv. 13. 1 Pet. iii. 12. 2 Pet. ii. 14. 1 John i. 1. ii. 11, 16. Rev. i. 7, 14. ii. 18. iii. 18. iv. 6, 8. v. 6. vii. 17. xix. 12. xxi. 4.
Plur., **sight**, Acts i. 9.

ὄφις.

serpent, Matt. vii. 10. x. 16. xxiii. 33. Mark xvi. 18(*ap*). Luke x. 19. xi. 11. John iii. 14. 1 Cor. x. 9. 2 Cor. xi. 3. Rev. ix. 19. xii. 9, 14, 15. xx. 2.

ὀφρύς.

brow (*marg.* **edge**), Luke iv. 29.

ὀχλέω.

vex, Luke vi. 18(ἐνοχλέω G~TTr*S*). Acts v. 16.

ὀχλοποιέω.

gather a company, Acts xvii. 5.

ὄχλος.

press, Mark ii. 4. v. 27, 30. Luke viii. 19. xix. 3.
multitude, Matt. iv. 25. v. 1. viii. 1, 18. ix. 8, 33, 36. xi. 7. xii. 15 (-LTrb*S*). xiii. 2*t*, 34, 36. xiv. 5, 14, 15, 19*t*, 22. 23. xv. 10, 30, 31, 32, 33, 35, 36, 39. xvii. 14. xix. 2. xx. 29, 31. xxi. 8, 9, 11, 46. xxii. 33. xxiii. 1. xxvi. 47, 55. xxvii. 20, 24. Mark ii. 13. iii. 9, 20, 32. iv. 1*t*, 36. v. 31. vii. 33. viii. 1, 2. ix. 14, 17. xiv. 43. xv. 8.
Luke iii. 7. v. 15, 19. vi 19. viii. 45. ix. 12, 16. xiv. 25. xviii. 36. xix. 39. xxii. 6 (*marg.* **tumult**), 47. John v. 13. vi. 2. Acts xiii. 45. xvi. 22. xix. 33. xxi. 34. xxiv. 18. Rev. vii. 9. xvii. 15. xix. 6.
company, Luke v. 29. vi. 17. ix. 38. xi. 27. xii. 13. John vi. 5. Acts vi. 7.
people, Matt. vii. 28. ix. 23, 25. xii. 23, 46. xiv. 13. xxi. 26. xxvii. 15. Mark v. 21, 24. vi. 33(*omS*), 34, 45. vii. 14, 17. viii. 6*t*, 34. ix. 15, 25. x. 1. xi. 18. xii. 12, 37, 41. xv. 11, 15.
Luke iii. 10. iv. 42. v. 1, 3. vii. 9, 11, 12, 24. viii. 4, 40, 42. ix. 11, 18, 37. xi. 14, 29. xii. 1, 54. xiii. 14, 17. xxiii. 4, 48.
John vi. 22, 24. vii. 12*t*, 20, 31, 32, 40, 43, 49. xi. 42. xii. 9, 12, 17,

18, 29, 34. Acts viii. 6. xi. 24, 26. xiv. 11, 13, 14, 18, 19. xvii. 8, 13. xix. 26, 35. xxi. 27, 35. xxiv. 12. Rev. xix. 1.
number of people, Mark x. 46.
number, Acts i. 15.

ὀχύρωμα.

stronghold, 2 Cor. x. 4.

ὀψάριον.

fish, John vi. 11. xxi. 9, 10p 13.
small fish, John vi. 9.

ὀψέ.

at even, Mark xiii. 35.
even, Mark xi. 19.
in the end, Matt. xxviii. 1.

ὄψιμος.

latter, Jas. v. 7.

ὄψιος, ὀψία.

ὀψία ὥρα, **eventide**, Mark xi. 11.

ὀψία, subst.

evening, Matt. xiv. 15, 23. xvi. 2.
even, Matt. viii. 16. xx. 8. xxvi. 20. xxvii. 57. Mark iv. 35. vi. 47. xv. 42. John vi. 16.
With γίνομαι p, **in the evening**, Mark xiv. 17. — **at even**, Mark i. 32.
See also ὤν fr. εἰμί.

ὄψις.

face, John xi. 44.
countenance, Rev. i. 16.
appearance, John vii. 24.

ὀψώνιον.

wages, Luke iii. 14pl (*marg.* **allowance**). Rom. vi. 23pl. 2 Cor. xi. 8.
charges, 1 Cor. ix. 7pl.

παγιδεύω.

entangle, Matt. xxii. 15.

παγίς.

snare, Luke xxi. 35. Rom. xi. 9. 1 Tim. iii. 7. vi. 9. 2 Tim. ii. 26.

πάγος.

With Ἄρειος, **Areopagus** (*marg.* **Mars' hill**), Acts xvii. 19. — **Mars' hill** (*marg.* **court of the Areopagites**), Acts xvii. 22.

πάθημα.

suffering, Rom. viii. 18. 2 Cor. i. 5, 6, 7. Phil. iii. 10. Col. i. 24. Heb. ii. 9, 10. 1 Pet. i. 11. iv. 13. v. 1.
affliction, 2 Tim. iii. 11. Heb. x. 32. 1 Pet. v. 9.
affection (*marg.* **passion**), Gal. v. 24.
motion (*Gr.* passion), Rom. vii. 5.

παθητός.

should suffercc, Acts xxvi. 23.

πάθος.

affection, Rom. i. 26.
inordinate affection, Col. iii. 5.
lust, 1 Thes. iv. 5.

παιδαγωγός.

schoolmaster, Gal. iii. 24, 25.
instructor, 1 Cor. iv. 15.

παιδάριον.

lad, John vi. 9.
child, Matt. xi. 16 (παιδίον GLTTr *S*).

παιδεία.

nurture, Eph. vi. 4.
instruction, 2 Tim. iii. 16.
chastening, Heb. xii. 5, 7, 11.
chastisement, Heb. xii. 8.

παιδευτής.

instructor, Rom. ii. 20.
which correcteth, Heb. xii. 9.

παιδεύω.

instruct, 2 Tim. ii. 25.
teach, Acts xxii. 3. Tit. ii. 12.
Pass., **learn**, 1 Tim. i. 20. — **be learned**, Acts vii. 22.
chasten, 1 Cor. xi. 32. 2 Cor. vi. 9. Heb. xii. 6, 7, 10. Rev. iii. 19.
chastise, Luke xxiii. 16, 22.

παιδιόθεν.

of a child, Mark ix. 21.

παιδίον.

little child, Matt. xviii. 2, 3, 4, 5. xix. 13, 14. Mark x. 14, 15. Luke xviii. 16, 17. 1 John ii. 13, 18.
young child, Matt. ii. 8, 9, 11, 13*t*, 14, 20*t*, 21. Mark x. 13.

child, Matt. xiv. 21. xv. 38. Mark vii. 28. ix. 24, 36, 37. Luke i. 59, 66, 76, 80. ii. 17, 21 (αὐτός GLTTr *S*), 27, 40. vii. 32. ix. 47, 48. xi. 7. John iv. 49. xvi. 21. xxi. 5 (*marg.* sir). 1 Cor. xiv. 20. Heb. ii. 13, 14. xi. 23.
damsel, Mark v. 39, 40*t*, 41.
Add Matt. xi. 16, for παιδάριον, G LTTr*S*. Mark vii. 30, for θυγατήρ, LTTr*S*.

παιδίσκη.

damsel, Matt. xxvi. 69. John xviii. 17. Acts xii. 13. xvi. 16.
maiden, Luke xii. 45.
maid, Mark xiv. 66, 69. Luke xxii. 56.
bondmaid, Gal. iv. 22.
bondwoman, Gal. iv. 23, 30*t*, 31.

παίζω.

to play, 1 Cor. x. 7.

παῖς.

child, Matt. ii. 16. xvii. 18. xxi. 15. Luke ii. 43. ix. 42. Acts iv. 27, 30.
son, John iv. 51.
Said of Christ, **Son**, Acts iii. 13, 26.
young man, Acts xx. 12.
maiden, Luke viii. 51.
maid, Luke viii. 54.
servant, Matt. viii. 6, 8, 13. xii. 18. xiv. 2. Luke i. 54, 69. vii. 7. xv. 26. Acts iv. 25.
man-servant, Luke xii. 45.

παίω.

smite, Matt. xxvi. 68. Mark xiv. 47. Luke xxii. 64. John xviii. 10.
strike, Rev. ix. 5.

πάλαι.

of old, Jude 4.
old[cc], 2 Pet. i. 9.
long ago, Matt. xi. 21.
a great while ago, Luke x. 13.
in time past, Heb. i. 1.
any while, Mark xv. 44 (ἤδη LTr).
Add 2 Cor. xii. 19, for πάλιν, LT*S*.

παλαιός.

old, Matt. ix. 16, 17. Mark ii. 21*t*, 22. Luke v. 36*t*, 37, 39. Rom. vi. 6. 1 Cor. v. 7, 8. 2 Cor. iii. 14. Eph. iv. 22. Col. iii. 9. 1 John ii. 7*t*.
παλαιά, **old things**, Matt. xiii. 52.
old [c]**wine**, Luke v. 39.

παλαιότης.

oldness, Rom. vii. 6.

παλαιόω.

make old, Heb. viii. 13.
Pass., **wax old**, Luke xii. 33. Heb. i. 11. — **decay**, Heb. viii. 13.

πάλη.

wrestle[cc], Eph. vi. 12.

παλιγγενεσία.

regeneration, Matt. xix. 28. Tit. iii. 5 (παλινγ. T*S*).

πάλιν.

again, Matt. iv. 7, 8. v. 33. xiii. 44 (-L[b]TTr*S*), 45, 47. xviii. 19 (ἀμήν L). xix. 24. xx. 5. xxi. 36. xxii. 1, 4. xxvi. 42, 43, 44, 72. xxvii. 50. Mark ii. 1, 13. iii. 1, 20. iv. 1. v. 21. vii. 31. viii. 13, 25. x. 1*t*, 10, 24, 32. xi. 27. xii. 4, 5(*om S*). xiv. 39, 40(*ap*), 61, 69, 70*t*. xv. 4, 12, 13. Luke xiii. 20. xxiii. 20.
John i. 35. iv. 3 (-G[o]T), 13, 46, 54. vi. 15(-G[o]). viii. 2(*ap*), 8(*ap*), 12, 21. ix. 15, 17, 26(-LTTr*S*), 27. x. 7, 17, 18, 19, 31, 39, 40. xi. 7, 8, 38. xii. 22 (*see* ἔρχομαι), 28, 39. xiii. 12. xiv. 3. xvi. 16, 17, 19, 22, 28. xviii. 7, 27, 33, 38, 40. xix. 4, 9, 37. xx. 10, 21, 26. xxi. 1, 16. Acts x. 15, 16 (εὐθύς LT*S*, -G[oo]). xi. 10. xvii. 32. xviii. 21. xxvii. 28.
Rom. viii. 15. xi. 23. xv. 10, 11, 12. 1 Cor. iii. 20. vii. 5. xii. 21. 2 Cor. i. 16. ii. 1. iii. 1. v. 12. x. 7. xi. 16. xii. 19 (πάλαι LT*S*), 21. Gal. i. 9, 17. ii. 1, 18. iv. 9, 19. v. 1, 3. Phil. i. 26. ii. 28. iv. 4. Heb. i. 5, 6. ii. 13*t*. iv. 5, 7. v. 12. vi. 1, 6. x. 30. Jas. v. 18. 2 Pet. ii. 20. 1 John ii. 8. Rev. x. 8, 11.
εἰς τὸ πάλιν, **again**, 2 Cor. xiii. 2.

πάλιν ἄνωθεν, **again**, Gal. iv. 9.
Add Mark vii. 14, for πάντα, G''L TTrS). viii. 1, *see* πάμπολυς. xi. 3 (. . hither), TrS. xiv. 40, *see* ὑποστρέφω. Luke vi. 43 (neither . .), L^bTTr^bS,

παμπληθεί.

all at once, Luke xxiii. 18.

πάμπολυς.

very great, Mark viii. 1 (πάλιν πολλοῦ G''LTrS).

πανδοχεῖον.

inn, Luke x. 34.

πανδοχεύς.

host, Luke x. 35.

πανήγυρις.

general assembly, Heb. xii. 23.

πανοικί.

with all one's house, Acts xvi. 34.

πανοπλία.

whole armor, Eph. vi. 11, 13.
all . . armor, Luke xi. 22.

πανουργία.

craftiness, Luke xx. 23. 1 Cor. iii. 19. 2 Cor. iv. 2.
cunning craftiness, Eph. iv. 14.
subtilty, 2 Cor. xi. 3.

πανοῦργος.

crafty, 2 Cor. xii. 16.

πανταχῇ, -χῆ L, every where.
Acts xxi. 28, for πανταχοῦ, G''LTS.

πανταχόθεν.

from every quarter, Mark i. 45 (πάντοθεν G''LT, παντόθεν Tr).

πανταχοῦ.

every where, Mark xvi. 20 (*ap*). Luke ix. 6. Acts xvii. 30. xxi. 28 (πανταχῇ G''LTS). xxviii. 22. 1 Cor. iv. 17.
in all places, Acts xxiv. 3.
Add Mark i. 28 (. . throughout), TTr^b.

παντελής.

εἰς τὸ παντελές, **to the uttermost** (*marg.* **evermore**), Heb. vii. 25.
μὴ εἰς τὸ παντελές, **in no wise**, Luke xiii. 11.

πάντῃ.

always, Acts xxiv. 3.

πάντοθεν.

on every side, Luke xix. 43.
round about, Heb. ix. 4.
Add Mark i. 45, *see* πανταχόθεν.

παντοκράτωρ.

Almighty, 2 Cor. vi. 18. Rev. i. 8. iv. 8. xi. 17. xv. 3. xvi. 7, 14. xix. 15. xxi. 22.
omnipotent, Rev. xix. 6.

πάντοτε.

always, Matt. xxvi. 11*t*. Mark xiv. 7*t*. Luke xviii. 1. John viii. 29. xi. 42. xii. 8*t*. xviii. 20 (G'', πάντες fr. πᾶς GLTTrS). Rom. i. 9(10). 1 Cor. i. 4. xv. 58. 2 Cor. ii. 14. iv. 10. v. 6. ix. 8. Gal. iv. 18. Eph. v. 20. Phil. i. 4, 20. ii. 12. Col. i. 3. iv. 12. 1 Thes. i. 2. iii. 6. 2 Thes. i. 3, 11. Phm. 4.
alway, John vii. 6. Phil. iv. 4. Col. iv. 6. 1 Thes. ii. 16. 2 Thes. ii. 13.
ever, Luke xv. 31. John xviii. 20. 1 Thes. iv. 17. v. 15. 2 Tim. iii. 7. Heb. vii. 25.
evermore, John vi. 34. 1 Thes. v. 16.
Add 2 Cor. vii. 14, for πάντα, L^m.

πάντως.

altogether, 1 Cor. v. 10. ix. 10.
by all means, Acts xviii. 21 (*ap*). 1 Cor. ix. 22.
at all, 1 Cor. xvi. 12.
surely, Luke iv. 23.
no doubt, Acts xxviii. 4.
οὐ πάντως, **in no wise**, Rom. iii. 9.
needs, Acts xxi. 22.

παρά.

I. With the Genitive.

from, Mark xii. 2. xiv. 43. Luke i. 45. ii. 1. viii. 49 (ἀπό L). John i. 6. v. 34, 41, 44. vii. 29. xv. 26*t*. xvi. 27, 28 (ἐκ LTTr). xvii. 8. Acts ix. 14. xxii. 5. xxvi. 10, 12(–G°L

S). Phil. iv. 18. 2 Pet. i. 17. 2 John 3*t*, 4.

of, Matt. ii. 4, 7, 16. xviii. 19. xx. 20 (ἀπό LTTr). Mark viii. 11. Luke vi. 34. xi. 16. xii. 48. John i. 14. iv. 9, 52. v. 44. vi. 45, 46. viii. 26, 40. ix. 16, 33. x. 18. xv. 15. xvii. 7. Acts ii. 33. iii. 2, 5. vii. 16. ix. 2. x. 22. xvii. 9. xx. 24. xxii. 30 (ὑπό G″L*S*). xxiv. 8. xxvi. 22(ἀπό LT*S*). xxviii. 22. Gal. i. 12. Eph. vi. 8. Phil. iv. 18. 1 Thes. ii. 13. iv. 1. 2 Thes. iii. 6. 2 Tim. i. 13, 18. ii. 2. iii. 14. Jas. i. 5, 7. 1 John iii. 22 (ἀπό LT*S*). v. 15 (ἀπό LT*S*). Rev. ii. 27. iii. 18.

out of, Luke vi. 19.

With art., **one's friends** (*marg.* **kinsmen**), Mark iii. 21. — **that one hath,** Mark v. 26. — **such things as one giveth,** Luke x. 7.

παρ' ἐμοῦ, **my,** Rom. xi. 27.

παρὰ Κυρίου, **the Lord's,** Matt. xxi. 42. Mark xii. 11.

παρά τινος, **any man's,** 2 Thes. iii. 8.

With ἀκούω, **hear one speak,** John i. 40(41).

Not rendered, John vii. 51.

Add Mark xvi. 9(*ap*). Luke i. 37, John viii. 38, *see* No. II.

II. With the Dative.

by, Luke ix. 47. John xix. 25. 1 Cor. xvi. 2.

with, Matt. xix. 26*t*. xxi. 25 (ἐν L Tr). xxii. 25. Mark x. 27*t*, 27(*ap*). Luke i. 30, 37 (*gen.* LᵐTTr*S*). ii. 52. xi. 37. xviii. 27*t*. xix. 7. John i. 39(40). iv. 40. viii. 38, 38 (*gen.* LTr*S*). xiv. 17, 23, 25. xvii. 5*t*. Acts ix. 43. x. 6. xviii. 3, 20(–LT *S*). xxi. 7, 8, 16. xxvi. 8. Rom. ii. 11. ix. 14. 1 Cor. iii. 19. vii. 24. 2 Cor. i. 17. Eph. vi. 9. 2 Thes. i. 6. 2 Tim. iv. 13. Jas. i. 17. 1 Pet. ii. 20. 2 Pet. iii. 8.

before, Rom. ii. 13. Jas. i. 27. 2 Pet. ii. 11(–G∞LT).

in the sight of, Gal. iii. 11.

among, Matt. xxviii. 15. Col. iv. 16. Rev. ii. 13.

of, Matt. vi. 1 (*marg.* **with**). 1 Pet. ii. 4.

Add Matt. viii. 10, *see* οὐδέ. Acts xxviii. 14, for ἐπί, L*S*.

See also ἑαυτοῖς fr. ἑαυτοῦ.

III. With the Accusative.

by . . side, Matt. xiii. 1, 4, 19. xx. 30. Mark ii. 13. iv. 1, 4, 15. x. 46. Luke viii. 5. xviii. 35. Acts x. 6, 32. xvi. 13.

With art., **those by . . side,** Luke viii. 12.

by, Matt. iv. 18. Mark i. 16. Luke v. 1, 2. Heb. xi. 12.

παρὰ τοῦτο, **therefore,** 1 Cor. xii. 15, 16.

at, Matt. xv. 30. Luke vii. 38. viii. 35, 41. x. 39 (πρός LᵐTTr*S*). xvii. 16. Acts iv. 35, 37. v. 2, 10 (πρός LT*S*). vii. 58. xxii. 3.

nigh unto, Matt. xv. 29. Mark v. 21.

above, Luke xiii. 2, 4. Rom. xiv. 5. Heb. i. 9.

past, Heb. xi. 11.

more than, Rom. i. 25. xii. 3.

than, Luke iii. 13. 1 Cor. iii. 11. Gal. i. 8, 9. Heb. i. 4. ii. 7 (*marg.* **to**), 9. iii. 3. ix. 23. xi. 4. xii. 24.

contrary to, Acts xviii. 13. Rom. xi. 24. xvi. 17.

against, Rom. i. 26. iv. 18.

save, 2 Cor. xi. 24.

Add Luke xviii. 14, for ἤ, LTr*S*. 2 Cor. viii. 3, for ὑπέρ, LT*S*.

παραβαίνω.

transgress, Matt. xv. 2, 3. 2 John 9 (προάγω LT*S*).

fall by transgression, Acts i. 25.

παραβάλλω.

compare, Mark iv. 30 (τίθημι LTTr *S*).

In navigation, **arrive,** Acts xx. 15.

παράβασις.

transgression, Rom. iv. 15. v. 14. Gal. iii. 19. 1 Tim. ii. 14. Heb. ii. 2. ix. 15.

breaking, Rom. ii. 23.

παραβάτης.

transgressor, Gal. ii. 18. Jas. ii. 9, 11.

who doth transgress, Rom. ii. 27.

breaker, Rom. ii. 25.

παραβιάζομαι.

constrain, Luke xxiv. 29. Acts xvi. 15.

παραβολεύομαι, expose one's self, venture.

Phil. ii. 30, for παραβουλεύ., GL*S*.

παραβολή.

comparison, Mark iv. 30.

parable, Matt. xiii. 3, 10, 13, 18, 24, 31, 33, 34*t*, 35, 36, 53. xv. 15. xxi. 33, 45. xxi. 1. xxiv. 32. Mark iii. 23. iv. 2, 10, 11, 13*t*, 33, 34. vii. 17. xii. 1, 12. xiii. 28. Luke v. 36. vi. 39. viii. 4, 9, 10, 11. xii. 16, 41. xiii. 6. xiv. 7. xv. 3. xviii. 1, 9. xix. 11. xx. 9, 19. xxi. 29.

figure, Heb. ix. 9. xi. 19.

proverb, Luke iv. 23.

παραβουλεύομαι.

regard not, Phil. ii. 30 (G′, παραβολεύομαι GL*S*).

παραγγελία.

commandment, 1 Thes. iv. 2. 1 Tim. i. 5.

charge, Acts xvi. 24. 1 Tim. i. 18.

Dat., **straitly,** Acts v. 28.

παραγγέλλω.

declare, 1 Cor. xi. 17[oc].

command, Matt. x. 5. Mark vi. 8. viii. 6. Luke viii. 29. ix. 21. Acts i. 4. iv. 18. v. 28, 40. x. 42. xv. 5. xvi. 18. xvii. 30. 1 Cor. vii. 10. 1 Thes. iv. 11. 2 Thes. iii. 4, 6, 10, 12. 1 Tim. iv. 11.

give commandment, Acts xxiii. 30.

charge, Luke v. 14. viii. 56. Acts xvi. 23. xxiii. 22. 1 Tim. i. 3. vi. 17.

give charge, 1 Tim. vi. 13.

give in charge, 1 Tim. v. 7.

Add Matt. xv. 35, παραγγείλας for ἐκέλευσε fr. κελεύω, LTr*S*.

παραγίνομαι.

Aorist, **be present,** Acts xxi. 18.

come. Matt. ii. 1. iii. 1, 13. Mark xiv. 43. Luke vii. 4[p], 20[p]. viii. 19. xi. 6. xii. 51. xiv. 21. xix. 16. xxii. 52. John iii. 23. viii. 2(*ap*). Acts v. 21, 22, 25. ix. 26[p], 39[p]. x. 32[p](*ap*), 33. xi. 23[p]. xiii. 14. xiv. 27[p]. xv. 4[p]. xviii. 27[p]. xx. 18. xxiii. 35. xxiv. 17, 24[p]. xxv. 7[p]. xxviii. 21. 1 Cor. xvi. 3. Heb. ix. 11.

come [c]thither, Acts xvii. 10.

go, Acts xxiii. 16.

Add 2 Tim. iv. 16, for συμπαραγίνομαι, L*S*.

παράγω.

pass by, Matt. xx. 30. Mark ii. 14[p]. xv. 21. John viii. 59(*ap*). ix. 1[p].

pass away, 1 Cor. vii. 31.

Mid., **pass,** 1 John ii. 8.—**pass away,** 1 John ii. 17.

pass forth, Matt. ix. 9[p].

depart, Matt. ix. 27[p].

Add Mark i. 16, for περιπατέω, G″ LTTr*S*. Luke xviii. 39, for προάγω, L[m].

παραδειγματίζω.

make a public example, Matt. i. 19 (δειγματίζω G′LTTr).

put to an open shame, Heb. vi. 6.

παράδεισος.

paradise, Luke xxiii. 43. 2 Cor. xii. 4. Rev. ii. 7.

παραδέχομαι.

receive, Mark iv. 20. Acts xvi. 21. xxii. 18. 1 Tim. v. 19. Heb. xii. 6.

Add Acts xv. 4, for ἀποδέχ., LT*S*.

παραδιατριβή.

Plur., **perverse disputings** (*marg.* **gallings one of another**), 1 Tim. vi. 5 (διαπαρατριβή GLT*S*).

παραδίδωμι.

give up, John xix. 30. Acts vii. 42. Rom. i. 24, 26.

give over, Rom. i. 28. Eph. iv. 19.

give, 1 Cor. xiii. 3. Gal. ii. 20. Eph. v. 2, 25.

be brought forth (*marg.* **be ripe**), Mark iv. 29.
deliver, Matt. v. 25, 25(-LTr^b S). xi. 27. xviii. 34. xx. 19. xxv. 14, 20, 22. xxvi. 15. xxvii. 2, 18, 26. Mark vii. 13. ix. 31. x. 33*t*. xv. 1, 10, 15. Luke i. 2. iv. 6. ix. 44. x. 22. xii. 58. xviii. 32. xx. 20. xxi. 12. xxiii. 25. xxiv. 7, 20. John xviii. 30, 35, 36. xix. 11, 16. Acts vi. 14. xii. 4. xvi. 4. xxi. 11. xxii. 4. xxvii. 1. xxviii. 16(*ap*), 17. Rom. iv. 25. vi. 17^cc. 1 Cor. v. 5. xi. 2, 23. xv. 3. 2 Cor. iv. 11. 1 Tim. i. 20. 2 Pet. ii. 4, 21. Jude 3.
deliver up, Matt. x. 17, 19, 21. xxiv. 9. Mark xiii. 9, 11. Acts iii. 13. Rom. viii. 32. 1 Cor. xv. 24.
cast into prison (*marg.* **deliver up**), Matt. iv. 12.
put in prison, Mark i. 14.
commit, Acts viii. 3.
Mid. or Pass., **commit** *one's self* (*marg. one's cause*), 1 Pet. ii. 23.
betray, Matt. x. 4. xvii. 22. xx. 18. xxiv. 10. xxvi. 2, 16, 21, 23, 24, 25, 45, 46, 48. xxvii. 3, 4^p. Mark iii. 19. xiii. 12. xiv. 10, 11, 18, 21, 41, 42, 44. Luke xxi. 16. xxii. 4, 6, 21, 22, 48. John vi. 64 (*with εἰμί*), 71. xii. 4. xiii. 2, 11, 21. xviii. 2, 5. xxi. 20. 1 Cor. xi. 23.
hazard, Acts xv. 26.
recommend, Acts xiv. 26. xv. 40.

παράδοξος.

Neut., **strange thing**, Luke v. 26.

παράδοσις.

tradition, Matt. xv. 2, 3, 6. Mark vii. 3, 5, 8, 9, 13. Gal. i. 14. Col. ii. 8. 2 Thes. ii. 15. iii. 6.
ordinance (*marg.* **tradition**), 1 Cor. xi. 2.

παραζηλόω.

provoke to jealousy, Rom. x. 19. xi. 11. 1 Cor. x. 22.
provoke to emulation, Rom. xi. 14.

παραθαλάσσιος.

With art., **which is upon the sea coast**, Matt. iv. 13.

παραθεωρέω.

to neglect, Acts vi. 1.

παραθήκη.

ἡ παρ. μοῦ, **that which I have committed unto** °**him**, 2 Tim. i. 12.
Add, for παρακαταθήκη, 1 Tim. vi. 20, 2 Tim. i. 14, GLT*S*.

παραινέω.

exhort, Acts xxvii. 22.
admonish, Acts xxvii. 9.

παραιτέομαι.

Mid., **entreat**, Heb. xii. 19.—**make excuse**, Luke xiv. 18.—**refuse**, Acts xxv. 11. 1 Tim. iv. 7. v. 11. Heb. xii. 25*t*.—**reject**, Tit. iii. 10.—**avoid**, 2 Tim. ii. 23.
Pass., **be excused**, Luke xiv. 18, 19.

παρακαθίζω.

With παρά, **sit at**, Luke x. 39.

παρακαλέω.

call for, Acts xxviii. 20.
entreat, Luke xv. 28. 1 Cor. iv. 13. 1 Tim. v. 1.
beseech, Matt. viii. 5, 31, 34. xiv. 36. xviii. 29. Mark i. 40. v. 10, 12, 23. vi. 56. vii. 32. viii. 22. Luke vii. 4. viii. 31, 32, 41. Acts xiii. 42. xvi. 15, 39. xxi. 12. xxv. 2. xxvii. 33. Rom. xii. 1. xv. 30. xvi. 17. 1 Cor. i. 10. iv. 16. xvi. 15. 2 Cor. ii. 8. v. 20^p. vi. 1. x. 1. xii. 8. Eph. iv. 1. Phil. iv. 2*t*. 1 Thes. iv. 10. 1 Tim. i. 3. Phm. 9, 10. Heb. xiii. 19, 22. 1 Pet. ii. 11.
desire, Matt. xviii. 32. Acts viii. 31. ix. 38. xix. 31. xxviii. 14. 1 Cor. xvi. 12. 2 Cor. viii. 6. xii. 18.
pray, Matt. xxvi. 53. Mark v. 17, 18. Acts xvi. 9. xxiv. 4. xxvii. 34.
exhort, Acts ii. 40. xi. 23. xiv. 22. xv. 32. Rom. xii. 8. 2 Cor. ix. 5. 1 Thes. iv. 1 and v. 14 (*marg.* **beseech**). 2 Thes. iii. 12. 1 Tim. ii. 1 (*marg.* **desire**). vi. 2. 2 Tim. iv. 2. Tit. i. 9. ii. 6, 15. Heb. iii. 13. 1 Pet. v. 1, 12. Jude 3.
exhort °**one another**, Heb. x. 25.

in one's exhortation, Luke iii. 18p.
With λόγῳ πολλῷ, **give much exhortation**, Acts xx. 2.
comfort, Matt. ii. 18. v. 4. Luke xvi. 25. Acts xvi. 40. xx. 12. 1 Cor. xiv. 31. 2 Cor. i. 4*tr*, 6. ii. 7. vii. 6*t*, 7, 13. Eph. vi. 22. Col. ii. 2. iv. 8. 1 Thes. ii. 11. iii. 2, 7. iv. 18 and v. 11 (*marg.* **exhort**). 2 Thes. ii. 17.
Pass., **be of good comfort**, 2 Cor. xiii. 11.
Add Acts xx. 1(. . embraced), L*S*.

παρακαλύπτω.

to hide, Luke ix. 45.

παρακαταθήκη.

that thing which is committed unto one, 2 Tim. i. 14 (παραθήκη GLT*S*).
that which is committed to one's trust, 1 Tim. vi. 20 (G′, παραθήκη GLT*S*).

παράκειμαι.

be present with, Rom. vii. 18, 21.

παράκλησις.

entreaty, 2 Cor. viii. 4.
exhortation, Acts xiii. 15. Rom. xii. 8. 1 Cor. xiv. 3. 2 Cor. viii. 17. 1 Thes. ii. 3. 1 Tim. iv. 13. Heb. xii. 5. xiii. 22.
comfort, Acts ix. 31. Rom. xv. 4. 2 Cor. i. 3, 4. vii. 4, 13.
consolation, Luke ii. 25. vi. 24. Acts iv. 36. xv. 31. Rom. xv. 5. 2 Cor. i. 5, 6*t*, 7. vii. 7. Phil. ii. 1. 2 Thes. ii. 16. Phm. 7. Heb. vi. 18.

παράκλητος.

advocate, 1 John ii. 1.
Comforter, John xiv. 16, 26. xv. 26. xvi. 7.

παρακοή.

disobedience, Rom. v. 19. 2 Cor. x. 6. Heb. ii. 2.

παρακολουθέω.

follow, Mark xvi. 17(*ap*).
With ᾗ fr. ὅς, **attain whereunto**, 1 Tim. iv. 6.
know fully (*marg.* **be a diligent follower of**), 2 Tim. iii. 10.
have perfect understanding of, Luke i. 3.

παρακούω.

neglect to hear, Matt. xviii. 17*t*.
Add Mark v. 36, for ἀκούω, TTr*S*.

παρακύπτω.

stoop down, Luke xxiv. 12(*ap*). John xx. 5, 11.
With εἰς, **look into**, Jas. i. 25. 1 Pet. i. 12.

παραλαμβάνω.

take with, Matt. xxvi. 37.
take unto, Matt. i. 20, 24.
take, Matt. ii. 13, 14, 20, 21. iv. 5, 8. xii. 45. xvii. 1. xviii. 16. xx. 17. xxiv. 40, 41. xxvii. 27. Mark iv. 36. v. 40. ix. 2. x. 32. xiv. 33. Luke ix. 10, 28. xi. 26. xvii. 34, 35, 36(*ap*). xviii. 31. John xix. 16 (*ap*). Acts xv. 39. xvi. 33. xxi. 24, 26, 32 (λαμβάνω L). xxiii. 18.
receive, Mark vii. 4. John i. 11. xiv. 3. 1 Cor. xi. 23. xv. 1, 3. Gal. i. 9, 12. Phil. iv. 9. Col. ii. 6. iv. 17. 1 Thes. ii. 13p. iv. 1. 2 Thes. iii. 6. Heb. xii. 28.
παραλήμψομαι, John xiv. 3, LTTr*S*.

παραλέγω.

Mid., *in navigation*, **sail by**, Acts xxvii. 13. — **pass**, Acts xxvii. 8.

παράλιος.

Subst., **sea coast**, Luke vi. 17.

παραλλαγή.

variableness, Jas. i. 17.

παραλογίζομαι.

beguile, Col. ii. 4.
deceive, Jas. i. 22.

παραλύω.

Pass., *perf. part.*, **taken with a palsy**, Luke v. 18. Acts viii. 7. — **sick of the palsy**, Luke v. 24 (παραλυτικός G″L*S*). Acts ix. 33. — **feeble**, Heb. xii. 12.

παραλυτικός.

that hath the palsy, Matt. iv. 24.
sick of the palsy, Matt. viii. 6. ix. 2*t*, 6. Mark ii. 3, 4, 5, 9, 10.

Add Luke v. 24, *see* παραλύω.

παραμένω.

abide, 1 Cor. xvi. 6.
continue, Heb. vii. 23. Jas. i. 25.
Add Phil. i. 25, for συμπαραμένω, G"L*S*.

παραμυθέομαι.

to comfort, John xi. 19, 31. 1 Thes. ii. 11. v. 14.

παραμυθία.

comfort, 1 Cor. xiv. 3.

παραμύθιον.

comfort, Phil. ii. 1.

παρανομέω.

contrary to the law, Acts xxiii. 3p.

παρανομία.

iniquity, 2 Pet. ii. 16.

παραπικραίνω.

provoke, Heb. iii. 16.

παραπικρασμός.

provocation, Heb. iii. 8, 15.

παραπίπτω.

fall away, Heb. vi. 6p.

παραπλέω.

sail by, Acts xx. 16.

παραπλήσιον.

nigh unto, Phil. ii. 27.

παραπλησίως.

likewise, Heb. ii. 14.

παραπορεύομαι.

pass by, Matt. xxvii. 39. Mark xi. 20p. xv. 29.
pass, Mark ix. 30 (πορεύομαι LTr).
go, Mark ii. 23.

παράπτωμα.

fall, Rom. xi. 11, 12.
fault, Gal. vi. 1. Jas. v. 16 (ἁμαρτία L*S*),
offence, Rom. iv. 25. v. 15*t*, 16, 17, 18, 20.
trespass, Matt. vi. 14, 15(-G∞T*S*), 15. xviii. 35(*om S*). Mark xi. 25, 26 (*ap*). 2 Cor. v. 19. Eph. ii. 1. Col. ii. 13.
sin, Eph. i. 7. ii. 5. Col. ii. 13.

παραρρέω.

let slip (*Gr.* run out as leaking vessels), Heb. ii. 1.

παράσημος.

whose sign °**was,** Acts xxviii. 11.

παρασκευάζω.

make ready, Acts x. 10p.
Mid., **prepare one's self,** 1 Cor. xiv. 8. —**be ready,** 2 Cor. ix. 2.—**ready,** 2 Cor. ix. 3p.

παρασκευή.

preparation, Matt. xxvii. 62. Mark xv. 42. Luke xxiii. 54. John xix. 14, 31, 42.

παρατείνω.

continue, Acts xx. 7.

παρατηρέω, -ομαι.

observe, Gal. iv. 10.
watch, Mark iii. 2. Luke vi. 7. xiv. 1 (*with* εἰμί). xx. 20. Acts ix. 24.

παρατήρησις.

observation (*marg.* **outward show**), Luke xvii. 20.

παρατίθημι.

set before, Mark vi. 41. viii. 6*t*, 7. Luke ix. 16. xi. 6. Acts xvi. 34. 1 Cor. x. 27.
τὰ παρατιθέμενα, **such things as are set before,** Luke x. 8.
put forth, Matt. xiii. 24, 31.
allege, Acts xvii. 3.
Mid., **commit,** Luke xii. 48. 1 Tim. i. 18. 2 Tim. ii. 2.—**commit the keeping of,** 1 Pet. iv. 19.—**commend,** Luke xxiii. 46. Acts xiv. 23. xx. 32.

παρατυγχάνω.

meet with, Acts xvii. 17.

παραυτίκα.

but for a moment, 2 Cor. iv. 17.

παραφέρω.

take away, Mark xiv. 36.
remove, Luke xxii. 42.
Add, for περιφέρω, Heb. xiii. 9, Jude 12, GLT*S*.

παραφρονέω.
as a fool, 2 Cor. xi. 23p.

παραφρονία.
madness, 2 Pet. ii. 16.

παραχειμάζω.
to winter, Acts xxvii. 12. xxviii. 11. 1 Cor. xvi. 6. Tit. iii. 12.

παραχειμασία.
With πρός, **to winter in**, Acts xxvii. 12.

παραχρῆμα.
presently, Matt. xxi. 19.
immediately, Luke i. 64. iv. 39. v. 25. viii. 44, 47. xiii. 13. xviii. 43. xix. 11. xxii. 60. Acts iii. 7. xii. 23. xiii. 11. xvi. 26.
forthwith, Acts ix. 18(*omS*).
straightway, Luke viii. 55. Acts v. 10. xvi. 33.
soon, Matt. xxi. 20.

πάρδαλις.
leopard, Rev. xiii. 2.

παρεδρεύω, sit near, serve.
1 Cor. ix. 13, for προσεδ., G''LT*S*.

πάρειμι.
be present, Luke xiii. 1. 1 Cor. v. 3p. 2 Cor. x. 2p, 11p. xi. 9(8)p. xiii. 2p, 10. Gal. iv. 18, 20.
present, 1 Cor. v. 3p. Heb. xii. 11p. 2 Pet. i. 12p.
be here present, Acts x. 33.
τὰ πάροντα, **such things as one hath**, Heb. xiii. 5.
ᾧ μὴ πάρεστι, **he that lacketh**, 2 Pet. i. 9.
be here, Acts xxiv. 19.
come, Matt. xxvi. 50. John vii. 6. xi. 28. Acts x. 21. xii. 20. xvii. 6. Col. i. 6.
Add 2 Pet. i. 8, for ὑπάρχω, L. Rev. xvii. 8, καὶ πάρεσται for καίπερ ἐστίν, GLTTr, καὶ πάλιν πάρεστε *S*.

παρεισάγω.
bring in privily, 2 Pet. ii. 1.

παρείσακτος.
brought in unawares, Gal. ii. 4.

παρεισδύνω.
creep in unawares, Jude 4.

παρεισέρχομαι.
come in privily, Gal. ii. 4.
enter, Rom. v. 20.

παρεισφέρω.
give, 2 Pet. i. 5.

παρεκτός.
except, Acts xxvi. 29.
With art., **those things that are without**, 2 Cor. xi. 28.
saving, Matt. v. 32.
Add Matt. xix. 9 (*ap*).

παρεμβολή.
army, Heb. xi. 34.
camp, Heb. xiii. 11, 13. Rev. xx. 9.
castle, Acts xxi. 34, 37. xxii. 24. xxiii. 10, 16, 32.

παρενοχλέω.
to trouble, Acts xv. 19.

παρεπίδημος.
pilgrim, Heb. xi. 13. 1 Pet. ii. 11.
stranger, 1 Pet. i. 1.

παρέρχομαι.
pass by, Mark vi. 48. Luke xviii. 37. Acts xvi. 8.
pass over, Luke xi. 42.
transgress, Luke xv. 29.
pass away, Matt. xxiv. 35*t*. xxvi. 42. Mark xiii. 31*t*. Luke xxi. 32, 33*t*. 2 Cor. v. 17. Jas. i. 10. 2 Pet. iii. 10. Rev. xxi. 1 (ἀπῆλθον GT, ἀπῆλθαν LTr*S*, fr. ἀπέρχομαι).
pass, Matt. v. 18*t*. viii. 28. xiv. 15. xxiv. 34. xxvi. 39. Mark xiii. 30. xiv. 35. Luke xvi. 17. Acts xxvii. 9.
past, 1 Pet. iv. 3p.
go, Luke xvii. 7.
come forth, Luke xii. 37.
come, Acts xxiv. 7(*ap*).

πάρεσις.
remission (*marg.* **passing over**), Rom. iii. 25.

παρέχω.
offer, Luke vi. 29.

minister, 1 Tim. i. 4.
give, Acts xvii. 31 (*marg.* **offer**). 1 Tim. vi. 17.
do for, Luke vii. 4.
bring, Acts xvi. 16.
show, Acts xxviii. 2.
Mid., **give,** Col. iv. 1. — **bring,** Acts xix. 24. — **show,** Tit. ii. 7.
keep, Acts xxii. 2.
See also κόπος.

παρηγορία.

comfort, Col. iv. 11.

παρθενία.

virginity, Luke ii. 36.

παρθένος.

virgin, Matt. i. 23. xxv. 1, 7; 11. Luke i. 27*t*. Acts xxi. 9. 1 Cor. vii. 25, 28, 34 (-G″L), 36, 37. 2 Cor. xi. 2. Rev. xiv. 4.

παρίημι.

Pass., **hang down,** Heb. xii. 12.

παριστάνω.

yield, Rom. vi. 13, 16. *Compare*

παρίστημι.

I. Present, 1st Aorist, and Future, *transitive.*

to present, Luke ii. 22. Acts ix. 41. xxiii. 33. Rom. xii. 1. 2 Cor. iv. 14. xi. 2. Eph. v. 27. Col. i. 22, 28.
give presently, Matt. xxvi. 53.
yield, Rom. vi. 13, 19*t*.
provide, Acts xxiii. 24.
commend, 1 Cor. viii. 8.
show, Acts i. 3. 2 Tim. ii. 15.
prove, Acts xxiv. 13.

II. Perfect, Pluperfect, and 2d Aorist, *intransitive.*

stand by, Mark xiv. 47, 69, 70. xv. 35. Luke xix. 24. John xviii. 22. xix. 26. Acts i. 10. ix. 39. xxiii. 2, 4. xxvii. 23.
assist, Rom. xvi. 2.
stand with, 2 Tim. iv. 17.
stand [c]**here,** Acts iv. 10.
stand up, Acts iv. 26.
stand, Mark xv. 39. Luke i. 19.
be brought before, Acts xxvii. 24.
come, Mark iv. 29.

III. Future Middle.

stand before, Rom. xiv. 10.

πάροδος.

way, 1 Cor. xvi. 7.

παροικέω.

to sojourn, Heb. xi. 9.
be a stranger, Luke xxiv. 18.

παροικία.

sojourning [c]**here,** 1 Pet. i. 17.
With ἐν, **when they**[c] **dwelt as strangers,** Acts xiii. 17.

πάροικος.

With εἰμί, **to sojourn,** Acts vii. 6.
stranger, Acts vii. 29. 1 Pet. ii. 11.
foreigner, Eph. ii. 19.

παροιμία.

proverb, John xvi. 25*t*, and 29, (*marg.* **parable.**) 2 Pet. ii. 22.
parable, John x. 6.

πάροινος.

given to wine, 1 Tim. iii. 3 (*marg.* **ready to quarrel and offer wrong, as one in wine**). Tit. i. 7.

παροίχομαι.

past, Acts xiv. 16[p].

παρομοιάζω.

be like unto, Matt. xxiii. 27 (ὁμοιάζω LTr).

παρόμοιος.

Neut. plur., **like things,** Mark vii. 8 (*ap*), 13.

παροξύνω.

Mid. or Pass., **be stirred,** Acts xvii. 16. — **be easily provoked,** 1 Cor. xiii. 5.

παροξυσμός.

With εἰς, **to provoke unto,** Heb. x. 24.
contention, Acts xv. 39.

παροργίζω.

to anger, Rom. x. 19.
provoke to wrath, Eph. vi. 4.
Add Col. iii. 21, for ἐρεθίζω, G′L*S*.

παροργισμός.

wrath, Eph. iv. 26.

παροτρύνω.

stir up, Acts xiii. 50.

παρουσία.

presence, 2 Cor. x. 10. Phil. ii. 12.
coming, Matt. xxiv. 3, 27, 37, 39. 1 Cor. xv. 23. xvi. 17. 2 Cor. vii. 6, 7. Phil. i. 26. 1 Thes. ii. 19. iii. 13. iv. 15. v. 23. 2 Thes. ii. 1, 8, 9. Jas. v. 7, 8. 2 Pet. i. 16. iii. 4, 12. 1 John ii. 28.

παροψίς.

platter, Matt. xxiii. 25, 26(–G∞T).

παῤῥησία.

boldness of speech, 2 Cor. vii. 4.
plainness (*marg.* **boldness) of speech**, 2 Cor. iii. 12.
boldness, Acts iv. 13, 29, 31. Eph. iii. 12. Phil. i. 20. 1 Tim. iii. 13. Heb. x. 19 (*marg.* **liberty**). 1 John iv. 17.
πολλὴν παρρησίαν ἔχω, **be much bold**, Phm. 8.
Dative, **boldly**, John vii. 26. — **openly**, Mark viii. 32. John vii. 13. xi. 54. xviii. 20. — **plainly**, John x. 24. xi. 14. xvi. 25, 29(*ἐν π.* LTTr*S*).
With ἐν, **boldly**, Eph. vi. 19. — **openly**, John vii. 4. Col. ii. 15.
With μετά, **boldly**, Heb. iv. 16. — **freely**, Acts ii. 29.
confidence, Acts xxviii. 31. Heb. iii. 6. x. 35. 1 John ii. 28. iii. 21. v. 14.

παῤῥησιάζομαι.

speak boldly, Acts xiv. 3. xviii. 26. xix. 8. Eph. vi. 20.
preach boldly, Acts ix. 27.
wax bold, Acts xiii. 46.
be bold, 1 Thes. ii. 2.
boldly, Acts ix. 29(28)p.
freely, Acts xxvi. 26p.

πᾶς.

Followed by ὅς[1], ὅστις[2], ὅσος[3].

1. *Sing.*, πᾶς, πᾶσα, πᾶν.

every, Matt. iii. 10. iv. 4. vii. 17, 19. ix. 35*t*. xii. 25*t*, 36. xiii. 47, 52. xv. 13. xviii. 16. xix. 3. Mark ix. 49(*ap*). xvi. 15(*ap*). Luke ii. 23. iii. 5*t*, 9. iv. 4(*ap*), 37. v. 17. x. 1. xi. 17. John i. 9. ii. 10. xv. 2. Acts ii. 5, 43. iii. 23[2]. x. 35. xiii. 27. xv. 21, 36. xviii. 4.
Rom. ii. 9. iii. 2, 4, 19. xiii. 1. xiv. 5, 11*t*. 1 Cor. i. 2. iv. 17. vi. 18. xi. 3, 4, 5. xv. 30. 2 Cor. ii. 14. iv. 2co. ix. 8. x. 5*t*. xiii. 1. Gal. v. 3. Eph. i. 21. iv. 14, 16. Phil. i. 3, 4, 18. ii. 9, 10, 11. iv. 21. Col. i. 10, 15, 28*tr*. 1 Thes. i. 8. 2 Thes. ii. 17. iii. 6, 17. 1 Tim. iv. 4. v. 10. 2 Tim. ii. 21. iv. 18. Tit. i. 16. iii. 1. Phm. 6.
Heb. ii. 2. iii. 4. v. 1. viii. 3. ix. 19. x. 11. xii. 1, 6. xiii. 21. Jas. i. 17*t*, 19. iii. 7, 16. 1 Pet. ii. 13. 1 John iv. 1, 2, 3. Rev. i. 7. v. 9, 13. vi. 14, 15, 15(–G∞LTTr*S*). xiv. 6. xvi. 3, 20. xviii. 2*t*, 17.
every one, Matt. vii. 8, 21, 26. xix. 29[1]. xxv. 29. Mark ix. 49. Luke vi. 40. xi. 4, 10. xviii. 14. xix. 26. John iii. 8, 20. vi. 40. xviii. 37. Rom. i. 16. x. 4. 1 Cor. xvi. 16. Gal. iii. 10, 13. 2 Tim. ii. 19. Heb. v. 13. 1 John ii. 29. iv. 7. v. 1.
every man, Luke vi. 30. xvi. 16. John vi. 45. Rom. ii. 10. xii. 3. 1 Cor. ix. 25. Heb. ii. 9. 1 Pet. iii. 15. 1 John iii. 3. Rev. xxii. 18.
every thing, 1 Cor. i. 5. 2 Cor. viii. 7. ix. 11. Eph. v. 24. Phil. iv. 6. 1 Thes. v. 18.
every c**branch**, John xv. 2.
ἐν παντί, **on every side**, 2 Cor. iv. 8. vii. 5. — **every where**, Phil. iv. 12. — **throughly**, 2 Cor. xi. 6.
any, Matt. xviii. 19. 2 Cor. i. 4. Heb. iv. 12. Rev. vii. 1(*τις* G′LTTr), 16. ix. 4*t*.
any one, Matt. xiii. 19.
any thing, Acts x. 14. Rev. xxi. 27.
With μή[1] *or οὐ*, **no**, Matt. xxiv. 22. Mark xiii. 20. Rom. iii. 20. 1 Cor. i. 29[1]. Gal. ii. 16. Eph. iv. 29[1]. v. 5. Heb. xii. 11. 2 Pet. i. 20. 1 John ii. 21. iii. 15. Rev. xviii. 22. — *οὐ πᾶν ῥῆμα*, **nothing**, Luke i. 37.

whosoever[cc], Matt. v. 22, 28. Luke vi. 47. xii. 8[1], 10[1], 48. xiv. 11, 33[1]. xvi. 18, 18 (-G[oo]LTTr). xx. 18. John iii. 15, 16. iv. 13. viii. 34. xi. 26. xii. 46. xvi. 2. xix. 12. Acts ii. 21[1]. x. 43. Rom. ii. 1. ix. 33(-G[oo] LT*S*). x. 11, 13[1]. 1 John ii. 23. iii. 4, 6*t*, 9, 10, 15. v. 1, 18. 2 John 9. Rev. xxii. 15.

whatsoever[cc], Matt. xv. 17. Rom. xiv. 23[1]. 1 Cor. x. 25, 27. Eph. v. 13. 1 John v. 4. Rev. xviii. 22.

whatsoever thing[cc], Mark vii. 18.

as many as, John xvii. 2[1].

all, Matt. ii. 3. iii. 5*t*, 15. vi. 29. xviii. 32, 34. xxi. 10. xxiii. 27, 35. xxvii. 25, 45. xxviii. 18. Mark i. 5. ii. 13. v. 33. vii. 14 (πάλιν G''LT Tr*S*). ix. 15. xi. 18. Luke ii. 1, 10. iii. 3, 6. iv. 13, 25. vi. 17. vii. 17, 29. viii. 47. ix. 13. x. 19. xii. 27. xiii. 17. xviii. 43. xx. 6 (ἅπας L[m]T Tr*S*), 45. xxi. 38. xxiv. 19. John v. 22. vi. 37, 39. viii. 2(*ap*). xvi. 13. xvii. 2. Acts i. 8, 21. ii. 17, 36. iii. 9, 11. iv. 29. v. 21, 34. vii. 14, 22. viii. 27. x. 2, 41. xi. 14. xii. 11. xiii. 10*tr*, 24, 39[cc]. xv. 12. xvii. 11, 26[cc], 26. xix. 26. xx. 18[cc], 19, 27, 28. xxi. 27. xxii. 5. xxiii. 1. xxiv. 3. xxv. 24 (ἅπας LT*S*). xxvi. 20[cc]. xxvii. 20. xxviii. 31.

Rom. i. 18, 29. iii. 19. iv. 16. ix. 17. x. 18. xi. 26. xv. 13, 14. 1 Cor. i. 5*t*. xiii. 2*t*. xv. 24*t*, 39. 2 Cor. i. 3, 4. vii. 1, 4. viii. 7. ix. 8*t*, 11. x. 6. xii. 12. Gal. v. 14. Eph. i. 3, 8, 21. ii. 21. iii. 19. iv. 2, 19, 31*t*. v. 3, 9. vi. 18*t*. Phil. i. 9, 20. ii. 29. iv. 7, 19. Col. i. 6, 9, 10, 11*t*, 19, 28. ii. 2, 9, 10, 19. iii. 16. iv. 12. 1 Thes. iii. 7, 9. v. 22. 2 Thes. i. 11. ii. 4, 9, 10. iii. 16. 1 Tim. i. 15, 16 (ἅπας LT*S*). ii. 2, 11. iii. 4. iv. 9. v. 2. vi. 1. 2 Tim. iii. 16, 17[cc]. iv. 2. Tit. ii. 10, 14, 15. iii. 2.

Heb. ii. 15. vi. 16. vii. 7. ix. 19*t*. Jas. i. 2, 21. iv. 16. 1 Pet. i. 24*t*. ii. 1*t*, 18. v. 7, 10. 2 Pet. i. 5. 1 John i. 7, 9. ii. 16. v. 17. Jude 3. Rev. v. 6. vii. 4[cc], 9[cc], 17[cc]. viii. 7. xi. 6[cc]. xiii. 7[cc], 12. xviii. 12, 17. xxi. 4[cc].

all things[cc], 2 Cor. vi. 4. vii. 11, 16. xi. 9.

all manner of, Matt. iv. 23*t*. v. 11. x. 1*t*. xii. 31. Luke xi. 42. Rom. vii. 8. 1 Pet. i. 15. Rev. xxi. 19.

all manner, Rev. xviii. 12*t*.

whole, Matt. viii. 32, 34. xiii. 2. Mark iv. 1. Luke i. 10. vi. 19. xxi. 35. Acts vi. 5. xiii. 44. Rom. viii. 22 (*marg.* **every**). Eph. iii. 15. iv. 16.

Not rendered, Matt. vii. 24[2]. x. 32[2]. Col. iii. 17[2], 23[2](-LT*S*). Rev. xxii. 3.

Add Matt. v. 32, πᾶς ὁ ἀπολύων for ὃς ἂν ἀπολύσῃ, G'LTr*S*. Luke iv. 7, πᾶσα for πάντα, GLTTr*S*. xii. 15, for τῆς, G''LTTr*S*. xxi. 4, for ἅπας, LTr*S*. Acts xxii. 30, for ὅλος, GLT *S*. Jude 25 (*ap*).

See also διά, διαπαντός, ἡμέρα, καιρός, οὐδέποτε, τόπος.

2. *Plural*, πάντες, πᾶσαι, πάντα.

all, Matt. i. 17. ii. 4, 16*t*. iv. 8, 9, 24. v. 15, 18. vi. 32, 33. viii. 16. ix. 35. x. 30. xi. 13, 28. xii. 15, 23. xiii. 32, 34, 44[3], 46[3], 51, 56*t*. xiv. 20, 35. xv. 37. xviii. 25[3], 26, 29 (-G[o]L[b]TTr*S*), 31. xix. 20, 27. xxi. 12, 26. xxii. 10[3], 27, 28. xxiii. 3[3], 5, 8, 36. xxiv. 2, 6(-G[o]LTr*S*), 8, 9, 14, 30, 33, 34, 47. xxv. 5, 7, 31, 32. xxvi. 1, 27, 31, 35, 52, 56, 70. xxvii. 1, 22. xxviii. 19.

Mark i. 5, 27 (ἅπας TTr*S*), 32. ii. 12*t*. iii. 28. iv. 13, 31, 32. v. 12 (-GL[b]Tr*S*), 26. vi. 33, 39, 41, 42, 50. vii. 3, 19, 23. ix. 35*t*. x. 20, 28, 44. xi. 17. xii. 22, 28, 29(*ap*), 33, 43, 44[3]. xiii. 4, 10, 30, 37. xiv. 23, 27, 29, 31, 50, 53, 64.

Luke i. 6, 48, 63, 65*t*, 66, 71, 75. ii. 3, 18, 19, 31, 38, 47, 51. iii. 15, 19, 20. iv. 5, 7 (πᾶσα GLTTr*S*), 15, 20, 22, 28, 36, 40[3]. v. 9. vi. 10, 19, 26(-G). vii. 1, 18, 35(-G[o]). viii. 40, 45, 52, 54(*ap*). ix. 1, 7, 17, 23,

43, 48. xi. 50. xii. 7, 18, 30, 31 (–G^{oo}L^{b}TTr*S*), 41, 44. xiii. 2, 3, 4, 5, 17*t*, 27, 28. xiv. 18, 29, 33. xv. 1, 14, 31. xvi. 14, 26. xvii. 10. xviii. 12^{3}, 21, 22^{3}, 28 (*τὰ ἴδια* G′ LT Tr). xix. 37. xx. 32(–G^{o}LTTr*S*), 38. xxi. 3, 15 (*ἅπας* TTr), 24, 29, 32, 35, 36. xxii. 70. xxiii. 48, 49. xxiv. 9*t*, 14, 21, 25, 27*t*, 47.

John i. 16. ii. 15. iii. 31, 31(*ap*). iv. 39^{3}. v. 28. vi. 45. vii. 21. x. 8^{3}, 29. xiii. 10, 11, 18. xv. 21. xvii. 10, 21. xviii. 40.

Acts i. 1, 14, 18, 19. ii. 7(–G^{o}LT, *ἅπας S*), 7 (*ἅπας* LT*S*), 12, 32, 39, 44. iii. 16, 18, 21(*πάντων τῶν* G′, *τῶν* GLT*S*), 24, 25. iv. 10*t*, 16, 24, 33. v. 5, 11, 17, 20, 23, 36^{3}, 37^{3}. vii. 10, 50. viii. 1, 10(–G^{o}T), 40. ix. 14, 21, 26, 35, 39, 40. x. 33, 36, 38, 43, 44. xi. 23. xiii. 22. xiv. 16. xv. 3, 17, 17 (*ap*), 18(*ap*). xvi. 26, 32, 33. xvii. 7, 21, 25, 30, 31. xviii. 2, 17, 23. xix. 7, 10, 17*t*, 34. xx. 25, 26, 32, 36, 37. xxi. 5, 18, 20, 21(–G^{o}L), 24. xxii. 3, 12, 15. xxiv. 5, 8. xxv. 24. xxvi. 3, 4, 14, 29. xxvii. 24, 35, 36, 37, 44. xxviii. 30.

Rom. i. 5, 7, 8. iii. 9, 12, 22, 22(*ap*), 23. iv. 11, 16. v. 12*t*, 18*t*. viii. 32, 37. ix. 5, 6, 7. x. 12*t*, 16. xi. 32*t*. xii. 4, 17 (*τῶν* L), 18. xiii. 7. xiv. 10. xv. 11*t*, 33. xvi. 4, 15, 24(*ap*), 26. 1 Cor. i. 10. iii. 22. vii. 7, 17. viii. 1. ix. 19, 24. x. 1*t*, 2, 3, 4, 11 (–L^{b}T), 17, 31. xii. 6*t*, 11, 12, 13*t*, 19, 26*t*, 29*f*, 30*tr*. xiii. 2, 3. xiv. 5, 18, 23, 24*tr*, 31*tr*, 33. xv. 7, 8, 10, 19, 22*t*, 25, 28*t*, 51*t*. xvi. 20, 24. 2 Cor. i. 1. ii. 3*t*, 5. iii. 2, 18. v. 10, 14(15)*t*, 15. vii. 13, 15. viii. 18. xi. 28. xiii. 2, 13(12), 14(13).

Gal. i. 2. ii. 14. iii. 8, 22, 26, 28. iv. 1, 26(–GL^{b}T*S*). vi. 6. Eph. i. 15, 23*t*. ii. 3. iii. 8, 18, 20, 21. iv. 6*f*, 10, 13. vi. 16*t*, 18, 24. Phil. i. 1, 4, 7*t*, 8, 13, 25. ii. 17, 21, 26. iv. 5, 18, 22, 23 (*τοῦ πνεύματος* LT*S*). Col. i. 4. ii. 3, 13, 22. iii. 8, 11*t*, 14, 17. iv. 7. 1 Thes. i. 2, 7. ii. 15. iii. 13. iv. 6, 10. v. 5, 26, 27. 2 Thes. i. 3, 4, 10. ii. 12 (*ἅπας* L^{m}T *S*). iii. 18. 1 Tim. ii. 1*t*, 2, 4, 6. iv. 10, 15 (*marg.* **all things**). v. 20. vi. 10. 2 Tim. i. 15. iii. 9, 11, 12. iv. 8(–G^{o}), 17, 21. Tit. ii. 11. iii. 2, 15*t*. Phm. 5.

Heb. i. 6, 11, 14. ii. 8, 11. iii. 16. iv. 4. v. 9. vii. 2. viii. 11. ix. 21. xi. 13, 39. xii. 8, 23. xiii. 4, 24*t*, 25. Jas. i. 8. ii. 10. 1 Pet. ii. 1. iii. 8. v. 5, 14. 2 Pet. iii. 9, 11, 16. 1 John ii. 19. 2 John 1. 3 John 12. Jude 15*f*. Rev. i. 7. ii. 23. v. 13. vii. 11. viii. 3. xii. 5. xiii. 8, 16. xiv. 8. xv. 4. xviii. 3, 19, 23, 24. xix. 5, 17, 21. xxi. 8. xxii. 21.

all men, Matt. x. 22. xix. 11. xxvi. 33. Mark i. 37. v. 20. xiii. 13. Luke xxi. 17. John i. 7. ii. 24. iii. 26. v. 23. xi. 48. xii. 32. xiii. 35. Acts i. 24. ii. 45. iv. 21. xix. 19. xxi. 28. Rom. xvi. 19. 1 Cor. ix. 19, 22. x. 33. 2 Cor. ix. 13. Gal. vi. 10. Eph. iii. 9 (–L^{b}*S*). 1 Thes. iii. 12. v. 14, 15. 2 Thes. iii. 2. 2 Tim. ii. 24. iv. 16. Heb. xii. 14. Jas. i. 5. 1 Pet. ii. 17. Rev. xix. 18.

all ^{c}**they,** Mark xii. 44.

all things, Matt. vii. 12^{3}. xi. 27. xi. 27. xiii. 41. xvii. 11. xix. 26. xxi. 22^{3}. xxii. 4. xxiii. 20. xxviii. 20^{3}. Mark iv. 34. vi. 30. vii. 37. ix. 12, 23. x. 27(*ap*). xi. 11. xiii. 23. xiv. 36. Luke i. 3. ii. 20. ix. 43. x. 22. xi. 41. xiv. 17(–L^{b}Tr^{b}*S*). xviii. 31. xxi. 22. xxiv. 44. John i. 3. iii. 35. iv. 25 (*ἅπας* TTr*S*), 29^{3}, 45^{1}. v. 20^{1}. x. 41^{3}. xiii. 3. xiv. 26, 26^{1}. xv. 15^{1}. xvi. 15^{3}, 30. xvii. 7^{3}. xviii. 4. xix. 28. xxi. 17. Acts iii. 21^{1}, 22^{3}. x. 33, 39^{1}. xiii. 39^{1}. xiv. 15. xvii. 22, 24, 25. xx. 35. xxii. 10. xxiv. 14. xxvi. 2^{1}.

Rom. viii. 28, 32. xi. 36. xiv. 2, 20. 1 Cor. ii. 10, 15. iii. 21. iv. 13. vi. 12*tr*. viii. 6*t*. ix. 12, 22, 25. x. 23*f*, 33. xi. 2, 12. xiii. 7*f*. xiv. 26, 40. xv. 27*tr*, 28*t*. xvi. 14. 2 Cor. ii. 9. iv. 15. v. 17(–G^{o}L*S*), 18. vi. 10.

vii. 14(πάντοτε Lm). ix. 8. xi. 6. xii. 19. Gal. iii. 10. Eph. i. 10, 11, 22*t*. iii. 9. iv. 10, 15. v. 13, 20. vi. 21. Phil. ii. 14. iii. 8*t*, 21. iv. 12, 13. Col. i. 16*t*, 17*t*, 18 (*marg.* **all**), 20. iii. 20, 22. iv. 9. 1 Thes. v. 21. 1 Tim. iii. 11. iv. 8. vi. 13, 17. 2 Tim. ii. 7, 10. iv. 5. Tit. i. 15. ii. 7, 9, 10.

Heb. i. 2, 3. ii. 8*t*, 10*t*, 17. iii. 4. iv. 13. viii. 5. ix. 22. xiii. 18. Jas. v. 12. 1 Pet. iv. 7, 8, 11. 2 Pet. i. 3. iii. 4. 1 John ii. 20, 27. iii. 20. 3 John 2. Rev. iv. 11. xviii. 14. xxi. 5, 7 (ταῦτα GLTTr*S*).

τὰ πάντα, **all these things**, Mark iv. 11.

all manner of, Acts x. 12.

διὰ πάντων, **throughout all quarters**, Acts ix. 32.

κατὰ πάντα, **in all points**, Heb. iv. 15.

everycc, Acts xxvi. 11.

every onecc, Luke ix. 43. Acts xvi. 26. xxviii. 2.

every one c**of you**, Mark vii. 14.

every mancc, 1 Cor. viii. 7.

every thingcc, Matt. viii. 33.

Not rendered, Mark xi. 24[3].

Add πάντα for τοῦτο, 1 Cor. ix. 23, G″LT*S*. Jude 5, LT*S*. — Matt. iii. 6 (. . baptized), Lb. Luke xiv. 10 (presence of . .), LTr*S*. John x. 4, for πρόβατα1st, LTTr. xviii. 20, πάντες for πάντοτε2d, GLTTr*S*. Rom. xvi. 16 (. . the churches), GLT*S*. 2 Tim. ii. 22 (with . .), L.

See also αἰών, ἅπας, ἡμέρα.

πάσχα.

passover, Matt. xxvi. 2, 17, 18, 19. Mark xiv. 1, 12*t*, 14, 16. Luke ii. 41. xxii. 1, 7, 8, 11, 13, 15. John ii. 13, 23. vi. 4. xi. 55*t*. xii. 1. xiii. 1. xviii. 28, 39. xix. 14. 1 Cor. v. 7. Heb. xi. 28.

Easter, Acts xii. 4.

πάσχω.

suffer, Matt. xvi. 21. xvii. 12. xxvii. 19. Mark v. 26. viii. 31. ix. 12. Luke ix. 22. xiii. 2. xvii. 25. xxii. 15. xxiv. 26, 46. Acts i. 3. iii. 18. ix. 16. xvii. 3. 1 Cor. xii. 26. 2 Cor. i. 6. Gal. iii. 4. Phil. i. 29. 1 Thes. ii. 14. 2 Thes. i. 5. 2 Tim. i. 12. Heb. ii. 18. v. 8. ix. 26. xiii. 12. 1 Pet. ii. 19, 20, 21, 23[2]. iii. 14, 17, 18 (ἀποθνήσκω G′L*S*). iv. 1p, 1, 15, 19. v. 10p. Rev. ii. 10.

feel, Acts xxviii. 5.

be vexed, Matt. xvii. 15(ἔχω LTr*S*).

πατάσσω.

strike, Matt. xxvi. 51.

smite, Matt. xxvi. 31. Mark xiv. 27. Luke xxii. 49, 50. Acts vii. 24. xii. 7, 23. Rev. xi. 6. xix. 15.

πατέω.

tread down, Luke xxi. 24.

tread under foot, Rev. xi. 2.

tread, Luke x. 19. Rev. xiv. 20. xix. 15.

πατήρ.

father, Matt. ii. 22. iii. 9. iv. 21, 22. viii. 21. x. 21, 35, 37. xv. 4*t*, 5, 6(5). xix. 5, 19, 29(*ap*) xxi. 31. xxiii. 9, 30, 32. Mark i. 20. v. 40. vii. 10*t*, 11, 12. ix. 21, 24. x. 7, 19, 29. xi. 10. xiii. 12. xv. 21.

Luke i. 17, 32, 55, 59, 62, 67, 72, 73. ii. 48. iii. 8. vi. 23, 26. viii. 51. ix. 42, 59. xi. 11, 47, 48. xii. 53*t*. xiv. 26. xv. 12*t*, 17, 18*t*, 20*t*, 21, 22, 27, 28, 29. xvi. 24, 27*t*, 30. xviii. 20.

John iv. 12, 20, 53. vi. 31, 42, 49, 58. vii. 22. viii. 38, 39, 41, 44*tr*, 53, 56. Acts iii. 13, 22(*ap*), 25. v. 30. vii. 2*t*, 4, 11, 12, 14, 15, 19, 20, 32, 38, 39, 44, 45*t*, 51, 52. xiii. 17, 32, 36. xv. 10. xvi. 1, 3. xxii. 1, 14. xxvi. 6. xxviii. 8, 25.

Rom. iv. 1 (προπάτωρ G″L*S*), 11, 12*t*, 16, 17, 18. ix. 5, 10. xi. 28. xv. 8. 1 Cor. iv. 15. v. 1. x. 1. Gal. iv. 2. Eph. v. 31. vi. 2, 4. Phil. ii. 22. Col. iii. 21. 1 Thes. ii. 11. 1 Tim. v. 1. Heb. i. 1. iii. 9. vii. 10. viii. 9. xii. 7, 9. Jas. ii. 21. 2 Pet. iii. 4. 1 John ii. 13, 14.

parent, Heb. xi. 23.

Said of God, **Father**, Matt. v. 16, 45, 48. vi. 1, 4, 6*t*, 8, 9, 14, 15, 18*t*, 26, 32. vii. 11, 21. x. 20, 29, 32, 33. xi. 25, 26, 27*tr*. xii. 50. xiii. 43. xv. 13. xvi. 17, 27. xviii. 10, 14, 19, 35. xx. 23. xxiii. 9. xxiv. 36. xxv. 34. xxvi. 29, 39, 42, 53. xxviii. 19.

Mark viii. 38. xi. 25, 26(*ap*). xiii. 32. xiv. 36. Luke ii. 49. vi. 36. ix. 26. x. 21*t*, 22*tr*. xi. 2, 13. xii. 30, 32. xxii. 29, 42. xxiii. 34(*ap*), 46. xxiv. 49.

John i. 14, 18. ii. 16. iii. 35. iv. 21, 23*t*. v. 17, 18, 19, 20, 21, 22, 23*t*, 26, 30(*omS*), 36*t*, 37, 43, 45. vi. 27, 32, 37, 39(*omS*), 44, 45, 46*t*, 57*t*. viii. 16, 18, 19*tr*, 27, 28, 29 (-G°°LTTr*S*), 38, 41, 42, 49, 54. x. 15*t*, 17, 18, 25, 29*t*, 30, 32, 36, 37, 38. xi. 41. xii. 26, 27, 28, 49, 50. xiii. 1, 3. xiv. 2, 6, 7, 8, 9*t*, 10*tr*, 11*t*, 12, 13, 16, 20, 21, 23, 24, 26, 28*t*, 31*t*. xv. 1, 8, 9, 10, 15, 16, 23, 24, 26*t*. xvi. 3, 10, 15, 16(*ap*), 17, 23, 25, 26, 27, 28*t*, 32. xvii. 1, 5, 11, 21, 24, 25. xviii. 11. xx. 17*tr*, 21. Acts i. 4, 7. ii. 33.

Rom. i. 7. vi. 4. viii. 15. xv. 6. 1 Cor. i. 3. viii. 6. xv. 24. 2 Cor. i. 2, 3*t*. vi. 18. xi. 31. Gal. i. 1, 3, 4. iv. 6. Eph. i. 2, 3, 17. ii. 18. iii. 14. iv. 6. v. 20. vi. 23. Phil. i. 2. ii. 11. iv. 20. Col. i. 2, 3, 12. ii. 2(*ap*). iii. 17. 1 Thes. i. 1, 1(*ap*), 3. iii. 11, 13. 2 Thes. i. 1, 2. ii. 16. 1 Tim. i. 2. 2 Tim. i. 2. Tit. i. 4. Phm. 3.

Heb. i. 5. xii. 9. Jas. i. 17, 27. iii. 9. 1 Pet. i. 2, 3, 17. 2 Pet. i. 17. 1 John i. 2, 3. ii. 1, 13, 15, 16, 22, 23, 24. iii. 1. iv. 14. v. 7(*ap*). 2 John iii. 3*t*, 4, 9. Jude 1. Rev. i. 6. ii. 27. iii. 5, 21. xiv. 1.

Add Matt. xxv. 41(*ap*). Luke ii. 33, *see* Ἰωσήφ. John vi. 40, for πέμπωρ, G″LTTr*S*. x. 38, for αὐτός, G′ LTTr*S*. xvi. 27, for θεός, Tr. Acts iv. 25(*ap*). 1 John ii. 23(*ap*).

πατραλῴας, πατρολῴας LT*S*.
murderer of a father, 1 Tim. i. 9.

πατριά.
lineage, Luke ii. 4.
family, Eph. iii. 15.
kindred, Acts iii. 25.

πατριάρχης.
patriarch, Acts ii. 29. vii. 8, 9. Heb. vii. 4.

πατρικός.
of one's fathers, Gal. i. 14.

πατρίς.
one's own country, Matt. xiii. 54, 57. Mark vi. 1, 4. Luke iv. 24.
country, Luke iv. 23. John iv. 44. Heb. xi. 14.

πατροπαράδοτος.
received by tradition from one's fathers, 1 Pet. i. 18.

πατρῷος.
of one's fathers, Acts xxiv. 14. xxviii. 17.
of the fathers, Acts xxii. 3.

παύω.
Mid., **cease**, Luke viii. 24. xi. 1. Acts v. 42. vi. 13. xiii. 10. xx. 1, 31. 1 Cor. xiii. 8. Eph. i. 16. Col. i. 9. Heb. x. 2. 1 Pet. iv. 1.—**refrain**, 1 Pet. iii. 10. — **leave**, Luke v. 4. Acts xxi. 32.

παχύνω.
Pass., **wax gross**, Matt. xiii. 15. Acts xxviii. 27.

πέδη.
fetter, Mark v. 4*t*. Luke viii. 29.

πεδινός.
With τόπος, **plain**, Luke vi. 17.

πεζεύω.
go afoot, Acts xx. 13.

πεζῇ.
afoot, Mark vi. 33.
on foot, Matt. xiv. 13.

πειθαρχέω.
obey a magistrate, Tit. iii. 1
obey, Acts v. 29, 32.
hearken unto, Acts xxvii. 21.

πειθός.
Plur.°°, **enticing** (*marg.* **persuasible**), 1 Cor. ii. 4 (πειθῷ G″).

πειθώ, persuasion.
1 Cor. ii. 4, *see* πειθός.

πείθω.

I. Present, 1st Aorist, and Future, *transitive*.
persuade, Matt. xxvii. 20. xxviii. 14. Acts xiii. 43. xiv. 19. xviii. 4. xix. 8, 26. xxvi. 28. xxviii. 23. 2 Cor. v. 11. Gal. i. 10.
assure(*Gr.* persuade), 1 John iii. 19.
make one's friend, Acts xii. 20.

II. Perfect and Pluperf., *intransitive*.
trust, Matt. xxvii. 43. Mark x. 24. Luke xi. 22. xviii. 9. 2 Cor. i. 9. x. 7. Phil. ii. 24. Heb. xiii. 18.
put one's trust, Heb. ii. 13(*with* εἰμί).
have whereof one might trust, Phil. iii. 4.
have confidence, 2 Cor. ii. 3. Gal. v. 10. Phil. i. 25. iii. 3. 2 Thes. iii. 4. Phm. 21.
be confident, Rom. ii. 19. Phil. i. 6.
wax confident, Phil. i. 14.

III. Passive and Middle.
be persuaded, Luke xvi. 31. xx. 6. Acts xxi. 14p. xxvi. 26. Rom. viii. 38. xiv. 14. xv. 14. 2 Tim. i. 5, 12. Heb. vi. 9. xi. 13(*omS*).
believe, Acts xvii. 4. xxvii. 11. xxviii. 24.
agree to, Acts v. 40.
yield unto, Acts xxiii. 21.
obey, Acts v. 36 (*marg.* **believe**), 37. Rom. ii. 8. Gal. iii. 1 (*ap*). v. 7. Heb. xiii. 17. Jas. iii. 3.

πεινάω.

to hunger, Matt. v. 6. xxi. 18. Luke iv. 2. vi. 21, 25. John vi. 35. Rom. xii. 20. 1 Cor. iv. 11. xi. 34. Rev. vii. 16.
be hungry, Mark xi. 12. 1 Cor. xi. 21. Phil. iv. 12.
hungry, Luke i. 53p.
be an hungered, Matt. iv. 2. xii. 1, 3. xxv. 35, 37, 42, 44. Mark ii. 25. Luke vi. 3.

πεῖρα.

trial, Heb. xi. 36.
With λαμβάνω, **assay**, Heb. **xi. 29.**

πειράζω.

try, Heb. xi. 17p. Rev. ii. 2, 10. iii. 10.
assay, Acts xvi. 7.
go about, Acts xxiv. 6.
examine, 2 Cor. xiii. 5.
prove, John vi. 6.
tempt, Matt. iv. 1. xvi. 1. xix. 3. xxii. 18, 35. Mark i. 13. viii. 11. x. 2. xii. 15. Luke iv. 2. xi. 16. xx. 23(*ap*). John viii. 6(*ap*). Acts v. 9. xv. 10. 1 Cor. vii. 5. x. 9 (ἐκπειράζω LmS), 13. Gal. vi. 1. 1 Thes. iii. 5. Heb. ii. 18*t*. iii. 9. iv. 15 (πειράω St G″T). xi. 37. Jas. i. 13p, 13*t*, 14.
tempter, Matt. iv. 3p. 1 Thes. iii. 5p.

πειρασμός.

With πρός, **to try**, 1 Pet. iv. 12.
temptation, Matt. vi. 13. xxvi. 41. Mark xiv. 38. Luke iv. 13. viii. 13. xi. 4. xxii. 28, 40, 46. Acts xx. 19. 1 Cor. x. 13*t*. Gal. iv. 14. 1 Tim. vi. 9. Heb. iii. 8. Jas. i. 2, 12. 1 Pet. i. 6. Rev. iii. 10.
temptations, 2 Pet. ii. 9.

πειράω.

to assay, Acts ix. 26.
go about, Acts xxvi. 21.
Add Heb. iv. 15, *see* πειράζω.

πεισμονή.

persuasion, Gal. v. 8.

πέλαγος.

sea, Acts xxvii. 5.
depth, Matt. xviii. 6.

πελεκίζω.

behead, Rev. xx. 4.

πέμπτος.

fifth, Rev. vi. 9. ix. 1. xvi. 10. xxi. 20.

πέμπω.

send, Matt. ii. 8. xi. 2. xiv. 10. xxii. 7. Mark v. 12. Luke iv. 26. vii. 6, 10, 19. xv. 15. xvi. 24, 27. xx. 11, 12, 13. John i. 22, 33. iv. 34. v. 23, 24, 30, 37. vi. 38, 39, 40 (p, πατήρ G″LTTr*S*), 44. vii. 16, 18, 28, 33. **viii. 16, 18, 26, 29. ix.**

4. xii. 44, 45, 49. xiii. 16, 20*t*. xiv. 24, 26. xv. 21, 26. xvi. 5, 7. xx. 21. Acts x. 5, 32, 33. xi. 29. xv. 22, 25. xix. 31. xx. 17. xxiii. 30. xxv. 21 (ἀναπέμπω LT*S*), 25, 27. Rom. viii. 3. 1 Cor. iv. 17. xvi. 3. 2 Cor. ix. 3. Eph. vi. 22. Phil. ii. 19, 23, 25, 28. iv. 16. Col. iv. 8. 1 Thes. iii. 2, 5. 2 Thes. ii. 11. Tit. iii. 12. 1 Pet. ii. 14. Rev. i. 11. xi. 10 (δίδωμι G''). xxii. 16.
thrust in, Rev. xiv. 15, 18.
Add Phm. 12, for ἀναπέμπω, G'.

πένης.

poor, 2 Cor. ix. 9.

πενθερά.

mother-in-law, Matt. x. 35. Luke xii. 53*t*.
wife's mother, Matt. viii. 14. Mark i. 30. Luke iv. 38.

πενθερός.

father-in-law, John xviii. 13.

πενθέω.

mourn, Matt. v. 4. ix. 15. Mark xvi. 10^p(*ap*). Luke vi. 25. 1 Cor. v. 2. Jas. iv. 9. Rev. xviii. 11.
wail, Rev. xviii. 15, 19.
bewail, 2 Cor. xii. 21.

πένθος.

mourning, Jas. iv. 9. Rev. xviii. 8.
sorrow, Rev. xviii. 7*t*. xxi. 4.

πενιχρός.

poor, Luke xxi. 2.

πεντάκις.

five times, 2 Cor. xi. 24.

πεντακισχίλιοι.

five thousand, Matt. xiv. 21. xvi. 9. Mark vi. 44. viii. 19. Luke ix. 14. John vi. 10.

πεντακόσιοι.

five hundred, Luke vii. 41. 1 Cor. xv. 6.

πέντε.

five, Matt. xiv. 17, 19. xvi. 9. xxv. 2*t*, 15, 16*t*, 20*f*. Mark vi. 38, 41. viii. 19. Luke i. 24. ix. 13, 16. xii. 6, 52. xiv. 19. xvi. 28. xix. 18, 19. John iv. 18. v. 2. vi. 9, 13, 19. Acts iv. 4. xx. 6. xxiv. 1. 1 Cor. xiv. 19. Rev. ix. 5, 10. xvii. 10.
See also ἑβδομήκοντα, μυριάς.

πεντεκαιδέκατος.

fifteenth, Luke iii. 1.

πεντήκοντα.

fifty, Luke vii. 41. xvi. 6. John viii. 57. xxi. 11. Acts xiii. 20.
See also ἀνά.

πεντηκοστή.

Pentecost, Acts ii. 1. xx. 16. 1 Cor. xvi. 8.

πέποιθα. See πείθω, II.

πεποίθησις.

trust, 2 Cor. iii. 4.
confidence, 2 Cor. i. 15. viii. 22. x. 2. Eph. iii. 12. Phil. iii. 4.

περ.

An enclitic particle, used for emphasis. *See* ἐάν (b), εἰ, III., ἐπειδήπερ, ἐπείπερ, ἤπερ, καθάπερ, καίπερ, ὅσπερ, ὥσπερ.

περαιτέρω, beyond, further.
Acts xix. 39, for περὶ ἑτέρων, LT.

πέραν.

beyond, Matt. iv. 15, 25. xix. 1. Mark iii. 8. John i. 28. iii. 26. x. 40.
over, John vi. 1, 17. xviii. 1.
on the other side of, John vi. 22, 25.
With art., **the other side**, Matt. viii. 18, 28. xiv. 22. xvi. 5. Mark iv. 35. v. 1, 21. vi. 45 (*marg.* **over**). viii. 13. Luke viii. 22.—**the farther side**, Mark x. 1.

πέρας.

end, Rom. x. 18. Heb. vi. 16.
utmost part, Luke xi. 31.
uttermost part, Matt. xii. 42.

περί.

I. With the Genitive.

about, John iii. 25. Acts xv. 2. xix. 23. xxv. 15, 24. Jude 9.
π. τούτου, **thereabout**, Luke xxiv. 4.
concerning, Matt. iv. 6. xi. 7. xvi.

11. Mark v. 16. vii. 17(-G″LTTr S). Luke ii. 17. vii. 24. xxiv. 19, 44. John vii. 12, 32. ix. 18. xi. 19. Acts i. 16. xix. 39 (*see* περαιτέρω). xxi. 24. xxii. 18. xxiii. 15. xxiv. 24. xxv. 16. xxviii. 21. Rom. i. 3. 1 Cor. vii. 25. xii. 1. xvi. 1. 1 Thes. iii. 2 (ὑπέρ GLTS). iv. 13. Heb. vii. 14. xi. 20, 22. 1 John ii. 26.

as concerning, Acts xxviii. 22. 1 Cor. viii. 4.

With art., **the things concerning,** Luke xxii. 37. xxiv. 27. Acts viii. 12. xix. 8. — **those things which concern,** Acts xxviii. 31. — **concerning,** Acts xxviii. 23. — **the things pertaining to,** Acts i. 3. — **one's affairs,** Eph. vi. 22. Phil. i. 27. — **one's state,** Phil. ii. 19, 20. — **one's estate,** Col. iv. 8. — **for,** Acts xxiv. 10. — **of,** Acts xxviii. 15.

of, Matt. xi. 10. xv. 7. xvii. 13. xxi. 45. xxii. 42. xxiv. 36. xxvi. 24. Mark i. 30. v. 27. vii. 6, 25. viii. 30. x. 10. xiii. 32. xiv. 21. Luke i. 1. ii. 33, 38. iii. 15. iv. 14, 37. v. 15. vii. 3, 17, 18, 27. ix. 9, 11, 45. xi. 53. xiii. 1. xvi. 2. xxi. 5. xxiii. 8. xxiv. 14.

John i. 7, 8, 15, 22, 30 (ὑπέρ LTTr S), 47(48). ii. 21, 25. v. 31, 32*t*, 36, 37, 39, 46. vii. 7, 13, 17, 39. viii. 13, 14, 18*t*, 26, 46. ix. 17. x. 25, 41. xi. 13*t*. xii. 41. xiii. 18, 22, 24. xv. 26. xvi. 8*tr*, 9, 10, 11, 19, 25. xviii. 19*t*, 23, 34. xxi. 24. Acts i. 1. ii. 29, 31. v. 24. vii. 52. viii. 34*tr*. ix. 13. xi. 22. xiii. 29. xv. 6. xvii. 32. xviii. 15, 25. xxi. 21. xxii. 10. xxiii. 6, 11, 20, 29. xxiv. 8, 22, 25. xxv. 9, 19*t*, 20, 26. xxvi. 26. xxviii. 21.

Rom. xiv. 12. xv. 14, 21. 1 Cor. i. 11. 2 Cor. x. 8. 1 Thes. i. 9. iv. 6. v. 1. 2 Tim. i. 3. Tit. ii. 8. Heb. iv. 4, 8. v. 11. vi. 9. ix. 5. x. 7. xi. 7, 22 (*see* μνημονεύω), 32. 1 Pet. i. 10*t*. iii. 15. 2 Pet. i. 12. iii. 16. 1 John i. 1. ii. 27. v. 9, 10. Jude 3, 15*t*.

περὶ αὐτοῦ, **thereof,** Matt. xii. 36.

περὶ τίνων, **whereof,** 1 Tim. i. 7.

περὶ οὗ (ἧς, ὧν), **whereof,** Acts xxiv. 13. 1 Cor. vii. 1. Heb. ii. 5. — **whereby,** Acts xix. 40. — **wherein,** Luke i. 4.

for, Matt. ii. 8. vi. 28. xxii. 16. xxvi. 28. Mark i. 44. xii. 14. xiv. 24 (ὑπέρ LTTrS). Luke ii. 27. iii. 19*t*. iv. 38. v. 14. xii. 26. xix. 37. xxii. 32. John ix. 21. x. 13, 33*t*. xii. 6. xv. 22. xvi. 26. xvii. 9*tr*, 20*t*. xix. 24. Acts viii. 15. xix. 40. xxiv. 21. Rom. viii. 3 (*marg.* **by a sacrifice for**). Eph. vi. 18. Col. i. 3 (ὑπέρ G′L). ii. 1 (ὑπέρ LS). iv. 3. 1 Thes. i. 2. iii. 9. v. 25. 2 Thes. i. 3, 11. ii. 13. iii. 1. Phm. 10. Heb. v. 3*t*. x. 6, 8, 18, 26. xi. 40. xiii. 11(-T), 18. 1 Pet. iii. 18. v. 7. 1 John ii. 2*t*. iv. 10. v. 16.

for . . sake, Acts xxvi. 7.

for the sins of°, 1 John ii. 2.

on . . behalf, 1 Cor. i. 4.

on, Matt. ix. 36. Acts x. 19.

touching, Acts xxiv. 21. xxvi. 2. Col. iv. 10.

as touching, Matt. xviii. 19. xxii. 31. Mark xii. 26. Acts xxi. 25. 1 Cor. viii. 1. xvi. 12. 2 Cor. ix. 1. 1 Thes. iv. 9.

at, Luke ii. 18. John vi. 41, 61.

with, Mark x. 41.

against, Matt. xx. 24. Acts xxv. 18.

over, Luke iv. 10. 1 Cor. vii. 37.

above, 3 John 2.

Not rendered, Luke ii. 17. Tit. iii. 8.

Add, for ὑπέρ, Luke vi. 28, TS. Acts xii. 5, xxvi. 1, G″LTS. Rom. i. 8, G′LTS. 1 Cor. i. 13, L. 2 Cor. i. 8, G′LS. Gal. i. 4, GLTS. Heb. v. 3, G′LTS. — Matt. xix. 17 (*ap*). Acts xix. 40 (of), LS.

See also ζήτησις.

II. With the Accusative.

about, Matt. iii. 4. viii. 18. xx. 3, 5, 6, 9. xxvii. 46. Mark i. 6. iii. 8, 32, 34(-G°). vi. 48. ix. 14, 42.

Luke x. 40, 41. xiii. 8. xvii. 2. Acts x. 9. xxii. 6*t*. 1 Tim. vi. 4. Jude 7.
With art., **they about**, Mark iii. 8. — **they that (which) were**[c] **about**, Mark iv. 10. Luke xxii. 49. — **how it will go with**, Phil. ii. 23.
οἱ περὶ τὸν Παῦλον, **we that were**[c] **of Paul's company**, Acts xxi. 8(*ap*). — **P. and his company**, Acts xiii. 13.
concerning, 1 Tim. i. 19. vi. 21. 2 Tim. ii. 18. iii. 8.
in, Tit. ii. 7.
of, Mark iv. 19.
Not rendered, John xi. 19(-LTr*S*).
Add Matt. xviii. 6, for ἐπί, LTr*S*. Acts x. 3 (about . .), L*S*.
See also περιζώννυμι, τοιοῦτος, τόπος.

περιάγω.

lead about, 1 Cor. ix. 5.
go about, Matt. iv. 23. ix. 35. Acts xiii. 11.
go round about, Mark vi. 6.
compass, Matt. xxiii. 15.

περαιρέω.

take away, Acts xxvii. 20. 2 Cor. iii. 16. Heb. x. 11.
In navigation, **take up** (*marg.* **cut**), Acts xxvii. 40[p].

περιάπτω, put around, apply. Luke xxii. 55, for ἅπτω, TTr*S*.

περιαστράπτω.

shine round, Acts xxii. 6.
shine round about, Acts ix. 3.

περιβάλλω.

cast about, Luke xix. 43.
put on, John xix. 2.
clothe, Matt. xxv. 36, 38, 43.
array in, Luke xxiii. 11.
Mid. or Pass., **cast about**, Acts xii. 8. — **have . . cast about**, Mark xiv. 51. — **be clothed(in**[1]**, with**[2]**,** τί, **wherewithal**[3]**)**, Matt. vi. 31[3]. Mark xvi. 5[1]. Rev. iii. 5, 18. iv. 4. vii. 9[2]. x. 1[2]. xi. 3[1]. xii. 1[2]. xviii. 16[1]. xix. 13[2]. — **be arrayed (in**[1]**)**, Matt. vi. 29. Luke xii. 27. Rev. vii. 13[1]. xvii. 4. xix. 8[1].

περιβλέπω.

Mid., **look round about**, Mark v. 32. ix. 8[p]. x. 23. — **look about on**, Mark iii. 34. — **look round about on (upon)**, Mark iii. 5. xi. 11[p]. Luke vi. 10.

περιβόλαιον.

vesture, Heb. i. 12.
covering (*marg.* **veil**), 1 Cor. xi. 15.

περιδέω.

bind about, John xi. 44.

περιδρέμω. See περιτρέχω.

περιεργάζομαι.

be a busy-body, 2 Thes. iii. 11.

περίεργος.

busy-body, 1 Tim. v. 13.
τὰ περ., **curious arts**, Acts xix. 19.

περιέρχομαι.

wander about, 1 Tim. v. 13. Heb. xi. 37.
vagabond, Acts xix. 13[p].
fetch a compass, Acts xxviii. 13.

περιέχω.

be contained, 1 Pet. ii. 6 (*see* ἐν).
after, Acts xxiii. 25[p] (ἔχω L*S*).
See also θάμβος.

περιζώννυμι.

Mid. or Pass, **gird one's self**, Luke xii. 37. xvii. 8. Acts xii. 8 (ζώννυμι G″LT*S*). — **have . . girt about**, Eph. vi. 14. — **be girded about**, Luke xii. 35. — **be girt**, Rev. i. 13. — *With* περί, **have . . girded**, Rev. xv. 6.

περίθεσις.

wearing, 1 Pet. iii. 3.

περιΐστημι.

stand round about, Acts xxv. 7.
stand by, John xi. 42.
Mid., **avoid**, Tit. iii. 9. — **shun**, 2 Tim. ii. 16.

περικάθαρμα.

filth, 1 Cor. iv. 13.

περικαθίζω, set down around. Luke xxii. 55, for συγκαθίζω, L.

περικαλύπτω.

to cover, Mark xiv. 65.
overlay, Heb. ix. 4.
blindfold, Luke xxii. 64[p].

περίκειμαι.

be hanged about, Mark ix. 42. Luke xvii. 2.

be compassed with, Heb. v. 2.

With ἔχω, **be compassed about with**, Heb. xii. 1p.

be bound with, Acts xxviii. 20.

περικεφαλαία

helmet, Eph. vi. 17. 1 Thes. v. 8.

περικρατής.

Lit. strong over, master of. *With* γίνομαι, **to come by**, Acts xxvii. 16.

περικρύπτω.

hide, Luke i. 24.

περικυκλόω.

compass round, Luke xix. 43.

περιλάμπω.

shine round about, Luke ii. 9. Acts xxvi. 13.

περιλείπω.

Pass., **remain**, 1 Thes. iv. 15, 17.

περίλυπος.

exceeding sorrowful, Matt. xxvi. 38. Mark xiv. 34.

exceeding sorry, Mark vi. 26.

very sorrowful, Luke xviii. 23, 24 (-TTrbS).

περιμένω.

wait for, Acts i. 4.

πέριξ.

round about, Acts v. 16.

περιοικέω.

dwell round about, Luke i. 65.

περίοικος.

neighbor, Luke i. 58.

περιούσιος.

peculiar, Tit. ii. 14.

περιοχή.

place, Acts viii. 32.

περιπατέω.

walk about, 1 Pet. v. 8.

walk, Matt. iv. 18. ix. 5. xi. 5. xiv. 25, 26, 29. xv. 31. Mark i. 16p (παράγω G″LTTrS). ii. 9. v. 42. vi. 48, 49. vii. 5. viii. 24. xvi. 12p(ap). Luke v. 23. vii. 22. xi. 44. xx. 46. xxiv. 17p. John i. 36p. v. 8, 9, 11, 12. vi. 19, 66. vii. 1t. viii. 12. x. 23. xi. 9, 10, 54. xii. 35t. xxi. 18. Acts iii. 6, 8t, 9, 12. xiv. 8, 10. xxi. 21.

Rom. vi. 4. viii. 1(ap), 4. xiii. 13. xiv. 15. 1 Cor. iii. 3. vii. 17. 2 Cor. iv. 2. v. 7. x. 2p, 3p. xii. 18. Gal. v. 16. Eph. ii. 2, 10. iv. 1, 17t. v. 2, 8, 15. Phil. iii. 17, 18. Col. i. 10. ii. 6. iii. 7. iv. 5. 1 Thes. ii. 12. iv. 1, 12. 2 Thes. iii. 6, 11. 1 John i. 6, 7. ii. 6t, 11. 2 John 4, 6t. 3 John 3, 4. Rev. ii. 1. iii. 4. ix. 20. xvi. 15. xxi. 24.

be walking, Mark xi. 27p.

be occupied, Heb. xiii. 9.

go, Mark xii. 38.

Add 1 Thes. iv. 1 (*ap*).

περιπείρω.

pierce through, 1 Tim. vi. 10.

περιπίπτω.

fall into, Acts xxvii. 41. Jas. i. 2.

fall among, Luke x. 30.

περιποιέω.

Mid., **purchase**, Acts xx. 28. 1 Tim. iii. 13. — *Add* Luke xvii. 33, for σώζω, TTr.

περιποίησις.

obtaining, 2 Thes. ii. 14.

With εἰς, **to obtain**, 1 Thes. v. 9. — **peculiar** (*marg.* **purchased**), 1 Pet. ii. 9.

purchased possession, Eph. i. 14.

saving, Heb. x. 39.

περιρρήγνυμι.

rend off, Acts xvi. 22.

περισπάω.

cumber, Luke x. 40.

περισσεία.

superfluity, Jas. i. 21.

abundance, Rom. v. 17. 2 Cor. viii. 2. — εἰς π., **abundantly**, 2 Cor. x. 15.

περίσσευμα.

abundance, Matt. xii. 34. Luke vi. 45. 2 Cor. viii. 14(13)t.

that wasc left, Mark viii. 8.

περισσεύω.

remain over and above, John vi. 13.
remain, Matt. xiv. 20. Luke ix. 17. John vi. 12.
be left, Matt. xv. 37.
redound, 2 Cor. iv. 15.
exceed, Matt. v. 20 (*with* πλεῖον). 2 Cor. iii. 9.
excel, 1 Cor. xiv. 12.
be the better (*marg.* **have the more**), 1 Cor. viii. 8.
abound, Rom. v. 15. xv. 13. 1 Cor. xv. 58. 2 Cor. i. 5*t.* viii. 2, 7*t.* ix. 8. Eph. i. 8. Phil. i. 9. iv. 12*t*, 18. Col. ii. 7.
abound more, Rom. iii. 7.
abundant, 2 Cor. ix. 12p.
abundance, Mark xii. 44p. Luke xii. 15inf. xxi. 4p.
be more abundant, Phil. i. 26.
With μᾶλλον, **abound more and more,** 1 Thes. iv. 1. — **increase more and more,** 1 Thes. iv. 10.
increase, Acts xvi. 5.
make abound, 2 Cor. ix. 8. 1 Thes. iii. 12.
have enough and to spare, Luke xv. 17 (*pass.* T).
Pass., **have abundance,** Matt. xxv. 29. — **have more abundance,** Matt. xiii. 12.

περισσός, περισσόν.

superfluous, 2 Cor. ix. 1.
more, Matt. v. 37, 47.
With ἐκ, **beyond measure,** Mark vi. 51 (-GoTrbS). — **vehemently,** Mark xiv. 31 (ἐκπερισσῶς G″LTTrS).
ὑπὲρ ἐκ περισσοῦ, **exceeding abundantly above,** Eph. iii. 20. — **exceedingly,** 1 Thes. iii. 10. — **very highly,** 1 Thes. v. 13 (*see* ὑπέρ, III).
more abundantly, John x. 10.
advantage, Rom. iii. 1.

Comp., περισσότερος, -ον.

more abundant, 1 Cor. xii. 23*t*, 24.
more abundantly, 1 Cor. xv. 10. Heb. vi. 17.
μᾶλλον π., **so much the more a great deal,** Mark vii. 36.
far more, Heb. vii. 15.
much more, Luke vii. 26.
the more, Luke xii. 48.
more, Matt. xi. 9. Luke xii. 4 (περισσόν L). 2 Cor. x. 8.
overmuch, 2 Cor. ii. 7.
greater, Matt. xxiii. 14 (13, *ap*). Mark xii. 40. Luke xx. 47.
Add Mark xii. 33, for πλεῖον, TrS.

περισσῶς.

exceedingly, Acts xxvi. 11.
out of measure, Mark x. 26.
the more, Matt. xxvii. 23.

Comp., περισσοτέρως.

the more exceedingly, Mark xv. 14 (περισσῶς GLTrS).
more exceedingly, Gal. i. 14.
exceedingly, 2 Cor. vii. 13.
the more abundantly, 2 Cor. xii. 15. 1 Thes. ii. 17.
more abundantly, 2 Cor. i. 12. ii. 4.
more abundant, 2 Cor. vii. 15. xi. 23.
much more, Phil. i. 14.
With προσέχω, **give the more earnest heed to,** Heb. ii. 1.
the rather, Heb. xiii. 19.
more frequent, 2 Cor. xi. 23.

περιστερά.

dove, Matt. iii. 16. x. 16. xxi. 12. Mark i. 10. xi. 15. Luke iii. 22. John i. 32. ii. 14, 16.
pigeon, Luke ii. 24.

περιτέμνω.

circumcise, Luke i. 59. John vii. 22. Acts vii. 8. xv. 1, 5, 24(*ap*). xvi. 3. xxi. 21. 1 Cor. vii. 18*t.* Gal. ii. 3. v. 2, 3. vi. 12, 13. Col. ii. 11.
*Pass.*cc, **have . . circumcised,** Gal. vi. 13.
Inf., **circumcising,** Luke ii. 21.

περιτίθημι.

set about, Mark xii. 1.
put about, Mark xv. 17.
put on (upon), Matt. xxvii. 28, 48. Mark xv. 36. John xix. 29.
bestow upon (*marg.* **put on**), 1 Cor. xii. 23.
See also φραγμός.

περιτομή.
circumcision, John vii. 22, 23. Acts vii. 8. x. 45. xi. 2. Rom. ii. 25*t*, 26, 27, 28, 29. iii. 1, 30. iv. 9, 10*t*, 11, 12*t*. xv. 8. 1 Cor. vii. 19. Gal. ii. 7, 8, 9, 12. v. 6, 11. vi. 15. Eph. ii. 11. Phil. iii. 3. Col. ii. 11*t*. iii. 11. iv. 11. Tit. i. 10.
Dat., **circumcised,** Phil. iii. 5.

περιτρέπω.
Lit. **turn about, pervert.** *With* εἰς μανίαν, **make mad,** Acts xxvi. 24.

περιτρέχω.
run through, Mark vi. 55.

περιφέρω.
bear about, 2 Cor. iv. 10.
carry about, Mark vi. 55. Eph. iv. 14. Heb. xiii. 9 and Jude 12 (παραφέρω GLT*S*).

περιφρονέω.
despise, Tit. ii. 15.

περίχωρος.
With γῆ *understood,* **region that lieth round about,** Acts xiv. 6.—**region round about,** Matt. iii. 5. Mark i. 28. vi. 55 (χώρα L[m]TTr*S*). Luke iv. 14. vii. 17.—**country about,** Luke iii. 3.—**country round about,** Matt. xiv. 35. Luke iv. 37. viii. 37.

περίψημα.
offscouring, 1 Cor. iv. 13.

περπερεύομαι.
vaunt one's self (*marg.* **be rash**), 1 Cor. xiii. 4.

πέρυσι.
With ἀπό, **a year ago,** 2 Cor. viii. 10. ix. 2.

πετάομαι, πέτομαι GLTTr*S*.
to fly, Rev. iv. 7. viii. 13. xiv. 6. xix. 17.

πετεινόν.
bird, Matt. viii. 20. xiii. 32. Luke ix. 58. Rom. i. 23. Jas. iii. 7.
fowl, Matt. vi. 26. xiii. 4. Mark iv. 4, 32. Luke viii. 5. xii. 24. xiii. 19. Acts x. 12. xi. 6.

πέτομαι.
to fly, Rev. xii. 14.
See also πετάομαι.

πέτρα.
rock, Matt. vii. 24, 25. xvi. 18. xxvii. 51, 60. Mark xv. 46. Luke vi. 48, 48(*ap*). viii. 6, 13. Rom. ix. 33. 1 Pet. ii. 8(7). Rev. vi. 15, 16.
Said of Christ, **Rock,** 1 Cor. x. 4*t*.

Πέτρος.
stone (*marg.* **Peter**), John i. 42(43).

πετρώδης.
τὰ π., **stony places,** Matt. xiii. 5, 20.
τὸ *or* τὰ π., **stony ground,** Mark iv. 5, 16.

πήγανον.
rue, Luke xi. 42.

πηγή.
fountain, Mark v. 29. Jas. iii. 11, 12(*ap*). Rev. vii. 17. viii. 10. xiv. 7. xvi. 4. xxi. 6.
well, John iv. 6*t*, 14. 2 Pet. ii. 17.

πήγνυμι.
to pitch, Heb. viii. 2.

πηδάλιον.
helm, Jas. iii. 4.
rudder, *adj.*, Acts xxvii. 40.

πηλίκος.
how great, Heb. vii. 4.
how large, Gal. vi. 11.

πηλός.
clay, John ix. 6*t*, 11, 14, 15. Rom. ix. 21.

πήρα.
scrip, Matt. x. 10. Mark vi. 8. Luke ix. 3. x. 4. xxii. 35, 36.

πῆχυς.
cubit, Matt. vi. 27. Luke xii. 25. John xxi. 8. Rev. xxi. 17.

πιάζω.
take, John vii. 30, 32, 44. x. 39. xi. 57. Acts iii. 7. Rev. xix. 20.
lay hands on, John viii. 20.
apprehend, Acts xii. 4[p]. 2 Cor. xi. 32.
catch, John xxi. 3, 10.

πιέζω.

press down, Luke vi. 38.

πιθανολογία.

enticing words, Col. ii. 4.

πικραίνω.

make bitter, Rev. viii. 11. x. 9.
Pass., **be bitter,** Col. iii. 19. Rev. x. 10.

πικρία.

bitterness, Acts viii. 23. Rom. iii. 14. Eph. iv. 31. Heb. xii. 15.

πικρός.

bitter, Jas. iii. 11, 14.

πικρῶς.

bitterly, Matt. xxvi. 75. Luke xxii. 62.

πίμπλημι, πλήθω.

fill, Matt. xxvii. 48. Luke i. 15, 41, 67. iv. 28. v. 7, 26. vi. 11. John xix. 29(*ap*). Acts ii. 4. iii. 10. iv. 8, 31. v. 17. ix. 17. xiii. 9, 45. xix. 29.
Pass., *with* χρόνος, **full time cometh,** Luke i. 57.
accomplish, Luke i. 23. ii. 6, 21, 22.
furnish, Matt. xxii. 10.
Add, for πληρόω, Luke i. 20, G'. xxi. 22, GLTTr*S*.

πίμπρημι.

Pass., **swell,** Acts xxviii. 6.

πινακίδιον.

writing-table, Luke i. 63.

πίναξ.

platter, Luke xi. 39.
charger, Matt. xiv. 8, 11. Mark vi. 25, 28.
Add Mark vi. 27 (to be brought ἐπὶ πίνακι), L[b].

πίνω.

to drink, Matt. vi. 25 (-G∞*S*), 31. xi. 18, 19. xxiv. 38, 49. xxvi. 27, 29*t*, 42. xxvii. 34*t*. Mark ii. 16(-L[b] *S*). xiv. 23, 25*t*. xv. 23(-TTr*S*). xvi. 18(*ap*). Luke i. 15. v. 30, 33, 39. vii. 33, 34. x. 7. xii. 19, 29, 45. xiii. 26. xvii. 8*t*, 27, 28. xxii. 18, 30. John iv. 7, 9, 10, 12, 13, 14. vi. 53, 54, 56. vii. 37. xviii. 11. Acts ix. 9. xxiii. 12, 21. Rom. xiv. 21. 1 Cor. ix. 4. x. 4*t*, 7, 21, 31. xi. 22, 25, 26, 27, 28, 29*t*. xv. 32. Heb. vi. 7. Rev. xiv. 10. xvi. 6. xviii. 3.
drink of, Matt. xx. 22*t*, 23. Mark x. 38*t*, 39*t*.

πιότης.

fatness, Rom. xi. 17.

πιπράσκω.

sell, Matt. xiii. 46. xviii. 25. xxvi. 9. Mark xiv. 5. John xii. 5. Acts ii. 45. iv. 34. v. 4[p]. Rom. vii. 14.

πίπτω.

to fall, Matt. vii. 25, 27. x. 29. xiii. 4, 5, 7, 8. xv. 14, 27. xvii. 6, 15. xxi. 44*t*(*ap*). xxiv. 29. xxvi. 39. Mark iv. 4, 5, 7, 8. v. 22. ix. 20. xiv. 35. Luke v. 12. vi. 39 (ἐμπίπτω LTTr), 49 (συμπίπτω TTr*S*). viii. 5, 6 (καταπίπτω TTr), 7, 8, 14. x. 18. xi. 17. xiii. 4. xvi. 21. xx. 18*t*. xxi. 24. xxiii. 30. John xii. 24. xviii. 6. Acts i. 26. ix. 4. xxii. 7. xxvii. 34 (ἀπόλλυμι GLT*S*).
Rom. xi. 11, 22. xiv. 4. 1 Cor. x. 8, 12. Heb. iii. 17. iv. 11. Jas. v. 12. Rev. i. 17. vi. 13, 16. vii. 11. viii. 10*t*. ix. 1. xi. 11 (ἐπιπίπτω G'' LTTr), 13, 16. xiv. 8, 8 (-Tr*S*[o]). xvi. 19. xvii. 10. xviii. 2, 2 (-Tr[b] *S*). xix. 10.
fall down, Matt. ii. 11. iv. 9. xviii. 26, 29. Luke viii. 41. xvii. 16. John xi. 32. Acts v. 5, 10. x. 25. xv. 16. xx. 9. 1 Cor. xiv. 25. Heb. xi. 30. Rev. iv. 10. v. 8, 14. xix. 4. xxii. 8.
light, Rev. vii. 16.
fail, Luke xvi. 17.
Add, for ἐκπίπτω, Mark xiii. 25, L TTr*S*. Rev. ii. 5, GLT*S*. For ἐμπίπτω, Luke xiv. 5, LTr*S*. For ἐπιπίπτω, Acts x. 44, L. xii. 11, L*S*. xix. 17, L. 1 Cor. xiii. 8, L.

πιστεύω.

believe, Matt. viii. 13. ix. 28. xviii. 6. xxi. 22, 25, 32*tr*. xxiv. 23, 26. xxvii. 42. Mark v. 36. ix. 23(-G[o]

TTrS), 23, 24, 42 (πίστιν ἔχω T). xi. 23, 24, 31. xiii. 21. xv. 32. xvi. 13 (*ap*), 14 (*ap*), 16 (*ap*), 17 (*ap*). Luke i. 20, 45. viii. 12, 13, 50. xx. 5. xxii. 67.

John i. 7, 12, 50(51). ii. 11, 22, 23. iii. 12*t*, 15, 16, 18*tr*, 36. iv. 21, 39, 41, 42, 48, 50, 53. v. 24, 38, 44, 46*t*, 47*t*. vi. 29, 30, 35, 36, 40, 47, 64*t*, 69. vii. 5, 31, 38, 39, 48. viii. 24, 30, 31, 45, 46. ix. 18, 35, 36, 38. x. 25, 26, 37, 38*t*, 38 (γινώσκητε LT Tr), 42. xi. 15, 25, 26*t*, 27, 40, 42, 45, 48. xii. 11, 36, 37, 38, 39, 42, 44*t*, 46, 47 (φυλάσσω G''LTTrS). xiii. 19. xiv. 1*t*, 10, 11*t*, 12, 29. xvi. 9, 27, 30, 31. xvii. 8, 20, 21. xix. 35. xx. 8, 25, 29*t*, 31*t*.

Acts ii. 44. iv. 4, 32. viii. 12, 13, 37*t* (*ap*). ix. 26, 42. x. 43. xi. 17, 21. xiii. 12, 39, 41, 48. xiv. 1, 23. xv. 5, 7, 11. xvi. 31, 34. xvii. 12, 34. xviii. 8*t*, 27. xix. 2p, 4, 18. xxi. 20, 25. xxii. 19. xxiv. 14. xxvi. 27*t*. xxvii. 25.

Rom. i. 16. iii. 22. iv. 3, 5, 11, 17, 18, 24p. vi. 8. ix. 33. x. 4, 9, 10cc, 11, 14*t*, 16. xiii. 11. xiv. 2. 1 Cor. i. 21. iii. 5. xi. 18. xiii. 7. xiv. 22*t*. xv. 2, 11. 2 Cor. iv. 13*t*. Gal. ii. 16. iii. 6, 22. Eph. i. 13p, 19. Phil. i. 29. 1 Thes. i. 7. ii. 10, 13. iv. 14. 2 Thes. i. 10*t*. ii. 11, 12. 1 Tim. i. 16. iii. 16. 2 Tim. i. 12 (*marg.* **trust**). Tit. iii. 8. Heb. iv. 3. xi. 6. Jas. ii. 19*t*, 23. 1 Pet. i. 8, 21 (p, πιστός LT). ii. 6, 7. 1 John iii. 23. iv. 1, 16. v. 1, 5, 10*t*, 13 (*ap*). Jude 5.

With εἰς, 1 John v. 10, ἐν, Mark i. 15, ἐπί, Luke xxiv. 25, **believe.**

Inf., **believing,** Rom. xv. 13.

believer, Acts v. 14p.

Pass., **be put in trust with,** 1 Thes. ii. 4. — *With* ἐγώ, **be committed to my trust,** 1 Tim. i. 11. — **be committed unto me,** Tit. i. 3.

commit to one's trust, Luke xvi. 11.

commit unto, John ii. 24. Rom. iii. 2cc. 1 Cor. ix. 17cc. Gal. ii. 7cc.

πιστικός.

Lit. true, genuine. *See* νάρδος.

πίστις.

faith, Matt. viii. 10. ix. 2, 22, 29. xv. 28. xvii. 20. xxi. 21. xxiii. 23. Mark ii. 5. iv. 40. v. 34. x. 52. xi. 22. Luke v. 20. vii. 9, 50. viii. 25, 48. xvii. 5, 6, 19. xviii. 8, 42. xxii. 32. Acts iii. 16*t*. vi. 5, 7, 8 (χάρις GLTS). xi. 24. xiii. 8. xiv. 9, 22, 27. xv. 9. xvi. 5. xx. 21. xxiv. 24. xxvi. 18.

Rom. i. 5, 8, 12, 17*tr*. iii. 3, 22, 25, 27, 28, 30*t*, 31. iv. 5, 9, 11, 12, 13, 14, 16*t*, 19, 20. v. 1, 2(–G°L^{b}T). ix. 30, 32. x. 6, 8, 17. xi. 20. xii. 3, 6. xiv. 1, 2, 23*t*. xvi. 26. 1 Cor. ii. 5. xii. 9. xiii. 2, 13. xv. 14, 17. xvi. 13. 2 Cor. i. 24*t*. iv. 13. v. 7, viii. 7. x. 15. xiii. 5.

Gal. i. 23. ii. 16*t*, 20. iii. 2, 5, 7, 8, 9, 11, 12, 14, 22, 23*t*, 24, 25, 26. v. 5, 6, 22. vi. 10. Eph. i. 15. ii. 8. iii. 12, 17. iv. 5, 13. vi. 16, 23. Phil. i. 25, 27. ii. 17. iii. 9*t*. Col. i. 4, 23. ii. 5, 7, 12. 1 Thes. i. 3, 8. iii. 2, 5, 6, 7, 10. v. 8. 2 Thes. i. 3, 4, 11. iii. 2. 1 Tim. i. 2, 4, 5, 14, 19*t*. ii. 7, 15. iii. 9, 13. iv. 1, 6, 12. v. 8, 12. vi. 10, 11, 12, 21. 2 Tim. i. 5, 13. ii. 18, 22. iii. 8, 10, 15. iv. 7. Tit. i. 1, 4, 13. ii. 2. iii. 15. Phm. 5, 6.

Heb. iv. 2. vi. 1, 12. x. 22, 38. xi. 1, 3, 4, 5, 6, 7*t*, 8, 9, 11, 13, 17, 20, 21, 22, 23, 24, 27, 28, 29, 30, 31, 33, 39. xii. 2. xiii. 7. Jas. i. 3, 6. ii. 1, 5, 14*t*, 17, 18*tr*, 20, 22*t*, 24, 26. v. 15. 1 Pet. i. 5, 7, 9, 21. v. 9. 2 Pet. i. 1, 5. 1 John v. 4. Jude 3, 20. Rev. ii. 13, 19. xiii. 10. xiv. 12.

belief, 2 Thes. ii. 13.

Gen., **of them that believe,** Heb. x. 39. — ὁ ἐκ πίστεως, **he which believeth,** Rom. iii. 26.

fidelity, Tit. ii. 10.

assurance (*marg.* **faith**), Acts xvii. 31.

Add Mark ix. 42, *see* πιστεύω. Eph. iv. 29, for χρεία, G'.

πιστός.

faithful, Matt. xxiv. 45. xxv. 21*t*,

23*t*. Luke xii. 42. xvi. 10*t*, 11, 12. xix. 17. Acts xvi. 15. 1 Cor. i. 9. iv. 2, 17. vii. 25. x 13. Gal. iii. 9. Eph. i. 1. vi. 21. Col. i. 2, 7. iv. 7, 9. 1 Thes. v. 24. 2 Thes. iii. 3. 1 Tim. i. 12, 15. iii. 11. iv. 9. vi. 2 (*marg.* **believing**). 2 Tim. ii. 2, 11, 13. Tit. i. 6, 9. iii. 8. Heb. ii. 17. iii. 2, 5. x. 23. xi. 11. 1 Pet. iv. 19. v. 12. 1 John i. 9. Rev. i. 5. ii. 10, 13. iii. 14. xvii. 14. xxi. 5. xxii. 6. — *Said of Christ*, **Faithful**, Rev. xix. 11.

Neut., **faithfully**, 3 John 5.

believing, John xx. 27. 1 Tim. vi. 2.

that (which) believeth, Acts x. 45. xvi. 1. 2 Cor. vi. 15. 1 Tim. iv. 3, 10. v. 16t (–[1st] G°L*S*).

believer, 1 Tim. iv. 12.

sure, Acts xiii. 34.

true, 2 Cor. i. 18. 1 Tim. iii. 1.

Add 1 Pet. i. 21, for πιστεύων[p], LT.

πιστόω.

Pass., **be assured of**, 2 Tim. iii. 14.

πλανάω.

Pass., **wander**, Heb. xi. 38. — **go astray**, Matt. xviii. 12*t*, 13. 1 Pet. ii. 25. 2 Pet. ii. 15. — **be out of the way**, Heb. v. 2. — **err**, Matt. xxii. 29. Mark xii. 24, 27. Heb. iii. 10. Jas. i. 16. v. 19.

seduce, 1 John ii. 26. Rev. ii. 20.

deceive, Matt. xxiv. 4, 5, 11, 24. Mark xiii. 5, 6. Luke xxi. 8. John vii. 12, 47. 1 Cor. vi. 9. xv. 33. Gal. vi. 7. 2 Tim. iii. 13*t*. Tit. iii. 3. 1 John i. 8. iii. 7. Rev. xii. 9. xiii. 14. xviii. 23. xix. 20. xx. 3, 8, 10.

πλάνη.

error, Matt. xxvii. 64. Rom. i. 27. Jas. v. 20. 2 Pet. ii. 18. iii. 17. 1 John iv. 6. Jude 11.

delusion, 2 Thes. ii. 11.

deceit, 1 Thes. ii. 3.

Gen., **to deceive**, Eph. iv. 14.

Add 1 Tim. iv. 1, for πλάνος, G′.

πλανήτης.

wandering, Jude 13.

πλάνος.

seducing, 1 Tim. iv. 1 (πλάνη G′).

deceiver, Matt. xxvii. 63. 2 Cor. vi. 8. 2 John 7*t*.

πλάξ.

table, 2 Cor. iii. 3*t*. Heb. ix. 4.

πλάσμα.

thing formed, Rom. ix. 20.

πλάσσω, -ττω.

to form, Rom. ix. 20. 1 Tim. ii. 13.

πλαστός.

feigned, 2 Pet. ii. 3.

πλατεῖα.

street, Matt. vi. 5. xii. 19. Luke x. 10. xiii. 26. xiv. 21. Acts v. 15 (*marg.*, *pl. with* κατά, **in every street**). Rev. xi. 8. xxi. 21. xxii. 2.

πλάτος.

breadth, Eph. iii. 18. Rev. xx. 9. xxi. 16*t*.

πλατύνω.

make broad, Matt. xxiii. 5.

enlarge, 2 Cor. vi. 11, 13.

πλατύς.

wide, Matt. vii. 13.

πλέγμα.

broided (*marg.* **plaited**, *in later eds., corruptly*, **broidered**) **hair**, 1 Tim. ii. 9.

πλείων, πλεῖον (πλέον[1]).

Comparative of πολύς.

With the Article[a]. Plural[2].

more, Matt. vi. 25. xx. 10. xxi. 36[2]. xxvi. 53[2]. Mark xii. 33 (περισσότερος Tr*S*), 43. Luke iii. 13[1]. ix. 13. xii. 23. xxi. 3. John iv. 1[2], 41[2]. vii. 31[2]. xv. 2. xxi. 15. Acts xxiii. 13[2], 21[2]. xxv. 6[2]. 2 Tim. ii. 16[cc]. Heb. iii. 3*t*. Rev. ii. 19[2].

the more, 1 Cor. ix. 19[a 2].

the more part, Acts xix. 32[a 2]. xxvii. 12[a 2].

more excellent, Heb. xi. 4.

most, Luke vii. 42, 43[a].

With ἐπί, **further**, Acts iv. 17. xxiv. 4. 2 Tim. iii. 9. — **long**, Acts xx. 9.

longer, Acts xviii. 20.
With οὐ, **yet but**[cc], Acts xxiv. 11[2].
above[cc], Acts iv. 22[2].
many,[2] Acts ii. 40. xiii. 31. xxi. 10. xxiv. 17. xxv. 14. xxvii. 20. xxviii. 23. 1 Cor. x. 5[a]. 2 Cor. ii. 6[a]. iv. 15[a]. Phil. i. 14[a]. Heb. vii. 23[a].
many things, Luke xi. 53[2].
very many, 2 Cor. ix. 2[a 2].
greater, Matt. xii. 41, 42. Luke xi. 31, 32. Acts xv. 28[1].
the greater part, 1 Cor. xv. 6[a 2].
See also περισσεύω.

Superlative, πλεῖστος.

most, Matt. xi. 20[a 2].
at the most, 1 Cor. xiv. 27[a].
very great, Matt. xxi. 8[a].
Add Mark iv. 1, for πολύς, TTr*S*.

πλέκω.

to plat, Matt. xxvii. 29[p]. Mark xv. 17. John xix. 2.

πλεονάζω.

abound, Rom. v. 20*t*. vi. 1. Phil. iv. 17[cc]. 2 Thes. i. 3. 2 Pet. i. 8.
abundant, 2 Cor. iv. 15[p].
With οὐ, **have nothing over,** 2 Cor. viii. 15.
make to increase, 1 Thes. iii. 12.

πλεονεκτέω.

get an advantage of, 2 Cor. ii. 11[cc].
make a gain of, 2 Cor. xii. 17, 18.
defraud, 2 Cor. vii. 2. 1 Thes. iv. 6 (*marg.* **oppress** *or* **overreach**).

πλεονέκτης.

covetous man, Eph. v. 5.
covetous, 1 Cor. v. 10, 11. vi. 10.

πλεονεξία.

covetousness, Mark vii. 22[pl]. Luke xii. 15. Rom. i. 29. 2 Cor. ix. 5. Eph. v. 3. Col. iii. 5. 1 Thes. ii. 5. 2 Pet. ii. 3.
covetous practice, 2 Pet. ii. 14.
greediness, Eph. iv. 19.

πλευρά.

side, John xix. 34. xx. 20, 25, 27. Acts xii. 7[cc].

πλέω.

to sail, Luke viii. 23[p]. Acts xxi. 3. xxvii. 6, 24.
sail by, Acts xxvii. 2.
Add Rev. xviii. 17 (*ap*).

πληγή.

stripe, Luke xii. 48. Acts xvi. 23, 33. 2 Cor. vi. 5. xi. 23.
wound, Rev. xiii. 3, 12, 14.
With ἐπιτίθημι, **to wound,** Luke x. 30.
plague, Rev. ix. 20. xi. 6. xv. 1, 6, 8. xvi. 9, 21*t*. xviii. 4, 8. xxi. 9. xxii. 18.
Add Rev. ix. 18 (these three . .), GLTTr, for τριῶν, *S*.

πλῆθος.

multitude, Mark iii. 7, 8. Luke i. 10. ii. 13. v. 6. vi. 17. viii. 37. xix. 37. xxiii. 1. John v. 3. xxi. 6. Acts ii. 6. iv. 32. v. 14, 16. vi. 2, 5. xiv. 1, 4. xv. 12, 30. xvii. 4. xix. 9. xxi. 22, 36. xxiii. 7. xxv. 24. Heb. xi. 12. Jas. v. 20. 1 Pet. iv. 8.
company, Luke xxiii. 27.
bundle, Acts xxviii. 3.

πληθύνω.

multiply, Acts ix. 31. 2 Cor. ix. 10. Heb. vi. 14*t*. 1 Pet. i. 2. 2 Pet. i. 2. Jude 2.
be multiplied, Acts vi. 1[p].
Pass., **multiply,** Acts vi. 7. vii. 17. xii. 24. — **abound,** Matt. xxiv. 12.

πλήθω. See πίμπλημι.

πλήκτης.

striker, 1 Tim. iii. 3. Tit. i. 7.

πλήμμυρα.

flood, Luke vi. 48.

πλήν.

than, Acts xv. 28.
except, Acts viii. 1.
save, Acts xx. 23.
but, Matt. xi. 22, 24. xviii. 7. Mark xii. 32. Luke vi. 24, 35. x. 14. xix. 27. xxii. 21, 22. xxiii. 28. John viii. 10(*ap*). Acts xxvii. 22. Rev. ii. 25.
but rather, Luke xi. 41. xii. 31.

nevertheless, Matt. xxvi. 39, 64. Luke xiii. 33. xviii. 8. xxii. 42. 1 Cor. xi. 11. Eph. v. 33. Phil. iii. 16.
notwithstanding, Luke x. 11, 20. Phil. i. 18. iv. 14.
Add Luke xvii. 1, for δέ[2d], LTr*S*.

πλήρης.

full, Matt. xiv. 20. xv. 37. Mark iv. 28. vi. 43 (πλήρωμα TTr*S*). viii. 19. Luke iv. 1. v. 12. John i. 14. Acts vi. 3, 5, 8. vii. 55. ix. 36. xi. 24. xiii. 10. xix. 28. 2 John 8.

πληροφορέω.

make full proof of (*marg.* **fulfill**), 2 Tim. iv. 5.
Pass., **be fully persuaded**, Rom. iv. 21. xiv. 5 (*marg.* **be fully assured**). —*Part. with art.*, **those things which are most surely believed**, Luke i. 1. — **be fully known**, 2 Tim. iv. 17.
Add Col. iv. 12, for πληρόω, G'LT*S*.

πληροφορία.

full assurance, Col. ii. 2. Heb. vi. 11. x. 22.
assurance, 1 Thes. i. 5.

πληρόω.

make full, Acts ii. 28.
Pass., **be full**, Matt. xiii. 48. John xv. 11. Phil. iv. 18. — **full**, John xvi. 24p. 1 John i. 4p. 2 John 12p. — **be filled with**, Phil. i. 11. — **fill**, Eph. i. 23. — **be full come**, John vii. 8. — **expire**, Acts vii. 30p. — **after**[ce], Acts xxiv. 27p. — **complete**, Col. ii. 10p. iv. 12p (*marg.* **filled**; πληροφορέω G'LT*S*). — **perfect**, Rev. iii. 2p.
preach[c] **fully**, Rom. xv. 19.
fill, Luke ii. 40. iii. 5. John xii. 3. xvi. 6. Acts ii. 2. v. 3, 28. xiii. 52. Rom. i. 29. xv. 13, 14. 2 Cor. vii. 4. Eph. iii. 19. iv. 10 (*marg.* **fulfill**). v. 18. Col. i. 9. 2 Tim. i. 4.
fill up, Matt. xxiii. 32.
supply, Phil. iv. 19.
fulfill, Matt. i. 22. ii. 15, 17, 23. iii. 15. iv. 14. v. 17. viii. 17. xii. 17. xiii. 35. xxi. 4. xxvi. 54, 56. xxvii. 9, 35(*ap*). Mark i. 15. xiv. 49. xv. 28(*ap*). Luke i. 20 (πίμπλημι G'). iv. 21. xxi. 22 (πίμπλημι GLTTr*S*), 24. xxii. 16. xxiv. 44. John iii. 29. xii. 38. xiii. 18. xv. 25. xvii. 12, 13. xviii. 9, 32. xix. 24, 36. Acts i. 16. iii. 18. ix. 23. xii. 25p. xiii. 25, 27. xiv. 26. Rom. viii. 4. xiii. 8. 2 Cor. x. 6. Gal. v. 14. Phil. ii. 2. Col. i. 25 (*marg.* **preach**[c] **fully**). iv. 17. 2 Thes. i. 11. Jas. ii. 23. Rev. vi. 11.
accomplish, Luke ix. 31.
end, Luke vii. 1. Acts xix. 21.
See also τεσσαρακονταετής.

πλήρωμα.

fulness, John i. 16. Rom. xi. 12, 25. xv. 29. 1 Cor. x. 26, 28(*ap*). Gal. iv. 4. Eph. i. 10, 23. iii. 19. iv. 13. Col. i. 19. ii. 9.
fulfilling, Rom. xiii. 10.
full, Mark viii. 20.
which is put in to fill up, Matt. ix. 16.
piece that filleth up, Mark ii. 21.
Add Mark vi. 43, for πλήρης, TTr*S*.

πλησίον.

near, John iv. 5.
With art., **neighbor**, Matt. v. 43. xix. 19. xxii. 39. Mark xii. 31, 33. Luke x. 27, 29, 36. Acts vii. 27. Rom. xiii. 9, 10. xv. 2. Gal. v. 14. Eph. iv. 25. Heb. viii. 11 (πολίτης GLT*S*). Jas. ii. 8.
Add Jas. iv. 12, for ἕτερος, G'LT*S*.

πλησμονή.

satisfying, Col. ii. 23.

πλήσσω, -ττω.

smite, Rev. viii. 12.

πλοιάριον.

small ship, Mark iii. 9.
little ship, Mark iv. 36 (πλοῖον GLTr*S*). John xxi. 8.
boat, John vi. 22, 22 (πλοῖον GLTTr*S*), 23 (πλοῖον L*S*).
Add, for πλοῖον, Luke v. 2, L[m]T. John vi. 24, LTTr.

πλοῖον.

ship, Matt. iv. 21, 22. viii. 23, 24. ix. 1. xiii. 2. xiv. 13, 22, 24, 29, 32, 33. xv. 39. Mark i. 19, 20. iv. 1, 36, 37. v. 2, 18, 21. vi. 32, 45, 47, 51, 54. viii. 10, 13(-G[oo]TTr[b]*S*), 14. Luke v. 2 (πλοιάριον L[m]T), 3*t*, 7*t*, 11. viii. 22, 37. John vi. 17, 19, 21*t*. xxi. 3, 6. Acts xx. 13, 38. xxi. 2, 3, 6. xxvii. 2, 6, 10, 15, 17, 19, 22, 30, 31, 37, 38, 39, 44. xxviii. 11. Jas. iii. 4. Rev. viii. 9. xviii. 17(*ap*), 19.

Plur., **shipping,** John vi. 24 (πλοιάριον LTTr).

Add Mark iv. 37, for αὐτό, G″LT Tr. *See also* πλοιάριον.

πλόος.

sailing, Acts xxvii. 9.
voyage, Acts xxvii. 10.
course, Acts xxi. 7.

πλούσιος.

rich, Matt. xxvii. 57. Mark xii. 41. Luke vi. 24. xii. 16. xiv. 12. xvi. 1, 19. xviii. 23. xix. 2. 2 Cor. viii. 9. Eph. ii. 4. 1 Tim. vi. 17. Jas. i. 10. ii. 5. Rev. ii. 9. iii. 17. xiii. 16.

rich man, Matt. xix. 23, 24. Mark x. 25. Luke xvi. 21, 22. xviii. 25. xxi. 1. Jas. i. 11. ii. 6. v. 1. Rev. vi. 15.

πλουσίως.

richly, Col. iii. 16. 1 Tim. vi. 17.
abundantly, Tit. iii. 6 (*Gr.* richly). 2 Pet. i. 11.

πλουτέω.

be rich, Luke xii. 21. Rom. x. 12. 1 Cor. iv. 8. 2 Cor. viii. 9. 1 Tim. vi. 9, 18. Rev. iii. 18.
rich, Luke i. 53[p].
wax rich, Rev. xviii. 3.
be made rich, Rev. xviii. 15, 19.
be increased with goods, Rev. iii. 17.

πλουτίζω.

make rich, 2 Cor. vi. 10.
enrich, 1 Cor. i. 5. 2 Cor. ix. 11.

πλοῦτος.

riches, Matt. xiii. 22. Mark iv. 19. Luke viii. 14. Rom. ii. 4. ix. 23. xi. 12*t*, 33. 2 Cor. viii. 2. Eph. i. 7, 18. ii. 7. iii. 8, 16. Phil. iv. 19. Col. i. 27. ii. 2. 1 Tim. vi. 17. Heb. xi. 26. Jas. v. 2. Rev. v. 12. xviii. 17(16).

πλύνω.

to wash, Rev. vii. 14.

Add Luke v. 2, for ἀποπλύνω, G′L Tr*S*. Rev. xxii. 14(*ap*).

πνεῦμα.

Said of the Divine Spirit[1]. Of demons[2]. Of other spirits[3]. The query (?) denotes an opinion of more or less weight, as of Calvin, De Wette, Tholuck, or Bruder.

wind, John iii. 8.
life (*Gr.* breath), Rev. xiii. 15.
spirit, Matt. iv. 1[1]. v. 3. viii. 16[2]. x. 1[2]. xii. 18[1], 43[2], 45[2]. xxii. 43([1]?). xxvi. 41. Mark i. 12[1], 23[2], 26[2], 27[2]. ii. 8. iii. 11[2], 30[2]. v. 2[2], 8[2], 13[2]. vi. 7[2]. vii. 25[2]. viii. 12. ix. 17[2], 20[2], 25[2]*t*. xiv. 38. Luke i. 17, 47, 80. ii. 40(-G[oo]LTTr*S*). iv. 33[2], 36[2]. vi. 18[2]. vii. 21[2]. viii. 2[2], 29[2], 55. ix. 39[2], 42[2], 55(*ap*). x. 20[2], 21. xi. 24[2], 26[2]. xiii. 11[2]. xxiii. 46. xxiv. 37[3], 39.[3]

John iii. 6. iv. 23, 24. vi. 63([1]?), 63. xi. 33. xiii. 21. Acts v. 16[2]. vi. 10. vii. 59. viii. 7[2]. xi. 12[1], 28[1]. xvi. 16[2], 18[2]. xvii. 16. xviii. 5(λόγος GLT*S*), 25. xix. 12[2], 13[2], 15[2], 16[2], 21. xx. 22([1]?). xxiii. 8[3], 9[3].

Rom. i. 4[1], 9. ii. 29. vii. 6. viii. 15, 16. xi. 8. xii. 11([1]?). 1 Cor. ii. 11, 12, 12([1]?). iv. 21. v. 3, 4, 5. vi. 17, 20(*ap*). vii. 34. xii. 10([3]?). xiv. 2, 14, 15*t*, 16, 32. xv. 45. xvi. 18. 2 Cor. ii. 13. iii. 6*t*, 8([1]?). iv. 13. vii. 1, 13. xi. 4. xii. 18. Gal. vi. 1, 18. Eph. i. 17. ii. 2. iv. 23. Phil. i. 27. iii. 3. Col. ii. 5. 1 Thes. v. 23. 2 Thes. ii. 2, 8. 1 Tim. iv. 1[2], 12(*om S*). 2 Tim. i. 7. iv. 22. Phm. 25.

Heb. i. 7[3], 14[3]. iv. 12. xii. 9, 23. Jas. ii. 26 (*marg.* **breath**). iv. 5. 1 Pet. iii. 4, 19[3]. iv. 6, 14([1]?). 1 John iv. 1*t*([3]?), 2([3]?), 3([3]?), 6*t*([3]?). v. 8

(¹?). Rev. i. 4(¹?). iv. 2¹. xvi. 13², 14². xvii. 3. xviii. 2². xix. 10. xxi. 10.

spiritual *gift* (*Gr.* spirit), 1 Cor. xiv. 12.

Gen., **spiritually**, Rom. viii. 6 (¹? *Gr.* of the Spirit).

ghost, Matt. xxvii. 50. John xix. 30.

Said of the Divine, **Spirit**, Matt. iii. 16. x. 20. xii. 28. Mark i. 10. Luke ii. 27. iv. 1, 14, 18. John i. 32, 33. iii. 5, 6, 8. 34 iv. 24. vii. 39. xiv. 17. xv. 26. xvi. 13. Acts ii. 4, 17, 18. v. 9. viii. 29, 39. x. 19. xvi. 7. xxi. 4.

Rom. viii. 1(*ap*), 2, 4, 5*t*, 9(¹?), 9*t*, 10, 11*t*, 13, 14, 15, 16, 23, 26*t*, 27. xv. 19, 30. 1 Cor. ii. 4, 10*t*, 11, 14. iii. 16. vi. 11. vii. 40. xii. 3, 4, 7, 8*t*, 9*t*, 11, 13*t*. 2 Cor. i. 22. iii. 3, 17*t*,* 18. v. 5. Gal. iii. 2, 3, 5, 14. iv. 6, 29. v. 5, 16(¹?), 17*t*(¹?), 18 (¹?), 22(¹?), 25*t*(¹?). vi. 8*t*(¹?). Eph. i. 13. ii. 18, 22. iii. 5, 16. iv. 3, 4. v. 9 (φῶς GLTS), 18. vi. 17, 18. Phil. 1. 19. ii. 1. Col. i. 8. 1 Thes. v. 19. 2 Thes. ii. 13. 1 Tim. iii. 16. iv. 1.

Heb. ix. 14. x. 29. 1 Pet. i. 2, 11, 22 (-G°°LTS). iii. 18. 1 John iii. 24. iv. 2, 13. v. 6*t*. Jude 19(¹?). Rev. i. 10. ii. 7, 11, 17, 29. iii. 1, 6, 13, 22. iv. 5. v. 6. xi. 11(¹?). xiv. 13. xxii. 17.

For the phrases **Holy Spirit, Holy Ghost**, *see* ἅγιος.

Add Acts iv. 25(*ap*). Phil. iv. 23, for πάντων fr. πᾶς, LTS. Rev. xxii. 6, for ἁγίος, GLTTrS.

πνευματικός.

spiritual, Rom. i. 11. vii. 14. 1 Cor. ii. 13. iii. 1. x. 3, 4*t*. xii. 1. xiv. 37. xv. 44*t*. Eph. i. 3. v. 19(-Lᵇ). vi. 12 (*marg.* **spirit**). Col. i. 9. iii. 16. 1 Pet. ii. 5*t*.

With art., **he that (which) is spiritual**, 1 Cor. ii. 15. Gal. vi. 1.—**that which is spiritual**, 1 Cor. xv. 46*t*.

Neut. plural, **spiritual things**, Rom. xv. 27. 1 Cor. ii. 13. ix. 11.—**spiritual** ᶜ**gifts**, 1 Cor. xiv. 1.

πνευματικῶς.

spiritually, 1 Cor. ii. 14. Rev. xi. 8.

πνέω.

to blow, Matt. vii. 25, 27. Luke xii. 55. John iii. 8. vi. 18. Rev. vii. 1.

wind (*sc.* αὔρα), Acts xxvii. 40ᵖ.

πνίγω.

choke, Mark v. 13.

take by the throat, Matt. xviii. 28.

πνικτός.

strangled, Acts xxi. 25(-G°).

things strangled, Acts xv. 20(-G°), 29(*plur.* LTS, -G°).

πνοή.

breath, Acts xvii. 25.

wind, Acts ii. 2.

ποδήρης.

garment down to the foot (*sc.* χιτών), Rev. i. 13.

πόθεν.

whence, Matt. xiii. 54, 56. xv. 33. xxi. 25. Mark xii. 37. Luke i. 43. xiii. 25, 27. xx. 7. John i. 48(49). ii. 9. iii. 8. vi. 5. vii. 27*t*, 28. viii. 14*t*. xix. 9. Rev. vii. 13.

from whence, Matt. xiii. 27. Mark vi. 2. viii. 4. John iv. 11. ix. 29, 30. Jas. iv. 1. Rev. ii. 5.

Add Jas. iv. 1(.. fightings), G'LTS.

ποιέω.

to make, Matt. iii. 3. iv. 19. v. 36. xii. 16, 33*t*. xvii. 4. xix. 4 (κτίζω Tr), 4. xx. 12. xxi. 13. xxii. 2. xxiii. 15*t*. xxv. 16 (κερδαίνω G'LTr). Mark i. 3, 17. iii. 12. vi. 21. vii. 37. viii. 25 (*see* διαβλέπω). ix. 5. x. 6. xi. 17. Luke iii. 4. v. 29, 34. ix. 33. xi. 40*t*. xiv. 12, 13, 16. xv. 19. xvi. 9. xix. 46.

John ii. 15ᵖ, 16. iv. 1, 46. v. 11, 15, 18. vi. 10, 15. vii. 23. viii. 53. ix. 6, 11, 14. x. 33. xii. 2. xiv. 23. xviii. 18. xix. 7, 12, 23. Acts ii. 36. iii. 12. iv. 24. vii. 40, 43, 44, 50. ix. 39. xiv. 15. xvii. 24, 26. xix. 24. xxiii. 13.

Rom. ix. 20, 21, 28. 1 Cor. vi. 15. x. 13. 2 Cor. v. 21. Eph. ii. 14, 15. 1 Tim. ii. 1. Heb. i. 2, 7. viii. 5, 9. xii. 13, 27. Jas. iii. 18. 1 John i. 10. v. 10. Rev. i. 6. iii. 9, 12. v. 10. xi. 7. xii. 17. xiii. 7(*ap*), 13 (-G), 14. xiv. 7. xvii. 16. xix. 19. xxi. 5. xxii. 15.

Mid., **make**, Luke v. 33. Acts i. 1. viii. 2. Rom. i. 9. xiii. 14. xv. 26. Eph. i. 16. iv. 16. Phil. i. 4. 1 Thes. i. 2. Phm. 4. 2 Pet. i. 10. — **give**, Jude 3. — *With* μνήμη, **have . . in remembrance**, 2 Pet. i. 15[cc]. — *With* λόγος, **move**[cc], Acts xx. 24.

cause, Matt. v. 32. John xi. 37. Acts xv. 3. Rom. xvi. 17. Col. iv. 16. Rev. xiii. 12, 15, 16.

cause to be, Rev. xii. 15.

bring forth, Matt. iii. 8, 10. vii. 17*t*, 18*t*, 19. xiii. 23, 26. xxi. 43. Luke iii. 8, 9. vi. 43*t* (*with* ἐστί).

bring, Acts xxiv. 17.

shoot out, Mark iv. 32.

bear, Luke viii. 8. xiii. 9. Jas. iii. 12. Rev xxii. 2.

yield, Jas. iii. 12. — **give**, Acts x. 2.

put, Acts v. 34.

show, Luke i. 51. x. 37. John vi. 30. Acts vii. 36[p]. Jas. ii. 13.

purpose[c], Eph. iii. 11.

mean, Acts xxi. 13[cc].

appoint (*Gr.* make), Heb. iii. 2.

ordain, Mark iii. 14.

gain, Luke xix. 18.

provide, Luke xii. 33.

work, Matt. xx. 12(*marg.* **continue**). Acts xv. 12. xix. 11. xxi. 19. Heb. xiii. 21 (*marg.* **do**). Rev. xvi. 14. xix. 20. xxi. 27.

do, Matt. i. 24. v. 19, 44, 46, 47*t*. vi. 1, 2*t*, 3[p], 3. vii. 12*t*, 21, 22, 24, 26. viii. 9*t*. ix. 28. xii. 2*t*, 3, 12, 50. xiii. 28, 41, 58. xvii. 12. xviii. 35. xix. 16. xx. 5, 15, 32. xxi. 6, 15, 21, 23, 24, 27, 31, 36, 40. xxiii. 3*tr*, 5, 23. xxiv. 46. xxv. 40*t*, 45*t*. xxvi. 12, 13, 19. xxvii. 22, 23. xxviii. 15.

Mark ii. 24, 25. iii. 8, 35. v. 19, 20, 32. vi. 5, 20, 30. vii. 8(*ap*), 12, 13, 37. ix. 13, 39. x. 17, 35, 36, 51. xi. 3(*ap*), 5, 28*t*, 29, 33. xii. 9. xiv. 7, 8, 9. xv. 8, 12, 14.

Luke i. 49. ii. 27. iii. 10, 11, 12, 14, 19. iv. 23. v. 6[p]. vi. 2, 2(-LTTr), 3, 10 (ἐκτείνω G'S), 11, 23, 26, 27, 31*t*, 33, 46, 47, 49. vii. 8*t*. viii. 21, 39*t*. ix. 10, 15, 43, 54(*ap*). x. 25[cc], 28, 37. xi. 42. xii. 4, 17, 18, 43, 47. xvi. 3, 4, 8. xvii. 9, 10*tr*. xviii. 18[cc], 41. xix. 48. xx. 2, 8, 13, 15. xxii. 19. xxiii. 22, 31, 34(*ap*).

John ii. 5, 11, 18, 23. iii. 2*t*, 21. iv. 29, 34, 39, 45, 54. v. 16, 19*f*, 20, 29, 30, 36. vi. 2, 6, 14, 28, 38. vii. 3, 4*t*, 17, 21, 31*t*, 51. viii. 28, 29, 38, 39, 40, 41, 44. ix. 16, 26, 31, 33. x. 25, 37, 38, 41. xi. 45, 46, 47*t*. xii. 16, 18, 37[p]. xiii. 7, 12, 15*t*, 17, 27*t*. xiv. 10, 12*tr*, 13, 14, 31. xv. 5, 14, 15, 21, 24*t*. xvi. 3. xvii. 4. xviii. 35. xix. 24. xx. 30. xxi. 25.

Acts i. 1. ii. 22, 37. iv. 7, 16, 28. vi. 8. viii. 6. ix. 6(*ap*), 6, 13, 36. x. 6(*ap*), 33, 39. xi. 30. xii. 8. xiv. 11, 15, 27. xv. 4, 17. xvi. 18, 30. xix. 14. xxi. 23, 33(*with* ἐστί). xxii. 10*t*, 26(*with* μέλλω). xxvi. 10.

Rom. i. 28, 32. ii. 3, 14. iii. 8, 12. vii. 15, 16, 19, 20, 21. x. 5. xii. 20. xiii. 3, 4. 1 Cor. v. 2 (πράσσω G''T S). vi. 18. vii. 36, 37, 38*t*. ix. 23. x. 31*t*. xi. 24, 25. xv. 29. xvi. 1. 2 Cor. viii. 10. xi. 12*t*. xiii. 7*t*. Gal. ii. 10. iii. 10, 12. v. 3. Eph. iii. 20. vi. 6, 8, 9. Phil. ii. 14. iv. 14. Col. iii. 17, 23. 1 Thes. iv. 10. v. 11, 24. 2 Thes. iii. 4*t*. 1 Tim. i. 13. v. 21. 2 Tim. iv. 5. Tit. iii. 5. Phm. 14, 21.

Heb. vi. 3. vii. 27. x. 7, 9, 36[p]. xiii. 6, 17, 19, 21. Jas. ii. 8, 12, 19. iv. 15, 17*t*. 1 Pet. ii. 22. iii. 11, 12. 2 Pet. i. 10[p], 19. 1 John i. 6. ii. 17, 29. iii. 7, 10(*ap*), 22. 3 John 5, 6, 10. Rev. ii. 5. xiii. 13, 14. xxii. 14 (*ap*).

in doing, Gal. vi. 9[p]. 1 Tim. iv. 16[p].

Inf. **doing**, 2 Cor. viii. 11.

can do, Gal. v. 17.

commit, Mark xv. 7. Luke xii. 48. John viii. 34. Acts xxviii. 17p. 2Cor. xi. 7. Jas. v. 15. 1 John iii. 4, 8, 9.
execute, John v. 27. Jude 15.
exercise, Rev. xiii. 12.
perform, Luke i. 72. Rom. iv. 21.
fulfill, Acts xiii. 22. Eph. ii. 3. Rev. xvii. 17.
keep, Matt. xxvi. 18. John vii. 19. Acts xviii. 21(*ap*). Heb. xi. 28.
observe, Acts xvi. 21.
hold, Mark xv. 1.
take, Mark iii. 6 (δίδωμι Tr).
With a dative (μοί, ἡμῖν), **deal with**, Luke i. 25. ii. 48.
abidec, Acts xx. 3.
continuec, Jas. iv. 13. Rev. xiii. 5 (–Goo, *add* ὃ θέλει *S*, *see* πόλεμος).
bec, 2 Cor. xi. 25.
Add Mark xiii. 22, for δίδωμι, T. Acts xxvi. 28, for γίνομαι, L*S*. 2 Thes. iii. 4 (*ap*). 1 John v. 2, for τηρέω, G′LT. Rev. xxii. 11, *see* δικαιόω.
See also ἀμέριμνος, ἀνομία, ἀποσυνάγωγος, γνώμη, δῆλος, ἐκβολή, ἐκδίκησις, ἔκθετος, ἐνέδρα, ἐπισύστασις, ἱκανός, καθαρισμός, λύτρωσις, μηδείς, ὁδός, πορεία, συστροφή, χρόνος.

ποίημα.

thing that is made, Rom. i. 20.
workmanship, Eph. ii. 10.

ποίησις.

deed (*marg.* **doing**), Jas. i. 25.

ποιητής.

doer, Rom. ii. 13. Jas. i. 22, 23, 25. iv. 11.
poet, Acts xvii. 28(–Go).

ποικίλος.

divers, Matt. iv. 24. Mark i. 34. Luke iv. 40. 2 Tim. iii. 6. Tit. iii. 3. Heb. ii. 4. xiii. 9. Jas. i. 2.
manifold, 1 Pet. i. 6. iv. 10.

ποιμαίνω.

feed cattle, Luke xvii. 7.
feed, John xxi. 16. Acts xx. 28. 1 Cor. ix. 7. 1 Pet. v. 2. Jude 12. Rev. vii. 17.
rule, Matt. ii. 6 (*marg.* **feed**). Rev. ii. 27. xii. 5. xix. 15.

ποιμήν.

shepherd, Matt. ix. 36. xxv. 32. xxvi. 31. Mark vi. 34. xiv. 27. Luke ii. 8, 15, 18, 20. John x. 2, 11*t*, 12, 14, 16.
Said of Christ, **Shepherd**, Heb. xiii. 20. 1 Pet. ii. 25.
pastor, Eph. iv. 11.

ποίμνη.

flock, Matt. xxvi. 31. Luke ii. 8. 1 Cor. ix. 7*t*.
fold, John x. 16.

ποίμνιον.

flock, Luke xii. 32. Acts xx. 28, 29. 1 Pet. v. 2, 3.

ποῖος.

what manner of, 1 Pet. i. 11.
what, Matt. xxi. 23, 24, 27. xxiv. 42, 43: Mark iv. 30 (τίς LTTr*S*). xi. 28, 29, 33. Luke vi. 32, 33, 34. xii. 39. xx. 2, 8. John xii. 33. xviii. 32. xxi. 19. Acts iv. 7*t*. vii. 49. xxiii. 34. Rom. iii. 27. 1 Cor. xv. 35. Jas. iv. 14. 1 Pet. ii. 20. Rev. iii. 3.
ποῖα, **what things**, Luke xxiv. 19.
what way (*sc.* ὁδός), Luke v. 19.
which, Matt. xix. 18. xxii. 36. Mark xii. 28. John x. 32.

πολεμέω.

make war, Rev. xiii. 4. xvii. 14. xix. 11.
war, Jas. iv. 2.
fight, Rev. ii. 16. xii. 7*t*.

πόλεμος.

war, Matt. xxiv. 6*t*. Mark xiii. 7*t*. Luke xiv. 31. xxi. 9. Jas. iv. 1. Rev. xi. 7. xii. 7, 17. xiii. 7(*ap*). xix. 19.
battle, 1 Cor. xiv. 8. Rev. ix. 7, 9. xvi. 14. xx. 8.
fight, Heb. xi. 34.
Add Rev. xiii. 5 (. . ποιῆσαι), ECm, (*marg.* **make war**).

πόλις.

city, Matt. ii. 23. iv. 5. v. 14, 35. viii. 33, 34. ix. 1, 35. x. 5, 11, 14, 15, 23*t*. xi. 1, 20. xii. 25. xiv. 13.

xxi. 10, 17, 18. xxii. 7. xxiii. 34t. xxvi. 18.' xxvii. 53. xxviii. 11. Mark i. 33, 45. v. 14. vi. 11(ap), 33, 56. xi. 19. xiv. 13, 16.
Luke i. 26, 39. ii. 3, 4t, 11, 39. iv. 29t, 31, 43. v. 12. vii. 11, 12t, 37. viii. 27, 34, 39. ix. 5, 10. x. 1, 8, 10, 11, 12. xiii. 22. xiv. 21. xviii. 2, 3. xix. 17, 19, 41. xxii. 10. xxiii. 19, 51 xxiv. 49. John i. 44 (45). iv. 5, 8, 28, 30, 39. xi. 54. xix. 20.
Acts v. 16. vii. 58. viii. 5, 8, 9, 40. ix. 6, x. 9. xi. 5. xii. 10. xiii. 44, 50. xiv. 4, 6, 13, 19, 20, 21. xv. 36. xvi. 4, 12t, 13 (πύλη G''LT*S*), 14, 20, 39. xvii. 5, 16. xviii. 10. xix. 29, 35. xxi. 5, 29, 30, 39. xxii. 3. xxiv. 12. xxv. 23. xxvi. 11. xxvii. 8.
Rom. xvi. 23. 2 Cor. xi. 26, 32. Heb. xi. 10, 16. xii. 22. xiii. 14. Jas. iv. 13. 2 Pet. ii. 6. Jude 7. Rev. iii. 12. xi. 2, 8, 13. xiv. 8(*omS*), 20. xvi. 19t. xvii. 18. xviii. 10t, 16, 18, 19, 21. xx. 9. xxi. 2, 10, 14, 15, 16t, 18, 19, 21, 23. xxii. 14, 19.
Add Acts iv. 27(*ap*).
See also κατά.

πολιτάρχης.

ruler of the city, Acts xvii. 6, 8.

πολιτεία.

freedom, Acts xxii. 28.
commonwealth, Eph. ii. 12.

πολίτευμα.

conversation, Phil. iii. 20.

πολιτεύω.

Mid., **one's conversation is,** Phil. i. 27.—**live,** Acts xxiii. 1.

πολίτης.

citizen, Luke xv. 15. xix. 14. Acts xxi. 39.
Add Heb. viii. 11, for πλησίον, GL T*S*.

πολλά. See πολύς.

πολλάκις.

often, Mark v. 4. 2 Cor. xi. 26, 27t. Phil. iii. 18. Heb. ix. 25, 26.
oft, Matt. xvii. 15. Acts xxvi. 11. 2 Cor. xi. 23. 2 Tim. i. 16. Heb. vi. 7.
oftentimes, Rom. i. 13. 2 Cor. viii. 22. Heb. x. 11.
ofttimes, Matt. xvii. 15. Mark ix. 22. John xviii. 2.
Add Rom. xv. 22, for τὰ πολλά, L.

πολλαπλασίων.

manifold more, Luke xviii. 30.
Add Matt. xix. 29, for ἑκατονταπλασίων, LTTr.

πολυεύσπλαγχνος, very compassionate or tender-hearted.

Jas. v. 11, for πολύσπλαγχνος, G'.

πολυλογία.

much speaking, Matt. vi. 7.

πολυμερῶς.

at sundry times, Heb. i. 1.

πολυποίκιλος.

manifold, Eph. iii. 10.

πολύς.

With the Article[a].

1. *Sing.*, πολύς, πολλή, πολύ.

much, Matt. vi. 30. xiii. 5. xxvi. 9. Mark iv. 5. v. 21, 24. vi. 34. Luke vii. 11, 47. viii. 4. ix. 37. x. 40. xii. 48tr. xvi. 10t. John vi. 10. vii. 12. xii. 9, 12, 24. xv. 5, 8. Acts xv. 7. xvi. 16. xviii. 10, 27. xxvii. 10.
Rom. iii. 2. v. 10, 15, 17. ix. 22. 1 Cor. ii. 3. xii. 22. 2 Cor. ii. 4. iii. 9, 11. vi. 4. viii. 4, 15, 22. Phil. ii. 12. 1 Thes. i. 5, 6. ii. 2. 1 Tim. iii. 8. Tit. ii. 3. Heb. xii. 9, 25. Jas. v. 16. 1 Pet. i. 7 (*see* πολύτιμος). Rev. xix. 1.
plenteous, Matt. ix. 37.
abundant (*Gr.* much), 1 Pet. i. 3[a].
the common, Mark xii. 37[a].
many, Acts xv. 32. Heb. v. 11.
Dat., **many,** John iv. 41.
ὥρας πολλῆς γενομένης, **when the day was far spent,** Mark vi. 35.
far passed, Mark vi. 35.
long, Matt. xxv. 19. John v. 6. Acts xxvii. 21.

μετὰ π., **long after**, Acts xxvii. 14.
great, Matt. ii. 18. v. 12. xiv. 14. xx. 29. xxiv. 30. xxvi. 47. Mark iii. 7, 8. iv. 1 (πλεῖστος TTr*S*). ix. 14. xiii. 26. xiv. 43(-L^b TTr*S*). Luke v. 6, 29. vi. 17, 23, 35. x. 2. xxi. 27. xxiii. 27. John v. 3 (-G^{o} L^b TTr *S*). vi. 2, 5. Acts vi. 7 xi. 21. xiv. 1. xvii. 4. xxi. 40. xxii. 28. xxiii. 10. xxiv. 2 (3), 7 (*ap*). xxv. 23. xxviii. 29(*ap*).
2 Cor. iii. 12. vii. 4*t*. viii. 2, 22. Eph. ii. 4ᵃ. Col. iv. 13. 1 Thes. ii. 17. 1 Tim. iii. 13. Phm. 7. Heb. x. 32. Rev. vii. 9. xix. 6.
greatly, Mark xii. 27.
ἐπὶ π., **a great while**, Acts xxviii 6.
With ἐν, **altogether**, Acts xxvi. 29 (μέγας G'LT*S*).
Add Mark viii. 1, *see* παμπόλλου. Acts viii. 8, for μέγας, LT*S*.
See also μᾶλλον, παρακαλέω, παρρησία.

2. *Plural*, πολλοί, πολλαί, πολλά.
many, Matt. iii. 7. vii. 13, 22*t*. viii. 11, 16, 30. ix. 10. x. 31. xiii. 17, 58. xv. 30. xix. 30. xx. 16(*ap*), 28. xxii. 14. xxiv. 5*t*, 10, 11*t*, 12ᵃ. xxvi. 28, 60(*ap*). xxvii. 52, 53, 55. Mark i. 34*t*. ii. 2, 15*t*. iii. 10. iv. 33(-G^o). v. 9, 26. vi. 2 (ᵃ G^{ph}T), 13*t*, 31, 33. vii. 4, 8(*ap*), 13. ix. 26. x. 31, 45, 48. xi. 8. xii. 5, 41. xiii. 6*t*. xiv. 24, 56. xv. 41.
Luke i. 1, 14, 16. ii. 34, 35. iii. 18. iv. 25, 27, 41. vii. 21*t*, 47ᵃ. viii. 3, 30. x. 24. xii. 7, 19. xiii. 24. xiv. 16. xv. 13. xxi. 8. xxii. 65. John ii. 12, 23. iv. 39. vi. 60, 66. vii. 31, 40(-LTTr*S*). viii. 30. x. 20, 32, 41, 42. xi. 19, 45, 47, 55. xii. 11, 42. xiv. 2. xix. 20. xx. 30. xxi. 25. Acts i. 3, 5. ii. 43. iv. 4. v. 12. viii. 7*t*, 25. ix. 13, 42. x. 27. xiii. 43. xv. 35. xvi. 18, 23. xvii. 12. xviii. 8. xix. 18. xx. 19(*om S*). xxiv. 10. xxv. 7. xxvi. 10. xxviii. 10.
Rom. iv. 17, 18. v. 15ᵃ*t*, 16, 19ᵃ*t*. viii. 29. xii. 4, 5ᵃ. xv. 23 (ἱκανός T). xvi. 2. 1 Cor. i. 26*tr*. iv. 15. viii. 5*t*. x. 17ᵃ, 33ᵃ. xi. 30. xii. 12*t*, 14, 20. xvi. 9. 2 Cor. i. 11*t*. ii. 4, 17ᵃ (λοιπός G'). vi. 10. ix. 12. xi. 18. xii. 21*t*. Gal. i. 14. iii. 16. iv. 27. Phil. iii. 18. 1 Tim. vi. 9, 10, 12. 2 Tim. ii. 2. Tit. i. 10. Heb. ii. 10. ix. 28. xii. 15(ᵃ LT*S*). Jas. iii. 1. 2 Pet. ii. 2. 1 John ii. 18. iv. 1. 2 John 7. Rev. i. 15. v. 11. viii. 11. ix. 9. x. 11. xiv. 2. xvii. 1. xix. 6, 12.
many things, Matt. xiii. 3. xvi. 21. xxv. 21, 23. xxvii. 19. Mark iv. 2. v. 26. vi. 20, 34. viii. 31. ix. 12. xv. 3. Luke ix. 22. x. 41. xvii. 25. xxiii. 8. John viii. 26. xvi. 12. Acts xxvi. 9. 2 Cor. viii. 22. Jas. iii. 2. 2 John 12. 3 John 13.
many ᶜ**stripes**, Luke xii. 47.
much, Mark i. 45. v. 10. Luke xii. 19. John iii. 23. xiv. 30. Acts x. 2. xiv. 22. xxvi. 24ᵃ. Rom. xv. 22ᵃ (*marg.* **many ways**, *or* **oftentimes**; πολλάκις L). xvi. 6, 12(*ap*). 1 Cor. xvi. 19. 2 Tim. iv. 14. Rev. v. 4 (πολύ G''LTTr*S*). viii. 3.
great, Matt. iv. 25. viii. 1, 18(-L *S*). xii. 15. xiii. 2. xv. 30. xix. 2, 22. Mark x. 22. Luke v. 15. xiv. 25.
greatly, Mark v. 23, 38. 1 Cor. xvi. 12.
sore, Mark ix. 26.
straitly, Mark iii. 12. v. 43.
oft, Matt. ix. 14(-L*S*).
Add Matt. xiv. 24 (*ap*).
See also προβαίνω, χρόνος.

πολύσπλαγχνος.

very pitiful, Jas. v. 11 (πολυεύσπλαγχνος G').

πολυτελής.

of great price, 1 Pet. iii. 4.
very precious, Mark xiv. 3.
costly, 1 Tim ii. 9.

πολύτιμος.

of great price, Matt. xiii. 46.
very costly, John xii. 3.
Add Matt. xxvi. 7, for βαρύτιμος, L*S*. 1 Pet. i. 7, πολυτιμότερος for πολὺ τιμιώτερος, GLT*S*.

πολυτρόπως.

in divers manners, Heb. i. 1.

πόμα.

drink, 1 Cor. x. 4. Heb. ix. 10.

πονηρία.

wickedness, Matt. xxii. 18. Mark vii. 22pl. Luke xi. 39. Rom. i. 29. 1 Cor. v. 8. Eph. vi. 12 (*gen.*, *marg.* **wicked**).

iniquity, Acts iii. 26.

πονηρός.

Sing. with the Article a.

evil, Matt. v. 45. vi. 23. vii. 11, 17, 18. xii. 34, 35*t*, 39. xv. 19. xx. 15. Mark vii. 22. Luke vi. 22, 45*t*. vii. 21. viii. 2. xi. 13, 29, 34. John iii. 19. vii. 7. Acts xix. 12, 13, 15, 16. Gal. i. 4. Eph. v. 16. vi. 13. 1 Tim. vi. 4. 2 Tim. iii. 13. iv. 18. Heb. iii. 12. x. 22. Jas. ii. 4. iv. 16. 1 John iii. 12. 2 John 11.

that which is evil, Luke vi. 45a. Rom. xii. 9a.

evil, *subst.*, Matt. v. 37a, 39a. vi. 13a. ix. 4pl. Luke iii. 19. vi. 35. xi. 4a(*ap*). 1 Thes. v. 22. 2 Thes. iii. 3a.

the evil, John xvii. 15a. [*S*).

π. ῥῆμα, **evil**, Matt. v. 11(–ῥ. LTr

Neut. pl., **evil things**, Matt. xii. 35. Mark vii. 23.

bad, Matt. xxii. 10.

harm, Acts xxviii. 21.

grievous, Rev. xvi. 2.

malicious, 3 John 10.

lewd, Acts xvii. 5.

wicked, Matt. xii. 45*t*. xiii. 49. xvi. 4. xviii. 32. xxv. 26. Luke xi. 26. xix. 22. Acts xviii. 14. Col. i. 21. 2 Thes. iii. 2.

that wicked person, 1 Cor. v. 13a.

the wicked one, Matt. xiii. 19a, 38a. 1 John ii. 13a, 14a. iii. 12a.

the wicked, Eph. vi. 16a.

that wicked one, 1 John v. 18a.

wickedness, 1 John v. 19a.

Add Acts xxv. 18 (. . accusation), G'L, πονηρά *S*.

πόνος.

pain, Rev. xvi. 10, 11. xxi. 4.

Add Col. iv. 13, for ζῆλος, GLT*S*.

πορεία.

With ποιέω, *mid.*, **to journey**, Luke xiii. 22.

way, Jas. i. 11.

πορεύω.

Passive deponent, πορεύομαι.

go away, Matt. xxviii. 16.

go one's way, Luke vii. 22. xvii. 19. John iv. 50*t*. Acts ix. 15. xxi. 5. xxiv. 25.

go forth, Luke viii. 14.

go, Matt. ii. 8, 20. viii. 9*t*. ix. 13. x. 6, 7p. xi. 4. xii. 1, 45. xvii. 27. xviii. 12. xxi. 2, 6. xxii. 9, 15. xxv. 9, 16. xxvi. 14. xxvii. 66. xxviii. 7, 9(*ap*), 19. Mark xvi. 10 (*ap*), 12p(*ap*), 15(*ap*).

Luke i. 39. ii. 3, 41. iv. 30, 42. v. 24. vii. 6, 8*t*, 11, 50. viii. 48. ix. 13, 51, 52, 53p, 56, 57p. x. 37, 38. xi. 5, 26. xiii. 32. xiv. 10, 19, 31. xv. 4, 15, 18. xvi. 30. xvii. 11, 14. xix. 12, 28, 36p. xxi. 8. xxii. 8, 22, 33, 39. xxiv. 13 (*with* εἰμί), 28*t*.

John vii. 35*t*, 53(*ap*). viii. 1(*ap*), 11(*ap*). x. 4. xi. 11. xiv. 2, 3, 12, 28. xvi. 28. xx. 17. Acts i. 11, 25. v. 20. viii. 26, 27, 36, 39. ix. 11. x. 20. xii. 17. xvi. 7, 16p, 36. xvii. 14. xviii. 6. xix. 21. xx. 1, 22. xxii. 5, 10. xxiii. 23, 32 (ἀπέρχομαι G'L*S*). xxv. 12, 20. xxvi. 12p. xxvii. 3. xxviii. 26.

Rom. xv. 25. 1 Cor. x. 27. xvi. 4*t*, 6. 1 Tim. i. 3p. Jas. iv. 13. 1 Pet. iii. 19, 22. Jude 11.

be going, Matt. xxviii. 11p.

go up, Acts i. 10p.

depart, Matt. ii. 9. xi. 7p. xix. 15. xxiv. 1. xxv. 41. Luke iv. 42. xiii. 31. John xvi. 7. Acts v. 41. xxii. 21. 2 Tim. iv. 10.

journey, Acts ix. 3. xxvi. 13.

make one's journey, Acts xxii. 6p.

take one's journey, Rom. xv. 24.

walk, Luke i. 6. xiii. 33. Acts ix. 31. xiv. 16. 1 Pet. iv. 3p. 2 Pet. ii. 10. iii. 3. Jude 16, 18.

Add Mark ix. 30, for παραπορεύομαι, LTr. Luke viii. 42 (*ap*). ix. 12, for ἀπέρχομαι, GLTTr*S*.

πορθέω.

to waste, Gal. i. 13.
destroy, Acts ix. 21. Gal. i. 23.

πορισμός.

gain, 1 Tim. vi. 5, 6.

πορνεία.

fornication, Matt. v. 32. xv. 19. xix. 9. Mark vii. 21. John viii. 41. Acts xv. 20, 29. xxi. 25. Rom. i. 29 (*omS*). 1 Cor. v. 1*t*. vi. 13, 18. vii. 2. 2 Cor. xii. 21. Gal. v. 19. Eph. v. 3. Col. iii. 5. 1 Thes. iv. 3. Rev. ii. 21. ix. 21. xiv. 8. xvii. 2, 4. xviii. 3. xix. 2.
Add Rev. xvii. 5, for πόρνη, C[m].

πορνεύω.

commit fornication, 1 Cor. vi. 18. x. 8. Rev. ii. 14, 20. xvii. 2. xviii. 3, 9. — **commit,** 1 Cor. x. 8.

πόρνη.

harlot, Matt. xxi. 31, 32. Luke xv. 30. 1 Cor. vi. 15, 16. Heb. xi. 31. Jas. ii. 25. Rev. xvii. 5 (πορνεία C[m], *marg.* **fornication**).
whore, Rev. xvii. 1, 15, 16. xix. 2.

πόρνος.

fornicator, 1 Cor. v. 9, 10, 11. vi. 9. Heb. xii. 16.
whoremonger, Eph. v. 5. 1 Tim. i. 10. Heb. xiii. 4. Rev. xxi. 8. xxii. 15.

πόῤῥω.

Comparative, ²πορρώτερω, -ρον LTTr.
far, Matt. xv. 8. Mark vii. 6.
further, Luke xxiv. 28².
a great way off, Luke xiv. 32.

πόῤῥωθεν.

afar off, Luke xvii. 12. Heb. xi. 13.

πορφύρα.

purple, Mark xv. 17, 20. Luke xvi. 19. Rev. xvii. 4 (πορφυροῦν GLTTr*S*). xviii. 12 (πορφύρεος G').

πορφύρεος, πορφυροῦς.

purple, *adj.*, John xix. 2, 5.
purple, *subst.*, Rev. xviii. 16.
Add, see πορφύρα.

πορφυρόπωλις.

seller of purple, Acts xvi. 14.

ποσάκις.

how often? Matt. xxiii. 37. Luke xiii. 34.
how oft? Matt. xviii. 21.

πόσις.

drink, John vi. 55. Rom. xiv. 17. Col. ii. 16 (*marg.* **drinking**).

πόσος.

how great? Matt. vi. 23.
how much? Matt. vii. 11. x. 25. xii. 12. Luke xi. 13. xii. 24, 28. xvi. 5, 7. Rom. xi. 12, 24. Phm. 16. Heb. ix. 14. x. 29.
Plural, **how many?** Matt. xv. 34. xvi. 9, 10. Mark vi. 38. viii. 5, 19, 20. Luke xv. 17. Acts xxi. 20. — *Neut.*, **how many things,** Matt. xxvii. 13. Mark xv. 4.
πόσος χρόνος, **how long ago?** Mark ix. 21.
what? 2 Cor. vii. 11.

ποταμός.

river, Mark i. 5. John vii. 38. Acts xvi. 13. Rev. viii. 10. ix. 14. xvi. 4, 12. xxii. 1, 2.
stream, Luke vi. 48, 49.
flood, Matt. vii. 25, 27. Rev. xii. 15, 16.
water, 2 Cor. xi. 26.
Add Matt. iii. 6 (.. Jordan), LTr*S*.

ποταμοφόρητος.

carried away of the flood, Rev. xii. 15.

ποταπός.

what manner of? Matt. viii. 27. Mark xiii. 1. Luke i. 29. vii. 39. 1 John iii. 1.
what manner of person, 2 Pet. iii. 11.
what, Mark xiii. 1.

ποτέ.

when, Luke xxii. 32.
sometime (sometimes²), Eph. ii. 13². v. 8². Col. i. 21. Tit. iii. 3². 1 Pet. iii. 20. — **some time,** Col. iii. 7.

once, Rom. vii. 9. Gal. i. 23.
in time (times[2]**) past**, Rom. xi. 30[2]. Gal. i. 13, 23[2]. Eph. ii. 2, 3[2], 11. Phm. 11. 1 Pet. ii. 10.
aforetime, John ix. 13.
in (the[1]**) old time**, 1 Pet. iii. 5[1]. 2 Pet. i. 21 (*marg.* at any time).
at length, Rom. i. 10.
at the last, Phil. iv. 10.
at any time, 1 Thes. ii. 5. Heb. i. 5, 13. ii. 1.
any time, 1 Cor. ix. 7.
ever, Eph. v. 29.
οὐ μή ποτέ, **never**, 2 Pet. i. 10.
See also δήποτε, μήποτε, ὁποῖος.

πότε.

In an indirect question [2].
when? Matt. xxiv. 3[2]. xxv. 37, 38, 39, 44. Mark xiii. 4, 33[2], 35[2]. Luke xii. 36[2]. xvii. 20[2]. xxi. 7. John vi. 25.
ἕως πότε; **how long?** Matt. xvii. 17*t*. Mark ix. 19*t*. Luke ix. 41. John x. 24. Rev. vi. 10.

πότερος.

Neut., **whether**, John vii. 17.

ποτήριον.

cup, Matt. x. 42. xx. 22, 23. xxiii. 25, 26. xxvi. 27, 39, 42(–G°°LTTr*S*). Mark vii. 4, 8(*ap*). ix. 41. x. 38, 39. xiv. 23, 36. Luke xi. 39. xxii. 17, 20*t*, 42. John xviii. 11. 1 Cor. x. 16, 21*t*. xi. 25*t*, 26, 27, 28. Rev. xiv. 10. xvi. 19. xvii. 4. xviii. 6.

ποτίζω.

give to drink, Matt. x. 42. xxvii. 48. Mark ix. 41. xv. 36.
give drink, Matt. xxv. 35, 37, 42. Rom. xii. 20.
make (to) drink, 1 Cor. xii. 13. Rev. [xiv. 8.
water, 1 Cor. iii. 6, 7, 8.
ἀπαγαγὼν ποτίζω, **lead away to watering**[co], Luke xiii. 15.
feed with, 1 Cor. iii. 2.

πότος.

banqueting, 1 Pet. iv. 3.

πού.

in a certain place, Heb. ii. 6. iv. 4.
about, Rom. iv. 19.
See also δήπου.

ποῦ.

In an indirect question [2].
where? Matt. ii. 2, 4[2]. viii. 20[2]. xxvi. 17. Mark xiv. 12, 14. xv. 47[2]. Luke viii. 25. ix. 58[2]. xii. 17[2]. xvii. 17, 37. xxii. 9, 11. John i. 38(39), 39(40). vii. 11. viii. 10(*ap*), 19. ix. 12. xi. 34, 57[2]. xx. 2[2], 13[2], 15[2]. Rom. iii. 27. 1 Cor. i. 20*tr*. xii. 17*t*, 19. xv. 55*t*. 1 Pet. iv. 18. 2 Pet. iii. 4. Rev. ii. 13[2].
whither? John iii. 8[2]. vii. 35. viii. 14[2]*t*. xii. 35[2]. xiii. 36. xiv. 5[2]. xvi. 5. Heb. xi. 8[2]. 1 John ii. 11[2].
Add Gal. iv. 15, for τίς, L*S*.

πούς.

foot, Matt. iv. 6. vii. 6. x. 14. xv. 30. xviii. 8*t*, 29 (–GLTr*S*). xxii. 13. xxviii. 9. Mark v. 22. vi. 11. vii. 25. ix. 45*t*. Luke i. 79. iv. 11. vii. 38*tr*, 44*t*, 45, 46(–G°). viii. 35, 41. ix. 5. x. 39. xv. 22. xvii. 16. xxiv. 39, 40(*ap*). John xi. 2, 32, 44. xii. 3*t*. xiii. 5, 6, 8, 9, 10 (–G°*S*), 12, 14*t*. xx. 12. Acts iv. 35, 37. v. 2, 9, 10. vii. 5, 33, 58. x. 25. xiii. 25, 51. xiv. 8, 10. xvi. 24. xxi. 11. xxii. 3. xxvi. 16.
Rom. iii. 15. x. 15. xvi. 20. 1 Cor. xii. 15, 21. xv. 25, 27. Eph. i. 22. vi. 15. 1 Tim. v. 10. Heb. ii. 8. xii. 13. Rev. i. 15, 17. ii. 18. iii. 9. x. 1, 2. xi. 11. xii. 1. xiii. 2. xix. 10. xxii. 8.
ὑποπόδιον τῶν ποδῶν, **footstool**, Matt. v. 35. xxii. 44. Mark xii. 36. Luke xx. 43. Acts ii. 35. vii. 49. Heb. i. 13. x. 13.
Add Luke x. 11(*ap*).

πρᾶγμα.

business, Rom. xvi. 2.
work, Jas. iii. 16.
matter, 1 Cor. vi. 1. 2 Cor. vii. 11. 1 Thes. iv. 6.
thing, Matt. xviii. 19. Luke i. 1. Acts v. 4. Heb. vi. 18. x. 1. xi. 1.

πραγματεία, -τία T*S*.

affair, 2 Tim. ii. 4.

πραγματεύομαι.
occupy, Luke xix. 13.

πραιτώριον.
Prætorium, Mark xv. 16.
palace (*marg.* Cæsar's court), Phil. i. 13.
common hall (*marg.* governor's house), Matt. xxvii. 27.
hall of judgment (*marg.* Pilate's house), John xviii. 28.
judgment-hall, John xviii. 28, 33. xix. 9. Acts xxiii. 35.

πράκτωρ.
officer, Luke xii. 58*t.*

πρᾶξις.
deed, Luke xxiii. 51. Acts xix. 18. Rom. viii. 13. Col. iii. 9.
works, Matt. xvi. 27.
office, Rom. xii. 4.

πρᾶος.
meek, Matt. xi. 29 (πραΰς LTTr*S*).

πρᾳότης.
πραΰτης T*S*[1], LT[2], LT*S*[3].
meekness, 1 Cor. iv. 21[3]. 2 Cor. x. 1[2]. Gal. v. 23[3]. vi. 1[1]. Eph. iv. 2[1]. Col. iii. 12[3]. 1 Tim. vi. 11 (πραϋπάθεια G''LT*S*). 2 Tim. ii. 25[3]. Tit. iii. 2[3].

πρασιά.
πρασιαὶ πρασιαί, in ranks, Mark vi. 40.

πράσσω, -ττω.
do, Luke xxii. 23. xxiii. 15, 41. John iii. 20. v. 29. Acts iii. 17. v. 35. xv. 29. xvi. 28. xvii. 7. xix. 36. xxvi. 9, 20, 26, 31. Rom. i. 32. ii. 1, 3. vii. 15, 19. ix. 11. xiii. 4. 1 Cor. ix. 17. 2 Cor. v. 10. Gal. v. 21. Eph. vi. 21. Phil. iv. 9. 1 Thes. iv. 11.
ἃ ἐπράξαμεν, our deeds, Luke xxiii. 41.
commit, Acts xxv. 11, 25. Rom. i. 32. ii. 2. 2 Cor. xii. 21.
use, Acts xix. 19.
keep, Rom. ii. 25.
require, Luke xix. 23.
exact, Luke iii. 13.
Add 1 Cor. v. 2, for ποιέω, G''T*S*.

πραϋπάθεια, suffering meekly.
1 Tim. vi. 11, for πρᾳότης, G''LT*S*.

πραΰς.
meek, Matt. v. 5. xxi. 5. 1 Pet. iii. 4.
Add Matt. xi. 29, for πρᾶος, LTTr*S*.

πραΰτης.
meekness, Jas. i. 21. iii. 13. 1 Pet. iii. 15. *Add, see* πρᾳότης.

πρέπω.
become, 1 Tim. ii. 10. Tit. ii. 1. Heb. vii. 26.
Impers., it becometh, Matt. iii. 15. Heb. ii. 10. — becometh, Eph. v. 3. — it is comely, 1 Cor. xi. 13.

πρεσβεία.
ambassage, Luke xiv. 32.
message, Luke xix. 14.

πρεσβεύω.
be an ambassador, 2 Cor. v. 20. Eph. vi. 20.

πρεσβυτέριον.
estate of elders, Acts xxii. 5.
elders, Luke xxii. 66.
presbytery, 1 Tim. iv. 14.

πρεσβύτερος, -τέρα.
elder, Luke xv. 25. 1 Pet. v. 5.
eldest, John viii. 9 (*ap*).
old man, Acts ii. 17.
elder woman, 1 Tim. v. 2.
elder, *subst.*, Matt. xv. 2. xvi. 21. xxi. 23. xxvi. 3, 47, 57, 59 (-G°°L Tr*S*). xxvii. 1, 3, 12, 20, 41. xxviii. 12. Mark vii. 3, 5. viii. 31. xi. 27. xiv. 43, 53. xv. 1. Luke vii. 3. ix. 22. xx. 1. xxii. 52. Acts iv. 5, 8, 23. vi. 12. xi. 30. xiv. 23. xv. 2, 4, 6, 22, 23. xvi. 4. xx. 17. xxi. 18. xxiii. 14. xxiv. 1. xxv. 15.
1 Tim. v. 1, 17, 19. Tit. i. 5. Heb. xi. 2. Jas. v. 14. 1 Pet. v. 1. 2 John 1. 3 John 1. Rev. iv. 4, 10. v. 5, 6, 8, 11, 14. vii. 11, 13. xi. 16. xiv. 3. xix. 4.

πρεσβύτης.
old man, Luke i. 18.
aged man, Tit. ii. 2.
aged, Phm. 9.

πρεσβῦτις.
aged woman, Tit. ii. 3.

πρηνής.
With γίνομαι, **fall headlong**, Acts i. 18.

πρίζω, πρίω.
saw asunder, Heb. xi. 37.

πρίν.
before, Matt. xxvi. 34, 75. Mark xiv. 72. Luke xxii. 61. John viii. 58. xiv. 29.
πρὶν ἤ, **before that**, Luke xxii. 34 (ἕως Tr*S*). Acts xxv. 16.—**before**, Matt. i. 18. Mark xiv. 30. Luke ii. 26. Acts ii. 20(−ἤ G°L*S*). vii. 2.
ere, John iv. 49.

πρό.
before, Matt. v. 12. viii. 29. xi. 10. xxiv. 38(−G°T). Mark i. 2. Luke i. 76. vii. 27. ix. 52. x. 1. xi. 38. xxi. 12. John v. 7. x. 8. xi. 55. xii. 1cc. xiii. 1. xvii. 5, 24. Acts v. 23 (ἐπί LT*S*), 36. xii. 6, 14. xiii. 24. xiv. 13. xxi. 38. Rom. xvi. 7. 1 Cor. ii. 7. iv. 5. Gal. i. 17. Eph. i. 4. Col. i. 17. 2 Tim. iv. 21. Heb. xi. 5. Jas. v 9, 12. 1 Pet. i. 20.
before, *adv.*cc, Matt. vi. 8. Luke ii. 21. xxii. 15. John i. 48(49). xiii. 19. Gal. ii. 12. iii. 23. 2 Tim. i. 9. Tit. i. 2.
or evercc, Acts xxiii. 15.
above, 1 Pet. iv. 8.
above (often misprinted *about*) . .
ago, 2 Cor. xii. 2.
Add Jude 25 (*ap*).

προάγω.
bring forth, Acts xii. 6. xxv. 26.
bring out, Acts xvi. 30.
go before, Matt. ii. 9. xiv. 22. xxi. 9, 31. xxvi. 32. xxviii. 7. Mark vi. 45. x. 32 (*with* ἦν). xi. 9. xiv. 28. xvi. 7. Luke xviii. 39 (παράγω Lm). 1 Tim. i. 18. v. 24. Heb. vii. 18.
Add Acts xvii. 5, for ἄγω, L*S*. 2 John 9, for παραβαίνω, LT*S*.

προαιρέω.
Mid., **to purpose**, 2 Cor. ix. 7.

προαιτιάομαι.
prove (*marg.* **charge**) **before**, Rom. iii. 9.

προακούω.
hear before, Col. i. 5.

προαμαρτάνω.
sin heretofore, 2 Cor. xiii. 2.
sin already, 2 Cor. xii. 21.

προαύλιον.
porch, Mark xiv. 68.

προβαίνω.
go on, Matt. iv. 21.
go farther, Mark i. 19p.
προβεβηκὼς ἐν ταῖς ἡμέραις αὐτοῦ, **well stricken in years**, Luke i. 7, 18.
προβ. ἐν ἡμέραις πολλαῖς, **of a great age**, Luke ii. 36.

προβάλλω.
put forward, Acts xix. 33.
shoot forth, Luke xxi. 30.

προβατικός.
sheep *market* (*marg.* **gate**), John v. 2.

προβάτιον, little sheep.
Jn. xxi. 16, 17, for πρόβατον, T, 17Tr.

πρόβατον.
sheep, Matt. vii. 15. ix. 36. x. 6, 16. xii. 11, 12. xv. 24. xviii. 12. xxv. 32, 33. xxvi. 31. Mark vi. 34. xiv. 27. Luke xv. 4, 6. John ii. 14, 15. x. 2, 3*t*, 4 (πάντα fr. πᾶς LTTr, −*S*), 4, 7, 8, 11, 12*t*, 12 (*ap*), 13, 15, 16, 26, 27. xxi. 16 and 17 (προβάτιον T, 17Tr). Acts viii. 32. Rom. viii. 36. Heb. xiii. 20. 1 Pet. ii. 25. Rev. xviii. 13.
See also αὐλή.

προβιβάζω.
With ἐκ, **draw out of**, Acts xix. 33 (συμβιβάζω L*S*).
instruct before, Matt. xiv. 8.

προβλέπω.
Mid., **provide** (*marg.* **foresee**), Heb. xi. 40.

προγίνομαι.
be past, Rom. iii. 25.

προγινώσκω.

know before, 2 Pet. iii. 17[p].
foreknow, Rom. viii. 29. xi. 2.
know, Acts xxvi. 5 (*with* ἄνωθεν).
foreordain, 1 Pet. i. 20.
Add Rom. xi. 1 (people ὃν προέγνω), L[b].

πρόγνωσις.

foreknowledge, Acts ii. 23. 1 Pet. i. 2.

πρόγονος.

Plural, **forefathers,** 2 Tim. i. 3. — **parents,** 1 Tim. v. 4.

προγράφω.

write aforetime, Rom. xv. 4 (γράφω L[m]).
write afore, Eph. iii. 3.
write, Rom. xv. 4 (γράφω G″LT*S*).
set forth evidently, Gal. iii. 1.
ordain before, Jude 4.

πρόδηλος.

manifest beforehand, 1 Tim. v. 25.
open beforehand, 1 Tim. v. 24.
evident, Heb. vii. 14.

προδίδωμι.

give first, Rom. xi. 35.

προδότης.

betrayer, Acts vii. 52.
traitor, Luke vi. 16. 2 Tim. iii. 4.

προδρέμω See **προτρέχω.**

πρόδρομος.

forerunner, Heb. vi. 20.

προεῖδον.

see before, Acts ii. 31.
foresee, Gal. iii. 8.

προεῖπον, -ερῶ, -είρηκα.

speak before, Acts i. 16. 2 Pet. iii. 2. Jude 17.
say before, Rom. ix. 29. 2 Cor. vii. 3. Gal. i. 9. Heb. x. 15 (εἴρηκα G″L*S*).
tell before, Matt. xxiv. 25. 2 Cor. xiii. 2.
foretell, Mark xiii. 23.
tell in time past, Gal. v 21.
forewarn, 1 Thes. iv. 6.
Add Heb. iv. 7, for εἴρηκα, G″LT*S*.

προελπίζω.

trust (*marg.* **hope**) **first,** Eph. i. 12.

προενάρχομαι.

begin before, 2 Cor. viii. 10.
begin, 2 Cor. viii. 6.

προεπαγγέλλω.

Mid., **promise afore,** Rom. i. 2.
Add 2 Cor. ix. 5, for προκαταγγέλλω, G″LT*S*.

προέπω, -ερῶ. See **προεῖπον.**

προέρχομαι.

go before, Luke i. 17. xxii. 47. Acts xx. 5, 13. 2 Cor. ix. 5.
go forward, Mark xiv. 35 (προσέρχομαι G′Tr).
go farther, Matt. xxvi. 39 (προσέρχομαι G′Tr*S*).
outgo, Mark vi. 33(*ap*).
pass on, Acts xii. 10.

προετοιμάζω.

prepare afore, Rom. ix. 23.
ordain (*marg.* **prepare**) **before,** Eph. ii. 10.

προευαγγελίζομαι.

preach the gospel before, Gal. iii. 8.

προέχω.

Mid., **be better,** Rom. iii. 9.

προηγέομαι.

prefer, Rom. xii. 10.

πρόθεσις.

purpose, Acts xi. 23. xxvii. 13. Rom. viii. 28. ix. 11. Eph. i. 11. iii. 11. 2 Tim. i. 9. iii. 10.
See also ἄρτος.

προθέσμιος.

Fem., **time appointed,** Gal. iv. 2.

προθυμία.

forwardness of mind, 2 Cor. ix. 2.
readiness of mind, Acts xvii. 11.
readiness, 2 Cor. viii. 11.
ready mind, 2 Cor. viii. 19.
willing mind, 2 Cor. viii. 12.

πρόθυμος.

ready, Mark xiv. 38. Rom. i. 15.
willing, Matt. xxvi. 41.

προθύμως.

willingly, 1 Pet. v. 2.

πρόϊμος. See πρώϊμος.

προϊνός. See πρωϊνός.

προΐστημι.

2nd Aorist,² or Middle.

be over, 1 Thes. v. 12.
rule, Rom. xii. 8. 1 Tim. iii. 4, 5², 12. v. 17².
maintain, Tit. iii. 8, 14 (*marg.* **profess**).

προκαλέω.

Mid., **provoke,** Gal. v. 26.

προκαταγγέλλω.

foretell, Acts iii. 24 (καταγγέλλω G LTS).
show before, Acts iii. 18. vii. 52.
Pass. part., *with art.*, **whereof** ᶜ**ye had notice before** (*marg.* **which hath been so much spoken of before**), 2 Cor. ix. 5 (προεπαγγέλλω G″LTS).

προκαταρτίζω.

make up beforehand, 2 Cor. ix. 5.

πρόκειμαι.

be set before, Heb. vi. 18. xii. 1, 2.
be set forth, Jude 7.
be first, 2 Cor. viii. 12.

προκηρύσσω, -ττω.

preach before, Acts iii. 20 (προχειρίζομαι GLTS).
preach first, Acts xiii. 24ᵖ.

προκοπή.

furtherance, Phil. i. 12, 25.
profiting, 1 Tim. iv. 15.

προκόπτω.

proceed, 2 Tim. iii. 9.
increase, Luke ii. 52. 2 Tim. ii. 16.
wax, 2 Tim. iii. 13.
profit, Gal. i. 14.
be far spent, Rom. xiii. 12.

πρόκριμα.

preferring one before another (*marg.* **prejudice**), 1 Tim. v. 21.

προκυρόω.

confirm before, Gal. iii. 17.

προλαμβάνω.

take before, 1 Cor. xi. 21.
overtake, Gal. vi. 1.
come aforehand, Mark xiv. 8.

προλέγω.

tell before, Gal. v. 21. 1 Thes. iii. 4.
foretell, 2 Cor. xiii. 2.

προμαρτύρομαι.

testify beforehand, 1 Pet. i. 11ᵖ.

προμελετάω.

meditate before, Luke xxi. 14.

προμεριμνάω.

take thought beforehand, Mark xiii. 11.

προνοέω.

provide for, 1 Tim. v. 8.
Mid., **provide,** Rom. xii. 17.—**provide for,** 2 Cor. viii. 21.

πρόνοια.

providence, Acts xxiv. 2.
provision for, Rom. xiii. 14.

προοράω.

see before, Acts xxi. 29 (*with* εἰμί).
Mid., **foresee,** Acts ii. 25.

προορίζω.

determine before, Acts iv. 28.
predestinate, Rom. viii. 29, 30. Eph. i. 5, 11.
ordain, 1 Cor. ii. 7.

προπάσχω.

suffer before, 1 Thes. ii. 2ᵖ.

προπάτωρ, forefather.

Rom. iv. 1, for πατήρ, G″LS.

προπέμπω.

conduct forth, 1 Cor. xvi. 11.
bring (forward¹) on one's journey, 1 Cor. xvi. 6. Tit. iii. 13. 3 John 6ᵖ¹.
bring on one's way, Acts xv. 3. xxi. 5. Rom. xv. 24. 2 Cor. i. 16.
accompany, Acts xx. 38.

προπετής.

heady, 2 Tim. iii. 4.
rashlyᶜᶜ, Acts xix. 36.

προπορεύομαι.

go before, Luke i. 76. Acts vii. 40.

πρός.

I. With the Genitive.

for, Acts xxvii. 34.

II. With the Dative.

at, Luke xix. 37. John xviii. 16. xx. 12*t*.

about, Rev. i. 13.

Add Mark v. 11, John xx.11, *see* No. III.

III. With the Accusative.

toward (to . . -ward^2), Luke xxiv. 29. Acts xxiv. 16. 2 Cor. i. 12^2, 18. iii. 4^2. vii. 4. Phil. ii. 30. Col. iv. 5. 1 Thes. i. 8^2. iv. 12. v. 14. Phm. 5 (εἰς L). 1 John iii. 21.

to, Matt. ii. 12. iii. 5, 14. vii. 15. x. 6, 13. xiv. 29. xvii. 14. xxi. 34. xxv. 9. xxvi. 18, 45, 57. xxvii. 4, 14. Mark i. 40, 45. iii. 7(G', εἰς G LT). iv. 41. v. 15, 19. ix. 14. x. 7 (–L*S*^{c}), 50. xi. 7, 27. xii. 2. xiv. 53.

Luke i. 27, 43, 55, 73. ii. 15. vi. 47. vii. 4, 6, 19, 44, 50. viii. 4, 19, 25, 35. ix. 14, 23. xi. 6. xii. 41, 58. xiv. 6, 7, 26. xv. 18, 20, 22. xvi. 26*t*. xix. 35. xx. 9, 10. xxi. 38. xxii. 45. xxiii. 4, 7, 15. xxiv. 17, 32.

John i. 42(43), 47(48). iii. 2, 20, 21, 26. iv. 33, 35. v. 40, 45. vi. 17, 35, 37*t*, 44, 68. vii. 45, 50. viii. 31. ix. 13. xi. 19, 45, 46. xiii. 3, 6. xiv. 18. xvi. 5, 10, 16(*ap*), 17, 28. xvii. 11, 13. xviii. 13. xix. 39. xx. 2*t*, 17*t*. xxi. 22, 23.

Acts ii. 7(–LT*S*), 12. iv. 23, 24. viii. 24. ix. 2, 10, 27, 32, 40. x. 3, 13, 21, 33. xi. 3, 30. xii. 20. xiv. 11. xvi. 36. xvii. 15. xx. 18. xxiii. 18, 22, 30. xxv. 16, 21. xxvi. 9. xxviii. 8, 23.

Rom. viii. 31. x. 1, 21. xv. 2, 22, 24(*ap*), 30. 1 Cor. ii. 1. iv. 18, 19. vi. 5. xiii. 12. xiv. 12. xv. 34. 2 Cor. ii. 1. iii. 1, 16. iv. 2. viii. 19. x. 4. xii. 14. xiii. 1, 7. Gal. i. 17. Eph. iv. 29. Phil. i. 26. ii. 25. Col. ii.23. 1 Thes. i. 9. Tit. iii. 1.

Heb. i. 13. vi. 11. ix. 13. Jas. iv. 5 (*see* φθόνος). 1 Pet. ii. 4. 2 John 12. 3 John 14. Rev. iii. 20.

πρὸς π., **which is to try**, 1 Pet. iv. 12.

πρὸς τό, *with an Infinitive*, **to**, Matt. v. 28. vi. 1. xiii. 30. Mark xiii. 22. — **for to**, Matt. xxiii. 5. — **to this end, that**, Luke xviii. 1. — **that . . may (might)**, Eph. vi. 11. 2 Thes. iii. 8. Jas. iii. 3 (εἰς LT*S*). — **that . . could**, 2 Cor. iii. 13. — **because . . would**, 1 Thes. ii. 9.

to do, 2 Cor. xi. 8.

to give, 1 Pet. iii. 15.

to answer, 2 Cor. v. 12.

unto, Matt. iii. 10, 13, 15(–L). xi. 28. xiii. 2. xiv. 25, 28. xix. 14. xxi. 1, 32, 37. xxiii. 34, 37. xxv. 36, 39. xxvi. 14, 40. xxvii. 19, 62. Mark i. 5, 32. ii. 3, 13. iii. 8, 13, 31. iv. 1. vi. 25, 30, 33 (*marg.* **against**), 45, 48, 51. vii. 1, 31 (εἰς GLTTr*S*). ix. 17, 19, 20. x. 1, 14. xii. 4, 6, 13, 18. xiv. 10. xv. 43.

Luke i. 13, 18, 19, 28, 34, 61, 80. ii. 20, 34, 48, 49. iii. 9, 12, 13, 14 (–LTTr). iv. 21, 23, 26*t*, 40, 43. v. 4, 10, 22, 31, 33, 34, 36. vi. 9. vii. 3, 7, 20*t*, 24, 40. viii. 21(–L), 22. ix. 3, 13, 33, 43, 50, 57, 59, 62(–T). x. 2, 23, 26, 29. xi. 1, 5*t*, 39, 53 (*ap*). xii. 1, 15, 16, 22, 41. xiii. 7, 23, 34. xiv. 3, 7, 23, 25. xv. 3. xvi. 1, 30. xvii. 1, 22. xviii. 3, 7(–TTr *S*), 9, 16, 31, 40. xix. 5, 8, 9, 13, 33, 39. xx. 2, 3, 23, 41. xxii. 15, 52, 70. xxiii. 14, 22, 28. xxiv. 5, 10, 17, 18, 25, 44.

John i. 29. ii. 3. iii. 4, 26. iv. 15, 30, 40, 47, 48, 49. v. 33. vi. 5*t*, 28, 34, 45, 65. vii. 3, 33, 37, 50. viii. 2 (*ap*), 3 (*ap*), 7 (*ap*), 57. x. 35, 41. xi. 3, 4, 15, 21, 29. xii. 32. xiii. 1. xiv. 3, 6, 12, 23, 28*t*. xvi. 7*t*. xviii. 24, 29, 38. xx. 10, 17.

Acts i. 7. ii. 29, 37, 38. iii. 11, 12, 22(*ap*), 22, 25. iv. 1, 8, 19, 23. v. 9, 35. vii. 3, 31(–G$^{\infty}$LT*S*). viii. 14, 20, 26. ix. 6(*ap*), 11, 15, 38. x. 15, 21(*ap*), 28. xi. 11, 20. xii. 5, 8, 15, 21. xiii. 15, 31, 32, 36. xv. 2, 7, 25,

33, 36. xvi. 37. xvii. 2, 15. xviii. 6, 14, 21. xix. 2*t*, 3(–G^{oo}LT*S*), 31. xx. 6. xxi. 11, 18, 37, 39. xxii. 1, 5, 8, 10, 13, 15, 21, 25. xxiii. 3, 15 (*εἰς* LT*S*), 17, 18, 24. xxv. 22. xxvi. 1, 6 (*εἰς* G″LT*S*), 14, 28. xxvii. 3. xxviii. 17, 21, 25, 26, 30.

Rom. i. 10, 13. x. 21. xv. 23, 29, 32. 1 Cor. iv. 21. xii. 2. xiv. 6, 26. xvi. 5, 11, 12. 2 Cor. i. 15, 16, 20. vi. 11. vii. 12. viii. 17. xii. 17. Gal. vi. 10*t*. Eph. ii. 18. iii. 14. v. 31 (–L*S*). vi. 9, 22. Phil. iv. 6. Col. iv. 8, 10. 1 Thes. i. 9. ii. 1, 2, 18. iii. 6, 11. 1 Tim. iii. 14. iv. 7, 8. 2 Tim. ii. 24. iii. 17. iv. 9. Tit. i. 16. iii. 2, 12*t*.

Heb. i. 8. v. 5, 7. vii. 21. ix. 20. xiii. 13. 2 Pet. iii. 16. 1 John v. 16*tr*, 17. 2 John 10, 12. Rev. x. 9. xii. 5, 12. xxi. 9(*om S*). xxii. 18 (*ἐπί* GLTTr*S*).

nigh unto, Mark v. 11 (*dat.* GLTTr*S*, –G^{o}).

at, Matt. xxvi. 18. Mark i. 33. v. 22. vii. 25. xi. 1. xiv. 54. Luke xvi. 20. xix. 29. John xx. 11(*dat.* GLTTr, *ἐν S*). Acts iii. 2. Rev. i. 17.

against, Matt. iv. 6. Mark xii. 12. Luke iv. 11. v. 30. xx. 19. Acts vi. 1. ix. 5(*ap*), 29. xix. 38. xxiii. 30. xxiv. 19. xxv. 19. xxvi. 14. 1 Cor. vi. 1. Eph. vi. 11, 12*five*. Col. iii. 13, 19. Heb. xii. 4. Rev. xiii. 6.

before, Acts xxvi. 26. Rom. iv. 2.

by, Mark iv. 1. xi. 4. Luke xxii. 56. Acts v. 10.

πρὸς ὅ, **whereby,** Eph. iii. 4.

with, Matt. xiii. 56. xxvi. 55(–G^{o}TTr^{b}*S*). Mark vi. 3. ix. 10, 16 (*marg.* **among**), 19. xi. 31. xiv. 49. Luke vi. 11. ix. 41. xviii. 11. xx. 5. John i. 1, 2. Acts ii. 47. iii. 25. xi. 2. xv. 2. xvii. 17. xxiv. 12. Rom. v. 1. 1 Cor. ii. 3. xvi. 6, 7, 10. 2 Cor. v. 8. vi. 14, 15. xi. 9(8). Gal. i. 18. ii. 5. iv. 18, 20. 1 Thes. iii. 4. 2 Thes. ii. 5. iii. 1, 10. Phm. 13. Heb. iv. 13. x. 16. 1 John i. 2. ii. 1.

to be compared with, Rom. viii. 18.

within, Mark xiv. 4.

in, Luke xii. 3. xxiv. 12(*ap*). 1 John v. 14 (*marg.* **concerning**).

between, Luke xxiii. 12. Acts xxvi. 31.

among, Mark i. 27. viii. 16. ix. 33 (–G^{oo}LTr*S*), 34. x. 26. xii. 7. xv. 31. xvi. 3. Luke iv. 36. xx. 14. xxii. 23. John vi. 52. vii. 35. xii. 19. xvi. 17. xix. 24. Acts iv. 15. xxviii. 4, 25. 2 Cor. xii. 21.

τὰ πρός, **the things which belong unto,** Luke xix. 42. — **those things which pertain to,** Rom. xv. 17. — **things that** *pertain* **unto,** 2 Pet. i. 3. — **in things pertaining** (*pertaining*²) **to,** Heb. ii. 17. v. 1². — **about,** Mark ii. 2. — **conditions of,** Luke xiv. 32. — **sufficient to,** Luke xiv. 28 (*τὰ εἰς* G′L*S*, *εἰς* GTTr). — **what one hath against,** Acts xxiii. 30 (*αὐτούς* for *τὰ πρὸς αὐτόν* LT*S*).

according to, Luke xii. 47. 2 Cor. v. 10. Gal. ii. 14.

for, Matt. xxvi. 12. Mark x. 5. Luke viii. 13. John v. 35. Acts iii. 10. xiii. 15. 1 Cor. vii. 5, 35*t*. x. 11. 2 Cor. ii. 16. vii. 8. Gal. ii. 5. Eph. iv. 12. 1 Thes. ii. 17. 1 Tim. i. 16. 2 Tim. iii. 16*f*. Phm. 15. Heb. xii. 10, 11.

π. τί, **for what intent,** John xiii. 28.

because of, Matt. xix. 8.

of, Heb. i. 7. xi. 18 (*marg.* **to**).

Not rendered, Luke ii. 18. iv. 4. vi. 3. xiv. 5. Acts xi. 14.

Add, for *εἰς*, Luke xxiv. 50, LTr*S*. Acts xvi. 40, GLT*S*. 1 Thes. i. 5, G′L. For *ἐπί*, Luke xvii. 4, LTr*S*. For *παρά*, Luke x. 39, L^{m}TTr*S*. Acts v. 10, LT*S*. — Mark ix. 14, *πρὸς αὐτούς* for *αὐτοῖς*, Tr*S*. xv. 42, *see προσάββατον*. Luke i. 30 (unto), L^{m}. x. 22(*ap*). xx. 25 (unto^{1st}), TTr*S*. 45 (*ap*). xxiv. 44 (unto^{1st}), L^{m}TTr*S*. John i. 19 (sent *πρὸς αὐτόν*), LTr. viii. 33 (. . him), LTTr*S*. xix. 2(*ap*). Acts v. 8(unto), LT*S*. xvii. 26, *see προτάσσω*. Rev. xii. 5 (to^{2d}), GLTTr*S*.

See also ἀλλήλων, διάκρισις, ἔνδειξις, κατάκρισις, μεθοδεία, ὀλίγος, παραχειμασία, συμφέρω, φωτισμός, χρεία.

προσάββατον.

the day before the sabbath, Mark xv. 42 (πρὸς σάββατον LTr).

προσαγορεύω.

to call, Heb. v. 10.

προσάγω.

bring, Luke ix. 41. Acts xvi. 20. 1 Pet. iii. 18.
draw near, Acts xxvii. 27°°.
Add Matt. xviii. 24, for προσφέρω, LTTr.

προσαγωγή.

access, Rom. v. 2. Eph. ii. 18. iii. 12.

προσαιτέω.

beg, Mark x. 46 (p, προσαίτης TTr*S*). Luke xviii. 35 (ἐπαιτέω LTTr*S*). John ix. 8.

προσαίτης, beggar.

Mark x. 46, for προσαιτέω^p, TTr*S*. John ix. 8, for τυφλός, GLTTr*S*.

προσαναβαίνω.

go up, Luke xiv. 10.

προσαναλίσκω.

spend, Luke viii. 43.

προσαναπληρόω.

to supply, 2 Cor. ix. 12 (*with* ἐστί). xi. 9.

προσανατίθημι.

Mid., **add in conference,** Gal. ii. 6. — **confer,** Gal. i. 16.

προσαπειλέω.

Mid., **threaten further,** Acts iv. 21p.

προσδαπανάω.

spend more, Luke x. 35.

προσδέομαι.

to need, Acts xvii. 25p.

προσδέχομαι.

receive, Luke xv. 2. Rom. xvi. 2. Phil. ii. 29.
accept, Heb. xi. 35.
take, Heb. x. 34.
allow, Acts xxiv. 15.
look for, Luke ii. 38. Acts xxiii. 21. Tit. ii. 13. Jude 21.
wait for, Mark xv. 43 (*with* ἦν). Luke ii. 25. xii. 36. xxiii. 51.
Add Heb. xi. 13, for λαμβάνω, L.

προσδοκάω.

look for, Matt. xi. 3. xxiv. 50. Luke vii. 19, 20. xii. 46. 2 Pet. iii. 12, 13, 14p.
look when, Acts xxviii. 6.
look, Acts xxviii. 6p.
expect, Acts iii. 5.
be in expectation (*marg.* **suspense**), Luke iii. 15p.
wait for, Luke i. 21 (*with* εἰμί). viii. 40. Acts x. 24 (*with* εἰμί).
tarry, Acts xxvii. 33.

προσδοκία.

looking after, Luke xxi. 26.
expectation, Acts xii. 11.

προσδρέμω. See προστρέχω.

προσεάω.

suffer, Acts xxvii. 7.

προσεγγίζω.

come nigh unto, Mark ii. 4.

προσεδρεύω.

wait at, 1 Cor. ix. 13 (παρεδρεύω G″LT*S*).

προσεργάζομαι.

to gain, Luke xix. 16.

προσέρχομαι.

come to, Matt. iv. 3p. viii. 25. ix. 14, 28. xiv. 15. xv. 1. xvii. 14, 19, 24. xviii. 21. xx. 20. xxi. 14, 28, 30. xxii. 23. xxiv. 1. xxvi. 17, 49. Mark x. 2. Luke viii. 24. xx. 27. xxiii. 36. Acts xxiii. 14. Heb. xi. 6.
come unto, Matt. v. 1. viii. 5. xiii. 36. xv. 30. xviii. 1. xix. 3. xxi. 23. xxiv. 3. xxvi. 7, 69, 73. Mark vi. 35. Acts x. 28. xviii. 2. xxiv. 23 (−G°°LT*S*). Heb. iv. 16. vii. 25. xii. 18, 22.
comer c**thereunto,** Heb. x. 1p.
come, Matt. iv. 11. viii. 19. ix. 20. xiii. 10, 27. xiv. 12. xv. 12, 23.

xvi. 1. xvii. 7. xix. 16. xxv. 20, 22, 24. xxvi. 50, 60p (*ap*), 60. xxviii. 2, 9, 18. Mark i. 31. xii. 28. xiv. 45p. Luke vii. 14. viii. 44. ix. 12. xiii. 31. John xii. 21. Acts xii. 13. xxii. 27. xxviii. 9. 1 Pet. ii. 4.
be a coming, Luke ix. 42p.
go to, Matt. xxvii. 58. Luke x. 34.
go unto, Luke xxiii. 52. Acts ix. 1.
go, Acts xxii. 26.
go near, Acts viii. 29.
draw near, Acts vii. 31p. Heb. x. 22.
consent to, 1 Tim. vi. 3.
Add, for ἔρχομαι, Matt. viii. 2, G′ LTTr*S*. ix. 18[1st], L*S*. For προέρχομαι, Matt. xxvi. 39, G′Tr*S*. Mark xiv. 35, G′Tr.
προσῆλθαν for προσῆλθον, Matt. v. 1, TTr*S*. ix. 28, xiii. 36, xiv. 15, LTTr. Luke xiii. 31, TTr.

προσευχή.

prayer, Matt. xvii. 21(*ap*). xxi. 13, 22. Mark ix. 29. xi. 17. Luke vi. 12. xix. 46. xxii. 45. Acts i. 14. ii. 42. iii. 1. vi. 4. x. 4, 31. xii. 5. xvi. 13, 16. Rom. i. 9(10). xii. 12. xv. 30. 1 Cor. vii. 5. Eph. i. 16. vi. 18. Phil. iv. 6. Col. iv. 2, 12. 1 Thes. i. 2. 1Tim. ii. 1. v. 5. Phm. 4, 22. 1Pet. iii. 7. iv. 7. Rev. v. 8. viii. 3, 4.
Dat., **earnestly**[c] (*marg.* **in his prayer**), Jas. v. 17.

προσεύχομαι.

pray, Matt. v. 44. vi. 5*t*, 6*t*, 7p, 9. xiv. 23. xix. 13. xxiv. 20. xxvi. 36, 39, 41, 42, 44. Mark i. 35. vi. 46. xi. 24p, 25. xiii. 18, 33 (-LT Tr[b]). xiv. 32, 35, 38, 39. Luke i. 10. iii. 21. v. 16. vi. 12, 28. ix. 18, 28, 29. xi. 1*t*, 2. xviii. 1, 10, 11. xxii. 40, 41, 44(*ap*), 46.
Acts i. 24. vi. 6p. viii. 15. ix. 11, 40. x. 9, 30. xi. 5. xii. 12. xiii. 3. xiv. 23. xvi. 25. xx. 36. xxi. 5. xxii. 17p. xxviii. 8. 1 Cor. xi. 4, 5, 13. xiv. 13, 14*t*, 15*t*. Eph. vi. 18. Phil. i. 9. Col. i. 3, 9. iv. 3. 1 Thes. v. 17, 25. 2 Thes. i. 11. iii. 1. 1 Tim. ii. 8. Heb. xiii. 18. Jas. v. 13, 14, 17, 18. Jude 20.
With μακρά fr. μακρός, **make long prayer (prayers**[2]**),** Matt. xxiii. 14(13, *ap*). Mark xii. 40[2]. Luke xx. 47[2].
pray for, Rom. viii. 26.
Add Jas. v. 16, for εὔχομαι, L.

προσέχω.

give heed to (unto[2]**),** Acts viii. 6[2], 10. 1 Tim. i. 4. iv. 1. Tit. i. 14.
take heed to (unto[2]**),** Luke xvii. 3. xxi. 34. Acts v. 35. xx. 28[2].
With ᾧ, **take heed whereunto,** 2 Pet. i. 19p.
take heed, Matt. vi. 1.
beware, Matt. vii. 15. x. 17. xvi. 6, 11, 12. Luke xii. 1 (*with* ἑαυτοῖς). xx. 46.
attend unto, Acts xvi. 14.
give attendance to (at[2]**),** 1 Tim. iv. 13. Heb. vii. 13[2].
have regard to, Acts viii. 11.
be given to, 1 Tim. iii. 8.
See also περισσῶς.

προσηλόω.

nail to, Col. ii. 14.

προσήλυτος.

proselyte, Matt. xxiii. 15. Acts ii. 10. vi. 5. xiii. 43.

πρόσκαιρος.

for a season, Heb. xi. 25.
With εἰμί, **dure for a while,** Matt. xiii. 21. — **endure but for a time,** Mark iv. 17.
temporal, 2 Cor. iv. 18.

προσκαλέω.

Middle, προσκαλέομαι.

call unto (to[1]**) one,** Matt. x. 1. xv. 32. xviii. 2. xx. 25. Mark iii. 13, 23. vi. 7. vii. 14. viii. 1, 34. x. 42[1]. xii. 43. xv. 44. Luke vii. 19(18). xvi. 5. xviii. 16. Acts vi. 2. xx. 1. xxiii. 17, 18, 23.
With ὅ, **call whereunto,** Acts xiii. 2.
call for, Acts xiii. 7. Jas. v. 14.
call, Matt. xv. 10. xviii. 32p. Luke xv. 26. Acts ii. 39. v. 40p. xvi. 10.

προσκαρτερέω.
continue steadfastly in, Acts ii. 42 (*with* εἰμί; *with* ἐν Lb).
continue instant in, Rom. xii. 12.
continue in, Acts i. 14 (*with* εἰμί). ii. 46 (*with* ἐν). Col. iv. 2.
continue with, Acts viii. 13 (*with* εἰμί).
attend continually upon, Rom. xiii. 6.
give one's self continually to, Acts vi. 4.
wait on continually, Acts x. 7.
wait on, Mark iii. 9.

προσκαρτέρησις.
perseverance, Eph. vi. 18.

προσκεφάλαιον.
pillow, Mark iv. 38.

προσκληρόω.
Pass., **consort with,** Acts xvii. 4.

πρόσκλησις, summons, charge. 1 Tim. v. 21. for πρόσκλισις, L.

προσκλίνω, incline towards. Acts v. 36, for προσκολλάω, G″LT*S*.

πρόσκλισις.
partiality, 1 Tim. v. 21 (πρόσκλησις L).

προσκολλάω.
Pass., **be joined unto,** Eph. v. 31 (*with* πρός StGT). — **join one's self to,** Acts v. 36 (προσκλίνω G″LT*S*).— **cleave to,** Matt. xix. 5 (κολλάω G″L TTr). Mark x. 7.

πρόσκομμα.
stumbling, 1 Pet. ii. 8(7).
stumbling-block, Rom. xiv. 13. 1 Cor. viii. 9.
offence, Rom. xiv. 20.
See also λίθος.

προσκοπή.
offence, 2 Cor. vi. 3.

προσκόπτω.
beat upon, Matt. vii. 27 (προσρήγνυμι Lm).
With πρός, **dash against,** Matt. iv. 6. Luke iv. 11.
stumble at, Rom. ix. 32. 1 Pet. ii. 8.
stumble, John xi. 9, 10. Rom. xiv. 21.

προσκυλίω.
roll to, Matt. xxvii. 60 (*with* ἐπί L).
roll unto, Mark xv. 46 (*with* ἐπί).

προσκυνέω.
With ἐνώπιον, **to worship** (*marg.* **fall down before**), Luke iv. 7.
worship, Matt. ii. 2, 8, 11. iv. 9, 10. viii. 2. ix. 18. xiv. 33. xv. 25. xviii. 26 (*marg.* **beseech**). xx. 20. xxviii. 9, 17. Mark v. 6. xv. 19. Luke iv. 8. xxiv. 52(*ap*). John iv. 20*t*, 21, 22*t*, 23*t*, 24*t*. ix. 38. xii. 20. Acts vii. 43. viii. 27. x. 25. xxiv. 11. 1 Cor. xiv. 25. Heb. i. 6(7). xi. 21. Rev. iii. 9. iv. 10. v. 14. vii. 11. ix. 20. xi. 1, 16. xiii. 4*t*. 8, 12, 15. xiv. 7, 9, 11. xv. 4. xvi. 2. xix. 4, 10*t*, 20. xx. 4. xxii. 8, 9.

προσκυνητής.
worshipper, John iv. 23.

προσλαλέω.
speak to, Acts xiii. 43.
speak with, Acts xxviii. 20.

προσλαμβάνω.
Mid., **take unto one,** Acts xvii. 5. xviii. 26. — **take,** Matt. xvi. 22. Mark viii. 32. Acts xxvii. 33, 34 (μεταλαμβάνω GLT*S*), 36. — **receive,** Acts xxviii. 2. Rom. xiv. 1, 3. xv. 7*t*. Phm. 12(-LT*S*), 17.

πρόσληψις (-λημψις LT*S*).
receiving, Rom. xi. 15.

προσμένω.
continue with, Matt. xv. 32.
continue in, 1 Tim. v. 5.
abide still, 1 Tim. i. 3.
tarry c**there,** Acts xviii. 18.
cleave unto, Acts xi. 23.
be with, Mark viii. 2.
Add Acts xiii. 43, for ἐπιμένω, GL [T*S*.

προσορμίζω.
Mid., **draw to the shore,** Mark vi. 53.

προσοφείλω.
owe besides, Phm. 19.

προσοχθίζω.
be grieved with, Heb. iii. 10, 17.

προσπαίω, strike or beat upon. Matt. vii. 25, for προσπίπτω, L. (A conjecture, allowed by the frequent use of ε for αι in early MSS.)

πρόσπεινος.
very hungry, Acts x. 10.

προσπήγνυμι.
crucify, Acts ii. 23.

προσπίπτω.
fall at, Mark vii. 25.
fall down at, Luke v. 8.
fall down before, Mark iii. 11. v. 33. Luke viii. 28, 47. Acts xvi. 29.
beat upon, Matt. vii. 25 (προσπαίω L). προσέπεσαν for -σον, TTr.

προσποιέω.
Mid., **make as though,** Luke xxiv. 28. — *With* μή, **as though** [c]**he heard them not,** John viii. 6[p](-StE, *omS*).

προσπορεύομαι.
come unto, Mark x. 35.

προσρήγνυμι.
beat vehemently upon (against[2]**),** Luke vi. 48, 49[2]. [L[m].
Add Matt. vii. 27, for προσκόπτω,

προστάσσω, -ττω.
to command, Matt. viii. 4. xxi. 6 (συντάσσω LTTr). Mark i. 44. Luke v. 14. Acts x. 33, 48.
bid, Matt. i. 24.
Add Acts xvii. 26, for προτάσσω, GT*S*.

προστάτις.
succorer, Rom. xvi. 2.

προστίθημι.
lay unto, Acts xiii. 36.
add, Matt. vi. 27, 33. Luke iii. 20. xii. 25, 31. xix. 11. Acts ii. 41, 47. v. 14. xi. 24. Gal. iii. 19 (G′, τίθημι G).
again[cc], Luke xx. 11, 12.
give more, Mark iv. 24(*ap*).
increase, Luke xvii. 5.
speak any[c] **more,** Heb. xii. 19.
proceed further, Acts xii. 3.
Add Mark xiv. 25, προσθῶ πιεῖν for πίω, G′.

προστρέχω.
run to, Mark ix. 15.
run [c]**thither to,** Acts viii. 30.
run, Mark x. 17.

προσφάγιον.
meat, John xxi. 5.

πρόσφατος.
new, Heb. x. 10.

προσφάτως.
lately, Acts xviii. 2.

προσφέρω.
bring to (unto[2]**),** Matt. iv. 24[2]. v. 23 (*with* ἐπί). viii. 16[2]. ix. 2, 32. xii. 22[2]. xiv. 35[2]. xvii. 16. xviii. 24[2] (προσάγω LTTr). xix. 13[2]. xxii. 19[2]. Mark x. 13. Luke xii. 11[2] (φέρω T, εἰσφέρω Tr*S*). xviii. 15[2]. xxiii. 14[2].
bring, Matt. xxv. 20. Mark x. 13 ([p], αὐτοῖς L[m]*S*).
put to, John xix. 29.
present unto (*marg.* **offer**), Matt. ii. 11.
offer, Matt. v. 24. viii. 4. Mark i. 44. Luke v. 14. xxiii. 36. Acts vii. 42. viii. 18. xxi. 26. Heb. v. 1, 3. viii. 3*t*, 4. ix. 7, 9, 14, 25, 28. x. 1, 2, 8, 11, 12[p]. xi. 4.
offer up, Heb. v. 7[p]. xi. 17*t*.
do, John xvi. 2.
deal with, Heb. xii. 7.

προσφιλής.
lovely, Phil. iv. 8.

προσφορά.
offering up (*marg.* **sacrificing**), Rom. xv. 16.
offering, Acts xxi. 26. xxiv. 17. Eph. v. 2. Heb. x. 5, 8, 10, 14, 18.

προσφωνέω.
speak to (unto[2]**),** Luke xxiii. 20. Acts xxi. 40[2]. xxii. 2.
call to (unto[2]**),** Matt. xi. 16[2]. Luke vii. 32.
call to (unto[2]**) one,** Luke vi. 13[2]. xiii. 12.

πρόσχυσις.
sprinkling, Heb. xi. 28.

προσψαύω.
to touch, Luke xi. 46.

προσωποληπτέω (-λημπτ - LTS).
have respect to persons, Jas. ii. 9.

προσωπολήπτης (-λήμπτ - LTS).
respecter of persons, Acts x. 34.

προσωποληψία (-λημψ - LTS).
respect of persons, Rom. ii. 11. Eph. vi. 9. Col. iii. 25. Jas. ii. 1.

πρόσωπον.
face, Matt. vi. 16, 17. xi. 10. xvi. 3. xvii. 2, 6. xviii. 10. xxvi. 39, 67. Mark i. 2. xiv. 65. Luke i. 76. ii. 31. v. 12. vii. 27. ix. 51, 52, 53. x. 1. xii. 56. xvii. 16. xxi. 35. xxii. 64(*ap*). xxiv. 5. Acts vi. 15*t*. vii. 45. xvii. 26. xx. 25, 38. 1 Cor. xiii. 12*t*. xiv. 25. 2 Cor. iii. 7, 13, 18. iv. 6. xi. 20. Gal. i. 22. ii. 11. Col. ii. 1. 1 Thes. ii. 17. iii. 10. Jas. i. 23. 1 Pet. iii. 12. Rev. iv. 7. vi. 16. vii. 11. ix. 7. x. 1. xi. 16. xii. 14. xx. 11. xxii. 4.
κατὰ π., **face to face**, Acts xxv. 16.
countenance, Luke ix. 29. Acts ii. 28. 2 Cor. iii. 7.
appearance (*Gr.* the face), 2 Cor. v. 12.
outward appearance, 2 Cor. x. 7.
fashion, Jas. i. 11.
presence, Acts iii. 13, 19. v. 41. 2 Cor. x. 1 (*marg.* **outward appearance**). 1 Thes. ii. 17. 2 Thes. i. 9. Heb. ix. 24.
πρὸ προσώπου, **before**, Acts xiii. 24.
εἰς π., **before**, 2 Cor. viii. 24.
person, Matt. xxii. 16. Mark xii. 14. Luke xx. 21. 2 Cor. i. 11. ii. 10 (*marg.* **sight**). Gal. ii. 6.
man's person, Jude 16.

προτάσσω, -ττω.
appoint before, Acts xvii. 26 (G', προστάσσω GTS, πρὸς τ. L).

προτείνω.
bind, Acts xxii. 25.

πρότερος.
former, Eph. iv. 22.
πρότερον, τὸ πρότερον, *adv.*
before, John vi. 62. ix. 8. 2 Cor. i. 15. 1 Tim. i. 13.
ἐὰν μὴ πρότερον (πρῶτον G'LTTrS), **before**, John vii. 51.
former, Heb. x. 32. 1 Pet. i. 14.
first, Heb. iv. 6. vii. 27.
at the first, Gal. iv. 13.
Add John vii. 50 (. . by night), LTTr.

προτίθημι.
Mid., **set forth**, Rom. iii. 25 (*marg.* **foreordain**). — **purpose**, Rom. i. 13. Eph. i. 9.

προτρέπω.
Mid., **exhort**, Acts xviii. 27.

προτρέχω.
run before, Luke xix. 4.
With τάχιον, **outrun**, John xx. 4.

προϋπάρχω.
be before, Luke xxiii. 12.
be . . beforetime, Acts viii. 9.

πρόφασις.
show, Luke xx. 47.
pretence, Matt. xxiii. 14(*ap*). Mark xii. 40. Phil. i. 18.
cloak, John xv. 22 (*marg.* **excuse**). 1 Thes. ii. 5.
color, Acts xxvii. 30.

προφέρω.
bring forth, Luke vi. 45*t*.

προφητεία.
prophecy, Matt. xiii. 14. Rom. xii. 6. 1 Cor. xii. 10. xiii. 8. 1 Tim. i. 18. iv. 14. 2 Pet. i. 20. 21. Rev. i. 3. xi. 6. xix. 10. xxii. 7, 10, 18, 19.
the gift of prophecy, 1 Cor. xiii. 2.
prophesying, 1 Cor. xiv. 6, 22. 1 Thes. v. 20.

προφητεύω.
to prophesy, Matt. vii. 22. xi. 13. xv. 7. xxvi. 68. Mark vii. 6. xiv. 65. Luke i. 67. xxii. 64. John xi. 51. Acts ii. 17, 18. xix. 6. xxi. 9.

1 Cor xi. 4, 5. xiii. 9. xiv. 1, 3, 4, 5*t*, 24, 31, 39. 1 Pet. i. 10. Jude 14. Rev. x. 11. xi. 3.

προφήτης.

prophet, Matt. i. 22. ii. 5, 15, 17, 23. iii. 3. iv. 14. v. 12, 17. vii. 12. viii. 17. x. 41*tr*. xi. 9*t*, 13. xii. 17, 39. xiii. 17, 35, 57. xiv. 5. xvi. 4 (-G°LTTr*S*), 14. xxi. 4, 11, 26, 46. xxii. 40. xxiii. 29, 30, 31, 34, 37. xxiv. 15. xxvi. 56. xxvii. 9, 35(*ap*). Mark i. 2 (G', Ἡσαίας (Ἡσ. L) ὁ προφήτης GLTTr*S*). vi. 4, 15*t*. viii. 28. xi. 32. xiii. 14(*ap*).
Luke i. 70, 76. iii. 4. iv. 17, 24, 27. vi. 23. vii. 16, 26*t*, 28(-G°LTr[b] *S*), 39. ix. 8, 19. x. 24. xi. 29(*om S*); 47, 49, 50. xiii. 28, 33, 34. xvi. 16, 29, 31. xviii. 31. xx. 6. xxiv. 19, 25, 27, 44. John i. 21, 23, 25, 45(46). iv. 19, 44. vi. 14, 45. vii. 40, 52. viii. 52, 53. ix. 17. xii. 38.
Acts ii. 16, 30. iii. 18, 21, 22, 23, 24, 25. vii. 37, 42, 48, 52. viii. 28, 30, 34. x. 43. xi. 27. xiii. 1, 15, 20, 27, 40. xv. 15, 32. xxi. 10. xxiv. 14. xxvi. 22, 27. xxviii. 23, 25.
Rom. i. 2. iii. 21. xi. 3. 1 Cor. xii. 28, 29. xiv. 29, 32*t*, 37. Eph. ii. 20. iii. 5. iv. 11. 1 Thes. ii. 15. Tit. i. 12. Heb. i. 1. xi. 32. Jas. v. 10. 1 Pet. i. 10. 2 Pet. ii. 16. iii. 2. Rev. x. 7. xi. 10, 18. xvi. 6. xviii. 20, 24. xxii. 6, 9.

προφητικός.

of the prophets, Rom. xvi. 26.
of prophecy, 2 Pet. i. 19.

προφῆτις.

prophetess, Luke ii. 36. Rev. ii. 20.

προφθάνω.

prevent, Matt. xvii. 25.

προχειρίζομαι.

make, Acts xxvi. 16.
choose, Acts xxii. 14.
Add Acts iii. 20, for προκηρύσσω, GLT*S*.

προχειροτονέω.

choose before, Acts x. 41.

πρύμνα.

hinder part of the ship, Mark iv. 38.
hinder part, Acts xxvii. 41.
stern, Acts xxvii. 29.

πρωΐ.

early, Mark xvi. 9(*ap*). John xx. 1.
ἅμα π., **early in the morning**, Matt. xx. 1.
λίαν π., **very early in the morning**, Mark xvi. 2.
in the morning, Matt. xvi. 3. Mark i. 35. xi. 20. xiii. 35.
morning, Mark xv. 1. Acts xxviii. [23.
Add, see πρωΐος.

πρώϊμος, πρόϊμος T*S*.

early, Jas. v. 7.

πρωϊνός, προϊνός T.

morning, Rev. ii. 28.
Add Rev. xxii. 16, for ὀρθρινός, GLTTr*S*.

πρωΐος.

early, John xviii. 28 (πρωΐ GLTTr *S*).
in the morning, Matt. xxi. 18(πρωΐ Tr*S*).
morning, Matt. xxvii. 1. John xxi. 4.

πρώρα.

foreship, Acts xxvii. 30.
forepart, Acts xxvii. 41.

πρωτεύω.

have the pre-eminence, Col. i. 18.

πρωτοκαθεδρία.

chief seat, Matt. xxiii. 6. Mark xii. 39.
highest seat, Luke xx. 46.
uppermost seats, Luke xi. 43.

πρωτοκλισία.

chief room, Luke xiv. 7. xx. 46.
highest room, Luke xiv. 8.
uppermost room (rooms[1]), Matt. xxiii. 6[1]. Mark xii. 39.
Add Luke xi. 43(*ap*).

πρῶτος.

1. πρῶτος, πρώτη, πρῶτον, *adj.*
first, Matt. x. 2. xii. 45. xvii. 27. xix. 30*t*. xx. 8, 10, 16*t*. xxi. 28, 31

(ὕστερος LTr), 36. xxii. 25, 38. xxvii. 64. Mark ix. 35. x. 31. xii. 20, 28, 29, 30(*ap*). xiv. 12. Luke ii. 2. xi. 26. xiii. 30*t*. xiv. 18. xvi. 5. xix. 16. xx. 29. John i. 41(42, *adv*. LTr). v. 4(*ap*). viii. 7(*ap*). xix. 32. xx. 4, 8. Acts xii. 10. xx. 18. xxvi. 23. xxvii. 43.

Rom. x. 19. 1 Cor. xiv. 30. xv. 45, 47. Eph. vi. 2. Phil. i. 5. 1 Tim. i. 16. ii. 13. v. 12. 2 Tim. iv. 16. Heb. viii. 7, 13. ix. 1, 2, 6, 8, 15, 18. x. 9. 1 John iv. 19. Rev. i. 11 (*ap*), 17. ii. 4, 5, 8, 19. iv. 1, 7. viii. 7. xiii. 12*t*. xvi. 2. xx. 5, 6. xxi. 1*t*, 19. xxii. 13.

that **are first**, Mark x. 31[pl].

ἐν πρώτοις, **first of all**, 1 Cor. xv. 3.

first [c]**day**, Matt. xxvi. 17. Mark xvi. 9(*ap*).

former, Acts i. 1. Rev. xxi. 4.

before, John i. 15, 30.

beginning, 2 Pet. ii. 20.

chief, Matt. xx. 27. Luke xix. 47. Acts xvi. 12 (*marg*. **first**). xvii. 4. xxv. 2. xxviii. 17. 1 Tim. i. 15.

chief man, Acts xiii. 50. xxviii. 7.

chief [c]**estate**, Mark vi. 21.

chiefest, Mark x. 44.

best, Luke xv. 22.

Add Mark iii. 16, πρῶτον Σίμωνα before καί, G[ph]. Acts xiii. 33, for δευτέρος, GLT.

2. πρῶτον, τὸ πρῶτον, *adv.*

first, Matt. v. 24. vi. 33. vii. 5. viii. 21. xii. 29. xiii. 30. xvii. 10, 11 (–G[oo]LTTr*S*). xxiii. 26. Mark iii. 27. iv. 28. vii. 27. ix. 11, 12. xiii. 10. xvi. 9(*ap*). Luke vi. 42. ix. 59, 61. x. 5. xi. 38. xiv. 28, 31. xvii. 25. xxi. 9. John xviii. 13. Acts iii. 26. vii. 12. xi. 26. xiii. 46. xxvi. 20.

Rom. i. 8, 16(–L[b]). ii. 9, 10. xv. 24. 1 Cor. xii. 28. xv. 46. 2 Cor. viii. 5. Eph. iv. 9(*om S*). 1 Thes. iv. 16. 2 Thes. ii. 3. 1 Tim. ii. 1. iii. 10. v. 4. 2 Tim. i. 5. ii. 6. Heb. vii. 2. Jas. iii. 17. 2 Pet. i. 20. iii. 3.

at first, John x. 40.

at the first, John xii. 16. xix. 39. Acts xv. 14.

first of all, Luke xii. 1. 1 Cor. xi. 18.

it first beginneth, 1 Pet. iv. 17.

at the beginning, John ii. 10.

before, John xv. 18.

chiefly, Rom. iii. 2.

Add John i. 41(42), *see* No. 1. vii. 51, for πρότερον, G'LTTr*S*.

πρωτοστάτης.

ringleader, Acts xxiv. 5.

πρωτοτόκια.

birthright, Heb. xii. 16.

πρωτότοκος.

first-born, Matt. i. 25 (–LTTr*S*). Luke ii. 7. Rom. viii. 29. Col. i. 15, 18. Heb. xi. 28. xii. 23.

first-begotten, Heb. i. 6. Rev. i. 5.

πταίω.

stumble, Rom. xi. 11.

fall, 2 Pet. i. 10.

offend, Jas. ii. 10. iii. 2*t*.

πτέρνα.

heel, John xiii. 18.

πτερύγιον.

pinnacle, Matt. iv. 5. Luke iv. 9.

πτέρυξ.

wing, Matt. xxiii. 37. Luke xiii. 34. Rev. iv. 8. ix. 9. xii. 14.

πτηνόν.

bird, 1 Cor. xv. 39.

πτοέω.

terrify, Luke xxi. 9. xxiv. 37.

πτόησις.

amazement, 1 Pet. iii. 6.

πτύον.

fan, Matt. iii. 12. Luke iii. 17.

πτύρω.

terrify, Phil. i. 28.

πτύσμα.

spittle, John ix. 6.

πτύσσω.

to close, Luke iv. 20.

πτύω.

spit, Mark vii. 33. viii. 23p. John ix. 6.

πτῶμα.

dead body, Rev. xi. 8, 9*t*.
carcass, Matt. xxiv. 28.
corpse, Mark vi. 29.
Add, for σῶμα, Matt. xiv. 12, G'L TrS. Mark xv. 45, LTTrS.

πτῶσις.

fall, Matt. vii. 27. Luke ii. 34.

πτωχεία.

poverty, 2 Cor. viii. 2, 9. Rev. ii. 9.

πτωχεύω.

become poor, 2 Cor. viii. 9.

πτωχός.

poor, Matt. v. 3. xi. 5. xix. 21. xxvi. 9, 11. Mark x. 21. xii. 42 (-G°), 43. xiv. 5, 7. Luke iv. 18. vi. 20. vii. 22. xiv. 13, 21. xviii. 22. xix. 8. xxi. 3. John xii. 5, 6, 8. xiii. 29. Rom. xv. 26. 2 Cor. vi. 10. Gal. ii. 10. Jas. ii. 3, 5, 6. Rev. iii. 17. xiii. 16.
poor man, Jas. ii. 2.
beggarly, Gal. iv. 9.
beggar, Luke xvi. 20, 22.

πυγμῇ.

oft (*marg.* **diligently**; *in the original*, with the fist; *Theophylact*, up to the elbow), Mark vii. 3.

πυκνός.

often, *adj.*, 1 Tim. v. 23.
πυκνά, **often,** Luke v. 33.—πυκνότερον, **the oftener,** Acts xxiv. 26.

πυκτεύω.

to fight, 1 Cor. ix. 26.

πύλη.

gate, Matt. vii. 13, 13 (-LS), 14 (-L^b). xvi. 18. Luke vii. 12. xiii. 24 (G', θύρα GLTTrS). Acts iii. 10. ix. 24. xii. 10. Heb. xiii. 12.
Add Acts xvi. 13, for πόλις, G''LTS.

πυλών.

gate, Luke xvi. 20. Acts x. 17. xii. 13, 14*t*. xiv. 13. Rev. xxi. 12, 12(*ap*), 13*f*, 15, 21*t*, 25. xxii. 14.
porch, Matt. xxvi. 71.

πυνθάνομαι.

ask, Luke xv. 26. xviii. 36. John xiii. 24(*ap*). Acts iv. 7. x. 18, 29. xxiii. 19.
inquire, John iv. 52. Acts xxiii. 20.
demand, Matt. ii. 4. Acts xxi. 33.
understand, Acts xxiii. 34p.

πῦρ.

fire, Matt. iii. 10, 11(-G°), 12. v. 22. vii. 19. xiii. 40, 42, 50. xvii. 15. xviii. 8, 9. xxv. 41. Mark ix. 22, 43(*ap*), 44(*ap*), 45(*ap*), 46(*ap*), 47 (-G°LTTrS), 48, 49. Luke iii. 9, 16, 17. ix. 54. xii. 49. xvii. 29. xxii. 55. John xv. 6. Acts ii. 3, 19. vii. 30. xxviii. 5.
Rom. xii. 20. 1 Cor. iii. 13*t*, 15. 2 Thes. i. 8. Heb. i. 7. xi. 34. xii. 18, 29. Jas. iii. 5, 6. v. 3. 1 Pet. i. 7. 2 Pet. iii. 7. Jude 7, 23. Rev. i. 14. ii. 18. iii. 18. iv. 5. viii. 5, 7, 8(-G°°). ix. 17, 18. x. 1. xi. 5. xiii. 13. xiv. 10, 18. xv. 2. xvi. 8. xvii. 16. xviii. 8. xix. 12, 20. xx. 9, 10, 14, 15. xxi. 8.
Gen., **fiery,** Heb. x. 27.
Add Rev. xx. 14.(*ap*).

πυρά.

fire, Acts xxviii. 2, 3.

πύργος.

tower, Matt. xxi. 33. Mark xii. 1. Luke xiii. 4. xiv. 28.

πυρέσσω, -ττω.

sick of a fever, Matt. viii. 14p. Mark i. 30p.

πυρετός.

fever, Matt. viii. 15. Mark i. 31. Luke iv. 38, 39. John iv. 52. Acts xxviii. 8.

πύρινος.

of fire, Rev. ix. 17.

πυρόω.

Pass., **be on fire,** 2 Pet. iii. 12.—**fiery,** Eph. vi. 16.—**burn,** 1 Cor. vii. 9. 2 Cor. xi. 29. Rev. i. 15p.—**be tried,** Rev. iii. 18.

πυῤῥάζω.

be red, Matt. xvi. 2, 3.

πυῤῥός.

red, Rev. xii. 3.
that is red, Rev. vi. 4.

πύρωσις.

burning, Rev. xviii. 9, 18.
fiery trial, 1 Pet. iv. 12.

πω.

An enclitic particle, *yet, even.* See μήπω, μηδέπω, οὔπω, οὐδέπω.

πωλέω.

sell, Matt, x. 29. xiii. 44. xix. 21. xxi. 12*t*. xxv. 9. Mark x. 21. xi. 15*t*. Luke xii. 6, 33. xvii. 28. xviii. 22. xix. 45. xxii. 36. John ii. 14, 16. Acts iv. 34, 37. v. 1. Rev. xiii. 17. — *Pass. part., with art.,* **whatsoever is sold,** 1 Cor. x. 25.

πῶλος.

colt, Matt. xxi. 2, 5, 7. Mark xi. 2, 4, 5, 7. Luke xix. 30, 33*t*, 35. John xii. 15.
Add Mark xi. 3(*ap*).

πώποτε.

at any time, John i. 18. v. 37. 1 John iv. 12.
With οὐ μή[1] *or* οὐδείς, **never,** Luke xix. 30. John vi. 35[1]. viii. 33.

πωρόω.

harden, Mark vi. 52. viii. 17. John xii. 40.
blind, Rom. xi. 7 (*marg.* **harden**). 2 Cor. iii. 14.

πώρωσις.

hardness (*marg.* **blindness**), Mark iii. 5.
blindness (*marg.* **hardness**), Rom. xi. 25. Eph. iv. 18.

πως.

by any means, Acts xxvii. 12. Rom. i. 10. xi. 14. 1 Cor. viii. 9. ix. 27. 2 Cor. xi. 3. Gal. ii. 2. Phil. iii. 11.
by some means, 1 Thes. iii. 5.
haply, 2 Cor. ix. 4.
perhaps, 2 Cor. ii. 7.
See also μήπως.

πῶς.

I. In a direct question, with the Indicative, Subjunctive[1], or Optative[2].

how? Matt. vii. 4. xii. 26, 29, 34. xxii. 12, 43, 45. xxiii. 33[1]. xxvi. 54[1]. Mark iii. 23. iv. 13. xii. 35. Luke i. 34. vi. 42. x. 26. xi. 18. xx. 41, 44. John iii. 4, 9, 12. v. 44, 47. vi. 52. vii. 15. viii. 33. ix. 10, 16, 19, 26. xii. 34. xiv. 5, 9. Acts ii. 8. viii. 31[2] (*with* ἄν). Rom. iii. 6. iv. 10. vi. 2. viii. 32. x. 14*t* ([1]L*S*), 14 ([1]L), 15([1]L*S*). 1 Cor. xiv. 7, 9, 16. xv. 12, 35. 2 Cor. iii. 8. Gal. iv. 9. 1 Tim. iii. 5. Heb. ii. 3. 1 John iii. 17. iv. 20 (οὐ L*S*).
how is it that? Matt. xvi. 11. Mark iv. 40 (*ap*). viii. 21(–T). Luke xii. 56. John iv. 9. vi. 42.
Add, for τί, Gal. ii. 14, GL*S*. For τίνι, Mark iv. 30[1], G″L[m]TTr*S*.

II. In an indirect question, with the Indicative or Subjunctive[1].

how, Matt. vi. 28. x. 19[1]. xii. 4. Mark ii. 26(–Tr[b]). v. 16. ix. 12. xi. 18. xii. 41. xiv. 1[1], 11[1]. Luke viii. 18. xii. 11[1], 27. xiv. 7. xxii. 2[1], 4[1]. John ix. 15. Acts iv. 21[1]. ix. 27*t*. xi. 13. xii. 17. xv. 36. 1 Cor. iii. 10. vii. 32([1]L*S*), 33([1]L*S*), 34([1]L*S*). Col. iv. 6. 1 Thes. i. 9. iv. 1. 2 Thes. iii. 7. 1 Tim. iii. 15. Rev. iii. 3.
after what manner, Acts xx. 18.
by what means, Luke viii. 36. John ix. 21.
that, Eph. v. 15.
Add, for ὡς, Mark xii. 26, TTr*S*. Luke vi. 4, LTr[b].

III. As an intensive exclamation.

how! Matt. xxi. 20. Mark x. 23, 24. Luke xii. 50. xviii. 24. John xi. 36.

ῥαββί, ῥαββεί T*S*.

Rabbi, Matt. xxiii. 7, 7(–G°LTr*S*), 8. John i. 38(39), 49(50). iii. 2, 26. vi. 25.
master, Matt. xxvi. 25, 49. Mark ix. 5. xi. 21. xiv. 45, 45(–G°LTr*S*). John iv. 31. ix. 2. xi. 8.

ῥαββονί, ῥαββουνί.
Rabboni, John xx. 16.
lord, Mark x. 51.

ῥαβδίζω.
beat with rods, 2 Cor. xi. 25.
beat, Acts xvi. 22.

ῥάβδος.
rod, 1 Cor. iv. 21. Heb. ix. 4. Rev. ii. 27. xi. 1. xii. 5. xix. 15.
staff, Matt. x. 10. Mark vi. 8. Luke ix. 3. Heb. xi. 21.
sceptre, Heb. i. 8*t*.

ῥαβδοῦχος.
serjeant, Acts xvi. 35, 38.

ῥαδιούργημα.
lewdness, Acts xviii. 14.

ῥαδιουργία.
mischief, Acts xiii. 10.

ῥακά.
raca, Matt. v. 22.

ῥάκος.
cloth, Matt. ix. 16. Mark ii. 21.

ῥαντίζω.
sprinkle, Heb. ix. 13, 19, 21. x. 22.

ῥαντισμός.
sprinkling, Heb. xii. 24. 1 Pet. i. 2.

ῥαπίζω.
smite with the palm of one's hand (*marg*. . . **a rod**), Matt. xxvi. 67.
smite, Matt. v. 39.

ῥάπισμα.
With βάλλω[1] *or* δίδωμι, **strike with the palm of one's hand**, Mark xiv. 65[1]. John xviii. 22 (*marg*. . . **a rod**). — **smite with one's hand**, John xix. 3.

ῥαφίς.
needle, Matt. xix. 24. Mark x. 25. Luke xviii. 25 (βελόνη G″LTTr*S*).

ῥέδα.
chariot, Rev. xviii. 13.

ῥέω.
to flow, John vii. 38.

ῥέω, ἐρρήθην or ἐρρέθην.
(Compare ἐρῶ, εἶπον.)
τὸ ῥηθέν, **that (it) which was spoken**, Matt. i. 22. ii. 15, 17, 23. iv. 14. viii. 17. xii. 17. xiii. 35. xxi. 4. xxii. 31. xxvii. 9, 35(*ap*). — **spoken of**, Matt. xxiv. 15. Mark xiii. 14(*ap*).—ὁ ῥηθ., **he that was spoken of**, Matt. iii. 3.
say, Matt. v. 21, 27, 31, 33, 38, 43. Rom. ix. 12, 26. Rev. vi. 11.
command, Rev. ix. 4.
make[c], Gal. iii. 16.

ῥῆγμα.
ruin, Luke vi. 49.

ῥήγνυμι, ῥήσσω.
rend, Matt. vii. 6.
Pass., **break**, Matt. ix. 17.
break forth, Gal. iv. 27.
burst, Mark ii. 22. Luke v. 37.
tear, Mark ix. 18 (*marg*. **dash**). Luke ix. 42.

ῥῆμα.
word, Matt. iv. 4. xii. 36. xviii. 16. xxvi. 75. xxvii. 14. Mark xiv. 72. Luke i. 38. ii. 29. iii. 2. iv. 4(*ap*). v. 5. xx. 26. xxiv. 8, 11. John iii. 34. v. 47. vi. 63, 68. viii. 20, 47. x. 21. xii. 47, 48. xiv. 10. xv. 7. xvii. 8. Acts ii. 14. v. 20. vi. 11, 13. x. 22, 37, 44. xi. 14, 16. xiii. 42. xvi. 38. xxvi. 25. xxviii. 25. Rom. x. 8*t*, 17, 18. 2 Cor. xii. 4. xiii. 1. Eph. v. 26. vi. 17. Heb. i. 3. vi. 5. xi. 3. xii. 19. 1 Pet. i. 25*t*. 2 Pet. iii. 2. Jude 17. Rev. xvii. 17 (λόγος GLTTr*S*).
saying, Mark ix. 32. Luke i. 65 (*marg*. **thing**). ii. 17, 50, 51. vii. 1. ix. 45*t*. xviii. 34.
thing, Luke ii. 15, 19. Acts v. 32.
See also πᾶς, πονηρός.

ῥήσσω. See ῥήγνυμι.

ῥήτωρ.
orator, Acts xxiv. 1.

ῥητῶς.
expressly, 1 Tim. iv. 1.

ῥίζα.
root, Matt. iii. 10. xiii. 6, 21. Mark iv. 6, 17. xi. 20. Luke iii. 9. viii. 13. Rom. xi. 16, 17, 18*t*. xv. 12. 1 Tim. vi. 10. Heb. xii. 15.

Said of Christ, **Root (root**[1]**)**, Rev. v. 5. xxii. 16[1].

ῥιζόω.

Pass. or Mid., **be rooted**, Eph. iii. 17(18). Col. ii. 7.

ῥιπή.

twinkling, 1 Cor. xv. 52(ῥοπή Lm).

ῥιπίζω.

toss, Jas. i. 6.

ῥιπτέω.

cast off, Acts xxii. 23.

ῥίπτω.

throw, Luke iv. 35p.
cast, Luke xvii. 2. Acts xxvii. 29.
cast down, Matt. xv. 30. xxvii. 5.
cast out, Acts xxvii. 19.
Pass., **be scattered abroad** (*marg.* **lie down**), Matt. ix. 36.

ῥοιζηδόν.

with a great noise, 2 Pet. iii. 10.

ῥομφαία.

sword, Luke ii. 35. Rev. i. 16. ii. 12, 16. vi. 8. xix. 15, 21.

ῥοπή, a sinking, a falling.

1 Cor. xv. 52, for ῥιπή, Lm.

ῥύμη.

street, Mt. vi. 2. Acts ix. 11. xii. 10.
lane, Luke xiv. 21.

ῥύομαι.

deliver, Matt. vi. 13. xxvii. 43. Luke xi. 4(*ap*). Rom. vii. 24. 2 Cor. i. 10*tr*. Col. i. 13. 1 Thes. i. 10. 2 Tim. iii. 11. iv. 18. 2 Pet. ii. 7, 9.
Deliverer, Rom. xi. 26p.
Aorist, ἐρρύσθην, **be delivered**, Luke i. 74. Rom. xv. 31. 2 Thes. iii. 2. 2 Tim. iv. 17.

ῥυπαίνω, befoul, defile.

ῥυπαρεύομαι, be filthy.

Rev. xxii. 11, *see* ῥυπόω.

ῥυπαρία.

filthiness, Jas. i. 21.

ῥυπαρός.

vile, Jas. ii. 2.
Add Rev. xxii. 11, *see* ῥυπόω.

ῥύπος.

filth, 1 Pet. iii. 21.

ῥυπόω.

be filthy, Rev. xxii. 11 (p, ῥυπαρός GLTTrb*S*), 11 (ῥυπαρεύομαι GTTrb, ῥυπαίνω, *pass.*, L*S*).

ῥύσις.

issue, Mark v. 25. Luke viii. 43, 44.

ῥυτίς.

wrinkle, Eph. v. 27.

ῥώννυμι.

Lit. strengthen. *Pass. imper.*, **farewell**, Acts xv. 29. xxiii. 30(–GoLT).

σαβαχθανί, -νεί Tr.

sabacthani, Matt. xxvii. 46 (-κθανί L). Mark xv. 34 (-κτανεί *S*).

σαβαώθ.

Sabaoth, Rom. ix. 29.
sabaoth, Jas. v. 4.

σαββατισμός.

rest (*marg.* **keeping of a sabbath**), Heb. iv. 9.

σάββατον.

The plural rendered by the singular[2].
Dative plural, σάββασι[3].

sabbath, Matt. xii. 5. xxviii. 1[2]. Mark ii. 27*t*, 28. xvi. 1. Luke vi. 1, 5, 6. xiii. 10[3], 15. xxiii. 54. John v. 9, 18. Acts xiii. 42 (*marg.* **week**). xviii. 4.
Gen., **sabbath**, *adj.*, Luke iv. 16. xiii. 14, 16. xiv. 5. John xix. 31. Acts xiii. 14. Col. ii. 16.
sabbath day, Matt. xii. 1[23], 2, 5[3], 8, 10[3], 11[23], 12[3]. xxiv. 20. Mark i. 21[23]. ii. 23[23], 24[23]. iii. 2[23], 4[3]. vi. 2. Luke iv. 31[3]. vi. 2[3], 7, 9[3]. xiv. 1, 3. xxiii. 56. John v. 10, 16. vii. 22, 23*t*. ix. 14, 16. xix. 31. Acts i. 12. xiii. 27, 44. xv. 21. xvii. 2.
week, Matt. xxviii. 1[2]. Mark xvi. 2[2], 9(*ap*). Luke xviii. 12. xxiv. 1[2]. John xx. 1[2], 19[2]. Acts xx. 7[2]. 1 Cor. xvi. 2[2].
Add Mark xv. 42, *see* προσάββατον.
See also ἡμέρα.

σαγήνη.
net, Matt. xiii. 47.

σαίνω, ἀσαίνω L, -ομαι.
move, 1 Thes. iii. 3.

σάκκος.
sackcloth, Matt. xi. 21. Luke x. 13. Rev. vi. 12. xi. 3.

σαλεύω.
shake, Matt. xi. 7. xxiv. 29. Mark xiii. 25. Luke vi. 48. vii. 24. xxi. 26. Acts iv. 31. xvi. 26. 2 Thes. ii. 2. Heb. xii. 26.
τὰ σαλευόμενα, **those things that are** (*marg.* **may be) shaken**, Heb. xii. 27. —τὰ μὴ σαλ., **those things which can not be shaken**, Heb. xii. 27.
shake together, Luke vi. 38.
stir up, Acts xvii. 13.
move, Acts ii. 25.

σάλος.
waves, Luke xxi. 25.

σάλπιγξ.
trump, 1 Cor. xv. 52. 1 Thes. iv. 16.
trumpet, Matt. xxiv. 31. 1 Cor. xiv. 8. Heb. xii. 19. Rev. i. 10. iv. 1. viii. 2, 6, 13. ix. 14.

σαλπίζω.
sound a trumpet (*marg.* **cause a trumpet to be sounded**), Matt. vi. 2.
a trumpet soundeth, 1 Cor. xv. 52.
sound, Rev. viii. 6, 7, 8, 10, 12, 13. ix. 1, 13. x. 7. xi. 15.

σαλπιστής.
trumpeter, Rev. xviii. 22.

σανδάλιον.
sandal, Mark vi. 9. Acts xii. 8.

σανίς.
board, Acts xxvii. 44.

σαπρός.
corrupt, Matt. vii. 17, 18. xii. 33*t*. Luke vi. 43*t*. Eph. iv. 29.
bad, Matt. xiii. 48.

σάπφειρος.
sapphire, Rev. xxi. 19.

σαργάνη.
basket, 2 Cor. xi. 33.

σάρδινος.
sardine, Rev. iv. 3 (*see* σάρδιος).

σάρδιος, σάρδιον.
sardius, Rev. xxi. 20.
Add Rev. iv. 3, for σάρδινος, GLT Tr*S*.

σαρδόνυξ.
sardonyx, Rev. xxi. 20.

σαρκικός.
fleshly, 2 Cor. i. 12. 1 Pet. ii. 11.
carnal, Rom. vii. 14 (σάρκινος GLT *S*). 1 Cor. iii. 1(-νος GLT*S*), 3 (-νος G″), 3, 4 (ἄνθρωπος LT*S*). 2 Cor. x. 4. Heb. vii. 16 (G′, -νος GLT*S*).
τὰ σαρκικά, **carnal things**, Rom. xv. 27. 1 Cor. ix. 11.

σάρκινος.
fleshy, 2 Cor. iii. 3.
Add, see σαρκικός.

σάρξ.
flesh, Matt. xvi. 17. xix. 5, 6. xxiv. 22. xxvi. 41. Mark x. 8*t*. xiii. 20. xiv. 38. Luke iii. 6. xxiv. 39. John i. 13, 14. iii. 6*t*. vi. 51, 52, 53, 54, 55, 56, 63. viii. 15. xvii. 2. Acts ii. 17, 26, 30(*ap*), 31.
Rom. i. 3. ii. 28. iii. 20. iv. 1. vi. 19. vii. 5, 18, 25. viii. 1(*ap*), 3*tr*, 4, 5*t*, 8, 9, 12*t*, 13. ix. 3, 5, 8. xi. 14. xiii. 14. 1 Cor. i. 26, 29. v. 5. vi. 16. vii. 28. x. 18. xv. 39*t*, 39 (*om**S*), 39(-G°), 50. 2 Cor. i. 17. iv. 11. v. 16*t*. vii. 1, 5. x. 2, 3*t*. xi. 18. xii. 7.
Gal. i. 16. ii. 16, 20. iii. 3. iv. 13, 14, 23, 29. v. 13, 16, 17*t*, 19, 24. vi. 8*t*, 12, 13. Eph. ii. 3*t*, 11*t*, 15. v. 29, 30(*ap*), 31. vi. 5, 12. Phil. i. 22, 24. iii. 3, 4*t*. Col. i. 22, 24. ii. 1, 5, 11, 13, 23. iii. 22. 1 Tim. iii. 16. Phm. 16.
Heb. ii. 14, v. 7. ix. 13. x. 20. xii. 9. Jas. v. 3. 1 Pet. i. 24. iii. 18, 21. iv. 1*t*, 2, 6. 2 Pet. ii. 10, 18. 1 John ii. 16. iv. 2, 3(*ap*). 2 John 7. Jude 7, 8, 23. Rev. xvii. 16. xix. 18*five*, 21.
Gen., **fleshly**, Col. ii. 18. — **carnal**,

Rom. viii. 7. Heb. ix. 10. — **carnally** (*Gr.* of the flesh), Rom. viii. 6.
Add 1 Cor. xv. 39(.. of fishes), LbT, σὰρξ πτηνῶν, ἄλλη δὲ ἰχθύων *S*.

σαρόω.

sweep, Matt. xii. 44. Luke xi. 25. xv. 8.

σάτον.

measure, Matt. xiii. 33. Luke xiii. 21.

σαυτοῦ. See σεαυτοῦ.

σβέννυμι.

quench, Matt. xii. 20. Mark ix. 44 (*ap*), 46(*ap*), 48. Eph. vi. 16. 1 Thes. v. 19 (ζβέννυμι T). Heb. xi. 34.
Pass., **go out** (*marg.* **be going out**), Matt. xxv. 8.

σέ. See σύ.

σεαυτοῦ, σαυτοῦ, -τῷ, -τόν.

thyself, Matt. iv. 6. viii. 4. xix. 19. xxii. 39 (ἑαυτόν G'). xxvii. 40. Mark i. 44. xii. 31. xv. 30. Luke iv. 9, 23. v. 14. x. 27. xxiii. 37, 39. John i. 22. vii. 4. viii. 13, 53. x. 33. xiv. 22. xxi. 18. Acts xvi. 28. xxvi. 1. Rom. ii. 1, 21. xiv. 22. Gal. vi. 1. 1 Tim. iv. 7, 16. v. 22. 2 Tim. ii. 15. Tit. ii. 7. Jas. ii. 8.
thine own self, John xvii. 5. Phm. [19.
thou thyself, Rom. ii. 19.
thy, Acts ix. 34cc.
unto thyself, Rom. ii. 5. 1 Tim. iv. 16.
thee, 2 Tim. iv. 11.
Add, for ἑαυτοῦ, -τόν, John xviii. 34, LTr*S*. Rom. xiii. 9, LT*S*. Gal. v. 14, GLT*S*.

σεβάζομαι.

to worship, Rom. i. 25.

σέβασμα.

that is worshipped, 2 Thes. ii. 4.
devotion (*marg.* **god that one worshippeth**), Acts xvii. 23.

σεβαστός, adj.

Augustus', Acts xxvii. 1.

σέβω.

Pass., **to worship**, Matt. xv. 9. Mark vii. 7. Acts xvi. 14. xviii. 7, 13. xix. 27. — **devout**, Acts xiii. 50p. xvii. 4p. — **devout person**, Acts xvii. 17p. — **religious**, Acts xiii. 43p.

σειρά.

chain, 2 Pet. ii. 4 (σειρός L*S*).

σειρός, pit, cavern.

2 Pet. ii. 4, for σειρά, L*S*.

σεισμός.

tempest, Matt. viii. 24.
earthquake, Matt. xxiv. 7. xxvii. 54. xxviii. 2. Mark xiii. 8. Luke xxi. 11. Acts xvi. 26. Rev. vi. 12. viii. 5. xi. 13*t*, 19(-Go). xvi. 18*t*.

σείω.

shake, Heb. xii. 26. Rev. vi. 13.
Pass., **shake**, Matt. xxviii. 4. — **quake**, Matt. xxvii. 51.
move, Matt. xxi. 10.

σελήνη.

moon, Matt. xxiv. 29. Mark xiii. 24. Luke xxi. 25. Acts ii. 20. 1 Cor. xv. 41. Rev. vi. 12. viii. 12. xii. 1. xxi. 23.

σεληνιάζομαι.

be lunatic, Matt. iv. 24. xvii. 15.

σεμίδαλις.

fine flour, Rev. xviii. 13.

σεμνός.

honest (*marg.* **venerable**), Phil. iv. 8.
grave, 1 Tim. iii. 8, 11. Tit. ii. 2.

σεμνότης.

honesty, 1 Tim. ii. 2.
gravity, 1 Tim. iii. 4. Tit. ii. 7.

σημαίνω.

signify, John xii. 33. xviii. 32. xxi. 19. Acts xi. 28. xxv. 27. Rev. i. 1.

σημεῖον.

sign, Matt. xii. 38, 39*tr*. xvi. 1, 3, 4*tr*. xxiv. 3, 24, 30. xxvi. 48. Mark viii. 11, 12*t*. xiii. 4, 22. xvi. 17 (*ap*), 20(*ap*). Luke ii. 12, 34. xi. 16, 29*tr*, 30. xxi. 7, 11, 25. John ii. 18. iv. 48. vi. 30. xx. 30. Acts ii. 19, 22, 43. iv. 30. v. 12. vii. 36.

viii. 13. xiv. 3. Rom. iv. 11. xv. 19. 1 Cor. i. 22. xiv. 22. 2 Cor. xii. 12*t*. 2 Thes. ii. 9. Heb. ii. 4. Rev. xv. 1.
token, 2 Thes. iii. 17.
wonder, Rev. xii. 1 and 3 (*marg.* **sign**). xiii. 13.
miracle, Luke xxiii. 8. John ii. 11, 23. iii. 2. iv. 54. vi. 2, 14, 26. vii. 31. ix. 16. x. 41. xi. 47. xii. 18, 37. Acts iv. 16, 22. vi. 8. viii. 6. xv. 12. Rev. xiii. 14. xvi. 14. xix. 20.

σημειόω.

Mid., **note** (*marg.* **signify**), 2 Thes. iii. 14.

σήμερον.

to-day, Matt. vi. 30. xvi. 3. xxi. 28. Luke v. 26. xii. 28. xiii. 32, 33. xix. 5. xxiii. 43. xxiv. 21(–Tr^b *S*). Heb. iii. 7, 13, 15. iv. 7*t*. v. 5. xiii. 8. Jas. iv. 13.
this day, Matt. vi. 11. xi. 23. xxvii. 8, 19. xxviii. 15. Mark xiv. 30. Luke ii. 11. iv. 21. xix. 9. xxii. 34. Acts iv. 9. xiii. 33. xix. 40. xx. 26. xxii. 3. xxiv. 21. xxvi. 2, 29. xxvii. 33. 2 Cor. iii. 14, 15. Heb. i. 5.
σήμερον ἡμέρα, **this day**, Rom. xi. 8.
Add Luke xxii. 61 (crow . .), TTr*S*.

σήπω.

to corrupt, Jas. v. 2.

σηρικός, σιρικός LTr*S*.

Neut., **silk**, Rev. xviii. 12.

σής.

moth, Matt. vi. 19, 20. Luke xii. 33.

σητόβρωτος.

moth-eaten, Jas. v. 2.

σθενόω.

strengthen, 1 Pet. v. 10.

σιαγών.

cheek, Matt. v. 39. Luke vi. 29.

σιγάω.

keep silence, Acts xv. 12. 1 Cor. xiv. 28, 34.
hold one's peace, Luke xx. 26. Acts xii. 17. xv. 13. 1 Cor. xiv. 30.
keep secret, Rom. xvi. 25.
keep close, Luke ix. 36.
Add Luke xviii. 39, for σιωπάω, L TTr.

σιγή.

silence, Acts xxi. 40. Rev. viii. 1.

σιδήρεος.

of iron, Rev. ii. 27. ix. 9. xii. 5. xix. 15.
iron, *adj.*, Acts xii. 10.

σίδηρος.

iron, Rev. xviii. 12.

σικάριος.

that is a murderer, Acts xxi. 38.

σίκερα.

strong drink, Luke i. 15.

σιμικίνθιον.

apron, Acts xix. 12.

σίναπι.

mustard seed, Matt. xiii. 31. xvii. 20. Mark iv. 31. Luke xiii. 19. xvii. 6.

σινδών.

fine linen, Mark xv. 46.
linen, Mark xv. 46. Luke xxiii. 53.
linen cloth, Matt. xxvii. 59. Mark xiv. 51, 52.

σινιάζω.

sift, Luke xxii. 31.

σιρικός. See σηρικός.

σιτευτός.

fatted, Luke xv. 23, 27, 30.

σιτίον, grain, corn.

Acts vii. 12, for σῖτος, G″LT*S*.

σιτιστός.

Neut., **fatling**, Matt. xxii. 4.

σιτομέτριον.

portion of meat, Luke xii. 42.

σῖτος.

wheat, Matt. iii. 12. xiii. 25, 29, 30. Luke iii. 17. xvi. 7. xxii. 31. John xii. 24. Acts xxvii. 38. 1 Cor. xv. 37. Rev. vi. 6. xviii. 13.
corn, Mark iv. 28. Acts vii. 12(*pl.*, σιτία fr. σιτίον G″LT*S*).
Add Luke xii. 18, for γέννημα, Tr.

σιωπάω.

hold one's peace, Matt. xx. 31. xxvi. 63. Mark iii. 4. ix. 34. x. 48. xiv. 61. Luke xviii. 39 (σιγάω LTTr). xix. 40. Acts xviii. 9.

Imper., **peace**, Mark iv. 39.

dumb, Luke i. 20p.

σκανδαλίζω.

offend, Matt. v. 29 (*marg.* **cause to offend**), 30. xi. 6. xiii. 21, 57. xv. 12. xvii. 27. xviii. 6, 8, 9. xxiv. 10. xxvi. 31, 33*t*. Mark iv. 17. vi. 3. ix. 42, 43 and 47 (*marg.* **cause to offend**), 45. xiv. 27, 29. Luke vii. 23. xvii. 2. John vi. 61. xvi. 1. Rom. xiv. 21(*ap*). 2 Cor. xi. 29.

make to offend, 1 Cor. viii. 13*t*.

σκάνδαλον.

occasion of stumbling (*Gr.* scandal), 1 John ii. 10.

stumbling-block, Rom. xi. 9. 1 Cor. i. 23. Rev. ii. 14.

occasion to fall, Rom. xiv. 13.

thing that offendeth (*marg.* **scandal**), Matt. xiii. 41.

offence, Matt. xvi. 23. xviii. 7*tr*. Luke xvii. 1. Rom. ix. 33. xvi. 17. Gal. v. 11. 1 Pet. ii. 8(7).

σκάπτω.

dig, Luke vi. 48. xiii. 8. xvi. 3.

σκάφη.

boat, Acts xxvii. 16, 30, 32.

σκέλος.

leg, John xix. 31, 32, 33.

σκέπασμα.

Plur., **raiment**, 1 Tim. vi. 8.

σκευή.

tackling, Acts xxvii. 19.

σκεῦος.

vessel, Mark xi. 16. Luke viii. 16. John xix. 29. Acts ix. 15. x. 11, 16. xi. 5. Rom. ix. 21, 22, 23. 2 Cor. iv. 7. 1 Thes. iv. 4. 2 Tim. ii. 20, 21. Heb. ix. 21. 1 Pet. iii. 7. Rev. ii. 27. xviii. 12*t*.

Plur., **stuff**, Luke xvii. 31.—**goods**, Matt. xii. 29. Mark iii. 27.

sail, Acts xxvii. 17.

σκηνή.

tabernacle, Matt. xvii. 4. Mark ix. 5. Luke ix. 33. Acts vii. 43, 44. xv. 16. Heb. viii. 2, 5. ix. 2, 3, 6, 8, 11, 21. xi. 9. xiii. 10. Rev. xiii. 6. xv. 5. xxi. 3.

habitation, Luke xvi. 9.

Add Heb. ix. 1 (*covenant*), St.

σκηνοπηγία.

of tabernacles, John vii. 2.

σκηνοποιός.

tent-maker, Acts xviii. 3(*ap*).

σκῆνος.

tabernacle, 2 Cor. v. 1, 4.

σκηνόω.

dwell, John i. 14. Rev. vii. 15. xii. 12. xiii. 6. xxi. 3.

σκήνωμα.

tabernacle, Acts vii. 46. 2 Pet. i. 13, 14.

σκιά.

shadow, Matt. iv. 16. Mark iv. 32. Luke i. 79. Acts v. 15. Col. ii. 17. Heb. viii. 5. x. 1.

σκιρτάω.

leap, Luke i. 41, 44.

leap for joy, Luke vi. 23.

σκληροκαρδία.

hardness of heart, Matt. xix. 8. Mark x. 5. xvi. 14(*ap*).

σκληρός.

hard, Matt. xxv. 24. John vi. 60. Acts ix. 5(*ap*). xxvi. 14. Jude 15.

fierce, Jas. iii. 4.

σκληρότης.

hardness, Rom. ii. 5.

σκληροτράχηλος.

stiff-necked, Acts vii. 51.

σκληρύνω.

harden, Rom. ix. 18. Heb. iii. 8, 15. iv. 7.

Pass. or Mid., **be hardened**, Acts xix. 9. Heb. iii. 13.

σκολιός.

crooked, Luke iii. 5. Phil. ii. 15.

untoward, Acts ii. 40.
froward, 1 Pet. ii. 18.

σκόλοψ.

thorn, 2 Cor. xii. 7.

σκοπέω.

look at, 2 Cor. iv. 18p.
look on, Phil. ii. 4.
mark, Rom. xvi. 17. Phil. iii. 17.
take heed, Luke xi. 35.
consider, Gal. vi. 1.

σκοπός.

mark, Phil. iii. 14.

σκορπίζω.

scatter, Luke xi. 23. John x. 12. xvi. 32.
scatter abroad, Matt. xii. 30.
disperse abroad, 2 Cor. ix. 9.

σκορπίος.

scorpion, Luke x. 19. xi. 12. Rev. ix. 3, 5, 10.

σκοτεινός.

dark, Luke xi. 36.
full of darkness, Matt. vi. 23. Luke xi. 34.

σκοτία.

darkness, Matt. x. 27. Luke xii. 3. John i. 5*t*. viii. 12. xii. 35*t*, 46. 1 John i. 5. ii. 8, 9, 11*tr*.
dark, John vi. 17. xx. 1.
Add Matt. iv. 16, for σκότος, LTTr.

σκοτίζω.

darken, Matt. xxiv. 29. Mark xiii. 24. Luke xxiii. 45. Rom. i. 21. xi. 10. Eph. iv. 18 (σκοτόω LT*S*). Rev. viii. 12. ix. 2 (σκοτόω LT).

σκότος, neut., masc.[1]

darkness, Matt. iv. 16 (σκοτία LT Tr). vi. 23*t*. viii. 12. xxii. 13. xxv. 30. xxvii. 45. Mark xv. 33. Luke i. 79. xi. 35. xxii. 53. xxiii. 44. John iii. 19. Acts ii. 20. xiii. 11. xxvi. 18. Rom. ii. 19. xiii. 12. 1 Cor. iv. 5. 2 Cor. iv. 6. vi. 14. Eph. v. 8, 11. vi. 12. Col. i. 13. 1 Thes. v. 4, 5. Heb. xii. 18[1] (ζόφος G''LT*S*). 1 Pet. ii. 9. 2 Pet. ii. 17. 1 John i. 6. Jude 13.

σκοτόω.

Pass., **full of darkness**, Rev. xvi. 10p.
Add, see σκοτίζω.

σκύβαλον.

Plural, **dung**, Phil. iii. 8.

σκυθρωπός.

of a sad countenance, Matt. vi. 16.
sad, Luke xxiv. 17.

σκύλλω.

to trouble, Mark v. 35. Luke viii. 49.
Mid., **trouble one's self**, Luke vii. 6.
Add Matt. ix. 36, for ἐκλύω, GLTTr*S*.

σκῦλον.

spoil, Luke xi. 22.

σκωληκόβρωτος.

eaten of worms, Acts xii. 23.

σκώληξ.

worm, Mark ix. 44(*ap*), 46(*ap*), 48.

σμαράγδινος.

emerald, Rev. iv. 3.

σμάραγδος.

emerald, Rev. xxi. 19.

σμύρνα.

myrrh, Matt. ii. 11. John xix. 39.

σμυρνίζω.

mingle with myrrh, Mark xv. 23.

σοί. See σύ.

σορός.

bier (*marg.* **coffin**), Luke vii. 14.

σός.

thy, thine, Matt. vii. 22*tr*. xiii. 27. xxiv. 3. Mark ii. 18. Luke v. 33. xv. 31. xxii. 42. John iv. 42. xvii. 6, 9, 10*t*, 17. Acts xxiv. 2, 4. 1 Cor. viii. 11. xiv. 16. Phm. 14.
thine own, Matt. vii. 3. John xviii. 35. Acts v. 4.
τὸ σόν, **that is thine**, Matt. xx. 14. xxv. 25.
οἱ σοί, **thy friends**, Mark v. 19.
τὰ σά, **thy goods**, Luke vi. 30.

σοῦ. See σύ.

σουδάριον

handkerchief, Acts xix. 12.

napkin, Luke xix. 20. John xi. 44. xx. 7.

σοφία.

wisdom, Matt. xi. 19. xii. 42. xiii. 54. Mark vi. 2. Luke ii. 40, 52. vii. 35. xi. 31, 49. xxi. 15. Acts vi. 3, 10. vii. 10, 22. Rom. xi. 33. 1 Cor. i. 17, 19, 20, 21*t*, 22, 24, 30. ii. 1, 4, 5, 6*t*, 7, 13. iii. 19. xii. 8. 2 Cor. i. 12. Eph. i. 8, 17. iii. 10. Col. i. 9, 28. ii. 3, 23. iii. 16. iv. 5. Jas. i. 5. iii. 13, 15, 17. 2 Pet. iii. 15. Rev. v. 12. vii. 12. xiii. 18. xvii. 9.

σοφίζω.

make wise, 2 Tim. iii. 15.

Mid., **devise cunningly**, 2 Pet. i. 16.

σοφός.

wise, Matt. xi. 25. Luke x. 21. Rom. i. 14, 22. xvi. 19, 27. 1 Cor. i. 19, 20, 25, 26, 27(*ap*). iii. 10, 18*t*, 19, 20. Eph. v. 15. 1 Tim. i. 17(*om S*). Jude 25(*om S*).

wise man, Matt. xxiii. 34. 1 Cor. vi. 5. Jas. iii. 13.

σπαράσσω, -ττω.

to tear, Mark i. 26p. ix. 20 (συσπαράσσω LTrm*S*). Luke ix. 39.

rend, Mark ix. 26.

σπαργανόω.

wrap in swaddling clothes, Luke ii. 7, 12.

σπάω.

Mid., **draw out**, Acts xvi. 27. — **draw**, Mark xiv. 47.

σπαταλάω.

live in pleasure, 1 Tim. v. 6 (*marg.* **live delicately**). Jas. v. 5.

σπεῖρα.

band, Matt. xxvii. 27. Mark xv. 16. John xviii. 12. Acts x. 1. xxi. 31. xxvii. 1.

band of men, John xviii. 3.

σπείρω.

to sow, Matt. vi. 26. xiii. 3, 4, 19, 24, 25 (ἐπισπείρω LTTr*S*), 27, 31, 37, 39. xxv. 24, 26. Mark iv. 3, 4, 14, 15*t*, 16, 18, 20, 31, 32. Luke viii. 5*t*. xii. 24. xix. 21, 22. John iv. 36, 37 (*with* ἐστί). 1 Cor. ix. 11. xv. 36, 37*t*, 42, 43*t*, 44. 2 Cor. ix. 6*t*. Gal. vi. 7, 8*t*. Jas. iii. 18.

sower, Matt. xiii. 3p, 18p. Mark iv. 3p, 14p. Luke viii. 5p. 2 Cor. ix. 10p.

Pass., **receive seed**, Matt. xiii. 19, 20, 22, 23.

σπεκουλάτωρ.

executioner (*marg.* **one of his guard**), Mark vi. 27.

σπένδω.

Mid., **be offered** (*Gr.* poured forth), Phil. ii. 17. — **be ready to be offered**, 2 Tim. iv. 6.

σπέρμα.

seed, Matt. xiii. 24, 27, 32, 37, 38. xxii. 24. Mark iv. 31. xii. 19, 20, 21, 22. Luke i. 55. xx. 28. John vii. 42. viii. 33, 37. Acts iii. 25. vii. 5, 6. xiii. 23. Rom. i. 3. iv. 13, 16, 18. ix. 7*t*, 8, 29. xi. 1. 1 Cor. xv. 38cc. 2 Cor. ix. 10 (σπόρος L). xi. 22. Gal. iii. 16*tr*, 19, 29. 2 Tim. ii. 8. Heb. ii. 16. xi. 11, 18. 1 John iii. 9. Rev. xii. 17.

issue, Matt. xxii. 25.

σπερμολόγος.

babbler (*marg.* **base fellow**), Acts xvii. 18.

σπεύδω.

haste unto (*marg.* **haste**), 2 Pet. iii. 12.

haste, Acts xx. 16.

make haste, Luke xix. 5, 6. Acts xxii. 18.

with haste, Luke ii. 16p.

σπήλαιον.

cave, John xi. 38.

den, Matt. xxi. 13. Mark xi. 17. Luke xix. 46. Heb. xi. 38. Rev. vi. 15.

σπιλάς.

spot, Jude 12.

σπῖλος.

spot, Eph. v. 27. 2 Pet. ii. 13.

σπιλόω.

to spot, Jude 23.

defile, Jas. iii. 6.

σπλάγχνα.
bowels, Acts i. 18. 2 Cor. vi. 12. Phil. i. 8. ii. 1. Col. iii. 12. Phm. 7, 12, 20.
bowels of compassion, 1 John iii. 17.
inward affection (*Gr.* bowels), 2 Cor. vii. 15.
tender (*marg.* **bowels**), Luke i. 78.

σπλαγχνίζομαι.
be moved with compassion, Matt. ix. 36. xiv. 14. xviii. 27. Mark i. 41. vi. 34.
have compassion, Matt. xv. 32. xx. 34. Mark viii. 2. ix. 22. Luke vii. 13. x. 33. xv. 20.

σπόγγος.
sponge, Matt. xxvii. 48. Mark xv. 36. John xix. 29.

σποδός.
ashes, Matt. xi. 21. Luke x. 13. Heb. ix. 13.

σπορά.
seed, 1 Pet. i. 23.

σπόριμος.
Neut. plur., **corn fields**, Mark ii. 23. Luke vi. 1. — **corn**, Matt. xii. 1.

σπόρος.
seed, Mark iv. 26, 27. Luke viii. 5, 11.
seed sown, 2 Cor. ix. 10.
Add 2 Cor. ix. 10, for σπέρμα, L.

σπουδάζω.
be forward, Gal. ii. 10.
be diligent, Tit. iii. 12. 2 Pet. iii. 14.
do diligence, 2 Tim. iv. 9, 21.
give diligence, 2 Pet. i. 10.
endeavor, Eph. iv. 3. 1 Thes. ii. 17. 2 Pet. i. 15.
labor, Heb. iv. 11.
study, 2 Tim. ii. 15.

σπουδαῖος.
forward, 2 Cor. viii. 17.
diligent, 2 Cor. viii. 22*t*.

σπουδαίως.
diligently, Tit. iii. 13.
instantly, Luke vii. 4.
Comp., σπουδαιοτέρως, -ότερον.
the more carefully, Phil. ii. 28.
very diligently, 2 Tim. i. 17 (σπουδαίως L*S*).

σπουδή.
haste, Mark vi. 25. Luke i. 39.
forwardness, 2 Cor. viii. 8.
diligence, Rom. xii. 8. 2 Cor. viii. 7. Heb. vi. 11. 2 Pet. i. 5. Jude 3.
business, Rom. xii. 11.
earnest care, 2 Cor. viii. 16.
care, 2 Cor. vii. 12.
carefulness, 2 Cor. vii. 11.

σπυρίς, σφυρίς[1].
basket, Matt. xv. 37. xvi. 10([1]L). Mark viii. 8([1]L*S*), 20. Acts ix. 25.

στάδιος, στάδιον[1].
furlong, Luke xxiv. 13. John vi. 19. xi. 18. Rev. xiv. 20. xxi. 16.
race, 1 Cor. ix. 24[1].
Add Matt. xiv. 28 (*ap*).

στάμνος.
pot, Heb. ix. 4.

στασιαστής, an insurgent.
Mark xv. 7, for συστατ., LTr*S*.

στάσις.
With ἔχω, **be standing**, Heb. ix. 8.
insurrection, Mark xv. 7.
sedition, Luke xxiii. 19, 25. Act xxiv. 5.
uproar, Acts xix. 40.
dissension, Acts xv. 2. xxiii. 7, 10

στατήρ.
piece of money (*marg.* **stater**), Matt xvii. 27.

σταυρός.
cross, Matt. x. 38. xvi. 24. xxvii. 32, 40, 42. Mark viii. 34. x. 21(–G L[b]Tr*S*). xv. 21, 30, 32. Luke ix. 23(*ap*). xiv. 27. xxiii. 26. John xix. 17, 19, 25, 31. 1 Cor. i. 17, 18. Gal. v. 11. vi. 12, 14. Eph. ii. 16. Phil. ii. 8. iii. 18. Col. i. 20. ii. 14. Heb. xii. 2.

σταυρόω.
crucify, Matt. xx. 19. xxiii. 34. xxvi. 2. xxvii. 22, 23, 26, 31, 3

38. xxviii. 5. Mark xv. 13, 14, 15, 20, 24, 25, 27. xvi. 6. Luke xxiii. 21*t*, 23, 33. xxiv. 7, 20. John xix. 6*tr*, 10, 15*t*, 16, 18, 20, 23, 41. Acts ii. 36. iv. 10. 1 Cor. i. 13, 23. ii. 2, 8. 2 Cor. xiii. 4. Gal. iii. 1. v. 24. vi. 14. Rev. xi. 8.

σταφυλή.

grapes, Matt. vii. 16 (*plur.* LTr*S*). Luke vi. 44. Rev. xiv. 18 (*sing.* G''T).

στάχυς.

ear of corn, Matt. xii. 1. Mark ii. 23. Luke vi. 1.
ear, Mark iv. 28*t*.

στέγη.

roof, Matt. viii. 8. Mark ii. 4. Luke vii. 6.

στέγω.

suffer, 1 Cor. ix. 12.
bear, 1 Cor. xiii. 7.
can forbear, 1 Thes. iii. 1p, 5p.

στεῖρος.

barren, Luke i. 7, 36. xxiii. 29. Gal. iv. 27.

στέλλω.

Mid. or pass., **withdraw one's self**, 2 Thes. iii. 6. — **avoid**, 2 Cor. viii. 20.

στέμμα.

garland, Acts xiv. 13.

στεναγμός.

groaning, Acts vii. 34. Rom. viii. 26.

στενάζω.

to sigh, Mark vii. 34.
groan, Rom. viii. 23. 2 Cor. v. 2, 4.
with grief, Heb. xiii. 17p.
grudge (*marg.* **groan**, *or* **grieve**), Jas. v. 9.

στενός.

strait, Matt. vii. 13, 14. Luke xiii. 24.

στενοχωρέω.

straiten, 2 Cor. vi. 12*t*.
distress, 2 Cor. iv. 8.

στενοχωρία.

distress, Rom. viii. 35. 2 Cor. vi. 4. xii. 10.
anguish, Rom. ii. 9.

στερεός.

steadfast, 1 Pet. v. 9.
sure (*marg.* **steady**), 2 Tim. ii. 19.
strong, Heb. v. 12, 14.

στερεόω.

establish, Acts xvi. 5.
make strong, Acts iii. 16.
Pass., **receive strength**, Acts iii. 7.

στερέωμα.

steadfastness, Col. ii. 5.

στέφανος.

crown, Matt. xxvii. 29. Mark xv. 17. John xix. 2, 5. 1 Cor. ix. 25. Phil. iv. 1. 1 Thes. ii. 19. 2 Tim. iv. 8. Jas. i. 12. 1 Pet. v. 4. Rev. ii. 10. iii. 11. iv. 4, 10. vi. 2. ix. 7. xii. 1. xiv. 14.

στεφανόω.

to crown, 2 Tim. 2, 5. Heb. ii. 7, 9.

στῆθος.

breast, Luke xviii. 13. xxiii. 48. John xiii. 25. xxi. 20. Rev. xv. 6.

στήκω.

to stand, Mark xi. 25. Rom. xiv. 4.
stand fast, 1 Cor. xvi. 13. Gal. v. 1. Phil. i. 27. iv. 1. 1 Thes. iii. 8. 2 Thes. ii. 15.

στηριγμός.

steadfastness, 2 Pet. iii. 17.

στηρίζω.

set steadfastly, Luke ix. 51.
fix, Luke xvi. 26.
establish (stablish[1]), Rom. i. 11. xvi. 25[1]. 1 Thes. iii. 2, 13[1]. 2 Thes. ii. 17[1]. iii. 3[1]. Jas. v. 8[1]. 1 Pet. v. 10[1]. 2 Pet. i. 12.
strengthen, Luke xxii. 32. Rev. iii. 2.
Add Acts xviii. 23, for ἐπιστ., L*S*.

στιβάς, twig, bough.

Mark xi. 8, for στοιβάς, LTTr*S*.

στίγμα.

mark, Gal. vi. 17.

στιγμή.

moment, Luke iv. 5.

στίλβω.
shine, Mark ix. 3.

στοά.
porch, John v. 2. x. 23. Acts iii. 11. v. 12.

στοιβάς.
branch, Mark xi. 8(στιβάς LTTr*S*).

στοιχεῖον.
element, Gal. iv. 3 and 9 (*marg.* **rudiment**). 2 Pet. iii. 10, 12.
rudiment (*marg.* **element**), Col. ii. 8, 20.
principle, Heb. v. 12.

στοιχέω.
walk orderly, Acts xxi. 24.
walk, Rom. iv. 12. Gal. v. 25. vi. 16. Phil. iii. 16.

στολή.
robe, Luke xv. 22. Rev. vi. 11. vii. 9, 13, 14.
long robe, Luke xx. 46.
long garment, Mark xvi. 5.
long clothing, Mark xii. 38.
Add Rev. vii. 14, στολὰς αὐτῶν for αὐτάς (Tr[b]), StTr.

στόμα.
mouth, Matt. iv. 4. v. 2. xii. 34. xiii. 35. xv. 8 (*ap*), 11*t*, 17, 18. xvii. 27. xviii. 16. xxi. 16. Luke i. 64, 70. iv. 22. vi. 45. xi. 54. xix. 22. xxi. 15. xxii. 71. John xix. 29. Acts i. 16. iii. 18, 21. iv. 25. viii. 32, 35. x. 34. xi. 8. xv. 7. xviii. 14. xxii. 14. xxiii. 2.
Rom. iii. 14, 19. x. 8, 9, 10. xv. 6. 2 Cor. vi. 11. xiii. 1. Eph. iv. 29. vi. 19. Col. iii. 8. 2 Thes. ii. 8. 2 Tim. iv. 17. Heb. xi. 33. Jas. iii. 3, 10. 1 Pet. ii. 22. Jude 16. Rev. i. 16. ii. 16. iii. 16. ix. 17, 18, 19. x. 9, 10. xi. 5. xii. 15, 16*t*. xiii. 2, 5, 6. xiv. 5. xvi. 13*tr*. xix. 15, 21.
στ. πρὸς στ., **face to face** (*Gr.* mouth to mouth), 2 John 12. 3 John 14.
edge, Luke xxi. 24. Heb. xi. 34.

στόμαχος.
stomach, 1 Tim. v. 23.

στρατεία.
warfare, 2 Cor. x. 4. 1 Tim. i. 18.

στράτευμα.
army, Matt. xxii. 7. Acts xxiii. 27. Rev. ix. 16. xix. 14, 19*t*.
men of war, Luke xxiii. 11[pl].
soldiers, Acts xxiii. 10.

στρατεύω.
Mid., **go a warfare,** 1 Cor. ix. 7. — **war,** 2 Cor. x. 3. 1 Tim. i. 18. 2 Tim. ii. 4. Jas. iv. 1. 1 Pet. ii. 11. — **soldier,** Luke iii. 14[p].

στρατηγός.
captain, Luke xxii. 4, 52. Acts iv. 1 (*marg.* **ruler**). v. 24, 26.
magistrate, Acts xvi. 20, 22, 35, 36, 38.

στρατιά.
host, Luke ii. 13. Acts vii. 42.

στρατιώτης.
soldier, Matt. viii. 9. xxvii. 27. xxviii. 12. Mark xv. 16. Luke vii. 8. xxiii. 36. John xix. 2, 23*t*, 24, 32, 34. Acts x. 7. xii. 4. 6, 18. xxi. 32*t*, 35. xxiii. 23, 31. xxvii. 31, 32, 42. xxviii. 16. 2 Tim. ii. 3.

στρατολογέω.
choose . . to be a soldier, 2 Tim. ii. 4.

στρατοπεδάρχης.
captain of the guard, Acts xxviii. 16(*ap*).

στρατόπεδον.
army, Luke xxi. 20.

στρεβλόω.
wrest, 2 Pet. iii. 16.

στρέφω.
to turn, Matt. v. 39. Acts vii. 42. Rev. xi. 6.
Mid., **turn one's self,** John xx. 14 16. — **turn one,** Luke x. 23(*ap*). — **turn,** Matt. xvi. 23. Luke vii. 44 ix. 55. xiv. 25. xxii. 61. xxiii. 28 John i. 38. Acts xiii. 46. — **turn again,** Matt. vii. 6. — **turn back again** Acts vii. 39. — **turn one about,** Luke vii. 9. — *With* γίνομαι, **be converted** Matt. xviii. 3.

Add, for ἀποστρέφω, Matt. xxvii. 3, TTr*S*. For ἐπιστρέφω, Matt. ix. 22, John xii. 40, LTTr*S*. — Luke x. 22 (*ap*).

στρηνιάω.

live deliciously, Rev. xviii. 7, 9.

στρῆνος.

delicacy, Rev. xviii. 3.

στρουθίον.

sparrow, Matt. x. 29, 31. Luke xii. 6, 7.

στρώννυμι, στρωννύω.

strew, Matt. xxi. 8. Mark xi. 8(*ap*).
spread, Matt. xxi. 8. Mark xi. 8.
With σεαυτῷ, **make thy bed**, Acts ix. 34.
furnish, Mark xiv. 15. Luke xxii. 12.

στυγητός.

hateful, Tit. iii. 3.

στυγνάζω.

be sad, Mark x. 22.
lower, Matt. xvi. 3.

στύλος.

pillar, Gal. ii. 9. 1 Tim. iii. 15. Rev. iii. 12. x. 1.

σύ.

1. *Nominative*, σύ.

thou, Matt. ii. 6. iii. 14. vi. 6, 17. xi. 3, 23. xiv. 28. xvi. 16, 18. xxvi. 25, 39, 63, 64, 69, 73. xxvii. 4, 11*t*. Mark i. 11. iii. 11. viii. 29. xiv. 36, 61, 67, 68. xv. 2*t*. Luke i. 28(*ap*), 42, 76. iii. 22. iv. 7, 41. vii. 19, 20. ix. 60. x. 15, 37. xv. 31. xvi. 7, 25 (-GTTr*S*), 25. xvii. 8. xix. 19, 42. xxii. 32, 58, 67, 70. xxiii. 3*t*, 37, 39, 40. xxiv. 18.

John i. 19, 21*t*, 25, 42 (43)*t*, 49 (50)*t*. ii. 10, 20. iii. 2, 10, 26. iv. 9, 10, 12, 19. vi. 30, 69. vii. 52. viii. 5 (*ap*), 13, 25, 33, 48, 52, 53, 53(*om S*). ix. 17, 28, 34*t*, 35. x. 24, 33. xi. 27, 42. xii. 34. xiii. 6, 7. xiv. 9. xvii. 5, 8, 21*t*, 23*t*, 25. xviii. 17, 25, 33, 34, 37*t*. xix. 9. xx. 15. xxi. 12, 15, 16, 17*t*, 22.

Acts i. 24. iv. 24. vii. 28. ix. 5. x. 15, 33. xi. 9, 14. xiii. 33. xvi. 31. xxi. 38. xxii. 8, 27. xxiii. 3, 21. xxv. 10. xxvi. 15. Rom. ii. 3, 17. ix. 20. xi. 17, 18, 20, 22, 24. xiv. 4, 10*t*, 32. 1 Cor. xiv. 17. xv. 36.

Gal. ii. 14. vi. 1. 1 Tim. vi. 11. 2 Tim. i. 18. ii. 1, 3 (*see* συγκακοπαθέω). iii. 10, 14. iv. 5, 15. Tit. ii. 1. Phm. 12 (σοί *LS*). Heb. i. 5, 10, 11, 12. v. 5, 6. vii. 17, 21. Jas. ii. 3*t*, 18, 19. iv. 12. 3 John 3. Rev. ii. 15. iii. 17. iv. 11. vii. 14.

Add Mark xiv. 30 (thou), GLTTr.

2. *Genitive*, σοῦ.

of thee, 1 Cor. xii. 21. Phm. 20.

thy, thine, Matt. i. 20. iv. 6, 7, 10. v. 23*t*, 24*tr*, 25, 29*tr*, 30*tr*, 33, 36, 39, 40, 43*t*. vi. 3*t*, 4*t*, 6*f*, 9, 10*t*, 13 (*ap*), 17*t*, 18*t*, 22*t*, 23*t*. vii. 3, 4*t*, 5. ix. 2, 6*t*, 14, 18, 22. xi. 10*t*, 26. xii. 2, 13, 37*t*, 47*t*. xv. 2, 4(*omS*), 28. xvii. 16. xviii. 8*t*, 9, 15*t*, 33. xix. 19(*omS*), 19. xx. 15, 21(-L*S*), 21. xxi. 5. xxii. 37*f*, 39, 44*t*. xxiii. 37. xxv. 21, 23, 25. xxvi. 42, 52, 73.

Mark i. 2*t*, 44. ii. 5(-L^b^), 9, 11*t*. iii. 5(-TTr^b^), 32*t*. v. 19, 34*t*, 35. vi. 18. vii. 5, 10*t*, 29. ix. 18, 38, 43, 45, 47. x. 19, 37, 37(-L^b^TTr), 37, 52. xii. 30*five*, 31, 36*t*. xiv. 70(*ap*).

Luke i. 13*t*, 36, 38, 42, 44, 61. ii. 29*t*, 30, 32, 35, 48. iv. 7, 8, 11, 12, 23. v. 5, 14, 20, 23, 24*t*. vi. 10, 29, 41, 42*tr*. vii. 27*t*, 44, 48, 50. viii. 20*t*, 48, 49. ix. 40, 41, 49. x. 17, 21, 27*six*. xi. 2*t*, 2(*ap*), 34*tr*, 36. xii. 20, 58. xiii. 12, 26, 34. xiv. 12*t*, 12 (*ap*). xv. 19*t*, 21*t*, 27*t*, 29, 30*t*, 32. xvi. 2(-G^oo^), 6, 7, 25*t*. xvii. 3, 19. xviii. 20, 20(-G^oo^LTr), 42. xix. 5, 16, 18, 20, 39, 42(-G^o^LTr*S*), 42(L^b^ Tr^b^*S*), 42, 43, 44*t*. xx. 43*t*. xxii. 32*t*. xxiii. 42, 46.

John ii. 17. iv. 16, 18, 50, 51(αὐτοῦ LTr*S*), 53. v. 8, 11, 12 (-TTr^b^ *S*). vii. 3. viii. 10(*ap*), 13, 19. ix. 10 (σοί L^m^), 17, 26. xi. 23. xii. 15, 28. xiii. 37, 38. xvii. 1, 1(-TTr*S*),

6*t*, 12, 14, 17(–G∞LTr*S*c), 26. xviii. 11(*omS*). xix. 26, 27. xx. 27*t*. xxi. 18. Acts ii. 27, 28, 35*t*. iii. 25. iv. 25, 27, 28, 28(–L), 29*t*, 30(–L), 30. v. 3, 4, 9. vii. 3*t*, 32, 33. viii. 20, 21, 22*t*. ix. 13, 14. x. 4*t*, 31*t*. xi. 14. xii. 8*t*. xiii. 35. xiv. 10. xvi. 31. xxii. 16, 18, 20. xxiii. 5, 35. xxvi. 16.

Rom. ii. 5, 25. iii. 4. iv. 18. viii. 36. x. 6, 8*t*, 9*t*. xi. 3*t*. xii. 20. xiii. 9. xiv. 10*t*, 15*t*, 21. xv. 9. 1 Cor. xv. 55*t*. Gal. iii. 16. v. 14. Eph. vi. 2. 1 Tim. iv. 12, 15. v. 23 (–L*S*), 23. 2 Tim. i. 4, 5*t*. iv. 5, 22. Phm. 2, 5, 6, 7, 13, 14, 21. Heb. i. 8*t*, 9*t*, 10, 12, 13*t*. ii. 7(*ap*), 12. x. 7, 9. Jas. ii. 8, 18, 18 (–G∞LT*S*). 2 John 4, 13. 3 John 2, 6. Rev. ii. 2, 2(–G∞LTTr), 2, 4, 5, 9, 13(*ap*), 19*tr*. iii. 1, 2, 8, 9, 11, 15, 18*t*. iv. 11. v. 9. x. 9*t*. xi. 17, 18*tr*. xiv. 15, 18. xv. 3*t*, 4*t*. xvi. 7. xviii. 10, 14, 23*t*. xix. 10*t*. xxii. 9*t*.

thine own, Matt. vii. 4, 5. Luke vi. 42*t*. viii. 39. xix. 22. John xvii. 11.

thee, Matt. ii. 6. iii. 14. iv. 6. v. 23, 29, 30, 42. vi. 2. xi. 10. xii. 38. xvii. 27. xviii. 8, 9, 15*t*, 16. xxi. 19. xxvi. 62. xxvii. 13. Mark i. 2(*om S*). xi. 14. xiv. 60. xv. 4. Luke i. 28, 35(GphLb, –StTTr*S*). iv. 10. vii. 27. viii. 28. ix. 38. xii. 20. xv. 18. xvi. 2. xxii. 32, 33. John iii. 26. ix. 37. xvii. 7, 8. Acts viii. 34. x. 22. xvii. 32. xviii. 10. xxi. 21, 24, 39. xxiii. 21, 30, 35. xxiv. 2, 19. xxv. 26. xxvi. 2, 3(–G∞LT*S*). xxvii. 24. xxviii. 21*t*, 22.

Rom. x. 8. xi. 21. 2 Cor. vi. 2. 1 Tim. iv. 16. vi. 21 (ὑμῶν L*S*). 2 Tim. i. 3. Tit. ii. 15. Phm. 4, 7. 3 John 3. Rev. ii. 4, 14, 20. iii. 8. xv. 4. xviii. 14*t*.

thoucc, Matt. vi. 3. xix. 21. Luke xiv. 8. Acts xxiv. 11.

τὰ σοῦ, **that thou** c**doest,** John vii. 3.

ὑπὸ σοῦ λ., **whereof thou speakest,** Acts xvii. 19.

Add, for σοί, Matt. ix. 5, GLTTr*S*. Mark ii. 9, GTTr*S*. For ὑμῶν, Matt. vi. 21*t*, G′LTTr*S*. — Matt. vi. 22 (. . eye), L*S*. xx. 21 (. . left), GL TTr*S*. Mark iii. 22(*ap*). x. 19 (. . mother), L*S*. Luke xi. 34(. . eye), G″LTTr*S*. John v. 10 (. . bed), L*S*. Acts x. 33 (. . God1st), G′. Rev. ii. 20 (. . woman), GprLT.

3. *Dative,* σοί.

to thee, Luke xiv. 9. John iv. 10. ix. 26. Acts xxi. 23. Rom. xiii. 4. xv. 9. Phm. 11*t*, 19. Heb. viii. 5. 3 John 14.

unto thee, Matt. v. 26. viii. 13. xi. 21*t*. xv. 28. xvi. 17, 18, 19, 22. xviii. 17, 22. xx. 14. xxi. 5. xxv. 44. xxvi. 34. Mark ii. 11. v. 41. x. 51. xiv. 30, 36. Luke i. 3. v. 24. vii. 14, 40, 47. viii. 39. x. 13*t*. xviii. 41. xxii. 11. xxiii. 43.

John i. 50(51). iii. 3, 5, 7, 11. iv. 26. v. 12, 14. xi. 40. xiii. 38. xviii. 30. xix. 11. xxi. 18. Acts ix. 17. x. 32(*ap*). xxiii. 18. xxiv. 14. xxiv. 16*t*. 1 Tim. i. 18. iii. 14. Phm. 16, 21. 2 John 5. 3 John 13. Rev. ii. 5, 16. xvii. 1.

for thee, Matt. v. 29, 30. xi. 24. xiv. 4. xvii. 4. xviii. 8, 9. xxvi. 17. Mark v. 19. vi. 18. ix. 5, 43 and 45 (σέ LTTr*S*), 47 (σέ TTr*S*). Luke ix. 33. John v. 10. Acts ix. 5(*ap*). xxii. 10. xxvi. 14. 2 Cor. xii. 9. Rev. xiv. 15(*omS*).

thee, Matt. ii. 13. iv. 9. v. 40. vi. 4, 6, 18, 23. viii. 19. ix. 2(–G′LT Tr*S*), 5 (σοῦ GLTTr*S*). xi. 23, 25. xii. 47. xviii. 26(–T), 29, 32. xix. 27. xxi. 23. xxvi. 33, 35. Mark i. 24. ii. 5 (G′, –GTTr*S*), 9 (σοῦ GTTr*S*). vi. 22, 23. ix. 25. x. 28. xi. 28. xiv. 31. Luke i. 13, 19, 35. iii. 22. iv. 6. v. 20, 23. ix. 57, 61. x. 21, 35. xi. 7, 35. xii. 59. xiv. 10*t*, 12, 14. xv. 29. xviii. 11, 28. xix. 43, 44*t*. xx. 2. xxii. 34.

John iv. 10. vi. 30. xi. 22, 41. xiii. 37. xvii. 5, 21. xviii. 34. xix. 11. xxi. 3. Acts iii. 6. vii. 3. viii. 20,

22. ix. 6. x. 6 (*ap*), 33. xvi. 18. xviii. 10. xxii. 10. xxvii. 24.

Rom. ix. 17. 2 Cor. vi. 2. Gal. iii. 8. Eph. v. 14. vi. 3. 1 Tim. iv. 14*t*. vi. 13. 2 Tim. i. 5*t*, 6. ii. 7. Tit. i. 5. Phm. 8. Jas. ii. 18. Jude 9. Rev. ii. 10. iii. 18. iv. 1. xi. 17. xvii. 7. xviii. 22*tr*, 23*t*. xxi. 9.

thy, Mark v. 9. Luke viii. 30. Rom. ix. 7. Heb. xi. 18.

thine, John xvii. 6, 9.

thine own, Acts v. 4.

μηδέν σοι καί, **have thou nothing to do with**, Matt. xxvii. 19.

thou^{cc}, Matt. xvii. 25. xxii. 16, 17. Mark iv. 38. x. 21 (*σέ* T*S*). Luke i. 14. x. 36, 40. xiv. 10, 14. xviii. 22. Acts viii. 21. xxvi. 1.

Not rendered, Mark xii. 14. 1 Cor. vii. 21.

Add Mark i. 11, for *ᾧ* fr. *ὅς*, G′LT Tr*S*. Luke xxii. 9 (prepare . .), L^{b}. John ix. 10, for *σοῦ*, L^{m}. Acts xiv. 10 (*ap*). xxiv. 13 (prove . .), L*S*. Phm. 11 (sent . .), G′. 12, for *σύ*, L*S*. 3 John 13 (to write . .), LT*S*.

See also ἐμοί, ἡμῖν, ἵλεως.

4. *Accusative, σέ.*

thee, Matt. iv. 6. v. 25, 25 (–LTr^{b} *S*), 29, 30, 39, 41, 42. ix. 22. xiv. 28. xviii. 8, 9, 15 (–L*S*), 33. xx. 13. xxv. 21, 23, 24, 37, 38, 39*t*, 44. xxvi. 35, 63, 68, 73. Mark i. 24, 37. iii. 32. v. 7, 19, 31, 34. ix. 17, 43, 45, 47. x. 49, 52. xiv. 31. Luke i. 19, 35. ii. 48. iv. 10, 11, 34. vi. 29, 30. vii. 7, 20, 50. viii. 20, 45, 48. xi. 27, 36. xii. 58*tr*. xiii. 31. xiv. 9, 10, 12, 18, 19. xvi. 27. xvii. 3 (–G^{o}LTTr*S*), 4, 4(–GT), 19. xviii. 42. xix. 21, 22, 43*tr*, 44. xxii. 64.

John i. 48(49)*t*, 50(51). vii. 20. viii. 10(*ap*), 11(*ap*). x. 33. xi. 8, 28. xiii. 8. xvi. 30. xvii. 1, 3, 4, 11, 13, 25*t*. xviii. 26, 35. xix. 10*t*. xxi. 15, 16, 17, 18, 20, 22, 23. Acts v. 9. vii. 27, 34, 35. ix. 34. x. 19, 22, 33. xi. 14. xiii. 11, 33, 47. xviii. 10. xxi. 37. xxii. 19. 21. xxiii. 3, 18, 20, 30. xxiv. 8(*ap*), 25. xxvi. 3, 16, 17*t*, 24.

Rom. ii. 4, 27. iv. 17. ix. 17. xi. 18, 22. xv. 3. 1 Cor. iv. 7. viii. 10(–L^{b}). Phil. iv. 3. 1 Tim. i. 3, 18. iii. 14. 2 Tim. i. 4, 6. iii. 15. iv. 21. Tit. i. 5. iii. 12, 15. Phm. 10, 18, 23. Heb. i. 5, 9. ii. 12. v. 5. vi. 14*t*. xiii. 5*t*. 2 Jn. 5, 13. 3 Jn. 14*t*. Rev, iii. 3(–G^{o}L TTr^{b}), 3, 9, 10, 16. xv. 4 (–G^{oo}LTTr).

thee . . ^{cc}**thou**, Acts xxii. 14. xxiv. 4.

thou^{cc}, Matt. xviii. 33. xxv. 27. Acts viii. 23. ix. 6. x. 6(*ap*). xiii. 47. xxiii. 11. xxiv. 4, 10. xxvi. 29. xxvii. 24. Rom. iii. 4. 1 Tim. vi. 14. Tit. iii. 8. 3 John 2. Rev. x. 11.

πρὸς σέ, **at thy house**, Matt. xxvi. 18.

Not rendered, Acts iv. 30(–T). v. 3.

Add, for *σοί*, Mark ix. 43, 45, LTTr *S*. 47, TTr*S*. x. 21, T*S*. For *μέ*, Rom. viii. 2, L^{m}*S*. — Mark x. 35 (desire . .), LTTr. John xxi. 18 (thee^{3d}), L^{b}. Acts v. 3 (. . to keep), T.

συγγένεια.

kindred, Luke i. 61. Acts vii. 3, 14.

συγγενής.

kin, Mark vi. 4 (*-νεῦσιν* TTr).

kinsman, Luke xiv. 12(*ap*). John xviii. 26. Acts x. 24. Rom. ix. 3. xvi. 7, 11, 21.

Plur., **kinsfolk**, Luke ii. 44. — **kinsfolks**, Luke xxi. 16.

cousin, Luke i. 36(*συγγενίς* L*S*), 58.

συγγενίς, kinswoman.

Luke i. 36, for *συγγενής*, L*S*.

συγγνώμη.

permission, 1 Cor. vii. 6.

συγκάθημαι.

sit with, Mark xiv. 54 (*with ἦν* fr. *εἰμί*). Acts xxvi. 30.

συγκαθίζω.

make sit together, Eph. ii. 6.

sit down together, Luke xxii. 55 (*περικαθίζω* L).

συγκακοπαθέω.

be partaker of afflictions, 2 Tim. i. 8.

Add 2 Tim. ii. 3, for *σὺ οὖν κακοπαθ.*, G″LT*S*.

συγκακουχέω.
Pass., **suffer affliction with,** Heb. xi. 25.

συγκαλέω.
call together, Mark xv. 16. Acts v. 21. — *Mid.*, Luke ix. 1. xv. 6, 9. xxiii. 13p. Acts x. 24. xxviii. 17.

συγκαλύπτω.
to cover, Luke xii. 2.

συγκάμπτω.
bow down, Rom. xi. 10.

συγκαταβαίνω.
go down with, Acts xxv. 5.

συγκατάθεσις.
agreement, 2 Cor. vi. 16.

συγκατατίθεμαι.
With εἰμί, **consent to,** Luke xxiii. 51.

συγκαταψηφίζω.
number with, Acts i. 26.

συγκεράννυμι.
Pass., **be mixed** (*marg.* **united**) **with,** Heb. iv. 2p.
temper together, 1 Cor. xii. 24.

συγκινέω.
stir up, Acts vi. 12.

συγκλείω.
conclude, Rom. xi. 32 (*marg.* **shut up together**). Gal. iii. 22.
shut up, Gal. iii. 23.
inclose, Luke v. 6.

συγκληρονόμος.
heir with, Heb. xi. 9.
heir together, 1 Pet. iii. 7.
joint heir, Rom. viii. 17.
fellow heir, Eph. iii. 6.

συγκοινωνέω.
communicate with, Phil. iv. 14p.
have fellowship with, Eph. v. 11.
be partaker of, Rev. xviii. 4.

συγκοινωνός.
partaker, Phil. i. 7.
With γίνομαι, **partake with,** Rom. xi. 17. 1 Cor. ix. 23.
companion, Rev. i. 9 (κοινωνός G′).

συγκομίζω.
carry *to one's burial*, Acts viii. 2.

συγκρίνω.
compare with, 1 Cor. ii. 13. 2 Cor. x. 12.
compare among, 2 Cor. x. 12.

συγκύπτω.
be bowed together, Luke xiii. 11.

συγκυρία.
chance, Luke x. 31.

συγχαίρω.
rejoice with, Luke i. 58. xv. 6, 9. 1 Cor. xii. 26. Phil. ii. 17, 18.
rejoice in (*marg.* **with**), 1 Cor. xiii. 6.

συγχέω, -χύνω.
confuse, Acts xix. 32.
confound, Acts ii. 6 (*marg.* **trouble in mind**). ix. 22.
stir up, Acts xxi. 27.
Pass., **be in an uproar,** Acts xxi. 31.

συγχράομαι.
have dealings with, John iv. 9.

συγχύνω. See συγχέω.

σύγχυσις.
confusion, Acts xix. 29.

συζάω.
live with, Rom. vi. 8. 2 Cor. vii. 3. 2 Tim. ii. 11.

συζεύγνυμι, -ζευγνύω.
join together, Matt. xix. 6. Mark x. 9.

συζητέω.
question with, Mark viii. 11. ix. 14.
question one with another, Mark ix. 10. — **question,** Mark i. 27. ix. 16.
inquire, Luke xxii. 23.
dispute with, Acts vi. 9.
dispute, Acts ix. 29.
reason together, Mark xii. 28.
reason, Luke xxiv. 15.

συζήτησις.
disputation, Acts xv. 2 (ζήτησις GL T*S*, - G°°). — **disputing,** Acts xv. 7.
reasoning, Acts xxviii. 29 (*ap*).

συζητητής.
disputer, 1 Cor. i. 20.

σύζυγος.
yoke-fellow, Phil. iv. 3.

συζωοποιέω.
quicken together with, Eph. ii. 5. Col. ii. 13.

συκάμινος.
sycamine tree, Luke xvii. 6.

συκέα, συκῆ.
fig-tree, Matt. xxi. 19*t*, 20, 21. xxiv. 32. Mark xi. 13, 20, 21. xiii. 28. Luke xiii. 6, 7. xxi. 29. John i. 48(49), 50 (51). Jas. iii. 12. Rev. vi. 13.

συκομωραία StG″,
συκομωρέα LT, συκομορέα EGTr*S*.
sycomore tree, Luke xix. 4.

σῦκον.
fig, Matt. vii. 16. Mark xi. 13. Luke vi. 44. Jas. iii. 12.

συκοφαντέω.
accuse falsely, Luke iii. 14.
take by false accusation, Luke xix. 8.

συλαγωγέω.
With εἰμί, **to spoil,** Col. ii. 8.

συλάω.
rob, 2 Cor. xi. 8.

συλλαλέω.
talk with, Matt. xvii. 3. Mark ix. 4. Luke ix. 30.
σ. πρός, **speak among,** Luke iv. 36.
commune with, Luke xxii. 4.
confer with, Acts xxv. 12p.

συλλαμβάνω.
catch, Acts xxvi. 21.
take, Matt. xxvi. 55. Mark xiv. 48. Luke v. 9. xxii. 54. John xviii. 12. Acts i. 16. xii. 3. xxiii. 27.
conceive, Luke i. 24, 31, 36. ii. 21. Jas. i. 15p.
Mid., **help,** Luke v. 7. Phil. iv. 3.

συλλέγω.
gather together, Matt. xiii. 30.
gather up, Matt. xiii. 28, 29p.
gather, Matt. vii. 16. xiii. 40, 41, 48. Luke vi. 44.

συλλογίζομαι.
σ. πρός, **reason with,** Luke xx. 5.

συλλυπέω.
grieve, Mark iii. 5.

συμβαίνω.
happen, Mark x. 32. Luke xxiv. 14. Acts iii. 10. 1 Cor. x. 11. 1 Pet. iv. 12. 2 Pet. ii. 22.
befall, Acts xx. 19.
συνέβη, **so it was,** Acts xxi. 35.

συμβάλλω.
confer, Acts iv. 15.
ponder, Luke ii. 19.
Mid., **help,** Acts xviii. 27.
meet with, Acts xx. 14.
encounter, Acts xvii. 18.
With εἰς, **make,** Luke xiv. 31.

συμβασιλεύω.
reign with, 1 Cor. iv. 8. 2 Tim. ii. 12.

συμβιβάζω.
Pass., **be compacted,** Eph. iv. 16.
knit together, Col. ii. 2, 19.
gather assuredly, Acts xvi. 10.
prove, Acts ix. 22.
instruct, 1 Cor. ii. 16.
Add Acts xix. 33, for προβιβ., L*S*.

συμβουλεύω.
to counsel, Rev. iii. 18.
give counsel, John xviii. 14.
Mid., **take counsel together,** John xi. 53 (βουλεύομαι LTr*S*). — **take counsel,** Acts ix. 23. — **consult,** Matt. xxvi. 4.

συμβούλιον.
council, Matt. xii. 14. Acts xxv. 12.
counsel, Matt. xxii. 15. xxvii. 1, 7. xxviii. 12. Mark iii. 6.
consultation, Mark xv. 1.

σύμβουλος.
counsellor, Rom. xi. 34.

συμμαθητής.
fellow disciple, John xi. 16.

συμμαρτυρέω.
bear witness with, Rom. viii. 16.
bear witness also (*marg.* **witness with**). Rom. ii. 15.
bear witness, Rom. ix. 1.
Mid., **testify unto,** Rev. xxii. 18 (μαρτυρέω GLTTr*S*).

συμμερίζω.
Mid., **be partaker with,** 1 Cor ix. 13.

συμμέτοχος.
partaker with, Eph. v. 7.
partaker, Eph. iii. 6.

συμμιμητής.
follower together, Phil. iii. 17.

συμμορφίζω, make of like form with. *See συμμορφόω.*

σύμμορφος.
conformed to, Rom. viii. 29.
fashioned like unto, Phil. iii. 21.

συμμορφόω.
make conformable unto, Phil. iii. 10 (*συμμορφίζω* G''LT*S*).

συμπαθέω.
have compassion of, Heb. x. 34.
be touched with the feeling of, Heb. iv. 15.

συμπαθής.
Plur., **having compassion one of another,** 1 Pet. iii. 8.

συμπαραγίνομαι.
come together, Luke xxiii. 48.
stand with, 2 Tim. iv. 16 (*παραγίνομαι* L*S*).

συμπαρακαλέω.
Pass., **be comforted together,** Rom. i. 12.

συμπαραλαμβάνω.
take with one, Acts xii. 25. xv. 37, 38. Gal. ii. 1.

συμπαραμένω.
continue with, Phil. i. 25 (*παραμένω* G''L*S*).

συμπάρειμι.
be here° present with, Acts xxv. 24.

συμπάσχω.
suffer with, Rom. viii. 17. 1 Cor. xii. 26.

συμπέμπω.
send with, 2 Cor. viii. 18, 22.

συμπεριλαμβάνω.
to embrace, Acts xx. 10.

συμπίνω.
drink with, Acts x. 41.

συμπίπτω, fall together.
Luke vi. 49, for *πίπτω*, TTr*S*.

συμπληρόω.
fill, Luke viii. 23.
Pass., **be fully come,** Acts ii. 1. — **come,** Luke ix. 51.

συμπνίγω.
choke, Matt. xiii. 22. Mark iv. 7, 19. Luke viii. 14.
throng, Luke viii. 42.

συμπολίτης.
fellow citizen, Eph. ii. 19.

συμπορεύομαι.
go with, Luke vii. 11. xiv. 25. xxiv. 15.
resort, Mark x. 1.

συμπόσιον.
συμπόσια συμπόσια, **by companies,** Mark vi. 39.

συμπρεσβύτερος.
also an elder, 1 Pet. v. 1.

συμφάγω. See *συνεσθίω.*

συμφέρω.
bring together, Acts xix. 19.
Intransitive, and impersonal[1].
be profitable, Matt. v. 29[1], 30[1]. Acts xx. 20. — *Part.*, **profit,** 1 Cor. vii. 35 and x. 33 (*σύμφορος* LT*S*). Heb. xii. 10. — *πρὸς τὸ σ.*, **to profit withal,** 1 Cor. xii. 7.
be expedient, John xi. 50[1]. xvi. 7[1]. xviii. 14[1]. 1 Cor vi. 12 (*marg.* **be profitable**). x. 23. 2 Cor. viii. 10[1]. xii. 1[1].
be good, Matt. xix. 10[1].
be better, Matt. xviii 6[1].

σύμφημι.
consent unto, Rom. vii. 16.

σύμφορος, profitable
1 Cor. vii. 35, x. 33, *see συμφέρω.*

συμφυλέτης.
countryman, 1 Thes. ii. 14.

σύμφυτος.
planted together, Rom. vi. 5.

συμφύω.
Pass., **spring up with**, Luke viii. 7.

συμφωνέω.
agree with, Matt. xx. 13. Luke v. [36.
agree together, Acts v. 9[oo].
agree, Matt. xviii. 19. xx. 2[p], 13. Acts xv. 15.

συμφώνησις.
concord, 2 Cor. vi. 15.

συμφωνία.
music, Luke xv. 25.

σύμφωνος.
ἐκ συμφ., **with consent**, 1 Cor. vii. 5.

συμψηφίζω.
to count, Acts xix. 19.

σύμψυχος.
like-minded, Phil. ii. 2.

σύν.
with, Matt. xxv. 27. xxvi. 35. xxvii. 38. Mark iv. 10. viii. 34. ix. 4. xv. 27. Luke i. 56. ii. 5, 13. v. 19. vii. 6, 12. viii. 1, 38. xix. 23. xx. 1. xxii. 14, 56. xxiii. 11, 32, 35 (-G°L[b]TrS). xxiv. 1(*ap*), 29, 44. John xviii. 1. xxi. 3.
Acts i. 14, 14(-G°°LS), 17 (ἐν GL TS), 22. ii. 14. iii. 4, 8. iv. 13, 14, 27. v. 1, 26. viii. 20, 31. x. 2, 20, 23. xiii. 7. xiv. 4*t*, 5, 13, 20, 28. xv. 22*t*, 25. xvi. 3. xvii. 34. xviii. 8, 18. xx. 36. xxi. 5, 16, 18, 24, 26, 29. xxii. 9. xxiii. 15, 27, 32. xxiv. 24. xxv. 23. xxvi. 13. xxvii. 2. xxviii. 16.
Rom. vi. 8. viii. 32. xvi. 14. 1 Cor. i. 2. v. 4. x. 13. xi. 32. xvi. 4, 19. 2 Cor. i. 1, 21. iv. 14. viii. 19 (ἐν G'LT). ix. 4. xiii. 4. Gal. iii. 9. v. 24. Eph. iii. 18. iv. 31. Phil. i. 1, 23. ii. 22. Col. ii. 5, 13, 20. iii. 3, 4, 9. iv. 9. 1 Thes. iv. 14, 17*t*. v. 10. Jas. i. 11. 2 Pet. i. 18.
ὁ (ἡ) σύν, **who (which) was° with**, 1 Cor. xv. 10. Gal. ii. 3.
οἱ σύν, **(they) that (which) are with**, Mark ii. 26. Luke v. 9. ix. 32. xxiv. 10, 24, 33. Acts v. 17, 21. xix. 38. Rom. xvi. 15. Gal. i. 2. Phil. iv. [21.
beside, Luke xxiv. 21.
Add, for διά, 2 Cor. iv. 14, G'LTS. For ἐν, Acts vii. 35[1st], G''LT. 2 Cor. xiii. 4, L[m]S. For καί, Acts xvi. 32[2d], GLTS. For μετά, Luke viii. 45, GL TTrS. — Matt. xxvii. 44 (with), L TrS. Mark xv. 32 (with), LS. Luke viii. 51(*ap*). John xii. 2, *see* συνανάκειμαι. — — *See also* ἔρχομαι.

συνάγω.
lead into, Rev. xiii. 10 (ἀπάγω G', -LTTrS).
gather together, Matt. xxii. 10. Luke xv. 13. John vi. 13. xi. 52. Acts xiv. 27. xv. 30[p]. Rev. xvi. 16. xx. 8.
gather up, John vi. 12.
gather, Matt. ii. 4[p]. iii. 12. vi. 26. xii. 30. xiii. 30, 47. xxv. 24, 26. xxvii. 27. Luke iii. 17. xi. 23. John iv. 36. xi. 47. xv. 6. Rev. xvi. 14.
bestow, Luke xii. 17, 18.
take in, Matt. xxv. 35, 38, 43.

Passive or Middle.
be gathered together, Matt. xiii. 2. xviii. 20. xxii. 41[p]. xxiv. 28. xxvii. 17[p]. Mark ii. 2. Luke xvii. 37 (ἐπισυνάγω TTrS). Acts iv. 6(5), 27. xx. 8. 1 Cor. v. 4[p]. Rev. xix. 19.
be gathered, Matt. xxii. 34. xxv. 32. Mark iv. 1. Acts iv. 26.
gather, Mark v. 21.
gather -selves together, Mark vi. 30. Rev. xix. 17.
be assembled together, Acts iv. 31.
be assembled, Matt. xxvi. 57. xxviii. 12[p]. John xx. 19(-G°LTTrS).
assemble together, Matt. xxvi. 3.
assemble themselves, Acts xi. 26.
come together, Matt. xxvii. 62. Mark vii. 1. Luke xxii. 66. Acts xiii. 44. xv. 6. xx. 7.
resort, John xviii. 2.

συναγωγή.
assembly (*Gr.* synagogue), Jas. ii. 2.
congregation, Acts xiii. 43.
synagogue, Matt. iv. 23. vi. 2, 5.

ix. 35. x. 17. xii. 9. xiii. 54. xxiii. 6, 34. Mark i. 21, 23, 29, 39. iii. 1. vi. 2. xii. 39. xiii. 9. Luke iv. 15, 16, 20, 28, 33, 38, 44. vi. 6. vii. 5. viii. 41. xi. 43. xii. 11. xiii. 10. xx. 46. xxi. 12. John vi. 59. xviii. 20. Acts vi. 9. ix. 2, 20. xiii. 5, 14, 42 (*ap*). xiv. 1. xv. 21. xvii. 1, 10, 17. xviii. 4, 7, 19, 26. xix. 8. xxiv. 12. Rev. ii. 9. iii. 9.

Plur., *with* κατά, **in every synagogue,** Acts xxii. 19. xxvi. 11.

συναγωνίζομαι.

strive together with, Rom. xv. 30.

συναθλέω.

strive together for, Phil. i. 27.
labor with, Phil. iv. 3.

συναθροίζω.

gather together, Luke xxiv. 33 (ἀθροίζω LTTr*S*). Acts xii. 12.
call together, Acts xix. 25.

συναίρω.

take, Matt. xviii. 23.
With λόγος, **reckon,** Matt. xxv. 19.
reckon, Matt. xviii. 24.

συναιχμάλωτος.

fellow prisoner, Rom. xvi. 7. Col. iv. 10. Phm. 23.

συνακολουθέω.

follow, Mark v. 37 (ἀκολουθέω L). Luke xxiii. 49.
Add Mark xiv. 51, for ἀκολουθέω, G'LTTr*S*.

συναλίζω.

Pass. or mid., **be assembled** (*marg.* **eat**) **together with,** Acts i. 4.

συναλλάσσω, bring together, reconcile. Acts vii. 26, *see* συνελαύνω.

συναναβαίνω.

come up with, Mark xv. 41. Acts xiii. 31.

συνανάκειμαι.

sit at the table (at meat[1]**) with,** Matt. xiv. 9[1]. Luke vii. 49[1]. xiv. 10[1], 15[1]. John xii. 2 (ἀνάκειμαι σύν GLTTr*S*).
sit down with, Matt. ix. 10.
sit together with, Mark ii. 15.
sit with, Mark vi. 22, 26 (ἀνάκειμαι TTr).

συναναμίγνυμι.

Pass. or mid., **have company with,** 2 Thes. iii. 14. — **company with,** 1 Cor. v. 9. — **keep company,** 1 Cor. v. 11.

συναναπαύω.

Mid., **be refreshed,** Rom. xv. 32 (*ap*).

συναντάω.

to meet, Luke ix. 37. xxii. 10. Acts x. 25. Heb. vii. 1, 10.
τὰ συναντήσοντα, **the things that shall befall,** Acts xx. 22.

συνάντησις.

With εἰς, **to meet,** Matt. viii. 34 (ὑπάντησις LTr*S*).

συναντιλαμβάνω.

Mid., **to help,** Luke x. 40. Rom. viii. 26.

συναπάγω.

lead away with, 2 Pet. iii. 17.
carry away with, Gal. ii. 13.
Pass., **condescend to** (*marg.* **be contented with**), Rom. xii. 16.

συναποθνήσκω.

die with, Mark xiv. 31. 2 Cor. vii. 3.
Aorist, **be dead with,** 2 Tim. ii. 11.

συναπόλλυμι.

Mid. or pass., **perish with,** Heb. xi. 31.

συναποστέλλω.

send with, 2 Cor. xii. 18.

συναρμολογέω.

join fitly together, Eph. iv. 16.
frame fitly together, Eph. ii. 21.

συναρπάζω.

catch, Luke viii. 29. Acts vi. 12. xix. 29. xxvii. 15p.

συναυξάνω.

Mid., **grow together,** Matt. xiii. 30.

συνβ., συνγ., συνζ., συνκ., etc.

In compounds of σύν and words beginning with β, γ, ζ, κ, λ, μ, π, σ, and ψ, the ν is often retained by

L, T, Tr, and *S;* e. g., *συνγενής* for *συγγενής*, *συνζάω* for *συζάω*.

σύνδεσμος.

band, Col. ii. 19.
bond, Acts viii. 23. Eph. iv. 3. Col. iii. 14.

συνδέω.

bind with, Heb. xiii. 3.

συνδοξάζω.

glorify together, Rom. viii. 17.

σύνδουλος.

fellow servant, Matt. xviii. 28, 29, 31, 33. xxiv. 49. Col. i. 7. iv. 7. Rev. vi. 11. xix. 10. xxii. 9.

συνδρομή.

With γίνομαι, **run together**, Acts xxi. 30cc.

συνεγείρω.

raise up together, Eph. ii. 6.
Pass., **rise with**, Col. ii. 12. iii. 1.

συνέδριον.

council, Matt. v. 22. x. 17. xxvi. 59. Mark xiii. 9. xiv. 55. xv. 1. Luke xxii. 66. John xi. 47. Acts iv. 15. v. 21, 27, 34, 41. vi. 12, 15. xxii. 30. xxiii. 1, 6, 15, 20, 28. xxiv. 20.

συνείδησις.

conscience, John viii. 9 (*ap*). Acts xxiii. 1. xxiv. 16. Rom. ii. 15. ix. 1. xiii. 5. 1 Cor. viii. 7 (*συνήθεια* G″ L*S*), 7, 10, 12. x. 25, 27, 28, 29*t*. 2 Cor. i. 12. iv. 2. v. 11. 1 Tim. i. 5, 19. iii. 9. iv. 2. 2 Tim. i. 3. Tit. i. 15. Heb. ix. 9, 14. x. 2. 22. xiii. 18. 1 Pet. ii. 19. iii. 16, 21.

συνεῖδον, σύνοιδα[1].

know by, 1 Cor. iv. 4[1].
be ware of, Acts xiv. 6.
be privy to, Acts v. 2[1].
consider, Acts xii. 12p.

σύνειμι.

be with, Luke ix. 18. Acts xxii. 11.

σύνειμι.

be gathered together, Luke viii. 4p.

συνεισέρχομαι.

go into with, John vi. 22.
go in with, John xviii. 15.

συνέκδημος.

companion in travel, Acts xix. 29.
to travel with, 2 Cor. viii. 19.

συνεκλεκτός.

elected together with, 1 Pet. v. 13.

συνελαύνω.

With εἰς εἰρήνην, **set at one again**, Acts vii. 26 (*συναλλάσσω* G′L*S*).

συνεπιμαρτυρέω.

bear witness also, Heb. ii. 4.

συνεπιτίθημι, *mid.*, join in assailing. Acts xxiv. 9, *see συντίθημι*.

συνέπομαι.

accompany, Acts xx. 4.

συνεργέω.

work with, Mark xvi. 20(*ap*). Jas. ii. 22.
work together, Rom. viii. 28.
worker together, 2 Cor. vi. 1p.
help with, 1 Cor. xvi. 16.

συνεργός.

fellow worker, Col. iv. 11.
work-fellow, Rom. xvi. 21.
fellow laborer, Phil. iv. 3. 1 Thes. iii. 2(*ap*). Phm. 1, 24.
laborer together with, 1 Cor. iii. 9.
companion in labor, Phil. ii. 25. [8.
fellow helper, 2 Cor. viii. 23. 3 John
helper, Rom. xvi. 3, 9. 2 Cor. i. 24.

συνέρχομαι.

come with, Luke xxiii. 55 (*with εἰμί*). John xi. 33. Acts x. 45.
come together, Matt. i. 18. Mark iii. 20. vi. 33(*ap*). Luke v. 15. Acts i. 6p. ii. 6. x. 27. xix. 32. xxi. 22. xxviii. 17p. 1 Cor. vii. 5 (*εἰμί* GLT*S*). xi. 17, 18p, 20p, 33p, 34. xiv. 23 (*ἔρχομαι* L), 26.
come, Acts v. 16. xxv. 17p.
company with, Acts i. 21.
accompany, Acts x. 23.
assemble with, Mark xiv. 53.
go with, Acts ix. 39. xi. 12. xv. 38. xxi. 16.
resort, John xviii. 20. Acts xvi. 13.
Add, for *ἔρχομαι*, Luke v. 17, L. Acts xxii. 30, GLT*S*.

συνεσθίω.
eat with, Luke xv. 2. Acts x. 41. xi. 3. 1 Cor. v. 11. Gal. ii. 12.

σύνεσις.
understanding, Mark xii. 33. Luke ii. 47. 1 Cor. i. 19. Col. i. 9. ii. 2. 2 Tim. ii. 7.
knowledge, Eph. iii. 4.

συνετός.
prudent, Matt. xi. 25. Luke x. 21. Acts xiii. 7. 1 Cor. i. 19.

συνευδοκέω.
have pleasure in (*marg.* **consent with**), Rom. i. 32.
be pleased, 1 Cor. vii. 12, 13.
consent unto, Acts viii. 1. xxii. 20.
allow, Luke xi. 48.

συνευωχέω.
Mid., **feast with,** 2 Pet. ii. 13p. Jude 12p.

συνεφίστημι.
rise up together, Acts xvi. 22.

συνέχω.
keep in, Luke xix. 43.
man that holdeth, Luke xxii. 63p.
stop, Acts vii. 57.
constrain, 2 Cor. v. 14.
press, Acts xviii. 5.
throng, Luke viii. 45.
Pass., **be straitened** (*marg.* **pained**), Luke xii. 50. — **be in a strait,** Phil. i. 23. — **be taken with,** Matt. iv. 24. Luke iv. 38. viii. 37. — **lie sick of,** Acts xxviii. 8.

συνήδομαι.
delight in, Rom. vii. 22.

συνήθεια.
custom, John xviii. 39. 1 Cor. xi. 16. *Add* 1 Cor. viii. 7, *see* συνείδησις.

συνηλικιώτης.
equal (*Gr.* eq. in years), Gal. i. 14.

συνθάπτω.
bury with, Rom. vi. 4. Col. ii. 12.

συνθλάω.
break, Matt. xxi. 44(*ap*). Luke xx. 18.

συνθλίβω.
to throng, Mark v. 24, 31.

συνθρύπτω.
break, Acts xxi. 13.

συνίημι.
consider, Mark vi. 52.
understand, Matt. xiii. 13, 14, 15, 19, 23, 51. xv. 10. xvi. 12. xvii. 13. Mark iv. 12. vii. 14. viii. 17, 21. Luke ii. 50. viii. 10. xviii. 34. xxiv. 45. Acts vii. 25*t*. xxviii. 26, 27. Rom. iii. 11. xv. 21. Eph. v. 17.
be wise, 2 Cor. x. 12 (*marg.* **understand**; – G∞).

συνίστημι, συνιστάω, -άνω.
I. Transitive.
make, Gal. ii. 18.
commend, Rom. iii. 5. v. 8. xvi. 1. 2 Cor. iii. 1. iv. 2. v. 12. x. 12, 18*t*. xii. 11.
approve, 2 Cor. vi. 4 (*Gr.* commend). vii. 11.
II. Intransitive.
stand with, Luke ix. 32.
stand (*Gr.* consist), 2 Pet. iii. 5.
consist, Col. i. 17.

συνοδεύω.
journey with, Acts ix. 7.

συνοδία.
company, Luke ii. 44.

συνοικέω.
dwell with, 1 Pet. iii. 7.

συνοικοδομέω.
build together, Eph. ii. 22.

συνομιλέω.
talk with, Acts x. 27p.

συνομορέω.
With εἰμί, **join hard to,** Acts xviii. 7.

συνοχή.
distress, Luke xxi. 25.
anguish, 2 Cor. ii. 4.

συντάσσω, -ττω.
appoint, Matt. xxvi. 19. xxvii. 10. *Add* Matt. xxi. 6, *see* προστάσσω.

συντέλεια.
end, Matt. xiii. 39, 40, 49. xxiv. 3. xxviii. 20. Heb. ix. 26.

συντελέω.
to end, Matt. vii. 28(τελέω LTTr*S*). Luke iv. 2p, 13p. Acts xxi. 27.
finish, Rom. ix. 28.
fulfill, Mark xiii. 4.
make, Heb. viii. 8.

συντέμνω.
cut short, Rom. ix. 28.
Pass. part., **short**, Rom. ix. 28(*ap*).

συντηρέω.
keep, Luke ii. 19.
observe, Mark vi. 20 (*marg.* **keep**, or **save**).
preserve, Matt. ix. 17. Luke v. 38 (-GoTTrb*S*).

συντίθημι.
Mid., **to covenant**, Luke xxii. 5.—**agree**, John ix. 22. Acts xxiii. 20.—**assent**, Acts xxiv. 9 (συνεπιτίθημι G LT*S*).

συντόμως.
a few words, Acts xxiv. 4.

συντρέχω.
run with, 1 Pet. iv. 4p.
run together, Acts iii. 11.
run, Mark vi. 33.

συντρίβω.
break in pieces, Mark v. 4.
break to shivers, Rev. ii. 27.
break, Mark xiv. 3. John xix. 36.
bruise, Matt. xii. 20. Luke ix. 39. Rom. xvi. 20 (*marg.* **tread**).
συντετριμμένος τὴν καρδίαν, **broken-hearted**, Luke iv. 18(*ap*).

σύντριμμα.
destruction, Rom. iii. 16.

σύντροφος.
which hadc **been brought up with** (*marg.* **foster-brother**), Acts xiii. 1.

συντυγχάνω.
come at, Luke viii. 19.

συνυποκρίνομαι.
dissemble with, Gal. ii. 13.

συνυπουργέω.
help together, 2 Cor. i. 11.

συνωδίνω.
travail in pain together, Rom. viii. 22.

συνωμοσία.
conspiracy, Acts xxiii. 13.

σύρτις, Σύρτις G, σῦρτις L.
quicksands, Acts xxvii. 17.

σύρω.
to draw, Acts xiv. 19. xvii. 6. Rev. xii. 4.
drag, John xxi. 8.
hale, Acts viii. 3.

συσπαράσσω, -ττω.
to tear, Luke ix. 42. [Trm*S*.
Add Mark ix. 20, for σπαράσσω, L

σύσσημον.
token, Mark xiv. 44.

σύσσωμος.
of the same body, Eph. iii. 6.

συστασιαστής.
that had madec **insurrection with**, Mark xv. 7 (στασιαστής LTr*S*).

συστατικός.
of commendation, 2 Cor. iii. 1, † (-GoL*S*).

συσταυρόω.
crucify with, Matt. xxvii. 44. Mark xv. 32. John xix. 32. Rom. vi. 6. Gal. ii. 20.

συστέλλω.
wind up, Acts v. 6.
Pass. part., **short**, 1 Cor. vii. 29.

συστενάζω.
groan together, Rom. viii. 22.

συστοιχέω.
answer to (*marg.* **be in the same rank with**), Gal. iv. 25.

συστρατιώτης.
fellow soldier, Phil. ii. 25. Phm. 2.

συστρέφω.
gather, Acts xxviii. 3p.
Add Matt. xvii. 22, for ἀναστρέφω, LTr*S*.

συστροφή.
ποιέω σ., **band together**, Acts xxiii. 12.
concourse, Acts xix. 40.

συσχηματίζω.
Mid. or pass., **fashion one's self ac-**

cording to, 1 Pet. i. 14.—**be conformed to**, Rom. xii. 2.

σφαγή.

slaughter, Acts viii. 32. Rom. viii. 36. Jas. v. 5.

σφάγιον.

slain beast, Acts vii. 42.

σφάζω, σφάττω.

slay, 1 John iii. 12*t*. Rev. v. 6, 9, 12. vi. 9. xiii. 8. xviii. 24.
kill, Rev. vi. 4.
wound (*Gr.* slay), Rev. xiii. 3.

σφόδρα.

greatly, Matt. xxvii. 54. Acts vi. 7.
very, Matt. xviii. 31. Mark xvi. 4. Luke xviii. 23.
sore, Matt. xvii. 6.
exceedingly, Matt. xix. 25.
exceeding, Matt. ii. 10. xvii. 23. xxvi. 22. Rev. xvi. 21.

σφοδρῶς.

exceedingly, Acts xxvii. 18.

σφραγίζω.

seal up, Rev. x. 4.
set a seal, Rev. xx. 3.
set to one's seal, John iii. 33.
seal, Matt. xxvii. 66. John vi. 27. Rom. xv. 28. 2 Cor. i. 22. Eph. i. 13. iv. 30. Rev. vii. 3, 4*t*, 5, 5*t*[1], 6*tr*[1], 7*tr*[1], 8*t*[1], 8. xxii. 10. ([1]-G∞LTTr[b]*S*.)
Add 2 Cor. xi. 10, for φράσσω, St.

σφραγίς.

seal, Rom. iv. 11. 1 Cor. ix. 2. 2 Tim. ii. 19. Rev. v. 1, 2, 5, 9. vi. 1, 3, 5, 7, 9, 12. vii. 2. viii. 1. ix. 4.

σφυρίς. See σπυρίς.

σφυρόν.

ankle-bone, Acts iii. 7.

σχεδόν.

almost, Acts xiii. 44. xix. 26. Heb. ix. 22.

σχῆμα.

fashion, 1 Cor. vii. 31. Phil. ii. 8.

σχίζω.

rend, Matt. xxvii. 51*t*. Mark xv. 38. Luke xxiii. 45. John xix. 24.
make a rent, Luke v. 36.
divide, Acts xiv. 4. xxiii. 7.
open (*marg.* **cleave** *or* **rend**), Mark i. 10.
break, John xxi. 11.
Add Luke v. 36 (man . .), G'TTr*S*.

σχίσμα.

rent, Matt. ix. 16. Mark ii. 21.
division, John vii. 43. ix. 16. x. 19. 1 Cor. i. 10 and xi. 18 (*Gr.* schism).
schism (*marg.* **division**), 1 Cor. xii. 25.

σχοινίον.

small cord, John ii. 15.
rope, Acts xxvii. 32.

σχολάζω.

give one's self to, 1 Cor. vii. 5.
empty, Matt. xii. 44[p].

σχολή.

school, Acts xix. 9.

σώζω.

to save, Matt. i. 21. viii. 25. x. 22. xiv. 30. xvi. 25. xviii. 11(*ap*). xix. 25. xxiv. 13, 22. xxvii. 40, 42*t*, 49. Mark iii. 4. viii. 35*t*. x. 26. xiii. 13, 20. xv. 30, 31*t*. xvi. 16(*ap*). Luke vi. 9. vii. 50. viii. 12. ix. 24*t*, 56 (*ap*). xiii. 23. xvii. 33 (περιποιέομαι TTr). xviii. 26, 42. xix. 10. xxiii. 35*t*, 37, 39. John iii. 17. v. 34. x. 9. xii. 27, 47. Acts ii. 21. iv. 12. xi. 14. xv. 1, 11. xvi. 30, 31. xxvii. 20, 31.
Rom. v. 9, 10. viii. 24. ix. 27. x. 9, 10. xi. 14, 26. 1 Cor. i. 18, 21. iii. 15. v. 5. vii. 16*t*. ix. 22. x. 33. xv. 2. 2 Cor. ii. 15. Eph. ii. 5, 8. 1 Thes. ii. 16. 2 Thes. ii. 10. 1 Tim. i. 15. ii. 4, 15. iv. 16. 2 Tim. i. 9. Tit. iii. 5. Heb. v. 7. vii. 25. Jas. i. 21. ii. 14. iv. 12. v. 15, 20. 1 Pet. iii. 21. iv. 18. Jude 5, 23. Rev. xxi. 24(*omS*).
Pass., **save one's self**, Acts ii. 40. —**be whole**, Matt. ix. 21. Mark v. 28. —**do well**, John xi. 12.
οἱ σωζόμενοι, **such as should be saved**, Acts ii. 47.
preserve, 2 Tim. iv. 18.
make whole, Matt. ix. 22*t*. Mark v.

34. vi. 56. x. 52 (*marg.* **save**). Luke viii. 48, 50. xvii. 19. Acts iv. 9.
heal, Mark v. 23. Luke viii. 36. Acts xiv. 9.

σῶμα.

body, Matt. v. 29, 30. vi. 22*t*, 23, 25*t*. x. 28*t*. xiv. 12 (πτῶμα G'LTr *S*). xxvi. 12, 26. xxvii. 52, 58, 58 (-Tr[b]*S*), 59. Mark v. 29. xiv. 8, 22. xv. 43, 45 (πτῶμα LTTr*S*). Luke xi. 34*tr*, 36. xii. 4, 22, 23. xvii. 37. xxii. 19. xxiii. 52, 55. xxiv. 3, 23. John ii. 21. xix. 31, 38*t*, 40. xx. 12. Acts ix. 50.
Rom. i. 24. iv. 19. vi. 6, 12. vii. 4, 24. viii. 10, 11, 13, 23. xii. 1, 4, 5. 1 Cor. v. 3. vi. 13*t*, 15, 16, 18*t*, 19, 20. vii. 4*t*, 34. ix. 27. x. 16, 17. xi. 24, 27, 29. xii. 12*tr*, 13, 14, 15*t*, 16*t*, 17, 18, 19, 20, 22, 23, 24, 25, 27. xiii. 3. xv. 35, 37, 38*t*, 40*t*, 44*tr*, 44 (-G°LT*S*). 2 Cor. iv. 10*t*. v. 6, 8, 10. xii. 2*t*, 3*t*.
Gal. vi. 17. Eph. i. 23. ii. 16. iv. 4, 12, 16*t*. v. 23, 28, 30. Phil. i. 20. iii. 21*t*. Col. i. 18, 22, 24. ii. 11, 17, 19, 23. iii. 15. 1 Thes. v. 23. Heb. x. 5, 10, 22. xiii. 3, 11. Jas. ii. 16, 26. iii. 2. 3, 6. 1 Pet. ii. 24. Jude 9.
Gen., **bodily**, 2 Cor. x. 10.
slave (*marg.* **body**), Rev. xviii. 13.

σωματικός.

bodily, Luke iii. 22. 1 Tim. iv. 8.

σωματικῶς.

bodily, Col. ii. 9.

σωρεύω.

to heap, Rom. xii. 20.
lade, 2 Tim. iii. 6.

σωτήρ.

saviour, Eph. v. 23.
Saviour, Luke i. 47. ii. 11. John iv. 42. Acts v. 31. xiii. 23. Phil. iii. 20. 1 Tim. i. 1. ii. 3. iv. 10. 2 Tim. i. 10. Tit. i. 3, 4. ii. 10, 13. iii. 4, 6. 2 Pet. i. 1, 11. ii. 20. iii. 2, 18. 1 John iv. 14. Jude 25.

σωτηρία.

saving, Heb. xi. 7.
that we° should be saved, Luke i. 71.
With εἰς, **that they° might be saved**, Rom. x. 1.
salvation, Luke i. 69, 77. xix. 9. John iv. 22. Acts iv. 12(*ap*). xiii. 26, 47. xvi. 17. Rom. i. 16. x. 10. xi. 11. xiii. 11. 2 Cor. i. 6*t*. vi. 2*t*. vii. 10. Eph. i. 13. Phil. i. 19, 28. ii. 12. 1 Thes. v. 8, 9. 2 Thes. ii. 13. 2 Tim. ii. 10. iii. 15. Heb. i. 14. ii. 3, 10. v. 9. vi. 9. ix. 28. 1 Pet. i. 5, 9, 10. 2 Pet. iii. 15. Jude 3. Rev. vii. 10. xii. 10. xix. 1.
With δίδωμι, **deliver**, Acts vii. 25.
health, Acts xxvii. 34. [T*S*.
Add 1 Pet. ii. 2(thereby εἰς σ.), GL

σωτήριος.

that bringeth salvation, Tit. ii. 11.
Neut., **salvation**, Luke ii. 30. iii. 6. Acts xxviii. 28. Eph. vi. 17.

σωφρονέω.

in one's right mind, Mark v. 15[p]. Luke viii. 35[p].
be sober minded (*marg.* **be discreet**), Tit. ii. 6.
be sober, 2 Cor. v. 13. 1 Pet. iv. 7.
εἰς τὸ σωφρονεῖν, **soberly** (*Gr.* to sobriety), Rom. xii. 3.

σωφρονίζω.

teach to be sober (*marg.* **wise**), Tit. ii. 4.

σωφρονισμός.

sound mind, 2 Tim. i. 7.

σωφρόνως.

soberly, Tit. ii. 12.

σωφροσύνη.

soberness, Acts xxvi. 25.
sobriety, 1 Tim. ii. 9, 15.

σώφρων.

sober, 1 Tim. iii. 2. Tit. i. 8.
temperate, Tit. ii. 2.
discreet, Tit. ii. 5.

ταβέρναι. See τρεῖς.

τάγμα.

order, 1 Cor. xv. 23.

τακτός.

set, Acts xii. 21.

ταλαιπωρέω.
be afflicted, Jas. iv. 9.

ταλαιπωρία.
misery, Rom. iii. 16. Jas. v. 1.

ταλαίπωρος.
wretched, Rom. vii. 24. Rev. iii. 17.

ταλαντιαῖος.
the weight of a talent, Rev. xvi. 21.

τάλαντον.
talent, Matt. xviii. 24. xxv. 15, 16, 16(-G°LTr), 20, 20(-Tr[b]), 20*t*, 22*tr*, 24, 25, 28*t*.
Add Matt. xxv. 18 (one . .), L.

ταλιθά.
talitha, Mark v. 41.

ταμεῖον.
store-house, Luke xii. 24.
secret chamber, Matt. xxiv. 26.
closet, Matt. vi. 6. Luke xii. 3.
ταμιεῖον, Matt. vi. 6, G.

ταννῦν. See νῦν.

τάξις.
order, Luke i. 8. 1 Cor. xiv. 40. Col. ii. 5. Heb. v. 6, 10. vi. 20. vii. 11*t*, 17, 21(*ap*).

ταπεινός.
lowly, Matt. xi. 29.
of low degree, Luke i. 52. Jas. i. 9.
Plur., with art., **men of low estate** (*marg.* **mean things**), Rom. xii. 16.
humble, Jas. iv. 6. 1 Pet. v. 5.
base, 2 Cor. x. 1.
cast down, 2 Cor. vii. 6.

ταπεινοφροσύνη.
lowliness of mind, Phil. ii. 3.
lowliness, Eph. iv. 2.
humbleness of mind, Col. iii. 12.
humility of mind, Acts xx. 19.
humility, Col. ii. 18, 23. 1 Pet. v. 5.

ταπεινόφρων, low-minded, base.
1 Pet. iii. 8, for φιλόφρων, GLT*S*.

ταπεινόω.
bring low, Luke iii. 5.
abase, Matt. xxiii. 12. Luke xiv. 11. xviii. 14. 2 Cor. xi. 7. Phil. iv. 12.
humble, Matt. xviii. 4. xxiii. 12. Luke xiv. 11. xviii. 14. 2 Cor. xii. 21. Phil. ii. 8. — *Mid.*, **humble one's self**, Jas. iv. 10. 1 Pet. v. 6.

ταπείνωσις.
low estate, Luke i. 48.
ἐν τῇ ταπεινώσει, **in that he[c] is made low**, Jas. i. 10.
humiliation, Acts viii. 33.
Gen., **vile**, Phil. iii. 21.

ταράσσω, -ττω.
to trouble, Matt. ii. 3. xiv. 26. Mark vi. 50. Luke i. 12. xxiv. 38. John v. 4(*ap*), 7. xii. 27. xiii. 21. xiv. 1, 27. Acts xv. 24. xvii. 8. Gal. i. 7. v. 10. 1 Pet. iii. 14.
ἐτάραξεν ἑαυτόν, **was troubled** (*Gr.* troubled himself), John xi. 33.
Add Acts xvii. 13 (up καὶ τ.), L*S*.

ταραχή.
troubling, John v. 4(*ap*).
trouble, Mark xiii. 8(-G°LTr*S*°).

τάραχος.
stir, Acts xii. 18. xix. 23.

ταρταρόω.
cast down to hell, 2 Pet. ii. 4.

τάσσω, -ττω.
ordain, Acts xiii. 48. Rom. xiii. 1 (*marg.* **order**).
set, Luke vii. 8.
appoint, Acts xxii. 10. — *Mid.*, Matt. xxviii. 16. Acts xxviii. 23p.
determine, Acts xv. 2.
addict, 1 Cor. xvi. 15.
Add Matt. viii. 9 (. . under), L*S*. Acts xvii. 26, *see* προτάσσω.

ταῦρος.
bull, Heb. ix. 13. x. 4.
ox, Matt. xxii. 4. Acts xiv. 13.

ταὐτά. See αὐτός, II.

ταῦτα, etc. See οὗτος.

ταφή.
With εἰς, **to bury in**, Matt. xxvii. 7.

τάφος.
sepulchre, Matt. xxiii. 27. xxvii. 61, 64, 66. xxviii. 1. Rom. iii. 13.
tomb, Matt. xxiii. 29.

τάχα.

peradventure, Rom. v. 7.
perhaps, Phm. 15.

ταχέως.

quickly, Luke xiv. 21. xvi. 6.
shortly, 1 Cor. iv. 19. Phil. ii. 19, 24. 2 Tim. iv. 9.
soon, Gal. i. 6. 2 Thes. ii. 2.
hastily, John xi. 31.
suddenly, 1 Tim. v. 22.

ταχινός.

swift, 2 Pet. ii. 1.
shortly[cc], 2 Pet. i. 14.

τάχιον, τάχιστα. See ταχύς.

τάχος.

Dat., **quickly**, Rev. ii. 5 (ταχύ ETr[b], G[oo]LT*S*).
With ἐν, **quickly**, Acts xii. 7. xxii. 18. — **speedily**, Luke xviii. 8. — **shortly**, Acts xxv. 4. Rom. xvi. 20. Rev. i. 1. xxii. 6.
Add 1 Tim. iii. 14, *see* ταχύς.

ταχύς.

swift, Jas. i. 19.

As an Adverb.

ταχύ, **quickly**, Matt. v. 25. xxviii. 7, 8. Mark xvi. 8(*omS*). John xi. 29. Rev. ii. 16. iii. 11. xi. 14. xxii. 7, 12, 20. — **lightly**, Mark ix. 39. — *Add* Luke xv. 22 (servants . .), L Tr[b]*S*. Rev. ii. 5, *see* τάχος.
τάχιον, **the sooner**, Heb. xiii. 19. — **quickly**, John xiii. 27. — **shortly**, 1 Tim. iii. 14 (ἐν τάχει L). Heb. xiii. 23. — *See also* προτρέχω.
ὡς τάχιστα, **with all speed**, Acts xvii. 15.

τε.

Followed by καί[1]; *by* δέ[2]; *by* γάρ[3].

and, Matt. xxiii. 6[1] (δέ LTTr*S*). xxvii. 48[1]. xxviii. 12. Mark xv. 36 (-LTr*S*). Luke ii. 16[1]. xii. 45[1]. xxi. 11*t*[1]. xxii. 66[1]. xxiv. 20[1]. John ii. 15[1]. iv. 42. vi. 18.
Acts ii. 3[1], 9[1], 33, 37, 40, 43[1], 46*t*. iii. 10[1](δέ L*S*). iv. 13, 33. v. 19, 35, 42. vi. 7, 12[1], 13. vii. 26 (G″, δέ G). viii. 1 (δέ LT, -*S*), 3, 6 (δέ LT*S*), 13, 25, 31. ix. 6[1](*ap*), 15[1], 18[1], 24 (δὲ καί LT*S*). x. 22, 28, 33, 48. xi. 13 (δέ L*S*), 21, 26. xii. 6, 8 (δέ L), 12. xiii. 1[1], 4. xiv. 12, 21[1]. xv. 4, 5, 39[1]. xvi. 11, 12 (κἀκεῖθεν for ἐκεῖθέν τε L*S*), 13, 23, 26[1] (δέ L*S*), 34. xvii. 4*t*, 5, 19, 26. xviii. 4[1], 11 (δέ L*S*), 26. xix. 3[2], 6[1], 11, 12, 18, 27[1](δέ St), 29. xx. 3, 7, 11(-LT*S*), 35. xxi. 11(-G[oo]LT*S*), 18, 20, 28[1], 30[1], 37. xxii. 7, 8[2], 28[2] (δέ L*S*, -T). xxiii. 10, 24, 35. xxiv. 5, 23(-G[oo] LT*S*), 23, 27. xxvi. 10, 11, 16, 20[1], 30. xxvii. 3*t*, 5, 8, 17, 20, 21, 43.
Rom. i. 27[1](δέ G″LT). ii. 19. xvi. 26. 1 Cor. i. 30[1]. iv. 21. Eph. iii. 19. Heb. i. 3. iv. 12[1]. vi 2*t*, 4[1], 5. ix. 1. xi. 32[1]. xii. 2. Jas. iii. 7[1]. Jude 6. Rev. i. 2 and xxi. 12(*omS*).
also, Heb. xi. 32[1].
both, Matt. xxii. 10[1]. Acts i. 1[1], 8[1], 13[1]. iv. 27[1]. v. 14[2]. viii. 12[1], 38[1]. x. 39[1]. xiv. 1[1], 5[1]. xix. 10[1]. xx. 21[1]. xxi. 12[1]. xxii. 4[1]. xxiv. 15[1]. xxv. 24[1]. xxvi. 16, 22[1]. xxviii. 23[1]. Rom. i. 12[1], 14*t*[1]. iii. 9[1]. 1 Cor. i. 2[1], 24[1]. Eph. i. 10[1](*omS*). Phil. i. 7[1]. Heb. ii. 4[1], 11[1]. v. 1[1], 14[1]. vi. 19[1]. ix. 9[1], 19[1]. x. 33[1].
τε καί, **whether . . or**, Acts ix. 2.
ἐάν τε . . ἐάν τε, **whether . . and wh.**, Rom. xiv. 8. — **whether . . or**, Rom. xiv. 8.
then, Acts xxiii. 5. xxvii. 29.
even, Rom. i. 26[3].
Not rendered, Luke xxiii. 12[1]. Acts i. 15. ii. 10*t*[1]. v. 24[1]. viii. 28. ix. 24[1], 29[1]. x. 2(-L*S*). xiii. 1[1], 2[1] (-LT*S*). xv. 9[1]. xvii. 10, 14. xviii. 5[1]. xix. 17[1]. xxi. 25[1]. xxiv. 3[1]. xxv. 23[1]. xxvi. 3[1], 22[1]. xxvii. 1[1]. xxviii. 23. Rom. i. 16[1], 20[1]. ii. 9[1], 10[1]. vii. 7[3]. x. 12[1]. 2 Cor. x. 8[1 3](-L[b]). Heb. iv. 12[1](-G[oo]L*S*). v. 7[1]. viii. 3[1]. ix. 2[1]. Jas. iii. 7[1].
Add, for δέ, Acts iv. 14, G″LT*S*. xii. 17[2d], xiii. 46[1], xiv. 11, 13 (ὅ τε for ὁ δέ), xxiii. 28, xxiv. 10, xxv. 2, **xxvi. 14, xxvii. 21, LT*S*. xiii.**

44, GT. xv. 32, StG*S*. xxviii. 2, LT. For καί, Acts ix. 3, LT*S*.
Luke xv. 2 (And . .), LTTr*S*. Acts xxiv. 4 (. . at), LT*S*. 10 (. . shut up), G'LT*S*. 23 (. . unto), LT*S*.
See also εἰ.

τεῖχος.

wall, Acts ix. 25. 2 Cor. xi. 33. Heb. xi. 30. Rev. xxi. 12, 14, 15, 17, 18, 19.

τεκμήριον.

infallible proof, Acts i. 3.

τεκνίον.

little child, John xiii. 33. Gal. iv. 19 (τέκνον L*S*). 1 John ii. 1, 12, 28. iii. 7, 18. iv. 4. v. 21.
Add Mark x. 24, for τέκνον, L.

τεκνογονέω.

bear children, 1 Tim. v. 14.

τεκνογονία.

child-bearing, 1 Tim. ii. 15.

τέκνον.

child, Matt. ii. 18. iii. 9. vii. 11. x. 21*t*. xi. 19 (ἔργον Tr*S*). xv. 26. xviii. 25. xix. 29. xxii. 24. xxiii. 37. xxvii. 25. Mark vii. 27*t*. x. 24 (τεκνίον L), 29, 30. xii. 19. xiii. 12. Luke i. 7, 17. iii. 8. vii. 35. xi. 13. xiii. 34. xiv. 26. xviii. 29. xix. 44. xx. 31. xxiii. 28. John viii. 39. xi. 52. Acts ii. 39. vii. 5. xiii. 33(32). xxi. 5. 21.
Rom. viii. 16, 17, 21. ix. 7, 8*tr*. 1 Cor. vii. 14. 2 Cor. vi. 13. xii. 14*t*. Gal. iv. 25, 27, 28, 31. Eph. ii. 3. v. 1, 8. vi. 1, 4. Col. iii. 20, 21. 1 Thes. ii. 7, 11. 1 Tim. iii. 4, 12. v. 4. Tit. i. 6. 1 Pet. i. 14. 2 Pet. ii. 14. 1 John iii. 10*t*. v. 2. 2 John 1, 4, 13. 3 John 4. Rev. ii. 23. xii. 4, 5.
son, Matt. ix. 2. xxi. 28*t*. Mark ii. 5. xiii. 12. Luke ii. 48. xv. 31. xvi. 25. John i. 12. 1 Cor. iv. 14, 17. Phil. ii. 15, 22. 1 Tim. i. 2, 18. 2 Tim. i. 2. ii. 1. Tit. i. 4. Phm. 10. 1 John iii. 1, 2.
daughter (*Gr.* child), 1 Pet. iii. 6.
Add Gal. iv. 19, for τεκνίον, L*S*.

τεκνοτροφέω.

bring up children, 1 Tim. v. 10.

τέκτων.

carpenter, Matt. xiii. 55. Mark vi. 3.

τέλειος.

perfect, Matt. v. 48*t*. xix. 21. Rom. xii. 2. Eph. iv. 13. Phil. iii. 15. Col. i. 28. iv. 12. Heb. ix. 11. Jas. i. 4*t*, 17, 25. iii. 2. 1 John iv. 18.
οἱ τ., **they that are perfect**, 1 Cor. ii. 6.
τὸ τ., **that which is p.**, 1 Cor. xiii. 10.
of full age (*marg.* **perfect**), Heb. v. 14.
man (*Gr.* perfect, *or* of a ripe age), 1 Cor. xiv. 20.

τελειότης.

perfectness, Col. iii. 14.
perfection, Heb. vi. 1.

τελειόω.

finish, John iv. 34. v. 36. xvii. 4. Acts xx. 24.
fulfill, Luke ii. 43p. John xix. 28.
make perfect, John xvii. 23. 2 Cor. xii. 9 (τελέω LT*S*). Heb. ii. 10. v. 9. vii. 19. ix. 9. x. 1. xi. 40. xii. 23. Jas. ii. 22. 1 John iv. 17, 18.
perfect, Luke xiii. 32. Heb. x. 14. 1 John ii. 5. iv. 12.
Pass., **be perfect**, Phil. iii. 12.
consecrate (*Gr.* perfect), Heb. vii. 28.

τελείως.

to the end (*Gr.* perfectly), 1 Pet. i. 13.

τελείωσις.

performance, Luke i. 45.
perfection, Heb. vii. 11.

τελειωτής.

finisher, Heb. xii. 2.

τελεσφορέω.

bring fruit to perfection, Luke viii. 14.

τελευτάω.

to die, Matt. xv. 4. Mark vii. 10. ix. 44(*ap*), 46(*ap*), 48. Luke vii. 2. Acts vii. 15. Heb. xi. 22p.
be dead, Matt. ii. 19p. ix. 18. Acts ii. 29.

decease, Matt. xxii. 25.
Add John xi. 39, for θνήσκω, G″L TTr*S*.

τελευτή.

death, Matt. ii. 15.

τελέω.

make an end, Matt. xi. 1.
finish, Matt. xiii. 53. xix. 1. xxvi. 1. John xix. 30. 2 Tim. iv. 7. Rev. x. 7. xi. 7. xx. 5.
Pass., **expire**, Rev. xx. 7 (*see* μετά).
go over (*marg.* **end** *or* **finish**), Matt. x. 23.
fulfill, Acts xiii. 29. Rom. ii. 27. Gal. v. 16. Jas. ii. 8. Rev. xv. 8. xvii. 17. xx. 3.
fill up, Rev. xv. 1.
accomplish, Luke xii. 50. xviii. 31. xxii. 37. John xix. 28.
perform, Luke ii. 39.
pay, Matt. xvii. 24. Rom. xiii. 6.
Add Matt. vii. 28, for συντελέω, LT Tr*S*. 2 Cor. xii. 9, for τελειόω, LT*S*.

τέλος.

end, Matt. x. 22. xxiv. 6, 13, 14. xxvi. 58. Mark iii. 26. xiii. 7, 13. Luke i. 33. xxi. 9. xxii. 37. John xiii. 1. Rom. vi. 21, 22. x. 4. 1 Cor. i. 8. x. 11. xv. 24. 2 Cor. i. 13. iii. 13. xi. 15. Phil. iii. 19. 1 Tim. i. 5. Heb. iii. 6(*ap*), 14. vi. 8, 11. vii. 3. Jas. v. 11. 1 Pet. i. 9. iv. 7, 17. Rev. ii. 26. xxi. 6. xxii. 13.
ending, Rev. i. 8(*om*).
finally[cc], 1 Pet. iii. 8.
With εἰς, **to the uttermost**, 1 Thes. ii. 16. — **continual**, Luke xviii. 5.
custom, Matt. xvii. 25. Rom. xiii. 7*t*.

τελώνης.

publican, Matt. v. 46, 47 (G′, ἐθνικός GLTTr*S*). ix. 10, 11. x. 3. xi. 19. xviii. 17. xxi. 31, 32. Mark ii. 15, 16. Luke iii. 12. v. 27, 29, 30. vii. 29, 34. xv. 1. xviii. 10, 11, 13.

τελώνιον.

receipt of custom, Matt. ix. 9. Mark ii. 14 (*marg.* **place where custom was**[c] **received**). Luke v. 27.

τέρας.

wonder, Matt. xxiv. 24. Mark xiii. 22. John iv. 48. Acts ii. 19, 22, 43. iv. 30. v. 12. vi. 8. vii. 36. xiv. 3. xv. 12. Rom. xv. 19. 2 Cor. xii. 12. 2 Thes. ii. 9. Heb. ii. 4.

τεσσαράκοντα, τεσσεράκοντα.

forty, Matt. iv. 2*t*. Mark i. 13. Luke iv. 2. John ii. 20. Acts i. 3. iv. 22. vii. 30, 36, 42. xiii. 21. xxiii. 13, 21. 2 Cor. xi. 24. Heb. iii. 9, 17. Rev. vii. 4. xi. 2. xiii. 5. xiv. 1, 3. xxi. 17.

τεσσαρακονταετής.

of forty years, Acts xiii. 18.
ἐπληροῦτο αὐτῷ τεσσ. χρόνος, **he was full forty years old**, Acts vii. 23.

τέσσαρες, -ρα, τέσσερες, -ρα.

four, Matt. xxiv. 31. Mark ii. 3. xiii. 27. Luke ii. 37. John xi. 17. xix. 23. Acts x. 11. xi. 5. xii. 4. xxi. 9, 23. xxvii. 29. Rev. iv. 4*t*, 6, 8, 10. v. 6, 8*t*, 14, 14(*omS*). vi. 1, 6. vii. 1*tr*, 2, 4, 11. ix. 13(–LTr[b] *S*), 14, 15. xi. 16. xiv. 1, 3*t*. xv. 7. xix. 4*t*. xx. 8. xxi. 17.

τεσσαρεσκαιδέκατος.

fourteenth, Acts xxvii. 27, 33.

τεσσεράκοντα. See τεσσαράκοντα.

τέσσερες. See τέσσαρες.

τεταρταῖος.

τετ. ἐστί, **hath been dead**[c] **four days**, John xi. 39.

τέταρτος.

fourth, Matt. xiv. 25. Mark vi. 48. Rev. iv. 7. vi. 7*t*. viii. 12. xvi. 8. xxi. 19.
fourth part, Rev. vi. 8.
ἀπὸ τετάρτης ἡμέρας, **four days ago**, Acts x. 30.

τετράγωνος.

foursquare, Rev. xxi. 16.

τετράδιον.

quaternion, Acts xii. 4.

τετρακισχίλιοι.

four thousand, Matt. xv. 38. xvi. 10. Mark viii. 9, 20. Acts xxi. 38.

τετρακόσιοι, -σια.
four hundred, Acts v. 36. vii. 6. xiii. 20. Gal. iii. 17.

τετράμηνος, -νον St.
four months, John iv. 35.

τετραπλόος, -οῦς.
fourfold, Luke xix. 8.

τετράπους.
Neut., **fourfooted beast**, Acts x. 12. xi. 6. Rom. i. 23.

τετράρχης.
tetrarch, Matt. xiv. 1. Luke iii. 19. ix. 7. Acts xiii. 1.

τετραρχέω.
(be[1]) tetrarch, Luke iii. 1[1], 1[p], 1[p].

τεφρόω.
turn into ashes, 2 Pet. ii. 6.

τέχνη.
art, Acts xvii. 29.
craft, Rev. xviii. 22.
occupation, Acts xviii. 3(*ap*).

τεχνίτης.
craftsman, Acts xix. 24, 38. Rev. xviii. 22.
builder, Heb. xi. 10.

τήκω.
Pass., **melt**, 2 Pet. iii. 12.

τηλαυγῶς.
clearly, Mark viii. 25.

τηλικοῦτος.
so great, 2 Cor. i. 10. Heb. ii. 3. Jas. iii. 4.
so mighty, Rev. xvi. 18.

τηρέω.
to watch, Matt. xxvii. 36, 54.
observe, Matt. xxiii. 3(-G°LTTr*S*), 3. xxviii. 20. Acts xxi. 25(*ap*).
keep, Matt. xix. 17. Mark vii. 9 (ἵστημι G″). John ii. 10. viii. 51, 52, 55. ix. 16. xii. 7. xiv. 15, 21, 23, 24. xv. 10*t*, 20*t*. xvii. 6, 11, 12, 15. Acts xii. 5, 6. xv. 5, 24 (*ap*). xvi. 23. xxiv. 23[cc]. xxv. 4, 21. 1 Cor. vii. 37. 2 Cor. xi. 9*t*. Eph. iv. 3. 1 Tim. v. 22. vi. 14. 2 Tim. iv. 7. Jas. i. 27. ii. 10. 1 John ii. 3, 4, 5. iii. 22, 24. v. 2 (ποιέω G′LT), 3, 18. Jude 6, 21. Rev. i. 3. ii. 26. iii. 8, 10*t*. xii. 17. xiv. 12. xvi. 15. xxii. 7, 9.
keeper, Matt. xxviii. 4[p].
hold fast, Rev. iii. 3(*ap*).
preserve, 1 Thes. v. 23. Jude 1.
reserve, Acts xxv. 21. 1 Pet. i. 4. 2 Pet. ii. 4 (*see* κολάζω), 9, 17. iii. 7. Jude 6, 13.

τήρησις.
keeping, 1 Cor. vii. 19.
hold, Acts iv. 3.
prison, Acts v. 18.

τίθημι.
to set, Acts xiii. 47. Rev. x. 2.
put, Matt. v. 15. xii. 18. Mark iv. 21. x. 16. Luke viii. 16. xi. 33. John xix. 19. Rom. xiv. 13. 1 Cor. xv. 25. 2 Cor. iii. 13. Rev. xi. 9.
lay, Matt. xxvii. 60. Mark vi. 29, 56. xv. 47. xvi. 6. Luke v. 18. vi. 48. xiv. 29[p]. xxiii. 53, 55. John xi. 34. xix. 41, 42. xx. 2, 13, 15. Acts iii. 2. iv. 37. v. 2, 15. vii. 16. ix. 37. xiii. 29. Rom. ix. 33. 1 Cor. iii. 10, 11. xvi. 2. 1 Pet. ii. 6.
lay down, Luke xix. 21, 22. John x. 15, 17, 18*t*. xiii. 37, 38. xv. 13. Acts iv. 35. 1 John iii. 16*t*.
lay aside, John xiii. 4.
Mid., **set**, 1 Cor. xii. 18, 28. — **put**, Matt. xiv. 3 (ἀποτίθημι LTr*S*). Acts i. 7. iv. 3. v. 18, 25. xii. 4. 1 Tim. i. 12. — **lay up**, Luke i. 66. — **let sink down**, Luke ix. 44. — **settle**, Luke xxi. 14 (*act.* LTTr*S*). — **commit** (*Gr.* put), 2 Cor. v. 19. — **appoint**, 1 Thes. v. 9. — **purpose**, Acts xix. 21. — **conceive**, Acts v. 4.
bow, Mark xv. 19.
set forth, John ii. 10.
give, John x. 11.
make, Matt. xxii. 44. Mark xii. 36. Luke xx. 43. Acts ii. 35. xx. 28. Rom. iv. 17. 1 Cor. ix. 18. Heb. i. 13. x. 13. 2 Pet. ii. 6.
appoint, Matt. xxiv. 51. Luke xii. 46. 2 Tim. i. 11. Heb. i. 2. 1 Pet. ii. 8.

ordain, John xv. 16. 1 Tim. ii. 7.

Add, for ἐπιτίθημι, Mark iv. 21, LTTr*S*. viii. 25, Tr. Luke viii. 16, LTTr*S*. Rev. i. 17, GLTTr. For κατατίθημι, Mark xv. 46, LTr*S*. For προστίθημι, Gal. iii. 19, G. For παραβάλλω, Mark iv. 30, LTTr*S*.

See also βουλή, γόνυ.

τίκτω.

bring forth, Matt. i. 21, 23, 25. Luke i. 31. ii. 7. Heb. vi. 7. Jas. i. 15. Rev. xii. 5, 13.

be delivered (of[1]**)**, Luke i. 57. ii. 6. Heb. xi. 11[1](G', *omS*). Rev. xii. 2, 4.

bear, Gal. iv. 27.

be born, Rev. xii. 4[cc]. — *Pass.*, **be born**, Matt. ii. 2 Luke ii. 11.

be in travail, John xvi. 21.

τίλλω.

to pluck, Matt. xii. 1. Mark ii. 23[cc]. Luke vi. 1.

τιμάω.

to honor, Matt. xv. 4, 6(5), 8. xix. 19. Mark vii. 6, 10. x. 19. Luke xviii. 20. John v. 23*f*. viii. 49. xii. 26. Acts xxviii. 10. Eph. vi. 2. 1 Tim. v. 3. 1 Pet. ii. 17 (*marg.* **esteem**), 17.

value, Matt. xxvii. 9, 9(*marg.* **buy**).

τιμή.

honor, John iv. 44. Acts xxviii. 10. Rom. ii. 7, 10. ix. 21. xii. 10. xiii. 7. 1 Cor. xii. 23, 24. Col. ii. 23. 1 Thes. iv. 4. 1 Tim. i. 17. v. 17. vi. 1, 16. 2 Tim. ii. 20, 21. Heb. ii. 7, 9. iii. 3. v. 4. 1 Pet. i. 7. iii. 7. 2 Pet. i. 17. Rev. iv. 9, 11. v. 12, 13. vii. 12. xix. 1(*omS*). xxi. 24 (-G[oo]LT*S*), 26.

price, Matt. xxvii. 6, 9. Acts iv. 34. v. 2, 3. xix. 19. 1 Cor. vi. 20. vii. 23.

precious (*marg.* **honor**), 1 Pet. ii. 7.

sum, Acts vii. 16.

τίμιος.

honorable, Heb. xiii. 4.

had in reputation, Acts v. 34.

precious, 1 Cor. iii. 12. Jas. v. 7. 1 Pet. i. 7 (*see* πολύτιμος), 19. 2 Pet. i. 4. Rev. xvii. 4. xviii. 12*t*, 16. xxi. 11, 19. — **dear**, Acts xx. 24.

τιμιότης.

costliness, Rev. xviii. 19.

τιμωρέω.

punish, Acts xxii. 5. xxvi. 11.

τιμωρία.

punishment, Heb. x. 29.

τίνω. See τίω.

τις, τι.

one, Matt. xii. 29, 47. Mark ix. 38. xv. 21. Luke vii. 36. viii. 49. ix. 19, 49. xi. 1, 45. xii. 13. xiii. 23. xiv. 1, 15. xvi. 30, 31. xxiii. 26. Acts v. 25, 34. vii. 24. ix. 43. x. 6. xix. 9(-LT*S*). xxi. 16. xxii. 12. xxv. 19. Rom. v. 7. 1 Cor. iii. 4. v. 1. xiv. 24. Tit. i. 12. Heb. ii. 6. Jas. ii. 16. v. 19.

one thing, Luke vi. 9 (EG', τί StG, εἰ LTTr*S*).

a, Luke xviii. 2*t*. John vi. 7 (-L[b] Tr). Acts v. 34(-G[o]LT*S*). xvi. 9. xviii. 14. xxvii. 8. 2 Cor. xi. 16. Gal. vi. 1. Heb. ii. 7 (*see* βραχύς), 9.

a kind of, Jas. i. 18.

a man, Matt. xviii. 12. xxii. 24. Mark viii. 4. xii. 19. Luke xii. 15[cc]. John iii. 3, 5. vi. 50. viii. 51, 52. xi. 10. xiv. 23. xv. 6, 13. Acts xiii. 41. Rom. viii. 24. 1 Cor. iv. 2. 2 Cor. viii. 12 (-G[oo]LT*S*). 1 Tim. i. 8. 2 Tim. ii. 5, 21. Jas. ii. 14, 18. 1 Pet. ii. 19. 2 Pet. ii. 19. 1 John iv. 20.

With οὐ, **no man**, Heb. v. 4. — **none**, Acts xxvi. 26. — **nothing**, Mark iv. 22(-G[o]L[b]Tr). 2 Cor. xiii. 8.

With οὐδέ, **nothing**, 1 Tim. vi. 7

a certain man, Luke ix. 57. x. 30. xiii. 6. John xi. 1. Acts xviii. 7. xix. 24. — *Pl.*, **certain men**, Jude 4.

a certain thing, Matt. xx. 20. Acts xxiii. 17.

certain, Matt. ix. 3. xii. 38. xxi. 33(*omS*). Mark ii. 6. v. 25(÷G[oo]LTr*S*). vii. 1. xi. 5. xii. 13. xiv. 51, 57. Luke i. 5. vi. 2. vii. 2, 41. viii. 2, 27. x. 25, 31, 33, 38*t*. xi. 1, 27,

37(–TTrS). xii. 16. xiii. 31. xiv. 2, 16. xv. 11. xvi. 1, 19, 20. xvii. 12. xviii. 9, 18, 35. xix. 12. xx. 9(om S), 27, 39. xxi. 2. xxii. 56. xxiii. 19. xxiv. 22, 24.

John iv. 46. v. 5. xii. 20. Acts iii. 2. v. 1, 2. vi. 9. viii. 9, 36. ix. 10, 19, 33, 36. x. 1, 11, 23, 48. xi. 5. xii. 1. xiii. 1(–G∞LTS), 6. xiv. 8. xv. 1, 2, 5, 24. xvi. 1, 1(omS), 12, 14, 16. xvii. 5, 6, 18, 20, 28, 34. xviii. 2, 24. xix. 1, 13, 31. xx. 9. xxi. 10. xxiii. 12(omS). xxiv. 1, 18, 24. xxv. 13, 14, 19. xxvii. 1, 16, 26, 39. Rom. xv. 26. Gal. ii. 12. Heb. iv. 7. x. 27.

certain c**others,** Luke xxiv. 1(*ap*).

divers, Mark viii. 3. Acts xix. 9.

some man, Acts viii. 31. 1 Cor. xv. 35.

somebody, Luke viii. 46. Acts v. 36.

some, Matt. xvi. 28. xxvii. 47. xxviii. 11. Mark vii. 2. ix. 1. xiv. 4, 65. xv. 35. Luke ix. 7, 8, 27. xi. 15. xiii. 1. xix. 39. xxi. 5. xxiii. 8. John vi. 64. vii. 25, 44. ix. 16. xi. 37, 46. xiii. 29. Acts v. 15. viii. 34. xi. 20. xv. 36. xvii. 4, 18, 21. xviii. 23. xxvii. 27.

Rom. i. 11, 13. iii. 3, 8. v. 7. xi. 14. 1 Cor. iv. 18. vi. 11. viii. 7. ix. 22. x. 7, 8, 9, 10. xv. 6, 12, 34, 37. 2 Cor. iii. 1. x. 2, 12. Gal. i. 7. Phil. i. 15*t*. 2 Thes. iii. 11. 1 Tim. i. 3, 6, 19. iv. 1. v. 15, 24*t*. vi. 10, 21. 2 Tim. ii. 18. Heb. iii. 4, 16 (τίς G LT). iv. 6. x. 25. xi. 40. xiii. 2. 2 Pet. iii. 9.

τις μέγας, **some great one,** Acts viii. 9.

something, Luke xi. 54. John xiii. 29. Acts iii. 5. xxiii. 18. Gal. vi. 3.

τινα, **some things,** 2 Pet. iii. 16.

somewhat, Luke vii. 40. Acts xxiii. 20. xxv. 26. 2 Cor. x. 8. Gal. ii. 6. Heb. viii. 3.

any man, Matt. xi. 27. xii. 19. xxi. 3. xxii. 46. xxiv. 23. Mark ix. 30. xi. 3, 16. xiii. 5, 21. Luke xiv. 8. xix. 8, 31. xx. 28. John iv. 33. vi. 46. 51. vii. 17, 37. ix. 22, 31, 32. x. 9, 28. xi. 9, 57. xii. 26*t*, 47. xvi. 30. Acts x. 47. xix. 38. xxiv. 12.

Rom. viii. 9. 1 Cor. v. 11. vii. 18. viii. 10. ix. 15 (*see* οὐδείς). x. 28. xiv. 27. 2 Cor. xii. 6. Eph. ii. 9. Col. ii. 4 (*see* μηδείς), 8. iii. 13. 2 Thes. iii. 8. Heb. iv. 11. xii. 15. 1 John ii. 1, 15, 27. v. 16. Rev. iii. 20. xxii. 18, 19.

any, Mark viii. 26. xi. 25. xvi. 18 (*ap*). Luke xxiv. 41. John i. 46(47). ii. 25. vii. 48. Acts iv. 34. ix. 2. xxv. 16. xxvii. 42. xxviii. 21*t*. Rom. viii. 39. ix. 11. xv. 18. 1 Cor. i. 15. vi. 1, 12. vii. 18. 2 Cor. xi. 21. xii. 17. Eph. v. 27. Col. ii. 23. iii. 13. 1 Thes. ii. 9. v. 15. 2 Thes. iii. 8. Heb. iii. 12, 13. iv. 1. xii. 15, 16. Jas. v. 12, 13*t*, 14, 19. 2 Pet. iii. 9.

any (τῳ *as* τινί for τῷ), 1 Thes. iv. 6 (G', τῷ GLT ; *marg.* **the**).

any thing, Matt. xxiv. 17 (τά GLT Tr, τό S). Mark xi. 13. xiii. 15. Luke xix. 8. xxii. 35. John vii. 4. xiv. 14. Acts xvii. 25. xix. 39. xxv. 11. Rom. xiv. 14. 1 Cor. ii. 2. iii. 7. viii. 2. x. 19(*ap*), 19. xiv. 35. 2 Cor. ii. 10. iii. 5. Gal. v. 6. vi. 15. 1 Thes. i. 8. Jas. i. 7. 1 John v. 14(*see* ὅστις).

any thing at all, Acts xxv. 8.

thing, Acts xxv. 26 (*see* τίς).

aught, Matt. v. 23. xxi. 3. Acts iv. 32. xxviii. 19. Phm. 18.

ἄν τις, **whosoever,** John xx. 23 (ἐάν τις L), 23 (ἐάν τις LS). — **every man,** Acts ii. 45.

ἐάν τις, **whosoever,** John xiii. 20 (ἄν τις LTTrS).

ἐὰν μή τι, **but what,** John v. 19.

whatsoever, 1 Cor. x. 31.

he, Acts iv. 35. Heb. x. 28.

hiscc, Acts xi. 29.

τι τῶν, **broken piece,** Acts xxvii. 44.

Not rendered, Mark xiv. 47(–LTr S). Luke vii. 19. xxii. 50, 59. John xi. 49. Acts xix. 14. xxi. 37(–G∘T). xxiii. 23. 1 Cor. ix. 12. 2 Cor. xii. 6(–LS). xiii. 5.

Add Matt. xxi. 28 (certain), G?L. Mark xv. 36, for εἷς, TrS. Luke viii.

51, *see* οὐδείς. ix. 8, for εἷς, TTr*S*. John xvi. 23, *see* ὅσος. Acts x. 5 (. . Simon), LT. xiii. 15(any), LT*S*. xvii. 21 (hear . .), L*S*. xxiii. 9 (*ap*). xxiv. 1 (. . elders), L*S*. xxviii. 3 (. . bundle), G′LT*S*?. 1 Cor. xii. 26, *see* εἴτε. 2 Cor. xi. 1 (a), C?EG′LT*S*. 3 John 9 (wrote . .), LT*S*. Rev. vii. 1, for πᾶς, G′LTTr.

See also ἄλλος, εἰ, εἰ μή, ἵνα, I., μέρος, μή, I., II., ὅς, VI., χείρων, χρόνος.

τίς, τί.

In an indirect question, followed by the Indicative[1]. Followed by the Subjunctive[2]; by the Optative[3].

who (whose, whom)? Matt. iii. 7. x. 11[1]. xii. 27, 48*t*. xvi. 13, 15. xvii. 25. xviii. 1(*with* ἄρα). xix. 25. xxi. 10, 23. xxii. 20, 28, 42. xxiv. 45. xxvi. 68. xxvii. 17. Mark i. 24[1]. ii. 7. iii. 33. v. 30, 31. viii. 27, 29. ix. 34[1]. x. 26. xi. 28. xii. 16, 23. xvi. 3.

Luke iii. 7. iv. 34[1]. v. 21*t*. vi. 47[1]. vii. 39[1], 49. viii. 45, 45(*ap*). ix. 9, 18, 20. x. 22*t*[1], 29. xi. 19. xii. 5[2], 14, 20, 42. xvi. 11, 12. xviii. 26. xix. 3[1]. xx. 2, 24, 33. xxii. 64.

John i. 19, 22. iv. 10[1]. v. 13[1]. vi. 60, 64*t*[1], 68. vii. 20. viii. 25, 53. ix. 2, 21[1], 36. xii. 34, 38*t*. xiii. 22[1], 24[3], 25. xviii. 4, 7. xix. 24[1]. xx. 15. xxi. 12. Acts vii. 27, 35. viii. 33, 34. ix. 5. xiii. 25. xix. 15. xxi. 33[3]. xxii. 8. xxvi. 15.

Rom. vii. 24. viii. 31, 33, 34, 35. ix. 19, 20. x. 6, 7, 16. xi. 34*t*, 35. xiv. 4. 1 Cor. ii. 16. iii 5. iv. 7. ix. 7*tr*. xiv. 8. 2 Cor. ii. 2, 16. xi. 29*t*. Gal. iii. 1. v. 7. 2 Tim. iii. 14[1]. Heb. iii. 17, 18. Jas. iii. 13. iv. 12. 1 Pet. iii. 13. v. 8[1]. 1 John ii. 22. v. 5. Rev. v. 2. vi. 17. xiii. 4*t*. xv. 4[2].

what? Matt. v. 46, 47. vi. 3[1], 25[2], 25[2](-G[oo]*S*), 25[2], 31*t*[2]. vii. 9. viii. 29. ix. 13[1]. x. 19[2], 19[1](*ap*). xi. 7, 8, 9. xii. 3[1], 7[1], 11. xvi. 26*t*. xvii. 25. xix. 16, 20, 27. xx. 21, 22[1], 32. xxi. 16[1], 28, 40. xxii. 17, 42. xxiv. 3. xxvi. 15, 65, 66, 70[1]. xxvii. 4, 22, 23.

Mark i. 24, 27(*ap*). ii. 25[1]. iv. 24[1]. v. 7, 9. 14[1]. vi. 2, 24. viii. 36, 37. ix. 6[2], 10[1], 16, 33. x. 3, 17, 36, 38[1], 51. xi. 5. xii. 9. xiii. 4, 11[2]. xiv. 36[1]*t*, 40[2], 63, 64, 68[1]. xv. 12, 14.

Luke iii. 10, 12, 14. iv. 34, 36. v. 22. vi. 11[3]. vii. 24, 25, 26, 31. viii. 9[3], 28, 30. ix. 25. x. 25, 26. xii. 11[2], 17, 22*t*[2], 29*t*[2], 49. xiii. 18. xiv. 31. xv. 4, 8, 26[3]. xvi. 3, 4[2]. xviii. 6[1], 18, 36[3], 41. xix. 48[2]. xx. 13, 15, 17. xxi. 7. xxii. 71. xxiii. 22, 31[2], 34[1](*ap*).

John i. 21, 22, 38(39). ii. 4, 18, 25. iv. 27. v. 12. vi. 6, 9, 28[2], 30*t*. vii. 51[1]. viii. 5(*ap*). ix. 17, 26. xi. 47, 56. xii. 27[2]. 49*t*[2]. xiii. 12[1]. xv. 15[1]. xvi. 17, 18, 18[1]. xviii. 21[1], 29, 35, 38. xxi. 21.

Acts ii. 12[3], 37. iv. 16. v. 35[1]. vii. 40, 49. viii. 36. ix. 6(*ap*), 6[1] (ὅστις G′LT*S*). x. 4, 6 (*ap*), 17[3], 21, 29. xi. 17. xii. 18[1](*with* ἄρα). xvi. 30. xvii. 18[3], 19[1], 20[3]. xix. 3, 35. xxi. 13, 22, 33. xxii. 10, 26. xxiii. 19.

Rom. iii. 1*t*, 3, 5, 9. iv. 1, 3. vi. 1, 15, 21. vii. 7. viii. 26[2], 27[1], 31. ix. 14, 30. x. 8. xi. 2[1], 4, 7, 15. xii. 2. 1 Cor. ii. 11. iv. 7, 21. v. 12. vii. 16. ix. 18. x. 19. xi. 22[2]. xiv. 6, 15, 16[1]. xv. 2 (*see* λόγος), 29, 32. 2 Cor. vi. 14*t*, 15*t*, 16. xii. 13.

Gal. iv. 30. Eph. i. 18*t*[1], 19[1]. iii. 9, 18[1]. iv. 9. v. 10[1], 17[1]. Phil. i. 18, 22. Col. i. 27[1]. 1 Thes. ii. 19. iii. 9. iv. 2. Heb. ii. 6. vii. 11. xi. 32. xii. 7. xiii. 6. Jas. ii. 14, 16. 1 Pet. i. 11. iv. 17. 1 John iii. 2[1]. Rev. ii. 7[1], 11[1], 17[1], 29[1]. iii. 6[1], 13[1], 22[1]. vii. 13. xviii. 18.

what is it which? Matt. xxvi. 62. Mark xiv. 60.

what is that? John xxi. 22, 23.

what thing? Mark i. 27. Luke xii. 11[2](-Tr[b]). John x. 6[1].

what manner of, Luke xxiv. 17. John vii. 36.

which? Matt. vi. 27. Luke vii. 42. ix. 46[3]. x. 36. xi. 5. xii. 25. xiv. 5, 28. xvii. 7. xxii. 23[3](*with* ἄρα),

24[1]. John viii. 46. xxi. 20. Acts vii. 52. Heb. i. 5, 13. v. 12[1].
whether? Matt. ix. 5. xxi. 31. xxiii. 17, 19. xxvii. 21. Mark ii. 9. Luke v. 23. xxii. 27.
τίς τί, *lit.* who . . what? **what every man,** Mark xv. 24[1].—**how much every man,** Luke xix. 15[1](-τίς Tr*S*).
any[co], Luke xi. 11.
With οὐ, **nothing,** Matt. xv. 32[2]. Mark vi. 36[2] (*see* ἄρτος). viii. 1[2], 2[2].
τί γίνομαι, **grow whereunto,** Acts v. 24[3].
where? Gal. iv. 15 (*marg.* **what?** ποῦ L*S*).
Dative, **whereunto?** Matt. xi. 16. Mark iv. 30[2](πῶς G″L[m]TTr*S*). Luke vii. 31. xiii. 18, 20.

Accusative, τί.

wherefore? John ix. 27. Acts xxii. 30[3]. Gal. iii. 19.
why? Matt. vi. 28. vii. 3. viii. 26. xvi. 8. xvii. 10. xix. 7, 17. xx. 6. xxii. 18. xxvi. 10. Mark ii. 7, 8, 24. iv. 40. v. 35, 39. viii. 12, 17. x. 18. xi. 3. xii. 15. xiv. 6. Luke ii. 48. vi. 2, 41, 46. xii. 26, 57. xviii. 19. xix. 33. xx. 23(*ap*). xxii. 46. xxiv. 5, 38. John i. 25. iv. 27. vii. 19. x. 20. xviii. 21, 23. xx. 13, 15. Acts i. 11. iii 12*t*. v. 4. ix. 4. xiv. 15. xv. 10. xxii. 7, 16. xxvi. 8, 14. Rom. iii. 7. viii. 24. ix. 19, 20. xiv. 10*t*. 1 Cor. iv. 7. x. 30. xv. 29, 30. Gal. ii. 14 (πῶς GL*S*). v. 11. Col. ii. 20.
how is it that? Luke xvi. 2.—**how is it?** Mark ii. 16(-TTr, διὰ τί for τί ὅτι *S*). Luke ii. 49. Acts v. 9. 1 Cor. xiv. 26.—**how,** Matt. xviii. 12. Luke i. 62[3]. John xiv. 22. 1 Cor. vii. 16. Eph.
wherewith, Luke xvii. 8[2]. [vi. 21.
Add Matt. vii. 14, for ὅτι, GLTr. Mark vi. 30[2], for ποῖος, LTTr*S*. Luke vi. 9, *see* τις. xx. 5, *see* διατί. John xiii. 18, for ὅς, Tr*S*. Acts xxiv. 20, for εἴ τις, GLT*S*. xxv. 26, τί γράψω for τι γράψαι, G″LT*S*. Heb. iii. 16, for τις, GLT.
See also ἄρα, διατί, εἰς, ἐν, ἕνεκα, ἱνατί, κατά, περί, περιβάλλω, πρός, χάρις.

τίτλος.

title, John xix. 19, 20.

τίω.

Lit. atone by, pay. *See* δίκη.

τοι, τοίγε.

See καιτοίγε, μέντοι, τοιγαροῦν, τοίνυν.

τοιγαροῦν.

therefore, 1 Thes. iv. 8.
wherefore, Heb. xii. 1.

τοίνυν.

therefore, Luke xx. 25. 1 Cor. ix. 26. Heb. xiii. 13.
then, Jas. ii. 24(*omS*).

τοιόσδε.

such, 2 Pet. i. 17.

τοιοῦτος.

such, Matt. ix. 8. xviii. 5. xix. 14. Mark iv. 33. vi. 2. vii. 8(*ap*), 13. ix. 37. x. 14. xiii. 19. Luke xviii. 16. John iv. 23. viii. 5(*ap*). ix. 16. Acts xvi. 24. xxvi. 29. Rom. xvi. 18. 1 Cor. v. 1. vii. 15, 28. xi. 16. xv. 48*t*. xvi. 16, 18. 2 Cor. iii. 4, 12. x. 11. xi. 13. xii. 3. Gal. v. 23. Phil. ii. 29. 2 Thes. iii. 12. 1 Tim. vi. 5(*ap*). Tit. iii. 11. Heb. vii. 26. viii. 1. xii. 3. xiii. 16. Jas. iv. 16. 3 John 8.
such an (a) one, 1 Cor. v. 5, 11. 2 Cor. ii. 7. x. 11. xii. 2, 5. Gal. vi. 1. Phm. 9.
such a man, 2 Cor. ii. 6.
such a fellow, Acts xxii. 22.
such thing, Luke ix. 9. xiii. 2 (οὗτος Tr*S*). Acts xxi. 25(*ap*). Rom. i. 32. ii. 2, 3. Gal. v. 21. Eph. v. 27. Heb. xi. 14.
περὶ τὰ τοιαῦτα, **of like occupation,** Acts xix. 25.
Add Rom. ii. 14, *see* οὗτοι.

τοῖχος.

wall, Acts xxiii. 3.

τόκος.

usury, Matt. xxv. 27. Luke xix. 23.

τολμάω.

be bold, 2 Cor. x. 2. xi. 21*t*. Phil. i. 14.

boldly, Mark xv. 43p.
dare, Matt. xxii. 46. Mark xii. 34. Luke xx. 40. John xxi. 12. Acts v. 13. vii. 32. Rom. v. 7. xv. 18. 1 Cor. vi. 1. 2 Cor. x. 12. Jude 9.

τολμηρότερον.

the more boldly, Rom. xv. 15.

τολμητής.

presumptuous, 2 Pet. ii. 10.

τομώτερος.

sharper, Heb. iv. 12.

τόξον.

bow, Rev. vi. 2.

τοπάζιον.

topaz, Rev. xxi. 20.

τόπος.

place, Matt. xii. 43. xiv. 13, 15, 35. xxiv. 15. xxvi. 52. xxvii. 33*t*. xxviii. 6. Mark i. 35, 45. vi. 31, 32, 35. xv. 22*t*. xvi. 6. Luke iv. 17, 37, 42. ix. 10(*ap*), 12. x. 1, 32. xi. 1, 24. xiv. 9. xvi. 28. xix. 5. xxii. 40. xxiii. 33. John iv. 20. v. 13. vi. 10, 23. x. 40. xi. 6, 30, 48. xiv. 2, 3. xviii. 2. xix. 13, 17, 20, 41. xx. 7. Acts i. 25. iv. 31. vi. 13, 14. vii. 7, 33, 49. xii. 17. xxi. 28*t*. xxvii. 8, 41. Rom. ix. 26. xii. 19. xv. 23. 1 Cor. i. 2. 2 Cor. ii. 14. Eph. iv. 27. 1 Thes. i. 8. Heb. viii. 7. xi. 8. xii. 17 (*marg*. **way**). 2 Pet. i. 19. Rev. ii. 5. vi. 14. xii. 6, 8, 14. xvi. 16. xx. 11.
ἐν παντὶ τόπῳ, **every where**, 1 Tim. ii. 8.
τὰ περὶ τὸν τόπον ἐκεῖνον, **the same quarters**, Acts xxviii. 7.
quarter, Acts xvi. 3.
coast, Acts xxvii. 2.
room, Luke ii. 7. xiv. 9, 10, 22. 1 Cor. xiv. 16.
license, Acts xxv. 16.
Add Mark vi. 11, 54, (*ap*). John xx. 25, for τύπος, LT. Acts i. 25, for κλῆρος, G'LT. 2 Thes. iii. 16, for τρόπος, G'L. Rev. xviii. 17(*ap*).
See also κατά, πεδινός, τραχύς.

τοσοῦτος.

so great, Matt. viii. 10. xv. 33. Luke vii. 9. Heb. xii. 1. Rev. xviii. 17.
so much, Matt. xv. 33. Acts v. 8*t*. Heb. i. 4. vii. 22. x. 25. Rev. xviii. 7.
as large, Rev. xxi. 16(*omS*).
so long, John xiv. 9. Heb. iv. 7.
Plural, **so many**, John vi. 9. xii. 37. xxi. 11. 1 Cor. xiv. 10.—**so many** (*marg*. **so great**) **things**, Gal. iii. 4.—**these many**, Luke xv. 29.

τότε.

then, Matt. ii. 7, 16, 17. iii. 5, 13, 15. iv. 1, 5, 10, 11. v. 24. vii. 5, 23. viii. 26. ix. 6, 14, 15, 29, 37. xi. 20. xii. 13, 22, 29, 38, 44, 45. xiii. 26, 36, 43. xv. 1, 12, 28. xvi. 12, 20, 24, 27. xvii. 13, 19. xviii. 21, 32. xix. 13, 27. xx. 20. xxi. 1. xxii. 8, 13, 15, 21. xxiii. 1. xxiv. 9, 10, 14, 16, 21, 23, 30*t*, 40. xxv. 1, 7, 31, 34, 37, 41, 44, 45. xxvi. 3, 14, 31, 36, 38, 45, 50, 52, 56, 65, 67, 74. xxvii. 3, 9, 13, 16, 26, 27, 38, 58. xxviii. 10.
Mark ii. 20. iii. 27. xiii. 14, 21, 26, 27. Luke v. 35. vi. 42. xi. 26. xiii. 26. xiv. 10, 21. xxi. 10, 20, 21, 27. xxiii. 30. xxiv. 45. John ii. 10(-L[b] Tr[b]*S*). vii. 10. viii. 28. xi. 14. xii. 16. xix. 1, 16. xx. 8. Acts i. 12. iv. 8. v. 26. vi. 11. vii. 4. viii. 17. x. 46, 48. xiii. 12. xv. 22. xvii. 14. xxi. 26, 33. xxiii. 3. xxv. 12. xxvi. 1. xxvii. 32. xxviii. 1.
Rom. vi. 21. 1 Cor. iv. 5. xiii. 10 (-G[∞]LT*S*), 12*t*. xv. 28, 54. 2 Cor. xii. 10. Gal. iv. 8, 29. vi. 4. Col. iii. 4. 1 Thes. v. 3. 2 Thes. ii. 8. Heb. x. 7, 9. xii. 26.
ὁ τότε, **that then was**, 2 Pet. iii. 6.
ἀπὸ τότε, **from that time**, Matt. iv. 17. xvi. 21. xxvi. 16.—**since that time**, Luke xvi. 16.
when[∞], Acts xiii. 3.
Not rendered, Luke xiv. 9. John xi. 6. xiii. 27. Acts xxvii. 21. 1 Cor. xvi. 2.
Add Luke xi. 24 (none, . .), L[b]. Acts xxi. 13 (. . answered), L*S*. Jude 9, for ὅτε, L.

τοὐναντίον.
contrariwise, 2 Cor. ii. 7. Gal. ii. 7. 1 Pet. iii. 9.

τοὔνομα. See ὄνομα.

τουτέστι. See ἐστί.

τοῦτο, etc. See οὗτος.

τράγος.
goat, Heb. ix. 12, 13, 19. x. 4.

τράπεζα.
table, Matt. xv. 27. xxi. 12. Mark vii. 28. xi. 15. Luke xvi. 21. xxii. 21, 30. John ii. 15. Acts vi. 2. Rom. xi. 9. 1 Cor. x. 21*t*. Heb. ix. 2.
meat, Acts xvi. 34.
bank, Luke xix. 23.

τραπεζίτης.
exchanger, Matt. xxv. 27.

τραῦμα.
wound, Luke x. 34.

τραυματίζω.
to wound, Luke xx. 12. Acts xix. 16.

τραχηλίζω.
to open, Heb. iv. 13.

τράχηλος.
neck, Matt. xviii. 6. Mark ix. 42. Luke xv. 20. xvii. 2. Acts xv. 10. xx. 37. Rom. xvi. 4.

τραχύς.
rough, Luke iii. 5.
τραχεῖς τόποι, **rocks,** Acts xxvii. 29.

τρεῖς, τρία.
three, Matt. xii. 40*f*. xiii. 33. xv. 32. xvii. 4. xviii. 16, 20. xxvi. 61. xxvii. 40, 63. Mark viii. 2, 31. ix. 5. xiv. 58. xv. 29. Luke i. 56. ii. 46. iv. 25. ix. 33. x. 36. xi. 5. xii. 52. xiii. 7, 21. John ii. 6, 19, 20. xxi. 11. Acts v. 7. vii. 20. ix. 9. x. 19(-G^{oo}T). xi. 11. xvii. 2. xix. 8. xx. 3. xxv. 1. xxviii. 7, 11, 12, 17. 1 Cor. x. 8. xiii. 13. xiv. 27, 29. 2 Cor. xiii. 1. Gal. i. 18. 1 Tim. v. 19. Heb. x. 28. Jas. v. 17. 1 John v. 7, 7(*ap*), 8*t*. Rev. vi. 6. viii. 13. ix. 18. xi. 9, 11. xvi. 13, 19. xxi. 13*f*.
Τρεῖς Ταβέρναι, **The three taverns,** Acts xxviii. 15.
Add Mark ix. 31, x. 34, μετὰ τρεῖς ἡμέρας for τῇ τρίτῃ ἡμέρᾳ, G″LTTr*S*.

τρέμω.
tremble, Mark v. 33. Luke viii. 47. Acts ix. 6(*ap*).
be afraid, 2 Pet. ii. 10.

τρέφω.
to feed, Matt. vi. 26. xxv. 37. Luke xii. 24. Rev. xii. 6 (ἐκτρέφω T).
nourish, Acts xii. 20. Jas. v. 5. Rev. xii. 14.
bring up, Luke iv. 16.
Add Luke xxiii. 29, for θηλάζω, L TTr*S*.

τρέχω.
to run, Matt. xxvii. 48. xxviii. 8. Mark v. 6 (1611 to 1687 **come,** probably a misprint). xv. 36. Luke xv. 20. xxiv. 12 (*ap*). John xx. 2, 4. Rom. ix. 16. 1 Cor. ix. 24*t*, 26. Gal. ii. 2*t*. v. 7. Phil. ii. 16. Heb. xii. 1. Rev. ix. 9.
have course (*Gr.* run), 2 Thes. iii. 1.

τρῆμα, a hole, eye.
Luke xviii. 25, for τρυμαλιά, LTTr*S*.

τριάκοντα.
thirty, Matt. xiii. 23. xxvi. 15. xxvii. 3, 9. Mark iv. 8. Luke iii. 23. John v. 5. vi. 19. Gal. iii. 17.
thirtyfold, Matt. xiii. 8. Mark iv. 20.

τριακόσιοι.
three hundred, Mark xiv. 5. John xii. 5.

τρίβολος.
thistle, Matt. vii. 16.
brier, Heb. vi. 8.

τρίβος.
path, Matt. iii. 3. Mark i. 3. Luke iii. 4.

τριετία.
space of three years, Acts xx. 31.

τρίζω.
gnash with, Mark ix. 18.

τρίμηνος.
Neut., **three months,** Heb. xi. 23.

τρίς.

thrice, Matt. xxvi. 34, 75. Mark xiv. 30, 72. Luke xxii. 34, 61. John xiii. 38. 2 Cor. xi. 25*t*. xii. 8.

ἐπὶ τρίς, **thrice**, Acts x. 16.—**three times**, Acts xi. 10.

τρίστεγος.

Neut., **third loft**, Acts xx. 9.

τρισχίλιοι.

three thousand, Acts ii. 41.

τρίτος.

third, Matt. xvi. 21. xvii. 23. xx. 3, 19. xxii. 26. xxvii. 64. Mark ix. 31 and x. 34 (*see* τρεῖς). xii. 21. xv. 25. Luke ix. 22. xii. 38. xviii. 33. xx. 12, 31. xxiv. 7, 21, 46. John ii. 1. Acts ii. 15. x. 40. xxiii. 23. 1Cor. xv. 4. 2 Cor. xii. 2. Rev. iv. 7. vi. 5*t*. viii. 10. xi. 14. xiv. 9(–G[o] *S*[c]). xvi. 4. xxi. 19.

τῇ τρίτῃ, **the third day**, Luke xiii. 32. Acts xxvii. 19.

τὸ τρίτον, **the third part**, Rev. viii. 7*t*, 8, 9*t*, 10, 11, 12*five*. ix. 15, 18. xii. 4. — ἐκ τρίτου, **the third time**, Matt. xxvi. 44 (–G[oo]L[b]).

Adv., (τὸ) τρίτον, **the third time**, Mark xiv. 41. Luke xxiii. 22. John xxi. 14, 17*t*. 2 Cor. xii. 14. xiii. 1.—**thirdly**, 1 Cor. xii. 28.

Add John xix. 14, for ἐκτός, G″. Rev. viii. 7(*ap*).

τρίχινος.

of hair, Rev. vi. 12.

τρόμος.

trembling, 1 Cor. ii. 3. 2 Cor. vii. 15. Eph. vi. 5. Phil. ii. 12.

With ἔχω, **tremble**[cc], Mark xvi. 8.

τροπή.

turning, Jas. i. 17.

τρόπος.

manner, Jude 7.

ὃν τρόπον, **in like manner as**, Acts i. 11.—**as**, Luke xiii. 34. Acts vii. 28. 2 Tim. iii. 8.—**even as**, Matt. xxiii. 37. — *With* κατά, **even as**, Acts xv. 11. xxvii. 25.

way, Rom. iii. 2. Phil. i. 18.

means, 2 Thes. ii. 3. iii. 16 (τόπος G′L).

conversation, Heb. xiii. 5.

τροποφορέω.

suffer one's manners, Acts xiii. 18 (G′, τροφοφορέω C[m]GLT ; *marg.* **bear** *or* **feed one, as a nurse beareth** *or* **feedeth her child**).

τροφή.

food, Acts xiv. 17. Jas. ii. 15.

meat, Matt. iii. 4. vi. 25. x. 10. xxiv. 45. Luke xii. 23. John iv. 8. Acts ii. 46. ix. 19. xxvii. 33. Heb. v. 12, 14.

Gen., **some meat**, Acts xxvii. 34, 36. — Not rendered, *with* κορέννυμι, Acts xxvii. 38.

τροφός.

nurse, 1 Thes. ii. 7.

τροφοφορέω, bring nourishment to, cherish. *See* τροποφορέω.

τροχιά.

path, Heb. xii. 13.

τροχός.

course, Jas. iii. 6.

τρύβλιον.

dish, Matt. xxvi. 23. Mark xiv. 20.

τρυγάω.

gather, Luke vi. 44. Rev. xiv. 18, 19.

τρυγών.

turtle-dove, Luke ii. 24.

τρυμαλιά.

eye, Mark x. 25. Luke xviii. 25 (τρῆμα LTTr*S*).

τρύπημα.

eye, Matt. xix. 24.

τρυφάω.

live in pleasure, Jas. v. 5.

τρυφή.

With ἐν, **delicately**, Luke vii. 25.

to riot[cc], 2 Pet. ii. 13.

τρώγω.

eat, Matt. xxiv. 38. John vi. 54[p] (*with art.*), 56, 57, 58. xiii. 18.

τυγχάνω.

obtain, Luke xx. 35. Acts xxvi. 22. 2 Tim. ii. 10. Heb. viii. 6. xi. 35.

enjoy, Acts xxiv. 2(3)p.

εἰ τύχοι, **it may chance,** 1 Cor. xv. 37. — **it may be,** 1 Cor. xiv. 10.

τυχόν, **it may be,** 1 Cor. xvi. 6.

Part., with οὐ, **no little,** Acts xxviii. 2. — **special,** Acts xix. 11.

Not rendered, Luke x. 30(-LTr*S*).

See also ἐπιμελεία.

τυμπανίζω.

to torture, Heb. xi. 35.

τυπικῶς, in figures, typically. 1 Cor. x. 11, for τύπος, L*S*.

τύπος.

print, John xx. 25, 25 (τόπος LT).

figure, Acts vii. 43. Rom. v. 14.

form, Rom. vi. 17.

fashion, Acts vii. 44.

manner, Acts xxiii. 25.

pattern, Tit. ii. 7. Heb. viii. 5.

ensample, 1 Cor. x. 11 (*marg.* **type**; τυπικῶς L*S*). Phil. iii. 17. 1 Thes. i. 7. 2 Thes. iii. 9. 1 Pet. v. 3.

example, 1 Cor. x. 6 (*Gr.* figure). 1 Tim. iv. 12.

τύπτω.

to beat, Luke xii. 45. Acts xviii. 17. xxi. 32.

strike, Luke xxii. 64(*ap*).

smite, Matt. xxiv. 49. xxvii. 30. Mark xv. 19. Luke vi. 29. xviii. 13. xxiii. 48. Acts xxiii. 2, 3*t*.

wound, 1 Cor. viii. 12.

τυρβάζω.

Pass. or Mid., **be troubled,** Luke x. 41 (θορυβάζω LTr*S*).

τυφλός.

blind, Matt. xi. 5. xii. 22, 22 (-LT Tr*S*). xv. 14*f*, 30, 31. xxi. 14. xxiii. 16, 17, 19, 24, 26. Mark x. 46. Luke iv. 18. vi. 39*t*. vii. 22. xiv. 13, 21. John v. 3. ix. 2, 8 (προσαίτης GLT Tr*S*), 18, 19, 20, 24, 25, 32, 39, 40, 41. x. 21. xi. 37. Acts xiii. 11. Rom. ii. 19. 2 Pet. i. 9. Rev. iii. 17.

which wasc **blind,** John ix. 1.

With art., **(he) that was**c **blind,** Luke vii. 21. John ix. 13.

blind man, Matt. ix. 27, 28. xx. 30. Mark viii. 22, 23. x. 49, 51. Luke xviii. 35. John ix. 6(-GoLbTr*S*), 17.

τυφλόω.

to blind, John xii. 40. 2 Cor. iv. 4. 1 John ii. 11.

τυφόω.

Pass., **be lifted up with pride,** 1 Tim. iii. 6. — **be proud** (*marg.* **be a fool**), 1 Tim. vi. 4.— **be high-minded,** 2 Tim. iii. 4.

τύφω.

Pass., **to smoke,** Matt. xii. 20.

τυφωνικός.

tempestuous, Acts xxvii. 14.

τυχόν. See τυγχάνω.

ὑακίνθινος.

of jacinth, Rev. ix. 17.

ὑάκινθος.

jacinth, Rev. xxi. 20.

ὑάλινος.

of glass, Rev. iv. 6. xv. 2*t*.

ὕαλος.

glass, Rev. xxi. 18, 21.

ὑβρίζω.

entreat spitefully, Matt. xxii. 6. Luke xviii. 32.

use despitefully, Acts xiv. 5.

entreat shamefully, 1 Thes. ii. 2.

reproach, Luke xi. 45.

ὕβρις.

reproach, 2 Cor. xii. 10.

hurt (*marg.* **injury**), Acts xxvii. 10.

harm, Acts xxvii. 21.

ὑβριστής.

despiteful, Rom. i. 30.

injurious, 1 Tim. i. 13.

ὑγιαίνω.

be in health, 3 John 2.

(be1**) whole,** Luke v. 311. vii. 10p.

wholesome, 1 Tim. vi. 3p.

be sound, Tit. i. 13. — **sound,** 1 Tim. i. 10p. 2 Tim. i. 13p. iv. 3p. Tit. i. 9p. ii. 1p, 2p.

safe and sound, Luke xv. 27[p].

ὑγιής.

whole, Matt. xii. 13. xv. 31. Mark iii. 5(*omS*). v. 34. Luke vi. 10(*ap*). John v. 4(*ap*), 6, 9, 11, 14, 15. vii. 23. Acts iv. 10.
sound, Tit. ii. 8.

ὑγρός.

green, Luke xxiii. 31.

ὑδρία.

water-pot, John ii. 6, 7. iv. 28.

ὑδροποτέω.

drink water, 1 Tim. v. 23.

ὑδρωπικός.

which had[c] the dropsy, Luke xiv. 2.

ὕδωρ.

water, Matt. iii. 11, 16. viii. 32. xiv. 28, 29. xvii. 15. xxvii. 24. Mark i. 8, 10. ix. 22, 41. xiv. 13. Luke iii. 16. vii. 44. viii. 24, 25. xvi. 24. xxii. 10. John i. 26, 31, 33. ii. 7, 9*t*. iii. 5, 23[pl]. iv. 7, 10, 11, 13, 14, 14(*ap*), 14, 15, 46. v. 3(*ap*), 4*t* (*ap*), 7. vii. 38. xiii. 5. xix. 34.
Acts i. 5. viii. 36*t*, 38, 39. x. 47. xi. 16. Eph. v. 26. Heb. ix. 19. x. 22(23). Jas. iii. 12. 1 Pet. iii. 20. 2 Pet. iii. 5*t*, 6. 1 John v. 6*tr*, 8.
Rev. i. 15. vii. 17. viii. 10, 11(–St), 11. xi. 6. xii. 15. xiv. 2, 7. xvi. 4, 5, 12. xvii. 1, 15. xix. 6. xxi. 6. xxii. 1, 17.

ὑετός.

rain, Acts xiv. 17. xxviii. 2. Heb. vi. 7. Jas. v. 7(–LT, καρπός *S*), 18. *See also* βρέχω.

υἱοθεσία.

adoption of sons, Gal. iv. 5.
adoption of children, Eph. i. 5.
adoption, Rom. viii. 15, 23. ix. 4.

υἱός.

son, Matt. i. 1*t*, 20, 21, 23, 25. ii. 15. vii. 9. ix. 27. x. 37. xii. 23. xiii. 55. xv. 22. xvii. 15. xx. 20, 21, 30, 31. xxi. 9, 15, 37*t*, 38. xxii. 2, 42, 45. xxiii. 35. xxvi. 37. Mark iii. 17, 28. vi. 3. ix. 17. x. 35, 46, 47, 48. xii. 6*t*, 35, 37.
Luke i. 13, 31, 36, 57. ii. 7. iii. 2, 23. iv. 22. v. 10. vii. 12. ix. 38, 41. x. 6. xi. 11, 19. xii. 53*t*. xv. 11, 13, 19, 21*t*, 24, 25, 30. xviii. 38, 39. xix. 9. xx. 13, 41, 44.
John i. 42(43), 45(46). iv. 5, 46, 47, 50, 53. vi. 42. ix. 19, 20. xvii. 12. xix. 26. Acts ii. 17. iv. 36. vii. 16, 21, 29. xiii. 21. xvi. 1. xix. 14. xxiii. 6, 16.
Rom. viii. 14, 19. ix. 9. 2 Cor. vi. 18. Gal. iv. 6, 7*t*, 22, 30*tr*. Eph. iii. 5. 2 Thes. ii. 3. Heb. ii. 6, 10. iii. 6. vii. 5(–L). xi. 21, 24. xii. 5, 6, 7*t*, 8. Jas. ii. 21. 1 Pet. v. 13. Rev. xxi. 7.
Said of Christ, with (τοῦ) θεοῦ, πατρός, ὑψίστου, εὐλογητοῦ, (¹); *with* (τοῦ) ἀνθρώπου (²), **Son**, Matt. iii. 17. iv. 3[1], 6[1]. viii. 20[2], 29[1]. ix. 6[2]. x. 23[2]. xi. 19[2], 27*tr*. xii. 8[2], 32[2], 40[2]. xiii. 37[2], 41[2]. xiv. 33[1]. xvi. 13[2], 16[1], 27[2], 28[2]. xvii. 5, 9[2], 12[2], 22[2]. xviii. 11[2](*ap*). xix. 28[2]. xx. 18[2], 28[2]. xxiv. 27[2], 30*t*[2], 37[2], 39[2], 44[2]. xxv. 13[2](*ap*), 31[2]. xxvi. 2[2], 24*t*[2], 45[2], 63[1], 64[2]. xxvii. 40[1], 43[1], 54[1]. xxviii. 19.
Mark i. 1[1], 11. ii. 10[2], 28[2]. iii. 11[1]. v. 7[1]. viii. 31[2], 38[2]. ix. 7, 9[2], 12[2], 31[2]. x. 33[2], 45[2]. xiii. 26[2], 32. xiv. 21*t*[2], 41[2], 61[1], 62[2]. xv. 39[1].
Luke i. 32[1], 35[1]. iii. 22. iv. 3[1], 9[1], 41[1]. v. 24[2]. vi. 5[2], 22[2]. vii. 34[2]. viii. 28[1]. ix. 22[2], 26[2], 35, 44[2], 56[2](*ap*), 58[2]. x. 22*tr*. xi. 30[2]. xii. 8[2], 10[2], 40[2]. xvii. 22[2], 24[2], 26[2], 30[2]. xviii. 8[2], 31[2]. xix. 10[2]. xxi. 27[2], 36[2]. xxii. 22[2], 48[2], 69[2], 70[1]. xxiv. 7[2].
John i. 18 (θεός L[m]Tr*S*, –G[o]), 34[1], 49(50)[1], 51(52)[2]. iii. 13[2], 14[2], 16, 17, 18[1], 35, 36*t*. v. 19*t*, 20, 21, 22, 23*t*, 25[1], 26, 27[2]. vi. 27[2], 40, 53[2], 62[2], 69[1](*ap*). viii. 28[2], 35, 36. ix. 35[1]. x. 36[1]. xi. 4[1], 27[1]. xii. 23[2], 34*t*[2]. xiii. 31[2]. xiv. 13. xvii. 1*t*. xix. 7[1]. xx. 31[1]. Acts vii. 56[2]. viii. 37[1](*ap*). ix. 20[1]. xiii. 33.
Rom. i. 3, 4[1], 9. v. 10. viii. 3, 29,

32. 1 Cor. i. 9. xv. 28. 2 Cor. i. 19[1] Gal. i. 16. ii. 20[1](*ap*). iv. 4, 6. Eph. iv. 13[1]. Col. i. 13. 1 Thes. i. 10. Heb. i. 2(1), 5*t*, 8. iv. 14[1]. v. 5, 8. vi. 6[1]. vii. 3[1], 28. x. 29[1]. 2 Pet. i. 17. 1 John i. 3, 7. ii. 22, 23, 24. iii. 8[1], 23. iv. 9, 10, 14, 15[1]. v. 5[1], 9, 10[1], 10, 11, 12, 12[1], 13[1](*ap*), 13[1], 20[1], 20. 2 John 3[1], 9. Rev. i. 13[2]. ii. 18[1]. xiv. 14[2].

child, Matt. v. 9, 45. viii. 12. ix. 15. xii. 27. xiii. 38*t*. xvii. 25, 26. xx. 20. xxiii. 15, 31. xxvii. 9, 56. Mark ii. 19. Luke i. 16. v. 34. vi. 35. xvi. 8*t*. xx. 34, 36*t*. John iv. 12. xii. 36. Acts iii. 25. v. 21. vii. 23, 37. ix. 15. x. 36. xiii. 10, 26.

Rom. ix. 26, 27. 2 Cor. iii. 7, 13. Gal. iii. 7, 26. Eph. ii. 2. v. 6. Col. iii. 6 (*ap*). 1 Thes. v. 5*t*. Heb. xi. 22. xii. 5. Rev. ii. 14. vii. 4. xii. 5. xxi. 12.

foal, Matt. xxi. 5.

Add Matt. xxiv. 36 (*ap*). Luke xiv. 5, for ὄνος, G″LTTr. 1 John ii. 23(*ap*). v. 10, for θεός, G′L.

ὕλη.

matter (*marg.* **wood**), Jas. iii. 5.

ὑμεῖς.

1. *Nominative*, ὑμεῖς.

ye(¹**you**, *ed.*1611), Matt. v. 13, 14, 48. vi. 9, 26. vii. 11, 12. ix. 4(-LTr*S*). x. 20, 31. xiii. 18. xiv. 16. xv. 3[1], 5, 16. xvi. 15. xix. 28, 28(αὐτοί Tr *S*). xx. 4, 7. xxi. 13, 32. xxiii. 8*t*, 13, 28, 32. xxiv. 33, 44. xxvi. 31. xxvii. 24. xxviii. 5. Mark vi. 31, 37. vii. 11, 18. viii. 29. xi. 17, 26[1](*ap*). xii. 27(-TTr*S*). xiii. 11, 23, 29.

Luke vi. 31(-L[b]). ix. 13, 20, 55 (*ap*). x. 23, 24. xi. 13, 39, 48. xii. 24, 29, 40. xvi. 15. xvii. 10. xix. 46. xxi. 31. xxii. 26, 28, 70. xxiv. 48, 49. John i. 26. iii. 28. iv. 20, 22, 32, 35, 38*t*. v. 20, 33, 34, 35, 38, 39, 44, 45. vi. 67. vii. 8, 28, 34, 36, 47. viii. 14, 15, 21, 22, 23*t*, 31, 38, 41, 44, 46, 47, 49, 54. ix. 19, 27, 30. x. 26, 36. xi. 49. xiii. 10, 13, 14, 15, 33, 34. xiv. 3, 17, 19*t*, 20(-L[b]), 20[1]. xv. 3, 4, 5, 14, 16, 16[1], 27, xvi. 20*t*, 22, 27. xviii. 31. xix. 6, 35.

Acts i. 5. ii. 15, 33, 36. iii. 13, 14, 25. iv. 7, 10. v. 30. vii. 4, 26(-G″ LT*S*), 51*t*, 52. viii. 24. x. 28, 37[1]. xi. 16. xv. 7. xix. 15. xx. 18, 25. xxii. 3. xxiii. 15. xxvii. 31.

Rom. i. 6. vi. 11. vii. 4. viii. 9. ix. 26. xi. 30. xvi. 17. 1 Cor. i. 30. iii. 17, 23. iv. 10*tr*. v. 2, 12. vi. 8[1]. ix. 1[1], 2. x. 15. xii. 27. xiv. 9[1], 12. xvi. 1, 6, 16. 2 Cor. i. 14. iii. 2. vi. 13, 16(ἡμεῖς L*S*), 18. viii. 9. ix. 4[1]. xi. 7[1]. xii. 11. xiii. 7, 9.

Gal. iii. 28, 29. iv. 12. v. 13. vi. 1. Eph. i. 13. ii. 11, 13, 22[1]. iv. 20. vi. 21. Phil. ii. 18. iv. 15*t*. Col. iii. 4, 7, 8[1], 13. iv. 1, 16. 1 Thes. i. 6. ii. 10, 14*t*, 19, 20. iii. 8. iv. 9. v. 4, 5. 2 Thes. i. 12. iii. 13. Jas. ii. 6. v. 8. 1 Pet. ii. 9. 2 Pet. iii. 17. 1 John i. 3. ii. 20, 24? 24, 27? iv. 4. Jude 17, 20.

ye yourselves, Luke xii. 36.

of you[cc], Eph. v. 33.

Not rendered, Mark xiii. 9. Luke ix. 44. 1 Pet. iv. 1. 1 John ii. 24? 27?

Add Gal. iv. 28, for ἡμεῖς, LT.

2. *Genitive*, ὑμῶν.

of you, Matt. xviii. 19. Mark x. 44 (ἐν ὑμῖν L*S*). Luke xi. 11. xiii. 15. xiv. 5. Acts ii. 22, 38. iii. 26[cc] (αὐτῶν L). xxvii. 34. Rom. i. 9, 12. 1 Cor. i. 12, 14. vi. 1. xii. 21. xiv. 26(-L*S*). xvi. 2. 2 Cor. ii. 3, 9. vii. 15. Eph. i. 16 (-L*S*). Phil. i. 3. 1 Thes. i. 2 (-L*S*). ii. 9, 11. iv. 4. 2 Thes. i. 3. iii. 8. Heb. iii. 12. vi. 11. Jas i. 5. 1 Pet. iv. 15.

your, Matt. v. 12, 16*tr*, 20, 37, 44, 45, 47, 48. vi. 1*t*, 8, 14, 15*t*, 21*t* (σοῦ G′LTTr*S*), 25*t*, 26, 32. vii. 6, 11*t*. ix. 4, 11, 29. x. 9, 13*t*, 14*t*, 20, 29, 30. xi. 29. xii. 27*t*. xiii. 16, 16(-L Tr[b]). xv. 3, 6. xvii. 20, 24. xviii. 14 (μοῦ LTr), 35. xix. 8*t*. xx. 26, 27. xxiii. 8, 9*t*, 10(-G′), 11, 32, 34, 38. xxiv. 20, 42. xxv. 8.

Mark ii. 8. vi. 11. vii. 13. viii. 17. x. 5, 43. xi. 25*t*, 26*t*(*ap*). xiii. 18

(-G°°LTTr*S*). Luke iii. 14. iv. 21. v. 4, 22. vi. 22, 23, 24, 27, 35*t*, 36, 38. viii. 25. ix. 5, 44. x. 6, 11, 20. xi. 13, 19*t*, 39, 46, 47, 48. xii. 7, 22 (-G°°LTTr*S*), 30, 32, 34*t*, 35. xiii. 35. xvi. 15. xxi. 14, 18, 19*t*, 28*t*, 34. xxii. 53. xxiii. 28. xxiv. 38.

John iv. 35. vi. 49, 58(-G°°LTTr *S*). viii. 21, 24*t*, 38(-G°°LTTr), 41, 42, 44, 54 (ἡμῶν G''TTr), 56. ix. 19, 41. x. 34. xiii. 14. xiv. 1, 27. xv. 11, 16. xvi. 6, 20, 22*t*, 24. xviii. 31. xix. 14, 15. xx. 17*t*. Acts ii. 17*f*, 39. iii. 17, 19, 22*t*. v. 28. vii. 37 (*omS*), 37, 43(-LT), 51, 52. xiii. 41. xv. 24. xvii. 23. xviii. 6. xix. 37.

Rom. i. 8. vi. 12, 13*t*, 19*tr*, 22. viii. 11. xii. 1*t*, 2(-G°°LT). xiv. 16. xv. 24(*Gr.* you). xvi. 19, 20. 1 Cor. i. 4, 26. ii. 5. v. 6. vi. 15, 19, 20, 20(*ap*). vii. 5, 14. ix. 11. xiv. 34 (-G°L*S*). xv. 14, 17*t*, 58. xvi. 3. 2 Cor. i. 6*t*, 14, 24*t*. iv. 5. v. 11. vii. 7*tr*, 13 (ἡμῶν LT*S*). viii. 14(13), 14, 19(G', ἡμῶν GLT*S*), 24*t*. ix. 2, 5, 10*t*, 13. x. 6, 8, 15. xi. 3. xii. 19. xiii. 9.

Gal. iv. 6 (G', ἡμῶν GLT*S*), 15, 16. vi. 18. Eph. i. 13, 18. iii. 13, 17. iv. 4, 23, 26, 29. v. 19. vi. 1, 4, 5, 9(*ap*), 14, 22. Phil. i. 5, 9, 19, 25, 26. ii. 17, 25, 30. iv. 5, 6, 7t, 17, 19. Col. i. 4, 8. ii. 5*t*, 13. iii. 3, 5, 8, 15, 16, 21. iv. 6, 8. 1 Thes. i. 3, 4, 8. ii. 17. iii. 2, 5, 6, 7, 10*t*, 13. iv. 3, 11. 2 Thes. i. 3, 4*t*. ii. 17. iii. 5. Phm. 22, 25.

Heb. iii. 8, 9, 15. iv. 7. vi. 10. ix. 14 (ἡμῶν G''L). x. 34, 35. xii. 3, 13. xiii. 17. Jas. i. 3, 21. ii. 2. iii. 14. iv. 1*t*, 3, 9, 14, 16. v. 1, 2*t*, 3*t*, 4, 5, 8, 12. 1 Pet. i. 7, 9(-T), 13, 14, 17, 18, 21, 22. ii. 12, 25. iii. 2, 7, 15, 16. v. 7, 8, 9. 2 Pet. i. 5, 10, 19. iii. 1. 1 John i. 4 (ἡμῶν StL*S*). Jude 12, 20. Rev. i. 9. ii. 23. xxii. 21 (τῶν ἁγίων GTr*S*, -G°LT).

With ἐκ, **your,** 2 Cor. viii. 7. ix. 2 (-ἐκ L*S*).

your own, Mark vii. 9. Acts xviii. 6. 2 Cor. vi. 12.

yours, 1 Cor. iii. 21, 22. xvi. 18. 2 Cor. xii. 14.

of yours, 1 Cor. viii. 9.

your things, 1 Cor. xvi. 14.

on your part, 1 Cor. xvi. 17 (ὑμέτερον LT).

τὰ περὶ ὑμῶν, **your affairs,** Phil. i. 27.—**your state (estate**[1]**),** Phil. ii. 19, 20. Col. iv. 8[1] (τὰ π. ἡμῶν G'L).

ὑμῶν αὐτῶν, **your own selves,** Acts xx. 30.—**yourselves,** 1 Cor. v. 13. —**your own,** 1 Cor. vii. 35.

yourselves, Matt. xxiii. 15. Eph. ii. 8.

you, Matt. v. 11, 12. vi. 27. vii. 9. xii. 11. xv. 7. xvii. 17*t*. xxi. 2, 43. xxiii. 11. xxvi. 21, 29. xxviii. 20. Mark vi. 11. vii. 6. ix. 19. xi. 2. xiv. 18. Luke ix. 41. x. 16. xi. 5. xii. 25. xiv. 28, 33. xv. 4. xvi. 26. xvii. 7, 21. xxi. 16. xxii. 15, 19, 20, 27, 53. xxiii. 14.

John i. 26. v. 45*t*. vi. 64, 70. vii. 19, 33. viii. 7(*ap*), 26, 46, 55 (ὑμῖν LTr). xii. 35 (ὑμῖν GLTTr*S*). xiii. 18, 21, 33. xiv. 9, 16, 30. xv. 18. xvi. 4, 5, 22, 26. Acts i. 7, 11. iii. 16. iv. 10, 11, 19. vi. 3. xviii. 14. xx. 18. xxiv. 21. xxv. 26. xxvii. 22.

Rom. i. 8. vi. 14. xii. 18. xv. 14, 24, 28, 33. xvi. 2, 20, 24(*ap*). 1 Cor. i. 11, 13. iv. 3. v. 2. vii. 28. ix. 12. xi. 24. xiv. 36. xvi. 23, 24. 2 Cor. i. 7(6), 16*t*, 23. iii. 1. vii. 4, 12 (ἡμῶν StLT), 13, 14. viii. 16. ix. 2, 3, 14. x. 13, 14, 16. xi. 8. xii. 11, 13, 14(-LT*S*). xiii. 11, 14(13).

Gal. iii. 2. iv. 12. Eph. i. 16. iii. 1, 13. iv. 31. Phil. i. 4, 7. iv. 9, 18, 23. Col. i. 3, 7 (ἡμῶν G''L*S*), 9, 24. ii. 1. iv. 9, 12*t*, 13, 18. 1 Thes. i. 2, 8. ii. 6, 7, 8, 17. iii. 6, 9. v. 12, 23, 28. 2 Thes. i. 3. 11. ii. 13. iii. 16, 18. 2 Tim. iv. 22(*ap*). Tit. ii. 8 (ἡμῶν GLT*S*). iii. 15.

Heb. iii. 13. iv. 1. vi. 9. xiii. 7, 17, 24, 25. Jas. ii. 6, 16. iv. 7. v. 4. 1 Pet. ii. 12. iii. 16(*ap*). v. 7. 2 John 3 (ἡμῶν St*S*). Rev. ii. 10. xviii. 20°°.

τῶν ψυχῶν ὑμῶν, **you**, 2 Cor. xii. 15 (*Gr*. your souls).

ye[cc]([1]**you**, 1611), Lk. xxii. 10. 1 Cor. v. 4. xi. 18, 20. xiv. 18[1]. 2 Cor. i. 11[1]. 1 Pet. iv. 4[1].—**ye** °**spake of**, Gal. iv. 15[1].

Add, for ἡμῶν, Mark ix. 40*t*, StGL. Luke ix. 50*t*, GLTTr*S*[1st]. Acts xiv. 17, GLT*S*. xix. 25, G″. xxviii. 25, LT*S*. Rom. xvi. 1, L[m]. 2 Cor. i. 11, T. v. 12, L[m]*S*. vii. 12, StLT*S*. 14, L. Eph. v. 2, T. Col. iii. 4, G″L[m] *S*. Tit. ii. 10, St. 1 Pet. ii. 21, C[m] GL*S*. 2 Pet. iii. 2, LT*S*.

Luke x. 11(*ap*). xi. 13(your), L. xii. 22 (. . body), L[b]. Acts ii. 38(. . sins), L*S*. Gal. iv. 14, for μοῦ τόν, G′L*S*. Eph. ii. 1 (. . trespasses), L T*S*. Phil. i. 28, for ὑμῖν, G′LT*S*. Col. iii. 19 (your), L. 1 Tim. vi. 21, for σοῦ, L*S*. 2 Pet. i. 10 (*ap*).

See also ὑπάρχω.

3. *Dative*, ὑμῖν.

to you, Matt. vii. 2, 12. xvi. 11. Mark iv. 24. xiii. 21. Luke vi. 31, 38. vii. 32(–Tr*S*). xvii. 23. xxi. 13. John xiii. 12, 15, 33. xix. 4. Acts xiii. 26, 46. Rom. i. 7, 15. xi. 13. 1 Cor. ix. 2. xi. 2, 22. xiv. 6. 2 Cor. i. 2. vii. 14. ix. 1. xi. 7. Gal. i. 3. iii. 5. Eph. i. 2. ii. 17. vi. 21. Phil. i. 28 (ὑμῶν G′LT*S*). iii. 1. 2 Thes. i. 7. Phm. 3. Heb. xiii. 19. Jas. iv. 8.

unto you, Matt. iii. 9. v. 18, 20, 22, 28, 32, 34, 39, 44. vi. 2, 5, 16, 25, 29, 33. vii. 7. viii. 10, 11. ix. 29. x. 15, 23, 42. xi. 9, 11, 17, 17(–LT Tr*S*), 22, 24. xii. 6, 31, 36. xiii. 11, 17. xvi. 28. xvii. 12, 20*t*. xviii. 3, 10, 13, 18, 19, 35. xix. 9, 23, 24, 28. xx. 32. xxi. 3, 21, 31, 43. xxii. 31. xxiii. 13, 14(*ap*), 15, 16, 23, 25, 27, 29, 36, 38, 39. xxiv. 2, 23, 26, 34, 47. xxv. 12, 40, 45. xxvi. 13, 15, 21, 29, 64. xxvii. 17, 21.

Mark iii. 28. iv. 11, 24(*ap*). vi. 11 (*ap*). viii. 12. ix. 1, 13, 41. x. 15, 29. xi. 3, 23, 24. xii. 43. xiii. 30, 37. xiv. 9, 18, 25. xv. 9. xvi. 7.

Luke ii. 11, 12. iii. 8. iv. 24. vi. 24, 25, 25(–G°TTr*S*), 26(*omS*), 27, 38. vii. 9, 26, 28, 32. viii. 10. x. 12, 19, 20. xi. 8, 9*t*, 41, 42, 43, 44, 46, 47, 51, 52. xii. 4, 5, 8, 22, 27, 31, 37, 44. xiii. 24, 25, 35*t*. xiv. 24. xv. 7, 10. xvi. 9. xviii. 17, 29. xix. 26. xxi. 3, 32. xxii. 16, 18, 29, 37. xxiv. 6, 36(*ap*).

John i. 51(52) ii. 5. iv. 35. v. 19, 24, 25. vi. 26, 27, 32, 36, 47, 53, 63, 65. vii. 22. viii. 24, 25, 34, 51, 58. x. 1, 7, 26(*ap*). xii. 24. xiii. 16, 20, 21, 34. xiv. 10, 12, 25, 26, 27*t*, 28. xv. 3, 7, 11, 15, 20, 21 (εἰς ὑμᾶς G′ LTTr, –*S*), 26. xvi. 1, 3(*om*), 4, 6, 12, 14, 15, 20, 23, 25*t*, 26, 33. xviii. 39*t*. xx. 19, 21, 26.

Acts ii. 14, 39. iii. 14, 20, 22, 26. iv. 10. v. 38. vii. 37. xiii. 38*t*, 41. xvii. 3, 23. xx. 27, xxviii. 28.

Rom. i. 11. xv. 15. xvi. 1. 1 Cor. i. 3. ii. 1. iii. 1. iv. 17. v. 9, 11. ix. 11. x. 28. xi. 23. xii. 31. xiv. 37. xv. 1*t*, 2, 3. 2 Cor. i. 13. ii. 3 (G°°LT*S*), 4. v. 12. vi. 18. vii. 12. xi. 9. xii. 19, 20.

Gal. i. 8*t*, 20. iv. 13. v 2. vi. 11. Eph. i. 17. Phil. i. 2, 29. ii. 19. iii. 15. Col. i. 2. iv. 7, 9. 1 Thes. i. 1. ii. 8. iv. 9, 15. v. 1. 2 Thes. i. 2. iii. 9. Phm. 22.

Heb. xii. 5. xiii. 7, 22. 1 Pet. i. 2, 12, 13. ii. 7. iv. 12. v. 12. 2 Pet. i. 2, 11, 16. iii. 1, 15. 1 John i. 2, 3, 4 (ἡμεῖς G′*S*), 5. ii. 1, 7, 8, 12, 13*tr*, 14*t*, 21, 26. v. 13. 2 John 12. Jude 2, 3*t*. Rev. i. 4. ii. 24. xxii. 16.

for you, Matt. xi. 22. xxv. 9, 34. Mark x. 36. Luke x. 14. John xiv. 2, 3. xvi. 7. Acts xxii. 25. 2 Cor. viii. 10. Phil. iii. 1. Col. i. 5. Heb. xiii. 17.

for yourselves, Matt. vi. 19, 20.

for your cause, 2 Cor. v. 13.

τὸ ἐφ' ὑ., **on your behalf**, Rom. xvi. 19.

against you, Luke x. 11.

with you, John xiv. 27. Acts xiv. 15.

of you[cc], Rev. ii. 23.

you, Matt. iii. 7. vi. 14. vii. 7. x 19(*ap*), 20, 27. xi. 21. xix. 8. xx

4, 26*t*, 27. xxi. 24, 27. xxiii. 3. xxiv. 25. xxviii. 7, 20. Mark x. 3, 5, 43*t*. xi. 25, 29, 33. xiii. 11, 23. xiv. 13, 15. Luke ii. 10. iii. 7, 13. iv. 25. vi. 28 (ὑμᾶς GLTr*S*), 47. ix. 27, 48. x. 8, 13, 24. xi. 9. xii. 5, 32, 51. xiii. 3, 5, 27. xvi. 12. xvii. 6, 10, 34. xviii. 8, 14. xix. 40. xx. 8. xxi. 15. xxii. 10, 12, 26, 67. xxiv. 44.

John iii. 12*t*. v. 38. vi. 32*t*. vii. 19. viii. 37, 40. ix. 27. x. 25, 32. xiii. 15, 19. xiv. 2, 16, 17*t*, 20, 25, 29. xv. 4, 7, 11, 14, 16, 17. xvi. 4*t*, 7, 13, 23, 25. xviii. 8. Acts v. 28. xiii. 26, 34. xv. 28. xx. 20, 26, 32(-LT*S*), 35. xxv. 5. xxvi. 8.

Rom. i. 12, 13. viii. 9, 10, 11*t*. xii. 3. xv. 5, 32(*ap*). 1 Cor. i. 4, 6, 10, 11. ii. 2. iii. 3, 16, 18. iv. 8. v. 1. vi. 2, 5, 7, 19. vii. 35. x. 27. xi. 18, 19*t*, 30. xii. 3. xiv. 25. xv. 12, 51. 2 Cor. i. 19, 21. iv. 12, 14. vii. 7, 11, 16. viii. 1. ix. 14. x. 1, 15. xii. 12. xiii. 3, 5.

Gal. i. 11. iii. 1(-G[oo]L*S*), 5. iv. 15, 16, 19, 20. v. 21. Eph. iii. 16. iv. 6 (ἡμῖν G, -G[oo]LT*S*), 32 (ἡμῖν G′ L). v. 3. Phil. i. 6, 25. ii. 5, 13, 17. iii. 18. Col. i. 6, 27. ii. 5, 13 (ἡμῖν StGLT*S*). iii. 13, 16. iv. 16. 1 Thes. i. 5. ii. 10, 13. iii. 4, 7. iv. 2, 6, 11. v. 12. 2 Thes. i. 4, 12. ii. 5. iii. 4 (-T*S*), 6, 7, 10, 11, 16. Phm. 6 (G′, ἡμῖν GLT).

Heb. xii. 7. xiii. 21. Jas. i. 26 (G′, *omS*). iii. 13. iv. 1. v. 3, 6, 13, 14, 19. 1 Pet. iii. 15. iv. 12. v. 1, 2, 14. 2 Pet. i. 8. ii. 1, 13. 1 John ii. 8 (ἡμῖν G′), 12, 14, 24*t*, 27. iv. 4. Jude 18. Rev. ii. 13. xviii. 6(*omS*).

your, Luke xvi. 11. xxi. 15. 1 Cor. vi. 5. xv. 34.

ὑμῖν αὐτοῖς, **yourselves**, 1 Cor. xi. 13.

ye[cc] ([1]**you**, *ed.* 1611), Matt. xviii. 12. xxi. 28[1]. xxii. 42. xxvi. 66. Mark xi. 24. xiv. 64. Luke vi. 32, 33, 34. John xi. 56. xviii. 39. Acts v. 9. xiii. 15. 2 Cor. viii. 13[1].

Not rendered, 1 Pet. iv. 12.

Add, for ἡμῖν, John xi. 50, TTr. Acts xiv. 17, GLT*S*. xvi. 17[2d], T*S*. Eph. vi. 12, L. 1 Pet. i. 12, GLT*S*. ii. 21, StGLT*S*. For ὑμῶν, John viii. 55, LTr. xii. 35, GLTTr*S*. — Mark x. 44, *see* ὑμῶν. John viii. 45 (you), L[b].

4. *Accusative*, ὑμᾶς.

you, Matt. iii. 11*t*. iv. 19. v. 11, 44*tr*(*ap*), 44, 46. vi. 30. vii. 6, 15, 23. x. 13, 14, 16, 17*t*, 19, 23, 40. xi. 28, 29. xii. 28. xxi. 24, 31, 32. xxiii. 34, 35. xxiv. 4, 9*t*. xxv. 12. xxvi. 32, 55(-G[o]TTr[b]*S*). xxviii. 7, 14. Mark i. 8*t*, 17. vi. 11. ix. 19, 41. xi. 29. xiii. 5, 9, 11, 36. xiv. 28, 49. xvi. 7.

Luke iii. 16*t*. vi. 9, 22*t*, 26, 27, 28, 32, 33. ix. 5, 41. x. 3, 6, 8, 9, 10, 11(*omS*), 16, 19. xi. 20. xii. 11, 12, 14, 28. xiii. 25, 27 (-L[b]TTr), 28. xvi. 9, 26. xix. 31. xx. 3. xxi. 12, 34. xxii. 31, 35. xxiii. 15 (*ap*). xxiv. 44, 49.

John iv. 38. v. 42. vi. 61, 70. vii. 7. viii. 32, 36. xii. 35. xiii. 34. xiv. 3, 18*t*, 26, 28. xv. 9, 12, 15*t*, 16*t*, 18, 19*t*, 20. xvi. 2*t*, 7*t*, 13, 22, 27. xx. 21. Acts i. 8. ii. 22, 29. iii. 22, 26. vii. 43. xiii. 32, 40(-LT*S*). xv. 24, 25. xviii. 21. xix. 13. xx. 20, 28, 29, 32. xxii. 1. xxiii. 15. xxvii. 22, 34. xxviii. 20.

Rom. i. 10, 11, 13*t*. ii. 24. x. 19*t*. xii. 1, 14(-T). xv. 13, 15, 22, 23, 24(*ap*), 24, 29, 30, 32. xvi. 16, 17, 19, 21, 22, 23*t*, 25. 1 Cor. i. 8, 10. ii. 1, 3. iii. 2. iv. 14, 15, 16, 17, 18, 19, 21. vii. 5, 32. x. 13*t*, 27. xi. 2, 3, 14, 22. xii. 1. xiv. 6*t*, 36. xvi. 5, 6, 7*t*, 10, 12, 15, 19*t*, 20. 2 Cor. i. 8, 12, 15, 16, 18. ii. 1, 2, 3, 4, 5, 8. iii. 1. vi. 11, 17. vii. 4, 8*t*, 12, 15. viii. 6, 17, 22, 23. ix. 4, 5, 8, 14. x. 1*t*, 9, 14. xi. 2*t*, 6, 9(8), 11, 20*t*. xii. 14*t*, 15, 16*t*, 17*t*, 18, 20, 21. xiii. 1, 3, 4, 13(12).

Gal. i. 6, 7, 9. ii. 5. iii. 1. iv. 11*t*, 17, 17 (ἡμᾶς EC[m]; *marg.* **us**), 18, 20. v. 2, 7, 8, 10*t*, 12. vi. 12, 13. Eph.

ii. 1. iii. 2. iv. 1. v. 6. vi. 22. Phil. i. 7(*see marg.*), 8, 24, 26, 27. ii. 25, 26. iv. 21, 22. Col. i. 6, 21, 22, 25. ii. 4, 8, 13, 16, 18. iv. 8, 10*t*, 12, 14. 1 Thes. i. 5, 9. ii. 1, 2, 9, 11, 12, 18. iii. 2, 2(-G°LT*S*), 4, 5, 6, 11, 12*t*. iv. 1, 10, 13. v. 4, 12*t*, 14, 18, 23, 24, 27. 2 Thes. i. 6, 10, 11. ii. 1, 3, 5, 13, 14 (*ἡμᾶς* L), 17 (-G°°LT*S*). iii. 1, 3, 4, 10.

Heb. v. 12. ix. 20. xiii. 21, 22, 23, 24. Jas. ii. 6. iv. 10. 1 Pet. i. 4 (*ἡμᾶς* StC[m]; *marg.* **us**), 10, 12, 15, 20, 25. ii. 9. iii. 13, 15. iv. 14. v. 6, 10(-G°LT*S*), 13. 2 Pet. i. 12, 13. ii. 3. 1 John ii. 26, 27*tr*. iii. 7, 13. 2 John 10, 12. Jude 5, 24 (*αὐτούς* St T). Rev. ii. 24. xii. 12.

δι' ὑμᾶς, **for your sakes (sake[1])**, John xi. 15. xii. 30. Rom. xi. 28. 1 Cor. iv. 6. 2 Cor. ii. 10. iv. 15. viii. 9. 1 Thes. i. 5[1]. iii. 9.

ἐφ' ὑμᾶς, **on your part**, 1 Pt. iv. 14(*ap*).

καθ' ὑμᾶς, **your**, Acts xviii. 15. Eph. i. 15.—**your own**, Acts xvii. 28.

τὰ καθ' ὑμᾶς, **the uttermost of your matter**, Acts xxiv. 22.

your[cc], John xiv. 26.

you . . [cc]**ye**, Acts xiv. 15.

ye[cc]([1]**you**, *ed.* 1611), Matt. vi. 8. Jn. iii. 7. Acts xvii. 22. xix. 36. Rom. i. 11[1]. vii. 4. xi. 25. xii. 2. xv. 13. 1 Cor. i. 7. x. 1, 13 (*om S*), 20. xiv. 5. 2 Cor. ii. 7. vi. 1. vii. 11 (-G°L *S*). xiii. 7. Eph. i. 18. iv. 17, 22. vi. 11. Phil. i. 7. 10, 12. Col. i. 10 (-GL*S*). ii. 1. iv. 6[1]. 1 Thes. i. 7. ii. 12. iv. 1, 3. 2 Thes. i. 5. ii. 2. iii. 6. Jas. ii. 7. iv. 2, 15. 2 Pet. i. 15[1]. iii. 11. Jude 5 (-G″LT).

Not rendered, 2 Pet. iii. 8.

Add, for *ἡμᾶς*, Rom. xv. 7, GLT*S*. xvi. 6, G″L*S*. 1 Cor. vii. 15, T*S*. Eph. v. 2, T*S*. 1 Thes. ii. 15, St. iv. 8, G″LT*S*. 1 Pet. iii. 18, T. 21, LT*S*. v. 10, G′LT*S*. 2 Pet. iii. 9, G″ LT*S*. — Matt. x. 23(*ap*). Luke vi. 28, for *ὑμῖν*, GLTr*S*. John xv. 21, *see ὑμῖν*. Col. ii. 13 (. . **hath he q.**), G′LT*S*. 1 Pet. ii. 11 (**you**), L.

ὑμέτερος.

your, John vii. 6. viii. 17. Acts xxvii. 34. Rom. xi. 31. 1 Cor. xv. 31 (*ἡμέτερος* StC[m]G′; *marg.* **our**). 2 Cor. viii. 8. Gal. vi. 13.

yours, Luke vi. 20. John xv. 20.

τὸ ὑμέτερον, **that which is your own**, Luke xvi. 12.

Add 1 Cor. xvi. 17, for *ὑμῶν*, LT.

ὑμνέω.

sing an hymn (*marg.* **psalm**), Matt. xxvi. 30[p]. Mark xiv. 26[p].

sing praise (praises[1]) unto, Acts xvi. 25[1]. Heb. ii. 12.

ὕμνος.

hymn, Eph. v. 19. Col. iii. 16.

ὑπάγω.

go away, John vi. 67. xii. 11. xiv. 28.

go one's way, Matt. v. 24. viii. 4, 13. xx. 14. xxvii. 65. Mark i. 44. ii. 11. vii. 29. x. 21, 52. xi. 2. xvi. 7. Luke x. 3. John viii. 21. xvi. 5. xviii. 8. Rev. xvi. 1.

go, Matt. v. 41. viii. 32. ix. 6. xiii. 44. xviii. 15. xix. 21. xx. 4, 7. xxi. 28. xxvi. 18, 24. xxviii. 10. Mark v. 19, 34. vi. 31, 38. xiv. 13, 21. Luke viii. 42(*ap*). xii. 58. xvii. 14. xix. 30. John iii. 8. iv. 16. vi. 21. vii. 3, 33. viii. 14*t*, 21, 22. ix. 7, 11. xi. 8, 31, 44. xii. 35. xiii. 3, 33, 36*t*. xiv. 4, 5. xv. 16. xvi. 5, 10, 16(*ap*), 17. xxi. 3. 1 John ii. 11. Rev. x. 8. xiii. 10. xiv. 4. xvii. 8, 11.

depart, Mark vi. 33. Jas. ii. 16.

ὕπαγε, **get thee hence**, Matt. iv. 10. —**get thee**, Matt. xvi. 23. Mark viii. 33. Luke iv. 8(*ap*).

ὑπακοή.

obedience, Rom. i. 5. v. 19. vi. 16. xvi. 19, 26. 2 Cor. vii. 15. x. 5, 6. Phm. 21. Heb. v. 8. 1 Pet. i. 2.

obeying, 1 Pet. i. 22.

With εἰς, **to obey**, Rom. vi. 16. — **to make obedient**, Rom. xv. 18.

Gen., **obedient**, 1 Pet. i. 14.

ὑπακούω.

hearken (*marg.* **ask who was**[c] **there**), Acts xii. 13.

obey, Matt. viii. 27. Mark i. 27. iv. 41. Luke viii. 25. xvii. 6. Rom. vi. 12, 16, 17. x. 16. Eph. vi. 1. Phil. ii. 12. Col. iii. 20, 22. 2 Thes. i. 8. iii. 14. Heb. v. 9. xi. 8. 1 Pet. iii. 6.

be obedient to, Acts vi. 7. Eph. vi. 5.

ὕπανδρος.

which hath an husband, Rom. vii. 2.

ὑπαντάω.

to meet, Matt. viii. 28. Luke viii. 27. John xi. 30. xii. 18.

go and meet, John xi. 20.

Add, see ἀπαντάω.

ὑπάντησις.

With εἰς, **to meet**, John xii. 13.

Add Matt. viii. 34, for συνάντησις, xxv. 1, for ἀπάντησις, LTr*S*.

ὕπαρξις.

substance, Heb. x. 34.

goods, Acts ii. 45.

ὑπάρχω.

to be, Luke viii. 41. ix. 48. xi. 13. xvi. 14, 23. Acts ii. 30. iv. 34 (εἰμί L*S*), 34. v. 4. vii. 55. viii. 16. x. 12. xiv. 8 (*omS*). xvi. 3, 20, 37. xvii. 24[p], 27, 29[p]. xix. 36, 40. xxi. 20. xxii. 3. xxvii. 12[p], 34. xxviii. 7, 18. Rom. iv. 19. 1 Cor. vii. 26. xi. 7[p], 18. xii. 22. 2 Cor. viii. 17. xii. 16. Gal. i. 14. ii. 14. Phil. ii. 6. iii. 20. Jas. ii. 15. 2 Pet. i. 8[p](πάρειμι L). ii. 19. iii. 11.

after[cc], Acts xxvii. 21[p].

live, Luke vii. 25.

have[cc], Acts iii. 6. iv. 37.

Not rendered, Luke xxiii. 50. Acts iii. 2.

τὰ ὑπάρχοντα.

the things which one possesseth, Luke xii. 15. Acts iv. 32.

that one hath, Matt. xix. 21 (*with* σοῦ). Luke xii. 33 (*with* ὑμῶν), 44. xiv. 33.

substance, Luke viii. 3.

goods, Matt. xxiv. 47. xxv. 14. Luke xi. 21. xvi. 1. xix. 8. 1 Cor. xiii. 3. Heb. x. 34.

ὑπείκω.

submit one's self, Heb. xiii. 17.

ὑπεναντίος.

contrary, Col. ii. 14.

adversary, Heb. x. 27.

ὑπέρ.

I. With the Genitive.

for, Matt. v. 44. Luke vi. 28 (περί T*S*). ix. 50. xxii. 19, 20. John vi. 51. x. 11, 15. xi. 4, 50, 51, 52. xv. 13. xviii. 14. Acts v. 41. viii. 24. xii. 5 (περί G″LT*S*). xv. 26. xxi. 13, 26. xxvi. 1 (περί G″LT*S*). Rom. i. 5, 8 (περί G′LT*S*). v. 6, 7*t*, 8. viii. 26 (–G°LT*S*), 27, 31, 32, 34. ix. 3. x. 1. xiv. 15. xv. 8, 9, 30. xvi. 4. 1 Cor. i. 13 (περί L). iv. 6. v. 7 (–G°°LT*S*). x. 30. xi. 24. xii. 25. xv. 3, 29*t*. 2 Cor. i. 6*t*, 11. v. 14 (15), 15*t*, 20, 21. vii. 12. viii. 16. ix. 14. xii. 8, 15, 19. xiii. 8. Gal. i. 4 (περί GLT*S*). ii. 20. iii. 13. Eph. i. 16. iii. 1, 13. v. 2, 20, 25. vi. 19, 20. Phil. i. 4, 7. Col. i. 7, 9, 24. iv. 12, 13. 1 Thes. v. 10. 2 Thes. i. 4, 5. 1 Tim. ii. 1, 2, 6. Tit. ii. 14. Heb. ii. 9. v. 1*t*, 3 (περί G′LT*S*). vi. 20. vii. 25, 27. ix. 7, 24. x. 12. xiii. 17. Jas. v. 16. 1 Pet. ii. 21. iii. 18. iv. 1 (–G°LT). 1 John iii. 16*t*.

on one's behalf, 2 Cor. i. 11. v. 12. viii. 24.

in the behalf of, Phil i. 29.

on one's part, Mark ix. 40.

for one's sake, John xiii. 37, 38. xvii. 19. Acts ix. 16. 2 Cor. xii. 10. Phil. i. 29. Col. i. 24. 3 John 7.

in one's stead, 2 Cor. v. 20. Phm. 13.

concerning, Rom. ix. 27.

of, 2 Cor. i. 7(6), 8 (περί G′L*S*). vii. 4, 14. viii. 23. ix. 2, 3. xii. 5*t*. Phil. ii. 13. iv. 10.

toward, 2 Cor. vii. 7.

by, 2 Thes. ii. 1.

Add, for περί, Mark xiv. 24, John i. 30, LTTr*S*. Col. i. 3, G′L. ii. 1, L*S*. 1 Thes. iii. 2, GLT*S*.

II. With the Accusative.
over, Eph. i. 22.
above, Matt. x. 24*t*. Luke vi. 40. Acts xxvi. 13. 1 Cor. iv. 6. x. 13. 2 Cor. i. 8. xii. 6. Gal. i. 14. Eph. iii. 20. Phil. ii. 9. Phm. 16.
beyond, 2 Cor. viii. 3 (παρά LT*S*).
more than, Matt. x. 37*t*. Phm. 21.
than, Luke xvi. 8. Heb. iv. 12.
to, 2 Cor. xii. 13.

III. As an Adverb.
more, 2 Cor. xi. 23 (ὑπερεγώ for ὑπὲρ ἐγώ L).
See also λίαν, περισσός.
ὑπερεκπερισσοῦ (-σῶς 1 Thes. v. 13, LT) for ὑπὲρ ἐκ περισσοῦ GLT.

ὑπεραίρω.
Mid., **exalt one's self**, 2 Thes. ii. 4. —**be exalted above measure**, 2 Cor. xii. 7, 7(*ap*).

ὑπέρακμος.
With εἰμί, **pass the flower of one's age**, 1 Cor. vii. 36.

ὑπεράνω.
far above, Eph. i. 21. iv. 10.
over, Heb. ix. 5.

ὑπεραυξάνω.
grow exceedingly, 2 Thes. i. 3.

ὑπερβαίνω.
go beyond, 1 Thes. iv. 6.

ὑπερβαλλόντως.
above measure, 2 Cor. xi. 23.

ὑπερβάλλω.
exceed, 2 Cor. ix. 14. Eph. i. 19. ii. 7.
excel, 2 Cor. iii. 10.
pass, Eph. iii. 19.

ὑπερβολή.
excellency, 2 Cor. iv. 7.
abundance, 2 Cor. xii. 7.
With κατά, **exceeding**, Rom. vii. 13. —**far more exceeding**, 2 Cor. iv. 17. —**beyond measure**, Gal. i. 13. —**out of measure**, 2 Cor. i. 8. —**more excellent**, 1 Cor. xii. 31.

ὑπερεγώ. See ὑπέρ, III.

ὑπερεῖδον.
wink at, Acts xvii. 30.

ὑπερέκεινα.
τὰ ὑ., **the regions beyond**, 2 Cor. x. 16.

ὑπερεκπερισσοῦ, -σῶς. See ὑπέρ.

ὑπερεκτείνω.
stretch beyond one's measure, 2 Cor. x. 14.

ὑπερεκχύνω.
Pass., **run over**, Luke vi. 38.

ὑπερεντυγχάνω.
make intercession for, Rom. viii. 26.

ὑπερέχω.
Part., **higher**, Rom. xiii. 1. —**supreme**, 1 Pet. ii. 13. —**excellency**, Phil. iii. 8. —**better**, Phil. ii. 3.
pass, Phil. iv. 7.

ὑπερηφανία.
pride, Mark vii. 22.

ὑπερήφανος.
proud, Luke i. 51. Rom. i. 30. 2 Tim. iii. 2. Jas. iv. 6. 1 Pet. v. 5.

ὑπερλίαν. See λίαν.

ὑπερνικάω.
be more than conqueror, Rom. viii. 37.

ὑπέρογκος.
Neut. plural, **great swelling words**, 2 Pet. ii. 18. Jude 16.

ὑπεροχή.
excellency, 1 Cor. ii. 1.
authority (*marg.* **eminent place**), 1 Tim. ii. 2.

ὑπερπερισσεύω.
abound much more, Rom. v. 20.
Pass., *with* τῇ χαρᾷ, **be exceeding joyful**, 2 Cor. vii. 4.

ὑπερπερισσῶς.
beyond measure, Mark vii. 37.

ὑπερπλεονάζω.
be exceeding abundant, 1 Tim. i. 14.

ὑπερυψόω.
exalt highly, Phil. ii. 9.

ὑπερφρονέω.
think highly, Rom. xii. 3.

ὑπερῷος.

Neut., **upper room**, Acts i. 13. — **upper chamber**, Acts ix. 37, 39, xx. 8.

ὑπέχω.

suffer, Jude 7.

ὑπήκοος.

obedient, 2 Cor. ii. 9. Phil. ii. 8. *With* γίνομαι, **obey**, Acts vii. 39.

ὑπηρετέω.

serve, Acts xiii. 36p.
minister, Acts xx. 34. xxiv. 23.

ὑπηρέτης.

servant, Matt. xxvi. 58. Mark xiv. 54, 65. John xviii. 36.
minister, Luke i. 2. iv. 20. Acts xiii. 5. xxvi. 16. 1 Cor. iv. 1.
officer, Matt. v. 25. John vii. 32, 45, 46. xviii. 3, 12, 18, 22. xix. 6. Acts v. 22, 26.

ὕπνος.

sleep, Matt. i. 24. Luke ix. 32. John xi. 13. Acts xx. 9*t*. Rom. xiii. 11.

ὑπό.

I. With the Genitive.

by, Matt. ii. 17 and iii. 3 (διά G′L TTr*S*). xxii. 31. xxvii. 35 (*ap*). Mark v. 4. xiii. 14(*ap*). Luke ii. 18, 26. iii. 19. v. 15(–G∞LTTr*S*). ix. 7(–G∞LᵇTTr*S*). xiii. 17. xvi. 22. xxi. 16. xxiii. 8. John viii. 9(*ap*). Acts iv. 36. x. 22. xiii. 4, 45. xv. 3, 40. xvi. 2. xxiv. 21 (ἐπί LT). xxv. 14. xxvii. 11.
Rom. iii. 21. xv. 24(ἀπό LT). 1 Cor. i. 11. 2 Cor. iii. 3. viii. 19, 20. Eph. ii. 11. v. 13. Phil. i. 28. Col. ii. 18. 2 Tim. ii. 26. Heb. ii. 3. iii. 4. 2 Pet. i. 21. iii. 2. Rev. ix. 18 (ἀπό GLTTr*S*).
with, Matt. viii. 24. xi. 7. xiv. 24. Luke vi. 18 (ἀπό GLTTr*S*). vii. 24. viii. 14. xxi. 20. Acts v. 16. xvii. 25. xxvii. 41. Jas. iii. 4. 2 Pet. ii. 7, 17. Rev. vi. 8.
from, Luke i. 26 (ἀπό TTr*S*). 2 Pet. i. 17.
among, Acts x. 22.

13*

of, Matt. i. 22. ii. 15, 16. iii. 6, 13, 14. iv. 1*t*. v. 13. vi. 2. x. 22. xi. 27. xiv. 8. xvii. 12. xix. 12. xx. 23. xxiii. 7. xxiv. 9. xxvii. 12. Mark i. 5, 9, 13. ii. 3. v. 26. xiii. 13. xvi. 11(*ap*). Luke ii. 21. iii. 7. iv. 2, 15. vii. 30. viii. 29, 43 (ἀπό LTTr). ix. 7, 8. x. 22. xiv. 8*t*. xvii. 20. xxi. 17, 24. John x. 14(*ap*). xiv. 21.
Acts ii. 24. iv. 11. x. 33 (ἀπό LT *S*), 38, 41, 42. xii. 5. xv. 4 (ἀπό T). xvi. 4, 6, 14. xvii. 13. xxi. 35. xxii. 11, 12. xxiii. 10, 27*t*. xxiv. 26. xxvi. 2, 6, 7.
Rom. xii. 21. xiii. 1. xv. 15. 1 Cor. ii. 12, 15. iv. 3*t*. vi. 12. vii. 25. viii. 3. x. 9, 10, 29. xi. 32. xiv. 24*t*. 2 Cor. i. 4, 16. ii. 6. iii. 2. v. 4. viii. 19. xi. 24. xii. 11. Gal. i. 11. iii. 17. iv. 9. v. 15. Eph. v. 12. Phil. iii. 12. 1 Thes. i. 4. ii. 4, 14*t*. 2 Thes. ii. 13. Heb. v. 4, 10. vii. 7. xi. 23. xii. 3, 5. Jas. i. 14. ii. 9. iii. 4, 6. 1 Pet. ii. 4. 3 John 12*t*. Jude 12, 17. Rev. vi. 13.
Not renderedcc, Acts viii. 6. xvii. 19. xx. 3. xxiii. 30(–LT*S*). 2 Cor. ii. 11. Heb. ix. 19.
Add, for ἀπό, Mark viii. 31, G″LT Tr*S*. Rom. xiii. 1, G″L*S*. For διά, Acts xii. 9, T. For ἐπί, Matt. xxviii. 14, LTr. For παρά, Acts xxii. 30, G″L*S*.

II. With the Accusative.

under, Matt. v. 15. viii. 8, 9*t*. xxiii. 37. Mark iv. 21*t*, 32. Luke vii. 6, 8*t*. xi. 33. xiii. 34. xvii. 24*t*. John i. 48(49). Acts ii. 5. iv. 12.
Rom. iii. 9, 13. vi. 14*t*, 15*t*. vii. 14. xvi. 20. 1 Cor. ix. 20*tr*. x. 1. xv. 25, 27. Gal. iii. 10, 22, 23, 25. iv. 2, 3, 4, 5, 21. v. 18. Eph. i. 22. Col. i. 23. 1 Tim. vi. 1. Jas. ii. 3. 1 Pet. v. 6. Jude 6.
into, Jas. v. 12 (*see* ὑπόκρισις).
in, Acts v. 21.
Add 1 Cor. ix. 20 (*ap*).

ὑποβάλλω.

suborn, Acts vi. 11.

ὑπογραμμός.
example, 1 Pet. ii. 21.

ὑπόδειγμα.
pattern, Heb. ix. 23.
ensample, 2 Pet. ii. 6.
example, John xiii. 15. Heb. iv. 11. viii. 5. Jas. v. 10.

ὑποδείκνυμι.
to show, Luke vi. 47. Acts ix. 16. xx. 35.
warn, Matt. iii. 7. Luke iii. 7.
forewarn, Luke xii. 5.

ὑποδέχομαι.
receive, Luke x. 38. xix. 6. Acts xvii. 7. Jas. ii. 25p.

ὑποδέω.
Mid., **bind on**, Acts xii. 8. —**be shod with**, Mark vi. 9. —**have . . shod**, Eph. vi. 15.

ὑπόδημα.
shoe, Matt. iii. 11. x. 10. Mark i. 7. Luke iii. 16. x. 4. xv. 22. xxii. 35. John i. 27. Acts vii. 33. xiii. 25.

ὑπόδικος.
guilty (*marg.* **subject to judgment**), Rom. iii. 19.

ὑποζύγιον.
ass, Matt. xxi. 5. 2 Pet. ii. 16.

ὑποζώννυμι.
undergird, Acts xxvii. 17.

ὑποκάτω.
under, Mark vi. 11. vii. 28. Luke viii. 16. John i. 50(51). Heb. ii. 8. Rev. v. 3, 13. vi. 9. xii. 1.
Add, for ὑποπόδιον, Matt. xxii. 44, G'LTTr*S*. Mark xii. 36, T.

ὑποκρίνομαι.
to feign, Luke xx. 20p.

ὑπόκρισις.
dissimulation, Gal. ii. 13.
hypocrisy, Matt. xxiii. 28. Mark xii. 15. Luke xii. 1. 1 Tim. iv. 2. 1 Pet. ii. 1.
Add Jas. v. 12, εἰς ὑπόκρισιν for ὑπὸ κρίσιν, St.

ὑποκριτής.
hypocrite, Matt. vi. 2, 5, 16. vii. 5. xv. 7. xvi. 3 (–G∞LTTr*S*c). xxii. 18. xxiii. 13, 14(*ap*), 15, 23, 25, 27, 29. xxiv. 51. Mark vii. 6. Luke vi. 42. xi. 44(*ap*). xii. 56. xiii. 15.

ὑπολαμβάνω.
receive, Acts i. 9.
answer, Luke x. 30.
suppose, Luke vii. 43. Acts ii. 15.
Add 3 John 8, for ἀπολαμβ., G'LT*S*.

ὑπόλειμμα, remnant, remainder. Rom. ix. 27, for κατάλειμμα, LT*S*.

ὑπολείπω.
to leave, Rom. xi. 3.

ὑπολήνιον.
wine-fat, Mark xii. 1.

ὑπολιμπάνω.
to leave, 1 Pet. ii. 21.

ὑπομένω.
abide, Acts xvii. 14.
tarry behind, Luke ii. 43.
endure, Matt. x. 22. xxiv. 13. Mark xiii. 13. 1 Cor. xiii. 7. 2 Tim. ii. 10. Heb. x. 32. xii. 2, 3, 7. Jas. i. 12. v. 11.
take patiently, 1 Pet. ii. 20*t*.
patient, Rom. xii. 12p.
suffer, 2 Tim. ii. 12.

ὑπομιμνήσκω.
put in remembrance (**of**[1]), 2 Tim. ii. 14[1]. 2 Pet. i. 12. Jude 5.
bring to remembrance, John xiv. 26.
put in mind, Tit. iii. 1.
remember, 3 John 10.
Mid., **remember**, Luke xxii. 61.

ὑπόμνησις.
remembrance, 2 Tim. i. 5. 2 Pet. i. 13. iii. 1.

ὑπομονή.
enduring, 2 Cor. i. 6.
patient waiting (*marg.* **patience**), 2 Thes. iii. 5.
patient continuance, Rom. ii. 7.
patience, Luke viii. 15. xxi. 19. Rom. v. 3, 4. viii. 25. xv. 4, 5.

2Cor. vi. 4. xii. 12. Col. i. 11. 1Thes. i. 3. 2 Thes. i. 4. 1 Tim. vi. 11. 2 Tim. iii. 10. Tit. ii. 2. Heb. x. 36. xii. 1. Jas. i. 3, 4. v. 11. 2 Pet. i. 6*t*. Rev. i. 9. ii. 2, 3, 19. iii. 10. xiii. 10. xiv. 12.

ὑπονοέω.

suppose, Acts xxv. 18.
deem, Acts xxvii. 27.
think, Acts xiii. 25.

ὑπόνοια.

surmising, 1 Tim. vi. 4.

ὑποπιάζω. See ὑπωπιάζω.

ὑποπλέω.

sail under, Acts xxvii. 4, 7.

ὑποπνέω.

blow softly, Acts xxvii. 13p.

ὑποπόδιον.

footstool, Matt. v. 35. xxii. 44(ὑποκάτω G'LTTr*S*). Mark xii. 36 (ὑποκάτω T). Luke xx. 43. Acts ii. 35. vii. 49. Heb. i. 13. x. 13. Jas. ii. 3.

ὑπόστασις.

substance (*marg.* **ground** *or* **confidence**), Heb. xi. 1.
person, Heb. i. 3.
confidence, 2Cor. xi. 17. Heb. iii. 14.
confidentcc, 2 Cor. ix. 4.

ὑποστέλλω.

withdraw, Gal. ii. 12.
Mid., **draw back**, Heb. x. 38.—**shun**, Acts xx. 27.—**keep back**, Acts xx. 20.

ὑποστολή.

Gen., **of them who draw back**, Heb. x. 39.

ὑποστρέφω.

turn back, Luke xvii. 15.
turn back again, Luke ii. 45.
return, Mark xiv. 40p(*ap*). Luke i. 56. ii. 39, 43. iv. 1, 14. vii. 10. viii. 39, 40. ix. 10p. xi. 24. xvii. 18. xix. 12. xxiii. 48, 56. xxiv. 9, 33, 52. Acts i. 12. viii. 25, 28. xii. 25. xiii. 13, 34. xx. 3. xxiii. 32. Heb. vii. 1.
return again, Luke x. 17. Acts xiv. 21. xxi. 6. Gal. i. 17.
return back again, Luke viii. 37.
come again, Acts xxii. 17p.
Add Luke ii. 20, for ἐπιστρέφω, G LTTr*S*. 2 Pet. ii. 21(*ap*).

ὑποστρωννύω, -ώννυμι.

spread, Luke xix. 36.

ὑποταγή.

subjection, 2 Cor. ix. 13. Gal. ii. 5. 1 Tim. ii. 11. iii. 4.

ὑποτάσσω, -ττω.

put under, 1 Cor. xv. 27*tr*, 28. Eph. i. 22. Heb. ii. 8.
put in subjection (unto[1]**, under**[2]**)**, Heb. ii. 5[1], 8, 8[2].
subject, Rom. viii. 20.
subdue unto, Phil. iii. 21.

Middle or Passive.

submit one's self to (unto), Rom. x. 3. 1 Cor. xvi. 16. Eph. v. 21, 22 (-G∞T). Col. iii. 18. Jas. iv. 7. 1 Pet. ii. 13. v. 5(-G°LT*S*).
(be) subject (to, unto), Luke ii. 51p. x. 17, 20. Rom. viii. 7. xiii. 1, 5. 1 Cor. xiv. 32. xv. 28. Eph. v. 24. Tit. iii. 1. 1 Pet. ii. 18. v. 5.
be in subjection to (unto), Heb. xii. 9, 1 Pet. iii. 1, 5.
be made subject to (unto), Rom. viii. 20. 1 Pet. iii. 22.
(be) obedient to (unto), Tit. ii. 5p, 9.
be under obedience, 1 Cor. xiv. 34.
be subdued unto, 1 Cor. xv. 28.

ὑποτίθημι.

lay down, Rom. xvi. 4.
Mid., **put in remembrance**, 1 Tim. iv. 6p.

ὑποτρέχω.

run under, Acts xxvii. 16.

ὑποτύπωσις.

pattern, 1 Tim. i. 16.
form, 2 Tim. i. 13.

ὑποφέρω.

to bear, 1 Cor. x. 13.
endure, 2 Tim. iii. 11. 1 Pet. ii. 19.

ὑποχωρέω.

withdraw one's self, Luke v. 16 (*with* εἰμί).

go aside, Luke ix. 10.

ὑπωπιάζω.

keep under, 1 Cor. ix. 27 (ὑπο. G'T).
weary, Luke xviii. 5.

ὗς.

sow, 2 Pet. ii. 22.

ὕσσωπος.

hyssop, John xix. 29. Heb. ix. 19.

ὑστερέω.

be behind, 2 Cor. xi. 5. xii. 11.
come short of, Heb. iv. 1.
lack, Matt. xix. 20. Mark x. 21. Luke xxii. 35.
part which lacked, 1 Cor. xii. 24p.
wantoc, John ii. 3p.
With ἀπό, **fail of** (*marg.* **fall from**), Heb. xii. 15.
Pass., **come behind,** 1 Cor. i. 7. — **come short of,** Rom. iii. 23. — **be destitute,** Heb. xi. 37. — **be in want,** Luke xv. 14. — **want,** 2 Cor. xi. 9 (8). — **suffer need,** Phil. iv. 12. — **be the worse,** 1 Cor. viii. 8 (*marg.* **have the less**; *ap*).

ὑστέρημα.

which is behind, Col. i. 24pl.
which is lacking, 1 Cor. xvi. 17. 2 Cor. xi. 9. 1 Thes. iii. 10pl.
lack, Phil. ii. 30.
want, 2 Cor. viii. 14(13), 14. ix. 12pl.
penury, Luke xxi. 4.

ὑστέρησις.

want, Mark xii. 44. Phil. iv. 11.

ὕστερος.

latter, 1 Tim. iv. 1.
Add Matt. xxi. 31, for πρῶτος, LTr.

ὕστερον, *adv.*

afterward (afterwards[1]**),** Matt. iv. 2. xxi. 29, 32. xxv. 11. Mark xvi. 14 (*ap*). Luke iv. 2(-GooLTTr*S*). John xiii. 36[1]. Heb. xii. 11.
at the last, Matt. xxvi. 60.
last, Matt. xxii. 27. Luke xx. 32.
last of all, Matt. xxi. 37.

ὑφαίνω, to weave.

Luke xii. 27 (*ap*).

ὑφαντός.

woven (*marg.* **wrought**), John xix. 23.

ὑψηλός.

high, Matt. iv. 8. xvii. 1. Mark ix. 2. Luke iv. 5(*ap*). Acts xiii. 17. Heb. vii. 26. Rev. xxi. 10, 12.
τὰ ὑψ., **high things,** Rom. xii. 16.
ἐν ὑψηλοῖς, **on high,** Heb. i. 3.
τὸ ὑψ., **that which is highly esteemed,** Luke xvi. 15.
Add **Rom.** xi. 20, *see* ὑψηλοφρονέω.

ὑψηλοφρονέω.

be high-minded, Rom. xi. 20 (ὑψηλὰ φρονέω Lm*S*). 1 Tim. vi. 17.

ὕψιστος.

most high (most High[1]**),** Mark v. 7. Luke viii. 28. Acts vii. 48[1]. xvi. 17. Heb. vii. 1.
Highest, Luke i. 32, 35, 76. vi. 35.
ἐν (τοῖς) ὑψίστοις, **in the highest,** Matt. xxi. 9. Mark xi. 10. Luke ii. 14. xix. 38.

ὕψος.

height, Eph. iii. 18. Rev. xxi. 16.
εἰς ὕψος, **on high,** Eph. iv. 8.
ἐξ ὕψους, **from on high,** Luke i. 78. xxiv. 49.
ἐν τῷ ὕψει αὐτοῦ, **in that he is exalted,** Jas. i. 9.

ὑψόω.

exalt, Matt. xi. 23. xxiii. 12*t*. Luke i. 52. x. 15. xiv. 11*t*. xviii. 14*t*. Acts ii. 33. v. 31. xiii. 17. 2 Cor. xi. 7. 1 Pet. v. 6.
lift up, John iii. 14, 14(-Lm). viii. 28. xii. 32, 34. Jas. iv. 10.

ὕψωμα.

high thing, 2 Cor. x. 5.
height, Rom. viii. 39.

φάγω.

eat, Matt. vi. 25, 31. xii. 4*t*. xiv. 16, 20. xv. 20, 32, 37. xxvi. 17, 26. Mark ii. 26*t*. iii. 20. v. 43. vi. 31, 36, 37*t*, 42, 44. viii. 1, 2, 8, 9(-GooT Trb*S*). xi. 14. xiv. 12, 14, 22(*om S*). Luke iv. 2. vi. 4*t*. vii. 36. ix.

13, 17. xii. 19, 22, 29. xiii. 26. xiv. 1, 15. xv. 23. xvii. 8*t*. xxii. 8, 11, 15, 16. xxiv. 43. John iv. 31, 32. vi. 5, 23, 26, 31*t*, 49, 50, 51, 52, 53, 58. xviii. 28. Acts ix. 9. x. 13, 14. xi. 7. xxiii. 12, 21.
Rom. xiv. 2, 21, 23. 1 Cor. viii. 8*t*, 13. ix. 4. x. 3, 7. xi. 20, 24(*om S*), 33. xv. 32. 2 Thes. iii. 8. Heb. xiii. 10. Jas. v. 3. Rev. ii. 7, 14, 17(*om S*), 20. x. 10. xvii. 16. xix. 18.
Inf., **eating**, 1 Cor. xi. 21. — **aught to eat**, John iv. 33. — **meat**, Matt. xxv. 35, 42. Luke viii. 55.

φαιλόνης, φελόνης GLT*S*.

cloak, 2 Tim. iv. 13.

φαίνω.

shine, John i. 5. v. 35. 2 Pet. i. 19. 1 John ii. 8. Rev. i. 16. viii. 12. xxi. 23.
Pass. or Mid., **shine**, Matt. xxiv. 27. Phil. ii. 15. Rev. xviii. 23. — **be seen**, Matt. vi. 5. ix. 33. — **appear**, Matt. i. 20. ii. 7, 13, 19. vi. 16, 18. xiii. 26. xxiii. 27, 28. xxiv. 30. Mark xvi. 9(*ap*). Luke ix. 8. Rom. vii. 13. 2 Cor. xiii. 7. Jas. iv. 14. 1 Pet. iv. 18. — φαινόμενα, **things which do appear**, Heb. xi. 3. — **seem**, Luke xxiv. 11. — **think**[cc], Mark xiv. 64.

φανερός.

manifest, Luke viii. 17. Acts iv. 16. Rom. i. 19. 1 Cor. iii. 13. xi. 19. xiv. 25. Gal. v. 19. Phil. i. 13. 1 John iii. 10.
ἐν τῷ φανερῷ, **openly**, Matt. vi. 4 (-G[oo]LTTr*S*), 6 (-LTTr*S*), 18 (*om S*). — **outwardly**, Rom. ii. 28. — **outward**, Rom. ii. 28.
With εἰμί, **appear**, 1 Tim. iv. 15.
With εἰς, **abroad**, Mark iv. 22. Luke viii. 17.
With γίνομαι, **be spread abroad**, Mark vi. 14.
known, Matt. xii. 16. Mark iii. 12. Acts vii. 13.

φανερόω.

make manifest, John i. 31. iii. 21. ix. 3. Rom. xvi. 26. 1 Cor. iv. 5. 2 Cor. ii. 14. iv. 10, 11. v. 11*t*. xi. 6. Eph. v. 13*t*. Col. i. 26. iv. 4. 2 Tim. i. 10. Heb. ix. 8. 1 John ii. 19. Rev. xv. 4.
manifest, Mark iv. 22. John xvii. 6. Rom. iii. 21. Tit. i. 3. 1 John i. 2*t*. iii. 5, 8. iv. 9.
manifest forth, John ii. 11.
declare manifestly, 2 Cor. iii. 3.
show, John vii. 4. xxi. 1. Rom. i. 19.
Pass. or Mid., **be manifest**, 1 Tim. iii. 16. 1 Pet. i. 20. — **show one's self**, John xxi. 1, 14. — **appear**, Mark xvi. 12(*ap*), 14(*ap*). 2 Cor. v. 10. vii. 12. Col. iii. 4*t*. Heb. ix. 26. 1 Pet. v. 4[p]. 1 John ii. 28. iii. 2*t*. Rev. iii. 18.

φανερῶς.

evidently, Acts x. 3.
openly, Mark i. 45. John vii. 10.

φανέρωσις.

manifestation, 1 Cor. xii. 7. 2 Cor. iv. 2.

φανός.

lantern, John xviii. 3.

φαντάζω.

Pass. part., **sight**, Heb. xii. 21.

φαντασία.

pomp, Acts xxv. 23.

φάντασμα.

spirit, Matt. xiv. 26. Mark vi. 49.

φάραγξ.

valley, Luke iii. 5.

φαρμακεία.

sorcery, Rev. ix. 21 (-κία T, φαρμακός *S*). xviii. 23 (-κία T).
witchcraft, Gal. v. 20.

φαρμακεύς.

sorcerer, Rev. xxi. 8(*see* φαρμακός).

φαρμακός.

sorcerer, Rev. xxii. 15.
Add Rev. xxi. 8, for -κεύς, GLTTr*S*.

φάσις.

tidings, Acts xxi. 31.

φάσκω.

affirm, Acts xxv. 19.

say, Acts xxiv. 9. Rev. ii. 2(*ap*).
profess, Rom. i. 22.

φάτνη.

manger, Luke ii. 7, 12, 16.
stall, Luke xiii. 15.

φαῦλος.

evil, Jas. iii. 16.
evil, *subst.*, John iii. 20pl. v. 29pl.
Neut., evil thing, Tit. ii. 8.
Add, for κακός, Rom. ix. 11, G″L TS. 2 Cor. v. 10, G′TS.

φέγγος.

light, Matt. xxiv. 29. Mark xiii. 24. Luke xi. 33 (φῶς LTrS).

φείδομαι.

to spare, Acts xx. 29. Rom. viii. 32. xi. 21*t*. 1 Cor. vii. 28. 2 Cor. i. 23. xiii. 2. 2 Pet. ii. 4, 5.
forbear, 2 Cor. xii. 6.

φειδομένως.

sparingly, 2 Cor. ix. 6*t*.

φελόνης. See φαιλόνης.

φέρω.

to bear, Luke xxiii. 26. John ii. 8*t*. xv. 2*t*, 4, 8. Heb. xiii. 13.
endure, Rom. ix. 22. Heb. xii. 20.
uphold, Heb. i. 3.
carry, John xxi. 18.
move, 2 Pet. i. 21p.
bring, Matt. xiv. 11*t*, 18. xvii. 17. Mark i. 32. ii. 3. vi. 27, 28. vii. 32. viii. 22. ix. 17, 19, 20. xii. 15, 16. xv. 22. Luke v. 18. xv. 23. xxiv. 1. John iv. 33. xviii. 29. xix. 39. xxi. 10. Acts iv. 34, 37. v. 2, 16. xiv. 13. 2Tim. iv. 13. 2Pet. ii. 11. 2John 10. Rev. xxi. 24, 26.
reach, John xx. 27.
reach °hither, John xx. 27.
lead, Acts xii. 10.
lay, Acts xxv. 7(*ap*).
bring forth, Mark iv. 8. John xii. 24. xv. 2, 5, 16.
Pass., be to be brought, 1 Pet. i. 13. — come, 2 Pet. i. 17p, 18, 21. — be (*marg.* be brought in), Heb. ix. 16.— *In navigation*, let drive, Acts xxvii. 15. — be driven, Acts xxvii. 17.
Mid., go on, Heb. vi. 1. — rush, Acts ii. 2.
Add, for ἄγω, Mark xi. 2, G″TTr S. 7, G″TTr. For ἐπιφέρω, Acts xxv. 18, G″LTS. For προσφέρω, Luke xii. 11, T.

φεύγω.

flee, Matt. ii. 13. iii. 7. viii. 33. x. 23. xxiv. 16. xxvi. 56. Mark v. 14. xiii. 14. xiv. 50, 52. xvi. 8. Luke iii. 7. viii. 34. xxi. 21. John x. 5, 12, 13(*ap*). Acts vii. 29. xxvii. 30. 1 Cor. vi. 18. x. 14. 1 Tim. vi. 11. 2 Tim. ii. 22. Jas. iv. 7. Rev. ix. 6. xii. 6.
flee away, Rev. xvi. 20. xx. 11.
escape, Heb. xi. 34. xii. 25 (ἐκφεύγω LS). — can escape, Matt. xxiii. 33 (*with* ἀπό).
Add Matt. x. 23(*ap*).

φήμη.

fame, Matt. ix. 26. Luke iv. 14.

φημί.

say, Matt. iv. 7. viii. 8. xiii. 28, 29. xiv. 8. xvii. 26. xix. 21 (λέγω L). xxi. 27. xxv. 21, 23. xxvi. 34, 61. xxvi. 11, 23, 65. Mark xiv. 29. Luke vii. 40, 44. xxii. 58, 70. xxiii. 3. John i. 23. ix. 38. Acts ii. 38(-L TS). vii. 2. viii. 36. x. 28, 30, 31. xvi. 30, 37. xvii. 22. xix. 35. xxi. 37. xxii. 2(3), 27, 28. xxiii. 5, 17, 18, 35. xxv. 5, 22(-LTS), 22, 24. xxvi. 1, 24, 25, 28 (-G∞LTS), 32. 1 Cor. vi. 16(-Lb). vii. 29. x. 15, 19. xv. 50. 2 Cor. x. 10. Heb. viii. 5.
affirm, Rom. iii. 8.
Add, for ἀποκρίνομαι, Mark ix. 38, TTrS. For εἶπον, Matt. xxii. 37, G LTTrS. Mark ix. 12, G″TTrS. x. 20, TrS. 29, TS. xii. 24, TTrS. Luke xv. 17, TS. John xviii. 29, TTrS. For λέγω, Matt. xix. 18, LS.

φθάνω.

prevent, 1 Thes. iv. 15.
attain, Rom. ix. 31. — *Aorist*, attain already, Phil. iii. 16.
come, Matt. xii. 28. Luke xi. 20. 2 Cor. x. 14. 1 Thes. ii. 16.

φθαρτός.
corruptible, Rom. i. 23. 1Cor. ix. 25. xv. 53, 54. 1 Pet. i. 23. — *Neut. pl.*, corruptible things, 1 Pet. i. 18.

φθέγγομαι.
speak, Acts iv. 18. 2 Pet. ii. 16, 18p.

φθείρω.
to corrupt, 1 Cor. xv. 33. 2 Cor. vii. 2. xi. 3. Rev. xix. 2 (διαφθείρω G″).
Mid., corrupt one's self, Jude 10.
Pass., be corrupt, Eph. iv. 22.
destroy, 1 Cor. iii. 17.
defile (*marg.* destroy), 1 Cor. iii. 17.
Add 2 Pet. ii. 12, *see* καταφθείρω.

φθινοπωρινός.
whose fruit withereth, Jude 12.

φθόγγος.
sound, Rom. x. 18. 1 Cor. xiv. 7 (*marg.* tune).

φθονέω.
to envy, Gal. v. 26.

φθόνος.
envy, Matt. xxvii. 18. Mark xv. 10. Rom. i. 29. Phil. i. 15. 1 Tim. vi. 4. Tit. iii. 3. Jas. iv. 5 (*marg.*, *with* πρός, enviously). 1 Pet. ii. 1.
envying, Gal. v. 21.

φθορά.
corruption, Rom. viii. 21. 1 Cor. xv. 42, 50. Gal. vi. 8. 2 Pet. i. 4. ii. 12, 19.
With εἰς, to perish, Col. ii. 22. — to be destroyed, 2 Pet. ii. 12.

φιάλη.
vial, Rev. v. 8. xv. 7. xvi. 1, 2, 3, 4, 8, 10, 12, 17. xvii. 1. xxi. 9.

φιλάγαθος.
lover of good men (*marg.* things), Tit. i. 8.

φιλαδελφία.
brotherly love, Rom. xii. 10 (*marg.* love of the brethren). 1 Thes. iv. 9. Heb. xiii. 1.
love of the brethren, 1 Pet. i. 22.
brotherly kindness, 2 Pet. i. 7*t*.

φιλάδελφος.
Plural, with εἰμί *understood*, love as brethren, 1 Pet. iii. 8 (*marg.* loving to the brethren).

φίλανδρος.
With εἰμί, love one's husband, Tit. ii. 4.

φιλανθρωπία.
love (*marg.* pity) toward man, Tit. iii. 4. — kindness, Acts xxviii. 2.

φιλανθρώπως.
courteously, Acts xxvii. 3.

φιλαργυρία.
love of money, 1 Tim. vi. 10.

φιλάργυρος.
covetous, Luke xvi. 14. 2 Tim. iii. 2.

φίλαυτος.
lover of one's own self, 2 Tim. iii. 2.

φιλέω.
to love, Matt. vi. 5. x. 37*t*. xxiii. 6. Luke xx. 46. John v. 20 (ἀγαπάω Lm). xi. 3, 36. xii. 25. xv. 19. xvi. 27*t*. xx. 2. xxi. 15, 16, 17*tr*. 1 Cor. xvi. 22. Tit. iii. 15. Rev. iii. 19. xxii. 15.
kiss, Matt. xxvi. 48. Mark xiv. 44. Luke xxii. 47.

φίλη.
friend, *fem.*, Luke xv. 9.

φιλήδονος.
lover of pleasures, 2 Tim. iii. 4.

φίλημα.
kiss, Luke vii. 45. xxii. 48. Rom. xvi. 16. 1 Cor. xvi. 20. 2 Cor. xiii. 12. 1 Thes. v. 26. 1 Pet. v. 14.

φιλία.
friendship, Jas. iv. 4.

φιλόθεος.
lover of God, 2 Tim. iii. 4.

φιλονεικία.
strife, Luke xxii. 24.

φιλόνεικος.
contentious, 1 Cor. xi. 16.

φιλοξενία.
hospitality, Rom. xii. 13.
to entertain strangers, Heb. xiii. 2.

φιλόξενος.
lover of hospitality, Tit. i. 8.
given to hospitality, 1 Tim. iii. 2.
With εἰμί understood, **use hospitality**, 1 Pet. iv. 9.

φιλοπρωτεύω.
love to have the pre-eminence, 3 John 9.

φίλος.
friend, Matt. xi. 19. Luke vii. 6, 34. xi. 5*t*, 6, 8. xii. 4. xiv. 10, 12. xv. 6, 9, 29. xvi. 9. xxi. 16. xxiii. 12. John iii. 29. xi. 11. xv. 13, 14, 15. xix. 12. Acts x. 24. xix. 31. xxvii. 3. Jas. ii. 23. iv. 4. 3 John 14(15)*t*.
Add Matt. v. 47, for ἀδελφός, G′.

φιλοσοφία.
philosophy, Col. ii. 8.

φιλόσοφος.
philosopher, Acts xvii. 18.

φιλόστοργος.
kindly affectioned, Rom. xii. 10.

φιλότεκνος.
With εἰμί, **love one's children**, Tit. ii. 4.

φιλοτιμέομαι.
strive, Rom. xv. 20.
study, 1 Thes. iv. 11.
labor (*marg.* **endeavor**), 2 Cor. v. 9.

φιλοφρόνως.
courteously, Acts xxviii. 7.

φιλόφρων.
courteous, 1 Pet. iii. 8.

φιμόω.
to muzzle, 1 Cor. ix. 9 (κημόω T). 1 Tim. v. 18.
put to silence, Matt. xxii. 34. 1 Pet. ii. 15.
Pass., **be speechless**, Matt. xxii. 12. — **hold one's peace**, Mark i. 25. Luke iv. 35. — **be still**, Mark iv. 39.

φλογίζω.
set on fire, Jas. iii. 6*t*.

φλόξ.
flame, Luke xvi. 24. Acts vii. 30. Heb. i. 7. Rev. i. 14. ii. 18. xix. 12.
Gen., **flaming**, 2 Thes. i. 8.

φλυαρέω.
prate against, 3 John 10.

φλύαρος.
tattler, 1 Tim. v. 13.

φοβέω.
Middle and Passive,
be afraid (of[1]**)**, Matt. ii. 22. xiv. 27, 30. xvii. 6, 7. xxv. 25. xxviii. 10. Mark v. 15, 36. vi. 50. ix. 32. x. 32. xvi. 8. Luke ii. 9. viii. 25, 35. xii. 4. John vi. 19, 20. xix. 8. Acts ix. 26[1]. xviii. 9. xxii. 29. Rom. xiii. 3[1], 4. Gal. iv. 11[1]. Heb. xi. 23[1]. 1 Pet. iii. 6, 14[1].
fear, Matt. i. 20. x. 26, 28 (*with* ἀπό), 28, 31. xiv. 5. xxi. 26, 46. xxvii. 54. xxviii. 5. Mark iv. 41. v. 33. vi. 20. xi. 18, 32. xii. 12. Luke i. 13, 30, 50. ii. 10. v. 10. viii. 50. ix. 34, 45. xii. 5*tr*, 7, 32. xviii. 2, 4. xix. 21. xx. 19. xxii. 2. xxiii. 40. John ix. 22. xii. 15. Acts v. 26. x. 2, 22, 35. xiii. 16, 26. xvi. 38. xxvii. 17, 24, 29. Rom. xi. 20. 2 Cor. xi. 3. xii. 20. Gal. ii. 12. Col. iii. 22. Heb. iv. 1. xi. 27. xiii. 6. 1 Pet. ii. 17. 1 John iv. 18. Rev. i. 17. ii. 10. xi. 18. xiv. 7. xv. 4. xix. 5.
reverence, Eph. v. 33.
Add Matt. ix. 8, for θαυμάζω, G″ LTTr*S*. Luke xxiv. 36(*ap*). Acts xxiii. 10, for εὐλαβέομαι, G′L*S*.

φοβερός.
fearful, Heb. x. 27.
Neut., **fearful thing**, Heb. x. 31.
terrible, Heb. xii. 21.

φόβητρον, -θρον LTTr.
fearful sight, Luke xxi. 11.

φόβος.
fear, Matt. xiv. 26. xxviii. 4, 8. Luke i. 12, 65. v. 26. vii. 16. viii. 37. xxi. 26. John vii. 13. xix. 38. xx. 19. Acts ii. 43. v. 5, 11. ix. 31. xix. 17. Rom. iii. 18. viii. 15. xiii. 7*t*. 1 Cor. ii. 3. 2 Cor. vii. 1, 5, 11, 15. Eph. v. 21. vi. 5. Phil. ii. 12. Heb. ii. 15. 1 Pet. i. 17. ii. 18. iii.

2, 15 (*marg.* **reverence**). 1 John iv. 18*tr.* Jude 23. Rev. xi. 11. xviii. 10, 15.
With ἔχω, **to fear**, 1 Tim. v. 20.
terror, Rom. xiii. 3. 2 Cor. v. 11. 1 Pet. iii. 14.
See also μέγας.

φοίνιξ.

palm-tree, John xii. 13.
palm, Rev. vii. 9.

φονεύς.

murderer, Matt. xxii. 7. Acts iii. 14. vii. 52. xxviii. 4. 1 Pet. iv. 15. Rev. xxi. 8. xxii. 15.

φονεύω.

do murder, Matt. xix. 18.
kill, Matt. v. 21*t.* xxiii. 31. Mark x. 19(–G°). Luke xviii. 20. Rom. xiii. 9. Jas. ii. 11*t.* iv. 2. v. 6.
slay, Matt. xxiii. 35.

φόνος.

murder, Matt. xv. 19. Mark vii. 21. xv. 7. Luke xxiii. 19, 25. Rom. i. 29. Gal. v. 21(–L^b^T*S*). Rev. ix. 21.
slaughter, Acts ix. 1.
See also ἀποθνήσκω.

φορέω.

to wear, Matt. xi. 8. John xix. 5. Jas. ii. 3.
bear, Rom. xiii. 4. 1 Cor. xv. 49*t.*

φόρος.

tribute, Luke xx. 22. xxiii. 2. Rom. xiii. 6, 7*t.*

φορτίζω.

to lade, Luke xi. 46.
Pass., **heavy laden**, Matt. xi. 28^p^.

φορτίον.

burden, Matt. xi. 30. xxiii. 4. Luke xi. 46*t.* Gal. vi. 5. [LT*S*.
Add Acts xxvii. 10, for φόρτος, G

φόρτος.

lading, Acts xxvii. 10 (*see* φορτίον).

φραγέλλιον.

scourge, John ii. 15.

φραγελλόω.

to scourge, Matt. xxvii. 26^p^. Mark xv. 15^p^.

φραγμός.

hedge, Mark xii. 1. Luke xiv. 23.
With περιτίθημι, **hedge round about**, Matt. xxi. 33.
partition, Eph. ii. 14.

φράζω.

declare, Matt. xiii. 36 (διασαφέω L Tr*S*). xv. 15.

φράσσω, -ττω.

to stop, Rom. iii. 19. Heb. xi. 33.
With εἰς, **stop of**^∞^, 2 Cor. xi. 10 (σφραγίζω St).

φρέαρ.

well, John iv. 11, 12. [2*t.*
pit, Luke xiv. 5. Rev. ix. 1, 2(*ap*),

φρεναπατάω.

deceive, Gal. vi. 3.

φρεναπάτης.

deceiver, Tit. i. 10.

φρήν.

Pl., **understanding**, 1 Cor. xiv. 20*t.*

φρίσσω, -ττω.

tremble, Jas. ii. 19.

φρονέω.

think, Acts xxviii. 22. Rom. xii. 3*t.* 1 Cor. iv. 6(–LT*S*). xiii. 11. Phil. i. 7.
be minded, Gal. v. 10. Phil. iii. 15*t.*
With τὸ αὐτό, **be of the same mind**, Rom. xii. 16. Phil. iv. 2.—**be of one mind**, 2 Cor. xiii. 11.—**be like-minded**, Rom. xv. 5. Phil. ii. 2.
With τὸ ἕν, **be of one mind**, Phil. ii. 2.
Pres. imper. pass., with τοῦτο, **let this mind be**, Phil. ii. 5.
mind, Rom. viii. 5. xii. 16. Phil. iii. 16(*ap*), 19.
savor, Matt. xvi. 23. Mark viii. 33.
regard, Rom. xiv. 6 (*marg.* **observe**), 6*t*(*ap*).—**set one's affection** (*marg.* **mind**) **on**, Col. iii. 2.
be careful, Phil. iv. 10.
Inf., **care**, Phil. iv. 10.
Add Rom. xi. 20, *see* ὑψηλοφρονέω.

φρόνημα.

mind, Rom. viii. 7 (*Gr.* minding), 27.

to be minded (*Gr.* minding), Rom. viii. 6*t*.

φρόνησις.

prudence, Eph. i. 8.
wisdom, Luke i. 17.

φρόνιμος.

wise, Matt. vii. 24. x. 16. xxiv. 45. xxv. 2, 4, 8, 9. Luke xii. 42. xvi. 8. Rom. xi. 25. xii. 16. 1 Cor. iv. 10. 2 Cor. xi. 19.
wise man, 1 Cor. x. 15.

φρονίμως.

wisely, Luke xvi. 8.

φροντίζω.

be careful, Tit. iii. 8.

φρουρέω.

keep, Gal. iii. 23. Phil. iv. 7. 1 Pet. i. 5.
keep with a garrison, 2 Cor. xi. 32.

φρυάσσω, -ττω.

to rage, Acts iv. 25.

φρύγανον.

stick, Acts xxviii. 3.

φυγή.

flight, Matt. xxiv. 20. Mark xiii. 18 (-G∞LTTr*S*).

φυλακή.

watch, Matt. xiv. 25. xxiv. 43. Mark vi. 48. Luke ii. 8pl (*marg.* **night watches**). xii. 38(-Tr*S*), 38.
ward, Acts xii. 10.
imprisonment, 2 Cor. vi. 5. Heb. xi. 36.
prison, Matt. v. 25. xiv. 3, 10. xviii. 30. xxv. 36, 39, 43, 44. Mark vi. 17, 27(28). Luke iii. 20. xii. 58. xxi. 12. xxii. 33. xxiii. 19, 25. John iii. 24. Acts v. 19, 22, 25. viii. 3. xii. 4, 5, 6, 17. xvi. 23, 24, 27, 37, 40. xxii. 4. xxvi. 10. 2 Cor. xi. 23. 1 Pet. iii. 19. Rev. ii. 10. xx. 7.
hold, Rev. xviii. 2.
cage, Rev. xviii. 2.

φυλακίζω.

imprison, Acts xxii. 19.

φυλακτήριον.

phylactery, Matt. xxiii. 5.

φύλαξ.

keeper, Acts v. 23. xii. 6, 19.

φυλάσσω, -ττω.

keep, Luke ii. 8. viii. 29cc. xi. 21, 28. John xii. 25. xvii. 12. Acts vii. 53. xii. 4. xvi. 4. xxi. 24. xxii. 20. xxiii. 35. xxviii. 16. Rom. ii. 26. Gal. vi. 13. 2 Thes. iii. 3. 1 Tim. vi. 20. 2 Tim. i. 12, 14. 1 John v. 21. Jude 24.
Mid., **keep one's self**, Acts xxi. 25 —**keep**, Matt. xix. 20. Luke xviii. 21. —**beware (of**[1]**)**, Luke xii. 15. 2 Tim. iv. 15[1]. 2 Pet. iii. 17.—**observe**, Mark x. 20.
observe, 1 Tim. v. 21.
save, 2 Pet. ii. 5. [LTTr*S*.
Add John xii. 47, for πιστεύω, G″

φυλή.

tribe, Matt. xix. 28. xxiv. 30. Luke ii. 36. xxii. 30. Acts xiii. 21. Rom. xi. 1. Phil. iii. 5. Heb. vii. 13, 14. Jas. i. 1. Rev. v. 5. vii. 4, 5*tr*, 6*tr*, 7*tr*, 8*tr*. xxi. 12.
kindred, Rev. i. 7. v. 9. vii. 9. xi. 9. xiii. 7. xiv. 6.

φύλλον.

leaf, Matt. xxi. 19. xxiv. 32. Mark xi. 13*t*. xiii. 28. Rev. xxii. 2.

φύραμα.

lump, Rom. ix. 21. xi. 16. 1 Cor. v. 6, 7. Gal. v. 9.

φυσικός.

natural, Rom. i. 26, 27. 2 Pet. ii. 12.

φυσικῶς.

naturally, Jude 10.

φυσιόω.

puff up, 1 Cor. viii. 1.—*Pass. or Mid.*, **be puffed up**, 1 Cor. iv. 6, 18, 19. v. 2. xiii. 4. Col. ii. 18.

φύσις.

nature, Rom. i. 26. ii. 14, 27. xi. 24*t*. 1 Cor. xi. 14. Gal. ii. 15. iv. 8. Eph. ii. 3. 2 Pet. i. 4.
With κατά, **natural**, Rom. xi. 21, 24.
kind (*Gr.* nature), Jas. iii. 7.
See also ἀνθρώπινος.

φυσίωσις.

swelling, 2 Cor. xii. 20.

φυτεία.

plant, Matt. xv. 13.

φυτεύω.

to plant, Matt. xv. 13. xxi. 33. Mark xii. 1. Luke xiii. 6. xvii. 6, 28. xx. 9. 1 Cor. iii. 6, 7, 8. ix. 7.

φύω.

spring up, Luke viii. 6p, 8. Heb. xii. 15.

φωλεός.

hole, Matt. viii. 20. Luke ix. 58.

φωνέω.

to crow, Matt. xxvi. 34, 74, 75. Mark xiv. 30, 68(-LbS), 72t. Luke xxii. 34, 60, 61. John xiii. 38. xviii. 27.

cry, Luke viii. 8. xvi. 24. xxiii. 46p. Acts xvi. 28. Rev. xiv. 18.

call (for[1]), Matt. xx. 32. xxvii. 47[1]. Mark iii. 31 (*καλέω* LTTr*S*, -G°). ix. 35. x. 49*tr*. xv. 35. Luke viii. 54. xiv. 12. xvi. 2. xix. 15. John i. 48(49). ii. 9. iv. 16. ix. 18, 24. xi. 28, 28[1]. xii. 17. xiii. 13. xviii. 33. Acts ix. 41p. x. 7, 18.

Add Mark i. 26, for *κράζω*, TTr*S*. John x. 3, for *καλέω*, G″LTTr*S*.

φωνή.

sound, Matt. xxiv. 31 (*marg.* **voice**). John iii. 8. 1 Cor. xiv. 7, 8. Rev. i. 15. ix. 9*t*. xviii. 22.

voice, Matt. ii. 18. iii. 3, 17. xii. 19. xvii. 5. xxvii. 46, 50. Mark i. 3, 11, 26. v. 7. ix. 7. xv. 34, 37. Luke i. 42 (*κραυγή* TTr), 44. iii. 4, 22. iv. 33. viii. 28. ix. 35, 36. xi. 27. xvii. 15. xix. 37. xxiii. 23*t*, 46. John i. 23. iii. 29. v. 25, 28, 37. x. 3, 4, 5, 16, 27. xi. 43. xii. 28, 30. xviii. 37. Acts ii. 14. iv. 24. vii. 31, 57, 60. viii. 7. ix. 4, 7. x. 13, 15. xi. 7, 9. xii. 14, 22. xiii. 27. xiv. 10. xvi. 28. xxii. 7, 9, 14. xxiv. 21. xxvi. 14, 24.

1 Cor. xiv. 10, 11. Gal. iv. 20. 1 Thes. iv. 16. Heb. iii. 7, 15. iv. 7. xii. 19, 26. 2 Pet. i. 17, 18. ii. 16. Rev. i. 10, 12, 15. iii. 20. iv. 1, 5. v. 2, 11, 12. vi. 6, 7(-GT), 10. vii. 2, 10. viii. 5, 13*t*. ix. 13. x. 3*t*, 4 (*om S*), 4, 7, 8. xi. 12, 15, 19. xii. 10. xiv. 2*f*, 7, 9, 13, 15. xvi. 1, 17, 18. xviii. 2(*ap*), 4, 22, 23. xix. 1, 5, 6*tr*, 17. xxi. 3.

voices, Luke xvii. 13. Acts xiv. 11. xxii. 22.

φωνὴ μία ἐγένετο ἐκ πάντων, **all with one voice cried out,** Acts xix. 34.

noise, Rev. vi. 1.

With γίνομαι, **be noised abroad** (*Gr.* voice be made), Acts ii. 6p.

Add Rev. xiv. 18, for *κραυγή*, LTr*S*.

φῶς.

light, Matt. iv. 16*t*. v. 14, 16. vi. 23. x. 27. xvii. 2. Luke ii. 32. viii. 16. xi. 35. xii. 3. xvi. 8. John i. 4, 5. iii. 19*t*, 20*t*, 21. v. 35. viii. 12*t*. ix. 5. xi. 9, 10. xii. 35*t*, 36*tr*, 46. Acts ix. 3. xii. 7. xiii. 47. xvi. 29. xxii. 6, 9, 11. xxvi. 13, 18, 23. Rom. ii. 19. xiii. 12. 2 Cor. iv. 6. vi. 14. xi. 14. Eph. v. 8*t*, 13*t*. Col. i. 12. 1 Thes. v. 5. 1 Tim. vi. 16. Jas. i. 17. 1 Pet. ii. 9. 1 John i. 5, 7*t*. ii. 8, 9, 10. Rev. xviii. 23. xxi. 24. xxii. 5.

Said of Christ, **Light,** John i. 7, 8*t*, 9.

fire, Mark xiv. 54. Luke xxii. 56.

Add Matt. xvii. 5, *gen.* for *φωτεινός*, G. Luke xi. 33, for *φέγγος*, LTr*S*. Eph. v. 9, for *πνεῦμα*, GLT*S*. Rev. xxii. 5 (. . [of] candle), G′LTrb*S*.

φωστήρ.

light, Phil. ii. 15. Rev. xxi. 11.

φωσφόρος.

day-star, 2 Pet. i. 19.

φωτεινός.

full of light, Matt. vi. 22. Luke xi. 34, 36*t*.

bright, Matt. xvii. 5 (G″, *see φῶς*).

φωτίζω.

give light, Luke xi. 36. Rev. xxii. 5.

light (lighten[1], enlighten[2]), John i. 9. Eph. i. 18[2]. Heb. vi. 4[2]. Rev. xviii. 1[1]. xxi. 23[1].

illuminate, Heb. x. 32p.
bring to light, 1 Cor. iv. 5. 2 Tim. i. 10.
make see, Eph. iii. 9.

φωτισμός.

πρὸς φ., to give **light**, 2 Cor. iv. 6.
light, 2 Cor. iv. 4.

χαίρω.

rejoice, Matt. ii. 10. v. 12. xviii. 13. Luke i. 14. vi. 23. x. 20*t*. xiii. 17. xv. 5. xix. 37. John iii. 29. iv. 36. xiv. 28. xvi. 20, 22. Acts v. 41. viii. 39. xv. 31. Rom. xii. 12, 15*t*. 1 Cor. vii. 30*t*. xiii. 6. 2 Cor. ii. 3. vi. 10. vii. 7, 9, 16. Phil. i. 18*t*. ii. 28. iii. 1. iv. 4*t*, 10. Col. i. 24. 1 Thes. v. 16. 1 Pet. iv. 13. 2 John 4. 3 John 3. Rev. xi. 10.
joy, 2 Cor. vii. 13. Phil. ii. 17, 18. Col. ii. 5. 1 Thes. iii. 9.
joyfully, Luke xix. 6p.
be glad, Mark xiv. 11. Luke xv. 32. xxii. 5. xxiii. 8. John viii. 56. xi. 15. xx. 20. Acts xi. 23. xiii. 48. Rom. xvi. 19. 1 Cor. xvi. 17. 2 Cor. xiii. 9. 1 Pet. iv. 13. Rev. xix. 7.
Imper., **hail!** Matt. xxvi. 49. xxvii. 29. Mark xv. 18. Luke i. 28. John xix. 3.—**all hail**, Matt. xxviii. 9. —**farewell**, 2 Cor. xiii. 11.
Inf., **greeting**, Jas. i. 1.—**send greeting**, Acts xv. 23. xxiii. 26.—**God speed**, 2 John 10, 11.

χάλαζα.

hail, Rev. viii. 7. xi. 19. xvi. 21*t*.

χαλάω.

let down, Mark ii. 4. Luke v. 4, 5. Acts xxvii. 30p. 2 Cor. xi. 33.
In navigation, **strike**, Acts xxvii. 17.
Not rendered, Acts ix. 25.

χαλεπός.

perilous, 2 Tim. iii. 1.
fierce, Matt. viii. 28.

χαλιναγωγέω.

to bridle, Jas. i. 26. iii. 2.

χαλινός.

bit, Jas. iii. 3.—**bridle**, Rev. xiv. 20.

χάλκεος, χαλκοῦς.

of brass, Rev. ix. 20.

χαλκεύς.

coppersmith, 2 Tim. iv. 14.

χαλκηδών.

chalcedony, Rev. xxi. 19 (καρχηδών G′).

χαλκίον.

brazen vessel, Mark vii. 4.

χαλκολίβανον.

fine brass, Rev. i. 15. ii. 18.

χαλκός.

brass, Matt. x. 9. 1 Cor. xiii. 1. Rev. xviii. 12.
money, Mark vi. 8. xii. 41.

χαμαί.

to the ground, John xviii. 6.
on the ground, John ix. 6.

χαρά.

joy, Matt. ii. 10. xiii. 20, 44. xxv. 21, 23. xxviii. 8. Luke i. 14. ii. 10. viii. 13. x. 17. xv. 7, 10. xxiv. 41, 52. John iii. 29. xv. 11*tr*. xvi. 20, 21, 22, 24. xvii. 13. Acts viii. 8. xiii. 52. xv. 3. xx. 24(-G∞LT*S*). Rom. xiv. 17. xv. 13, 32. 2 Cor. i. 24. ii. 3. vii. 13. viii. 2. Gal. v. 22. Phil. i. 4, 25. ii. 2. iv. 1. 1 Thes. i. 6. ii. 19, 20. iii. 9. 2 Tim. i. 4. Phm. 7 (χάρις StG″T). Heb. xii. 2. xiii. 17. Jas. i. 2, iv. 9. 1 Pet. i. 8. 1 John i. 4. 2 John 12. 3 John 4.
Gen., **joyous**, Heb. xii. 11.
joyfulness, Col. i. 11.
μετὰ χαρᾶς, **joyfully**, Heb. x. 34.
gladness, Mark iv. 16. Acts xii. 14. Phil. ii. 29.
Dat., **greatly**c, John iii. 29.
See also ὑπερπερισσεύω.

χάραγμα.

mark, Rev. xiii. 16, 17. xiv. 9, 11. xv. 2(*ap*). xvi. 2. xix. 20. xx. 4.
Dat., **graven**, Acts xvii. 29.

χαρακτήρ.

express image, Heb. i. 3.

χάραξ.

trench, Luke xix. 43.

χαρίζομαι.

give freely, Rom. viii. 32.
τὰ χαρισθέντα, **the things that are freely given,** 1 Cor. ii. 12.
give, Luke vii. 21. Acts xxvii. 24. Gal. iii. 18. Phil. i. 29. ii. 9. Phm. 22.
grant, Acts iii. 14.
deliver, Acts xxv. 11, 16.
forgive, Luke vii. 43. 2 Cor. ii. 7, 10*tr*. xii. 13. Eph. iv. 32*t*. Col. ii. 13. iii. 13*t*.
forgive frankly, Luke vii. 42.

χάρις.

grace, Luke ii. 40. John i. 14, 16*t*, 17. Acts iv. 33. xi. 23. xiii. 43. xiv. 3, 26. xv. 11, 40. xviii. 27. xx. 24, 32. Rom. i. 5, 7. iii. 24. iv. 4, 16. v. 2, 15*t*, 17, 20, 21. vi. 1, 14, 15. xi. 5, 6*tr*, 6(*ap*). xii. 3, 6. xv. 15. xvi. 20, 24(*ap*). 1 Cor. i. 3, 4. iii. 10. x. 30 (*marg.* **thanksgiving**). xv. 10*tr*. xvi. 23. 2 Cor. i. 2, 12. iv. 15. vi. 1. viii. 1, 6, 7, 9, 19. ix. 8, 14. xii. 9. xiii. 14(13).
Gal. i. 3, 6, 15. ii. 9, 21. v. 4. vi. 18. Eph. i. 2, 6, 7. ii. 5, 7, 8. iii. 2, 7, 8. iv. 7, 29. vi. 24. Phil. i. 2, 7. iv. 23. Col. i. 2, 6. iii. 16. iv. 6, 18. 1 Thes. i. 1. v. 28. 2 Thes. i. 2, 12. ii. 16. iii. 18. 1 Tim. i. 2, 14. vi. 21. 2 Tim. i. 2, 9. ii. 1. iv. 22 (*ap*). Tit. i. 4. ii. 11. iii. 7, 15. Phm. 3, 25. Heb. ii. 9. iv. 16*t*. x. 29. xii. 15, 28. xiii. 9, 25. Jas. iv. 6*t*. 1 Pet. i. 2, 10, 13. iii. 7. iv. 10. v. 5, 10, 12. 2 Pet. i. 2. iii. 18. 2 John 3. Jude 4. Rev. i. 4. xxii. 21.
Gen., **gracious,** Luke iv. 22.
favor, Luke i. 30. ii. 52. Acts ii. 47. vii. 10, 46. xxv. 3.
pleasure, Acts xxiv. 27. xxv. 9.
liberality (*Gr.* gift), 1 Cor. xvi. 3.
gift, 2 Cor. viii. 4.
benefit (*marg.* **grace**), 2 Cor. i. 15.
thanks (thank[1]**),** Luke vi. 32[1], 33[1], 34[1]. 1 Cor. xv. 57. 2 Cor. ii. 14. viii. 16. ix. 15.
With ἔχω, **to thank,** Luke xvii. 9. 1 Tim. i. 12. 2 Tim. i. 3.
χάρις τῷ Θεῷ, **God be thanked,** Rom. vi. 17.
thankworthy, 1 Pet. ii. 19.
acceptable (*marg.* **thank**), 1 Pet. ii. 20.
Add Acts vi. 8, for πίστις, GLTS. Rom. vii. 25, for εὐχαριστέω, G″LT S. Phm. 7, for χαρά, StG″T.

Accusative, χάριν,

for . . sake, Tit. i. 11.
τούτου χάριν, **for this cause,** Eph. iii. 1, 14. Tit. i. 5.
because of, Gal. iii. 19. Jude 16.
οὗ χάριν, **wherefore,** Luke vii. 47.
χάριν τίνος, **wherefore?** 1 John iii. 12.
See also λοιδορία.

χάρισμα.

free gift, Rom. v. 15, 16.
gift, Rom. i. 11. vi. 23. xi. 29. xii. 6. 1 Cor. i. 7. vii. 7. xii. 4, 9, 28, 30, 31. 2 Cor. i. 11. 1 Tim. iv. 14. 2 Tim. i. 6. 1 Pet. iv. 10.

χαριτόω.

Pass. part., **highly favored** (*marg.* **graciously accepted** *or* **much graced**), Luke i. 28.
make accepted, Eph. i. 6.

χάρτης.

paper, 2 John 12.

χάσμα.

gulf, Luke xvi. 26.

χεῖλος.

lip, Matt. xv. 8. Mark vii. 6. Rom. iii. 13. 1 Cor. xiv. 21. Heb. xiii. 15. 1 Pet. iii. 10.
shore, Heb. xi. 12.

χειμάζω.

Pass., **be tossed with a tempest,** Acts xxvii. 18.

χείμαρρος.

brook, John xviii. 1.

χειμών.

tempest, Acts xxvii. 20.
foul weather, Matt. xvi. 3.
winter, Matt. xxiv. 20. Mark xiii. 18. John x. 22. 2 Tim. iv. 21.

χείρ.

hand, Matt. iii. 12. iv. 6. v. 30.

viii. 3, 15. ix. 18, 25. xii. 10, 13, 49. xiv. 31. xv. 2, 20. xvii. 22. xviii. 8*t*. xix. 13, 15. xxii. 13. xxvi. 23, 45, 50, 51. xxvii. 24. Mark i. 31, 41. iii. 1, 3, 5*t*. v. 23, 41. vi. 2, 5. vii. 2, 3, 5, 32. viii. 23*t*, 25. ix. 27, 31, 43*t*. x. 16. xiv. 41, 46. xvi. 18(*ap*). Luke i. 66, 71, 74. iii. 17. iv. 11, 40. v. 13. vi. 1, 6, 8, 10*t*. viii. 54. ix. 44, 62. xiii. 13. xv. 22. xx. 19. xxi. 12. xxii. 21, 53. xxiii. 46. xxiv. 7, 39, 40(*ap*), 50.

John iii. 35. vii. 30, 44. x. 28, 29, 39. xi. 44. xiii. 3, 9. xx. 20, 25*t*, 27*t*. xxi. 18. Acts ii. 23. iii. 7. iv. 3, 28, 30. v. 12, 18. vi. 6. vii. 25, 35, 41, 50. viii. 17, 18, 19. ix. 12, 17, 41. xi. 21, 30. xii. 1 (*see* ἐπιβάλλω), 7, 11, 17. xiii. 3, 11, 16. xiv. 3. xvii. 25. xix. 6, 11, 26, 33. xx. 34. xxi. 11*t*, 27, 40. xxiii. 19. xxiv. 7(*ap*). xxvi. 1. xxviii. 3, 4, 8, 17.

Rom. x. 21. 1 Cor. iv. 12. xii. 15, 21. xvi. 21. 2 Cor. xi. 33. Gal. iii. 19. vi. 11. Eph. iv. 28. Col. iv. 18. 1 Thes. iv. 11. 2 Thes. iii. 17. 1 Tim. ii. 8. iv. 14. v. 22. 2 Tim. i. 6. Phm. 19. Heb. i. 10. ii. 7(*ap*). vi. 2. viii. 9. x. 31. xii. 12. Jas. iv. 8. 1 Pet. v. 6. 1 John i. 1. Rev. i. 16, 17(*om S*). vi. 5. vii. 9. viii. 4. ix. 20. x. 2, 5, 8, 10. xiii. 16. xiv. 9, 14. xvii. 4. xix. 2. xx. 1, 4.

Not rendered, Acts xv. 23.

Add Mark xiv. 20 (dippeth . .), L. xvi. 18(καὶ ἐν ταῖς χερσὶν they[1st]), Tr.

χειραγωγέω.

lead by the hand, Acts ix. 8. xxii. 11.

χειραγωγός.

Pl., **some to lead by the hand**, Acts xiii. 11.

χειρόγραφον.

handwriting, Col. ii. 14.

χειροποίητος.

made with (by[1]) hands, Acts vii. 48. xvii. 24. Eph. ii. 11[1]. Heb. ix. 11, 24.

With art., **that is made with hands**, Mark xiv. 58.

χειροτονέω.

choose, 2 Cor. viii. 19.

ordain, Acts xiv. 23[p].

χείρων, χεῖρον.

worse, Matt. ix. 16. xii. 45. xxvii. 64. Mark ii. 21. Luke xi. 26. 1 Tim. v. 8. 2 Pet. ii. 20.

εἰς τὸ χεῖρον, **worse**, Mark v. 26.

ἐπὶ τὸ χεῖρον, **worse and worse**, 2 Tim. iii. 13.

χεῖρόν τι, **a worse thing**, John v. 14.

sorer, Heb. x. 29.

χήρα.

widow, Matt. xxiii. 14(*ap*). Mark xii. 40, 42, 43. Luke ii. 37. iv. 25. vii. 12. xviii. 3, 5. xx. 47. xxi. 2, 3. Acts vi. 1. ix. 39, 41. 1 Cor. vii. 8. 1 Tim. v. 3*t*, 4, 5, 9, 11, 16*t*. Jas. i. 27. Rev. xviii. 7.

that was[c] a widow, Luke iv. 26.

χθές, ἐχθές LTTr*S*.

yesterday, John iv. 52. Acts vii. 28. Heb. xiii. 8.

χιλίαρχος.

chief captain, Acts xxi. 31, 32, 33, 37. xxii. 24, 26, 27, 28, 29. xxiii. 10, 15, 17, 18, 19, 22. xxiv. 7(*ap*), 22. xxv. 23. Rev. vi. 15.

high captain, Mark vi. 21.

captain, John xviii. 12. Rev. xix. 18.

χιλιάς.

Plural, **thousands**, Rev. v. 11*t*. — **thousand**, Luke xiv. 31*t*. Acts iv. 4. 1 Cor. x. 8. Rev. vii. 4, 5*tr*, 6*tr*, 7*tr*, 8*tr*. xi. 13. xiv. 1, 3. xxi. 16.

χίλιοι.

thousand, 2 Pet. iii. 8*t*. Rev. xi. 3. xii. 6. xiv. 20. xx. 2, 3, 4, 5, 6, 7.

χιτών.

coat, Matt. v. 40. x. 10. Mark vi. 9. Luke iii. 11. vi. 29. ix. 3. John xix. 23*t*. Acts ix. 39.

garment, Jude 23.

Plural, **clothes**, Mark xiv. 63.

χιών.

snow, Matt. xxviii. 3. Mark ix. 3 (-G[∞]TTr*S*). Rev. i. 14.

χλαμύς.
robe, Matt. xxvii. 28, 31.

χλευάζω.
mock, Acts ii. 13 (διαχλευάζω GLT*S*). xvii. 32.

χλιαρός.
lukewarm, Rev. iii. 16.

χλωρός.
green, Mark vi. 39. Rev. viii. 7.
Neut. **green thing**, Rev. ix. 4.
pale, Rev. vi. 8.

χξς'.
six hundred three-score and six, Rev. xiii. 18 (ἑξακόσιοι (-αι *S*) ἑξήκοντα ἕξ LTr*S*, ἑξακόσιοι δεκαέξ L[m]).

χοϊκός.
earthy, 1 Cor. xv. 47, 48, 49.
οἱ χοϊκοί, **they that are earthy**, 1 Cor. xv. 48.

χοῖνιξ.
measure, Rev. vi. 6*t*.

χοῖρος.
swine, Matt. vii. 6. viii. 30, 31, 32, 32(−GLTr*S*). Mark v. 11, 12, 13, 14 (αὐτός GLTTr*S*), 16. Luke viii. 32, 33. xv. 15, 16.

χολάω.
be angry, John vii. 23.

χολή.
gall, Matt. xxvii. 34. Acts viii. 23.

χόος, χοῦς.
dust, Mark vi. 11. Rev. xviii. 19.

χορηγέω.
to minister, 2 Cor. ix. 10.
give, 1 Pet. iv. 11.

χορός.
dancing, Luke xv. 25.

χορτάζω.
to feed, Luke xvi. 21.
fill, Matt. v. 6. xiv. 20. xv. 33, 37. Mark vi. 42. vii. 27. viii. 8. Luke vi. 21. ix. 17. John vi. 26. Phil. iv. 12. Jas. ii. 16. Rev. xix. 21.
satisfy, Mark viii. 4.

χόρτασμα.
sustenance, Acts vii. 11.

χόρτος.
grass, Matt. vi. 30. xiv. 19. Mark vi. 39. Luke xii. 28. John vi. 10. Jas. i. 10, 11. 1 Pet. i. 24*tr*. Rev. viii. 7. ix. 4.
blade, Matt. xiii. 26. Mark iv. 28.
hay, 1 Cor. iii. 12.

χράω.
1. κίχρημι, **lend**, Luke xi. 5.
2. *Mid.*, χράομαι, **use**, Acts xxvii. 17. 1 Cor. vii. 21, 31. ix. 12, 15. 2 Cor. i. 17. iii. 12. xiii. 10. 1 Tim. i. 8. v. 23. — **entreat**, Acts xxvii. 3.
3. *Impers.*, χρή, **ought**[cc], Jas. iii. 10.

χρεία.
use, Eph. iv. 29 (*marg.* **profitably**[cc]; πίστις G'). Tit. iii. 14.
business, Acts vi. 3.
need, Matt. iii. 14. vi. 8. xxi. 3. xxvi. 65. Mark ii. 17, 25. xi. 3. Luke ix. 11. xix. 31, 34. John xiii. 29. Acts ii. 45. iv. 35. 1 Cor. xii. 21*t*, 24. Phil. iv. 19. 1 Thes. v. 1. Heb. v. 12*t*. vii. 11. x. 36. 1 John iii. 17. Rev. iii. 17. xxi. 23.
With ἔχω, **to need**, Matt. ix. 12. xiv. 16. Mark xiv. 63. Luke v. 31. xv. 7. xxii. 71. John ii. 25. xiii. 10. xvi. 30. Eph. iv. 28. 1 Thes. i. 8. iv. 9. 1 John ii. 27. Rev. xxii. 5 (G', −ἔχω GT).
needful[cc], Luke x. 42.
necessity, Acts xx. 34. Rom. xii. 13. Phil. iv. 16.
τὰ πρὸς τὴν (τὰς LT*S*) χ., **such things as are necessary**, Acts xxviii. 10.
want, Phil. ii. 25.
lack, 1 Thes. iv. 12.

χρεωφειλέτης, χρεοφ. LTTr*S*.
debtor, Luke vii. 41. xvi. 5.

χρή. See χράω.

χρήζω.
to need, Luke xi. 8. 2 Cor. iii. 1.
have need of, Matt. vi. 32. Luke xii. 30. Rom. xvi. 2.

χρῆμα.
Plur., **riches**, Mark x. 23, 24. Luke

xviii. 24. — **money**, Acts viii. 18, 20. xxiv. 26.
money, Acts iv. 37.

χρηματίζω.
Pass., **be warned of (from) God**, Matt. ii. 12, 22. Acts x. 22. Heb. xi. 7. — **be admonished of God**, Heb. viii. 5.
reveal, Luke ii. 26 (*with* εἰμί).
call, Acts xi. 26[cc]. Rom. vii. 3.
speak, Heb. xii. 25.

χρηματισμός.
answer of God, Rom. xi. 4.

χρήσιμος.
Neut., **profit**, 2 Tim. ii. 14.

χρῆσις.
use, Rom. i. 26, 27.

χρηστεύομαι.
be kind, 1 Cor. xiii. 4.

χρηστολογία.
good words, Rom. xvi. 18.

χρηστός.
good, 1Cor. xv. 33. — *Comp.*, **better**, Luke v. 39 (*positive* TTr*S*).
Neut., **goodness**, Rom. ii. 4.
kind, Luke vi. 35. Eph. iv. 32.
gracious, 1 Pet. ii. 3.
easy, Matt. xi. 30.
Add Phil. i. 21, for χριστός, G′.

χρηστότης.
goodness, Rom. ii. 4. xi. 22*tr*.
good, *subst.*, Rom. iii. 12.
kindness, 2 Cor. vi. 6. Eph. ii. 7. Col. iii. 12. Tit. iii. 4.
gentleness, Gal. v. 22.

χρίσμα.
anointing, 1 John ii. 27*t*.
unction, 1 John ii. 20.

χριστός. See Proper Names.

χρίω.
anoint, Luke iv. 18. Acts iv. 27. x. 38. 2 Cor. i. 21. Heb. i. 9.

χρονίζω.
delay, Matt. xxiv. 48. Luke xii. 45
tarry, Matt. xxv. 5[p]. Luke i. 21. Heb. x. 37.

χρόνος.
time, Matt. ii. 7, 16. xxv. 19. Luke i. 57. iv. 5. John v. 6. xiv. 9. Acts i. 6, 7. iii. 21. vii. 17. xiii. 18. xiv. 28. xvii. 30. xviii. 20. xxvii. 9. Gal. iv. 4. 1 Thes. v. 1. Heb. iv. 7. v. 12. xi. 32. 1 Pet. i. 17, 20. iv. 2, 3. Jude 18. Rev. x. 6.
With ἱκανός, **(of) long time**, Acts viii. 11. xiv. 3. — *Plur.*, **for a long time**, Luke xx. 9. — *With* ἐκ, **long time**, Luke viii. 27.
πολλοῖς χ., **oftentimes**, Luke viii. 29.
ἐν παντὶ χρόνῳ ἐν ᾧ, **all the time that**, Acts i. 21.
With ποιέω, **spend some time** [c]**there**, Acts xviii. 23[p]. — **tarry there**[c] **a space**, Acts xv. 33[p].
ὅσον χρόνον (*with* ἐπί[1]), **as long as**, Mark ii. 19(*ap*). Rom. vii. 1[1]. 1 Cor. vii. 39[1]. Gal iv. 1[1].
while, Luke xviii. 4. John vii. 33. xii. 35.
χρόνον τινά, **a while**, 1 Cor. xvi. 7.
season, Acts xix. 22. xx. 18. Rev. vi. 11. xx. 3.
space, Rev. ii. 21.
Add Luke xxiii. 8, *see* ἱκανός.
See also αἰώνιος, πόσος, τεσσαρακονταετής.

χρονοτριβέω.
spend the time, Acts xx. 16.

χρύσεος, χρυσοῦς.
of gold, 2 Tim. ii. 20. Rev. iv. 4. ix. 20.
golden, Heb. ix. 4*t*. Rev. i. 12, 13, 20. ii. 1. v. 8. viii. 3*t*. ix. 13. xiv. 14. xv. 6, 7. xvii. 4. xxi. 15.
Add Rev. ix. 7, for ὅμοιος χρυσῷ, G.

χρυσίον.
gold, Acts iii. 6. xx. 33. Heb. ix. 4. 1 Pet. i. 7, 18. iii. 3. Rev. iii. 18. xxi. 18, 21.
Add, *see* χρυσός.

χρυσοδακτύλιος.
with a gold ring, Jas. ii. 2.

χρυσόλιθος.
chrysolite, Rev. xxi. 20.

χρυσόπρασος.
chrysoprasus, Rev. xxi. 20.

χρυσός.
gold, Matt. ii. 11. x. 9. xxiii. 16, 17*t*. Acts xvii. 29. 1 Cor. iii. 12. 1 Tim. ii. 9 (χρυσίον L). Jas. v. 3. Rev. ix. 7 (G', *see* χρύσεος). xvii. 4 (χρυσίον GLTTr). xviii. 12, 16(χρυσίον GLTTr).

χρυσόω.
to deck, Rev. xvii. 4 (*Gr.* gild). xviii. 16.

χρώς.
body, Acts xix. 12.

χωλός.
lame, Matt. xi. 5. xv. 30, 31. xxi. 14. Luke vii. 22. xiv. 13. Acts iii. 2.—**that is lame**, Acts viii. 7.
τὸ χ., **that which is lame**, Heb. xii. 13.
lame man, Acts iii. 11 (*see* ἰάομαι).
being a cripple, Acts xiv. 8.
halt, Matt. xviii. 8. Mark ix. 45. Luke xiv. 21. John v. 3.

χώρα.
country, Matt. ii. 12. viii. 28. Mark v. i. 10. Luke ii. 8. viii. 26. xv. 13, 15. xix. 12. xxi. 21. John xi. 54, 55. Acts xii. 20. xviii. 23. xxvii. 27.
region, Matt. iv. 16. Luke iii. 1. Acts viii. 1. xiii. 49. xvi. 6.
land, Mark i. 5. Luke xv. 14. Acts x. 39.
coasts, Acts xxvi. 20.
field, John iv. 35. Jas. v. 4.
ground, Luke xii. 16.
Add Mark vi. 55, *see* περίχωρος.

χωρέω.
be room to receive, Mark ii. 2.
can receive, Matt. xix. 11.
receive, Matt. xix. 12*t*. 2 Cor. vii. 2.
can contain, John xxi. 25.
contain, John ii. 6.
have place, John viii. 37.
go, Matt. xv. 17.—**come**, 2 Pet. iii. 9.

χωρίζω.
put asunder, Matt. xix. 6. Mark x. 9.
separate, Rom. viii. 35, 39.—*Pass. part.*, **separate**, Heb. vii. 26.

14

Mid., **depart**, Acts i. 4. xviii. 1, 2. 1 Cor. vii. 10, 11, 15*t*. Phm. 15.

χωρίον.
place, Matt. xxvi. 36. Mark xiv. [32.
field, Acts i. 18, 19*t*.
parcel of ground, John iv. 5.
land, Acts iv. 34. v. 3, 8.
possessions, Acts xxviii. 7.

χωρίς.
by °**itself**, John xx. 7.
without, Matt. xiii. 34. Mark iv. 34. Luke vi. 49. John i. 3. xv. 5 (*marg.* **severed from**). Rom. iii. 21, 28. iv. 6. vii. 8, 9. x. 14. 1 Cor. iv. 8. xi. 11*t*. Eph. ii. 12. Phil. ii. 14. 1 Tim. ii. 8. v. 21. Phm. 14. Heb. iv. 15. vii. 7, 20, 21(20). ix. 7, 18, 22, 28. x. 28. xi. 6, 40. xii. 8, 14. Jas. ii. 18 (ἐκ StC[m]E ; *marg.* **by**), 20, 26*t*.
beside, Matt. xiv. 21. xv. 38. 2 Cor. xi. 28.
Add 2 Cor. xii. 3, for ἐκτός, LT.

χῶρος.
north-west, Acts xxvii. 12.

ψάλλω.
sing, Rom. xv. 9. 1 Cor. xiv. 15*t*.
sing psalms, Jas. v. 13.
make melody, Eph. v. 19.

ψαλμός.
psalm, Luke xxiv. 44. Acts xiii. 33. 1 Cor. xiv. 26. Eph. v. 19. Col. iii. 16.—*Plural*, **Psalms**, Luke xx. 42. Acts i. 20.

ψευδάδελφος.
Plural, **false brethren**, 2 Cor. xi. 26. Gal. ii. 4.

ψευδαπόστολος.
Plur., **false apostles**, 2 Cor. xi. 13.

ψευδής.
false, Acts vi. 13.
liar, Rev. ii. 2. xxi. 8 (ψεύστης L).

ψευδοδιδάσκαλος.
Plur., **false teachers**, 2 Pet. ii. 1.

ψευδολόγος.
speaking lies, 1 Tim. iv. 2.

ψεύδομαι. See ψεύδω.

ψευδομάρτυρ.
false witness, Matt. xxvi. 60(*ap*), 60(-TTr*S*). 1 Cor. xv. 15.

ψευδομαρτυρέω.
bear false witness, Matt. xix. 18. Mark x. 19. xiv. 56, 57. Luke xviii. 20. Rom. xiii. 9 (*om*).

ψευδομαρτυρία.
false witness, Matt. xv. 19. xxvi. 59.

ψευδοπροφήτης.
false prophet, Matt. vii. 15. xxiv. 11, 24. Mark xiii. 22. Luke vi. 26. Acts xiii. 6. 2 Pet. ii. 1. 1 John iv. 1. Rev. xvi. 13. xix. 20. xx. 10.

ψεῦδος.
lie, John viii. 44. Rom. i. 25. 2 Thes. ii. 11. 1 John ii. 21, 27. Rev. xxi. 27. xxii. 15.
lying, Eph. iv. 25.—*Gen.*, **lying,** *adj.*, 2 Thes. ii. 9.
Add Rev. xiv. 5, for δόλος, GLTTr*S*.

ψευδόχριστος.
Plur., **false Christs,** Matt. xxiv. 24. Mark xiii. 22 (-T).

ψεύδω.
Mid., **to lie (to¹),** Acts v. 3¹ (*marg.* **deceive**), 4. Rom. ix. 1. 2 Cor. xi. 31. Gal. i. 20. Col. iii. 9. 1 Tim. ii. 7. Heb. vi. 18. Jas. iii. 14. 1 John i. 6. Rev. iii. 9.—**falsely,** Matt. v. 11ᵖ (*Gr.* lying; -G∞LTTrᵐᵇ).

ψευδώνυμος.
falsely so called, 1 Tim. vi. 20.

ψεῦσμα.
lie, Rom. iii. 7.

ψεύστης.
liar, John viii. 44, 45. Rom. iii. 4. 1 Tim. i. 10. Tit. i. 12. 1 John i. 10. ii. 4, 22. iv. 20. v. 10.
Add Rev. xxi. 8, for ψευδής, L.

ψηλαφάω.
Pass. part., **that might° be touched,** Heb. xii. 18.
handle, Luke xxiv. 39. 1 John i. 1.
feel after, Acts xvii. 27.

ψηφίζω.
to count, Luke xiv. 28. Rev. xiii. 18.

ψῆφος.
stone, Rev. ii. 17*t*.—**voice,** Acts xxvi. 10 (*lit.* pebble, *hence* vote).

ψιθυρισμός.
whispering, 2 Cor. xii. 20.

ψιθυριστής.
whisperer, Rom. i. 29(30).

ψιχίον.
crumb, Matt. xv. 27. Mark vii. 28. Luke xvi. 21 (-LᵇTTrᵇ*S*).

ψυχή.
life, Matt. ii. 20. vi. 25*t*. x. 39*t*. xvi. 25*t*. xx. 28. Mark iii. 4. viii. 35, 35(-G°). x. 45. Luke vi. 9. ix. 24*t*, 56 (*ap*). xii. 22, 23. xiv. 26. xvii. 33. John x. 11, 15, 17. xii. 25*t*. xiii. 37, 38. xv. 13. Acts xv. 26. xx. 10, 24. xxvii. 10, 22. Rom. xi. 3. xvi. 4. Phil. ii. 30. 1 John iii. 16*t*. Rev. viii. 9. xii. 11.
soul, Matt. x. 28*t*. xi. 29. xii. 18. xvi. 26*t*. xxii. 37. xxvi. 38. Mark viii. 36, 37. xii. 30, 33(*ap*). xiv. 34. Luke i. 46. ii. 35. x. 27. xii. 19*t*, 20. xxi. 19. John xii. 27. Acts ii. 27, 31(*omS*), 41, 43. iii. 23. iv. 32. vii. 14. xiv. 22. xv. 24. xxvii. 37. Rom. ii. 9. xiii. 1. 1 Cor. xv. 45. 2 Cor. i. 23. 1 Thes. ii. 8. v. 23. Heb. iv. 12. vi. 19. x. 38, 39. xiii. 17. Jas. i. 21. v. 20. 1 Pet. i. 9, 22. ii. 11, 25. iii. 20. iv. 19. 2 Pet. ii. 8, 14. 3 John 2. Rev. vi. 9. xvi. 3. xviii. 13, 14. xx. 4.
heart, Eph. vi. 6.
With ἐκ, **heartily,** Col. iii. 23.
mind, Acts xiv. 2. Phil. i. 27. Heb. xii. 3. — *See also* ἡμῶν, ὑμῶν.

ψυχικός.
natural, 1 Cor. ii. 14. xv. 44*t*.
τὸ ψ., **that which is n.,** 1 Cor. xv. 46.
sensual, Jas. iii. 15 (*marg.* **natural**). Jude 19.

ψύχος.
cold, John xviii. 18. Acts xxviii. 2. 2 Cor. xi. 27.

ψυχρός.
cold, Rev. iii. 15*t*, 16.
cold water, Matt. x. 42.

ψύχω.
Pass., **wax cold,** Matt. xxiv. 12.

ψωμίζω.
bestow to feed, 1 Cor. xiii. 3.
feed, Rom. xii. 20.

ψωμίον.
sop, John xiii. 26 (*marg.* **morsel**), 26, 27, 30.

ψώχω.
to rub, Luke vi. 1.

Ω.
Omega, Rev. i. 8, 11(*ap*). xxi. 6. xxii. 13.

ὦ.
O, Matt. xv. 28. xvii. 17. Mark ix. 19. Luke ix. 41. xxiv. 25. Acts i. 1. xiii. 10. xviii. 14. Rom. ii. 1, 3. ix. 20. xi. 33. Gal. iii. 1. 1 Tim. vi. 20. Jas. ii. 20.
Not rendered, Acts xxvii. 21.

ὦ, ᾖς, ᾖ. See εἰμί.

ὧδε.
hither, Matt. viii. 29. xiv. 18. xvii. 17. xxii. 12. Mark xi. 3. Luke ix. 41(-G°). xiv. 21. xix. 27. John vi. 25. xx. 27. Acts ix. 21. Rev. iv. 1. xi. 12.
here, Matt. xii. 41, 42. xiv. 8, 17. xvi. 28. xvii. 4*t*. xx. 6. xxiv. 2, 23. xxvi. 38. xxviii. 6. Mark vi. 3. viii. 4. ix. 1, 5. xiii. 21. xiv. 32, 34. xvi. 6. Luke iv. 23. ix. 12, 27 (αὐτοῦ TTr*S*), 33. xi. 31, 32. xvii. 21, 23. xxii. 38. xxiv. 6. John vi. 9. xi. 21, 32. Acts ix. 14. Col. iv. 9. Heb. vii. 8. xiii. 14. Jas. ii. 3(-G°° LT*S*), 3. Rev. xiii. 10, 18. xiv. 12, 12(*om S*). xvii. 9.
ὧδε..ὧδε, **here..there,** Matt. xxiv. 23.
in this place, Matt. xii. 6.
ἕως ὧδε, **to this place,** Luke xxiii. 5.
Add Mark xiii. 2 (left . .), G′LTr*S*. Luke xv. 17 (perish . .), GLTTr*S*. xvi. 25, for ὅδε, G″LTTr*S*. xxi. 6 (another . .), L*S*.

ᾠδή.
song, Eph. v. 19. Col. iii. 16. Rev. v. 9. xiv. 3*t*. xv. 3*t*.

ὠδίν.
travail, 1 Thes. v. 3.
pain, Acts ii. 24.
sorrow, Matt. xxiv. 8. Mark xiii. 8 (*Gr.* pain of a woman in travail).

ὠδίνω.
to travail in birth (of[1]**),** Gal. iv. 19[1]. Rev. xii. 2.—**travail,** Gal. iv. 27.

ὦμος.
shoulder, Matt. xxiii. 4. Luke xv. 5.

ὤν, οὖσα, ὄν. See εἰμί.

ὠνέομαι.
to buy, Acts vii. 16.

ᾠόν.
egg, Luke xi. 12.

ὥρα.
hour, Matt. viii. 13. ix. 22. x. 19 (*ap*). xv. 28. xvii. 18. xx. 3, 5, 6 (-G°°LTTr*S*), 9, 12. xxiv. 36, 42 (ἡμέρα LTTr*S*), 44, 50. xxv. 13. xxvi. 40, 45, 55. xxvii. 45*t*, 46. Mark xiii. 11, 32. xiv. 35, 37, 41. xv. 25, 33*t*, 34. Luke vii. 21. x. 21. xii. 12, 39, 40, 46. xx. 19. xxii. 14, 53, 59. xxiii. 44*t*. xxiv. 33. John i. 39(40). ii. 4. iv. 6, 21, 23, 52*t*, 53. v. 25, 28. vii. 30. viii. 20. xi. 9. xii. 23, 27*t*. xiii. 1. xvi. 21, 32. xvii. 1. xix. 14, 27. Acts ii. 15. iii. 1. v. 7. x. 3, 9, 30, 30(-G°°LT*S*). xvi. 18, 33. xix. 34. xxii. 13. xxiii. 23. 1 Cor. iv. 11. xv. 30. Gal. ii. 5. Rev. iii. 3, 10. ix. 15. xi. 13 (ἡμέρα G″). xiv. 7. xvii. 12. xviii. 10, 17 (16), 19.
time, Matt. xiv. 15. xviii. 1 (ἡμέρα G″L). Mark vi. 35. Luke i. 10. xiv. 17. John xvi. 2, 4, 25. 1 John ii. 18*t*. Rev. xiv. 15.
high[c] **time,** Rom. xiii. 11.
season, John v. 35. 2 Cor. vii. 8. Phm. 15.
instant, Luke ii. 38.
Gen., **short,** 1 Thes. ii. 17.

Add Luke xiii. 31, for ἡμέρα, G'T*S*. *See also* ὄψιος, πολύς.

ὡραῖος.

beautiful, Matt. xxiii. 27. Rom. x. 15. — **Beautiful,** Acts iii. 2, 10.

ὠρύομαι.

to roar, 1 Pet. v. 8.

ὡς.

In notation of time[1]. Of number[2].

as, Matt. i. 24. vi. 10, 12. vii. 29*t*. viii. 13. x. 16*tr*, 25*t*. xiii. 43. xiv. 5. xvii. 2*t*, 20. xviii. 3, 4, 33. xix. 19. xx. 14. xxi. 26. xxii. 30, 39. xxvi. 19, 39*t*, 55. xxviii. 9[1](*ap*), 15. Mark i. 2 (καθώς TTr*S*), 22*t*. iii. 5 (*om S*). iv. 26. vi. 15, 34. vii. 6. viii. 24. ix. 3(-G[∞]TTr*S*). x. 1, 15. xii. 25, 31, 33. xiii. 34. xiv. 48.

Luke ii. 15[1]. iii. 4, 23. vi. 10(*ap*), 22, 40. ix. 54 (*ap*). x. 3, 18, 27. xi. 2(*ap*), 36, 44. xiv. 22. xv. 19, 25[1]. xvii. 6, 28 (*see* καθώς). xviii. 11, 17. xxi. 35. xxii. 26*t*, 27, 31, 52. xxiii. 14, 26[1]. John i. 14. xv. 6. xx. 11[1]. Acts ii. 15. iii. 12. vii. 51 (καθώς L). viii. 32, 36[1]. x. 25[1]. xi. 17. xiii. 25[1], 33. xvi. 4[1]. xvii. 28. xxii. 5, 25[1]. xxiii. 11, 15, 20. xxv. 10. xxvii. 30.

Rom. i. 21. iii. 7. iv. 17. v. 15, 16, 18. vi. 13 (ὡσεί L*S*). viii. 36. ix. 27, 29. xiii. 9, 13. xv. 15. 1 Cor. iii. 1*tr*, 10, 15. iv. 1, 7, 13, 14, 18. v. 3*t*. vii. 7, 8, 17*t*, 25, 29, 30*tr*, 31. viii. 7. ix. 20*t*, 21, 22(-L[b]T*S*), 26*t*. x. 7 (ὥσπερ G'LT*S*), 15. xiii. 11*tr*. xiv. 33. xvi. 10. 2 Cor. ii. 17*tr*. iii. 1, 5. v. 20. vi. 4, 8, 9*tr*, 10*tr*, 13. vii. 14. ix. 5. x. 2, 14. xi. 3, 15, 16. xiii. 2, 7.

Gal. i. 9. iii. 16*t*. iv. 12*t*, 14*t*. v. 14. vi. 10. Eph. ii. 3. iii. 5. v. 1, 8, 15*t*, 22, 23, 28. vi. 5, 6*t*, 7(-St), 20. Phil. i. 20. ii. 8, 12, 15, 22. Col. ii. 6, 20. iii. 12, 18, 22, 23. iv. 4. 1 Thes. ii. 4, 7, 11, 13(-StEGLT*S*). v. 2, 4, 6. 2 Thes. ii. 2*t*, 4(*om S*). iii. 15*t*. 1 Tim. v. 1*t*, 2*t*. 2 Tim. ii. 3, 9, 17. iii. 9. Tit. i. 5, 7. Phm. 9, 16, 17.

Heb. i. 11. iii. 2, 5, 6, 8, 15. iv. 3. vi. 19. vii. 9. xi. 9, 27, 29. xii. 5, 7, 16, 27. xiii. 3*t*, 17. Jas. i. 10. ii. 8, 9, 12. v. 3, 5(-LT*S*). 1 Pet. i. 14, 19, 24(-L, ὡσεί *S*), 24. ii. 2, 5, 11, 12, 14, 16*t*, 25. iii. 7*t*, 16(*ap*). iv. 10, 11*t*, 12, 15*t*, 16, 19 (-L*S*). v. 3, 8, 12. 2 Pet. i. 19. ii. 1, 12. iii. 8*t*, 9, 10, 16*t*. 1 John i. 7. ii. 27. 2 John 5. Jude 10.

Rev. i. 10, 14*t*, 15*t*, 16, 17. ii. 24, 27*t*. iii. 3, 21. iv. 1, 7(G', -G). v. 6. vi. 11, 12*t*, 13, 14. ix. 2, 3, 5, 7, 8*t*, 9, 17. x. 1, 7, 9, 10. xii. 15. xiii. 2*t*, 11. xiv. 2*t*. xvi. 3, 15. xvii. 12. xviii. 6. xix. 6(-L), 6, 12(-G[∞]T*S*). xx. 8. xxi. 2. xxii. 1.

as . . as, Matt. xxvii. 65.

according as, Rom. xii. 3. 2 Pet. i. 3. Rev. xxii. 12.

even as, Matt. xv. 28. Mark iv. 36. 1 Cor. iii. 5. Eph. v. 33. 1 Pet. iii. 6. Jude 7.

ὡς ἄν, **even as,** 1 Cor. xii. 2. — **as,** 2 Cor. x. 9. 1 Thes. ii. 6 (7, ὡς ἐάν LT). — **as soon as**[1], Phil. ii. 23. — **when**[1], 1 Cor. xi. 34.

ὡς καί, **as well as,** 1 Cor. ix. 5.

like as, Matt. xii. 13.

like, Matt. vi. 29. xxviii. 3. Mark iv. 31. Luke xii. 27. John vii. 46 (*ap*). Acts viii. 32. Rev. xviii. 21.

even like, Rev. xxi. 11.

like unto, Acts iii. 22. vii. 37(*marg.* **as**). Rev. ii. 18.

unto, Rom. ix. 29.

for, Matt. xxi. 46 (εἰς G''LTTr*S*). 1 Pet. ii. 16.

as it were (had been), John vii. 10. xxi. 8[2]. Acts x. 11. xi. 5. xvii. 14 (ἕως L*S*). Rom. ix. 32. 1 Cor. iv. 9. 2 Cor. xi. 17. Phm. 14. Jas. v. 3. Rev. iv. 1. vi. 1. viii. 8, 10. ix. 7, 9. x. 1. xiii. 3. xiv. 3(-GT*S*). xv. 2. xix. 6. xxi. 21.

as soon as[1], Luke i. 23, 44. xxii. 66. John xi. 20, 29. xviii. 6. xxi. 9.

when[1], Luke i. 41. ii. 39. iv. 25. v. 4. vii. 12. xi. 1. xii. 58. xix. 5, 29, 41. xx. 37. John ii. 9, 23. iv.

1, 40. vi. 12, 16. vii. 10. viii. 7(*ap*). xi. 6, 32, 33. xix. 33. Acts v. 24. vii. 23. x. 7. xiii. 29. xiv. 5. xvi. 15. xvii. 13. xviii. 5. xix. 9. xx. 14, 18. xxi. 12, 27. xxii. 11. xxv. 14. xxvii. 1, 27. xxviii. 4.

ὡς ἐάν, **whensoever**[1], Rom. xv. 24 (ὡς ἄν LT*S*).

while[1], Luke xxiv. 32*t*. Acts i. 10. x. 17.

after[1], Acts xvi. 10. xix. 21. xxi. 1[cc].

after that[1], Acts ix. 23.

since[1], Mark ix. 21.

about[2], Mark v. 13. viii. 9. Luke ii. 37 (ἕως LTTr*S*). viii. 42. John i. 39(40). vi. 19(ὡσεί L). xi. 18. Acts i. 15. v. 7. xiii. 18, 20. xix. 34. Rev. viii. 1. xvi. 21.

how, Mark iv. 27[cc]. xii. 26 (πῶς T Tr*S*). Luke vi. 4 (πῶς LTr[b]). viii. 47. xxii. 61. xxiii. 55. xxiv. 6 (ὅσα fr. ὅσος L[m]), 35. Acts x. 28, 38. xi. 16. xx. 20. Rom. x. 15. xi. 2, 33. 2 Cor. vii. 15. Phil. i. 8. 1 Thes. ii. 10, 11.

so, Heb. iii. 11.

so that, Acts xx. 24.

that, Luke xvi. 1[cc]. Acts xvii. 22[cc]. xxviii. 19. Rom. i. 9. 2 Tim. i. 3.

Add, for ἕως, John xii. 35, LTTr. 36, LTTr*S*. For καθώς, Acts x. 47, LT*S*. For ὅμοια, Rev. xvi. 13, GL TTr. For οὐ, Mark xiv. 72, LTTr*S*. For ὡσεί, ὥσπερ, *see* ὡσεί, ὥσπερ.

Heb. i. 12, *see* ἱμάτιον. Rev. iv. 6 (. . a sea), GLTTr*S*. vi. 6 (. . a voice), LTr*S*. xiv. 2 (. . of harpers), GLTTr*S*. xix. 1 (. . a great voice), GLTTr*S*.

See also ὅτι, I., τάχιστα fr. ταχύς.

ὡσαννά.

Hosanna, Matt. xxi. 9*t*, 15. Mark xi. 9, 10. John xii. 13.

ὡσαύτως.

after the same manner, 1 Cor. xi. 25.

even so, 1 Tim. iii. 11.

in like manner, Luke xx. 31. 1 Tim. ii. 9.

likewise, Matt. xx. 5. xxi. 30, 36. xxv. 17. Mark xii. 21. xiv. 31. Luke xiii. 3 (ὁμοίως LTr*S*). xxii. 20. Rom. viii. 26. 1 Tim. iii. 8. v. 25. Tit. ii. 3, 6.

Add Luke xiii. 5, for ὁμοίως, TTr *S*. xx. 31 (took her .), L[b].

ὡσεί.

as it were (had been), Luke xxii. 44 (*ap*). Acts vi. 15. ix. 18 (ὡς L*S*).

as, Matt. ix. 36 (ὡς Tr). xxviii. 3 (ὡς LTr*S*), 4 (ὡς LTTr*S*). Mark ix. 26. Luke xxiv. 11. Heb. i. 12. xi. 12 (ὡς GLT*S*).

like as, Acts ii. 3.

like, Matt. iii. 16. Mark i. 10 (ὡς GLTTr*S*). Luke iii. 22 (ὡς LTr*S*). John i. 32 (ὡς GLTTr*S*). Rev. i. 14 (ὡς GLTr*S*).

about, Matt. xiv. 21. Mark vi. 44 (*om*, ὡς *S*). Luke i. 56 (ὡς LTr*S*). iii. 23. ix. 14, 28. xxii. 41, 59. xxiii. 44. John iv. 6 (ὡς LTTr*S*). vi. 10 (ὡς Tr*S*). xix. 14 (ὡς G″LTTr*S*), 39 (ὡς GLTTr*S*). Acts ii. 41. iv. 4 (ὡς L[b], -T*S*). v. 36 (ὡς LT). x. 3. xix. 7.

Add, for ὡς, John vi. 19, L. Rom. vi. 13, L*S*. — Luke ix. 14 (. . by fifties), L[b]Tr[b]*S*.

ὥσπερ.

even as, Matt. v. 48 (ὡς LTr*S*). xx. 28.

as, Matt. vi. 2, 5 (ὡς LTr*S*), 7, 16 (ὡς LTr*S*). xii. 40. xiii. 40. xviii. 17. xxiv. 27, 37, 38 (ὡς LTTr*S*). xxv. 14, 32. Luke xvii. 24. xviii. 11 (ὡς LTr). John v. 21, 26. Acts ii. 2. iii. 17. xi. 15. Rom. v. 12, 19, 21. vi. 19. xi. 30. 1 Cor. viii. 5. xi. 12. xv. 22. xvi. 1. 2 Cor. i. 7 (ὡς L T*S*). viii. 7. ix. 5 (ὡς GLT*S*). Gal. iv. 29. Eph. v. 24 (ὡς LT*S*). 1 Thes. v. 3. Heb. iv. 10. vii. 27. ix. 25. Jas. ii. 26.

like as, Rom. vi. 4.

as when, Rev. x. 3.

Add 1 Cor. x. 7, for ὡς, G′LT*S*.

ὡσπερεί.

as, 1 Cor. xv. 8.

ὥστε.

so that, Matt. viii. 28. xiii. 2, 32. Mark iii. 20. iv. 1, 32, 37. xv. 5. Luke v. 7. Acts xvi. 26. xix. 10, 12, 16. Rom. xv. 19. 1 Cor. i. 7. xiii. 2. 2 Cor. ii. 7. iii. 7. vii. 7. Phil. i. 13. 1 Thes. i. 7, 8. 2 Thes. i. 4. ii. 4. Heb. xiii. 6.

insomuch that, Matt. viii. 24. xii. 22. xiii. 54. xv. 31. xxiv. 24. xxvii. 14. Mark i. 27, 45. ii. 2, 12. iii. 10. ix. 26. Luke xii. 1. Acts v. 15. 2 Cor. i. 8. Gal. ii. 13.

insomuch as, Acts i. 19.

that, John iii. 16. Acts xiv. 1. xv. 39.

With an Infinitive, **to,** Matt. x. 1. xxvii. 1. Luke ix. 52 (ὡς L^m^*S*). — **as to,** Matt. xv. 33. — **that . . might,** 1 Pet. i. 21. — **that . . should,** Rom. vii. 6. 1 Cor. [illegible] 1.

so then, Mark x. 8. 1 Cor. iii. 7. vii. 38. 2 Cor. iv. 12. Gal. iii. 9.

therefore, Mark ii. 28. Rom. xiii. 2. 1 Cor. iii. 21. iv. 5. v. 8. xv. 58. 2 Cor. v. 17. Gal. iv. 16. Phil. iv. 1.

wherefore, Matt. xii. 12. xix. 6. xxiii. 31. Rom. vii. 4, 12. 1 Cor. x. 12. xi. 27, 33. xiv. 22 39. 2 Cor. v. 16. Gal. iii. 24. iv. 7. Phil. ii. 12. 1 Thes. iv. 18. Jas. i. 19 (ἴστε G'L, ἰστω *S*, fr. εἶδον). 1 Pet. iv. 19.

Add, for εἰς τό, Luke iv. 29, GLT Tr*S*. xx. 20, LTTr*S*.

ὠτάριον, an ear.

Mark xiv. 47, etc. *See* ὠτίον.

ὠτίον.

ear, Matt. xxvi. 51. Mark xiv. 47 (ὠτάριον G'LTTr*S*). Luke xxii. 51. John xviii. 10 (ὠτάριον TTr*S*), 26.

ὠφέλεια.

profit, Rom. iii. 1.

advantage, Jude 16.

ὠφελέω.

to profit, Mark viii. 36. John vi. 63. Rom. ii. 25. 1 Cor. xiii. 3. xiv. 6. Gal. v. 2. Heb. iv. 2.

Mid. or Pass., **be profited,** Matt. xv. 5. xvi. 26. Mark vii. 11. — **profit**^oc^, Heb. xiii. 9. — **be advantaged,** Luke ix. 25. — **be bettered,** Mark v. 26.

prevail, Matt. xxvii. 24. John xii. 19.

ὠφέλιμος.

profitable, 1 Tim. iv. 8. 2 Tim. iii. 16. Tit. iii. 8.

With εἰμί, **to profit,** 1 Tim. iv. 8.

NOTE. — Besides the few cases of omission marked *S*^c^, the Sinaitic Manuscript lacks the context also in the following instances of substitution, and thus fails to support either reading; viz., Mark iv. 37, πλοῖον for αὐτό. vi. 4, συγγενεύς for -νῆς. Luke xiv. 15, ἄριστον for ἄρτος. xx. 28, ᾖ fr. εἰμί for ἀποθνήσκω. John vi. 55, ἀληθής for ἀληθῶς. Acts ii. 21, ἐάν for ἄν. 1 John v. 15, ἄν for ἐάν. Rev. iv. 5, ἐστί for εἰσί. xx. 5, ζάω for ἀναζάω, ἄχρι for ἕως. See also the Appendix, Mark xvi. 9 – 20; John vii. 53 – viii. 11.

PROPER NAMES.

'Ααρών, **Aaron**, Luke i. 5. Acts vii. 40. Heb. v. 4. vii. 11. ix. 4.
'Αβαδδών, **Abaddon**, Rev. ix. 11.
'Αβελ, **Abel**, Matt. xxiii. 35. Luke xi. 51. Heb. xi. 4. xii. 24.
'Αβιά, **Abia**, **1**, king, Matt. i. 7*t*. —**2**, priest, Luke i. 5.
'Αβιάθαρ, **Abiathar**, Mark ii. 26.
'Αβιληνή, **Abilene**, Luke iii. 1.
'Αβιούδ, **Abiud**, Matt. i. 13*t*.
'Αβραάμ, **Abraham**, Matt. i. 1, 2, 17. iii. 9*t*. viii. 11. xxii. 32. Mark xii. 26. Luke i. 55, 73. iii. 8*t*, 34. xiii. 16, 28. xvi. 22, 23, 24, 25, 29, 30. xix. 9. xx. 37. John viii. 33, 37, 39*tr*, 40, 52, 53, 56, 57, 58. Acts iii. 13, 25. vii. 2, 16, 17, 32. xiii. 26. Rom. iv. 1, 2, 3, 9, 12, 13, 16. ix. 7. xi. 1. 2 Cor. xi. 22. Gal. iii. 6, 7, 8, 9, 14, 16, 18, 29. iv. 22. Heb. ii. 16. vi. 13. vii. 1, 2, 4, 5, 6, 9. xi. 8, 17. Jas. ii. 21, 23. 1 Pet. iii. 6.
Aceldama. *See* 'Ακελδαμά.
'Αγαβος, **Agabus**, Acts xi. 28. xxi. 10.
'Αγαρ, **Agar**, Gal. iv. 24, 25(-G' [L*S*).
'Αγρίππας, **Agrippa**, Acts xxv. 13, 22, 23, 24, 26. xxvi. 1, 2, 7(-G°° LT*S*), 19, 27, 28, 32.
Achaia, etc. *See* 'Αχαΐα, *etc.*
'Αδάμ, **Adam**, Luke iii. 38. Rom. v. 14*t*. 1 Cor. xv. 22, 45*t*. 1 Tim. ii. 13, 14. Jude 14.
'Αδδί, -εί TTr*S*, **Addi**, Luke iii. 28.
'Αδμείν. *See* 'Αράμ.
'Αδραμυττηνός, **of Adramyttium**, Acts xxvii. 2.
'Αδρίας, **Adria**, Acts xxvii. 27.
Æneas, **Ænon**. *See* Αἰνέας, *etc.*
'Αζώρ, **Azor**, Matt. i. 13, 14.
'Αζωτος, **Azotus**, Acts viii. 40.
'Αθῆναι, **Athens**, Acts xvii. 15, 16. xviii. 1. 1 Thes. iii. 1.
'Αθηναῖος, **Athenian**, Acts xvii. 21. —**of Athens**, Acts xvii. 22.
Αἰγύπτιος, **Egyptian**, Acts vii. 22, 24, 28. xxi. 38. Heb. xi. 29.
Αἴγυπτος, **Egypt**, Matt. ii. 13, 14, 15, 19. Acts ii. 10. vii. 9, 10*t*, 11, 12, 15(-T), 17, 34*t*, 36, 39, 40. xiii. 17. Heb. iii. 16. viii. 9. xi. 26, 27. Jude 5. Rev. xi. 8. —*Add* Acts vii. 18 (arose ἐπ' Αἴγυπτον), L*S*.
Αἰθίοψ, **Ethiopian**, Acts viii. 27. —**of Ethiopia**, Acts viii. 27.
Αἰνέας, **Æneas**, Acts ix. 33, 34.
Αἰνών, **Ænon**, John iii. 23.
'Ακελδαμά, -δαμάχ LT*S*, **Aceldama**, Acts i. 19.
'Ακύλας, **Aquila**, Acts xviii. 2, 18, 26. Rom. xvi. 3. 1 Cor. xvi. 19. 2 Tim. iv. 19.
'Αλασσα. *See* Λασαία.
'Αλεξανδρεύς, **Alexandrian**, Acts vi. 9. —'Αλεξ. τῷ γένει, **born at Alexandria**, Acts xviii. 24.
'Αλεξανδρῖνος, **of Alexandria**, Acts xxvii. 6. xxviii. 11.
'Αλέξανδρος, **Alexander**, **1**, son of Simon, Mark xv. 21. —**2**, a high priest, Acts iv. 6. —**3**, of Ephesus, Acts xix. 33*t*. —**4**, the coppersmith, 1 Tim. i. 20. 2 Tim. iv. 14.
'Αλφαῖος, **Alpheus**, *or* -**æus**, **1**, father of James, Matt. x. 3. Mark iii. 18. Luke vi. 15. Acts i. 13. —**2**, father of Levi, Mark ii. 14.
'Αμιναδάβ, 'Αμειναδάβ T, **Aminadab**, Matt. i. 4, 4(-αδάμ *S*). Luke iii. 33 ('Αδάμ *S*).
'Αμπλίας, 'Αμπλιᾶτος L^m^*S*, **Amplias**, Rom. xvi. 8.
'Αμφίπολις, **Amphipolis**, Acts xvii. 1.
'Αμών, 'Αμώς LTTr*S*, **Amon**, Matt. i. 10*t*.

Ἀμώς, Amos, Luke iii. 25.

Ἀνανίας, Ananias, 1, of Jerusalem, Acts v. 1, 3, 5. — 2, of Damascus, Acts ix. 10*t*, 12, 13, 17. xxii. 12. — 3, high priest, Acts xxiii. 2. xxiv. 1.

Ἀνδρέας, Andrew, Matt. iv. 18. x. 2. Mark i. 16, 29. iii. 18. xiii. 3. Luke vi. 14. John i. 40(41), 44(45). vi. 8. xii. 22*t*. Acts i. 13. [xvi. 7.

Ἀνδρόνικος, Andronicus, Rom.

Ἄννα, Anna, Luke ii. 36.

Ἄννας, Annas, Luke iii. 2. John xviii. 13, 24. Acts iv. 6.

Ἀντιόχεια, Antioch, 1, of Syria, Acts xi. 19, 20, 22, 26(25), 26, 27. xiii. 1. xiv. 26. xv. 22, 23, 30, 35. xviii. 22. Gal. ii. 11. — 2, of Pisidia, Acts xiii. 14. xiv. 19, 21. 2 Tim. iii. 11. [5.

Ἀντιοχεύς, of Antioch, Acts vi.

Ἀντίπας, Antipas, Rev. ii. 13.

Ἀντιπατρίς, Antipatris, Acts xxiii. 31.

Ἀντίχριστος. See p. 32.

Ἀπελλῆς, Apelles, Rom. xvi. 10.

Ἀπολλύων. See p. 41.

Ἀπολλωνία, Apollonia, Acts xvii. 1.

Ἀπολλώς, Apollos, Acts xviii. 24. xix. 1. 1 Cor. i. 12. iii. 4, 5, 6, 22. iv. 6. xvi. 12. Tit. iii. 13.

Ἀππίου φόρον, Appii forum, Acts xxviii. 15.

Ἀπφία, Apphia, Phm. 2.

Aquila. *See* Ἀκύλας.

Ἀραβία, Arabia, Gal. i. 17. iv. 25.

Ἀράμ, Aram, Matt. i. 3, 4. Luke iii. 33 (Ἀδμείν, τοῦ Ἀρνεί T*S*).

Ἄραψ, Arabian, Acts ii. 11.

Archelaus, etc. *See* Ἀρχ., *etc.*

Ἄρειος Πάγος. *See* πάγος, p. 305.

Ἀρεοπαγίτης, -είτης T, Areopagite, Acts xvii. 34.

Ἀρέτας, Aretas, 2 Cor. xi. 32.

Ἀριμαθαία, Arimathea, *or* -æa, Matt. xxvii. 57. Mark xv. 43. Luke xxiii. 51. John xix. 38.

Ἀρίσταρχος, Aristarchus, Acts xix. 29. xx. 4. xxvii. 2. Col. iv. 10. Phm. 24(23).

Ἀριστόβουλος, Aristobulus, Rom. xvi. 10.

Ἀρμαγεδδών, Ἀρ. LT, -εδών LTTr *S*, Μαγεδών G′, Armageddon, Rev. xvi. 16.

Ἀρνεί. *See* Ἀράμ.

Ἀρτεμᾶς, Artemas, Tit. iii. 12.

Ἄρτεμις, Diana, Acts xix. 24, 27, 28, 34, 35.

Ἀρφαξάδ, Arphaxad, Lk. iii. 36.

Ἀρχέλαος, Archelaus, Mt. ii. 22.

Ἄρχιππος, Archippus, Col. iv. 17. Phm. 2.

Ἀσά, -άφ LTr*S*, Asa, Matt. i. 7, 8.

Ἀσήρ, Aser, Luke ii. 36. Rev. vii. 6.

Ἀσία, Asia, Acts ii. 9. vi. 9(–L). xvi. 6. xix. 10, 22, 26, 27. xx. 4, 16, 18. xxi. 27. xxiv. 18. xxvii. 2. 1 Cor. xvi. 19 (18). 2 Cor. i. 8. 2 Tim. i. 15. 1 Pet. i. 1. Rev. i. 4, 11(*om S*). — *Add* Rom. xvi. 5, for Ἀχαΐα, GLT*S*.

Ἀσιανός, of Asia, Acts xx. 4.

Ἀσιάρχης, chief of Asia, Acts xix. 31.

Ἄσσος, Assos, Acts xx. 13, 14. — *Add* Acts xxvii. 13, for ἆσσον, St.

Ἀσύγκριτος, Asyncritus, Rom. xvi. 14.

Athens, etc. *See* Ἀθῆναι, *etc.*

Ἀττάλεια, Attalia, Acts xiv. 25.

Αὔγουστος, Augustus, Luke ii. 1. — *See also* Σεβαστός.

Ἄχαζ, Achaz, Matt. i. 9*t*.

Ἀχαΐα, Achaia, Acts xviii. 12, 27. xix. 21. Rom. xv. 26. xvi. 5 (Ἀσία GLT*S*). 1 Cor. xvi. 15. 2 Cor. i. 1. ix. 2. xi. 10. 1 Thes. i. 7, 8.

Ἀχαϊκός, Achaicus, 1 Cor. xvi.

Ἀχείμ, Achim, Matt. i. 14*t*. [17.

Ἄψινθος, Wormwood, Rev. viii. 11.

Azor, etc. *See* Ἀζώρ, *etc.*

Βάαλ, Baal, Rom. xi. 4.

Βαβυλών, Babylon, Matt. i. 11, 12, 17*t*. Acts vii. 43. 1 Pet. v. 13. Rev. xiv. 8. xvi. 19. xvii. 5. xviii. 2, 10, 21.

Βαλαάμ, Balaam, 2 Pet. ii. 15. Jude 11. Rev. ii. 14.

Βαλάκ, Balak, Rev. ii. 14.

Βαραββᾶς, Barabbas, Matt. xxvii. 16, 17, 20, 21, 26. Mark xv. 7, 11, 15. Luke xxiii. 18. John xviii. 40t.

Βαράκ, Barak, Heb. xi. 32.

Βαραχίας, Barachias, Matt. xxiii. 35.

Βαρθολομαῖος, Bartholomew, Matt. x. 3. Mark iii. 18. Luke vi. 14. Acts i. 13.

Βαριησοῦς, Bar-jesus, Acts xiii. [6.

Βὰρ Ἰωνᾶ, βὰρ Ἰωνᾶ G, Βαριωνᾶ LT, Bar-jona, Matt. xvi. 17.

Βαρνάβας, Barnabas, Acts iv. 36. ix. 27. xi. 22, 25(-G°°LTS), 30. xii. 25. xiii. 1, 2, 7, 43, 46, 50. xiv. 12, 14, 20. xv. 2t, 12, 22, 25, 35, 36, 37, 39. 2 Cor. ix. 6. Gal. ii. 1, 9, 13. Col. iv. 10.

Βαρσαβᾶς, -ββᾶς LTS, Barsabas, **1**, Joseph, Acts i. 23. — **2**, Judas, Acts xv. 22.

Βαρτίμαιος, Bartimeus, *or* -æus, Mark x. 46.

Βεελζεβούβ, -βούλ StEGLTTrS, Beelzebub, Matt. x. 25. xii. 24, 27. Mark iii. 22. Luke xi. 15, 18, 19.

Βελίαλ, Βελίαρ StGTS, Belial, 2 Cor. vi. 15.

Βενιαμίν, Benjamin, Acts xiii. 21. Rom. xi. 1. Phil. iii. 5. Rev. vii. 8.

Βερνίκη, Bernice, Acts xxv. 13, 23. xxvi. 30. [10, 13.

Βέροια, Berea, *or* -œa, Acts xvii.

Βεροιαῖος, of Berea, Acts xx. 4.

Βηθαβαρά, Bethabara, John i. 28 (G'', Βηθανία GLTTrS).

Βηθανία, Bethany, **1**, near Jerusalem, Matt. xxi. 17. xxvi. 6. Mark xi. 1, 11, 12. xiv. 3. Luke xix. 29. xxiv. 50. John xi. 1, 18. xii. 1. — *Add* Mark viii. 22, *see* Βηθσαιδάν. — **2**, beyond Jordan, *see* Βηθαβαρά.

Βηθεσδά, Bethesda, John v. 2 (Βηθσαϊδά Lm, Βηθζαδά S).

Βηθλεέμ, Bethlehem, Matt. ii. 1, 5, 6, 8, 16. Luke ii. 4, 15. John vii. 42.

Βηθσαϊδά, -δάν, Bethsaida, **1**, of Galilee, Matt. xi. 21. Mark vi. 45. viii. 22 (Βηθανία G'). Luke x. 13 (Βηδσαϊδά Lm). John i. 44 (45). xii. 21. — *Add*, *see* Βηθεσδά. — **2**, of Gaulonitis, Luke ix. 10.

Βηθφαγή, Βηθφαγῆ, -σφαγή, Bethphage, Matt. xxi. 1. Mark xi. 1 (-G'LT). Luke xix. 29.

Βιθυνία, Bithynia, Acts xvi. 7. 1 Pet. i. 1.

Βλάστος, Blastus, Acts xii. 20.

Βοανεργές, -ηργές LTTrS, Boanerges, Mark iii. 17.

Βοόζ, Βοός, Booz, Matt. i. 5t. Luke [iii. 32.

Βορρᾶς. See p. 63.

Βοσόρ, Bosor, 2 Pet. ii. 15.

C. *See* K., X. — Ch. *See* X.

Castor. *See* Διόσκουροι. [13.

Γαββαθᾶ, Gabbatha, John xix.

Γαβριήλ, Gabriel, Luke i. 19, 26.

Γάδ, Gad, Rev. vii. 5.

Γαδαρηνός, Gadarene, Mark v. 1 (Γερασηνός G''LTTrS). Luke viii. 26 (Γερασηνός G''LTTr, Γεργεσηνός S), 37 (Γερασηνός LTTr, Γεργεσηνός S). — *Add*, *see* Γεργεσηνός.

Γάζα, Gaza, Acts viii. 26.

Γάϊος, Gaius, **1**, of Macedonia, Acts xix. 29. — **2**, of Derbe, Acts xx. 4. — **3**, of Corinth, Rom. xvi. 23. 1 Cor. i. 14. — **4**, a Christian, 3 John 1.

Γαλάτης, Galatian, Gal. iii. 1.

Γαλατία, Galatia, 1 Cor. xvi. 1. Gal. i. 2. 2 Tim. iv. 10. 1 Pet. i. 1.

Γαλατικός, of Galatia, Acts xvi. 6. xviii. 23.

Γαλιλαία, Galilee, Matt. ii. 22. iii. 13. iv. 12, 15, 18, 23, 25. xv. 29. xvii. 22. xix. 1. xxi. 11. xxvi. 32. xxvii. 55. xxviii. 7, 10, 16. Mark i. 9, 14, 16, 28, 39. iii. 7. vi. 21. vii. 31. ix. 30. xiv. 28. xv. 41. xvi. 7. Luke i. 26. ii. 4, 39. iii. 1. iv. 14, 31, 44. v. 17. viii. 26. xvii. 11. xxiii. 5, 6, 49, 55. xxiv. 6. John i. 43(44). ii. 1, 11. iv. 3, 43, 45, 46, 47, 54. vi. 1. vii. 1, 9, 41, 52t. xii. 21. xxi. 2. Acts ix. 31. x. 37. xiii. 31.

Γαλιλαῖος, Galilean, *or* -æan,

Mark xiv. 70. Luke xiii. 1, 2*t*. xxii. 59. xxiii. 6. John iv. 45. Acts ii. 7. —of Galilee, Matt. xxvi. 69. Acts i. 11. v. 37.

Γαλλίων, Gallio, Acts xviii. 12, 14, 17.

Γαμαλιήλ, Gamaliel, Acts v. 34. xxii. 3.

Γεδεών, Gedeon, Heb. xi. 32.

Γεθσημανῆ, -εῖ LTr, -εί T, -ι, -ει *S*, Gethsemane, Matt. xxvi. 36 (-εί G''). Mark xiv. 32.

Γεννησαρέτ, Γενησαρέτ, Gennesaret. Matt. xiv. 34(-ρέθ LT). Mark vi. 53. Luke v. 1.

Γεργεσηνός, Γερασηνός G''L, Γαδαρηνός G'TTr, Γαζαρηνός *S*, Gergesene, Matt. viii. 28.

Γολγοθᾶ, Golgotha, Matt. xxvii. 33. Mark xv. 22. John xix. 17.

Γομόρρα, Γόμορρα, Gomorrha, *or* -rah, Matt. x. 15. Mark vi. 11 (*ap*). Rom. ix. 29. 2 Pet. ii. 6. Jude [7.

Γώγ, Gog, Rev. xx. 8.

Δαβίδ, Δαυίδ G, Tr in Apoc., Δαυείδ LT*S*, Tr in Gospels, David, Matt. i. 1, 6*t*, 17*t*, 20. ix. 27. xii. 3, 23 xv. 22. xx. 30, 31. xxi. 9, 15. xxii. 42, 43, 45. Mark ii. 25. x. 47, 48. xi. 10. xii. 35, 36, 37. Luke i. 27, 32, 69. ii. 4*t*, 11. iii. 31. vi. 3. xviii. 38, 39. xx. 41, 42, 44. John vii. 42*t*. Acts i. 16. ii. 25, 29, 34. iv. 25. vii. 45. xiii. 22*t*, 34, 36. xv. 16. Rom. i. 3. iv. 6. xi. 9. 2 Tim. ii. 8. Heb. iv. 7. xi. 32. Rev. iii. 7. v. 5. xxii. 16.

Δαλμανουθά, Dalmanutha, Mark viii. 10. [10.

Δαλματία, Dalmatia, 2 Tim. iv.

Δάμαρις, Damaris, Acts xvii. 34.

Δαμασκηνός, Damascene, 2 Cor. xi. 32.

Δαμασκός, Damascus, Acts ix. 2, 3, 8, 10, 19, 22, 27. xxii. 5, 6, 10, 11. xxvi. 12, 20. 2 Cor. xi. 32. Gal. i. 17.

Δανιήλ, Daniel, Matt. xxiv. 15. Mark xiii. 14(*ap*).

Δεκάπολις, Decapolis, Matt. iv. 25. Mark v. 20. vii. 31.

Δερβαῖος, of Derbe, Acts xx. 4.

Δέρβη, Derbe, Acts xiv. 6, 20. xvi. 1.

Δημᾶς, Demas, Col. iv. 14. 2 Tim. iv. 10. Phm. 24.

Δημήτριος, Demetrius, 1, the silversmith, Acts xix. 24, 38.—2, a Christian, 3 John 12.

Diana. *See* Ἄρτεμις.

Δίδυμος, Didymus, John xi. 16. xx. 24. xxi. 2. [34.

Διονύσιος, Dionysius, Acts xvii.

Διοπετής. See p. 91.

Διόσκουροι, Castor and Pollux, Acts xxviii. 11.

Διοτρεφής, Diotrephes, 3 John 9.

Δορκάς, Dorcas, Acts ix. 36, 39.

Δρούσιλλα, Drusilla, Acts xxiv. 24.

Ἔβερ, Ἐβέρ, Heber, Luke iii. 35.

Ἑβραϊκός, of Hebrew, Luke xxiii. 38(*op*).

Ἑβραῖος, Hebrew, Acts vi. 1. 2 Cor. xi. 22. Phil. iii. 5*t*.

Ἑβραΐς, Hebrew, Acts xxi. 40. xxii. 2. xxvi. 14.

Ἑβραϊστί. See p. 100.

Egypt, etc. *See* Αἴγυπτος, *etc.*

Ἐζεκίας, Ἐζεκείας LT, Ezekias, Matt. i. 9, 10.

Ἐλαμίτης, Ἐλαμείτης T, Elamite, Acts ii. 9(-*S*).

Ἐλεάζαρ, Eleazar, Matt. i. 15*t*.

Ἐλιακείμ, Eliakim, Matt. i. 13*t*. Luke iii. 30.

Elias. *See* Ἡλίας.

Ἐλιέζερ, Eliezer, Luke iii. 29.

Ἐλιούδ, Eliud, Matt. i. 14, 15.

Ἐλισάβετ, Elisabeth, Luke i. 5, 7, 13, 24, 36, 40, 41*t*, 57.

Ἐλισαῖος, Ἐλ. LT, -ισσαῖος StEGT, Eliseus, *or* -æus, Luke iv. 27.

Ἑλλάς, Greece, Acts xx. 2.

Ἕλλην, Greek, John xi. 20. Acts xiv. 1. xvi. 1, 3. xvii. 4. xviii. 4, 17 (-G∞LT*S*). xix. 10, 17. xx. 21. xxi. 28. Rom. i. 14, 16. x. 12. 1 Cor. i. 22, 23 (ἔθνος GLT*S*), 24. Gal. ii. 3. iii. 28. Col. iii. 11.—Gentile, John vii. 35 (*marg.* Greek), 35. Rom. ii. 9 and 10 (*Gr.* Greek). iii. 9. 1 Cor. x. 32 and xii. 13 (*Gr.* Greek).—*Add* Acts xi. 20, *see* Ἑλληνιστής.

Ἑλληνικός, Greek, Rev. ix. 11. — of Greek, Luke xxiii. 38(*ap*).
Ἑλληνίς, Greek, Mark vii. 26 (*marg.* Gentile). Acts xvii. 12.
Ἑλληνιστής, Grecian, Acts vi. 1. ix. 29. xi. 20 (Ἕλλην GLT, εὐαγγελιστής *S*).
Ἑλληνιστί, in Greek, John xix. 20. — Greek, Acts xxi. 37.
Ἐλμωδάμ, Ἐλ. L, -μαδάμ LTTr*S*, Elmodam, Luke iii. 28.
Ἐλύμας, Elymas, Acts xiii. 8.
Ἐμμανουήλ, Emmanuel, Matt. i. 23. [13.
Ἐμμαούς, Emmaus, Luke xxiv.
Ἐμμόρ, Ἐμμώρ LT*S*, Emmor, Acts vii. 16.
Ἐνώς, Enos, Luke iii. 38.
Ἐνώχ, Enoch, Luke iii. 37. Heb. xi. 5. Jude 14.
Ἐπαίνετος, Epenetus, *or* Epænetus, Rom. xvi. 5.
Ἐπαφρᾶς, Epaphras, Col. i. 7. iv. 12. Phm. 23.
Ἐπαφρόδιτος, Epaphroditus, Phil. ii. 25. iv. 18.
Ἐπικούρειος, Epicurean, Acts xvii. 18.
Er. *See* Ἤρ.
Ἔραστος, Erastus, Acts xix. 22. Rom. xvi. 23. 2 Tim. iv. 20.
Ἑρμᾶς, Hermas, Rom. xvi. 14.
Ἑρμῆς, 1, in mythology, Mercurius, Acts xiv. 12. — 2, a Christian, Hermes, Rom. xvi. 14.
Ἑρμογένης, Hermogenes, 2Tim. i. 15.
Ἐρυθρὰ Θάλασσα. See p. 169.
Esaias, Esau. *See* H.
Ἐσλί, -εί TTr*S*, Esli, Luke iii. 25.
Ἐσρώμ, Esrom, Matt. i. 3. Luke iii. 33.
Ethiopia, etc. *See* Αἰθίοψ.
Εὔα, Εὔα St[2], Εὔα G[1]LT, Eve, 2Cor. xi. 3[1]. 1 Tim. ii. 13[2].
Εὔβουλος, Eubulus, 2Tim. iv. 21.
Εὐνίκη, Eunice, 2 Tim. i. 5.
Εὐωδία, Εὐοδία GLT*S*, Euodias, *properly* Euodia, Phil. iv. 2.
Εὐροκλύδων, Εὐρυκ. G, Εὐρακύλων L*S*, Euroclydon, Acts xxvii. 14.
Εὔτυχος, Eutychus, Acts xx. 9.
Εὐφράτης, Euphrates, Rev. ix. 14. xvi. 12.
Ἐφεσῖνος, of Ephesus, Rev. ii. 1 (ἐν Ἐφέσῳ, GLTTr*S*).
Ἐφέσιος, Ephesian, Acts xix. 28, 34, 35*t*. xxi. 29.
Ἔφεσος, Ephesus, Acts xviii. 19, 21, 24. xix. 1, 17, 26. xx. 16, 17. 1 Cor. xv. 32. xvi. 8. Eph. i. 1 (-T[b]*S*). 1 Tim. i. 3. 2 Tim. i. 18. iv. 12. Rev. i. 11. — *Add.* Rev. ii. 1, *see* Ἐφεσῖνος.
Ἐφραίμ, -αίμ GLT, Ephraim, John xi. 54.
Ezekias. *See* Ἐζεκίας.
Ζαβουλών, Zabulon, Matt. iv. 13, 15. Rev. vii. 8.
Ζακχαῖος, Zaccheus, *or* -æus, Luke xix. 2, 5, 8.
Ζαρά, Zara, Matt. i. 3.
Ζαχαρίας, Zacharias, 1, son of Barachias, Matt. xxiii. 35. Luke xi. 51. — 2, father of John the Baptist, Luke i. 5, 12, 13, 18, 21, 40, 59, 67. iii. 2.
Ζεβεδαῖος, Zebedee, Matt. iv. 21*t*. x. 2. xx. 20. xxvi. 37. xxvii. 56. Mark i. 19, 20. iii. 17. x. 35. Luke v. 10. John xxi. 2.
Ζεύς, Jupiter, Acts xiv. 12, 13.
Ζηλωτής, Zelotes, Luke vi. 15. Acts i. 13.
Ζηνᾶς, Zenas, Tit. iii. 13.
Ζοροβάβελ, Zorobabel, Matt. i. 12, 13. Luke iii. 27.
F., G. *See* Φ., Γ.
fair havens, The. See p. 242.
Gentile. *See* Ἕλλην, Ἑλληνίς.
Gnidus. *See* Κνίδος.
Greece, etc. *See* Ἑλλάς, *etc.*
Heber, etc. *See* Ἔβερ, *etc.*
Ἡλί, Ἡλ. GTTr, -εί TTr*S*, Heli, Luke iii. 23.
Ἡλίας G, Ἡ. LTTr, St *varies*, Elias, Matt. xi. 14. xvi. 14. xvii. 3, 4, 10, 11, 12. xxvii. 47, 49. Mark vi. 15. viii. 28. ix. 4, 5, 11, 12, 13. xv. 35, 36. Luke i. 17. iv. 25, 26. ix. 8, 19, 30, 33, 54 (*ap*). John i. 21, 25. Rom. xi. 2. Jas. v. 17.

Ἤρ, Ἢρ L, **Er**, Luke iii. 28.

Ἡρώδης, **Herod**, **1**, the Great, Matt. ii. 1, 3, 7, 12, 13, 15, 16, 19. 22. Luke i. 5. Acts xxiii. 35.—**2**, Antipas, Matt. xiv. 1, 3, 6*t*. Mark vi. 14, 16, 17, 18, 20, 21, 22. viii. 15. Luke iii. 1, 19*t*. viii. 3. ix. 7, 9. xiii. 31. xxiii. 7*t*, 8, 11, 12, 15. Acts iv. 27. xiii. 1.—**3**, Agrippa, Acts xii. 1, 6, 11, 19, 20(*om S*), 21.

Ἡρωδιανός, **Herodian**, Matt. xxii. 16. Mark iii. 6. xii. 13.

Ἡρωδιάς, **Herodias**, Matt. xiv. 3, 6. Mark vi. 17, 19, 22. Luke iii. 19.

Ἡρωδίων, Ἡροδ. St. *err.*, **Herodion**, Rom. xvi. 11.

Hierapolis. *See* Ἱεράπολις.

Hierusalem. *See* Ἱεροσόλυμα.

Hymenæus. *See* Ὑμέναιος.

Ἡσαΐας, Ἠσαΐας L, **Esaias**, Matt. iii. 3. iv. 14. viii. 17. xii. 17. xiii. 14. xv. 7. Mark vii. 6. Luke iii. 4. iv. 17. John i. 23. xii. 38, 39, 41. Acts viii. 28, 30. xxviii. 25. Rom. ix. 27, 29. x. 16, 20. xv. 12.—*Add* Mark i. 2, τῷ (–Tr[b]) Ἡσαΐᾳ τῷ προφήτῃ for τοῖς προφήταις, GLTTr*S*.

Ἡσαῦ, **Esau**, Rom. ix. 13. Heb. xi. 20. xii. 16.

Θαδδαῖος, **Thaddeus**, *or* **-æus**, Matt. x. 3(–G[o]T). Mark iii. 18.

Θάμαρ, **Thamar**, Matt. i. 3.

Θάρα, **Thara**, Luke iii. 34.

Θεόφιλος, **Theophilus**, Luke i. 3. Acts i. 1.

Θεσσαλονικεύς, **Thessalonian**, Acts xx. 4. 1 Thes. i. 1. 2 Thes. i. 1. —**of Thessalonica**, Acts xxvii. 2.

Θεσσαλονίκη, **Thessalonica**, Acts xvii. 1, 11, 13. Phil. iv. 16. 2 Tim. iv. 10.

Θευδᾶς, **Theudas**, Acts v. 36.

Θυάτειρα, **Thyatira**, Acts xvi. 14. Rev. i. 11. ii. 18, 24.

Θωμᾶς, **Thomas**, Matt. x. 3. Mark iii. 18. Luke vi. 15. John xi. 16. xiv. 5. xx. 24, 26, 27, 28, 29(–GLTTr, καί *S*). xxi. 2. Acts i. 13.

Ἰάειρος, **Jairus**, Mark v. 22(–G[o]). Luke viii. 41.

Ἰακώβ, **Jacob**, **1**, son of Isaac, Matt. i. 2*t*. viii. 11. xxii. 32. Mark xii. 26. Luke i. 33. iii. 34. xiii. 28. xx. 37. John iv. 5, 6, 12. Acts iii. 13. vii. 8*t*, 12, 14(–G[o]). 15, 32, 46. Rom. ix. 13. xi. 26. Heb. xi. 9, 20, 21.—**2**, father of Joseph, Matt. i. 15, 16.

Ἰάκωβος, **James**, **1**, son of Zebedee, Matt. iv. 21. x. 2(3). xvii. 1. Mark i. 19, 29. iii. 17*t*. v. 37, 37(αὐτός G′). ix. 2. x. 35, 41. xiii. 3. xiv. 33. Luke v. 10. vi. 14. viii. 51. ix. 28, 54. Acts i. 13. xii. 2.—**2**, son of Alphæus, Matt. x. 3. xxvii. 56. Mark iii. 18. xvi. 1. Luke vi. 15, 16. xxiv. 10. Acts i. 13*t*. xii. 17. xv. 13. xxi. 18. 1 Cor. xv. 7. Gal. ii. 9, 12. Jas. i. 1. Jude 1.—**3**, (2?) brother of Jesus, Matt. xiii. 55. Mark vi. 3. xv. 40. Gal. i. 19.

Ἰαμβρῆς, **Jambres**, 2 Tim. iii. 8.

Ἰαννά, -ναί LTTr*S*, **Janna**, Luke iii. 24.

Ἰαννῆς, **Jannes**, 2 Tim. iii. 8.

Ἰαρέδ, Ἰάρεθ L, -ρετ *S*, **Jared**, Luke iii. 37.

Ἰάσων, **Jason**, Acts xvii. 5, 6, 7, 9. Rom. xvi. 21.

Iconium. *See* Ἰκόνιον.

Ἰδουμαία, **Idumea**, *or* **-æa**, Mark iii. 8.

Jechonias. *See* Ἰεχονίας.

Jephthae. *See* Ἰεφθάε.

Ἰεζαβήλ, Ἰεζάβελ GTTr, Ἰεζάβελ L, Ιαζαβελ *S*, **Jezebel**, Rev. ii. 20.

Ἱεράπολις, **Hierapolis**, Col. iv. 13.

Ἱερεμίας, **Jeremias**[1], **Jeremy**, Matt. ii. 17. xvi. 14[1]. xxvii. 9(Ἰ. St).

Ἱεριχώ, Ἱερειχώ T *except*[1], **Jericho**, Matt. xx. 29. Mark x. 46, 46 (*see* ἐκεῖθεν). Luke x. 30. xviii. 35. xix. 1. Heb. xi. 30[1].

Ἱεροσόλυμα, Ἱερουσαλήμ[2], **Jerusalem**, **Hierusalem** *ed.* 1611, *etc.*, Matt. ii. 1, 3. iii. 5. iv. 25. v. 35. xv. 1. xvi. 21. xx. 17, 18. xxi. 1, 10. Mark iii. 8, 22. vii. 1. x. 32, 33. xi. 11, 15, 27. xv. 41. Luke ii. 22, 42(–G[oo]TTr[b]*S*). xviii. 31([2]TTr *S*). xix. 28. xxiii. 7. John i. 19.

ii. 13, 23. iv. 20, 21, 45. v. 1, 2. x. 22. xi. 18, 55. xii. 12. Acts i. 4. viii. 1, 14. xi. 2(²LTS), 22(²LTS), 27. xiii. 13. xviii. 21(*ap*). xx. 16 (²TS). xxi. 17. xxv. 1, 7, 9, 15, 24. xxvi. 4, 10, 20. xxviii. 17. Gal. i. 17, 18. ii. 1. — *Add, see* Ἱερουσαλήμ.

Ἱεροσολυμίτης, –μείτης TS, of Jerusalem, Mark i. 5. John vii. 25.

Ἱερουσαλήμ, Ἱεροσόλυμα¹, Jerusalem, Hier. *ed.* 1611, *etc.*, Matt. xxiii. 37*t*. Mark xi. 1(¹GLTTrS). Luke ii. 25, 38 (*marg.* Israel), 41, 43, 45. iv. 9. v. 17. vi. 17. ix. 31, 51, 53. x. 30. xiii. 4, 22(¹L^m S), 33, 34*t*. xvii. 11. xix. 11. xxi. 20, 24. xxiii. 28. xxiv. 13, 18, 33, 47, 49 (*om*S), 52. Acts i. 8, 12*t*, 19. ii. 5, 14. iv. 6(5), 16. v. 16, 28. vi. 7. viii. 25 (¹LTS), 26, 27. ix. 2, 13, 21, 26, 28. x. 39. xii. 25. xiii. 27, 31. xv. 2, 4. xvi. 4(¹LTS). xix. 21 (¹LTS). xx. 22. xxi. 4 (¹GLTS), 11, 12, 13, 15(¹G″LTS), 31. xxii. 5, 17, 18. xxiii. 11. xxiv. 11. xxv. 3, 20(¹LTS). Rom. xv. 19, 25, 26, 31. 1 Cor. xvi. 3. Gal. iv. 25, 26. Heb. xii. 22. Rev. iii. 12. xxi. 2, 10. — *Add, see* Ἱεροσόλυμα.

Ἰεσσαί, Jesse, Matt. i. 5, 6. Luke iii. 32. Acts xiii. 22. Rom. xv. 12.

Ἰεφθάε, Jephthae, Heb. xi. 32.

Ἰεχονίας, Jechonias, Matt. i. 11, 12.

Ἰησοῦς, Jesus, Matt. i. 1, 16, 18 (–G^o TTr), 21, 25. ii. 1. iii. 13, 15, 16. iv. 1, 7, 10, 12(–G^{oo}TTrS), 17, 18(*om*S), 23(–TTr^b). vii. 28. viii. 3(–LTTrS), 4, 5 (αὐτός GLTTrS), 7(–LTTr^b S), 10, 13, 14, 18, 20, 22, 29(*om*S), 34. ix. 2, 4, 9, 10, 12(–L Tr^b S), 15, 19, 22, 23, 27, 28, 30, 35. x. 5. xi. 1, 4, 7, 25. xii. 1, 15, 25 (–LTTrS). xiii. 1, 34, 36(–G^{oo}LTTr S), 51(*ap*), 53, 57. xiv. 1, 12, 13, 14 (–G^{oo}LTTrS), 16, 22 (*om*S), 25 (*om*S), 27, 29, 31. xv. 1, 16(–LTTr S), 21, 28, 29, 30 (αὐτός G′LTTrS), 32, 34. xvi. 6, 8, 13, 17. 20(*om*S), 21, 24. xvii. 1, 4, 7, 8, 9, 11(–G^{oo}L TTrS), 17, 18, 19, 20(–LTTrS), 22, 25, 26. xviii. 1, 2(–TrS), 22. xix. 1, 14, 18, 21, 23, 26, 28. xx. 17, 22, 25, 30, 32, 34. xxi. 1, 6, 11, 12, 16, 21, 24, 27, 31, 42. xxii. 1, 18, 29, 37(–LTTrS), 41. xxiii. 1. xxiv. 1, 2 (ἀποκριθείς LTTrS), 4. xxvi. 1, 4, 6, 10, 17, 19, 26, 31, 34, 36, 49, 50*t*, 51, 52, 55, 57, 59, 63, 64, 69, 71, 75. xxvii. 1, 11*t*, 17, 20, 22, 26, 27, 37, 46, 50, 54, 55, 57, 58. xxviii. 5, 9, 10, 16, 18.

Mark i. 1, 9, 14, 17, 24, 25, 41(–L TTrS). ii. 5, 8, 15, 17, 19. iii. 7. v. 6, 7, 13(–G^{oo}L^b TrS), 15, 19(–G^{oo}L^b TTrS), 20, 21, 27, 30, 36. vi. 4, 30, 34(–GL^b TTrS). vii. 27(–LTTrS). viii. 1(*om*S), 17(–TTr^b), 27. ix. 2, 4, 5, 8, 23, 25, 27, 39. x. 5, 14, 18, 21, 23, 24, 27, 29, 32, 38, 39, 42, 47*t*, 49, 50, 51, 52, 52(αὐτός GLTrS). xi. 6, 7, 11(–G^{oo}LTTrS), 14(*om*S), 15 (*om*S), 22, 29, 33*t*. xii. 17, 24, 29, 34, 35, 41(–L^b TTrS). xiii. 2, 5. xiv. 6, 18, 22 (–L^b TTr^b S?), 27, 30, 48, 53, 55, 60, 62, 67, 72. xv. 1, 5, 15, 34, 37, 43. xvi. 6.

Luke i. 31. ii. 21, 27, 43, 52. iii. 21, 23. iv. 1, 4, 8, 12, 14, 34, 35. v. 8, 10, 12, 19, 22, 31. vi. 3, 9, 11. vii. 3, 4, 6, 9, 19, 22(–L^b TTrS), 40. viii. 28, 28(–G^o), 30, 35*t*, 38(–G^{oo}L^b TTrS), 39, 40, 41, 45, 46(–G^{oo}), 50. ix. 33, 36, 41, 42, 43 (–G^{oo}TTrS), 47, 50, 58, 60(–G^{oo}L^b TTrS), 62. x. 21 (–LTrS), 29, 30, 37, 39 (Κύριος LTTrS), 41 (Κύριος L^m TS). xiii. 2 (–L^b TTrS), 12, 14. xiv. 3. xvii. 13, 17. xviii. 16, 19, 22, 24, 37, 38, 40, 42. xix. 3, 5, 9, 35*t*. xx. 8, 34. xxii. 47, 48, 51, 52, 63(αὐτός G″LTTrS). xxiii. 8, 20, 25, 26, 28, 34(*ap*), 42, 43 (–TTr^b S), 46, 52. xxiv. 3(–T), 15, 19, 36(*om*S).

John i. 17, 29, 36, 37, 38, 42(43), 43 (44, *om*S), 45 (46), 47 (48), 48 (49), 50 (51). ii. 1, 2, 3, 4, 7, 11, 13, 19, 22, 24. iii. 2 (αὐτός GLTTr S), 3, 5, 10, 22. iv. 1, 2, 6, 7, 10, 13, 16(–L^b TTr^b), 17, 21, 26, 34, 44, 46(*om*S), 47, 48, 50*t*, 53, 54. v. 1,

6, 8, 13, 14, 15, 16, 17, 19. vi. 1, 3, 5, 10, 11, 14 (–TTr*S*), 15, 17, 19, 22, 24*t*, 26, 29, 32, 35, 42, 43, 53, 61, 64, 67, 70(–G^{oo}T). vii. 1, 6, 14, 16, 21, 28, 33, 37, 39. viii. 1(*ap*), 6(*ap*), 9(*ap*), 10(*ap*), 11(*ap*), 12, 14, 19, 20 (*omS*), 21(–G^{oo}LTTr*S*), 25, 28, 31, 34, 39, 42, 49, 54, 58, 59. ix. 3, 11, 14. 35, 37, 39, 41. x. 6, 7, 23, 25, 32, 34. xi. 4, 5, 9, 13, 14, 17, 20, 21, 23, 25, 30, 32, 33, 35, 38, 39, 40, 41, 44, 45(*om*), 46, 51, 54, 56. xii. 1, 3, 7, 9, 11, 12, 14, 16, 21, 22, 23, 30, 35, 36, 44. xiii. 1, 3(–$G^{oo}L^{b}$TTr*S*), 7, 8, 10, 21, 23*t*, 25, 26, 27, 29, 31, 36, 38. xiv. 6, 9, 23. xvi. 19, 31. xvii. 1, 3. xviii. 1, 2, 4, 5, 5(–TTr), 7, 8, 11, 12, 15*t*, 19, 20, 22, 23, 28, 32, 33, 34, 36, 37. xix. 1, 5, 9*t*, 11, 13, 16 (*ap*), 18, 19, 20, 23, 25, 26, 28, 30, 33, 38*t*, 38 (*αὐτός* LTr, *αὐτόν*, –*σῶμα*, *S*), 39(*αὐτός* LTTr), 40, 42. xx. 2, 12, 14*t*, 15, 16, 17, 19, 21 (–TTr*S*), 24, 26, 29, 30, 31. xxi. 1(–T), 4*t*, 5(–L^{b}), 7, 10, 12, 13, 14, 15, 17, 20, 21, 22, 23, 25.

Acts i. 1, 11, 14, 16, 21. ii. 22, 32, 36, 38. iii. 6, 13, 20, 26(*omS*). iv. 2, 10, 13, 18, 27, 30, 33. v. 30, 40, 42. vi. 14. vii. 55, 59. viii. 12, 16, 35, 37(*ap*). ix. 5, 17(–G^{oo}), 27, 29(28, –LT*S*), 34. x. 36, 38. xi. 17, 20. xiii. 23, 33(32). xv. 11, 26. xvi. 18, 31. xvii. 3, 7, 18(*ap*). xviii. 5, 28. xix. 4, 5, 10(*omS*), 13*t*, 15, 17. xx. 21, 24, 35. xxi. 13. xxii. 8. xxv. 19. xxvi. 9, 15. xxviii. 23, 31.

Rom. i. 1, 3(4), 6, 7, 8. ii. 16. iii. 22, 24, 26(–G^{o}T). iv. 24. v. 1, 11, 15, 17, 21. vi. 3, 11, 23. vii. 25. viii. 1, 2, 11, 39. x. 9. xiii. 14. xiv. 14. xv. 5, 6, 8 (–G^{oo}LT*S*), 16, 17, 30. xvi. 3, 18 (*omS*), 20, 24, 25, 27. 1 Cor. i, 1, 2*t*, 3, 4, 7, 8, 9, 10, 30. ii. 2. iii. 11. iv. 15. v. 4*t*, 5 (*ἡμῶν Ἰησοῦ Χριστοῦ* L^{b}, –T). vi. 11. viii. 6. ix. 1. xi. 23. xii. 3*t*. xv. 31, 57. xvi. 22(–G^{oo}LT*S*), 23, 24. 2 Cor. i. 1, 2, 3, 14, 19. iv. 5*t*, 6 (–LT), 10*t*, 11*t*, 14*t*. v. 18 (–G^{oo}LT*S*). viii. 9. xi. 4, 31. xiii. 5, 14(13).

Gal. i. 1, 3, 12. ii. 4, 16*t*. iii. 1, 14, 22, 26, 28. iv. 14. v. 6. vi. 14, 15 (*ap*), 17, 18. Eph. i. 1*t*, 2, 3, 5, 15, 17. ii. 6, 7, 10, 13, 20. iii. 1, 9(*ap*), 11, 14(*ap*), 21. iv. 21. v. 20. vi. 23, 24. Phil. i. 1*t*, 2, 6, 8, 11, 19, 26. ii. 5, 10, 11, 19, 21. iii. 3, 8, 12 (*om*), 14, 20. iv. 7, 19, 21, 23. Col. i. 1, 2(*ap*), 3, 4, 28(*omS*). ii. 6. iii. 17.

1 Thes. i. 1, 1(*ap*), 3, 10. ii. 14, 15, 19. iii. 11, 13. iv. 1, 2, 14*t*. v. 9, 18, 23, 28. 2 Thes. i. 1, 2, 7, 8, 12*t*. ii. 1, 14, 16. iii. 6, 12, 18. 1 Tim. i. 1*t*, 2, 12, 14, 15, 16. ii. 5. iii. 13. iv. 6. v. 21. vi. 3, 13, 14. 2 Tim. i. 1*t*, 2, 9, 10, 13. ii. 1, 3, 8, 10. iii. 12, 15. iv. 1, 22(–T*S*). Tit. i. 1, 4. ii. 13. iii. 6. Phm. 1, 3, 5, 6(–L*S*), 9, 23, 25.

Heb. ii. 9. iii. 1. iv. 14. vi. 20. vii. 22. x. 10, 19. xii. 2, 24. xiii. 8, 12, 20, 21. Jas. i. 1. ii. 1. 1 Pet. i. 1, 2, 3*t*, 7, 13. ii. 5. iii. 21. iv. 11. v. 10, 14(–G^{oo}LT). 2 Pet. i. 1*t*, 2, 8, 11, 14, 16. ii. 20. iii. 18. 1 John i. 3, 7. ii. 1, 22. iii. 23. iv. 2, 3, 15. v. 1, 5, 6, 20(–G^{o}). 2 John 3, 7. Jude 1*t*, 4, 17, 21. Rev. i. 1, 2, 5, 9(–G″), 9. xii. 17. xiv. 12. xvii. 6. xix. 10*t*. xx. 4. xxii. 16, 20, 21.

Add, for Κύριος, Acts xviii. 25, LT*S*. Jude 5, G″L. After Lord, Mark xvi. 19, LTr. 2 Thes. ii. 8, G^{pr}LT*S*. For *Χριστός*, Acts ix. 20, GLT*S*. After Christ, Acts xxiv. 24, L*S*. Rom. viii. 11, L^{b}*S*. 34, L^{b}*S*. 1 Cor. iv. 17, L*S*. Gal. v. 24, L^{b}T*S*. Eph. iii. 6, LT*S*. Col. i. 2, L. iv. 12, LT*S*. For he, Matt. iv. 19, L^{b}. viii. 32, L^{b}. xvi. 15, L^{b}. xxii. 20, LT. xxvi. 38, G^{ph}T. Mark v. 34, L. Luke v. 34, Tr*S*. John xii. 1, LTTr*S*.—John i. 43 (44, . . saith), LTTr*S*. Acts x. 48, *see* Κύριος. xiv. 10(*ap*). xvi. 7 (Spirit . .), G^{pr}LT*S*. Rom. xv. 32, *see* θεός. Jude 25(*ap*).

Ἰησοῦς, Jesus, **1**, son of Nun, Acts vii. 45. Heb. iv. 8(*marg.* Joshua).—**2**, Justus, Col. iv. 11.—**3**, son of Eliezer, *see* Ἰωσῆς.

Ἰκόνιον, Iconium, Acts xiii. 51. xiv. 1, 19, 21. xvi. 2. 2 Tim. iii. 11.

2 Cor. iii. 7, 13. Gal. vi. 16. Eph. ii. 12. Phil. iii. 5. Heb. viii. 8, 10. xi. 22. Rev. ii. 14. vii. 4. xxi. 12.

Ἰσραηλίτης, -λεί-TTrS, Israelite, John i. 47(48). Rom. ix. 4. xi. 1, 1. 2 Cor. xi. 22.—of Israel, Acts ii. 22. iii. 12. v. 35. xiii. 16. xxi. 28.

Ἰταλία, Italy, Acts xviii. 2. xxvii. 1, 6. Heb. xiii. 24.

Ἰταλικός, *fem.*, Italian °band, Acts x. 1.

Ἰτουραία, Iturea, *or* -æa, Luke iii. 1.

Ἰωάθαμ, Joatham, Matt. i. 9*t*.

Ἰωάννα, Joanna, Luke viii. 3. xxiv. 10.

Ἰωαννᾶς, Ἰωανάς LTTr, Ἰωνάς S, Joanna, *properly* as, Luke iii. 27.

Ἰωάννης, John, 1, the Baptist, Matt. iii. 1, 4, 13, 14(-LTr[b]S). iv. 12. ix. 14. xi. 2, 4, 7, 11, 12, 13, 18. xiv. 2, 3, 4, 8, 10. xvi. 14. xvii. 13. xxi. 25, 26, 32. Mark i. 4, 6, 9, 14. ii. 18*t*. vi. 14, 16(-G[oo]), 17, 18, 20, 24, 25. viii. 28. xi. 30, 32. Luke i. 13, 60, 63. iii. 2, 15, 16, 20. v. 33. vii. 18, 19, 20, 22, 24*t*, 28, 29, 33. ix. 7, 9, 19. xi. 1. xvi. 16. xx. 4, 6. John i. 6, 15, 19, 26, 28, 29(*om*S), 32, 35, 40(41). iii. 23, 24, 25, 26, 27. iv. 1. v. 33, 36. x. 40, 41*t*. Acts i. 5, 22. x. 37. xi. 16. xiii. 24, 25. xviii. 25. xix. 3, 4.

2, the Apostle, Matt. iv. 21. x. 2 (3). xvii. 1. Mark i. 19, 29. iii. 17. v. 37. ix. 2, 38. x. 35, 41. xiii. 3. xiv. 33. Luke v. 10. vi. 14. viii. 51. ix. 28, 49, 54. xxii. 8. Acts i. 13. iii. 1, 3, 4, 11. iv. 13, 19. viii. 14. xii. 2, 12. Gal. ii. 9. Rev. i. 1, 4, 9. xxi. 2(*om*S). xxii. 8.

3, Mark, Acts xii. 25. xiii. 5, 13. xv. 37.—4, chief priest, Acts iv. 6. — 5, father of Peter, *see* Ἰωνᾶς, 2.

Ἰώβ, Job, Jas. v. 11.

Ἰωήλ, Joel, Acts ii. 16(-L).

Ἰωνάν, -άμ TTrS, Jonan, Luke iii. 30.

Ἰωνᾶς, Jonas, Jona[1], 1, the prophet, Matt. xii. 39, 40, 41*t*. xvi. 4. Luke xi. 29, 30, 32*t*.—2, Ἰωάνης LTr, Ἰωάννης TS, father of Peter, John i. 42(43)[1]. xxi. 15, 16, 17.—*Add* Matt. xvi. 17, *see* Βαριωνᾶ.

Ἰωράμ, Joram, Matt. i. 8*t*.

Ἰωρείμ, Jorim, Luke iii. 29.

Ἰωσαφάτ, Josaphat, Matt. i. 8*t*.

Ἰωσῆς, Joses, Jose[1], 1, son of Eliezer, Luke iii. 29[1] (Ἰησοῦς LTTrS).—2, brother of James, Matt. xxvii. 56. Mark xv. 40, 47.—3, (2?) brother of Jesus, Matt. xiii. 55. Mark vi. 3.—4, Barnabas, Acts iv. 36 (Ἰωσήφ G'LTS).

Ἰωσήφ, Joseph, 1, son of Jacob, John iv. 5. Acts vii. 9, 13*t*, 14, 18. Heb. xi. 21, 22. Rev. vii. 8.—2, 3, 4, ancestors of Jesus, Luke iii. 24, 26, 30.—5, husband of Mary, Matt. i. 16, 18, 19, 20, 24. ii. 13, 19. Luke i. 27. ii. 4, 16, 33 (G', πατὴρ αὐτοῦ GTTrS), 43(*ap*). iii. 23. iv. 22. John i. 45(46). vi. 42.—6, of Arimathæa, Matt. xxvii. 57, 59. Mark xv. 43, 45. Luke xxiii. 50. John xix. 38.—7, *see* Ἰωσῆς, 4.

Ἰωσίας, Josias, Matt. i. 10, 11.

Judæa, etc. *See* Ἰουδαία, *etc.*

Jupiter. *See* Ζεύς.

Καϊάφας, Caiaphas, Matt. xxvi. 3, 57. Luke iii. 2 (Καίφας L). John xi. 49. xviii. 13, 14, 24, 28. Acts iv. 6.

Κάϊν, Cain, Heb. xi. 4. 1 John iii. 12. Jude 11.

Καϊνάν, Cainan, 1, son of Enos, Luke iii. 37.—2, son of Arphaxad, Luke iii. 36 (-άμ TS).

Καῖσαρ, Cæsar, Matt. xxii. 17, 21'*r*. Mark xii. 14, 16, 17*t*. Luke ii. 1. iii. 1. xx. 22, 24, 25*t*. xxiii. 2. John xix. 12*t*, 15. Acts xi. 28 (*om* S). xvii. 7. xxv. 8, 10, 11, 12*t*, 21. xxvi. 32. xxvii. 24. xxviii. 19. Phil. iv. 22.

Καισάρεια, Cesarea, *or* Cæsarea, 1, Philippi, Matt. xvi. 13. Mark viii. 27.—2, of Palestine, Acts viii. 40. ix. 30. x. 1, 24. xi. 11. xii. 19. xviii. 22. xxi. 8, 16. xxiii. 23, 33. xxv. 1, 4, 6, 13.

Καλοὶ λιμένες. See p. 242.

Κανᾶ, Cana, John ii. 1, 11. iv. 46. xxi. 2.

Καναανίτης, καν. G, Canaanite, Matt. x. 4 (Καναναῖος, G'LTTr). Mark iii. 18 (-αῖος LTTrS).

Κανδάκη, Candace, Acts viii. 27.

Καπερναούμ, Καφαρναούμ LTTrS, G''[1], Capernaum, Matt. iv. 13[1]. viii. 5. xi. 23. xvii. 24. Mark i. 21. ii. 1. ix. 33. Luke iv. 23, 31. vii. 1. x. 15. John ii. 12. iv. 46. vi. 17, 24, 59.

Καππαδοκία, Cappadocia, Acts ii. 9. 1 Pet. i. 1.

Κάρπος, Carpus, 2 Tim. iv. 13.

Κεγχρεαί, Cenchrea, Acts xviii. 18. Rom. xvi. 1.

Κέδρος *plur.* StTTr, Κεδρών GLS, Cedron, John xviii. 1.

Κηφᾶς, Cephas, John i. 42(43). 1 Cor. i. 12. iii. 22. ix. 5. xv. 5. Gal. ii. 9 (Πέτρος G'). — *Add*, for Πέτρος, Gal. i. 18, G'LTS. ii. 11, 14, G''LTS.

Κιλικία, Cilicia, Acts vi. 9. xv. 23, 41. xxi. 39. xxii. 3. xxiii. 34. xxvii. 5. Gal. i. 21.

Κίς, Cis, Acts xiii. 21.

Κλαύδη, Καῦδα LS, Clauda, Acts xxvii. 16.

Κλαυδία, Claudia, 2 Tim. iv. 21.

Κλαύδιος, Claudius, **1**, Cæsar, Acts xi. 28. xviii. 2. — **2**, Lysias, Acts xxiii. 26.

Κλεόπας, Cleopas, Luke xxiv. 18.

Κλήμης, Clement, Phil. iv. 3.

Κλωπᾶς, Cleophas, *marg.* Clopas, John xix. 25.

Κνίδος, Cnidus, Gnidus *ed.* 1611 *etc.*, Acts xxvii. 7.

Κολοσσαί, Κολασσαί StG'', Colosse, Col. i. 2.

Κορέ, Core, Jude 11.

Κορίνθιος, Corinthian, Acts xviii. 8. 2 Cor. vi. 11.

Κόρινθος, Corinth, Acts xviii. 1. xix. 1. 1 Cor. i. 2. 2 Cor. i. 1, 23. 2 Tim. iv. 20.

Κορνήλιος, Cornelius, Acts x. 1, 3, 7 (αὐτός GLTS), 17, 21 (*ap*), 22, 24, 25, 30, 31.

Κούαρτος, Quartus, Rom. xvi. 23.

Κρήσκης, Crescens, 2 Tim. iv. 10.

Κρής, *pl.* Κρῆτες, Cretes, Acts ii. 11. — Cretians, Tit. i. 12.

Κρήτη, Crete, Acts xxvii. 7 (*marg.* Candy), 12, 13, 21. Tit. i. 5.

Κρίσπος, Crispus, Acts xviii. 8. 1 Cor. i. 14.

Κύπριος, of Cyprus, Acts iv. 36. xi. 20. xxi. 16.

Κύπρος, Cyprus, Acts xi. 19. xiii. 4. xv. 39. xxi. 3. xxvii. 4.

Κυρηναῖος, Cyrenian, Mark xv. 21. Luke xxiii. 26. Acts vi. 9. — of Cyrene, Matt. xxvii. 32. Acts xi. 20. xiii. 1.

Κυρήνη, Cyrene, Acts ii. 10.

Κυρήνιος, Κυρίνος L, Cyrenius, Luke ii. 2.

Κυρία. *See* κυρία, p. 234.

Κῶς, Coos, Acts xxi. 1.

Κωσάμ, Cosam, Luke iii. 28.

Λάζαρος, Lazarus, **1**, of Bethany, John xi. 1, 2, 5, 11, 14, 43. xii. 1, 2, 9, 10, 17. — **2**, in the parable, Luke xvi. 20, 23, 24, 25.

Λάμεχ, Lamech, Luke iii. 36.

Λαοδίκεια, Laodicea, Col. ii. 1. iv. 13, 15, 16. Rev. i. 11. — *Add*, *see* Λαοδικεύς.

Λαοδικεύς, Laodicean, Col. iv. 16. Rev. iii. 14 (ἐν Λαοδικείᾳ C[m]GL TS, *marg.* in Laodicea).

Λασαία, -έα T, -σσαία S, Ἄλασσα L, Lasea, *or* -æa, Acts xxvii. 8.

Latin. *See* Ῥωμαϊκός, Ῥωμαϊστί.

Λεββαῖος, Lebbeus, *or* -æus, Matt. x. 3 (-G°LTrS).

Λευί, Λευεί TTrS, Levi, **1**, son of Jacob, Heb. vii. 5, 9. Rev. vii. 7. — **2**, son of Simeon, Luke iii. 29. — **3**, son of Melchi, Luke iii. 24.

Λευίς, Λευίς TTr[1], Levi, the apostle, Mark ii. 14. Luke v. 27[1], 29[1].

Λευίτης, -ίτης TTr, Levite, Luke x. 32. John i. 19. Acts iv. 36.

Λευϊτικός, Λευιτ. T, Levitical, Heb. vii. 11.

Λιβερτῖνοι, Libertines, Acts vi. 9.

Λιβύη, Libya, Acts ii. 10.

Λιθόστρωτον, Pavement, John xix. 13.

Λῖνος, Λίνος LT, Linus, 2 Tim. iv. 21.
Λίψ. See p. 243.
Λουκᾶς, Lucas[1], Luke, Col. iv. 14. 2 Tim. iv. 11. Phm. 24(23)[1].
Λούκιος, Lucius, Acts xiii. 1. Rom. xvi. 21.
Λύδδα, Lydda, Acts ix. 32, 35, 38.
Λυδία, Lydia, Acts xvi. 14, 40.
Λυκαονία, Lycaonia, Acts xiv. 6.
Λυκαονιστί, in the speech of Lycaonia, Acts xiv. 11.
Λυκία, Lycia, Acts xxvii. 5.
Λυσανίας, Lysanias, Luke iii. 1.
Λυσίας, Lysias, Acts xxiii. 26. xxiv. 7(*ap*), 22.
Λύστρα (ἡ, τά[2]), Lystra, Acts xiv. 6, 8[2], 21. xvi. 1, 2[2]. 2 Tim. iii. 11[2].
Λωΐς, Lois, 2 Tim. i. 5.
Λώτ, Lot, Luke xvii. 28, 29, 32. 2 Pet. ii. 7.
Μαάθ, Maath, Luke iii. 26.
Μαγδαλά, Μαγαδάν LTTr*S*, Magdala, Matt. xv. 39.
Μαγδαληνή, Magdalene, Matt. xxvii. 56, 61. xxviii. 1. Mark xv. 40, 47. xvi. 1, 9(*ap*). Luke viii. 2. xxiv. 10. John xix. 25. xx. 1, 18.
Μαγεδών. *See* Ἁρμαγεδδών.
Μαγώγ, Magog, Rev. xx. 8.
Μαδιάμ, Madian, Acts vii. 29.
Μαθουσάλα, Mathusala, Luke iii. 37.
Μαϊνάν, Μεννά L[b]TTr*S*, Menan, Luke iii. 31.
Μακεδονία, Macedonia, Acts xvi. 9, 10, 12. xviii. 5. xix. 21, 22. xx. 1, 3. Rom. xv. 26. 1 Cor. xvi. 5*t*. 2 Cor. i. 16*t*. ii. 13. vii. 5. viii. 1. xi. 9. Phil. iv. 15. 1 Thes. i. 7, 8. iv. 10. 1 Tim. i. 3.
Μακεδών, Macedonian, Acts xxvii. 2.—(man[1]) of Macedonia, Acts xvi. 9. xix. 29[1]. 2 Cor. ix. 2, 4.
Μαλελεήλ, Maleleel, Luke iii. 37.
Μάλχος, Malchus, John xviii. 10.
Μαμμωνᾶς. See p. 248.
Μαναήν, Manaen, Acts xiii. 1.
Μανασσῆς, Manasses, **1**, son of Joseph, Rev. vii. 6.—**2**, king of Judah, Matt. i. 10*t*.
Μάρθα, Martha, Luke x. 38, 40, 41*t*. John xi. 1, 5, 19, 20, 21, 24, 30, 39. xii. 2.
Μαρία[1], Μαριάμ[2], Mary, **1**, mother of Jesus[1 2], Matt. i. 16, 18, 20. ii. 11. xiii. 55. Mark vi. 3. Luke i. 27, 30, 34, 38, 39, 41, 46, 56. ii. 5, 16, 19, 34. Acts i. 14.—**2**, mother of James, etc.[1], Matt. xxvii. 56, 61. xxviii. 1. Mark xv. 40, 47. xvi. 1. Luke xxiv. 10. John xix. 25.—**3**, Magdalene[1], Matt. xxvii. 56, 61. xxviii. 1. Mark xv. 40, 47. xvi. 1, 9(*ap*). Luke viii. 2. xxiv. 10. John xix. 25. xx. 1, 11, 16, 18.—**4**, sister of Martha[1], Luke x. 39, 42. John xi. 1, 2, 19, 20, 28, 31, 32, 45. xii. 3. —**5**, mother of John Mark[1], Acts xii. 12.—**6**, of Rome[2], Rom. xvi. 6 (Μαρίαν L).
Μάρκος, Marcus[1], Mark, Acts xii. 12, 25. xv. 37, 39. Col. iv. 10[1]. 2Tim. iv. 11. Phm. 24[1]. 1Pet. v. 13[1].
Ματθαῖος, Μαθθαῖος LTTr*S*, Matthew, Matt. ix. 9. x. 3. Mark iii. 18. Luke vi. 15. Acts i. 13.
Ματθάν, Μαθ. LTTr, Matthan, Matt. i. 15*t*.
Ματθάτ, Μαθ.TTr[1]*S*, Matthat, **1**, **2**, Luke iii. 24(-άθ *S*), 29[1](-άαθ *S*).
Ματθίας, Μαθ. T, Matthias, Acts i. 23, 26.
Ματταθά, Mattatha, Luke iii. 31.
Ματταθίας, Mattathias, Luke iii. 25, 26.
Μελεᾶς, Melea, Luke iii. 31.
Μελίτη, Melita, Acts xxviii. 1.
Μελχί, -εί TTr*S*, Melchi, **1**, **2**, Luke iii. 24, 28.
Μελχισεδέκ, Melchisedec, Heb. v. 6, 10. vi. 20. vii. 1, 10, 11, 15, 17, 21(*ap*).
Mercurius. *See* Ἑρμῆς.
Μεσοποταμία, Mesopotamia, Acts ii. 9. vii. 2.
Μεσσίας, Μεσίας G'', Messias, John i. 41(42). iv. 25.
Μῆδος, Mede, Acts ii. 9.
Μίλητος, Miletus, -tum[1], Acts xx. 15, 17. 2 Tim. iv. 20[1].
Μιτυλήνη, Mitylene, Acts xx. 14.

Μιχαήλ, Michael, Jude 9. Rev. xii. 7.

Μνάσων, Mnason, Acts xxi. 16.

Μολόχ, Moloch, Acts vii. 43.

Μύρα, -ρρα L, Myra, Acts xxvii. 5.

Μυσία, Mysia, Acts xvi. 7, 8.

Μωσῆς St G L[3], Μωϋσῆς (St[1]G[2]) or Μωυσῆς LTTrS, Moses, Matt. viii. 4[2"]. xvii. 3, 4. xix. 7, 8. xxii. 24. xxiii. 2. Mark i. 44. vii. 10. ix. 4, 5. x. 3, 4. xii. 19, 26. Luke ii. 22. v 14. ix. 30, 33. xvi. 29, 31. xx. 28, 37. xxiv. 27, 44. John i. 17, 45(46). iii. 14. v. 45, 46. vi. 32. vii. 19, 22*t*, 23. viii. 5(*ap*). ix. 28, 29. Acts iii. 22. vi. 11, 14[12]. vii. 20, 22, 29, 31, 32, 35[12], 37[12], 40, 44. xiii. 39. xv. 1[12], 5[12], 21. xxi. 21. xxvi. 22. xxviii. 23. Rom. v. 14. ix. 15[3] x. 5, 19. 1 Cor. ix. 9. x. 2. 2 Cor. iii. 7, 13, 15. 2 Tim. iii. 8[12]. Heb. iii. 2, 3, 5, 16. vii. 14. viii. 5. ix. 19[12]. x. 28. xi. 24. xii. 21. Jude 9. Rev. xv. 3.

Ναασσών, Naasson, Matt. i. 4*t*. Luke iii. 32.

Ναγγαί, Naggai, Luke iii. 25.

Ναζαρέτ, -ρέθ, -ράθ, -ρά, Nazareth, Matt. ii. 23. iv. 13. xxi. 11. Mark i. 9. Luke i. 26. ii. 4, 39, 51. iv. 16. John i. 45(46), 46(47). Acts x. 38.

Ναζαρηνός, of Nazareth, Mark i. 24. xiv. 67. xvi. 6. Luke iv. 34.

Ναζωραῖος, Nazarene, Matt. ii. 23. Acts xxiv. 5. — of Nazareth, Matt. xxvi. 71. Mark x. 47. Luke xviii. 37. xxiv. 19. John xviii. 5, 7. xix. 19. Acts ii. 22. iii. 6. iv. 10. vi. 14. xxii. 8. xxvi. 9. — *Add* Acts ix. 5 (Jesus . .), L[b].

Ναθάν, Nathan, Luke iii. 21.

Ναθαναήλ, Nathanael, John i. 45(46), 46(47), 47(48), 48(49), 49 (50). xxi. 2.

Ναΐν, Nain, Luke vii. 11.

Ναούμ, Naum, Luke iii. 25. [11.

Νάρκισσος, Narcissus, Rom. xvi.

Ναχώρ, Nachor, Luke iii. 34.

Νεάπολις, Neapolis, Acts xvi. 11.

Νεεμάν, Ναιμάν LTTrS, Naaman, Luke iv. 27.

Νεφθαλείμ, Nephthalim, Matt. iv. 13, 15. Rev. vii. 6 (Nepthali *ed.* 1611, Nepthalim *in mod. eds.*).

Νηρεύς, -έας L[m], Nereus, Rom. xvi. 15.

Νηρί, -εί TTrS, Neri, Luke iii. 27.

Νίγερ, Niger, Acts xiii. 1.

Νικάνωρ, Nicanor, Acts vi 5.

Νικόδημος, Nicodemus, John iii. 1, 4, 9. vii. 50. xix. 39.

Νικολαΐτης, Nicolaitan, -ane *a misprint of mod. eds.*, Rev. ii. 6, 15.

Νικόλαος, Nicolas, Acts vi. 5.

Νικόπολις, Nicopolis, Tit. iii. 12.

Νινευΐ, -ή T, Nineve, Luke xi. 32 (Νινευῖται, G'LTrS).

Νινευΐτης, -ίτης, -ειτης, Ninevite, Luke xi. 30. — of Nineveh, Matt. xii. 41. — *Add*, *see* Νινευΐ.

Νότος. See p. 268.

Νυμφᾶς, Νύμφας L, Nymphas, Col. iv. 15.

Νῶε, Noe, Noah[1], Matt. xxiv. 37, 38. Luke iii. 36. xvii. 26, 27. Heb. xi. 7[1]. 1 Pet. iii. 20[1]. 2 Pet. ii. 5[1].

Obed, Osee. *See* Ὠβήδ, Ὠσηέ.

Ὀζίας, Ozias, Matt. i. 8, 9.

Ὀλυμπᾶς, Olympas, Rom. xvi. 15.

Ὀνήσιμος, Onesimus, Col. iv. 9. Phm. 10.

Ὀνησίφορος, Onesiphorus, 2 Tim. i. 16. iv. 19.

Οὐρβανός, Urbane, Rom. xvi. 9.

Οὐρίας, Urias, Matt. i. 6.

Παμφυλία, Pamphylia, Acts ii. 10. xiii. 13. xiv. 24. xv. 38. xxvii. 5.

Πάρθος, Parthian, Acts ii. 9.

Παρμενᾶς, Parmenas, Permenas *ed.* 1611, *etc.*, Acts vi. 5.

Πάταρα, Patara, Acts xxi. 1.

Πάτμος, Patmos, Rev. i. 9. [14.

Πατρόβας, Patrobas, Rom. xvi.

Παῦλος, 1, Paulus, Acts xiii. 7. — 2, Paul, Acts xiii. 9, 13, 16, 43, 45, 46, 50. xiv. 9, 11, 12, 14, 19. xv. 2*t*, 12, 22, 25, 35, 36, 38, 40. xvi. 3, 9, 14, 17, 18, 19, 25, 28, 29, 36, 37. xvii. 2, 4, 10. 13, 14, 15, 16, 22, 33. xviii. 1(-LTS), 5, 9, 12, 14, 18. xix. 1, 4, 6, 11, 13, 15, 21, 26, 29, 30. xx. 1, 7, 9, 10, 13, 16, 37. xxi. 4, 8,

11, 13, 18, 26, 29, 30, 32, 37, 39, 40. xxii. 25, 28, 30. xxiii. 1, 3, 5, 6, 10, 11(*omS*), 12, 14, 16*t*, 17, 18, 20, 24, 31, 33. xxiv. 1, 10, 23(*αὐτός* GLT*S*), 24, 26, 27. xxv. 2, 4, 6, 7(*ap*), 9, 10, 14, 19, 21, 23. xxvi. 1*t*, 24, 28, 29. xxvii. 1, 3, 9, 11, 21, 24, 31, 33, 43. xxviii. 3, 8, 15, 16, 17 (*αὐτός* GLT*S*), 25, 30(*omS*).

Rom. i. 1. 1 Cor. i. 1, 12, 13*t*. iii. 4, 5, 22. xvi. 21. 2 Cor. i. 1. x. 1. Gal. i. 1. v. 2. Eph. i. 1. iii. 1. Phil. i. 1. Col. i. 1, 23. iv. 18. 1 Thes. i. 1. ii. 18. 2 Thes. i. 1. iii. 17. 1 Tim. i. 1. 2 Tim. i. 1. Tit. i. 1. Phm. 1, 9, 19. 2 Pet. iii. 15.—*Add* Acts xxv. 8, for *αὐτός*, LT*S*. xxvi. 25(he), L*S*.

Πάφος, Paphos, Acts xiii. 6, 13.

Πέργαμος, Pergamos, Rev. i. 11. ii. 12.

Πέργη, Perga, Acts xiii. 13, 14. xiv. 25.

Περσίς, Persis, Rom. xvi. 12(*ap*).

Πέτρος, Peter, Matt. iv. 18. viii. 14. x. 2. xiv. 28, 29. xv. 15. xvi. 16, 18, 22, 23. xvii. 1, 4, 24, 26(*ap*). xviii. 21. xix. 27. xxvi. 33, 35, 37, 40, 58, 69, 73, 75. Mark iii. 16. v. 37. viii. 29, 32, 33. ix. 2, 5. x. 28. xi. 21. xiii. 3. xiv. 29, 33, 37, 54, 66, 67, 70, 72. xvi. 7. Luke v. 8. vi. 14. viii. 45, 51. ix. 20, 28, 32, 33. xii. 41. xviii. 28. xxii. 8, 34, 54, 55, 58, 60, 61*t*, 62(–GTr*S*). xxiv. 12(*ap*). John i. 40(41), 44(45). vi. 8, 68. xiii. 6, 8, 9, 24, 36, 37. xviii. 10, 11, 15, 16*t*, 17, 18, 25, 26, 27. xx. 2, 3, 4, 6. xxi. 2, 3, 7*t*, 11, 15, 17, 20, 21. Acts i. 13, 15. ii. 14, 37, 38. iii. 1, 3, 4, 6, 11, 12. iv. 8, 13, 19. v. 3, 8, 9, 15, 29. viii. 14, 20. ix. 32, 34, 38, 39, 40*t*. x. 5, 9, 13, 14, 17, 18, 19, 21, 23 (*ἀναστάς* fr. *ἀνίστημι* GLT*S*), 25, 26, 32, 34, 44, 45, 46. xi. 2, 4, 7, 13. xii. 3, 5, 6, 7, 11, 13(*αὐτός* GLT*S*), 14*t*, 16, 18. xv. 7. Gal. i. 18(*Κηφᾶς* G'LT*S*). ii. 7, 8, 11 and 14 (*Κηφᾶς* G''LT*S*). 1 Pet. i. 1. 2 Pet. i. 1. — *Add* John i. 42(43), *see* p. 326. Gal. ii. 9, for *Κηφᾶς*, G'.

Phalec, etc. *See* *Φαλέκ*, *etc.*

Πιλάτος, *Πιλᾶτος* LTTr, Pilate, Matt. xxvii. 2, 13, 17, 22, 24, 58*t*, 62, 65. Mark xv. 1, 2, 4, 5, 9, 12, 14, 15, 43, 44. Luke iii. 1. xiii. 1. xxiii. 1, 3, 4, 6, 11, 12, 13, 20, 24, 52. John xviii. 29, 31, 33, 35, 37, 38. xix. 1, 4, 6, 8, 10, 12, 13, 15, 19, 21, 22, 31, 38*t*. Acts iii. 13. iv. 27. xiii. 28. 1 Tim. vi. 13.

Πισιδία, Pisidia, Acts xiii. 14. xiv. 24.

Ποντικός, *with τῷ γένει*, born in Pontus, Acts xviii. 2.

Πόντιος, Pontius, Matt. xxvii. 2(–Tr*S*). Luke iii. 1. Acts iv. 27. 1 Tim. vi. 13.

Πόντος, Pontus, Acts ii. 9. 1 Pet. i. 1. [7, 8.

Πόπλιος, Publius, Acts xxviii.

Πόρκιος, Porcius, Acts xxiv. 27.

Ποτίολοι, Puteoli, Acts xxviii. 13.

Πούδης, Pudens, 2 Tim. iv. 21.

Πρίσκα[1], *Πρίσκιλλα*, Prisca, Priscilla, Acts xviii. 2, 18, 26. Rom. xvi. 3 ([1]GLT*S*). 1 Cor. xvi. 19. 2 Tim. iv. 19[1].

Πρόχορος, Prochorus, Acts vi. 5.

Πτολεμαΐς, Ptolemais, Acts xxi. 7.

Πύθων, *πύθ*. G'LT, divination, *marg.* Python, Acts xvi. 16.

Πύρρος, Acts xx. 4 (Sopater . .), GprLT*S*.

Quartus. *See* *Κούαρτος*.

'Ραάβ, Rahab, Heb. xi. 31. Jas. ii. 25. — *Compare* *'Ραχάβ*.

'Ραγαῦ, Ragau, Luke iii. 35.

'Ραμᾶ, Rama, Matt. ii. 18.

'Ραχάβ, Rachab, Matt. i. 5.

'Ραχήλ, Rachel, Matt. ii. 18.

'Ρεβέκκα, Rebecca, Rom. ix. 10.

Red sea. See p. 169.

'Ρεμφάν, *'Ρεφάν* G'LT, *'Ρομφάν* *S*, Remphan, Acts vii. 43.

'Ρήγιον, Rhegium, Acts xxviii.

'Ρησά, Rhesa, Luke iii. 27. [13.

'Ροβοάμ, Roboam, Matt. i. 7*t*.

'Ρόδη, Rhoda, Acts xii. 13.

'Ρόδος, Rhodes, Acts xxi. 1.

'Ρουβήν, Reuben, Rev. vii. 5.

'Ρούθ, **Ruth**, **Matt. i. 5.**

'Ροῦφος, Rufus, Mark xv. 21. Rom. xvi. 13.

'Ρωμαϊκός, of Latin, Luke xxiii. 38(*ap*).

'Ρωμαῖος, Roman, John xi. 48. Acts xvi. 21, 37, 38. xxii. 25, 26, 27, 29. xxiii. 27. xxv. 16. xxviii. 17.—of Rome, Acts ii. 10.

'Ρωμαϊστί, in Latin, John xix. 20.

'Ρώμη, Rome, Acts xviii. 2. xix. 21. xxiii. 11. xxviii. 14, 16. Rom. i. 7, 15. 2 Tim. i. 17.

Σαδδουκαῖος, Sadducee, Matt. iii. 7. xvi. 1, 6, 11, 12. xxiii. 22, 34. Mark xii. 18. Luke xx. 27. Acts iv. 1. v. 17. xxiii. 6, 7, 8.

Σαδώκ, Sadoc, Matt. i. 14*t*.

Σαλά, Sala, Luke iii. 35.

Σαλαθιήλ, Salathiel, Matt. i. 12*t*. Luke iii. 27.

Σαλαμίς, Salamis, Acts xiii. 5.

Σαλείμ, Salim, John iii. 23.

Σαλήμ, Salem, Heb. vii. 1, 2.

Σαλμών, Salmon, Matt. i. 4, 5. Luke iii. 32.

Σαλμώνη, Salmone, Acts xxvii. 7.

Σαλώμη, Salome, Mark xv. 40. xvi. 1.

Σαμάρεια, Samaria, Luke xvii. 11. John iv. 4, 5, 7. Acts i. 8. viii. 1, 5, 9, 14. ix. 31. xv. 3.

Σαμαρείτης, Samaritan, Matt. x. 5. Luke ix. 52. x. 33. xvii. 16. John iv. 39, 40. viii. 48. Acts viii. 25.

Σαμαρεῖτις, of Samaria, John iv. 9*t*.

Σαμοθράκη, Samothracia, Acts xvi. 11.

Σάμος, Samos, Acts xx. 15.

Σαμουήλ, Samuel, Acts iii. 24. xiii. 20. Heb. xi. 32.

Σαμψών, Samson, Heb. xi. 32.

Σαούλ, Saul, **1**, the king, Acts xiii. 21.—**2**, Paul, Acts ix. 4*t*, 17. xxii. 7*t*, 13. xxvi. 14*t*. *See* Σαῦλος.

Σαπφείρη, -α L, Sapphira, Acts v. 1. [1, 4.

Σάρδεις, Sardis, Rev. i. 11. iii.

Σάρεπτα, Sarepta, Luke iv. 26.

Σαρούχ, Σερούχ LTTr*S*, Saruch, Luke iii. 35.

Σάρρα, Sara[1], Sarah, Rom. iv. 19. ix. 9. Heb. xi. 11[1]. 1 Pet. iii. 6[1].

Σαρών, Saron, Acts ix. 35.

Σατᾶν[1], Σατανᾶς, Satan, Matt. iv. 10. xii. 26. xvi. 23. Mark i. 13. iii. 23, 26. iv. 15. viii. 33. Luke iv. 8 (*ap*). x. 18. xi. 18. xiii. 16. xxii. 3, 31. John xiii. 27. Acts v. 3. xxvi. 18. Rom. xvi. 20. 1 Cor. v. 5. vii. 5. 2 Cor. ii. 11. xi. 14. xii. 7[1]. 1 Thes. ii. 18. 2 Thes. ii. 9. 1 Tim. i. 20. v. 15. Rev. ii. 9, 13*t*, 24. iii. 9. xii. 9. xx. 2, 7.

Σαῦλος, Saul, Acts vii. 58. viii. 1, 3. ix. 1, 8, 11, 19(*omS*), 22, 24, 26(*omS*). xi. 25, 30. xii. 25. xiii. 1, 2, 7, 9. *See also* Σαούλ.

Σεβαστός, Augustus, Acts xxv. 21, 25. *See also* p. 359.

Σεκοῦνδος, Secundus, Acts xx. 4.

Σελεύκεια, Seleucia, Acts xiii. 4.

Σεμεί, -είν L, -εείν TTr*S*, Semei, Luke iii. 26.

Σέργιος, Sergius, Acts xiii. 7.

Σήθ, Seth, Luke iii. 38.

Σήμ, Sem, Luke iii. 36.

Σιδών, Sidon, Matt. xi. 21, 22. xv. 21. Mark iii. 8. vii. 24 (-G°T), 31. Luke iv. 26 (Σιδώνιος G'LTr*S*). vi. 17. x. 13, 14. Acts xxvii. 3.

Σιδώνιος, of Sidon, Acts xii. 20. —*Add, see* Σιδών.

Σίλας[1], Σιλουανός, Silas, Silvanus, Acts[1] xv. 22, 27, 32, 34(*ap*), 40. xvi. 19, 25, 29. xvii. 4, 10, 14, 15. xviii. 5. 2 Cor. i. 19. 1 Thes. i. 1. 2 Thes. i. 1. 1 Pet. v. 12.

Σιλωάμ, Siloam, Luke xiii. 4. John ix. 7, 11.

Simeon. *See* Συμεών.

Σίμων, Simon, **1**, Peter, Matt. iv. 18. x. 2. xvi. 16, 17. xvii. 25. Mark i. 16, 29, 30, 36. iii. 16, 18. xiv. 37. Luke iv. 38*t*. v. 3, 4, 5, 8, 10*t*. vi. 14. xxii. 31. xxiv. 34. John i. 40, 41, 42. vi. 8, 68. xiii. 6, 9, 24, 36. xviii. 10, 15, 25. xx. 2, 6. xxi. 2, 3, 7, 11, 15*t*, 16, 17. Acts x. 5, 18, 32. xi. 13. 2 Pet. i. 1 (Συμεών StGT*S*).—*Add* Mark i. 16, for αὐτός G''LTTr*S*. iii. 16, *see* πρῶτος.—

2, Zelotes, Matt. x. 4. Mark iii. 18. Luke vi. 15. Acts i. 13. —3, brother of Jesus, Matt. xiii. 55. Mark vi. 3. —4, the leper, Matt. xxvi. 6. Mark xiv. 3. —5, the Pharisee, Luke vii. 40, 43, 44. —6, of Cyrene, Matt. xxvii. 32. Mark xv. 21. Luke xxiii. 26. —7, father of Judas, John vi. 71. xii. 4. xiii. 2, 26. —8, Magus, Acts viii. 9, 13, 18, 24. — 9, the tanner, Acts ix. 43. x. 6, 17, 32.

Σινᾶ, Sina, Sinai², Acts vii. 30, 38. Gal. iv. 24², 25².

Σιών, Sion, Matt. xxi. 5. John xii. 15. Rom. ix. 33. xi. 26. Heb. xii. 22. 1 Pet. ii. 6. Rev. xiv. 1.

Σκευᾶς, Sceva, Acts xix. 14.

Σκύθης, Scythian, Col. iii. 11.

Σμύρνα, Smyrna, Rev. i. 11. — *Add, see* Σμυρναῖος.

Σμυρναῖος, in Smyrna, Rev. ii. 8 (ἐν Σμύρνῃ GLTTr*S*).

Σόδομα, Sodoma¹, Sodom, Matt. x. 15. xi. 23, 24. Mark vi. 11(*ap*). Luke x. 12. xvii. 29. Rom. ix. 29¹. 2 Pet. ii. 6. Jude 7. Rev. xi. 8.

Σολομών, -ῶν, Solomon, Matt. i. 6, 8. vi. 29. xii. 42*t*. Luke xi. 31*t*. xii. 27. John x. 23. Acts iii. 11. v. 12. vii. 47.

Σουσάννα, Susanna, Luke viii. 3.

Σπανία, Spain, Rom. xv. 24, 28.

Στάχυς, Stachys, Rom. xvi. 9.

Στεφανᾶς, Stephanas, 1 Cor. i. 16. xvi. 15, 17.

Στέφανος, Stephen, Acts vi. 5, 8, 9. vii. 59. viii. 2. xi. 19. xxii. 20 (-G°).

Στωϊκός, Stoic, Acts xvii. 18.

Συμεών, Simeon, 1, son of Jacob, Rev. vii. 7. —2, son of Juda, Luke iii. 30. —3, a devout Jew, Luke ii. 25, 34. —4, Peter, Acts xv. 14.— *See also* Σίμων.—5, Niger, Acts xiii. 1.

Συντύχη, Syntyche, Phil. iv. 2.

Συράκουσαι *or* -ακοῦσαι, Syracuse, Acts xxviii. 12.

Συρία, Syria, Matt. iv. 24. Luke ii. 2. Acts xv. 23, 41. xviii. 18. xx. 3. xxi. 3. Gal. i. 21.

Σύρος, Syrian, Luke iv. 27.

Συροφοίνισσα, -φοινίκισσα L*S*, Συραφοινίκισσα G, Σύρα Φοινίκισσα TTr, Syrophenician, *or* Syrophœnician, Mark vii. 26.

Σύρτις. See p. 377.

Συχάρ, Sychar, John iv. 5.

Συχέμ, Sychem, 1, son of Emmor, 2, city of Ephraim, Acts vii. 16*t*.

Σώπατρος, Sopater, Acts xx. 4.

Σωσθένης, Sosthenes, 1, Acts xviii. 17. —2 (1?), 1 Cor. i. 1.

Σωσίπατρος, Sosipater, Rom. xvi. 21.

Ταβέρναι. *See* τρεῖς, p. 390.

Ταβιθά, Tabitha, Acts ix. 36, 40.

Ταρσεύς, of Tarsus, Acts ix. 11. xxi. 39.

Ταρσός, Tarsus, Acts ix. 30. xi. 25. xxii. 3.

Τέρτιος, Tertius, Rom. xvi. 22.

Τέρτυλλος, Tertullus, Acts xxiv. 1, 2.

Thaddæus, etc. *See* Θαδδαῖος, *etc.*

Τιβεριάς, Tiberias, John vi. 1, 23. xxi. 1.

Τιβέριος, Tiberius, Luke iii. 1.

Τίμαιος, Timeus *or* -æus, Mark x. 46.

Τιμόθεος, Timotheus, Timothy², Acts xvi. 1. xvii. 14, 15. xviii. 5. xix. 22. xx. 4. Rom. xvi. 21. 1 Cor. iv. 17. xvi. 10. 2 Cor. i. 1², 19. Phil. i. 1. ii. 19. Col. i. 1. 1 Thes. i. 1. iii. 2, 6. 2 Thes. i. 1. 1 Tim. i. 2², 18². vi. 20². 2 Tim. i. 2². Phm. 1². Heb. xiii. 23².

Τίμων, Timon, Acts vi. 5.

Τίτος, Titus, 2 Cor. ii. 13 (12). vii. 6, 13, 14. viii. 6, 16, 23. xii. 18*t*. Gal. ii. 1, 3. 2 Tim. iv. 10. Tit. i. 4.

Τραχωνῖτις, Trachonitis, Luke iii. 1.

Τρόφιμος, Trophimus, Acts xx. 4. xxi. 29. 2 Tim. iv. 20.

Τρύφαινα, Tryphena, *or* -æna, Rom. xvi. 12. [12.

Τρυφῶσα, Tryphosa, Rom. xvi.

Τρωάς, Troas, Acts xvi. 8, 11. xx. 5, 6. 2 Cor. ii. 12. 2 Tim. iv. 13.

Τρωγύλλιον, Trogyllium, Acts xx. 15(*ap*).

Τύραννος, Tyrannus, Acts xix. 9.

Τύριος, of Tyre, Acts xii. 20.

Τύρος, Tyre, Matt. xi. 21, 22. xv. 21. Mark iii. 8. vii. 24, 31. Luke vi. 17. x. 13, 14. Acts xxi. 3, 7.

Τυχικός, Tychicus, Acts xx. 4 Eph. vi. 21. Col. iv. 7. 2 Tim. iv. 12. Tit. iii. 12.

Urbane, Urias. *See* Οὐρβανός, *etc.*

Ὑμέναιος, Hymeneus, *or* -æus, 1 Tim. i. 20. 2 Tim. ii. 17.

Wormwood. *See* Ἄψινθος.

Φαλέκ, Φάλεκ LTr, Φάλεγ Lm, Phalec, Luke iii. 35.

Φανουήλ, Phanuel, Luke ii. 36.

Φαραώ, Pharaoh, Acts vii. 10, 13, 21. Rom. ix. 17. Heb. xi. 24.

Φαρές, Phares, Matt. i. 3*t*. Luke iii. 33.

Φαρισαῖος, Pharisee, Matt. iii. 7. v. 20. ix. 11, 14, 34. xii. 2, 14, 24, 38(-L). xv. 1, 12. xvi. 1, 6, 11, 12. xix. 3. xxi. 45. xxii. 15, 34, 41. xxiii. 2, 13, 14(*ap*), 15, 23, 25, 26, 27, 29. xxvii. 62. Mark ii. 16 (τῶν Φ. for καὶ οἱ Φ. LmTr*S*), 18(οἱ Φ. GL TTr*S* for οἱ τῶν Φ. StG',), 18, 24. iii. 6. vii. 1, 3, 5. viii. 11, 15. x. 2. xii. 13. Luke v. 17, 21, 30, 33. vi. 2, 7. vii. 30, 36*t*, 37, 39. xi. 37, 38, 39, 42, 43, 44(*ap*), 53. xii. 1. xiii. 31. xiv. 1, 3. xv. 2. xvi. 14. xvii. 20. xviii. 10, 11. xix. 39. John i. 24. iii. 1. iv. 1. vii. 32*t*, 45, 47, 48. viii. 3 (*ap*), 13. ix. 13, 15, 16, 40. xi. 46, 47, 57. xii. 19, 42. xviii. 3. Acts v. 34. xv. 5. xxiii. 6*t*, 6 (*pl.* G''LT*S*), 7, 8, 9. xxvi. 5. Phil. iii. 5. — *Add* Matt. vii. 28 (scribes καὶ οἱ Φ.), L. Mark ix. 11 (οἱ Φ. καὶ the s.), Lb*S*.

Φῆλιξ, Felix, Acts xxiii. 24, 26. xxiv. 3, 22, 24, 25, 27*t*. xxv. 14.

Φῆστος, Festus, Acts xxiv. 27. xxv. 1, 4, 9, 12, 13, 14, 22, 23, 24. xxvi. 24, 25, 32.

Φιλαδελφεία, Philadelphia, Rev. i. 11. iii. 7.

Φιλήμων, Philemon, Phm. 1.

Φιλητός, Philetus, 2 Tim. ii. 17.

Φιλιππήσιος, Philippian, Phil. iv. 15.

Φίλιπποι, Philippi, Acts xvi. 12. xx. 6. Phil. i. 1. 1 Thes. ii. 2.

Φίλιππος, Philip, Philippi[2], 1, the apostle, Matt. x. 3. Mark iii. 18. Luke vi. 14. John i. 43(44), 44(45), 45(46), 46(47), 48(49). vi. 5, 7. xii. 21, 22*t*. xiv. 8, 9. Acts i. 13. —2, the evangelist, Acts vi. 5. viii. 5, 6, 12, 13, 26, 29, 30, 31, 34, 35, 37(*ap*), 38, 39, 40. xxi. 8. —3, Herod, Matt. xiv. 3(-T). Mark vi. 17. Luke iii. 19(*om* *S*). —4, tetrarch, Matt. xvi. 13[2]. Mark viii. 27[2]. Luke iii. 1.

Φιλόλογος, Philologus, Rom. xvi. 15.

Φλέγων, Phlegon, Rom. xvi. 14.

Φοίβη, Phebe, *or* Phœbe, Rom. xvi. 1.

Φοινίκη, Phenice, *or* Phœnice, -cia[2], Acts xi. 19. xv. 3. xxi. 2[2].

Φοινίκισσα. *See* Συροφοίνισσα.

Φοίνιξ, Phenice, Acts xxvii. 12.

Φόρον. *See* Ἀππίου φόρον.

Φορτουνᾶτος, Fortunatus, 1 Cor. xvi. 17.

Φρυγία, Phrygia, Acts ii. 10. xvi. 6. xviii. 23.

Φύγελλος, -ελος LT*S*, Phygellus, 2 Tim. i. 15.

Χαλδαῖος, Chaldean, *or* -æan, Acts vii. 4.

Χαναάν, Chanaan, Acts vii. 11. xiii. 19.

Χαναναῖος, of Canaan, Matt. xv. [22.

Χαρράν, Charran, Acts vii. 2, 4.

Χερουβίμ, -βείν LT, cherubims, Heb. ix. 5.

Χίος, Chios, Acts xx. 15.

Χλόη, Chloe, 1 Cor. i. 11.

Χοραζίν, -ζείν TTr*S*, Chorazin, Matt. xi. 21. Luke x. 13 (Χω. St).

Χουζᾶς, Chuza, Luke viii. 3.

Χριστιανός, Christian, Acts xi. 26. xxvi. 28. 1 Pet. iv. 16.

Χριστός, *lit.* anointed; commonly with the article in the Gospels, denoting *the Messiah*; e.g., John i. 20, 25, 41(42). iv. 29. vii. 26. xx. 31.

Christ, Matt. i. 1, 16, 17, 18. ii. 4. xi. 2. xvi. 16, 20. xxii. 42. xxiii. 8(*om* *S*), 10. xxiv. 5, 23. xxvi. 63,

68. xxvii. 17, 22. Mark i. 1. viii. 29. ix. 41. xii. 35. xiii. 21. xiv. 61. xv. 32. Luke ii. 11, 26. iii. 15. iv. 41(*omS*), 41. ix. 20. xx. 41. xxii. 67(66). xxiii. 2, 35, 39. xxiv. 26, 46. John i. 17, 20, 25, 41(42, *marg.* anointed). iii. 28. iv. 25, 29, 42 (–G°°LTTr*S*). vi. 69(*ap*). vii. 26, 27, 31, 41*t*, 42. ix. 22. x. 24. xi. 27. xii. 34. xvii. 3. xx. 31.

Acts ii. 30(*ap*), 31, 36, 38. iii. 6, 18, 20. iv. 10, 26. v. 42. viii. 5, 12, 37(*ap*). ix. 20 (Ἰησοῦς GLT*S*), 22, 34. x. 36. xi. 17. xv. 11(–GT*S*), 26. xvi. 18, 31(–LT*S*). xvii. 3*t*. xviii. 5, 28. xix. 4(*omS*). xx. 21(–LT). xxiv. 24. xxvi. 23. xxviii. 31.

Rom. i. 1, 3(4), 6, 7, 8, 16(*omS*). ii. 16. iii. 22, 24. v. 1, 6, 8, 11, 15, 17, 21. vi. 3, 4, 8, 9, 11, 23. vii. 4, 25. viii. 1, 2, 9, 10, 11, 17, 34, 35, 39. ix. 1, 3, 5. x. 4, 6, 7. xii. 5. xiii. 14. xiv. 9, 10(θεός G′LT*S*), 15, 18. xv. 3, 5, 6, 7, 8, 16, 17, 18, 19, 20, 29, 30. xvi. 3, 5, 7, 9 (Κύριος L), 10, 16, 18, 20, 24(*ap*), 25, 27.

1 Cor. i. 1, 2*t*, 3, 4, 6, 7, 8, 9, 10, 12, 13, 17*t*, 23, 24, 30. ii. 2, 16(Κύριος L). iii. 1, 11, 23*t*. iv. 1, 10*t*, 15*t*, 17. v. 4(–LT), 4(–LT*S*), 7. vi. 15*t*. vii. 22. viii. 6, 11, 12. ix. 1(–LT*S*), 12, 18(–G°°LT*S*), 21. x. 4, 9(Κύριος G″L*S*), 16*t*. xi. 1, 3*t*. xii. 12, 27. xv. 3, 12, 13, 14, 15, 16, 17, 18, 19, 20, 22, 23*t*, 31, 57. xvi. 22(–G°°LT*S*), 23(–T*S*), 24. 2 Cor. i. 1, 2, 3, 5*t*, 19, 21. ii. 10, 14, 15, 17. iii. 3, 4, 14. iv. 4, 5, 6. v. 10, 14, 16, 17, 18, 19, 20*t*. vi. 15. viii. 9, 23. ix. 13. x. 1, 5, ., 7(–GT*S*), 14. xi. 2, 3, 10, 13, 23, 31(–LT*S*). xii. 2, 9, 10, 19. xiii. 3, 5, 14(13).

Gal. i. 1, 3, 6(–G°), 7, 10, 12, 22, ii. 4, 16*tr*, 17*t*, 20*t*, 21. iii. 1, 13, 14, 16, 17(–G°°LT*S*), 22, 24, 26, 27, 28, 29. iv. 7(*ap*), 14, 19. v. 1, 2, 4, 6, 24. vi. 2, 12, 14, 15(*ap*), 18. Eph. i. 1*t*, 2, 3*t*, 5, 10, 12, 17, 20. ii. 5, 6, 7, 10, 12, 13*t*, 20. iii. 1, 4, 6, 8, 9 (*ap*), 11, 14 (*ap*), 17, 19, 21. iv. 7, 12, 13, 15, 20, 32. v. 2, 5, 14, 20, 23, 34, 25, 32. vi. 5, 6, 23, 24. Phil. i. 1*t*, 2, 6, 8, 10, 11, 13, 15, 16, 18, 19, 20, 21 (χρηστόν G′), 23, 26, 27, 29. ii. 1, 5, 11, 16, 21, 30 (–G°T, Κύριος *S*). iii. 3, 7, 8*t*, 9, 12, 14, 18, 20. iv. 7, 13(*omS*), 19, 21, 23. Col. i. 1, 2, 2 (*ap*), 3, 4, 7, 24, 27, 28. ii. 2(*ap*), 5, 6, 8, 11, 17, 20. iii. 1*t*, 3, 4, 11, 13 (Κύριος L, θεός *S*), 16, 24. iv. 3, 12.

1 Thes. i. 1, 1(*ap*), 3. ii. 6, 14, 19 (–G°°LT*S*). iii. 2, 11 (–LT*S*), 13 (–G°°LT*S*). iv. 16. v. 9, 18, 23, 28. 2 Thes. i. 1, 2, 8(–L^{b}T), 12(–L^{b}T*S*), 12. ii. 1, 2(Κύριος GLT*S*), 14, 16. iii. 5, 6, 12, 18. 1 Tim. i. 1*t*, 2, 12, 14, 15, 16. ii. 5, 7(*om*). iii. 13. iv. 6. v. 11, 21. vi. 3, 13, 14. 2 Tim. i. 1*t*, 2, 9, 10, 13. ii. 1, 3, 8, 10, 19 (Κύριος GLT*S*). iii. 12, 15. iv. 1, 22 (–LT*S*). Tit. i. 1, 4. ii. 13. iii. 6. Phm. 1, 3, 6, 8, 9, 23, 25.

Heb. iii. 1(*omS*), 6, 14. v. 5. vi. 1. ix. 11, 14, 24, 28. x. 10. xi. 26. xiii. 8, 21. Jas. i. 1. ii. 1. 1 Pet. i. 1, 2, 3*t*, 7, 11*t*, 13, 19. ii. 5, 21. iii. 16, 18, 21. iv. 1, 11, 13, 14. v. 1, 10, 14. 2 Pet. i. 1*t*, 8, 11, 14, 16. ii. 20. iii. 18. 1 John i. 3, 7(–LT*S*). ii. 1, 22. iii. 23. iv. 2, 3(*ap*). v. 1, 6, 20 (–G°). 2 John 3, 7, 9, 9(–G°LT*S*). Jude 1*t*, 4, 17, 21. Rev. i. 1, 2, 5, 9(–LTTr*S*), 9(–G°°LTTr*S*). xi. 15. xii. 10, 17(*om*, θεός *S*). xx. 4, 6. xxii. 21(–LT*S*).

Add, for θεός, Rom. x. 17, L*S*. Eph. v. 21, Col. iii. 15, GLT*S*. 1 Pet. iii. 15, G′LT*S*. For Κύριος, Eph. v. 29, Phm. 20^{2d}, GLT*S*. Phil. ii. 19, L. After Jesus, Acts iv. 33, L^{b}*S*. 1Cor. vi. 11, L*S*.—Mark iii. 12(*ap*). Acts x. 48, *see* Κύριος. xiv. 10(*ap*). 1 Cor. v 5, *see* Ἰησοῦς. Gal. ii. 20 (*ap*). Jude 25(*ap*).

Χωραζίν. *See* Χοραζίν.

Χῶρος. See p. 417.

Ὠβήδ, Obed, Matt. i. 5. Luke iii. [32.

Ὡσηέ, Ὡ. T, Osee, Rom. ix. 25.

Zabulon, etc. *See* Ζαβουλών, *etc.*

INDEX.

***The letter *m* denotes a *marginal* translation; *p*, a *phrase* not given entire in the Index. The *p* is not always added where it might have been. The letters *t* and *tr* refer to *two* or *three* Greek words in the same page.

APPENDIX

OF VARIOUS READINGS IN LARGER CLAUSES.

MATT. v. 44, –*εὐλογεῖτε τοὺς καταρωμένους ὑμᾶς, καλῶς ποιεῖτε τοὺς μισοῦντας ὑμᾶς*, G^{oo}LTTr*S*. –*ἐπηρεαζόντων ὑμᾶς, καὶ* G^{o}LTTr*S*.

vi. 13, *ὅτι σοῦ ἐστιν ἡ βασιλεία καὶ ἡ δύναμις καὶ ἡ δόξα εἰς τοὺς αἰῶνας. ἀμήν.* om*S*.

x. 19, –*δοθήσεται γὰρ ὑμῖν ἐν ἐκείνῃ τῇ ὥρᾳ τί λαλήσετε·* G^{o}L^{b}. — 23, *ἑτέραν* for *ἄλλην* GLTr*S*. add *κἂν ἐκ ταύτης* (*ἐν τῇ ἑτέρᾳ* L) *διώκωσιν ὑμᾶς, φεύγετε εἰς τὴν ἄλλην.* G^{pr}L^{b}.

xiii. 51, –*Λέγει αὐτοῖς ὁ Ἰησοῦς*, G^{oo}LTTr*S*.

xiv. 24, *σταδίους πολλοὺς ἀπὸ τῆς γῆς ἀπεῖχεν*, for *μέσον τῆς θαλάσσης ἦν*, Tr.

xv. 5, –*ἢ τὴν μητέρα αὐτοῦ* L*S*. — 8, *Ἐγγίζει μοι* and *τῷ στόματι αὐτῶν καὶ* om*S*.

xvii. 21, –*the verse* Tr^{b}*S*. — 26, *εἰπόντος δέ* LTr, *ὁ δὲ ἔφη S*, for *λέγει αὐτῷ ὁ Πέτρος*. –*ὁ Πέτρος* G^{oo}T.

xviii. 11, –*the verse* G^{oo}LTTr*S*.

xix. 9, *παρεκτὸς λόγου πορνείας* for *εἰ μὴ ἐπὶ πορνείᾳ* L. –*εἰ* GTTr*S*. –*καὶ ὁ ἀπολελυμένην γαμήσας μοιχᾶται.* Tr^{b}*S*. — 17, *Τί με ἐρωτᾷς περὶ τοῦ ἀγαθοῦ; εἷς ἐστὶν ὁ ἀγαθός.* for *Τί με λέγεις ἀγαθόν; οὐδεὶς ἀγαθός, εἰ μὴ εἷς, ὁ Θεός* (G′). GLTTr*S*. — 29, *ἢ γονεῖς*, for *ἢ πατέρα, ἢ μητέρα*, L^{m}.

xx. 7, –*καὶ ὃ ἐὰν ᾖ δίκαιον λήψεσθε* G^{oo}LTTr*S*. — 16, –*πολλοὶ γάρ εἰσι κλητοί, ὀλίγοι δὲ ἐκλεκτοί.* Tr^{b}*S*. — 22, *καὶ τὸ βάπτισμα, ὃ ἐγὼ βαπτίζομαι, βαπτισθῆναι* om*S*. — 23, *καὶ τὸ βάπτισμα, ὃ ἐγὼ βαπτίζομαι, βαπτισθήσεσθε* om*S*.

xxi. 44, –*the verse* G^{o}L^{b}TTr^{m}.

xxiii. 14(13), –*the verse* G^{oo}LTTr*S*.

xxiv. 36, after *οὐρανῶν*, add *οὐδὲ ὁ υἱός* L*S*.

xxv. 13, *ἐν ᾗ ὁ υἱὸς τοῦ ἀνθρώπου ἔρχεται* om*S*. — 29, *τοῦ δὲ . . ἀπ' αὐτοῦ* for *ἀπὸ δὲ τοῦ . . ἀπ' αὐτοῦ* G″LTTr*S*. — 41, *ὃ ἡτοίμασεν ὁ πατήρ μου* for *τὸ ἡτοιμασμένον* G′.

xxvi. 60, –*πολλῶν ψευδομαρτύρων προσελθόντων* G^{o}.

xxvii. 4, *δίκαιος* for *ἀθῶος* G′. — 35, *ἵνα πληρωθῇ τὸ ῥηθὲν ὑπὸ τοῦ προφήτου, Διεμερίσαντο τὰ ἱμάτιά μου ἑαυτοῖς, καὶ ἐπὶ τὸν ἱματισμόν μου ἔβαλον κλῆρον.* om*S*.

xxviii. 9, –*ὡς δὲ ἐπορεύοντο ἀπαγγεῖλαι τοῖς μαθηταῖς αὐτοῦ*, G^{oo}LTTr*S*.

MARK i. 27, –*Τί ἐστι τοῦτο;* G′, –*ὅτι* G′. *διδαχὴ καινή·* (, Tr) *κατ' ἐξουσίαν* LTr, *διδαχὴ καινὴ κατ' ἐξουσίαν·* T*S*, for *τίς ἡ διδαχὴ ἡ καινὴ αὕτη, ὅτι*

ii. 19, –*ὅσον χρόνον μεθ' ἑαυτῶν ἔχουσι τὸν νυμφίον, οὐ δύνανται νηστεύειν·* G^{o}. *αὐτῶν* for *ἑαυτῶν* TTr*S*. — 22, –*ἀλλὰ οἶνον νέον εἰς ἀσκοὺς καινοὺς βλητέον·* TTr^{b}, –*βλητέον S*.

iii. 12, after *ποιήσωσι* add *, ὅτι ᾔδεισαν τὸν χριστὸν αὐτὸν εἶναι* L^{b}. — 32, after *ἀδελφοί σου* add *καὶ αἱ ἀδελφαί σου* G^{ph}LTTr^{mb}.

iv. 15, *ἐν αὐτοῖς* G″L*S*, *εἰς αὐτούς* TTr, for *ἐν ταῖς καρδίαις αὐτῶν* — 24, –*καὶ προστεθήσεται ὑμῖν* G. *τοῖς ἀκούουσιν* om*S*. — 31, –*τῶν ἐπὶ τῆς γῆς* L^{b}. — 40, *; οὔπω* G′LTr*S*, *; οὕτως οὔπω* G″, for *οὕτω; πῶς οὐκ*

vi. 11, *ὃς ἂν* (*ἐὰν* L) *τόπος μὴ δέξηται* for *ὅσοι ἂν μὴ δέξωνται* TTr*S*. –*ἀμὴν λέγω ὑμῖν, ἀνεκτότερον ἔσται Σοδόμοις ἢ Γομόρροις ἐν ἡμέρᾳ κρίσεως, ἢ τῇ πόλει ἐκείνῃ.* GL^{b}TTr*S*. — 33, before *ἐκεῖ* add *καὶ ἦλθον* G′. –*καὶ προῆλθον αὐτούς*, G. –*καὶ συνῆλθον πρὸς αὐτόν.* GLTr*S*. — 54, after *αὐτόν* add *οἱ ἄνδρες τοῦ τόπου ἐκείνου* L^{b}.

Mark vii. 8, –*βαπτισμοὺς ξεστῶν καὶ ποτηρίων, καὶ ἄλλα παρόμοια τοιαῦτα πολλὰ ποιεῖτε* Tr^{b}*S*. — 16, –*the verse* Tr^{b}*S*:

viii. 24, *ὅτι ὡς δένδρα ὁρῶ* for *ὡς δένδρα* StG′LTTr*S*.

ix. 38, –*ὃς οὐκ ἀκολουθεῖ ἡμῖν* G*S*. –*ὅτι οὐκ ἀκολουθεῖ ἡμῖν* G^{oo}TTr^{b}.—43, –*εἰς τὸ πῦρ τὸ ἄσβεστον* G^{o}. — 45, –*εἰς τὸ πῦρ τὸ ἄσβεστον* G^{oo}L^{b}TTr*S*. — 44, 46, –*the verses* G^{o}TTr^{b}*S*. — 49, –*καὶ πᾶσα θυσία ἁλὶ ἁλισθήσεται* Tr^{b}*S*.

x. 27, –*πάντα γὰρ δυνατά ἐστι παρὰ τῷ Θεῷ*. G^{o}. –*ἐστι* Tr*S*.

xi. 3, *λύετε τὸν πῶλον* for *ποιεῖτε τοῦτο* L^{m}. — 8, –*καὶ ἐστρώννυον εἰς τὴν ὁδόν* TTr*S*. — 10, *ἐν ὀνόματι Κυρίου om**S*. — 26, –*the verse* TTr*S*.

xii. 14, before *ἔξεστι* add *εἰπὲ οὖν ἡμῖν*, L. — 21, *μὴ καταλιπὼν* for *καὶ οὐδὲ αὐτὸς ἀφῆκε* L^{m}Tr*S*. — 29, *πρώτη πάντων ἐντολή* G, *πρώτη ἐστίν* G″TTr *S*, *πάντων πρώτη* G′, *πρώτη ἐντολή ἐστιν* L^{b}, for *πρώτη πασῶν τῶν ἐντολῶν* — 30, –*αὕτη πρώτη ἐντολή*. T*S*. — 33, –*καὶ ἐξ ὅλης τῆς ψυχῆς*, L^{b}*S*.

xiii. 14, –*τὸ ῥηθὲν ὑπὸ Δανιὴλ τοῦ προφήτου*, GL^{b}TTr*S*.

xiv. 19, –*καὶ ἄλλος, Μή τι ἐγώ;* G^{o} Tr*S*. — 40, *πάλιν* (–G^{oo}Tr) *ἐλθὼν εὗρεν αὐτοὺς* for *ὑποστρέψας εὗρεν αὐτοὺς πάλιν* LTr*S*. — 70, –*καὶ ἡ λαλιά σοῦ ὁμοιάζει* G^{oo}LTTr*S*.

xv. 28, –*the verse* G^{oo}TTr^{b}*S*.

xvi. 9–20, –*the verses* G^{oo}T*S*.

This passage is *contained* in most of the uncial MSS. now extant, including A (the Alexandrine, 5th cent.), C (Ephraemi, 5th cent.), and D (Bezæ, or Cantabrigiensis, 6th cent.). Also in the cursive MSS. and the ancient versions, except as stated below. It is *omitted* in ℵ (the Sinaitic) and B (the Vatican), each of the 4th cent., and in the Arabic codex in the Vatican, apparently based on an ancient Greek text. Of the cursives, 137 and 138 mark the passage with an asterisk; and about twenty five others, in marginal scholia, note its omission in *many*, *most*, *more ancient*, or *more correct* copies.

The uncial L (8th cent.) gives *another* passage as found in some MSS., adding the one in question as also found after ver. 8. This other passage appears for substance in the Latin *k*, and the statement in L is supported by the cursive 274 and by a scholium in the Harclean Syriac. In B a *blank space* — the only one in the MS. — is left instead of the passage. All critics agree that the Gospel would end at ver. 8 very abruptly, and that Mark could not have intended thus to close the book. And all confess that the following verses differ in *style* from the rest of the book, seventeen words or phrases occurring in them either not found elsewhere in the New Testament, or not elsewhere in Mark, or used in a peculiar sense. These facts have led to various conjectures.

The patristic testimony is divided. The passage is cited as genuine by Irenæus (flor. A.D. 167), Hippolytus (A.D. 220), in the Apostolical Constitutions (4th cent.?), by Cyril of Jerusalem (A. D. 350), Ambrose (A. D. 374), Augustine (A.D. 396), and Nestorius (A.D. 428). It is *not* cited by Justin Martyr (A. D. 140), Clement of Alexandria (A.D. 194), or Origen, the critic of his time (A. D. 230). Victor of Antioch (A. D. 401) and Severus of Antioch (A. D. 513) speak of it as wanting in many MSS. Eusebius (A.D. 315) and Jerome (A.D. 392) say the same of "nearly all" the Greek copies. Eusebius and Gregory Nyssen (A. D. 371) assert its absence from the more accurate copies. Nor is it reckoned in the "sections" of Ammonius (A.D. 220) or Eusebius.

The modern critics are likewise divided. The passage is retained by Simon, Mill, Bengel, Matthæi, Storr, Eichhorn, Kuinoel, Guericke, Scholz, Feilmoser, Knapp, Vater, Rinck, Lachmann, Olshausen, Ebrard, De Wette, Bloomfield, Scrivener, Stuart, and others. J. D. Michaelis and Hug regard it as a later addition of Mark himself. Tregelles thinks it *canonical*, but not written by Mark. It is questioned or omitted, besides Griesbach and Tischendorf, by Rosenmüller, Bertholdt, Gratz, Schott (Isagoge), Schulz, Fritzsche, Credner, Wieseler, Neudecker, Theile, Reuss, Meyer, Davidson, Green, Norton, and others.

xvi. 14, after *ἐγηγερμένον* add *ἐκ νεκρῶν* L. — 18, before *ὄφεις* add *καὶ ἐν ταῖς χερσὶν* Tr.

Luke i. 28, –*εὐλογημένη σὺ ἐν γυναιξίν* G^{o}TTr^{b}*S*.

ii. 43, *ἔγνωσαν οἱ γονεῖς* for *ἔγνω Ἰωσὴφ καὶ ἡ μήτηρ* G′LTTr*S*.

iii. 16, after *βαπτίζω ὑμᾶς* add *εἰς μετάνοιαν* L.

iv. 4, –*ἀλλ' ἐπὶ παντὶ ῥήματι Θεοῦ* TTr^{b}*S*. — 5, –*ὁ διάβολος* G^{oo}TTr*S*, –*εἰς ὄρος ὑψηλὸν* L^{b}TTr*S*. — 8, –*Ὕπαγε ὀπίσω μου, Σατανᾶ*. GL^{b}TTr*S*. — 18, –*ἰάσασθαι τοὺς συντετριμμένους τὴν καρδίαν* GL^{b}TTr*S*.

vi. 10, *ὑγιὴς om**S*, –*ὡς ἡ ἄλλη* G″ L^{b}Tr*S*. — 35, after *πολύς* add *ἐν τοῖς οὐρανοῖς* L^{b}. — 45^{21}, –*θησαυροῦ τῆς* *καρδίας αὐτοῦ* G^{oo}L^{b}TTr*S*. — 49, *διὰ τὸ καλῶς οἰκοδομεῖσθαι αὐτήν* for *τεθεμελίωτο γὰρ ἐπὶ τὴν πέτραν* TTr*S*.

Luke vii. 31, *εἶπε δὲ ὁ Κύριος*, om*S*.

viii. 42, *καὶ ἐγένετο ἐν τῷ πορεύεσθαι* for *ἐν δὲ τῷ ὑπάγειν* LT. — 45, – *καὶ λέγεις, Τίς ὁ ἁψάμενός μου;* G^{o} Tr^{b}*S*. — 51, *τινὰ σὺν αὐτῷ* for *οὐδένα* LTTr. — 54, – *ἐκβαλὼν ἔξω πάντας, καὶ* G^{o}LTTr*S*.

ix. 10, – *τόπον ἔρημον* G′TTr, – *πόλεως καλουμένης* G″*S*. — 23, – *καὶ ἀράτω τὸν σταυρὸν αὐτοῦ* G^{o}, – *καθ' ἡμέραν* G^{oo}L. — 54, – *ὡς καὶ 'Ηλίας ἐποίησε* G^{o}TTr*S*. — 55, – *καὶ εἶπεν, Οὐκ οἴδατε οἵου πνεύματός ἐστε ὑμεῖς·* G^{oo} LTTr*S*. — 56, *ὁ γὰρ υἱὸς τοῦ ἀνθρώπου οὐκ ἦλθε ψυχὰς ἀνθρώπων ἀπολέσαι, ἀλλὰ σῶσαι.* om*S*.

x. 11, after *ὑμῶν* add *εἰς τοὺς πόδας* LTTr*S*, . . . *ὑμῶν* T. — 22, before *Πάντα* add *Καὶ στραφείς πρὸς τοὺς μαθητὰς εἶπε*, StC^{m}LT.

xi. 2, – *ἡμῶν ὁ ἐν τοῖς οὐρανοῖς* GT Tr*S*. – *γενηθήτω τὸ θέλημά σου*, GT Tr, – *ὡς ἐν οὐρανῷ, καὶ ἐπὶ τῆς γῆς.* GL^{b}TTr. — 4, – *ἀλλὰ ῥῦσαι ἡμᾶς ἀπὸ τοῦ πονηροῦ* GTTr*S*. — 43, after *ἀγοραῖς* add *καὶ τὰς πρωτοκλισίας ἐν τοῖς δείπνοις* L^{b}. — 44, – *γραμματεῖς καὶ Φαρισαῖοι, ὑποκριταί*, GL^{b}TTr*S*. — 53, *Καὶ* G″, *Κἀκεῖθεν ἐξελθόντος αὐτοῦ*, TTr*S*, for *Λέγοντος δὲ αὐτοῦ ταῦτα πρὸς αὐτούς*, — 54, – *ἵνα κατηγορήσωσιν αὐτοῦ* G^{oo}TTr^{b}*S*.

xii. 27, *οὔτε νήθει οὔτε ὑφαίνει* for *αὐξάνει· οὐ κοπιᾷ, οὐδὲ νήθει* T.

xiv. 12, – *μηδὲ τοὺς συγγενεῖς σου*, G^{o}.

xvii. 24, – *ἐν τῇ ἡμέρᾳ αὐτοῦ* L. — 36, – *the verse* St, om*S*.

xix. 45, – *ἐν αὐτῷ καὶ ἀγοράζοντας* G^{oo}TTr*S*.

xx. 23, – *Τί με πειράζετε;* G^{oo}TTr*S*. — 24, after *δηνάριον* add *οἱ δὲ ἔδειξαν (αὐτῷ S)· καὶ εἶπεν*, L^{b}*S*. — 30, – *ἔλαβεν* and *τὴν γυναῖκα, καὶ οὗτος ἀπέθανεν ἄτεκνος* G′TTr*S*. — 45, *πρὸς αὐτούς* for *τοῖς μαθηταῖς αὐτοῦ* T.

xxii. 31, – *Εἶπε δὲ ὁ Κύριος*, TTr^{b}. — 43, 44, – *the verses* L^{b}. — 64, – *ἔτυπτον αὐτοῦ τὸ πρόσωπον, καὶ* L^{b}TTr*S*.

xxiii. 15, *ἀνέπεμψε γὰρ αὐτὸν πρὸς ἡμᾶς* for *ἀνέπεμψα γ. ὑμᾶς π. α.* G′*S*. — 17, – *the verse* G^{oo}L^{b}TTr. — 34, – *ὁ δὲ 'Ιησοῦς ἔλεγε, Πάτερ, ἄφες αὐτοῖς· οὐ γὰρ οἴδασι τί ποιοῦσι.* L^{b}. — 38, – *γράμμασιν 'Ελληνικοῖς καὶ 'Ρωμαϊκοῖς καὶ 'Εβραϊκοῖς* L^{b}TTr. – *Οὗτος ἐστιν* L^{b}.

xxiv. 1, – *καί τινες σὺν αὐταῖς* G^{o}L TTr*S*. — 12, – *the verse* L^{b}TTr^{b}. – *κείμενα μόνα* Tr*S*. *αὐτὸν* for *ἑαυτὸν* Tr. — 36, – *καὶ λέγει αὐτοῖς, Εἰρήνη ὑμῖν.* T. add *ἐγώ εἰμι, μὴ φοβεῖσθε.* L^{b}. — 40, – *the verse* TTr^{b}. *ἔδειξεν* for *ἐπέδειξεν* LTr*S*. — 42, – *καὶ ἀπὸ μελισσίου κηρίου* G^{o}LTr^{b}*S*. — 51, – *καὶ ἀνεφέρετο εἰς τὸν οὐρανόν* G^{o}T*S*. — 52, – *προσκυνήσαντες αὐτόν* G^{o}T. — 53, – *αἰνοῦντες καὶ* Tr^{b}*S*, – *καὶ εὐλογοῦντες* T.

John i. 27, – *ὃς ἔμπροσθέν μου γέγονεν* GL^{b}TTr*S*. — 36, after *Θεοῦ* add *ὁ αἴρων τὴν ἁμαρτίαν τοῦ κόσμου* L^{b}.

iii. 13, – *ὁ ὢν ἐν τῷ οὐρανῷ* G^{o}*S*. — 15, – *μὴ ἀπόληται, ἀλλ'* G^{oo}L^{b}TTr*S*. — 31, 32, – *ἐπάνω πάντων ἐστί, καὶ* G^{oo}*S*.

iv. 14, – *οὐ μὴ διψήσῃ εἰς τὸν αἰῶνα· ἀλλὰ τὸ ὕδωρ ὃ δώσω αὐτῷ* L^{b}.

v. 3, 4, – *ἐκδεχομένων* to *νοσήματι.* G^{boo}TTr*S*. — 16, – *καὶ ἐζήτουν αὐτὸν ἀποκτεῖναι*, GL^{b}TTr*S*.

vi. 11, – *τοῖς μαθηταῖς, οἱ δὲ μαθηταὶ* G^{oo}LTTr*S*. — 22, *ἐκεῖνο εἰς ὃ ἐνέβησαν οἱ μαθηταὶ αὐτοῦ* *om*, *τοῦ 'Ιησοῦ* for *αὐτοῦ* *S*. — 51, – *ἣν ἐγὼ δώσω* G^{o}LTr*S*. — 69, *ὁ ἅγιος τοῦ Θεοῦ* GL TTr*S*, for *ὁ Χριστὸς ὁ υἱὸς τοῦ Θεοῦ τοῦ ζῶντος* G′.

vii. 46, – *ὡς οὗτος ὁ ἄνθρωπος* G^{o}L TTr^{b}.

vii. 53 – viii. 11, – *the passage* G^{booo} LTTr*S*.

This narrative is *contained* in uncials D, F (9th cent.), G and H (11th cent.), K (9th cent.), U (9th or 10th cent.), and in more than 300 cursives. It is found also in some copies of the Old Latin version, and in the Vulgate, the Æthiopic, the Jerusalem Syriac Lectionary, and the Arabic. In E (8th cent.), M (9th or 10th cent.), and about sixty cursives it is *marked as doubtful* (with * or †), entire or from ch. viii. 3. More than fifteen cursives place it at the end of the Gospel; one after vii. 36; and four after Luke xxi. It is *omitted* by ℵ, A, B, C, T (5th cent.), L, X

16*

(9th or 10th cent.), Δ (9th cent.), and by more than fifty cursives, including codex 33. Also by some copies of the Old Latin, by the Peshito and Harclean Syriac, the good MSS. of the Memphitic, and the Thebaic, Gothic, and Armenian versions.

In D the passage differs widely from the received text, and other MSS. vary still from this and from each other. It seems *out of its place*; its style is peculiar; and Augustine speaks of those who thought its doctrine lax, while some who omit it still regard it as genuine tradition and history.

It is cited in the Apostolical Constitutions, but without John's name. Also by Euthymius (A. D. 1116), but with the remark that accurate copies either omit it or mark it as doubtful. It is recognized by the Latin Fathers Ambrose, Jerome and Augustine with note of its omission in some early copies, and by others since the 4th century. On the other hand Tertullian (A.D. 200), Cyprian (A.D. 248), and Juvencus (A. D. 330) do not use it, and it is omitted by the Greek Fathers Origen, Chrysostom (A.D. 398), Theodore of Mopsuestia (A.D. 407), and Theophylact (A.D. 1077) in their Commentaries, by Nonnus (A.D. 410) in his Paraphrase, and by Apollinaris and Basil (A.D. 370), Cyril of Alexandria (A.D. 412), and Cosmas (A. D. 535).

It is retained by Mill, Whitby, Lampe, Bengel, Michaelis, Heumann, Stäudlin, Storr, Kuinoel, Hug, Hahn, Maier, Ebrard, Hilgenfeld, Stier, Lange, Bloomfield, Stuart, and others. It is questioned or omitted by Erasmus, Beza, Calvin, Grotius, Wetstein, Semler, Paulus, Tittmann, Wegscheider, De Wette, Brückner, Knapp, Theile, Lücke, Feilmoser, Credner, Tholuck, Baumgarten-Crusius, Bleek, Olshausen, Hitzig, Baur, Luthardt, Ewald, Hengstenberg, Meyer, Porter, Davidson, Alford, Scrivener, Green, Norton, and others.

JOHN viii. 59, *διελθὼν διὰ μέσου αὐτῶν· καὶ παρῆγεν οὕτω. om*S.

x. 12, –*τὰ πρόβατα* L^{b}Tr*S*.—13, –*ὁ δὲ μισθωτὸς φεύγει* G^{oo}L^{b}Tr*S*.—14, *γινώσκουσίν με τὰ ἐμά* for *γινώσκομαι ὑπὸ τῶν ἐμῶν* LTr*S*.—26, –*καθὼς εἶπον ὑμῖν* G^{o}L^{b}Tr*S*.

xi. 41, *οὗ ἦν ὁ τεθνηκὼς κείμενος om*S.

xiii. 24, *καὶ λέγει αὐτῷ, Εἰπὲ τίς ἐστιν* for *πυθέσθαι τίς ἂν εἴη* LTTr.—32, –*εἰ ὁ Θεὸς ἐδοξάσθη ἐν αὐτῷ* L^{b}Tr*S*.

xvi. 16, –*ὅτι ἐγὼ ὑπάγω πρὸς τὸν πατέρα* G^{o}L^{b}TTr*S*, –*ἐγὼ* GL.

xix. 2, after *αὐτόν*, add *καὶ ἤρχοντο πρὸς αὐτόν*, LTTr*S*.—16, –*Παρέλαβον δὲ τὸν Ἰησοῦν καὶ ἀπήγαγον*. G^{o}, *ἤγαγον* for *ἀπήγαγον* G, –*καὶ ἀπήγαγον* LTTr.—29, *σπόγγον οὖν μεστὸν τοῦ ὄξους ὑσσώπῳ* for *οἱ δέ, πλήσαντες σπόγγον ὄξους, καὶ ὑσσώπῳ* LTr*S*.

ACTS ii. 30, *τὸ κατὰ σάρκα ἀναστήσειν τὸν Χριστόν om*S.

iii. 22, –*γὰρ πρὸς τοὺς πατέρας* G^{oo}LT*S*, –*γὰρ* G.

iv. 12, –*καὶ οὐκ ἔστιν ἐν ἄλλῳ οὐδενὶ ἡ σωτηρία·* G^{o}.—25, *ὁ τοῦ πατρὸς ἡμῶν διὰ πνεύματος ἁγίου στόματος* for *ὁ διὰ στόματος* L*S*.—27, after *ἀληθείας* add *ἐν τῇ πόλει ταύτῃ* GLT*S*.

viii. 37, *the verse om*S.

ix. 5, 6, *σκληρόν* to *αὐτόν*, *om*S.

x. 6, *οὗτος λαλήσει σοι τί σε δεῖ ποιεῖν. om*S.—21, *τοὺς ἀπεσταλμένους ἀπὸ τοῦ Κορνηλίου πρὸς αὐτόν om*S.—32, –*ὃς παραγενόμενος λαλήσει σοι*. G^{o}L*S*.

xiii. 42, *αὐτῶν* for *ἐκ τῆς συναγωγῆς τῶν Ἰουδαίων* GLT*S*.

xiv. 10, after *φωνῇ*, add *Σοὶ λέγω ἐν τῷ ὀνόματι τοῦ κυρίου Ἰησοῦ Χριστοῦ*, L.

xv. 17, *πάντα*^{2d} *om*S.—18, –*ἐστι τῷ Θεῷ πάντα τὰ ἔργα αὐτοῦ* GT*S*.—24, –*λέγοντες περιτέμνεσθαι καὶ τηρεῖν τὸν νόμον*, G^{oo}LT*S*.—34, –*the verse* G^{oo}LT*S*.

xvii. 18, –*ὅτι* to *εὐηγγελίζετο*. G^{o}.

xviii. 3, –*ἦσαν γὰρ σκηνοποιοὶ τὴν τέχνην*. G^{o}.—21, –*Δεῖ με πάντως τὴν ἑορτὴν τὴν ἐρχομένην ποιῆσαι εἰς Ἱεροσόλυμα·* G^{oo}LT*S*.

xx. 15, –*καὶ μείναντες ἐν Τρωγυλλίῳ*, G′′L*S*.—18, after *αὐτόν*, add *ὁμοῦ ὄντων αὐτῶν*, L.

xxi. 8, *οἱ περὶ τὸν Παῦλον om*S.—25, –*μηδὲν τοιοῦτον τηρεῖν αὐτούς, εἰ μὴ* G^{oo}L*S*.

xxiii. 9, *τινες τῶν γραμματέων τοῦ μέρους* G′*S*, *τινὲς* L, for *οἱ γραμματεῖς τοῦ μέρους*

xxiv. 6, 7, 8, –*καὶ κατὰ τὸν ἡμέτερον νόμον* to *ἔρχεσθαι ἐπὶ σέ*. G^{oo}LT*S*.—26, –*ὅπως λύσῃ αὐτόν* G^{oo}LT*S*.

xxv. 6, *ἡμέρας οὐ πλείους ὀκτὼ ἢ δέκα* (–*οὐ* G′, *οὐ πλ. ἡμ. etc.* *S*) for *ἡμέρας πλείους ἢ δέκα* GLT*S*.—7, *αἰτιώματα* (G) *καταφέροντες* for *αἰτιάματα φέροντες* LT*S*, –*κατὰ τὸν Παῦλον* G^{oo}LT*S*.

ACTS xxvi. 30, *Καὶ ταῦτα εἰπόντος αὐτοῦ*, (G'') *omS*.
xxviii. 16, –*ὁ δὲ ἑκατόνταρχος παρέδωκε τοὺς δεσμίους τῷ στρατοπεδάρχῃ·* G''LT*S*. — 29, –*the verse* G°°LT*S*.

ROM. iii. 22, –*καὶ ἐπὶ πάντας* G°°L*S*.
vi. 12, *αὐτῇ ἐν omS*, –*ταῖς ἐπιθυμίαις αὐτοῦ* G.
viii. 1, *μὴ κατὰ σάρκα περιπατοῦσιν, ἀλλὰ κατὰ πνεῦμα omS*.
ix. 28, –*ἐν δικαιοσύνῃ· ὅτι λόγον συντετμημένον* L*S*: [LT*S*.
x. 1, *αὐτῶν* for *τοῦ Ἰσραήλ ἐστιν* G
xi. 6, –*εἰ δὲ ἐξ ἔργων, οὐκ ἔτι ἐστὶ χάρις· ἐπεὶ τὸ ἔργον οὐκ ἔτι ἐστὶν ἔργον*. GL*S*.
xii. 17, after *καλὰ* add *ἐνώπιον τοῦ Θεοῦ καὶ* L[b].
xv. 24, –*ἐλεύσομαι πρὸς ὑμᾶς* GL*S*.
— 32, –*καὶ συναναπαύσωμαι ὑμῖν* G°L.
xvi. 12, –*ἀσπάσασθε Περσίδα τὴν ἀγαπητήν, ἥτις πολλὰ ἐκοπίασεν ἐν Κυρίῳ*. L[b]. — 24, –*the verse* L*S*.

1 COR. i. 27, –*ἵνα τοὺς σοφοὺς καταισχύνῃ· καὶ τὰ ἀσθενῆ τοῦ κόσμου ἐξελέξατο ὁ Θεός*, L[b].
vi. 20, *καὶ ἐν τῷ πνεύματι ὑμῶν, ἅτινά ἐστι τοῦ Θεοῦ omS*.
vii. 38, *γαμίζων* G', *γαμίζων τὴν παρθένον ἑαυτοῦ* (*ἑ. π.*) L*S*, for *ἐκγαμίζων*
viii. 8, *μὴ φάγωμεν, ὑστερούμεθα* (*περισσεύομεν* L), *οὔτε ἐὰν φάγωμεν, περισσεύομεν* (*ὑστερούμεθα* L) LT, for *φ., περισσ.· οὔτε ἐὰν μὴ φ., ὑστερ.*
ix. 10, *ἐπ' ἐλπίδι τοῦ μετέχειν* for *τῆς ἐλπ. αὐτοῦ μετέχειν ἐπ' ἐλπίδι* GLT*S*.
— 20, after *νόμον*[2d], add *μὴ ὢν αὐτὸς ὑπὸ νόμον*, GLT*S*.
x. 19, –*ὅτι εἴδωλον τί ἐστιν ; ἢ* G°°*S*.
— 28, *τοῦ γὰρ Κυρίου ἡ γῆ καὶ τὸ πλήρωμα αὐτῆς*. *omS*.
xv. 51, *κοιμηθησόμεθα· οὐ* for *οὐ κοιμηθησόμεθα·* G'L*S*.

2 COR. i. 20, *διὸ καὶ δι' αὐτοῦ* for *καὶ ἐν αὐτῷ* G'L*S*.
xii. 1, *δεῖ, οὐ συμφέρον μέν, ἐλεύσομαι δὲ καὶ* for *δὴ οὐ συμφέρει μοι· ἐλεύσομαι γὰρ* L*S*. — 7, –*ἵνα μὴ ὑπεραίρωμαι* G°L[b]*S*.

GAL. ii. 20, *Θεοῦ καὶ Χριστοῦ* for *υἱοῦ τοῦ Θεοῦ* L.
iii. 1, *τῇ ἀληθείᾳ μὴ πείθεσθαι omS*.
iv. 7, *διὰ Θεοῦ* LT*S* for *Θεοῦ διὰ Χριστοῦ* –G°°.
v. 1, –*οὖν* T, place after *στήκετε* G'' L*S*.
vi. 15, *οὔτε γὰρ* for *ἐν γὰρ Χριστῷ Ἰησοῦ οὔτε* G''T.

EPH. iii. 9, *διὰ Ἰησοῦ Χριστοῦ omS*.
— 14, –*τοῦ Κυρίου ἡμῶν Ἰησοῦ Χριστοῦ* G°°LT*S*.
v. 30, –*ἐκ τῆς σάρκος αὐτοῦ, καὶ ἐκ τῶν ὀστέων αὐτοῦ* G°L*S*.
vi. 9, *αὐτῶν* (*ἑαυτῶν S*) *καὶ ὑμῶν* for *ὑμῶν αὐτῶν* C[m]G'LT*S*.

PHIL. iii. 16, *κανόνι, τὸ αὐτὸ φρονεῖν omS*. — 21, *εἰς τὸ γενέσθαι αὐτὸ omS*.

COL. i. 2, –*καὶ Κυρίου Ἰησοῦ Χριστοῦ* GL[b]T. — 14, *διὰ τοῦ αἵματος αὐτοῦ omS*.
ii. 2, *καὶ πατρὸς καὶ τοῦ om*, –*Χριστοῦ* GT, *πατρὸς Χριστοῦ S*.
iii. 6, –*ἐπὶ τοὺς υἱοὺς τῆς ἀπειθείας* L[b]T. — 17, *Ἰησοῦ Χριστοῦ* L, *Κυρίου Ἰ. Χ. S*, for *Κυρίου* (–G°°) *Ἰησοῦ*

1 THES. i. 1, –*ἀπὸ Θεοῦ πατρὸς ἡμῶν καὶ Κυρίου Ἰησοῦ Χριστοῦ* G°L[b]T.
iii. 2, *συνεργὸν* (*διάκονονS*) *τοῦ Θεοῦ* for *διάκονον τοῦ Θεοῦ καὶ συνεργὸν ἡμῶν* GLT*S*.
iv. 1, after *Θεῷ*, add *καθὼς καὶ περιπατεῖτε*, G'LT*S*.

2 THES. iii. 4, *ὑμῖν καὶ ἐποιήσατε καὶ ποιεῖτε* for *ὑμῖν, καὶ ποιεῖτε* L[b].

1 TIM. vi. 5, –*ἀφίστασο ἀπὸ τῶν τοιούτων*. G°°LT*S*.

2TIM. iv. 22, –*ἡ χάρις μεθ' ὑμῶν*. G°.

HEB. ii. 7, –*καὶ κατέστησας αὐτὸν ἐπὶ τὰ ἔργα τῶν χειρῶν σου* GL[b]T.
iii. 6, –*μέχρι τέλους βεβαίαν* T. — 9, *ἐν δοκιμασίᾳ* for *ἐδοκίμασάν με* G' LT*S*.
vii. 21, –*κατὰ τὴν τάξιν Μελχισεδέκ* G°T*S*[c].
xii. 20, *ἢ βολίδι κατατοξευθήσεται omS*.

Jas. iii. 12, –οὕτως, G°°LT, οὔτε (οὐδὲ *S*) ἁλυκὸν for οὐδεμία πηγὴ ἁλυκὸν καὶ GLT*S*.

1 **Pet.** iii. 16, –ὑμῶν ὡς κακοποιῶν T. iv. 14, –κατὰ μὲν αὐτοὺς βλασφημεῖται, κατὰ δὲ ὑμᾶς δοξάζεται. G°°LT*S*.

2 **Pet.** i. 1, ἡμῶν not rendered with Θεοῦ; add after σωτῆρος BC?E.—10, after σπουδάσατε add ἵνα διὰ τῶν καλῶν ὑμῶν (–ὑμῶν *S*) ἔργων L*S*.

ii. 21, ὑποστρέψαι ἀπὸ L, εἰς τὰ ὀπίσω ἀνακάμψαι ἀπὸ *S*, for ἐπιστρέψαι ἐκ

1 **John** ii. 23, after πατέρα ἔχει. add ὁ ὁμολογῶν τὸν υἱὸν καὶ τὸν πατέρα ἔχει. C(*in italics*)GLT*S*.

Though given as doubtful in C, the omission in some MSS. plainly arose from the similar ending of the previous clause.

iii. 10, ὢν δίκαιος for ποιῶν δικαιοσύνην L.

v. 7, 8, ἐν τῷ οὐρανῷ, ὁ Πατήρ, ὁ Λόγος, καὶ τὸ Ἅγιον Πνεῦμα· καὶ οὗτοι οἱ τρεῖς ἕν εἰσι. καὶ τρεῖς εἰσιν οἱ μαρτυροῦντες ἐν τῇ γῇ, om*S*.

The words are found in no Greek MS. before the 15th or 16th century, and in no early version. "Unless," says Alford, "pure caprice is to be followed in the criticism of the sacred text, *there is not a shadow of reason for supposing them genuine*." Tischendorf says, "That this spurious addition should continue to be published as a part of the Epistle, I regard as an impiety," etc. And President T. D. Woolsey, "Do not truth and honesty require that such a passage should be struck out of our English Bibles, a passage which Luther would not express in his translation, and which did not creep into the German Bible until nearly fifty years after his death?" See Orme's "Memoir of the Controversy on 1 John v. 7," edited by Ezra Abbot. New York, 1866.

v. 13, τοῖς πιστεύουσιν εἰς τὸ ὄνομα τοῦ υἱοῦ τοῦ Θεοῦ om*S*.

Jude 22, 23, ἐλέγχετε (ἐλεᾶτε *S*) διακρινομένους(*S*), οὓς δὲ σώζετε ἐκ πυρὸς ἁρπάζοντες, οὓς δὲ ἐλεᾶτε (-εῖτε G) ἐν φόβῳ G″LT, for ἐλεεῖτε διακρινόμενοι· οὓς δὲ ἐν φόβῳ σώζετε, ἐκ τοῦ πυρὸς ἁρπάζοντες (–ἐν φόβῳ add οὓς δὲ ἐλεᾶτε ἐν φόβῳ *S*).—25, after ἡμῶν add διὰ Ἰησοῦ Χριστοῦ τοῦ κυρίου ἡμῶν G^pr^LT*S*. after ἐξουσία, add πρὸ παντὸς τοῦ αἰῶνος, G′LT*S*.

Rev. i. 11, Ἐγώ εἰμι τὸ Α καὶ τὸ Ω, ὁ πρῶτος καὶ ὁ ἔσχατος· om*S*.

ii. 2, λέγοντας ἑαυτοὺς ἀποστόλους (εἶναι T) for φάσκοντας εἶναι ἀποστόλους GLTTr*S*.—3, καὶ οὐ κεκοπίακες (-κας Tr, ἐκοπίασας G*S*) for κεκ. καὶ οὐ κέκμηκας GLTTr*S*.—13, –τὰ ἔργα σου καὶ G°LTTr*S*.—21, καὶ οὐ θέλει (οὐκ ἠθέλησεν L^m^) μετανοῆσαι ἐκ . . αὐτῆς (ταύτης *S*) for ἐκ . . α., καὶ οὐ μετανόησεν (–*S*) GLTTr.

iii. 3, –καὶ ἤκουσας, καὶ τήρει, G°°.

iv. 3, –καὶ ὁ καθήμενος G°°Tr^b^, ἦν om*S*.—8, ἓν καθ' ἓν (ἓν ἕκαστον *S*) αὐτῶν (–αὐτῶν G′) for ἓν καθ' ἑαυτό GLTTr*S*.—11, ὁ Κύριος καὶ ὁ Θεὸς ἡμῶν for Κύριε LTTr*S*.

v. 11, –καὶ ἦν ὁ ἀριθμὸς α. μ. μ. St. —14, ζῶντι εἰς τοὺς α. τῶν α. om*S*.

vii. 10, καθημένῳ ἐπὶ τοῦ θρόνου τοῦ Θεοῦ ἡμῶν for Θ. ἡ. καθ. . . θρόνου St.

viii. 7, after γῆν· add καὶ τὸ τρίτον τῆς γῆς κατεκάη, GLTTr*S*.

ix. 2, –καὶ ἤνοιξε τὸ φρέαρ τῆς ἀβύσσου G°Tr^b^*S*.—19, ἐξουσίαι for -ία St, –καὶ ἐν ταῖς οὐραῖς αὐτῶν St.

x. 6, –καὶ τὴν θάλασσαν καὶ τὰ ἐν αὐτῇ L^b^Tr^b^*S*.

xi. 1, –καὶ ὁ ἄγγελος εἱστήκει St, om*S*.

xiii. 3, ἐθαυμάσθη (LTr) ἐν for ἐθαύμασεν St.—7, –Καὶ to αὐτούς· L.

xiv. 1, after ὄνομα add αὐτοῦ καὶ τὸ ὄνομα GLTTr*S*.—4, ἐνώπιον τοῦ θρόνου τοῦ Θεοῦ om*S*.

xv. 2, ἐκ τοῦ χαράγματος αὐτοῦ om*S*.

xvii. 17, –καὶ ποιῆσαι LTTr, –μίαν γνώμην L.

xviii. 2, ἰσχυρᾷ φωνῇ GLTTr*S*, ἰσχύϊ G′, for ἰσχύϊ, φωνῇ μεγάλῃ—17, ὁ ἐπὶ τόπον πλέων for ἐπὶ τῶν πλοίων ὁ ὅμιλος GLTTr*S*.

xix. 12, after ἔχων add ὀνόματα γεγραμμένα καὶ T.

xx. 14, ὁ θάνατος ὁ δεύτερός ἐστιν ἡ λίμνη τοῦ πυρός for ἐστιν ὁ δεύτερος θάνατος G′LTTr*S*.

xxi. 12, –καὶ ἐπὶ τοῖς πυλῶσιν ἀγγέλους δώδεκα, LTr.

xxii. 14, πλύνοντες τὰς στολὰς αὐτῶν for ποιοῦντες τὰς ἐντολὰς αὐτοῦ G′LTTr*S*.

SUPPLEMENT.

THE READINGS OF TISCHENDORF'S VIIIth EDITION WHICH VARY FROM THOSE OF HIS VIIth EDITION.

**The Sinaitic MS. accords with these readings when not otherwise noted. In those which here stand alone the change is in the form or the order of words, or in the addition of the article or conjunction. S* denotes the Sinaitic MS. as first written, S[a] as altered by a corrector of the fourth century, S[c] of the seventh.

MATT. i. 4, Ἀμιναδάβ, -ὰβ 5*t*, Βοὲς 7, Ἀσάφ, 8, Ἀσὰφ 18, Ἰησοῦ before Χριστοῦ ‖ –γὰρ 24, ἐγερθεὶς for διεγερθεὶς ‖ –ὁ before Ἰωσὴφ

ii. 21, εἰσῆλθεν fr. εἰσέρχομαι for ἦλθεν 22, –ἐπὶ ‖ τοῦ πατρὸς αὐτοῦ Ἡρώδου,

iii. 2, –καὶ 6, ποταμῳ after Ἰορδάνῃ 7, –αὐτοῦ 14, –Ἰωάννης 16, βαπτισθεὶς δὲ for καὶ β. ‖ –αὐτῷ ‖ πνεῦμα θεοῦ for τὸ πνεῦμα τοῦ θεοῦ ‖ –καὶ[4th] 17, ηὐδόκησα.

iv. 1, ὁ Ἰησοῦς 2, τεσσερ. νύκτας, 4, ἐπὶ for ἐν 5, ἔστησεν 9, εἶπεν for λέγει 10,–ὀπίσω μου 13, Ναζαρὰ for Ναζαρὲθ *S* 16, σκότει 18, 19, ἁλεεῖς 23, ἐν ὅλῃ τῇ Γαλιλαίᾳ (–ὅλῃ *S*) for ὅλην τ. Γ. 24, καὶ δαιμον.

v. 9, –αὐτοὶ 11, πᾶν πονηρὸν καθ' ὑμῶν ψευδόμενοι for καθ' ὑμ. πᾶν πο. ῥῆμα 13, βληθὲν ‖ –καὶ 21, etc., ἐρρέθη 22, ῥαχά, 23, κἀκεῖ 25, –σὲ παραδῷ[2d] 28, –αὐτὴν[1st] 32, πᾶς ὁ ἀπολύων for ὃς ἂν ἀπολύσῃ ‖ μοιχευθῆναι for μοιχᾶσθαι 39, ῥαπίζει εἰς for -σει ἐπὶ ‖ –σοῦ 42, δανίσασθαι 46, τὸ αὐτὸ for οὕτως 48, ὡς for ὥσπερ

vi. 1, –τοῖς 4, ἡ σοῦ ἐλεημοσύνη ᾖ ‖ –αὐτὸς 5, 16, ὡς for ὥσπερ 6, ταμεῖόν 7, βατταλ. 22, –οὖν ‖ ᾖ ὁ ὀφ. σου ἁπλοῦς, 25, –καὶ τί πίητε 33, –τοῦ θεοῦ

vii. 4, ἐκ for ἀπὸ 9, 10, –ἐὰν 12, ἐὰν for ἂν 13, –ἡ πύλη T[b] 14, –ἡ πύλη (*S*) T[b] 15, –δὲ[1st] 16, σταφυλὰς 18*t*, ἐνεγκεῖν fr. φέρω for ποιεῖν 21, τοῖς οὐρανοῖς 24, ὁμοιωθήσεται for ὁμοιώσω αὐτὸν

viii. 5, εἰσελθόντος δὲ αὐτοῦ 5, 8, ἑκατοντάρχης 8, ἀποκριθεὶς δὲ for καὶ ἀπ. 12, ἐξελεύσονται fr. ἐξέρχομαι for ἐκβληθήσονται fr. ἐκβάλλω 13, –καὶ[2d] ‖ –αὐτοῦ 22, –Ἰησοῦς 25, –οἱ μαθηταὶ 27, αὐτῷ ὑπακού. 28, ἐλθόντος αὐτοῦ (-των αὐτῶν *S*) 32, ἀπῆλθον ‖ τοὺς χοίρους for τὴν ἀγέλην τῶν χοίρων ‖ –τῶν χοίρων[2d] 34, ὑπάντησιν τοῦ for συνάντησιν τῷ

ix. 1, –τὸ 2, 5, ἀφίενταί 3, εἶπον 4, ἱνατί for Ἵνα τί ὑμεῖς 9[2d], 19, ἠκολούθει 10, –καὶ[2d] 11, ἔλεγον fr. λέγω for εἶπον 12, 22, –Ἰησοῦς ‖ ἀλλ' 14, –πολλά 17, ἀπόλλυνται 18, –ὅτι 22, θύγατερ, 28, προσῆλθον 30, ἀνεῴχθησαν

x. 2, καὶ Ἰάκωβος 5, Σαμαριτῶν 8, after θεραπεύετε, add νεκροὺς ἐγείρετε, 9, μηδὲ ἄργυρον (see pp. 45, 260), 10, ῥάβδον· 14, ἂν for ἐὰν ‖ ἔξω after ἐξερχόμενοι ‖ ἐκ before τῶν ποδῶν 15, Γομόρρων 19, παραδῶσιν ‖ λαλήσητε·[2d] 23, ἑτέραν for ἄλλην ‖ –ἂν 28, φοβεῖσθε 33, κἀγὼ αὐτὸν

xi. 8, ἀνθρ. ἰδεῖν ‖ –εἰσίν 10, ὃς for καὶ 11, αὐτοῦ ἐστίν. 14, Ἡλείας for Ἡλίας *S* 16, ταῖς ἀγοραῖς, 19, ἔργων for τέκνων 23, μὴ . . ὑψωθήσῃ; for ἡ . . ὑψώθης, ‖ καταβιβασθήσῃ for καταβήσῃ fr. καταβαίνω ‖ ἔμεινεν 26, εὐδοκία ἐγένετο

xii. 4, ἔφαγον, 10, θεραπεῦσαι; 11, ἔσται after τίς 15, –ὄχλοι 18, –εἰς (*see note*) ‖ ηὐδόκησεν 29, διαρπάσῃ for ἁρπάσει 31 –τοῖς ἀνθρώποις[2d] 35, τὰ ἀγαθά, 44, ἐλθὸν ‖ καὶ σεσαρωμένον 46, –δὲ 47, –*the verse* T[b] (*S* omits from ζη-

τοῦντες in ver. 46). 48, *λέγοντι* for *εἰπόντι* 49, –*αὐτοῦ* 50, *ποιήσῃ*

xiii. 1, –*δὲ* ‖ *ἐκ* for *ἀπὸ* 2, –*τὸ* 4, *ἦλθεν* ‖ *καὶ κατέφαγεν* 7, *ἔπνιξαν* fr. *πνίγω* for *ἀπέπνιξαν* 11, –*αὐτοῖς* 17, –*γὰρ* ‖ *ἴδαν*, 18, *σπείραντος* 24, *σπείραντι* 27, *ἔσπειρας* 28, *δοῦλοι λέγουσιν αὐτῷ* for *αὐτῷ λέγουσιν* 30, *εἰς* before *δεσμὰς* 35, *'Ησαίου* after *προφήτου* 36, *προσῆλθον* 40, *κατακαίεται* for *καίεται* 48, –*αὐτὴν* ‖ *καὶ καθίσαντες* 55, *οὐχ* for *οὐχὶ* 56, *ταῦτα πάντα;* 57, *ἰδίᾳ πατρίδι* for *πατ. αὐτοῦ*

xiv. 1, *τετραάρχης* 3, –*αὐτὸν* ‖ *ἐν φυλ. ἀπέθετο* for *ἔθετο ἐν τῇ φ.* ‖ *Φιλίππου* after *γυναῖκα* T^b. 4, *'Ιωάννης αὐτῷ* for *αὐτῷ ὁ 'Ιω.* 12, *πτῶμα* for *σῶμα* 13, *ἀκούσας δέ* for *καὶ ἀκούσας* 15, *προσῆλθον* ‖ *παρῆλθεν ἤδη·* 16, 27, –*'Ιησοῦς* 18, *ὧδε αὐτούς.* 19, *τοῦ χόρτου,* ‖ *εὐλόγησεν* 22, –*εὐθέως* 25, *ἦλθεν* for *ἀπῆλθεν* 26, *ἰδόντες δὲ* for *καὶ ἰδ.* ‖ –*οἱ μαθηταὶ* ‖ *τῆς θαλάσσης* 27, *εὐθὺς* 29, –*ὁ*^{2d} 30, –*ἰσχυρὸν* 32, *ἀναβάντων* for *ἐμβάντων* 33, –*ἐλθόντες* 34, *ἐπὶ τὴν γῆν εἰς Γεννησαρέτ* for *εἰς τ. γ. Γεννησαρέθ*

xv. 1, –*οἱ* ‖ *Φαρισαῖοι καὶ γραμματεῖς* 2, –*αὐτῶν* 5, –*καὶ* 15, –*ταύτην* 22, *ἔκραξεν* fr. *κράζω* for *ἐκραύγασεν αὐτῷ* 30, *ἔριψαν* 31, *ἐδόξαζον* 35, *παραγγείλας* for *ἐκέλευσεν* ‖ *τῷ ὄχλῳ* 36, *ἔλαβεν* for *καὶ λαβὼν* ‖ *καὶ εὐχαριστήσας* ‖ *ἐδίδου* 38, *παιδίων καὶ γυναικῶν* 39, *ἐνέβη* fr. *ἐμβαίνω* for *ἀνέβη*

xvi. 1, *ἐπηρώτων* 2, 3, –*ὀψίας* to *δύνασθε;* T^b. 12, after *ζύμης* add *τῶν Φαρισαίων καὶ Σαδδουκαίων* 14, *'Ηλείαν* (*S* *Ηλιαν*) 16, –*καὶ*^{1st} ‖ *κλεῖδας* 23, *εἶ ἐμοῦ* for *μοῦ εἶ* 28, *ὅτι* before *εἰσίν* ‖ *τῶν ὧδε ἑστώτων*

xvii. 3, etc., *'Ηλείας* 3, *συνλαλοῦντες μετ' αὐτοῦ* 7, *προσῆλθεν . . καὶ ἁψάμενος αὐ.* for *προσελθὼν . . ἥψατο αὐ. καὶ* 12, *ἀλλ'* 14, –*αὐτῶν* 20, *ὀλιγοπιστίαν* for *ἀπιστίαν* 21, –*the verse.* 22, *συστρεφομένων* for *ἀναστ.* 24, –*τὰ*^{2d} 25, *εἰσελθόντα* for *ὅτε εἰσῆλθεν* 26, *εἰπόντος δὲ* for *λέγει αὐτῷ* 27, *σκανδαλίζωμεν*

xviii. 2, –*ὁ 'Ιησοῦς* 5, *τοιοῦτο* 6, *περὶ* for *εἰς* (*ἐπὶ* St). 7, –*ἐκείνῳ* 8, *κυλλὸν ἢ χωλὸν,* 15, –*εἰς σὲ* 16, *σεαυτοῦ* for *σοῦ* 17, *εἰπὸν* 18*t*, –*τῷ* 19, –*ἀμήν* ‖ *συμφ. ἐξ ὑμῶν* for *ὑμ. συμφ.* 21, *ὁ Π. εἶπεν αὐτῷ* 22, *ἀλλ'* 24, *προσηνέχθη* fr. *προσφέρω* for *προσήχθη* fr. *προσάγω* ‖ *εἰς αὐτῷ* 25, –*αὐτοῦ*^{2d} ‖ *εἶχεν,* 26, *σοι* after *ἀποδώσω* 29, –*εἰς τοὺς πόδας αὐτοῦ* 30, –*οὐ* 31, *οὖν* for *δὲ* 35, *οὐράνιος* for *ἐπουράνιος*

xix. 3, –*ἀνθρώπῳ* 5, *ἕνεκα* 9, *ὅτι* before *ὃς ἂν* ‖ –*καὶ ὁ ἀπολελυμένην γαμήσας μοιχᾶται* 14, *αὐτοῖς* after *εἶπεν* ‖ *ἐμέ* for *μέ* 17, *τήρησον* 18, *ποίας; φησίν.* for *λέγει αὐτῷ Ποίας;* 21, –*τοῖς* ‖ *οὐρανῷ* 22, –*τὸν λόγον* 24, *ὅτι* after *ὑμῖν* 26, *δυνατὰ πάντα.* 28, *παλινγ.* ‖ *αὐτοὶ* for *ὑμεῖς* 29, *ἕνεκα τοῦ ἐμοῦ ὀνόματος,*

xx. 4, *καὶ ἐκείνοις* 10, *ἐλθόντες δὲ* for *καὶ ἐλθ.* ‖ *πλείονα* ‖ *ἔλαβον τὸ ἀνὰ δην. καὶ αὐτοί.* 12, *αὐτοὺς ἡμῖν* 13, *ἑνὶ αὐτῶν εἶπεν·* 15, *ἢ* for *εἰ* 16, –*πολλοὶ γάρ εἰσιν κλητοί, ὀλίγοι δὲ ἐκλεκτοί.* 17, –*μαθητὰς* 18, *εἰς θάνατον* for *θανάτῳ* 20, *παρ'* for *ἀπ'* 21, –*σου*^{1st} 26, 27, *ἔσται* for *ἔστω* 27, *ἂν* for *ἐὰν* 30, –*Κύριε* ‖ *υἱὲ* 31, *σιωπήσωσιν.* ‖ *ἔκραξαν* ‖ *υἱὲ* 33, *ἀνοιγῶσιν* ‖ *οἱ ὀφθαλμοὶ ἡμῶν.* 34, *ὀμμάτων* for *ὀφθαλμῶν* *S.* ‖ –*αὐτῶν οἱ ὀφθαλμοί*

xxi. 1, *Βηθφαγὴ* 2, *πορεύεσθε* ‖ *κατέναντι* for *ἀπέναντι* 2, 3, *εὐθὺς* 4, –*ὅλον* 5, *καὶ ἐπιβεβηκὼς* 6, *προσέταξεν* for *συνέταξεν* 7, *ἐπ'* for *ἐπάνω*^{1st} ‖ –*αὐτῶν*^{2d} 8, *ἔστρωσαν* 11, *ὁ προφήτης 'Ιησοῦς* 18, *Πρωὶ* for *Πρωΐας* 22, *ἂν* for *ἐὰν* 23, *ἐλθόντος αὐτοῦ* 24, *ἀποκριθεὶς δὲ* 27, *εἶπαν·* 29, –*δὲ*^{2d} 45, *ἀκούσαντες δὲ* for *καὶ ἀκού.* 46, *ἐπεὶ* for *ἐπειδὴ*

xxii. 7, *ὁ δὲ βασιλεὺς* for *καὶ ἀκούσας ὁ βασιλεὺς ἐκεῖνος* 10, *νυμφὼν* for *γάμος* 13, *ὁ βασιλεὺς εἶπεν* ‖ *ἐκβάλετε αὐτὸν* for *ἄρατε αὐτὸν καὶ ἐκ.* 16, *λέγοντας·* 20, *καὶ λέγει* ‖ *ἡ εἰ-*

κὼν αὕτη καὶ ἡ ἐπιγραφή; 21, –αὐτῷ 23, –οἱ 27, –καὶ 30, γαμίζονται for ἐκγαμ. ‖ –τοῦ 32, –ὁ θεὸς after ἐστιν 35, –καὶ λέγων 39, –δὲ 43, καλεῖ κύριον αὐτόν, 44, –ὁ

xxiii. 1, ὁ 'Ιησοῦς 4, –καὶ δυσβάστακτα (μεγάλα before βαρέα *S*) ‖ αὐτοὶ δὲ τῷ for τῷ δὲ 5, γὰρ for δὲ[2d] 7, –ῥαββεί[2d] 9, ὑμῶν ὁ πατὴρ 18, ἂν for ἐὰν 21, κατοικοῦντι 23, –δὲ 30, κοινωνοὶ αὐτῶν 36, ταῦτα πάντα 37, ὄρνις ἐπισυνάγει ‖ –αὐτῆς[2d]

xxiv. 1, ἀπὸ τοῦ ἱεροῦ ἐπορεύετο, 2, ταῦτα πάντα; 6, –πάντα 7, ἐπ' ἔθνος ‖ –καὶ λοιμοὶ 17, καταβάτω 18, τὸ ἱμάτιον 21, οὐκ ἐγένετο 24, πλανηθῆναι, 28, –γὰρ 29, ἐκ for ἀπὸ 30, –τῷ ‖ –τότε[2d] 31, –φωνῆς 33, ταῦτα πάντα, 36, after οὐρανῶν add οὐδὲ ὁ υἱός ‖ –μου 38, πρὸ before κατακλυσμοῦ ‖ γαμίζοντες for ἐκγ. 39, ἔσται καὶ 40, ἔσονται δύο 43, διορυχθῆναι 45, –αὐτοῦ[1st] 48, –ἐκεῖνος 49, αὐτοῦ after συνδούλους

xxv. 1, αὐτῶν for ἑαυτῶν ‖ ὑπάντησιν for ἀπάντ. 2, ἐξ αὐτῶν ἦσαν μωραὶ καὶ πέντε φρονιμοί. 3, αἱ γὰρ for αἵτινες ‖ –αὐτῶν 4, –αὐτῶν[1st] ‖ ἑαυτῶν for αὐτῶν[2d] 6, –αὐτοῦ 9, οὐκ for οὐ μὴ ‖ –δὲ[2d] 15, 16, εὐθέως πορευθεὶς for εὐθέως. πορ. δὲ 17, –καὶ ‖ –καὶ αὐτὸς 18, γῆν for ἐν τῇ γῇ 20, 22, –ἐπ' αὐτοῖς 22, –δὲ 27, τὰ ἀργύριά ‖ τραπεζείταις 32, ἀφορίσει 37, εἴδομεν 41, –οἱ

xxvi. 7, ἔχουσα ἀλάβ. μύρου ‖ πολυτίμου for βαρυτίμου ‖ τῆς κεφαλῆς 9, –τοῖς 10, ἠργάσατο 15, καὶ ἐγὼ 17, –αὐτῷ 23, τὴν χεῖρα ἐν τῷ τρ. 26, –τὸν ‖ δοὺς τοῖς μαθηταῖς εἶπεν· 36, ἐκεῖ προσεύξ. 38, –ὁ 'Ιησοῦς 39, προσελθὼν for προελθὼν 44, πάλιν after εἰπὼν 52, τὴν μαχ. σου 53, ἄρτι put after παραστ. μοι ‖ λεγιώνων 58, –ἀπὸ 59, –καὶ οἱ πρεσβύτεροι 61, αὐτὸν before οἰκοδομ. 69, ἐκάθητο ἔξω 70, –αὐτῶν 71, τοῖς for αὐτοῖς ‖ –καὶ

xxvii. 2, –αὐτὸν[2d] ‖ –Ποντίῳ ‖ Πειλάτῳ 3, –τοῖς[2d] 4, εἶπον 5, εἰς τὸν ναὸν for ἐν τῷ ναῷ 11, ἐστάθη ‖ –αὐτῷ 12, –τῶν[2d] 13, Πειλᾶτος 21, τὸν Βαραββᾶν. 29, ἐνέπαιξαν 31, ἐκδύσαντες αὐ. τ. χλ. ἐνέδ. 34*t*, πειν (πιν *S*). ‖ οἶνον for ὄξος 35, βαλόντες 40, καὶ κατάβηθι 42, πιστεύσωμεν 43, –αὐτὸν[1st] 44, σὺν before αὐτῷ 46, ἠλεὶ ἠλεὶ (ηλωι *t S*) λεμὰ σαβαχθανεί; 47, ἑστηκότων ‖ 'Ηλείαν (-λίαν *S*) 49, 'Ηλείας (-λίας *S*) 51, –ἀπὸ 54, ἑκατοντάρχης 56, 'Ιωσὴφ 57, ἐμαθητεύθη 58, Πειλάτῳ Πειλᾶτος (Πιλ. *t S*) 59, –ἐν 61, Μαριὰμ ἡ Μαγ. 62, Πειλᾶτον (Πιλ. *S*) 64, –αὐτοῦ

xxviii. 1, Μαριὰμ ἡ Μαγ. 2, καὶ προσελθὼν 3, ὡς for ὡσεὶ 9, ὑπήντησεν for ἀπήντ. 10, καὶ ἐκεῖ 11, ἀνήγγειλαν for ἀπήγγ. 14, –αὐτὸν 15, ἐφημίσθη for διεφ. 17, –αὐτῷ

Mark **i.** 1, –υἱοῦ θεοῦ 2, ἐγὼ before ἀποστέλλω 4, ὁ βαπτίζων 5, 'Ιεροσολυμεῖται 8, ἐν bef. πνεύματι 9, Ναζαρὲτ 11, –ἐγένετο 14, Μετὰ δὲ for Καὶ μετὰ ‖ ὁ 'Ιησοῦς 15, 25, –λέγων 16, 17, ἁλεεῖς (ἁλιεῖς[1st] *S*) 18, 21, εὐθὺς 18, –αὐτῶν 24, –ἔα 25, –λέγων 27, αὐτοὺς for πρὸς ἑαυτ. 31, –εὐθέως 36, κατεδίωξεν ‖ –ὁ 39, ἦλθεν for ἦν 40, –αὐτὸν καὶ[2d] 41, καὶ for ὁ δὲ 'Ιησοῦς ‖ –αὐτῷ 45, εἰς πόλιν φαν. εἰσελθεῖν, ἀλλ'

ii. 1, ἐν οἴκῳ for εἰς οἶκον 2, –εὐθέως 4, προσενέγκαι fr. προσφέρω for προσεγγίσαι ‖ ὅπου for ἐφ' ᾧ 5, καὶ ἰδὼν for ἰδὼν δὲ ‖ ἀφίενταί (ἀφέωνταί *S*) 8, –αὐτοὶ 9, ἀφίενταί ‖ καὶ ἆρον τὸν κράβαττόν σου ‖ ὕπαγε for περιπάτει 10, ἐπὶ τ. γ. ἀφ. ἁμ. 12, ἔμπροσθεν for ἐναντίον 13, εἰς for παρὰ 15, –ἐν τῷ 15, 16, καὶ ἠκολούθουν αὐτῷ καὶ γραμ. τῶν Φαρισαίων. καὶ 16, ὅτι ἤσθιεν for αὐτὸν ἐσθίοντα ‖ τελων. καὶ ἁμαρ. *t* 22, ῥήξει 23, αὐτὸν ἐν τοῖς σάβ. παρ. ‖ καὶ οἱ μαθ. αὐτοῦ ἤρξαντο 25, λέγει 26, τοὺς ἱερεῖς, 27, καὶ οὐχ

iii. 1, –τὴν[1st] 2, ἐν bef. τοῖς σάβ. ‖ κατηγορήσωσιν 3, τῷ τ. ξηρὰν χ.

ἔχοντι· for τῷ ἐξηραμμένην ἔχ. τὴν χ. 4, ἀγαθὸν ποιῆσαι for ἀγαθοποιῆσαι 6, ἐποίησαν 7, καὶ ἀπὸ τ. 'Ιου. ἠκολ. 8, –οἱ 11, λέγοντες 16, add καὶ ἐποίησεν τοὺς δώδεκα, before καὶ ἐπέθηκεν 19, ἔρχεται 20, –ὁ ‖ μήτε for μηδὲ 25, σταθῆναι 26, ἑαυτόν, ἐμερίσθη. καὶ for ἑαυτὸν καὶ μεμέρισται, 27, εἰς τ. οἰκίαν τ. ἰσχ. εἰσελθὼν τὰ σκεύη (εἰσελθὼν bef. εἰς *S*). 28, ἂν for ἐὰν 29, ἔσται 31, καὶ ἔρχεται (–οὖν) ἡ μήτηρ αὐ. καὶ οἱ ἀδ. αὐτοῦ, 33, καὶ οἱ ἀδελφοί μου for ἢ οἱ ἀδ. 34, περιβλεψ. τοὺς περὶ αὐτὸν κύκλῳ 35, –μου$^{\text{2d}}$

iv. 1, εἰς πλοῖον ἐμβ. 3, –τοῦ 8, ἄλλα 10, ἠρώτουν 11, –τὰ 15, ἐν αὐτοῖς for εἰς αὐτούς 16, ὁμοίως εἰσὶν 18, ἐπὶ for εἰς 22, ἵνα bef. φανερωθῇ 26, –ἐὰν 28, εἶτεν 31, κόκκῳ ‖ μικρότερον ὂν (–ἐστὶν) 32, μεῖζον πάντων τῶν λαχάνων, ‖ κατασκηνοῦν. 33, ἠδύναντο 36, πλοῖα for πλοιάρια ‖ ἦσαν for ἦν$^{\text{2d}}$ 38, ἐγείρουσιν for διεγείρουσιν

v. 2, ἐξελθόντος αὐτοῦ ‖ ὑπήντησεν for ἀπήντησεν 5, διαπαντὸς 6, αὐτῷ 10, αὐτὰ (*S* αὐτὸν) 12, –πάντες οἱ δαίμονες 13, –εὐθέως ὁ 'Ιησοῦς 15, –καὶ$^{\text{3d}}$ 21, εἰς τὸ πέραν πάλιν 25, –τις ‖ δώδεκα ἔτη 26, ἑαυτῆς for αὐτῆς 27, τὰ περὶ 33, ἐπ' 34, θύγατερ 36, –εὐθέως 40, αὐτὸς δὲ for ὁ δὲ

vi. 2, διδάσκειν ἐν τῇ συναγωγῇ ‖ τούτῳ for αὐτῷ 4, ἑαυτοῦ for αὐτοῦ$^{\text{1st}}$ 6, ἐθαύμασεν 14, ἐγήργερται ἐκ νεκρῶν for ἐκ νεκρῶν ἀνέστη 15, 'Ηλείας (*S* 'Ηλίας) 20, ἠπόρει for ἐποίει 27, ἐνέγκαι (*S* ενεγκε) 29, αὐτὸν for αὐτὸ 30, –καὶ$^{\text{3d}}$ ‖ –ὅσα$^{\text{2d}}$ 33, αὐτοὺς after ἐπέγνωσαν ‖ –καὶ συνῆλθον πρὸς αὐτόν 35, γινομένης ‖ –αὐτῷ ‖ ἔλεγον 36, τί φάγωσιν. for ἄρτους· τί γὰρ φάγ. οὐκ ἔχουσιν. 37, δώσωμεν 38, ἄρτους ἔχετε; 43, κλασμάτων 49, ἐπὶ τῆς θαλ. περιπατοῦντα ‖ ὅτι φαντασμά ἐστιν, for φάντ. εἶναι, 50, ὁ δὲ for καὶ$^{\text{2d}}$ 51, –καὶ ἐθαύμαζον 52, ἀλλ' ἦν for ἦν γὰρ 53, ἐπὶ τὴν γῆν ἦλθον ‖ εἰς before Γεννησαρὲτ 55, περιέδραμον ‖ καὶ ἤρξαντο ‖ –ἐκεῖ 56, ἐὰν for ἂν ‖ εἰς before πόλεις ‖ εἰς before ἀγρούς, ‖ ἐτίθεσαν ‖ ἥψαντο

vii. 2, ὅτι after αὐτοῦ ‖ ἐσθίουσιν 3, πυκνὰ for πυγμῇ 4, ἀπὸ ‖ –καὶ κλινῶν 5, διατί 6, –ὅτι before καλῶς ‖ ὅτι before οὗτος 8, –γὰρ ‖ –βαπτισμοὺς *to end of verse.* 12, –καὶ ‖ –αὐτοῦ$^{\text{1st and 2d}}$ 15, αὐτόν after κοινῶσαι ‖ –ἐκεῖνα 16, –*the whole verse.* 17, εἰς τὸν οἶκον 24, ἐκεῖθεν δὲ for καὶ ἐκεῖθεν ‖ ὅρια for μεθόρια ‖ ἠθέλησεν ‖ ἠδυνάσθη 25, ἀλλὰ ‖ εἰσελθοῦσα for ἐλθοῦσα 26, Συροφοινικίσσα ‖ ἐκβάλῃ 28, –γὰρ 32, καὶ μογιλάλον 33, –αὐτοῦ$^{\text{1st}}$ 35, –εὐθέως ‖ εὐθὺς before ἐλύθη 36, –αὐτὸς

viii. 1, πάλιν πόλλου for παμπόλλου 3, νῆστις ‖ ἥκασιν for εἰσίν 7, εὐλογήσας αὐτὰ παρέθηκεν for ταῦτα *to end of verse.* 8, καὶ ἔφαγον for ἔφ. δὲ 16, ἔχομεν 17, –ἔτι (see note) 19, καὶ πόσους 20, καὶ for δὲ ‖ –αὐτῷ 23, βλέπει 25, δηλαυγῶς for τηλαυγῶς ‖ ἅπαντα for πάντα 26, μὴ for μηδὲ$^{\text{1st}}$ ‖ –μηδὲ$^{\text{2d}}$ *to end of verse.* 28, 'Ηλείαν 35, ψυχὴν αὐτοῦ for ἑαυτοῦ ψυχὴν (see note) 37, add δοῖ ἄνθρωπος after γὰρ

ix. 2, τὸν 'Ιωάννην 3, ἐγένετο 4, 'Ηλείας (*S* 'Ηλίας) ‖ Μωϋσεῖ (*S* Μωϋσῇ) 5, τρεῖς σκηνάς ‖ Μωϋσεῖ ‖ 'Ηλείᾳ (*S* 'Ηλίᾳ) 6, ἀποκριθῇ (*S* απεκριθη) for λαλήσει 7, ἐγένετο for ἦλθεν 9, καὶ καταβ. for καταβ. δὲ 11, add οἱ Φαρισαῖοι καὶ before οἱ γραμ. ‖ 'Ηλείαν (*S* 'Ηλίαν) 12, 'Ηλείας (*S* 'Ηλίας) ‖ ἐξουθενωθῇ 13, 'Ηλείας (*S* 'Ηλίας) 14, ἐλθόντες ‖ εἶδον ‖ πρὸς αὐτούς (*S* πρὸς ἑαυτούς) for αὐτοῖς 18, –αὐτόν$^{\text{2d}}$ 20, τὸ πνεῦμα εὐθὺς συνεσπάραξεν for εὐθ. τ. π. ἐσπάραξεν 22, ἀλλὰ 25, ὁ ὄχλος 27, –αὐτὸν$^{\text{1st}}$ ‖ αὐτοῦ after χειρὸς 28, εἰσελθόντος αὐτοῦ 33, –πρὸς ἑαυτοὺς 37, ἂν$^{\text{1st}}$ for ἐὰν ‖ παιδίων τούτων for τοιούτων παιδ. ‖ ἂν$^{\text{2d}}$ for ἐὰν 38, –λέγων ‖ ἐν before τῷ ὀνόματι ‖ add ὅτι οὐκ ἠκολούθει ἡμῖν after αὐτόν 41, μου after *ὀνόματι* ‖ *ἀπολέσῃ* 42, *ἂν* for *ἐὰν* ‖ *τούτων τῶν πιστευόντων* for *τῶν πίστιν ἐχόντων* ‖ *μύλος ὀνικὸς* for *λίθος μυλικὸς* 43, *εἰσελθεῖν εἰς τὴν ζωὴν* 47, *σε* before *ἐστὶν* ‖ *τὴν γέενναν* 49, –*καὶ πᾶσα to end of verse.* 50, *ἄλα* twice for *ἅλας* (*S* *ἅλας*$^{\text{1st}}$)

x. 1, *Καὶ ἐκεῖθεν* 2, *οἱ Φαρ.* 5, *ὁ δὲ* for *καὶ ἀποκρ. ὁ* 7, *αὐτοῦ* after *μητέρα* ‖ –*καὶ προσκολ. to end of verse.* 11, *ἂν* for *ἐὰν* 12, *αὐτὴ ἀπολύσασα* for *γυνὴ ἀπολύσῃ* ‖ *γαμήσῃ ἄλλον* for *καὶ γαμηθῇ ἄλλῳ* 15, *ἂν* for *ἐὰν* 16, *κατευλόγει, τιθ. τὰς χεῖρ. ἐπ' αὐτά* ‖ –*αὐτά*$^{\text{3d}}$ 19, *σου* after *μητέρα* 20, *ἔφη* for *ἀποκ. εἶπεν* 21, *τοῖς πτωχοῖς* ‖ –*ἄρας τὸν σταυρόν.* 24, –*τοὺς πεποιθ. ἐπὶ χρήμασιν* 27, –*ἐστιν* 32, *οἱ δὲ* for *καὶ*$^{\text{3d}}$ 34, *καὶ ἐμπτύσουσιν αὐτῷ καὶ μαστιγ.* ‖ –*αὐτόν*$^{\text{2d}}$ 35, *οἱ υἱοὶ* 36, *ποιήσω* 37, *σου* after *εἷς*$^{\text{2d}}$ 43, *ἂν* for *ἐὰν* ‖ *μέγας γενέσθαι* 44, *ἂν* for *ἐὰν* 47, *υἱὲ* for *ὁ υἱὸς* 51, *σοι θέλεις ποιήσω;* 52, *αὐτῷ* for *τῷ Ἰησοῦ*

xi. 2, *οὔπω* before *κεκάθικεν* 3, *πάλιν* before *ὧδε* 4, *τὸν πῶλον* ‖ *τὴν θύραν* 11, *ὀψὲ* for *ὀψίας* 17, *αὐτοῖς* after *ἔλεγεν* 18, *ἐξεπλήσσοντο* 31, *διατί* ‖ *οὖν* before *οὐκ*

xii. 1, *ἄνθρωπος ἐφύτ.* 3, *καὶ* for *οἱ δὲ* 4, –*λιθοβολήσαντες* ‖ *ἐκεφαλίωσαν* ‖ *ἠτίμασαν* for *ἀπέστειλαν ἠτιμωμένον* 8, *ἐξέβαλον* 14, *καὶ* for *οἱ δὲ* ‖ *ἀλλ'* 15, *ἰδὼν* for *εἰδὼς* 17, *αὐτοῖς* after *εἶπεν* ‖ *ἐξεθαύμαζον* 21, *μὴ καταλιπὼν* for *καὶ οὐδὲ αὐτὸς ἀφῆκεν* 22, *ἔσχατον* 25, –*οἱ* 26, *ὁ θεὸς*$^{\text{3d}}$ and 4th 27, *ὁ θεὸς* 28, *ἰδὼν* for *εἰδὼς* 32, *εἶπες* 33, –*καὶ ἐξ ὅλης τῆς ψυχῆς* ‖ *περισσότερον* for *πλεῖον* ‖ *τῶν θυσιῶν* 35, *Δαυείδ ἐστιν;* 36, *εἶπεν* for *λέγει* ‖ *κάθου* ‖ *ὑποπόδιον* for *ὑποκάτω* 40, *κατεσθίοντες* 43, *εἶπεν* for *λέγει*

xiii. 1, –*ἐκ* before *τῶν* 2, *ἐπὶ λίθον* 3, *ὁ Πέτρος* 4, *μέλλῃ* 7, *ἀκούσητε* 8, *ἐπ' ἔθνος* ‖ –*καὶ ταραχαί* 9, *ἀρχὴ* 10, *πρῶτον δεῖ* 11, –*μηδὲ μελετᾶτε* 15, –*εἰς τὴν οἰκίαν* ‖ *ἆραί τι* 16,–*ὢν* 19, *ἣν* 22, *δὲ* for *γὰρ* ‖ *ψευδόχριστοι καὶ* before *ψευδοπροφ.* 28, *γινώσκετε* 29, *ἴδητε ταῦτα* 32, *οἱ ἄγγελοι* 37, *ὃ* for *ἃ*

xiv. 3, *τὸν* for *τὴν* 5 *ἐνεβριμοῦντο* 7, –*αὐτοὺς* 10, –*ὁ*$^{\text{1st}}$ ‖ *Ἰσκαριώθ,* 15, *κἀκεῖ* 16, –*αὐτοῦ* 18, *ὁ Ἰης. εἶπεν* 19, –*καὶ ἄλλος Μήτι ἐγώ;* 20, –*ἐκ* 29, *εἰ καὶ* 31, –*μᾶλλον* ‖ *ἀπαρνήσωμαι.* 36, *τοῦτο ἀπ' ἐμοῦ* 40, *αὐτῶν οἱ ὀφθ.* 41, *τὸ λοιπὸν* 42, *ἤγγισεν* 43, –*ὢν* ‖ –*τῶν*$^{\text{4th}}$ 44, *σύνσημον* 45, –*ῥαββεί*$^{\text{2d}}$ 49, *ἐκρατήσατε* 51, –*οἱ νεανίσκοι* 52, –*ἀπ' αὐτῶν* 53, –*αὐτῷ* 54, *συνκαθ.* 55, *εὕρισκον·* 68, *οὔτε*$^{\text{1st}}$ for *οὐκ* 72, *εὐθὺς* before *ἐκ δευτέρου* ‖ *τρίς με ἀπαρνήσῃ.*

xv. 1, –*ἐπὶ τὸ* ‖ *ἑτοιμάσαντες* for *ποιήσ.* ‖ *τῶν γραμματέων* ‖ *Πειλάτῳ* 2, 4, *Πειλᾶτος* 4, –*λέγων* 5, *Πειλᾶτον.* 6, *ὃν παρῃτοῦντο* for *ὅνπερ ᾐτοῦντο* 7, *στασιαστῶν* for *συνστασ.* 8, –*ἀεὶ* 9, 12, 14, 15, *Πειλᾶτος* 12, *πάλιν ἀποκρ.* ‖ *ἔλεγεν* for *εἶπεν* 14, *περισσῶς* 15, *ποιῆσαι τὸ ἱκ. τῷ ὄχλῳ* 16, *συνκαλ.* 18, *βασιλεῦ* 20, *τὰ ἰδ. ἱματ. αὐτοῦ.* ‖ –*αὐτόν*$^{\text{4th}}$ 21, *ἀπ'* 22, *τὸν Γολγ.* 23, *ὃς δὲ* for *ὁ δὲ* 30, *καταβὰς* for *καὶ κατάβα* 32, –*τοῦ*$^{\text{1st}}$ ‖ *σὺν* before *αὐτῷ* 34, *τῇ ἐνάτῃ ὥρᾳ* ‖ *λεμὰ σαβαχθανεί* (*S* *σαβακτανει*), ‖ *μου* after *θεός*$^{\text{1st}}$ 35, *παρεστώτων* ‖ *Ἠλείαν* 36, *τις* for *εἷς* ‖ –*τε* ‖ *Ἠλείας* 39, –*κράξας* 41, –*καὶ*$^{\text{1st}}$ 43, *Πειλᾶτον* 44, *Πειλᾶτος ἐθαύμαζεν* 46, *μνήματι* for *μνημείῳ*

xvi. 2, *τῇ μιᾷ τῶν σαβ.* ‖ *μνῆμα* for *μνημεῖον* 5, *εἰσελθοῦσαι* for *ἐλθ.* ‖ *εἶδον* 8, *γὰρ* for *δὲ*

Luke i. 6, *ἐναντίον* for *ἐνώπιον* 9, *ἔλαχε* 17, *Ἠλεία* 21, *αὐτὸν ἐν τῷ ναῷ.* 25, *ἐπεῖδεν* 28, *ὁ ἄγγελος* before *εἶπεν* 36, *συγγενίς* 43, *ἐμέ* for *μέ* 44, *ἐν ἀγαλ. τὸ βρέφος* 49, *μεγάλα* for *μεγαλεῖα* 56, *ὡς* for *ὡσεὶ* 62, *αὐτό* 66, *γὰρ* after *καὶ*$^{\text{2d}}$ 70, –*τῶν*$^{\text{2d}}$

ii. 2, –*ἡ* ‖ *ἐγέν. πρώτη* 3, *ἑαυτοῦ* for *ἰδίαν* 5, –*γυναικί* 7, –*τῇ* 9, –*ἰδοὺ* 12, –*κείμενον* 15, –*καὶ οἱ ἄνθρωποι* ‖ *ἐλάλουν* for *εἶπον* 17, ἐγνώρισαν for διεγν. 19, Μαρία ‖ συνβάλλ. 22, παραστῆσαι 24, τῷ νόμῳ 25, ἄνθρωπος ἦν 26, ἂν after πρὶν ἢ 33, αὐτοῦ after μήτηρ 36, μετὰ ἀνδρ. ἔτη 37, ἀπὸ (*S* ἐκ for ἀπὸ) ‖ δεήσεσι 38, –αὐτη ‖ θεῷ for κυρίῳ 39, πάντα for ἅπ. ‖ –τὰ ‖ ἐπέστρεψαν for ὑπεστρ. 48, εἶπεν πρ. αὐτ. ἡ μήτηρ 51, –ταῦτα 52, ἐν τῇ before σοφ.

iii. 1, Πειλάτου ‖ τετρααρχοῦντος 3, τὴν περίχ. 11, ἔλεγεν 14, πρὸς αὐτοὺς for αὐτοῖς ‖ μηδένα[2d] for μηδὲ 16, λέγων πᾶσιν (for ἅπασιν) ὁ 'Ιωάννης 17, –καὶ[1st] ‖ διακαθᾶραι ‖ συναγαγεῖν 19, τετραάρχης 20, –καὶ[2d] ‖ –τῇ 22, ὡς for ὡσεὶ 23, –ὁ ‖ –τοῦ before 'Ιωσήφ 24, Μαθθὰθ 29, Μαθθὰθ 31, Ναθὰμ 32, Σαλὰ for Σαλμὼν 33, 'Αμιναδὰβ (*S* 'Αδὰμ) ‖ 'Εσρὼμ 37, 'Ιάρετ ‖ Μελελεὴλ ‖ Καϊνὰμ

iv. 8, ὁ 'Ιησ. εἶπ. αὐτῷ 16, –τὴν[1st] ‖ Ναζαρά ‖ ἀνατεθραμμένος 20, οἱ ὀφθ. ἐν τῇ συναγ. ἦσαν 24, ἑαυτοῦ for αὐτοῦ 25, ὅτι after ὑμῖν ‖ 'Ηλείου (*S* Ἡλιου) 26, 'Ηλείας ‖ Σιδωνίας 27, 'Ελισαίου ‖ ἐκαθαρίσθη 35, τὸ μέσον 40, ἐθεράπευεν 41, ἐξήρχοντο

v. 2, ἁλεεῖς ‖ ἔπλυναν for ἀπέπλυναν 3, ἐν τῷ πλοίῳ ἐδίδ. for ἐδίδ. ἐκ τοῦ πλ. 5, –αὐτῷ ‖ τὰ δίκτυα 6, διερήσσετο (*S* διερρήσσετο) for διερήγνυτο ‖ τὰ δίκτυα 7, ἦλθαν 10, –ὁ 'Ιησ. 11, πάντα for ἅπ. 12, ἰδὼν δὲ for καὶ ἰδὼν 17, αὐτόν 24, ἀφιέναι 26, εἴδομεν 28, πάντα for ἅπ. 29, πολ. τελωνῶν 30, καὶ ἁμαρτωλῶν after τελ. 34, 'Ιησ. after ὁ δὲ ‖ νηστεῦσαι 36, τὸ ἐπίβλημα after συμφων.

vi. 2, ποιεῖν after ἔξεστιν 3, ὁ 'Ιησ. πρὸς αὐτ. εἶπ. 6, –καὶ[1st] 7, κατηγορεῖν for κατηγορίαν 10, –ὡς ἡ ἄλλη. 11, ποιήσαιεν 12, ἐξελθεῖν αὐτὸν for ἐξῆλθεν 17, πολὺς after ὄχλ. 18, –καὶ[21] 25, νῦν after ἐμπεπλησμ. 26, εἶπ. ὑμᾶς 28, ὑμᾶς[1st] for ὑμῖν 29, εἰς for ἐπὶ 30, –δὲ τῷ before αἰτοῦντι 33, γὰρ after καὶ[1st] ‖ ἀγαθοποίητε ‖ –γὰρ after καὶ[2d] 34, δανίσητε 35, μηδένα ‖ ἀπελπ. 36, –οὖν ‖ –καὶ 38, ᾧ γὰρ μέτρῳ for τῷ γ. αὐτ. μέτρ. ᾧ 40, –αὐτοῦ[1st] 45, –αὐτοῦ[1st] 48, οἰκοδομῆσθαι

vii. 4, ἠρώτων for παρεκάλουν 6, –ἀπὸ ‖ –πρὸς αὐτ. ‖ ἑκατοντάρχης ‖ –αὐτῷ 10, εἰς τ. οἰκ. οἱ πεμφθ. ‖ –ἀσθενοῦντα 11, ἐπορεύθη 12, μονογ. υἱὸς ‖ ἦν after αὕτη ‖ ἦν after ἱκανὸς 13, ἐπ' αὐτὴν 16, ἠγέρθη 17, –ἐν[2d] 28, –γὰρ 32, –ὑμῖν[2d] 33, μὴ for μήτε[1st] ‖ ἐσθίων ‖ μηδὲ for μήτε[2d] 34, ἐσθίων 38, ὀπ. παρ. τ. πόδ. αὐτ. ‖ τ. δάκρ. ἤρξ. βρέχ. τ. πόδ. αὐτοῦ ‖ ἐξέμαξεν 42, –εἰπέ ‖ ἀγαπ. αὐτόν; 43, –ὁ[1st] 44, μου ἐπὶ τοὺς πόδας 45, διέλειπεν 46, μου τ. πόδας. 47, αὐτ. αἱ ἁμαρτ.

viii. 5, αὐτοῦ for ἑαυτοῦ 7, συνφυεῖσαι 9, –λέγοντες ‖ αὕτη εἴη ἡ παραβ. 12, ἀκούσαντες 13, τὴν πέτραν 17, μὴ after οὐ[3d] ‖ γνωσθῇ 18, ἂν γὰρ for γὰρ ἐὰν ‖ ἂν for ἐὰν[2d] 19, Παρεγένετο ‖ μήτ. αὐτοῦ 20, ἀπηγγ. δὲ for καὶ ἀπ. ‖ –λεγόντων ‖ ὅτι ἡ μήτ. 26, Γεργεσηνῶν for Γερασ. 27, –αὐτῷ[2d] ‖ ἔχων for ὃς εἶχεν ‖ –ἐκ ‖ καὶ χρόνῳ ἱκανῷ οὐκ ἐνεδύσατο (for ἐνεδιδύσκετο) ἱμάτιον 28, –καὶ[1st] 29, ἐδεσμεύετο ‖ δαιμονίου 30, ὄνομά ἐστιν; ‖ λεγιών ‖ εἰσῆλθ. δαιμ. πολλὰ 31, παρεκάλουν 34, ἔφυγον 35, ἦλθον ‖ εὗρον ‖ ἐξῆλθεν for ἐξεληλύθει 36, –καὶ 37, Γεργεσηνῶν for Γερασ. ‖ εἰς πλοῖον 39, σοι ἐποί. 40, ὑποστρέφειν 42, ἐν δὲ τῷ ὑπάγειν for καὶ ἐγένετο ἐν τῷ πορεύεσθαι 45, –καὶ λέγ. *to end of verse.* 48, θύγατερ 49, –αὐτῷ ‖ μηκέτι for μὴ 51, ἐλθὼν for εἰσελθ.

ix. 1, Συνκαλεσάμενος 5, ἂν for ἐὰν ‖ ἀποτινάσσετε 7, τετραάρχης ‖ ἠγέρθη 8, 'Ηλείας 12, –τοὺς before ἀγρ. 13, ἄρτ. πέντε 14, δὲ[1st] for γὰρ 15, κατέκλ. for ἀνέκλ. 19, 'Ηλείαν 21, λέγειν for εἰπεῖν 22, ἐγερθῆναι for ἀναστῆναι 26, λόγους after ἐμοὺς 27, ἑστηκότων 30, 'Ηλείας 31, ἤμελλεν 32, εἶδαν 33, ὁ Πέτρ. ‖ 'Ηλείᾳ 36, ἑώρακαν (*S* ἑωράκασιν) 37, –ἐν 38, ἐβόησεν for ἀνεβ. ‖ μοι ἐστίν 47, εἰδὼς 48, ἂν for ἐὰν^{2d} (*S* – ἐὰν^{2d}) 49, ὁ Ἰωάνν. 50, εἶπ. δὲ for καὶ εἰπ. ‖ –ὁ 52, αὐτοῦ for ἑαυτοῦ ‖ πόλιν for κώμην ‖ Σαμαριτῶν 54, –αὐτοῦ 57, ἂν for ἐὰν ‖ –κύριε 59, –Κύριε ‖ πρωτ. ἀπελθ. 62, πρὸς αὐτὸν after δὲ

x. 2, ἐκβαλῃ 4, μὴ^{3d} for μηδὲ ‖ –καὶ 6, ἐπαναπαήσεται 8, –δ' 11, –ἡμῶν 12, λέγω δὲ 15, μὴ for ἡ ‖ ὑψωθήσῃ ‖ –τοῦ 20, ἐνγέγρ. 21, ἐν τῷ πν. τῷ ἁγίῳ ‖ ἐγέν. εὐδοκ. 24, ἴδαν 25, –καὶ^{2d} 27, ἐν ὅλῃ τῇ ψυχῇ ‖ ἐν ὅλῃ τῇ ἰσχύϊ ‖ ἐν ὅλῃ τῇ διανοίᾳ 30, –δὲ ‖ –τυγχάνοντα 33, Σαμαρίτης 34, πανδοκίον 35, –ἐξελθὼν ‖ πανδοκεῖ 38, τὴν οἰκίαν. ‖ –αὐτῆς 39, Μαριάμ 40, κατέλιπεν 41, θορυβάζῃ for τυρβ. 42, γὰρ for δὲ^{2d} ‖ –ἀπ'

xi. 2, προσεύχησθε 8, φίλ. αὐτοῦ ‖ ἀναιδίαν 12, –ἐὰν 15, εἶπον 17, διαμ. ἐφ' ἑαυτ. 19, αὐτ. κριτ. ἐσ. ὑμῶν. 22, –ὁ 25, ἐλθὸν 26, εἰσελθόντα for ἐλθ. 28, μενοῦν for Μενοῦνγε 30, Νινευεῖταις 32, Νινευεῖται for Νινευὴ 33, –δὲ 36, τι μέρος 44, οἱ περιπατ. 47, καὶ οἱ for οἱ δὲ 54, –αὐτόν

xii. 11, εἰσφέρωσιν for φέρωσιν ‖ μεριμνήσητε 13, ἐκ τ. ὄχλ. αὐτ. 14, κριτὴν for δικαστὴν 21, αὐτῷ for ἑαυτῷ 25, μεριμνῶν after ὑμῶν ‖ προσθ. ἐπὶ τ. ἡλικ. αὐτ. 26, οὐδὲ for οὔτε 38, κἂν for καὶ ἐὰν ‖ –ἔλθῃ^{1st} –φυλακῇ^{1st} ‖ –ἐκεῖνοι 39, –ἐγρηγόρησεν ἂν καὶ ‖ οὐκ ἂν ἀφ. 40, οὖν 42, καὶ εἶπ. ‖ –δὲ 47, αὐτοῦ^{1st} for ἑαυτοῦ ‖ ἢ for μηδὲ 49, ἐπὶ for εἰς 52, ἑνὶ οἴκῳ 53, –τὴν$^{1st\ and\ 2d}$ ‖ –αὐτῆς$^{1st\ and\ 2d}$ 54, –τὴν ‖ ἐπὶ for ἀπὸ ‖ ὅτι before ὄμβρ. 59, –οὐ ‖ τὸ for τὸν

xiii. 1, Πειλᾶτος 2, ταῦτα for τοιαῦτα 3, μετανοῆτε ‖ ὁμοίως for ὡσαύτως 4, δεκαοκτώ for δέκα κ. ὀκτώ, 7, ἀφ' οὗ after ἔτη ‖ ἱνατί 9, εἰς τὸ μέλλον· εἰ δὲ μήγε, 11, δεκαοκτώ for δέκα κ. ὀκτώ ‖ συνκύπτουσα 12, ἀπὸ before τῆς ἀσθ. 15, δὲ for οὖν 19, –μέγα 22, Ἱεροσόλυμα 27, ὑμᾶς after οἶδα ‖ –τῆς 28, ὄψεσθε (*S* ἴδητε) 29, –ἀπὸ^{2d} 34, ὄρνιξ 35, –δὲ

xiv. 5, πεσεῖται for ἐμπεσ. ‖ –τῇ 6, –αὐτῷ 10, πάντων after ἐνώπ. 14, δέ for γὰρ 15, ὅστις for ὃς 16, μέγα 17, εἰσιν ‖ –πάντα 18, πάντ. παραιτ. ‖ ἐξελθὼν 22, ὃ for ὡς 26, αὐτοῦ for ἑαυτοῦ^{1st} ‖ δὲ for τε 27, –καὶ^{1st} 31, βουλεύσεται 33, εἶναί μου 34, ἅλα^{2d} 35, –ἀκούειν

xv. 5, αὐτοῦ for ἑαυτοῦ 6, συνκαλεῖ ‖ συνχάρητέ 7, ἐν τῷ οὐρ. ἔσται 9, συνκαλεῖ ‖ συνχάρητέ 17, περισσεύουσιν ‖ λιμῷ ὧδε 20, αὐτοῦ^{1st} for ἑαυτοῦ ‖ εἶδεν 21, αὐτῷ ὁ υἱὸς 30, –τῶν 32, –καὶ^{3d}

xvi. 2, δύνῃ 4, ἐκ before τῆς 9, ἐκλίπῃ 12, δώσει ὑμῖν 14, –καὶ^{1st} 26, ἐν for ἐπὶ ‖ πᾶσι 27, οὖν σε 29, –αὐτῷ (*see note*) ‖ ἔχουσι

xvii. 1, αὐτοῦ after μαθ. 4, πρός σε after ἐπιστρ. 9, –οὐ δοκῶ. 11, –αὐτὸν ‖ μέσον Σαμαρίας 12, ὑπήντησαν 16, Σαμαρίτης 17, –οἱ^{2d} 24, –ἡ^{2d} 28, καθὼς for καὶ ὡς 33, –αὐτήν^{2d} 35, ἡ μία

xviii. 1, –καὶ^{1st} 4, δὲ ταῦτα ‖ οὐδὲ ἄνθρωπον for καὶ ἄνθ. οὐκ 10, ὁ εἷς 11, –πρὸς ἑαυτὸν 12, ἀποδεκατεύω 13, ὁ δὲ for καὶ ὁ ‖ –εἰς^{2d} 16, προσεκαλέσατο αὐτὰ ‖ λέγων· for εἶπεν· 17, ἂν for ἐὰν 19, –ὁ^{2d} 22, –τοῖς before οὐρ. 26, εἶπαν 29, –ὅτι ‖ εἵνεκεν 40, ὁ Ἰησ.

xix. 2, –οὗτος 4, εἰς τὸ ἔμπρ. ‖ συκομορέαν 5, –εἶδεν αὐτὸν καὶ 9, –ἐστιν. 15, δεδώκει 23, διατί ‖ κἀγὼ ‖ αὐτὸ ἔπραξα. 26, –γὰρ (*S* –γὰρ ὑμῖν) ‖ –ἀπ' αὐτοῦ. 31, διατί ‖ –αὐτῷ 34, ὅτι ὁ κύρ. 35, αὐτῶν for ἑαυτ. 38, –ἐρχόμενος 43, παρεμβαλοῦσιν for περιβαλοῦσιν 44, λίθ. ἐπὶ λίθον ἐν σοί 48, ἐξεκρέμετο

xx. 2, λέγ. πρ. αὐτ. 4, τὸ before Ἰωάν. 5, διατί 10, ἐξαπ. αὐτ. δείρ. κενόν. 13 –ἰδόντες 20, ἐνκαθέτους 24, –ἀποκριθέντες ‖ οἱ δὲ 25, –τῷ^{1st} 28, ᾖ for ἀποθάνῃ^{2d} 31, ἀπέθανον 34, γαμίσκονται for ἐκγαμίζ. 35, γαμίζ. for ἐκγαμ. 42, –καὶ ‖ αὐτὸς γὰρ 44, κύρ. αὐτ. 45, τοῖς μαθηταῖς (*S* τοῖς μαθ. αὐτοῦ) for πρ. αὐτ.

xxi. 2, –καὶ 8, –ὅτι ‖ –οὖν 9, ταῦτα γεν. 10, ἐπ' ἔθνος 11, λιμ. καὶ λοιμ. ‖ φόβητρά 12, τὰς συναγ. 13, –δὲ 17, ὑπὸ πάντων διὰ τὸ ὄν. μου 19, κτήσασθε 20, –τὴν 24, μαχαίρης 35, ἐπεισελεύσεται for ἐπελεύσεται 36, κατισχύσητε for καταξιωθῆτε ‖ ταῦτα πάντα

xxii. 10, εἰς ἣν for οὗ 13, εἰρήκει 16, αὐτὸ for ἐξ αὐτοῦ 18, ὅτι before οὐ ‖ ἀπὸ τ. νῦν after πίω 19, –τὴν (*by accident*) 26, γινέσθω 27, δὲ ἐν μέσ. ὑμ. εἰμὶ 30, καθήσεσθε for καθίσεσθε 36, ὁ δὲ εἶπ. ‖ –οὖν 37, –ἔτι ‖ τὸ^{3d} for τὰ 42, παρενέγκαι 44, καὶ ἦν ‖ –δὲ ‖ καταβαίνοντος 52, πρὸς for ἐπ' 53, ἀλλ' ‖ ἐστὶν ὑμῶν 62, –ὁ Πέτρ. 66, ἀπήγαγον for ἀνήγ. ‖ αὐτῶν for ἑαυτ.

xxiii. 1, Πειλᾶτον. 2, καὶ^{2d} before λέγ. 3, Πειλᾶτος 4, Πειλᾶτος 6, Πειλᾶτος ‖ –Γαλιλαίαν 8, ἐξ ἱκανῶν χρόνων θέλων 11, καὶ^{1st} after αὐτὸν^{1st} ‖ Πειλάτῳ 12, 'Ηρώδης καὶ ὁ Πειλᾶτος ‖ αὐτούς. for ἑαυτ. 13, Πειλᾶτος ‖ συνκαλ. 14, οὐθὲν 15, ἀνέπεμψεν ‖ αὐτὸν πρὸς ἡμᾶς for ὑμᾶς πρ. αὐτ. 18, τὸν 20, δὲ for οὖν ‖ Πειλᾶτος 23, –καὶ τῶν ἀρχ. 24, Πειλᾶτος 25, –τὴν 27, –καὶ^{2d} 29, αἱ κοιλ. αἳ 33, –ἐξ after δὲ (*by accident*) 35, –καὶ^{2d} ‖ –σὺν αὐτοῖς 36, ἐνέπαιξαν 45, τοῦ ἡλίου ἐκλιπόντος for καὶ ἐσκ. ὁ ἥλιος ‖ ἐσχίσθη δὲ for καὶ ἐσχίσθη 47, ἑκατοντάρχης 49, ἀπὸ after αὐτῷ^{1st} 50, καὶ after ἄρχ. 51, συνκατατιθέμενος ‖ –καὶ^{2d} ‖ –καὶ αὐτὸς 52, Πειλάτῳ 53, –αὐτὸ^{1st} ‖ οὐδέπω for οὔπω 54, παρασκευῆς καὶ 55, ἐκ. τ. Γαλ. αὐτῷ

xxiv. 1, ἐπὶ τὸ μν. ἦλθ. 3, τοῦ κυρίου 'Ιησοῦ added after σῶμα 4, ἐσθῆτι ἀστραπτούσῃ 10, ἦσαν ‖ –αἱ^{2d} 11, ταῦτα for αὐτῶν 13, ἐν αὐτῇ τῇ ἡμ. ἦσαν πορ. 17, ἐστάθησαν for ἐστε 19, Ναζαρηνοῦ 21, –σήμερον (*S* –ἄγει σήμ.) 22, γενόμεναι 23, ἦλθον 27, διερμήνευσεν ‖ ἑαυτοῦ for αὐτ. 28, προσεποιήσατο πορρωτέρω 29, ἤδη ἡ ἡμ. 34, ὄντως ἠγ. ὁ κύρ. 38, διατί 39, σάρκας 42, –καὶ ἀπὸ μελ. κηρ. 47, εἰς for καὶ^{2d} ‖ ἀρξάμενοι 49, κἀγὼ for κ. ἰδ. ἐγὼ 50, –ἔξω ‖ πρὸς for εἰς 53, διαπαντὸς

John i. 4, ἐστιν for ἦν^{1st} 12, ἔλαβον 20, ἐγὼ οὐκ εἰμί 21, 'Ηλείας ‖ σύ after εἶ ‖ –καὶ^{2d} 24, –οἱ 25, 'Ηλείας 26, στήκει (*S* ἑστήκει) 28, ὁ 'Ιωάν. 31, –τῷ^{2d} 37, –καὶ^{1st} ‖ ἤκουσ. οἱ δύο μαθ. αὐτοῦ 38, –δὲ 40, οὖν after ἦλθαν 46, –τὸν^{2d} 47, –καὶ^{1st} ‖ –ὁ 50, αὐτῷ after ἀπεκρίθη 52, –ἀπ' ἄρτι

ii. 3, οἶνον οὐκ εἶχον, ὅτι συνετελέσθη ὁ οἶνος τοῦ γάμου. for ὑστερ. οἴνου ‖ εἶτα before λέγει ‖ οἶνος οὐκ ἔστιν. 8, οἱ δὲ for καὶ^{3d} 10, –τότε 22, ὃν for ᾧ

iii. 5, τῶν οὐρανῶν. for τοῦ θεοῦ. 16, –αὐτοῦ 17, –αὐτοῦ^{1st} 18, –δὲ 24, –ὁ 26, ἦλθον ‖ εἶπον 31, –ἐπάνω πάντων ἐστίν· after ἐρχόμ.^{2d} 32, –τοῦτο 36, –δὲ

iv. 1, 'Ιησοῦς for κύ. 3, πάλιν after ἀπῆλθ. 4, 5, and 7, Σαμαρίας 5, ὃ for οὗ 9, –οὖν ‖ Σαμαρῖτις· ‖ Σαμαρίτιδος ‖ –οὐ γὰρ συνχρ. 'Ιουδ. Σαμ. 11, –οὖν 14, ἐγὼ before δώσω^{2d} 15, διέρχωμαι for ἔρχομαι 16, φών. τ. ἄνδ. σου 17, εἶπεν· ἄνδ. οὐκ ἔχω. ‖ εἶπες 24, –αὐτόν ‖ προσκ. δεῖ 27, ἦλθαν 29, ἃ for ὅσα 37, –ὁ^{2d} 38, ἀπέσταλκα 39, Σαμαριτῶν ‖ ἃ for ὅσα 40, Σαμαρῖται, 45, ὡς for ὅτε ‖ ἃ for ὅσα 46, 'Ην δὲ for καὶ ἦν 50, ὃν for ᾧ 51, –αὐτοῦ^{2d} ‖ ἤγγειλαν for ἀπήγγ. λέγοντες ‖ αὐτοῦ^{2d} for σου 53, –ἐν^{1st} ‖ –ὅτι^{2d}

v. 1, ἡ ἑορτὴ 2, τὸ λεγόμενον for ἡ ἐπιλ. ‖ Βηθζαθά, 9, –εὐθέως 10, καὶ before οὐκ 15, εἶπεν for ἀνήγγ. 17, –'Ιησ. 18, –οὖν 19, ἔλεγεν for εἶπεν ‖ ἂν^{1st} for ἐὰν ‖ ποιεῖ ὁμοίως 20, θαυμάζετε. 23, τιμῶσι$^{1st\ and\ 2d}$ 25, ἀκούσουσιν (*S* ἀκούσωσι) 26, οὕτως καὶ τῷ υἱῷ ἔδωκεν (*S* –οὕτως ἔδωκε *to end of verse*) 27, –καὶ^{2d} 28, ἀκούσουσιν (*S* ἀκούσωσιν) 32, οἴδατε 37, πώποτε ἀκηκ. 40, ἔχητε. 42, οὐκ ἔχ. τὴν ἀγ. τοῦ θεοῦ

vi. 3, ἐκαθέζετο 5, – τὸν 6, ἔμελλεν 7, ἀποκρίνεται ‖ ὁ Φίλ. 9, –ἓν 10, ὡς for ὡσεὶ 11, εὐχαρίστησεν καὶ ἔδωκεν for εὐχαριστήσας διέδωκεν 14, εἰς τὸν κόσμ. ἐρχ. 15, φεύγει for ἀνεχώρησεν 17, – τὸ ‖ κατέλαβεν δὲ αὐτοὺς ἡ σκοτία for καὶ σκοτία ἤδη ἐγεγόνει ‖ οὔπω for οὐκ ‖ ἐληλ. 'Ιησ. (– ὁ) πρ. αὐτούς 18, διηγείρετο for διεγείρετο 19, στάδια 21, ἐπὶ τὴν γῆν 22, εἶδον (*S* εἶδεν) for ἰδὼν ‖ πλοῖον for πλοιάριον^{2d} 23, – δὲ ‖ ἦλθον (*S* ἐπελθόντων οὖν τῶν πλοίων for ἀλλα δὲ ἦλθε πλοιάρια) 27, δίδωσιν ὑμῖν for ὑμ. δώσει 29, πιστεύητε 33, ὁ after ἄρτος 35, οὖν after εἶπεν ‖ ἐμὲ for με 36, – με 37, ἐμὲ for με 38, ποιήσω 44, με for ἐμὲ 45, ἀκούσας ‖ ἐμέ for με. 46, θεὸν for πατέρα. 51, ἐκ τοῦ ἐμοῦ ἄρτου for ἐκ τούτου τ. ἀρ. ‖ ζήσει ‖ δώσω ὑπὲρ τῆς τοῦ κόσμου ζωῆς, ἡ σάρξ μου ἐστίν, for δώσω ἡ σ. μ. ἐ., ἣν ἐγὼ δ. ὑπ. τ. τ. κόσμ. ζωῆς. 52, ἡμῖν οὗτος 54, – ἐν 65, ἐμὲ for με 66, οὖν after τούτου ‖ πολλοὶ τ. μαθ. αὐτ. ἀπῆλθον (*S* – αὐτοῦ) 70, ὁ 'Ιησ. after αὐτοῖς (*see note; not so S*) 71, ἔμελλεν (*S* – λον) ‖ αὐτὸν παραδιδ.

vii. 1, – Καὶ 4, τι ἐν κρυπτῷ 6, – οὖν 10, εἰς τὴν ἑορτήν after οἱ ἀδ. αὐτοῦ and om. after ἀνέβη ‖ ἀλλ' for ἀλλὰ ὡς 12, ἦν περὶ αὐτοῦ ‖ ἐν τῷ ὄχλῳ 16, – ὁ 17, – τοῦ 22, – διὰ τοῦτο ‖ ὁ Μ. 23, ὁ Μ. 29, ἀπέσταλκεν. 31, Πολλοὶ δὲ ἐπιστ. ἐκ τ. ὄχλ. εἰς αὐτ. ‖ – ὅτι ‖ μὴ for μήτι ‖ ποιεῖ for ἐπ. 32, οἱ ἀρχ. καὶ οἱ Φαρ. 35, – ἡμεῖς 37, ἔκραζεν ‖ – πρὸς μὲ 40, τούτων after τῶν λόγων 41, ἄλλοι^{2d} for οἱ δὲ 42, ὁ χρ. ἔρχεται; 45, διατί 46, λαλεῖ after οὗτος 50, – ὁ ἐλθὼν πρὸς αὐτ. πρότερον 52, προφ. ἐκ τ. Γαλ. ‖ ἐγείρεται.

viii. 14, – δὲ 16, – πατήρ. 17, γεγραμμένον ἐστὶν for γέγραπται 23, ἐκ τ. κόσμ. τούτου ἐστε 38, ἃ ἐγὼ (*see note*) for ἐγὼ ὃ ‖ ἃ ἠκούσατε (*S* ἑωράκ.) παρὰ τοῦ πατρὸς for ὃ ἑωρ. παρὰ τῷ πατρὶ 39, ἐστε for ἦτε 41, εἶπαν 43, 46, διατί 48, Σαμαρίτης 52, εἶπαν 55, κἂν for καὶ ἐὰν 56, εἴδη 57, εἶπαν

ix. 1, εἶδεν 4, ἡμᾶς (2*t*) for ἐμὲ and με 6, – τοῦ τυφλοῦ 9, ἀλλὰ 11, ὁ ἄνθρ. ὁ λεγ. ‖ καὶ νιψάμ. 17, λέγ. οὖν 20, ἀπεκρ. οὖν 21, ἑαυτοῦ for αὐτοῦ^{2d} 23, ἐπερωτήσατε for ἐρωτήσ. 28, εἶπαν 30, ἤνοιξεν (*S* – ξε) 35, – ὁ ‖ – αὐτῷ ‖ ἀνθρώπου for θεοῦ 37, ἑώρακας 40, – ταῦτα ‖ εἶπαν

x. 7, – πάλιν αὐτοῖς 8, – πρὸ ἐμοῦ 12, – δὲ (*not S*) ‖ ἐστὶν ‖ – τὰ πρόβατα^{3d} 13, – ὁ δὲ μισθ. φεύγει 14, γινώσκουσί με τὰ ἐμά for γινώσκομαι ὑπὸ τ. ἐμ. 16, δεῖ με 20, οὖν for δὲ 22, – τοῖς (*see note*) 24, εἰπὸν 25, – αὐτοῖς 26, ὅτι οὐκ for οὐ γάρ ‖ – καθὼς εἶπον ὑμῖν. 27, ἀκούουσιν 28, δίδ. αὐτοῖς ζωὴν αἰών. 29, – μου ‖ ὃ for ὃς ‖ μεῖζον (*S* μείζων) 31, – οὖν 32, ἔργα καλὰ 36, – τοῦ 38, πιστεύετε (2^{d}) for πιστεύσατε 39, – πάλιν 42, πολλ. ἐπίστευσαν

xi. 1, τῆς Μαρ. 12, οἱ μαθηταί after αὐτῷ 18, – ἡ 21, – τὸν ‖ ἀπέθανεν ὁ ἀδ. μου for ὁ ἀδ. μου ἐτεθνήκει. 22, – ἀλλὰ 31, δόξαντες for λέγοντες 32, πρὸς for εἰς 33, εἶδεν 38, ἐμβριμούμενος 44, αὐτοῖς ὁ 'Ιησ. for 'Ιησ. αὐτοῖς 46, εἶπαν 53, ἐβουλεύσαντο for συνεβ. 56, ἔλεγαν.

xii. 1, – ὁ τεθνηκώς, ‖ – ὁ before 'Ιησ. 4, δὲ for οὖν 5, διατί 6, ἔχων for εἶχεν καὶ 9, ὁ ὄχλος 13, ὡσαννά for 'Ωσαννά, ‖ καὶ ὁ βασ. 16, αὐτοῦ οἱ μαθ. 20, προσκυνήσωσιν 23, ἀποκρίνεται 25, ἀπολλύει for ἀπολέσει 29, – καὶ 34, ἀπεκρίθη οὖν 48, – ἐν (*by mistake*) 50, ἐγὼ λαλῶ,

xiii. 3, ἔδωκεν 10, – ἢ τοὺς πόδας 15, δέδωκα 18, τίνας for οὓς ‖ ἐπῆρκεν 19, ἀπάρτι 25, ἐπιπεσὼν οὖν for ἀναπεσὼν 26, – οὖν^{1st} ‖ ὁ 'Ιησ. 32, αὐτῷ^{2d} for ἑαυτῷ 33, ἐγὼ before ὑπάγω 37, διατί

xiv. 3, τόπον ὑμῖν, 7, ἐγνώκατε ‖

ἐμέ for μέ ‖ γνώσεσθε for ἐγνώκειτε ἄν
‖ ἀπάρτι 9, ὁ Ἰησ. ‖ τοσούτῳ χρόνῳ ‖
– καὶ before πῶς 10, ὁ ἐν ἐμοὶ μένων
‖ αὐτοῦ for αὐτός. 14, με after αἰτήσητέ
15, τηρήσετε (*S* – σητε) 16, μεθ' ὑμῶν ᾖ
xv. 4, μένῃ ‖ μένητε. 6, μένῃ ‖ αὐτὸ
10, κἀγὼ for ἐγὼ ‖ μου after πατρός
13, – τις 14, ἃ 16, δῷ (*S* δώσει) 18,
– ὑμῶν 24, ἐποίησεν, ‖ ἑωράκασιν 26, – δὲ
xvi. 7, – ἐγὼ^{3d} 13, ἀκούει 16, οὐκέτι
for οὐ 17, εἶπον ‖ – ἐγὼ 20, ἀλλ' 22,
νῦν μὲν λύπην
xvii. 1, – ὁ before Ἰησ. ‖ ἐπάρας ‖ – καὶ
before εἶπεν 2, δώσῃ (*S* δώσω) 4,
τελειώσας· 6, ἔδωκας ‖ καὶ ἐμοὶ for κἀμοὶ
‖ ἔδωκας 11, αὐτοὶ for οὗτοι ‖ – καὶ before ἡμεῖς. 13, ἑαυτοῖς for αὐτοῖς. 17,
– σου 19, – ἐγὼ 21, πιστεύῃ
xviii. 1, τοῦ κέδρου for τῶν κέδρων
3, ἐκ τῶν before Φαρ. 5, Ἰησοῦς after
αὐτοῖς 6, – ὅτι 7, αὐτοὺς ἐπηρ. 13,
ἤγαγον for ἀπήγ. ‖ – αὐτὸν 14, ἀποθανεῖν for ἀπολέσθαι 15, – ὁ before ἄλλος
18, καὶ after δὲ ‖ ὁ Π. μετ. αὐτ. 24,
ἀπέστειλεν οὖν (*S* δὲ) 28, ἀλλὰ for
ἀλλ' ἵνα 29, Πειλᾶτος (*S* Πιλ. so elsewhere ch. xviii., xix.) ‖ ἔξω after
Πειλ. ‖ – κατὰ 31, ὁ Πειλ. ‖ – αὐτόν^{2d}
after κρίν. ‖ εἶπον οὖν 33, εἰς τὸ πρ.
πάλιν ‖ Πειλ. (so 37, 38) 37, ὁ Ἰησ.
‖ – ἐγὼ^{1st} 39, ἀπολύσω ὑμῖν ‖ ἀπολ.
ὑμῖν 40, – πάντες
xix. 1, Πειλ. 4, ὁ Πειλ. ἔξω ‖ οὐχ for
ἐν αὐτῷ οὐδεμίαν 5, ἰδοὺ for Ἴδε
6, – λέγοντες ‖ Πειλ. 7, – αὐτῷ ‖ – ἡμῶν
8, 10, Πειλ. 11, ἔχεις ‖ δεδομ. σοι
‖ παραδοὺς ‖ με σοὶ 12, ὁ Πειλ.
ἐζήτει 13, 15, Πειλ. 17, ἑαυτῷ for
αὐτῷ 19, 21, 22, Πειλ. 23, τέσ-
σερα 24, – ἡ λέγουσα 25, Μαριὰμ 2*t*
26, – αὐτοῦ 27, αὐτ. ὁ μαθ. 29, – οὖν
after σκεῦος (*S* δὲ for οὖν) ‖ σπόγγον
οὖν μεστὸν ὄξους for οἱ δὲ πλήσαντες
σπ. ὄξους καὶ 30, – ὁ Ἰησ. 31, ἐπεὶ
παρασκ. ἦν after Ἰουδαῖοι ‖ Πειλ. 35,
πιστεύητε. 38, Μετὰ δὲ ‖ Πειλ. 2*t* ‖
ἦλθον ‖ ἦραν ‖ αὐτόν for τὸ σῶμα τ.
Ἰησ. 40, – ἐν
xx. 1, 11, Μαριὰμ 11, ἔξω (*S* om.)
κλαίουσα. 13, – καὶ^{1st} 18, ἑώρακα 19, ὁ
Ἰησ. 20, – καὶ^{2d} 23, ἀφέωνται (*S*
ἀφεθήσεται) 25, ἑωράκαμεν ‖ μου τ.
δάκτ. 31, πιστεύητε

xxi. 1, Ἰησοῦς after πάλιν (*S* π. ἑαυτ.
ὁ Ἰησ.) 4, ἐπὶ for εἰς 5, – ὁ 6, λέγει
for ὁ δὲ εἶπεν 11, εἰς τὴν γῆν for ἐπὶ
τῆς γῆς 12, δὲ after οὐδεὶς 17, λέγει
for εἶπεν^{2d} ‖ – Ἰησοῦς 21, οὖν after
τοῦτον 23, οὗτος ὁ λόγος ‖ – τί πρὸς
σέ; 25, *omits the whole verse.*
Acts i. 1, ὁ Ἰησ. 5, δὲ ἐν πνεύματι
βαπτ. ἁγ. 7, – δὲ (not *S*) 8, ἐν before
πάσῃ ‖ Σαμαρίᾳ 10, ἐσθήσεσι 11,
βλέποντες for ἐμβλέπ. 14, – σὺν^{2d} 15,
ὡσεὶ for ὡς 16, – ταύτην 19, ὁ before
καὶ ‖ πᾶσι ‖ Ἀχελδαμάχ, 22, ἄχρι for
ἕως
ii. 2, καθήμενοι for καθεζόμενοι 3, καὶ
ἐκάθισεν for ἐκ. τε 4, πάντες for ἅπ. 5,
εἰς for ἐν 7, πάντες (ἅπαντες *S**) after
δὲ ‖ οὐχ for Οὐχὶ 12, θέλει (θέλοι *S*) for
ἂν θέλοι 14, ὁ Πέτρος ‖ πάντες for ἅπ.
16, Ἰωήλ· after προφήτου 17, καὶ
ἔσται 20, – ἢ after πρὶν ‖ – καὶ ἐπιφανῆ
21, ἂν for ἐὰν (*S** omits the verse, but
S^{a} restores it) 22, δυνάμεσι ‖ τέρασι
25, μου after κύριον ‖ διαπαντός, 26,
ἐλπίδι for ἐλπ. 27, ἐνκαταλείψεις
(ἐγκατ. *S*) 31, ἐνκατ. 34, – ὁ 37,
ποιήσωμεν, 38, φησίν, after μετανοήσ-
ατε, ‖ τῶν ἁμαρτιῶν ὑμῶν for ἁμ. simply
40, αὐτοὺς after παρεκάλει 43, πολλὰ
δὲ for πολλά τε ‖ after ἐγίνετο^{2d} adds
ἐν Ἱερουσαλήμ, φόβος τε ἦν μέγας ἐπὶ
πάντας. 44, καὶ πάντες ‖ πιστεύσαντες
47, – τῇ ἐκκλησίᾳ, adding ἐπὶ τὸ αὐτό,
from iii. 1.
iii. 1, Ἐπὶ τὸ αὐτὸ transferred to ii.
49 ‖ Πέτρος δὲ 6, – ἔγειρε καὶ 7, adds
αὐτόν after ἤγειρεν ‖ αἱ βάσεις αὐτοῦ ‖
σφυδρά, 8, καὶ αἰνῶν 10, δὲ for τε ‖
αὐτὸς for οὗτος 11, τὸν Ἰωάν. ‖
Σολομῶντος 13, ὁ θεὸς added before
Ἰσαὰκ and before Ἰακώβ, ‖ – αὐτὸν ‖
Πειλάτου (Πιλ. *S*), 19, πρὸς for εἰς
22, ἡμῶν for ὑμῶν after θεὸς
iv. 4, – ὁ 5, εἰς for ἐν 6, Ἄννας ὁ
ἀρχιερεὺς καὶ Καϊάφας καὶ Ἰωάννης
καὶ Ἀλέξανδρος 7, ἐν τῷ μέσῳ ‖ τοῦτο
ἐποιήσατε 8, – τοῦ Ἰσραήλ, 9, σέσωται,
16, ποιήσωμεν ‖ ἀρνεῖσθαι 17, – ἀπειλῇ
18, – τὸ 19, εἶπον 25, ὁ τοῦ πατρὸς
ἡμῶν διὰ πνεύματος ἁγίου στόματος for
ὁ διὰ στόμ. ‖ ἱνατί 27, Πειλᾶτος 29,
ἔπιδε 30, σε after ἐκτείνειν 32, – ἡ
(twice) 33, δυνάμει μεγάλῃ ‖ Ἰησοῦ

Χριστοῦ τοῦ κυρίου for τ. κ. Ἰησ. 34, ἦν for ὑπῆρχεν 37, πρὸς for παρὰ

v. 3, διατί ‖ –σε$^{\text{2d}}$ 8, ἀπεκρίθη δὲ ‖ –ὁ before Πέτρος 10, εὗρον 12, πολλὰ ἐν τῷ λαῷ· ‖ Σολομῶντος (Σαλ. *S*) 15, καὶ εἰς for κατὰ 16, –εἰς before Ἱερ. 24, –ἱερεὺς καὶ ὁ 26, ἦγεν for ἤγαγεν ‖ –ἵνα (*see note*) 31, τοῦ δοῦναι 32, –αὐτοῦ before μάρτ. ‖ –δὲ after πνεῦμα 38, ἄφετε for ἐάσατε

vi. 3, δέ, for οὖν, 9, τῶν λεγομένων 13, λαλῶν ῥήματα 15, πάντες for ἅπ. ‖ εἶδον

vii. 1, –ἄρα 3, ἐκ before τῆς συγ. 7, ὁ θεὸς εἶπεν, 8, –ὁ before Ἰσ. and before Ἰακ. 10, ἔναντι for ἐναντίον ‖ ἐφ' before ὅλον 11, Αἴγυπτον for γῆν Αἰγύπτου 13, αὐτοῦ for Ἰωσήφ$^{\text{2d}}$ 15, εἰς Αἴγυπτον after Ἰακὼβ 16, ἐν Συχέμ for τοῦ Σ. 18, ἐπ' Αἴγυπτον after ἕτερος 21, ἐκτεθέντος δὲ αὐτοῦ 26, συνήλλασσεν for συνήλασεν ‖ ἱνατί 30, ἐν φλογὶ πυρὸς 39, ἐν ταῖς καρδίαις for τῇ καρδίᾳ 40, ἐγένετο for γέγονεν 43, Ῥομφάν for Ῥεφάν, 45, ἐξέωσεν 46, οἴκῳ for θεῷ 47, Σαλωμὼν 50, ταῦτα πάντα 51, καρδίαις for τῇ καρδίᾳ 58, αὐτῶν after ἱμάτια

viii. 1, –δὲ after πάντες ‖ Σαμαρίας 2, ἐποίησαν 5, εἰς τὴν πόλιν ‖ Σαμαρίας (Καισαρίας *S**) 7, πολλοὶ for πολλῶν 9, Σαμαρίας 10, πάντες after προσεῖχον 13, σημεῖα καὶ δυνάμεις ‖ μεγάλας γινομένας for γινόμενα 14, Σαμαρία 25, Σαμαριτῶν 27, –ὃς before ἐληλύθει 28, –καὶ before ἀνεγίνωσκεν 33, –αὐτοῦ$^{\text{1st}}$ ‖ –δὲ 40, –αὐτὸν (*by accident*) ‖ Καισαρίαν.

ix. 2, ἂν for ἐάν ‖ ὄντας τῆς ὁδοῦ, 3, αὐτὸν περιήστραψεν 8, ἠνοιγμένων 12, χεῖρας, 13, ἤκουσα 18, ὡς for ὡσεὶ 21, εἰς for ἐν ‖ ἐληλύθει, 22, συνέχυννεν (–υνε *S*) ‖ –τοὺς before Ἰουδαίους 25, αὐτὸν (*omitted accidentally in ed.* 7, *see note*) after καθῆκαν 26, εἰς for ἐν ‖ ἐπείραζεν for ἐπειρᾶτο 30, Καισαρίαν 31, Σαμαρίας 34, –ὁ$^{\text{2d}}$ 36, ἀγαθῶν ἔργων 37, ἔθηκαν αὐτὴν 40, καὶ before θεὶς 43, –αὐτὸν

x. 1, Καισαρίᾳ 2, –τε ‖ διαπαντός, 3, περὶ before ὥραν 9, αὐτῶν for ἐκείνων 11, –δεδεμένον καὶ 15, ἐκαθάρισεν 17, –καὶ ‖ ὑπὸ for ἀπὸ 19, ζητοῦντες 24, εἰσῆλθαν for –θεν ‖ Καισαρίαν· 26, καὶ ἐγὼ for κἀγὼ 30, –νηστεύων καὶ 32, –ὃς παραγενόμενος λαλήσει σοι 33, ὑπὸ for ἀπὸ 37, ἀρξάμενος 39, ἐν before Ἱερ. 40, ἐν before τῇ τρίτῃ ἡμ. 48, δὲ for τε ‖ αὐτοῖς ‖ Ἰησοῦ Χριστοῦ for τοῦ κυρίου

xi. 9, ἐκαθάρισεν 11, ἦμεν ‖ Καισαρίας 12, μηδὲν διακρίναντα (–νοντα *S**) after αὐτοῖς 13, δὲ for τε ‖ –αὐτῷ 16, τοῦ κυρίου 17, –δὲ 18, ἐδόξασαν ‖ ἄρα for Ἄραγε ‖ εἰς ζωὴν ἔδωκεν. 20, καὶ before πρὸς 22, οὔσης before ἐν Ἱερ. ‖ –διελθεῖν 23, τὴν χάριν τὴν 26, πρώτως for πρῶτον 28, –καὶ

xii. 1, ὁ βασ. Ἡρώδης 3, –αἱ 5, ἐκτενῶς for ἐκτενὴς 9, διὰ for ὑπὸ 19, –τὴν before Καισ. (*see note*) ‖ Καισαρίαν 21, –καὶ 25, –καὶ$^{\text{2d}}$

xiii. 1, τετραάρχου 4, –τὴν$^{\text{1st}}$ ‖ Σελευκίαν ‖ –τὴν$^{\text{2d}}$ 6, Βαριησοῦ, 11, τε for δὲ ‖ ἔπεσεν for ἐπέπεσεν 14, ἐλθόντες for εἰσελθ. 15, ἐν ὑμῖν λόγος 17, Ἰσραὴλ after τούτου 19, –αὐτοῖς 20, καὶ μετὰ ταῦτα transposed after πεντήκοντα. ‖ –τοῦ 25, –ὁ before Ἰωάν. (*see note*) ‖ τί ἐμὲ for Τίνα με 26, ἡμῖν for ὑμῖν$^{\text{2d}}$ 28, Πειλᾶτον (Πιλ. *S*) 32, ἡμῶν for αὐτῶν ἡμῖν 39, –καὶ 43, αὐτοῖς after προσλαλ. 44, δὲ for τε ‖ ἐρχομένῳ for ἐχομένῳ 45, –τοῦ ‖ λαλουμένοις for λεγομένοις 46, –δὲ 49, καθ' for δι' 52, δὲ for τε

xiv. 3, ἐπὶ before τῷ λόγῳ ‖ διδόντος 7, εὐαγγ. ἦσαν. 8, ἀδύνατος ἐν Λύστροις (*so intended, but the text and note are both wrong*) 10, –τῇ 12, Δία, 17, καίτοι (so *S*^{c}) for καίτοιγε (so *S**) ‖ αὐτὸν for ἑαυτὸν 25, εἰς τὴν Πέργην for ἐν Πέργῃ

xv. 1, τῷ after ἔθει 3, Σαμαρίαν, 4, ὑπὸ for ἀπὸ 6, δὲ for τε 7, ζητήσεως for συνζητ. 16, κατεστραμμένα for κατεσκαμμένα 17, –ὁ 20, –ἀπὸ 22, ἔδοξε 23, –καὶ οἱ before ἀδελφοὶ 26, παραδεδωκόσι 28, τῷ πνεύματι τῷ ἁγίῳ for τ. ἁγ. πν. ‖ τούτων after πλὴν 30, κατῆλθον for ἦλθον 32, ἐπεστήριξαν (so *S*^{a}; *S** omits καὶ ἐπ.) 37, ἐβούλετο ‖ τὸν Ἰωάννην

xvi. 1, εἰς before Λύστραν 6, διῆλθον 7, δὲ after ἐλθόντες 9, καὶ before παρακαλῶν 10, –τὴν ‖ συμβιβάζοντες

‖ θεὸς for κύριος 11, – τῆς ‖ δὲ for τε ‖ Νέαν πόλιν for Νεάπολιν 12, κἀκεῖθεν for ἐκεῖθέν τε ‖ κολωνία. ‖ ταύτῃ for αὐτῇ 13, ἐνομίζομεν (–ζεν *S*) προσευχὴν 14, – τοῦ 15, μένετε· 17, κατακολουθοῦσα ‖ ἔκραζεν (*for* ἔκραξεν, *misprint in 7th ed.*) 18, – ὁ 19, τὸν Σίλαν 24, λαβὼν 26, ἠνοίχθησαν ‖ δὲ for τε 28, φωνῇ μεγάλῃ ‖ – ὁ 29, τῷ Σίλᾳ, 33, ἅπαντες for πάντες 34, ἠγαλλιάσατο 38, τε for δὲ 40, ἀπὸ for ἐκ ‖ ἰδόντες παρεκάλεσαν τοὺς ἀδελφούς, for ἰδ. τ. ἀδ. παρ. αὐτούς, ‖ ἐξῆλθαν.

xvii. 1, τὴν ᾿Απολ. ‖ – ἡ 2, διελέξατο 3, – ὁ (also Χριστὸς ᾿Ιησοῦς, for Χριστός, ᾿Ιησοῦς) 5, ζηλώσαντες δὲ οἱ ᾿Ιουδαῖοι καὶ προσλαβ. for προσλαβ. δὲ οἱ ᾿Ιουδαῖοι οἱ ἀπειθοῦντες ‖ τινὰς ἄνδρας καὶ ἐπιστάντες for ἐπ. τε ‖ προαγαγεῖν for ἀγαγεῖν 6, – τὸν 7, ἕτερον λέγοντες 10, τῶν ᾿Ιουδαίων ἀπῄεσαν· 11, – τὸ 13, καὶ ταράσσοντες after σαλεύοντες 14, ἕως for ὡς ‖ ὑπέμειναν 15, τὸν Τιμ. 18, ᾿Επικουρίων 19, ῎Αριον 20, τίνα θέλει for τί ἂν θέλοι 21, τι after ἀκούειν 22, – ὁ ‖ ᾿Αρίου 26, – αἵματος 30, ἀπαγγέλλει for παραγγέλλει ‖ πάντας

xviii. 1, – δὲ 2, τεταχέναι for διατετ. 3, ἠργάζοντο· 5, εἶναι after ᾿Ιουδαίοις 7, εἰσῆλθεν for ἦλθεν ‖ Τιτίου (*S* Τιτου) before ᾿Ιούστου 9, ἐν νυκτὶ δι᾿ ὁράματος 11, δὲ for τε 12, ἀνθυπάτου ὄντος for ἀνθυπατεύοντος 14, – οὖν ‖ ἀνεσχόμην 18, Κενχρεαῖς 19, διελέξατο 22, Καισαρίαν, 23, στηρίζων for ἐπιστηρίζων 26, Πρίσκιλλα καὶ ᾿Ακύλας (*S* –λα) ‖ τὴν ὁδὸν τοῦ θεοῦ.

xix. 1, κατελθεῖν for ἐλθεῖν 2, οὐδ᾿ for οὐδὲ 3, ὁ δὲ εἶπεν for εἶπέν•τε 4, – μὲν 6, ἦλθε 7, δώδεκα for δεκαδύο. 8, τὰ before περὶ 11, ὁ θεὸς ἐποίει 14, – οἱ 15, αὐτοῖς after εἶπεν 16, ἐφαλόμενος 22, – τὴν^{1st} 24, οὐκ ὀλίγην ἐργασίαν, 27, τῆς μεγαλειότητος 30, Παύλου δὲ for τοῦ δὲ Π. 32, συγκεχυμένη, ‖ ἕνεκα for –κεν 33, συνεβίβασαν for προεβίβ. 34, κράζοντες 37, ἡμῶν for ὑμῶν. 38, ἔχουσι 39, περὶ ἑτέρων for περαιτέρω 40, οὐ after περὶ οὗ ‖ ἀποδοῦναι for δοῦναι ‖ περὶ before τῆς συστρ. (*see note*)

xx. 1, μεταπεμψάμενος for προσκαλεσάμενος ‖ παρακαλέσας (*S.* παρ. καὶ), before ἀσπασάμενος ‖ πορεύεσθαι ‖ – τὴν 3, γνώμης 4, – ἄχρι τῆς ᾿Ασίας 5, οὗτοι δὲ 6, ὅπου for οὗ 13, διατεταγμένος ἦν, 14, συνέβαλλεν (*S* –λλον) 15, – καὶ μείναντες•ἐν Τρωγυλίῳ ‖ τῇ δὲ ἐχ. 16, εἴη for ἦν 21, – τὴν after πίστιν ‖ Χριστόν after ᾿Ιησοῦν. 22, ἐμοὶ for μοι 23, λέγον 26, διότι for διὸ ‖ εἰμι for ἐγὼ 27, ὑμῖν transposed after θεοῦ 28, – οὖν 29, – γὰρ ‖ – τοῦτο, 30, ἑαυτῶν for αὐτῶν. 32, οἰκοδομῆσαι for ἐποικ. ‖ τὴν κληρονομίαν

xxi. 3, ἀναφάναντες ‖ κατήλθομεν for κατήχθημεν ‖ τὸ πλοῖον ἦν 5, ἡμᾶς ἐξαρτίσαι ‖ γυναιξὶ 8, ἤλθομεν ‖ Καισαρίαν 9, θυγ. τεσ. παρθένοι 13, τότε ἀπεκρίθη for ἀπ. τε ‖ καὶ εἶπεν after Παῦλος 16, Καισαρίας 18, τε for δὲ 20, εἶπαν ‖ – ἐν τοῖς ᾿Ιουδαίοις 25, – μηδὲν τοιοῦτον τηρεῖν αὐτοὺς εἰ μὴ 31, συγχύννεται 33, ἁλύσεσι δυσί, ‖ – ἂν 37, τι after εἰπεῖν 40, γενομένης

xxii. 2, προσεφώνει 3, – μέν 8, ἐμέ· 9, – καὶ ἔμφοβοι ἐγένοντο 13, ἐμὲ 16, ἀπόλυσαι (*misprint for* ἀπόλουσαι) 18, ἴδον ‖ – τὴν 23, δὲ for τε 28, δὲ after ἀπεκρίθη 29, αὐτὸν ἦν 30, ὑπὸ for παρὰ

xxiii. 1, τῷ συνεδρίῳ ὁ Παῦλος 5, ὅτι before ἄρχοντα 8, μήτε for μηδὲ ‖ τινὲς τῶν γραμματέων for γραμματεῖς 10, γινομένης ‖ φοβηθεὶς for εὐλαβηθεὶς 11, οὕτω 14, μηδενὸς 16, τὴν ἐνέδραν for τὸ ἔνεδρον ‖ παραγενόμενος 17, ἄπαγε 22, ἀπέλυσε ‖ ἐμέ. 23, τινας δύο ‖ Καισαρίας, 24, διασώσωσι 25, ἔχουσαν for περιέχ. 27, – αὐτόν 28, – αὐτὸν 30, – μέλλειν ‖ ἐξ αὐτῶν after ἔσεσθαι ‖ – ἐξαυτῆς 32, ἀπέρχεσθαι for πορεύεσθαι 33, Καισαρίαν 34, ἐπαρχείας 35, τοῦ ῾Ηρώδου

xxiv. 1, πρεσβ. τινῶν for τῶν πρεσβ. 3, διορθωμάτων for κατορθωμάτων 5, στάσεις for στάσιν 11, δώδεκα for δεκαδύο 12, ἐπίστασιν for ἐπισύστασιν 13, οὐδὲ for οὔτε ‖ σοι after δύνανται 14, πᾶσι ‖ τοῖς ἐν before τοῖς προφ. 15, πρὸς for εἰς 16, διαπαντός. 18, αἷς for οἷς 20, – ἐν ἐμοὶ 24, ἰδίᾳ before γυναικὶ (so S^a, not S^*) ‖ ᾿Ιησοῦν after Χριστὸν (so S^*, omitted by S^c and apparently S^a) 25, – ἔσεσθαι 27, χάριτα ‖ κατέλιπε

xxv. 1, ἐπαρχείῳ (*S** -χιω) for ἐπαρχίᾳ || Καισαρίας, 4, Καισαρίαν, 5, ἄτοπον for τούτῳ 6, Καισαρίαν, 7, αὐτὸν after περιέστησαν 10, ἑστὼς transposed before ἐπὶ τ. β. || ἠδίκηκα, 13, Καισαρίαν || ἀσπασάμενοι 17, αὐτῶν after οὖν 18, ἐγὼ ὑπενόουν πονηράν (*S** -ρα), for ὑπ. ἐγώ, 20, -εἰς 24, βοῶντες for ἐπιβ. || αὐτὸν ζῆν 25, κατελάβομην (*S*[c], but *S** καταλαβόμενος) || -καὶ before αὐτοῦ

xxvi. 1, ἀπελογεῖτο transposed after χεῖρα 2, ἐπὶ σοῦ μέλλων σήμ. ἀπολ. 3, σε ὄντα 4, τὴν ἐκ νεότ. || ἴσασι || πάντες οἱ 5, θέλωσι || θρησκίας 6, ἡμῶν after πατέρας 7, ἐκτενείᾳ 12, -καὶ[1st] || -παρὰ 14, λέγουσαν for λαλοῦσαν || -καὶ λέγουσαν 20, -εἰς before πᾶσαν 21, -οἱ || ὄντα after συλλαβ. 25, Παῦλος after ὁ δὲ 28, ποιῆσαι for γενέσθαι. 29, εὐξάμην 30, συνκαθήμενοι 31, ἢ δεσμῶν ἄξιον || τι after ἄξιόν

xxvii. 2, εἰς after πλεῖν 3, πορευθέντι 5, Μύρρα (*S* Λύστραν) 8, πόλις ἦν || Λασαία (*S** Λασσ-). 11, -τοῦ 12, πλείονες || ἐκεῖθεν for κἀκεῖθεν, 14, εὐρακύλων for εὐροκλύδων· 16, Κλαῦδα 19, ἔριψαν for ἐρρίψαμεν· 23, ἐγώ, after εἰμὶ 27, ἐγένετο for ἐπεγένετο 30, πρῴρης (*S*[c]; πλωρης *S**) 33, ἡμέρα ἔμελλεν for ἤμελλεν ἡμ. 39, ἐβουλεύοντο || δύναιντο for δυνατὸν 41, πρῷρα 43, ἀπορίψαντας

xxviii. 3, ἐξελθοῦσα for διεξ. 4, εἶδον 5, ἀποτινάξας 6, ἐμπιπρᾶσθαι for πίμπρασθαι || μεταβάλλομενοι 14, παρ' for ἐπ' 15, ἔλαβε 16, εἰσήλθομεν || τὴν Ῥώμην, 17, ἔθεσι 20, εἵνεκεν for ἕνεκ. 21. περὶ (*S* κατὰ) σοῦ ἐδεξ. 22, ἡμῖν ἐστὶν 23, ἦλθον for ἧκον 25, τε for δὲ 31, -Χριστοῦ

ROMANS i. 24, -καὶ 27, τε for δὲ || ἄρρενες 2*t* (so *S**, but *S*[a] ἄρσενες for 2d ἀρ.) || ἄρρεσιν (so *S**, but *S*[a] ἀρσ.) 29, κακίᾳ πλεονεξίᾳ

ii. 2, γὰρ for δὲ 8, ἀπειθοῦσι || -μὲν 16, Χριστοῦ Ἰησοῦ (so *S**, not *S*[a]) 26, οὐχ for οὐχὶ 29, ἀλλ'

iii. 4, καθάπερ for καθὼς || νικήσεις 7, δὲ for γὰρ 12, ὁ ποιῶν 22, -καὶ ἐπὶ πάντας 26, Ἰησοῦ after πίστεως. 28, γὰρ for οὖν 30, εἴπερ for ἐπείπερ

iv. 1, εὑρηκέναι transposed after ἐροῦμεν || προπατόρα (with *S**) for πατέρα (*S*[a]) 5, ἀσεβῆν, 9, -ὅτι 11, δι' for διὰ || -καὶ before αὐτοῖς || -τὴν 15, δὲ for γὰρ after οὐ 18, ἐπ' for ἐφ' 19, -οὐ 21, καὶ πληροφορηθεὶς

v. 1, ἔχωμεν 2, τῇ πίστει after ἐσχήκαμεν || ἐπ' for ἐφ' 6, ἔτι after ἀσθενῶν 8, εἰς ἡμᾶς ὁ θεὸς 12, ἡ ἁμαρτία εἰς τὸν κόσμον 12, adds ὁ θάνατος after ἀνθρώπους 17, τῷ τοῦ ἑνὸς for ἐν ἑνὶ

vi. 11, εἶναι after ἑαυτοὺς 13, ὡσεὶ for ὡς

vii. 13, ἐγένετο for γέγονεν 15, τοῦτο before πράσσω 16, σύνφημι 17, ἐνοικοῦσα for οἰκοῦσα

viii. 2, σε for με 11, τὸν Ἰησοῦν || ἐκ νεκρῶν Χριστὸν for Χρ. ἐκ νεκρ. || Ἰησοῦν after Χριστὸν || διὰ τοῦ ἐνοικοῦντος αὐτοῦ πνεύματος 15, δουλίας for -λείας 21, διότι for ὅτι || δουλίας 23, ἡμεῖς before καὶ[2d] 26, προσευξώμεθα 27, ἐραυνῶν 34, Ἰησοῦς after Χριστὸς || -καὶ before ἐγερθείς, also before ἐστιν

ix. 15, Μωϋσεῖ for -σῇ (*see note in 7th edition*) 18, ἐλεεῖ 19, -οὖν after τί 20, ὦ ἄνθρωπε, μενοῦνγε 28, -ἐν δικαιοσύνῃ, ὅτι λόγον συντετμημένον 29, ἐνκατέλιπεν || ὡμοιώθημεν. 31, -δικαιοσύνης[2d] 32, διατί; || -γὰρ

x. 5, ὅτι placed after γράφει || -τοῦ || -αὐτὰ || αὐτῇ for αὐτοῖς. 14, ἐπικαλέσωνται || πιστεύσωσιν || 14, ἀκούσονται 15, κηρύξωσιν || -εἰρήνην, τῶν εὐαγγελιζομένων 17, Χριστοῦ for θεοῦ 19, ἐπ' ἔθνει

xi. 2, Ἠλείᾳ (*S* Ηλια) 6, -εἰ δὲ ἐξ ἔργων, οὐκέτι ἐστιν χάρις, ἐπεὶ τὸ ἔργον οὐκέτι ἐστιν ἔργον. 8, καθάπερ for καθὼς 10, διαπαντὸς 13, δὲ for γὰρ || οὖν after μὲν 17, -καὶ after ῥίζης 19, -οἱ 20, ὑψηλὰ φρόνει for ὑψηλοφρόνει 21, -μήπως 22, ἐπιμένῃς || 23, ἐπιμένωσιν 25, παρ' for ἐν 31, νῦν before ἐλεηθῶσιν

xii. 1, τῷ θεῷ εὐάρεστον 4, πολλὰ μέλη 5, τὸ δὲ for ὁ δὲ 14, ὑμᾶς after διώκοντας 20, ἀλλὰ ἐὰν for ἐὰν οὖν

xiii. 1, ὑπὸ for ἀπὸ after εἰ μὴ 11, ἤδη ὑμᾶς for ἡμᾶς ἤδη

xiv. 5, γὰρ after μὲν 6, -καὶ ὁ μὴ φρονῶν τὴν ἡμέραν κυρίῳ οὐ φρονεῖ. 14, ἑαυτοῦ for αὐτοῦ 19, διώκομεν 21, -ἢ *σκανδαλίζεται ἢ ἀσθενεῖ.* 22, *ἣν* after *πίστιν*

xv. 4, *διὰ* after *καὶ* 14, *τῆς γνώσεως* 15, –*ἀδελφοί*, ‖ *ἀπὸ* for *ὑπὸ* 18, *κατειργάσατο* 19, *θεοῦ* after *πνεύματος* 23, *κλίμασι* ‖ *πολλῶν* for *ἱκανῶν* 24, –*ἐλεύσομαι πρὸς ὑμᾶς* ‖ *ὑφ'* for *ἀφ'* 26, also 27, *ηὐδόκησαν* 30, *ἀδελφοί*, after *ὑμᾶς*, 31, *τοῖς ἁγ. γένηται* 32, *ἐλθὼν ἐν χαρᾷ* for *ἐν χαρᾷ ἔλθω* ‖ –*καὶ*

xvi. 2, *αὐτὴν προσδέξ.* 6, *ὑμᾶς* for *ἡμᾶς*. 8, *'Αμπλίατον* for *'Αμπλίαν* 14, *'Ασύνκριτον* 17, *ἐκκλίνετε* 20, –Χριστοῦ 24, *omits the verse.* 27, *τῶν αἰώνων* after *αἰῶνας*

1 Corinthians i. 2, *τῇ οὔσῃ ἐν Κορίνθῳ* placed after *θεοῦ* ‖ –*τε* 14, –*τῷ θεῷ* 25, –*ἐστίν*^2d^

ii. 2, *εἰδέναι τι* 3, *κἀγὼ* for *καὶ ἐγὼ* 9, *ἃ* for *ὅσα* 10, *δὲ* for *γὰρ* ‖ –*αὐτοῦ*. 15, –*τὰ*

iii. 3, *σαρκικοί ἐστε.* 5, *τί twice* for *τίς* ‖ –*ἀλλ' ἢ* 10, *ἔθηκα*, 11, *'Ιησοῦς Χριστός*. 12, –*τοῦτον* ‖ *χρυσίον* for *χρυσόν*, ‖ *ἀργύριον* for *ἄργυρον*, 19, *τῷ θεῷ*

iv. 6, *'Απολλῶν* (so *S**, but –*λω* *S*[a]) 14, *νουθετῶν.* 17, *αὐτὸ* after *τοῦτο* ‖ *'Ιησοῦ* after *Χριστῷ*

v. 3, –*ὡς* 4, –*ἡμῶν*[1st] 5, *'Ιησοῦ* after *κυρίου.*

*** Tischendorf's eighth edition of the Greek Testament is still in course of publication. When it is finished, the account of its new readings will be completed, and will be furnished in a separate form, on application, to those who have it here incomplete.

THE END.

www.ingramcontent.com/pod-product-compliance
Lightning Source LLC
LaVergne TN
LVHW010740120826
845150LV00009B/521

9781425558697